John Platter SOUTH AFRICAN WINES 2002

THE GUIDE TO CELLARS, VINEYARDS

WINEMAKERS, RESTAURANTS

AND ACCOMMODATION

The John Platter SA Wine Guide (Pty) Ltd
www.platterwineguide.co.za

Publisher
Andrew McDowall

Editor
Philip van Zyl

Tasters
Michael Fridjhon, Angela Lloyd, Jabulani Ntshangase, Neil Pendock, Dave Swingler; Cape Wine Masters Tim James, Tony Mossop, Irina von Holdt; honor- ary members of the Institute of Cape Wine Masters Colin Frith, Dave Hughes.

Contributors
David Biggs, Graham Howe, Lindsaye McGregor

Sales
Alison Worrall

Co-ordination
Ann Bomford, Ina de Villiers, Helene Scott, Meryl Weaver

Maps
Tim James/Gawie du Toit

Photography
Dennis Gordon

PO Box 53212, Kenilworth 7745

E-mail: publisher@platterwineguide.co.za; editor@platterwineguide.co.za
Website: www.platterwineguide.co.za
Tel: (021) 761-8773
Fax: (021) 762-5914

ISBN 0-9583898-9-6

Typeset by Zebra Publications, Hout Bay
Printed and bound in South Africa by NBD, Cape Town, South Africa

Foreword

Less than a decade after the end of South Africa's economic isolation, it seems our wine industry has come of age. With the advent of democracy and the opening up of new markets and exposure to global trends, we are now better equipped than ever to compete with confidence on the world wine stage.

Perhaps it's a question of maturity and learning to contain what can sometimes appear to be contradictory forces. We have become simultaneously outward-looking and introspective. We have become serious about being taken seriously, but we have become more relaxed about doing so. We are focused but without losing sight of the fact that wine should be fun and an expression of enjoyment.

We have been keen to learn, to experiment and to consolidate, and we are secure enough to listen to good advice and act on it, without forfeiting our own identity.

More and more of our winemakers are young, adventurous and, above all, passionate about their pursuit. Building from a sound academic foundation supplied by the University of Stellenbosch and the Elsenburg College of Agriculture, they travel abroad gaining exposure to the techniques and styles of their counterpars in other countries. At the same time, many local winemakers are participating in joint ventures with counterparts from France, the US and Australia.

While these overseas contacts have awakened South African winemakers to new possibilities, they are not afraid to express the uniqueness of what is their own.

The enormous biodiversity of the Cape with its varied soils and microclimates means that we are in a position to produce a whole range of wine styles that reflect the individuality of terroir. And site-specific wines are assuming an increasing importance in the South African portfolio.

We are better at understanding the potential of our vineyards, and our winemakers are devoting much of their focus to viticultural practices to keep intervention in the cellar to a minimum.

Better preparation of soils, improved crop management, more appropriate use of water, and the harvesting of riper grapes, together with the greater availability of plant material free of known viruses, are all contributing to a better starting point in the cellar.

In other words, there has been a shift from grape farming to wine growing.

And this shift has taken us to new wine-growing areas, well suited to the production of outstanding wines that take advantage of the cooling effect of high altitudes and maritime breezes. It has also resulted in a dramatic swing to the planting of red varieties.

At the same time, SA has assumed a leading role in developing controls to protect the environment and its natural resources. Through the

Integrated Production of Wine (IPW), we are beginning to produce grapes profitably but in an environmentally sensitive way. The only other country in the world to operate a similar system is New Zealand.

And our advances are being widely acknowledged. The number of international accolades our wines are winning grows every year. Most recently, South African winemakers earned several major awards that included the Robert Mondavi Trophy for Winemaker of the Year, and the Château Pichon-Longueville Comtesse de Lalande trophy for best red blend (most often the preserve of the French) at the 2001 International Wine & Spirit Competition in London.

We also brought home a bigger collection of trophies and gold medals on the 2001 International Wine Challenge than ever before, and more of our wines are scoring 90+ in *Wine Spectator* and Robert Parker's *Wine Advocate*.

These successes are also the mark of greater collaboration among producers, marketers, researchers and industry bodies. The collective goal is for SA to become a main-stage world player as opposed to a chorus member performing on the fringes. We present a more united front because we have become more united in our resolve to keep getting better at what we do.

For the first time we are working together as a team. That doesn't mean domestic rivalry has stopped. As you will see from the increased number of listings in this edition of the guide, there are many more contenders in the local industry. But we have begun to see the larger gains that come from working together to build South Africa. We understand more readily the overarching allure of this generic brand, which melds old and new world, classicism and innovation, and sophistication and the exotic. It provides the context for the individuality of our winemakers, a stage on which they can play and a gateway through which new consumers can enter.

Exports are climbing, both in turnover and in value, as our wines earn greater respect from foreign palates. They delight in the quality, diversity and value from which they can select. The UK remains the biggest destination for our exports, but other traditional markets, such as the Benelux countries and Germany are strengthening their already considerable support. At the same time, Scandinavian consumers, as well as those from the US, Canada, Japan, Hong Kong, Singapore and India are discovering our vinous charms.

The Cape's growing attraction as a wine tourism destination also brings us into contact with global demands, trends and ideas. And that is how it should be. To come of age is one thing, but to stay dynamic, relevant and interesting is altogether another.

Su Birch
CEO, Wines of South Africa

Editor's note

CHRONICLING, as we annually do, what's what and who's who in the winelands, we find ourselves snap-shooting an industry wildly in love with change. Renewal is in the air – our own fuller body reflects the sixty-something brands that have emerged in the past year, as well as the dizzying number of start-ups and spin-offs, take-overs and buy-outs (some opt-outs, too) vying for attention. The more significant developments and trends are thumbnailed in these pages, along with pointers of a more general nature such as top-performing wines, vintage notes, grape varieties and wine styles, winegrowing areas, wine terms and a potted picture of the local wine industry. Also noteworthy are the Stay-over and Eat-out sections, featuring upmarket accommodation and hospitality in wine country.

New in this edition is a survey of wineries in the most important vinotourism areas as viewed from the perspective of the disabled. Our collaborator in this ongoing project is Guy Davies, a disability consultant who's visited some 150 cellars at our request to assess how friendly these are to the disabled. His conclusions are presented in the section Disabled access in SA wineries, and reflected in the A-Z.

Not entirely new, but reincorporated by overwhelming demand is the 'A-code list', which provides a clue to the provenance of otherwise anonymous bottles by identifying the holder of the unique 'A-number' on the label.

Updates on wineries and wines appear in the A-Z section. As always, we've tried to feature every SA-bottled or boxed wine available during the currency of the book (while we've made every effort to be comprehensive, a few examples have doubtless slipped past us; we'll try to reflect these dropped catches as well as new releases in the next edition). Included in the A-Z are release dates (where none is mentioned, it's safe to assume wines are already obtainable from retailers, the cellars or the hospitality trade, or even sold out), quantities produced and general style indicators. Technical details – alcohol, acid, sugar levels, time in wood etc – are provided only where they are useful in giving clues to the character of the wine.

A word about our rankings: we cover the full spectrum, from wines we consider 'somewhat less than ordinary' (and award 0 stars) to the 'superlative Cape classics', worthy of a full 5. Wines rated ✵ or higher are listed first in each entry, with a general rating in the margin. Vintages deviating from the general rating are individually starred in the text. 'Good everyday drinking' wines and more modest examples (✵ or fewer) are included in the 'run-on' listing at the end of the entry. Look for the ✓ icon for exceptional quality vs price among the more serious wines, and the ☻ symbol for bargain quaffing. See also How to use the guide.

Because of early deadlines, many wines in the guide are tasted freshly bottled or as works-in-progress; any considered unrateable as a result are noted in the text. It's worth mentioning in relation to the star-ratings that we taste from mid-June to mid-August – somewhat earlier than in the past. Because of the subjective element associated with wine assessment, we strongly recommend you view the ratings as adjuncts to the tasting notes (and the results of other professional tastings mentioned in the descriptions and the section on Top performers), rather than oracular pronouncements.

Wines featured in the guide are assessed by a team of internationally experienced tasters whose professionalism and unflagging enthusiasm we gratefully acknowledge. They are Michael Fridjhon, Colin Frith, Dave Hughes, Tim James, Angela Lloyd, Tony Mossop, Jabulani Ntshangase, Neil Pendock, Dave Swingler and Irina von Holdt. Their initials appear below the wines they tasted. Warm thanks to contributor-in-chief Lindsaye McGregor; also to David Biggs and Graham Howe; co-ordinators Meryl Weaver, Helene Scott, Ina de Villiers, Ann Bomford and Linda Hunt; sales consultant Alison Worrall, photographer Dennis Gordon; and layout/design ace Gawie du Toit. Special thanks to the wine producers, without whose support the book could not be produced. Personal thanks to long-suffering Cathy, and Luke, still in a beer phase.

Finally, for updates and extra information not included in this guide, an invitation to visit our website, www.platterwineguide.co.za.

Le Prix du Champagne Lanson

In a year marked by wide acclaim for SA wine, our 2001 edition was named Best Wine Guide by the international judges of the Champagne Lanson Awards, which recognise winewriting excellence in print and electronic media world-wide. The 12th annual awards drew a record number of entries, and these were judged by Masters of Wine David Molyneux-Berry, Rosemary George and Laura Jewell, wine consultant Pamela Gregory, winewriters Stephen Brook and Charles Metcalfe, wine merchant Gerald Duff, and the MD of Champagne Lanson, Georges Alnot. Though five top-selling titles from Australia, Europe and SA were shortlisted, this "compact, clear and concise" guide was the unanimous choice because it offers "reliable information and opinions". The judges concluded: "A really good reference book – the essential guide to South African wines."

How to use this guide

Ratings

(Subjective choices in a South African wine context)

★★★★★	Superlative. A Cape classic	★★★★½	Outstanding
★★★★	Excellent	★★★½	Very good/promising
★★★	Good everyday drinking	★★½	Pleasant drinking
★★	Casual quaffing	★½	Plain and simple
★	Very ordinary	No star	Somewhat less than ordinary
✓	Good value	☻	Exceptionally drinkable and well priced

Symbols & abbreviations

- Bottles own wine on property
- Visiting hours, tasting details (no tasting fee unless noted)
- Restaurant/refreshments
- Accommodation
- Other tourist attractions/amenities on the property

Veritas	SA National Bottled Wine Show
VVG	Veritas double-gold medal
VG	Veritas gold medal
SAYWS	SA Young Wine Show
SAA	Selected for South African Airways (First & Business Class)
IWC	International Wine Challenge
IWSC	International Wine & Spirit Competition
WOM	Wine of the Month Club (Reserve/Value) winner

See also section on SA wine competitions

Wine ★	Stars in SA *Wine* magazine
CWG	Cape Winemakers Guild
WO	Wine of Origin
Bdx	Bordeaux
MCC	Methode cap classique; sparkling wine by methode champenoise (see SA wine styles)
NLH	Noble Late Harvest
SLH	Special Late Harvest
LBV	Late Bottled Vintage
NV	Non-vintage. Year of harvest not stated on label
Malo	Malolactic fermentation (see Winemaking terms)
g/ℓ	Grams per litre
% alc	Percentage of alcohol by volume

Assumptions

Unless stated otherwise, the following are implied:

- Cabernet = cabernet sauvignon; pinot = pinot noir; chenin = chenin blanc; sauvignon = sauvignon blanc; riesling = Rhine/weisser riesling; touriga = touriga naçional; tinta = tinta barocca (tinta r = tinta roriz; tinta f = tinta francisca)
- Red wines oaked; whites not
- Case = 12 × 750 ml bottles
- All wines dry unless noted
- 'Malo' denotes full malolactic fermentation unless noted

See also Editor's Note for more about using the guide.

Contents

Disabled access in SA wineries

In line with its policy of encouraging excellence in wine and related areas, the guide commissioned me to undertake the first disabled access audit of South Africa's wine tasting centres and cellar tour facilities. The aim is to visit, and objectively assess how friendly they are to the disabled.

Given the scope of the project, the audit is being done in phases. For this edition the most popular vinotourism areas of Constantia, Stellenbosch, Franschhoek and Paarl have been visited. It would just not have been feasible to visit every establishment in time for this edition. This certainly does not mean that producers not yet visited do not have good disabled facilities; it merely means that we are not yet in the position to be able to comment on these farms.

The intention is to complete the whole audit by the next edition, and then to update the information continually as facilities improve. It is important to realise that this audit is very much a snapshot in time; it can only be as accurate as the last visit. Many establishments are undertaking renovations and improvements, and every effort is being taken to incorporate any changes taking place. I am in a wheelchair, and visit each producer myself. Not just wheelchair access is assessed though; the audit also covers other disabilities, such as sight, or hearing impairment. There are stringent building regulations concerning these issues, but often it would be impractical to enforce these regulations in every case. A practical balance needs to be sought. A copy of the audit is given to each producer, which highlights any problem areas. Hopefully this will create a greater awareness of this issue, and improve access for all the disabled.

Disabled access is not exclusive; indeed, many people not generally regarded as disabled will benefit from improvements made. There are many fine examples within the wine industry where the requirements of the disabled have been successfully addressed, but some establishments deserve special recognition. The House of JC le Roux in the beautiful Devon Valley of Stellenbosch is a magnificent example, where the needs of the disabled have been fully integrated into the establishment.

Hopefully, like a good wine, disabled access will improve over time. Awareness is the first stage in any improvement. I am finding the audit both challenging and satisfying; many producers are aware of these issues and have facilities that make visiting their premises much easier not only for disabled people, but for the public in general. Unfortunately, there are still many obstacles, and the disabled person needs to know which premises have fully addressed these problems. The results of the first phase of the audit are given in the table below.

The industry has the opportunity to set a good example to other areas of tourism, and everyday life in South Africa.

Guy Davies
Tel (021) 872-1101 • Fax (021) 872-9675 • Email east19@cis.co.za

Winery accessibility ratings

	Parking	Tasting	Toilet	Tour
Constantia				
Buitenverwachting	●	●		
Constantia Uitsig	●			
Groot Constantia	●	●		
Klein Constantia	●	●		
Steenberg	●	●	●	
Franschhoek/Groot Drakenstein				
Agusta	●	●		
Boschendal	●	●		

	Parking	Tasting	Toilet	Tour
Cabrière	●	●		●
Cape Chamonix		●		
Dieu Donné	●			
Franschhoek Vineyards	●			●
La Couronne				
La Motte	●	●	●	
La Petite Ferme				
Mont Rochelle				
Môreson	●	●		●
Plaisir de Merle	●			
Rickety Bridge				
Stony Brook				
Paarl				
Ashanti	●	●		●
Avondale	●	●		
Backsberg	●	●	●	●
Bernheim	●	●		
Boland	●			
De Villiers				
De Zoete Inval	●	●		
Fairview	●	●	●	
Glen Carlou	●	●		●
Kleine Draken	●	●		
Laborie	●	●		
Landskroon	●			
Nederburg	●	●	●	
Nelson's Creek	●	●	●	●
Perdeberg	●			
Rhebokskloof	●	●		●
Ruitersvlei	●	●	●	
Seidelberg	●			
Simonsvlei	●	●	●	
Vendôme	●	●		
Villiera	●	●		
Welgemeend	●	●		●
Windmeul				
Stellenbosch				
Alto	●			
Amani	●	●		●
Asara			●	●
Audacia	●	●		●
Avontuur	●	●		
Bergkelder	●	●	●	
Beyerskloof	●	●		
Bilton	●	●	●	
Blaauwklippen	●	●		
Camberley	●			
Carisbrooke	●			
Clos Malverne				
Delaire		●		
Delheim	●	●		
De Meye				

	Parking	Tasting	Toilet	Tour
Eikendal	●	●		●
Fort Simon	●	●		
Hartenberg	●			
Hazendal	●		●	
Helderkruin	●	●		
J C le Roux	●	●	●	●
Jordan	●	●		
Kaapzicht	●			
Kanonkop	●	●		
Kanu	●			
Ken Forrester	●	●		
Klawervlei	●	●		●
Kleine Zalze	●	●		
Knorhoek	●	●		
Koelenhof	●	●		
Laibach				
Lanzerac	●	●	●	●
L'Avenir	●			
Le Bonheur	●		●	
L'Emigré				
Lievland	●	●		
Louiesenhof	●	●		
Louisvale	●	●		
Middelvlei	●	●		
Morgenhof	●	●	●	●
Muratie				
Neethlingshof	●	●	●	
Neil Ellis	●			
Oude Libertas/Distell Adam Tas Cellar	●	●		●
Overgaauw	●	●		
Rustenberg	●	●	●	
Rust en Vrede	●			
Saxenburg	●			
Simonsig	●	●		●
Somerbosch	●	●		
Spier	●	●		
Sylvanvale	●	●	●	●
Thelema	●	●		
Uiterwyk	●			
Uitkyk		●		
Vergelegen	●	●	●	
Vlottenburg	●	●		
Vredenheim	●	●		
Warwick	●			
Waterford	●	●		●
Welmoed	●			
Zevenwacht	●	●		●

A brief industry profile

IN WORLD TERMS, the South African wine industry is still a small one. It ranks 16th, with less than 1.5% of the global hectarage, though in output it is a stronger 7th, accounting for about 3% of total international wine production.

There are 117 066 ha under vines in SA, of which 105 566 ha are used for the production of wine (2000 figures). Of the ±314- million wine-vines, more than one-fifth are chenin blanc; sultana (also used for non-alcohol purposes) is the second biggest white grape, followed by colombard and chardonnay; the biggest plantings of red are cabernet (just 8.4% of the total vineyard), followed by pinotage and shiraz (for further details see also sections Winegrowing areas and Grape varieties). Here it is relevant to note that while the ratio of red to white varieties overall remains heavily skewed towards the latter, the gap is narrowing from roughly 15% red to 85% white in 1990, to about 32% to 68% today. More than 80% of all new plantings in 2000 were reds (shiraz, cabernet and merlot at the head of the list); conversely, 87% of all grubbings were white (led by chenin, white french and colombard).

The total grape crop in 2000 was ±1-million tons, from which ±830-million litres of wine were made. Of these, ±540 000-million litres (±65%) were made into 'good wine' (i.e. not channelled into brandy production, spirit distillation or non-alcoholic beverages). Just over 32% of good wine was sold in bottle in 2000 (down from 35% the previous year), ±36% in boxes or bags and ±25% in plastic (balance in "other containers").

SA's wine is produced, according to official 2000 statistics, by 355 active cellars – 185 non-estate 'private producers'; 92 registered 'estates', 69 co-operatives and 9 producing wholesalers.

National annual per capita wine consumption has declined steadily in the past 20 years (as have brandy and other spirits), and now stands at ±9 litres (beer remains the alcoholic beverage of choice, with nearly 45% market share; natural wine slots in at ±16%). While SA has slid to 30th position in the world rankings, Luxembourg (61 litres), France (57) and Portugal (52) have tippled their way to the very distant top; Australia and Chile rank 18th and 26th, with 19 and 14 litres a person a year.

Though locals imbibe less of the grape national crop, the upside is that foreigners continue to lap up more. Exports of SA natural, sparkling and fortified wine now top 139-million litres or just over 25% of 'good-wine' production. This presents a dramatic rise since the country's post 1994-ballot return to the international arena. That year ±50-million litres – just 12% of the 'good' fraction – were exported. Encouragingly, just over 66% is now exported in bottle (as opposed to bulk).

Winegrowing areas

FROM A 17TH-CENTURY experimental vineyard in the Dutch East India Company gardens below Table Mountain, South Africa's vignoble over more than 340 vintages has spread over a large area. Grapes are now grown in close to 60 officially declared appellations covering in excess of 100 000 hectares. Since the introduction of the Wine of Origin scheme in 1972/3, production zones have been designated 'regions', 'districts' and 'wards' – the latter being smaller geographical units whose soil, climate and ecological factors are officially, though perhaps not universally, considered distinctive. 'Estates', the smallest category of the WO system, are normally single farms. In this guide, only officially registered estates – at press time there were close to 100, though some do not produce under their own label and some do not make wine at all – are referred to as 'estates'. This distinguishes them from what in officialese are 'private wine cellars', 'co-operatives' and 'producing wholesalers'. Below are the important grape cultivation zones. Note: Figures relating to the areas under vine mentioned here are kindly supplied by SA Wine Industry Information & Systems (SAWIS). They reflect the current (2000) status for the *official WO areas*, and as such may differ from other published figures based on the old District Council demarcations or 'KWV districts' (including – confusingly – SAWIS' own excellent annual booklet, *SA Wine Industry Statistics*, available from Debbie Wait, tel 021-807 5711).

Cape Point Exciting new cool-climate district within the catchall Coastal Region, situated on the western ridges of the Cape Peninsula mountain spine (the Constantia vineyards are on the opposite side). Shot to prominence when the first and as yet sole producer, Cape Point Vineyards, clinched a recent Young Wine Show championship trophy, for sauvignon. 56% red 44% white. Major varieties (ha): cabernet (10), shiraz (4), pinot (4); sauvignon (11), chardonnay (3), semillon (1).

Constantia Ward within the umbrella Coastal Region on the eastern gradients of the Peninsula massif, summer-cooled by south-easters from False Bay. A premier-league viticultural area, focused since the earliest days on fine wine production. Recognised for whites generally, sauvignon in particular. 37% red 63% white. Major varieties (ha): cabernet (52), merlot (34), shiraz (21); sauvignon (105), chardonnay (63), hanepoot (26).

Durbanville A Coastal ward in transition, poised between rustic tradition and headlong development. Some of the earliest farmland in Cape to be planted with vines, these rolling hills are moving out of the anonymous shadow of bulk-wine production into the glare of solo stardom. Important quality factors include deep, moisture-retentive soils, cooling summer night-time mists and climatic influences from Table Bay and, marginally, False Bay. Recognised for sauvignon blanc, merlot. 59% red, 41% white. Major varieties (ha): cabernet (214), shiraz (173), merlot (135); sauvignon (216), chenin (106), chardonnay (84).

Elim Youngest of the new crop of maritime vineyards, situated around the old mission village of Elim near Cape Agulhas, Africa's southern extremity. Officially a standalone ward within the WO scheme, its still tiny hectarage is among the most promising and closely watched in the Cape. 65% red 35% white. Major varieties (ha): cabernet (16), merlot (5), petit verdot (1); sauvignon (12), semillon (2).

Little Karoo Once fringed by a prehistoric ocean, this now semi-arid scrubland is perfect for ostrich farming but something of a challenge for wine growers who rely on irrigation for their vineyards. Similarities (in climate, if not soil) with the Douro Valley of Portugal have inspired some local vintners, principally around the quaint village of Calitzdorp, to apply their talents to 'port' with results that impress even the Portuguese. Recognised for 'port' styles, other fortifieds. 17% red 83% white. Major varieties: (ha) ruby cabernet (110), red muscadel (104), pinotage (96); colombard (839), chenin (748), hanepoot (343).

Olifants River Quality moves are afoot in these north-westerly Cape grape growing areas, both in the Olifants Valley and the cooler uplands, including the vineyards of the Cederberg. Piekenierskloof, an eyrie ward officially appellated in 1999, is a promising development. Recognised for everyday reds, fortifieds. 26% red 74% white. Major varieties (ha): shiraz (669), pinotage (498), merlot (448); chenin (2 206), colombard (1 697), hanepoot (875).

Northern Cape This is the hottest, most northerly Cape growing area, and the 4th largest, with more than 15 000 ha (close to 15% of the national vineyard) along the Orange River. Overwhelmingly a white grape area. But plantings of reds, especially merlot, shiraz and pinotage, are spreading five times faster than white. 0.9% red 99.1% white. Major varieties (ha): ruby cabernet (36), red muscadel (21), cabernet franc (20); sultana (10 292), colombard (2 147), chenin (666).

Wine of Origin-defined production areas

Region	District	Ward
Breede River Valley	Robertson	Agterkliphoogte
		Bonnievale
		Boesmansrivier
		Eilandia
		Hoopsrivier
		Klaasvoogds
		Le Chasseur
		McGregor
		Vinkrivier
	Swellendam	Buffeljags
		Stormsvlei
	Worcester	Aan-de-Doorns
		Goudini
		Nuy
		Scherpenheuvel
		Slanghoek
Little Karoo	–	Montagu
	–	Tradouw
	Calitzdorp	–
Coastal	Cape Point	–
	–	Constantia
	Tygerberg	Durbanville
	Paarl	Franschhoek Valley
		Wellington
	Stellenbosch	Jonkershoek Valley
		Papegaaiberg
		Simonsberg–Stellenbosch
		Bottelary
		Devon Valley
	Swartland	Groenekloof
		Riebeekberg
	Tulbagh	–
Olifants River	Lutzville Valley	Koekenaap
	–	Spruitdrift
	–	Vredendal
	–	Piekenierskloof
–	Overberg	Walker Bay
		Elgin
–	Douglas*	–
–	Piquetberg	–
–	–	Cederberg
–	–	Ceres
–	–	Elim NEW
–	–	Hartswater*
–	–	Herbertsdale
–	–	Lower Orange*
–	–	Rietrivier (Free State)*
–	–	Ruiterbosch
–	–	Swartberg
Boberg (fortified wines from Paarl & Tulbagh)		

*Production zones within the officially designated Northern Cape Geographical Unit; all other areas are part of the Western Cape Geographical Unit.

Source: SAWIS

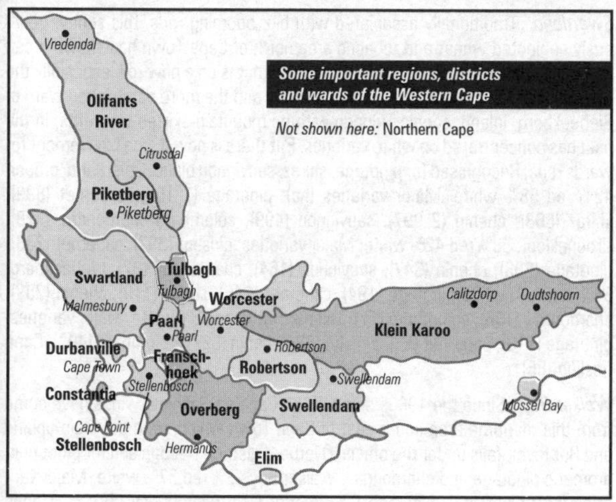

Paarl This district has many different mesoclimates, soils and aspects and thus succeeds with a wide range of styles/varieties. The ward of Wellington has shed its Sleepy Hollow image with some promising wines, especially reds, from properties mostly on higher ground. The other ward, Franschhoek, founded by 17th-century Huguenots and now a millionaire's playground, falls within this viticultural district. Paarl proper is recognised for shiraz and, more recently, viognier/mourvèdre grown on warmer slopes; Franschhoek for chenin, semillon; Wellington for shiraz and gutsy red blends generally. Paarl 'proper': 49% red 51% white. Major varieties (ha): cabernet (1 441), pinotage (893) cinsaut (725); chenin (2 484), sauvignon (580), chardonnay (565). Franschhoek: 35% red 65% white. Major varieties: cabernet (168), merlot (104), shiraz (78); sauvignon (238), chardonnay (175), chenin (157). Wellington: 47% red 53% white. Major varieties: cabernet (599), cinsaut (582), pinotage (298); chenin (1 404), Cape riesling (200), sauvignon (189).

Robertson Though a warmer area, the 'valley of vines and roses' traditionally has been white wine country. However, there have been flashes of red-wine brilliance, especially shiraz but recently also cabernet. Significant features include cooling late afternoon south-easters during summer, and limestone soils. Recognised for chardonnay, colombard for brandy, everyday whites, sparkling. 27% red 73% white. Major varieties (ha): cabernet (903), shiraz (652), ruby cabernet (515); colombard (2 334), chenin (2 249), chardonnay (1384).

Stellenbosch To many, this intensively farmed district around the town of Stellenbosch is *the* red-wine producing area in South Africa. Yet many of its whites (and bubblies and fortifieds) also feature in the SA premier league. Key contributors to quality are the cooler mountain slopes, variegated soil types and breezes off False Bay which help moderate summer temperatures. Officially designated wards within the district are Jonkershoek Valley east of Stellenbosch town; Simonsberg-Stellenbosch, encompassing the south-western foothills of Simonsberg mountain; and Bottelary, Devon Valley and Papegaaiberg north-west of the town. Further subdivisions are likely in the future. Recognised for cabernet, pinotage, shiraz, chenin, sparkling. 55% red 45% white. Major varieties (ha): cabernet (2 697), merlot (1 400), pinotage (1 315); chenin (2 515), sauvignon (1 573), chardonnay (949).

Swartland Traditionally associated with big, booming reds, this sunny, previously neglected wheat and tobacco area north of Cape Town has shown it can make top-table white wines too. Now the district is on a new roll, especially the Groenekloof ward nearer the cooling Atlantic, and the more established ward of Riebeekberg. Inland, scenic Tulbagh with its mountain-skirted vineyards, in the past has concentrated on white varieties. But there is now a small movement towards reds. Recognised for pinotage, shiraz, sauvignon blanc. Swartland 'proper' 42% red 58% white. Major varieties (ha): pinotage (1 152), cabernet (899), shiraz (568); chenin (2 997), sauvignon (499), colombard chardonnay (318). Groenekloof: 58% red 42% white. Major varieties: cinsaut (297), cabernet (288), pinotage (205); chenin (347), sauvignon (164), chardonnay (82). Riebeekberg: 54% red 47% white pinotage (194), cabernet (146), shiraz (119); chenin (282), chardonnay (136), colombard (77). Tulbagh: 18% red 82% white. Major varieties: pinotage (110), cabernet (82), cinsaut (63); chenin (822), colombard (407), Cape riesling (85).

Walker Bay Since the 1980s some of the Cape's splashiest wines have come from this maritime area south-east of Cape Town which, with the Elgin upland and Bot River, falls under the official Overberg district. Recognised for pinot noir, aromatic pinotage and chardonnay. Walker Bay 43% red 57% white. Major varieties (ha): pinot (27), pinotage (15), merlot (10); chardonnay (38), sauvignon (33) chenin (21) Elgin: 40% red, 60% white. Major varieties: pinot (19), cabernet (10), merlot (8); sauvignon (27), chardonnay (18), riesling (5).

Worcester The colossus of SA winedom, measured by the number of vines planted (nearly 60-million, or nearly 20% of the national vineyard). Production is chiefly for brandy, and most of the rest goes directly to wholesaling producers. But small quantities are bottled under own labels, and these often represent good value for money. Traditionally vineyards were sited in fertile alluvial soils; now they are starting to move up into the hills. Recognised for fortified muscadel, hanepoot. 27% red 73% white. Major varieties (ha): cinsaut (826), pinotage (789), shiraz (714); chenin (4 363), colombard (2 222), hanepoot (1 329).

Grape varieties

LEGISLATION requires the presence in the wine of only 75% of the stated variety (85% if exported). Blends may only name component parts if those components were vinified separately, prior to blending; then they are listed with the larger contributor(s) named first. If one of the blend partners is less than 20%, percentages for all the varieties must be given. Figures given for proportion of national vineyard are for 2000 (latest available).

Red-wine varieties

Cabernet sauvignon Adaptable and internationally planted black grape making some of the world's finest and longest-lasting wines. And retaining some of its inherent qualities even when overcropped in poorer soils and climates. Can stand alone triumphantly, but frequently blended with a wide range of other varieties: traditionally, as in Bordeaux, with cab franc, merlot and a few minor others, but also in South Africa, for example, sometimes partnering varieties such as shiraz and pinotage. Number of different clones, with differing characteristics. 8.4% of total vineyard area, steadily increasing (3.8% in 1990).

Cabernet franc Like its close relative cabernet sauvignon, with which it is often partnered, a classic part of the bordeaux blend, but in SA and elsewhere also used for varietal wines – particularly on the Loire. Tiny vineyard area (0.5%), increasing.

Carignan Hugely planted in the south of France, where it is not much respected. But there, as in SA, older, low-yielding vines can produce pleasant surprises. Insignificant vineyard area.

Cinsaut Cinsault in France. Another of the mass, undistinguished plantings of southern France, which only occasionally comes up trumps. Used to be known locally as hermitage, the name reflected in its offspring (with pinot noir), pinotage. 3.3% of vineyard area, decreasing (5.7% in 1990).

Gamay noir Although it produces some serious long-lived wines in Beaujolais, its use for (mainly) early- and easy-drinking Beaujolais, often using carbonic maceration, is the model mostly copied in SA. Insignificant vineyard area.

Grenache (noir) The international (ie French) name for the Spanish grape garnacha. Widespread in Spain and southern France, generally used in blends (as in Rioja and Chateauneuf), but occasionally by itself. A favourite for rosés. When restrained, capable of greatness, but this is rare. Tiny plantings here. (White and pink versions also occur.)

Merlot Classic blending partner (as in Bordeaux) for cabernet, now wildly fashionable around the world, where it tends to be seen as an 'easier' version of cab – although this is perhaps because it is often made in a less ambitious manner. Merlot varietal wines increasingly common in SA too. 4.6% of vineyard area, strongly increasing (0.9% in 1990).

Mourvèdre Internationally known by its French name, though originally Spanish (monastrell). In Australia and California also called mataro – which is, strangely, its official name in SA. Particularly successful in some serious southern French blends, and increasingly modish internationally. Miniscule plantings here.

Nebbiolo Perhaps the greatest red grape to have scarcely ventured from its home – Piedmont in this case, where it makes massive, tannic, long-lived wines. Minute plantings here.

Petit verdot Use of this excellent variety in Médoc limited by its late ripening. Now appearing in some local blends, and a few varietals. Tiny quantities.

Pinotage South Africa's 'national grape' is a 1920s cross between pinot noir and cinsaut ('hermitage'). Became unfashionable in the 80s, with only a few champions, but now has cachet and some international success. Made in a range of styles, from simply fruity to ambitious, well-oaked examples. Particularly expressive in Stellenbosch's 'golden crescent' from Simonsberg to Kuils River. 6.2% of vineyard area, steadily increasing (2.1% in 1990).

Pinot noir Notoriously difficult grape to succeed with outside its native Burgundy, but SA, along with the rest of the New World, now producing excellent examples, especially as use of BK5 'champagne' clone wanes. Usually matured in wood; seldom at bargain price. Still very small proportion of the vineyard (0.5%).

Ruby cabernet US cross between cabernet sauvignon and carignan, designed for heat tolerance. Rather rustic, used mostly in cheaper blends. 1.9% of vineyard area.

Shiraz Better known as syrah outside SA and Australia (and on some local labels too). Internationally increasing in popularity, with northern Rhône and now also Australia as its major domiciles. Clearly happy in warmer climates, shiraz is seen by many as the great hope for SA wine. Made here in a variety of styles – generally wooded, often with American oak. 5.3% of vineyard area, sharply up from 0.7% in 1990.

Tinta barocca Elsewhere spelt 'barroca'. One of the important Portuguese port-making grapes, which is now its primary role in SA, usually blended. Also used for some varietal unfortified wines, and namelessly in some 'dry reds'. Insignificant vineyard area.

Touriga naçional Important Portuguese port-making grape, now usefully grown here for similar ends, along with tinta francisca, tinta roriz (tempranillo) and souzão. Tiny plantings.

Zinfandel The quintessential Californian grape (of European origin, and the same as Italy's primitivo), used here in a small way for some big wines. Tiny plantings.

White wine varieties

Chardonnay In the Cape, as elsewhere, many new vineyards of this grape have come onstream in recent years, with wines showing a wide range of styles, quality and price. Generally used varietally, but also in blends. Often heavily wooded in more ambitious wines. 5.7% of vineyard area, has increased greatly (1.5% in 1990), now stabilising.

Chenin blanc South Africa has more chenin (locally also called steen) vineyards than even France's Loire Valley, the variety's home. Used here for everything from generic 'dry whites' though to ambitious sweet wines, to brandy. Some notable table-wine successes in recent years, in a sea of overcropped mediocrity. 21.4% of vineyard area, declining fast (31.9% in 1990).

Colombar(d) One of the mainstays of brandy production in the Cape, colombard (usually without the 'd' in SA) also used for numerous varietal and blended wines, ranging from dry to sweet – seldom wooded. Now 10.8% of vineyard area, after peaking at 11.2% in 1999.

Gewürztraminer Readily identifiable from its rose petal fragrance, best known in its Alsatian guise. In the Cape usually made in sweeter styles. Insignificant vineyard area.

Hanepoot Traditional Afrikaans name for muscat d'Alexandrie, the Cape's most planted muscat variety (see also muscadel below). 3.8% of vineyard area (some for raisins and table grapes), declining.

Muscadel Name used here for both muscat de Frontignan and muscat blanc à petits grains (both red and white versions). The grape associated with the famous Constantia dessert wines of the 18th century today is used chiefly for dessert and fortified wines and for touching up blends. Red and white versions together ±1.2% of vineyard area.

Muscat See Hanepoot and Muscadel.

Riesling The name a source of confusion to consumers, and of distress to the producers of what is known in its great homeland, Germany, simply as riesling and here officially as Rhine or weisser riesling. In SA, standing alone, 'riesling' usually, and officially, refers to Cape riesling (sometimes called Paarl or SA riesling), a much inferior grape properly known as crouchen blanc, mostly used here anonymously in blends, and sometimes varietally. Rhine/weisser riesling frequently in off-dry style here, in blends or varietally, some noteworthy botrytised dessert examples – and developing terpene character much earlier in SA than in cooler climates. Cape riesling 2% of vineyard area, decreasing; Rhine/weisser 0.5%, down from 1.1% in 1990. Note: in this guide 'riesling' without qualification refers to the latter.

Sauvignon blanc Prestigious vine most associated with eastern Loire regions, Bordeaux and, increasingly, New Zealand – whose wines have helped restore fashionability to the grape. The Cape version no longer a poor relation of these. Usually dry, but some sweet wines; sometimes wooded, more often not (former sometimes called fumé blanc/blanc fumé). 5.1% of vineyard area, stabilising.

Semillon The present small hectarage devoted to semillon is a far cry from the early 19th century, when the grape, also known as 'groen' (green) grape, a reference to its bright foliage, represented 93% of all Cape vines. Sometimes heavily wooded. Since 1997, 1% of vineyard area.

Viognier Increasingly fashionable noble variety internationally, spreading out from its home in the northern Rhone, now showing promise here. Usually only lightly wooded, if at all. Insignificant vineyard area.

Recent Cape vintages

SA WINES do not exhibit the major vintage variations seen in cooler northern regions such as Burgundy or Bordeaux. There are, nevertheless, significant variations from year to year, albeit within an SA context. (These, in terms of reds, relate more to relative ageing potential than the declaration of generally poor vintages; whites, if anything, are more prone to vintage variation, summer heatwaves leaching them of freshness and flavour.) Dry, hot summers are the norm but a variety of factors make generalisations both difficult and dangerous. Allowances should be made for the widely scattered growing areas – 350 km north and east, and now increasingly spreading west and south. These, and a harvest spread over the best part of three months, see significant changes in weather. Further, modern vineyard practices and new winemaking techniques tend to minimise variations. Also important for reds if the virus status of vine; virus-free material ripens more easily than virus-infected. Then there are the exceptions: in a year such as 96 (with rains during the harvest), some producers 'declassified' wines or did not release their flagships, while a few others delivered reds with grace and power. All of which underlines the fact that there is no substitute for sensitive and intelligent winemaking, increasingly evident among winemakers able to 'read' the vintage before harvest.

2001 Estimates indicate a still smaller crop than the already reduced 00 vintage, but with a corresponding increase in quality. Factors of note are decreased production after intensive uprooting of high-yielding vines and a higher red:white ratio. The hot summer that followed the third consecutive parched winter was one of the driest ever, resulting in very few problems with disease. A series of heatwaves at harvest time led to rapidly increasing sugar levels and many varieties ripened simultaneously. Red: Some excellent wines, massively fruity and concentrated, possibly long-lived. White: Producers able to time picking between heatwaves have delivered stylish whites packed with flavour and distinguished by high alcohols. Arguably the best in the past five years for sauvignon.

2000 A small harvest, ±540-million litres (this, below, designates 'good wine' production only) and a difficult year with patchy quality. The third hot summer in a row, following yet another warm, dry winter which led to uneven budding. Fires on Stellenbosch's Simonsberg damaged and even destroyed some vineyards. Red: Predictably powerful with excellent concentration and ripe, sometimes overripe, fruit with softer acidity. Many reds, pinotage especially, show massive tannin structures. The best should keep very well. White: Less stellar than reds; the bigger, bolder wines such as chardonnay and semillon fared better, the rest seem to have been more affected by the heat which destroyed aroma. Not for long keeping.

1999 A large harvest of ±595-million litres, and another warm vintage following a dry winter. Red: Near-perfect conditions for ripening of reds meant fat, alcoholic wines with an attractive juiciness. Tannins are much softer than in 1998 and generally will be ready earlier. Drink 99s while waiting for 98. An excellent vintage for restaurants. White: Some attractive fruity whites from chardonnay, semillon and chenin but generally lacking flavour and concentration.

1998 A significantly smaller harvest, from which a total of ±540-million litres was produced. A cool wet winter in 1997 before a warm ripening season and sustained heat during the harvest in almost all areas. Generally, smaller berries led to less juice recovery and higher tannins. Red: The warm vintage translated into big, dark-coloured, robust wines bursting with fruit but distinguished by tough tannins. Most will need long cellaring before they soften, but generally there is sufficient fruit to justify extended keeping. White: Less exciting and frequently lacking aroma, as one would expect in a hot year. Full-bodied wines such as chardonnay particularly good, but seem not to be lasting as well as expected.

1997 A slightly larger vintage at ±545-million litres and one of the coolest. Showers during budding and berry-set meant serious problems with downy mildew, while the ongoing cool weather led to the latest harvest on record. Red: Altogether more slender and supple, rather than light. Impatient winemakers who harvested too early made unbalanced wines with harsh, green tannins. The best wines show pristine fruit and smooth tannins; they are beautifully elegant and should be approaching drinkability. White: Some excellent, stylish wines with beautiful aromas, showing refinement and balance; yet only the best have kept well.

1996 A large crop, ±575-million litres, which ripened in near-perfect conditions until late January when a series of showers spoiled the harvest. The continuing damp weather was perfect for the development of botrytis, a negative factor for reds but sublime for sweet whites. Red: Generally poorly balanced and awkward, lacking fruit and concentration. Without doubt a lesser vintage, yet still produced some stars. Not for keeping. White: Wines lack concentration, most already consumed. An important year for botrytis, some excellent NLHs now reaching maturity.

Older vintages

1995 Very dry and hot; ripe, big but concentrated reds with good maturation potential. **1994** Hottest, driest vintage in decades; variable quality, though new-clone cabernets and early ripening reds fared well. **1993** Year without serious mishaps; some excellent sauvignons; above-average reds. **1992** Coolish year favouring whites, especially sauvignon; reds also very good to outstanding; first- rate pinotage vintage **1991** Dry, warm to hot year, favouring early to mid-season ripeners; some exceptionally concentrated, long- lasting reds. **1990** Uneven year, alternatively cool and warm; average year for whites; middling reds with some very characterful examples; good cabernets. The **1980**s: as a rough rule, the even years were usually more favourable for reds (82, 84, 86); the uneven years, marginally cooler, favoured whites, but uneven 'white' years 87 and especially 89 produced some remarkable reds. The **1970**s: again, even years generally favoured reds. The best of the 70s was undoubtedly 74; but it's rare to find any that have hung in. The **1960**s and earlier vintages of only academic interest now, though some reds have aged astonishingly well. For real excitement, rewind to the **1790**s: a recently-broached dessert from 1791 still stunning! (see Klein Constantia).

SA wine styles

Blanc de blancs White wine made from white grapes only; also used for champagne and **methode cap classique**.

Blanc fumé or **fumé blanc** Dry white made from sauvignon blanc, not necessarily finished in wood (nor smoked, smoky).

Blanc de noir A pink wine (shades range from off-white through peach to pink) made from red grapes.

Brut See **sugar or sweetness**, **sparkling wine**.
Cap classique See **methode cap classique**.
Carbonated See **sparkling wine**.
Cultivar Grape variety (a contraction of 'cultivated variety').
Cuvee French term for the blend of a wine.
Demi-sec See **sugar or sweetness**.
Dessert wine A sweet wine, often to accompany the dessert but sometimes pleasurably prior, as in Sauternes/Barsac/Jurancon- style sweets with foie gras.
Dry to sweet See **sugar or sweetness**.
Fortified wines Increased in alcoholic strength by the addition of spirits, in SA to 15% or more alcohol by volume.
Jerepiko or **jeripigo** A red or white wine, produced without fermentation; grape juice is fortified with grape spirit, thereby preventing fermentation; very sweet, with considerable unfermented grape flavours.
Late Harvest Sweet wine made from late harvested and therefore sweeter grapes. See **sugar or sweetness**.
Methode cap classique (MCC) See **sparkling wine**.
Noble Late Harvest (NLH) Sweet dessert wine exhibiting a noble rot (botrytis) character, from grapes infected by the botrytis cinerea fungus. This mould, in warm, misty autumn weather, attacks the skins of ripe grapes, causing much of the juice to evaporate. As the berries wither, their sweetness and flavour become powerfully concentrated. These nobly-rotten grapes yield some stunning dessert wines. SA law dictates that grapes for NLH must be harvested at a minimum of 28° Balling and residual sugar must exceed 50 g/ℓ.
Nouveau Term originated in Beaujolais for fruity young and light red, usually from gamay and made by the carbonic maceration method. Bottled a few weeks after vintage to capture youthful, fresh flavour of fruit and yeasty fermentation.
Premier grand cru Unlike in France, not an officially recognised rating in SA – usually an austerely dry white.
Perlant, perlé, pétillant Lightly sparkling, carbonated wine.
Port Fortified dessert with improving quality record in Cape since late 1980s, partly through efforts of SA Port Producers' Association which recommends use of word 'Cape' to identify the local product. Following are SAPPA-defined styles: **Cape White**: non-muscat grapes, wood aged min 6 mths, any size vessel; **Cape Ruby**: blended, fruity, components aged min 6 mths, up to 3 years depending on size of vessel. Average age min 1 year. **Cape Vintage**: fruit of one harvest; dark, full-bodied, vat- aged (any size); **Cape Vintage Reserve**: fruit of one harvest in year of "recognised quality". Preferably aged min 1 year, vats of any size, sold only in glass; **Cape Late Bottled Vintage** (LBV): fruit of single "year of quality", dark, full-bodied, slightly tawny colour, aged 3-6 years (of which min 2 years in oak); **Cape Tawny**: wood-matured, amber-orange (tawny) colour, smooth, slightly nutty taste (white grapes not permitted); **Cape Dated Tawny**: single-vintage tawny.
Residual sugar See **sugar or sweetness**.
Rosé Pink wine, made from red or a blend of red and white grapes. The red grape skins are removed before the wine takes up too much colouring.
Sparkling wine Bubbly, or 'champagne', usually white but sometimes rosé and even red, given its effervescence by carbon dioxide – allowed to escape in the normal winemaking process. **Champagne** is sparkling wine that undergoes its second fermentation in the bottle. Under an agreement with France, SA does not use the term 'champagne', which properly is a geographic appellation describing the sparkling wines from the Champagne

area. Instead, **methode cap classique** (MCC) is the SA term to describe sparkling wines made by the classic methode champenoise. **Charmat** undergoes its second, bubble-forming fermentation in a tank and is bottled under pressure. **Carbonated** sparklers are made by the injection of carbon dioxide bubbles (as in fizzy soft drinks). See also **sugar or sweetness**.

Special Late Harvest (SLH) SA designation for a dessert style. Grapes must be harvested at a minimum of 22° Balling sugar (quite normal for even dry wines) and have a maximum of 50 g/ℓ of residual sugar.

Stein Semi-sweet white wine, usually a blend and often confused with steen, a grape variety (chenin blanc), though most steins are made partly from steen grapes.

Sugar or sweetness In still wines: extra-dry or bone-dry are wines below 2,5 g/ℓ in residual sugar content, undetectable to the taster. A wine legally is dry up to 4 g/ℓ. Taste buds will begin picking up a slight sweetness, or softness, in a wine – depending on its acidity – at about 5-6 g/ℓ, when it is still off-dry. But by about 8-9 g/ℓ a definite sweetness can usually be noticed. However, an acidity of 8-9 g/ℓ can render a sweet wine fairly crisp even with a sugar content of 20 g/ℓ plus. Official sweetness levels in SA wine are:

Still wines	Sugar (g/ℓ)	Sparkling wines	Sugar (g/ℓ)
Extra dry	≤ 2,5	Extra dry/brut	≤ 15
Dry	≤ 4	Dry/sec	15-35
Semi-dry	4-12	Semi-sweet/demi-sec	35-50
Semi-sweet	4-30	Sweet/doux	> 50
Late Harvest	20-30		
Special Late Harvest (SLH)[1]	≤ 50		
Natural Sweet (or Sweet Natural)	> 30		
Noble Late Harvest (NLH)[2]	> 50		
Naturally dried grape wine (straw wine)[3]	> 30		

[1] Grapes must be harvested at 22° Balling or more, i.e. ripe.
[2] Must have at least 30 g/ℓ sugar-free extract, grapes harvested at 28° Balling or more.
[3] Potential alcohol must be at least 16% by volume.

Varietal wine From single variety of grape. In SA must consist of 75% or more of the stated grape – but 85% or more if exported.

Vintage In SA primarily used to denote year of harvest. Not a substantive quality classification (a 'vintage' port in Europe means one from an officially declared great port grape year).

Winetasting terms

Short of a ready description? Here are a few frequently used words, phrases and explanations that may be helpful. See also Winemaking terms; SA wine styles.

Accessible, approachable Flavours and feel of the wine are harmonious, easily recognised; it is ready to drink.

Aftertaste The lingering flavours and impressions of a wine; its persistence – the longer, the better.

Alcoholic 'Hot' or, in excess, burning character caused by imbalanced or excessive alcohol. Also simply spiritous.

Astringent Mouth-puckering sensation in the mouth, associated with high tannin (and sometimes acid); also bitter, sharp.

Aroma Smells in the bouquet, or nose, especially the odours associated with the grape, rather than the winemaking process.

Attack First sensations on palate/nose – pungent, aggressive, quiet, etc.

Attractive Having some (modest) positive attributes; pleasant.

Austere Usually meaning unyielding, sometimes harsh.

Backbone The wine's well formed, firm, not flabby or insipid.

Baked 'Hot', earthy quality. Usually from scorched/shrivelled grapes which have been exposed too long to the sun, or from too warm a barrel fermentation, especially in some whites.

Balance Desirable attribute. The wine's chief constituents – alcohol, acid, tannin, fruit and wood (where used) – are in harmony.

Bead Bubbles in sparkling wine; a fine, long-lasting bead is the most desirable. See also **mousse**.

Big Expansive in the mouth, weighty, full-bodied, as a result of high alcohol or fruit concentration.

Bite or **grip** Imparted by tannins and acids (and alcohol in fortified wines); important in young wines designed for ageing. If overdone can impart undesirable bitterness, harshness or spirity 'glow'.

Bitter Sensation perceived mainly on the back of the tongue, and in the finish of the wine. Usually unpleasant, though an accepted, if not immediately admired character of certain Italian wines. Sometimes more positively associated with the taste of a specific fruit or nut, such as cherry-kernel or almond.

Body Fullness on the palate.

Botrytis/ed Exhibits a noble rot/botrytis character, from grapes infected by the *Botrytis cinerea* fungus.

Bottle age Negative or positive, depending on context. Positively describes development of aromas/flavours (i.e. complexity) as wine moves from youth to maturity. Much prized attribute in fine whites and reds. Negatively, bottle-age results in a wine with stale, empty or even off odours.

Buttery Flavour and texture associated with barrel-fermented white wines, especially chardonnays; rich, creamy smoothness.

Charming Usually used in the context of lighter, simpler wines. Sometimes synonymous with 'sweet' (both as in 'sugary' and 'dear').

Classic Showing characteristics of the finest examples of European classics of bordeaux, burgundy etc; usually associated with balance, elegance, subtlety.

Coarse Rough, unbalanced tannins, acid, alcohol or oak.

Complexity Strong recommendation. A complex wine has several layers of flavour, usually developing with age/maturation. See bottle age.

Concentration See intensity.

Confected Over-elaborately constructed, artificial, forced; also overly sweet.

Corked Wine is faulty; its flavours have been tainted by yeast, fungal or bacterial infections from the cork. It smells of damp, mouldy bark in its worst stages – but sometimes it's barely detectable. In a restaurant, a corked wine should be rejected and returned immediately; producers are honour-bound to replace corked wine.

Creamy Not literally creamy, of course; more a silky, buttery feel and texture.

Crisp Refers to acidity. Positively, means fresh, clean; negatively, too tart, sharp.

Deep and depth Having many layers; intense; also descriptive of a serious wine.

Dense Well-padded texture, flavour-packed.

Deposits (also sediment or crust) Tasteless and harmless tartrates, acid crystals or tannin in older red wines. Evidence that wine has not been harshly fined, filtered or cold-stabilised.

Dried out Bereft of fruit, harder constituents remaining; tired.

Earthy Usually positive, wine showing its origins from soil, minerally, damp leaves, mushrooms etc.

Easy Undemanding (and hopefully inexpensive).

Elegant Stylish, refined, 'classic'.

Esters Scents and smells, usually generated by alcohols and acids in wine. A wine can be described as 'estery' when these characteristics are prominent.

Extract An indication of the 'substance' of a wine, expressed as sugar-free or total extract (which would include some sugars). 18 g/ℓ would be low, light; anything much above 23 g/ℓ in whites is significant; the corresponding threshold for reds is around 30 g/ℓ.

Fat Big, full, ample in the mouth.

Finesse Graceful, polished. Nothing excessive.

Finish The residual sensations – tastes and textures – after swallowing. Should be pleasant (crisp, lively) and enduring, not short, dull or flat. See also **length**.

Firm Compact, has good **backbone**.

Flabby Usually, lacking **backbone**, especially acid.

Flat Characterless, unexciting, lacking acid. Or bubbly which has lost its fizz.

Fleshy Very positive, meaning a wine is well fleshed out with texture and grape flavours.

Flowery Floral, flower-like (i.e. the smell of rose, honeysuckle, jasmine etc). Distinct from **fruity** (i.e. smell/taste of papaya, cantaloupe, grape! etc)

Forward rather than shy; advancing in age too; mature.

Fresh Lively, youthful, invigorating. Closely related to the amount of acid in the wine and absence of oxidative character: a big, intensely sweet dessert without a backbone of acidity will taste flat and sickly; enough acid and the taste is fresh and uncloying.

Fruity See **floral.**

Full High in alcohol and extract.

Gamey Overripe, decadent; not universally unattractive.

Gravel/ly With suggestions of minerally, earthy quality; also firm texture.

Green Usually unripe, sour; sometimes simply youthful.

Grip Often almost literally gripping, firm on palate, in finish. Acid, tannin, alcohol are contributors.

Heady Usually refers to the smell of a wine. High in alcohol; intense, high-toned.

Herbaceous Grassy, hay-like, heathery, can also indicate under-ripeness.

Hollow Lacking substance, flavours.

Honey or **honeyed** Sometimes literally a honey/beeswax taste or flavour; a sign of developing maturity in some varieties or more generally a sign of bottle age.

Hot Burning sensation of alcohol in finish.

Intensity No flab, plenty of driving flavour; also deep colour.

Lean Thin, mean, lacking charm of ample fruit; also, more positively, compact, sinewy.

Lees/leesy Taste-imparting dead yeast cells (with grape skins and other solid matter) remaining with wine in tank/barrel (or bottle in the case of methode champenoise sparkling wines) after fermentation. The longer the wine is 'on its lees' (sur lie) the more richness and flavour it should absorb.

Light/lite Officially wines under 10% alcohol, also light in body (and often short on taste); a health-conscious trend in both reds and whites.

Lively Bouncy, fresh flavours.

Long or **length** Enduring; wine's flavours reverberate in the palate long after swallowing.

Maderised Wine smells/tastes oxidised and flat; colour is often brownish. Overmature.

Meaty Sometimes suggesting a general savouriness; but also literally the aroma of meat – raw, smoked etc. Often applied to merlot, shiraz, sometimes cabernet.

Mousse Fizz in sparkling wines; usually refers also to quality, size and effervescence of the bubbles. See also **bead**.

Mouthfeel, **mouthfilling** Texture, feel; racy, crispness (fine with appropriate dishes) or generous, supple, smooth.

Neutral What it says, neither here nor there.

New world Generally implies accessible, bold, often extrovert (in terms of fruit and use of oak). **Old world** embraces terms like subtle, complex, less oaky, more varied and generally more vinous (than fruity). See also **classic**.

Oaky Having exaggerated oak aromas/flavours (vanilla, spice, char, woodsmoke etc). Young wines can outgrow oakiness, older ones less readily. Oak balanced by fruit in young wines may lessen with age, but over-oaked young wines (where fruit is not in balance) will become over-oaked old wines.

Palate Combination of flavour, taste and texture of a wine.

Pebbly See gravelly.

Perfumed or **scented** Strong fragrances (fruity, flowery, animal etc)

Plump Well fleshed in a charming, cherubic way.

Porty Heavy, over-ripe, stewed; a negative in unfortified wine.

Rich Flavourful, intense, generous. Not necessarily sweet.

Robust Strapping, full bodied (but not aggressive).

Rough Bull-in-a-china-shop wine, or throat sand-papering quality.

Round Well balanced, without gawkiness or jagged edges.

Sharp or **tart** All about acid, usually unbalanced. But occasionally sharpish, fresh wine is right for the occasion.

Short or **quick** Insubstantial wine, leaving little impression.

Simple One-dimensional or no flavour excitement.

Stalky Unripe, bitter, stemmy.

Stewed Over-ripe, cooked, soft, soggy fruit.

Structure Vague word, usually refers to the wine's make up (acid, tannin, alcohol) in relation to its ageing ability; if a wine is deemed to have 'the structure to age' it suggests these principal preservatives are in place.

Stylish Classy, distinguished; also voguish.

Supple Very desirable (not necessarily subtle), yielding, refined texture and flavours. See also **mouthfeel**.

Tannic Tannins are prominent in the wine, imparting, positively, a mouth-puckering, grippy, tangy quality; negatively, a harsh, unyielding character.

Tension Racy, nervous fruity-acid play on the palate. Often associated with German riesling.

Terpene(s)/terpenoid Strong, floral compounds influencing the aromas of especially riesling, gewürztraminer and the muscats; with bottle-age, terpenes often develop a pungent resinous oiliness.

Texture Tactile 'feel' in the mouth: hard, acidic, coarse and alcoholic; or, smooth, velvety, 'warm'.

Toasty Often used for barrel-fermented and aged wines showing a pleasant biscuity, charry character.

Vegetal Grassy, leafy, herby – in contrast to fruity, flowery, oaky. Overdone, a no- no.

Yeasty Warm bread or bakery smells, often evident in barrel-fermented whites and methode champenoise sparkling wines, where yeasts stay in contact with the wine after fermentation.

Winemaking terms

A few brief reference explanations. See also Winetasting terms, SA wine styles.

Acid and **acidity** The fresh – or, in excess, sharp or tart – taste of wine. Too little acid and the wine tastes dull and flat. In South Africa, winemakers are permitted to adjust acidity, either by adding acid – at any stage before bottling – or by lowering the acid level with the use of calcium carbonate. See also **volatile acid** and **malolactic**.

Alcohol An essential component of wine, providing fullness, richness and, at higher levels, sometimes an impression of sweetness. Also a preservative, helping keep wines in good condition. Produced by yeasts fermenting the sugars in the grape. Measured by volume of the total liquid. Most unfortified table wines in SA vary between 11% and 14% by vol; fortifieds range from about 16% to 21%.

Barrels (barrel-aged; barrel-fermented) Wines are transferred into barrels to age, pick up oaky flavours, etc. When must or fermenting must is put into barrels, the resulting wine is called barrel-fermented. A barrel or cask is generally a 225-500 ℓ oak container; barrique is a French word for a 225 ℓ barrel; a pipe, adapted from the Portuguese *pipa*, usually indicates a vessel of 530-630 ℓ; vat is a term generally used for larger (2 000-5 000 ℓ) wooden vessels.

Batonnage See **lees**.

Blend A wine made from two or more different grape varieties, vintages, vineyards or containers. Some of the world's finest wines are blends.

Carbonic maceration or **maceration carbonique** Method of fermenting wine without crushing grapes first. Whole clusters with stalks, etc are put into closed vat; **fermentation** occurs within the grape berries which then burst.

Chaptalisation Originally French term for the addition of sugar to grape must to raise the alcohol of a wine. Not permitted in South Africa. Legal in only parts of France, Germany, where they are not usually permitted to make the **acid** adjustments allowed in South Africa. Winemakers in both hemispheres bend the rules.

Charmat method of making sparkling wine in a sealed tank (cuvee close) under pressure. Easier, cheaper than **methode champenoise** manner of creating bubbles.

Cold ferment Cold is a relative term; applied to fermentation of mainly white wines in temperature-controlled tanks, it refers to a temperature around usually 13-16 °C. The benefits, especially important in a country such as South Africa, where grapes may come into a cellar anything up to 30 °C, include conserving the primary fruit aromas and ensuring fermentation is carried out steadily and thoroughly.

Cold soak or cold maceration. Red winemaking method carried out prior to alcoholic **fermentation**. Skins and juice of grapes are held, usually for a few days, at a sufficiently cool temperature to prevent fermentation. The theory is that it extracts more favourable colour and aromas than after fermentation.

Cold stabilisation Keeping a wine at about –4°C for a week or more to precipitate tartaric **acid** and "clean up" the wine, preventing later formation of (harmless) tartrate crystals in bottle. Some winemakers believe this process damages flavour and prefer to avoid it.

Dosage The sugar added to **methode champenoise** or MCC after the second **fermentation**.

Fermentation The conversion of sugar in grapes into alcohol and carbon dioxide, a function of enzymes secreted by **yeasts**. Wild yeasts occur in vineyards and wineries, but in modern Cape winemaking cultured yeasts are normally added to secure the process. Beyond about 15% of alcohol, yeasts are overwhelmed and fermentation ceases, although it usually is stopped (for instance by cooling, **filtration** or the addition of alcohol) before this stage. See also **malolactic**.

Filtration Removes last impurities including **yeast** cells. Done excessively, can thin a wine. Some traditionalists bottle without **cold-** or **protein stabilisation** or filtration.

Fining and **protein stabilisation** Not to be confused with **filtration**. Fining is ridding wine of suspended particles by adding substances that attract and draw the particles from the wine.

Free run After grapes have been de-stalked and crushed, juice runs freely (without pressing). This juice is the cleanest, and some believe the purest, making fruitier wines.

Glycerol Minor product of alcoholic **fermentation**. Glycerol – the name derives from the Greek for sweet – has an apparent sweetening effect on even dry wines and also gives them a viscous, mouth-filling character.

Lees Spent **yeast** cells and other matter which collect at the bottom of any container in winemaking. Yeast autolysis, or decomposition, can impart richness and flavour to a wine, sometimes referred to as leesy. Lees stirring or batonnage involves mixing the bed of lees in a barrel or tank through the wine, which is said to be **sur lie**; it is employed primarily on barrel-fermented white wines. The main effects of mixing lees and wine are to prevent off-odours (mainly the rotten eggs smell of hydrogen sulphide) developing from lack of oxygen, to limit the amount of wood **tannin** and flavour extracted, and to increase flavour.

Malolactic fermentation (malo) Occurs when bacteria convert malic into lactic **acids**. This reduces the acidity of a wine, a normal and healthy process, especially in reds – provided, of course, it occurs before bottling.

Maturation Ageing properties are closely related to **tannin** and fixed **acid** content of a wine. A relatively full red wine with tannin has lasting power. With age, it will often develop complexity, subtlety and smooth mellowness. Lighter wines with lower tannins are drinkable sooner but probably will not reach the same level of complexity. A number of Cape whites, especially chardonnays and rieslings, now mature well over several years, but most are best drunk in their fruity youth, up to 18 months.

Methode champenoise Classic method of making champagne by inducing secondary **fermentation** in the bottle and producing fine bubbles. Due to French restrictions on terminology, Cape sparkling wines made in this way are called methode cap classique (MCC).

Micro-oxygenation Relatively new (1990) vinification technique enabling introduction of precise, controlled doses of oxygen to must/wine. Advocates claim softer **tannin**, more stable colours among the advantages.

Oak chips of several kind of *quercus*, either placed in used **barrels** or stainless steel tanks, are used increasingly in South Africa, as are oak staves. Frowned on by some purists still, the 'additives' approximate those of a new barrel, far cheaper, more easily handled.

Oak-matured See barrels.

Organic viticulture/winemaking Increasingly popular alternative to 'conventional' or 'industrialised' winegrowing, emphasising natural and sustainable farming methods and cellar techniques.

Oxidation Change (usually for the worse) due to exposure to air, in whites often producing dark yellow or yellowish colour (called maderisation), altering, 'ageing' the taste. Controlled aeration is used to introduce acceptable and desirable development in wine.

pH A chemical notation, used in winemaking and evaluation. The pH of a wine is its effective, active **acidity** – not in volume but by strength or degree. The reading provides a guide to a wine's keepability. The optimum pH in a wine is somewhere between 3,1 and 3,4 – which significantly improves a wine's protection from bacterial spoilage, so permitting it to mature and develop if properly stored.

Racking Drawing or pumping wine off from one cask or tank to another, to leave behind the deposit or **lees**.

Reductive Wine in an unevolved, unoxidised state is said to be 'reductive'; usually with a tight, sometimes unyielding character. The absence of air (in a bottled wine) or the presence of substantial (anti-oxidant) sulphur dioxide levels, will inhibit both **oxidation** and reduction processes, which are linked and complementary.

Skin contact After crushing and de-stemming, white grapes may be left for a period with the juice, remaining in contact with skins (before being moved into the press, from which the grape juice is squeezed). A number of winemakers believe the colours and flavours in and under the grape skins should be maximised in this way; others believe extended (or any) contact can lead to coarseness, even bitterness.

Sur lie See **lees**.

Tannin Vital preservative in wine, which derives from the grape skins. Necessary for a red wine's longevity. A young wine's raw tannin can give it a harshness, but no red wine matures into a great one without tannin, which itself undergoes change, combines with other substances and mellows. Tannin leaves a mouth-puckering dryness about the gums, gives 'grip' to a wine. A wooded wine will also contain wood tannin. Various types or qualities of tannin are increasingly commented on.

Tartrates Harmless crystals formed by tartaric **acid** precipitating in non-**cold-stabilised** wine. Because of lack of public acceptance, usually avoided through cold stabilisation.

Unfiltered See **filtration**.

Volatile acid (VA) That part of the **acidity** which can become volatile. A high reading indicates a wine is prone to spoilage. Recognised at high levels by a sharp, 'hot', vinegary smell. In South Africa, most wines must by law be below 1,2 g/ℓ of VA; in practice, the majority are well below 1 g/ℓ

Whole-bunch pressing or **cluster pressing** Some Cape cellars use this age-old process of placing whole bunches directly in the press and gently squeezing. The more usual method is to de-stem and crush the grapes before pressing. Whole bunch pressing is said to yield fresher, cleaner must, and wine lower in polyphenols, which, in excess, tend to age wines faster and render them coarser.

Wood-fermented/matured See barrels.

Yeasts Micro-organisms that secrete enzymes which convert or ferment sugar into alcohol. Naturally present in vineyards and on grapes but locally, wild yeasts are usually killed by addition of sulphur, and cultured yeasts are used. The wild yeasts in the Cape were generally thought unsuitable in the past, especially for white musts. Lately, a few growers have begun to experiment with 'wild' fermentations, i.e. using natural vineyard yeasts, for both red and white wines. There have been some excellent results.

SA wine competitions

An increasing number of wine competitions are run by liquor industry bodies, independent companies and, now, individuals, to promote the standard of SA wine. The following are the main national events:

Air France-Preteux Bourgeois Classic Staged by French cork merchant Preteux Bourgeois, with Air France, under the rules of the Office Internationale de la Vigne et du Vin (OIV) to recognise old world-inclined SA wines with ageing potential. International judges.

ABSA Bank/PPA Top Ten Run by the local Pinotage Producers' Association with a major financial institution to set international quality targets for vintners of SA's home-grown variety, pinotage. Local palates.

Chenin Blanc Challenge SA *Wine* and a corporate sponsor annually anoint SA's top chenin. Wooded and unwooded wines are judged by an SA panel in the drier (max 20 g/ℓ sugar) spectrum.

Diners Club Winemaker of the Year A different category is chosen each year for this competition, inaugurated in 1981, whose schedules give local producers enough time to experiment, fine-tune and even plant new vineyards. Local panel with some overseas representation.

Juliet Cullinan Wine Masters Awards New, controversially-named national competition judged by *Cape* Wine Masters (CWMs) – not to be confused with the savants graduating from the antedating international Master of Wine (MW) education programme.

Michelangelo International Inaugurated in 1997 and run under the rules of the OIV, these Gauteng-based selections are judged by a combined international/local panel. Highest accolade is the Grand Medaille d'Or.

SAA Selections Not a competition, but an annual singling-out of wines to fly with South African Airways. A panel of local and overseas judges evaluates entries from across the winelands. Drinkability in flight conditions is an important consideration. The top-scoring red, white, bubbly and 'port' receive the SAA Trophy.

South African Young Wine Show Inaugurated in 1975 to gauge the quality of infant wines prior to finishing and bottling, thereby also allowing recognition to wineries that sell in bulk and would otherwise remain unsung. Local judges rate five categories and 70 classes. The Grand Champion receives the General Smuts Trophy.

Veritas Major competition hosted by the South African National Wine Show Association, recognising top market-ready wines across a range of categories. Double-gold, gold, silver and bronze medals are awarded. Star-performers may affix the Veritas logo to their winning bottles. Local palates with some overseas input.

The Cape's top performers

THE FOLLOWING are the leading South African wines in 1999-2001, as measured by their showing in some of the leading annual local wine awards, as well as this guide. These awards are: Veritas (we indicate only double-gold medallists – score of 17/20 or higher by 5 of the 7 judges); SAA Selections (1st/Business Class Top Ten red and white wines, with SAA Trophy winners – the top-scoring red, white, sparkling and 'port' wines that year – indicated by ✪); and SA *Wine* magazine (only four stars and above indicated). Our own ⁂ ratings also flagged. Results of other local and international competitions are included in the A-Z section under individual producers and brands. Be aware that some wineries do not enter competitions, thus they might not be represented here. Also see section SA wine competitions. Note: this is not a comprehensive list.

	Vintage	Veritas Dbl Gold	SAA	Wine 4-5 Stars	Platter 20 01	Platter 2002
Cabernet Franc						
Avontuur Avon Ridge	99		●			
Bellingham Spitz	96			●		
Blaauwklippen	98		●			
Cabernet Sauvignon						
Agusta	98			●		
Allesverloren	96			●		
Ashwood	99		●			
Avondale	99		●			
Avontuur	99		●	●		
Blue Creek	98			●		
Boekenhoutskloof	99					●
Boekenhoutskloof	98			●	●	
Boland	99	●				
De Heuvel	99			●		
De Trafford	98			●		
Delaire Botmaskop	98	●		●		
Delheim	99	●				
Delheim	97			●		
Devon Hill	00	●				
Devonair	00	●				
Eikendal Reserve	99			●		
Fairview	00		●			
Flagstone	99			●		
Fleur du Cap	97			●		
Fleur du Cap Unfiltered	97			●		
Goede Hoop	97			●		
Graham Beck	99		●			
Grangehurst CWG	98			●		
Havana Hills Du Plessis Reserve	99	●		●		
Hoopenburg	98		●			
Kanu	98	●				
Klein Constantia	97			●		
Kleine Zalze Barrel Matured	99	●				
KWV Cathedral Cellars Paarl	97		●			
Laborie	00	●				
Laborie	98		●			
Landskroon Reserve	98		●			
L'Avenir	97		●	●		
Le Riche	99		●			
Le Riche	98		●			
Le Riche Reserve	99				●	
Longridge	98		●			
Longridge	97		●	●		
Môreson Pinehurst	98		●			
Morgenhof Reserve	98	●		●	●	
Mouton-Excelsior Huguenot Reserve	87		●			
Neil Ellis Reserve	98	●		●		
Saxenburg	97		●			

	Vintage	Veritas Dbl Gold	SAA	Wine 4-5 Stars	Platter 20 01	Platter 2002
Somerbosch	98			●		
Spier IV Spears Reserve	98			●		
Stark	98					●
Stellenbosch Vineyards Genesis	97		●			
Stony Brook Reserve	98			●		
Thelema	98			●		
Thelema	97			●	●	
Thelema	96			●		
Vergelegen	98		●			
Vriesenhof	98			●		
Waterford	98			●		
Wellington Wine Cellar	98	●				
Woolworths Reserve (Villiera)	97			●		
Merlot						
Amani	99			●		
Boschendal	97		●	●		
Buitenverwachting	99	●				
Coppoolse Finlayson Sentinel	00	●				
De Trafford	99			●		
Devon Hill	00	●				
Dieu Donné	99		●	●		
Fleur du Cap Unfiltered	97			●		
Graham Beck	98		●	●		
Hartenberg	96	●		●		
Jacaranda	99			●		
Jordan	99	●				
Kanu	99	●				
Koelenhof	99	●				
Koelenhof	98			●		
Longridge	98		●	●		
Makro Babbling Brook	99			●		
Morgenhof	98		●	●		
Overgaauw	99			●		
Rhebokskloof	98			●		
Ruggeri	00	●				
Saxenburg Private Collection	98			●		
Saxenburg Private Collection	97			●		
Simonsvlei Hercules Paragon	98			●		
Spice Route Flagship	99			●	●	
Spier IV Spears Reserve	98			●		
Thelema	98		●	●		
Thelema Reserve	99					●
Veenwouden	98	●		●		
Veenwouden	97			●		
Vergelegen	98			●		
Vergenoegd	98			●		
Villiera Reserve	98			●		

	Vintage	Veritas Dbl Gold	SAA	Wine 4-5 Stars	Platter 20 01	Platter 2002
Vlottenburg	99			●		
Woolworths Terroir (Wildekrans)	97			●		
Pinotage						
Ashanti	99		●			
Avontuur	99		●	●		
Bellingham Spitz	99		●			
Bellingham Spitz	98		●			
Bergsig	99			●		
Blaauwklippen	98			●		
Bouwland	98		●			
Cape Levant	96		●			
Clos Malverne	99					
Darling Cellars Groenekloof	98		●	●		
Devon Hill	99		●			
Diemersdal	98		●	●		
Douglas Green	98		●			
Fairview Primo	00					●
Graham Beck	98		●	●		
Groene Cloof	98			●		
Groene Cloof	99			●		
Groot Constantia	99			●		
Hidden Valley	97			●		
JP Bredell	98			●		
Kaapzicht	98			●		
Kaapzicht Reserve	97			●		
Kaapzicht Steytler	99			●		
Kaapzicht Steytler	98			●		
Kanonkop	99			●		
Kanonkop	98		●	●		
Kanonkop	97		●	●		
Kanonkop CWG	99			●		
KWV Cathedral Cellar	98		●			
Laibach	97			●		
Lanzerac	98		●			
L'Avenir	00	●				
L'Avenir	99	●	●	●		
L'Avenir	97			●		
Longridge	98			●		
Mont Rochelle	99			●		
Môreson	99			●		
Morgenhof	99			●		
Neethlingshof Lord Neethling	98			●		
Neethlingshof Lord Neethling	97			●		
Nietvoorbij	99			●		
Rijk's Private Cellar	00	●				
Savanha Reserve	98			●		
Simonsig Red Hill	99			●		
Simonsig Red Hill	97		●			
Slaley Broken Stone	00			●		

	Vintage	Veritas Dbl Gold	SAA	Wine 4-5 Stars	Platter 20 01	Platter 2002
Slaley Broken Stone	98			●		
Somerbosch Reserve	99			●		
Southern Right	97			●		
Spice Route Flagship	98			●		
Stellenzicht	98			●		
Stonewall	00			●		
Stony Brook	00	●				
Stony Brook	98			●		
Thelema	98			●		
Tukulu	00	●				
Uiterwyk Top of the Hill	00	●				
Uiterwyk Top of the Hill	97	●		●		
Villiera	97			●		
Vinfruco Rock Ridge	99		●			
Zevenwacht	97			●		
Pinot Noir						
Bouchard Finlayson Galpin Peak	97		●			
De Trafford	99			●		
Hamilton Russell Vineyards	00	●				
Hamilton Russell Vineyards	99	●				
Hamilton Russell Vineyards	98			●		
Ruby Cabernet						
Goudini Ruby Cabernet Reserve	99	●				
Shiraz						
Asara Theresa	97			●		
Bartho Eksteen	00	●		●		
Boekenhoutskloof	97			●		
Boland	00			●		
Bolpaas Reserve	99		●			
Boschendal	97			●		
Coleraine	99			●		
Coppoolse Finlayson	98			●		
Darling Cellars 'DC'	99			●		
De Trafford	98			●		
Delheim	98			●		
Delheim Vera Cruz	98					●
Fairview Cyril Back	98		●			
Gilga	00					●
Gilga	98			●		
Graham Beck	98		●			
Graham Beck Coastal	99		●	●		
Graham Beck The Ridge	98		●	●		
Groot Constantia	99		●	●		
Havana Hill Du Plessis Reserve	00	●				
Havana Hill Du Plessis Reserve	99	●		●		
JP Bredell	99			●		
Kanu Limited Release	98			●		

	Vintage	Veritas Dbl Gold	SAA	Wine 4-5 Stars	Platter 2001	Platter 2002
Kevin Arnold	99		●			
Klein Constantia	97			●		
KWV Cathedral Cellar	98		●			
KWV Cathedral Cellar	97		●			
Landskroon	98			●		
Lievland	98			●		
Longridge Bay View	98		●			
Muratie	00					●
Neil Ellis	99		✪			
Neil Ellis	98		✪			
Neil Ellis Reserve	99	●				
Neil Ellis Stellenbosch	99			●		
Nitida	98			●		
Plaisir de Merle	98			●		
Rickety Bridge	99			●		
Rust en Vrede	98			●		
Saxenburg Select	98				●	
Simonsig Merindol	98			●		
Simonsig Merindol	97			●		
Slaley	00			●		
Slaley	98			●		
Spice Route Flagship Syrah	99			●		
Spice Route Flagship Syrah	98			●		
Stellenzicht Syrah	99			●		
Stellenzicht Syrah	98			●		
Stellenzicht Syrah	97		●	●		
Swartland	99			●		
Vergelegen	99		●	●		
Vergenoegd	98			●		
Vergenoegd	97			●		
Red Blends						
Avondale Dry Red	99	●				
Avontuur Baccarat	99			●		
Bellevue Tumara	99			●		
Beyerskloof	98	●		●		
Beyerskloof	97			●		
Beyerskloof	99	●				
Blaauwklippen Barouche	00	●				
Boschkloof Reserve Cabernet Sauvignon-Merlot	98	●				
Bouwland Cabernet-Merlot	98		●			
Cederberg Cederberger	98			●		
Clos Malverne Auret	98					●
Clos Malverne Auret	97			●		
Clos Malverne Cabernet-Merlot	98		●			
Clos Malverne Cabernet-Pinotage	98			●		
Clos Malverne Devonet	97			●		
Cordoba Crescendo	97			●		
De Toren Fusion V	99			●		
Delaire Cabernet-Merlot	99			●		

	Vintage	Veritas Dbl Gold	SAA	Wine 4-5 Stars	Platter 20 01	Platter 2002
Delaire Cabernet-Merlot	98		●			
Devon Hill Bluebird	00	●				
Fairview Shiraz-Mourvèdre	98			●		
Flagstone Longitude	00	●				
Flagstone Strata Series George's Blend	00	●				
Glen Carlou Grand Classique	96		●	●		
Grangehurst Cabernet-Merlot	98			●		
Havana Hills Du Plessis Reserve	00					●
Jordan Chameleon Cabernet-Merlot	98	●				
Jordan Cobblers Hill Reserve	98			●		
Kaapzicht Steytler Vision	00	●				
Kanonkop Paul Sauer	98	●		●		●
Kanonkop Paul Sauer	97	●				
Kanonkop Paul Sauer	96			●		
Kanu Keystone	99	●		●		
Kanu Red	98			●		
Klein Gustrouw Cabernet-Merlot	98			●		
Klein Gustrouw Cabernet-Merlot	97			●		
KWV Cathedral Cellar Triptych	97		●	●		
Lanzerac Classic	00	●				
L'Avenir L'Ami Simon	97			●		
Le Bonheur Prima	96			●		
Meerlust Rubicon	95		●	●		
Meinert Cabernet-Merlot	97			●		
Morgenhof Cabernet-Cabernet Franc	00			●		
Morgenhof Merlot-Malbec	99			●		
Morgenhof Première Sélection	97			●		
Morgenhof Première Sélection	96			●		
Nitida Calligraphy	99			●		
Overgaauw Tria Corda	98			●		
Rozendal	98			●		
Ruitersvlei Cabernet-Merlot	99			●		
Rust en Vrede Estate Wine	98			●		●
Rust en Vrede Estate Wine	97	●				
Rust en Vrede Estate Wine	96	●		●		
Rust en Vrede Estate Wine	95	●				
Rustenberg Brampton Cabernet-Merlot	99		●			
Rustenberg John X Merriman	99			●		
Rustenberg Stellenbosch	96		●			
Simonsig Frans Malan Reserve	97		●			
Simonsig Tiara	98			●		
Slaley Cabernet-Shiraz	98			●		
Spice Route Cabernet-Merlot	98			●		
Stonewall Ruber	99			●		
Stony Brook Reserve	00			●		
Uiterwyk Estate Wine	97			●		
Uitkyk Cabernet-Shiraz	96		●			

	Vintage	Veritas Dbl Gold	SAA	Wine 4-5 Stars	Platter 20 01	Platter 2002
Veenwouden Classic	99			●		
Veenwouden Classic	98	●		●	●	
Veenwouden Classic	96			●		
Veenwouden Vivat Bacchus	99	●		●		
Vergelegen	98		●	●	●	
Vergelegen Cabernet Franc-Merlot	99			●		
Vergelegen Estate Wine	99					●
Vergelegen Mill Race Red	99		●	●		
Vergelegen Mill Race Red	98		●			
Villiera Merlot-Pinotage	99			●		
Woolworths Cabernet-Merlot (Neil Ellis)	99			●		
Yonder Hill iNanda	98			●		
Zevenwacht Cabernet-Merlot	96			●		
Chardonnay						
Agusta	98			●		
Agusta Haute Provence Reserve	98			●		
Amani	99			●		
Amani	98			●		
Asara	99		●			
Avontuur Avon Ridge	99			●		
Avontuur Reserve	99			●	●	
Boschendal Reserve	98		●			
Cathedral Cellar	00	●				
Constantia Uitsig Reserve	97			●		
Constantia Uitsig Reserve	00			●		
Constantia Uitsig Reserve	98		●			
Danie de Wet Limestone Hill	00	●				
De Wetshof D'Honneur	99	●				
De Wetshof Finesse	98		●			
Delaire	99		●			
Dellrust	99			●		
Eikendal	98		●	●		
Fairview Akkerbos	00			●		
Fort Simon	99		●			
Glen Carlou	98		●	●		
Goedgeloof Kanu	98		●	●		
Graham Beck Lonehill	99		●			
Groote Post	99			●		
Hartenberg	98		●			
Jordan	00			●		
Jordan	99		●			
Jordan	98		●			
Kanu	00			●		
Kanu	98			●		
L'Avenir	99			●		
Linton Park	99			●		
Longridge	98			●		
L'Ormarins	98		●			
Louisvale	99		●			

	Vintage	Veritas Dbl Gold	SAA	Wine 4-5 Stars	Platter 20 01	Platter 2002
Mont Rochelle Oak Matured	99		●	●		
Mulderbosch (wooded)	99			●		
Mulderbosch (wooded)	98			●		
Neil Ellis Elgin	99	●				
Nitida	98			●		
Oak Village Barrel Selection	99	●				
Paul Cluver	98		●			
Seidelberg	99	●				
Slaley	99	●				
Spier	00			●		
Stellenryck	99			●		
Stellenzicht	98		●			
Uitkyk Reserve	99		●			
Vergelegen	99		●	●		
Vergelegen	98		●			
Vergelegen Reserve	99	●		●		
Vergelegen Reserve	97		●	●		
Vinfruco Rock Ridge	01	●				
Warwick	99		●			
Chenin Blanc						
Asara	99		●			
Blue White	97			●		
Boland	01	●				
Boschendal	00		●	●		
Cederberg	00	●				
Kanu Limited Release Wooded	00			●		
Kanu Limited Release Wooded	99			●		
Kleine Zalze Barrel Fermented	98		●			
Longridge Bay View	99			●		
Morgenhof	98		●			
Robusto	00			●		
Seidelberg	01	●				
Simonsig	01	●				
Spice Route	99			●		
Villiera	01	●				
Villiera	99		●			
Gewürztraminer						
Nederburg Gewürztraminer	97		●			
Villiera Gewürztraminer	99		●			
Zevenwacht	99		●			
Pinot Blanc						
Nederburg Reserve	98		●			
Riesling						
Rhebokskloof	97		●			
Simonsig	98		●			
Villiera	99		●			
Weltevrede	98		●			

	Vintage	Veritas Dbl Gold	SAA	Wine 4-5 Stars	Platter 20 01	Platter 2002
Sauvignon Blanc						
Asara	99		●			
Avontuur	00		●			
Backsberg	99		●			
Bartho Eksteen	01			●		
Bon Courage	00		●			
Cape Point	00			●		
Darling Cellars 'DC'	00			●		
Durbanville Hills	99	●				
Excelsior	00		●			
Fairview	00		●			
Groote Post	99			●		
Jordan	99			●		
Jordan Blanc Fumé	98		●			
Ken Forrester	00		●			
Klein Constantia	97		●			
Klein Constantia	99		●			
L'Avenir	99		●			
Long Mountain	00			●		
Neil Ellis Elgin	99		●			
Neil Ellis Groenekloof	00		●			
Neil Ellis Groenekloof	99			●		
Nitida	00		●			
Rickety Bridge	00			●		
Rijk's Private Cellar	00	●		●		
Robertson Wide River Reserve	00			●		
Simonsig	00		●			
Simonsig Vin Fumé	99		●			
Spier IV Spears	99		●			
Springfield Life from Stone	99		●			
Steenberg Reserve	01	●				
Steenberg Reserve	99		✪	●		
Steenberg Select	00		●			
Stellenbosch Vineyards Kumkani	99			●		
Vergelegen	00		●			
Vergelegen	99			●		
Vergelegen	98		●			
Vergelegen Reserve	00		●			
Vergelegen Reserve	01					●
Vergelegen Reserve	99		●			
Villiera	99		●			
Villiera Blanc Fumé	99			●		
Villiera Bush Vine	99		●			
Woolworths Vin de Cuvée (Robertson)	00			●		
Semillon						
Boschendal Jean le Long	99			●		
Constantia Uitsig Reserve	98		●	●		
Eikehof Bush Vine	00			●		
Fairview	99		●			

	Vintage	Veritas Dbl Gold	SAA	Wine 4-5 Stars	Platter 20 01	Platter 2002
Fairview Oom Pagel	00					●
Steenberg	98		●	●		
Steenberg (oaked)	99			●		
Viognier						
Fairview	99			●		
White Blends						
Boland Bon Vino Dry	01	●				
Jordan Chameleon	00		●			
Jordan Chameleon	99		●			
L'Avenir Vin d'Erstelle	98		●			
Neil Ellis Inglewood	99		●			
Simonsig Mustique	99		●			
Vergelegen Vin de Florence	99		●			
Desserts						
Avontuur Above Royalty	00					●
Avontuur Above Royalty	99				●	
Boland Century 00 NLH	98			●		
Bon Courage Gewürztraminer SLH	00	●				
Bon Courage Natural Sweet	01	●				
Bon Courage NLH	00			●		
De Trafford Vin de Paille	99			●		
De Wetshof NLH	00				●	
Fairview La Beryl	99			●		
Kanu NLH	99			●		
Klein Constantia NLH	98	●				
Klein Constantia NLH	98			●		
Klein Constantia Vin de Constance	96			●	●	
Klein Constantia Vin de Constance	95			●		
Morgenhof NLH	98			●		
Neethlingshof NLH	98			●		
Paul Cluver NLH	99			●		
Paul Cluver Riesling SLH	99			●		
Robertson Wide River Almond Grove NLH	99			●		
Signal Hill Crême de Tête	98			●		
Signal Hill Vin de Glacière	98			●		
Signal Hill Vin de l'Empereur	NV			●		
Slanghoek NLH	99			●		
Spier IV Spears NLH	98			●		
Stellenzicht Weisser Riesling NLH	98			●		
Vergelegen Semillon NLH	98			●		
Woolworths Fields of Gold (Ashanti)	NV			●		
Methode Cap Classique						
Ambeloui	98			●		
Avontuur Brut	NV			●		
Boschendal Brut	95			●		
Graham Beck Brut	NV		✪	●		
Laborie Brut	93			●		

	Vintage	Veritas Dbl Gold	SAA	Wine 4-5 Stars	Platter 2001	Platter 2002
Morgenhof Brut Reserve	97	●		●		
Pongràcz	NV		✪	●		
Rustenberg Brut	NV			●		
Simonsig Cuvée Royale	92	●				
Simonsig Kaapse Vonkel	96			●		
Twee Jonge Gezellen Krone Borealis Brut	94			●		
Villiera Tradition Brut Rosé	NV			●		
Fortified desserts						
Bakenskop Red Muscadel	99	●				
Boland Red Muscadel	97	●				
Boland White Muscadel	97	●				
Boland White Muscadel	95	●				
Doornkraal Pinta	NV	●				
Du Toitskloof Hanepoot Jerepigo	99	●		●		
Du Toitskloof Hanepoot Jerepigo	97			●		
Du Toitskloof Hanepoot Jerepigo	95			●		
Excelsior Vlakteplaas White Muskadel	00	●				
Klawer Red Muskadel	01	●				
Monis Moscato	92	●				
Nuy Red Muskadel	99	●				
Nuy Red Muskadel	98	●				
Nuy White Muskadel	99	●				
Nuy White Muskadel	98	●				
Slanghoek Red Jeripiko	00	●				
Swartland Red Jeripiko	01	●				
'Port'						
Allesverloren	93			●		
Axe Hill Cape Vintage	99			●		●
Axe Hill Cape Vintage	98				●	
Bergsig LBV	97			●		
Boplaas Cape Vintage Reserve	99			●		
Boplaas Cape Vintage Reserve	97	●				
Bredell & Nel Cape Vintage Reserve	97			●		
Bredell's Cape Vintage Reserve	98	●				
Bredell's Cape Vintage Reserve	97	●				
JP Bredell Cape Vintage Reserve	98			●	●	
KWV	97		✪			
Landskroon	97			●		
Masters Cape Vintage Reserve	98			●		
Monis Tawny Port	NV	●				
Morgenhof Cape Vintage	98	●				
Morgenhof Centenaire Cape Vintage Reserve	98					
Morgenhof Centenaire Cape Vintage Reserve	98	●		●		
Overgaauw Cape Vintage	98			●		
Swartland Vintage	99	●				

Wine routes, trusts & associations

For localised information about regional official wine routes and wineries, contact these organisations:

Calitzdorp Wine Route Tel (044) 213-3312 (ask for Tourism Information) • Fax (044) 213-3302.

Constantia Wine Route Tel (021) 794-1810 (ask for André Badenhorst) • Fax (021) 794-1812 • E-mail badenhorst@icon.co.za.

Durbanville Wine Route Tel 083-310-1228 (cellular) • Fax 976-5631 • E-mail nitida@mweb.co.za.

Franschhoek see Vignerons de Franschhoek.

Helderberg Wine Route Tel (021) 852-6166 • Fax (021) 851-1497 • E-mail hwr@mweb.co.za • Website www.helderbergwineroute.co.za.

Little Karoo Wine Trust Tel/fax (028) 572-1284 (Riaan Marais) • E-mail info@kleinkaroowines.co.za.

Northern Cape Vintners Tel 082-924-7254 (cellular) • Fax (051) 448-6076 • E-mail wineworx@bigfoot.com.

Olifants River Wine Trust Tel/fax (027) 213-3126 • Cell 083-701-9146 • E-mail olifantsrivwineroute@kingsley.co.za

Paarl Vintners Tel (021) 872-3605 • Fax (021) 872-3841 • E-mail paarl@wine.co.za Website www.paarlwine.co.za.

Robertson Wine Valley Tel (023) 626-3167 • Fax (023) 626-1054 • E-mail info@robertsonwinevalley.co.za • Website www.robertsonwinevalley.co.za.

Stellenbosch Wine Route Tel (021) 886-4310 • Fax (021) 886-4330 • E-mail info@wineroute.co.za Website www.wineroute.co.za.

Swartland Wine Route Tel (022) 487-1133 • Fax (022) 487-2063 • E-mail swartlandinfo@westc.co.za.

Tulbagh Wine Trust Tel/fax (023) 230-1348 • E-mail readers@iafrica.com • Website www.tulbagh.com.

Vignerons de Franschhoek Tel (021) 876-3062 • Fax (021) 876-2964/2768 • E-mail franschhoek@wine.co.za • Website www.franschhoekwines.co.za.

Wellington Wine Route Tel (021) 873-4604 • Fax (021) 873-4607 • E-mail welltour@cis.co.za Website www.visitwellington.com.

Worcester Winelands Association Tel (023) 342-8710 or (023) 342-8720 • Fax (023) 342-2294 • E-mail manager@worcesterwinelands.co.za • Website www.worcesterwinelands.co.za.

Winelands tourism offices

For additional accommodation options, brochures and local advice, contact the information offices and/or publicity associations of the wine areas you plan to visit.

Franschhoek Publicity Association Tel (021) 876-3062 • Fax (021) 876-2768 • E-mail info@franschhoek.org.za.

Helderberg Tourism Bureau Tel (021) 851-4022 • Fax (021) 851-1497 • E-mail info@helderbergtourism.co.za

Hermanus Tourism Bureau Tel (028) 312-2629 • Fax (028) 313-0305 • E-mail infoburo@itec.co.za

McGregor Publicity Association Tel (023) 625-1954 • Fax (023) 625-1630

Northern Cape Tourism Tel (053) 832-2657 Fax (053) 831-2937 E-mail tourism@northercape.org.za

Paarl Publicity Association Tel (021) 872-4842 • Fax (021) 872-9376 • E-mail paarl@cis.co.za

Robertson Tourism Bureau Tel (023) 626-4437 • Fax (023) 626-4290 • E-mail info@robertson.org.za

Stellenbosch Publicity Association Tel (021) 883-3584 • Fax (021) 883-8017 • E-mail eikestad@iafrica.com

Wellington Tourism Bureau Tel (021) 873-4604 • Fax (021) 873-4607 • E-mail welltour@cis.co.za

West Coast Tourism Bureau Tel (022) 714-2088 • Fax (022) 714-4240 • E-mail bureau@kingsley.co.za

Worcester Tourism Bureau Tel (023) 348-2795 • Fax (023) 347-4678 • E-mail records@worcmun.org.za

Some specialist tour operators

Adamastor & Bacchus John Ford conducts tailor-made tours for small groups to wine farms not usually accessible to the public. Photography an additional speciality. Tours can be conducted in German and Norwegian. Tel (021) 439-3169 • Cell 083-229-1172 • E-mail johnford@iafrica.com.

André Morgenthal Offers specialist wine tours to off-the-beaten-track cellars, and conducts innovative 'out-tastings' in your home or venue of choice. Carefully chosen wines and food create a synergistic experience, with cigars and all trimmings. Tel (021) 887-6583/082-658-3883 • E-mail wynsacci@hotmail.com.

Gourmet Wine Tours NEW Exploratory tours for individuals or small groups covering principal wine areas and estates in the Western Cape, combined with meals in selected leading restaurants. By Stephen Flesch, Satour-registered guide, former chair of the Wine Tasters Guild of South Africa and secretary of the Cape Town Slow Food Convivium. Some French and German spoken. Tel (021) 705-4317 • Fax (021) 706-0766 • Cell 083-229-3581 • E-mail sflesch@iafrica.com.

The Capevine Special-interest tour operator Annette Stals will organise the consummate Cape winelands experience to facilitate your enjoyment of wine, architecture, history, gardens, regional cuisine and beautiful scenery. Tel (021) 913- 6611 • Tel/fax (021) 913- 4580 • E-mail capevine@iafrica.com.

Vineyard Ventures Super-experienced guides Gillian Stoltzman (082-893-5387) and Glen Christie (082-920-2825) specialise in small groups, tailor-making each sipping-safari to visitors' tastes – off the tourist beat. Tel (021) 434-8888 • Fax (021) 434-9999 • E-mail vinven@iafrica.com • Website www.vineyardventures.co.za

Vintage Cape Tours Private and tailor-made tours for the discerning food and wine lover, conducted by specialist wine guides in English, German, French and Afrikaans. Tel (021) 872-9252 • Tel/fax (021) 862-1484 • Cell 082-553-8928 or 082-656-3994 • E-mail vctours@adept.co.za • Website www.vintagecape.co.za.

Vintour NEW Helmut Feil, Satour-qualified guide with 37 years' experience in the wine industry, offers small tailor-made tours for the serious wine and food connoisseur or professional, in German or English. Tel/fax (021) 976-5709 • Cell 083-626-0029 • E-mail helmut@vintour.co.za.

Window on Cape Wine Meryl Weaver, Satour-registered (and passionate about wine), specialist guide for: personally tailored full or half-day excursions; tutored tastings; a quality, visual winelands presentation, which includes a tasting. Ideal for conference entertainment or tourgroups (1 hour). Tel/fax (021) 889-1002 • Cell 082-782-5198 • E-mail mvweaver@iafrica.com.

Armchair tours of the winelands

Sovereign Video *Winelands of the Cape.* This popular video presentation includes 28 top estates and covers the main production areas. Tel (021) 423-3043 • Fax (021) 423-3056.

Wine education

Accolade Wine Appreciation Experienced Cape Town-based wine taster/educator Claude Felbert offers his introductory wine appreciation course, which includes ± 11 hours of tuition and an exam for those who wish to write it, at least 8 times a year. Higher-level individual 'varietal courses' are also offered, along with twice-yearly detailed tasting programmes with sections on common wine faults. Courses for 10 or more people are held in other centres by arrangement. Tel (021) 712-4245 or 083-261-8863 • Fax (021) 712- 6220 • E-mail accolade@ibox.co.za.

Cape Wine Academy Official education body for the SA wine industry, headquartered in Stellenbosch with a branch in Johannesburg and centres in Durban, Pretoria, Bloemfontein, Port Elizabeth, Knysna, Windhoek and Harare. Runs theory and tasting courses with examinations at several levels. New courses include wine service, an introduction to wines of the world, and skills workshops for cellar workers. The principal is Christine Rudman.

Stellenbosch: tel (021) 809-7597/7547, fax (021) 883-9179 • Johannesburg: tel (011) 783-4585/6, fax (011) 883-2356 • Durban: tel/fax (031) 564-5067 • Pretoria tel/fax (012) 333-1978 • Bloemfontein: tel (051) 403-8500, fax (051) 448-6076 • Port Elizabeth (Jaco Schoeman): tel (041) 504-3872, fax (041) 504-3744 • Harare: tel (09263) 913538-40 • E-mail capewineacademy@hotmail.com • Website www.capewineacademy.co.za.

Cape Wine Master Successful completion of examinations set since 1983 by the Cape Wine & Spirit Education Trust have qualified 45 wine aficionados and professionals for the title of Cape Wine Master. Their Institute holds seminars, runs tasting workshops, charts trends, names a Wine Personality of the Year, and more. Chair Christine Rudman is also principal of the Cape Wine Academy (above). Tel (021) 809-7591, fax (021) 883-9179. The members are:

Chris Bargmann • Margie Barker • F C 'Duimpie' Bayly • Paul Benade • Cathy Brewer • Robin Brown • Sue Brown • Gert Burger • Gulio Cecchini • Michael Claasens • Marilyn Cooper • Bill Cooper-Williams • Henry Davel • Dick Davidson • Greg de Bruyn • Stephan du Toit • Pieter Esbach • Frith Colin (Hon) • Margaret Fry • Loraine Fuller-Drury • Peter Gebler • Penny Gold • Jeff Grier • Phyllis Hands (Hon) • Bennie Howard • Dave Hughes (Hon) • Tim James • Dave Johnson • Val Kartsounis • Peter Koff • Gerald Ludwinski • Marietjie Marais-Brown • Alf Mauff • Tony Mossop • Allan Mullins • Boets Nel • Carel Nel • Elsie Pels • Christine Rudman • Lynne Sheriff • Cornel Spies • Clive Torr • Charl van Teijlingen • Sue van Wyk • Irina von Holdt • Cathy White • Geoff Willis

Stay-over in the winelands

Featured below are guest lodges, hotels, country inns, B&Bs and self-catering cottages in the winelands, many of them on wine farms: look for the 🛏 symbol below the individual entries in this guide. All these establishments have restaurants, swimming pools, gardens/terraces, parking and televisions et al (unless stated to the contrary). All rates are for standard double rooms unless otherwise specified, for example per person (pp), breakfast included (B&B) or on a dinner, bed and breakfast basis (DB&B). The stay-overs featured below describe their own attractions.

Constantia

Constantia Uitsig Country Hotel Spaanschemat River Road • From R1 188-R1 788 room only • Major credit cards accepted • Owners David & Marlene McCay • Tel (021) 794-6500 • Fax (021) 794-7605 • E-mail zinta@uitsig.co.za • Website www.uitsig.co.za

Nestled in the Constantia Valley, Constantia Uitsig, meaning Constantia view, is where you will encounter peace and tranquillity on a working wine farm, just 20 minutes from the hustle and bustle of the city centre and Waterfront. The Hotel boasts 16 garden rooms, all individually furnished with elegant simplicity. The interiors are furnished with stylish antiques and exude warmth and comfort. Facilities include 2 award-winning restaurants (see separate Eat-out entry), 2 swimming pools, a world-renowned cricket oval and an exclusive conference venue.

Hampshire House 10 Willow Road • R470 B&B • No restaurant • Major credit cards accepted • Non-smoking residence • Owners Ricky & Carole Chapman • Tel (021) 794-6288 • Fax (021) 794-2934 • E-mail stay@hampshirehouse.co.za • Website www.hampshirehouse.co.za

Set in the idyllic Constantia wine valley, Hampshire House was a 99/00 finalist in the AA/SAA Accommodation Awards. It provides the perfect base from which to explore the picturesque Cape Peninsula, with easy motorway access to Table Mountain, the V&A Waterfront, the winelands and beaches, as well as excellent local restaurants. Five individually decorated en suite bedrooms have king-sized or twin beds, satellite television, CD player, radio alarm, bar fridge, overhead fan and cosy underfloor heating in winter. There's a pool and secure off-street parking. English and continental buffet breakfasts are available. You can enjoy a drink in the Hampshire Arms, a cosy pub with a comprehensive winelist.

The Cellars-Hohenort Hotel 193 Brommersvlei Road • From R1 445 B&B • Major credit cards accepted • Owner Liz Mc Grath • Tel (021) 794-2137 • Fax (021) 794-2194 • E-mail cellars@ct.lia.net • Website www.cellars-hohenort.com

The hotel is adjacent to the world-famous Kirstenbosch Botanical Gardens and minutes away from Constantia Wine Route. It has 9 acres of magnificently landscaped gardens and a small vineyard. In its renaissance as one of the great country hotels of the Cape, the five-star Cellars-Hohenort is a member of the international Relais & Chateaux Association. There's also a tennis court, beauty spa, hair salon, putting green and gift shop. (See separate Eat-out entries for The Cellars Restaurant and The Cape Malay Restaurant.)

Elgin/Walker Bay

Wildekrans Country House Opposite Houw Hoek Farm Stall on the N2 • R350 B&B • Meals available on request • Major credit cards accepted • Owners Barry Gould & Alison Green • Tel (028) 284-9827 • Fax (028) 284-9624 • E-mail wildekrans@kingsley.co.za

Wildekrans is on a fruit farm in the peaceful and scenic Houw Hoek Valley, surrounded by mountains, just an hour's drive from Cape Town. Three en suite bedrooms in the old homestead (1811) are furnished with four-poster beds. Two cottages are set in the tranquil garden and pear orchard. All are also available for self-catering holidays. Relax in the large English country garden or at the pool. Leisurely walks, hikes and mountain bike trails begin at the foot of the garden. Appreciate the Wildekrans collection of contemporary South African art. Visit the Walker Bay wine route and beaches.

Franschhoek

Auberge Clermont Robertsvlei Road • Tel (021) 876-3700 • Fax (021) 876-3701 • E-mail clermont@mweb.co.za • Website www.clermont.co.za

This magnificent auberge has been created in a historic wine cellar surrounded by chardonnay vineyards. The scent of roses, lavender and rosemary is everywhere. The 6 luxe en suite rooms have been individually decorated in Provençal style with great attention to detail. Underfloor heating and ceiling fans ensure year-round comfort. The generous bathrooms have double basins, heated towel rails and separate showers. There is a pool and tennis court on the premises, and a three-bedroomed self-catering villa alongside a formal French garden. Clermont is 1 km from the village centre and close to its associate restaurant, Haute Cabrière (see separate Eat-out entry).

Auberge du Quartier Français Cnr Berg & Wilhelmina Streets • R1 700 room only • Major credit cards accepted • Tel (021) 876-2151 • Fax (021) 876-3105 • E-mail res@lqf.co.za • Website www.lequartier.co.za

Le Quartier Français is a sanctuary of intimacy and comfort. Set behind a bright Provençal façade with whitewashed stone walls, the 15 luxury rooms are fully air-conditioned and decorated in a modern Cape Provençal style, individually furnished with brightly coloured fabrics, deep-down designer duvets, king-sized beds wrapped in Egyptian linen and log fireplaces for winter. The two suites have separate living rooms, air conditioning and private swimming pools set in secluded gardens. Le Quartier Français also features a trendy cigar bar, a lounge, a patio restaurant, the main restaurant (see separate Eat-out entry for Le Quartier Français), an intimate courtyard and a well-stocked library.

Ballon Rouge 7 Reservoir Street • Tel (021) 876-2651 • Fax (021) 876-3743 • Major credit cards accepted • E-mail info@ballon-rouge.co.za • Website www.ballon-rouge.co.za

Ballon Rouge was purchased by current owner Henry de Necker in June 2001. The guesthouse has been extensively refurbished and exquisitely decorated to ensure guests a comfortable and memorable stay. Guests are pampered and made to feel at home. Ballon is well situated within walking distance of all Franschhoek attractions and a short drive from most of the top wine estates. A full English breakfast is served with a buffet of fresh fruits, pastries and cereals. The secluded swimming pool brings refreshing relief from the summer heat, and the rooms are warm and cozy in winter with log fires in the bar and dining area. A private lounge with library is available for the enjoyment of the guests.

Cathbert Country Inn Franschhoek Road, Simondium • R350 pp sharing • Major credit cards accepted • Owners Robert & Ann Morley • Tel/fax (021) 874-1366 • E-mail info@cathbert.co.za • Website www.cathbert.co.za

Wake up to country quiet, clean air and glorious views, just 40 minutes from Cape Town. Cathbert Country Inn – a 99/00 AA/SAA Accommodation Awards finalist – is in the heart of the winelands at the foot of the majestic Simonsberg mountains, perfectly placed for touring Paarl, Stellenbosch and Franschhoek. Individually appointed suites, all with private verandas, opening onto dam, vineyard and mountain views, have all the trimmings: a comfortable sitting area, TV, mini-bar, underfloor heating, fireplace and ceiling fans. Breakfast at leisure on a sunny garden deck or in the restaurant overlooking the pool; gourmet dinners are also served. Mountain walks, bird watching and many fine golf courses nearby take care of the great outdoors. Airport transfers can be arranged.

Franschhoek Country House Main Road • From R275 pp B&B (R550 per room) • Major credit cards accepted • Tel (021) 876-3386 • Fax (021) 876-2744 • E-mail fch@mweb.co.za • Website www.ecl.co.za

Wallow in luxury and some serious indulgence at this upmarket country house in the fetching Franschhoek Valley. The restored manor house and former perfumery, which dates back to 1890, has 14 rooms and suites, most with fireplaces and balconies, with all the expected comforts and amenities, including satellite television. A swimming pool is set in tranquil gardens with mountain vistas. Guests can enjoy lunch or dinner at the famous in-house Monneaux restaurant (see separate Eat-out entry), which is known for its exquisite menu and wine selection.

La Couronne Hotel Robertsvlei Road • R1 560 B&B • Major credit cards accepted • Tel (021) 876-2770 • Fax (021) 876-3788 • E-mail reservations@lacouronnehotel.co.za • Website www.lacouronnehotel.co.za

La Couronne, 'the crown' of Franschhoek, is positioned in what is undoubtedly one of the most beautiful settings in the world. The small luxury hotel, set among the vines of the La Couronne wine estate, offers a complete winelands experience, with fine dining and a vast selection of South African and international wines (see separate Eat-out entry). Guests are invited to a private tasting in the estate cellar, and can enjoy a horse ride, a walk through the vineyards, or trout fishing in one of their mountain ponds. During the harvest season guests are encouraged to become involved in the winemaking process.

La Petite Ferme Pass Road • From R425 pp sharing B&B • Owners Mark & Josephine Dendy • Tel (021) 876-3016/8 • Fax (021) 876-3624 • E-mail lapetite@iafrica.com

La Petite Ferme is set high above Franschhoek (a vantage point from which it catches the last rays of the afternoon sun) with breathtaking views of orchards, vineyards and the lush valley below. Luxury, elegance and comfort are paramount, with 3 delightful private cottages set among the vineyards, each with private patio and plunge pool; the spacious bedrooms have fireplaces, TV, bar fridges, heaters and ceiling fans, and bathrooms with roomy oval tubs and showers. Country-style breakfasts are served in the cottage, cooked farm breakfasts in the restaurant (see separate Eat-out entry).

Résidence Klein Oliphants Hoek 14 Akademie Street • R285 pp B&B • Major credit cards accepted • Owners Ingrid & Camil Haas • Tel/fax (021) 876-2566 • E-mail info@kleinoliphantshoek.com • Website www.kleinoliphantshoek.com

The Résidence Klein Oliphants Hoek is named after the original name for Franschhoek, once the foraging place of roaming elephants. The guesthouse is a beautifully renovated 1888 English missionary station, with 6 spacious en suite rooms and a private garden suite. Splendid views of the surrounding mountains and garden. There are fireplaces in both the lounge and restaurant. Your multilingual hosts Camil and Ingrid, who have international catering experience, will host your dinner on request. Cooking classes in the open kitchen at the old wood stove will inspire you to explore European-African cuisine in combination with the best wines of the valley.

Houw Hoek (see Elgin/Walker Bay)

Montagu

Mimosa Lodge Church Street, Montagu • R405 pp DB&B • Green Season from R185 pp B&B • Breakfast R40, dinner R105 for non-residents • Owners Yvette & Andreas Küng • Tel (023) 614-2351 • Fax (023) 614-2418 • E-mail mimosa@lando.co.za • Website www.mimosa.co.za

Firmly established in Montagu, this carefully restored historic building exudes charm, warmth and friendliness. The decor is vibrant and colourful. The 9 comfortable en suite bedrooms have modern facilities, while the 3 suites offer luxury and tranquillity. The garden with its black-marbled pool is surrounded by the Lodge's own apricot orchards. Mimosa Lodge is renowned for its creative cuisine by owner Andreas Küng. The highly acclaimed table d'hôte changes daily, and special dietary requirements are gladly catered for. The Lodge's own wine cellar provides the perfect match for an excellent dinner.

Paarl

Grande Roche Hotel Plantasie Street • R1 750 B&B • Major credit cards accepted • Tel (021) 863-2727 • Fax (021) 863-2220 • E-mail reserve@granderoche.co.za • Website www.granderoche.co.za

Grande Roche has become a legend in South Africa with an array of awards including the 1995 'Tourism Hotel of the Year Award' for "incredible attention to detail, impeccable grounds, excellent food and superb levels of luxury" and the American-based international Andrew Harper Award given to outstanding country estates exuding warmth, charm and excellence. This South African gem overlooks vineyards and rugged mountains, and its sprawl of individually decorated suites are a gentle alternative to the hurly-burly of big city life. You can relax in the pools, go biking or play tennis on site, enjoy excellent golf nearby, go to the gym or indulge in a massage given by the hotel's private masseur. It's the ideal base from which to explore the entire Cape region. (See separate Eat-out entry for Bosman's.)

Lanquedoc Guest Cottages Klein Drakenstein • Self-catering cottages: 2 en suite bedrooms R825 per night in season, R600 per night out of season; 1 en suite bedroom R495 per night in season, R360 per night out of season • Continental breakfast on request, R25 pp • Major credit cards accepted • Tel (021) 862-3368/ 3190 • Fax (021) 862-3258/6300 • E-mail lanque@iafrica.com

The historic Lanquedoc Farm invites you to experience a working olive farm in the heart of the Cape winelands. Set at the foothills of the Klein Drakenstein mountains in the fertile Paarl Valley, luxurious self-catering cottages provide accommodation of the highest standard for the discerning traveller. There's a magnificent pool with covered pavilion, braai facilities in the garden, spectacular mountain bike and hiking trails through olive groves, vineyards and buchu plantations, as well as easy country walks, crackling log fires and unforgettable scenery. Lanquedoc's superior extra virgin olive oil and black mission olives – processed on the farm – are available for purchase by guests.

Pontac Manor Hotel & Restaurant 16 Zion Street • R790 B&B • Major credit cards accepted • Owners Desire & Tim Orill-Legg; Stanley Carpenter • Tel (021) 872-0445 • Fax (021) 872-0460 • E-mail pontac@iafrica.com • Website www.pontac.com

Tucked beneath Paarl Rock, Pontac Manor, dating back to 1723, has been beautifully restored to its original Victorian splendour. The hotel, with its warm, old-world atmosphere and air of timeless sophistication, offers 16 tastefully decorated and spacious bedrooms with en suite bathrooms, set in a large, sculpted garden with pool. From the broad terrace, guests can enjoy a magnificent view over the valley to the mountains beyond. The newly opened 'Restaurant at Pontac' offers fine dining with a New World flair. Interesting dishes with delicate sauces please every palate. Light meals and refreshments are served throughout the premises. Well- equipped meeting facilities for up to 22 people are offered in the new Conference Suite, while the Board Room accommodates up to 12 delegates. (See separate Eat-out entry.)

Robertson

Fraai Uitzicht 1798 Klaas Voogds East, on R60 between Robertson & Ashton/Montagu • R400-R590 B&B, R470 self-catering • Major credit cards accepted • Owners Axel Spanholtz & Mario Motti • Tel/fax (023) 626-6156 • E-mail info@fraaiuitzicht.com • Website www.fraaiuitzicht.com

This historic wine and guest farm, and restaurant (see separate Eat-out entry), at the foothills of the Langeberg mountains in the Klaas Voogds Valley, is a delightful place. With long farm walks, a wealth of bird life and spectacular views across the Robertson 'Valley of Wine and Roses', it is the perfect place to relax and experience the beauty and tranquillity of nature. Attentive hosts and luxury guest cottages, each with open fireplace, braai facilities and a big private veranda, await you. There's a lovely pool, a bamboo forest, and beautiful herb, flower and rose gardens surrounded by vineyards and fruit orchards. Try the fine 'wine and dine menu', a six-course meal, complemented by selected wines that incorporate some of the Robertson Valley's finest.

Somerset West (see Stellenbosch)

Stellenbosch

Aan die Oewer Guesthouse Jonkershoek Valley • R340 pp B&B • Major credit cards accepted • No restaurant • Tel (021) 887-9385, Fax (021) 887-2418 • E-mail aandieoewer@iafrica.com • Website www.aandeoever.co.za

This riverside guesthouse is situated just outside historic Stellenbosch in the lush Jonkershoek valley. A perfect place to relax in cushioned comfort. Cool down in the lovely swimming pool or enjoy a bottle of wine in the park-like garden under century-old oak trees. This is the best possible setting for a guesthouse in the winelands and it's positioned right opposite the Neil Ellis winery, with Lanzerac just down the road. The area is ideal for hiking and cycling, and the nature reserve is a mere 2km away. Aan die Oewer is only 3.5 km from the buzzy town of Stellenbosch with its excellent restaurants, surrounding wine estates and tradition of hospitality.

Bordeaux Place @ 33° South Vlottenburg Road (off R310), Vlottenburg • From R175-R220 B&B (double pp sharing), R250 B&B (single) • Conference facilities • No pool •Major credit cards accepted • Owner Simon Lavarack • Tel (021) 881-3791 • Fax (021) 881-3740 • E-mail bordeauxplace@mweb.co.za • Website www.bordeauxplace.co.za

Bordeaux place lies only a few kilometres from historic Stellenbosch. Each stylish bedroom has a lovely view of the winelands, spacious bathroom and bar fridge. Enjoy leisurely meals while surrounded by gracious old oaks and mountain vistas (see separate Eat-out entry for The Restaurant @ 33° South). A wide variety of the winelands' very best products are for sale, with the added bonus for overseas or upcountry visitors of having their wines delivered to their door.

Devon Valley Hotel Devon Valley Road • R650, including full farmhouse breakfast • Major credit cards accepted • Owners David & Lee Ann Nathan-Maister • Tel (021) 882-2012 • Fax (021) 882-2610 • E-mail devon@iafrica.com

A Stellenbosch landmark for over 50 years, the Devon Valley Hotel offers stunning views, cosy rooms, innovative Cape country cuisine and the finest winelist in the winelands (see separate Eat-out entry for The Vineleaf). Walk through the beautiful gardens, gaze over their own vineyards or just sit on the patio, admire the view and sip a glass of their award-winning Sylvanvale wine. At night, sit in front of the log fire at the Cat & Moose bar, and savour one of their 120 single malt whiskies – the largest selection in Africa!

Die Ou Pastorie Country House & Restaurant 41 Lourens Street, Somerset West • R410 pp B&B • Major credit cards accepted • Owner Garry Roberts Tel (021) 852-2120 • Fax (021) 851-3710 • E-mail info@dieoupastorie.co.za • Website www.dieoupastorie.co.za

This historical monument with its gracious period antiques dates back to 1819, yet offers every modern convenience for the discerning traveller of today. Situated in the Helderberg basin, which is central to all the major tourist attractions in and around the Cape Town area, Die Ou Pastorie lies close to the winelands routes of Stellenbosch, Franschhoek, Paarl and Helderberg. The 16 en suite bedrooms are located in the well-manicured gardens in two 'pavilions' separated by the extensive herb garden. The rooms are classically decorated in Victorian style, capturing the spirit of luxury. The restaurant with its elegant dining rooms, situated in the original parsonage, has a warm and intimate atmosphere where continental cuisine and an award-winning winelist provide a memorable dining experience (see separate Eat-out entry).

Knorhoek Guest House Knorhoek Wine Farm, Knorhoek Road (off R44 between Stellenbosch/Paarl) • From R220 pp B&B • Major credit cards accepted • Meals on request • Owners The Van Niekerk family • Tel (021) 882-2114 • Fax (021) 882-2115 • E-mail guesthouse@knorhoek.co.za • Website www.knorhoek.co.za

Tucked in a beautiful valley at the foot of the Simonsberg lies this historic Stellenbosch wine farm with freehold deeds dating back to 1710. Your hosts, Ingrid and Carol, invite you to savour the tranquillity of this magnificent setting while enjoying all the comforts of home (these include underfloor heating and coffee-/tea-making facilities). There's a tennis court, rock pool and barbecue area, and scenic vineyard walks. Wake up to birdcalls and farmyard bustle, and let them spoil you with a traditional breakfast that's a fitting start to an exciting day of exploring the Boland.

L'Avenir Wine Estate Guest House Klapmuts Road (R44), north of Stellenbosch towards Paarl • R330 B&B • Meals on request • Major credit cards accepted • Owners L'Avenir Wine Estate Pty Ltd • Tel (021) 889-5001 • Fax (021) 889-5258 • E-mail lavenir@adept.co.za • Website adept.co.za/lavenir/

This is a wine lover's heaven: 9 en suite bedrooms set around a large pool on a wine estate with 70 hectares of prime vineyards to wander in, cellar tours and award-winning wines at cellar prices. Relaxed and unhurried luxury, only 5 minutes from Stellenbosch, 20 minutes from the airport and the beaches of the Strand, 50 minutes from Cape Town. Conference facilities are available.

Natte Valleij Farm Klapmuts Road (44), 12 km north of Stellenbosch towards Paarl • R160 pp, including full breakfast • Self-catering cottages: Vineyard Cottage from R375 per day; Cellar Cottage R250 per day • Owners Charles & Charlene Milner • Tel (021) 875-5171 • Fax (021) 875-5475 • E-mail milner@intekom.co.za

The historic Natte Valleij farm is situated in the prime winegrowing Muldersvlei bowl, renowned for its award-winning reds. The farm nestles under the Simonsberg mountains and is surrounded by many well-known estates. There's a B&B option as well as two self-catering cottages: Vineyard Cottage (circa 1714) can sleep 6 in 3 double bedrooms, with 2 bathrooms, sitting room and dining room; Cellar Cottage sleeps 2 to 4. Both cottages have their own stoep and braai facilities. The secluded swimming pool is set in a large garden. You can fish for bass in the farm dam or go for long walks through forests or up the mountain. Charles and Charlene Milner offer friendly hospitality and welcome the opportunity to share with you the ambience of a bygone era.

Tulbagh

Lemberg Wine Estate and Guest House Off the R46 • R350 per couple per night, excl food (R100 discount for South Africans) • Owners Uschi and Klaus Schindler • Tel (023) 230-0659 • Fax (023) 230-0661 • E-mail schindler@lando.co.za • Website www.kapstadt.de/lemberg

The guesthouse is a magnificent rondavel, set on 21 ha next to a lake, perfectly appointed for privacy. This is an exclusive suite, tastefully decorated, with a fully equipped kitchen, bedroom with king-sized bed, en suite bathroom with shower, cosy lounge, fresh flowers and fruits, veranda and garden leading to the lake. Breakfasts, gourmet lunches or evening dinners are served in the guesthouse or at the lake's edge. The ideal place from which to explore the beautiful Cape in all directions and good advice is offered on enjoyable half-day or day trips to the many places of interest around the estate. Visitors will enjoy a personal wine tasting and informative cellar tour – they produce 3 distinctive and carefully crafted wines. Let the hedonist in you enjoy being pampered with personal, attentive service.

Wellington

Diemersfontein Country House On R301, between Paarl & Wellington • R350 pp sharing, R400 pp single B&B • Meals on request • Major credit cards accepted • Owners David & Sue Sonnenberg • Tel (021) 873-2671 • Fax (023) 864-2095 • E-mail diemers@kingsley.co.za • Website www.diemers.co.za

The elegant Diemersfontein Country House, a much-loved family home, offers you warm hospitality in a gracious setting. Laze beside the pine-sheltered pool amidst idyllic gardens or experience the magnificent fynbos mountain scenery on horseback. Fifteen beautifully appointed en suite bedrooms. Weddings, conferences and functions.

Klein Rheboksskloof Country & Guest House Hildenbrand Wine & Olive Estate, Horseshoe Drive • From R380 B&B pp sharing • Major credit cards accepted • Owner Reni Hildenbrand • Tel/fax (021) 873-4115 • E-mail info@wine-estate-hildenbrand.co.za • Website www.wine-estate-hildenbrand.co.za

Situated on an historical 40ha farm, you'll find this a tranquil retreat offering exquisite wine and olive oil from the estate. After a breakfast with a 'difference', you'll be invited to join a cellar tour through the farm's 19th-century wine cellar and also be introduced to table olive and olive oil processing. Meet the farmyard animals or lounge by the pool overlooking the vineyards, olive groves and peaceful valley of Wellington. Stroll through the vineyards and orchards or along the river bank and discover a natural pool for a cooling dip. Have a delicious lunch in the estate's restaurant (see separate Eat-out entry for Hildenbrand's Table) or arrange for a special dinner or barbecue. A haven of hospitality that will be an unforgettable experience.

Eat-out in the winelands

Many wineries offer light lunches or picnics: look for the 🍴 symbol above the individual entries in this guide. The restaurants featured below describe their own culinary styles, menus and attractions.

Constantia

Cloete's at Alphen Alphen Drive • Classic cuisine • Lunch/dinner daily • Major credit cards accepted • Convenient parking • Tel (021) 794-5011 • Fax (021) 794-5710 • E-mail reservations@alphen.co.za • Website www.alphen.co.za

Cloete's at Alphen is in the elegant 18th-century manor house, a national monument, on the historic Alphen Estate at the gateway to the Constantia Valley. Enjoy classic à la carte meals in an atmosphere of past intrigue, surrounded by antiques and paintings from the Cloete family collection. The restaurant specialises in small private functions. If you are looking for something more casual, try the memorabilia-filled Boer 'n Brit in the Jonkershuis or the terrace in the dappled shade of ancient oaks.

Constantia Uitsig Spaanschemat River Road • Mediterranean influences • Lunch 12:30-14:00, dinner 19:30-21:00 (every day in season) • Booking essential • Fully licensed • Corkage R20 • Children welcome • Wheelchair-friendly • Major credit cards accepted • Non-smoking in dining rooms • Tel (021) 794-4480 • Fax (021) 794-3105 • E-mail frank@uitsig.co.za • Website www.uitsig.co.za

Constantia Uitsig Restaurant is housed in the original Manor House under the shade of 100-year-old oaks with sweeping views of the Constantia Valley. Constantia Uitsig Restaurant has consistently been amongst the top 10 restaurants in South Africa since its inception, and offers widely varied Mediterranean Provençal cuisine. To complement your meal, their winelist offers the best of the Cape, with the wines of the Constantia valley well represented. **La Colombe**, tel (021) 794-2390, fax (021) 794-7914 or e-mail lc@uitsig.co.za, their second restaurant, was recently voted the top restaurant in South Africa. La Colombe serves traditional French Provençal cuisine. French-born chef, Franck Dangereux, changes the menu daily according to the season and what is available from the market. (See separate Stay-over entry.)

Parks 114 Constantia Main Road • Global cuisine • Dinner Mon-Sat • Booking advised • Corkage R25 • Children welcome • Wheelchair-friendly • Major credit cards accepted • Non-smoking • Tel (021) 797-8202 • Fax (021) 797-8233 • E- mail bibendum@iafrica.com • Website www.parksgroup.com

New visitors and large numbers of regulars are assured of a warm welcome and professional service at Michael and Madeleine Olivier's popular Constantia restaurant. Guests dine in the rooms of the beautifully restored house, set in a pretty garden. The atmosphere is elegant but relaxed. Parks's signature dishes – blackened fish and slow-roast duck – are retained by popular demand while the rest of the menu offers interesting and unusual dishes using fresh, seasonal ingredients. Desserts are scrumptious and, while fresh fruits and sorbets always feature, the main emphasis here is, quite frankly, sinful. Both the food and the extensive winelist offer flair and quality at a fair price.

Peddlars-on-the-Bend Spaanschemat Road • Country fare • Open daily 11:00-23:00 (pub), 12:00-23:00 (restaurant) • Closed Christmas Day • Booking advised • Corkage R10 • Children welcome • Wheelchair-friendly • Major credit cards accepted • Non-smoking 80% • Tel (021) 794-7747/50 • Fax (021) 794-2730

Peddlars-on-the-Bend has become one of Cape Town's most popular destinations for locals and visitors alike. Warm country charm, a lovely garden setting under a huge oak tree and a reputation for quality service make this an irresistible venue. The menu offers generous (but reasonably priced) portions of wholesome country food: hearty casseroles in winter, good steaks, fresh linefish and tasty pasta. Award-winning winelist (Diners Club) showcases the area but ventures further afield too; includes some special buys from private cellars and auctions. Good selection of local brandy; cognac and cigars.

The Cape Malay Restaurant The Cellars-Hohenort Hotel, 93 Brommersvlei Road • Cape Malay • Dinners only 19:00-21:30 • Closed Sun in season; closed Mon & Tue out of season • Closed Jul-Sep • Booking advised • Wheelchair-friendly • Major credit cards accepted • Non-smoking • Tel (021) 794-2137 • Fax (021) 794-2149 • E-mail cellars@ct.lia.net • Website www.cellars-hohenort.com

Cape Malay cuisine is unique to the Western Cape. It dates back to the 17th century and has evolved to reflect the influences of the times. Originally a product of the early Indian and Malay settlers in the Cape, it has since been adapted by the creative indigenous cooks of this area. The cuisine is now noted for its mild spice and aromatic character. For a taste of the specialities on the menu here, try snoek soup, a traditional 'chowder-style' fish soup, for starters; move on to a Cape Malay mild chicken curry seasoned with cumin, turmeric, fennel seeds and finished with plain yoghurt; round off with malva pudding, a warm sponge pudding soaked in caramel syrup. Award-winning winelist (Diners Club Platinum 99, Diamond 00 & 01). (See separate Stay-over entry.)

The Cellars Restaurant The Cellars-Hohenort Hotel, 93 Brommersvlei Road • Contemporary international • Breakfast 7:00-10:00; Lunch 12:00-14:30; Dinner 19:00-21:30 • Booking advised • Wheelchair-friendly • Major credit cards accepted • Non-smoking • Tel (021) 794-2137 • Fax (021) 794- 2149 • E-mail cellars@ct.lia.net • Website www.cellars-hohenort.com

Regarded as one of the Top 10 in South Africa, The Cellars Restaurant is a gastronomic delight with contemporary, international fare, featuring the freshest of local produce. The elegant blue-and-gold appointed room affords sweeping views of some of the most beautiful gardens in the country. In these luxurious surrounds, be it a light lunch on the sunny patio or an 'occasion' dinner, the atmosphere is always relaxed and the service friendly. For a healthy lunch choice try the Cellars Chicken Salad – chicken dusted with sesame seeds, fresh garden greens, and a honey and soya dressing. A favourite on the dinner menu is char-grilled saddle of springbok with roasted root vegetables, pommes anna and juniper berry sauce. The award-winning winelist (Diners Club Platinum 99, Diamond 00 & 01) boasts some 300 wines carefully selected by an accomplished sommelier and rarer Cape vintages are brought from the rustic cellar on request. (See separate Stay-over entry.)

Franschhoek

Ballon Rouge 7 Reservoir Street • Modern continental cuisine with South African influences • Open 7 days a week, 8:00-21:30 • Booking advised • Corkage R10 • Children welcome • Major credit cards accepted • Non-smoking section • Tel (021) 876-2651 • Fax (021) 876-3743 • E-mail info@ballon-rouge.co.za • Website www.ballon-rouge.co.za

Ballon is comfortably niched as an elegant country-styled restaurant with a wide-ranging continental menu. The restaurant has undergone major refurbishment with a fresh new look and menu. Ably assisted by an energetic and talented team, chef-patron Bradley Tyler conjures exciting meals with an accent on simplicity from the freshest of locally sourced produce. Staff are trained to ensure that your dining experience is memorable in what can only be described as one of Franschhoek's most warm and friendly establishments. The winelist has won a Diners Club award each year since 94, and the restaurant is currently placed as one of the top 100 in South Africa. (See separate Stay-over entry.)

Boschendal You'll be spoilt for choice with three culinary options on this historic wine farm: Boschendal Restaurant, Le Café and Le Pique-Nique. See separate listings.

Boschendal Restaurant Pniel Road (R310), 1,5km from junction with R45 • Cape-French cuisine with extensive buffet • Open 7 days a week, 12:15 for 12:30, guests to be seated by 13:30 • Closed Good Friday, 1 May, 16 Jun • Booking advised • Corkage R15 • Children welcome (half-price for ages 2-10) • Wheelchair-friendly • Major credit cards accepted • Non-smoking • Smart-casual dress code • Tel (021) 870-4274 • Fax (021) 874-2137 • E-mail reservations@boschendal.com • Website www.boschendal.com

Housed in the original cellar, the Boschendal Restaurant serves delicious buffet-style lunches. Heap your plate with expertly prepared Cape-French cuisine, steaming roasts, local seafood specialities, imaginative salads and sinful desserts from tables groaning with these tantalising treats, complemented by fine Boschendal wines, including the Jean le Long range, available only in this restaurant. (Diners Club Winelist awards for 98, 99 & 00.) Beautifully restored and well appointed, this is an ideal place to settle back and savour the food, the ambience and the company. The Manor House is a National Monument and museum with fascinating artworks, Cecil Rhodes memorabilia, Kraak porcelain, furniture and displays.

Bread & Wine Happy Valley Road, La Motte • Modern country fare • Open Wed-Sun, except during season • Booking advised • Children welcome • Wheelchair- friendly • Major credit cards accepted • Tel (021) 876-3692 • Fax (021) 876-3105 • E-mail linda@lqf.co.za • Website www.moreson.co.za

Surrounded by vineyards and lemon orchards, the newly spruced up Bread & Wine restaurant on the Môreson wine farm is a place to indulge the senses. Modern country fare tempts the palate with flirtatious combinations of food and award-winning wines. Feast on delicious local produce, home-made breads, sausages, cured meats and pickles. Bread & Wine is a relaxed and rustic setting for informal family lunches, business lunches and dinners, weddings and larger functions.

Haute Cabrière Cellar Restaurant Pass Road • International cuisine • Closed for 2 weeks annually, usually in July • Booking advised • Children welcome •

Wheelchair-friendly • Major credit cards accepted • Non-smoking • Tel (021) 876-3688 • Fax (021) 876-3691 • E-mail hautecab@iafrica.com

High up on the Franschhoek Pass and overlooking the beautiful valley you'll find the award-winning Haute Cabrière Restaurant in a magnificent mountain cellar. Here two prodigious winelands talents, chef-patron Matthew Gordon and winegrower Achim von Arnim, present a true marriage of food and wine. The cuisine is international, the standard world class. All dishes are available in full- and half- portions – try several to mix and match with the wines, which are all available by the glass or bottle. Wonderful fresh fish, succulent lamb, fresh home-made pasta, salads from the farm and a great selection of delicious modern cuisine will take you into a new dimension in eating out. (See separate Stay-over entry for Auberge Clermont).

La Couronne Robertsvlei Road • New World cuisine • Open daily • Booking advised • Corkage R25 • Children welcome • Major credit cards accepted • Non-smoking • Tel (021) 876-2770 • Fax (021) 876-3788 • E-mail reservations@lacouronnehotel.co.za • Website www.lacouronnehotel.co.za

Situated on the slopes of the Franschhoek foothills and blessed with spectacular views of the valley, this small luxury hotel's restaurant conveys true elegance, and has already been voted one of the top 50 most exciting restaurants in the world by Condé Nast Traveler. Patrons can relish modern international cuisine and an intelligently structured winelist. Alfresco dining on the terrace completes the romantic setting that is the hallmark of the La Couronne experience. Undoubtedly one of the most beautiful locations in the world. (See separate Stay-over entry.)

La Petite Ferme Pass Road • French country cuisine • Open Mon-Sun • Booking advised • Corkage R8 • Children welcome • Major credit cards accepted • Non-smoking • Tel (021) 876-3016/8 • Fax (021) 876-3624 • E-mail lapetite@iafrica.com

Three generations of the Dendy Young family have been involved in the restaurant. Natalie, Mark's cousin, manages the restaurant enabling him to concentrate on the increased wine production. Mark manages to welcome patrons in between the pressing of his next ton of grapes. The wines made here are exclusively available on the winelist or in limited quantities to patrons. The menu features everything from favourite recipes from past generations to more sophisticated and innovative cuisine. Carol Dendy Young still remains active in the kitchen while assisting resident chef Lizette Crabtree. Seasonal fresh produce from the valley includes rainbow trout, a house speciality, deboned and smoked on the farm, and Plum Crazy, home- grown Santa Rosa plums in a port wine sauce. Traditional Malay influences also feature regularly as do lighter summer sensations. Enthusiastic service and magnificent views of the valley below make for an unforgettable winelands experience. (See separate Stay-over entry.)

Le Café at Boschendal Pniel Road (R310) • Breakfasts, teas & Cape-French light lunches • Open Mon- Sun, 10:00-17:00 • Closed Good Friday, 1 May, 16 Jun & Christmas Day • No bookings accepted • Corkage R15 • Special children's menu • Wheelchair-friendly • Major credit cards accepted • Indoor-outdoor seating • Tel (021) 870-4274/82/ 83 • Fax (021) 874-2137

Tucked away in the original slave quarters, Le Café serves tasty breakfasts, light lunches and country-style teas with the best scones and muffins in the valley. Enjoy traditional bobotie in the cosy restaurant in winter; in summer, relax outdoors with a glass of wine, a slice of quiche or a baguette and a salad under the dappled shade of ancient oaks.

Le Pique-Nique at Boschendal Pniel Road (R310) • French-style picnic hampers • Open Mon-Sun, mid-Oct to Apr, 12:15-13:30 for collection of baskets • Closed May to mid-Oct & Good Friday • Booking advised • Corkage R15 • Special children's hampers • Wheelchair-friendly • Major credit cards accepted • Tel (021) 870- 4274 • Fax (021) 874-2137 • E-mail reservations@boschendal.com

During the summer months Le Pique-Nique, at the foot of the majestic Simonsberg mountain, provides the perfect setting for an al fresco lunch. Collect your hamper filled with pâtés, French baguettes, home-cooked cold meats and crispy salads from the gazebo and spread your picnic at tables in the shade of fragrant pine trees or on the lawn beside a pond. For those who can't resist, ice-cream and coffee are served from the gazebo. Guests may linger in the gardens as long as they wish.

Le Quartier Français 16 Huguenot Street • Innovative Cape-Provençal cuisine • Open 7 days a week, breakfast, lunch & dinner • Booking advised • Corkage R20 • Children welcome • Wheelchair-friendly • Major credit cards accepted • Non-smoking • Air-conditioned • Tel (021) 876-2151 • Fax (021) 876-3105 • E-mail linda@lqf.co.za • Website www.lequartier.co.za

Le Quartier Français, with its vibrant and colourful cigar bar, spacious, airy restaurant, panoramic view of the mountains and lavender-filled gardens, lends itself to chef Margot Janse and her team tickling your taste buds. Innovative dishes such as olive oil poached salmon trout with a smoked salmon fritter, cucumber and seaweed, or grilled springbok loin in a balsamic broth with roast onions, mushrooms and curried gnocchi, are served in the restaurant. In the bar or on the terrace, try the lamb burger with creamed avocado, marinated tomato and pickled cucumber on a toasted foccacia. Meals are complemented by an award-winning winelist (Diners Club Winelist Platinum Award 00) featuring local wines. (See separate Stay-over entry for Auberge du Quartier Français.)

Monneaux Franschhoek Country House Main Road • Fusion with Eastern influences • Open 7 days a week, breakfast, lunch & dinner • Booking advised • Corkage R20 • Wheelchair-friendly • Children welcome • Major credit cards accepted • Non-smoking section • (021) 876-3386 • (021) 876-2744 • fch@mweb.co.za • Website www.ecl.co.za

Situated at the Franschhoek Country House (see separate Stay-over entry), the Monneaux Restaurant is named after the building, which was once a perfume- producing factory. Voted one of the top restaurants in SA, the modern French fusion cuisine is innovative, prepared with fresh well-sourced ingredients and exquisitely presented. Lunches are served under a spreading pepper tree in the gardens while dinner is served in the understated yet elegant dining room or enclosed verandah. The extensive winelist emphasises local wines.

Greyton

Greyton Lodge 46 Main Street • African/Continental • Open Mon-Sun 7:30-23:30 • Closed for lunch Mon • Booking advised • Corkage R12 • Children welcome • Major credit cards accepted • Non-smoking section (cigar-friendly) • Tel (0282) 549-876 • Fax (0282) 549 672 • E-mail greytonlodge@kingsley.co.za • Website www.greytonlodge.com

Revel in the historic surroundings created by hospitable owners Philip and Sandra Engelen. Emphasis is on refined country cooking, complemented by award- winning winelists (Diners Club Winelist awards for 93, 96, 97 98, 99, 00 & 01). In summer, breakfast and lunch are served in the garden, while in winter you can dine by candlelight beside one of the cavernous log fires. Nailed to the ceiling in the Royal Bar are some 20 000 corks, while on the wall are signatures of winemakers and wine industry luminaries (including John Platter). The 17 rooms and suites make the lodge an ideal relaxing getaway or conference breakaway.

Groot Drakenstein (see Franschhoek)

Paarl

Bosman's Grande Roche Plantasie Street • Global cuisine with 'Flavours of the Cape' menu • Open daily, all day • Closed Jun, Jul & Aug • Booking essential • Wheelchair-friendly • Major credit cards accepted • Tel (021) 863-2727 • Fax (021) 863-2220 • E-mail christine@granderoche.co.za

Wind your way through the winelands and stop at Bosman's for light, elegant, informal lunches complemented by splendid wines from the superbly stocked cellar (Diners Club Winelist Diamond award in 00). Bosman's is a world-class restaurant providing contemporary Cape gourmet cuisine in the refined atmosphere of a magnificent manor house. The Grande Roche, a five-star estate hotel (see separate Stay-Over entry), has become a legend on the hospitality scene, winning a formidable array of awards and culinary accolades. Latest achievements include being ranked among the 10 top wine country hotels of the world in America's Food & Wine magazine and Satour's first Hotel of the Year award for its "incredible attention to detail, impeccable grounds, excellent food and superb levels of luxury". The first and only hotel-restaurant in Africa to achieve Relais Gourmand status, one of the world's highest Relais & Chateaux culinary appellations.

Cotage Fromage – The Cheese & Olive Oil Speciality Shop Vrede en Lust Farm, intersection of Klapmuts & R45, Simondium • Informal deli-style with fresh ingredients • Open daily, 9:00-17:00 (closed for dinner except for pre-booked groups or special functions) • Closed Christmas Day, New Year's Day & Easter Monday • Corkage R10 • Children welcome • Wheelchair-friendly • Major credit cards accepted • Tel (021) 874-3991 • Fax (021) 874-3992 • E-mail tania.bouwer@cotagefromage.co.za; tracy.vanmaaren@ixchange.com

The focus is on local cheeses, olive oils and olives. Some of the most popular items on the menu are the 3 cheese boards. A 'normal', goat and connoisseur version each showcase the best of South African cheeses, served with delectable deli products like marinated mushrooms, artichokes de angelo, sun-dried tomatoes, feta and freshly baked bread, all made by Cotage Fromage. Patrons have the option of eating next to the fire in winter or outside under the oaks in summer. Well positioned adjacent to the new cellar and vineyards of working wine farm Vrede and Lust, is has a warm and relaxed atmosphere, an ideal setting for lazy lunches. Wines from the area, including those of neighbouring farms, are served.

Il Casale Ashanti Wine Farm, Klein Drakenstein • Mediterranean & SA influences • Open Sep-May, 6 days a week lunch & dinner; mid-Aug to Sep, lunch Wed-Sun, dinner Fri-Sat • Closed mid-Jun to mid-Aug (special bookings only) • Booking advised • Corkage R20 • Children welcome • Wheelchair-friendly • Major credit cards accepted • Non-smoking section • Tel (021) 862-6288 • Fax (021) 862-2864/863-3325 • E-mail casale@intekom.co.za

An exciting new venue on a very Mediterranean note, Il Casale offers breathtaking views of the Drakenstein mountains from the heart of Ashanti wine farm. Marc Friederich and his team use the freshest ingredients and some very typical South African delights to produce a tasty combination of Italian and Provençal cuisine. Home-made bread is baked daily. In winter, the fireplace creates a very warm and relaxed atmosphere in the arty lounge. In summer, the lovely terrace and lawn overlooking the 25ha dam makes it the ideal setting for lazy lunches and weddings.

The Restaurant at Pontac 16 Zion Street • New World cuisine • Sep-Apr, open 7 days a week lunch & dinner; May-Aug, closed Tue • Booking advised • Children welcome • Wheelchair access • Major credit cards accepted • Tel (021) 872-0445 • Fax (021) 863-8906 • E-mail pontac@iafrica.com • Website www.pontac.com

Housed in the renovated former estate barn, 'The Restaurant at Pontac' offers fine dining with a New World flair. A varied and unique selection of interesting dishes are specially prepared by their talented young South African-born chef, who trained in restaurants locally as well as in a Michelin-rated restaurant in Europe. The speciality of the house: delicate sauces with mouthwatering flavours guaranteed to please every palate. This contemporary cuisine is served in an elegant yet cosy environment, with the historic character of the building retained in its original wooden floors and restored brickwork. Antique window frames and deep-set window ledges lend an air of nostalgia. The restaurant with its Koi fish pond and gardens offers an unrivalled view of Paarl Rock and is an inviting venue for candlelit dinners or casual lunches. In winter, the fireplace adds a warm glow. (See separate Stay-over entry.)

Rhebokskloof Restaurant Rhebokskloof Wine Estate, Wine Route No 8 • Global cuisine • Open 7 days a week for tea and lunch (closed for dinner Tue & Wed) • Booking advised • Tel (021) 869- 8606 • Fax (021) 869-8906 • E-mail rhebok@iafrica.com • Website www.rhebokskloof.co.za

Rhebokskloof Restaurant offers an opportunity to enjoy top quality wines from a award-winning winelist that highlights Rhebokskloof Estate's wines, accompanied by superb global cuisine (one of South Africa's top 100 restaurants), all in one of the most stunning settings in the Cape winelands.

The Olive and Vine Seidelberg Wine Estate, Suid-Agter Paarl Road • Eclectic cuisine • Open Mon-Fri 10:00-16:00; Sat-Sun 10:00-15:00 for teas/lunches; closed Christmas Day & Good Friday • Booking advised in summer • Tel (021) 863-3495/6, Fax (021) 863-3797 • E-mail ebr@new.co.za

Fast becoming one of Paarl's most popular winelands eateries. Intimate cellar-style restaurant or outdoor seating with magnificent views. Varied menu and daily specials, including the best wild trout in the winelands, caught on the farm – smoked to order on the premises – makes this a must-visit. Sinful desserts made on the farm. Picnic baskets available on a pre-booked basis. Dinner by appointment for groups of 15 to 30 people.

Wagon Wheels 57 Lady Grey Street • Steakhouse par excellence • Tue-Fri 12:00-14:00; Tue-Sat 18:00-late • Closed Sun-Mon • Dinner only public holidays • Booking advised • Wheelchair-friendly • Major credit cards accepted • Smoking and a non-smoking section • Tel (021) 872-5265

Pierre and Sandra van der Merwe's famous Wagon Wheels is no ordinary steakhouse. This switched-on couple serves the most extraordinary steaks in the winelands, impeccably grilling sumptuously matured cuts with accompaniments to faint for – awesome chips, unbelievably crisp (and elegant) garden salads, superb alternatives for the carnivorously challenged, and a decidedly classy winelist featuring local heroes and some high-powered non-citizens. All in a relaxed, friendly ambience, much loved by locals and international visitors. Also caters for smokers and non-smokers alike, with a welcoming smile for children.

Robertson

Branewynsdraai Restaurant & Wine Sales 1 Kromhout Street • Traditional & à la carte • Open Mon-Sat 10:00-16:00, 19:00-late, all year round; Sun 12:00-14:30 (winter months & functions only) • Booking advised • Corkage R5 • Children welcome • Wheelchair access • Major credit cards accepted • Tel (023) 626-3202 • Fax (023) 626-1031 • E-mail branewynsdraai@xpoint.co.za

Situated just off the main road on the Worcester side of Robertson, this restaurant offers three venues: shady garden tables under the ancient pepper trees, the tranquil dining room, as well as an enclosed courtyard which hosts private functions, tour groups and weddings. The menu encompasses Cape traditional cuisine, superb steaks and seafood. Other features include an award-winning winelist (Diners Club Winelist awards 96, 98, 99, 00 & 01), a TV room and children's menu, cosy fires in winter and an adjacent wine shop.

Fraai Uitzicht 1798 Klaas-Voogds East (R60), between Robertson & Ashton/Montagu • Country fare • Open for lunch & dinner, Wed-Sun • Closed Jun & Jul • Booking advised • Corkage R10 • Major credit cards accepted • Non-smoking inside • Tel/fax (023) 626-6156 • E-mail info@fraaiuitzicht.com • Website www.fraaiuitzicht.com

This historic wine and guest farm (see separate Stay-over entry) was recently restored and a restaurant opened, much to the delight of local residents. Attentive hosts provide a friendly, relaxed ambience for fine dining. The varied menu consists of hearty home-cooked dishes using fresh produce from their vegetable and herb garden. Starters such as Black Forest rolls with spinach, ham and feta, or springbok carpaccio, main dishes that include tequila chicken, braised lamb in phyllo pastry or fillet Fraai Uitzicht, followed by not-to-be-missed desserts, especially the dream of chocolate. The inside fireplace is a delight in winter, and the outside verandah has spectacular views across the Breede River Valley. The food is complemented by a winelist that incorporates some of the Robertson Valley's finest.

Somerset West (see Stellenbosch)

Stellenbosch

Avontuur Wine Estate R44 between Stellenbosch & Somerset West • Cape country cuisine • Buffet lunch Mon-Fri 12:30-17:00, closed Sat-Sun • Booking advised • Children welcome • Wheelchair-friendly • Major credit cards accepted • Tel (021) 855-3450 • Fax (021) 855-4600 • E-mail avonwine@mweb.co.za • Website www.avontuurestate.co.za

This intimate restaurant with its views over the winelands towards Table Mountain offers delicious Cape country buffet-style lunches. A friendly relaxed ambience is the perfect setting in which to sample the extensive range of award-winning wines. The menu offers a variety of traditional dishes including smoked snoek, Cape Malay chicken, venison and glazed gammon together with succulent vegetables and superb salads. These are complemented by wonderful desserts including pumpkin pie, followed by a unique cheese board. Seasonal variations allow guests to enjoy this experience beside the log fire or under the vines on the terrace.

Die Ou Pastorie Restaurant 41 Lourens Street, Somerset West • Continental cuisine • Lunch Tue-Fri, dinner Mon-Sat; closed Sun • Booking advised • Corkage R20 • Major credit cards accepted • Non-smoking (except in bar) • Tel (021) 852-2120 • Fax (021) 851-3710 • E-mail info@dieoupastorie.co.za • Website www.dieoupastorie.co.za

This characterful restaurant has been offering consistency in service and quality of food for many years. The combination of good food, excellent service and dedication to guests' satisfaction are the cornerstones here. Owner Garry Roberts, aided by chef Carmen Truter, provides an innovative modern-styled à la carte menu, which changes seasonally, with flavours and textures that are harmoniously blended. This has earned Die Ou Pastorie the reputation of being one of the top restaurants in the Western Cape. It also features an award-winning winelist (Diners Club Winelist awards in 96, 97, 98, 99 & 00). This elegant restaurant, set in the historic former Dutch Reformed Church parsonage (circa 1819), offers the warmth, elegance and tranquillity of a bygone era and ensures an unforgettable experience. (See separate Stay-over entry.)

Hermitage at Hazendal, Bottelary Road, Kuils River • Unique combination of SA, Russian and Mediterranean cuisine • Picnics during season (Nov-Mar) • Open Mon-Sun, 12:00-14:30 • Closed Good Friday, Christmas Day, New Year's Day • Booking advised • Children welcome • Wheelchair-friendly • Major credit cards accepted • Non-smoking • Tel (021) 903-5112 ext 210 • Fax (021) 903-0057 • E-mail info@hazendal.co.za

This intimate restaurant is situated between the original cellar, which has now been renovated into a tasting centre and restaurant, and the new state-of-the-art cellar, built in 1996. A lovely fireplace in the lounge creates a warm welcome, and is a great place to relax after mealtimes. There's seating for about 50 people in the restaurant, with two adjoining courtyards. Outdoor seating on the patios affords beautiful views of the surrounding mountains and hills. Meals vary from light fresh salads, hearty home-made soups and specialities, to pasta and traditional Cape Malay dishes. Hazendal also offers this superb venue for functions. Russian-born owner Dr Mark Voloshin's passion for his homeland's culture saw him establish the Marvol Museum of Russian Art, which is situated inside the wine cellar, along with the conference facility, which can host up to 40 people. Here you can see a display of Russian icons and paintings by well-known Russian artists – Mark Voloshin's private collection of Fabergé eggs and jewellery are also on permanent display.

Lady Phillips Restaurant Vergelegen Farm, Lourensford Road, Somerset West • Cosmopolitan cuisine • Open Mon-Sun, lunch 12:00-14:30; tea 10:00-11:30, 15:00-16:00 • Booking advised • Corkage R10 • Children welcome • Wheelchair-friendly • Major credit cards accepted • Non-smoking • No cellphones • Tel/fax (021) 847-1346 • E-mail ladyphillips@vergelegen.co.za • Website www.vergelegen.co.za

A delightful daytime venue all year round, with open-air patio and newly redecorated interior, filled with fresh flowers. The small innovative à la carte menu makes imaginative use of the large variety of herbs picked daily from the garden. Country lunches range from quiches to home-made gourmet pies and pastas, as well as continental dishes. Interesting vegetarian dishes are also a feature. In summer, from Nov to Apr, 9:30-16:00 daily, the nearby **Rose Terrace** is open for alfresco lunches of pâté, salads and baguettes.

L'Auberge du Paysan Off the R44 between Somerset West & Stellenbosch; turn into Winery Road, follow signs into Raithby Road • French cuisine • Lunch Tue- Sat, dinner Mon-Sat • Booking advised • Corkage R15 • Children over 10 • Wheelchair-friendly • Major credit cards accepted • Tel/fax (021) 842-2008 • Website www.aubergedupaysan.co.za

Patron Frederick Thermann's style and panache highlight the discreet charms of this chic French country restaurant, among the finest in the country. The elegant appointments, decor and ambience complement the traditional classic French menu with specialities from Alsace and Provence. In summer, sip pre-dinner drinks on the shady patio, and in winter, wine and dine in the romantic warmth of the open log fire. Tempting terrine of pheasant Cumberland, a casserole of fruits de mer or delicate and piquant quails followed by a finalé of crème brulée are specialities of the house. In winter, oysters, venison and duckling, and in summer, crustaceans and fresh Stellenbosch berries are seasonal delights. You may want to treat yourself to crêpe Suzette or sabayon prepared at your table by the patron. Superb winelist with L'Auberge du Paysan Pinotage now available.

Le Pommier Helshoogte Pass, Banhoek • Country fare • Lunch/dinner Tue-Sat; lunch only Sun • Closed Mon out of season • Booking advised • Tel (021) 885-1269 • Fax (021) 885-1274

Rooted high up on the Helshoogte Pass overlooking the lush Banhoek Valley, you'll find Le Pommier Restaurant. This old converted farm-shed offers not only spectacular views but also a sense of timeless charm, warmth and personality. Like the mountains, forever suggesting different moods, Le Pommier offers cosy log fires in winter with snow-capped mountains in the distance and cool rolling greenery in the endless summer. These allures, combined with personal service, add to a sense of wellbeing not often experienced. Facilities include a conference/ function centre, art gallery and guesthouse.

Oude Libertas Restaurant & Conference Centre Oude Libertas Road, opposite Distell off Adam Tas Road • Intercontinental cuisine • Lunch Mon-Fri 1200-15:00, dinner Mon-Sat 18:00-22:00 • Closed Sun • Booking advised • Corkage R16 • Wheelchair-friendly • Major credit cards accepted • Tel (021) 809-7429 • Fax (021) 886-6908 • E-mail oudelib@adept.co.za • Website www.oudelibertas.co.za

Seated in an intimate alcove at Oude Libertas Restaurant Cellar, surrounded by 7 000 bottles of maturing red wine, you can prepare for an eating experience that will excite the palate. You will be treated to the best of intercontinental cuisine, complemented by your choice of award-winning Distell wines. Oude Libertas Restaurant provides the ideal venue for a relaxed meal, business lunch or romantic dinner. In the Vineyard Hall, they cater for exquisite weddings, corporate functions and gala dinners. Oude Libertas conference centre consists of a theatre-style auditorium that will meet all your conference needs.

The Duck Pond R310, Welmoed Winery, Lynedoch • Country fare • Open 7 days a week in summer for lunch, 12:00-15:00 • Closed Mon during winter • Booking advised • Fully licensed • Corkage R9 • Children welcome • Wheelchair access • Major credit cards accepted • Non-smoking section • Tel/fax (021) 881-3310

The Duck Pond serves country-style food focusing on a lighter, healthier approach and using the freshest ingredients sourced from the area. Known for its personal friendly service and lovely setting – children especially love the ducks at the pond – it is the perfect place for long, lazy lunches. Specialities include ostrich bobotie, fragrant chicken and mushroom pie, fresh mussels, and roast duck with a port and berry sauce. They also cater for weddings, birthdays, parties and general functions. The restaurant is fully licensed and promotes Welmoed's award-winning wines at very reasonable prices. They also cater for weddings, birthday parties and general functions.

The Restaurant @ 33° South Vlottenburg Road (off R310), Vlottenburg • Real food • Lunch Mon-Sun, dinner Fri-Sat (except for pre-booked groups or functions) • Booking advised • Corkage R15 (though not encouraged as wine markups are minimal) • Children welcome • Wheelchair-friendly • Major credit cards accepted • Tel (021) 881-3793 • Fax (021) 881-3740 • E-mail restaurant@33south.co.za • Website www.33south.co.za

Anne Pearson's brilliance in the kitchen drew fans from as far afield as Durban and even Johannesburg to her Pietermaritzburg restaurants, La Provence and White Mischief. Their loss is definitely the winelands' gain but come and find out for yourself why many regard her food as the best in the country... And with wine prices so incredibly reasonable you'll probably feel inclined to order more than one to match the food. (See separate Stay-over entry for Bordeaux Place @ 33° South.)

The Vineleaf Devon Valley Hotel, Devon Valley Road • Innovative Cape cuisine • Booking advised • Corkage R12 (no charge on rare/unusual wines) • Children welcome • Wheelchair-friendly • Major credit cards accepted • Non-smoking section • Tel (021) 882-2012 • Fax (021) 882-2610 E-mail devon@iafrica.com

The Vineleaf at the historic Devon Valley Hotel (see separate Stay-over entry) serves innovative Cape cuisine, with the emphasis on home-grown and organic produce. The menu changes daily to highlight whatever is fresh, exciting or seasonal. Head chef Isaac Monaheng aims to combine the best of South African ingredients with originality and style – just-caught stumpnose on home-made squid-ink tagliatelle in a saffron broth gives you a taste of what to expect. In summer, enjoy a light lunch on the patio or enjoy a winelands pizza prepared in the wood-fired oven. In winter, savour one of their own Sylvanvale wines in front of the roaring log fire – the award-winning winelist (Diners Club Winelist merit awards in 98, 99 and Diamond award in 00) offers the full range of Devon Valley wines together with a representative selection of the Cape's finest.

96 Winery Road Restaurant Zandberg Farm, Winery Road (off the R44 between Somerset West & Stellenbosch) • Country fare with Cape, Provençal and Eastern influences • Lunch Mon-Sun, dinner Mon-Sat; lunch only Sun • Booking advised • Corkage R10 • Children welcome • Wheelchair-friendly • Major credit cards accepted • Non-smoking section • Tel (021) 842-2020 • Fax (021) 842-2050 • E-mail wineryrd@mweb.co.za

From the start in 1996 it has been their goal to delight each guest with a superb dining experience in their warm, relaxing venue in the heart of the glorious Helderberg winelands. A sort of food HQ for, in particular, local and international wine luminaries. Food is fresh, colourful, uncomplicated, mostly organic, cooked with care and generosity. The menu changes frequently according to the whim and creativity of chef Natasha Harris and mother nature. The winelist is extensive with choices from the Helderberg region and the 'rest of the world' with something to suit every pocket and palate.

Stellenbosch/Kuils River (see Stellenbosch)

Wellington

Hildenbrand's Table Hildenbrand Wine & Olive Estate, Klein Rhebokskloof Country & Guest House, Horseshoe Road • Cape country • Open 7 days a week, 11:30-15:00 (dinners by arrangement) • Booking advised • Children welcome • Wheelchair-friendly • Major credit cards accepted • Tel/fax (021) 873-4115 • Cell (082) 774-7249 • E-mail info@wine-estate-hildenbrand.co.za • Website www.wine-estate-hildenbrand.co.za

"Country meals with a touch of class, cosy atmosphere and fantastic hosts," is how their guests describe them. Situated on a historical 40ha wine and olive estate, they change the menu seasonally. The traditional Cape and Mediterranean influence is retained through the use of their superior olive products and fresh herbs from the farm and accentuated by their own home-made chutneys and breads. Their speciality, ostrich bobotie, fresh salads, ploughman's platter and a 'pasta surprise' are all very popular and can be enjoyed under a charming shady tree or inside their *gemütliche* tasting room adjacent to the wine cellar. A growing variety of the estate's wines can be tasted or chosen to complement you meal. Bon appetit! (See separate Stay-over entry.)

Wine and food partners

Here are some recommendations on matching cuisine and wine:

Artichokes Make most wines taste metallic. Drink water, or squeeze lemon onto the chokes, which seems to tone down the tinny edges, and team with a high-acid, fresh dry white.

Asparagus A difficult customer. A dry white with lots of flavour, like fresh sauvignon.

Avocado Riesling, white port.

Barbecue See Braai below.

Beef Roast: Cape Bdx blend, cabernet, cabernet franc, merlot, pinot, just about any serious red. Cold roast beef: room for a bit of light here, reds that can take a spot of chilling, pinot, also rosé, blanc de noir, sparkling dry rosé. See also Stews below.

Biltong (savoury air-dried meat snack, usually sliced) Not usually partnered with wine, but try robust shiraz (or beer).

Bobotie (spicy ground-meat, usually lamb) Many possible wine-partners: try dry sparkling, fresh young chenin, riesling, pinotage or other reds made in fruity, easy- drinking styles.

Bouillabaisse Fresh young white, sauvignon, dry rosé.

Braai (the traditional barbecue, a national institution) The wine partner would depend on what's being braaied, but whether meat, fish or fowl, choose a wine with character and muscle, not a fragile little thing that would be overwhelmed by the smoke for a start.

Carpaccio Meat: Just about any red. Fish: chardonnay, MCC.

Charcuterie Simple fresh reds.

Cheese A good cheddar can be very good with an elegant red or ruby port. Cream cheese is better with full-bodied whites – try semillon or chardonnay. Goat's cheese: full-bodied white or dry red. Blue cheese: as long as it's not too powerful, good with rich dessert whites such as NLH and port.

Chicken Roast: best red or white. Pie: try light to medium shiraz or young pinotage.

Chinese MCC, dry (or dryish) white with flavour; riesling.

Chocolate Difficult. Demi-sec bubbly, red muscadel, Cape Pineau des Charentes (see Laborie, Louwshoek-Voorsorg). Or wait and have a glass of dry champagne after the choc mousse.

Crudités Simple dry white.

Curry Pinotage-punting Beyers Truter of Kanonkop recommends (what else?) pinotage; Giorgio Dalla Cia of Meerlust suggests cabernet or a Cape Bdx blend. Fish curry: chardonnay is good, especially when coconut milk is an ingredient. A cheerful, slightly off-dry (and slightly petillant) chenin blend is fine too. Also blanc de noir. Sweetish Cape-Malay curries: try matching the spice with gewürz or young riesling or contrasting with sauvignon.

Desserts See Chocolate above.

Duck Fruity young red, champagne, shiraz, off-dry riesling, pinot.

Eggs Not great for or with any wine, but a simple omelette calls for a simple glass of red.

Foie gras Sweet white, NLH/SLH, MCC, merlot.

Fruit MCC, sweet sparkling wine, Late or Special Late Harvest, hanepoot jerepiko or rosé. Strawberries: with cream: NLH; without cream: Uiterwyk's Pieter de Waal recommends a light red. Beware of citrus fruits as they can overpower/sour a wine.

Game birds Rosé, pinot or Cape Bdx blend. Remember, the darker the meat, the darker/stronger the wine. Guinea fowl: pinot, merlot or powerful oaked chenin.

Ham Young pinot; fresh, juicy red.

Hamburgers Dry, simple red.

Ice-cream (If not too sweet) Good bubbly.

Karoo lamb and mutton Roast: best red (cabernet, merlot etc.). Chops: shiraz or young cabernet. Try to avoid mint sauce – it distorts the taste of even minty, new-clone cabs. Stews: light red.

Kidneys Full red, riesling, chardonnay.

Liver Fruity, forceful young red, maybe pinotage.

Mushrooms Pinot.

Mustard sauce Light red, pinotage.

Nuts Port after a meal; sherry before; nutty desserts: MCC.

Oxtail Shiraz.

Pasta Seafood: sauvignon, down-table chardonnay; cream, cheese, egg, meat, tomato sauces: sturdy red.

Pastries and cakes SLH.
Pâté Champagne, gewürz, riesling, pinot.
Phutu or mealie meal (SA equivalent of polenta) Sturdy red.
Pizza Depends on ingredients, but also see pasta above.
Pork Off-dry white, fruity red, rosé, zinfandel. Pinotage with spare ribs. In Portugal, roast sucking pig is often teamed with bubbly.
Quiche Full fruity white, riesling, gewürz, sylvaner.
Rabbit Depends on how it's cooked, and the ingredients. Anything from great to simple, red or white.
Ratatouille Light, fruity red, rosé, blanc de noir.
Risotto Fish: medium-bodied dry white; mushrooms: pinot.
Salads Go easy on the vinaigrette – vinegar (or even too much lemon juice) affects wine. A prickly fresh white or rosé with a salade Niçoise. Chardonnay with a grand shellfish salad. Or something non-serious like a blanc de noir. Or top up one's water table.
Seafood Caviare MCC.
Fish Kurt and Lyn Ammann of Rozendal recommend dry red. If that doesn't appeal, dry sparkling, MCC or dry white (sauvignon or chardonnay/chardonnay blend) are safe choices for saltwater; more delicate white or MCC for freshwater. Grilled: sauvignon; cream sauce: chardonnay, chardonnay blend. With red-wine sauce: red used in recipe, or pinot. Smoked: crisp aromatic white, sauvignon, full-bodied (wooded) chardonnay, gewürz or riesling, dry or with a touch of sugar. Sushi: a not-too-grand (nor too rich) chardonnay.
Salmon Chardonnay or fruity non-tannic young red.
Sardines (grilled) Crisp petillant white, young red.
Smoorvis (braised fish, usually lightly spicy) Frisky (off-dry) chenin, chardonnay or young pinotage.
Snoek Assertive dry white, young red or pinotage.
Sole Grilled: sauvignon or Cape riesling. Sauced: chardonnay.
Trout Young riesling
Shellfish Grilled, boiled, steamed or cold (with mayonnaise): sauvignon, crisp young chenin or off-dry riesling. Rich sauce: MCC or chardonnay-sémillon blend. Piri-piri: this spicy/hot sauce calls for a light petillant white.
Calamari (squid) Sauvignon, dry white blend or light red.
Cape salmon (geelbek) Racy sauvignon.
Crab Riesling or off-dry chenin.
Crayfish (Cape rock lobster or kreef) Sauvignon or chardonnay.
Elf (shad) Chardonnay, dry chenin or Cape riesling.
Galjoen Sauvignon, chardonnay or cabernet blanc de noir.
Kingklip Chardonnay or wood-matured white.
Langoustine (deep-sea, from SA's East Coast) MCC, chardonnay.
Mussels Sauvignon or chenin. Smoked: wooded chardonnay
Oysters MCC, sauvignon, lightly wooded or unwooded chardonnay.
Perlemoen (abalone) Chardonnay or sauvignon.
Prawns Chardonnay or sauvignon.
Snacks Of the canapé sort: aperitif white, fruity, dry to off-dry, kir, sparkling white/ rosé, blanc de noir, dry sherry.
Snails Chardonnay, pinot, dry riesling.
Sosaties As for curry.
Soufflés Cheese: red; fish: white; dessert: dessert white.
Steak Red wine: cabernet, merlot, shiraz – take your pick. Robert and Gabi Christianus of Wagon Wheels & Gabi's recommend vintage champagne. Pepper steak: somehow smoothes tannins, so doesn't need a mellow old bottle.

Stews and bredies Hearty red. Fish casserole: fresh young white, sauvignon or dry rosé. Waterblommetjie bredie: sauvignon, chardonnay, young pinotage or merlot.

Sweetbreads Chardonnay, or fine claret, pinot.

Thai Draughts of cool fresh dry white for the chilli-hot dishes. Lemon grass, coconut milk and good chardonnay go surprisingly well together. A chilled nouveau style could hold its own.

Tongue Gently dry white, fruity red.

Tripe Hearty red, simple dry white or dry rosé. With tomato: dry red. With onions or white sauce: off-dry chenin or chenin-blend.

Turkey Zinfandel, dry rosé, pinot.

Veal Take your pick, depending on preparation. With vitello tonnato try a chilled, light red.

Vegetables Sauvignon.

Venison Powerful pinot, pinotage, shiraz or mature Cape Bdx blend.

See also *Wine styles* for more about the styles mentioned here.

Maps

The maps on the following pages show wineries and other locales where wine may be tasted (at times indicated under the relevant entries in the A–Z). The areas covered by the individual maps are not necessarily those of the official Wine of Origin areas — which are indicated on a separate map (see Winegrowing areas). Note that the maps are not to scale, and a few are not to scale at all.

Areas covered by the maps

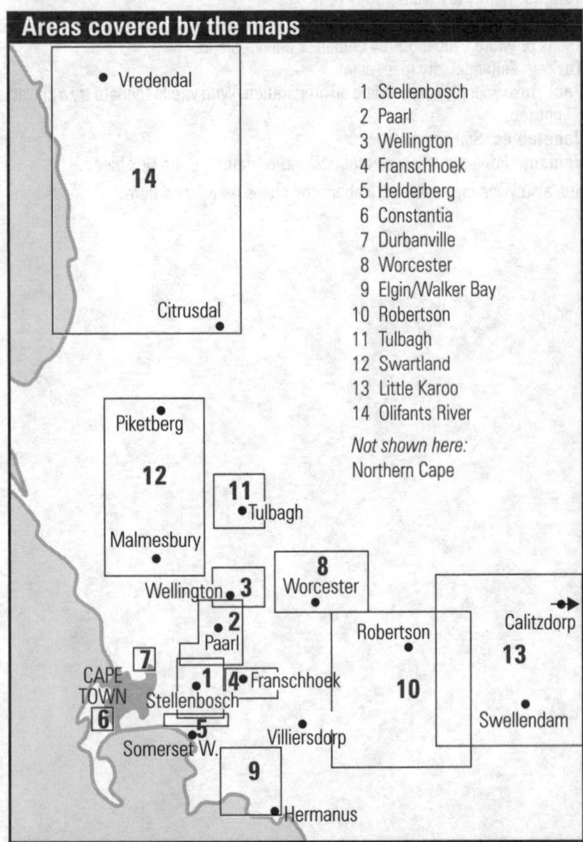

Some distances from Cape Town (kilometres)

Calitzdorp	370	Paarl	60	Tulbagh	120
Franschhoek	75	Robertson	160	Worcester	110
Hermanus	120	Stellenbosch	45	Vredendal	300

Key for maps

Main access roads	R62 R60 Road numbers
Roads	Towns
Gravel roads	18 Tasting facilities

Constantia

1 Ambeloui
2 Buitenverwachting
3 Constantia Uitsig
4 Groot Constantia
5 High Constantia
6 Klein Constantia
7 Steenberg

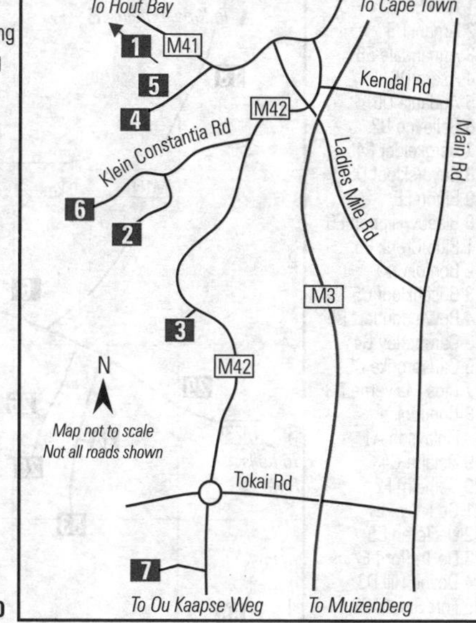

Constantia Wine Route
Tel: (021) 794-1810

Durbanville

1 Altydgedacht
2 Bloemendal
3 Diemersdal
4 Durbanville Hills
5 Meerendal
6 Nitida

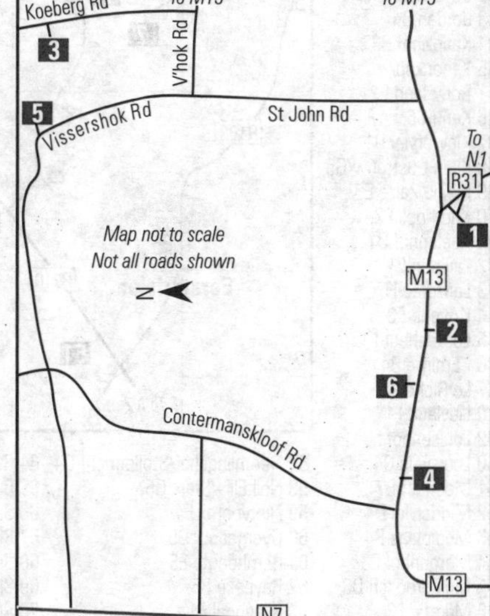

Durbanville Wine Route
Tel: 083-310-1220

Stellenbosch

1 Alto E7
2 Amani B5
3 Annandale E6
4 Asara D5
5 Audacia D6
6 Bellevue B2
7 Bergkelder E4
8 Beyerskloof D3
9 Bilton E6
10 Blaauwklippen E6
11 Blue Creek E6
12 Bonfoi C4
13 Boschkloof C5
14 Bowe Joubert B5
15 Camberley G4
16 Carisbrooke C5
17 Clos Malverne D3
18 Coppoolse Finlayson A1
19 Delaire G4
20 Delheim F2
21 De Meye E1
22 De Toren B5
23 De Trafford F7
24 Devon Hill D3
25 Fort Simon B3
26 Goede Hoop B3
27 Graceland E6
28 Hartenberg D3
29 Hazendal A3
30 Helderkruin E7
31 Hoopenburg E1
32 JC le Roux D3
33 Jordan B4
34 Kaapzicht B3
35 Kanonkop/ Bouwland E2
36 Kanu C5
37 Klawervlei D1
38 Klein Gustrouw G5
39 Kleine Zalze E5
40 Knorhoek F2
41 Koelenhof D1
42 Laibach E1
43 Lanzerac F5
44 L'Avenir E3
45 Le Bonheur F1
46 L'Emigré B4
47 Le Riche G5
48 Lievland F1
49 Louisenhof E3
50 Louisvale C4
51 Meerlust B7
52 Middelvlei D4
53 Mooiplaas B4
54 Morgenhof E3
55 Mulderbosch D3
56 Muratie F2

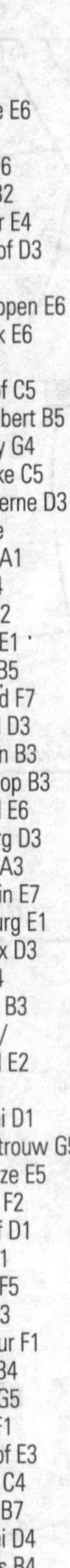

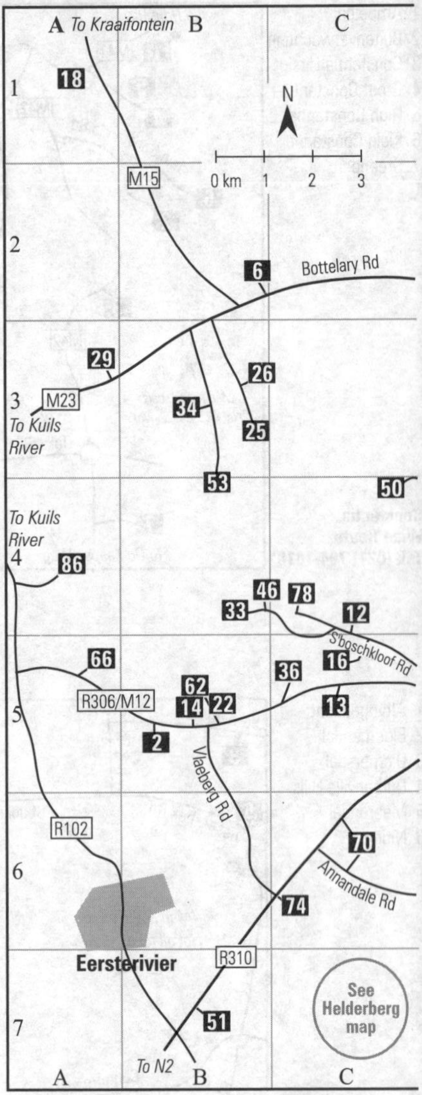

57 Neethlingshof/Stellenzicht D4
58 Neil Ellis/Stark G5
59 Nietvoorbij E4
60 Overgaauw D5
61 Remhoogte E3
62 Reyneke B5
63 Rozendal F4
64 Rustenberg F3
65 Rust en Vrede E7
66 Saxenburg A5
67 SFW/Distell E4
68 Simonsig D2
69 Slaley E2
70 Spier/Savanha C6

Stellenbosch

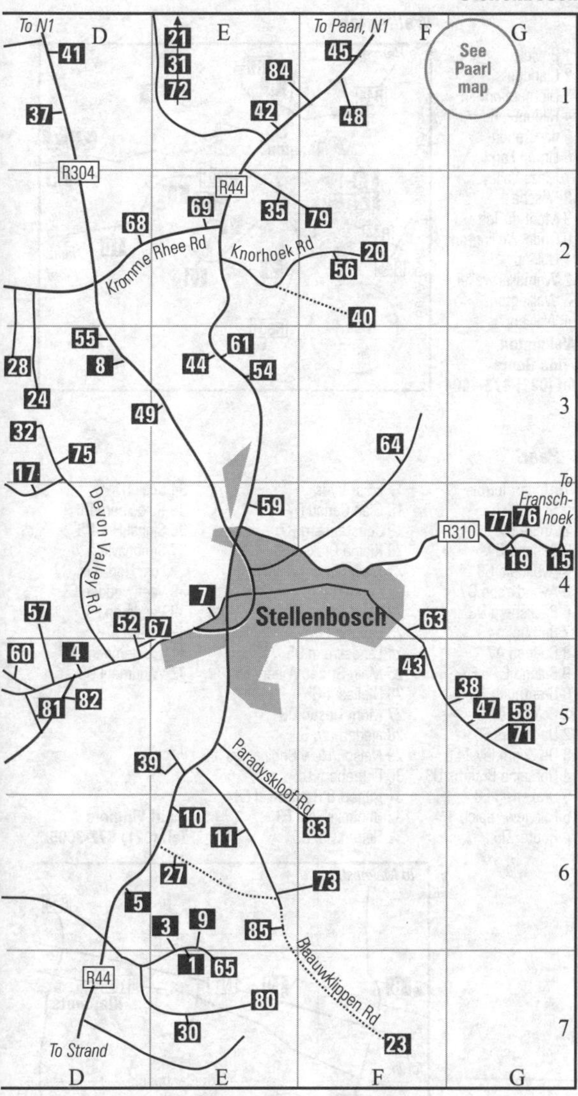

71 Stark G5
72 Starke E1
73 Stellekaya F6
74 S'boschVyds/ Welmoed C6
75 Sylvanvale (Devon Valley Hotel) D3
76 Thelema G4
77 Tokara G4
78 Uiterwyk C4
79 Uitkyk F2
80 Uva Mira E7
81 Vlottenburg D5
82 Vredenheim D5
83 Vriesenhof/Talana Hill F6
84 Warwick E1
85 Waterford E6
86 Zevenwacht A4

Stellenbosch Wine Route
Tel: (021) 886-4310

Wellington

1 Bovlei
2 Claridge
3 Diemersfontein
4 Hildenbrand
5 Jacaranda
6 Linton Park
7 Maze Valley
8 Mischa
9 Mont du Toit
10 Oude Wellington
11 Upland
12 Wamakersvallei
13 Wellington
14 Welvanpas

Wellington Wine Route
Tel (021) 873-4604

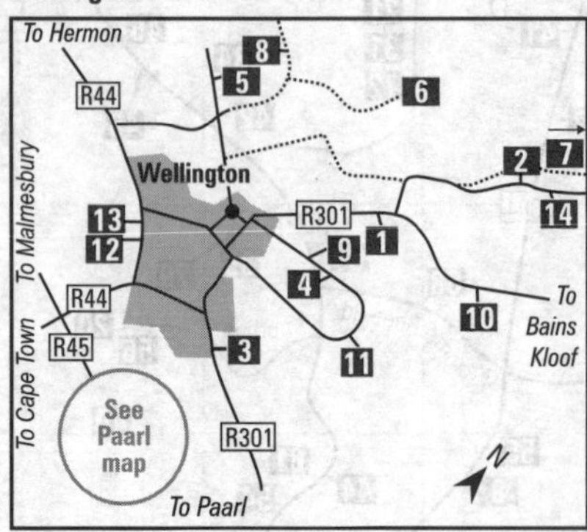
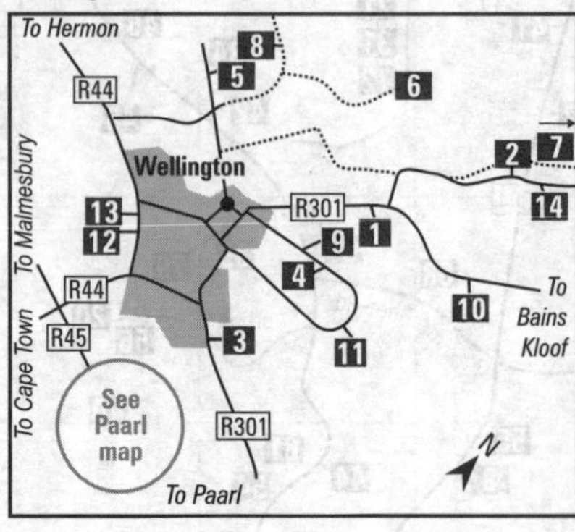

Paarl

1 African Terroir/ Sonop D1
2 Anura D7
3 Ashanti G4
4 Avondale G6
5 Avondvrede D7
6 Backsberg D8
7 Bernheim F3
8 Bodega A7
9 Boland E3 & F3
10 Brenthurst E6
11 Coleraine E6
12 De Villiers E3
13 De Zoete Inval E6
14 Domaine Brahms D3
15 Drakensig E8
16 Fairview/ Spice Route D6
17 Frost Vyds
18 Glen Carlou D7
19 Joostenberg B7
20 Kleine Draken E6
21 Klein Simonsvlei/ Niel Joubert D7
22 KWV E5
23 Laborie E6
24 Landskroon D5
25 Main Street Winery E5
26 Mellasat G5
27 Mont Destin D8
28 Nederburg G4
29 Nelson/New Beginnings E2
30 Perdeberg D2
31 Rupert & Rothschild E8
32 Rhebokskloof E3
33 Ruitersvlei D5
34 Scali D1
35 Seidelberg D6
36 Signal Hill D8
37 Simonsvlei/ Lost Horizons D7
38 Veenwouden F3
39 Vendôme F5
40 Villiera A8
41 Welgemeend D7
42 Windmeul D3

Paarl Vintners
Tel: (021) 872-3605

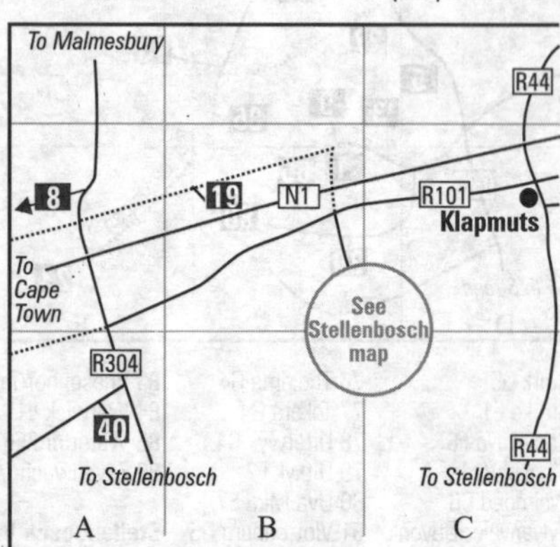

Paarl

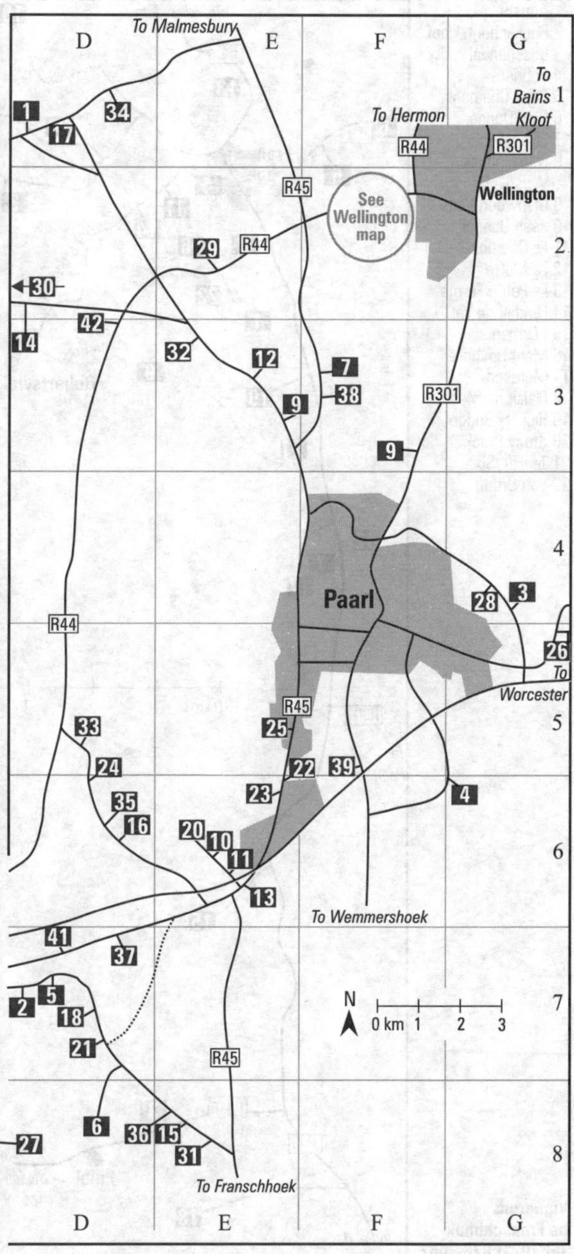

D
E
F
G
D
E
F
G
1
2
3
4
5
6
7
8
To Malmesbury
To Hermon
To Bains Kloof
R44
R301
R45
See Wellington map
Wellington
R44
R301
Paarl
R44
R45
To Worcester
To Wemmershoek
R45
To Franschhoek
N
0 km 1 2 3
1
34
17
29
30
42
14
32
12
7
38
9
9
28
3
26
33
25
24
22
39
23
4
35
16
20
10
11
13
41
37
5
2
18
21
6
36
15
31
27

Franschhoek

1 Agusta
2 Boekenhoutskloof
3 Boschendal
4 Cabrière
5 Cape Chamonix
6 Dieu Donné
7 Eikehof
8 Franschhoek Vyds/La Bri
9 Glenwood Vyds
10 Jean Daneel
11 La Couronne
12 La Motte
13 La Petite Ferme
14 Landau du Val
15 L'Ormarins
16 Mont Rochelle
17 Môreson
18 Plaisir de Merle
19 Rickety Bridge
20 Stony Brook
21 TenFiftySix
22 Von Ortloff

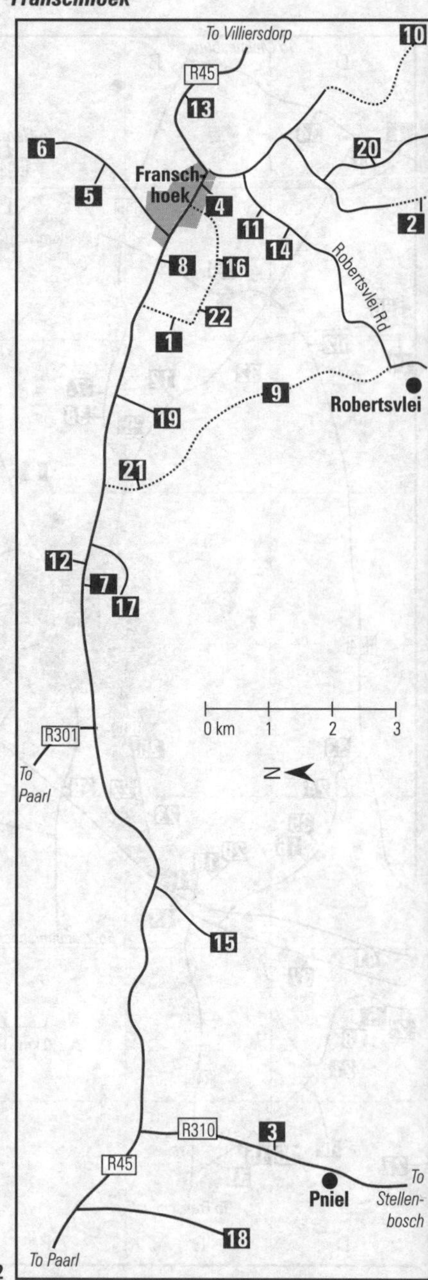

Vignerons de Franschhoek
Tel: (021) 876-3062

Helderberg

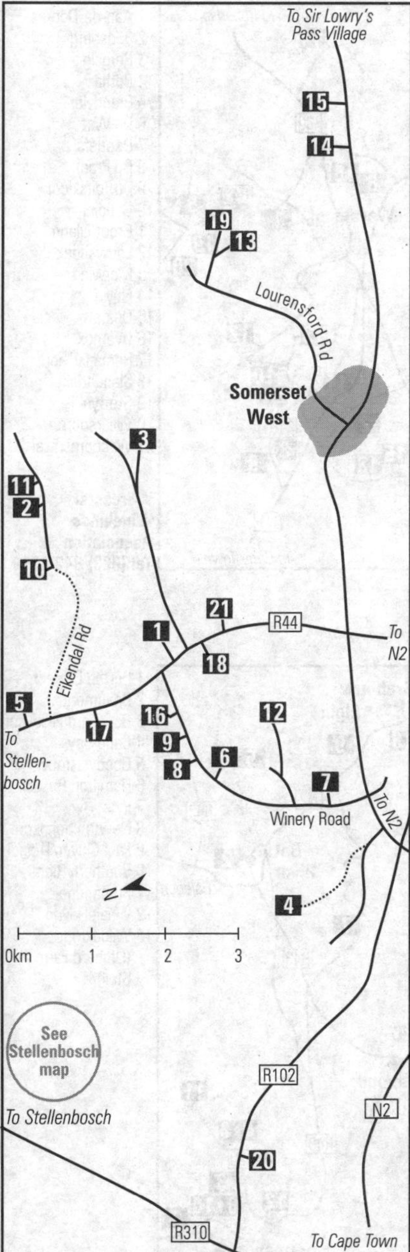

1 Avontuur
2 Clos du Ciel
3 Cordoba
4 Dellrust
5 Eikendal
6 Helderberg/ S'bosch Vyds
7 JP Bredell
8 Ken Forrester/ Meinert (96 Winery Rd)
9 L'Auberge
10 Longridge
11 Lushof
12 Lyngrove/ Baarsma
13 Morgenster
14 Mount Rozier
15 Onderkloof
16 Post House
17 Somerbosch
18 Stonewall
19 Vergelegen
20 Vergenoegd
21 Yonder Hill

Helderberg Wine Route
Tel: (021) 852-6166

Worcester

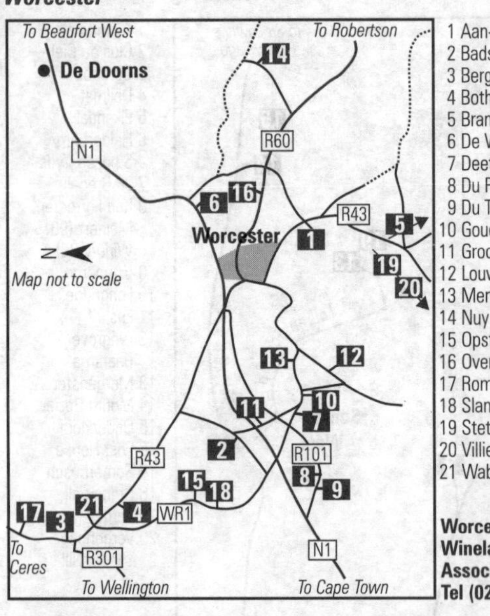

1 Aan-de-Doorns
2 Badsberg
3 Bergsig
4 Botha
5 Brandvlei
6 De Wet
7 Deetlefs
8 Du Preez
9 Du Toitskloof
10 Goudini
11 Groot Eiland
12 Louwshoek
13 Merwida
14 Nuy
15 Opstal
16 Overhex
17 Romansrivier
18 Slanghoek
19 Stettyn
20 Villiersdorp
21 Waboomsrivier

Worcester Winelands Association Tel (023) 342-8710

Elgin/Walker Bay

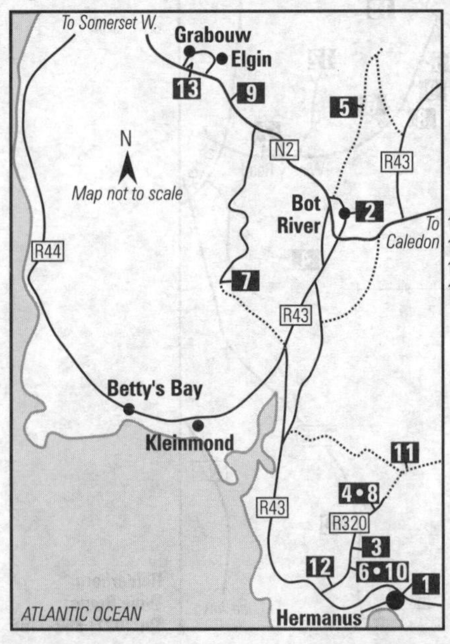

1 Bartho Eksteen
2 Beaumont
3 Bouchard Finlayson
4 Cape Bay
5 Goedvertrouw
6 Hamilton Russell
7 Iona
8 Newton Johnson
9 Paul Cluver/Thandi
10 Southern Right
11 Sumaridge
12 WhaleHaven
13 Wildekrans (Orchard Farm Stall)

Robertson

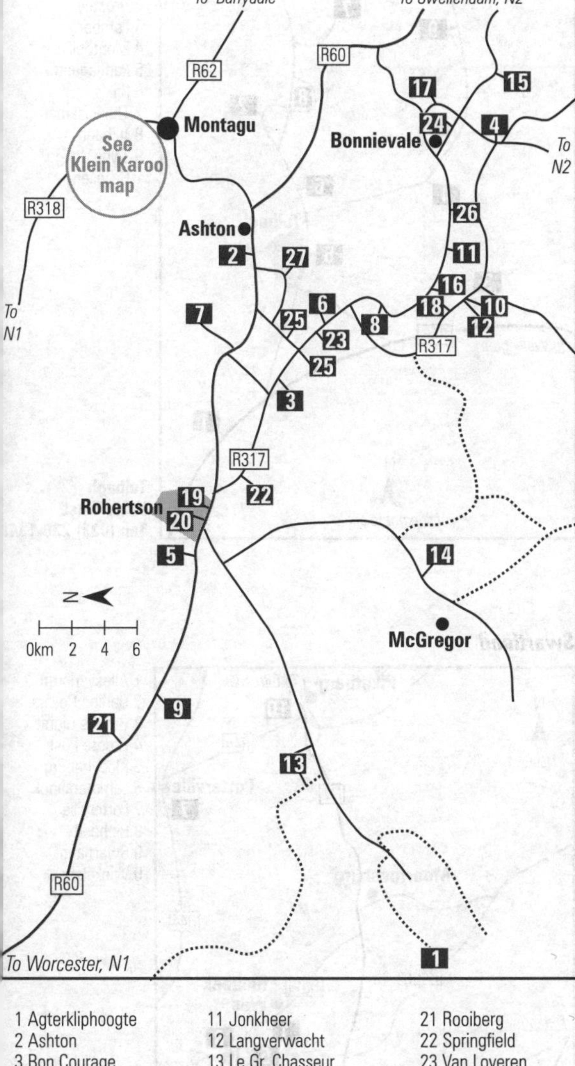

1 Agterkliphoogte
2 Ashton
3 Bon Courage
4 Bonnievale
5 Clairvaux/Appelsdrift
6 De Wetshof
7 Fraai Uitzicht
8 Goedverwacht
9 Graham Beck
10 Janéza
11 Jonkheer
12 Langverwacht
13 Le Gr. Chasseur
14 McGregor
15 Merwespont
16 Mooiuitsig
17 Nordale
18 Quando
19 Robertson
20 Roodezandt
21 Rooiberg
22 Springfield
23 Van Loveren
24 Van Zylshof
25 Viljoensdrift
26 Weltevrede
27 Zandvliet

Robertson Wine Valley
Tel: (023) 626-3167

Tulbagh

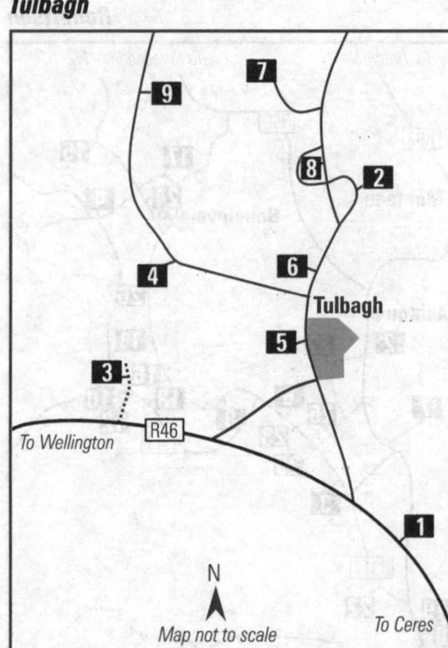

1 De Heuvel
2 Drostdy
3 Lemberg
4 Montpellier
5 Paddagang
6 Rijk's
7 Theuniskraal
8 Tulbagh
9 Twee Jonge Gezellen

Tulbagh Wine Trust
Tel: (023) 230-1348

Swartland

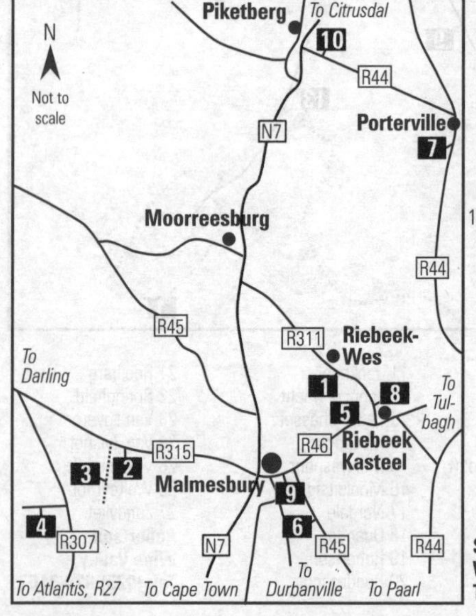

1 Allesverloren
2 Darling Cellars
3 Groene Cloof
4 Groote Post
5 Kloovenburg
6 Lammershoek
7 Porterville
8 Riebeek
9 Swartland
10 Winkelshoek

Swartland Wine Route
Tel: (022) 487-1133

Little Karoo

1 Andrew Jonker
2 Axe Hill
3 Barrydale
4 Bloupunt
5 Boplaas
6 Calitzdorp
7 Die Krans
8 Die Poort
9 Domein Doornkraal
10 Grundheim
11 Joubert-Tradouw
12 Kango
13 Ladismith
14 Mons Ruber
15 Montagu
16 Rietrivier
17 Uitvlucht

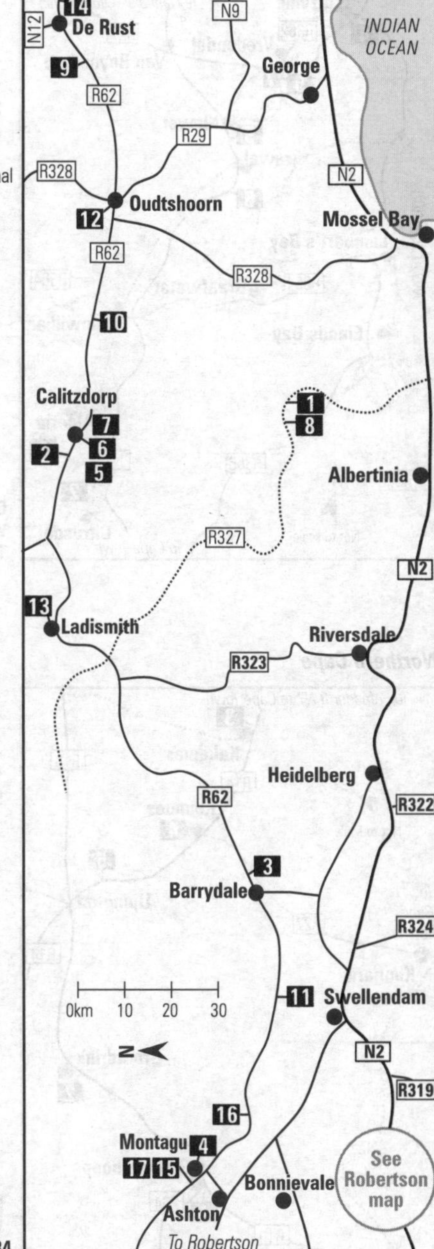

Little Karoo Wine Trust
Tel: (028) 572-1284

Olifants River

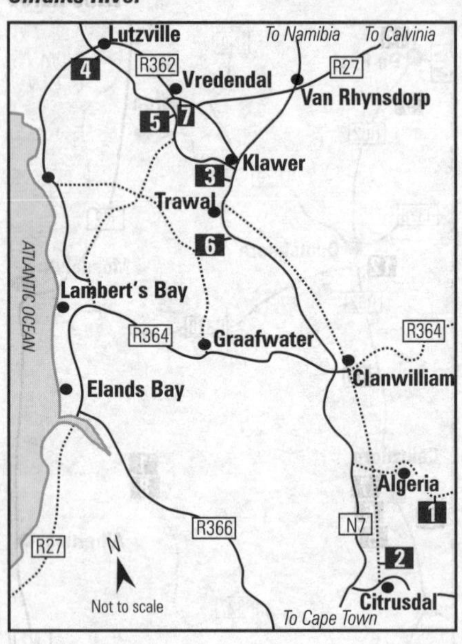

1 Cederberg
2 Goue Vallei
3 Klawer
4 Lutzville
5 Spruitdrift
6 Trawal
7 Vredendal

Olifants River Wine Trust
Tel: (027) 213-3126

Northern Cape

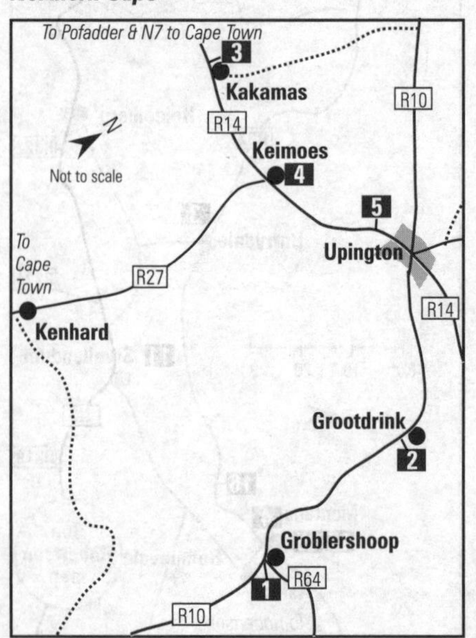

1 Groblershoop
2 Grootdrink
3 Kakamas
4 Keimoes
5 Upington

Northern Cape Vintners
Tel: 082-924-7254

Aan de Doorns Winery

*Worcester • Tasting & sales Mon-Fri 8-5 • Cellar tours by appointment • Owners 52 members • Cellarmaster Johan Morkel • Winemaker Gert van Deventer • Vineyards 1 154 ha • Production ± 17 500 tons • PO Box 235 Worcester 6849 • **Tel (023) 347-2301** • Fax (023) 347-4629 • E-mail aded@intekom.co.za*

TUCKED AWAY off the busy road between Worcester and Robertson, this co-operative cellar offers plenty of reasons to take a short detour. With tasting facilities on the Breede River, you can combine wine sampling and canoe tripping or, if you're adventurous, bush-bashing on one of three 4×4 trails in the area (we recommend you refrain from tasting until afterwards). And if wine is all you have in mind, you'll be delighted by their modest prices: the super-quaffing Colombar-Chardonnay costs about R10 a bottle! Be sure to catch these attractions from Monday to Friday, however. The doors are shut on weekends (affording cellarmaster Johan Morkel time to indulge his enthusiasm for golf). The wines below are all NEW to this edition.

Red Muscadel ✓ **00** very smooth; raisin hints and lengthy muscat finish; pleasantly tingly alc (16.5%). 258 cases (× 6, as are all of these) .

Colombar-Chardonnay ☻ **01** white-peach/tropical fruit succulence finishes bone dry with fresh lemony farewell. 13.6% alc. 520 cases.

Pinotage **00** nostalgic old-Cape pinotage with estery/savoury tones; well disguised ±14% alc. 500 cases. **Doornroodt** Black pepper, clove and floral sniffs in **00**, ruby cab/merlot (70/30); Am oak-chipped, which obvious, though high alc (14%) is not. 1 420 cases. **99** VG. **Blanc de Noir** Coral-orange **01**, with red muscadel's muscat/honeysuckle perfumes, very sweet and smooth. 13.1% alc. 500 cases. **Colombar** Drink-now **01** bone dry guava tastes, Granny Smith apple zest to finish. 13.1% alc. 520 cases. **Clairette Blanche** Lunch-time-light **01**, lively dry-hay/guava hints; dry finish. Screwcap. 260 cases. **Sparkling Demi-Sec** Salmon pink semi-sweet with soda-pop sparkle; light and candyflossy. **NV** (00). Colombard/ruby cab. 230 cases. **Muscat d'Alexandrie** Honeysuckle fragranced full-sweet fortified, **01** appears quite spiritous though analysis not especially high (16.4%). 440 cases. **Port** Old-style SA 'port', **99** sweet and only moderately alcoholic (16.5%). Tinta's earthy aromas, candy/toffee tastes. 250 cases. —*DH*

@blaauwklippen see Makro
A Few Good Men see Arlington, Riebeek

African Dawn

WILDLIFE-THEMED range by a partnership of Breede River cellars. The 'Big Five' front label paintings are by Cape artist Tony Butler. The wines, available from some game parks, guest houses, duty free shops and retailers, untasted.

African Legend see Sonop
African Sky see Drostdy
African Sunset see Clairvaux

African Terroir

Paarl/Stellenbosch (see Paarl map) • Tasting, sales, cellar/vineyard tours by appointment • Bed & breakfast at Sonop Farm • Owner Jacques Germanier Group/ SAVISA (Pty) Ltd • Managing director Bernard Fontannaz • Winemaker Alain Cajeux • Vineyards 74 ha (own) Production 120 000 cases 60% red 40% white •

African Terroir

PO Box 1142 Stellenbosch 7599 • ***Tel (021) 887-2409*** • *Fax (021) 886-4838* • *E-mail office@sonop.co.za*

THIS INNOVATIVE operation, part of a Swiss-based multinational negociant business, has undergone a minor makeover and come out suitably enhanced, with the spotlight firmly on shiraz. Crowning new project Azania on the West Coast (they've grown from one farm to several, with wineries and long-term partnerships with growers all over the Cape), a red-grape-only cellar, is the finishing touch to a process that started in the vineyards three years ago. "Results have surpassed the spirit of hope put into this new venture," says motivated MD Bernard Fontannaz. The range has been freshly groomed under a new trading name, African Terroir. Then there are two special projects close to Fontannaz's heart. Leading with an approach that's still a small component in SA, Organic Terroir sees 40 hectares at Sonop in Paarl fully converted to organics with a projected target of 750 ha. The Winds of Change label, described by Fontannaz as a "business proposition with a social dimension", is just that: families living on Sonop now own 12 ha of land and the houses on it, and a percentage of earnings goes directly back into community upliftment projects.

Azania range NEW

Shiraz 'Lavished with attention' hardly hints at treatment accorded this newcomer, with specifically built cellar to coax precisely this sort of **01** brooding depth from coddled West Coast fruit. Deepest, densest hues emitting supercharged aromas of cherry, choc, briar and nettle; in palate all these plus oakchar and vanilla in surprisingly sappy format, though finish is quite firm and correctly dry. Drinkable now, enough structure to merit cellaring (given lack of track record, regular monitoring advised). Am/Fr oak-matured.

Big Five Collection NEW

Cabernet Sauvignon Immediate impression of refinement and balance; **01** almost unbelievably smooth for such a young lion (the animal emblazoned in a handsome stylised visual on the front-label); full of flavour, juicy yet contained; doesn't strive for effect – and admirably moderate alc (13.1%).

Pinotage (Elephant) Pachyderm allusion appropriate because of **01**'s large dimensions: forward, punchy style; very full-flavoured (plums, red berries) with charry oak touches. Though accessible, this the only animal in Collection that really needs taming-time in bottle. 13.3% alc.

Merlot (Buffalo) Variety in Cape all too often uptight and ungenerous; this **01** gives its aromas/flavours munificently: lovely floral tones to start, then choc-coated cherries and sweet tannins beautifully attuned to the fruit. Lightly Allier-oaked, 2nd fill.

Chardonnay (Leopard) This winery's creamy tones again evident here, with hints marmalade, lees, lime in smooth toasty palate. After the richness, a properly dry, firm conclusion. **01** 30% oaked, first fill, small portion Am barrels.

Sauvignon Blanc ☆ Here's the Rhino, with decidedly fleet-footed acidity racing through **01**'s green grass/pepper palate to a clean, long finish. 13.2% alc.

Bredasdorp range

Exclusive to German market.

> **Ruby Cabernet** ☻ ☆ Good few steps up on pvs. Versatile **01** full of sappy berry fruit yet enough body, soft tannins and acidity for comfortable pairing with pizza, pasta and alfresco-style salads. 13.6% alc.

Sauvignon Blanc ☆ Very lively, refreshing **01** nicely padded with varietal fruit, balanced acidity and lingering Granny Smith apple tastes.

Diemersdal range

Cabernet Sauvignon Sophisticated wine with beautiful balance, showing refinement of Dbnville fruit. **99**, generous, fleshy, fine-tannined. **00** wonderfully ripe, giving; expansively constructed (13.5% alc) yet classic. Already fairly accessible but begs at least a few yrs to grow; should peak around 2008.

Pinotage Returns to form with big-and-beautiful **00**, reflecting the modern Cape densely extracted, oak-slathered style (which sits well with many overseas palates). Lots of sappy fruit, choc textures, soft tannins which should carry good 4-6 yrs. **99** rustic with forbidding tannins.

Harmony NEW Balanced, complex, compatible Cape Red blend with big toasty structure that will need time to show its best. Cab s/f, shiraz and pinotage, with attributes of each present and ready to knit over the next 6-8 yrs.

Chardonnay 99 fat juicy mouthful, disciplined by powerful oak. Follow-up **01** vintage, as elsewhere in these ranges, better structured, firmer and more satisfying. House's viscous mouthfeel evident, here with butterscotch and marmalade embellishments.

Sauvignon Blanc 01 generally super sauvignon yr for Dbnville, origin of this range. Effusively flavoured with sweet varietal figs, peppers and greengage; full-bodied, zesty. Delicious now, with promise of short-term maturation. **00**.

Kersfontein range

Pinotage Well made, balanced **01** highlights variety's fullness, richness; tannins dextrously extracted to showcase ripe plum/banana fruit without losing vinosity. Better structure than intensely ripe, chewy **00**.

Morgan range

Cabernet Sauvignon Stepped-up barrelled portion (to 50%) gives extra resonance to **01** compared to pvs. Tones as dark as the stylish packaging: blackcurrant, milk choc and some toffee deliciousness. Smooth yielding tannins provide accessibility now with something in reserve for ageing. Allier casks. 13.5% alc.

Cabernet Franc Svelte, lightish-toned **99** followed by slightly firmer, more structured **01** with attractive spice-emporium aromas and supple tannins. Hint of fresh earth in lengthily tapering finish. 13.5% alc.

Merlot Yet another improved player in this team. **01** impresses with pure varietal aromas/flavours, good plummy sap sprinkled with sweet-violets. Unlike **99**, tannins well managed, almost sweet.

Chardonnay As above, notched-up oaking (to 50%, in Allier wood) lifts **01** into higher echelon. More conducive yr also reflected in sleeker frame compared with **00**, with sparkly acidity helping to maintain balance between sweet vanilla oak and ripe-peachy/leesy tones. 13.% alc.

Pinotage Fine cross-over style, balancing ripe accessible fruit and enough heft to confidently bring to table. Plummy/mulberry fruit with banana nuance. **Sauvignon Blanc** Youthful, bright **01** offers pleasing ripe tropical flavours with a green pepper bite; finishes briskly clean.

Out of Africa range

Cabernet Sauvignon 01, with emphatic new-clone cab profile, raises the bar for this label; cassis perfume and spicy oak harmoniously blended with green peppers and toasted almonds. Tannins comfortable, well padded for good 4/5 yrs' ageing. 13.3% alc. This, below, unfiltered, so with time may throw a sediment. Big step up from homely **99** with some older-clone dryness.

Pinotage Latest **01** mirrors romantic front-label in its seductive oaky tones of creamy choc, vanilla and char over super-ripe berry fruit. 40% oaked, older Allier barrels. 13.4% alc. **99** fragrant, also velvet-textured.

★**Shiraz** NEW Exciting debut for this label in **01**, aromatic style with mouthfilling fruit and gamey/herby whiffs over light earthy tones. Not overly big (13.3% alc), boisterous or showy; ripe but well proportioned/controlled. Good development potential over 4-6 yrs, though we suspect the cork will be pulled long before.

★**Chardonnay** Latest **01** bears virtually no resemblance to **00** ★ (difficult chardonnay yr). Fresher, firmer, more lively in the mouth, not too potent (13.2%) yet generously favoured with high-toned pineapple nuances and cinnamon snatches in lemony conclusion. 20% new oak, 4 mths.

★**Sauvignon Blanc** Again, little comparison between this **01** and pvs **00** ★; latest absolutely billows tropical fruit then turns citric in palate with complicated layers of bell pepper, green apple and guava; excellent limey acidity invigorates, brings you back for more. 13.6% alc.

Sonop Organic Terroir range

★**Shiraz** NEW Modern, expressive style; **01** sweet-spicy with sappy blackcurrant fruit and deep whiffs of varietal smoke and pepper; balanced tannins end with tasty lick of vanilla. Oaked, 80/20 Fr/Am casks.

Pinotage ★ **01** very good ambassador for Brand Pinotage: unwooded, so fruit jumps out in all its juicy freshness, slightly sweet mulberry/redcurrant tastes and no hint of harshness or astringency. For current enjoyment. 13.2% alc. **Chardonnay** ★ Fr-oaked **01** tasted young yet already balanced, creamy; satisfying flow of mixed fruits through palate concluding with lovely lemon-vanilla flourish. 13.5% alc. **Sauvignon Blanc** ★ Miles better than pvs. **01** super-clean, popping with varietal 'green' aromas and complementary tropical flavours. 13.2% alc.

Tribal range

Cape Red NEW ☻ ★ Trio of fruity grapes makes delightful **01** combo, fresh and juicy with touches warm-earth and tannin holding it all together. **Cape White** NEW ☻ ★ Real summer salad flavours in lively **01** with breezy lemon acidity. Clever mix chenin, colombard, sauvignon.

Winds of Change range

★**Semillon-Chardonnay 01** only partially barrelled to preserve ripe, vibrant tropical/citrus fruits. Just enough toasty vanilla to accent the already smooth lemony textures. **99** super ripe, rounded, palate-expanding.

Merlot-Pinotage ☻ ★ Highly compatible varietal marriage results in full juicy mouthful of plums, cherries and the scent of violets. Good toasty tannin background from brief spell in cask.

Pinotage-Cabernet Sauvignon ★ Cab's firmish structure evident in **01** finish, through the start is soft and ripe-berried with hints of sweet spice and vanilla. Good now, and enough guts for 2-4 yrs. Partially oaked. **Pinotage-Shiraz** ★ Intended as drinkable-off-the-shelf wine, which **01** certainly is. Abundant ripe cherry/plum flavours folded with some oak-spice and undemanding tannins. **Chardonnay** ★ This label bound to win plenty of fans with **01**, creamy toasted pine-nuts chopped into ripe peaches and pears. Refreshing grapefruit finish quickly has you reaching for the glass.

Following not tasted for this ed (pvs ratings in brackets): African Legend range: **Cabernet Sauvignon (00** ★**)**, **Merlot (99** ★**)**, **Pinot Noir (00** ★**)**, **Pinotage (00** ★**)**, **Shiraz (00** ★**)**, **Chardonnay (00** ★**)**, **Chenin Blanc (00** ★**)**, **Colombard (00** ★**)**, **Sauvignon Blanc (00** ★**)**; Bredasdorp range: **Rosé (00** ★**)**; Cape Levant range: **Cabernet Sauvignon (97** ★**)**, **Merlot (99** ★**)**, **Pinotage (**★**)**; Cape Soleil range: **Merlot (00** ★**)**, **Pinotage (00** ★**)**, **Shiraz (00** ★**)**, **Chardonnay (00** ★**)**,

Sauvignon Blanc (**00** ★★★); Diemersdal range: **Merlot** (**99** ★★★), **Shiraz** (**99** ★★★); Kersfontein range: **Cabernet Sauvignon** (**00** unrated), **Cabernet Franc** (**00** ★★★); Morgan range: **Shiraz** (**99** ★★★), **Chenin Blanc 00** ★★; Sonop Organic Terroir range: **Cabernet Sauvignon 00** ★★★, **Merlot 99** ★★★, **Chenin Blanc 00** ★★★; Tribal range: **Sparkling Wine** (**NV** ★★★), **Elixir** (**NV** ★★★). — *DH*

African Wines & Spirits

Constantia • Directors Mike Cox, James McLachlan, André van Wyk, Chris Weeden • PO Box 389 Constantia 7848 • ***Tel (021) 794-6697*** *• Fax (021) 794-3990*

MARKETING company that owns a number of established brands such as Craighall, Bertrams and Cinzano. Also S/SW (South/South West) easy drinkers, and international rights for the Alphen range (see separate entries).

Agterkliphoogte Winery 

Robertson (see Robertson map) • Tasting, sales, cellar tours Mon-Fri 8-12.30; 1.30-5 • Owners 22 members • Winemaker Helmard Hanekom (since 1986) • Consulting viticulturist Briaan Stipp (VinPro) • Vineyards 398 ha • Production 6 500 tons (500 cases own label) 67% white 11% red 22% fortified & other • PO Box 267 Robertson 6705 • ***Tel (023) 626-1103*** *• Fax (023) 626-3329 • E-mail akhwyn@lando.co.za*

PLAYING FIRST FIDDLE in what has been pretty much a one-man band is Helmard Hanekom, now backed by a secretary and cellar assistant. With a revamp of the cellar complex and a tasting facility facelift completed, this co-op in the secluded Agterkliphoogte Valley near Robertson has acquired a clean-lined contemporary look. New agents have been appointed to handle exports for the Wandsbeck range. "Things look promising," says a delighted Hanekom, who may have his hands full but will nonetheless still be nipping off for a spot of underwater harvesting of the perlemoen and crayfish variety on weekends. The range not ready for tasting. Previous, all 00s, included **Ruby Cabernet** (★★★), **Shiraz** (★★), **Chardonnay** (★★★), **Sauvignon Blanc** (★★), **Red Muscadel** (★★).

Agulhas see Merwespont

Agusta Wines 

Franschhoek (see Franschhoek map) • Tasting & sales daily 10-6 Tasting fee R5 for 5 wines • Cellar tours by appointment • Le Provençal Restaurant re-opening this year • Informal restaurant opening soon for lunches & dinners • Luxury 5-bedroom guest house • Conferences • Facilities for children • Tourgroups • Wheelchair-friendly • Owner Count Riccardo Agusta • Winemaker Alastair Rimmer • Consultant winemaker Bruwer Raats • Consulting viticulturist Kevin Watt (since end 2000) • Vineyards 40 ha • Production 400 tons 60 000-80 000 cases 85% white 15% red • PO Box 393 Franschhoek 7690 • ***Tel (021) 876-3195*** *• Fax (021) 876-3118 • E-mail orders@agustawines.co.za*

THINGS are getting back on track for Agusta and its Italian owner, ex-racing driver Count Riccardo Agusta, after a somewhat gravelly transition period. Seems that previous cellar teething problems have been smoothed out with a bigger press and more tanks in the line-up. Newly-appointed Stellenbosch graduate Alastair Rimmer is heading up the harvest this year with Bruwer Raats as consultant, part of the game plan to elevate this winery to new heights. And, just in case the R17-million cellar revamp wasn't enough of a shake-up, an informal eatery was built to complement the flagship restaurant, re-launching in fittingly Italian guise. Boding well for the future are new reds – merlot, cabernets sauvignon and franc, pinot noir, shiraz and petit verdot – planted on the cooler southern slopes across the road at recently acquired farm La Terra du Luc. New viticultural consultant Kevin Watt is paying "pedantic" attention to the vines.

Count Agusta range

Cabernet Sauvignon Festooned with young wine show ribbons: national champ in **97**, **98** (not tasted); local hero in **96**, **95**. Pvs **99** tour de force marred by perceptible sweetness, which properly absent in current **00**, very classic, seriously structured; refined spicy/cedary oak over black-fruit depths; dry but ripe tannins. 100% cab, yr oaked. 3 800 (× 6) cases.

Chardonnay Opulent, blockbustery example; 100% barrel-fermented (Fr, Am, Russian cooperage), aged 9 mths, which blatant in current **99**, hedonistic lime-butterscotch swanning in perceptibly sweet (5.2 g/ℓ sugar) palate; VG, WOM Reserve selection (though we suggest this for fans of oakier, low-acid styles). Incoming **00** dry, subtly oaked, balanced. These half-notches down from pvs **98** VG, with 15% unwooded portion for freshness, and **97** SAA.

Muscat du Provençal ✓ Muscat d'alexandrie's powerful perfumes tamed by light oaking in this very unusual fortified **NV**; smoky sugarcane, honey/marmalade sweetness showing some oxidation (which some palates appreciate). 16,4% alc.

Merlot NEW 100% merlot, portion Vredendal fruit; **00** green-minty, nose very soft and ripe, palate still unyielding mid-01, give 2-3 yrs to grow. Yr oaked. **Sauvignon Blanc** Latest **01** unoaked (unlike pvs, which partly barrelled); sample offers lightish passionfruit/gooseberry flavours. 1 200 (× 6) cases.

Agusta range

Franschhoek Fine White Easy dry sipping **01**, unoaked 60/40 sauvignon, chardonnay from Grande Provence farm; med-bodied. 1 680 cases. NEW to this ed, as is ... **Franschhoek Misty** 'Bouquet'-style semi-dry **00**, fragranced with apples, melons, muscat; simple med-bodied quaffing. Partly cask-aged.

Angels' Tears range

Red ☻ Easy red/black fruity jumble; **99** partly oaked for comfortable quaffing. Med-bodied blend cab (80%), merlot.

White Ever popular fruity mouthful, just beyond semi-dry. Chenin (50%) holding its own against hanepoot's grapiness. **Sparkling** NEW Spumante-style floral semi-sweet, mouthfilling fizz, lightish young-crowd pleaser. Hanepoot/sauvignon. All above **NV.** Discontinued: in Haute Provence range: **Chardonnay Reserve** (**98** VVG); **Semillon Reserve** (**98**); **Semillon** (**97** ★); **Blanc Fumé** (**98** VG); also **Count Agusta Semillon 99** (); in Agusta range: **Chardonnay** (**99**); **Sauvignon Blanc** (**99**); **Bianco** (**NV** no stars); **Brut** (**NV**). — *JN*

Allesverloren Estate

Swartland (see Swartland map) • Tasting & sales Mon-Fri 8.30-5 Sat 8.30-12.30 On public holidays phone (022) 461-2589 • Cellar tours by appointment • Owners/winemakers Danie & Fanie Malan • Vineyards 160 ha • Production 1 400 tons • PO Box 23 Riebeek West 7306 • ***Tel (022) 461-2320*** *• Fax (022) 461-2444 • E-mail dmalan@wcaccess.co.za*

Serious devotees of winemaker Danie Malan's manly reds need no longer feel the pinch of the ongoing stock shortage situation (especially Shiraz), with the release of more wines in 2001. Extensive planting of red wine grapes a decade ago is paying dividends. "Selection is just as strenuous," assures Malan, "but there will be more wine available." Further cause for celebration is a limited first-time release of a Vintage Port scheduled for this year. Malan, whose family has farmed here since 1870, often travels extensively as "part of the job". Having clocked up air miles to Singapore, the UK and several other EU countries (luckily before the carnivorous ban kicked in, so he wasn't too deprived of his favourite roast beef), he grounded himself last year because he simply had "too much to do at home". Which bodes even better for die-hard fans ...

Cabernet Sauvignon ✓ Strapping, fruit-packed cab with, recently, silkier tannins for earlier approachability. **96** among most substantial, promising cabs from often ethereal yr. SAA, *Wine*. Potential for 8-10 yrs' development. **97** lighter colour/body, reflecting cool vintage. Latest **98**, warmer yr, more generous, almost plump. These ±18 mths Fr oak, 50% new.

Shiraz ✓ Big, full-textured, reflecting warmer climate vyds. **96** Highly rated by 98 Diners Club judges. No **97**. **98** unexpectedly slim ('only' 13,6% alc), well oaked (only 30% new wood). Latest **99** packs familiar Allesverloren clout (14.3% alc); unyielding mid-01 yet plenty of roasty fruit for good ageing. 18 mths oak, 10% new.

Tinta Barocca Since **95**, in full-blown hearty-fruity style hinted at in **90**, **91**. **96** SAA. **97** showed complexity, lower (definitely not insubstantial) 13,4% alc from cooler vintage; some fresh-earthiness, as in latest **98**, which bigger (14.6% alc), firmer textured but more foursquare (so closer to Drink now or keep 4-8 yrs. Fr oak 18 mths, 50/50 2nd/3rd fill.

Port ✓ Reliable, ready on release LBV, deservedly ubiquitous in restaurants, pubs etc. Latest **95** continues trend to Portuguese dryness (99 g/ℓ sugar) though lowish alc (±17.5%), probably more attuned to SA than Iberian palates. First to feature dash tempranillo, with standard mix tintas francisca & barocca, souzao, pontac, malvasia rey. Old-oak aged. No **94**. Pvs **93** SAPPA/Peter Schultz trophy, *Wine*. — *IvH*

Alphen Mondial

COLLABORATION between the Cloete-Hopkins family, original owners of the old-Cape Alphen label, and African Wines & Spirits. The range, all 99s, not tasted for this ed (previous ratings in brackets): **Pinotage** (), **Chardonnay** (), **Sauvignon Blanc** ().

Alto Estate

*Stellenbosch (see Stellenbosch map) • Tasting & sales Mon-Fri 9-5 Sat 10-4 Closed Sun • Owner Lusan Holdings • Winemaker Schalk van der Westhuizen (since 2000) • Vineyards 100 ha • Production 459 tons 33 174 cases • PO Box 104 Stellenbosch 7599 • **Tel (021) 881-3884** • Fax (021) 881-3894*

THERE's "not a lot happening" at this venerable property high in the Helderberg, reports gentle giant Schalk van der Westhuizen, then promptly owns up to a dash of stagefright at his first – and unusually late, dry and hot – harvest here. "The grapes took so long to ripen that I started to worry," he says, "but it all turned out well and I am very pleased with the quality." Barrels were purchased and adjustments made to the cellar because wines are going to be aged on the estate for the first time in many years (they were traditionally matured at Bergkelder). VdW and team are also sorting out the cellar insulation and replacing some old vines with cabernet franc. Will he be putting his signature to that old Cape wine institution Alto Rouge? A management decision has been taken to have no signature on the label for now. "Old Schalk must first prove himself," laughs this self-effacing winemaker, who notched up a good few awards (especially for his gorgeous NLH desserts) at Neethlingshof, his birthplace and previous winemaking arena.

Cabernet Sauvignon Ageworthy cab, classically structured, needing time to reach peak. Never more so than **98** whose refined, fragrant charms should be resisted at least 5 yrs, preferably 10. Fabulous cedar-and-violets perfume, inky depths of cassis, melting tannins. Recalls opulence of **95** ★★, with mouth-expanding concentration. *Wine* ★. **97** silky, satisfying and – again – deserving time. **96** ★ reflects difficult vintage, lighter-bodied yet balanced. These ±13,3 alc; 18-20 mths new Fr oak. No **92-94**.

★**Rouge** ✓ One of the grand old SA wine institutions with, in recent yrs, something approaching claret intensity, structure; seriousness underlined by 25-30% new oaking. Current **98** probably finest of the 90s; beautifully balanced, fine-grained; sweet Helderberg fruit ascendant. Higher proportion shiraz (18%) than pvs, but again merlot-driven (47%, cab 23%, cab f 12%). ±13% alc. **97**, with no cab f and merlot at 65%, fragrant, spicy, slighter. **96** VG bigger-bodied yet seemingly lighter.

★**Port** Modern and rather delicious. **97** approaching Portuguese-style balance (18,2 alc; 92 g/ℓ sugar), but Cape-style varietal composition: 100% shiraz. First in old 300 ℓ barrels 36 mths, now in expensive 500 ml bottles. Only from cellar. — *IvH*

Altydgedacht Estate 

Durbanville (see Durbanville map) • Tasting & sales Mon-Fri 9-5 Sat 9-1 • Cellar tours by appointment • Owners Parker family • Winemaker Oliver Parker (since 1980) • Viticulturists John Parker (since 1976) & Gerhard Fourie (since 1997) • Vineyards 130 ha • Production 1 000 tons (5 500 cases own label) 50/50 red/white • PO Box 213 Durbanville 7551 • ***Tel (021) 976-1295*** *• Fax (021) 976-8521*

"Nothing dramatically new has happened," shrugs Oliver Parker. Then again, it probably wouldn't be allowed to on this purist property in Durbanville, with its old-world soul, where memorabilia and traditions from as far back as 1710 have been preserved. The Parker family have been making wine for five generations and continue to do so in spite of the urban creep in this business-is-booming area. The emphasis now is on expanding their vineyards to meet the demand for cool climate grapes: they're increasing production of the 'big 6' as well as cabernet franc and smaller plantings of viognier, and virus-free barbera clones have also come into bearing.

★**Cabernet Sauvignon** ✓ Highly rated since first **82**, gold medallist on SAYWS. Invariably coolly refined, sometimes lean. **97** classically styled; tannic brio preceeds sweet fruit to very dry finish. Suggest cellar 3-4 yrs, then watch it bloom into ★. 14% alc. 175 cases. Released ahead of **98**, which all but sold out mid-01.

★**Barbera** ✓ An original; still Cape's only wine made from this Italian grape. Upcoming **99** (ex barrel) best since maiden **92** (all pvs paired with shiraz in deliciously named Barbiraz, later known as Tintoretto – this blend ripe for 21st century revival?) **99** offers more refined version of usual wild berry/ scrubby/ minty array; mouthfilling sweet-spicy palate, length. Am-oaked, as always, 18 mths, which obvious mid-01, so bottle-age 4-5 yrs. 13.8% alc. Only 220 cases.

★★**Merlot** ✓ Another canny switch sees a later vintage released aread of an earlier (cf Cab above). Here it's immediately accessible **00** striding out before discipined, even stern **99** ★, which will need bottle age and then probably grow only knee-hight to towering **00**, with more of everything. Best thing in this winery; enjoy in 3-5 yrs.

★**Pinotage** Accessible new-style pinotage since **93**. **97** ★ best of recent vintages; Latest **99** booms banana and plum, turning creamy in mouth with pinotage's not infrequent tannin rejoinder. Yr oaked. 700 cases. 13.6% alc.

★**Shiraz** ✓ **99**, back-tasted mid-01, holding; fragrant menthol, wild scrub add to spicy allure; tenacous but not rude tannins which should soften, carry 6 yrs+. 14 mths oaked. 13% alc. 510 cases. Pvs **96** unrated.

☆**Gewürztraminer** ✓ Since maiden 86, resolutely dry, alluding to Alsace styles (rare in Cape). Sometimes demure to start, as in **00** ☆, though nothing coy about 01, which assails you with a thousand talcum puffs. Shimmering blush colour entices, incense fragrance bewitches, bone dry palate bids arresting farewell. 13.7% alc. 258 cases.

Chatelaine ☻ ☆ Prettily floral anytime quaff; **01** bit sweeter than pvs, but balanced. 50/50 buket/gewürz. Comfortable 12.6% alc.

Chardonnay Returns to the guide with **01** sample; difficult to read: almost no oak impact (yet 50% barrelled); some leesy/citrus impressions. Possible ☆ rating on release early 02. 14% alc. 380 cases. **Sauvignon Blanc** ☆ Classic Dbnville aromatics (capsicum/cat's pee/green tea) in **01**; vibey fruit but arrestingly dry. Individual style has its adherents. 13,3% alc. 685 cases. **Chenin Blanc-Sauvignon Blanc** ☆ NEW It's possible to read the blend fractions in the **01** bouquet: 60% ripe guava (chenin), 40% capsicum (sauvignon). Fresh, if a little quick. 13% alc. 250 cases. — *DH*

Amabokobokho see Bovlei

Amani

Stellenbosch (see Stellenbosch map) • Tasting, sales & cellar tours Tue-Sat 10-4 • 'Sit down' tastings, including cellar tour/barrel tasting by arrangement (max 20 people) • Views • Gallery • Fine-art exhibitions year-round • Wheelchair-friendly • Owners Mark & Hillary Makepeace • Winemaker Mark Makepeace (since 2000) • Vineyards 18.4 ha • Production 85 tons 6 000 cases 60% white 40% red • PO Box 12422 Die Boord 7613 • ***Tel (021) 905-1126*** *• Fax (021) 905-4404 • E-mail wine@amani.co.za*

'100% Sold Out' signs outside this winery for two vintages in a row forced Mark and Hillary Makepeace to close their tasting room for several months. In the cellar, good friend Rod Easthope and partner Emma Williams still guide them, ensuring they "work hard at extracting every bit of idiosyncratic charm from our particular bit of Polkadraai terroir – but also have fun doing it". The winemaking philosophy is simple: If you really make your wine in the vineyard, then you'll be able to watch the quality grow in the cellar. Amani keeps its African roots showing, combining contemporary and ethnic in roughcast desert-shaded walls, corrugated iron roofs and steel awnings that borrow their design straight from the townships. A new association with Elizabeth Miller Art ensures the tasting room-cum-gallery is filled with local artists' work.

☆**Chardonnay** ✓ Latest release nicknamed Bulldog, tongue-in-jowl reference to "aggressive" batonnage regime. Yet **00** surprisingly elegant. Soft, ripe-peachy fruit, gentle apple-toned farewell. Could go few yrs. **99** ☆ understated, satiny. These barrel fermented/aged 9 mths, 1st/2nd fill Fr oak; 13-13.5% alc. 1 000 cases. Maiden **98** snapped up by US buyers.

☆**Merlot** ✓ Here's the real bulldog in this range: gutsy, needing food or time's discipline. **00** cinnamon-spicy; rich; chunky tannins. 500 cases. Impressive follow-up, potential to trounce maiden **99** which, retasted mid-01, softening, another yr/2 to go. Fruit ex-Helderberg. *Wine* ☆. These ±13,8% alc; 100% barrel-fermented/matured, 35% new, 18 mths; splash cab or cab/f.

☆**Sauvignon Blanc** ✓ Partially barrel-fermented **01** exhilaratingly tart, fruity; nettley parting. Try with lightly chilled smoked salmon pasta, suggests Mark Makepeace. 13.2% alc. 2 500 cases.

Brushed Chardonnay NEW ☆ Partially Fr oak-fermented/matured version of above; **00** with (what else?) brush of sweet vanilla. Well priced. 13.5% alc; 800

cases. **Charlotte** ★ NLH named after the Makepeaces' young daughter. **00** recognisably chenin, zestily sweet. Fr oaked 9 mths; 12,5% alc. 375 ml. 500 cases. Discontinued: **Chenin Blanc**, **Sculpted Blanc.** — *DH*

Ambeloui Wine Cellar

*Hout Bay (see Constantia map) • Tasting, sales & cellar tours "by appointment but very welcome" • Groups welcome • Owners Nick & Ann Christodoulou • Winemaker/viticulturist Nick Christodoulou • Vineyard 0,6 ha • Production 400 cases 100% MCC • PO Box 26800 Hout Bay 7872 • **Tel 082-441-6039** • Fax (021) 790-7873 • E-mail ambeloui@icon.co.za • Website www.ambeloui.co.za*

"We're running out of children to name vintages after," laughs Nick Christodoulou, whose passions are of the sparkling variety – wine and sea – both of which he's lucky enough to have close at hand. "The 2001 was named after the youngest, Alexis. I guess it's Ann and Christo for the next two, then we'll have to start at Lisa all over again," he concludes. New is the introduction of the disgorgement date on the bottle, one of the first MCC producers to do so. "By 2003 we'll have 2- and 3-year-olds available," says Christodoulou, who's been holding some base-wine in reserve to make manifest a dream of releasing sparklers with 3 or more years on the lees. Last year they opened harvesting days to clients and friends for the first time, which culminated in an exuberant harvest party, a tradition they intend to uphold.

★**Miranda Brut MCC** Serious, classically styled, varietally correct (pinot noir/ chardonnay). Still-available **99** ('Miranda') 60/40 blend; hints at ★ potential. Latest **00** ('Christo'), tasted soon after disgorgement Aug 5th 01, more black fruit apparent than pvs (70% pinot component); baker's shop tones; extra complexity from barrel fermentation of 15% of base-wine. Clearly these slow starters, give ample time to develop. — *DH*

Andrew Jonker Wines

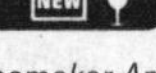

*Albertinia (see Little Karoo map) • Tasting Mon-Fri 8-5 • Owner/winemaker Andrew Jonker (since 1994) • Vineyards 22 ha • Production ± 300 tons 90% white 10% red • PO Box 9 Albertinia 6695 • **Tel/fax (028) 735-2102***

Andrew Jonker makes his wines "very simply, in a converted store" on his farm beside the Gouritz River – right next-door to brother Jannie, winemaker and distiller at Die Poort. Elsenburg-trained Andrew Jonker specialises in sweet whites and reds (a Pinotage, Tinta Barocca and Pinotage-Ruby Cabernet are among the current releases), and though these were unavailable for tasting as the guide went to press, Andrew Jonker is clearly delighted to be realising a long-time dream. "Love of wine," he confides, is the reason he decided to make his own 22 ha into wine – and an esteem for Grundheim's Danie Grundling, the master-distiller and vintner who plies his trade near Calitzdorp on the opposite side of the Langeberg Mountains. Though tucked away in secluded valley, these cellar doors are wide open for tasting and sales weekdays during office hours. If you're in the Albertinia area or passing through on the Garden Route, they'd be delighted to receive you.

Angels' Tears see Agusta

Annandale

*Stellenbosch (see Stellenbosch map) • Tasting & sales by appointment • Owner/ winemaker Hempies du Toit • **Tel (021) 881-3560/1** or 082 895 8960 • Fax (021) 881-3562 • E-mail annandale@telkomsa.net*

Genial winemaker Hempies du Toit is in his element on his own Helderberg property. The cellar is operational and though somewhat rudimentary (he describes it as "about two years after the Stone Age"), it's certainly environmentally friendly.

With no cooling plant yet, this resourceful mountain of a man directed water from the nearby stream into a dam, from the dam into the cooling jackets and then back into the stream again: "I was really scared of trying it, but it worked!" The roof leaks, but his own special brand of logic prevails: "If the wine doesn't leak out of the tanks, the water can't leak into them ... " A new "non-bordeaux style" red blend, Cavalier, is a nod to the proud equestrian history of the property. Also new is the first Port (untasted), which du Toit proclaims as "spot on".

Cabernet Sauvignon Improving by the vintage. Latest **98** well and elegantly structured, with modest 12.5% alc. Forthcoming attractive nose, savoury and smoky, touch vanilla behind the berries. Fr oak-matured, 2/3 new. 1 500 cases. Deserves another few years to develop, as does weightier **97** (13.2% alc). **96** lighter and lower keyed.

Cavalier NEW Shiraz/cab blend striding out from the stable. Leathery shiraz dominates **99**, with lurking blackberries. Powerful palate, 13.4% alc, plenty of fruit and tannin, finish made rather stern by acid. Needs time to find its pace. — *TJ*

AntHill NEW

Somerset West • Not open to the public • Owners Mark Howell, Hylton Schwenk • Winemaker/viticulturist ("self-appointed") Mark Howell • Production 250 cases • 26 Topaz Street Somerset West 7130 • ***Tel (021) 852-6349*** *• Fax (021) 855-5086 • E-mail howellg@freemail.absa.co.za*

Mark Howell, who's been rolling out the barrels for the local wine industry for the past two years, makes his wine at a friend's cellar "on the sneak" (suitably clandestine for a founder member of the Society of Garage Winemakers). AntHill is more than just a combination of Howell's 'official' first name, Anthony, and that of Hylton Schwenk, his financial partner. According to an interesting piece of research that Howell stumbled upon, some of the best vineyards are on old termite mounds or where termite activity has taken place over the last few centuries. Which "fitted in nicely with the name". He chose to make Pinotage as it's uniquely South African; and he's in no rush, slowly finding his own individual style and experimenting with this single wine (the first vintage, made from grapes bought in from Darling, was wild yeast fermented). "There will only ever be a Pinotage under the AntHill label!" says an emphatic Howell.

Pinotage "This is a food wine," insists Mark Howell, and he's right. **00** still puckery from ageing in barrels, 60% new; smooth with full-bodied cuisine (vintner suggests venison) or bottle-age few yrs to liberate the minerally red-berry fruit. 13.5% alc. 550 (× 6) cases. — *DH*

Anura Vineyards NEW

Paarl (see Paarl map) • Tasting & sales by appointment • Owner/winemaker Tymen Bouma • Vineyard manager Hannes Kloppers (since Jun 1997) • Assistant winemaker Piet September (since Feb 2001) • Vineyards 102 ha • Production 475 tons (60 tons 5 000 cases own label) 67% red 23% white • PO Box 192 Simondium 7670 • ***Tel (021) 875-5360*** *• Fax (021) 875-5657 • E-mail info@anuravineyards.co.za • Website www.anuravineyards.co.za*

When Tymen Bouma retired from the optics business to his 240 ha prime site in the same lustrous Simonsberg surroundings as Backsberg and Glen Carlou, he set his sights on making wine from some 60 t of the 500 t of top fruit he sells off (the vision is to build up to 1 000 t, 70 for own use). Harvest 2001 was vinified in a converted shed. "It was fun!" says winemaker-in-the-making Bouma, who was guided through the process by a "master winemaker" who must remain nameless. Both premier label Anura and second tier Frog Hill are amphibious references to nearby landmark Paddabult. The focus is on reds – pinotage, cabernet, merlot and shiraz. With graftings of sangiovese, mourvèdre and grenache, there's a European-style blend in the future line-up, as well as plans to produce cheese and develop the tasting facilities.

Note: following wines tasted as unfinished samples. **Cabernet Sauvignon** Attention-grabbing **01**; massive palate (14.4% alc), dry, minerally. Shows ✱ potential. Nevers/Allier oak, 50% new. This, all below, to be casked min 18 mths. ±1 800 cases. **Merlot** Potentially first-rate example (✱?). **01**, with drop cab, exhales classy perfumes of mint/damson; implacably black; forthcoming but balanced; nascent dark-choc tastes should become more obvious with bottle age; Nevers/Allier barriques, 40% new.) 13.6% alc. ±1 000 cases. **Pinotage** Modern take on hoary *dikvoet* style. **01** estery; mulberry coulis sweetness; power alc; yet intelligent, focused, unjammy; massed fine-grain tannins for short-term imbibing or cellaring. 27% Am oak, some new; remainder Fr Nevers/Allier. Should rate min ✱ on release. ±3 000 cases. **Shiraz** Extraordinary **01** (unrated) analogous to Europe's dried-grape styles; dizzying 15.2% alc, super-dense (not raisiny) fruit, sweet acidity. *Vino da meditazione* – to be approached slowly, contemplatively. New Am oak. ± 120 cases. — *TM*

Apostles Falls see International Wine Services

Appelsdrift Co-op Winery

Robertson (see Robertson map) • Tasting & sales Mon-Fri 8-5.30 Sat 9-12.30 Public holidays 9-4.30 • Cellar tours by arrangement • Gifts • Walks • Owner Wouter de Wet • Winemaker Kobus van der Merwe • PRO Ria de Wet • Vineyards 60 ha • Production 800 tons 60% red 40% white • PO Box 179 Robertson 6705 • ***Tel (023) 626-3842*** *• Fax (023) 626-1925 • E-mail clairvaux@xsinet.co.za*

This is the new-look Clairvaux winery, a familiar landmark at the entrance to Robertson town, remodelled, renamed and repossessed, so to speak, by the proud De Wet family, who built the original cellar 70 years ago and became so famous for Muscadel and Hanepoot, they had to truffle grapes in vineyards as far away as Montagu. After the family sold out in the 1960s, Clairvaux became a co-op. But now it's a de Wet domain once more, with Wouter de W of nearby Appelsdrift farm linking up with part-of-the-furniture Kobus van der Merwe, winemaker here for over a quarter-century, to adrenalise a venerable brand. At the time of writing, the cellar revamp was approaching completion and the new-generation wines below were about to be launched. Fortunately showers of cement-dust failed to dim Kobus vdM's famously quick wit. Asked what occasion would cause him to break out a bottle of his new Sandberg blend, he deadpans: "When [international wine superstars] Robert Mondavi and Edmund de Rothschild come visiting".

Clairvaux range

✱**Madonna's Kisses** ✓ **01** jerepigo with fiery gold robe and sultry jasmine perfume, satin texture. 17% alc. 50 cases.

> **Soleil** ● ✱ **01** Lightish perfumed mouthful from muscadel; semi-sweet muscatty tones brightened by fruity acids. 100 cases.

Cabernet Sauvignon-Shiraz ✱ Outgoing fresh-fruity style, oak influenced with enough oomph, tannic acerbity in **01** to need a hearty dish. 13.5% alc. 100 cases. **Sandberg Purple** NEW ✱ Name/colours evoke sunset splashing on extraordinary dune-like Sandberg mountain nearby; **01** fleshy, full-bodied dry red, ruby cab lifted by pinotage. 13.8% alc. 100 cases. **Rosé** ✱ Confected, ultra-light (8.5% alc), very sweet **01**, with exotic 'pollen' aromas. Colombard/pinotage. 100 cases. **Chardonnay-Colombar** NEW ✱ **01** Jolly, unwooded dryish tipple; hints of peach and lime zest. 13% alc. 100 cases. **Port** NEW ✱ More 'dessert wine' than

'Port'; ruby cab's mulberries trumpet in **01** Bushveld fireside fortifier. Lowish alc for this style – 16%. 50 cases.

Discontinued (pvs ratings in brackets): Clairvaux range: **Vin Rouge** (☆), **Sauvignon Blanc** (★), **Rhine Riesling** (☆), **Red Muscadel Jerepiko** (★★); **Golden Muscadel Jerepiko** (★★); NV African Sunset range: **Ruby Red** ★; **Rosé** (☆); **Blanc de Blanc** ★★; **Late Harvest** ★★. — *TM*

Arcady see Bovlei

Arlington Beverage Group

Stellenbosch • Managing director Richard Addison • Production 100 000 cases (40 000 own labels) • PO Box 1376 Stellenbosch 7599 • ***Tel (021) 794-6697*** *• Fax (021) 794-3990 • E-mail avi@dial.pipex.com or abg@adept.co.za • Website www.arlingtonbeverage.com*

ARLINGTON is involved in product development, sales, marketing and export of SA wines to Europe and America. The own-label wines A Few Good Men and Hutton Ridge are made by Riebeek Winery (see that entry); Millbrook, Lansdowne and Rocheburg (untasted) are by Darling Cellars. Arlington also represents a number of top SA wine properties in the international market.

Arniston Bay see Vinfruco

Asara Estate

Stellenbosch (see Stellenbosch map) • Tasting & sales Mon-Fri 9-5 Sat 10-5 (Nov-Apr) 10-2 (May-Oct) Tasting fee R10 p/p (includes tasting glass) • Cellar tours by appointment • BYO picnic by arrangement • Play area for children • Walks by arrangement • Views • Owner Markus Rahmann • Winemaker Jan van Rooyen (since 1999) • Viticulturist Pieter Rossouw (since 1997) • Sales & marketing manager Twiggy Tolken (since 2000) • Vineyards 120 ha • Production ± 500 tons 75% red 25% white • PO Box 79 Vlottenburg 7604 • ***Tel (021) 888-8000*** *• Fax (021) 888-8001 • E-mail info@AsaraWine.com • Website www.AsaraWine.com*

HONG KONG-BASED German businessman Markus Rahmann knows exactly what he wants. He flew in to see this historic estate, drove up the lush fynbos-fringed driveway in the morning and left that afternoon as the new owner – a decision made easier by the revitalisation the property has undergone since Francois Tolken bought it from the Roux family in 1995. In a reversal of roles, the Tolkens intend to travel the world and Rahmann, together with his wife Christiane and two young children, Henry and Lisa, are planning to settle here soon, completing a circle: his Namibian-born mother went to school in Stellenbosch. Asara derives its name from three African gods – Asis (Sun), Asase (Earth) and Astar (Sky) – to the Rahmanns – a far more harmonious association than the battlefield connotation of Verdun. In the meantime, winemaker Jan van Rooyen reports that the 98 reds "surpassed all expectations".

★★**Cabernet Sauvignon** Immaculately, classically structured **98** ★★★ announces this label as big-league player. Very ripe-picked, a la mode, yielding massed dark savoury fruit, soaring 14% alc. Yet sparkly acidic edge, crunchy mineral texture impart bright, aerial tone for refined overall effect. Inaugural **97** slimmer at 12,7% alc, chiming with cooler vintage. Ample fine-grained tannins suggest there's no rush to uncork either of these. 18/15 mths Fr oak. 2 415/770 cases.

★★**Merlot** Above vintage-dictated variance apparent here, too. First **97**, in cooler yr, vinous rather than varietally typical. **98** ★★ reflects warmer conditions in ampler body (13.5% alc), bigger structure of tannin, acidity, needing 3-4 yrs bottle ageing. 18 mths Fr oak. 607 cases.

Estate Wine (Theresa in pvs ed) Flagship claret of this revitalised estate, debuted splendidly with **97** cab/merlot (80/20) blend, lauded by several judging panels. Step-up **98** (70/30) stuns with its velvety hues; classy cassis/blackberry spiciness; burnished tannic tension. Achieves lightness despite heft of alc. Approachable, yet immeasurably better in 5-10 yrs. These 18 mths new Fr oak. Alcs 13/14%, 970/755 cases.

Chardonnay Serious contender, cask-fermented/aged 12 mths, **99** applauded by SAA judges. **00** (sample) finer, min on mid-01 form. Oak subjugated to persistent cling-peach/citrus fruit; shiny, almost flinty acids for sophisticated, light tone. 818 cases.

Noble Late Harvest NEW First ever made on this estate. From chenin, barrel-fermented, impressively endowed with towering 14% alc, piercing 7.5 g/ℓ acid, sauternes-style low sugar (85 g/ℓ) which sets **01** (sample) apart in Cape. Glistening yellow-gold glints, botrytis-perfumed honey-pineapple crisped with lime, all-pervading mountain breeze freshness. Profoundly pleasurable. Only 379 cases of 375 ml.

White Port NEW One of small handful in Cape, sensibly in 375 ml, setting refined tone. From chenin, 18 mths Fr oak, all new (unique in SA), fortified with barrel matured spirit; modish lower 17% alc. **98** (sample tasted, rating provisional) shows exotic toasted walnut tastes fleshed with generous peach/papaya. Viscous but uncloying texture. Innovative, delicious – deserves to be successful. 968 cases.

Pinotage 00 not ready for tasting. 1 100 cases. Pvs **99**. **Gamay Noir** (under discontinued Interlude range in pvs ed) The 'old' estate's speciality, made in **97** for first time since 1983. Newest **01** (sample) bright purple robes; minty, bright red/dark fruit, unwooded. Tasty. 660 cases. **Dry Red** and **Rosé**, both NEW, not ready for tasting. Neither were **Chenin Blanc 00** (pvs **99** SAA), **Sauvignon Blanc 01** 1 000 cases (pvs **99** SAA. **Dry White** (Interlude Blanc in pvs ed). Latest version not ready for tasting. Pvs **99**. — *JN*

Ashanti

Paarl (see Paarl map) • Tasting & sales Mon-Fri 9-5 Sat 10-4 Tasting fee R5 refundable with purchases • Cellar tours by appointment • Il Casale Restaurant (see Eat-out section) • Views • Wheelchair-friendly • Owner Ashanti Estates (Pty) Ltd • Winemaker Sydney Burke (since 2001 harvest) with assistant winemaker Nelson Buthelezi • Viticulturist Louis Hitchcock (since 1992) • Vineyards 96 ha • Production 500 tons 34 000 cases 70% red 30% white • PO Box 934 Huguenot 7645 • ***Tel (021) 862-0789*** *• Fax (021) 862-2864 • E-mail info@ashantiwines.com sales@ashanti-wines.com • Website http://ashantiwines.com*

THE POWERFUL Ashanti empire in West Africa was built mainly on the gold that lay beneath its soil. This property on the slopes of the Drakenstein mountains has riches that flourish from below the ground upwards, with vineyards embracing some of the most diverse terroirs in Paarl. All the intrinsics are in place for a sharp new focus on red wine, allied to a stratification of the range into a *grand vin*, a South African blend and a convivium of easy drinkers including Sunset Blush, popular at restaurants Ashanti Dôme in Shanghai and Ashanti in Hong Kong, both owned by international art dealer Manfred Schoeni, who heads the syndicate that owns this farm. Going with the flow is buoyant Sydney Burke, who is intent on upgrading the vineyards with a more scientific approach. Gastronomic appeal comes in the form of Il Casale, a Cape-Mediterranean restaurant with sun-washed yellow walls overlooking an enormous dam, complete with hyperactive bird life. All the signs that Ashanti is entering its own golden age are there.

Dôme NEW Californian showpiece Opus One and its international peers are Sydney Burke's lofty quality aspirations for this headily aromatic flagship, bdx quartet cabs s/f, malbec, petit verdot. **00** enticing potpourri bouquet; frustratingly shy palate (which will open with time); enthalling spicy acidity. Previewed from barrel; potential ★ on release in March 02. 2-6 yr maturation horizon. 15 mths Fr oak. 13.9% alc. 500 cases.

Varietal wines

★**Cabernet Sauvignon** Broad-shouldered Paarl cab (13.7% alc), but like all these reds, not inelegant. **00** still boarded up mid-01 but hinting at good development; probably early-ish peaking (±5 yrs). Yr Fr oak. 2 250 cases. **99** untasted. **98** ready, pleasant to drink now. WOM selection.

★**Pinotage** ✓ Fast establishing itself as one of Cape's top examples. **99** luscious, velvety; vigorous tannins for ageing 4-6 yrs. **00** deeply, densely flavoured with lip-smacking caramel core; delicious now but better in yr/2. 10 mths casked. 13.9% alc. 3 000 cases.

★★**Shiraz 00**, unrated barrel sample from pvs ed, now delivering spectacularly on early promise. Veritable UN of flavour associations: France, Australia, SA (even Thailand, in fresh coriander whiffs), but symbiotic, not overwrought, beautifully oaked (yr Fr/Am). 13.9% alc. This and above to be phased out in favour of …

Ashanti NEW … sexy blend pinotage, cab, shiraz blend, well-fused. Fuchsia coloured **01** buoyed by percentage carbonic maceration, manifesting deliciously as sweet plum jam. Sample too unformed mid-01 to rate conclusively; possible ★ on release March 02. Probably longer term wine than Dôme above. Yr oaked. 14% alc. 20 000 cases.

Concept wines NEW

Joseph's Hat ★ Different, quaffable blend pinotage, cab, mourvèdre; bright almost jammy fruit, briefly oaked. 14% alc. 3 000 cases. **Sunset Blush** ★ Assertive, individual; pungent and very dry. Demands food. 13.5% alc. 2 000 cases. **Nicole's Hat** Chenin, riesling, chardonnay, unwooded; Moderate 12.3% alc. Not tasted. 11 000 cases. Discontinued: **Malbec** (pvs ★), **Zinfandel** (★), **Red Dragon** (★), **Chenin Blanc Reserve** (★), **Peak** (★). — *TM*

Ashbourne

Hamilton Russell Vineyards discontinued these single-site 'terroir' bottlings (Pinot Noir 96, 97; Chardonnay 96, 98, all ★★), "after it became apparent that they were being interpreted as 'flagships' rather than simply wines with a different personality." Fruit previously set aside for Ashbourne now blended with the standard range, though occasionally portions might appear in CWG Auction reserves.

Ashton Co-operative Winery

Ashton (see Robertson map) • Tasting & sales Mon-Fri 8-12.30; 1.30-5 Sat 9-12.30 • Cellar tours by arrangement • Owners 60 members • Winemakers Marna Brink (since 1995), Philip Louw (since 2000) • Consulting viticulturist Briaan Stipp (VinPro) • Vineyards 1 000 ha • Production ±18 000 tons (10 000 cases own label) 32% white 18% red 50% grape concentrate • PO Box 40 Ashton 6715 • ***Tel (023) 615-1135*** *• Fax (023) 615-1284*

Stalwart Marna Brink and her new cellar-mate Philip Louw (ex Simonsvlei) are making sweet music at this co-operative winery near Ashton village. They have a large orchestra of varieties and sites to play with, including sauvignon in the cooler Langeberg hills, chardonnay in chalky valley soils and noble reds in heavier ochre clays. Colombard and other old-time workhorses, dwindling to some 60% of the good-wine crop, are also vinified for sale to the merchant houses (you'll usually find something of Ashton in Craighall and S/SW, among others), for distilling or for production of grape concentrate (Ashton is SA's only supplier of this sweetening agent). Handling selected blocks separately, Brink and Louw made the promising Cabernet, Merlot and Shiraz below in 2001 for possible release as cellar Reserves, "but only if the quality is right".

'Reserve' range NEW

Cabernet Sauvignon Too unformed to rate; looks like step up from standard version below. **Merlot** Unmistakably merlot; fruity, already quite mellifluous, full of potential, could rate ❋ on release. Ditto **Shiraz** Sweet fruited, lots of charry oak. These **01**s previewed ex cask (Fr/Am, 30-40% new) mid-01; alcs 13.6-14%; 300-500 cases.

'Regular' range

❋**Chardonnay ✓ 00** ripening attractively in bottle; ready, could go yr/2. Barrel fermented/aged new 300 ℓ Fr/Am casks. 14% alc. 3 000 cases.

❋**White Muscadel** Latest **98** regains heights of some pvs; velvet smooth, raisiny mouth, lovely springtime fragrances. 750 cases. **97** ⁂ losing youthful zing though still good, soft mouthful. **96** SAYWS gold.

Blanc de Noir NEW ☻ ⁂ Charming **01** picnic partner (roses on label double as instant alfresco decor); light muscat sweetness cut by prickly acidity. Red muscadel. 3 000 cases. **Colombard** ☻ ⁂ **01** perfumed tropical fruits unfettered by oak, briskly dry finish. 13% alc. 3 000 cases. **Pétillant Blanc** ☻ ⁂ Delightful soft, fragrant **00** mouthful; energetic spritz scythes through sweetness for clean, lightish taste. Colombard/white muscadel (60/40). Screwtop. 4 500 cases. **Late Harvest** ☻ ⁂ **01** Rolling tropical/muscat sweetness uplifted by acid. Muscadel/colombard. 13% alc. 3 500 cases.

Cabernet Sauvignon ⁂ **99** Ripe red/black berry bouquet with spicy oak (yr casked), med-bodied. 3 000 cases. **Ruby Cabernet 98** (in magnum) also available; not tasted for this ed; pvs rating: ⁑. **Shiraz** ⁂ **99** rung up from pvs; generous old-clone flavours; smoky vanilla from 6 mths oak, could go 2-3 yrs. 13,2% alc. 3 000 cases. **Satyn Rooi** ⁂ Latest **00** anything but satiny blend ruby cab/pinotage (50/50), unwooded; big burry tannins need time or something extravagantly barbecued. 3 000 cases. **Sauvignon Blanc** NEW ⁂ **01** from Langeberg slopes; picked early for crispness; firm dry finish; med-bodied. 1 500 cases. **Colombar-Chardonnay** ⁑ **00** relaxed summer dry-swigging; suggestion of oak; now with some drink-me-soon honeyed tones. 51/49 blend. 1 500 cases. **Special Late Harvest** ⁂ Light textured **00** has held well, but suggest drink soon to catch fragile spring-blossom fragrances. Muscat de frontignan. 4 500 cases. **Red Muscadel** ⁂ **99** Copper hued fortified; oodles fresh muscat fruit (not a raisin in sight), zingy acidic tang. 16.5% alc. 750 cases. **Port** ⁑ Old-style **98**, backtasted mid-01, earth/fruitcake tastes from fortification with 3 yr old brandy. Ruby cab. 16% alc. 650 cases. — *DH*

Ashwood see Winecorp Private Label Services

Assegai NEW

Stellenbosch • Owners Woodlands Import Export (Josef Ressi & Raimund Buchner) • Production ± 2 250 cases • PO Box 2033 Dennesig 7601 Stellenbosch • ***Tel (021) 855-2249*** *• Fax (021) 855-4924 • E-mail rbuchner@worldonline.co.za*

Austria, Germany and Estonia are the markets initially targeted by wine-partners Raimund Buchner and Josef Ressi for their young export range, whose name is steeped in earthy African associations (the traditional iron-tipped spear, and an indigenous hardwood that proliferates in Stellenbosch's Jonkershoek Valley, among them). Grapes for the wines below are ferreted out of various Western Cape vineyards (the red vines a relatively mature 18-25 years) and brought to

Devon Hill for vinification by Kosie Möller, ex-KWV cellar headman and now operations chief of West Coast Vineyards.

Cabernet Sauvignon ✓ Classically styled, like all these reds; 2 yrs Fr oak; 13% alc. **98** deep-coloured, forceful but balanced; satisfying tannic structure builds to good savoury finish. Drinkable now, will keep a few yrs. 350 cases.

Pinotage ✓ **98** juicy and savoury, but well-structured rather than gushingly fruity. Balanced if slightly lean-finishing. Elegant 12.5% alc. 18 mths Fr oak. 700 cases.

Shiraz ✓ Spicy, peppery **98** bouquet. Round and ripe to taste, soft ripe tannins and layers of fruit. Mouthwatering acidity. 18 mths equal Fr/Am oak; 13.5% alc. 700 cases.

Merlot 98 ★ Med-bodied, well flavoured, with good tannins. Dry, but a touch acid in conclusion; tone down with Raimund Buchner's food suggestion of duck, lamb or tongue. 13% alc. 18 mths Fr oak. **Sauvignon Blanc 01** ★ Contains its scary 14.5% alc better than many. Forward grassy/tropical fruit, balanced and juicy, crisp finish. — *TJ*

Astonvale see Zandvliet

Audacia Wines

Stellenbosch (see Stellenbosch map) • Tasting & sales Mon-Fri 9-5 Sat 9.30-5 Sun 12-4 Open public holidays except Christian religious days and New Year • Cellar tours by appointment • Wheelchair-friendly • Owners Trevor & Diane Strydom • Winemaker/general manager Elsa Carstens (since 1999) assisted by William Thiart • Viticulturist Elsa Carstens assisted by Willem Booysen • Marketing manager/PRO Lana Engelbrecht (since Jan 2001) • Vineyards 15 ha with 3 ha producing • Production 70 tons 100% red • PO Box 12679 Die Boord 7613 • ***Tel (021) 881-3052*** *• Fax (021) 881-3137 • E-mail audacia@icon.co.za • Website www.wine.co.za*

If you like your wine experience cushioned in comfort, Trevor and Diane Strydom's winery may be just your speed. You can disappear into vast couches (the *kaggel* adds to the warm atmosphere in winter) at the Victorian tasting locale with its mountain views and inspiring exhibitions of local artists' work. Expect quirky comments from committed winemaker/viticulturist Elsa Carstens, who leads all the cellar tours herself. "Audacia's like a rose bush that grew too wildly," she observes. "With loving care and serious pruning the first roses are now blooming." Red wine fermentation capacity has doubled, the first Shiraz in the farm's history produced (it and the Cabernet won gold medals on the 2001 National Young Wine Show) and a limited amount of Merlot, the first since 1997, released (with a freshly refined label design).

Cabernet Sauvignon ✓ Elsa Carstens' sure hand showing in latest **99** richer, more mouthfilling than pvs; rightsized tannins for now or 3-6 yrs. Predecessors less interesting. **98**, **97** both ★; the former relaxed, chocolaty; the latter firmer, slenderer. These Fr oak-aged, 6-14 mths, none new; 500 cases.

Merlot NEW **00** with 15% cab; yr Fr oak, none new; 14% alc. Untasted. 400 cases. **Chardonnay** Casualty of farm's focus on reds. Pvs **98** ★. — *DH*

Autumn Harvest

Forerunner of mid-priced wines in SA; by Distell.

Crackling ★ **NV** blend with tingly petillance; soft, not overly sweet; moderate 11% alc. Screwcap. Not tasted for this ed: **Grand Cru** (pvs rating 2), **Stein** (★), **Late Vintage** (★). — *IvH*

Avoca see Douglas Winery

Avondale

Paarl (see Paarl map) • Tasting & sales Mon-Fri 8-5 Sat 9-1 • Views • Owner Avondale Trust • Winemaker Dewaldt Heyns (since 1998) • Viticulturist Jonathan Grieve (since 2000) • Vineyards 60 ha • Production 250 tons (7 000 cases own label) 80% red 20% white • PO Box 602 Suider-Paarl 7624 • **Tel (021) 863-1976** • Fax (021) 863-1534 • E-mail wine@avondalewine.co.za

THE CRITICALLY acclaimed cuvee Julia from this immaculately restored 18th-century property was originally intended for easy drinking and labelled Dry Red in an after-the-fact sort of way. All that changed when it promptly won a Veritas double-gold and was re-named in memory of matriarch Julia Grieve, who had died shortly before. The last in this long lineage, Michaelis-trained Jonathan Grieve joined his hands-on father, John, on the farm about four years ago and has now replaced Peter Sewell, who left for London last year, as viticulturist. With an additional 20 ha planted, reds are represented by shiraz, cabernets sauvignon and franc, and merlot; whites by chenin, chardonnay and sauvignon. This should help alleviate the rather embarrassing (though flattering) position they found themselves in last year when stocks ran dry. Unspoiled by success, switched-on marketer Brian Robertson declares: "If we make the best possible Avondale wine, we have achieved our objective. If we make just another wine with no sense of place, we've missed the boat completely."

'Reserve' range NEW

The new flagships, yet to be named; essentially cask selections, necessarily limited quantities.

Merlot Delivers what many other Cape merlots lack: ripeness (no hint of green), flavour, amplitude. **00** unblended merlot, fermented 100% new Fr oak, to be bottle-aged 2 yrs on property. Ripe picked, attention-grabbing (as are all these reds), abundantly proportioned; tannins subordinate to mouthwatering fresh-baked mince-pie flavours. 14% alc. 240 cases.

'Reserve Blend' (To be named) Shimmering cab/cab f/merlot (53/25/22) cuvee, lavished with attention (cold macerated, matured 100% new Fr oak), destined for 2004 release. **00** unbridled opulence, enveloping warmth; ethereal floral notes from cab f. 14% alc. 200 cases.

Avondale range

Cabernet Sauvignon ✓ Big-hearted, ripe cab with classically styled tannins and, in latest **00**, extra enticement of heathery/fresh-herbal fragrances from 12% cab f (these unobscured by dint of thoughtful new-oak reduction – 80% vs 100% for pvs). Fuller figured than pvs (14.4%) alc but not ungainly. Impressive debut **99** fruitily dense, sweet, buttressed by mouth-gripping tannin.

Shiraz ✓ If Paarl needed a poster to advertise claim to shiraz eminence, this new-barrel-fermented example, with dash cab, could well be it. Two releases to date, crystallising different aspects of grape: 99 smoky, oak-spicy, scrubby; 00 sample absolutely crammed with plum cake-and-brandy flavour, mellifluous tannin; super-ripe 14.5% alc (vs pvs 13,4%); smoothed with texturising rather than sweetening 3.3 g/ℓ sugar. Release July 02. New casks, aged 60% new Fr, rest used Am. 800 cases.

Julia ✓ Dry Red of pvs ed has ripened into delicious mouthful. **99**, with adroitly managed 42% ruby cab (plus cab/cab f (52/6), 80% new Fr oak, remainder 2nd fill. Seriously tasty, piquant berries, satisfying tannins. Follow-up **00** lighter feel (though 14.8% alc hardly a pushover), more fruit-driven (only 20% new casks); already integrated. Mid-01 rated ✵, should grow into ✵ in time. 2 200 cases.

❁Chenin Blanc ✓ Mouthfilling fruity style, peaches-and-cream impression from smidgeon fermented in new Fr oak. **99** with lemon freshness; **00** marginally finer; bright, zesty; latest **01** floral; racy acid meliorated by ripe fruit. 13.1% alc. 390 cases.

❁Sauvignon Blanc ✓ Fruit from cooler Stbosch for zestier profile. **01** best of these. Classy bouquet (the whole sauvignon scenario – chilli to passionfruit), crunching acidity which needs food. Light-bodied/toned, to enjoy right now. **99**, contrastingly, needed time. These partially wooded. 300-500 cases. **00** untasted.

❁Muscat Blanc ✓ Pvsly Muscat du Cap. Individual, limited release (200-500 cases) jerepiko from top-performing low-cropped (3-4 t/ha) block muscat de f. **00** fragrant, luscious, unexpectedly zippy despite low 4 g/ℓ acid, powerfully sweet 238 g/ℓ sugar. **01** (similar analysis) perfumed, nougat like, sophisticated apricot kernel finish. 16% alc.

Chardonnay 00 too young to rate for pvs ed (but hinted at ❁ future); follow-up **01** not ready for tasting. Discontinued: **Eclipse** Pvs **99** ❁. — *TM*

Avondvrede

Stellenbosch (see Stellenbosch map) • Tasting & sales by appointment • Owners Enthoven family • Farm manager Dorothea Crafford • Winemaker Gerda Willers • Vineyards 8,2 ha • PO Box 152 Klapmuts 7625 • ***Tel 083 658-0595****/082 854-5953 • Fax (021) 875-5609*

Growth is the word that encapsulates the spirit of steady improvement and slow expansion at this property in the viticulturally favoured Simonsberg neighbourhood, where owners John and Christine Enthoven at first kept their cabernet all to themselves, sharing it with only a few lucky customers and restaurants in Belgium, John's birthplace. The Enthovens and their farm manager and viticulturist, Dorothea Crafford, are brushing up on oenology to gain their independent winemaking wings (to date wine has been made under Gerda Willers' freelance supervision). Building of the winery and the house itself is complete and the focus has shifted to planting – both garden and vineyards. In the meantime, chenin blanc bought from a neighbour with similar terroir has resulted in Elegance 2000 (untasted), also available only from the farm.

❁Koningshof Cabernet Sauvignon Sturdy, unflashy almost austere style Medoc red. Latest **00** still palpably tannic with ample evidence of 12 mths barrel-ageing; blackcurrant fruit lifted by 13% alc. Needs time to settle down, harmonise and evolve. 350 cases. **99** ❁ Koningshof Noble Red in pvs ed. — *MF*

Avontuur Estate

Stellenbosch (see Helderberg map) • Tasting & sales Mon-Fri 8.30-5 Sat 9-1 Tasting fee R10 for 5 samples • Restaurant (see Eat-out section) Buffet lunches • Views • Wheelchair-friendly • Owner Tony Taberer • Winemaker Lizelle Gerber (since 1999) • General manager Pippa Mickleburgh (since 1999) • Vineyards 50 ha • Production ± 420 tons (35 000 cases own label) 65% red 35% white • PO Box 1128 Somerset West 7129 • ***Tel (021) 855-3450*** *• Fax (021) 855-4600 • E-mail avonwine@mweb.co.za*

Women winemakers in SA collected more awards last year than ever before. One of these shining sisters who are doing it for themselves is gutsy Lizelle Gerber, who works with an all-women team, from the winery through to the thoroughbred stud, that seems to have really shaken things up on former Zimbabwean tobacco baron Tony Taberer's prime Helderberg spread. Three harvests later, this poised young winemaker has garnered enough medals for wines across the style spectrum to satisfy her military bent (she was set for an army career before a visit to Elsenburg College caused an about-turn). There's a spirit of camaraderie here and Gerber is adamant that it's teamwork that's turning potential into reality at this revitalised estate. Avontuur is also one of the newest stops on the Brandy Route.

Cabernet Sauvignon 99 takes label up a level (and into air: SAA First/Business class plaudits). Yielding style packed with mineral/walnut sophistication; fruit elongated by unobtrusive 3.2 g/ℓ sugar. 14% alc. 900 cases. Glimpse at **00** presages riper concentration and . Yr oak, 20% new.

Merlot Stylistic leap from med-bodied, taut, meat-toned **98** VG, WOM, to fuller **99** with fleshy plum ripeness; fine acid tension; carefully managed tannins ensure boldness doesn't get out of hand. Yr/2 in bottle should bring more relaxed harmony. 14% alc. Yr Fr oak, 20% new. 800 cases. Barrel sample **00** develops theme.

Pinotage Gongs aplenty for **99**, SAA red wine trophy runner-up, ABSA Top Ten. With extra yr has gained more suave harmony; fine but still distinct pinotage astringency that 4-5 yrs' bottle ageing should sort out. Next **00**, still in barrel, more readily recognisable dried bananas/summer pud nuances; big in all departments, including youthful tannins, which should calm down after spell in bottle. 12 mths casked, 10-15% new, 5% Am oak. 14% alc. 1 100 cases.

Baccarat Medoc blend resurrected with **99** after 3 yr gap, to resounding Michelangelo applause. Cigarbox/cedary oak/tobacco whiffs brightened with cassis/mulberry ripeness. Creamy concentration folded into sinewy but malleable tannins; refined Helderberg fruit pumped up – some would say transformed – by 18 mths 100% new Fr oak. 14% alc. 800 cases. Preview **00** promises similar high quality.

Chardonnay Reserve (to be renamed Luna de Miel). From nowhere, **99** (first solo vintage for Lizelle Gerber and first at Avontuur) took SAA judges – and us – by storm. **00** demonstrates this no chance success; thumbprint super-dense lemon/lime texture embroidered with rich lees, delicious toasty hazelnut from beautifully absorbed 100% new Fr oak (Burgundian cooper Gillet key component). If anything, shows greater refinement, poise than pvs thanks to minerally acid vitality (though analysis much the same). 14% alc. 330 cases.

Chenin Blanc NEW ✓ Winery's first ever Chenin (eyeing 01 Diners Club trophy?). Bold, beautifully modern **01**; pre-bottling sample concentrated though unflashy; leesy/yeasty features; some arresting acidity keeps whole party under control. 13% alc. 500 cases.

Sauvignon Blanc 00 part of Avontuur's 2000 SAA haul. **01**, sampled pre-bottling, in higher league than pvs: fine chalky, fumé aromas, undeveloped but ample flavour; incisive fruity acids. Could rate higher on release. 12.5% alc. ±600 cases.

Above Royalty ✓ Label launched with **90** (resounding name actually that of one of farm's thoroughbreds). Then a Natural Sweet, now full-fledged NLH from riesling. **00** rare beneficiary of noble rot in tenaciously dry yr, but not so much as to swamp variety's seductive white peach/mineral personality. Riveting acid slices through oak-brushed, luxurious sweetness to vibrating clean finish. **99** VG, Michelangelo gold. 7 200 375 ml bottles from miserly 2 t/ha yield. 12% alc. These cask-fermented/aged 9 mths, two-thirds new; ±113 g/ℓ sugar, 8.6 g/ℓ acid.

Brut ✓ (MCC 2000 in pvs ed) Fine example of methode champenoise sparkling style. Classic cuvee pinot noir/chardonnay reflected in pink-tinged wheaten hue. 3 yrs on lees imparts delicate yeasty richness, ginger biscuit tang; these more apparent in creamy/leesy palate; superfine tingling mousse invigorates. *Wine* ✵. ±1 000 cases.

Avon Rouge ☻ ✵ Decade on, still cheerleader for red-and-ready styles. Rollicking fresh-picked blackberries set perfect uncork-now tone in **00**, usual cab/merlot mix. To drink rather than store. 13,5% alc. 5 000 cases.

Cabernet Franc ✵ Variety unusually sparky in this neighbourhood (cf SAA listing for lightly oaked **99**). Next **00** expressive yet unshowy fragrance; open texture encircled by tannins. 6 mths used Fr oak. 13.5% alc. 600 cases. **Pinot Noir 00** (barrel sample) suggests more attractive cherry-like freshness than pvs **99** ✵; firmer, riper tannins and slightly higher rating. Yr Fr oak. 13.5% alc. 340 cases. **Frantage** ✵ Cab f/pinotage, less distinctive than this partnership can be; lightish, fleeting somewhat rustic flavours in current **98**. Yr used casks. 1 000 cases. **Ruby Blush** ✵ **00** med-bodied rosé from ruby cab, with true-to-name soft ruby tinge; unobtrusive wild strawberry fruits encouraged by balanced sweetness. 2 000 cases. **Chardonnay** ✵ Unpretentious, drinkable **00**; bright lemony hue reflected in unflashy, fresh citrusy nose; palate fleshed out by subtle oak. 1 800 cases. **Dolcetto** ✵ An individual for individuals: semi-sweet red, latest **NV** from ruby cab/merlot/pinot (Italian variety cheekily featured in name, conspicuously absent). 18 g/ℓ sugar insufficient to tame, especially, ruby cab's wilder elements. 13,5% alc. **Insensata** ✵ Gentle semi-sweet chenin, **99** limited quantity still available; not re-tasted for this ed. Discontinued: **Sauvignon Blanc-Chardonnay**. *—AL*

Axe Hill

Calitzdorp (see Little Karoo map) • Open to the public by appointment • Sales from Queens Bottle Store, Voortrekker Road (R62), Calitzdorp • Owners Tony & Lyn Mossop • Winemaker Tony Mossop (since 1996) • Vineyard manager Sydney Cooper (since 1996) • Vineyard 1 ha • Production 6-8 tons 400 cases 100% 'port' • PO Box 43942 Scarborough 7975 • **Tel (021) 780-1051** (farm 044 213-3585) • Fax (021) 780-1178 • E-mail tony@axehill.co.za

At this specialist 'port' cellar on the cusp of Calitzdorp, where the grapes are hand-sorted and foot-trodden in the traditional way, Tony and Lyn Mossop produce only the one singular wine in its tall, dark, handsome (and justly lauded) packaging. "We don't market a 'reserve' port. With Axe Hill, what you see is what you get, and we like to feel it's always a 'reserve' even if the 'r' word doesn't appear on the bottle." contends Cape Wine Master Tony Mossop, a taster for this guide (discerning taste buds run in the family: wife Lyn's a corporate caterer supreme, son Miles is debuting as winemaker at Tokara). The 2001 harvest was a bit smaller: "Accordingly, I feel this one may be our best yet – cooler harvest conditions, no rot, good sugar/acid balance and tremendous colour, all the things you look for in a vintage port." Plantings of souzao, which performs well in Calitzdorp, will add spice to the touriga nacional and tinta barocca.

✵**Cape Vintage Port** ✓ Since sensational maiden **97**, one of the Cape's finest and most 'correct': varieties per the Douro, properly foot-trodden, old-oak-aged, fortified to around 20% alc. Fragrant, individual, beautiful. **98** fractionally sweeter, touch more tinta b; probably longer-term wine than pvs. New **99** best of this exulted trio; subtle, more deeply layered than pvs, will need extra time to fully develop (10 yrs min – though doubtful if many will resist its charms). Touriga nacional/tinta b (75/25), yr 500 ℓ old Fr oak, plus 10 mths tank; alc 20.2%. ±8 000 bottles. WOM selection. **97**, **99** *Wine* ✵. *— CF*

Azania see African Terroir

Baarsma SA

Stellenbosch • Owners Baarsma Holdings • MD Chris Rabie (since Jul 01) • Winemaker/viticulturalist Danie Zeeman (since Nov 1998) • Vineyards 76 ha • Production 550 tons (5 000 cases own label) • 80% red 20% white • Luxury guest house • Restaurant/kitchen facilities by arrangement • PO Box 7275 Stellenbosch 7599 • Tel (021) 880-1221 • Fax (021) 880-0851 • E-mail chris@ baarsma.co.za

BAARSMA SA is a subsidiary of the Dutch Wine group, top importer of SA wine into the Benelux countries. The organisation's Stellenbosch offices are near its 76-hectare vineyards on the Lyngrove property, with its neighbouring luxury guest house.

Lyngrove Collection

Cabernet Sauvignon 01 eager sweet cab fruit, unoaked to show off ripe mulberry/raspberry tones, drink-easy supple tannins. 13.4% alc. 400 half-cases.

Pinotage Massive sweet Paarl/Malmesbury fruit in smooth, slightly smoky **00**, plum/banana glossed with oak; sustained flavours for now and ±4 yrs. 10 mths oak. 14.5% alc.

Lyngrove Collection Sauvignon Blanc ★ For those who prefer a lighter style, **01**'s moderate alc (±12%) offers a good option with no skimping on varietal flavour; crisp finish revitalises. 4 000 cases. Not ready for tasting: **Cinsaut-Pinotage 01**, **Chardonnay 01**.

Lyngrove Reserve range

Cabernet Sauvignon-Merlot Balanced **00** with plum, cassis, red cherry aromas topped with vanilla; mouth-warming ripe fruit, succulent tannins and enduring length create instant drinkability and promise of 3-5 yrs' development. 10 mths oak. 13.5% alc .

Shiraz-Pinotage ★ Individualistic **00**, merger Stbosch/Malmesbury terroirs. Warm meaty tones, woodsmoke over ripe plums and dried prunes; contrasting sweet firmness in finish. 10 mths oak. 14% alc. 1 700 cases. **Chardonnay 01** not ready for tasting. Also available, not ready for tasting: Ancient Africa range NEW: **Cabernet Sauvignon 00, Merlot 00, Shiraz 00, Sauvignon Blanc 01** Lazy Bay range NEW: **Sunset Red 01, Wave White 01**. — *DH*

Babbling Brook see Makro

Backsberg Estate

Paarl (see Paarl map) • Tasting & sales Mon-Fri 8.30-5 Sat 9-2 Sun 11-2.30 Tasting fee R5 p/p • Self-guided cellar tour with audio-visual presentation • Tastings for groups of max 20 by arrangement • Restaurant facilities "Tables at Backsberg" Tue-Fri 10-4 Sat & Sun 11-3 • Play area for children • Maze • Gifts • Wheelchair-friendly • Owner Michael Back • General manager Charles Withington • Winemaker Hardy Laubser (since 1988) • Viticulturist Clive Trent • Vineyards 160 ha • PO Box 537 Paarl 7624 • ***Tel (021) 875-5141*** *• Fax (021) 875-5144 • E-mail info@backsberg.co.za • Website www.backsberg.co.za*

IF BACKSBERG were a website it would read 'under construction'. But a wine farm is infinitely more tangible than cyber. Part of the new approach is the large-scale establishment of high-density vineyards and the installation of small tanks for selective lots, an intensive analysis of grape performance, and the introduction of organic vineyards and new varieties. Then it's off with the old: long-standing Backsberg supporters will have to hurry to snap up the very last vintage of Hanepoot (available only on the estate in its special 500 ml bottle). And on with the new: they've bottled the first viognier, petit verdot and kosher chardonnay (winemaker Hardy Laubser was behind SA's earliest varietal malbec). Even the traditional tourist video from the early 70s didn't escape unnoticed: it's been replaced by a slick slide presentation. There've been structural changes too, with a new tasting facility in the heart of the winery, and the old tasting room transformed into a restaurant serving hearty country fare. An added family attraction is the largest living maze in the world. Meanwhile the four-year Freedom Road project to fund housing for long-employed staff has run its full course (it concluded with the 1999 vintage, now sold out). Sufficient funds have been raised and they've already laid the foundations for the first homes. Initially, 20 houses are being built and, in most cases, the houses will be handed over to prospective new homeowners entirely mortgage-free!

✵**Merlot** ✓ Elegant rather than blockbuster style gets coffee/choc-mint injection in latest **99**. Vibrant ruby, rich mocha nuances preface decadent pulpy mouthful, sweet black berry fruit concentrated alongside fine-grained tannins, fresh finish. Stylistic consonance with ripe **98** ✵ which geared up from mulberry-fruited **97**. A Laubser favourite; enthusiasm shared by drinking public. Yr oak casks.

✵**Pinotage** ✓ Upgrade for ever-reliable dowager from increasing new-clone fruit component (young vines on-stream from **98**, now 1/5 of total, balance from 33-yr-old vyds). Current **99** prominent, focused yellow plum, red cherry fruit give vibrancy to wake-up-call edgy tannins. Needs further bottle ageing. Yr oak. 13.7% alc.

✵**Shiraz** A style that has done yeoman service but begs for an infusion of more modern fruit. **99** maintains old-clone palette; smoky, leathery fruit, prune characters tautly strung between supportive wood, 13.7% alc and firm tannins. Like **98**, ripe but fruit curiously unyielding. **97** ✵ richer, most intense Backsberg red of that yr.

✵**Klein Babylonstoren** ✓ Part of the Cape furniture, as so often here, an innovation in its day. Parochial, to some unpronounceable, name joined on label by subtitle Cabernet Sauvignon-Merlot, which it always is. **98** mid-ruby, exuberant waves blackcurrant, mint jostle with fragrant new oak. Tangy, chewy, firm and elegant; youthful ripe tannins settling; clean pencil lead tail. Balanced, by far the most exciting red in the range. **97** untasted. **96** ✵ easy rather than intense; from troubled harvest. Components separately Fr oak-matured 15 mths before blending.

✵**Chardonnay Reserve** ✓ Selection highly concentrated fruit courtesy of Backsberg's doyen chardonnay vyds, tiny production only several hundred cases. Sample 2nd release **00** ✵ quieter fruit aromas, flavour, gentle pear/citrus upstaged by seamless oak. Classier, more elegant than standard bottling below. Maiden **99** more generous, expansive. New Fr casks.

✵**John Martin** ✓ Barrel-fermented sauvignon, one of first in Cape, named for late, venerable GM. Characteristic bold flavours, dry, full-bodied track record but not heavy/blowsy. Excels at table, especially with sea-fresh fish. Tank sample **01**, like pvs, individual; has ability to age a bit. Oak matured 6 mths.

Chenin Blanc ✵ ☻ Reliably charming, quaffable, **01** doesn't disappoint. Ripe guava/pear-drop aromas, bracing acidity counters off-dry finish. Light, fruity, fresh.

Cabernet Sauvignon ✵ Legions of supporters for enduring favourite won't be disappointed by upcoming **99**. Gentle ruby; moist, sappy old-clone cab nose, leafy depth and solid late fillip in mouth. **Malbec** ✵ Individual curiosity, one of handful in Cape. Produced when 1 ha vyd generous enough to crop, packaged with Back father-and-son motifs, sold cellar door only. Current **98** smoky, oaky, dusty fruit, sinuous; bigger than lighter **97**. **Dry Red** ✵ Not truly dry in **01** (4.6 g/ℓ sugar) but as ripe, packed with sweet plums, as ever. Based on pinotage, blend of all farm's reds plus some volume-extending chenin at times. **Rosé** ✫ **01** introduces vintaging to pvs **NV** offering; cherry red, cherry fruit, semi-sweet, from pinotage.

Chardonnay ☆ One of the Cape's first. Latest **00** as tasty as early wines two decades ago; generous lime zest freshens butterscotch nose, full buttery palate, 14% alc. lifted by racy finish. Partially oak-fermented, some new casks. **Rhine Riesling** ☆Semi-sweet **00** scented with musky evening flowers, tinge honey, pleasant sweetness tempered by lively acidity. **Sauvignon Blanc** ☆ Tropical whiffs, melons, gooseberry ahead of grass aroma/flavour; very dry, brisk; high evident 14% alc in finish of **01** tank sample. **99** SAA. **Semillon** ☆ Back on the road with unwooded **00**, in different guise to pvs barrel-fermented **98**. Alluring ginger/cardamom counter to pineapple fruit, bracing, bone-dry finish. Ready.

Special Late Harvest ☆ **00** developing secondary aromas, earthy complexion to pineapple, mimosa, touches honey. Straightforward sweetness, trenchant acidity sweeps clean. 90/10 chenin/hanepoot. **Sparkling Brut** ☆ MCC back with **98**, first since **93**. Colour holding, nose caramelised peanut brittle, palate still lively, tapers to pleasant creaminess, fullness mid-palate. 2 yrs on lees (though back label asserts 5, which mathematically impossible!). Chardonnay/ pinot noir. **Hanepoot** ☆ Old retainer re-emerges in new clothes – natty 500 ml bottle with modern label offers respectability to fortified favourite. **00** full ripe, honeyed, grapey richness forged with 17% alc. Fireside fare.

Freedom Road range

Label of Backsberg worker-management project, now discontinued as "mission accomplished" (see intro). A single **Sauvignon Blanc (99** ☆).

Simsberg range

Includes **Pinot Noir**, **Cabernet Sauvignon-Merlot** and **Chardonnay**, for export. — *DS*

Badsberg Co-op Winery

Worcester (see Worcester map) • Tasting & sales Mon-Fri 8-5 Sat 10-1 Closed onn Sundays & Public holidays • Tasting fee R5 p/p for groups of more than 10 • Cellar tours by arrangement • Owners 26 members • Cellar master Willie Burger (since 1998) • Winemaker Hugo Conradie (since 1996) • Viticulturist Jurie du Plessis (since 2000) • Vineyards 1 000 ha • Production 15 000 tons 94% white 6% red • PO Box 72 Rawsonville 6845 • ***Tel (023) 349-3021*** *• Fax (023) 349-3023 • E-mail badsberg@lando.co.za*

This co-op in Rawsonville celebrated its centenary last year with several changes including a tasting locale a hop away from the hot springs at Goudini. Everything's chugging along nicely according to winemaker/manager Willie Burger who, despite feeling the squeeze of an abnormally low rainfall and subsequent decline in grape tonnage, proclaims the quality of the 2001 harvest as good. They've released their freshly gilded Red Jerepigo cellar star, and stepping out of the wings are a Sauvignon and Rosé. Now they're working on the problem of too few reds (only merlot and pinotage so far): "I hope we're not too late," chuckles Burger.

- ✬**Red Jerepigo** NEW ✓ Fascinating expression of pinotage, with fine tea-leaf character in **00**, Young Wine Show gold. Heavily delicate, luscious sweetness balanced by lower alcohol than Hanepoot above (16.7 vs 17.5%), and the better for it. One sip goes a long, long way.
- ✬**Hanepoot Jerepigo** ✓ **99** retasted mid-01 no longer quite as balanced – touch fiery from acid, spirit; still lovely fresh flowery, grapey flavours; long, delicious finish. 17.5% alc.

Pinotage ✯. **00** step down from pvs. Attractive red-fruited nose, lifted by hint of wood (chip) influence, leads to initially warmly pleasant palate, but high acidity, some bitterness take over. 13.2% alc. **Rosé** NEW ⁑ Sunset pink **01** from merlot flaunts choc-coated cherries. Light, semi-sweet, with saving acidity. **Chardonnay Sur Lie** ✯ **00** less satisfying than pvs. Buttery, limey notes, with some sugar, unobtrusive wooding adding touch richness, offset by crisp acidity. **Sauvignon Blanc** NEW ✯ **01** Huge gusts of aromas and flavour tamed by racy acidity, dry crisp finish. Modest 12.2% alc. **Badsberger** ⁑ A refreshingly dry pleasure. **01**, from chenin, packed with grassy guava flavour. **Special Late Harvest** ⁑ Mouthfilling marmalade taste in this pleasant med-bodied **01** hanepoot sweetie. **Vin Doux Sparkling** ⁑ **01** From the foam come the unmistakeably grapey floral aromas of hanepoot. Light-bodied (10% alc); cheerfully sweet, acidity controlling the 60 g/ℓ sugar. **Port** ⁑ **99**, mostly from pinotage, green-leafy qualities, little of port about it; lean, slightly bitter finish. — *TJ*

Bakenskop see Jonkheer

Barefoot Wine Company see BWC

Barrydale Winery

Tradouw Valley (see Little Karoo map) • Tasting & sales Mon-Fri 8-5 Sat & public holidays 9-1 • Cellar tours by appointment. • Picnic baskets by arrangement (24 hours' notice needed) or BYO • Play area for children • Tourgroups • Owners 53 members • Manager/winemaker Riaan Marais (since 1999) • Consulting viticulturists Willem Botha, Briaan Stipp (VinPro) • Vineyards 350 ha • Production 3 400 tons (400 tons, 25 000 cases own label) 20% white 20% red, 60% spirits • PO Box 59 Barrydale 6750 • ***Tel (028) 572-1012*** *• Fax (028) 572-1541 • E-mail barrywine@dorea.co.za*

They've been reshuffling the decks at this winery on the crest of the ruggedly beautiful Tradouw Pass in their bid to become a more focused fine wine producer (confirmation of potential comes in frequent cross-border quests for prime fruit from this underrated area). The new Seven Falls label replaces the Barrydale range, a Pinotage joins the Misty Point duo, and a Pinot Noir is released under the premier Tradouw labél. Situated on Route 62, which winds its way through Barrydale and the cool Tradouw Valley, it has also been a distillery for the past 60 years (producer of the Joseph Barry Potstill Brandy). Which seems only fitting, as brandy was considered essential on the transport wagons of old as they journeyed through the contrasting Little Karoo landscape into the interior.

Tradouw range

✵**Reserve** This label often very good, if early maturing; pvs were bdx blends (first from this area); current **00** unblended cab, yr small-oaked; delicious, accessible, but better in yr/2. Future will be cab/merlot. Pvsly tasted **97** ✯. 500 cases.

✵**Chardonnay Sur Lie** Continues new world course set with **99** ✯, **98** VG. Newest **00** toothsome peachy/leesy tastes, fresh, not over-full (13.2% alc); 11 mths barriqued, 50% malo. Suggest drink soonish. 400 cases.

✵**Sauvignon Blanc** ✓ Back in guide with a cracking **01**, cat's pee and the whole aromatic petshop; technically off-dry, but racy acidity cuts any incipient sugariness. Value at ±R18 ex cellar. 1 200 cases.

Merlot Flies out the cellar. **00** sold out; **01** Pvsly rated **98** ⁑. **Pinot Noir** ✯ "Difficult customer; last made in 97!" says winemaker. Latest **01** turned out nicely – farmyard, cherries; juicy flavours/tannins for succulent early drinking. Comfortable 12% alc. 400 cases. Discontinued: **Cap Classique NV** (95) ✵.

Seven Falls (Barrydale) range

Blanc de Noir ☆ Barely-blush-pink semi-sweet **00**; red muscadel's honeysuckle scents; tangy cherry flavours. Light 11.5% alc. 600 cases. **Chardonnay-Chenin Blanc** Unwooded **00** blend not rated. 600 cases. Pvs **99** ☆☆.

Misty Point range

Red ☻ ☆☆ High-energy ruby cab/merlot combo (90/1) again in latest **01**, seriously gulpable; well-pitched 13% alc). Partly oaked. 2 000 cases.

Pinotage NEW **01** not ready for tasting. **White** ☆ Tropical/floral sniffs in off-dry **NV**, lightish honeycomb tastes. 500 cases. — *DH*

Bartho Eksteen Wines

Walker Bay (see Walker Bay map) • Tasting & sales Mon-Fri 9-6 Sat 9-2 (business hours will be altered for peak season) at Wine & Company 7 High Street Hermanus • Wide range of hand made cheeses & wine gifts for sale • Mediterranean style lunches served in wine garden • Owners Bartho Eksteen & Ailsa Butler (UK) • Winemaker Bartho Eksteen • Production 23 tons 1 500 cases 84% white 16% red • Suite 47 Private Bag X15 Hermanus 7200 • ***Tel (028) 313-2047*** *• Fax (028) 312-4029 • E-mail winenco@mweb.co.za*

WHAT'S THIS, an identity crisis? When 'M. Sauvignon' himself describes the highlight of his year as the release of his first own-label red, it's enough to grab attention (though he had put Wildekrans in the pound seats with his Cabernet Sauvignon 96 before flying off solo). Hermanus-based Bartho Eksteen made only 2 880 bottles of his Shiraz 00 and the back-label, in characteristic family man mode, pays tribute to his warm and close-knit brood. But he hasn't lost an ounce of his enthusiasm for his favoured sauvignon and continues to monitor quality with his annual benchmark tasting. Equally wine-focused wife Suné owns friendly Wine & Company. They recently moved both house and shop into bigger premises – a row of converted Victorian cottages with an enclosed garden where you can enjoy a Mediterranean-style meal and a generous splash of wine. Next up is his own cellar (he currently makes the Sauvignon at nearby Cape Bay, the Shiraz at Sumaridge).

☆☆☆☆ **Sauvignon Blanc** ✓ Packaging hints at Bdx, but styling of latest **01** and most pvs alludes to the Loire's racy flint. **01** strikes coolly, quickly gathers speed to steely dry, bright fruity finish; mouthcoating, serious sauvignon, full-flavoured but light-tripping. 13.2% alc. **00** reverted to classic mode, after detour into plump tropicality in **99** ☆☆☆, with soupcon semillon ex Beaumont.

☆☆☆ **Shiraz** Potential only hinted at in pvs ed now beginning to actualise, though **00** still yrs away from peak; nose closed, fruit compact but myriad-layered; well oaked. Enormous (14.6% alc) but balanced. — *TM*

Baynsvalley see Bovlei
Bay View see Longridge

Beaumont Wines

Walker Bay (see Walker Bay map) • Tasting, sales, cellar tours Mon-Fri 9.30-12. 30; 1.30-4.30 Sat morning by appointment • Tasting/tours for groups by appointment • Fee quoted on enquiry • BYO picnic on special open days (also art exhibits on these days) • Self-catering cottages • Owners Raoul & Jayne Beaumont • Winemaker Niels Verburg (since 1995) • Viticulturist Sebastian Beaumont (since 1999) • Vineyards 38 ha • Production 250 tons • PO Box 3 Bot River 7185 • Office tel (028) 284-9194 • Cellar tel (028) 284-9450 • Fax (028) 284-9733 • E-mail beauwine@netactive.co.za

Being lapped up in London at the likes of Gary Rhodes' and 'Naked Chef' Jamie Oliver's restaurants are the wines from this quirky Bot River winery (even the dog is mainly wolf – with delightfully unlupine floppy ears!). Seems the Brits have latched onto the Chenin, and the Pinotage was selected for longstanding UK wine merchant Berry Bros' own label after a protracted search, reports Jayne Beaumont, resident wine stylist, marketer, artist, mother and more. Upping the UK tempo, the barrel-matured Jackals River Pinotage was chosen by Oddbins. The symbiotic relationship that's developed between vineyards (viticulturist son Sebastian Beaumont) and cellar (passionate winemaker Niels Verburg) has delighted farmer, father and avid biker Raoul Beaumont. Jeweller daughter Ariane has stepped in to speed up the admin and marketing. For a Beaumont Wine Experience, book a day of pruning, cellar touring, tasting and lunching. Or stay over in one of the guest cottages (you'll feel like you've temporarily slipped off the planet).

Pinotage ✓ New-wave SA pinotage incorporating cool Walker Bay influence; individuality heightened by naturally fermented portion. **99**, very good pinotage yr here, touch Am oak (8%) for interesting sweet-dry effect. 8 mths casked, some new. **00** higher proportion (20%) Am oak. 675 cases only (crop thinned by hail – see also below), flew out of cellar on release. Big, bold, lashed with tannin; needs 2-3 yrs minimum. **01** fruitier, power packed (14% alc), more obviously pinotage. 1 600 cases. **Jackals River Pinotage** NEW "A more serious attempt," explains Niels Verburg. Half of above **99** returned to cask for extra lie-in (6 mths new/2nd fill, equal Fr/Am). Thunderously oaky mid-01, rating nearer on present form. Brave experiment which deserves time to run its course. 13.5% alc. 500 cases.

Mourvèdre Collector's item: first varietal bottling in SA. Dramatic debut **99** startlingly intense for immature vines; inky, dense, puckeringly tannic on release. Current **00** just one new Fr barrel, 18 mths; spunky fruit on firm tannic base, serious length. 3-5 yrs from optimum pleasure. Niels Verburg declares upcoming **01** his "special monster"; we wonder: are the casks in his cellar strong enough to contain it ...?

Shiraz Move to spicier, more refined mode announced with **98**, **99** scales new peaks in **00**, markedly richer, weightier than pvs (14% alc) but harmonious; Beaumontesque tannins (with fruit to match) need 2-3 yrs minimum; preview of upcoming **01** on track, finer fruit structure (so watch for it in next yr's 5 star line). **99** much lighter, savoury. These 8-12 mths oak, mainly Fr casks, none new; portion fruit ex Bottelary; 700-1 500 cases.

Hope Marguerite Chenin Blanc Barrel Reserve ✓ Designer wine, tweaked in vyd/cellar to appeal to "serious chenin fans"; intense, ageworthy. Ancient single vyd, over 40 yrs old, low-cropped (4-6 t/ha), entirely Fr oak fermented, sur lie 16-19 mths. First release **97**. **99**, back-tasted mid-01, honeyed, waxy. **00** sensitively oaked, delicious apple crunch in finish; **01** first with new-oak fraction, gorgeously smooth, smoky.

Chenin Blanc ✓ Taut classicism from old low-yielding vyds on own farm; new Fr barrelled portion blended-in for fatter profile. **99** citrusy freshness from high natural acidity. **00** intense, nervy on release. Signature wet wool character less overt in **01** unfinished sample (rated mid-01). These ±500 cases.

Chardonnay ✓ Steely elegance the hallmark here, not a gram of flab; needs time and oysters. Barrel-fermented/aged 12 mths, 25% new Allier. **00** bigger than usual (14% alc), lemon-cream tastes, zingy tail. Give 4-5 yrs. **01** shrouded in fermentation aromas, impossible to rate; appears similar. 13.5% alc. 500 cases, May 02 release.

Sauvignon Blanc ✓ **01**, with dash semillon, has pvs **00**'s racy fullness, plus tropical tones for extra complexity, satisfaction. Good match for rich linefish. 13.2% alc. 500 cases.

Goutte d'Or Honeyed botrytis dessert, oaked, which rare in Cape. **98** unblended chenin, not quite up to **99** with 40% semillon; holding mid-01; marmalade viscosity with edgy sherbet finish. No **00**. **01** sauternes-style semillon/sauvignon (80/20), berry selection, 100% new Fr oak; billowing cloud botrytis (80%); an infant, impossible to appraise conclusively, but very promising. These ±150 cases. 375 ml.

Ariane Since **99**, Bdx cuvee with house's firm tannins; needs 4-6 yrs to become velvety. ±8 mths Fr oak, some new. **01** preview most promising to date; greater concentration; probable on release. **Raoul's Old Basket Press Rustic Red** Spicy, ripe, earthy (like Raoul?); muscular tannins and fabulous 15% alc in latest **01**. Tinta, unwooded. 1 500 cases. **Jayne's Old Basket Press Walker Bay White** Charming easy drinker; **01** again unwooded chenin, zesty and fresh. 13.5% alc. 200 cases. **Port** To enjoy "on cold nights with port lovers or lovers", chuckles Niels Verburg. **00** preview enormous, power-packed; demands cellaring through 2030; tinta/pinotage/cab; ultra-traditional methods. 20% alc. 100 cases. — *DH*

Bellevue Estate

*Stellenbosch • Tasting Mon-Fri 8-4 Sat & public holidays 9-3 Closed on Sundays • Cellar tours by appointment • Owner Houdamond Trust • Winemakers/viticulturists Dirkie Morkel (since 1979) with ACF van der Merwe (since 2000) • Vineyard manager J Pypers (since 1985) • Marketing manager Heidi Kritzinger • Vineyards 190 ha • Production 1 200 tons (± 113 tons own label) 75% red 25% white • PO Box 33 Koelenhof 7605 • **Tel (021) 882-2055** • Fax (021) 882-2899 • E-mail bellevue1@global.co.za*

A SUCCESSFUL joint-venture export range with KWV gave unassuming fourth-generation Dirkie Morkel, who for more than 20 years had quietly made wine and indulged his passion for horseriding on this family farm in Bottelary, the confidence to enter the local market in 2000. Joining the first trio of reds are an untasted Shiraz and Pinot Noir ("to which I've lost my heart," sighs Dirkie Morkel). A Chardonnay and Sauvignon bring whites into the line-up. They've also installed a potstill with the aim of producing their first estate brandy. With 190 ha under vine and 17 mostly red varieties to play with, the first petit verdot is destined for the blend. A freshly tiled new tasting room lets you taste wines inside a tank, literally: the front walls have been removed from the old cellar's *kuipe* (open cement tanks) to create intimate seating.

Pinotage ✓ This pioneer – world's first commercial pinotage, SA national champ of 1959 (released 1961 under Lanzerac label) – still showing the way. Ancient bushvines; oaked ±yr, 50/50 Fr/Am, half new. **99** maiden vintage under estate label, SAYWS gold; bounded out of the cellar. Back-tasted mid-01 quieter than pvsly, nearer on present streamlined form; whereas follow-up **00** deserves its higher rating: bigger, fuller in every respect. Including variety's puissant tannins (which better controlled in pvs), so will need further bottle ageing. 13.2% alc. 800 cases.

Tumara ✓ Hedonistic red, showcasing Bottelary's sweet sunshiny fruit; approachable early but so complex, merits up to 10 yrs to develop fully. The pair of releases under estate label both Medoc style cuvees, cab from top performing block (75%), with merlot, cab f (15/10) in pvs **99** *Wine*; current **00** with malbec in place of merlot (future might include petit verdot). **00** marginally slenderer than pvs (13.1 vs 13,8% alc), but similar attention-grabbing cinemascope of aromas/flavours (spice rack to forest floor). These ±yr Fr oak-matured, 50% new. 1 000 cases.

✱**Malbec** ✓ Vivacious plummy mouthful, eucalyptus afterthoughts, translucent tannins for instant accessibility. Pour **00** within 3-5 yrs with your best roast. 8 mths 300 ℓ Fr casks, 2nd fill. 14% alc. 1 000 cases.

Chardonnay NEW From top performing block. Fermented partially in Fr casks, malo in tank. Generous peachy fruit structure suggests **01** sample will rate ✱ on release. 13% alc. 330 cases. **Sauvignon Blanc** NEW Two blocks, harvested for seamless spread grass/green fig and tropical tones. **01** med-bodied, zesty apple-like palate, very dry finish. Unfinished sample unrateable. 13% alc. 330 cases. — *DH*

Bellingham

Franschhoek • Closed to the public • Tasting & sales at Franschhoek Vineyards • Owner DGB (Pty) Ltd • Oenologist Jaco Potgieter • Winemaker Graham Weerts (since Sep 2001) • Marketing Vera Orffer • Production 350 000 cases • PO Box 79 Groot Drakenstein 7680 • ***Tel (021) 874-1011*** *• Fax (021) 874-1690 • E-mail exports@dgb.co.za • Website www.dgb.co.za*

The 2001 vintage was the last one to be made by Charles Hopkins, winemaker at Graham Beck's Coastal Cellar, on Bellingham (previous owner Beck sold his interests to DGB). Newly appointed full-time winemaker Graham Weerts (ex Devon Hill in Stellenbosch, he picked up some California know-how as part of the red wine programme at Kendall-Jackson) is sure to keep this respected range flying high. He'll be strongly backed by astute oenologist Jaco Potgieter, who ensures that only the best of the bunch from contract growers in widespread vineyards get delivered to the cellar.

Premium range

✱**Cabernet Franc Spitz** Refined wine, aromatic and immensely satisfying on release with excellent ageing potential. First release **95** placed it in the first league; rich, densely fruity; VVG; **96** more open, earlier accessible; SAA, *Wine* ✱; **97** elegant, light textured, chiming with cool vintage; **98** riper, aromatic, with nutmeg/eucalyptus spicing; latest **99** ✱✱ finest of all; superb concentration and balance, vintage's punchy alc (13.6%) sheathed in velvet glove of beautifully ripe, spicy fruit. An undersung gem of the harvest. 15 yr old vines; 13 mths Fr oak, some new.

✱**Pinotage Spitz** Has never looked back since first **96** Perold Trophy winner for best Pinotage on 1997 IWSC; VVG, like follow-up **97**. Slow-starting **98** ✱ labelled 'Limited Edition', signed by winemaker. **99** reverts to form with sweet-spicy, savoury elegance; mint/bluegum redolence; stringent oak regime (13 mths 100% new Am casks) needs 4-5 yrs' bottle ageing; the investment will be richly repaid over the following decade.

'Big Six' range

✱**Shiraz** Where generous, spicy **99** was irresistibly accessible on release, sturdily constructed **00** needs time to internalise its more bracing tannin structure, bigger scaffolding of oak. Likely 10-15 yr maturation window. Six Coastal vyds; 13 mths Am oak, 80% new. 13,2% alc.

✱**Merlot** Emphatically new world **00** trounces rather stern, firm-tannined **99**. Latest will grow into ✱ if allowed to develop all its ripe, sweet characters, savoury/perfumed nuances. Start drinking in 04, should evolve until 08. WO Paarl. 13.2% alc.

✱**Cabernet Sauvignon** Serious, carefully constructed cab, yr oaked in 50% new casks; big, quite firm tannins for 6-8 yrs' good development. **00** ripe with choc/sweet summer-berry-pudding flavours. 13.3% alc.

Pinotage ★★ Modern-Cape style; fruity with light oak backdrop, supple dry tannins. **00** enjoyable but better in 2-3 yrs. 13.6% alc. Quality in quantity here – 33 000 cases. **Sauvignon Blanc** ★★ Contrast of shiny green peppers/tropical fruits in **01**; soft but not lacking character or zest. Med-bodied. **Chardonnay 00** (unrated) a big, punchy mouthful of grapefruit and lemon, spicy vanilla equally (but no more) prominent; racy acidity craves food. New Fr oak-fermented/matured 9 mths.

'Blended' range

Sauvenay ☻ ☆ Happily married sauvignon/chardonnay; **01** bright, lip-smacking, as always; med-bodied dry, unwooded.

Classic Cabernet Sauvignon-Merlot ☆ **99** mulberry, liquorice/fennel, strict tannins, give few yrs to soften; drink after 5-7 yrs. Med/full-bodied. **Rosé** First in Cape; usually solid ☆ though light, semi-dry **01** sample uncharacteristically subdued; should perk up presently. Cinsaut/pinotage. **Chardonnay-Semillon** NEW ☆ **01** tastes crisp and dry; partly oaked chardonnay component adds peachy depth, semillon limey breadth. ±13% alc. **Premier Grand Cru** ☆ SA's first dry white table wine, still top seller in its class: 31 000 cases. **NV** Rousing, fruity blend sauvignon, chenin, Cape riesling, colombard; light bodied. **Johannisberger** ☆ Launched 1957, still SA's best selling semi-sweet – 100 000 cases. (Export label Cape Gold.) Light-bodied **NV** (11% alc), tastily tropical and fresh-finishing. **Brut** ☆ Chardonnay-based extra-dry bubbles with dash sauvignon for zest; refreshing generous mousse. **NV** charmat. 13% alc. — *DH*

Bergkelder

Stellenbosch (see Stellenbosch map) • Tasting Mon-Fri 8-5 Sat 9-1 Tasting fee R10 p/p Sales Mon-Fri 9-4.30 Sat 9-12.30 • Tours Mon-Fri 10, 10.30, 3; Sat 10, 10.30, 11 (includes audio-visual presentation available in 6 languages) • Owner Distell • Cellarmaster Callie van Niekerk • Senior winemakers Coenie Snyman (reds, since 1995), Karl Lambour (whites, since 2000) • PO Box 184 Stellenbosch 7599 • ***Tel (021) 809-8492*** *• Fax (021) 887-9081 • Website www.bergkelder.co.za*

LITERALLY 'Mountain Cellar', after the maturation halls cut into Stellenbosch's Papegaaiberg, Bergkelder is responsible the following ranges listed separately in this guide: Fleur du Cap, Grünberger, Here XVII, Kupferberger and Stellenryck. See also Distell.

Bergsig Estate

Worcester (see Worcester map) • Tasting & sales Mon-Fri 8-5 Sat 9-1 • Cellar tours by arrangement • Portion of farm is sanctuary for rare suurpootjie tortoise • Owners Lategan family • Winemaker De Wet Lategan (since 1992) • Vineyards 230 ha • Production ±3 000 tons, ±30 000 cases (15 000 cases own label) 70% white 30% red • PO Box 15 Breede River 6858 • ***Tel (023) 355-1603/355-1721*** *• Fax (023) 355-1658 • E-mail wine@bergsig.co.za • Website www.bergsig.co.za*

LEAN AND KEEN is the modus operandi of the younger generation Lategan family at their estate in the scenic Breede River Valley. Blazing a trail towards total independence, they intend to stop selling bulk wine within the next few years (done here since 1843). Encouraging others in the valley to break the mainly co-operative mould (and bringing home medals by the score as extra sway), they're the only winery in the area to bottle on-site – they've installed their own Italian bottling line so there's no more queuing up. "Importers take note if you can deliver on short notice. First invest then the orders will come," suggest these fine young optimists. Staking their claim to the international market, a whistle-stop trip to North America and Europe saw them literally knocking on people's doors (they did an e-mail blitz before they left). Now they've appointed "good agents everywhere" and orders are rolling in.

Pinotage ✓ Critically acclaimed example (show medals in SA, France, Hong Kong for breakthrough **99**), from two ±30 yr old shy-bearing vyds. Step-up **00** ⁂, WOM Value, with spruced-up label, slimmer profile (12.9% alc vs **99**'s 13.6), more refined, yet appears plushy through cleverly used Am oak.

Chardonnay ✓ Ascends to higher league with latest **00**, oaked comprehensively (new 300 ℓ cask fermented, yr aged; malo completed) but sensitively; should go ±2 yrs. 13.5% alc. WOM selection. **99** ⁂ step up on pvs.

Sauvignon Blanc Brut ✓ Now vintaged (pvs were NV), **01** energetic carbonated dry sparkler always farm-dew fresh (picked early morning), smilingly priced. Could even be aged a bit. 12.6% alc.

Sweet Hanepoot ✓ Face-lifted **99**, in stylish and manageable 375 ml bottle, retains its light, bright lemony charm; bit smoother now, moderate 16.8% alc even better integrated.

Noble Late Harvest ✓ Unoaked NLH, made intermittently; pvs **99** chenin, gewürz, sauvignon, riesling; back-tasted mid-01 shows bigger botrytis dimension. **01** ⁂ buket/kerner; similar dryish profile, intriguing forest-track nuances need ±2 yrs bottle ageing to develop. 375 ml.

Cape Ruby ✓ Young but already starry label. Multi-vintage (97/99) blend tinta b, touriga, large-oak aged 12 mths; warming coffee/toffee tones, balanced spirit/acid. **NV**.

Late Bottled Vintage Port ✓ Low cropping single block tinta; 3 yrs 3 000 ℓ oak vats. Current standout **97** (VG, *Wine* ⁂, WOM Reserve) growing richer, more christmas cakey. 95 g/ℓ sugar, 18% alc.

Cabernet Sauvignon ☻ ⁂ Yr in bottle has mellowed **99**; med/light-bodied fruits turning lightly savoury, so suggest drink soon. Oaked. **Ruby Cabernet-Merlot** ☻ ⁂ Ruby cab's spice, merlot's plums crammed into succulent med-bodied **00**, unoaked and for early enjoyment. **Chenin Blanc** ☻ ⁂ Chill and drink within yr to catch **01**'s charming lemonade quaffability at peak. 13% alc. **Pinotage Blanc de Noir** ☻ ⁂ Chatty alfresco sip; **01** light fairground candy, pear-drop and frisky sweetness.

Sauvignon Blanc ⁂ Never a shouter; **01** lightish toned, fresh finishing for satisfying early drinking. 13.1% alc. **Gewürztraminer** ⁂ Invariably in traditional semi-sweet drink-soon style; perfumed **01** with Golden Delicious apple finish. 13.5% alc. **Bouquet Light** ⁑ **01** delicate, refreshing semi-sweet perlé with ripe tropical tones; from early harvested morio muscat. Low 9.4% alc. **Chenin Blanc Special Late Harvest** Untasted. Last was **99** ⁑. **Painted Lady** ⁂ Well made sweet carbonated pink **NV**, from pinotage; not sugary. Lowish 11.3% alc. — *DH*

Bernheim

Paarl (see Paarl map) • Tasting, sales & cellar tours Mon-Fri 8.30-5 Sat/Sun by appointment • Light snacks by arrangement • Birding (official aviary sanctuary faces onto this Berg River fringing farm) • Owners Schwulst Family Trust • Winemaker Gisela Kolar • Assistant winemaker Norbert Kolar • Viticulturist George Schwulst • Marketing/sales Brigitta Schwulst 082-888-3223 • Production 60 tons 4 000 cases 70% red 25% white 5% rosé • PO Box 7274 Noorder-Paarl 7623 • ***Tel/fax (021) 872-5618*** *• E-mail bernheim@iafrica.com • Website www.bernheimwines.com*

"We're totally self-sufficient at last," says ex-Gautenger Bernice Schwulst, who has taken to the Boland like the proverbial duck to water (frequent flyers from the nearby bird sanctuary include ibis, fish eagles and, in a spectacular sunset sighting, a pink cloud of flamingoes). From humble beginnings, the hands-on Schwulst family has worked wonders on their small Berg River family farm, located in loudhailer distance of class act Veenwouden. There's oodles of energy, a new project constantly in motion. Young winemaker-daughter Gisela Kolar (helped during harvest by husband Norbert Kolar, who's completing a doctorate in biochemistry) notched up their first three Veritas silvers, proudly displayed in the tasting room – a converted storage dam – with its new circular tasting counter. Keeping things in the family, older daughter Brigitta Schwulst is now co-ordinating marketing and building small-volume exports to Germany, Denmark, Belgium and Mauritius.

Philip's Pinotage ☻ ⁂ **01** fruitier than pvs; bright, quaffable (though big 13,8% alc needs watching). Briefly oaked. 900 cases.

Eureka Cabernet Sauvignon ★ Highly individual (as are all these); **00** some varietal character; curious sweet-sour tannins in full throated style (14,6% alc). Unoaked. 900 cases. **Pinotage Reserve** NEW Fr staved, 6 mths. 13.8% alc. 250 cases. **'Shiraz'** NEW To be named. 13.4% alc. 280 cases. Tank sample too unformed to rate, as was **'Merlot-Cabernet Sauvignon'** NEW To be named. Briefly oaked. 14% alc. 150 cases. **Serendipity** Rose-bud pink semi-sweet rosé **01**; light-bodied pinotage/chenin. 600 cases. **Sauvignon Blanc** NEW ★ Water-white **01**, brazen acidity, some neutral fruity flavour. 13.9% alc. 350 cases. **Reminisce** ⁑ Unlike pvs, full bodied (13% alc), **01** uncomplicated dry chenin. 400 cases **Abendsglück** ⁑ **01** dry, fruity, crisp colombard; med-bodied. 460 cases. **Morgentau** ★ Very ripe picked, naturally sweet chenin (no concentrate added); **01** with usual lowish alc (11,7%). 500 cases. **Wilhelm V Port** Honours quartet of Wilhelms in this close-knit family. **NV** from cab, portion oaked. 14% alc. 200 cases. — *DH*

Bertrams Wines

VENERABLE BRAND established by Robert Fuller Bertram at the end of the 19th century – now under aegis of African Wines & Spirits.

- ⁂ **Cabernet Sauvignon** ✓ Pleasingly restrained **98** now offers some dusty red berries in lightweight but well-constructed package. 8 mths Fr oak, 50% new. This, below Stbosch/Paarl fruit. 4 000 cases. **96** VG.
- ⁂ **Shiraz** ✓ **98** warm, outgoing but not brash. Smoky/spicy ripe fruit, mocha hints; balanced by firm but gentle tannin, savoury acidity; drink now or keep few yrs. Well integrated Fr oak, 80% new. 3 000 cases. **96** *Wine* ⁂.
- ⁂ **Robert Fuller Reserve** ✓ Classically minded bdx blend cab/merlot (70/30); **97** drinks very well. Balanced; satisfying tannic grip; sweet touch from Am component of oaking (also Fr, 6 mths). Lightish 12% alc. 3 000 cases.

Bertrams Ruby Port ⁑ Old-style **NV** offering from pinotage; latest (01) less persuasive than previous: acid/alc dominate mid-palate and soft, slightly bitter fruit the finish. 17% alc. 3 000 cases. — *TJ*

Beste Wense see West Coast Vineyards

Beyerskloof

Stellenbosch (see Stellenbosch map) • Tasting & sales Mon-Fri 9-4.30 Sat 9-12.30 • Wheelchair-friendly • Owners Beyers Truter, Simon Halliday, Johann & Paul Krige • Winemaker/viticulturist Beyers Truter (since 1989) • Own vineyards ±5 ha • Production 70 000 cases 100% red • PO Box 107 Koelenhof 7605 • ***Tel (021) 882-2135*** *• Fax (021) 882-2683*

WITH NO TIME to rest on his heap of laurels, Beyers Truter approached winemaking at this pocket of a property, with a charming pinotage-hued tasting room, as a "10-year experimental phase" (first vintage was 89). "If you stop learning as a craftsman, that's the day they have to 'spit' you away," says the überwinemaker, here in partnership with Johann and Paul Krige of Kanonkop, where Truter full-times). "You must never stop trying. Which doesn't mean to say you don't know what you're doing!" he chortles. Now he's busy with the next 'experimental phase': "If we talk about a South African style, we talk somewhere between classic (for me bordeaux) and new world. We're in the middle, a market not a lot of people can play in. My wines are going that route: I like that style." Seems everybody else does too: the very affordable signature Pinotage, a sellout from its 35 000-case first release in 1995, is approaching the 100 000 cases-a-year mark.

Beyerskloof Cape tourist attraction in own right, stunning no matter how variable/hot the vintage. Own pristine 5 hectares, harvested as a block, 80/20 cab/merlot combo; 2 yrs new Nevers barriques. Current **99** breathtaking, textbook bdx blend; wafting pencil shavings, tobacco leaf, cigarbox, cedar lead to tailored cassis fruit, formed by merlot's savoury/meat fibre; beauty is in the soft, fully ripe tannins that coat the mouth rather than dessicate it. Finer (marginally less 'chunky') than very ripe **98** (which, notably, less spiritous: 13% vs **99**'s 13.7% alc). Personal best still stunning **97** *Wine*, Air France trophy (as was **96**), 91 Robert Parker rating. Deeper, fuller, more lengthy, less obvious (in an already refined context); roundly delicious. Good when young, these gems deserve 5 quiet yrs from release.

Pinotage ✓ Any wine purveyor's dream: accessible on release, ageable, affordable, individual, available! Amazing consistency too; quality despite soaring volumes. Sample upcoming **01** concentrated colour, blackberry fruit pastille nose, superb medley plum fruits; gentle tannins, fortifying but moderate 13.3% alc focus, sustain palate. Will be as popular as ever. **00** more overt sweet pinotage character than **99**, best to date. Mature (20 yrs+) old dryland bushvine fruit/wine from various 'quality partners'. — *DS*

Bianco see De Heuvel
Big Five Collection see African Terroir

Bilton Wines

Stellenbosch (see Stellenbosch map) • Tasting & sales Mon-Fri 8.30-4.30 Sat 10-4 or by appointment • Light refreshments (bookings only) • BYO picnic • Conferencing for 20-25 delegates • Walks • Mountain biking • Views • Wheelchair-friendly • Owner Mark Bilton • Consulting winemaker Pierre Wahl • Viticulturist/estate manager Adrean Naudé (since 1996) • Vineyards 60 ha • Production 500 tons (30 tons 1 600-1 700 cases own label) 70% red 30% white • PO Box 60 Lynedoch 7603 • ***Tel (021) 881-3714/082 804-2224*** *Fax (021) 881-3721 • E-mail blyhoek@mweb.co.za • Website www.bilton.co.za*

"It was with great pleasure that I harvested the last of the pears – with a chainsaw!" announces ex-industrial chemist and deciduous fruit expert Adrean Naudé with a decidedly wicked undertone. His transition to winemaker is complete: he's well and truly hooked. With its privileged position high on the Helderberg slopes and neighbours that include Alto, Stellenzicht and Rust en Vrede, Bilton's salad days are over (owner Mark Bilton used to grow gourmet greens for Woolies) and some of those fertile lands are lying fallow ("like a tabletop, it's totally flat!"), just waiting for more vines. In the past two years an additional 30 ha were planted with noble reds. Naudé hopes to have the cellar housed in a new building soon, although he maintains the focus is on "making beautiful wines, not just getting the place looking snazzy" (though it looks none too shabby now, with the tasting room and offices incorporated in a beautifully renovated old building).

Merlot Just 80 cases of maiden **98** prickled select group of tastebuds with vivid, full-bore style (harvested 27 B); more will get their tongues around follow-up **99**, of which 500 cases made; slightly slimmer-fruited (though marginally broader-framed at 14.5% alc), so ✵; easy, not unsatisfying sweet/smoky/savoury spread. This and below ±15 mths Fr barriques.

✵**Cabernet Sauvignon 99**, sampled fresh from bottling line for pvs ed, has perked up as envisaged. Modern juicy cassis tastes, already rounded; well meshed cedary oak. Ready, should go ±5 yrs. 13,5% alc. 500 cases. — *TM*

Birdfield see Klawer
Bisweni see Havana Hills

Blaauwklippen

Stellenbosch (see Stellenbosch map) • Tasting & sales Mon-Fri 9-5 Sat 9-4 Tasting fee R10 • Cellar tours Mon-Thu 11, 3; Fri 11 • Coachman's lunch Mon-Sat 12-4 • Museum of antique carriages, cars & furniture • Owner Farmers Markt Landhandel Gmbh • Winemaker Paul Engelbrecht (since 2001) • Vineyard manager Kowie Kotze (since 1987) • Vineyards 100 ha • Production 600 tons (500 tons 35 000 cases own label) 60% red 40% white • PO Box 54 Stellenbosch 7599 • ***Tel (021) 880-0133*** *• Fax (021) 880-0136 • E-mail mail@blaauwklippen.com*

This sleeping beauty of an estate on the fringes of Stellenbosch's burgeoning suburbia has woken up to some world-class treatment. Blaauwklippen's new owner, an international player in the property development arena, struggles to keep a low profile: he's the face behind the plushy Arabella Country Estate near Hermanus for one, the mega Cape Town Convention Centre, scheduled for completion in 2003, and the Paulaner Brauhaus in the brand-new Clock Tower at the Waterfront for another. Part of the positive transition process at this farm includes restoring existing historic buildings, and opening new restaurants and a deli with the emphasis on family entertainment, all tastefully in keeping with their 'inspired by the past and in love with the future' tag line, of course. In the midst of this hullabaloo, the real focus hasn't shifted: vineyards bulldozered and extensive replantings almost complete, all they're waiting for is their new winemaker, Paul Engelbrecht, to seriously apply those special skills (gained training students in cellar practices and experimental vinifications at Stellenbosch University) to produce supreme wines.

Barrel Selection range NEW

The flagships; limited quantities, only exceptional yrs.

✵**Cabernet Sauvignon** (Cabernet Sauvignon Reserve in pvs ed) Gone is the dusty/tobacco B'klippen leanness of yore; next-generation **99**, revisited for this guide, exudes sweet red fruits, luxurious vanilla touches; good weight and sleek, tucked-away tannins for now and 5-8 yrs. New Fr oak, 2 yrs. 13.5% alc. Pvs were made for CWG auction.

✵**Merlot** Combo Stbosch (70%), Paarl-area grapes; 30% casked (of which 70% new Fr). Promising **00**, with floral/eucalyptus dimension; sweet-spicy non-aggressive tannins; long gliding finish. 13% alc.

✵**Shiraz** Broad-shouldered, though not a blockbuster, **00** subdued and tight mid-01 from yr new Fr oak; some ripe plum/prune, green-leaf nuances; suggest bottle-age 2-3 yrs, then monitor development. Own fruit. 13.5% alc. Above 1 000-1 500 cases.

Blaauwklippen range

✵**Pinotage** Style change in **00** to sweet-tannined juiciness; lighter than pvs (12% alc), accessible; suavely oaked (8 mths new Fr casks). Earlier peaking than pvs. **98** *Wine* ✵. **99** ✵ less generous than either.

✵**Zinfandel** This cellar's signature; **99** vinified for fruity brightness (pvs more classically vinous). Fresh commercial feel accentuated by punchy 14% alc, ingratiating 4 g/ℓ sugar, vanillin fillip from 7 mths Am oak. 1 500 cases. Pvs **Reserve** ✫ **98** richer, concentrated; Am oak barrelling well contained by dry tannins.

✫**Barouche Cape Blend** NEW **00** winner of 2000 Blaauwklippen Blending Competition, pinotage/shiraz/cab cuvee (50/30/20), 6 mths new Fr oak; proceeds to farm's pre-school. Accessible, friendly. 560 cases.

✫**Red Landau** ✓ (Bordeaux Blend in pvs ed) Latest **99** raises this stalwart out of steerage. Bdx blend (cab f/cab/merlot, small cask aged, Fr/Am), succulent, sweet-tannined for off-the-shelf accessibility plus ±4 yrs' maturation potential. 13.2% alc. 3 000 cases.

White Landau Chardonnay-Semillon ☻ ⁂ Citrus-fragrant **00**, with limey flavours broadened by brief Fr barrelling. 13% alc. 2 500 cases.

Shiraz ⁂ **00** bit friendlier than Barrel Selection above; herbal touches, chunky tannins; should gain interest in 2-3 yrs. Am oak. 13.5% alc. 2 000 cases. **Sauvignon Blanc** ⁑ Undemanding picnic style; **01** offers the usual light tropical tones, crisp dry finish. 13.5% alc. 3 000 cases. **Port** ⁑ Returns to the guide with ruby-style (though vintaged) **97**; dry, spiritous, medicinal tastes. From zinfandel, pontac. Strapping 21.5% alc.

Following to be discontinued: 'Regular' **Cabernet Sauvignon** (Pvs **99** ⁂); **Cabernet Franc** (**98** ⁂); **Chardonnay Reserve** (**99** ⋆); **Chardonnay** (**00** unrated). — *DH*

Bloemendal Estate

Durbanville (see Durbanville map) • Tasting & sales Mon-Fri 9-5 Sat 9-1 • Bloemendal Restaurant tel (021) 975-2525/7575 (also conferences) • Owner/winemaker Jackie Coetzee • Vineyards 150 ha • Production 1 000 tons (5 000 cases own label) 80% red 20% white • PO Box 466 Durbanville 7551 • ***Tel/fax (021) 976-2682***

Jackie Coetzee is slacking a knot or two. Instead of windsurfing, he's into more family-oriented fishing, horseriding and roughing it in the Richtersveld. "I'll leave the surfing to youngsters like Eben Sadie," laughs Coetzee. Back on the family farm, with its head-turning views, his passion for wine remains intact. Blowing him away in the cellar is the first Shiraz from their cool-climate vineyards, though he assures "there will always be a Cabernet". In the vineyards are new merlot and, contrary to fashion dictates, no chardonnay – they've whisked it all out. Cellar tweakings include switching from traditional *kuipe* (open cement tanks) to more easily controlled enclosed vessels for half of the merlot and new-clone cabs (which he deems "way better"). Coetzee is a stakeholder in local rising star Durbanville Hills ("I don't believe in putting all my grapes in one basket," he quips), adding lustre to this underplayed area only minutes from Cape Town.

✫**Cabernet Sauvignon** As individual as its maker. Slow starting, usually best 5-7 yrs after vintage (and should keep well for 15). Current **98**, back-tasted mid-01, still tight-wound, needing time. Ripe red berry, cassis, classically dry finish augur well. Yr Fr oak. 13.4% ac.

✫**Merlot 99**, revisited for this ed, ripening into finest of the recent vintages. Plenty of extract, long ripe tannins, deep cherry plushness. Good structure, already quite soft, approachable. 40% new Fr oak well absorbed, as is sturdy 13,7% alc. Promise of ✫, given time.

✫**Shiraz** NEW All-American oak-barrelled **99** pick of this cellar's reds; quince-like piquancy to long ripe-plum flavours, concluding with fragrant Karoo bush whiffs. Chunky but sweet tannins accessible now and promising development over decade or more.

☆**Sauvignon Blanc 'Suider Terras'** Variety on this farm shows distinctive dusty pungency, sometimes with sweet pepper, ripe-fig overtones, depending on vintage. Both these nuances, plus snatch tobacco pouch in attention-grabbing **01**, from single vyd on southerly ridge. Excellent concentration of cool fruit, complex, exciting. This limited-release 'reserve' (500 cases) only in standout vintages. Good now; track record suggest it will grow (into ☆☆) over several yrs. "Hit it right on the head this time," smiles Jackie Coetzee. Standard **Sauvignon Blanc** Similar to **01** above; racy, figgy, slightly grassier tones; will keep several yrs but probably not reach sibling's heights. 500 cases.

☆**Semillon** Latest release reflects increasing vine maturity. Smoky, mouthfilling, almost sweet **01** flavours of lime, lemonade; bracing acidity and endless zesty finish prefigure good development. Partial barrelling contributes interest rather than oak character. 250 cases. — *DH*

Bloupunt Wines

Montagu (see Little Karoo map) • Tasting & sales Mon-Fri 9-5 Sat 9-4 Nominal tasting fee for tourgroups • Cellar visits by arrangement • Views • Owner Phil Hoffman • Winemakers/viticulturists Paul & Phil Hoffman (since 1997) • Vineyards 3 ha • Production 55 tons (±4 000 cases own label) 100% white • 12 Long Street Montagu 6720 • ***Tel/fax (023) 614-2385*** *• E-mail bloupunt@lando.co.za • Website www.bloupuntwines.co.za*

"Dixie and I decided to take a sabbatical last year. As luck would have it, the quality of the fruit was the best we've ever had," laments retired bank manager Phil Hoffman (although he and his simpatica wife, often found behind the wheel of the tractor, don't seem to be slowing down). Bloupunt, which is literally in Montagu village (one of the Long Street farms), takes its name from the hazy 'blue point' mountain peak visible from the winery's stoep. This enthusiastic family of wine lovers (son Paul deftly sidestepped a future in finance) initially specialised only in chardonnay. Now they've diversified: the uncertified 99 Merlot was a cellar sellout; the duly certified 00 was released at last year's Little Karoo Arts Festival, and during the 2001 'breather' (the chardonnay crop was sold off) they doubled the bought-in merlot production (planned 3,5 hectares will be split between the two varieties). Now Paul Hoffman has been hard at work launching a new website when not at the controls of his remote-controlled helicopters.

☆**Chardonnay** ✓ Two versions, both equally attractive, moderately priced, cuisine-friendly (sushi, Thai curries are some Hoffman recommendations; we'd add Moroccan). **Wooded** Fragrant peachy fruit embroidered with clean, spicy vanilla oak, dry finish. Latest **00** starting quietly, but should follow pattern of **99**, showing good bottle development. Fermented/matured Fr barrels/staves, 6 mths; no malo. **Unwooded** ☆ More straightforward; some peachy aromas. Latest is **00**, 6 wks sur lie. These from mature vyd on property. Big alcs 13-14%. 370-1 900 cases.

Merlot First release **99** flew out of the cellar; samples of **00** (featured in pvs ed), latest **01** too young to rate conclusively. Bought-in grapes. ±13% alc. ±500 cases. — *DH*

Blueberry Hill

Franschhoek's Brian and Lindy Heyman call on medico-turned-winemaker Nigel McNaught to make this wine at his next-door Stony Brook cellar. PO Box 580 Franschhoek 7690 • **Tel (021) 876-3362** • Fax (021) 876-2114

Sauvignon Blanc ☆ Juicy, uncomplicated **00** with fruit salad/pear-drop aromas; gentle fruit-acid balance for aperitif sipping. 13,7% alc. 400 cases. — *DH*

Blue Creek

Stellenbosch (see Stellenbosch map) • Tasting, sales, cellar tours Mon-Fri by appointment • Tourgroups • Views • Owners Rabie & Piet Smal • Winemaker Piet Smal (since 1998) • Consulting viticulturist Andrew Teubes • Vineyards 5 ha • Production 20 tons 1 000 cases 100% red • PO Box 3247 Matieland Stellenbosch 7602 • ***Tel (021) 887-6938/880-0522*** *• Fax (021) 886-5462*

DENTIST PIET SMAL has reason to smile. From small beginnings (Euro-inspired Smal realised the family's 5 ha smallholding was plenty big enough to produce wines) and a single-label range (a winning cabernet), this boutique winery has sprouted in new directions. Last year, he decided to try his hand at Pinotage from a tiny block that came into bearing. Tucked into the viticulturally blessed Blaauwklippen valley, this property has a natural spring bubbling up to create a fountain in the middle of one of the vineyard blocks – an abundance used to occasionally irrigate the vines, in the cellar and for household consumption (there are so many frogs serenading loudly here at night their label narrowly missed being called Paddavlei). Everything Smal does is with "a little help from my friends" and there's been plenty to keep his retired father, Rabie Smal, busy too. They've upgraded the cellar extensively and made "quite dramatic aesthetic improvements" which have led to an innovation for busy working people: Wednesday evening wine tastings (by prior appointment).

✯**Cabernet Sauvignon** ✓ Comfortable, giving style, critically acclaimed. First was **96**. **97** (also unrated) made with Jacques Kruger, selected by Wine of the Month Club. **98** ✯ plump, almost succulent; ready but will keep 5-6 yrs. Current **99** more claret-like, concentrated; best in 5-7 yrs. Grapes ex Helderberg (Eikendal), Devon Valley, Bottelary. Yr Nevers barriques, mainly 2nd fill. Unfiltered. 14% alc. 700 cases.

Pinotage NEW Piet Smal pleased with first attempt ("very user friendly"), though we feel **00** (unrated sample) probably too robustly tannic for most palates. 13.5% alc. 450 cases. — *DH*

Blue Mountain see Breëvallei

Blue Ridge see Villiera

Blue White see Old Vines

Bodega

Paarl (see Paarl map) • Tasting & sales by appointment • "Occasional" B&B • BYO picnic • Walks • Owners Julianne Barlow & Jeremy Squier • Winemaker/viticulturist Julianne Barlow advised by Eugene van Zyl, Paul Wallace • Vineyards 14 ha • Production ±60 tons (±1 500 cases own label) 100% red • PO Box 590 Kraaifontein 7569 • ***Tel (021) 988-2929*** *• Fax (021) 988-3527 • E-mail austinwine@iafrica.com*

"THERE'S SOMETHING good in the sandy swathes of Joostenbergvlakte!" laughs Julianne Barlow, who grows grapes and wine on a "little patch of paradise" near Villiera (UK-based brother Jeremy Squier, a retired farmer, is the other pole of this bi-hemispheric family operation). New in the boutique cellar is a Pinotage, made for the first time for six years "due to some requests". Mostly, however, the merlot and cabernet grapes are sold off, and Julianne Barlow invariably gets "excellent feedback from the cellars who bought them".

✯**Merlot** Moves into more mainstream idiom with latest **99**; fresh ripe plums, cherries in sweet-fruited palate. Soft tannins for early pleasure. Own grapes ex "Jeremy's favourite vineyard". 7 mths 2nd fill Fr oak. 700 cases. **98** ⁂ holding, meaty/savoury tones, berry fruity finish.

Cabernet Sauvignon ☆ **98**'s initial fruity ripeness fading, growing porty with some chunky tannins still. Single vyd. 10 mths new Fr oak. 14% alc. 50 of 320 cases remain. — *DH*

Boekenhoutskloof

Franschhoek (see Franschhoek map) • Tasting by appointment • Sales Mon-Fri 9-5 • Owner Boekenhoutskloof Investments (Pty) Ltd • Winemaker Marc Kent (since 1994) • Viticulturist Pieter Siebrits (since 1997) • PO Box 433 Franschhoek 7690 • ***Tel (021) 876-3320*** *• Fax (021) 876-3793 • E-mail boeken@mweb.co.za*

"Big bucks just flew into my back pocket!" chuckles Marc Kent, whose Monty Pythonesque humour guarantees a laugh a minute. He's car-hunting (the trusty farm wheels having long passed their sell-by date) and what he'd really like is one of those only-in-your-dreams Latin numbers with cruising speeds of Mach II. But he's leaning towards something more practical and, mock-delighted about all the money he's going to save, guffaws: "It's like a fortune suddenly landed in my wallet!" All wonderfully wacky and refreshingly unpretentious for a young man who's surfing a wave of international recognition. "Marc Kent ... combines the power and ripeness of the new world with the elegance and precision of the old", bubbles American reputation-maker Robert Parker; the Conran Group places what amounts to a standing order for PR Cabernet, and the PR Merlot is poured at the swanky Grand Hotel, Stockholm. Yet while his wines are toasted by the vinous elite, the genial ex Natalian retains his baggies-and-beach-thongs style. "I've been incredibly lucky," shrugs the winemaker, whose dogs Pétrus and Gaia sometimes run foul of the porcupines that roam this pristine mountain sanctuary.

☆☆ **Cabernet Sauvignon** Brilliant **98**, with Robert Parker 90-point seal of approval, deservedly placed this all-F'hoek cab on winner's podium alongside media-hyped Syrah below (also with Parker imprimatur). Follow-up **99** equally dazzling. Much bigger, plusher tones than pvs; seriously substantial – in richness, ripe-fruited density rather than alc (13.6%); probing, classic, terroir-reflective blackberry/cassis flavours in fine, insistent tannin wrapping. Appropriately classic cellar treatment: egg-white fining, no filtration, generous 27 mths new Fr oak, mostly Sylvain chateau (extra thin stave). 530 cases. **98** concentrated, complex fruit purity, minerally chic. **97** ☆☆ unusually delicate despite powerful thrust, complexity. VVG. All from single F'hoek hillside vyd.

☆☆ **Syrah** Tempting to call third edition of in-demand, personality-packed Cape Shiraz 'coming of age wine' – ever-questing Marc Kent, certainly, not indulging in laurel-resting. Yet **99** something of a milestone in its sheer pleasurableness. Recalls trumpeting pepperiness of internationally swooned-over **97** ☆☆, (here in richer black tones rather than vintage-hallmark white), **98**'s deep throated rumblings, tight structure. Latest combines, augments both with more punchy penetration, savoury substance. Most complete, classic (a Kent goal) and probably long-lived of trio; vibrant grape tannins, though balanced, really mean business. Same Wellington vyd as **98**, similarly massive (14.8% alc) yet well-controlled. **97** from now grubbed-up S/West vyd. Traditionally vinified: no yeast inoculation; 18 mths Fr oak, none new. 420 cases.

☆ **Semillon** ✓ Idiosyncratic, food-orientated wine with own Cape classic status (though "still grossly underrated on local market", Marc Kent bemoans). **00** ☆☆ probably biggest to date (in substance – alc remains 13%). Concentration, mouthcoating opulence balanced by lively freshness (partly ex barrel sauvignon blended in, a la Graves, to prevent flabbiness en route to mature stardom); light citrus lilt encourages youthfully approachable nose, minerally palate tension. 330 cases **99** silkily viscous, persistent. **98** distinctive, slightly austere baked sponge pudding character of maturing older-vine semillon. From F'hoek bushvines. Fermented/aged new Burgundy casks; through malo.

Porcupine Ridge range

✵**Cabernet Sauvignon** ✓ Latest **00** ✵ typifies this range: quality, structure with greatest possible fruit appeal Delicious choc-berry sophistication secured by fine, insistent background tannin. Oak (25%) a conduit for fruit flow. Still sufficiently firm to require, say, homemade steak, kidney & mushroom pie for max enjoyment; but should soften, improve over 4-5 yrs. 13.3% alc. Stbosch, F'hoek fruit.

✵**Syrah** Gut-warming **00**, big (13.6% alc), soft, round; in same 'comfort food' mould as **99**, though slightly fresher, grippier; insinuating smoky/gamey infusions lifted by spice. Has drink-me-now penned all over it. Wellington/F'hoek grapes rounded 8 mths in Fr oak.

✵**Sauvignon Blanc 01** elevates F'hoek's usually so-so sauvignons up the flavour ladder, but retains essential 2-bottle drinkability. Inviting cool scents, vivacious freshness, emphatic length. 12.7% alc keeps within realms of Marc Kent's sensible lunchtime parameters. 3 F'hoek vyds. 10 500 cases, which fly out of the cellar.

Merlot ✭ Honest, well-made **00**; ripe, dark-berried fruit intensity well to fore, rich, mouthfilling with firming nip tannin augmenting overall pleasing dryness. Good length, now and for ±3 yrs. Mainly own young vyds, some Stbosch, Wellington; portion unwooded. 13,9% alc. **Pinotage Reserve 99**, exclusive to Makro, not retasted for this ed. Pvs rating ✵. — *AL*

Boland Kelder

Paarl (see Paarl map) • Tasting & sales Mon-Fri 8-5 Sat 8.30-1 • Cellar tours by appointment • Picnic lunches during December holidays • Play area for children • Underground cellar venue for private functions & tastings • Owner Boland Kelder • Cellarmaster & manager Altus le Roux • Winemakers Naudé Bruwer, Daljosafat cellar (since 1999); Johan Joubert and assistant Bernard Smuts, Northern Paarl cellar (since 1997) • Viticulturist Jurie Germishuys (since 1998) • Vineyards ± 2 000 ha • Production 17 100 tons • PO Box 7007 Noorder-Paarl 7623 • ***Tel (021) 862-6190*** *(Daljosafat) (021) 872-1747 (Northern Paarl) • Fax (021) 862-5379 • E-mail boland@wine.co.za • Website www.bolandwines.co.za*

DAB-HAND Altus le Roux isn't at all stooped, but if he were it would surprise noone. The *chef* of this enterprising *cave* (it sprawls over two premises in Paarl) had enough show medals pinned to his chest in 2001 to alter even a ramrod posture such as his (weightiest of all was the king-of-the-castle International Winemaker of the Year award, for most impressive performance overall at the International Wine & Spirit Competition). Yet part-of-the-masonry le Roux, winemaker and now cellarmaster here since 1984, and his team, vine-minded Jurie Germishuys and cellar-centered Johan Joubert and Naudé Bruwer, believe it's all part of "a chain of quality" that begins in the vineyard and ends with the bottle in the consumer's hands. Which may account for why the beach-thonged quaffers here are as likely to be called to the rostrum as their cravatted counterparts.

✵**Cabernet Sauvignon** ✓ Noteworthy stylistic leap from earthy/meaty **98** to modern, bright, cassis-themed **99**; motif more vividly expressed (with volatile uplift) in current **00**. All characterised by well-paced dry tannins, complementary oak; **99** probably most immediately appealing (to IWSC judges, too, who awarded Cabernet Sauvignon Trophy in 01); new oak embroidery, freshness, ripe accessibility should hold yr min; SAYWS gold, VVG. 14.2% alc. **98** SAA.

✵**Pinotage** ✓ **00** quieter (in youth) than ebullient yet well-constructed **99**, first pinotage in Top Ten reds on Air France 00 competition, member of above IWSC winning team. **00** also delicious; dark-fruited succulence, very well tempered tannins providing rounded savouriness. Pleasing spicy extras from careful oaking. 13.5% alc. **97** *Wine* ✵.

Shiraz ✓ Generous Am oak adds to new world profile of cellar's consumer-friendly style. **98** ⁂, with booming 15% alc, hit with 01 IWSC judges, who awarded Shiraz trophy. Current **00** more focused, multi-layered, probably best to date; needs time to meld/mellow, ample smoky savoury notes to open up. 14.5% alc. **99** SAYWS classwinner.

Red Muscadel ✓ Latest **00** fortified dessert weighs in at now permissible low 15% alc (same as IWSC-lauded Shiraz above!), which gives fuller rein to cold tea leaf/dried herb fragrance without diminishing essential lusciousness of style. **99** similar idiom; very low 3.1 g/ℓ acidity.

White Muscadel ✓ Tangy-smooth **97** still available (at giveaway R18/bottle). Rich grape, honeysuckle, nascent nuttiness mingle in expansive perfumed, viscous, fruitly sweet palate. 17.5% alc.

Chenin Blanc ☻ ⁂ Purists may scorn its ephemeral, dryish, swiggable style, but **01**'s sure to be another consumers smash. No fancy oak or cellar tricks, just the genuine thing. WOM Value. **Brut** ☻ ⁂ Crowd-pleasing **01** from sauvignon; lively fizz topped with gentle green grass/fresh fig; non-aggressively dry. Carbonated.

Merlot ⁂ Simple, straightforward **00**; probably best before second birthday. Forward but not brash warm plum-jam/choc notes. Hefty 14% alc. **Pinotage-Cinsaut** ⁂ Cheerful see-through purple-crimson in **01**; mashed ripe banana mingles with smoky/spicy aromas; lip-smacking style set to party as soon as it's uncorked. **Chardonnay** ⁑ Cellar's white flagship clanks with show medals, yet **00** lacks distinction, reveals only light lemony touches and texturising effect of high 14% alc. **Sauvignon Blanc** ⁑ Simple, herbaceous tones in full-bodied **01**; lacks zing, but sweetish fruit/alcohol offer acceptable quaffing in short term. 13. 5% alc. **Riesling** ⁑ **01** forthcoming ripe, dry hay aromas; good flavour intensity, balanced dry mouthful. **Bukettraube** Off-dry, easy style. Pvs was **00** ⁑. **Noble Late Harvest** ⁂ Veritas and Michelangelo golds mirrored in vivid aureate hue of **00** dessert, muscat de f in eye-catching curvilinear turquoise bottle; feather-textured, but lacks acid raciness for greater memorability. **Vin Doux** ⁑ Honeyed tropical, grassy notes in **00** from sauvignon; sweetness tempered by brisk, lively bubble. **Port** ⁂ Fruity, ruby-style **97**; good intensity; sweeter-toned choc/black cherry flavours rounded by yr oak. Lowish 16,7% alc.

Bon Vino range

Now in 500 ml 'bordeaux lite' bottles; 2 ℓ and 5 ℓ packs. All **NV**.

Dry Red ☻ ⁂ Candidate for superquaffer of the year; soft, juicy, forward; sensible 13% alc. Unbelievable R7.70/bottle. New merlot/cab/pinotage combo makes commendable Cape blend too. **Dry White** ☻ ⁂ Deliberately unpretentious, yet VG in 99, 00! Latest (01) gentle herbaceous/lime/lemongrass fragrance; soft, full; drinkability lifted by soupcon sugar. Chenin/sauvignon/Cape riesling. Ultra-friendly R6.35/bottle.

Semi-Sweet ⁑ Juicy, soft balanced sweetness; quiet grapey infusion from 8% hanepoot, balance chenin. —*AL*

Bon Courage Estate

Robertson (see Robertson map) • Tasting & sales Mon-Fri 8.30-5 Sat 9.30-1 Tasting fee for groups of more than 10 • Cellar tours by appointment during tasting hours • Light meals, coffees during tasting hours, "indoors or under the pepper tree" • Conferences • Walks • Views • Birdlife • Play area for children • Tourgroups • Owner André Bruwer • Winemaker Jacques Bruwer (since 1992)

• *Viticulturists André & Jacques Bruwer • Vineyards 150 ha • Production 1 700-2 000 tons • PO Box 589 Robertson 6705 •* ***Tel (023) 626-4178*** *• Fax (023) 626-3581 • E-mail boncourage@minds.co.za*

CRAGGY André Bruwer struck gold eleven years ago with a Diners Club trophy for his Gewürztraminer SLH, but winemaking scion Jacques is uncovering hidden treasure in a parallel vein of their 150 hectare Robertson terroir. Constant experimentation with Shiraz since 1989, and more recently vinification with some new oak, led to the breakthrough 1999 vintage, lauded by the SAA Selections panel. Now there's a 'Reserve', matured in new oak and fashionably labelled Syrah, to add a fresh chapter to the history of the farm, established in 1927 by Jacques Bruwer's grandfather Willie. Also new here is a blanc de blancs cap classique (untasted), set for mid-year release. Originally from the Loire, these champagne-admiring Bruwers still believe MCC is "the ultimate in winemaking". No doubt a bottle of their favourite bubble was broached to toast the arrival of 4th generation André Jnr in 2001.

'Syrah Inkara' NEW (Name being finalised at press time). Expansive, modern **00** richly, firmly structured, though more around acid than tannin; sweetening influence of 100% new Am oak. Still young – extra star-wattage possible with yr/2 in bottle. 13.2% alc. 300 cases.

Shiraz More serious contender since **98**. Latest **00**'s ripe red-fruit/smoke aromas lead on to firm structure; plummily sweet conclusion. Yr Am oak, 20% new. 13% alc. 500 cases. Not as winning as **99** SAA, best ever non-fortified red from farm.

Cabernet Sauvignon-Shiraz ✓ Dusty spice, smoke; red berries (from 60% cab) in wooded version of **99**. Gentle tannins, juicy, bright sweetish finish. Unoaked version (not tasted for this ed) with lively hedgerow scents. **98** VG.

Chardonnay Prestige Cuvée ✓ **99** offers butterscotch/melon for starters; more evidence of yr Fr oak accompanying rich, flavoursome main course; more austere finale. (Another **99** version had only 4 mths oak.) **00** perhaps lighter hearted, fruitier, more zippy; wears 6 mths oak well. Both 13.5% alc. 300/500 cases.

Noble Late Harvest ✓ Lusciously sweet botrytis dessert from riesling, made intermittently. **00** VG best since standout **91** VVG (pvs **99**, rest of 90s not quite as head-turning). Latest now ready – big aromas, flavours of marmalade, raisin, honey; long clean finish. Lowish 10% alc. 200 cases.

Jacques Bruére Brut Some finesse and panache in current **NV** (98) pinot/chardonnay MCC sparkler; touch appley richness, dry finish. Usual lowish 11% alc. WOM Reserve. 300 cases.

Red Muscadel ✓ Grapey/floral character in pale red **01**, but perhaps not the usual intensity of flavour. Long clean finish. Restrained 16% alc, in keeping with more modern style. **99** unusually deep colours, scents. **94** Wine.

Wit Muscadel ✓ Bemedalled classic of this fortified style. Trademark beeswax/barley sugar in newest **01**; massive rich power without undue unctuousness, despite 227 g/ℓ sugar. Needs time, though, for components to marry. 17% alc. This, above, 300 cases.

Colombard Poolside pleasure – and dipping-safe (only 11% alc in **01**). Light altogether, but with lingering flavour, charm aplenty. 1 000 cases. **Colombard-Chardonnay** 'Smart casual' would be this wine's dress-code. 70% colombard in **01**, soupcon chardonnay oaked. Warmly friendly, yet elegantly poised (if touch dilute). WOM Value. 1 000 cases. **Gewürztraminer Special Late Harvest** Rose petals/marmalade flavours blossom in **01**. Sweet, but delicate; like a nice old lady's powdered and soft-wrinkled cheek. 300 cases.

Cabernet Sauvignon ✯ Honest fruity rusticity now dominates med-bodied **99**; notes green olive/spice. Easy-going tannins, savoury acidity. 8 mths oak. 500 cases. **Pinot Noir** Not tasted for this ed. Pvs **99** ✯. **Sauvignon Blanc** ⁑ Crisply straightforward tropical **01**, lightweight body leading to tart, green conclusion. 1 000 cases. **Riesling** ★ **01** unremarkable, light off-dry from crouchen blanc. 500 cases. **Blush Vin Doux** ⁑ Back in guide with pinot/muscadel **NV** sparkler. Decent backbone of acidity keeps foaming cloy at bay.

Three Rivers range

Ruby Cabernet-Pinotage ☻ ✯ Unwooded, easy-drinking **00** with baked jam aromas, lively juiciness. 13% alc. 500 cases.

Chardonnay ⁑ Unwooded version. "For all occasions; not too serious", says winemaker, fairly enough. Dry, limey, full-flavoured **01**; chunky 13.5% alc. 1 000 cases. **Chenin Blanc** ⁑ NEW Bold, forthright simplicity of flavour in **01**; lingering tropical fruit, but short on crispness/zing. 500 cases. — *TJ*

Bonfoi Estate

Stellenbosch (see Stellenbosch map) • Tasting & sales Mon-Fri 9-12.30; 1.30-5 Sat 10-12.30 • Owner/winemaker/viticulturist Johannes van der Westhuizen (since 1990) • Vineyards ±100 ha • Production 700 tons (30 tons 1 850 cases own label) 55% white 45% red • PO Box 9 Vlottenburg 7604 • ***Tel/fax (021) 881-3604*** *• E-mail bonfoi@mweb.co.za*

Most of the plums on the van der Westhuizens' Stellenboschkloof estate have been grubbed up and this year will be replaced by cabernet franc and merlot – further evidence of the transformation under tireless owners Johannes and Ilze vd Westhuizen, who have masterminded an extensive replanting of the auspiciously-sited 100 hectares, dizzily sweeping up the Bottelary Hills. Upgrades to the vinification facilities include a brand-new vat-ageing hall, where a future Cape Red is currently incubating. You can view these and other developments at first hand from the new tasting room while sampling the latest addition to the family: a Sauvignon from a lofty vineyard looking out over False Bay.

✯ **Cabernet Sauvignon** Current **98** revisited mid-01, showing good bottle development; med-bodied plum pudding, spicy vanilla flavours against soft smoky tannins. Drinks well now, though should hold good few yrs. Fr oak-aged, 18 mths, 60% new. 500 cases. **97** ✯ tauter, tannic; more old-Cape style.

Sauvignon Blanc NEW ✯ Creditable maiden **01** from 190-240 m high block; shy dusty/grapefruity tones, green nettle/greengage tinges; sweet impression from high 13.7% alc. Augurs well for future. 320 cases. — *TM*

Bonnievale Cellar

Bonnievale (see Robertson map) • Tasting & sales Mon-Fri 8-5 Sat 10-1 • Cellar tours by arrangement • Views • Owners 60 members • Manager/winemaker Henk Wentzel (since 1999) • Assistant winemaker Francois Agenbag (since 2001) • Vineyards 790 ha • Production ±10 000 tons (25 000 cases own label) 70% white 30% red • PO Box 206 Bonnievale 6730 • ***Tel (023) 616-2795/2359*** *• Fax (023) 616-2332 • E-mail winemaker@bonnievalecellar.co.za • Website www.bonnievalecellar.co.za*

"Chance of a lifetime," declared Christopher Rigg, visionary Barberton gold baronet, property developer and founder of Bonnievale, in his early 1900s sales pitch to prospective farm owners of this scenic swathe of Breede River basin. Those words gain a contemporary resonance as the members of this co-op launch a fresh assault on the international market (2001 saw winemaker/manager Henk Wentzel and team unveil their revamped range below at the London Wine & Spirits Fair) as well as the local arena. They've added 20 000 cases in the past year to the quantities sold in their own bottles, and they're looking to increase exports of bulk products too. An exciting prospect is the Breede River's first organic range, from an eco-tweaked member-farm hoping to gain full certification around 2003.

Cabernet Sauvignon-Merlot NEW ✓ An unheralded pleasure! Well-made/priced **01** lightly oaked 67/33 blend; minerally background to delicious summer pud palate, dry tannins control the sweet fruit now and for 3-5 yrs. 13% alc. 20 000 cases.

Shiraz Venison and other aromatic meats will go with **00**'s scrubby, peppery, smoky tones. Lightly oak-staved. 13.7% alc. 1 000 cases. **Kelkierooi** New smarter livery for **00**, lightish but tasty unwooded cinsaut/ruby cab with very slight peppery grip. 500 ml. 1 000 cases. **CCC** NEW Acronym for varietal triumvirate colombard, chenin, chardonnay in this billowing tropical blend, partly oaked, light. 3 000 cases.

Sauvignon Blanc High-toned **01** with lightish nettles and fruits, piercing acidity. For early drinking. 1 500 cases. **Kelkiewit** **NV**. Colombard, chenin, chardonnay in this dryish, lightweight libation. 500 ml. 1 000 cases. **Special Late Harvest** **NV** (00) lightish honeyed chenin; botrytis and fungi hints; unexpectedly dry for style. 1 000 cases. Discontinued: **Cabernet Sauvignon** (**99**); **Pinotage** (**00** untasted); **Riggton Red** (**00**); **Chenin Blanc** (**00** untasted); **Pik 'n Wyntjie** (**00** untasted); **Riggton White** (**00**). — *DH*

Boplaas

Calitzdorp (see Little Karoo map) • Tasting & sales Mon-Fri 8-5 Sat 9-3 • Cellar tours by appointment • Tourgroups • Views • Permanent exhibition of San artefacts • Carel Nel part owner of 47 000 ha Rooiberg Conservancy nearby • Owners Carel & Jeanne Nel • Winemaker Carel Nel • Viticulturist Pieter Terblanche • Vineyards 67 ha • Production 900 tons 25 000 cases 50/50 red/white • PO Box 156 Calitzdorp 6660 • ***Tel (044) 213-3326*** *• Fax (044) 213-3750 • E-mail boplaas@mweb.co.za • Website www.boplaas.co.za*

"I HAVE MET many of the world's great winemakers," says Carel Nel, "but it was from Robert Mondavi that I learned it is possible to build a great reputation in just one generation." If this Cape Wine Master from Calitzdorp earns a place in SA's oenological pantheon, it will be partly because he's been wine-focused since he was at school. In fact, winegrowing seems to be in his genes: "I think I inherited my father's love of wine." An abiding preoccupation is port – it was the subject of Nel's CWM thesis, and it inspired him to become the catalyst for a number of key innovations, such as the annual Calitzdorp Port Festival and the SA Port Producers' Association. These have helped raise the calibre of not just Nel's own 'ports' but also those of his fellow growers'. And it seems the best it yet to come: harvest 2001 was exceptionally favourable for port varieties, Nel reports, resulting in grapes with deep colours and intense flavours. "It promises to be a real vintage year."

Pinotage Reserve Unblended pinotage ex Stbosch, showing complexity, balance, suppleness. Roasty/charry dimension developing in **99**, contrasting well with sweet fruit. 8 mths Fr oak, 50% new. 250 cases. Regular **Pinotage** , from own grapes, no new oak. **99** lighter than Reserve (12.8% vs 13.5% alc), fruitier; ready.

Cabernet Sauvignon Reserve 99 tasted for pvs ed holding; ready, though blackcurrant/ripe-plum flesh, soft tannins suggest could go few more yrs;

Stbosch grapes vinified in C'dorp; oaking as above. 250 cases. Regular **Cabernet Sauvignon** ☆ **00** no new oak; more open, accessible; not for extended ageing. 1 800 cases. Similar analyses; alcs ±12.5%.

Merlot Reserve Sinewy, almost austere style. **98**, back-tasted mid-01, dry, puckering; needs time/food to tone down present astringency. Stbosch fruit; barrelling per Reserves above. 250 cases. Regular **Merlot** ☆, from C'dorp vyds; **00** more open-textured than stablemate, bigger (13.7% alc), ready to drink. No new casks. 1 500 cases.

Muscadel ✓ **00** velvety fortified white dessert developing with distinction; overall delicacy reflected in light raisin tone with piquant lemon uplift. 15.4% alc low for this style.

Cape Vintage Reserve Port ✓ Ageworthy 'port', made only in exceptional yrs. Stylistic fine-tuning brings forth a gem in **99** ☆, Carel Nel's finest since **91** ☆ and breakthrough **86**, which announced cellar's Portuguese-inspired lofty aspirations. **99** gains extra fillip from maturing touriga vyd, ungrafted 30-yr-old block tinta, plus excellent sugar:alc ratio (90 g/ℓ, 19% vs 94.5, 18.8 of pvs). Result is punchier, edgier style; spiritous and introverted now, but tight-packed bluegummy/peaty core set to unfold thrillingly over 10-20 yrs. *Wine* ☆, SAYWS gold, local show classwinner. 18 mths 500 ℓ Portuguese pipes. 400 cases. No **98**.

Cape Tawny Port SA benchmark for this style. Wood-matured **NV**, 80% tinta b, balance touriga; avg age 8 yrs, freshened before bottling with dash younger touriga. Limpid tawny-orange hues; satin palate. String of awards, of which Best SA Tawny in SA *Wine* 2 yrs running. 105 g/ℓ sugar, 18,8% alc. 150 cases. **Cape Dated Tawny Vintner's Selection** NEW **80** more concentrated version of above, slightly sweeter. Tinta b. 10 yrs Portuguese oak; 106 g/ℓ sugar, 18% alc.

Blanc de Noir ☺ ☆ Rose-bud pink semi-sweet outdoor companion; **01**, like pvs, pinotage/cab/shiraz blend, moderate 12% alc. **Golden Harvest** ☺ ☆ Low alc Natural Sweet white; delicate grapefruit/honeysuckle aromas in **01**; brisk acidity ensures uncloying finish. Colombard/ muscadel.

Sangiovese Last was **99** ☆. Aged 10 mths new Fr oak. **Shiraz Reserve** ☆ Second vintage **99** flew SAA Business Class. Toasty smokiness now apparent; structure for further 3-5 yrs. Stbosch grapes, 10 mths new Fr oak. 250 cases. **Dry Red** ☆ Varietal miscellany with soft, light-bodied dried-fruit flavours, appetising savoury tang. Honest everyday stuff. **Chardonnay** ☆ **00** lauded by national/local young wine show judges; undemanding, some sweet-tropical nuances. Not oaked. **Sauvignon Blanc** ☆ Invariably well behaved example. **01** med-bodied with boiled sweet/pear-drop easiness, fresh finish. 1 400 cases. **Late Harvest** ☆ Perfumed **01**, usual low 10% alc, dry-tasting. **Pinot Noir Brut** ☆ Light-bodied **00** showing bottle age, earthy tones. Carbonated. **Sweet Sparkling** ☆ Festive **NV** bubble, sweet, grapey; from hanepoot/colombard. Low 10% alc. **Red Dessert** ☆ Russet hued **NV** blend tinta b/muscadel, fortified to 16.5% alc. Unusual, attractive savoury/stewed fruit contrast. **Sweet Hanepoot** ☆ **00** golden fortified dessert, ethereal grapey sweetness, good thread of acidity. 15.5% alc. **Cape Vintage Port** ☆ This 'standard' version produced annually, usually tinta b/touriga/souzao mix, aged 18-24 mths old 500 ℓ Portuguese pipes. 'Correct' lower level sugars – 94 g/ℓ in latest **98**; earthier than pvs, not as youthfully grippy; approachable. SAYWS gold. 18.8% alc. 1 500 cases. **Cape Ruby Port** ☆ Still SA's best selling **NV** ruby, in drier Portuguese style. Satisfying, attractively priced blend tinta b/touriga. 18% alc. **Cape White Port** ☆ Not too sweet **NV** fortified from colombard; popular (lightly chilled) as aperitif. 750 cases. — *DH*

Boschendal Wines

Franschhoek (see Franschhoek map) • Tasting & sales Nov-Apr: Mon-Sat 8.30-4.30 Sun 9.30-12.30 May-Oct: Mon-Sat 8.30-4.30 Tasting fee R6 p/p • Combined cellar/vineyard tour Nov-Apr 10.30 & 11.30 (weather dependent) • Cellar tours May-Oct 10.30 & 11.30 (booking essential) • Restaurants, picnics, also children's picnics Nov-Apr (see Eat-out section) • Tourgroups • Gifts • Views • Tours of restored 1812 manor house • Wheelchair-friendly • Owner Anglo American Farms (MD: Don Tooth) • Senior winemaker JC Bekker (since 1996) • Assistant winemakers Lionell Leibrandt & Henry Kotze • Viticulturist Spekkies von Breda (since 1995) with André Lambrechts • Vineyards 344 ha • Production 240 000 cases 49% white 32% red 14% pink 5% sparkling • PO Groot Drakenstein 7680 • Restaurant: Tel (021) 870-4274 • Fax (021) 874-1864 • E-mail reservations@boschendal.com • Winery: ***Tel (021) 870-4200*** *• Fax (021) 874-1531 • E-mail bekkerjc@amfarms.co.za • Websites www.boschendal.com and www.boschendalwines.co.za*

THIS WAKING beauty, at the time of going to press, was waiting for a suitor to keep her in the style to which she'd grown accustomed as belle of the present owner, Anglo American. Strategic realignment sees Amfarms looking for a suitable buyer for these immensely prestigious 3 500 hectares, stretching from Simonsberg to the Groot Drakenstein mountains, wine-farmed since at least 1685. Given the scale, the deal could take two years or longer to complete. In the meantime, it's (very big) business as usual. Vintage 2001 was "the largest and most hectic ever", and a quarter of the crop arrived in one week! After crushing around the clock ("for four weeks we didn't close at all"), the team say they're "very excited" about the quality. Frenetic activity in the cellar is matched in the vineyards, revolutionised on a scale unmatched in the Cape. A staggering 176 ha of white and virus-infected red varieties have been uprooted and replanted, mostly with red classics. Amid the hubbub, cellar commodore J C Bekker completed an honours degree in oenology while second-in-command Henry Kotze found time to get married.

☆ **Grand Reserve** Classically crafted flagship won't wow show judges – too demure for that – but reward patient cellar enthusiasts. 2nd release **98** ☆☆ Medoc-profile cab s/f, merlot (50/25/25); resounding if shy meaty/earthy, tomato cocktail aromas; palate mid-01 very closed, tight choc, bramble fruit under guard. Unavailable for instant gratification but clearly big wine, big time. **97** VG cask selection of equal merlot, cab f. These yr Fr oak, 50% new, rest 2nd fill. Limited filtration.

☆ **Merlot** Follows, if anything can, Big Brother above in tasting line-up. Denser yet more accessible in **99**, full ruby shimmers alongside open, plump mocha, gamey meat features. Rich, delicious mouthful, soft tannins guide without interfering. Flagrantly easy in youth but deserves 5 more yrs. 100% merlot picked ripe, fermented up to 30 °C, 3 wks on skins, yr Fr oak, 30% new. Bigger **98** similar gamey/meaty fruit, terrific superstructure, luscious plums/cherries beckon beneath. 13,9% alc. Both more perfumed, intense, mouthfilling than lavishly decorated **97**.

☆ **Jean le Long Merlot 99** returns label to range, 1st since **94**. Opaque dense blue-black colour; delicate, echoing bouquet violets, roasted nuts, nutmeg, paprika-spiced goulash. Tense, tapered palate merlot mocha but more elegant, less obvious, more alluring than 'standard' above. Loads of tannins, pots of alcohol (14.5%), rapid-fire intensity of flavour.

☆ **Shiraz** Style changed in **97**; packaging (to curvaceous Rhone bottle) in **98**; now quality leaps ahead in **99** ☆☆: constantly unfurling aromas of milled pepper, savoury black olive/pimento spice with terrific firm, structured mouthful packed with mulberry/chocolate fruit, hemmed in by mineral thread. Restrained, refined. 95% malo in steel, yr Fr oak. 14.5% alc. Showstopping **98** cocked an ear to Australia: full, robust, fat-fruited. **97** VVG, *Wine* ✵, not as voluminous. These from low 4.5 t/ha cropped single vyd.

✵**Lanoy** Nicolas de Lanoy, 17th century owner of part of property, would also be wondering where his namesake goes next. Developed more gravity with recent releases; now that above stars are coming out, morphs back into original cab-suffused incarnation in latest **99** ✵ (66% with 21% shiraz, dashes cab f, merlot) which shows with 'Boschendal fynbos' fragrance, sappy brambles, smoky pepper spice. Well constructed but less serious than merlot-based **98** which shared oaking regimen (25% new, rest 2nd/3rd fill barriques, 12 mths). **97** Diners Club finalist.

✵**Pinot Noir-Chardonnay** ✓ Characteristically first to market (the SA style pioneered here), boldly packaged as red yet pouring white, with legions of fans (local and foreign): **00** sold out before it could be tasted! Sample upcoming **01** true to form: senior partner pinot (portion cask fermented) offers cherry fruit, broad gamey texture leavened by pink grapefruit twist from oaked chardonnay. Tantalising aperitif. No **99**. Limited production – act early or miss out …

✵**Chardonnay Reserve** While purists (and its winemakers, we suspect) may seek some restraint, the public will love **00**, bumptious in cellar, brash (not harsh) in bottle. Glass almost too small for its delights: brilliant golden patina, massively rich nose of apple-pie, vanilla, baker's butter; herculean ripe fruitonly just controlled by zinging acid; serious alc (14.6%) the crescendo. Wow. 3 t/ha yield (only dinky thing about it), 50% natural fermentation (over 5 mths!), half malo, barrelled 11 mths, 25% new. Successor to bold **99**. Standard **Chardonnay** quieter (could hardly be anything else), not without own significant charms: sample **01** fresh, lemon/lime intensity under wraps, will open (as has **00**) to reveal bursts zesty lime fruits sparking creamy melting butter in palate. 14.3% alc. Good food accompaniment. Portion oaked (60%, some new casks); no malo, for freshness.

✵**Jean le Long Sauvignon Blanc** 'WO Coastal' despite grapes from own pedigreed single dryland block, 22 yrs old. **01** vintage maximises consistently good fruit: resounding pepper, green pea, olive herbaceous lucidity; firm, structured mouthful, racy finish. Closed mid-01, promises gooseberry fruits over 18 mths. 14.2% alc. Pvs **99** inimitably Boschendal: herbaceous nettle/heather wafts, tropical fruit flavours.

✵**Sauvignon Blanc 01** maintains rating threatened by stylistic pendulum: back to opulent tropical melon/soft peach, albeit with feisty grassy chord, crisp finish (belying 4 g/ℓ sugar); less obvious scrub character that marked unique, herbaceous **00**. Both better suited to tables than showcase. Farm fruit: low-yielding, slow-ripening 400 m high site, ultra-reductive handling. 14.1% alc.

✵**Jean le Long Semillon** Single 400 m high (slow-ripening) vyd's meagre 2 t/ha yield gives winemakers – more used to directing volume blends – crack at boutique crafting: "Very, very special" they aver. Always single vyd, after property's Huguenot founder. No problems ripening in **00**: Am oak (50%) plays cymbal, alc (15.2%) beats drum. Leek-green lights to straw; vanilla-sugar nose with lanolin depth; bold palate bucked by mulish alc. Demands food. Cask-fermented/aged 8 mths. **99** better balanced, full but tapered palate. *Wine* ✵.

✵**Grand Vin Blanc** Best of cellar's trio sauvignon-based blends; endured 16 yrs since intended one-off for 300th anniversary. Oaked sauvignon (85%, barriques 6 mths; 15% cask-fermented chardonnay), subtitled Sauvignon Blanc on label (call it Blanc Fumé – which it is – and nobody would buy it!). **01** retains signet 'Boschendal buchu' – grassy/herby flavours injected with spice; soft, just-sweet (5 g/ℓ sugar); full enough for food, just enough grip to tighten the belt. 13,7% alc.

✵**Vin d'Or** Gentle, painstaking handling reflected in elegant **98** (first since **94**). Induced berry concentration (stems lightly crushed) preserved by careful harvesting at 18.5% potential alc, bunch-pressing, cool fermentation. Developing golden shards, bouquet ripe with lemon-zest cut honey, plush apricot/soft peach flavours, brush botrytis. Candied orange-peel twist to tail. 100% semillon. 103 g/ℓ sugar contained by 8 g/ℓ acid. 12,8% alc.

Brut 2000 Premium MCC bubbly launched for Y2K; wise punters who abstained will be rewarded: delightfully open, rich yeasty aromas to luxurious, plush, seasoned-leather palate, hints caramel. All integrated, wonderful now. (Collector's note: technical gremlins see three labels in market: rare embossed; standard 'vertical-strip', black rectangle – latter more mundane, does duty on more recent stocks). Carries disgorging date (May 99). Equal chardonnay/pinot, low sulphured; complexity geared up by total 3 yrs on lees. Bone-dry. Less than 2 000 bottles. VG, *Wine*.

Brut Not the flash label in sparkling triumvirate, but next **96** showcases best of the house: yellow shot with saffron; upholstered biscuity texture, black-grape body, tropical tones, yeasty richness from 4 yrs on lees. Remarkably fresh, complex. Degorging date (Nov 00) now shown. More racy, longer legs than millennium whizz-fizz above, both ready. Residual sugars (8.6 g/ℓ) marginally higher than pvs. 60/40 pinot/chardonnay. No **94**.

Blanc de Noir Venerable stalwart since first into Cape market two decades ago. Possibly under threat of corporate realignment (old vines grubbed up, 40% production cut in 00) but consumers keep baying for more. Consistency a hallmark, blend pinot, merlot (66/33). Sample **01** salmon pink, tawny tints; red cherries, quince plump out easy off-dry mouthful. **Chenin Blanc** Style seemingly set by nature, who appears to be halting fermentation early for off-dry profile with formidable alc. **01** again 7.4 g/ℓ sugar, 14.3% alc, both obscure honeyed fruit in mouth. Sweet, simple. **Blanc de Blanc** Brand builder likely to trounce newbies and other pretenders. Sample **01** confirms change to now sauvignon-dominated refreshing white quaff, albeit more tropical, pulpy, sweeter than pvs' grassy, heather tones. Breadth, depth from splash chardonnay. Unoaked. ± 13% alc. **Riesling** (Cape) **99** was to be swansong, casualty of sweeping upgrade, but rescued by marketing men: demand just too great! **01** evokes nights in game farm rondavel; heady thatch, hint of winter-melon, otherwise undemanding. **Sauvignon Blanc-Semillon** NEW Does Boschendal, with stated focus on quality reds, need another new, sauvignon-based white? Time will tell. **01** herbal grass, ripe gooseberry/tropical lift. Semillon (20%) adds roundness. No oak, just-dry 3.5 g/ℓ sugar. 13% alc. **Le Bouquet** Decidedly muscat-driven semi-sweet, though riesling (36%), gewürz (20%) add sensorial spice in **00**. Pungent aromatic muscat esters, honeyed pineapple amplified in mouth, all napped in dusty spice. Tastes drier than 14.8% g/ℓ. 13,15% alc. Note: **Jean le Long Pinot Noir** Excellent debut **97** a once-off.

Le Pavillon range

Le Grand Pavillon Serious MCC; properly brut. **NV** (96) 70/30 chardonnay/pinot (promised, correct name change dropping 'Blanc de Blancs' still to work its way onto market) enjoys extra pinot weight from pvs. Creme brulee, nutcrackle aromas, resonating mousse. Toasty but tiring; enjoy now.

Rouge Lots of competitors at R20 price point, but latest **00** holds own: baked, toasted, meaty, smoky character, less cassis/cherry, milled pepper than pvs, good grip without being hard. Tannins respond to gentle cooling. Now 70% merlot leads 20% cab, 10% pinot. **Blanc** **00** chardonnay, chenin blend; developed colour, neutral nose, residual sugar (6.8 g/ℓ) adds allure. Not as fruity as pvs. — *DS*

Boschkloof Wines

Stellenbosch (see Stellenbosch map) • Tasting, sales, cellar tours Mon-Sat 8-6 by appointment • Play area for children • Views • Owners/winemakers Reenen Furter & Jacques Borman • Viticulturist Reenen Furter • Vineyards 16 ha • Pro-

duction 180 tons • PO Box 1340 Stellenbosch 7599 • ***Tel (021) 881-3293*** *• Fax (021) 881-3032 • E-mail boschkloof@adept.co.za*

"WHAT STARTED OUT six years ago as a semi-retirement venture has developed into a full-time occupation," remarks former radiologist Reenen Furter cheerfully, using his x-ray vision to create "one of a kind wines" (son-in-law Jacques Borman of La Motte the other half of this boutique partnership in Stellenbosch's Polkadraai Hills). Their aim is to grow the finest grapes possible, and they're expanding their repertoire with 2.5 hectares of shiraz and cabernet franc. New in the range is a limited-release Reserve, dashingly outfitted (as are all these) in white and gold. The inspirational 'Grail' logo on the front labels symbolises "the cup of abundance, the best in food and drink, the quest for perfection".

✱**Cabernet Sauvignon-Merlot** Stylish Nevers-matured blend; **99** sweet and long; fleshy; wonderfully balanced and brimming with potential. Would be shame to open too early. 68/32 ratio, 14 mths oak. 13,6% alc. 2 600 cases. Good step up from pvs ultra-lean styles, epitomised by **98** ✱, with dry tannic frame needing copious time.

✱**Chardonnay** Serious oaked example; recent vintages show pleasing improvement. Latest **00** smoky, vanilla tones; 100% malo well judged, emphasising richness without flab. Barrel-fermented/aged 11 mths, Fr/Am oak (70/30), 50% new. 1 500 cases. **99** stepped into mainstream with delicious grapefruit-marmalade toast flavours.

Cabernet Sauvignon ✱ Current **98**, back-tasted mid-01, still much quieter than pvs, though retains signature elegance. Own, Paarl/Stbosch fruit, 14 mths oak, 50% new. **Merlot** ✱ **99**, revisited mid-01, sedate, sweet-fruited and unexpectedly dry. Reenen Furter enjoys his with saddle of springbok. Portion sourced-in grapes. Yr oak. 13,5% alc. WOM. 2 500 cases. **Boschkloof Reserve** ✱ NEW Just 640 cases of a special selection, and a different take on above bdx theme. Cab, merlot in 88/12 proportion, 24 mths Fr-barrelled, 100% new oak. Very aptly named 'Reserve': reticence, firmness are current hallmarks, but **98**'s tannins are ripe, auguring well for good long-term development. VVG. — *DH*

Botha Wine Cellar

Worcester (see Worcester map) • Tasting & sales Mon-Fri 7.30-12.30; 1.30-5.30 Sat 9-12.30 • Cellar tours by appointment • BYO picnic • Tourgroups by appointment • Views • Owners 32 members • Manager/ cellarmaster Dassie Smith (since 1996) • Winemaker Johan Linde (since 1996) & Michiel Visser (since 2000) • Viticulturist Francois Nel (since 2001) • Production 24 000 tons (15 000 cases own label) 78% white 22% red • PO Box 30 Botha 6857 • ***Tel (023) 355-1740*** *• Fax (023) 355-1615*

THIS close-knit team really know how to keep their customers happy. Their range has something to suit many tastes and occasions (including a fireside warming Port, which you'll no doubt find tucked into cellarmaster Dassie Smith's bag when on one of his hunting trips); they open bright and early; and their front door is virtually on the main Worcester-Ceres road, so you don't waste time getting to the tasting centre or the picnic spot, encircled by glorious mountains that sometimes become magically snow-capped in winter.

Dassie's Reserve range

✱**Cabernet Sauvignon** ✓ Among the best-value oak-matured co-op cabs. **99** 14 mths Fr barriques, which well support ripely generous, suavely textured black fruit. Good dry finish. 13.2% alc not overblown. 250 cases. **98** also highly concentrated. **97** SAYWS gold.

Pinotage ✓ Pvs **97** not a patch on next-up **98**, yr Fr oak. Packed with pulpy red berries/cherries, held together by calm tannins. Moderate 13.1% alc. Drink soon to catch the fruity fireworks. 350 cases.

Special Late Harvest ✓ Latest **01** not tasted for this ed. **99** first release set high standard, followed by **00**, with botrytis hints. Lightish alcs for easier pleasure. ±300 cases.

Colombard ☻ Exuberant, assertive **01** an uncomplicated tropical pleasure; enjoy in zingy youth. 12.2% alc. 300 cases.

Merlot New to the guide in **99**; intense colours/tastes matched by forceful tannins needing bit of time. Good effort showing some seriousness. 300 cases. **Shiraz** Attractive, generously red-fruited **99**; full (13.8% alc), grain invisible sugar for smoothness. Oaked. 450 cases. **Chardonnay** Unwooded **01** improves on pvs with creamy lemon/lime persistence, tangy finish. Powerful alc (13,7%). 300 cases. **Chenin Blanc** NEW Off-dry **01** shy, retiring, melon/spice nuances in compact, med-bodied fruity palate. 300 cases.

Standard range

Merlot ✓ Latest not as high-vaulting as deep-piled **99**. Unwooded **01** lusty, strapping (± 14% alc) but also rough, needing 6-12 mths' smoothing. 300 cases.

Red Jerepigo ✓ **00** improving with bottle age, still-youthful hay/port-like nuances knitting with the spirit; now shows more delicacy, balance than white version below. 17.2% alc.

Hanepoot Jerepigo ✓ This traditional Cape fortified dessert a speciality of the house; pour solo in winter, over crushed ice in summer. **99** with unusual bitter-marmalade tang. Latest **00** more pedestrian, lacks acidic vibe to counter the sweetness. 16.6% alc. 500 cases.

Port ✓ **97** ageing with aplomb; succulent Christmas pudding flavours well meshed with tangy spirit. Nods to a Vintage style. Pinotage/shiraz, 2 yrs old casks. 19,6% alc.

Dassie's Rood ☻ Slurpable **00** braai-side companion (to be slugged seated: 13.6% alc) or table auxiliary. Cinsaut, ruby cab, cab, plumped with smidgeon sugar. 5 000 cases.

Cabernet Sauvignon Back in firmer mode in **01** after pvs (**99**) easy swigging; dry tannins offset by ripe unwooded fruit, smidgeon sugar. 13,6% alc. **Pinotage** Unoaked version unexpectedly subdued in **01**; give bit of time to unfurl (and note the high 13.9% alc). 300 cases. **Shiraz** NEW Creditable **01** debut; good varietal character, smooth, well fleshed. Big 13.9% alc; not oaked. 300 cases. **Blanc de Blanc** Best in yr of harvest. **01** med/full-bodied blend chenin, colombard, crouchen quieter than pvs; tastes bone-dry. 500 cases. **Chardonnay Brut Sparkling** Busy-bubbled **01** expansive (at 13.7% alc), non-aggressively dry. 300 cases. Carbonated. **Sparkling Chardonnay Demi-sec** Appealing carbonated fizz with delicate boiled-sweets nuances, broad mouthfeel; not overpoweringly sweet. **NV**. — *IvH*

Bouchard Finlayson

Walker Bay (see Walker Bay map) • Tasting & sales Mon-Fri 9.30-5 Sat 9.30-12.30 Closed public holidays • Fynbos tours by arrangement • Owner Bouchard Finlayson (Pty) Ltd • Winemaker/viticulturist Peter Finlayson (since 1990) • Vineyards 15 ha • Production 12 000 cases 85% white 15% red • PO Box 303

*Hermanus 7200 • **Tel (028) 312-3515** • Fax (028) 312-2317 • E-mail info@bouchardfinlayson.co.za • Website www.bouchardfinlayson.co.za*

"It's a bit like SA winning the figure skating in the Winter Olympics," sighs Peter Finlayson. "A big deal, actually, and yet only a handful of locals even notice. "Pinot noir, in many respects, has been regarded as a sideshow in SA." For Finlayson, by contrast, it's an enduring passion and a personal crusade that he's pursued with vigour and brio for more than two decades, latterly on this immaculate domaine in the Hemel-en-Aarde Valley. Which is why his star-turn on the 2000 International Wine Challenge dais, with prestigious Burgundy & Pinot Noir Trophy aloft, was for him a winemaking coming-of-age: "I've always said that I'd have arrived the day I competed successfully against a top burgundy." And for SA, too, a joyful affirmation that local pinot can set off flashlights around the world. While a family trust under Stanley and Bea Tollman has taken ownership of the property, shareholder Finlayson remains the winemaker and *primum mobile*. Meanwhile the components for a future sangiovese/nebbiolo-containing cuvee are evolving alongside their other burgundian preoccupation, chardonnay.

Galpin Peak Pinot Noir Path-blazing SA pinot, stylistic compass set to Burgundy (Burgundian clone 113, dense-planted, pruned in Fr double guyot mode, new-oak regime rightsized to 25% to not overpower). From own vyds overlooked by Galpin Peak, now reaching early adulthood, which reflected in **00**, probably biggest to date (in substance, not alc, a moderate 13%). House's tannic tautness, pvsly matter of some controversy, here balanced by ripe-fruit saturation. Uncompromising, introspective in youth, yet with aura of grandeur, great vinosity auguring well for long journey to maturation around 08. Meantime enjoy softer **99**, with more moderate 12.8% alc. **98** difficult pinot year, quieter. **97** milestone from super vintage (see also below).

Tête de Cuvée Galpin Peak Pinot Noir Occasional bottling, only from the greatest years, always a limited release barrel selection. **96** (20 cases!) set tone, triumphantly followed by **97**, Pinot trophy at IWC; emphatic vindication of Peter F's pinot obsession, now fuelled by maturing vines. (No **98**). Latest **99** softer, less weighty; vintage elegance, charm beautifully expressed in languid silkiness; black-cherry/forest-floor kernel gently brushed with oak (Fr, 70% new). Likely to peak earlier than **97** but enough backbone to reach own 06/07 maturity date. 13% alc. 200 cases. **97** nowhere near best. 120 cases, 300 magnums.

Missionvale Chardonnay Flagship white imbued, like rest of range, with individuality; most classically styled of these. **00** as thrilling as pvs, another triumph of balance, finesse. Gorgeous mineral, lemon delicacy spotlighted by careful oaking. Youthfully tight yet penetrating. **99** also slow developer. Own grapes, harvested for intensity without breathtaking alcs (±12.5%); barrel-fermented; 100% malo. 650 cases.

Kaaimansgat Chardonnay 'Crocodile's Lair' from, according to PF, "fabulous" 600 m high Villiersdorp vyd, vinified to preserve crystalline fruit. **00** fresh, pretty citrus, toasted hazelnuts aromas; initial fruity suppleness slightly blunted by touch alc in farewell. **99** now enriched by developing honeyed bouquet, nutty weight. Half barrel-fermented; whole oak-matured 8 mths. 13,5% alc. 3 500 cases.

Sans Barrique Chardonnay Those who decry unwooded styles knoweth not this delicious unadorned wine; subtler, perhaps more expressive of ethereal Kaaimansgat fruit than the above. **00** lingering smoky, flinty clarity; sweeping breadth, yet cool, poised timbre, deliberately styled to accompany seafood. 13% alc. 1 000 cases.

Pinot Blanc-Chardonnay 99 a burgundian concoction (pinot b originally from, through no longer widely planted in, that Fr wine region) with varieties acknowledged on front-label a la new world. Also distinctly unburgundian are **00**'s bold buttered toast flavours, youthful sweetish sensation (partly from substantial alc). Could mellow beneficially, given 1/2 yrs. Home pinot b, barrel-fermented, matured; Kaaimansgat chardonnay unwooded. 500 cases.

Sauvignon Blanc ☆ Premium-priced **01** step up from **00** but, tasted just post-bottling, unsettled. Lively, herbaceous; fills out in palate; whistle clean. 13% alc. Home vyd. **Blanc de Mer** ☆ Eccentric unwooded blend rare-in-Cape kerner (50%), equal dollops gewürz, riesling, sauvignon, chardonnay from Elgin/Villiersdorp's cool climes. Hence **00**'s freshness, delicate piquancy. Natural liaison with food, especially oysters (Knysna Oyster Company is biggest customer). 2 000 cases. —*AL*

Bouwland

Stellenbosch (see Stellenbosch map) • Not open to the public, but tasting & sales at Kanonkop, Beyerskloof (see those entries) • Owners Johann & Paul Krige, Beyers Truter • Winemaker Beyers Truter • Viticulturist Koos du Toit (since 1996) • Vineyards 80 ha • Production 30 000 cases 100% red • PO Box 74 Koelenhof 7605 • ***Tel/fax (021) 882-2447*** *• E-mail wine@kanonkop.co.za*

CANNY Johann and Paul Krige and Beyers Truter (of Kanonkop and Beyerskloof) know good vineyard prospects when they see them, and they've been busy redeveloping these 80 Bottelary hectares since 1997, planting mostly pinotage with dashes of cabernet and merlot. Meantime, even before their vines grow up, this is a success story: buying in fruit from nearby farms, which produce the same sort of personality-packed wines their own vineyards will eventually deliver, the Bouwland brand name is already established in 20 countries.

☆ **Cabernet Sauvignon-Merlot** ✓ So drinkable in youth, it's highly unlikely to get the few yrs cellaring it deserves, or the more thoughtful contemplation its commands. Latest **00** ☆ retains complex smoky oak, barbecue-spice aromatic interest, but more chunky fruit than **99**, which offered meaty aromas, soft mouthful plums. —*DS*

Bovlei Winery

Wellington (see Wellington map) • Tasting & sales Mon-Fri 8.30-12.30, 1.30-5 Sat 8.30-12.30 • No cellar tours during harvest • Views • Owners ±50 members • Winemaker Hendrik de Villiers (since 1996) • Assistant winemaker Albertus Louw (since 1998) • Consulting viticulturist Dawie le Roux (VineWise) • Vineyards 560 ha • Production 7 500 tons, 135 000 cases 60% red 40% white • PO Box 82 Wellington 7654 • ***Tel (021) 873-1567/864-1283*** *• Fax (021) 864-1483 • E-mail lizl@bovlei.co.za • Website www.bovlei.co.za*

HENDRIK DE VILLIERS and his deputy Albertus Louw are the fired-up team in charge of this trusty cellar, established in 1907 in an area with a winemaking tradition dating back to the Huguenots at the end of the 17th century. On the duo's and vine-wise Dawie le Roux's advice, the growers have been focusing on one of the current Cape preoccupations – improved fruit ripeness – and their efforts are bearing good results. Marthinus Broodryk, winemaker and cellarmaster for more than a decade, has left to run his own negociant company. He continues to manage Bovlei's international brands, however, including Amabokobokho, Arcady, Baynsvalley, Hawekwa Peaks, Marthinus and Peaks View, and as well as the export business of the joint-venture company Cape Wine Cellars. Bovlei fans can taste the range Mon-Sat at the cellar below Bainskloof Pass, or during the annual Wellington Wine Festival which is held in Spring.

☆ **Cabernet Sauvignon** ✓ The flagship, accessible on release with promise of short term development. Latest **00**, 4 mths oak staved; striking colours/textures; modern, juicy, balanced. 13% alc. ±1 000 cases.

Shiraz Millennium NEW ✓ **99** millennium release in striking tapered bottle showing exceptionally well mid-01; sweet ripe fruits/tannins throughout, strong herbal/sweet-spicy oak tones, smoky swirl in finish; 7-10 yr lifespan; best from 2003/4.

Shiraz ☆ ☻ **00** cherry/dried prune, light savoury unwooded flavours; supple, swiggable. 13% alc. 750 cases. **Pinotage** ☻ ☆ Lovely plummy fruit unadorned by oak; **00** good now, soft tannins for 4-5 yrs. 13.5% alc. 1 040 cases. **Grand Rouge** ☻ ☆ Easy everyday fare. **00** plummy cab f/merlot blend, oaked, airy feel despite 13% alc. 1 000 cases. **Chenin Blanc** ☻ ☆ **01** returns to form of pvs with light-bodied but persistent guava/passionfruit flavours; bright lemony dry finish. 2 500 cases.

Special Late Harvest ★ Usually from chenin; smooth, clean dessert; for early enjoyment. Current is **99**. **Natural Sweet** ☆ NEW Almondy, light, brisk-finishing **00**, for drinking now. Chenin. 500 cases. Following **NV** sparkles from sauvignon: **Baynsvalley Brut** ☆ Lightish, extra-dry carbonated fizz with mouthwatering freshness. Splash semillon for broader feel. 500 cases. Latest (**01**) bottlings of **Sec** and **Demi-sec**not ready for tasting. Pvs ☆. **Red Hanepoot** ☆ Lightish, still-lively **90** (☆) fortified dessert; raisins from nose through to clean, spirity tail. 800 cases. **Muscat d'Alexandrie** ☆ Another fortified oldie: **90** still golden: brilliant 24-carat sheen, penetrating molten barley sugar sweetness. 800 cases. **Port** ★ Ruby cab/cab-based **97** offers unexceptional earthy/savoury tastes. 1 200 cases.

500 ml **NV** 'Wellington Dumpies': **Vin Rouge** Cinsaut/cab/merlot; latest not ready for tasting; pvs ☆. **Vin Blanc** ☆ Well made, lightish dry from sauvignon. Clubhouse quick quaff. 11.5% alc. **Stein** From sauvignon; not ready for tasting. In 5 ℓ casks: **Dry Red** ☆ Unpretentious, quaffable bunch of softies (cinsaut/pinotage/merlot). Moderate 12.5% alc. **Dry White** ☆ Lightish, fresh swigger from chenin. Discontinued: **Blanc Imperial**. — *DH*

Bowe Joubert NEW

*Stellenbosch (see Stellenbosch map) • Tasting & cellar tours by appointment • Owners Alphonso Bowe, Andrew Hilliard, Jannie & Lukas Joubert • Winemaker Jannie Joubert • Viticulturist Lukas Joubert • Vineyards 75 ha • Production 750 tons 20 000 cases own label 50% red 50% white • PO Box 1114 Stellenbosch 7599 • **Tel (021) 881-3103** • Fax (021) 881-3377 • E-mail info@bowejoubert.com • Website www.bowejoubert.com*

Bringing some West Indian hip-sway to Stellenbosch's Polkadraai Hills is Bahaman entrepreneur Alphonso Bowe, who's joined hands with American investors and the local Joubert family to buy the old Veelverjaaght property and set it tripping to an international beat. With the experienced Jouberts hands-on (Jannie in cellar, Lukas in vineyard and Fanie in the operations hot-seat), they've added a red wine cellar and rolled in new oak while keeping cool with state-of-the-art chilling equipment. Meanwhile the 62 False Bay-cooled hectares are rustling with new cabernet and shiraz, and merlot, cabernet franc, pinot noir and more cabernet are set for planting. Export engines are revving, and "a significant number of the 45 000 cases" are expected to go to the Bahamas, Caribbean, US, Canada and Europe. Their vision, explains Alphonso Bowe, "is to make the property a flagship producer, a benchmark for quality". The following range, untasted, was being unveiled as this guide went to press: Cabernet Sauvignon, Merlot, Pinotage, Shiraz, Cabernet Sauvignon-Merlot, Mach 1.0 (bordeaux blend), Rosé, Chardonnay, Chenin Blanc (oaked and unwooded versions), Sauvignon Blanc and Mosaic (blended white).

Bradgate see Jordan

Brampton see Rustenberg

Brandvlei Winery

Worcester • Tasting & sales Mon-Thu 8-12.30; 1.30-5 Fri 8-12.30; 1.30-4.30 • Cellar tours by arrangement • Reception facilities for ± 150 guests • Owners 32 members • Manager/winemaker Jean le Roux with assistant winemaker Jandré Human • Viticulturist Pierre Snyman (since 2000) • Vineyards 1 270 ha • Production 20 000 tons (4 000 cases own label) 90% white 10% red • PO Box 595 Worcester 6849 • ***Tel (023) 349-4215*** *• Fax (023) 349-4332 • E-mail brandvlei@cybertrade.co.za*

THIS CO-OPERATIVE near a thermal spring is really cooking. Not only vintning-wise (though brand-new Italian fermenters form part of a high-tech array that's "among the most modern in the industry", according to winemaker Jean le Roux). In the labour-relations arena, farm workers are being trained in basic viticultural techniques ("we're leaders in this regard") while in the vineyard, eco-cordial practices are followed in line with IPW (Integrated Production of Wine) guidelines. Key to success (sauvignon and ruby cab-merlot blends a particular emphasis) is their 'estate within a co-op' philosophy, enabling top-performing blocks to be nurtured and vinified individually.

Ruby Cabernet-Merlot ☻ ⁂ Juicy, quaffable **00** sensitively fermented with oak chips, giving nice charry background to ripe-plum/pepper tastes. Med-bodied. 1 058 cases. **Chenin Blanc** ☻ ⁂ Award-winning block billows tropical fruit salad in **01** (sample), med-bodied dry early-drinking available virtually free (±R8/bottle) from cellar. 700 cases. **Bacchante** ⁂ ☻ Charming semi-sweet drops with honeysuckle/mimosa fragrances. **01** lightish, for early enjoyment. Colombard, hanepoot blend. 280 cases.

Chardonnay ⁂ Grapefruity **01**, light feel (though 13.4% alc), lemon-zesty finish. Not oaked. 500 cases. **Sauvignon Blanc** ★ Evanescent, bone-dry **01**, early picked (19° B) for racy freshness. 11% alc. 1 000 cases. **Hanepoot Jeripiko** ⁂ Pleasurable **99** fortified dessert, revisited mid-01, now shows pepper nuance to original lemon meringue pie. 17% alc. 280 cases. **Sec Sparkling** ⁑ Hyperkinetic **99** chardonnay/hanepoot fusion acquiring light honeyed tone; suggest drink up. 249 cases. — *DH*

Bredasdorp see Sonop

Bredell & Nel

THIS STARTED OFF as a lark, with two of the Cape's leading 'port' exponents, Anton Bredell and Carel Nel, disputing the merits of their respective vintage reserves. As a compromise, the two were combined and the blend judged better than the sum of the parts (more recently by Veritas and SAA panels who awarded, respectively, a double-gold medal and the prestigious Port Trophy). The result is the collector's item (only 225 cases) below. Enquiries Boplaas tel (044) 213-3326 • JP Bredell Wines tel (021) 842-2478. See also Boplaas and J P Bredell Wines entries for further details.

⁂**Cape Vintage Reserve** Douro-style blend of finished wines made in Calitzdorp (Boplaas), Helderberg (J P Bredell). Crimson-edged **97** maturing beautifully; mouthfilling plummy, minty flavours edged with vanilla and peach kernel. Surprisingly good now, but much bigger pleasures await around 2010. 2 yrs Fr oak. ±19% alc, 95 g/ℓ sugar. — *DH*

Bredell see J P Bredell

Breëvallei Wines 

*Worcester (see Worcester map) • Sales Mon-Fri 8-5 Sat 8-1 • Owners Breëvalley Wines (Pty) Ltd • MD Koos van Rensburg • PO Box 5300 Worcester 6849 • **Tel (023) 342-2335** • Fax (023) 342-8764 • E-mail nobo@nobo.co.za • Website nobo@nobo.co.za*

INSPIRED by the natural beauty of their surroundings, a number of cellars around Worcester and Rawsonville pool their vinous gems under the Blue Mountain label, which they consider "typical of the wines of the region". Seasoned Cape Wine Master Dick Davidson assists with the selection and blending.

Blue Mountain range

Fronté ☻ ☆ Powder-puff pretty muscat aromas in **00** petillant semi-sweet, smiled upon by the SA Heart Foundation (only 8.4% alc). Soft and delicious. 2 000 cases.

Cabernet Sauvignon 01 not ready for tasting. 1 500 cases. **Pinotage** ☆ Action centres on palate and sweetish crushed red-berry fruits; adroitly oaked and not too strenuously tannic. 13.7% alc. 1 000 cases. **Shiraz** ☆ **00** lightly oaked, so attention dwells on generous, pristine fruit with white pepper, smoked meat subtleties. Rather nice; just missed ☆. 13.2% alc. 1 500 cases. **Chardonnay** ☆ Unoaked, honest **00**; balanced med-bodied dry white with fresh fruity finish. 2 000 cases. **Chenin Blanc** ☆ For when the focus is elsewhere eg watching *Big Brother*. Lightish, dry **00** retains some quiet freshness. 4 000 cases. **Sauvignon Blanc** ☆ Should appeal to fans of the softer, lighter sauvignon style; undemanding green pepper nuances in dry palate. 2 000 cases. — *IvH*

Brenthurst Winery 

*Paarl (see Paarl map) • Tasting & sales by appointment • Owner Adv SA Jordaan • Winemaker Adv SA Jordaan, with consultants • Consulting viticulturist Johan Wiese • Vineyards 5 ha • Production 50-70 tons 3 000-5 000 cases 100% red • PO Box 6091 Main Road Paarl 7622 • **Tel (021) 863-1154/424-6602** • Fax (021) 424-5666*

"JUST ABOUT the whole of the 2000 vintage has already been reserved by overseas clients," reports José Jordaan, Cape Town senior counsel and after-hours vintner (with expert consultants) on a bijoux property below Paarlberg. Though Jordaan's cellar is anchored in stone (it's set among granite boulders in what used to be a quarry), its elegantly packaged produce has always soared far and wide (the maiden 94 flew to the US and Europe). And though the stylistic orientation has changed from Right to Left Bank Bordeaux, customers keep coming back for more (including global carrier Lufthansa). Range not taste for this edition. Previous included: **Cabernet Sauvignon-Merlot (98** ☆), **Cabernet Sauvignon Reserve (97** ☆).

Broken Stone see Slaley

Buitenverwachting 

Constantia (see Constantia map) • Tasting & sales Mon-Fri 9-5 Sat 9-1 • Cellar tours by appointment • Buitenverwachting Restaurant Tel (021) 794-3522 Also light lunches/cakes & coffee served on terrace, picnic lunches in summer • Play area for children • Views • Jazz concerts • Teddy Bear Fair May 1st • Valentine's Picnic • Owner Richard & Sieglinde (Christine) Mueller, Lars Maack • Winemaker Hermann Kirschbaum (since 1992) • Farm/vineyard manager Peter Reynolds (since 1997) • Own vineyards 100 ha • Production 70 000 cases 80%

white 20% red • *PO Box 281 Constantia 7848* • ***Tel (021) 794-5190*** • *Fax (021) 794-1351* • *E-mail buiten@pixie.co.za*

THE INIMITABLE winemaker who this year celebrates a decade at this historic, rejuvenated Constantia property is modest about his laudatory achievements. "The farm is bigger than the winemaker," says Hermann Kirschbaum. "You have to play second fiddle." While legion admirers might strongly disagree, they're only too happy about the new strings in his bow – malbec, pinot noir and petit verdot – which have brought the red-vine population up to 30% and added to the maestro's already expressive cool-climate palette. Now Kirschbaum and co-owner Lars Maack are going high-tech in pursuit of their ecological goals. "We've installed a weather station to recover more data about humidity, rainfall, wind and temperatures," reveals Maack. "This will further our aim of becoming 100% organic producers. We've also bought new vineyard implements and tractors for the same purpose." Also 'green', and budding with promise, is new assistant winemaker Jacques Moelans, who swept in fresh from Elsenburg (where he was top of his class) in time for the 2001 crush – a remarkable harvest, reports Kirschbaum, with "brilliant quality fruit".

Christine One of the original SA claret blends pursuing international form and class. Individual, neither new world nor old; composition vintage-dependant – usually 80% cab, 15% cab f, splash merlot, from low-yield vyds. Usually 18 mths barrique aged, high fraction new oak, though next-up **98**, not ready for tasting, breaks mould with more rigorous regimen: all-new casks 30 mths! Will be eagerly awaited by punters who, due to in-house declassification, will be deprived of cool-vintage **97**. "Not good enough," shrugs Hermann Kirschbaum. Fans will find comfort in **96**, lighter yr and probably earliest- peaking of recent vintages. **95**, swathed in quiet class, softening but not yet *à point*. **94** also very fine.

Merlot 95 first release in 4 yrs. Soft but manicured; burnished tannins and great persistence for long, good maturation. Follow-up **99** not ready for tasting. **Selection Alexander von Essen** NEW (Export blend for German agent) classic cool-climate merlot. **99** bright ruby-plum; spicy cassis, pencil box and faraway fennel whiffs. Tight-wound, savoury; elegant fruit acids balance well-delineated, cedary redcurrant fruit.

Cabernet Sauvignon Returned from sabbatical with **95** to rapturous welcome by fans still impressed by **92** VVG, SAA, and **91**, **90**, both VG. **95** inky colours, enticing blueberry, cigarbox perfumes, tapered tannins – all made for wonderfully welcome return. Fast-forward to next-up **99**, not ready for tasting.

Pinot Noir Foretaste of **01** barrel reveals tremendous structure, deep colour, massed cherry/strawberry fruit. Concentration increased by 'bleeding' some juice prior to fermentation. Powerful tannins, too, acknowledged by Hermann K who may back-blend *saignée* portion.

Buiten Keur Stylish bdx blend from barrels not quite making stringent Christine selection cut. **96** last under this label; name change to Meifort reflects owners Richard & Christine Mueller's German ancestral history. Mainly merlot (50%), cab s/f (30/20). Lightish, synchronous with vintage, very savoury; maraschino cherries and *filet bleu* in palate; cultured tannic almond twist in finish. **97** (preview) cab f's herbal spice in foreground, generous redcurrant accompaniment; very poised. These usually 18 mths small wood, 2nd/3rd fill.

Sauvignon Blanc Established its pedigree over years of consistent delivery. Always tight, restrained on release; payback is rewarding bottle maturation. **01** ideal ripening conditions show in fragrant greengage, grass, backed by something riper (yellow pear/melon?). Bright rhubarb fruit in palate; brisk acidity hold attention as figs/gooseberries race to gunflinty finish. Among best of vintage. **00** 'fire-storm yr' broader shouldered but trademark rapier finesse; developing well. **Selection Alexander von Essen** (WO Coastal) Exclusive for German buyer; Cecil Skotnes art-label. **01** more floral than above, very fragrant; subtle lavender scents and flavours of dried peach, fig, lime.

✵**Chardonnay** Hermann K poured all his perfectionism into extraordinary **00** – hedonism cloaked in triumphant yellow-gold, oozing toast-and-butterscotch deliciousness. Not for the faint-hearted, however: ±14% alc bolstering big extract, punchy lime-marmalade fruit, though firm mineral finish keeps weight in check. Punctilious vinification: 24 hour skin-contact, mix cultured/natural yeasts, two-thirds Fr oak-fermented, equal 1st/2nd fill. This latest chimes with flamboyant Kirschbaum style, only recent deviation being chablis-like, cool-vintage **97** *Wine* ✵.

✵**Rhine Riesling** Racy, off-dry style made here. 18 yr old vines, whole-bunch pressed, cool-fermented for delicacy, varietally pure pepperiness. Bouquet of latest **01** ✵ shy, herb-fragrant; palate livelier with focused, concentrated grapefruit tastes, arresting fruit acids. These, plus lowish alc and sugar (11.3% 7.9 g/ℓ) create dry impression. Should age well. **00** less reserved than above and pvs releases.

✵**Buiten Blanc** ✓ Omnipresence of this dry white on chic restaurant lists now stretching cellar to its limits: "I need more tanks!" pleads Hermann K, eyeing 40 000 cases. **01** mainly sauvignon, as usual with dashes riesling, chenin (HK "likes to play a bit each year to keep people guessing", so we won't divulge any secrets); maintains now expected standard with whiffy, grassy aromas, tensioned balance among ripe gooseberry, melon, tropical fruits. Smidgeon sugar adds suppleness to bracing finish. Grapes ex-Durbanville/Darling.

✵**Semillon-Sauvignon Blanc** NEW Bone-dry, full-bodied, minerally blend, unwooded. **01** already showing some development; attractive, slightly oily thatch/herb aromas; semillon's lanolin texture, lime flavours dominate.

✵**Brut MCC** Traditionally bottle-fermented **NV** sparkle; 50% pinot noir with chardonnay, pinot gris. Lazy bubbles and spicy, floral aromas ripening into warm, almost meaty toasty buttered brioche tones. Surprisingly assertive, firm in mouth, almost austerely dry. Ready, but plenty of life left. Currently a multi-vintage blend (97/98/99), disgorged as required. **00** to be vintaged ("Deserves preservation on its own").

Natural Sweet Maiden **00** (unrated) from barrel fermented Dbnville sauvignon. Follow-up **01** not ready for tasting. **Blanc de Noir** NEW "Helps improve colour in our reds," says Hermann K. "We drain some juice, and this is the result." **01** preview tangy, just-pink; strawberry flavours. Cab s/f, merlot, with thimble sugar for smoothing rather than sweetening. — *TM*

Bushman's Creek see Devon Hill

BWC (pvsly Barefoot Wine Company)

Stellenbosch • Tasting & sales by appointment • Owners Catherine Marshall, Jeff Jolly, Greg Mitchell, Peter Oxenham • Winemaker/logistician Catherine Marshall (since 1997) • Production 20 tons 1 400 cases 100% red • PO Box 13404 Mowbray 7705 • ***Tel/fax (021) 887-9910*** *• E-mail wine@barefoot.co.za • Website www.barefoot.co.za*

THIS NOMADIC TRIBE of friends in wine has put down temporary roots at Agusta's revamped cellar where they're renting space (self-proclaimed vagabond winemaker Cathy Marshall also moonlights from here for two other clients). For me flavour is the essence of a wine," she enthuses, leaving herself room to roam in search of isolated pockets of grapes (including grenache, mourvèdre, viognier) to blend more complex, classic wines. This freewheeling attitude belies a serious intent to create an "icon" wine from selected rows and barrels in the next four years. The maiden vintage of their dessert-style wine (name-switch from Pineau des Charentes to

Myriad sidesteps wine-political complications) was released in special 375 ml bottles. "They're snapping it up in Johannesburg," announces Marshall.

Shiraz Grown-up and handsome in ebony bottle with original artwork by Hannetjie de Clerq. Rhoneward glances since maiden **99**, Fr oak, 6 mths 3rd/4th fill, then 6 mths new. Next up **01** just popped out of the toaster! Real breakfast aromas: fresh coffee, basket damson fruit, prosciutto on the side. Absolutely mouthwatering. Juicy supportive tannins for now or keeping (we challenge you!); potential for on release in Apr 02. Shows class of Agter-Paarl fruit. All new Fr oak, mainly Burgundian cooperage. 14% alc. 750 cases. No **00**.

Pinot Noir Up and coming label; latest features fruit ex Muratie, pinot's original SA home. **97** (unrated) was first, Devon Valley grapes; **99**, first with Muratie infusion, smoky, cherry/strawberry-toned. Latest **00** most serious (100% new oak), finest to date; restrained, almost cerebral now; will gain harmony, opulence with time. **01** (preview) more immediately appealing; deftly wooded to showcase graceful fruit; needs 2-3 yrs minimum to grow (into ?). ±yr 2nd fill. 14% alc. 400 cases.

Myriad Jerepigo formula (unfermented pinot noir fortified with brandy) "with some individual manipulations," chortles Cathy Marshall. Highly individual; tautly tensioned between vinosity, sweetness. First (and current) **00** lavender-perfumed; drier than ±50 g/ℓ sugar suggests. **01** preview riper, sweeter; pine-fragranced; potential on release. Serve (chilled, if preferred) as aperitif or with creamy cheeses. 16.9% alc. 410 bottles, 375 ml. — *TM*

Caap Mooi see Wiese Portfolio
Cabernet Company see Claridge

Cabrière Estate

*Franschhoek (see Franschhoek map) • Tasting Mon-Fri 11 & 3 Tour & tasting Sat 11 Fee R20 p/p (incl tour) • Sales Mon-Fri 9-4.30 Sat 11-1 • Cellar tours by Achim von Arnim every Sat 11 or by appointment • Haute Cabrière Cellar Restaurant (see Eat-out section) • Owner Clos Cabrière Ltd • Winegrower Achim von Arnim (since 1984) • Viticulturist Sakkie Lourens • Production 420 tons 30 000 cases • PO Box 245 Franschhoek 7690 • **Tel (021) 876-2630** • Fax (021) 876-3390 • E-mail cabriere@iafrica.com • Website www.cabriere.co.za*

It's virtually impossible not to be swept up by the bubbling enthusiasm of Cabrière's Achim von Arnim. And it all revolves around bubbles, of course. His chardonnay and pinot noir were planted specifically to produce sparkling wines in the traditional style. There have been offshoots too, and all in the traditional manner. While only the very best free-run juice is used in the production of the Pierre Jourdan MCC range, the second pressing goes to make their heady Fine de Jourdan potstill brandy. To complete the circle, there's the unusual (for South Africa) Petit Pierre Ratafia, a blend of the potstill brandy and sweet chardonnay juice. The name derives from the fact that similar drinks were traditionally served to seal a treaty (or 'ratify' it). Achim von Arnim's Saturday morning cellar tours are a tourist attraction in themselves.

Haute Cabrière range

Pinot Noir Since **94** (in this guide on release), standout in SA context. New burgundian clones, densely planted, kid-gloved in cellar with gentle pressing; fermentation in closed tanks; 8-10 mths ageing in hand-picked Troncais cooperage. Rubicund **00** vividly hued; ripe morello fruit and pancetta savouriness, lively acids to absorb alcoholic punch (14%). **99** somewhat attenuated, lighter (13% alc); quick, sweet gamey flavours. Toasty nuances from 35% new oak (vs **00**'s 30%, reflected in oak-enhanced rather than -imparted bouquet of violets, cherries).

✵Chardonnay-Pinot Noir Characterful, cuisine-comfortable just-dry white, blended from juice not required for sparklers below; so effectively 'still' cap classique; same whole bunch pressing, unoaked. **01** 50/50 blend; gossamer salmon hues; salt-grass bouquet; firm, lightish (12% alc) palate. Sugar:fruit ratio better judged than in herby **00** ★★.

Pierre Jourdan range

Mostly sparkling wines, honouring the French Huguenot who founded the estate in 1694.

✵Cuvée Belle Rose Superb cap classique with delicate yet generous, persistent flavours. Whole-bunch pressed, early picked pinot noir; berries macerated 3 days for 'blanc de noir' robe. Raspberry-toned crispness outstanding with Atlantic salmon, crayfish, duck. Latest release 99 (**NV** on label) fractionally sweeter than previous (7 vs 5.5 g/ℓ sugar) for extra richness to balance less opulent fruit. Like most of Achim von Arnim's bubbles, rewards cellaring good few years.

✵Cuvée Reserve NEW **NV** Uncommon richness, complexity from extraordinary 60 mths on lees. 60/40 chardonnay, pinot noir; former imparting chalky tones to latter's red berries. Vibrant mousse, not over-effervescent; long, dry finish. Earthy, full and autolytic nose.

✵Blanc de Blancs First fraction of bunch-pressed chardonnay, barrelled 4-5 mths, adding toasty stratum to cream-layered palate. Rich mouthfeel, balance from ripe-vintage fruit (98, though **NV** on label). Slightly sweeter than pvs (6 g/ℓ sugar vs 4.5).

Brut ★★ 60/40 chardonnay, pinot with former's elegance and cut, latter's more assertive thrust. Extremely energetic, almost frothy mousse. Apple tones and heightened richness, mouthfeel from slightly higher sugar (6.5 g/ℓ vs pvs 3.8). *Wine Enthusiast* Top 10 sparkling wine survey. Excellent with abalone, Parma ham. **NV**. **Brut Sauvage** ★★ House austerity reaches its zenith in this nervous ultra-brut cap classique, with as many devotees as detractors. No alleviating sugar dosage brings chardonnay, pinot interplay (60/40) into riveting focus. Really needs food, preferably fine fresh salty oysters. **NV**; mainly for on-consumption trade. **Brut Tranquille** NEW ★★ Only non-sparkling member of this range – essentially "a still champagne – lunchtime wine to be enjoyed on the terrace, relaxing," says AvA, who feels this unique in cellar because "it's not necessary to pair it off with food". We disagree: racy acidity, slightly brittle finish need a mollusc or something finned. Lightish body (11.5%), salmon hue; fragrant almost perfumed palate toned with raspberry. **NV**. — *NP*

Calitzdorp Winery

Calitzdorp (see Little Karoo map) • Tasting & sales Mon-Fri 8-5 Sat 8-12 Cellar tours during tasting hours • Terrace with panoramic views • Owners 66 members • Winemaker Alwyn Burger (since 1990) • Consulting viticulturists Stephan Joubert, Briaan Stipp (VinPro) • Vineyards 150 ha • Production 3 000 tons (38 tons, 3 000 cases own label) 93% white 7% red • PO Box 193 Calitzdorp 6660 • ***Tel (044) 213-3301*** *• Fax (044) 213-3328*

If Calitzdorp is the 'port' capital of SA (as its adherents claim), then this is the value-shopping mall. Here you'll find three Portuguese-inspired Cape ports, characterful and delicious, at prices that cause them to fly out the cellar faster than you can say ostrich – which two-legged tourist attractions happen to be part of the scenery from the airy view deck outside the tasting room, never more buzzy than during the annual Port Festival. Alwyn Burger, First Citizen of the cellar for more than a decade, styles the fortified gems and a range of natural wines from 150 hectares spread under a perennially blue sky. Expect the mercury to rise notch or two when young rows of shiraz spice up the varietal mix. The range not ready for tasting for this ed; previous ratings in brackets: **Gamka Cabernet Sauvignon (99 ✵)**, **Merlot (99 ✵)**,

Grand Vin Rouge (**NV** ★), **Blanc de Noir** (**NV** ★), **Chardonnay** (**00** ★), **Sauvignon Blanc** (**00** ★), **Vin Blanc** (**NV** ★), **Golden Jerepiko** (**NV** ★★), **Sweet Hanepoot** (**99** ★★), **White Muscadel** (**99** ★★), **Vintage Port** (**98**★★), **LBV Port** (**97** ★★), **Ruby Port** (**NV** ★★).

Camberley Wines

Stellenbosch (see Stellenbosch map) • Tasting, sales, cellar tours Mon-Sat 9-5 Sun by appointment • B&B guest cottages • Tourgroups • Views • Owners John & Gaël Nel • Winemaker John Nel • Consulting viticulturist Aidan Morton • Vineyards 2.4 ha • Production 16-17 tons 2 000 cases (500 ml) 100% red • PO Box 6120 Uniedal 7612 • ***Tel/fax (021) 885-1176*** *• E-mail camberleywines@hotmail.com*

EVERYTHING about this Helshoogte winery is diminutive and handcrafted. Even their (500 ml) packaging, a feature since the maiden 96 vintage, is down-scaled. So it's not surprising that owners John and Gaël Nel and their new viticultural savant Aidan Morton intend to trim production on the original two-and-a-half hectares to a Lilliputian 5 tons/ha. This to bolster the already impressive quality the energetic couple (he a Cape Town quantity surveyor, she a professional caterer who also runs the delightful guest cottages on the property) achieve from year to year. Cabernet, merlot and shiraz on a leased property come into production this year, and an additional half-hectare is being prepared for a port variety. Further cheer for fans is the first Pinotage, from grapes sourced in the Knorhoek area. They're aiming for a February release, though John Nel adds a question mark: "Here's hoping ...? The variety's so bloody temperamental!"

★★**Cabernet Sauvignon-Merlot** Great charm, elegance in pre-bottling sample of **00**, gushing sweet red berry fruit but firmly underpinned by fine tannin, savoury acidity, clever oaking (14 mths Fr/Russian barriques, 70% new). Delicious now, but deserves some yrs to develop. 80% cab. 13.5% alc. Debut **99** showed intriguing baked-earth/savoury nuances. (**98** and pvs mainly or exclusively cab).

Merlot To date only exceptional **99** ★★★. — *TJ*

Cameradi Wines

Wellington • Sales & cellar tours by appointment • Owners Stelvest BK (Pieter Laubscher, Niel Smith, Nic Swingler, Hendrik du Preez & Casper Lategan) • Winemaker Casper Lategan (since Jan 2000) • Production 1 ton 65 cases 100% red • Bainstraat 48 Wellington 7655 • ***Tel (021) 873-1225*** *• Cell 082-880-2382 • Fax (021) 873-4910 • E-mail latsement@cybertrade.co.za*

LIKE MANY bright SA sparks, this boutique winery sprang from a conversation beside a braai-fire. The five student-mates present intended to play the financial markets and later diversify into real estate. A change of plan saw them branch into "liquid assets" instead and a small-scale foray into winegrowing, first experimentally and now for gain. These comrades in wine, generalled by winemaker Casper Lategan, hand-craft their (untasted by us) Cabernet and Shiraz in a Wellington home-cellar with a maturation area attached. "We neither filter nor fine," remarks Casper Lategan. "We make only reds, and buy grapes mostly from Stellenboschkloof. Everyone helps with the bottling and labelling." Activities which fortunately shouldn't impact too much on braai-time: in true *garagiste* fashion their total output is a bijou 260 cases.

Cape Bay Wines

CAPE WINE MASTER and negociant Dave Johnson is expanding the scope of this venture with the purchase a 40 ha property in the Hemel-en-Aarde Valley near Hermanus. Planned plantings in the next two years include pinot, for which the area has gained a good reputation, Rhone varieties and sauvignon. See also Newton Johnson and Sandown Bay.

Pinotage ✓ Latest oak-influenced **01** gutsier (14% alc), grippier than pvs (which unoaked); massed charry fruits need a plate (Dave Johnson recommends spicy oriental, BBQ rib or roast) or yr/2 in your cellar.

Cabernet Sauvignon-Merlot ✓ Sappy red fruit makes **01** unoaked 60/40 blend very easy to quaff now; pliable tannins will stretch the pleasure over 2-3 yrs. 13.2% alc. Pvs (**NV** ☆) sterner, less approachable in youth.

Mellow Red ☻ ☆ Unwooded ruby cab, cinsaut, dash merlot. Berries, fresh earth and just enough tannin to control the juiciness. "Steakhouse wine," says vintner, "lightly chill if needed." **NV**.

Chardonnay ☆ Unwooded **01** zinger offers exotic papaya, guava to taste; finishes crisply. 13% alc. **Chenin Blanc** ☆ Sweet-smelling **01** tastes lemony-dry, brisk acidity calls for something freshly landed. 13% alc. **Sauvignon Blanc** ☆ Bright citrus/tropical food wine. **01** less pushy than pvs; lightish, gently dry. **Bouquet Blanc** ☆ Lovely light floral **01**; smooth rather than sweet, lemon-tangy finish. Colombard, gewürz, fernão pires, white muscadel. *— DH*

Cape Chamonix Wine Farm

*Franschhoek (see Franschhoek map) • Tasting & sales daily 9-5 Tasting fee R10 p/p for 5 wines. Also tasting & sales of farm-distilled fruit spirits & mountain spring Eau de Chamonix • Cellar tours by appointment • La Maison de Chamonix Restaurant (see Eat-out section) • Fully equipped self-catering cottages **Tel (021) 876-2494** • Weddings by arrangement (tables outside if weather permits) **Tel (021) 876 2393** • Gifts • Views • Tourgroups by appointment • Wheelchair-friendly • Owner Chris Hellinger • Winemaker/viticulturist Peter Arnold (since 1992) • Export & marketing Manager Uschi van Zweel • Vineyards 50 ha • Production 240 tons (180 tons 15 000 cases own label) 60% red 38% white 2% MCC • PO Box 28 Franschhoek 7690 • **Tel (021) 876-2494/8** office (021) 876-3241 tasting/sales • Fax (021) 876-3237 • E-mail marketing@chamonix.co.za • Website www.chamonix.co.za*

On the heights above Franschhoek, Chamonix has become a popular destination for visitors from all over the world. The atmosphere is relaxed, and the lunches under the spreading oaks are exactly what visitors want to find when exploring the winelands. If the meal lingers too long, there are handily near sleep-overs (sleep-it-offs?) on the property with views to intoxicate you all over again. And if, perchance, romance were to blossom around Peter Arnold's internationally celebrated wines (made in the passionate French style), they'll spread a wedding reception for you, alfresco if you prefer. To be toasted, naturally, with their cap classique, and a promise to return to this eyrie and its charming ambience.

Pinotage NEW Crossover style with wide appeal. **00** fruity but not in-your-eye-juicy; some restraint and nice dry finish tastes good on its own and in company of various cuisines. Doesn't take itself too seriously. 280 cases.

Pinot Noir 99 developing with some distinction; from own vyds, 14 mths barrelled, 50% new oak; ripe fruit, good varietal character and gamey farewell. Easy 12,5% alc. 120 cases.

Chardonnay Reserve Showy, individual style, definite oak character will appeal to many – as to Chardonnay du Monde judges, who awarded a prestigious gold to **97**, now ripening into butterscotch, honeycomb richness. Follow-up **98** SAA very similar but more substantial (13,% alc); should also age well. Entirely barrel-fermented, new Fr/German oak, 16 mths lees-suffused, full malo. 400

cases. Regular **Chardonnay** ✵ **98** not as fresh as above, already some good honeyed notes creeping in, nice toasty finish. Air France laureate. 13% alc. 1 400 cases.

✵**Courchevel Méthode Cap Classique** Back in the guide in a new bottle-fermented incarnation (pvs carbonated); **NV**, 100% chardonnay from own vyds. Bone dry (2 g/ℓ sugar), pleasingly austere tones, steely lemon flavours and contrasting leesy richness (min 19 mths bottle aged) which highly versatile with food.

Cabernet Sauvignon ⁂ Has come off the boil since tasted for last ed; **97** leanish; dry tarry finish which now better with food than unpartnered. Med/light bodied, 26 mths oak. 4 000 cases. **Sauvignon Blanc Reserve** ⁂ Fumé blanc-style **00** not its usual puissant self (**98** ✵). Usual bone dry, vinous old-world style, but only some vague peachy flavours mid-01. Fermented/aged in barrique, full malo. Suitable for "extremely long 'girls' lunches, says Uschi van Zweel, "with dill-sauced smoked salmon on the menu". 13.5% alc. 2 000 cases. Discontinued: **Chenin Blanc Oak Matured** Pvs **98** ⁂. Also available: **Rouge NV**, **Sauvignon Blanc 00** pvsly rated ✵. — *TM*

Cape Classics

Stellenbosch • Owners Gary & André Shearer, with non-active shareholders • Winemaker Barry Kok (since 2000) • Production 60 000 cases 60% red 40% white • PO Box 5421 Cape Town 8000 • ***Tel (021) 881-3810*** *• Fax (021) 881-3814 • E-mail gary@capeclassics.co.za • Website www.natural.co.za*

Brothers Gary and André Shearer are maestros when it comes to marketing some of SA's hottest wine properties. They've had a year with so many positives there's not enough space to list them, so we'll start with the latest high note: their US-based Cape Classics (the entire operation is now consolidated under this name) has been named 'Best Wine Importer' in Food & Wine magazine's American Wine Awards ("a small ray of joy" for their NY-based marketer Molly Choi in the midst of last year's shocking events). Last year saw the launch of the Merlot, Shiraz, and Blush in the US and, for the second year in a row, in Robert Parker's *The Wine Advocate* tasted through their portfolio. Their own-brand Cape Indaba Merlot, Sauvignon Blanc and Shiraz received scores of 86, 86 and 85 respectively and were designated 'excellent value'. The Indaba Merlot will also be flying First and Business Class on SAA. But we've saved the best for last: 2001 was the graduation year of their first Indaba Scholarship student, Mzukhona Mvemve, who'll soon be winging his way around the wine world. Another promising recipient, Alison Adams, is sailing through her third year, also at Stellenbosch University.

Cape Indaba range

✵**Shiraz** ✓ **00** appealing, generous style with varietally correct spiciness; smooth, undaunting tannins. 14% alc. 5 000 cases. Bought in ex Paarl/Worcester.

✵**Sauvignon Blanc** ✓ Biggest seller in this range – 14 000 (well priced) cases; best in youth. **00** was standout; latest **01** ⁑ more commercial, undemanding, yet varietally correct. 13% alc. Rbtson fruit.

Pinotage-Cinsaut ☻ ⁑ Easy, satisfying; lightly chill for summer quaffing. **00** lightly oaked, lowish 12.4% alc. 4 000 cases.

Cabernet Sauvignon ⁑ **00** competently made from Malmesbury fruit, balanced. 70% Fr oak. 13.2% alc. 6 000 cases. **Merlot** ⁂ **00** plenty of choc/char flavour, mouthfilling; ready but won't fall apart over 2-3 yrs. 13.5% alc. 9 000 cases. **Pinotage** ⁂ Fr-oaked **00** splashed with ruby cab, med/light-bodied enjoyment now with pizza, richer pasta; or in 2-3 yrs. 7 500 cases. **Blush** ★ NEW Unusual grenache/sauvignon mix; **00** lightish semi-sweet, fruity; like pop-soda. Bought in from Olifants R/Paarl. 1 500 cases. **Chardonnay** ⁑ Am/Fr-oaked **00** has lost its fresh appeal; some citrus/vanilla tastes. 13% alc. 7 000 cases. **Chardonnay** ⁑ Unwooded version; **00** undemanding, delicate but not meagre pear/grapefruit flavours. 13% alc. 2 800 cases. **Chenin Blanc** ⁑ Pear-toned **01**; ordinary but not unsatisfying; lowish 12% alc. Lightly oaked. 9 000 cases. **Chenin-Chardonnay** ★ Lightly oaked **00** lacks zing, better in yr of vintage. 12% alc. 2 000 cases. **Discontinued: Brut Sparkling** Once-off **NV** ⁂. — *JN*

Cape Gables

AFFORDABLE easy-drinking range made for Ocean Traders International by Franschhoek Vineyards. **Tel (021) 557-3799** • Fax (021) 557-3742 • E-mail craigoti@mweb.co.za • Website www.oti-africa.com

Cabernet Sauvignon ⁑ Unwooded, med-bodied **00**'s blackberry fruits still served with mouthcoating tannins; cut with hearty winter stew or something barbecued. **Merlot** ⁑ Unoaked, med/full-bodied **00** shows strict tannin, little of its initial fruit. 13% alc. **Pinotage** ⁂ Full bodied **00** unencumbered by oak; sweet-fruited, slightly estery; pleasant now with spicy foods or flavourful cheeses. 14% alc. **Grand Vin Rouge** ⁑ Light, almost rosé **NV** gravitates naturally to pizza/pasta; uncomplicated, quaffable. **Rosé** Jazzy pink **NV**; sweet, honeyed. **Blanc de Blanc** ⁑ Dry, lightish **NV** from chenin, colombard, semillon. **Sauvignon Blanc** ⁂ **01** step up from pvs; bright, grassy/peppery, full-bodied (14% alc), dry finishing. **Chenin Blanc** ⁂ Guava toned off-dry **01**; crisp and easy; for early drinking. 13.5% alc. **Venestia Blanc** ★ Honeyed semi-sweet **NV**, equal hanepoot/chenin partnership. 13% alc. — *DH*

Cape Indaba see Cape Classics

Capelands

BUDGET-priced, quality-driven range by Winecorp.

Classic Cape Red ☻ ⁂ Latest **01** unoaked mix cinsaut, pinotage; attractive cinnamon, wild strawberry confiture aromas; vibrant flavours offset by unaggressive tannins; dry finish. Among first in modish 1 000 ml bottle. **Classic Cape White** ☻ ⁂ **01** (preview, as is above) now duo chenin, sauvignon (pvs a quartet); still highly quaffable, mouthfilling, dry. Sized for every occasion (187, 750, 1 000 ml; bag-in-box; wine-by-glass dispenser).

Following export-only; none ready for tasting, pvs ratings ⁂-⁂: **Merlot**, **Pinotage** NEW, **Ruby Cabernet**, **Chenin Blanc** NEW. **Chardonnay** discontinued. — *AL*

Cape Levant see Sonop
Capell's Court see Linton Park
Cape Mouton see Mouton-Excelsior

Capenheimer

SA's original perlé wine, launched 1962. Based on the Italian lambrusco style, with a light, crisp sparkle. From Monis. **NV** not tasted for this ed, but on track record good ⁂ quality.

Cape Point Vineyards 

Cape Point • Tasting by appointment • Owner Sybrand van der Spuy • Winemaker Emmanuel Bolliger (since Jun 1996) • Viticulturist/farm manager Japie

*Bronn (since 1999) with R du Plessis • Vineyards 35 ha • Production 100 tons 60% red 40% white • PO Box 37700 Valyland 7978 • **Tel (021) 785-7660** • Fax (021) 785-7662 • E-mail info@cape-point.com*

THESE maritime vineyards in one of the Cape's newest wine wards are pushing the frontiers of viticulture about as far as grapes can grow – anything further south would have to be kelp! Leading the way are these daring young vineyards, red and white, planted scientifically to specific soils and sites in Redhill, Noordhoek and Fishhoek. Youthful, but already feted by National Young Wine Show judges, who plucked the 2000 Sauvignon from anonymity and showered it with glory. Now Emmanuel Bolliger is overgrafting chardonnay to more sauvignon, some destined for their new sauternes-style dessert. Punters will have to wait longer for the reds. Though the first Cabernet is in the barrel, the winemaker believes Cape reds are released far too young – he intends to hold back at least five years. "We haven't produced our best yet," he asserts. "But the soils are so rich, and the vines grow so quickly, we've been able to speed up the whole process as they do Down Under."

- ✵**Chardonnay** Within refined frame, maiden **00** packs plentiful flavour/style. Taut, minerally backbone lends inviting freshness to richer textural notes, emphasises lime-fruit purity. Shouldn't need more than 2 yrs to fully evolve, harmonise. Fermented/aged 13 mths Fr oak, 60% new; partial malo. This, Scarborough below, barrel selections from same (young) vyd.
- ✵**Sauvignon Blanc** Coolly elegant **01**, follow-up to rampant **00** SAYWS grand champion, tweaked with dashes barrel-fermented semillon, sauvignon, "for palate breadth, not oak flavour". Tasted pre final blending, likely ✵ rating. **00** with similar power, graceful fruit crescendo – good food-friendly style; but ultimately younger vintage will have the edge.
- ✵**Semillon Noble Late Harvest** Sauternes is Bolliger's benchmark: semillon, barrel fermentation, maturation and lower residual sugar level are his tools in **00**. Though touch sweet (112 g/ℓ sugar vs Bdx benchmarks' 90-100), but doesn't detract from peachy/apricot intensity with dusty botrytis/oak enrichment. Luscious, flavoursome and, thanks to gorgeous acidity, uncloying. Carries 14.5% alc with commendable lightness.

Scarborough range

Chardonnay NEW ★ Reconciles accessibility and interest. **00** lively spice, pickled limes combination, broadened by tropical, leesy tones, all elegantly pure; juicy, clean, rounded finish. Oak important but supportive. Fr barrels, some new. 13.2% alc. **Sauvignon Blanc** ★ Designed for immediate enjoyment, goal well in reach of **01** preview, with generous fig fragrance; good juicy weight balanced by invigorating, fine acid. Could rate higher on release. 13,5% alc. —*AL*

Cape Safari see Cape Wine Cellars
Cape Salute see Coppoolse Finlayson-Sentinel
Cape Soleil see Sonop
Cape Table see Riebeek
Cape View see Kaapzicht, International Wine Services

Cape Vineyards

*Rawsonville • Not open to the public for tasting • Enquiries Henriëtte Jacobs • PO Box 106 Rawsonville 6845 • **Tel (023) 349-1585/1466** • Fax (023) 349-1592 • E-mail henriette@cape-vineyards.com • Website www.wine.co.za/Cape Vineyards*

EXPORTING to Europe, the US and Canada, this joint venture among several progressive Breede River wineries handles mainly bulk wine but also bottles small quantities under its own labels. One of these recalls the Scot Andrew Geddes Bain, pioneer road engineer whose projects include the pass that links the Breede and Berg valleys and bears his name.

✪**Rawson's Cabernet Sauvignon** Good example of the unwooded style. Med-bodied **99** minty whiffs from dash merlot, smidgeon ruby cab adds spicy note. Enough guts to go 3-4 yrs. 2 000 cases.

✪**Andrew Bain Chardonnay** Several cellars' wines blended for med-bodied **00**, sensitively oak-staved to cosset citrus fruit. Wood better integrated here than in Rawson's version below. 2 000 cases.

Rawson's Ruby Cabernet-Merlot ⁂ Increasingly popular blend in Cape; harmonious **00** features equal proportions for good spread of pruney, plummy tastes. Unwooded. WOM Value. 13.3% alc. 3 000 cases. **Rawson's Chardonnay** ⁂ Though sparingly wood-staved, **00** tastes oaky, sweetish (which not unappealing). Try with traditional apricot-sauced braai snoek. 13% alc. 3 000 cases. Also available, not tasted: **Andrew Bain Cabernet Sauvignon-Merlot**. — *JN*

Cape Wine Cellars

Wellington • Sales from S.A.D Dried Fruit shop 21 Main Road Wellington (no tasting) Mon-Fri 9-1; 2-5 Sat 9-12.30 • Owners Boland Wine Cellar, Bovlei Winery, Wamakersvallei Winery, Wellington Wine Cellar • Marketing manager Tinus Broodryk • Master blender Jeff Wedgwood (since 1995) with cellarmasters from above wineries • Production 250 000 cases 50% white 45% red 5% rosé • PO Box 386 Wellington 7654 • ***Tel (021) 873-0230*** *• Fax (021) 873-6909 • E-mail tinus@bovlei.co.za or info@sadgroup.co.za • Website www.capewinecellars.co.za*

This Wellington organisation is suffused with sunshiny fruit: its shareholders, all local wineries (Boland, Bovlei, Wamakersvallei and Wellington Cellar), contribute wines for blending by master-assembler Jeff Wedgwood. The S.A.D Group, synonymous with dried fruit, no longer are a shareholder but their Foods division still distribute the flagship Kleinbosch brand in SA (supermarkets being the main focus). The export arena, which snaps up most of the 250 000 annual cases, is now under the command of Tinus Broodryk, long-time Bovlei cellar chief whose terroir-stained hands are well equipped to help drive this low-profile yet high-impact business into the future. The range is for sale (though not for tasting) at S A D's famous store on Wellington's high street. If you can't make the detour, click to CWC's outlet on the Internet for on-line orders and information.

Kleinbosch range

Allusion to untrellised bush vines, a common sight around Wellington.

Cabernet Sauvignon ⁑ Oak-touched **00** baked-prune flavours; unsophisticated but perfectly acceptable with rustic foods. 13.4% alc. 10 000 cases. **Shiraz** ⁂ **01** (sample) trip down old-Cape lane: Bushveld-fire aromas; very ripe, vividly flavoured fruit. Rustic wine for unceremonious occasions. 10 000 cases. **Merlot** ⁂ **98** packs warm-country punch of spicy fruit, alc (14.7%); big tannins need time or something fatty coiled on a grill. 10 000 cases. **Pinotage** ⁂ 10 000 cases of **00** crushed red cherries/raspberries, lightly oaked, slightly astringent still but rather nice. **Rouge** ⁂ Uncomplex but gluggable **99**, 75/25 cinsaut/cab blend with lively tart fruit in lightish frame. 3 000 cases of 1 000 ml. **Chardonnay** ⁂ Unwooded, med-bodied **01** not short on flavour, interest; ripe lemons, limes and gentle acidity to serve with summer buffets. 15 000 cases. **Chenin Blanc** ⁂ Satisfying **01** standalone drink, not too alcoholic, abundant appley/melony flavours finish cleanly dry. 20 000 cases. To be discontinued: Kleinbosch **Special Late Harvest**; Cape Safari range (all **NV**): **Late Sun Red**, **Blush**, **Stardust**, **Late Harvest**. — *IvH*

Cape Wine Exports

*Walker Bay • Not open to the public • Tasting for overseas guests by appointment • Cellar tours by appointment • Directors Ben Chowney, Des Dall, KM Chowney • Production 7 000-8 000 cases 60% red 40% white • PO Box 898 Hermanus 7200 • **Tel (028) 313-0137/8** • Fax (028) 313-0139 • E-mail cwe@itec.co.za • Website www.cwe.co.za*

FROM its Hermanus headquarters, CWE focuses mainly on the export of quality red and white table wine to Australia, Europe, the US and South America. Its Fernkloof range not available for tasting for this ed; previous have included **Cabernet Sauvignon** (pvs **98** ⁂), **Merlot** (**98** ⁂), **Pinotage** (**98** ⁂), **Chardonnay** (**00** ✵), **Chenin Blanc** (**00** ⁂), **Sauvignon Blanc** (**00** ⁂).

Cardouw see Goue Vallei

Carisbrooke

*Stellenbosch (see Stellenbosch map) • Tasting & sales Mon-Fri 9-5 Nov-Jan Sat mornings • Owner Willem Pretorius • Winemaker/viticulturist Kowie du Toit (Vlottenburg Winery) • Vineyards 6 ha • Production 40 tons 1 500 cases 100% red • PO Box 25 Vlottenburg 7604 • Tel (021) 881-3034 home • **Tel (021) 881-3798** fax/office • E-mail wjpret@mweb.co.za*

CARISBROOKE, after the town in Alan Paton's *Cry the Beloved Country* is owned by senior counsel Willem Pretorius who, honouring the ideals of quality and equity espoused by the famous SA author, has set up an empowerment scheme whereby the farm staff share in the profits from the single wine, made by Kowie du Toit of Vlottenburg.

✵**Cabernet Sauvignon** Modern Cape cab, well structured, soft; **99** fragrant with cassis/plum, not as complex as **98** ✵, earlier peaking. Own fruit ex Stellenboschkloof, matured in 100% new Fr oak. 13% alc. 1 000 cases. — *CF*

Carneby Liggle

VENTURE between SA wine author/entrepreneur Graham Knox and German-owned Blaauwklippen, for export to UK. PO Box 54 Stellenbosch 7599 • **Tel (021) 880-0135** • E-mail doolhof@mweb.co.za

Old Bush Vine Red ⁂ First **00** a wine with attitude – "blackberry juice with balls" said a UK wine buyer, memorably; follow up **01** (sample) another viniferous United Nations (zinfandel, shiraz, cinsaut, ruby cab, carignan, tinta, pinotage!) promising more of the same – and then some. Zin's clarion raspberries again ring loud, clear; this time accompanied by more palate-caressing softness, sweet spicy substance. **Old Bush Vine White** NEW ⁂ **01** (sample) with plenty of presence, character, though insinuating vinosity rather than full-frontal fruit. Mere whiffs citrus, tropical fruits, fleeting spice from original chenin, sauvignon, semillon, gewürz composition. Vintage's concentration in abundance, plus creamy dry smoothness. — *AL*

Carnival

THESE are the Spar chain of convenience stores' boxed wines, available in 1, 3 and 5 ℓ packs. All **NV** (00/01). See also Country Cellars and Spar.

Rosé ★ Petally semi-sweet, mostly from chenin; ruby cab gives the rose lights. (24 g/ℓ sugar). **Grand Cru** ★ Properly bone-dry no-frills glug; med-bodied; from chenin. **Stein** ⁑ Unpretentious semi-sweet; pleasant ripe-apple, honey tastes; lowish 11% alc. **Late Harvest** ★ Similar to Stein, but sweeter; some floral, honeydew melon nuances. Chenin, med-bodied.

Classic Red ☻ ✵ Crowd-pleasing, fruit-juicy style; lightly oaked. Ruby cab, pinotage in lightish frame which takes well to light chilling. To enjoy "after you've mown the lawn," suggest winemakers. — *JN*

Cathedral Cellar see KWV International

Cederberg Wine

Cederberg (see Olifants River map) • Tasting & sales Mon-Sat 8-12.30; 2-5 (tasting fee) • BYO picnic • Fully equipped self-catering cottages • Gifts • Walks/hikes • Views • Proclaimed conservation area • 4×4 trail • Mountain biking • Private observatory nearby tel (027) 482-2825 • Owners Nieuwoudt family • Winemaker David Nieuwoudt (since 1996) • Viticulturist Ernst Nieuwoudt • Vineyards 28 ha • Production 160 tons (8 000 cases own label) 60% red 40% white • PO Box 84 Clanwilliam 8135 • ***Tel (027) 482-2827*** *• Fax (027) 482-1188 • E-mail cederwyn@iafrica.com*

These spectacular vineyards (at ±1 000 m above sea level they're the highest in the Cape) have produced their first crop of shiraz. The wine is still in barrels, where it will remain for about 14 months. Winemaker David Nieuwoudt is excited about this latest addition to the critically acclaimed range. He promises: "This will definitely be something worth waiting for." And travelling for, he might add, to the Nieuwoudts' mountain sanctuary for a tasting-visit, or a stay-over (comfortable cottages are conveniently near), wonderful hiking trails and recently-established 4×4 and mountain bike tracks. It would take at least a weekend to do the area full justice.

✵**Cabernet Sauvignon 99** coming-of-age for this delicious, elegant cab; has evolved splendidly over past yr, pure cassis mulberry/cedary oak in classy marriage. Rich-fruited, fleshy within sleek, streamlined frame. Firmness, legs to improve over 3-4 yrs. **00** similar but greater intensity, breadth; Fr oak entirely complementary though still youthfully exuberant; should settle, integrate over next yr, continue to grow for much longer. 13.5% alc. 14 mths 60% new oak.

✵**Pinotage** Annual improvements evident in this flavoursome, full-bodied pinotage. **99**'s initial sharpness replaced by unusual tasty gamey notes (shared by many 99 pinotages), conventional redcurrant/raspberry. **00** ✵ altogether bigger (14.5% alc); deeper ruby brilliance; ripe cherry, spice fragrance; generous Am oak seasoning (60% vs pvs 50%). Flavour purity focused by hallmark lightness; exceptionally polished tannins (no hint of bitterness) will nevertheless benefit from 4-5 yrs' mellowing. Remainder Fr, total 75% new, 14 mths. Maiden **97** ABSA Top 10, WOM Reserve.

✵**V Generations** NEW Tribute to the kin who have farmed this wild mountain land since 1893. Cab lavishly adorned with classy cedary tones from 14 mths 100% new Fr oak; this, mid-01, holds sway over **00**'s plush cassis, mulberry; fine, vibrant dry tannins similarly rule fully ripe, creamy flavours. Should have settled by June 02 release, though further ageing (5-6 yrs) strongly advised. Impressive newcomer, trumpeting yet another undersung area's class. Single 20 yr old vyd, one of oldest on farm.

✵**Chardonnay 01** with carefully regulated new world flair: rich yellow-peach, buttered toast smells. Similar complexities in full-bodied, juicy palate. More obvious excess of 14.5% alc contained by fruit concentration, lively acid backbone. Best within 18 mths of harvest. **00** understated, complex citrus, melon, yellow peach fruit. 100% barrel-fermented/aged 5 mths.

✵**Sauvignon Blanc 01** introverted when sampled just post-bottling (not unusual for variety); gooseberry, fumé qualities lurking, should perk up in due course; moderate 12.5% alc, assertive acid thread spotlights flavour purity of these elevated vyds.

Chenin Blanc Barrel Fermented Latest **01** repeats sensitive oak seasoning achieved with pvs. Imparts spice to soft peach/mango bouquet, gently enriches pure-fruited flavours. Concentration, structure to absorb somewhat edgy acidity evident just post-bottling. Fr cask-fermented/aged 4 mths. 13% alc.

Chenin Blanc Unwooded Tongue-tingling **01** with vivacious papaya, melon juiciness; smidgeon balancing sugar adds to overall daintiness, charm. **Bukettraube** Elsewhere-ignored variety gets cinderella transformation into fresh, refined **01**. Merest whiff muscat, more (unusual) dried Provencal herbs bouquet. Scintillating, zingy natural acidity effortlessly balances fairly sturdy alc (13%), fruit-enhancing sugar.

Cederberger Drinking – rather than thinking – style **00**; dark-hued, soft redberry fragrance, silky texture, fruitily rounded in ready-to-uncork harmony. Pinotage, ruby cab, merlot, polished yr in Fr oak, none new. 14% alc. — *AL*

Cellar Cask

Budget-priced boxed/screwcap range by Distell. The range not available for tasting but, on track record, dependable quality. **Premier Claret Dry Red**, **Select Johannisberger** (semi-sweet red), **Premier Grand Cru, Premier Semi-Sweet**, **Premier Late Harvest**, **Select Johannisberger**. All **NV**.

Cellar Reserve see Shoprite Checkers
Chamonix see Cape Chamonix Wine Farm
Chardonnay Company see Claridge

Chateau Libertas

SA's biggest selling cork-closed red, launched 1932 (when it retailed for a shilling a bottle). Special dispensation allows it to retain French 'chateau' appellation. By Distell.

Chateau Libertas **99** Blend cab, cinsaut, merlot, shiraz (65/20/10/5), cab portion oaked 22-24 mths, some new casks. Welcoming, homely; leafy quality to well-fleshed palate. Epitome of drinkability, unobtrusively oaked, lacks neither substance (13.5% alc) nor flavour. — *IvH*

Cheetah Valley see Winecorp Private Label Services
Chiwara see International Wine Services
Christo Wiese see Wiese Portfolio
Cilliers Cellars see Stellendrift

Cinzano

Popular lowish-alcohol range of carbonated sparklers. African Wines & Spirits is SA agent for this famous Italian brand. NVs below not re-tasted; descriptions/ratings from pvs ed.

Spumanté Good example of this light-bodied style. Smiling muscat nose; sweet softness livened by pert bubble. **Tiziano** Rose-coloured, strawberry/cherry toned sweet fizz; lively mouth-expanding mousse.

Clairvaux see Appelsdrift

Claridge Wines

Wellington (see Wellington map) • Tasting & sales, cellar/distillery tours by appointment • Private luncheons for 6-60 guests by appointment • Owners Roger &

Maria Jorgensen, with Michael Loubser • Winemaker/viticulturist Roger Jorgensen (since 1991) • Production 10 000 cases 95% red 5% white • PO Box 407 Wellington 7654 • ***Tel (021) 864-1241*** *• Fax (021) 864-3620 • E-mail claridge@ezinet.co.za*

"Grape and wine prices *must* come down," declares Roger Jorgensen, "if we are to have a dog's chance against Chile et al in the UK market." He should know. This Wellington-based wine-farmer/entrepreneur is the energy behind the innovative Pinotage Wine Company, which sources grapes and wines from the Swartland and Paarl for European and US supermarket chains. Their Bush Vine Pinotage, styled to show off "only the consumer friendly aspects" of the all-SA grape, has been a smash. It's offered in more than 3 000 stores, and Jorgensen frets because he can hardly meet the demand. Undaunted, he's also registered Chardonnay, Cabernet and, now, Shiraz companies. While he continues to strive for wines as "up-market as possible", he warns that SA must be realistic when it comes to prices. "You may quote me," he emphasises. Meanwhile multi-dimensional Jorgensen continues to offer the characterful Claridge wines, from own-farm fruit, and a Pinot from neighbour and SAA long-haul pilot Naas Ferreira, crop organically managed by Jorgensen ("No tractor, no 'bag-muck' – only mulch and compost").

✬**Claridge Red Wellington** ✓ Assertive claret style, dark as ink; always cab/merlot/cab f in 60/30/10 vyd ratio. First **91** helped put Wellington on red wine map; following releases all individuals, powerfully structured. Latest **00** (sample) jam-packed with warm fruit; puckering. 14 mths Fr cooperage, some new. 13.5% alc not as high as some pvs. 440 cases. No **97**. **98**, **99** not tasted.

Claridge Chardonnay Gutsy, individual style; old vines, mix Californian, Burgundian, Swiss clones, bunch-pressed, barrel-fermented. Current **98** ✬ another burly number (14% alc); some lees/honey tones but not as interesting as some pvs. No **97**, **00**. **99** untasted. **Klein Optenhorst Pinot Noir 00** (unfinished sample, not rated) extraordinary colour, almost opaque; dense palate tightly shut, offers only vague roasted-nut tones. No **98**. **99** bottled but not tasted. **97** ✬. **The Pinotage Company Selected Bush Vine Pinotage** Concept wine for early/easy drinking, fruit-focused. First **98** and following **99** both ✬; latest **00** ✬ spicy red fruit abundance, deft oaking. Note: **Cabernet/Shiraz Company 00**s not ready for tasting. — *JN*

Clos du Ciel

Stellenbosch (see Helderberg map) • Tasting, sales, cellar tours by appointment • Small tourgroups by arrangement • Views • Owner Peter Aschke • Winemaker André Morgenthal (since 1999) • Vineyard 1.53 ha • Production 9 tons 62% white 38% red • PO Box 12830 Die Boord 7613 • ***Tel/fax (021) 855-2573***

On a clear day you can see as far as Cape Point from Clos du Ciel, stunningly placed in a mountain bowl on the Helderberg, with the distinctive gabled shape of the Simonsberg to one side and Table Mountain outlined in the distance. André Morgenthal, who made the wines, stayed local last harvest (with loads of help from near-neighbour Tjuks Roos, a new basket press and an open fermenter), buying in red grapes from nearby vineyards (last year's came from the Simonsberg). More shiraz and cabernet made up for not finding a suitable parcel of pinot. The chardonnay vineyard on the property was low on yield, big on concentration. Now he's "keeping the wines happy" in between his many other commitments as communications manager for Wines of South Africa.

✬**Chardonnay** Inspired intuitive winemaking by philosophy/drama graduate André Morgenthal. Operatically proportioned **00** collector's item, just 550 cases. Power packed (14.1% alc), off-dry (9 g/ℓ sugar) yet – miraculously – skips lightly, even elegantly, charms utterly. Portion barrique-fermented, aged; Damy, Billon cooperage. — *DH*

Clos Malverne

Stellenbosch (see Stellenbosch map) • Tasting & sales Mon-Fri 10-1, 2-4.30 • Owner Seymour Pritchard • Winemaker/viticulturist Isak 'Ippie' Smit (since Nov 1997) • Production 370 tons 26 000 cases 92% red 8% white • PO Box 187 Stellenbosch 7599 • ***Tel (021) 882-2022*** *• Fax (021) 882-2518 • E-mail closma@mweb.co.za*

PINOTAGE-POWERED Seymour Pritchard, owner of this hot property in cool Devon Valley with its seasonal mists rolling in from the Indian Ocean, is ever concerned with the future of this grape (2001 was a notable vintage for SA's indigenous variety, which has been seen seriously wooing some foreign palates). The future of pinotage will possibly be greater as a blended wine rather than a straight cultivar itself, is the current viewpoint here. Creating the right recipe for the quintessential Cape blend, they've learnt from experience, depends on flag-flying pinotage being the lesser varietal – 30% or lower – and used subtly in the blend (although their single varietal version is not being neglected by any means: the award-winning Pinotage 2000 was boldly spruced up with a new burgundy bottle and fashionably low-slung label). But you won't find a trace of tunnel vision here – the family-backed team is very excited about the maiden Shiraz and reports that demand is double the supply when it comes to the Sauvignon.

✲ **Auret** ✓ Stylish, laurel-wreathed Cape Red (VVG, SAA, Diners Club shortlist, Wine ✲✲✲✲, WOM etc etc) featuring pinotage in supportive role, reaches its zenith in **98** ✲✲✲✲, brilliantly realised blend cab, pinotage, merlot (64/21/15), proportions fine-tweaked to maximise cab's structure, pinotage's vibrant-fruited palate coverage, merlot's curvaceous body. Some gamey/organic sniffs to add complexity to big concentration, body (±14% alc). Sensitively oaked: 20% new Fr barriques, rest 2nd/3rd fill, 2 mths. Traditional vinification in open fermenters, basket pressed (a Seymour Pritchard mantra). 1 600 cases. **97**, with soupcon more of the local star (60/25/15), better weighted, balanced, than pvs, with vintage's more refined allures. Some Am oak (25%, remainder Fr). **96** ✲✲✲ in modern, approachable style, first announced with **95**.

✲ **Pinotage Reserve** Showy, deep-flavoured barrel selection bristling with show awards. Pvs craved time to soften, develop (±3 yrs), but latest seamlessly-tannined **99** ✲✲✲✲ marvellously accessible now. Swashbuckling, as are all these, but essentially classically styled; 'serious' cigarbox smells, blackcurrants and plums, even hints of Burgundy amid the muscles. Approachable, but deserves (rather than demands) 4-5 yrs to attain peak. Partly Am-oaked (20%), rest Fr, 20% new casks, 12 mths. 2 700 cases. **98** first with inbuilt accessibility; **97** very tightly wound initially, needing plenty of time. Regular **Pinotage** Lighter oaking (4-6 mths Fr casks) designed to showcase grape's ample charms. After silk-textured, loudly-praised **98**, latest **00** ✲✲✲ feels somewhat rustic, leaden-footed; sweetish plum cake tastes and big tannins need food. 8 500 cases.

✲ **Cabernet Sauvignon** Steadily improving label, showing purer, stronger varietal character, succulence. Tempo increased with **97** ✲, **98** SAA. Newest **99** shy; some eucalyptus/herbal whiffs; palate more open, nicely tweaked with tannin, but needs bit of time. 13.9% alc. 1 000 cases.

✲ **Shiraz** NEW Blockbusting, attention-commanding style, but not over-manipulated for effect. Jam-packed with good shiraz fruit; deftly controlled Am oak imparts creaminess rather than sweet character. Promising **99** debut. 30% insourced fruit. 13.3% alc. 900 cases.

✲ **Cabernet Sauvignon-Merlot** Chic, lightly wooded, highly drinkable blend. **98** flew with SAA. Cleverly constructed **99** more satisfying than now stand-alone Cab above, more definition, flavour. Christmas cake tones complemented by 6 mths new Fr oaking. 13,5% alc. 4 000 cases.

Cabernet Sauvignon-Shiraz ✓ Attractive spicy/savoury blend with, in 3rd release **99**, some peppercorn nuances to ripe redcurrant fruit. Fairly restrained style (despite beefy 13.4% alc), lightish oak (6 mths older Fr) well woven. 2 500 cases. Less tannic than **98** VG. **97** *Wine* ✯.

Cabernet Sauvignon-Pinotage Punchy new-world style, loads of personality; 100% own fruit. Newest **99** big mouthful blackcurrant fruit (and alc: 13.7%); 36% pinotage coats every cranny with ripe plums and pepper; savoury, almost gamey tones, too. Harmonious, succulent blend, well oaked (yr Fr casks, some new). 3 000 cases. **98** *Wine* ✯.

Sauvignon Blanc ✓ Auspiciously-sited vyd beside farm dam ±5°C cooler than property's higher-lying plots. Helps explain why **00** ✯ retained some zest in notoriously hot yr. In cooler **01**, fairly crackles with delicious flavour; racy sweet pepper tones underpinned by very ripe gooseberry. Dab sugar smoothes. 13.3% alc. 2 700 cases. — *TM*

Clovelly Wines

Stellenbosch • Guesthouse • Owners Deon Toerien, Jacques Fourie & Mineke Toerien-Fourie • Consulting winemaker/vineyard manager Jacques Fourie (since Nov 2000) • Vineyards 3 ha • Production 28 tons 500 cases 90% red 10% white • Private Bag X5061 Stellenbosch 7599 • ***Tel/fax (021) 882-2511*** *• Cell 082-853-7190 (J Fourie) • E-mail mwpetina@mweb.co.za*

If you don't find action-man Jacques Fourie offroad racing or mountain biking, or cellar chiefing at Mount Rozier, where he now full-times, try calling at home in Stellenbosch's Devon Valley. He and wife Mineke have always yearned for their own wine label and now, with vinously inclined in-laws Deon and Alma Toerien, they've reached their dream. Their boutiquey 3 hectares of cabernet will provide a single vineyard wine when their contract with Distell expires in 2007. Meanwhile their inaugural Cabernet was made from insourced grapes and vinified in Franschhoek. It proved an instant hit upcountry, and in Japan and the UK. For good measure, they've also introduced a Chardonnay and a Dry Red. Next is their own cellar ("still in planning") and, on the wish-list, an audience with visionary wine czar Robert Mondavi "to find out where he thinks the world of wine is headed". Then, for after-action satisfaction, a braai chez Fourie "with our family, friends and very good wine".

Cold Duck (5th Avenue)

POPULAR low-alcohol pink sparkle with origins in Germany, where leftover wine in the pubs ('kalte ente') was poured into jugs and sold at reduced prices. At around 8% alcohol, can be flung back with more than usual gusto. By Distell.

NV ✯ Ferdinand de Lesseps grapes give their heady pineapple fragrance, pinotage their candyfloss tones (and rosy colour) to charming, gently sweet carbonated sparkle with piquant fizz. — *IvH*

Coleraine Wines

Paarl (see Paarl map) • Tasting & sales by appointment • Views • Owners Kerr family • Winemaker Clive Kerr (since 1999, with consultant Loftie Ellis (since 1998) • Viticulturist Clive Kerr (since 1980) • Vineyards 30 ha • Production 130 tons (100 tons total) 100% red • PO Box 579, Suider-Paarl 7624 • ***Tel (021) 863-3443/2073*** *• Fax (021) 863-3443 • E-mail colerain@mweb.co.za*

THE NAME and the Celtic imagery of the front label come from ancestral Ireland, but owner Clive Kerr wears the hats of several other nationalities when he makes the wines below. The critically acclaimed Shiraz and promising bordeaux blend courtesy to France, while the jolly quaffing 'Cape red' is as local as the Paarl fire brigade, which it honours. Kerr started his career on these 42 hectares twenty-one years ago, and always nurtured the dream of producing wine from his own grapes. His first vintage (1999) was with winemaker Graham Weerts (who's since moved to Bellingham); now Weerts cellarmasters while kid-gloving the new plots of mourvèdre, petit verdot and viognier. Already his wines have found markets in Europe and the US. Local marketing is in the hands of energetic Wine Worx, so we're likely to encounter these labels more frequently in the future.

Shiraz 99 long sold out, though highly regarded first release, back-tasted mid-01, still impresses with deep cerise red, chocolatey raspberry aromas, succulent and richly textured palate. Wine, SAYWS gold, WOM Reserve. Fr/Am oak, 35% new; 14,1% alc. 1 000 cases. Note: **00**s, **01**s of this, below not ready for tasting.

Cabernet Sauvignon-Merlot Destined to become a benchmark Paarl red. **99** deep mulberry tones, pure cassis aromas layered with vanilla whiffs, hints of plum, slight choc-cherry tones; ripe but not blowsy, firm-tannined elegant finish. 60/40 blend, 13,6% alc; open fermenters; 40% new Fr/Am oak. 1 000 cases.

Fire Engine Red Latest **00** blend merlot/ruby cab/cinsaut (47/33/20). **99**, same varieties, ruby cab ringing the bell. — *MF*

Constantia Uitsig

*Constantia (see Constantia map) • Tasting & sales Mon-Sat 9-5 Tasting fee discretionary • Cellar tours by appointment • Constantia-Uitsig & La Colombe restaurants, Spaanschemat River Café (see Restaurant section) • Luxury Constantia Uitsig Country Lodge (see Stay-over section) • Tourgroups • Gifts • Conference facilities • Views • Owners Dave & Marlene McCay • Wine director André Badenhorst (since 1988) • Viticulturist André Rossouw (since 1997) • Vineyards 35 ha • Production 280 tons 22 000 cases 60% white 40% red • PO Box 402 Constantia 7848 • **Tel (021) 794-1810** • Fax (021) 794-1812 • E-mail wine@icon.co.za • Website www.constantiauitsig.co.za*

Half of this trophy Constantia wine farm is up for grabs for a cool R97-million at the time of writing. The up-for-sale 40 hectares exclude some vineyard, the manor house, wine shop, cricket oval (owner David McCay's a former WP cricket all-rounder) and restaurants, top-of-the-food-chain Constantia Uitsig, La Colombe and the Spaanschemat River Café, still madly in fashion. In the meantime, it's business as usual. Wine director André Badenhorst will now be making the wines himself at neighbouring Steenberg's cellar. Their Chardonnay already a success story, Badenhorst is delighted with their SAYWS-applauded Cabernet. "Lots of people say this area cannot produce red wines. We're proving them wrong!" Ongoing in-depth discussions and analysis are aimed at improving viticulture and pinpointing their strengths and weaknesses. (Life's always interesting at this idyllic property: Badenhorst had to cut short our conversation, as a Russian speaker of parliament and his delegation were coming for a tasting – seems that what he deems one of wine's best kept secrets got let out of the bag.)

Merlot Steadily delivering on potential as best in this cool valley. Ruby-robed **99**, tasted pre-bottling for pvs ed, now quite generously fruited with damsons, prunes; spicy nuance from 14 mths Fr oak. Needs extra yr's ageing though won't attain plushness of **98**. with christmas cake tones.

Cabernet Sauvignon **99**, pvsly tasted from barrel, has unfurled to reveal soft red-berry fruit, refined cedar, tobacco leaf bouquet; lip-smacking graphite core. Pacier than minty **98** with green finish.

Chardonnay Reserve Pvs standout **97** (sole SA chardonnay to garner both 1999 VVG and London Wine Challenge gold; also SAA, *Wine*) trumped by latest **00**, first to be new-oak-fermented, yr lees-aged. Operatically flavoured (melons & lemons slathered with honey, butterscotch) yet beautifully controlled, harmonious. Bigger, more overtly oaked than **98**. **99** bolder, in mould of **97**. Versatile with food (of the airborne variety, too: these SAA, KLM frequent flyers). **Chardonnay Barrel Select** A further blending of only the best barrels, 100 cases for property's restaurants/cellar door. Last tasted was **99**.

✵**Sauvignon Blanc** Maturing vines upping the ante with each vintage. Astonishingly concentred **01** ✵ pungently aromatic with peppers, grass, assorted green fruits. Wells of flavour buoyed by needle-fine acidity. **00** leapfrogged out of pond into different class.

✵**Semillon Reserve** André Badenhorst convinced variety has natural home here; judging panels seem to agree: *Wine* ✵, SAA for **98**. VG for **00**. Character epitomised by **99**: stunningly scented; beeswax, fresh thatch, new-cream initially aerated by bracing freshness. Retasted mid-01, deliciously creamy with lime undertones which **00**, with extra kumquat fragrance, should acquire given the time it deserves. Barrel-fermented/aged 12 mths, new Fr wood.

✵**Semillon Noble Late Harvest** Riveting botrytis dessert with immediate claim to excellence with maiden **00**. Only three barriques, harvested at 39°B, gently pressed into barrel.

✵**Uitsig Blanc** ✓ Good sauvignon yr lifts latest **01** into higher bracket. Fresh, green-vegetable aromas and complementary fruit salad tastes. Mostly sauvignon, with dash West Coast chenin. Stylishly packaged unwooded easy-drinker. **99** ★★.

Cabernet Sauvignon-Merlot Not tasted for ed. Pvs **97** ★★. **Chardonnay Unwooded** ★★ Latest **01** faithful to chablis style that has won it UK followers. Chalky hints with zesty cantaloupe counterpoint. Breadth from ripe fruit and 13.5% alc. — *NP*

Coppoolse Finlayson-Sentinel Winery

Stellenbosch (see Stellenbosch map) • Visits by appointment • Owners Rob Coppoolse, Walter Finlayson, Viv Grater • Managing & marketing director Rob Coppoolse (since 1991) • Cellarmaster Walter Finlayson (since 1992) • Winemakers Adele Dunbar & Riaan Möller (since 1998) • Production: 500 tons 600 000 cases (100 000 cases own label) 60% red 35% white 5% rosé • PO Box 4028 Old Oak 7537 • ***Tel (021) 982-6175*** *• Fax (021) 982-6296 • E-mail wine@sentinel.co.za*

If you're wanting a typical Cape winery, this certainly isn't the place to look! This rapidly expanding negociant company now occupies some 13 warehouses in a modern industrial park in Brackenfell, and is growing almost daily. New developments include plans for a 1 500 m² cooled warehouse, an additional maturation cellar for 1 000 barrels and a new tank hall with a 600 000 ℓ capacity. Since the last visit a second bottling line has been installed. Emphasis is now on the Sentinel and Kaya ranges (the latter resurrected and re-launched in London in 2001). A new facet of the business is the provision of analytical services to other wineries, though exports remain the main drive. The vista from the cellar (or should we say 'factory') has not improved, but cellarmaster Walter Finlayson reports that it now includes a fine view of a cash loan office.

Sentinel range

✵**Shiraz** Standout **98**'s ✵ luminance (VVG, *Wine* ✵✵, Air France) unmatched by later releases. Latest **00** dominated by smoked/charred quality – not unattractively; firm structured, rich, savoury. 18 mths mix of Fr/Am oak. 13% alc. 3 000 cases (× 6, as everywhere below).

Cabernet Sauvignon ★★ Toasty plumminess leads to big (13.3% alc) palate; **99** sweetish but mouth-drying tannic finish. 18 mths Fr oak. 13.5% alc. 1 200 cases **Merlot** ★★ **99** shows cherries, hint mocha on well-constructed tannin/acid base

13% alc. 2 000 cases. **Pinotage** ★★☆ Charred wood, red berry aromas/flavours in **00**; med-bodied, savoury, with dry tannins; yr in barrel. 1 500 cases. **Chardonnay 01** not ready for tasting; pvs ★☆. **Sauvignon Blanc** ★ **01**'s mild, watery fruitiness tightens to mild acid grip in finish. 5 500 cases.

Kaya range

Wines bought in and blended.

Shiraz ★★☆ Friendly aromas of red-fruit jam/smoke in **00**; pleasantly balanced palate; lingering. 13% alc. 9 950 cases. **Shaka** ★☆ Light-bodied **00** red blend; soft tannins/acid smeared lightly with jammy fruit. 1 460 cases. **Chenin Blanc** ★☆ Acidic fringe to simple soft fruitiness in **01**. 3 500 cases. **Cabernet Sauvignon**, **Pinotage**, **Sauvignon Blanc** not ready for tasting.

Kaapse Pracht range

For the Netherlands market.

Cinsaut-Pinotage Latest not tasted for this ed. Pvs **99** ★★☆. **Droë Steen** ★☆ Med-bodied **01**, straightforward dry, crisp and lightly fruity chenin. 13% alc. 2 500 cases.

Kaapse Vreugd range

For Dutch market; wines bought in and blended.

Cinsaut-Pinotage ★☆ Lunchtime-light ruby **00**, with moderate alc (12%), light berry character; unwooded. 2 500 cases. **Chenin Blanc-Chardonnay** ★☆ Easy-going dry **01**, with chardonnay offering a bit of weight to softly balanced chenin. 13% alc. 2 500 cases.

Also available, not tasted for this ed: Kaaps Genoegen range, Kaaps Geskenk range NEW; discontinued: Cape Salute range: **Cabernet Sauvignon** (pvs rating ★★☆), **Pinotage** (★★☆), **Chenin Blanc-Chardonnay**, **Chenin Blanc** (★☆); Mount Disa range: **Shiraz 98** (★★★☆), **Cabernet Sauvignon** (★★☆), **Pinotage** (★★☆), **Cape Salute** (★☆), **Chardonnay** (★☆), **Sauvignon Blanc** (★☆). — *TJ*

Cordoba

Stellenbosch (see Helderberg map) • Tasting & cellar tours by appointment Mon-Fri 8.30-5 Sales Mon-Fri 8.30-5 • Owner Jannie Jooste • Winemaker/viticulturist Christopher Keet (since 1993) • Vineyards 31 ha • Production 100 tons, 7 000 cases 70% red, 30% white • PO Box 5609 Helderberg 7135 • ***Tel (021) 855-3744*** *• Fax (021) 855-1690 • E-mail cordoba@adept.co.za*

You have to be fit to tackle the steep slopes of Cordoba, where vineyards and cellar cling to the mountainside like swifts' nests. Athletic Chris Keet is certainly up to the challenges, keeping in tone by regular strenuous paddle-skiing. His mover-shaker style transfers easily from the False Bay breakers to dining rooms and show halls, where his wines – led by the stunning Crescendo – continue to make waves. But, reveals Keet, Crescendo's initial success is just a starting point. "We've spent a lot of effort identifying the vast variety of sites on Cordoba, with their individual soils, aspects and altitudes. We've also focused on selecting the most suitable varieties and clones," he says. Cabernets sauvignon and franc have already been added. Now extra cab franc is being established (the variety a high-flyer in the Helderberg, it seems) along with merlot – all focused on making Crescendo an even better wine. Small quantities of Shiraz, cabernet sauvignon and chardonnay will also form part of the future picture. The excitement is almost tangible.

★★★★☆ **Crescendo** A Cape touchstone aiming to compete with St Emilion's best. Individual, powerful cab f fleshed out, now, by only merlot – cab not a feature of latest **98**, brooding, minerally, deep-flavoured and still rapier-taut. 65/35 blend, new Fr oak 18 mths. Powerful 13.8% alc, sweet mouthcoating tannins for sound keeping. "Allow 10 yrs before touching," implores Chris Keet, "will then give the total pleasure it was created for." 500 cases only. New Cape star since maiden

95 ★★, *Wine* ★, Air France trophy winner, 70/20/10 cab f/cab/merlot, **96** 80/20 cab f/merlot marginally lighter in difficult yr; **97** same assemblage as **95**.

★★**Merlot** Understudy to Crescendo fanfare, but could easily top the bill elsewhere. **98**, in fact, very similar to superstar above, slightly sweeter, without the complexity. Violets, dark coffee and toasty vanilla tannins. Extra succulence should come with 1-3 yrs in bottle. 18 mths Fr oak, 20% new. 800 cases. **97** utterly delicious; **96** extraordinarily concentrated for generally lighter harvest; **95** gutsy, more outspoken than **94**. These to fill the time (luxuriously) waiting for big brother above to mature.

★**Cabernet Sauvignon** Cellar philosophy of cool understatement epitomised here. Current **97** ripening in bottle, now with light minty whiffs to original cigarboxy blackcurrant. Fr oak, 18 mths, 50% new. 700 cases. Pvs **95** with puckering tannic tail, needed time. Above both improved on austere **96,** leaner **94**. ±12,5% alcs.

★**Chardonnay** Latest **00** maintains 50% new-oak elaboration, partial natural fermentation of pvs for fuller, creamier profile with extra complexity. Wholebunch pressed, Fr oak. Good deal bigger than **99** (13.5% alc vs 12,5), toasty vanilla-fudge with contrasting piquant citrus. 800 cases.

Shiraz Barrel Reserve Last was **97** ★, not retasted for this ed. Discontinued: **Sauvignon Blanc** Pvs **99** ★.

Mount Claire range

Mountain Red ☻ ★ Latest **NV** (99) version quaffably cab-based, with merlot and smidgeon shiraz adding cracked-pepper interest; lightish, to drink now or keep 2-3 yrs.

Discontinued: **Mountain White** Pvs **99** ★. — *DH*

Count Agusta see Agusta

Country Cellars

THESE are the Spar chain of convenience stores' cork-closed wines. See Carnival for the boxed range; see also Spar for further details.

Limited Edition range

★**Cabernet Sauvignon Nyathi** Well-made, tasty **99** ripening in bottle; spicy black fruits and hint of tannin to enjoy now or keep 3-4 yrs. 6 mths new 300 ℓ Fr barriques (as are all reds in range); moderate 12.5% alc. 2 000 cases.

★**Merlot Narrabos 98** ready, but still-sweet fruit suggests another good 3 yrs ahead. 13% alc. 1 500 cases. Follow-up **99** not ready for tasting.

★**Shiraz Bayete** Robust style with expansive plummy/herby flavours, earthy/toasty undertones. **99** easy feel from sweet fruit and lenient tannins; clean finish. 13% alc. 2 000 cases.

Chardonnay Narina 00 not ready for tasting. Pvs **99** ★.

Varietal range

So called, but includes a blend.

Cabernet Sauvignon ★ **00** in the savoury taste spectrum with green pepper tones, some undaunting tannins; generous extract, alc (13.5%). **Merlot** ★ Med-bodied. **99** pleasing spicy/fruity tones, some softish tannins and more spice in palate. 3 000 cases. **Pinotage** ★ Full-bodied **99** classically structured, fairly dry, should flesh out, given yr/2. 13% alc. 2 000 cases. **Ruby Cabernet** NEW ★ **00** with 15% alc, spicy, tobacco-leaf character and red fruits; oak-chipped. 2 000 cases. **Claret** ★ Sweet-oaky **99** offers upfront red fruit, charry/smoky aromas from partia new Fr oaking, 3 mths cab, merlot, pinotage. 2 500 cases. **Chardonnay** ✯ Honest, well-made unwooded **01**, well-expressed varietal character. 13.2% alc. ±2 000 cases. **Sauvignon Blanc** ✯ **01** refreshing, lively grassy tastes. Med-bodied. ±2 000 cases. **Blanc de Blanc** ⁑ Lower Orange River fruit in **01**, from chenin; fresh dry melony tastes and big 13.8% alc. **Special Late Harvest** Not tasted. Discontinued: **Chenin Blanc** (pvs **00** unrated).

Generic range

Classic Red ☻ ⁑ Smooth red-fruited vin ordinaire from pinotage, ruby cab; needs a fire to sip beside; lightly wooded.

Rosé ★ Semi-sweet picnic/alfresco wine with delicate plum tones; chenin, and ruby cab for colour; med-bodied. **Dry White** ★ Ripe-fruity tones over grassy hints; very dry finish. 13.8% alc not to be thrown back. **Low Alcohol Dry White** Not tasted. **Stein** ⁑ Plain and simple but easy, med-bodied; good ripe tropical fruit. **Late Harvest** ★ No-frills semi-sweet; some muted honeyed flavours. Discontinued: **Sparkling Brut** (pvs ✯), **Doux** (⁑). Above all **NV**. —*JN*

Craighall

Reliable, popular value-for-money range from African Wines & Spirits. Styled for early/easy drinking.

Cabernet Sauvignon-Merlot ✯ To drink while watching sport on TV, suggest the makers, reasonably, for **00**. Jammy fruit, enough tannin/acid to balance it for easy pleasure. Lightly oaked; med-bodied. 19 000 cases. **Chardonnay-Sauvignon Blanc** ✯ Simple, outdoorsy **01** is 50/50 blend, but dominated by sauvignon flavour-wise. Fresh, fruity; zippy finish. 70 000 cases. **Sauvignon Blanc** ⁑ NEW Fresh, tangy **01** offers plenty of flavour and no complications. Med-bodied. 10 000 cases. Fruit above ex Rbtson. —*TJ*

Culemborg

Good value range from DGB in 2 ℓ screwtop glass jugs. All **NV**.

Dry Red ☻ ✯ Bouncy scarlet charmer with lithe tannin for extra-easy quaffing. Med-bodied.

Blanc de Noir Coral-saronged blush, lighter-bodied for relaxed summery occasions. Untasted (pvs rating ✯). **Grand Cru** ⁑ Light-bodied no-frills glug, extra-dry finish chimes with style. **Light** ⁑ Coastal market only. 9,8% alc. Light tropical fruit, agreeably dry and undemanding. **Stein** ⁑ True to style: soft, delicate flavours, non-sticky finish, undaunting 11% alc. **Late Harvest** ✯ Port Elizabeth/East London only. 1 000 ml. Smoothly muscatty, sweet, lightweight and easy. **Diamanté Crystal Blanc** ⁑ Perlé-style snappy sip with dryish finish; soft, lively mousse. **Diamanté Blanc de Noir** ⁑ Med-bodied, spritzy semi-dry blush; candyfloss ethereality which refreshes.

Export range

Cape Red ☻ ✯ **00** merry mix cinsaut/ruby cab with red-grapey core; party held together by light grip of tannin; softly dry. Med-bodied.

Cabernet Sauvignon ✯ **00** slightly charry from fleeting oak contact, sweetish fruit; easy. 13.2% alc. **Cinsaut** ✯ Undemanding, unwooded **00**, light textured but (like rest of range) just enough tannin for versatile table-mating. **Merlot** ✯ **00** rewarding ripe-plum/mocha varietal tones, frisky but not unmannered tannins, fruity-sweet farewell. 13.8% alc. **Pinotage** ✯ **00** unwooded cherry/strawberry tastes braced with sturdy tannin; counter with full-bore cuisine such as venison casseroles. ±13% alc. **Blanc de Noir** ✯ **01** slightly built sip in pale coppery robes; delicate tropical fruits in off-dry palate. **Chardonnay** ✯ Still-fresh **00** unwooded, dry; ripe peach, pear, estery whiffs, fresh finish. Drink soon. 13.4% alc. **Chenin Blanc** ✯ **00** Fresh-fruity style, piquant dry finish, for early enjoyment. 13.2% alc. **Sauvignon Blanc** ✯ **01** Recognisably sauvignon, surprisingly weighty (only 11.4% alc); styled to quaff right now. **Cape White** ✯ **01** lightish no-frills slurp; crisp, almost brisk dry finish. Miscellaneous grapes with muscat. **Blanc de Blanc** ★ **00** swiftly fading into honeyed age. — *DH*

Cullinan View

Export range for Matthew Clark, UK, by Vinimark (see also that entry).

✯**Cabernet Sauvignon 00** smooth and soft; easy; lightly-oaked style for drinking young. Lots of cab flavour. 13% alc.

Sauvignon Blanc ☻ ✯ **01** vibrant fruity example, made reductively to capture freshness. Drink now to catch the nice chalky tones. 13,5% alc.

Pinotage ✯ **01** (sample) quite earthy, rustic, dry; needs a braai-mate to bring out the fruit. 13% alc. **Chardonnay** ✯ Lightly-wooded **01** with tropical-toned buttery vanilla palate, clean dry citrus finish. 13,6% alc. **Chenin Blanc** ✯ Lightish **01**, gentle just-dry swig; lemonade flavours best right now. **Colombard** ✯ Off-dry in **01**, though impression is smooth rather than sweet. Lightish tropical/pineapple tones. — *DH*

Darling Cellars

West Coast (see Swartland map) • Tasting & sales Mon-Thu 8-5 Fri 8-4 Sat 8-12 Tasting fee R5 p/p • Cellar tours by appointment • BYO picnic • Seasonal wildflowers • 4×4 Trail on Oude Post farm • Owners 24 shareholders • General Manager John Sheppard • Winemakers Abé Beukes (since 1997), Johan Nesenberend & Martin Stevens • Viticulturist Abé Beukes (since Dec 1997) • Production manager Jacques van Niekerk • Quality control Marius Botha • Sales & marketing Richard Hilton • Vineyards 1 500 ha • Production 8 000 tons 500 000 cases 55% white 45% red • PO Box 114 Darling 7345 • ***Tel (022) 492-2276*** *• Fax (022) 492-2647 • E-mail info@darlingcellars.co.za*

Like the West Coast flamingos, the wines from this export-driven cellar migrate north (and west and east) in one of the Cape's bigger brand-building success stories. The completion of a new vatting cellar brings the total capacity to 1 500 casks – enough to accommodate the big-volume demands of a 500 000-cases-a-year operation. But also to serve the barrel-development needs of the winery's limited-quantity ranges, now proudly joined by the new top range, Onyx – an allusion to the granite bedrock found in the flagship Groenekloof vineyard. "This," enthuses Abe Beukes, "is our pride and joy. Bushvines predominate, and yields are low – as low as 3 tons/hectare." The apex of the range is a red with pinotage. "A rare devil", says this minister's son, which he's tamed by blending it with some of their bemedalled shiraz. Doing their bit to ensure the wines fly out of the cellar are brand new labelling and packing lines.

Onyx range

✯✯**Kroon** ('Red Blend' in pvs ed). Cellar's flagship is has equal portions pinotage, shiraz. While inspiration is local, execution is more evocative of bdx. **00** starts more quietly than pvs (but should attain heights of **99** in 3-4 yrs); mineral-led nose, ripe cherry/plum tones and ripe-banana whiff; fresh, juicy palate, fruit sweetness nicely controlled for satisfying dry finish. Like more open, lush-fruited **99**, can be broached now but better around 06.

Chardonnay NEW Refined example, showing cool Groenekloof fruit, though **99**'s unexpectedly advanced for its age; probably best drunk soonish. Vanilla/barley-sugar tones, finishing with hint of toast. 13.1% alc.

For export only; not tasted for this ed: **Pinotage** (pvs rating), **Merlot**, **Shiraz**.

Groenekloof range

Cabernet Sauvignon Retasted mid-01 still taut, with some dry tannins, though still-healthy fruit, generous alc (13,5%) suggest **98**'s structure should see it through to maturity 6-8 yrs away. **97** *Wine* .

Shiraz Bigger, more 'serious' than DC below. **99**, from 2 hillside vyd sites, mellowing; minerally, smoky black olive/choc in broad palate. Very good now, promises to be sensational in ±5 yrs. 14.4% alc.

Pinotage NEW Streamlined **99** unusual, attractive beetroot character (feature of several of these wines), juicy tannins, airy feel despite heavy 13.6% alc; persistent.

Also available, not tasted for this ed: **Chardonnay** (pvs rating), **Sauvignon Blanc** ().

DC range

Cabernet Sauvignon ✓ Soft, ripe instant drinkability; cherries, walnuts, tobacco in **99** full, 'sweet' palate. Generous, ready, but will hold couple of years. Flies off shelves in Sweden. Combo Fr oak barrels/staves. 13,6% alc. **98** sold out. **97** SAA.

Merlot ✓ Drinkability the main feature of **99** (like most of these reds), thanks to lively but not flagrant juiciness; rounded tannins; plums and some good savoury, beetroot, green bean tones; unusual woodsmoky finish. ±14% alc.

Pinotage ✓ Benefit of mature vines felt even in this mid-tier range. Compared to pvs, banana-toned **99** surprisingly firm tannin grip, turning almost rigid in finish; demands ageing 2-5 yrs. 13.5% alc. Oaked, unlike mouthfilling, pleasantly tart **98**. **97** SAA.

Shiraz ✓ Refined, pleasingly structured **99**; warm, easy spread of savoury, herbaceous, spice tones and sweet, soft fruit. Substantial but not tiringly chunky as some modern Cape shirazes can be. Well managed oak (±60% staves, rest casks). Probably shade better now than Groenekloof above, and lots of life ahead. 13.8% alc. **98** VG, **97** SAA.

Sauvignon Blanc ✓ **01** riper than pvs; bright and refreshing without being insubstantial; passion fruit tones and touches of litchi. Best in yr of harvest. **00** with nettly/flinty tang.

Chardonnay Not quite up to speed of pvs. **00** more angular, insubstantial. Not for ageing. 13.8% alc.

Lagoon Rosé ☻ Fresh, not oversweet **00**. Gulpable strawberries and plums in med-bodied, flamingo-pink blend cinsaut, chenin. Instant consumer hit in see-through 1 000 ml lipped bottle.

Flamingo Bay range

Cinsaut-Cabernet Sauvignon ☻ Cleverly made swig; easy but not simple **01**; designed for now-drinking but could go 18-24 mths. Watch the 13.9%. **Chenin Blanc-Sauvignon Blanc** ☻ Charming no-worries quaff. Lemonade and guavas in zesty, low-priced **01**. — *DH*

Daschbosch see Louwshoek-Voorsorg
David Frost see Frost Vineyards
DC Wines see Darling Cellars

Deetlefs Estate

*Worcester (see Worcester map) • Tasting & sales Mon-Fri 8.30-4.30 • Traditional 'lapa' entertainment area for functions • Owner/winemaker Kobus Deetlefs • Cellar manager Johan Lotz (since 2000) • PO Box 36 Rawsonville 6845 • **Tel (023) 349-1260** • Fax (023) 349-1951 • E-mail deetlefs@wine.co.za • Website www.wine.co.za/deetlefs*

These personality-packed wines, released under the estate's label since 1997, have been well received in export markets from the US to Europe and the East. Sixth generation winemaker Kobus Deetlefs has been focusing on semillon (the 50 year old bushvines on his Du Toitskloof farm are his pride and passion). He reports: "Our emphasis is paying dividends worldwide." Mouthfeel is the mantra of this thoughtful and vital young man who believes: "You drink a wine, you don't sniff it". Coming soon, wines for vegans and vegetarians (polished with specially selected fining agents), the estate's first MCC sparkling, the first malbec rows and a maiden Merlot (for a sneak preview, see below). A portion of sales from all Deetlefs wines are donated to the International Campaign to Ban Land Mines.

✵**Pinotage** Pvs **98** SAYWS reserve champ, flew BA Business Class. Current **99** growing in bottle, initial tight tannins softening, revealing ripe red-berry concentration, suggestion of fruit sweetness, could go few more yrs. 50% oak. SAYWS gold. **00** (sample), like all these 00s, distinct improvement. Watch this space ...

✵**Semillon 00**, tasted as sample for pvs ed, still quite spry; good, light honey veneer to ripe, sweet peach/apricot tones and tangy lemon/herb. Finishes briskly with suggestion of smoky vanilla. Combo new Australian clones, ±50 yr old bushvines. 50% barrelled; 8 mths on lees. 13,2% alc. **99** growing in bottle, turning viscous. SAYWS gold.

✵**Chardonnay** Full leesy style, supple and full-flavoured. **99** ⁂ ready and should hold another yr/2. Portion barrel-aged, remainder sur lie in tank. 13,5% alc. **00** distinct improvement. Delicious lime-lees platform stacked with peaches, lemons, spicy oak. Balanced, already drinkable; should hold 3-4 yrs.

✵**Chenin Blanc** Full-bodied, serious dry chenin, unwooded, 90 days sur lie for creamier mouthfeel. **99** ⁂ acidity beginning to taper, suggest drink up. **00** similar vinification but immediately more striking; nice leesy feel, apple, lemon finish; balanced. 13% alc.

Stonecross Pinotage ☻ ⁂ Modern, juicy style, lightly oaked to showcase generous sweet plummy fruit. **01** also with banana bounce and lively fruit tannins, preventing flab. Drink within 3 yrs. 13% alc.

Merlot First crop **00** not released. Taste from **01** barrel (unrated) shows mouth-expanding cherry-plum flavour, massive tannins with lots of sweet fruit behind; promising. 6 mths oak. 13.5% alc. **Shiraz** ⁂ Light-toned, sweet fruited, supple style. Maiden **00** aromatically leathery, heathery. Ready, could go ±5 yrs. 40% casked. **01** preview step up in fruit; almost fruit-cordial character mid-palate. Could crack✵ on release. 14% alc. **Sauvignon Blanc** ⁂ Differential picking results in spread of green-to-ripe flavours; **00** full-bodied (13.2% alc), tasty. **Weisser Riesling** NEW ⁂ Unusual sweet spice/dry herb character; off-dry with bright fruit acid, light terpenes in **01** background. Deserves 18-24 mths to develop. 2 500 cases. **Philippus Petrus Deetlefs Muscat d'Alexandrie** Striking, modern packaging for a venerable oak-aged fortified dessert, designed to showcase ageability of hanepoot. Occasional label: first is **74**, released end 2000; next will be 2024! Highly individual style; for more specialised palates. Unrated. R165/bottle ex farm. 2 000 bottles, 375 ml. — *DH*

De Forellen see Lanzerac Farm & Cellar

De Heuvel Estate

Tulbagh (see Tulbagh map) • Tasting, sales & cellar tours Mon-Fri 9.30-12.30 1.30-5 Sat 10-1 • Olive oil/olive products produced/sold ex-cellar • Facilities for children • Proclaimed conservation area • Owners Leonardo Antonio Bianco & Sons • Winemaker Antonio Bianco, with Mark Carmichael-Greene • Viticulturist Craig Bianco • Viticultural consultant Paul Wallace • Vineyards 15 ha • Production up to 70 tons 4 500 cases (for 2001) 100% red • PO Box 103 Tulbagh 6820 • ***Tel (023) 231-0350*** *• Fax (023) 231-0938 • E-mail bianco@lando.co.za*

The extended Bianco family rustles up those Mediterranean staples – red wine and olive oil – on their 45 hectare estate in the secluded Tulbagh valley. Deep family ties that exert a pull from hilly Piedmont are made tangible in the distinctive European styling of their *rosso* range. Cabernet was first up, followed by a Shiraz, the first ever bottled in this area (a visiting French winemaker snapped some up for a blind tasting back home. "At least he was impressed," chuckles modest Toni Bianco, who is "not unpleased" with their first attempt). Next up was local hero Pinotage, also getting a touch of old world treatment. Consultant Paul Wallace now adds expert viticultural advice. After a foray to gauge the international market, Bianco reports their wines were very well received, particularly in Germany, where he found an open-minded attitude towards trying new wines.

Bianco range

★**Cabernet Sauvignon** Individual, aromatic style with loads of personality. Latest **00** with unheralded strong tannic framework; exotic lantana and herbs bouquet. Bottle-age 2-3 yrs, drink up to 10. ±13% alc. 1 600 cases. Yr oak, mostly Fr. Total contrast to soft, plump, **99** succulent on release.

★**Shiraz** NEW Another big Bianco rosso (13.5% alc); **00**'s tannins somewhat toned down by sweet fruit. Plummy/savoury qualities should complement game and hearty beef casseroles. Start drinking in 3-4 yrs. Yr Fr oak. 300 cases.

Pinotage NEW ★ Long-haul **00** sweet fruited, aromatic; underpinned by variety's socking tannins. Cellar or serve with osso bucco. Fr oak. 13% alc. — *DH*

De Hoopen NEW

Napier • Tasting/sales at Vindigo Wine & Décor Co, Napier. Mon-Thu 9.30-5.30 Fri 9.30-6.30 Sat & Sun 9.30-4.30 • Fee R10 for 3 different wine tastings plus De Hoopen tasting glass • Owners Nick Yell & Joe Toweel • Production 100 cases • 108 Sarel Cilliers Street Napier 7270 • ***Tel (028) 423-3069*** *• Fax (028) 423-3070 • E-mail vindigo@isat.co.za*

Beaumont's beefy Niels Verburg makes these 100 cases for far-flung wine-mates Joe Toweel, anchored in Gauteng, and thirtysomething Nick Yell, honourably self-discharged from a "pretty successful career in advertising and marketing" and now whooping it up in postcardy Napier. After scouring the Elgin/Walker Bay wineries for a house brand for their new wineshop-cum-collectibles gallery (as well as selected restaurants and stockists), the Yells collared Verburg to style the Special Reserve below to their easy/early drinking specs.

★**Pinotage Special Reserve** Serious, well endowed pinotage in the Beaumont mould; mouthfilling, smoky fruitcake bits and upfront oak tannins, which suggest **00** best with strapping food now or bottle-aged yr/2 for greater pleasure (and more stars). 13% alc. — *DH*

Dekkersvlei see Mellasat

Delaire Winery

Stellenbosch (see Stellenbosch map) • Tasting & sales Mon-Sun 10-5 Tasting fee R12 p/p plus R12 glass deposit which is refundable • Cellar tours by appointment • The Green Door Restaurant (see Eat-out section); picnics Oct-Apr (booking essential) • Two self-catering mountain lodges • Views • Owner Agrifarm International (Pty) Ltd, headed by Masoud Alikhani • Winemaker/marketing Bruwer Raats (since 1997) • Vineyard manager Jaco van der Westhuizen (since 1997) • Consulting viticulturist Paul Wallace (VineWise) • Production 150 tons 10 000 cases 60 % red 40% white • PO Box 3058 Stellenbosch 7602 • ***Tel (021) 885-1756*** *• Fax (021) 885-1270 • E-mail delaire@iafrica.com • Website www.delairewinery.co.za*

This lofty winery's name may mean 'in the sky' but rock-solid Bruwer Raats' winemaker's boots are firmly planted in these high-altitude soils. An enthusiastic proponent of single-vineyard wines, he's long been isolating blocks with premium potential. To prove his head isn't in the clouds, the maiden Botmaskop cabernet (under a label reserved for peak vintages from vineyards on the slopes of Botmas Peak) and Merlot have been scaling the heights, justification enough for this single-mindedness. He's keyed up about their first cabernet franc coming on line, sensing potential for another single-site release. "I think it's a variety that can consistently produce top quality in the Cape," says Raats (and several others). A marketing jamboree to Korea and Japan saw orders waiting in the cellar when Raats returned (though the Merlot and Botmaskop are currently the most expensive SA wines in Japan), a visit to New York added two wine stores in the upmarket Hamptons to their client base, and Disney's African-themed Animal Kingdom selected the entire range.

✵**Botmaskop** Explosive statement wine reserved for exceptional years; after the mountain peak behind the farm. First was **98**, 100% cab, black, oozing sweet fruit, dense palate packed with savoury spice and blackcurrant. Huge mouthful shored up with stacked tannins, classic dry persistence. Russian, Am oak, 60% new. (No **99**.) **00**, released July 02, again all cab, similar; aged mainly Fr oak (80%), remainder Russian/Am.

✵**Merlot** Delaire's flagship red, notable for its exuberance and limit-nudging price. Latest **00** evokes massive style set by pvs **98**, with striking spearmint/mocha flavours, bracing acidity adding rousing freshness to ripe-tannin base. Initially austere and inaccessible, demands (and will richly reward) patience – 10 yrs min. **97** VG. (No **99**; blended in Cab-Merlot below). Grapes from single site with easterly aspect, shielded by trees, only 4 hrs daily sun in height of summer. 18 mths new oak. 13,5% alc.

✵**Cabernet Sauvignon-Merlot** Returns to form after dip in difficult **99** ✵, admired by double-gold awarding Michelangelo judges. **00** with splash cab f for final 67:29:4 ratio; ripe berries deliciously embroidered by spectrum of oaks: spice from Russian (5%), oak, vanilla, toast from Am (10%), choc ex Fr. **98** SAA. **97** VG, SAA.

✵**Chardonnay** Rather deliciously settled into critically-acclaimed broad butterscotchy style with, in latest **00**, toasted nuts nuance to apple/tropical tones and vanilla. 20% unoaked for freshness; rest 9 mths Fr casks (mixed age). **99** butteriness cut by citric tang, gravelly finish. **98** Michelangelo gold, in same mould, with fresh-picked peaches-and-pears core, vanilla pod and malty/caramel palate. **97** *Wine* ✵.

✵**Chardonnay Unwooded** NEW ★ Bruwer Raats' fruit focus gets ultimate expression in **01**, concentration of sweet fruit, lively acids for fresh, clean tastes. Some appley suggestions from 6 mths lees-ageing.

✵**Sauvignon Blanc Barrel-Matured** Toast and buttery wood flavours combine harmoniously with gooseberry, asparagus, grapefruit fruit in **00**; powerful cool-climate acidity (bushvines among highest in Stbosch at ±500 m) makes this a food wine, compared to solo-sippable **99**, with gooseberry, thatchy grass flavours sharing stage with wood. These ±50% Fr oak, 3 mths.

✵**Sauvignon Blanc** Unwooded version; graduated power from differentially harvested parcels all showing their wares. **01** ✵ flavour spectrum ranges from grassy lemon and lime to honey-melon and kiwi. Complex, intellectual wine for aficionados, deserving time to mature 2/3 yrs. Less tropical than **99**, with intense 'sweet-ripe gooseberry. **98** not as big, WOM selection.

Chenin Blanc ⁂ Easy-quaffing **01** pear-drops and grapefruit bouquet. Bought-in fruit ex Kuils River. Discontinued: Green Door range. Pvs included: **Merlot Alternative** (**99** ✵), **Sauvignon Blanc** (**99** ✵), **Grand Vin Blanc** (**00** ⁂), **Chenin Blanc** (**00** ⁂), **Weisser Riesling** (**00** ⁂), **Bubbly** ⁂ **NV** (99). — *NP*

De Leuwen Jagt see Seidelberg

Delheim

Stellenbosch (see Stellenbosch map) • Tasting & sales Mon-Fri 9-5 Sat 9-3 Sun 11-3.30 (Oct-Apr) Tasting fee R15 • Closed 1 Jan, Good Fri, Easter Sun, 25 Dec • Cellar tours Mon-Fri 10.30 & 2.30 Sat 10.30 • Formal tastings for groups of 15-50 in vat cellar by appointment • Delheim Garden Restaurant Mon-Sun 12.00-2.30 (Oct-Apr) Tel (021) 882-2297 • Owners Hans Hoheisen & MH 'Spatz' Sperling • Winemaker Conrad Vlok (since Aug 2000) • Viticulturist Victor Sperling (since 1993) • Vineyards 120 ha • Production 700 tons 60 000 cases 60% red 40% white • PO Box 10 Koelenhof 7605 • ***Tel (021) 882-2033*** *• Fax (021) 882-2036 • E-mail delheim@delheim.com • Website www.delheim.com*

It's 30 years since Spatz Sperling (and a handful of other progressive wine producers) founded the Stellenbosch Wine Route, changing the pace of the SA wine industry forever. Undimmed, the ebullient 'Duke of Delheim' continues his quest to spread the wine message – most recently as guest on the fabled QE 2, on the 50th anniversary of Sperling's arrival in SA on the Winchester Castle. Back home, Delheim's tasting area and farm-restaurant (first of its kind in the area) are getting a bright new look for the annual influx of summer visitors. The gewürztraminer vineyard destroyed by fire two years ago has been repopulated with sauvignon and the area of fynbos that was burnt has been re-established. With daughter Nora (Thiel) continuing the tradition as spinner of the magical marketing web ("The Sperling family is still 100% involved in making the Delheim experience one to remember," she assures), focused brother Victor Sperling as general manager and viticulturist, and their artistic mother Vera, a universal energising presence, this wine business – more than ever – is a family affair.

✵**Grand Reserve** Long-time flagship shows results of attention to vyd management, selective picking. Rises to fresh heights in **98** ✵✵, again mainly cab, splash (6%) merlot from the Vera Cruz vyds. Dark garnet shards introduce mustard-seeds bouquet and round, full palate with beautifully expressive and vinous fruit. Oak (18 mths small Fr, 50% new) balanced by fruit ripeness. Same density as **97**, whose fruitiness showed an almost essencey quality. *Wine* ✵. These for long keeping (some still impress after 15 yrs). **96** 92 points in UK *Wine*.

✵**Cabernet Sauvignon** ✓ Continues impressive run of fine value, quality. Latest **00** riper, fuller than pvs, but presently shy, gripping. Cassis perfumes should unfurl within yr, continue improving for min 10. **99** with 10% merlot softening, more overtly oaked, reflecting 9 mths Fr barrique ageing. Also structured for the long haul. Standout **98** VVG, Michelangelo gold, *Wine* ✵.

✵**Merlot** Returns to plusher mode with **00** (barrel sample) after pvs meander along slimmer, leafy lanes. Choc-plum aromas and minty hints; though med-bodied, feels more substantial thanks to generously ripe fruit. **99** ☆ revisited mid-01, more sinuous than pvsly, some white-pepper whiffs from yr Fr oak. Drier than gushingly flavoursome **98** VG.

☆**Pinotage** Touch of acetone in **00** bouquet, raspberries and sweetness from ripe fruit. Balanced Am (33%), Fr (66%) oak, 11 mths. Keep a few yrs. Fatter than **99**, textbook example of new bright-fruited SA style. **98** harking back to older modes (but liked by ABSA Top Ten, Veritas judges).

☆**Shiraz** ✓ **00** among biggest of the recent vintages (14%+ alc), with deep-piled flavours to match. Aniseed, meat, gamut of black berries in full, chewy package with firm tannins; these should relax with extra yr in bottle, drink for further 5 yrs min. Returns to style of multi-gonged **98** ☆, WOM selection. Both richer than taut-on-release **99** with Rhonish characters needing time to unpack.

☆**Rhine Riesling Natural Sweet** ✓ **00**, yr on, showing gilded lights, hair-dressing-salon bouquet and honeyed pineapples tastes. 85 g/ℓ sugar tastes smoothly luscious, rather than sweet. Excellent value-for-money dessert with long life ahead. Good notch above maiden **99** ☆.

☆**Chardonnay 00** commercial style, well made, not over-wooded. Melange of fruit in palate, protracted limey finish. **99** ☆ with dash chenin, similarly sensitively oaked (this the style since grapefruity **98**). **01** not ready for tasting.

☆**Sauvignon Blanc 01** raises the bar for variety at this property in cooler yr. Fresh, crisp, ripe Cape gooseberry fruit plumps the acidity for racy but not bracing conclusion. Leap up from **00** ☆ with delicate pear/floral whiffs, hints of green pea.

☆**Edelspatz Noble Late Harvest** A Cape dessert institution. **00** lusciously sweet but elegant chenin (±120 g/ℓ) sugar); revisited mid-01 oozes honey-melon and a bright citrus tang, botrytis adds opulent touch. **98** ☆ in similar style, but from riesling, bukettraube.

Pinotage Rosé ☻ ☆ Light and flavoursome **01**, semi-dry (pvs was sweeter) fragrant Blackpool-rock tones, vibey pink shades.

Chenin Blanc ☆ **01** pear-drop bouquet expands to full, fruity palate with slightly sharp finish. Inexpensive poolside quaff. **Pinot Blanc Brut** ☆ **00** light (11.5% alc), energetic charmat fizz; dry, fruity though not overly complex. Also available, untasted for this ed: **Dry Red** (Pvs **00** ☆), **Heerenwijn** (**NV** ☆), **Goldspatz Stein** (**00** ☆), **Spatzendreck Late Harvest** (**00** ☆).

Vera Cruz Estate range

These warmer-climate vineyards, long the source of some of Delheim's top wines, now show their class less anonymously. Always a cellarmaster's selection, the range may vary from vintage to vintage.

☆**Shiraz** Mid-01 found these maturing into showstoppers. **99** gets fireworks going with strikingly deep ruby hues; heady aromatic bouquet swirls into palate with nuances of spice, pepper and game. Wonderfully satisfying finish, with echoes of exquisitely judged oak (13 mths Fr). Already captivating, will continue to seduce well into the next decade. Michelangelo double-gold. Maiden **98**, held back for extended bottle ageing at the cellar; emerges with triumphant ☆ rating. Stunning complexity, concentration of exotically savoury fruit. Hickory-smoked ham, coffee, breakfast bacon plus fabulous spices. Chewy but ripe tannins. 15 mths Fr oak, brilliantly attuned to the fruit. IWSC gold.

☆**Pinotage 98** back-tasted for this ed has evolved a singular bouquet of dill, cherries and woodsmoke. Vanilla nuances, too, from Am oak (19 mths). Typical sweetish pinotage entry, sappy fruit; supple impression aided by sturdy alc, lowish acid, sweetness in finish (13,7% alc, 5,4 g/ℓ acid, 3,2 g/ℓ sugar). — *NP*

Dellrust Wines

*Stellenbosch (see Stellenbosch map) • Tasting & sales Mon-Fri 8-5 Tasting R5 for 6 wines R8 for whole range • Cellar tours during tasting hours by appointment • Play area for children • Tourgroups by arrangement • Walks by arrangement • Owner/winemaker Albert Bredell • Viticulturist Gerjo Ben van der Merwe (since 1996) • Vineyards 100 ha • Production 800-900 tons (80 tons own label) 65% red 35% white • PO Box 5666 Helderberg 7135 • **Tel (021) 842-2752** • Fax (021) 842-2456 • E-mail dellrust@cybertrade.co.za • Website www.dellrust.co.za*

It seems the Bredell family just can't help making a splash wherever they surface in the wine world. After many years of anonymity supplying grapes to KWV, Albert Bredell surprised the experts by launching his own label with a range of highly individual wines that have won immediate friends. A welcome change from commercialised touristy wineries, this simple, rustic farm in Firgrove, with its cafe under the trees, run by Elmarie Bredell, is a delight to visit. Children are very welcome, the atmosphere is relaxed and informal, the fare home-made and tasty.

Merlot Swashbuckling style packed with mouthfilling fruit. New **00** with extra earth/eucalyptus suggestion, dark-choc finish. Tannins tight still, give yr/2 to become more supple. 14 mths Fr casks, some new. 13,5% alc. 1 200 cases. **99** SAYWS gold.

Merlot-Pinotage-Shiraz NEW Cellar's flagship, a well thought-out blend which, Albert Bredell correctly notes, "contains all the characters expected from the various varieties". **00** wildflower perfume over fresh earth, mouthcoating/filling (13.5% alc) sweet-sour plums, smoky hints and white pepper sprinkle. Bit of choc to chew on. Selection from 3 vyds, Fr small-oaked, 14 mths. 1 200 cases.

Vintage Port NEW ✓ Port-making must be in the Bredell genes (Albert Bredell's brother Anton a celebrated exponent of the style). 100% tinta's thumbprint stewed-plum, prune aromas in delicious **00** (sample tasted, rating provisional); also snatches cured bacon and contrasting cocoa in farewell. Classically correct formula (19% alc, 94 g/ℓ sugar, 18 mths oak) sets scene for fascinating development (Albert Bredell envisages peak around 2010. 200 cases.

Chenin Blanc ☻ **01** maintains slurpability of pvs. Sugar again tweaked to just off-dry to showcase generous unoaked fruit salad flavours. 13.5% alc. 1 100 cases. **Tinta Barocca-Cinsaut** ☻ Juicy braai-friendly style. **00** with sweetish, smoky fruit. Oak-staved/barrelled. Especially popular with foreign customers, reports Albert Bredell. 3 000 cases.

Pinotage Untasted. Pvs **99**. **Chardonnay** Untasted. Pvs **99**. **Sauvignon Blanc** **01** more subdued than pvs despite 14% power-alc (possibly sullen phase – variety notoriously fickle); some light mown-lawn tones. 1 100 cases. — *TM*

De Meye Wines

*Stellenbosch (see Stellenbosch map) • Tasting, sales & cellar tours by appointment Tel (021) 884-4131 • Owner Jan Myburgh Family Trust • Winemaker Marcus Milner (since 1999) • Vineyard manager Philip Myburgh • Vineyards 60 ha • Production 12 000 cases 90% red 10% white • PO Box 20 Muldersvlei 7607 • **Tel (021) 884-4131** • Fax (021) 884-4154 • E-mail demeye@cybertrade.co.za*

Cycling-mad Marcus Milner knows a thing or two about balance (with remarkable poise, he famously proposed to wife Cathy atop the last murderous hill of the Argus Cycle Tour), so it's entirely fitting that the new flagship of this range is a red named Trutina, a Latin word associated with equilibrium and symmetry. "The whole essence of a blend is balance," reflects Milner, who in 1999 pedalled over the hill from Warwick to join Jan and Philip Myburgh (the latter an old school friend) on this lovely family farm (named after a river in Holland, origin of the first Myburghs to emigrate to the Cape). Fresh from a star turn at the Wine of the Month Club selections – their 2000 Chardonnay was judged best out of 90 – they've decided to further focus their energies by switching from regular sales/tasting hours to visits by appointment. Vinophiles remain assured of a warm welcome.

✵**Cabernet Sauvignon 99** very attractive now, and with structure of tannin/acid to develop good few years. Honest varietal character, ripe but not pushy. Balanced, with 16 mths integrated Fr oak. 13% alc. 2 000 cases. More presence than **98** ✯, easy, savoury, most drinkable but lower-keyed.

✵**Shiraz 00** still youthfully shy, but clearly fleshy and ripe, with firm tannic structure, and suggestive of the smoked meat, raspberries and earthiness of **99** – though **00**'s alc level more massive at 13.9%. From 20 yr old vines, 10 mths Fr oak. 2 200 cases.

✵**Trutina** NEW Opaquely dark **00** still holding back, but this cab-shiraz blend shows exciting promise. Ripe, rich and powerful (13.8 alc), but an authority deriving from fine-textured tannins and good balance – and balance is what the name means in Latin. One to watch. 700 cases.

✵**Chardonnay 01** shows debut **00**, WOM Reserve, was no flash in the pan. Confident nutty, citrus aromas preface a powerful (14% alc), balanced, intense tasting experience, with integrated oak and long finish. Strangely like sampling a fine, very light brandy. 1 200 cases.

Pinotage ✯ Behind the bright, original label are old bushvines speaking in a rather restrained style, **00** only hinting at jammy fruitiness. Suggest keep and improve a few years. 6 mths Fr barriques. 2 000 cases. Debut **99** ✯ we characterised as 'a charming nostalgic quaff'. — *TJ*

Destiny see Ruitersvlei

De Toren

*Stellenbosch (see Stellenbosch map) • Tasting, sales & cellar tours by appointment. • Views • Owner Kleine Uitzicht Wines (Pty) Ltd/Emil den Dulk • Winemaker Albie Koch (since 1999) • Viticulturists Emil den Dulk, Albie Koch (since 1999) • Viticultural consultant Johan Pienaar (since 1994) • Vineyards 19.9 ha • Production 100 tons (60 tons 3 100 cases own label) 100% red • PO Box 48 Vlottenburg 7604 • **Tel (021) 881-3119** • Fax (021) 881-3335 • E-mail info@de-toren.com • Website www.de-toren.com*

In a dream debut, the bordeaux blend from this little property in the Polkadraai Hills of Stellenbosch registered 90 points on kingmaker Robert Parker's rating scale – "a world-first for a maiden wine from anywhere", exult entrepreneur-turned-vintner Emil den Dulk and switched-onto-wine wife Sonette. Next, Virgin Wines UK flew into raptures: "It's … a brilliant blend of new world energy and old world panache." Now the den Dulks are taking their prodigy to France (along with hand-harvested vineyard snails for the Gallic gourmet trade – enough to make a Frenchman weep into his beret). Back home, with phase two of the gravity-fed winery complete, it boasts a "V I P tasting centre" and an underground cellar where the 2001 vintage ("best season for quality wines in the past ten years", raves Albie Koch) waits to spring.

✵**Fusion V** Suave, sleek **00** tasted prior to fining, bottling; but remarkably approachable, tasty already; very ripe jammy fruit lurking in opaquely dark, heavily extracted and dense texture. Good acidity, ripe soft tannins handle yr in oak well – 60% new; 10% of older wood is Am. Likely to appeal to US guru Robert Parker, as did similarly styled **99** (also gold on IWSC). 5 bdx varieties involved (hence name): cab, merlot, malbec, cab f, petit verdot (60/13/13/10/4). 13.5% alc. — *TJ*

De Trafford Wines 

Stellenbosch (See Stellenbosch map) • Tasting, sales, cellar tours Fri & Sat 10-1, otherwise by appointment • Owner/winemaker David Trafford • Vineyard manager Mavis Trafford • Production 60 tons 3 000 cases 80% red 20% white • PO Box 495 Stellenbosch 7599 • ***Tel (021) 880-1611*** *• Fax (021) 880-1611*

Architect-turned-winemaker David Trafford gained his winemaking experience in France, so he and wife Rita recall last year's visit to the Loire Valley (two tickets the prize for wining the 2000 Chenin Challenge) as very special, a second honeymoon spent sipping wines and learning from dedicated, forthcoming vignerons. Back home at the top of the long and winding road that leads to the below-ground *cave* (a study in simplicity that suits his hand-crafted approach) on Mont Fleur farm, in the saddle between the Stellenbosch and Helderberg mountains, they seem to be on a bit of a roll with shiraz: the 98 was rated top in the southern hemisphere in an extensive tasting by the French magazine *GaultMillau* ("It was a joy to see nearby Stellenzicht come in second!" Trafford laughs; "together we really beat the Aussies!") and they participated in their first CWG Auction, where Trafford was "astounded" at the price the 99 Shiraz fetched (R200 a bottle). Recently contracted Aidan Morton is managing the vineyards, including the small parcels from which they buy grapes, in his characteristic hands-on style.

✮**Cabernet Sauvignon** Cab at its regal best; always with hand-crafted feel allowed by boutique quantities – 950 cases only of **00** (from barrel), massively concentrated, ripe with densely layered tannins, suitably lavish oaking; needs lots of patience but worth it. **99** fine cab fragrance/flavours, authoritative tannins; sleek, intense. Indisputably in Cape's top echelon. Low-yield Stbosch vyds, 50/50 bought in/home grown. A collectible stayer – probably beyond 2010. **97** ✮ Air France plaudit. Oaked ±20 mths, ±50% new barrels, tiny portion Am oak. **00** sample from 3 yr old Keerweder vyd, 100 cases to be bottled separately, more black/red fruit fragrance, lighter texture (though higher alc 15.3% vs 14.8%), lively dryness.

✮**Merlot** Ageworthy example, worth of standalone status in range. **00** notch up on intense, deep **99**; latest more sultry, introverted though beautifully built to hide even lofty 14.5% alc. Extremely rich, deep bitter-choc flavours carefully cloaked in 18 mths oak seasoning (40% new, 5% Am); ripe chunky tannins; already smoothly drinkable, needs 5-7 yrs to reach impressive potential. 850 cases.

✮**Pinot Noir** Nothing contrived about David T's pinots (nor, in fact, any of his wines) **00**, for CWG Auction, given carte blanche to choose own evolution, hence gorgeous wild cherry, mushroom, spicy leafy flamboyance; matching strong ruby lights. Soft, sweet-fruited flesh, fine yielding tannin; impressive presence from fully effective 14.3% alc. Mix young Burgundy clones, old Swiss BK5. 16 mths Fr oak, 33% new. Unfined/unfiltered. 65 cases only. **99** leap forward on pvs. Delicious, as are all these, fragrant, softly mouthcoating. Pvs, specially **96**, firm, less yielding.

✮**Shiraz** Hard to believe giant **00** (Barossa of the Cape?), tasted just pre-bottling, tips scales at 15.5% alc – you'd never guess on tasting. Ripeness (immediately evident in multi-hued brilliance) balanced by wonderful fresh intensity. Perfectly proportioned, though full of 'grunt'; melted dark-choc with spicy, cedary oak (which Cape rather than Barossa); abundant but uninhibiting tannin. Needs plenty time to settle. 120 cases. **99** (15.3% alc) exclusively for CWG auction. Evolving, with clear blackberry, clean leather fragrance; richly textured, still youthfully firm. 70 cases. These ex young home vyds; oak-matured, portion new Fr/Am, 16-19 mths, malo in cask. First **98** topped *Wine*'s tasting of Cape shiraz.

✮**Elevation 393** (Reserve in pvs ed – allusion to height above sea level of architect David T's home) Most miserly, in terms of quantity, of already bijoux range:

mere 94 cases of **99** (magnums only); best barrels, exclusively ex vyds surrounding Trafford's home. Closed down a bit since last yr; more savoury, cedary spice elements overtaken by minerally tautness; greater tannin grip. This temporary – quite usual – phase in young, ageworthy red. Plentiful ripe fruit will wake in own time (later rather than sooner, in view of large-format bottle). 50% cab, balance equal merlot, shiraz. 14.2% alc. 20 mths Fr oak, 85% new. Unfined, so may throw a sediment.

De Trafford Chenin Blanc 00 light-yrs away from traditional Cape chenin, though doesn't pretend to be Loire either; is its own style: emphatically ripe (due to partial natural yeast fermentation?), distinctively individual. Oakspice and deep, dried-honeysuckle scents; uncompromisingly dry, bold, firm; yet amazingly delicate, too, though still some way off full bloom. Signature style also achieved through low yields (5-7 t/ha), laudably non-interventionist cellar regimen. 8 mths oak, 30% new, mostly Am; partial malo. 13.8% alc. 330 cases. **99** topped *Wine*'s Chenin Challenge though we, like David T, prefer **00**, agree about when to drink (now to 03). 2 different blocks, high/lower Helderberg slopes.

Keermont Chenin Blanc (Keerweder Chenin Blanc in pvs ed) Single 28 yr old Helderberg vyd, distinctly different from above (though also forms part of that blend). **00** vivid spicy citrus, herbal tang, repeated at end. Rich, fluid feel, lively piquant interjections, with Trafford's thumbprint firm dryness. Barrelling, natural yeast treatment as above. 13.3% alc. 150 cases.

Vin De Paille Cape pioneer of time-consuming, barely economical, magical chenin dessert: hand picked bunches, individually laid out on racks, air-dried 3 wks for supercharged concentration. Latest **00** contains experimental 15% chardonnay (plus a barrel of **99**, which didn't finish fermenting in time for that bottling. Unaided, these can ferment up to yr!), which variety also used in Jura, where similar style produced. Among sweetest at 235 g/ℓ sugar, giving puppy-fat feel to powerful kumquat marmalade flavours. Will settle, slim down (and probably regain extra half-star); also gain more sleek tension from racy 7.4 g/ℓ acid. **99** *Wine* drier, finer, sleeker; **98** with similar sugar to **00**, Air France plaudit. Oaked, mostly new, 50/50 Fr/Am. 209 cases of 500 ml. — *AL*

De Villiers Wines

Paarl (see Paarl map) • Tasting Mon-Fri 9-5 • Sales Mon-Fri 8-5 Sat 9-1 • BYO picnic • Views • Owner/viticulturist Villiers de Villiers • Winemaker Dominique Waso (since 1999) • Vineyards 75 ha • Production 30 000 cases 60% red 40% white • PO Box 714 Noorder-Paarl 7623 • ***Tel (021) 863-8480*** *• Fax (021) 863-8755 • E-mail devwines@mweb.co.za*

As Paarl Mountain descends from its granite heights it passes through the seldom-mentioned Vale of Nantes, and if you haven't discovered its secluded charms then Villiers de Villiers, owner of this historic family farm, will show you around. Obvious attraction is the renovated and open-for-tasting/sales Cape Dutch homestead with its original rietdak, inviting fireplace and warm yellowwood fittings (the tasting counter is made from original pieces found in the house). But it's from the stoep that the "secret of Nantes" is revealed: an intoxicating view to savour while you taste the wines or linger over a BYO picnic.

Cabernet Sauvignon ✓ Step up from **00** lightish easy drinker to **01** (sample); latest more serious, tannic, complex; structure (including muscle-bound 14% alc) for some development. 1 000 cases (× 6, as are all these).

Cabernet Franc ✓ Deep colours announce serious intent in **01** (sample), flagship of this range with liquorice fragrance, dry but malleable tannins. Balanced; potential for 3-4 yrs' ageing. 1 000 cases.

Merlot ☻ ⁑ **99** has mellowed into lovely gentle quaff; pretty violet scents, plummy tastes. 1 000 cases.

Shiraz ⁂ **01** preview not as dramatic as red stablemates above, but far from charmless; ample tannin, bit of juice, med-bodied. Give yr/2 to meld. 13.5% alc. 1 000 cases. **Pinotage** ★ **99** not an easy drink mid-01; fairly tannic, savoury, sweet-sour finishing. **Cabernet Franc-Merlot Reserve** ⁂ These invariably flavoursome, satisfying reds for early/early enjoyment. Current **99** med-bodied; nice minerally oak. **Chardonnay** ⁑ Latest **01** (fruit ex Bonnievale) not as exciting as some pvs; sweet tropical aromas, dry finish. 13% alc. 1 000 cases. **Paarl Riesling 00**, from crouchen blanc, past best. Also available, not ready for tasting: **Blanc de Noir**, **Sauvignon Blanc**. — *DH*

Devonair

Stellenbosch • Tasting by arrangement • Owners Bernie & Zolia Rumble • Consulting winemaker Danie Steytler (Kaapzicht, since 1999) • Viticulturist Manus Lotter (since 1997) • Vineyards 3.5 ha • Production 22 tons ± 900 cases own label 100% red • PO Box 148 Koelenhof 7605 • ***Tel (021) 882-2353*** *• Fax (021) 981-4517 • E-mail rumble@icon.co.za*

BRICK making to vintning is the leap of faith being made by Bernie and Zolia Rumble, proud owners of 3,5 hectares of cabernet in Stellenbosch's scenically endowed Devon Valley. Quantum-leaping with the vinously wide-eyed couple are experienced Danie Steytler, of Kaapzicht repute, and walking vine-handbook Manus Lotter. All are delighted with the first 900 cases, made in 2000 with extra help from "the farmers and community around us who are generous with their support and advice". Conceding that the learning curve is extremely steep, the sporty Rumbles aren't certain who most influenced their budding wine venture: "Ask us next year when we know what we don't know now!"

Cabernet Sauvignon ⁂ Expansive **00**, very generous 14.3% alc not out of kilter with ripe brambly fruit. Still-tight tannins, lengthy flavours augur well for longer-term cellaring. — *NP*

Devon Hill

Stellenbosch (see Stellenbosch map) • Tasting & Cellar tours Mon-Fri 8-5 • Views • Winemaker Kosie Möller (since Feb 2001) • Viticulturists Johan Wiese • Vineyards 60 ha • Production 270 tons 30 000 cases own label 80% red, 20% white • PO Box 541 Stellenbosch 7599 • ***Tel (021) 865-2453*** *• Fax (021) 865-2444 • E-mail devhill@mweb.co.za*

IT may not have been a major consideration, but one perk of moving to this immaculate Swiss-owned property in Devon Valley is that Kosie Möller now has some of the best views in winedom (his old Paarl office overlooked a weighbridge). The much-medalled young winemaker was tapped by Devon Hill co-owner Jean Vogel to take over the running of the property after Möller's departure from KWV, where he'd cellar-mastered (and globe-trotted) since 1993. He and his new partners (which include up-and-coming Paarl-based negociant house West Coast Vineyards) will be looking to infuse the ranges below with some flashbulb-popping Möller magic, and they seem to be off to a fine start. "The challenge is to make world-class wines in a more serious style," says the freshly enthused winemaker. With only noble varieties mountaineering 270 m up the Bottelary Hills, this cool property certainly gives him plenty to work with. See also West Coast Vineyards.

Devon Hill range

✪**Bluebird** NEW Intelligent, seamless pinotage-led blend, with cab f, merlot (40/30/30), yr Fr oak; **00** masterpiece of restrained understatement; whiffs cedar, cigarbox, earthy notes; mineral textures layered between raspberry, black cherry, hints cassis, mint, fine tannins beautifully integrated.

✪**Cabernet Sauvignon 00** shows gamey notes overlaying blackcurrant, raspberry, whiffs strawberry. Soft tannins, gentle textures; fat, almost sweet finish belies ageing potential. Yr Fr casks. 13,5% alc. 2 500 cases.

✪**Sauvignon Blanc** In Kosie Möller's hands **01** becomes a flamboyantly over-the-top statement of bulging tropical fruit, super-ripe gooseberry, peach, grapefruit, intoxicating honeysuckle and cantaloupe. 14,5% alc adds a headiness of a different sort. 2 000 cases.

Merlot ✫ Oak matured **00** light on fruit; some mulberry/baked apple sniffs; solid oak tannins dominate finish. 13,5% alc. 2 000 cases. **Pinotage** ✫✫ Slight Provencal feel to **00**'s raspberry/black cherry fragrance, light varnishy spice, mushroom/farmyard aromas. Plummy tannins for early quaffability, food cordiality. Fr oak-aged. 2 000 cases.

Devon View range NEW

✪**Pinotage** Precocious **01** impresses with sumptuous plum, loganberry aromas, textures of velvet and brocade; ends with bon-bon/Ribena sweetness. 3 000 cases.

Sauvignon Blanc ✫✫ **01** in Loire-like herbal style, green fig, grassy notes; crisp, food-friendly. **Cabernet Sauvignon** ✫ Oaked **00** shows mineral/earth tones, in keeping with austere tannins, lean gamey finish. 12% alc. 2 500 cases.

Bushman's Creek range NEW

✪**Shiraz** Larger-than-life Barossa style, **98** jam-packed with loganberry, raspberry fruit, coffee, caramel, intense black cherry flavours. 18 mths Fr/Am oak. 13,8% alc.

✪**Sauvignon Blanc 01** slightly downsized version of hugely tropical Devon Hill bottling; super-ripe pineapple, spanspek aromas; great amplitude of succulent gooseberry/peach salad flavours. 1 250 cases.

Cabernet Sauvignon ✫ Oaked **98** tight-fruited, lean; some cassis/eucalyptus notes; herbal/limey mouthfeel. **Merlot** ✫✫ Straightforward, accessible red; dense plum/mulberry notes make **98** quaffable yet ageworthy. Robust tannins cushioned with fruit sweetness, full but not fat finish. 18 mths Fr oak. 13,6% alc. **Pinotage** ✫✫ Med-full bodied **98** fragrant compote Xmas pudding, caramel, cloves, cassia; dense leafy tannins mingle with southern French gaminess. Oaked. **Cabernet Sauvignon-Merlot** ✫ Wooded **98** black-edged cerise hues, herbal/minty whiffs; leafy, austere mineral textures with elusive spices in tail. 13,3% alc. — *MF*

Devon View see Devon Hill above

De Wet Co-op

*Worcester (see Worcester map) • Tasting & sales Mon-Fri 8-5 Sat 9-12 Tasting fee 50c/wine • Cellar tours by appointment • Owners 60 members • Winemakers Piet le Roux (since 1995), André van Dyk (since 2000) • Vineyards 900 ha • Production 14 500 tons 94% white 6% red • PO Box 16 De Wet 6853 • **Tel (023) 349-2710** • Fax (023) 349-2762 (New contact no's from mid-2002 **Tel (023) 341-2710** Fax (023) 341-2762) • E-mail dewetwynkelder@mweb.co.za*

Piet le Roux and André van Dyk are spearheading this unpretentious winery's leap into red wine. While some hold back, anticipating an eventual upturn in demand for whites, these 60 growers are boosting their red crop from the present 6% to 16% of total by 2004. In the mean time they're focused on pinpointing the most promising red parcels and blocks of sauvignon within the 900 hectare vignoble. "And," they report, "though we have been forced by the bottle manufacturers to change from a [transparent] flint bottle to a green screwcap, our Petillant Fronté is still our best selling wine locally." Good news for not only the winery but also the national Heart Foundation, which applauds this light, low-alcohol spritz.

Red Muscadel 97 fortified dessert a standout; muscat intensity, honeysuckle, freesia fragrance. Follow-up **98** more workmanlike; some cherry, raisins in uncloying sweet palate.

Cabernet Sauvignon **99** improving in bottle; cassis and red/black cherries in gentle tannic embrace; fairly light tone despite robust 13,5%. Yr used casks. **Pinotage** NEW Instantly mature **98** soft, ready to drink. Liquorice/cherries in med-bodied, oaked palate. **Dry Red** Formulation changes every yr, but gulpability quotient remains high. Splash 99 blend joins 00 cab f/ruby cab in **00**, which has softened since last tasted. **Blanc de Noir** Striking orange-pink **00**, lively summer party semi-sweet from pinotage. 13% alc. **Chardonnay** Oak-chipped **00** too assertive for solo consumption; tame with (winemakers' suggestion) hearty seafood casseroles. 13% alc. **Clairette Blanche** Usually shows personality here (elsewhere bland). Apple fragrances in lightish-bodied **01**, bright clean dry finish. Screwtop. **Riesling** Always swiggably light, tasty. **01** some varietal (crouchen blanc) character; fruitily dry. **auvignon Blanc** NEW Gentle grassy tastes in uncomplicated, lightish **01**. **Bouquet Blanc** Off-dry picnic partner; **00** with spicy muscat aromas. Lightish-bodied white varietal miscellany. **Petillant Fronté** Lightly spritzy, extra-low alc (8,5%) **NV** charmer gallops out of the cellar. 100% muscat de f. **Special Late Harvest** **00** from chenin (pvs gewürz). Sampled mid-01, not its usual charming self. **Cuveé Brut** Fresh uncomplicated **NV** carbonated sparkler from sauvignon; lowish 11% alc. **Vin Doux** Lightish, soft, sweet-fruity **NV** freshened by acidity. **Hanepoot** Lighter, more fragrant version of the traditional fortified dessert; **01** for earlier drinking. 16.8% alc. **Ruby Port** **99** (different bottling to pvsly reviewed 99, which rated) lighter-style fireside warmer from touriga. ±18% alc, 95.5 g/ℓ sugar. — *CF*

De Wetshof Estate

Robertson (see Robertson map) • Tasting & sales Mon-Fri 8.30-4.30 Sat 9.30-12.30 • Cellar tours by appointment • Mountain/vineyard views • Owner Danie de Wet • Winemaker Danie de Wet with Willie Stofberg • Viticulturist George Thom (since 1996) • Vineyards 140 ha • Production 1 800 tons • PO Box 31 Robertson 6705 • ***Tel (023) 615-1853/ 7*** *• Fax (023) 615-1915 • E-mail info@dewetshof.co.za • Website www.dewetshof.co.za*

This prestigious Robertson estate, with its chateau-like headquarters amid serried vines, has built its fine international reputation on white wine (genial giant Danie de Wet a Diners Club laureate for chardonnay). And though reds are on the agenda (and in barrels – the second small black-grape crop was taken in during 2001), the aim is to stay 95% white. In a further countertrend, they're planning to remain predominantly a chardonnay house, with roughly 60% of the 38 000 annual cases given to this grape. Encouragingly, demand for chardonnay is perking up, reveals the engaging Bennie Stipp, stalwart of De Wetshof's marketing team. "We've always done well in this category because of our quality." If that sounds like PR spin, there's the International World Quality Commitment Star Award, recently presented by Business Initiative Directions, to underline their credentials. They're keeping on a winning roll by working with Californian viticultural wizard Phil Freese to select and performance-tune suitable vineyard blocks for their various chardonnay styles. Meanwhile they're directing some of their seemingly boundless energy into developing a local niche for the internationally-established Danie de Wet range.

Danie de Wet Bateleur Chardonnay This estate's enduring flagship, always a personal Danie de Wet barrel selection – finesse, complexity the aims, which seldom better expressed than in latest **00** absolutely gorgeous; packed with marmalade and unusual whisky-like smoky flavours. Ripe-fruit concentration effortlessly absorbs strong vein of acidity (8.1 g/ℓ). 1 000 cases. **98** rich toasted nut, smoky citrus array. Delicate peach/apricot fragrances in well-oaked, classically dry palate. 8-10 mths mixed Fr cooperage. ±13% alc.

Chardonnay D'Honneur Bolder, more flamboyant understudy of Bateleur. **00** big but soft, with smoothing grain sugar. Fr barrel-fermented/aged. 1 300 cases. **99**, with chunky oak, lime-chalky zip, structured for keeping. Fr barrel fermented/aged 8-10 mths. Generous 14% alcs.

Finesse Chardonnay ✓ Historically most elegant of trio barrel fermented chardonnays, though latest **01** bigger, fuller than usual; direction hinted at in **00**, peach/apricot aromas suffuse cinnamon-spicy citrus palate; luscious, sweet-fruited flourish. **99** more demure. **98** SAA.

Bon Vallon Chardonnay ✓ Unwooded version, maiden **91** first in this style in SA. **98** first ever VVG in category, WOM selection; **99** leesy, powerful; **00** initially lower keyed. **01** chalky, thrillingly fresh and drinkable peach-lime combo. 14.5% alc. 10 000 cases.

Lesca Chardonnay NEW Stylish slimmed-down version of Bateleur. Barrel-fermented, briefly-aged **01** features house's pristine peach/apricot fruit; bright sweet-oak, lemon zesty finish. Tasted young, shows potential to develop into . 13.5% alc. 5 000 cases.

Danie de Wet Limestone Hill Chardonnay NEW Should convert many non-fans of the unwooded style with striking, showy **01**; deliciously chalky palate layered with citrus-orchard flavours; peach-almond whiffs to persistent sweet fruit, piquant apple-sour finish. 13.5% alc. 3 000 cases.

Danie de Wet Call of the African Eagle Chardonnay Reserve NEW **01** similar to Limestone Hill but bigger, barrique-fermented and briefly aged for more rounded, less challenging (and slightly less interesting) tone. Should age well. 14.4% alc. 15 000 cases.

Blanc Fumé Lightly wooded sauvignon with enthusiastic following; very good food style. **01** brisk limey/chalky fruit broadened by seamless oaking (portion casked). Usual bone-dry finish. 13,5% alc. 1 200 cases.

Rhine Riesling ✓ Among more convincing, individual examples in Cape, worthy of a little bottle ageing to show best. Off-dry **00** developing beautifully, acquiring ripe pineapple overtone; 5-7 yrs ahead. Latest **01** more tropical, knife-edge sugar/acid balance (7 g/ℓ, 2 g/ℓ); intense spicy lemon-lime bouquet, enduring finish. 1 000 cases.

Edeloes Gorgeous, full-blown botrytis dessert from riesling, with plausible claim to Cape premiership. IWSC gold medal/trophy for best NLH style, VG, *Wine* for stunning **98**. Topped by triumphant **00** , opulent crushed pineapple, wild-honey intensity checked by riveting nervous acidity. Luscious yet still wonderfully fresh, elegant despite intensity and sturdy weight of alc (13,9%). 11,5 g/ℓ acid, 129 g/ℓ sugar. Chic 50 cl flint bottle. 700 half-cases of 500 ml.

Danie de Wet Cape Muscadel NEW Excellent new-wave Cape fortified: refined, smartly packaged, with lower-level alcohol now permitted for these styles (15.2%). **00** perfumes of almond, marmalade, jasmine; smooth, uncloying mouthfeel. 15% alc. 1 500 half-cases of 500 ml.

Sauvignon Blanc Attractive early/easy-drinker. **01** passion fruit, touch melon, dry lemony finish. 2 200 cases. **Blanc De Wet** Fresh, no-pretensions sauvignon/chardonnay blend, to drink young. Chalky 01's piercing acidity better now with rich seafood or after mid-02. 1 500 cases. **Mine d'Or** (Natural Sweet) Light-bodied/toned extra-low-alc riesling dessert (name translation of Goudmyn, the original farm). **01** lemon-lime, sherbet/lemonade tastes; sweet but not cloying. 9% alc. Enjoy in flush of youth. **Gewürztraminer** ☆ Delicate, exotically-scented Natural Sweet dessert. **99**, follow-up **00** unexpectedly ephemeral in palate after billowing rosepetal bouquet. 11.7% alc. 700 half-cases of 500 ml. — *DH*

De Zoete Inval Estate

Paarl (see Paarl map) • Tasting & sales Mon-Sat 9-5 • BYO picnic • Wheelchair-friendly • Owner Adrian Frater Trust • Winemakers/viticulturists Gerard & John Robert Frater • Production 250 tons 50/50 red/white • PO Box 591 Suider-Paarl 7624 • ***Tel (021) 863-2375*** *• Fax (021) 863-2817 • E-mail dezoeteinval@wine.co.za • Website www.dezoeteinval.co.za*

The Fraters, making wine here in Paarl for 120 years, burst with character – and their wines are no little grey numbers either. Approachable and welcoming, they offer a standing invitation to "taste our wines when you are in our neck of the woods". Winegrowing is now shared between fifth generation Gerard and his younger brother John Robert. And though modernism encroaches (they are well aware that "the onslaught of global competition has lifted the bar in terms of quality and competitiveness"), the ambience reminds of a kinder, gentler age. Which you can take home, if you fancy, in the form of Cabernets from the early 80s. "These wines are remnants of the great Cape reds," remarks John Robert Frater, and will remind you of the 'good old days'."

Blush ☻ ☆ 'Blush' almost an overstatement. **01** mere suggestion of pink, belies a lot of taste, blackcurrant mostly, and fresh leaves. Very different, very characterful. 2 000 cases.

Cabernet Sauvignon Vintages **80**, **81**, **84** all still available. "Well-aged in the traditional style." Unrated. **Grand Rouge** ☆ Latest **00** mainly cab, yr older oak. Pleasantly savoury, almost bacon-biscuity; light-bodied (11.2% alc); tannins need yr/2. 150 cases. **Chardonnay** ☆ Diffident **00**, light lemony flavours and slender body. Very subtly oaked. 1 500 cases. **Late Harvest** Current **99** untasted. **Port** ☆ "Mixture of old port varieties" fortified with 3 yr old brandy. Old-Cape style **99** pale garnet, warm nutty aromas; tasty and not oversweet. Low 16.8% alc. But not very port-like. 300 cases. — *IvH*

Die Krans

Calitzdorp (see Little Karoo map) • Tasting & sales Mon-Fri 8-5 Sat 9-3 (9-4 during holidays) Private tasting for tourgroups by arrangement • Cellar tours by appointment (December school holiday every hour on the hour) • Vintners platters 12-2 Sat & Wed during Feb (pick your own Hanepoot); rest of year for groups of more than 10 by prior arrangement • BYO picnic • Extra virgin olive oil sold • Self-guided vineyard walks year round • Views • Owners/winemakers/viticulturists Boets Nel (since 1982) & Stroebel Nel (since 1988) • Vineyards 40 ha • Production 400-500 tons 15 000-20 000 cases 40% red 20% white 40% port & fortified desserts • PO Box 28 Calitzdorp 6660 • ***Tel (044) 213-3314*** *• Fax (044) 213-3562 • E-mail diekrans@mweb.co.za*

Boets and Stroebel Nel have tweaked their wine list, but declare there's no change in their stated ambition to become South Africa's top port-style wine producers. "On the contrary, we feel we are closer than ever to our vision, with a whole range of quality ports being offered." Including, for the first time in about five years, a White Port, reintroduced in response to European visitors, especially from Germany and Holland. Changes to their red wine portfolio include a new unfortified flagship Touriga Nacional (first varietal bottling in SA) and an upcoming Tinta Roriz. Both have good export potential, believes Boets Nel, who remarks that the range as a whole is now more widely available in SA and internationally through agents in Europe and America. See also under Masters Port.

✵**Touriga Nacional** NEW ✓ Sauve, subtly oaked (5 mths) **00**; nice savoury addition to inky fruit; no earthy/porty tones. Friendly (as are all these reds – though 14.5% alc better sipped than slugged); should develop interestingly. Only 300 cases, sure to be snaffled by collectors. Exclusive to Makro (see also that entry.)

✵**White Muscadel Jerepigo** ✓ Benchmark of this fortified dessert style in Cape: concentrated, long-lived and sweet, yet uncloying. Latest **00** with luscious honey-macerated pineapple flavours. 1 000 cases. Similar to **99**, identical 17% alc, 190 g/ℓ sugar. Frequent show medallist.

✵**White Muscadel Reserve** ✓ "Very popular in Europe," reveals Boets Nel, who's fine-tuned the formula for drier, lower alc profile. This tinkering delivers a cracker in **00** ✵, wonderfully uncloying dried-fig/pineapple nuances, sweet-sour finishing twist. 800 cases. This, **99** ✵ and **98** *Wine* ✵ in elegant flint half-bottle. ±16% alcs, ±190 g/ℓ sugars.

✵**Vintage Reserve Port** Cellar's standard-bearer, and since inaugural **90** stand-out in increasingly competitive Portuguese-inspired field. Latest **99** blend 50/30/15/5 tinta, touriga (slightly higher proportion than pvsly), souzao, tinta r. Superlative presence, generosity; oak quietly tucked away; already velvety but 3-4 yrs minimum needed to open. Fortified with unmatured spirit; 16 mths 4 000 ℓ vats. 94 g/ℓ sugar, 19.5% alc. VG, SAYWS gold, local show champion. 700 cases. 'Declared' in only outstanding vintages: no **98**, **96**. Widely lauded: **97** ✵, VVG, *Wine* ✵, Schulz/SAPPA trophy. **95** *Wine* ✵.

✵**Cape Vintage Port** ✓ Made annually, one of SA's soundest standard vintage 'ports'. **99** ✵ reflects power, generosity of yr. 16-18 mths old 500 ℓ oak. 18.5% alc. 1 000 cases admired by SAYWS judges, served on Air Namibia. **98** ★★ lighter than **97**, excellent vintage.

✵**Cape Tawny Port** ✓ Gorgeous **NV** from tinta (80%) with touriga (15%) tinta r/cinsaut (5%), ripening in bottle. Showing array of clean-cut flavours (biscuits, pine kernels). Ready now (though Boets Nel envisages 10 yr future). Avg age 8 yrs. 19,5% alc, 106 g/ℓ sugar. 1 000 cases.

✵**Cape Ruby Port** ✓ Portuguese-styled **NV** with enough amplitude for a vintage port, yet light toned, even delicate. Still modestly priced at around R20 ex cellar. VG, regional show gold, WOM Value. 50/40/5/5 tinta, touriga, souzao, tinta r. 18,5% alc, 95 g/ℓ sugar. ±4 000 cases. Also in 250 ml screwcaps.

Golden Harvest ☻ ★★ Sweet, lightish **NV** late harvested gewürz, hanepoot. Non-cloying and delicious. 11.5% alc. 1 500 cases.

Cabernet Sauvignon ★★ Discreetly oaked cab with tobacco pouch aroma, nice winey tastes in **00**. 12,5% alc (earlier harvested than usual because of floods). ±2 000 cases. **Pinotage** ★★ Sunshiney unwooded **00** with medicinal snatches; tannic still, give 12-18 mths. Mix 27/5 yr old vines. 1 500 cases. **Tinta Barocca** ★★ **00** granny's cupboard smells; light-toned (but 13.8% alc), fruity, easy drinker. Chill in summer. ±1 500 cases. **Chenin Blanc** ★ Unoaked **01** with splash chardonnay, spicy, undemanding. 13.8% alc. 800 cases. **Chardonnay (unwooded)** ★★ Afrikaans label ("Very popular in Belgium, Netherlands"). **01** simple but not artless. Big 14% alc. Good with roast pork and apple sauce. 1 000 cases. **Spumanté** ★ Featherlight semi-sweet fizz, **NV** carbonated version of Golden Harvest. "For happy occasions." 500 cases. **Heritage Collection White Jerepigo** ★ Unctuous chenin dessert with botrytis whiff. Distinctive 'eco' label (profits to nature conservation education). Latest is **99**. 17% alc. 250 cases. **White Port** ★★ Returns to range with familiar oxidative nutty character, yet drier than pvs. Try over ice with twist lemon. Chenin, 12 mths old casks. **NV**. 19.5% alc. 500 cases. Discontinued: **Chardonnay Wooded** (Pvs **99**). — *IvH*

The next time you're looking for a quality bottle of wine, stop at your local SPAR, SUPERSPAR or KWIKSPAR and try a bottle of Country Cellars. Chosen by SPAR's expert wine panel, Country Cellars wines are easy-drinking, equally enjoyable with a meal or on their own. Savour our everyday drinking or exotic wood matured wines which will gracefully improve in the bottle. So here's to outstanding wine: Cheers!

SPAR

VINTAGE BANKING

A robust, well-matured blend of banking services for the wine industry.

Nedbank for Business is there to serve all kinds of companies. From major corporations to one-man bands, the bank delivers flexible, relevant banking solutions that work. They are particularly active in certain niche industries – one of which is wine.

They know that behind every luscious bottle of buttery Chardonnay and every glass of full-bodied Cabernet there are tireless farmers, innovative cellarmasters, competitive marketers and experienced distributors. People who know exactly what they are doing – but need the help and advice of an informal financial partner.

The people at Nedbank for Business will bring the same degree of skill and commitment to your banking requirements as you give to your wines.

A FULL BANKING SERVICE FOR WINEMAKERS, DISTRIBUTORS AND EXPORTERS

Nedbank for Business offers a comprehensive range of banking services, which they can customise to suit the client. They:

- structure finance for capital equipment and infrastructure;
- help exporters to manage the risks of trading overseas;

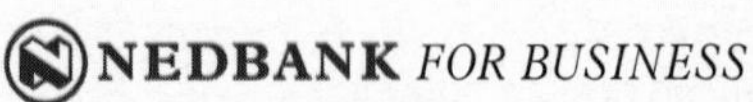

- handle foreign exchange formalities;
- introduce clients to appropriate, internationally recognised financial products and;
- provide access to secure, time-saving electronic banking facilities.

THE CREAM OF THE CROP

John Barnardt, Nedbank's Specialist Relationship Manager for the fruit and wine industries, is based at the bank's Commercial Division in Cape Town. With a BSc from the University of Stellenbosch (majoring in Agricultural Economics), as well as five years' experience as a farmer and nine years as a banking consultant to agriculture, John is completely at home in the winelands, and was instrumental in building Nedbank's successful Wine Industry portfolio which has been functional for five years.

Stephen Baker, Nedbank's other Specialist Relationship Manager for your industry, is an experienced commercial banker who has been a member of the fruit and wine team for the past three years.

They share Nedbank's commitment to getting South African wines into as many countries, homes, shops and restaurants as possible – and in helping you to harvest the rich rewards.

Call John or Stephen on (021) 469-9500 to arrange a personal appointment.

NEDBANK *FOR BUSINESS*

A division of Nedcor Bank Limited (Reg No 1951/000009/06)

Gently persuading Gauteng vinophiles to release their inner hedonists is **Noni Torrent**, *stylish proprietor of The Wine Room in trendy Melville's upmarket Bamboo shopping centre. She and her wine-enthused and knowledgeable staff offer a very special selection of local and imported wines, with designer accessories to further enhance the experience. They are, after all, 'dedicated to the pure enjoyment of wine'.*

Actively involved in the

We like to think of ourselves as more than just supporters of the Sc
prestigious Diners Club Winemaker or Winelist of the Year Awards,
Wine Society, our hands-on involvement helps in the creation of m

Cape Wine Master ***Christine Rudman****, principal of the Cape Wine Academy, is as integral a part of the Cape wine scene as Mon Repos, their historic Stellenbosch HQ. The Academy offers everything from fun food and wine pairing, to sommelier training and in-depth courses for those with serious career intent. Convenient satellites in all the major South African centres and correspondence courses make studying this fascinating subject available to everyone.*

Committed to the promotion of South African wine, **Dr Thandi Ndlovu** *is a board member of Wines of South Africa (WOSA). She swapped her career as a medical doctor for one in the construction industry and now chairs the Motheo Group in Johannesburg, a city as vibrant and dynamic as she is.*

Diemersdal Estate

Durbanville (see Durbanville map) • Tasting & sales Mon-Fri 9-5 Sat 9-3 • Cellar tours by appointment • Meals for groups of up to 35 by arrangement • Conferences • Walks • Mountain biking • Owner Tienie Louw • Winemaker Tienie Louw • Viticulturist Div van Niekerk (since 1980) • Vineyards 180 ha • Production 1 800 tons 80% red 20% white • PO Box 27 Durbanville 7551 • ***Tel (021) 976-3361*** *• Fax (021) 976-1810 • E-mail joelouw@iafrica.com*

Traditionally the wine farms in this area sent most of their production to the big wholesalers, which meant the Durbanville vineyards strutted their stuff behind their cordon of leaves. Now the curtain is lifting, and the vineyards taking their rightful place centre-stage. Here at Diemersdal, a new cellar has been commissioned and for the first time all the grapes are going into the cellar's own wines. "We're no longer selling a berry to the trade," says Tienie Louw, assisted in 2001 by Graham Weerts (Div van Niekerk, viticulturist since 1980, still very much in situ). There's certainly no problem about selling Diemersdal wines. Perspicacious Tienie Louw was one of the first to grasp the export opportunities that materialised post apartheid, and strong international ties mean Diemersdal wines will continue to be enjoyed in most European countries.

✵**Cabernet Sauvignon** New **99** continues fast pace set by **98**, which flew with SAA. Lively supple tannins bring sweet-fruit flavours into focus. 5 clones vinified/raised separately 12 mths before blending, 13.4% alc. 1 500 cases. This, reds below, traditionally open-tank fermented.

✵**Pinotage** ✓ Modern, fruity but not overblown style, latest with shiraz-like bushfire aromas; **99** unquiet tannins needing yr/2 to settle. Still-feisty 32 yr old block; yr small oak. 13.6% alc. 1 800 cases. **98** *Wine* ✵, SAA.

✵**Shiraz** ✓ Elegant style; in these maritime hills, shows high-toned pepper, wild scrub aromatics. **99** ✵ very soft, sweet-tannined. Mix old/new clones, fermented open/closed vessels ("Good combination that works for me," notes winemaker). 13.8% alc. 1 800 cases. Almost certainly earlier-maturing than generously flavoured **98**, with feisty acidity.

✵**Private Collection** Good vinous qualities in this cab-led blend with merlot cab f. Pvs **98** SAA bold, deep-flavoured; upcoming **99** savoury rather than fruity; powerful but ripe tannic platform for long (9-10 yrs) ageing. Start drinking from 2003. 13.4% alc. 1 800 cases.

✵**Sauvignon Blanc** Even in area renowned for 'sauvage' varietal character night-harvested **01**'s full-frontal nettle, green pepper punch delivers a surprise knockout. Wonderfully racy palate, nicely fleshed with ripe fruit. Could age, though very good now solo or with the day's catch. 13% alc. 1 500 cases Improves on **00** ✵ debut.

Matys ☻ NEW ✵ Should come with pronunciation guide: say mah-*tays,* not mateys (!) though it's very easy to befriend this swiggable bdx blend flaunting sweet cassis, plum fruits. Cab/merlot, wood-staved. 13% alc. 1 000 **NV** cases.

Chardonnay NEW Promising **01** debut for this label, oozing personality from arresting ripe mango/spicy oak contrast, sweet-fruited finish. Tasted in infancy (as was Sauvignon above) so hard to call, but should rate ✵ on present form Bunch-pressed, barrique-fermented. 13.5% alc. 500 cases, well priced ex cellar One to watch. — *DH*

Diemersfontein Wines

Wellington (see Wellington map) • Tasting, sales & cellar tours by appointment Fee R10 p/p • Light meals by appointment Booking essential • Conferences • Walks • Mountain biking • Guesthouse and B&B (see Stay-over section) •

Owners David & Sue Sonnenberg • Manager/contact person Anzill Adams • Winemaker/viticulturist Bertus Fourie (since Oct 2000) • Consulting winemaker Lofty Ellis • Consulting viticulturist Eben Archer • Vineyards 37 ha • Production 110 tons (250 tons 2002) 4 144 cases 100% red • PO Box 41 Wellington 7654 • ***Tel (021) 873-4447*** *• Fax (021) 864-2095 • E-mail wine@diemersfontein.co.za • Website www.diemersfontein.co.za*

INSPIRED by the rising standard of wines out of Wellington, and reassured of the suitability of their hillside soils, power-couple David and Sue Sonnenberg are channelling their energies into their own brand, after supplying Bovlei co-op for more than 20 years. To help them reach their lofty goal of "establishing a top red wine estate brand and produce a South African icon within the next 5-10 years", they've locked onto some major talents – winemaker Bertus Fourie, role-modelling his vinous philosophy on that of the late John Goschen ("not just a job, but a way of living"); viniferous databanks Eben Archer and Lofty Ellis; and Anzill Adams, switched-on co-ordinator of the original SA wine empowerment project, New Beginnings. Together, they're striding into a brave new world of not only wining but also sharing and caring – a portion of the proceeds will go to an in-house trust for the educational and training needs of the Diemersfontein staff and the community.

✲**Cabernet Sauvignon** Promising **01** radiates pure well-handled cassis fruit; inky plum shades presage assertive but ripe tannic backbone, carrying to unjammy finish. Deserves 2-3 yrs' ageing; should go further 7. Potential ✲ (this, below tasted in youth mid-01; ratings are provisional).

✲**Merlot** Avoids meanness of many SA merlots; **01** very ripe; fruit tones contrast pleasingly with damp thatch/fennel aromas, integrated oak. Wears majestic 15% alc quite lightly. 70% new casks, mainly Fr.

Pinotage 01, too, manages to hide its 15.5% alc well, so feels almost refined, neither overweight nor flabby. Arresting black hues; meaty/gamey flavours burnished by powdery tannins. Enough structure for 8-10 yrs' good ageing. Too young to rate – possible ✲ (lauded by 01 SAYWS judges, who named it class winner).

First Release range

✲**Shiraz** Modern SA style, heavily oaked but not inharmonious; lots of ripe bouncy fruit in **01**, controlled by acidity and peppery/toasty tones; gutsy alc (14.5%). 30% oaked in new Am barriques.

Cabernet Sauvignon ★ **01** popular style, licked with dollop sugar (6.9 g/ℓ) for effortless drinking; bright jammy fruit balanced by firm acidity; lightish feel (though alc very high: 14.5%). Grapes for this, below ex Doolhof. **Merlot** ★ Partly Am-oaked **01** lighter, brighter profile compared to namesake above, more exuberant; good drinking now, lubrication provided by smidgeon sugar and ruddy 14% alc. **Pinotage** ★ Oak-staved **01**, more overtly pinotage than above; soft, ripe in-face fruit; mite oaky (sample tasted) though blackcurrant fruit powers through finish. 14.5% alc. — *TM*

Die Poort

Herbertsdale (see Little Karoo map) • Tasting & sales Mon-Fri 9-5 • Cellar tours by appointment • Views • Owner JPW Jonker • Winemaker/viticulturist Jannie Jonker • PO Box 99 Herbertsdale 6505 • ***Tel (028) 735-2406*** *• Fax (028) 735-2347*

A 40-minute detour inland from Mossel Bay will land you up at the only winery on the Garden Route. At the foot of the Outeniqua mountains near Herbertsdale, the farm has been in the Jonker family for two generations. You're guaranteed a warm welcome with home-grown wines and country cuisine in the satisfying traditional boerekos mode. Die Poort has its own potstill and produces brandy (which rocks the socks off holidaymakers – and local show judges, who recently awarded it a gold medal; for good measure they also crowned Jannie Jonker's Pinotage Little Karoo champion). Apple brandy and unmatured witblits are other attractions. The range, unavailable for tasting, has included: red: **Cabernet Sauvignon**, **Pinotage**, **Hemelrood**; dry white: **Premier Grand Cru**, **Blanc de Blanc**, **Cape St Blaize**; semi-sweet white: **Late Harvest**, **Frölich Stein**, **Camilla** (perlé); sparkling: **Vin Doux**; fortifieds: **Selected Red Jerepigo**, **Red Jerepigo**, **Sweet Jerepigo**, **Selected White Jerepigo**, **White Jerepigo**, **Golden Jerepigo**, **Raisin Jerepigo**, **Lissa Jonker Hanepoot**, **Port Pinotage**, **White Port**.

Dieu Donné Vineyards

Franschhoek (see Franschhoek map) • Tasting & sales Mon-Fri 8.30-4.30 • Cellar tours by arrangement • BYO picnic • Views • Owner Robert Maingard • Winemaker Stephan du Toit (since 1996) • Viticulturist Hennie du Toit • Vineyards 40 ha • Production 16 500 cases 60% red 35% white 3% rosé 2% sparkling • PO Box 94 Franschhoek 7690 • ***Tel (021) 876-2493*** *• Fax (021) 876-2102 • E-mail dieudonne@zsd.co.za*

Visitors to this eagle-nest in Franschhoek will see plenty of changes when the new tasting area is completed in the not too distant future. Plans are afoot to link this venue to a viewing point overlooking some of the Cape's most spectacular vineyards. Next will be picnic lunches to complement the wines. The merlot vineyard, on a steep south-west aspect, is being extended to cater for demand from several countries, including Japan and Norway. The farm's first Shiraz represents one more step toward winemaker Stephan du Toit's goal of producing a 70:30 red-white wine ratio.

✯**Cabernet Sauvignon** Seriously minded, smoke-tinged **99** step up from pvs; plenty dark fruit in tight, hard tannic casing; 30% new wood 18 mths. 13.5% alc. 4 000 cases. **98** lighter toned, easier. **Cabernet Sauvignon Reserve** NEW **99** brighter fruit than regular; big dry tannins, fruit sweetness linger; herbaceous edge; should soften somewhat with a few yrs. 20 mths new Fr oak. 13.3% alc. 250 half-cases (as are all these).

✯**Merlot** Refined classical styling; dusty herbaceous notes in **00** pre-bottling sample. Austere dry tannins/finish, might soften with few yrs. 16 mths Fr oak, 30% new. 2 600 cases. Critically acclaimed **99** untasted. **98** ✯ choc-mint complexity, violet hints.

✯**Noble Late Harvest** Rich, honeyed, raisined dessert from botrytised chenin; **97** still developing well. 7,8 g/ℓ acid, 124 g/ℓ sugar. 450 cases.

Pinotage ★★ Inviting, friendly aromas in oaked **00** lead on to strapping tannins/acid; lots of spicy fruit; dry, slightly bitter farewell. 13% alc. 550 cases. **Shiraz** ★★ NEW Smoky/jammy aromas/flavours with spicy edge; characteristic Dieu Donné firmness of structure in **00**. Yr 2nd fill Fr barrels. 350 cases. **Cabernet Sauvignon-Merlot** ★★ Sternly styled **97** 85/15 blend; showing smoky meat with the berries; spartan tannins, savoury finish. 20 mths new Fr oak. 13,7% alc. 260 cases. **Rosé** ★★ Perfect for pleasant pink picnics. **00** sweetish but light, crisp; from chardonnay/cab. 650 cases. **Chardonnay** (wooded) ★★ **00** boasts immodestly of its 50% new Fr oak background, over which it spreads a crisp, lemony richness. Slight afterburn from big 14% alc. 950 cases. **Chardonnay Unwooded** ★ **00** fresh butterscotch-hinting quaffer; well-textured lemony taste, dry, near-sour finish. 13,2% alc. 2 500 cases. **Sauvignon Blanc** ★★ Food-friendly, flavoursome **01**; crisp acid almost masks 5.5 g/ℓ sugar, which adds richness, soft finish. 13.4% alc. 2 000 cases. **Special Late Harvest** ★ **98** still drinks nicely; gently sweet tropical richness. Chenin. 13% alc. 600 cases. **Methode Cap Classique NV** (98) brut from chardonnay, not ready for tasting. Discontinued: **Chenin Blanc** Pvs **99** ★. — *TJ*

Distell

Stellenbosch • PO Box 184 Stellenbosch 7599 • ***Tel (021) 809-7000***

THE marriage of wine colossi Distillers Corporation and Stellenbosch Farmers' Winery (SFW) has created this strapping young buck, singly responsible for just under 30% of the Cape's annual table-wine output of some 340-million litres. A listed group with a market capitalisation of about R1.5-billion, Distell covers the full wine spectrum through a singularly diversified product range (other beverage interests, including liqueurs, brandies, sherries, white spirits and fruit juices fall beyond the scope of this book). Brands individually listed in the guide are: 5th Avenue Cold Duck, Allesverloren, Alto, Autumn Harvest, Capenheimer, Cellar Cask, Chateau Libertas, Drostdy-Hof, Durbanville Hills, Fleur du Cap, Fort Simon, Golden Alibama, Graça, Grand Mousseux, Grünberger, Here XVII, Honey Blossom, J C le Roux, Jacobsdal, Jacques Pinard, Kellerprinz, Kupferberger Auslese, Lanzerac, Le Bonheur, Lieberstein, Monis, Nederburg, Neethlingshof, Oom Tas, Overmeer, Plaisir de Merle, Pongrácz, Rietvallei, Roodendal, Sedgwick's, Ship Sherry, Stellenryck, Stellenzicht, Tassenberg, Taverna, Theuniskraal, Tukulu, Two Oceans, Uitkyk, Virginia and Zonnebloem. Another facet of operations is the Vinoteque cellaring scheme for buyers purchasing young wine at an annual pre-release event. For a fee, these wines can be stored in perfect cellar conditions in Stellenbosch. Distell recently raised some local eyebrows by appointing a young Australian, Linley Schultz, its winemaker-in-chief. Some interpreted the internationally seasoned oenologist's advent as a logical next step for an organisation whose stated objective is "to be a leader and innovator in the world beverage market". Can a strategic linkage with an offshore (Antipodean?) corporate partner be far behind?

Distillers Corporation see Distell

Domaine Brahms

Paarl (see Paarl map) • Tasting & sales by appointment • Owners Braam & Gesie Lategan • Winemaker/viticulturist Gesie Lategan (since 1999) • Vineyards 30 ha • Production 100 tons 1 500 cases 100% red • PO Box 2136 Windmeul 7630 • ***Tel/fax (021) 863-8555*** *• E-mail brahms@iafrica.com*

GESIE Lategan's first name may mean 'little spirit', but there's nothing small about her or the dreams slowly being realised here. She and husband (fellow jurist) Braam have 27 ha of cabernet, merlot, pinotage and some ruby cabernet on the lower foothills of Paarl Mountain. Not to forget Gesie Lategan's favourite, "mystical" shiraz, which is the majority grape in the first bottle under the flagship label, Brahms. A Pinotage (untasted) and a future blend appear under an alternative marque. Quantities will always be limited, foresees Gesie Lategan, who shook off the shackles of a distinguished career as a Cape High Court advocate to follow her vinous dream. While studying cellar technology at Elsenburg, a serious car crash almost shattered her hopes. At last, in 1998, the family built a basic cellar and the following year crushed their first grapes. Now they're unstoppable, planning tasting facilities to join the existing guesthouse on the farm.

✰**Shiraz** There's more Rhone than Barossa to this shiraz, with dash cab, made for the long haul though showing well now. **99** from low-yielding (6 t/ha) bushvine vyds; plump raspberry/blackfruit aromas, youngberry notes layered with sweet gamey whiffs, hints liqueur chocolate; firm but not heavy tannins, spicy sweet finish. Hand selected fruit, prolonged skin contact, yr mainly 2nd/3rd fill Fr oak. 14% alc. 700 cases. — *MF*

Domein Doornkraal

De Rust (see Little Karoo map) • Tasting & sales Mon-Fri 9-5 (8-5.30 during school holidays) Sat 8-1 Also at Jemima's, Baron von Rheede Str, Oudtshoorn • Cellar tours by appointment • Meals for groups of 10 or more by arrangement • Tourgroups • Gifts • Owners/winemakers Swepie & Piet le Roux with Maria le Roux (2001 vintage) • Vineyards ±29 ha • Production 200 tons (4 000 cases own label) 45% white 25% red 10% rosé 20% sparkling/desserts • PO Box 14 De Rust 6650 • ***Tel/fax (044) 251-6715*** *• E-mail doornkraal@xsinet.co.za*

THE industrious le Roux family are doing all they can to introduce the wines and foods of the Little Karoo to a wider audience. Two of Swepie le Roux's daughters run the popular Jemima's Restaurant in Oudtshoorn, where only the traditional dishes – and the wines – of the region are offered. Now winemaking son Piet has opened a wine sales office next door to Jemima's to showcase the wide range produced in his cellar. He says: "We may also offer a few wines from local producers who do not have sales facilities of their own." In the pipeline is a bordeaux blend, untasted by us, which should be available for sale soon.

- ☆**Pinta** ✓ Latest (00) version of this jerepigo style dessert features familiar good earthy, porty tones, rich chocolatey smoothness. Pinotage, tinta. **NV**.
- ☆**Diep Tanige Port** ✓ Tawny 'port' with plum, toasted hazelnuts bouquet, gamey hints; touriga, tinta blended across 92, 94, 96 vintages, large Fr cask-aged. "Mends a broken heart", asserts romanticist Swepie le Roux. 200 cases.

Merlot ☆ Lightly oaked **00** quaffably soft, fruity; cellar's signature earthiness in background. Limited release of 500 cases. **Merlot-Pinotage** NEW **00** easy drinker features contribution of ancient pinotage vines; supple sweet fruit flavours, hints of oak char. 13.5% alc. **Kannaland** ☆ Recommended by Swepie le R for summer enjoyment; could be lightly chilled; pvsly tasted **00** still satisfying, smooth. Tinta, merlot, pinotage. 500 cases. **Semillon Reserve** Oak-staved **99** past best. 500 cases. **Tickled Pink** ☆ Friskily-foamy, blush-pink carbonated bubbly; gently sweet; lightish (11,5% alc). **NV**. 500 cases. **Jerepigo** ☆ Muscat de f fortified to 16.5%, partially old-oaked; **00** with splashes 94, 99; delicious and not too dauntingly sweet. 16.5% alc. Also available, not ready for tasting (pvs ratings in brackets, **NV** unless noted): **Kuierwyn Effe-droog** (☆), **Tinta Bianca Effe-droog** (☆), **Tinta Bianca Soet Natuurlik** (**99** ☆), **Majoor** (☆), **Kaptein** (☆), **Luitenant** (☆), **Korporaal** (untasted). Discontinued: **Cabernet Sauvignon** (**97** ☆). *— DH*

Doolhof see Maze Valley Wines

Dornier Wines

Stellenbosch • Not open to the public • Owner Christoph Dornier, Switzerland • Winemaker Ian Naudé (since Jan 2001) • Viticulturist Lucas de Kock (since Jan 2001) • Vineyards 80 ha • Production ± 500 tons 80% red 20% white • PO Box 7518 Stellenbosch 7599 • ***Tel (021) 880-0557*** *• Fax (021) 880-1499 • E-mail info@dornierwines.co.za • Website www.dornierwines.co.za*

THESE Helderberg foothills are alive with the sound of money – a cool R100-million – transforming three sleepy old properties into a showplace wine and cultural spread. Applying the make-over is – appropriately – a fine-artist, internationally reputed Christoph Dornier, who perpetuates summer by swallowing to Stellenbosch at the first sign of Swiss snow. When in residency, you'll find him on the Keerweder portion of the property (which dates back to 1694), from where he's orchestrating the construction of an ultramodern, Johan Malherbe-designed cellar, a conference centre to accommodate 200 people and an open-air summer concert courtyard. In a masterstroke, Dornier has included vibrant ex Linton Park winemaker Ian Naudé in this wide-stretching canvas. A brilliant colourist in own right, internationally seasoned Naudé's aims are "stylish but fun wines" with, probably uniquely in the Cape, "a sense of humour". The first experimental vinifications took place in a neighbouring cellar in 2001. Expect a very different sort of laughing, singing wine to emerge from these hands.

Douglas Green 

Wellington • Not open to the public • Owner DGB (Pty) Ltd • Winemaker Cassie du Plessis • Wine buyer Arend Adriaanse • Oenologist Jaco Potgieter • Production 100 000 cases • PO Box 79 Groot Drakenstein 7680 • ***Tel (021) 874-1011*** *• Fax (021) 874-1690 • E-mail exports@dgb.co.za*

From well-managed sites in far-flung areas to the committed co-operation of the various cellars where the wines are made (the new Wellington cellar is used for blending and bottling), the modus operandi here is teamwork. At the hardworking core of the team, you'll find oenologist Jaco Potgieter, winemaker Cassie Carstens and wine buyer Arend Adriaanse, guided by dynamic winemaker John Worontchak. Australian born and trained, London-based Worontchak makes wine in a staggering seven different countries each year. The latest vintage reflects the team's serious focus on new world styling. See also Bellingham.

Douglas Green range

⁂**Merlot** NEW **00** fruit-essencey style with pyrethrum, violets bouquet; minerally concentration of plum, vanilla, oak-char, mint; highly accessible now and could age a bit.

⁂**Chardonnay** Partially oaked **01** ⁂ lacks complexity, keeping qualities of pvs **00** but has its own allures: rounded peach/vanilla nuances, piquant finish. Full bodied (13,5% alc), as was pvs.

Cabernet Sauvignon ⁂ Generous, drink-now dry red. Slightly smoky/toasty tannins in **00** for teaming with a range of foods. 13% alc. **Pinotage** ⁂ Characterful, unmistakably pinotage; cinnamon spice in **00** and loads of variety's sometimes stroppy tannins, needing ±18 mths to sober down. 13,2% alc. **St Augustine** ⁂ Favourite in SA since the 40s; made-over in **98**, though still mainly cab (with merlot, ruby cab, cab f, cinsaut); still full-bodied (13+% alc). Current **99** ripe, sweet, rotund; quaffable with guts for 3-5 yrs. **Cinsaut-Pinotage** NEW ⁑ All the succulent, plummy characters of the varieties in one sweet, almost sugary **01** mouthful. Gossamer tannins rescue from decadence. 13% alc. **Sauvignon Blanc** ⁂ Juicy **01**'s tangy greeting, sherbety adieu are charming now and should be enjoyed within the yr. Lightish 11.8% alc. **Colombard-Chardonnay** NEW ⁑ Ethereal pear/guava tones in lightish, sherbety **01** easy drink, which should be quaffed soon, solo or with, say, seafood. **Blanc de Blanc** ⁂ **01** crisply dry fruity mouthful; with tingly tropical farewell. Light/med-bodied. Not tasted for this ed: **Ruby Port** Pvs **NV** ⁂.

The Saints by Douglas Green

This range offers reliability, value and the added attraction of moderate-to-low alcohols. All **NV**.

St Raphael ☻ ⁂ Smooth dry red with fruity/savoury tones, mildly grippy tannins for versatile food partnering. Unwooded. 12% alc. **St Claire** ☻ ⁂ Blush-pink rosé with very low alc (8%) and balanced sweetness. Honeysuckle fragrances; soft, grapey tastes. Chenin, gewürz, pinotage.

St Vincent ⁑ Light, just-dry sauvignon, chenin blend with rousing tropical zing. **St Morand** ⁂ Drier than pvs; retains perfumed bouquet, light tropical fruitiness, brisk finish. **St Anna** ⁂ Chenin, gewürz with nervy acid to cleanse the subtropical palate, bring it back for more. Low alc (8,15%). — *DH*

Douglas Winery

*Northern Cape • Tasting & sales Mon-Fri 8-1; 2-5 • Owner GWK Ltd (2 000 shareholders) • Winemakers WH 'Pou' le Roux (since 1978) & Danie Kershoff (since 1992) • Viticulturist Danie Kershoff • Vineyards 533 ha • Production 6 700 tons (8 000-10 000 cases own label) • PO Box 47 Douglas 8730 • **Tel (053) 298-8314** • Fax (053) 298-1845 • E-mail wynkelder@gwk.co.za*

Avoca, a Latin word associated with the confluence of waters, is the apposite new identity of this cellar at the intersection of the Orange, Vaal and Riet Rivers. Water is a constant preoccupation in these warm northerly climes, and viticulture is possible only through irrigation. Translating these aqueous themes into visual imagery, Cape Town's creative fountainhead Anthony Lane has produced a striking new look for the spruced-up range (all pvs Douglas Winery labels to be phased out). Included in the new portfolio are a certified and an uncertified range, including the winery's signature fortifieds (their Red Jerepiko national class champ of 95). Amid all the changes, there's a very steady constant: winemaker 'Pou' le Roux. "We had a 60% crop loss in 2001 due to various natural causes," reports the unflappable veteran of 30 harvests. "Luckily the quality is much better than in previous years."

Avoca certified range

Ruby Cabernet ⁑ **00** high-toned jammy fruit; softly dry; Unwooded, moderate 12% alc. Don't hesitate to chill in summer. 350 cases. **Chardonnay** ⁑ Unoaked **00** fairly one-dimensional but not unattractive, med-bodied. Drink soon. 400 cases. **Red Muscadel** ⁂ **99** floral bouquet, sweetness cut by dried-fruit tang. 16.5% alc. 300 cases. Also available, not ready for tasting: **Merlot**, **Cabernet Sauvignon**, **Gewürztraminer**. All **01**.

Avoca Uncertified range

In 750 ml, 1 ℓ and 2 ℓ packs. **NV**.

Sweet Hanepoot ✓ (99) Brilliant gold glints; lively apricot, peach, mango fruit basket; richness balanced by bright acidity. 16.5% alc. 500 cases.

Classic White ☻ ⁑ Light floral summer celebrator, fruitily dry. From chenin, splashed with colombard. Exotic litchi scents. 600 cases. **Classic Gold** ☻ ⁑ Sippable spicy/floral semi-sweet with crisp uncloying finish. Gewürz/hanepoot. Lowish 10.8% alc. 600 cases.

Classic Red ⁑ (01) Uncomplicated, unwooded fruity tipple. Shiraz, merlot, ruby cab blend, med-bodied; spicy. **Classic Rosé** ★ Ruby cab, chenin; similar to above but sweeter, like pop-soda. Similar lowish alc (11.5% alc). **Cape Red Jerepigo** ⁑ Unusual malt/molasses tones, not tooth-achingly sweet; from ruby cab; (00). 16.5% alc. 400 cases. **Ruby Port** ⁂ Light (17%) alc for this style. Ruby cab/pinotage; stewed plum/prune aromas; honeycomb tastes. 500 cases. — *JN*

Drakensig

NEW

*Paarl (Simondium) • Tasting & sales 10 Dec-12 Jan Mon-Fri 9-5; Sat 9-1 • Closed public & religious holidays • Owner Marais Viljoen • Winemaker Ben Janse (since Jan 1999) • Viticulturist Marais Viljoen • Vineyards 13 ha • Production 30 ton 2 300 cases (own label) 80% red 20% white • PO Box 22 Simondium 7670 • **Tel (021) 874-3881** • Fax (021) 874-3882 • E-mail drakensig@mweb.co.za*

This brand new cellar in the Simondium area near Paarl is the realisation of a dream for owner Marais Viljoen, who has been producing export table grapes for many years and has always wanted to run a boutique winery. Encouraged by his long-time friend and mentor, Nico Vermeulen, Marais appointed Ben Janse as his winemaker and made his first wines in the Nuwe Hoop cellar in 2000. The Drakensig cellar is now up and running, and Viljoen Marais says his aim is to produce good quality wines at affordable prices. The range is small, as only four varieties are grown on the 20 hectare farm, but future plans include a Reserve range.

Shiraz ✓ Likeable, drinkable **00** rich and plummy; mace, clove and cracked peppercorn hold the attention, late-palate woodsmoky notes. 13.1% alc not aggressively high. 800 cases.

Sauvignon Blanc ✓ More stylish than an everyday quaff, yet deliciously drinkable (and in fact should be broached soon). **00** ★ green fig, peppery aromas with herby nettle nuances in sweetish palate; clean finish. **01** notch up, zingier; similar green flavours joined by riper gooseberry; balanced. Grapes ex-Dbnville/F'hoek. 500/900 cases.

Cabernet Sauvignon ★ "A fireside goblet," feels Marais Viljoen. Sweet impression enhances **99**'s already welcoming style, though bit of background tannin should ensure 4-5 yrs' maturation. Fr oak. 13.5% alc. 800 cases. **Pinotage** ★ Bought-in Wellington fruit highlights variety's darker, more rustic spectrum: **00** earthy, dark-choc flavours; astringent tannin. Am oak 9 mths. 800 cases.
— *DH*

Drostdy Wines

Tulbagh (see Tulbagh map) • Tasting & sales Mon-Fri 8-12; 1.30-5 Sat 9-12.30 • Cellar tours Mon-Fri 11, 3; Sat 11 • Owner Distell • Winemaker Frans du Toit (since 1968) • PO Box 9 Tulbagh 6820 • ***Tel (023) 230-1086*** *• Fax (023) 230-0510*

The low alcohol Extra Light, ideal for weight-watching vinophiles, is one of this venerable winery's top sellers. Less dainty, but just as evergreen, are the Cape Red and Chardonnay – both lunchtime favourites with a very wide appeal. The range is named after Tulbagh's old magistracy, now a national monument, and created under the very seasoned eye of Frans du Toit, keen believer in the two cornerstones: "selection and blending". Also made here are Two Oceans (see entry) and African Sky (export range, not tasted), all marketed by Distell.

Drostdy-Hof range

Ruby Cabernet ★ Oak-brushed **99** advertises itself with brilliant ruby gloss, near tannin-free succulence. Irresistible and, like all below, to be enjoyed soon. 13.2% alc. 30 000 cases.

Cabernet Sauvignon ★ Lovely old-clone cab; soft, pruney flavours; **98** like pvs, gently wooded and flavoursome. 10 000 cases. **Merlot** ★ Oaked **99** unusually puckery, needs yr/2 to ease into its usual svelte-textured drinkability; sweetish plummy tastes augur well. 13.5% alc. Massive volumes. **Pinotage** ★ Latest **98** total contrast to soft, easy **97**; give time to smooth in bottle or subdue with spicy ribs. 20 000 cases. **Cape Red** ★ Unwooded **01** quintet of varieties; med-bodied, sweetish, fruity. Lightly chill for summer barbecues. 13% alc. 400 000 cases. **Claret Select** ★ Lightish **NV** blend; structured for unproblematic pleasure; now with sweetish choc-boxy tones from 10 g/ℓ sugar. **Chardonnay** ★ **00** as modestly flavoured as priced; smooth, slightly creamy from subtly oaked portion. **Sauvignon Blanc** ★ **00** Uncharacteristically light, almost insubstantial; lacks variety's pleasing kick. **Extra Light** ★ Nicely pungent aromas in this **NV** soft, crisp and dry best seller – all at low level 9.8% alc. **Steen/Chenin Blanc** ★ No flashing lights but no disappointments either in **01**; soft and round, but dry, with spicy flick in tail. **Premier Grand Cru** ★ **NV** with particularly pleasant aromas, uncompromising dry finish. Salad of varieties; moderate alc. **Stein Select** ★ Latest **NV** slender in every respect; delicate semi-sweet tastes, barest suggestion of bouquet. **Late Harvest ★ NV** Sweeter version of Stein; from chenin ex Stbosch/Worcester. **Adelpracht ★** 800 000 ℓ (!) of Stbosch, Paarl, Swtland chenin, SLH style (±45 g/ℓ sugar); lightish, always balanced by fruity acidity as in **00** for pleasant sipping. — *IvH*

Dumisani see Winecorp Private Label Services
Duncan's Creek see Rickety Bridge
Du Plessis see Havana Hills

Du Preez Estate

Rawsonville (see Worcester map) • Tasting & sales Mon-Fri 8-5 Fee R5 p/p • Cellar tours by appointment • BYO picnic • Play area for children • Tourgroups • Walks • 4×4 trail • Owner HL du Preez • Winemaker/viticulturist Hennie du Preez • Vineyards 130 ha • Production 1 700 tons 65% white 35% red • PO Box 12 Rawsonville 6845 • ***Tel/fax (023) 349-1642*** *• E-mail dupreezestate@intekom.co.za*

Two Hennies grow these characterful wines on a family spread near Rawsonville: Jnr looks after the cellar and the 130 hectares (35% planted with reds, including 'discovery' grape petit verdot) while Snr … well, he's the owner. Between them they seem to have it all under control. In answer to our question, what's new in your winery? they rapid-fire: "Nothing new or newsworthy". But with export channels open to Europe and the Far East, and eager buyers for their 7 000 own-label cases, they're probably just too exhausted to reply. Though Hennie Jnr would no doubt perk up considerably if he met Delheim's irrepressible Spatz Sperling, whom Hennie du Preez admires for his "wonderful character steeped in wine".

★**Shiraz** NEW ✓ Fuchsia-edged **00**, understated tar/woodsmoke whiffs over concentrated red berry aromas; quite restrained style (within parameters of boisterous 13.9% alc) with nice sour-plum flavour; oak better integrated than Merlot below. 1 500 cases.

★**Pinotage** ✓ Big and ripe **00** with floral scents and ripe berries; cigarbox nuances from yr oak ageing and pinotage's palate-coating fruit in finish. 14% alc. 500 cases.

★**Hanepoot** ✓ Senior-citizen bushvines bear the grapes for this smooth fortified dessert. **99** filling out in bottle, turning brilliant yellow-gold; complex, almost overpowering aromas of ripe grapes, honeysuckle, cinnamon; unusual desiccated coconut twist. Not too alcoholic 17% fortification. 600 cases.

Polla's Red ☻ ★ Tasty **00** with hint hillside scrub in plummy finish. Oaked blend shiraz, pinotage, petit verdot, ruby cab. Med-bodied, harmonious. 8 000 cases. **Sauvignon Blanc** ☻ ★ Hennie du Preez should patent his formula for easy to enjoy, varietally correct sauvignon; med-bodied **01** flinty, bone dry, crisp finishing. 1 500 cases.

Merlot NEW ★ **00** overtly oaky; toffee-like wood tones dominate mulberries-and-cream aromas; turn quite astringent in finish. 13.2% alc. 350 cases. — *TM*

Du Preez Wine see Migration

Durbanville Hills

Durbanville (see Durbanville map) • Tasting & sales Mon-Fri 9-4.30 Sat & Sun 10-2.30 Fee R5 • Cellar tours Mon-Fri 11 and 3 • Groups private, informal and formal tastings & tours by arrangement • Lunches from 12-2.30 Mon-Sun booking essential • Picnic lunches available Nov-Feb • Venue for corporate and private functions • Owners Distell with 7 local farmers & workers trust • Winemaker Mar-

*tin Moore (since 1999) with Riaan Oosthuizen • Vineyards 550 ha, rising to 640 ha • Production 8 000 tons (total capacity) 51% red 49% white • PO Box 3276 Durbanville 7551 • **Tel (021) 558-1300** • Fax (021) 558-9658 • E-mail dhills@distell.co.za • Website www.durbanvillehills.co.za*

"IT'S OUR GOAL to make *the* South African breakthrough on the global market," say this super-energised team, who play in a computerised cellar straight out of Star Trek. Commanding the enterprise is Martin Moore, recently beamed up from Constantia to these "not just cool, almost cold" hills – and clearly relishing the chill. "Now that we've mastered the technology," Moore and co-pilot Riaan Oosthuizen say, "we're sticking to a contemporary style of winemaking. Keeping up the quality in quantity, that's the challenge." Which, judging from their high-volume Premium range, they're doing with aplomb. Now they're aiming their technology at expressing their terroir in the limited-release Rhinofields (named after the indigenous fynbos) and 'Single Vineyard' ranges. "Making these Reserve wines," super-confident Moore says, "is easy once you get to know the quality and potential of each vineyard." Will these techies conquer Planet Earth? Watch this space ...

'Single Vineyard' range NEW

Merlot Consider rating for this idiocyncratic **99** (sample) a provisional one, very much a love or hate style. Similar themes expressed here and in Premium version: super-ripe cherry slathered with choc and powerful eucalyptus scents with touches of meat; big, savoury palate with vanilla-mulberry – all delivered with treacly intensity. Extraordinary. Will raise eyebrows and, no doutb cheers too) while Martin M tucks into his portion with his favoured ossobucco. 18 mths new Fr oak. 13.3% alc. 650 cases.

Sauvignon Blanc "Made to make a statement," says Martin M, "SA, being between New Zealand and Sancerre, can produce the best of both worlds." **01** (sample) conveys the point in riveting, convincing fashion: emormous concentration of pure varietal fruit, almost 'sauvignon essence', leaning, if anything, towards Europe in flinty/racy tones but also showcasing Dbnville's hallmark 'dusty' sweet-pepper tones. Fruit from 2 producers, selected vyds, "not just cool, almost cold". Just 800 cases which, winemaker reluctantly concedes "will be fashionable at wine tastings!"

Rhinofields range NEW

Merlot 99 more serious than Premium below, not as immediately acessible or plasurable; yet promise of plenty of delayed pleasure in ripe, supple fruit with telltale wild-scrubby nuance; very dry tannins need good few yrs' softening. 2 vyds, 10% from higher-lying site. 18 mths new Fr oak, mostly Burgundian coopers. 2 500 cases.

Chardonnay Delicious ripe yellow peach flesh the attention grabber here, like biting into the actual fruit, complete with tactile dimension of light viscousness in palate. Weighty 00 (13.6% alc) 40% new Fr oak fermented/aged 8 mths, back-blended with splash oaked 99 "to add balance without being forced to stay in wood too long". 2 500 cases.

Sauvignon Blanc Fruit from 2 producers, selected vyds. **01** (sample) lower alc (13% alc) than Premium version below, but more concentration in good sauvignon yr, mouthwatering acidity; aromatic version with sweet peppers and hints khaki bush. Restrained, undeveloped, needs time (winemaker says first yr in bottle should "serve as part of the winemaking process". 2 500 cases.

Premium range NEW

Cabernet Exciting newcomer which showcases cabernet potential of this appellation. Big structure, intense flavours in **99**. Serious cab for keeping min 5 yrs. **00** (sample) less 'serious', for earlier drinking; warm, ripe, juicy with lovely soft tannins. Will win many friends for cellar/area. 100% Fr oak, 50% new. 8 900 cases. Martin M partners his with oxtail.

✵**Merlot** Big, fleshy **99** introduced this label's trademark ultra-intense varietal choc-cherry-mint ensemble. Hedonistic follow-up **00** ✵ (sample) embroiders theme with endless layers of plush fruit contrasting pleasantly with wild herby hillside whiffs in a palate almost eerily free of tannin. 3 Dbnville vyds. 18 mths oak, 60% new. 8 300 cases.

✵**Pinotage** "Very friendly, accessible wine" the goal, cleverly attained in **99** and again in **00** ✵ (sample), from 2 Dbnville farms, Fr oak aged, 55% new Burgundian cooperage. Extrovert sweet berry fruit, very tender tannins and acidity. Slight hint of wildness adds interest. 8 000 cases.

✵**Shiraz** Exciting shiraz, **99** picked very ripe and fruit-driven with very little of variety's more outspoken aromatics. Unheralded, this 'hidden' side leaps out the **00** ✵ (sample) glass with roasty, toasty, smoky abandon. "Deliberately encouraged development of peppery flavour in the cellar," reveals Martin M, "results even more outspoken than expected." Wonderfully showy wine, will appeal to hard-core shiraz fans, though this essentially an easier/earlier drinking style. 20% new Am oak, 30% new Fr, balance older casks. 7 000 cases.

✵**Sauvignon Blanc** "We got a clear message from restaurants & speciality wine shops," says Martin Moore, "customers don't want an overly serious style in this volume range. So we held back in good 01 vintage and listened to the market." If this is 'holding back', then hang onto your tastebuds! **01** (sample) absolutely packed with full-house of extrovert sauvignon aromas/flavours, from dusty sweet pepper to fig-leaf to gooseberry; concentrated, fresh (but not bracing), wonderfully persistent, lovely bone-dry finish. Dbnville fruit. 13.5% alc. 11 000 cases. Vibier than **00**, which well handled in tricky sauvignon vintage.

Chardonnay Not tasted for this ed. Pvs Slow starting **00** ✵. — *IvH*

Du Toitskloof Winery

Worcester (see Worcester map) • Tasting & sales Mon-Fri 8-5 Sat 8.30-12 • Cellar tours by arrangement • Formal tasting for groups max 40 • Views • Owners 12 members • Winemakers Philip Jordaan (since 1983), Shawn Thomson (since 1999), Jaco Brand (since 1999), Derick Cupido • Consulting viticulturist Schalk du Toit (VinPro) • PRO Arina le Roux • Accountant Verna Kotze Production 11 000 tons • PO Box 55 Rawsonville 6845 • ***Tel (023) 349-1601*** *• Fax (023) 349-1581 • E-mail dutoitcellar@intekom.co.za*

The N1 highway may now bypass this delightful cellar, which was once at the roadside, but faithful customers are more than willing to drive the extra kilometre or two to get their favourite drops, now with spruced-up new labels "to suit the new corporate image". And while some of the drive of the dynamic wine-making team is being directed toward elegant dry reds, more good news is that the easy-drinking whites and sweet fortifieds are being given as much care as ever. Once you're hooked on Philip Jordaan's delicious bottled sunshine, you'll find it hard not to turn off at that Rawsonville exit …

✵**Shiraz** One of the new-generation stars of this cellar. Good varietal black pepper, plum, red berry array in **00**. Big but not worrisome 13.6% alc. This, varietal reds below all oaked ±8 mths. 2 400 cases (approximate number, as are all these). **99** ✵ but Michelangelo gold.

✵**Noble Late Harvest** Impressive **99** debut botrytised dessert from muscat, chenin; Dried-peach, apricot, tropical sweetness cut by racy acidity. SAYWS champ. Low level 93 g/ℓ sugar closer to Sauternes than traditional Cape. 13.5% alc. 4 500 bottles of 375 ml.

✵**Red Muscadel** ✓ Among the Cape's top fortified muscats: opulent, elegant – and always a bargain. Latest **00** just like biting a fresh muscadel grape: sappy, vibrant, youthful; tangy farewell. 16.1% alc. 600 cases. **99** billows rosepetals and honeysuckle; **98** ☆ unexpectedly subdued.

✪ **Hanepoot Jerepigo** ✓ So decorated, it needs its own trophy hall. Current **99** ☆ shimmering brassy-gold, intriguing botrytis hints and silky palate with limpid spirity warmth. Low-cropping bushvines from farm owned by T C Botha. Low 15.3% alc. Astounding ±R15 ex-cellar price. 1 000 cases poised to age rewardingly. *Wine* ✪, Michelangelo gold – as was **95** VG; **97** VG, *Wine* ✪, SAYWS champion. These ±4 g/ℓ acid, 200-230 g/ℓ sugar.

Merlot ☻ ☆ Partial carbonic maceration helps explain effortlessly drinkable **00**, sweet plum flavours balanced by downy dry tannins. Fairly modest alc. 1 600 cases. **Blanc de Noir** ☻ ☆ Snazzy coral colour; **01** with juicy strawberry fruit that finishes gently dry. Easy 11,7% alc. 300 cases. **Special Late Harvest** ☻ ☆ Honeysuckle and tropical perfumes, ripe fruit salad tastes in gentle, lightish semi-sweet **01**; pleasingly zingy finish. Chenin, muscat. 1 600 cases. **Sparkles Brut** ☻ ☆ Light, undemanding carbonated **NV** with bracing muscat/lemon tones, huge fizz, crisp dry finish. Chardonnay, chenin, muscadel. 480 cases.

Cabernet Sauvignon ☆ Becoming more serious by the vintage, still excellent value. SAYWS champion **00** savoury tones, supple 'sweet' flavours/tannins. Philip Jordaan drinks his with pasta carbonara. **Pinotage** ☆ Sweet ripe plums, berries in **00** value-quaff, good juicy mouthful with matching tannins. 13.7% alc. 1 800 cases. **Dry Red** ☆ "Braaivleis wine," says Philip Jordaan, no doubt nosing the smoky tones; gluggable fleshy strawberries from ruby cab, cinsaut; unwooded. **NV** 500 ml screwcap.

Chardonnay ☆ Partially Fr cask-fermented **01**, big (14,1% alc) but balanced; creamy ripe-peach and toasty tastes. 1 250 cases. **Chenin Blanc** ☆ Fruit-packed lightish lunchtime sip; **01** with lemon excitement, piquant finish. 1 300 cases. **Colombard** Untasted. Pvs **00** ☆. **Sauvignon Blanc** ☆ Uncomplicated, value quaff with touch gooseberry, guava and grass in **01**. 13% alc. 1 520 cases. **Riesling** ★ Lightish dry **01** from Cape riesling; demure peardrop, green apple tones. 1 370 cases. **Semillon-Chardonnay** Untasted. Pvs 00 ☆. **Blanc de Blanc** ☆ Delicate floral/pear scents, not too dry, light. **NV** chenin in 500 ml screwcap. **Bukettraube** ☆ Gentle, light floral semi-sweet **01**. Good, Philip Jordaan says, with fresh ripe strawberries. 540 cases. **Late Vintage** Untasted. Pvs **NV** ★. **Cape Vintage Port** ☆ More ruby than vintage character, but perfectly acceptable **99**; some dried prunes, ripe plums with light tannin undertone. Quite dry at 74 g/ℓ sugar. From pinotage. 18.3% alc. — *DH*

EagleVlei

Stellenbosch • Not open to the public • Tasting & sales for trade by appointment • Owners Steve & Jean Weir, André & Tess van Helsdingen • Winemaker André van Helsdingen • Consulting viticulturist Paul Wallace (VineWise) • Vineyards 7 ha • Production 1 500 cases 100% red • PO Box 969 Stellenbosch 7599 • ***Tel/fax (021) 880-1846*** *• E-mail avanhels@adept.co.za • Website www.eaglevlei.co.za*

While many Cape wineries are opening their hearts and doors to tourists, EagleVlei remains a private place, selling all of their small production to the trade or overseas. The addition of 4 hectares of cabernet and pinotage, all under drip irrigation, brings the total area under vine to around 10 ha – which is all they need "to produce top, exclusive red wine," says André van Helsdingen, civil engineer, winemaker and co-owner here with wife Tessa, and Steve and Jean Weir, now living in London. Until these young vines reach maturity, grapes are being bought in from selected Stellenbosch farms. Their first releases, a Cabernet and a

Pinotage, have been well received and earned orders from the UK, Germany and Switzerland. Meanwhile the "sporty, active and busy" van Helsdingens hope someday to welcome visitors: "Who knows, perhaps as we grow this will happen," says Tessa van Helsdingen.

- **Cabernet Sauvignon** Announced itself in style with great-looking/tasting **97**, showcasing elegance of cooler yr. **98** richer, more concentrated, in line with warmer vintage. **99**, tasted at same stage of development, not as impressive. Now there's scintillating **00** to keep the punters smiling: classically correct styling, minerally/flinty textures, elastic tannins gently hugging massed sweet fruit (ex Stbosch's super-starry Slaley farm). Deserves spell in cellar, say 3-4 yrs, to unfurl; should still be stunning in 10 yrs. Fr-oaked, 12 mths. 750 cases.
- **Pinotage** ✓ Returns to high-flying form in **00**, richly perfumed with raspberry/mulberry aromas and generously endowed with persistent sweet fruit. Bottelary grapes, yr Fr oak. Pvs **99** (sampled just post bottling, hence a qualified rating) less exciting than dream-debut **98**, with glossy tannins to match the designer-chic front label. 13,4% alc. These ±500 cases to enjoy with – the van Helsdingens' recommendation – game pie. — *DH*

Eddie Barlow Wines see Windfall

Edonia

Stellenbosch • Not open to the public • Owners GAM Audy • Winemaker Ernst Gouws • Production 4 000 cases own label 80% red 20% white • PO Box 1233 Stellenbosch 7599 • ***Tel (021) 884-4221*** *• Fax (021) 884-4904 • E-mail hoopen@new.co.za*

HOOPENBURG's wine-and-marriage partners Ernst & Gwenda Gouws are the considerable energies behind this export-only brand owned by French negociant house GAM Audy. Made by Ernst Gouws from grapes ex his own vineyard in Stellenbosch plus selected sites in the larger WO Coastal appellation, and exported to Europe and the Far East.

- **Merlot 00** similar to Hoopenburg's own version but slightly lighter/brighter timbre (despite enormous 15% alc); healthy tannin structure accessible but will benefit from 4-6 yrs' bottle ageing. 10 mths new/2nd fill Fr oak. 500 cases.
- **Shiraz 00** wonderfully drinkable example, new world-inclined with lovely lifted fruit from (partial) new Fr oaking (10 mths), palate-broadening alc (14.3%). We'd drink soonish, with (Gwenda Gouws' food suggestion) oxtail casserole. 1 000 cases.
- **Chardonnay** Very attractive, mouthfilling **00**. Peachy fruit flows cleanly through palate to sparkling slightly sweet finish. Potentially heavy 13.7% alc buoyed up by light-toned lemon/lime piquancy. Clever winemaking. 500 cases.

Ruby Cabernet Showcase for variety's attractive qualities in Cape. **00** unwooded; earthy green pepper, ripe plum/cassis combo, plus smoky extras; dry tannic grip leavened by apparent sweetness in finish. Creamy pastas would be good food matches. 13.7% alc. 1 000 cases. — *DH*

Eersterivier Cellar see Stellenbosch Vineyards

Eikehof

Franschhoek (see Franschhoek map) • Tasting, sales, cellar tours by appointment • Owner F Malherbe • Winemaker Francois Malherbe (since 1992) • Vineyards 40 ha • Production 70 tons 4 000 cases 70% red 30% white • PO Box 222 Franschhoek 7690 • ***Tel/fax (021) 876-2469***

This serene father-and-son winery in Franschhoek (its name alludes to the oaks that spread their reviving shade) is home to venerable semillon bushvines that celebrate their centenary this year. They're the pride and joy of fourth-generation winemaker Francois Malherbe, whose forefather Gideon Malherbe planted the first vines on the nearby farm Normandie in 1688. "A few years ago, my father wanted to rip up the old vines and replant. I insisted, 'No, I'll make a very special wine with these old grapes'." And so he does. Semillon, the sometime ubiquitous-in-Cape *groendruif*, is now Eikehof's proud signature, though newer shiraz and merlot are showing the way forward in a predominantly red wine drinking world.

☆**Cabernet Sauvignon** ✓ Since debut **93**, densely packed, showy, sturdily tannined for long keeping. **00** cast in this mould but step up in quality: cherries/mulberries in ripe profusion, sweet/spicy oak and muscular tannins that will help elevate the wine to, on current form, ☆☆ maturity around 2010. 13,5% alc. 2 200 cases. Youthfully astringent **99** ☆, not as serious as some pvs, though not without charm.

☆**Shiraz** ✓ **00** from pvs ed still being raised in Nevers small-oak (so consider rating provisional). Plums and muted whiffs wild scrub, sweet tannins with parting dark-choc hints. Confident start, looks like needing ±5 yrs development, will be very good. Own vyds. Tiny quantities: 80 cases.

☆**Bush Vine Semillon** ✓ Deep-flavoured dry white, with distinction of springing, with admirable verve and freshness, from ancient low-cropped bush vines. **99**, WOM selection, re-tasted mid-01, punchy, sweetly fruited almost rich; contrast with **00** ☆, light asrtringency noted in pvs ed now more overt; perhaps a temporary feature but suggest monitor regularly. These whole-bunch pressed, 50% oak fermented/aged 6-8 mths, Fr/Am casks; tank-fermented portion sur lie. 13-13,5% alc. ±600 cases. Regular **Semillon** ☆ Mix ancient/youthful, bush/trellised vines, briefly oaked, similar smells/tastes but notch less intense, faster-maturing. **00** drinks well now; clean limey freshness, some buttery oak roundness. 13,5% alc. 500 cases.

☆**Chardonnay** ✓ This will appeal to those to prefer the fruitier style. **99** melon/lemon aromas; full, creamy mouth, tapered citrus zesty finish. Latest **00** delightfully soft and gentle, citrusy; mere suggestion of vanilla-oak. Whole bunch pressed, cask-fermented 50/50 Fr/Am but not matured. ±13% alc. 800 cases.

Merlot ☆ Charming, silk-tannined **00** offers sweet violets in ripe, pruney palate. Francois M likes to drink his with springbok steaks or lamb casseroles. Oak-aged. 13% alc. 2 200 cases. — *DH*

Eikendal Vineyards

Stellenbosch (see Helderberg map) Tasting & sales Mon-Fri 9-5 Sat 9-4 (Oct-Apr); 9-1 (May-Sep) Sun 10-4 Tasting fee R10 p/p • Cellar tours Mon-Fri 11.30 & 2.30 (Dec-Feb) • Summer picnic baskets or country platter (Oct-Apr) Mon-Fri & Sun (mid-Nov to mid-Apr) Booking essential • Friday evening fondue (Jun-Sep) Book ahead • Eikendal Lodge B&B • Function facilities • Owners Substantia AG (Switzerland) • General manager Hennie Pool (since 2001) • Cellarmaster/production manager Josef Krammer (since 1987) • Production 500 tons 30 000 cases • PO Box 2261 Dennesig 7601 • ***Tel (021) 855-1422*** *• Fax (021) 855-1027 • E-mail eikendal@netactive.co.za • Website www.eikendal.com*

One of the Cape's best-kept secrets, Eikendal's wines are seldom advertised or puffed with self-praise. But this Swiss-owned gem, with Austrian-born stalwart Josef Krammer orchestrating the cellar (long-time deputy Anneke Burger now West Coasting at Groene Cloof) produces consistently fine wines. The whole tone of Eikendal is modest and understated. The team prefer to allow their products to speak for themselves. And what poetry they speak! Those who hear them for the first time simply can't believe their luck. "Why have I never tasted these wines?" they sigh. And there are other secrets to yodel about – the elegant picnic lunches beside the little lake, the cosy winter fondues, the vine-ringed B&B. New chief-of-staff Hennie Pool assures the tone will not change "despite organisational changes and a few new faces". Indeed, why tweak a winning formula? With new shiraz and merlot coming into production, there's more excitement in store...

Cabernet Sauvignon Reserve Made only in exceptional years and then released when up to demanding scratch; only from cellar door. **99**'s initially strong tannic barrier yielding, releasing fragrant spices, red cherry/cassis fruits – all in Eikendal's restrained display; powerful 14,2% alc folded away. 17 mths new barriques. 150 cases. *Wine* ✵. Pvs was **96**. 100% cab, 2 yrs casked. Regular **Cabernet Sauvignon** ✓ ✵ Back-taste of still-available **98** reveals a more sophisticated, complex individual. Tannins softening, energising the fruit; extra whiffs of funghi, sweet spice and toast. Enough substance for 3-4 more yrs. ±24 mths used oak, some Am for spice. 2 000 cases.

Merlot ✓ Eikendal has led Cape merlot direction since first **91**. Latest **00** stumps most pvs from this property with finely controlled display of luscious ripe fruit, toasty oak seasoning (Fr casks, 12 mths). Recent vintages more assertively tannic than pvs, yet here balanced by fruit sweetness, smidgeon actual sugar (3 g/ℓ) for pleasurable smoothness. 13.5% alc. 1 200 cases. **99** less luxuriant than pvs, still irresistibly charming. WOM Reserve. **98** ripe blackberry flesh, venison/roast coffee scents.

Classique Blend cab, merlot, cab f (60/22/8) in **99**; livelier than pvs; more generous berry-cherry fruits yet still firmish, full (13.6% alc). Needs 2/3 yrs to settle/grow (possibly into higher star rating). 1 200 cases. **98** merlot-led, with puckering tannins needing time in bottle to soften. WOM Reserve. These ±20 mths new/2nd fill Fr barrels.

Rossini NEW Suave entrant to burgeoning red blend scene. Sleek, understated in the Eikendal manner, not too full (13% alc); yet generously proportioned, sweet-fruited and ripe, also savoury and very smooth, almost creamy. **99** blend cab s/f, shiraz, merlot; 20 mths oak. Bit unsettled still; keep 2-3 yrs then drink for further 3 min. 500 cases.

Chardonnay Bulging chest of awards for this consistently excellent example since **92** (SA champion young white wine of yr). Current **00** maintains the excitement: immediate impression of sweet, smooth fruit; lovely clean-cut seamless flavours and vanilla-spicy oak, which deeply embedded in core of citrus fruit. Track record for good development over 3-5 yrs. Barrel-fermented, 100% new wood, 7 mths. 2 000 cases. **Reserve 99** becoming deliciously creamy while retaining wonderful chalky complexity with hints of marmalade, sweet caramel. Fantastic finish. cellar door only. Cask-fermented/aged 10 mths. 12. 9% alc. 150 cases.

Sauvignon Blanc ✓ Well priced, med-bodied refreshment for those who prefer less grassy bite in their sauvignon. **01** delightfully crisp, clean, very lively but unaggressive. 1 000 cases. Level above **00**.

Pinot Noir **00** reflects influence of French cellar assistant, Christian Cardet: incredible colour extraction from unfashionable BK5 clone. Revisited mid-01 shows good development, complexity; now some savoury hints, suppler tannins. Drink or keep yr/2. 13.3% alc. 400 cases. **Cabernet Sauvignon-Merlot** Last was **99** ✵, not retasted for this ed. **Blanc Fumé** Uncorking **00** yr on suggests these counter-trendy individuals (40% barrel fermented) improve with age; nicely round, gentle toast/lees accents developing; original intriguing thatchy aromas intact. WOM Value. **01** preview shows benefit or cool yr. ±13% alc. 1 000 cases. **Blanc de Blanc** Invariably fresh, undemanding drink-young dry chenin/sauvignon blend. Med-bodied **01** rousing tropical/lemony flavours, generous beyond price level. **Verdi** NEW Charming, crisp, just-dry aperitif; sauvignon, chenin, chardonnay; lightly oaked and uncomplicatedly drinkable. 500 cases. **Stein** Not retasted for this ed. Pvs **99** ☆. **Chenin Blanc-Sauvignon Blanc Demi-Sec** ★ Unwieldy name for simple, lightish fruity sparkler, not over-sweet, balanced; foamy mousse. 300 cases.

Rouge ☻ ☆ Best seller with bearing. **99** clean tangy/savoury melange of 5 varieties, ±6 mths Slovenian large wood. Refreshingly lowish 12% alc. "Also very good for glühwein," reminds Josef Krammer. 5 000 cases. **Chenin Blanc** ☻ ☆ Part barrel-fermented **01** (sample) perhaps best value in Stbosch. Usual off-dry tones with extra frisson from cooler growing season. 13.5% alc. 1 000 cases. **Special Late Harvest** ☻ ☆ Even determined dry white drinkers can't resist these ingeniously proportioned drops. Like pvs, **01** packed with tangerine, pink grapefruit medley. Refreshing late-gripping, cleansing acid for cloy-free quaffing. From chenin, botrytis-brushed. **Sauvignon Blanc Brut** ☻ ☆ Carbonated bubbly with grassy nose, refreshing crisp finish. **NV**. Moderate alc for aperitif sipping. WOM Value. 500 cases. — *DH*

Eikestad see Vinfruco
Elements see Hartswater

Elephant Pass Vineyards

Franschhoek • Closed to the public. • Self-catering guest cottage Tel (021) 876-3280/082-937-3789 • Owners Peter & Ann Wrighton • Consulting winemaker Jean Daneel (since 1998) • Viticulturist Steve Smith (since 1998) • Vineyards 5 ha • Production ±800 cases 50/50 red/white • PO Box 415 Franschhoek 7690 • ***Tel (021) 876-3666*** *• Fax (021) 876-2219*

Peter Wrighton, owner of the attractive little farm, Oude Kelder, is concerned (he certainly isn't alone) about the high alcohol levels being reached in SA wines. "Because of our high sugar levels, we're getting wines with 14% or more alcohol," he says. "In France they're more used to about 12%. Our high levels could have a detrimental effect on sales." This retired industry captain has no problems selling his own boutique quantities, which travel to Europe and the US from their birthplace beside the old elephant trail in Franschhoek.

☆ **Merlot** Refined style, characterised by purity of fruit, superlative oak management (forte of Diners Club-ovationed Jean Daneel). **98** set the scene, now followed by **99** ☆, which appears less substantial (despite much higher alc: 14.2%), more streamlined; oak very well integrated. Perhaps in a trough, give yr/2 to integrate, unfold. These 20 mths Fr oaked, 40% new. 200 cases.

☆ **Blanc Fumé** Returns to guide with **00**, 100% sauvignon, matured in 2nd fill Fr oak, vinified for Fr profile "rather than flinty New Zealand style, requiring use of relatively unripe grapes in our climate". Understated; atypical sauvignon with snow-pea bouquet; unusually substantial palate (not attained via alc, which only 12.7%); intuitively oaked. Will appeal greatly to sauvignon aficionados.

Chardonnay Reserve ☆ Beginning to show bottle maturation character, probably at peak; med-bodied **99** with nice butterscotch and honey to complement the piquant lemon-peel. Fr oak-matured, 40% new. 75 cases only. **Celebration** Toasts this property's miraculous escape from 99 raging forest fire. Limited stocks still available at press time. **NV** not restated for this ed. Pvs rating ☆. — *CF*

Elixir see African Terroir
Emerald Glen see Stellekaya
Equus see Zandvliet
Eventide see Mischa

Excelsior Estate

Robertson • Not open to the public • Cellar tours by appointment • Owners/viticulturists Stephen & Freddie de Wet • Winemaker Jaco Marais (since 1996) • Vineyards 250 ha • Production 2 500 tons 60% red 40% white • PO Excelsior Estate Ashton 6715 • ***Tel (023) 615-2050/1980*** *• Fax (023) 615-2019 • E-mail stephendewet@hotmail.com*

MOST SA wineries start local, then consider going global. Brothers Stephen and Freddie de Wet have excelled by bucking convention. Most of their cases travel overseas (and onto the shelves of UK mega-chains Waitrose and Tesco, among others). Their local presence is quite recent "but highly successful," says Stephen de Wet. Their world – and now SA – conquering recipe is, they reveal, "affordable quality". And if you think you've heard that line before, consider (more trend-dodging here) they're actually planning to establish white varieties to meet the demand for their Sauvignon and Chardonnay. In the meantime they're not neglecting reds: 34 hectares of shiraz have been planted recently, and they've released their first Merlot. This, focused young Jaco Marais feels, is a good lunchtime option that complements "the full spectrum of foods". And if Excelsior isn't on your favourite restaurant winelist, you can always pop into The Wine Boutique in nearby Ashton, where the full range of Robertson Valley wine is available at cellar prices.

Special Reserve ✓ Flavour-packed, sweetish from ripe plum/mulberry fruits and big alc (14%); yet well controlled by oak; **98** mellowing, still enough tannins for 5-7 yrs' good development. Yr Fr/Am casks, portion unwooded. 2 400 cases.

Cabernet Sauvignon 00 property's first single vyd wine, specifically for estate label (other blocks blended for customers' private labels); promising, balanced; fruit/tannin for now and 5-7 yrs. 9 mths oak, 80% Fr, rest Am. 10 000 cases. Trumps **99** with plummy baked-fruit quality. 14% alc.

Merlot NEW **00** first from this winery, aged 9 mths Fr/Am oak. Light tints, violets and mocha fragrances, then some unexpectedly chunky tannins needing bit of time or strongly flavoured cuisine. 13.5% alc. 8 000 cases. **Chardonnay 01** not ready for tasting. Pvs **00**. **Sauvignon Blanc** **01** compelling mix of tropical tones and aromatic 'cool climate' crispness. Frisky, fun wine, easy to drink and well priced. Commendable quality given the volumes. 13,5% alc. 20 000 cases. — *DH*

Excelsior-Vlakteplaas see Kango

Fairseat Cellars

Not open to the public • Owner Dick Davidson • PO Box 53058 Kenilworth 7745 • ***Tel (021) 797-1951*** *• Fax (021) 762-9656 • E-mail fairseat@mweb.co.za*

NEGOCIANT and Cape Wine Master Dick Davidson sources wines locally for export to Europe. The range, not tasted for this ed, features a widely praised label with original oil by well known Cape artist James Yates.

Fair Valley

Not open to the public • Wines mainly for export, but may be available ex-Fairview (see that entry). • Owner Fair Valley Workers Association • Winemaker Awie Adolph • Production 1 500 cases • PO Box 583 Suider Paarl 7624 • ***Tel (021) 863-2450*** *• Fax (021) 863-2591*

The Fair Valley Workers Association, one of the first farmworker empowerment initiatives in the Western Cape, took some time to get off the ground initially because of some bureaucratic hiccups. Now they're positioned for take-off: last year they showed their wines at a Dutch trade show, all part of the drive spearheaded by export manager Marlene Fortuin, to increase their overseas base (Oddbins in the UK is already a regular customer), and winemaker Awie Adolph proudly introduced the maiden Pinotage 2001. It bears the new label, which sums it all up beautifully: "The hands that work the soil feed the soul ... " Construction of the first eight homes on the 17-hectare Fair Valley farm adjacent to Fairview is underway, and next up are the winery and own-vineyards. The range not tasted for this ed. Last was a **Chenin Blanc 00** (☆).

Fairview

*Paarl (see Paarl map) • Tasting & sales Mon-Fri 8.30-5 Sat 8.30-1 Closed Good Friday, Christmas, New Year's Day • Groups by appointment • Cheese and wine tasting/sales Fee R10 p/p • Play area for children • Views • Wheelchair-friendly • Owner Charles Back • Winemakers Anthony de Jager (since 1996) & Charles Back • Viticulturist Johan Botha • Marketing Jeremy Borg • PO Box 583 Suider-Paarl 7624 • **Tel (021) 863-2450** • Fax (021) 863-2591 • E-mail fairback@iafrica.com • Website www.fairview.co.za*

This is the supercharged HQ for the Wines of Charles Back. The unorthodox winemaker-turned-phenomenon spends most of his time in the vineyards, where he's long been successfully experimenting with non-traditional varieties, or tasting in his cellars (here in Paarl, at Spice Route in the Swartland and the adjacent micro-winery on the Kalbaskraal road, from which Back intends to produce a single iconic blend). When his three talented winemakers fly off for crushes in climates warmer, Back gets left in charge, "a measure of their trust in me," he quips, without irony. A new 600 ton red wine cellar was completed just in time for the 2001 vintage. There's space pressure even with it, announces unflappable winemaker Anthony de Jager, but "hectares and hectares of space out there", he enthuses of untapped local vineyards, Agter-Paarl being the current playground of choice. "We have world-class wines on our doorstep, all that's needed is some tweaking and attention to detail." Which happens to be the forte of resident marketing virtuoso Jeremy Borg, who's masterminded a treat for Britons foraging through their 'Naked Chef' Jamie Olivier gourmet Christmas hampers: bottles of irreverently named Goats do Roam, soon to be joined in the range by the equally saucy Goat Roti.

☆**Malbec** ✓ Glow-inducer, real 'bistro wine' with extra exotic appeal from scarcity of variety in Cape; **00** thumbprint gutsy sweet summer fruits, juicy textures/tannins, long food-friendly finish. Best young. Fairview grapes, lightly Fr-oaked. 13.7% alc. More exciting than **99** ☆.

☆☆**Primo Pinotage** ✓ Assured, non-interventionist winemaking immediately apparent in **00**'s stunning 'grainy' robes reflecting pristine purple fruit within (unfined/unfiltered). Massively flavourful, complex; layered sweet mulberry/cherry tones bestrewn with cloves, vanilla and coffee. Bountiful tannins, still quite overt, organise and focus the sumptuousness, bring it to classically bone-dry conclusion. Grapes ex bushvines on Jan Greef's eponymous Agter-Paarl farm. 9 mths new oak. Deserved IWSC gold. 14.8% alc.

☆☆**Amos Pinotage** Malmesbury bushvines bestow their bounty on **99**, glowing purple in fleshy glassful of choc-dipped black cherries. Pervasive hints of violets, vanilla in ripe-tannined dry finish. Fruit ex Klein Amos Kuil farm, harvested at 25°B. 14 mths new barrels; unfined/unfiltered. 13.7% alc.

☆**Shiraz** ✓ This winery's signature and Cape bellwether since benchmark **74**. Latest **00** (sample) plummy with sweet-violets perfume and suggestion of mint; early-approachable tannins; should develop spicily over 5 yrs or more. Variety of clones grown on own farm, 7 t/ha yield. 14 mths mostly Fr oak, some Am. **99** similar qualities; **98** complex smoked-meat, fennel accents to concentrated red-berry flavours.

☆☆ **Cyril Back Shiraz** Salute to Charles Back's late father, shiraz pioneer; in modern, expressive mode as above but classically styled, not a blockbuster. **98** Michelangelo gold. Crimson-edged **99** developing into something extraordinary; dark mulberry glow; bouquet of plums, pepper, mixed-spice and ginger; deep, powerful, creamy flavours delicious now and for anything up to 10 yrs. Own-farm fruit. Yr Am/Fr casks. 14,3% alc.

☆ **Zinfandel 00** not quite as massive as brace-yourself **97** ☆, which packed California-esque 16,4% alc. Latest more contained yet retains some of variety's signature 'wildness', brawn (15.2% alc); ripe, packed with pulpy summer berries which, though off-dry (9.4 g/ℓ sugar), taste rich rather than sweet. Paarl bushvines, 20+ yrs old, harvested 27°B.

☆ **Zinfandel-Cinsault** ✓ Another bit of creative blending, eagerly snaffled in quantity by canny UK retail chains. Lovely sweet strawberry jam, stewed prune flavours of **99** ☆ reprised in **00**'s soft, juicy mouthful; sweet spicy fruit oozes from every crevice yet ample tannins and gentle oak keep it all under control. Paarl-area grapes, fermented together on oak staves. 14% alc.

☆ **Goats do Roam** Fairview's cheeky riposte to the much-hyped Cotes-du-Rhone styles, brilliantly packaged and marketed, and a smash in the UK especially. Red blend 7 varieties "personal selection by the rampant Fairview Goats as they Roam the vineyards for the ripest fruit", according to the Back label. Suitably southern Fr air about **00**, liquorice and sweet spices to succulent plum fruit; best in blooming youth (though could easily go 2/3 yrs). Very lightly oaked. 13,1% alc. More concentration, persistence than **99** ☆. Exceptional, unsurprisingly, with Fairview's goats milk cheese.

☆ **Goats do Roam Rosé** ✓ Natural companion to red billy above; in juicy-dry style. Features super-youthful fruit selected by "in-house cheese-making family goatherd". Drink-young **01** friskier than first-out **00** (top dry rosé at Sydney IWC), more presence, flavour; shimmering pink shades mirror fleshy cherries, raspberries, rosepetal wisps. Firm finish excellent with food. Partly oak-fermented. Mostly bushvines ex 4 areas (including rising-star Piekenierskloof), lightly oaked. 13.2% alc.

☆ **Akkerbos Chardonnay** Top-drawer Cape chardonnay, name an allusion to the numerous English oaks shading the property (acorns pvsly tasty snacks for the farm pigs). Own grapes given full Burgundian oak treatment (fermented/sur lie 14 mths Fr barrels; malo). **99** ripe pineapple, passion fruit tastes and firm, concentrated citrus; endless toasty finish. WOM Reserve. **00** ☆☆ rivetingly complex, creamy; already beautifully harmonious with promise of growth over 3-5 yrs. 13,9% alc.

☆ **Chardonnay** ✓ **99** from AdJ's favourite vyd: "Consistent thread of citrus from this block". Lime-grapefruit juiciness wrapped in vanilla (from Fr/Am oak, equal new/2nd fill); firm, muscular finish with butterscotch twist. **01** (sample) similar but spicier, sweeter-fruited, already balanced for current drinking and potential for 2-4 yrs ageing. Bone-dry finish. Fermented/aged 6 mths new/2nd fill Fr/Am barriques. 14% alc.

☆ **Chenin Blanc** ✓ Gorgeous sweet-oak backing to soft ripe fruits; **01** mouthfilling, clean leesy undertone which good now and could age interestingly. Paarl/Malmesbury bushvines; cask-fermented/sur lie 6 mths. 14.4% alc. **99** ☆ new-oak fermented, muscular lime/peach flavours.

☆☆ **Oom Pagal Semillon** Shimmering green-gold hues of **00** exude sophistication and class. Introduced with smoky citrus aromas and toasted hazelnuts; sweet citrus fruits and lees sweep into palate with controlled power; variety's beeswax tones add complexity, richness to sumptuous yet balanced wine. Hot vintage reflected in ripe 14.7% alc, seamlessly absorbed. Superb now and anything up to 9 yrs. Barrel-fermented/aged new med-toast barrels, 7 mths. **99** Michelangelo gold.

✵**Semillon** ✓ **00** attractive combo lemons/limes, creamy beeswax and leesy textures suffused with elegant sweet fruit; good lemon-zest finish offsets weightiness of big 14.4% alc. Paarl grapes, whole-bunch pressed; cask-fermented/aged 7 mths, new oak. **99** ✵ oak-fermented, substantial (14,5% alc), with dash sauvignon for extra perk on palate. Michelangelo gold.

✵**Viognier** Now a signature wine for this cellar; hailed as among the finest in the new world from this tricky Rhone grape. Maiden **98** praised by wine eminence Jancis Robinson as "triumph of world class". *Wine* ✵, IWSC gold. Greater concentration in subsequent releases as vines mature. **00** Michelangelo gold. Latest **01** breathtakingly full (14.4% alc), round, stacked with variety's peach/apricot tones and hints orange; delicious (and arguably best) now, though structure to keep 2/4 yrs. Barrel-fermented/aged 2nd fill Fr oak. Excellent with Fairview's La Beryl Pont l'Eveque-style cheese.

✵**La Beryl Blanc** Riesling 'straw wine', one of the new-breed Cape desserts (ripe grapes given extra oomph by allowing to air-dry on straw mats). First was **99** ⁂ creamy fruit-salad aromas and touches spice; soft, juicy-sweet flavours. *Wine* ✵. Upscale **00**, from chenin, exotic dried peach, apricot whiffs over massively concentrated sweet/sour palate, braced by rapier acidity for whistle-clean finish (250 g/ℓ sugar, 9 g/ℓ acid).

✵**La Beryl Rouge** ('Straw Wine' in pvs ed) ⁂ Red version of above, from cinsaut; medium garnet-ruby hues, initially shyer than counterpart, more effusive with strawberry/peanut brittle nuances. **00** lacks concentration, richness, balance of white version; drier at 122 g/ℓ.

Gamay Noir ☻ ⁂ Invariably charming and harmoniously quaffable; fruitily dry; latest purple-hued **01** refreshes with blackcurrant zest, hint of gingerbread in juicy palate. Drink chilled (with braaied fish or chicken) – and soon. 12.5% alc.

Carignan ⁂ Dense purple hues in **00**, with splash shiraz; crimson edge previews sweet raspberries and cinnamon; smoky firm finish. Yr barrelled. Vyd "accidentally found whilst looking for old-vine pinotage"! 14.1% alc. **Pinotage** ⁂ Variety's forwardly robust aspects – lively tannins, dark smoky fruit – nicely balanced in **00** by ripe juicy tones of plum and cherry. Easy/early drink with legs for 2-4 yrs. 8 mths new oak. 13.5% alc. **Shiraz-Mourvèdre** ⁂ New to this ed in **00**, emblazoned with opulent fruit and some dark choc/truffle tones; tannins invisible until the very end, materialise smoothly dry. 75/25 blend, grapes ex Fairview. 8 mths new Fr/Am oak. 13.9% alc. **Sauvignon Blanc** ⁂ **01** step above pvs; well padded with ripe gooseberry/fig and hints nettle; acid nicely pitched to invigorate non-aggressively. Malmesbury fruit. 13.1% alc. **Goats do Roam White** NEW ⁂ Delightful addition to the Goats family, featuring quartet of grapes including viognier and uniquely (with special permission from the authorities) grenache blanc. **01** big-boned (14% alc) yet very easy to drink; smoothly dry, balanced; aromatic thyme/rosemary counterpoints to unwooded peach/lime fruits. For current drinking. 14% alc. Not tasted for this ed: **Cabernet Sauvignon** (Pvs **98** ⁂), **Merlot** (**99** ✵), **Anthony's Chardonnay** (**98** ✵), **Special Late Harvest** (**99** ⁑), **Hanepoot** (**99** ⁂). — *DH*

Fat Bastard

Enquiries: Richard Kelley at Vinimark (see that entry).

Tongue-in-cheek international label created by European wine-partners Thierry Boudinaud and Guy Anderson. After a long afternoon's blending, one cuvee stood out as being truly exceptional, and Anderson commented that it was reminiscent of a good Batard-Montrachet; Boudinaud retorted that it was more of a "fat bastard of a chardonnay" and the name stuck. In 1995, some 1 800 cases were produced and soon snapped up; this year about 250 000 cartons will be shipped to Europe, America and the Far East (a Syrah, unavailable locally, is also made). South Africa's own FB is from the Robertson Valley.

✵**Chardonnay** Latest **01**, like maiden **99**, strikes with bracing fruity verve. Presently outspoken tone needs food riposte or yr/2 bottle age. Partly barrel-fermented. 750/1 500 ml. No **00**. — *DH*

Fernkloof see Cape Wine Exports
Five Heirs see Wiese Portfolio

Flagstone Winery & Vineyards

Cape Town • Tasting, sales, cellar tours by appointment • Owners Jack family • Winemakers Bruce Jack, Dudley Wilson, Matt Orton, Gerald Cakijana, Themba Mtiya • Viticulturist Bruce Jack • Production 400 tons 28 000 cases 50% red 44% white 6% blanc de noir • ***Tel (021) 425-3766*** *• Fax (021) 425-3764 • E-mail terraceroad@icon.co.za • Website www.flagstonewines.com*

Wine of Origin Waterfront? You'd be forgiven for thinking so – this company has its cellar at Cape Town's world-famous V&A dockyard. During the crush, don't be surprised to see a 24-hours-a-day tribe with purple hands, wide-eyed on coffee, scurrying about from cellar to vineyard to advanced cold storage facility (the reason they're here in the very spot where Jan van Riebeeck is thought to have waded ashore in 1652). This inveterate bunch go 'cherry picking' in vineyards everywhere (gently persuading growers to hand over management of selected parcels in the process). Bruce Jack and his fellow "bungee jumpers" have heard some of their choices described as risky, even extreme. They drop 80% of the crop in some of their vineyards, cold-soak their reds for up to a month and encourage natural, wild ferments. Then they frown on the use of sulphur. "This could be deemed a little excessive but never risky," counters Jack. For them, seeing their hard work and uncompromising attitude recognised with consumer high-fives is vindication enough. For the rest, they're content to carry on sleeping, drinking, loving and living wine. The wines not tasted for this edition. Currently available are: Foundation Range: **The Music Room** (cab), **Writer's Block** (pinotage), **BK5** (pinot noir), **Poetry Collection** (pinot noir), **Longitude** ("crafted red blend"), **Dragon Tree** (cab/pinotage); **Resolute 166** (chardonnay), **Two Roads** (chardonnay), **Semaphore** (pinot gris); **Free Run** (sauvignon), **Heywood House** (barrel-fermented sauvignon), **Noon Gun** (dry white blend); Strata Series ("experimental, once-off, seriously adventurous wines"): **Rockwood** (cab), **The Shindig** (shiraz), **George's Blend** (pinot/merlot), **Strata** (wild barrel-fermented chenin), **The Discovery** (pinot meunier), **The Rumour Mill** (viognier).

Flamingo Bay see Darling Cellars
Fleermuisklip see Lutzville

Fleur du Cap

Tasting & sales at Bergkelder (see that entry).

"Don't call me a white winemaker", skyscraper Karl Lambour says impishly. "People might get the wrong end of the stick. I happen to make the white wines." Iconoclastic Lambour makes up a sparky duo with Coenie Snyman, the wise young man of the cellar who makes the reds for this very established, freshly energised range – and happened to come up with the idea of the critically acclaimed, new expanded Unfiltered Collection. "We want to make wines with outspoken varietal character," Snyman explains, "that give the best possible expression to a specific site. That means avoiding filtration, which strips away flavour, as part of a non-interventionist approach."

Unfiltered Collection

Cabernet Sauvignon 96 revealed intentions for a modern, sophisticated cab to lead this unfiltered, unstabilised range – which may throw harmless deposits if given the few yrs it deserves. Deeply coloured **97** good flesh supported by 100% new oak. Same oak regime for latest **98** (entirely Fr casks – pvs 20% Am), Helderberg fruit; like Merlot below, unshowy, controlled; cedary dark-berried depths needing time to develop. 13% alc chimes with more restrained tone. 600 cases.

Merlot Exotically spiced **96** began this vinous journey in remarkable fashion; **97** showed a richer, darker-toned nuance; stylish **98**, ex Bottelary, 18 mths oaked, 50% new Fr, classically inclined with lead-pencil whiffs, spicy tannins, ripe damson fruit. Big wine (±14% alc) but feels more contained. Bdx-like touch tar in finish. 600 cases.

Chardonnay NEW Hedonistic **00** barrique-fermented; flavour packed, with sweet, juicy yellow-peaches piled onto spicy new oak. Breakfasty bouquet of lime marmalade toast. Another Lambour-sized number (harvested 24/25°B for power alc around 14.5%; technically off-dry at 4.1 g/ℓ sugar) yet somehow attains an aura of grace.

Sauvignon Blanc ✓ On retaste mid-01, higher rating for exceptional **00**, ripening in bottle and gaining terrific sweet (not honeyed) tones from highly concentrated gooseberry fruit; some dusty/peppery whiffs (Dbnville fruit making its presence felt). Rich, full in mouth, big but soft acidity, big yet unintimidating alc (13.6%).

Semillon NEW Classically constructed **00** eloquent expression of varietal; high-toned citrus, lanoline and deeper accents of limestone cliff, damp cellar; all clean-cut, pure rather than opulent (despite munificent ±14% alc) but satisfying nonetheless. Somewhat shy mid-01, doubtless in dumb phase, try again half-way through 02.

Standard range

Cabernet Sauvignon "**97** was an excellent vintage," enthuses Coenie Snyman. We agree: rating for this stylish, classic cab, 18 mths barrelled, 50% new, mostly Fr; lightish-bodied but wonderfully deep flavoured, cedary; cassis/dark berries woven into fine, cool tannins. Stunning now and, we suggest, in the shorter term. Outstanding performance given the high quantities (35 000 cases). **96** successful in generally light yr. Probably readier for drinking than previous few vintages. Both WOM selections.

Merlot Many show awards for this label, though to us recent vintages more workmanlike. Latest **99** spicy, nice poise between fruit, oak; chunky tannins, though, needing yr/2 to settle. Yr barrelled, 35% new oak. 35 000 cases. **98** softer, dark fruited. Fairly high alcs (±13,5%).

Pinotage Smidgeon new oak for **98**, big (13.7% alc), packed with ripe red fruits; contrasting fruit-sweetness, very dry finish. 20 000 cases. **97** somewhat tart, dryly tannic. WOM selection.

Shiraz Somewhat shy **99**, med-bodied; warm baked fruit, roast beef sniffs; good savoury tannins. Yr/2 needed for flavours to become fully fleshed. 18 mths oak. 15 000 cases. **98** firmly structured, dominating acidity.

Chardonnay ✓ Probably best price:quality ratio for variety in Cape. Mastercrafted **00** shimmers bright lemon-gold, tastes creamily of vanilla-biscuit, finishes harmoniously with citrus tang. Delicious. Still slightly powdery from 9 mths oak, 50% new, so probably best kept yr/2. 13.5% alc. Wood-fermented **99** rich, limey, balanced. **98** low-keyed, elegant yet rich.

Chenin Blanc NEW Introduced ahead of Diners Club 01 competition, 100% barrelled **00** certainly in showstopping style (golds at Michelangelo, Juliet Cullinan competitions): very ripe, massive (15.5% alc), concentrated; dominated by oak mid-01, but should knit and ripen very well over 2-3 yrs (and become starrier). 70 cases.

Sauvignon Blanc ✓ Hits the spot in cooler **01** vintage with full-house of asparagus, cat's pee, pepper tones; full (13.6% alc.), broad-textured with persistent, freshening acidity. Should keep yr/2.

Riesling Unusually sweet **01** very light bodied, floral. From Cape riesling. **Natural Light** Not insubstantial despite low 10% alc. **01** round, soft with ample lemony/grassy flavours. Mostly from chenin. **Noble Late Harvest** Still-available **96** not retasted for this ed. Pvs rating . — *IvH*

Fontein see International Wine Services
Forge Mill see Franschhoek Vineyards
Forrester Vineyards see Ken Forrester

Fort Simon Estate

Stellenbosch (see Stellenbosch map) • Tasting & sales Mon-Fri 9.30-5 Sat 10-2 & public holidays 10-4 Tasting fee R5 for 5 wines • Cellar tours by arrangement • Light meals for up to 50 by appointment • Locale for receptions for 40-50 guests by arrangement • Views • Wheelchair-friendly • Owners Renier & Petrus Uys • Winemaker Marinus Bredell (since 1997) • Viticulturist Renier Uys (since 1983) • Vineyards 61 ha • Production 20 000 cases 60% red 40% white • PO Box 43 Sanlamhof 7532 • ***Tel (021) 906-0304*** *• Fax (021) 906-0304 • E-mail fortsim@iafrica.com*

For the first-time visitor, Fort Simon comes as something of a surprise. You round a bend in the road and are faced with a huge medieval fortress, complete with battlements, moat and drawbridge. Hardly the sort of thing one expects in the sleepy Boland hills. But don't be fooled by the whimsical setting. Behind the fairytale facade is a state-of-the-art winery where Marinus Bredell has been producing some seriously good wines for owners Renier and Petrus Uys. The range will soon be expanded following new plantings of malbec, shiraz and pinotage. This is a great venue for receptions and parties, and they can accommodate up to 4 000 guests. It's wheelchair friendly too. Wines from Fort Simon have found a ready market in several countries, including Estonia.

Pinotage First-release **98** raspberry/plum flavours joined by banana, cinnamon, brush tar. Relaxed sweetish tannins and thumping 14% alc. Follow-up **99** lighter in alc (13.2%), extract; tight tannins noted pvsly need yet more time. ±9 mths Fr/Am oak, 2nd fill. 14 000 cases.

Merlot ✓ **98** first release introduced pleasingly soft, richer style with bouquet of blackcurrant, violets and distinctive sweetish impression, very full alc (14%). **99** in similar mould with slightly sterner tannins, needing yr/2 to soften. Extra roasty/toasty dimension to go with grilled meats. These 9 mths 300 ℓ Fr oak (**99** 30% Am), 2nd fill.

Anna Simon Merlot-Pinotage 98 launched this label in fine fashion with VVG, Diners Club shortlisting. Multi-fruited **99** offered cherries, plums, blackberries, whiff tomato from the vegetable patch. Distinctive sweetness cut short by drying tannins. **00** high-toned, plummy; edgy acidity needs time to tone down. 13.4% alc. Combo oak chips/barrels 4-6 mths. 5 500 cases.

Chardonnay ✓ Marinus Bredell has a great affinity with this grape. Again evident in **00** with delectable tones of butterscotch, caramel and toast; pervasively, persistently flavoured. Bright, fresh core of lemony fruit augurs well for development. 2 300 cases. **98** VG, *Wine* . These fermented/aged 8 mths new 300 ℓ Fr oak. ± 13,5% alc. Aussie smoothing trick – touch imperceptible sugar (± 3,5 g/ℓ) – used.

Chenin Blanc Barrel Fermented ✓ Deftly oaked to highlight delicate fruit. **98** SAA. **99** WOM selection. **00** lemon piquancy layered with smoky oak. Latest **01** (sample) finest to date; particularly well oaked, adds Eastern spices, touch vanilla to lovely quince/lime tones; smooth, delicious. 4 800 cases. These fermented/aged ± 4 mths Fr/Am oak. Alcs ±14%. **Barrel Fermented Chenin Blanc Reserve** NEW Limited release of 570 cases; bushvine vyd in stony soils. **01** (sample) identical cellar regime but markedly richer, gutsier; retains elegance of the regular version but needs time to show its more opulent charms.

Sauvignon Blanc Latest **01** mouthwatering without sauvignon's sometimes aggressive raciness; full-flavoured/bodied (13.5% alc); bone-dry yet balanced. Reductively subdued **99** needed time to get going.

Barrel Fermented Sauvignon Blanc NEW **00** not ready for tasting. Untasted for this ed: **Shiraz 98**, **Restelle Sauvignon Blanc-Chardonnay-Chenin Blanc** (**99**). — *IvH*

Fraai Uitzicht 1798

Robertson (see Robertson map) • Sales at Fraai Uitzicht restaurant Wed-Sun during restaurant hours (also see Eat-out section) • Cellar tours during restaurant hours • B&B/self-catering chalets • Gifts • Walks • Views • Birding • Art • Mountain biking • Owners Axel Spanholtz & Mario Motti • Winemaker Pieter Ferreira (consulted in pvt capacity for 2000 harvest only) • Viticulturist Laing Vermeulen • Vineyards 9 ha • Production 500 cases • PO Box 97 Robertson 6705 • ***Tel/fax (023) 626-6156*** *• E-mail info@fraaiuitzicht.com • Website www.fraaiuitzicht.com*

The name of this retreat on the heights above Klaasvoogds alludes to the pretty vista, but multi-talents Axel Spanholtz and Mario Motti have ensured it's no longer just the view that's enticing. The partners have taken a new broom (and brush and trowel) to every corner of their delightful old farm, nipping and tucking its rustic charms into a chic country spread for themselves and their mostly international guests. Above the duck-noisy dam is the terraced restaurant (Mario Motti himself chefs a cosmopolitan menu designed to complement top local wines); attached is the compact cellar, painstakingly refurbished and now equipped with a cooling plant "to provide the optimal conditions for bottle maturation". The purple walls tell you this is a shrine to hedonistic merlot: maiden-vintage 00 (made from their own rows with help from their enthusiastic winemaker friends) was such a success, they decided to extend the cellar for the next crush. Strikingly minimalist, the 'palm print' front label tells you the contents are, like everything here, hand-made, hands-on.

Merlot Traditionally-made **00** deliciously rich, though textures and tastes still tight-furled mid-01, needing some bottle maturation or, as seems more likely, Mario Motti's cuisine to bring forth the presently-hidden depths. Easy 12.5%. 900 half-cases. — *CF*

Franschhoek Vineyards

Franschhoek (see Franschhoek map) • Tasting & sales Mon-Fri 9.30-5 Sat 10-4 Sun 11-3 Closed Christmas Day, New Year's Day & Good Friday Tasting fee R10 p/p (Group tasting includes 20 min audio-visual presentation) • Restaurant open for lunch and dinner Tue-Sun • Owners 96 shareholders • Winemaker Deon Truter (since 1980) • Consulting viticulturist Pietie le Roux • Vineyards ±400 ha • Production 3 000 tons 80 000 cases • PO Box 52 Franschhoek 7690 • ***Tel (021) 876-2086*** *• Fax (021) 876-3440 • E-mail inf@franschhoek-vineyards.co.za • Website www.franschhoek-vineyards.co.za*

The traditional old image of a 'co-op winery' is a far cry from this 85-member operation, where the drive is always toward better quality and individuality of style. New equipment for making red wine was used for the first time in 2001, and veteran winemaker Deon Truter's white wines have been highly rated by British buyers. To consolidate the existing ranges, the Franschhoek Vineyards label will be expanded to include a full range of both red and white varietals. The La Cotte label has been re-positioned as a good value range. Keeping right up with the latest trends, the Franschhoek Vineyards wine shop has launched its own on-line wine-retailing website offering not only their range but a wide range of wines from the Franschhoek Valley.

Franschhoek Vineyards range

✵**Merlot** NEW Cherry/mulberry tastes in **00**, showing more oomph than elsewhere in the red range. Good now, promise of 3 yrs' development. Emblematic of new-found pep within these ranges.

Cabernet Sauvignon ⁂ Generally lighter style, yet **00** more forthcoming; nice plummy fruit for smooth quaffing. 2 000 cases. **Pinotage** ⁂ **00** step up on pvs; more supple, friendlier. 200 cases. **Chardonnay** ⁑ NEW Very lightweight peachy **00**, for early drinking. 200 cases. **Chenin Blanc Barrel Fermented 01** not ready for tasting. **98** ⁑. **Sauvignon Blanc** ⁂ Drink-soon **01** bright, juicy; ultra-clean lemonade flavours. 13,5% alc. 2 000 cases. **Semillon Barrel Fermented 97** very tired now. Best young and fresh. 13% alc. 1 000 cases.

La Cotte range

Sauvignon Blanc ⁑ Uncomplicated **01** styled for outdoor enjoyment. 13.5% alc. 2 000 cases. **Blanc de Blanc** ⁑ **NV** (**01**) youthfully floral, crisply dry, med-bodied. Blend semillon, chenin, colombard. 10 000 cases. Semi-Sweet ⁂ Equal chenin/hanepoot blend, light muscat wafts in semi-sweet **NV**. The following sparkles all carbonated: **Chardonnay Brut** ⁂ Hugely fizzy, mouthfilling; some varietal character in **00**. Well priced. **Sauvignon Blanc Brut** ⁂ Bracingly frothy **00**, just off-dry, distinct sauvignon character. 2 000 cases. **Demi Sec** ⁑ Expansive, decidedly sweet NV fizz, broad foamy mouthful. Chenin/ hanepoot. 1 000 cases. **Port** ⁂ Light, pleasant drops from pinotage, unoaked. **99** slightly less sugar (73 g/ℓ) than pvs, higher alc at 19% alc. Screwcap.

Not tasted for this ed (pvs ratings in brackets): **Cabernet Sauvignon Special Reserve** (**97** ⁂), **Merlot** (**99** ⁑), **Grand Rouge** (**99** ⁑), **Ros** (**99** ⁂), **Chardonnay Unwooded** (**00** ⁑), **Chenin Blanc** (**00** ⁑), **Light** (**00** ⁑).

Forge Mill range NEW

Export range.

Cinsaut-Cabernet Sauvignon ⁂ Eagerly forthcoming **01** ripe strawberry flavours, pleasantly grippy tannins; ready, could go 2-3 yrs. **Chenin Blanc-Sauvignon Blanc** NEW ⁑ Don't keep **01** hanging about; styled for effortless sipping. **Sauvignon Blanc-Semillon** ⁑ Lightweight, lemonadey **01**, ready when you are. — *DH*

Frasers Bay see International Wine Services
Fredericksburg see Rupert & Rothschild Vignerons
Freedom Road see Backsberg
Friends see Lutzville
Friesland see Kaapzicht

Frost Vineyards NEW

Paarl (see Paarl map) • Tasting, sales & cellar tours by appointment • Owners David & Michel Frost • GM (USA) Simon Gers • Winemaker Jason Fisher (since Jan 1998) • Viticulturist Michel Frost • Vineyards 17 ha • Production 150 tons 5 418 cases 69% red 31% white • PO Box 2067 Windmeul 7630 • ***Tel (021) 863-8339*** *•*

Fax (021) 863-8732 • E-mail frostms@global.co.za, simon-gers@frostwine.com • Website www.frostwine.com

PROFESSIONAL golfer David Frost and his brother Michel have combined their passion for vineyards and links in an unusual way. The two grew up on a grape farm in Stellenbosch and always dreamed of producing their own wines. In 1994 the brothers bought a 300 hectare farm, St Clements, near Paarl. Jason Fisher, winemaker at Cosentino Winery in California's Napa Valley was enlisted to help them get established. Part of David Frost's dream is to put something back into the community, so all future vintages of his wines will be dedicated to a golfing legend. And $1 from every bottle of wine sold will be donated to a charity selected by that golfer. First to be recognised was Sam Snead; the wines released in 2001 are dedicated to Arnold Palmer.

☆**Cabernet Sauvignon Reserve 99**, with splash merlot, dusty red berry fruit, mint-edged. Balanced, on largeish scale (13.7% alc) and firmly structured, with sour-cherry note to lingering finish. Needs bit of time. Supportive 22 mths Fr oaking. ±1 800 cases (also in 1.5, 3 ℓ).

☆**Merlot Reserve** Powerful rather than concentrated **99**; whiffs plum pud, spicy smoked meat. Good savoury acidity and big soft tannins, leading to bright refreshing finish. 22 mths Fr oak. 14.5% alc. ±1 800 cases.

☆**Chardonnay** Serious, barrel-fermented **00**, offering butterscotch, lime with spicy, toasty edge. Firm, balanced, rich mouthful, yr Fr oak integrated. We'd drink soonish while deliciously harmonious. 13.2% alc. Fruit ex Asara, Stbosch. 850 cases.

Sauvignon Blanc 01 not ready for tasting. 855 cases. —*TJ*

Gecko Ridge

Stellenbosch • Owner Pernod Ricard SA • Group wine development director Robin Day • Managing Winemaker Jacques Kruger (since 1998) • Production 270 000 cases • PO Box 1324 Stellenbosch 7599 • Tel (021) 880-1688 • Fax (021) 880-1691 • E-mail jacques@prsa.co.za

Consumer-friendly range in bright, attractive packaging.

African Red NEW ☆☆ Bright, juicy cherry/mulberry fruit; uncomplex, lightish **NV** with pleasing acidic twist to stand up to rich cuisine. **Rosé** ☆ Commercial style semi-sweet **NV**; purple-pink hues, shy herbal/strawberry-lozenge nose, zippy fruit. Not too sugary or alcoholic. **Chardonnay** ☆ Unoaked **00** carefree quaffer with citrus zest finish. ±13% alc. **Chenin Blanc** ☆☆ **00**'s sweet-fruit smells, quince-like tastes carry though to the bone-dry finish. 12.6% alc. **Sauvignon Blanc** ☆ In **00**'s light frame (11.5% alc) lurk quite assertive, unusual flavours of talcum powder/honey, which should be savoured soon. **Dry White** ☆☆ Acidity holds honeyed bottle age in check in unpretentious, med-bodied **NV**. Creamy dry pineapple flavours ready to drink. **Chardonnay Brut Sparkling NV** carbonated bubbles not retasted for this ed. Pvsly ☆☆. —*TM*

Genesis see Stellenbosch Vineyards

Gilga

Stellenbosch • Not open to the public • Owner/winemaker Chris Joubert • Production 300 cases 100% red • PO Box 28746 Danhof 9310 • ***Tel 082-579-6282*** *• Fax (051) 436-9029*

THE shy young maiden who, in a Persian legend, discovered the pleasures of fermented grape juice, is smiling on Chris Joubert. The Overgaauw cellar chief, here in part-time role, making the Shiraz below for his own account, immediately attracted a cult following for his debut 98. Deciding that 99 was too light a vintage ("Gilga will only be released when it's good enough. The goal always is a five-star"), he skipped that year. Now he's back with a cracker – the discipline of self-imposed declassification multi-rewarded with a shower of stars. No back-patting, however, for the self-effacing Joubert. "What began as a hobby has received a phenomenal response," he remarks. "I want to thank the friends Gilga made in the past two years, and remind them this is a hand-crafted product. Please accord it special treatment and allow it to mature."

Shiraz A small chip off the big block on Overgaauw estate, Stbosch, "personally attended to" by Chris Joubert; latest **00** unblended shiraz (pvs with thimble cab), complicatedly vinified/aged (8 mths 100% new oak, equal Am/Fr; then 7 mths 2nd fill Fr). Stark purple-black hues; penetrating cracked pepper bouquet with whiffs balsam, clove; wide-framed palate slathered with chocolately tannins. Strapping (like its creator), mouthfilling (14% alc) yet finely poised. Abstain (won't be easy) min 5 yrs, preferably 8-10. SAYWS gold for this, *Wine* for debut **98** similarly intense, powerful, interminably long. No **99**. — *DH*

Glen Carlou Vineyards

Paarl (see Paarl map) Tasting & sales Mon-Fri 8.45-4.45 Sat 9-12.30 Tasting fee R5 p/p • Tasting/sale of home-made cheese • Cellar tours by appointment • Wheelchair-friendly • Owners Walter & David Finlayson/Hess Holdings, Switzerland • Winemaker David Finlayson (since 1994) with Arco Laarman (since 2000) • Viticulturist Marius Cloete (since 2000) • Vineyards 65 ha • Production 35 000 cases 60% white 40% red • PO Box 23 Klapmuts 7625 • ***Tel (021) 875-5528*** *• Fax (021) 875-5314 • E-mail glencarl@mweb.co.za • Website www.glencarlou.co.za*

The first day of last year's harvest was marked by the birth of David and Lizel Finlayson's first child, Daniella. Otherwise it was a laidback (except for lack of sleep), slow-ripening affair – unlike the marketing, which is frenetic. Both local and export markets are "on fire" and they've been sold out within six months of release (which is why they've now doubled cellar space). Their sought-after chardonnay is still the biggest SA premium wine export to the US and was shown once again at the ultra A-list New York Wine Experience. Back home, they're an integral part of the regional drive (dad Walter Finlayson, when not crafting gourmet cheeses or consulting at Coppoolse-Finlayson, is chairman of the freshly enthused Paarl Vintners' Wine Committee) for quality – and recognition as prime syrah territory. David F irreverently likens Paarl's relationship with Stellenbosch to Sonoma vs Napa: "Stellenbosch has big reputations, big names but isn't as highly activated. Better wines often come from the smaller Paarl producers, who're taking more and more honours," challenges this newly elected chairman of the CWG, who insists that private wineries must now take the lead in SA.

Pinot Noir String of top-rank releases to date; flavour concentration aided by Glen C's "continental climate", higher-density plantings (±7000 vines/ha), mature vines (16+ yrs). Latest **00** with warm-vintage sweet youngberry fruit, richness checked by sturdy structure of tannin, alc (14%). Though succulent enough to drink now, we'd delay the pleasure couple of yrs: these invariably slow starters. **99**, with ripe cherries kept taut by waxy richness, delicious now, will keep improving. **98** vibrant youngberry fruit framed by non-intrusive grape/oak tannins. ±Yr new Dargaud & Jaegle Fr oak. **96** *Wine*.

Shiraz NEW Crackerjack **00** sprinted out of cellar straight into winner's enclosure at Paarl Vintners' Shiraz Challenge 00. Full-bore new-world style (Francophiles beware), enormous concentration and alc (14.5%); coffee, new-leather, spice aromas and endless plummy, chewy fruit. 8 mths 2nd fill barrels (50/50 Am/Fr).

Grand Classique The flagship, classic red infused with David F's cellar experience at Ch Margaux. Malbec, petit verdot, come online (just) in latest **99**, cab uppermost as always, with merlot, cab f for final 55/35/5/4/1 ratio. 2 yrs Fr oak, 70% new. Opulent ripe fruit in big but balanced body (14% alc), bone-dry finish.

Like pvs, begs bottle ageing to develop its potential (optimal drinking around 08). Somewhat lighter **98**, scented, stony mineral core lifted by dark-roast coffee richness. 13,5% alc. **97** Air France laureate; **96** VVG, SAA, *Wine* ☆).

☆**Tortoise Hill** David F's "spicy flavourful Mediterranean-style red" establishing itself as fun, tasty wine egging on the party but dense enough tannins to be taken seriously. Extra pizzazz from piquant choice of varieties. Latest **00** ☆ blend merlot, shiraz, zinfandel, touriga (45/20/20/15), stamped with vintage's super-ripe fruit, nut-kernel tones. Well-made, med-bodied, trattoria-friendly; ripeness helps it step up from **99**, with splash touriga dizzying up cab/merlot base. **98** more Fr than local despite 36% pinotage infusion. Name suggests tortoise shape of hill dominating the farm. ±Yr mainly 2nd fill Fr/new Am oak.

☆**Chardonnay Reserve** New-Cape benchmark, making waves in US where this punchy style highly sought after. From best fruit (paradoxically "worst-looking" site – mix quartz/clay), natural yeast fermentation; yr new Fr oak, 100% malo – all add breadth/width to creamy finish. Best 18 mths after bottling, can last 10 yrs. Frustratingly small quantities. Latest **00** ☆☆ for CWG Auction, comfort-zone wine: rich, warm, toasty; one to cellar min 3 yrs. Deep draughts of citrus, toasted nuts, chalk in clotted-cream texture. Pvs similarly styled. Oak, often prominent in youth, softens with time, as in **98**; oak/fruit have harmonised. Standard **Chardonnay** More readily accessible (and available – 18 000 cases); led by lemon/lime fruit as in **00**, little sharp mid-01 but should mellow with time. **99** densely chalky. **98** SAA, *Wine* ☆. Partial natural yeast ferment. ±8 mths mix 1st/3rd fill Fr cooperage.

☆**Cape Vintage** Correctly labelled (the word 'port' does not appear) for both export/domestic markets. Classic (Portuguese) 'vintage' formula: 'correct' varieties – touriga, tintas b/r; ±90 g/ℓ sugar, solid 19% alc. 2 yrs seasoned Fr oak. **99** not ready for tasting. **98**, revisited mid-01, ageing beneficially; gaining coffee/mocha overtones to plump prune fruit; hints of choc, liquorice in mouth; youthful complexity augurs well for good long-term ageing. **97** ☆ now not showing well, fruit/alc standing apart. **96** ☆ (*Wine* ☆) slightly volatile, hints fennel and leather.

Not tasted for this ed: **Pinot Noir Reserve** For CWG Auction. **99** ☆☆; **Devereux** Occasional label. Last was **00** ☆. — *NP*

Glenhurst NEW

Stellenbosch • Cellar tours by appointment • Owner Dave King • Winemaker Rod Easthope (since Oct 1999) • Viticulturists Rod Easthope and Jaco van der Westhuizen • Vineyards 22 ha • Production 200 tons 90% red 10% white • PO Box 1193 Stellenbosch 7599 • Cell 083-395-7929

"To fill the vacant position of SA's 'first growth' wine producer" is the challenge ringing from these high Simonsberg vineyards owned by Gauteng businessman David King, whose natural progression has been from "avid consumer of fine wine" via contact and consultation with wine industry luminaries to winegrower in own right. He's enlisted the services of "top-notch technical personnel", notably hotwired consultant Rod Easthope to energise the 20 hectares of classic varieties – cabernets sauvignon/franc, merlot, shiraz and sauvignon blanc – to produce, Easthope says, "ultra-premium wines that will cement Stellenbosch's reputation as one of the world's finest wine regions". A cellar has been built and the first wines were about to be bottled as the guide went to press. "It's difficult to establish when Glenhurst wines will be released. We'll only start crowing when we believe we have something to crow about!" This also applies, Easthope says, to the wines to be produced from house-owned vineyards near Agulhas and released under the label Quoin Rock.

Glenview

Owner Robin Marks • Production 6 000 cases (own label) 60% red 40% white • PO Box 32234 Camps Bay 8040 • ***Tel (021) 438-1080*** *• Fax (021) 438-3167 • E-mail bayexport@kingsley.co.za*

CAPETONIAN Robin Marks has established this brand "to offer wine lovers a product they can enjoy every day with little effect on their monthly budget". Most of the 6 000 cases go to restaurants (including establishments in Thailand and the Netherlands) but some are available from retail outlets around Cape Town. The wines can be enjoyed "on their own or as a complement to most dishes", says Marks, whose base in Camps Bay is convenient for those occasions when he breaks away for a spot of wind-surfing.

Dry Red ★ NV Vin ordinaire from mostly cinsaut, cab, splashes chenin, shiraz, pinotage. **Dry White ⁑ NV** Refreshing, well-made casual dry quaff; med-bodied, from chenin. — *DH*

Glenwood

Franschhoek • Tasting, sales & cellar tours to be established • Owner Dontair (Pty) Ltd • Winemaker/viticulturist DP Burger (since Apr 1992) • Vineyards 22 ha • Production ± 180 tons 350 cases 50% red 50% white • PO Box 204 Franschhoek 7690 • ***Tel/fax (021) 876-3338*** *• E-mail glenwood@adept.co.za*

AT this fledgling winery in Franschhoek, the only thing viticulturist-turned-winemaker D P Burger (with freelance winemaker Gerda Willers consulting) is missing about a decade spent nurturing vines (the fruit was traditionally sold to DGB and Winecorp) is having a holiday in April. Now they're building their own cellar (its initial 25 ton capacity will slowly increase) to be ready for this year's harvest, by which time the merlot planted a few years back will be in production. Retired UK business consultant and owner Alastair Wood is still based in London but plans to eventually live on the farm.

Shiraz ⁂ 00 finished wine bought from Brenthurst, Paarl; leaner style with firm acidity; puckering now, needs 2-3 yrs. Medium-weight (though should feel bigger – 13.5% alc). Excellent with lamb or tongue, advises D P Burger. 800 cases (× 6, as are all these). **Sauvignon Blanc ⁂ 01** harvested at 5 am for crispness. Grassy, undemanding yet satisfying. 13% alc. 750 cases. **Chardonnay Wooded ⁂** Lemon, buchu tones in **00**, lightish-flavoured but not ungenerous; harmonious with lift of acidity which good with richer cuisine. 13% alc. 340 cases. **Semillon Wooded ⁂** Understated, food-cordial example, med-bodied; **00** warm bakery smells; firm dry finish. Fruit/oak well knit. Barrel fermented, matured 8 mths. 200 cases. **Semillon ⁑** Unoaked version. Some green-peach, pear flavours in **01**; not in same league as above. 13% alc. 244 cases. — *DH*

Goat Roti see Fairview

Goats du Roam see Fairview

Goede Hoop Estate

Stellenbosch (see Stellenbosch map) • Tasting, sales, cellar tours by appointment • Self catering facilities by arrangement • BYO picnic • Conferencing for small groups (10-15 people) • Owner Pieter Bestbier • Winemakers Pieter Bestbier (since 1988), with Willie Malherbe (since 2000) • Viticulturist Johan de Beer (since 2000) • Vineyards 80 ha • Production 700 tons (345 tons 12 000 cases own label) 56% red 44% white • PO Box 25 Kuils River 7579 • ***Tel (021) 903-6286*** *• Fax (021) 906-1553 • E-mail goede@adept.co.za • Website www.goedehoop.co.za*

Winegrower Pieter Bestbier loves his vocation but what he loves more are the people who enjoy his wines. Which is why he receives visitors himself – no impersonal self-guided tours here – by appointment. If that's not reason enough to make the journey into the Bottelary Valley, then the unpretentious ambience and scenic beauty certainly are. Not forgetting the wines themselves, which are charming and affordable, and admired by customers in several countries. As we keep saying, if you're seeking the antithesis of today's over-hyped wine world, it's right here at this tranquil, very welcoming estate.

✺**Cabernet Sauvignon** ✓ **97** *Wine* ✺ first cab release from this property since **91**. Latest **98** more vibrant new world style with wider spread of aromas/flavours including cocoa, hints of dried fruit; latter's piquancy joined in palate by bright acidity, lifting the ripe wild-berry fruit. Thoughtfully made wine; will appeal widely. These yr new barrels. Moderate ±13% alcs. 2 000 cases.

✺**Shiraz** ✓ Track record over past few vintages places this shiraz in the Cape's upper crust. **98** finely layered intensity, some classy whiffs of truffle, smoky oak. **99** lighter (12,5% alc) but tasty, plenty of prune/fennel flavours. Drink or age further. Mix new/old clones; ±6 mths Fr casks, none new. 1 500 cases. **00** not ready for tasting.

✺**Vintage Rouge** ✓ Now a Right merlot/cab (60/40) – pvs were variations on cab, shiraz, pinotage); new rather than old-world. Upfront blackberries/cherries in **98** ✺, 'sweet' fruit supported by good tannins. WOM selection. **99** back on quality track of **97** VG; more classical, better managed tannins. 4 mths 2nd/3rd fill casks. 14,2% alc. **00** not ready for tasting.

✺**Pinotage** ✓ Estate's pinotage pvsly went into Vintage Rouge above; from **99** solo-starring and showing good form. Lightly oaked (6 mths 2nd/3rd fill). 2nd release **00** in completely different mode: overpoweringly aromatic – exotic incense, fennel, eucalyptus billow from glass of super-extracted fruit. Not unattractive, just needs yr/2 to settle. 1 000 cases.

Chardonnay ★ New-oak fermented **00** creamy, buttery style; undemanding but good for food-partnering with richly-sauced cuisines. Med-bodied. 400 cases. **Sauvignon Blanc** ★ **01** (sample tasted, rating provisional) not an earth shatterer, but will appeal to fans of a lighter, gentler sauvignon. Pineapple, guava tones, supple but crisp acidity. 500 cases. — *TM*

Goedgeloof see Kanu

Goedvertrouw Estate

Walker Bay (see Elgin/Walker Bay map) • Tasting, sales, cellar tours "all hours by appointment" • art gallery • Elreda Pillmann's home-cooked meals by arrangement. • Play area for children • Small conferences • Walks • Views • Proclaimed conservation area • Owners Arthur & Elreda Pillmann • Winemaker Arthur Pillmann • Vineyards 8 ha • Production 25 tons 70% red 30% white • PO Box 37 Bot River 7185 • ***Tel (028) 284-9769*** *• Fax (028) 284-9443*

Nature is allowed to take its course on this little hands-on wine estate near Bot River – not always with happy results. A violent hail storm completely destroyed the 2000 grape crop. "You can't fight nature," sighs Arthur Pillmann. Fortunately harvest 2001 was relatively uneventful, and now the eightysomething engineer turned organic winefarmer is back with a batch of releases, including a Cabernet to rival his signatures, Pinot Noir and Chardonnay. Wife Elreda still provides warm hospitality and home-cooked cuisine, and the tasting room has been expanded to include a well-appointed art gallery, which is available for use by any talented local artist.

✺**Cabernet Sauvignon 99**, tasted in 00 as promising barrel sample, emerges in extraordinarily fine fettle. Pitch black robe; bouquet booms dense clouds of cassis, almost raisiny ripe, touches molasses amid the berries; vibrant blackcurrant/Ribena flavours in powerfully concentrated form (yet alc not high at 12.

8%). Beautiful bright acidity energises the ensemble; closes with whiffs violets, fennel and twist choc. Yr 2nd fill Fr oak.

Pinot Noir These all individuals, fragrant and very dry, acquiring surprisingly authentic burgundian tones with age. **99** shows a russet edge and tar/truffle bouquet over chewy cherry/beetroot flavours; somewhat rustic, earthy (partly from plodding 14.2% alc), yet engaging – fascinating development ahead. Unwooded. **98** with posy of violets and palate of stone fruits; delicious, fine tannins. These fermented with natural yeasts.

Chardonnay Major style change to unwooded from pvs finely-oaked, butterscotchy styles. True to form, **01** suffers from none of the blandness that dogs many unadorned Cape examples; good concentration from low-cropped 4 t/ha vines). **Sauvignon Blanc** Invariably characterful; **01** retiring floral/perfumed nose, unusual quince/pear flavours; not overtly sauvignon but a well-made, different, 'white wine'. — *TM*

Goedverwacht Estate

Robertson (see Robertson map) • Tasting & sales Mon-Fri 9.30-4 Sat 10-1 • Cellar tours by appointment • BYO picnic • Tourgroups • Owner/winemaker Jan du Toit • Viticulturist Danie Visser (since 1990) • Vineyards 110 ha Production 1 300 tons 80% white 20% red • PO Box 128 Bonnievale 6730 • ***Tel (023) 616-3430*** *• Fax (023) 616-2073 • E-mail goedverwachtestate@lando.co.za*

"I'm not one of those well-to-do people who farm *with* money," says Jan du Toit. "I farm *for* money." Which is why this hardworking Bonnievale grower and wife Marianne are on a mission to make the best wine they can at the lowest price possible. "If we don't give consumers value for money, who will?" they wonder, genuinely concerned about spiralling wine prices generally. They're countering by not only keeping prices low (their Colombard, which helps fund endangered Blue Crane research, is only R13 ex cellar) but also making a visit to their Breede River-fronting estate as pleasurable as possible (adding extra allure is the new tasting centre, the epitome of understated chic). The adjacent winery is squeaky-clean (Jan du Toit a cellar-hygiene fanatic) and, beyond, a second farm with cool southerly aspects is being planted with shiraz, for a future oak-matured flagship, and cabernet franc to extend the current bordeaux blend.

Cabernet Sauvignon-Merlot ✓ New (Fr) oak component upped to 25% in **01** (sample) to complement sweet-ripe, almost cordial-like blueberry fruit, from maturing vyd. 13.8% alc. 2 650 cases. Serious intent announced with **00**, 10% new Fr oak.

Colombard ✓ Candidate for best colombard of vintage. **01** lightish bodied but super-intense, complex, with estate's signature 'brut' finish. Old colombard clone, mollycoddled in cellar. 5 000 cases to go with creamy-sauced mussels, bouillabaisse, Mediterranean platters.

Crane Red Merlot NEW Chalky shales of this vyd seem to favour the variety; **01** barrel sample shows potential to grow into over 2-3 yrs. Ultra-ripe fruit; chunky, slightly sweet mouthfeel. Briefly oaked. 13.5% alc. 3 100 cases. **Chardonnay Wooded** Floral **00** with fresh liveliness that many other oaked chardonnays lack. 13.5% alc. 1 000 cases. **Chardonnay Sur Lie** Unwooded version, lees-aged 75-90 days – style increasingly in demand internationally. **01** pleasantly creamy, full, balanced. 13.5% alc. 1 000 cases. **Sauvignon Blanc** From riverside vyd; **01** light-bodied yet well padded with fresh green fruit, mouthwatering acidity. 3 000 cases. — *IvH*

Golden Alibama

Big-volume wine brand of Distell, available in various pack sizes.

NV Very dry no-frills drop; deep amber glints. — *IvH*

Goudini Winery

Worcester (see Worcester map) • Tasting & sales Mon-Fri 8-5 Sat 10-1 Tasting fee R2 p/p • Cellar tours by appointment • Closed religious public holidays • Light meals for larger groups (20-plus) by appointment • Reception facilities for functions/conferences • Tourgroups • Owners 42 members • Winemakers Hennie Hugo (since1985) & Willem Louw (since 1999) • Vineyards 1 018 ha • Production 20 000 tons (8 000 cases own label) 80% white 20% red • PO Box 132 Rawsonville 6845 • ***Tel (023) 349-1090*** *• Fax (023) 349-1095 • E-mail cellar@goudiniwine.co.za winesales@goudiniwine.co.za • Website www.goudiniwine.co.za*

THESE value-priced wines come to you from the cellar beside the Smalblaar ('Narrow Leaf') River – a reference to the fragrant trees that grow here and impart a special character to the local honey (which, in turn, is alluded to in the name Goudini, meaning 'fragrant honey'). If you care to taste or buy some of the produce, made by Hennie Hugo and Willem Louw, the cellar-attached Goudini Wine House is where it all happens.

Chardonnay ✓ Light-hearted rather than serious, briefly oaked for bit of complexity; but essentially for fun. **01** brimming peaches/pears; keen acidity maintains the bounce. 13,7% alc. 600 cases. Up from **00**.

Chenin Blanc ✓ "Delicious springy wine," says back-label, and so it is. Ripe passion fruit, guava, mere suggestion of sweetness; **01** med-bodied for early drinking. 12% alc. WOM selection. 1 000 cases.

Hanepoot Regular award-winning full-sweet fortified dessert, back up to speed in **01** with intricate honeysuckle, muscat, herb, mint and jasmine fragrances. Warming and nice. 17% alc. 300 cases.

Rodini NEW Pinotage/cinsaut combo; peppers, plums and choc mingle with verve; some tannins to stand up to richer savoury cuisines. 500 ml screwcap. **Rosé** NEW Cinsaut in full fruity flight; coral **01** gulpable and not too sweet. Enjoy (with quiche, ventures winemaker) in blush of youth. 200 cases. **Umfiki** Appropriately named 'Newcomer' early-release semillon, chardonnay, unwooded; lightish and quaffble, with bright acidity. Just-dry **01** must be drunk "immediately", instructs winemaker. 270 cases.

Blanc de Noir 01 semi-sweet from cinsaut. Not tasted. 200 cases. **Riesling** Traditional Cape riesling, frequent local show accolades. Clean white-peach, lemon tastes in med-bodied **01**, to be enjoyed in fruity youth. 300 cases. **Sauvignon Blanc** Lightweight **01** simple, easy drinking; finishes very dry. 600 cases. **Semillon Reserve** Not ready for tasting. 200 cases of **01**. **Colombar** NEW Variety's guava tastes in **01**, smooth, gentle, not too full at 13% alc. 500 ml screwcap. 200 cases. **Blanc de Blanc** NEW **01**, dry white from clairette blanche, not ready for tasting. 300 cases. **Special Late Harvest** **01** fresh guava nose mirrored in palate with tropical fruit salad and bits of apple. Attractive, lightish and not oversweet. Enjoy soon. 800 cases. **Sauvignon Blanc Sparkling Brut** Unbelievably fizzy and, given its generous sauvignon character, something akin to drinking atomised grass cuttings! Latest **01**, unlike pvs, is vintaged. Lowish 10,8% alc. 200 cases. WOM Value. **Demi Sec** NEW Above fizz in sweeter guise. 10.6% alc. 200 cases. Also available, not tasted: **Pinotage** (Pvs **99**), **Ruby Cabernet Reserve** (**98**), **Shiraz 01** NEW, **Ruby Cabernet-Merlot** (**99**), **Port** (**99**). Following may be available: **Clairette Blanche** (Pvs **00**), **Late Harvest Steen** (**99**). — *DH*

Goudveld Estate

Orange Free State • Tasting & sales Mon-Sat 8-6 • Cellar tours by appointment • Light refreshments by arrangement • Conference/reception locale for 100-120 *guests • Barbecue area • Owner Jan Alers • Winemaker/viticulturist Merkil Alers (since 1985) • Vineyards18 ha • Production 174 tons (2 000 cases own label) 75% red 25% white • PO Box 1091 Welkom 9460 • **Tel (057) 352-8650** • Fax (057) 353-2140*

ALWAYS first with the Free State goodies, this cellar with its unique cycad garden (about 300 specimens, some believed to be more than 2000 years old), was the first to add Pinot Noir, Ruby Cabernet and Chardonnay to its range. Now they're grubbing up 12 hectares and establishing fernao pires and colombard, to satisfy the demand for the light, refreshing styles that go down so well in their warm part of the country. Aside from the above-mentioned wines, the range, untasted for this ed, includes: **Cabernet Sauvignon**, **Pinotage**, semi-sweet **Rosé**, **Semi-Sweet Red**, **Kellertrots** (sweet colombard), **Late Harvest**, **Golden Nectar Hanepoot**, **Red Muscadel**, **Port**.

Goue Vallei Wines

*Olifants River (see Olifants River map) • Tasting & sales Mon-Fri 8-5 Sat 9-12.30 • Cellar tours by appointment • BYO picnic • Proclaimed conservation area • Owner Goue Vallei Wines (Pty) Ltd • Winemaker Johan Delport • Consulting viticulturists VinPro • Vineyards ± 1 300 ha • Production 8 000 tons 85% white 15% red • PO Box 41 Citrusdal 7340 • **Tel (022) 921-2233** • Fax (022) 921-3937 • E-mail gouwin@yebo.co.za*

PROMISING new wines from the recently proclaimed Piekenierskloof area now account for almost 40% of the total production from this cellar. "Those high-altitude vineyards provide conditions very suitable for the production of great shiraz," rhapsodises new winemaker Johan Delport. Hence the new shiraz vines nesting in cool eyries, some as high as 750 m above sea level. Delport, who moved here recently from Klawer, hopes to increase the percentage of reds from 20% to 40% in the next few years. The 2001 harvest was small, following a very dry growing season. But, Delport says, things are looking good for a bumper 2002 vintage after a winter of cooler, wet weather.

Piekenierskloof Cabernet Sauvignon NEW **00** unfinished sample showcases soft cool-climate mulberry fruit; firm but sweet tannin. 18 mths 2nd fill Fr oak. Indicator of class of the area; potential to develop into ★. 13.5% alc. 500 cases.

Cardouw range

Premium range for export; named after locally well-known Cardouw ('Shortcut') farm.

Cabernet Sauvignon ✓ Slow-starting **98** only now beginning to show its potential. Concentrated dark-berried fruit, dried-prune/savoury touches; long tannins for 4-6 yrs' good development. 13,8% alc. 700 cases.

Pinotage ★★ **98** with warm spicy plums, sweet fruit to quell powerful dry tannins. Med-bodied, 8 mths oak. 13,2% alc. Latest **00** not ready for tasting.

Chardonnay ★★ Cask-fermented/aged **99** with relaxed peachy tones for easy glugging now. 13.4% alc. 600 cases.

Goue Vallei range

Cabernet Sauvignon ✓ Investments in vyds/cellar evident in notch-up **00**; snips mint, succulent tannin for 4-5 yrs' good ripening. 13.9% alc. 200 cases. **99** ★★ foursquare, earlier-maturing.

Classique Rouge ★★ ☻ Charming drink-now red; Latest **NV** (01) lively, tangy. Med-bodied varietal quintuplet, unwooded. 5 000 cases.

Pinotage ★ Fr/Am-oaked **00** sullen, astringent; table partner rather than stand-alone drink. 13,5% alc. 2 800 cases. **Chianti** ★ Latest bottling of med-bodied **NV**

(99) quaffer back on track; sweet ripe plums nicely oaked. 800 cases. **Rosé** ☆ NEW Deep-hued **00** smooth pomegranate tastes; sweetness clipped by tannin/acid. Chenin/cab. 700 cases. **Blanc de Noir** ☆ Offbeat grenache-based semi-sweet; exotic shell-pink **00**. Med-bodied. 1 000 cases.

Chardonnay ☆ Partly wooded **01** has dried-peach tastes, firmly dry finish. 13.4% alc. 2 000 cases. **Chenin Blanc** ☆ Well priced around R11 from cellar. **01** plenty of zesty-dry chenin flavour. 13.9% alc. 1 800 cases. **Sauvignon Blanc** ☆ Night-harvested **01** lightish-toned/bodied, like pvs, fresh and dry. 1 000 cases. **Blanc de Blanc** ☆ Keenly fresh, light-bodied dry **01**. For salad days. Colombard. 2 000 cases. **Bukettraube** ☆ Unpretentious smooth semi-sweet white with honeysuckle fragrance. **01** lightish 11,5% alc. 1 500 cases. **Late Vintage** ☆ Back in the guide with **01**, from Cape riesling; haystack aromas, better sugar/acid balance than SLH below. 1 500 cases. **Special Late Harvest** ☆ Chenin's ripe-guava tones, gentle sweetness in drink-soon **01**. 1 000 cases. Following bubblies **NV**: **Brut** ☆ Straightforward light perk-me-up from chardonnay. 500 cases. **Vin Doux** ☆ Chenin-based sweet sparkler; fine carbonation. Very moderate 11.5% alc. 2 000 cases.

Red Jerepiko ☆ NEW Unusual, pleasant **NV** (99), with earthy/tarry tastes. Lowish 15.2% alc; not oversweet. 1 000 cases. **Hanepoot Jerepiko** ☆ Latest bottling of lively, well made fortified **NV** among recent bests from this cellar; bright lemonade tang. 18.9% alc. 900 cases. **White Muskadel** ☆ **NV** (98) Very sweet fortified improving in bottle, gaining warm toffee tones. 17.2% alc. 2 000 cases. **Port NV** Reappears in the guide with challenging tar/damp-earthy tones. 18.2% alc. 1 500 cases.

Sonnigdal range

Boxed range available in 2 and 5 ℓ. Untasted.

Dry Red, **Grand Cru**, **Stein**.

Impala range

Exclusive to UK market. Not tasted.

Pinotage, **Cabernet Sauvignon-Merlot**, **Ruby Cabernet-Pinotage**, **Chardonnay**, **Chenin Blanc**, **Sauvignon Blanc**. — *DH*

Graça

Vinho verde-inspired petillant quaffer, still SA's top selling cork-closed wine, with carefully cultivated brand persona. Ubiquitous on local wine lists. By Distell.

Rosé ☺ ☆ Varieties below with pinotage for pink prettiness. Semi-sweet earthy tones, lightly spritzed. Lowish 11% alc. **Graça** ☺ ☆ Latest bottling semi-dry, as always, blend sauvignon, semillon, Cape riesling (60/20/20); light, lemony, quaffable. 310 000 cases. These crowd-pleasing **NV**s also in pot-bellied 375 ml 'dinkies'. — *IvH*

Graceland Vineyards

*Stellenbosch (see Stellenbosch map) • Tasting, sales & cellar tours by appointment • Two-room B&B with many amenities and expansive views • Owners Graceland (Pty) Ltd • Consulting winemaker Rod Easthope (since 1999) • Viticulturists Susan McNaughton & Rod Easthope • Vineyards 9 ha • Production 25 tons 1 500 cases 100% red • PO Box 7066 Stellenbosch 7599 • **Tel (021) 881-3121** • Fax (021) 881-3341 • E-mail pmcn@iafrica.com • Website www.gracelandvineyards.com*

The 2001 vintage on this Stellenbosch property was abundant in more ways than one: their largest crop so far (30 t) all seemed to ripen at once, so everyone on the farm got roped in (even some of the guests staying in their deluxe B&B volunteered) and quickly learnt how to use those vineyard shears. Not to be outdone

Purdy, their German short-haired pointer, promptly joined the harvest party by having 11 puppies in the cellar. "Their yelping helped hasten fermentation," laugh Paul and Susan Mc Naughton. Responsible for the vineyards (with assistance from consulting Kiwi Rod Easthope), Susan Mc Naughton hopped hemispheres on a wine marketing foray last year and this red-only winery now exports to several EU countries as well as the UK and Canada.

✵**Cabernet Sauvignon** ✓ Restrained rather than flamboyant, with bdx-like austerity most evident in **99**'s ✵ cassis whiffs, dry but not too lean tannins, elegant dense-fruited finish. A mere 600 cases, aged 15 mths in Fr oak, 30% new. 13.8% alc. Maiden **98** altogether more showy, more forward youngberry aromas, creme brulee notes, fuller and fatter textures.

✵**Merlot** ✓ **99** plumper and more showy than first release **98**. Latest offering now has fuller plum/mulberry aromas, cassia spice, softer tannins, slight hint of bouillon. 13,5% alc. 15 mths Fr oak, 25% new. Pvs more austere now, though initially hailed for fruit opulence. Note: **00**s of above not ready for tasting. — *MF*

Graham Beck Wines

Robertson cellar

See Robertson map • Tasting & sales Mon-Fri 9-5 Sat 10-3 • Cellar tours by appointment • BYO picnic • Gifts • Views • Private game park • Owner Graham Beck • Cellarmaster Pieter Ferreirà (since 1990) • Winemaker Jacques Conradie (since 2001) • Viticulturist Leon Dippenaar, advised by Johan Wiese • Vineyards 186 ha • Production 152 000 cases • PO Box 724 Robertson 6705 • ***Tel (023) 626-1214*** *• Fax (023) 626-5164 • E-mail cellar@grahambeckwines.co.za • Website www.grahambeckwines.co.za*

Coastal Cellar (Franschhoek)

Not open to the public • Cellar tours by appointment • Owner Graham Beck • Cellarmaster Charles Hopkins (since 1999) • Viticulturist Johan Dippenaar, advised by Johan Wiese • Vineyards 130 ha • Production 90 000 cases • PO Box 134 Franschhoek 7690 • ***Tel (021) 874-1258*** *• Fax (021) 874-1712 • E-mail coastal@grahambeckwines.co.za • Website www.grahambeckwines.co.za*

Mining tycoon Graham Beck's wine interests are so high powered, they need two cellars (one, named Coastal, on Bellingham farm, Franschhoek, the other on Madeba, Robertson), a pair of cellarmasters (Cape standouts Charles Hopkins and Pieter Ferreira respectively), several appellations (including maritime-swept Firgrove, where Graham Beck now owns two prime farms) and a quarter of a million cases (far and widely exported) to contain them. Plus a staircase of quality – sweeping up from the crowd-roarers like Railroad Red (48 000 cases and climbing) through the single varieties (now also featuring viognier, first harvested in commercial quantity in 2001) and world-class sparkling; to the swanky single-vineyard wines (including a new Cabernet from the Firgrove dream-home). Then there's the new pinnacle, a blend of classic reds from both cellars. Within all this diversity is a (dual) constant: "The identities and styles of our accomplished cellarmasters," explains marketing director Jacques Roux, "they are the keys to our strategy to establish Graham Beck Wines as a competitive brand on the international market."

✵**'Estate Blend'** NEW One for the 'Wine of Origin' scholars: made by two individual winemakers, in two geographically separate cellars, with fruit of three varieties grown in as many different 'appellations', and known in-house as 'Estate Blend'. Likely to see the market as 'Wine of Origin Coastal', but no conundrum for the contents – a premium blend cab, cab f, merlot, each parcel wine vinified 'at home' prior to collaborative blending. **99** radiant full ruby; nose offers ground deep-roast coffee beans, cassis; closed palate pledges ripe fruit within gentle tannins, marked by cool spearmint freshness. New, 2nd fill Fr oak, 14% alc. 1 000 cases.

Coastal Cellar range

Cornerstone Cabernet Sauvignon NEW Latest (more to come?) release of named, single vyd site 'reserves', separating out best from big blends for boutique style handling, marketing. 5 t/ha grapes from Firgrove's Vredenhof farm of unique coffeestone, decomposed granite, lavished with new Fr oak 21 mths. **99** unpushy savoury scents – wild mushrooms, spicy leather, game birds – precede palate closed in youth. Promise of dense blackberry fruit, plush tannins, complex flavour to come. Needs min 5 yrs from harvest to yield. 'C for serious' the playful cellar blurb. For sure. 13.4% alc. 500 cases.

Cabernet Sauvignon With plethora of Am oak in cellar for other, fruitier varieties, mainstay cabernet demands Fr cask, gets it, holds fort while upstarts venture into frontier territory. **99** classic mould but accessible, aromatic coffee/ choc bouquet, supple yet succulent blackcurrant palate, ripe tannic grip. **98** handsome, dense, firmly structured for long haul. Latest less oak (14 mths) all Fr, 95% new. 13,6% alc. 2 500 cases.

Old Road Pinotage Further proof of value of best vyd site identification for 'reserve' bottlings – paradoxically possible for large outfit because of ability to manoeuvre volume components. No problem with its lineage: single dryland bushvine location, planted 1963, Beck-owned from 1998. **99** statement wine in all respects: rich colour, smoky, pan-roasted spice aromas, clove-cherry plum fullness incised by orange-skin tang, excellent balance – fruit, wood, acid and gentle 12.2% alc in formation. Opulent yr new Am casks. 1 000 cases. Loudly praised **98** SAA, ABSA Top 10, *Wine* ☆☆, eucalyptus, bold cherry. 13% alc. 800 cases.

Pinotage Summer-ripe, unambiguous pinotage fruit gets transatlantic 50:50 Am/Fr treatment (2nd fill) in **00** bottling of Firgrove/F'hoek crop: rich, warm baked-plum-pud aromas laced with clove. 'Pears-in-red-wine' palate bolstered by pithy, tropical fruit, cut with late acid brush. Bags of flavour; 13.6% alc less confined than compact. Inky **99**, whiffs spice, mint, red cherry, firm ripe tannins, 12,2% alc. 4 000 cases. "Potjie/braai on patio" wine, says Charles H.

Shiraz ✓ Powered by fruit of dryland, mature vines (60% beyond their teens) ex Firgrove, F'hoek. **00** riper, bolder than pvs; smouldering mulberry fruit, broadening 14.5% flick-flack with Am oak vanilla. Pugnacious successor to lighter, leather-spicy **99**, massive yet refined **98**, both bristling with awards. Submerged cap fermentation, 14 mths new Am oak.

Merlot ☆ Concentrated style more sappy, austere in latest **00**, vinous tension, taut fruit interplay with pepper spice, fennel in spite of full body (13,5% alc), sweeter Am oak. Mineral finish. 50/50 Am/Fr oak, 2nd fill, 14 mths. 1 250 cases.

Sauvignon Blanc ☆ Super fruit concentration, flavour intensity in **01**: grass, nettles the vehicle, juicy tropical flavours the content. Excellent varietal character, length of flavour beyond modest pricing. WOM selection.

Robertson Cellar range

The Ridge Shiraz Some wines say 'drink me!' This tall poppy (in the increasingly crowded parking lot of serious Cape examples) is one. **99**, more Fr styling, more pimento, spice, white pepper, less bursting fruit but fine component intensity, balanced, succulent dry finish. Named for single rich, red limestone vyd (opposite *avant garde* tasting room), Rbtson version of Coonawarra's famous *terra rossa*. Sustained award haul for pvs **98** (VG, SAA, *Wine* ☆☆). Partial barrel-fermentation (last 3% alc in new Am casks), 14 mths 80/20 new Am/Fr; 13,8% alc. 1 500 cases.

Merlot Now housed in Coastal Range. Pvs **99** 15+% alc. 2nd/3rd fill 60% Am, 40% Fr.

Chardonnay Elegant chardonnay enjoying premium oak management. **00** casualty of lesser year, somewhat oxidative hues; prominent wood (barrel-fermented, matured 11 mths, 80% new Fr oak), flatters palate, only nudging dry at 4.2 g/ℓ sugar. **99** spicy minerals/fruit, seamlessly oaked. 100% whole-bunch-pressed. 2 700 cases.

Blanc de Blancs Vintaged chardonnay brut MCC, amongst Cape's classiest. 50% of whole-bunch-pressed base wine favoured with fermentation in traditional oak, lends creamy, toasty hallmark to style more restrained than Brut below. **96** full straw hues, quiet nose offset by rich, broad mouthful tensioned with acid brace. Excellent enduring length. Fresh, finessed, will gather more complex flavour with 1-2 yrs maturation. WOM selection. 1 500 cases. **93** prominent secondary characteristics.

Brut Champagne launches liners, this MCC has sent a premium brand into international seas: from maiden bottling selected for inauguration of Nelson Mandela, through BBC 'Food & Drinks' selection as Best Sparkling Wine, golds at IWC, Veritas, to SAA trophy in 00, a consistent winner. Current **NV** as good: luminous ochre; languid bead, leesy biscuit aromas belt out of the glass; wonderful pinot richness firms up poised palate, ready to stimulate gastronomy, fraternity. 50/50 chardonnay/pinot noir, 24 mths on lees. Clean commercial style (25 000 cases) with panache.

Rhona Muscadel Bold aperitif or dessert (chilled with biscotti, sabayon-napped summer fruits), launched waves as regeneration of trusty fortified muscat de f, in packaging fit for elegant courts (problems inserting cork into pvs elegant, swan-neck sees this now in more conservative, squatter container). **97** honeyed muscat nose, menthol spears fresh palate, spirit rush reminds this is 'sweet dessert liqueur wine'. **96** *Wine* with bottle-aged complexity, balanced sugar. "Natural enzymatic fermentation." 174 g/ℓ sugar. 17% alc. 1 500 half-cases 500 ml.

Waterside White ☻ Clever entry-level quaffer from Rbtson folds wood-matured (3 mths) 51% chardonnay breadth, body in with fresh, breezy tropical fruit of colombard. **01** energised by brisk acidity, fruit provokes a second glass. Volumes approach 30 000 cases a yr. Enjoy in flush of youth.

Railroad Red For bistros and winebars' suggests Pieter F. **00** sees pinotage enter blend, offering pulpier damson plum counterpoint to smoky shiraz, seamed by dusty cab backdrop. Integrated fruit, tannin, 13.5% alc. Blooming to 48 000 cases. **Sparkling Pinotage MCC** (Cap Classique Sparkling Red in pvs ed) Bottle-fermented pinotage, "a world first", not for the faint hearted. Upcoming release marked by trenchant pinotage fruit, fermentation character vying for the lead. Unambiguous rusticity will find fans. 18 mths lees, dry but not brut 18 g/ℓ sugar. Discontinued: **Fleury Cabernet Sauvignon-Merlot** Last was **98**. — *DS*

Grand Mousseux

Since 1929, SA's affordable, dependable sparkler for all occasions. NVs by Distell.

Vin Sec Least sweet of these; fresh clean bubbles, mouthfilling, fruity. Equal clairette/chenin blend, as is ... **Vin Doux** Big, creamy fizz; brisk acidity; fine carbonation. **Spumante** Muscat, tropical, floral tones; lowish 10,5% alc nicely fleshed by fruity sweetness. From white muscadel. Good with ice cream. **Grand Rouge** Not tasted for this ed. Pvs. — *IvH*

Grangehurst 

Stellenbosch • Sales Mon-Fri 9-5 • Owner/winemaker Jeremy Walker • Grapes from 4 Stellenbosch areas (Helderberg, Firgrove, Stellenbosch Kloof & Devon Valley) • Production 85 tons 5 500 cases 100% red • PO Box 206 Stellenbosch 7599 • **Tel (021) 855-3625** • Fax (021) 855-2143 • E-mail winery@grangehurst.co.za

It's been 10 harvests since Jeremy Walker, a traditionalist at heart, made his maiden vintage on his family's Helderberg smallholding in a converted squash court, which initially served as the winery. That sporty start will remain etched in local wine lore, even though a cellar's subsequently been built. With a decade of memories behind him – and legends, like the one about him falling into an open fermenting tank while dutifully punching down the skins (the wine went on to win a gold medal!), Walker's vision remains clear: small, specialised and red, with pinotage playing an important part. While he'll continue to buy in grapes from selected parcels, new Grangehurst-owned prime slopes north of Stellenbosch are to be planted this year with cabernet and merlot, followed by pinotage and shiraz. Back to the future, last harvest was particularly good for reds and could even live up to his personal *annus mirabilis*, the 95 vintage. "I want every year to be like that!" he sighs.

✵✵**Nikela** Grangehurst's flagship, a thoughtful – and delicious – contribution to the Cape Red debate; the Xhosa name, meaning 'tribute', for Jeremy Walker's late parents. Formula evolving, as Walker (and fellow *pinotagistes*) refine their ideals: "Perhaps a minimum of 30% pinotage, up to a maximum 70%", he suggests. Stunning latest **98**, as it happens, contains close to self-imposed min (33%, with 57/10 cab/merlot), less than Diners Club-gonged maiden **97** (45/46/9). Latest leans to cab's cassis, sweet pepper, fennel tones, pinotage provides mulberry, palate-covering richness; all zipped in spicy oak envelope (80/20 Fr/Am). Strong musculature, compact black-fruits-and-cream finish. 780 cases, 1 000 (highly collectible) magnums. **97** softer, more seductive and fleshy, in line with blend, yet also for long haul – 10 yrs min. Grapes ex Stbosch, Devon Valley.

✵✵**Cabernet Sauvignon-Merlot** Strong allusions to bdx in **98**'s rich plum cake aromas and signature inky dustiness of well-wooded, ripe cab. Usual recipe 70/30 changes to 80/20 cab/merlot, delivering more structured, disciplined claret tones oozing class, longevity and backbone. Fennel, choc, cassis integrate seamlessly with vanilla-tinged oak (Fr/Am, 77/23, new/old, 23 mths. 1 225 cases, 500 magnums. Quartet Stbosch area vyds. **97** (71/29 blend) more austere, leafy and tannic. **96** still youthful, vibrant. **95** ✵✵ (which confirmed Grangehurst on serious Cape wine map), classic claret profile. SAA, UK *Decanter* lauded **94** voted top overall in recent G'hurst retrospective.

✵**Pinotage** Benchmark status in Cape affirmed at recent Pinotage Association 'vintage preview', where **01** sample swept the popular vote. Current **98**, back-tasted (and re-rated) mid-01, showcases grape's burgundian qualities (cherry, strawberry fruits and game/undergrowth whiffs); super-elegant style with wrap-around flavour, good grip, soft fine tannins. **97** *Wine* ✵; **96** more herbaceous, savoury/farmyard style. **95** *Wine* ✵ and landmark yr, now shows almost jammy but vibrant cassis notes, bright fruit; still needs some time! Leavened with splash (8-15%) cab since initial **92**. These barrel-aged, about 25% new, 65% Fr, rest Am, 10-15 mths.

✵**CWG Auction Reserve Cabernet Sauvignon** Only 'straight' cab from this cellar. **98**, gavelled at 00 Auction, blockbuster raised in 5 new 225 ℓ Fr barriques giving firm but silky frame to compact, chewy, ripe blackberry core, with hint of violets. Favourite of four (**95-98**) Reserves at above retrospective. Shows cigarbox, some almost meaty whiffs, classic Medoc lead-pencil notes from exquisite oak. Trio Stbosch sites; 23 mths oak. 140 cases. **97** also deluxe version, cedary wafts with cassis flesh; mocha, fennel, green pepper flavours, similar at early stage to **95** which swept boards as sole *Wine* ✱ from that star vintage.

✱**CWG Auction Pinotage** Collaboration with Dave Hidden, owner of excellent Devon Valley vyd. **00**, for 01 Auction, untasted. Pvs was **97**, a statement wine, 18 mths new wood. Also, like 'regular' above, with dash cab. No **96**. **95** fetched remarkable (in 1996) R100/bottle. —*TM*

Granite Creek see Laborie

Green on Green 

"Quixotic venture" between envelope-pushing winemaker Bruce Jack of Flagstone and winewriting entrepreneur Graham Knox "to find out why Semillon had been the grape of choice of ancient artisanal winemakers, pre-stainless steel, pre-enzymes and fancy yeast strains". The answer was found in a gnarly and unkempt Wellington vineyard which, miraculously, produced "a ripe crop of sugar-sweet grapes with racy flavours". Using only nature's own protections, the vintners' challenge was "to lose as little as possible between vineyard and bottle". See Flagstone for tasting/sales details.

✱**Green on Green** Nearly everything about this delicious **01** individual is green – groendruif ('green grape', old-Cape term for formerly ubiquitous semillon) from Groenberg (Green Mountain); green bdx bottle and label adornment. Only wine itself isn't 'green'/unripe (though non-interventionist vinification accords with 'green' eco-principles). Immediately obvious from gorgeous sunny-ripe colour; concentrated honey-lemon fruit enriched by fine spicy/vanilla oak. Lushness battened down by enough substance, structure to see 'rabble' grape to blue-blooded maturity in 3-5 yrs. —*AL*

Griekwaland West Co-op see Douglas
Groblershoop see Oranjerivier Wine Cellars

Groene Cloof 

Swartland (see Swartland map) • Tasting & sales Mon-Do 10-4 Fri 10-1 Sat 10-1 • Cellar tours by appointment • Views • Proclaimed conservation area • Owner Johan van der Berg • Winemaker Anneke Burger (since 2001) • Consulting viticulturist Paul Wallace (VineWise) • Vineyard manager Hardie van den Heever • Vineyards ±200 ha • Production 20 000 cases (10 000 cases own label) 60% red 40% white • PO Box 125 Darling 7345 • ***Tel (022) 492-2839*** *• Fax (022) 492-3261 • E-mail cloofwines@intekom.co.za*

The steady swing toward red wines continues at this West Coast winery with the planting, during 2001, of shiraz and merlot, bringing the total area under vines to 200 ha. Bukettraube and colombard have been uprooted to make way for the new reds, but, significantly, 10 ha of old chenin have been retained. In the cellar Anneke Burger, formerly of Eikendal, has taken over from Frikkie Botes. Her plans include "a truly South African cabernet-merlot-shiraz blend". Enthusiastic owner Johan van der Berg, who bought the farm in 94 and completed the cellar in 97, believes bushvines are the way to go. "At present only 20 ha of chardonnay vines are still on trellises," he remarks, no doubt feeling vindicated by the splash made by his Pinotage 99, which scooped the most recent SA Pinotage Championships.

✱**Cabernet Sauvignon** Modern, well made cab showing considerable presence and heft. Recent releases more elegant than milestone **98**, first wine bottled in new cellar, despite **99**'s higher alc (14% vs 13,5%). **99** sophisticated strawberries-and-cream texture, fine dry tannins. **00** strong green pepper overtones, hints choc, coffee. Bushvines; 9-12 mths casked.

Pinotage First release **98** had *Decanter* panel see four stars, but we preferred follow-up **99**, as did SA *Wine*/ABSA judges who named it their 01 Pinotage Champion. Super wine, not nearly as flamboyant as 14,5% alc suggests. **00** bigger, even, at 15%, but not 'hot'; should rise to height of pvs in 3-5 yrs. 3 500 cases. Bushvines, oaking as above.

Chenin Blanc Good everyday quaff, fruity and bone dry. Unoaked **01** well priced at R18 ex cellar.1 500 cases. Discontinued: **Bush Vine 99** untasted. — *DH*

Groenekloof see Darling Cellars, Neil Ellis, Woolworths

Groot Constantia Estate

Constantia (see Constantia map) • Tasting & sales daily except Christmas Day, Good Friday & 1 Jan. Tasting 9-5.30 Dec-Apr; 10-5 May-Nov Fee includes glass Sales 9-6 Dec-Apr; 10-5 May-Nov • Cellar tours between 10-4 in summer; 11-3 in winter Booking essential Large groups can book times to suit. • Two restaurants • Gift shop • Conference facilities • Walking trail • Museum • Manor house • Managed by Groot Constantia Trust • General manager Jean du Toit • Winemaker Boela Gerber with Roger Arendse • Vineyard manager Callie Bröcker • Vineyards 90 ha • Production 601 tons 45 000 cases 55% red 45% white • Private Bag X1 Constantia 7848 • ***Tel (021) 794-5128*** *• Fax (021) 794-1999 • E-mail pro@grootconstantia.co.za, enquiries@grootconstantia.co.za*

FUN-loving winemaker Boela Gerber, who says he arrived in the cellar (from Rickety Bridge in Franschhoek) "at the same time as the grapes", is settling in happily after his first season at this wine estate (the oldest on the Cape block, and they now have a new specialised tour, tasting and lunching dripping with history to go with the status). Being small, the Constantia Wine Route community is close-knit, and neighbourly Hermann Kirschbaum at Buitenverwachting has been an "absolute gem". When things get extreme in the cellar, there's always his mountain bike and the nearby Tokai forest, where he holds his breath and takes off on the "awesome!" downhills. While Gerber's paying attention to the valley's reputation for sauvignons, he'd like to see their reds on a par, to which end they're moving towards small-oak vatting (with some "stunning merlots" resting in them as we speak). Exports to Germany, Holland, Japan and the US are flowing fast. Now Gerber's game plan for this year is pampering the vineyards, isolating quality blocks and checking out the rest of his new turf.

Pinotage ✓ Constantia valley's only varietal bottling of the grape – and a most unusual one. Minty cool-climate fruit a hallmark of **99**; ripe unjammy plum fruits, nicely rounded and full. Modern, delicious (a fact which did not escape Veritas, ABSA Top Ten, WOM selectors). 3 000 cases. Several steps up on last-tasted **97**.

Shiraz ✓ Selected block of mature vines. **99** showing more oak than when tasted for pvs ed (75/25 US/Fr, 6 mths); underlying smoky, chocolatey fruit still healthy, sweet and probably best around 05. 13.7% alc. 5 000 cases.

Gouverneurs Reserve Estate's standard-bearing red, since inception a cellarmaster's selection of best-performing blocks, irrespective of variety. **99** smells like classic bdx (flinty 'cold stones' bouquet) but it's a blend with dollop pinotage, ±30% merlot, ±55% cab. Latter uppermost in ripe dark berry fruits, still slathered with 14 mths Fr oak. Huge alcohol (±14%) will mellow into rich, warm sensory experience within ±2 yrs, continue drinking well for another 10. WOM Reserve. 1 200 cases.

Merlot-Shiraz ✓ Modern, compatible couple dominated by shiraz in **99** (though junior partner in 60/40 blend), supplying generous spice, pepper tones. Lovely grip, balance between fruit/wood (40% new, 10 mths). For earlier drinking: now to 05. 3 500 cases.

Chardonnay ✓ Deeply-flavoured barrel-fermented chardonnay, 100% malo for rich buttery profile. **01** (sample) even in extreme youth generous, full, complex; toasty butterscotch textures from 100% new Fr oak (anticipated 10 mths). Give yr/2 to settle, then drink until 06. **00** similar toasty profile with ginger-cream texture.

✪**Sauvignon Blanc** ✓ Fermentation 'pear-drops' still in bouquet of **01** (sample), plus citrus aromas, green pepper flavours. Not over-aggressive. Pvs **00**, with splash semillon, more tropical, softer.

✪**Weisser Riesling** ✓ Welcome return in **01** after short break – quality of unreleased **00** not up to exalted standard of powerfully botrytised (50%) **99** ✪✪. Latest shows why this one of Cape's top rieslings. Full, scintillating ripe apple fruit, extra richness, as always, from well-pitched sugar (22 g/ℓ slightly drier than **99**'s 28). Botrytis, often a feature, adds complexity. 1 500 cases. Still great match for spicy Cape-Malay cuisine.

✪**Constantia Blanc** New broom Boela Gerber sweeps in with new formulation, fresh verve for this old retainer. **01** mostly sauvignon, dab semillon (a Gerber favourite). Lively grassy tastes, ample in palate, long lipsmacking dry finish. **00** ✪ delicately floral, finishes with juicy twist.

✪**Port** More 'serious' contender, following transfusion with Douro aristocrat touriga (10%, balance tinta). Now vintaged (**99**) nice light style, well fruited, 12 mths 300 ℓ barrels very well woven. Succulence concludes with pleasing firm, dry finish (70 g/ℓ sugar).

Bouquet Blanc ☻ ✪ **00** ageing gracefully in bottle. Spicy/petally blend gewürz, morio muscat (75/25). Ripe, flavoursome; finishes gently dry. Should be enjoyed soonish.

Cabernet Sauvignon ✪ Well-oaked **99** offers round drinkability; variety's blackcurrant joined by mulberry in approachable palate. 5 500 cases. **Merlot** Current **99** not retasted for this ed. Pvsly ✪. **Constantia Rood** ✪ Cabs s/f with splashes merlot, shiraz. **99** light, lively though just a tad green. ±8 mths Fr barrelled. — *NP*

Grootdrink see Oranjerivier Wine Cellars

Groot Eiland Winery

Worcester (see Worcester map) • Tasting & sales Mon-Fri 8.30-12.30; 1.30-5 Sat by appointment • Cellar tours during tasting hours • Walks • Views • Owners 17 members • Winemaker Erik Schlünz (since 2000) with Marthinus Joubert (since 1965) • Consultant viticulturist Schalk du Toit (VinPro) • Vineyards 600 ha • Production 10 600 tons 90% white 10% red • *PO Box 93 Rawsonville 6845 •* ***Tel (023) 349-1140*** *• Fax (023) 349-1801 • E-mail grooteiland@lando.co.za*

"New reception area" is all the news we got from Erik Schlünz, who's clearly settled into his managing/winemaking role here after hopping over the mountain from Spruitdrift in time for the 2001 crush (with his penchant for bundu-bashing, Schlünz might have been tempted to follow the crow's route!). His arrival gives further impetus to this co-op's thrust into red wine (a personal Schlünz goal is to made "champion reds") as well as a more aggressive marketing drive locally and overseas (exports already flow to America and Europe). And though Schlünz has no time to be interviewed for the guide, it's safe to say he'd spare a moment for Sandra Bullock, the Hollywood iconette he'd like to meet more than anyone in the world of wine "because she's better looking than winemakers". The range, not ready for tasting for this edition, includes: **Cabernet Sauvignon** (pvs **98** ✪), **Pinotage** (**99** ✪), **Merlot** NEW, **Shiraz** (**00** ✪), **Rosé** (**NV**/00 ✪), **Chardonnay** (**00** ✪), **Chenin Blanc** (**00** ✪), **Sauvignon Blanc** (**00** ✪), **Meander** (**00** ✪), **Hönigtraube** (**NV** ✪).

Groote Post Vineyards

Darling (see Swartland map) • Tasting & sales Mon-Fri 8-12, 2-5 Sat 8-12 • Owners Peter & Nicholas Pentz • Winemaker Lukas Wentzel • Viticulturist Johan Pienaar (VinPro) • Vineyard manager Jannie de Klerk (since 1996) • Vineyards 85 ha • Production 280 tons 13 000 cases 40% red 60% white • Private Bag X1 Bloubergrant 7441 • ***Tel (021) 557-0606*** *(office) (022) 492-2825 (winery) • Fax (021) 557-8280 (office) (022) 492-2693 (winery) • E-mail gpwines@iafrica.com*

COMING across this wine and dairy farm on an off-the-beaten track in the Darling Hills is a delightful surprise: the old homestead is a relaxed picnic spot on the world famous West Coast Spring Flower Route. Tastings take place in an atmospheric old fort, a crucible of Cape history – the outpost once provisioned the fleets sailing around the Cape of Good Hope. The vineyards have been replanted for the first time since the 19th century by co-owner and vineyard chief Nick Pentz (his and viticultural cornerman Johan Pienaar's meticulousness recognised by judges of the 2001 Vineyard Block Competition). New pinot, cabernet franc and shiraz complete a decade-long programme and bring the total area under vine to 120 ha. Now shepherding the fruits of these cool climate plots (the chilly Atlantic Ocean just 7 km away) through cellar to bottle is ex La Motte winemaker, Lukas Wentzel.

✵**Sauvignon Blanc** ✓ Groenekloof terroir yields more Loire-style high-fruited sauvignons. **00**, mid-01, grassy/green fig notes, lime/grapefruit finish; ideally paired with West Coast crayfish. **99** equally herbaceous. WOM selections. Latest **01** ✵ full, sweet-fruited; could age yr/2. 13,4% alc. ±5 700 cases.

✵**Chardonnay** Part barrel-fermented **00**, reminiscent of Maconnais white (though now showing more oak). Lime/grapefruit more ebullient than cinnamon/vanilla notes from oak vinification. Young bushvines; partial malo, 8 mths lees ageing, 1st/2nd fill Fr barrels. 1 000 cases.

Merlot ★★ Pungently aromatic **00**, greengage layered with smoky oak, plums/mulberries leap from glass; light caramel, butterscotch add weight to elegant, almost herbal palate. More power (14,5% alc) than evident in quite spartan finish. **Pinot Noir** ★★ **00** black cherry notes, elegant but elusive spice; light herbal aromas and vanilla whiffs from 9 mths oaking add their own dimension. 12,8% alc. 2 400 cases. **Chardonnay Unwooded** Not tasted for this ed. Pvs was **00** (★★). **Chenin Blanc** ☆ **00** whiffs lemon/pear, delicate fruit-drop spice, crisp finish. 12% alc. 1 000 cases. — *MF/DH*

Groot Geluk see Vinfruco

Grünberger

POPULAR Bergkelder range with a Germanic inspiration that extends to the Frankish flagon-type 'bocksbeutel' bottle used for the non-spritzy wines.

Rosenlese ☆ Pale coral **01**, earthy nuances, sweet red-winey tastes; from sauvignon, ruby cab. 7,9% alc. **Freudenlese** ★★ **01** sauvignon, gewürz flaunting honeysuckle *and* honey aromas; slight (7.5% alc) yet feels substantial, balanced. Like Rosenlese, made in Natural Sweet style. **Stein** ★ Soft, off-dry **00**; light-bodied/flavoured, delicately scented. Not as satisfying as pvs. **Spritzenlese** ★★ Natural Sweet-style spritzy sauvignon, chenin. **01** with meaty richness in bouquet, palate. 8.1% alc. In tall 'tower' screw-topped bottle. **Spritziger** ★★ **01** packaged and carbonated similarly to above, but more delicate, off-dry. Floral touches, gently sweet, refreshing. — *IvH*

Grundheim Wines

Oudtshoorn (see Little Karoo map) • Tasting & sales Mon-Fri 8-5 Sat 8-1 • Cellar tours on request • Distilling demonstrations Mar-Apr • Owner Danie Grundling •

Winemaker Dys Grundling • Vineyards 20 ha • Production 300 tons 50/50 red/ white • PO Box 400 Oudtshoorn 6620 • ***Tel/fax (044) 272-6927***

Dys Grundling, admirer of Australian muscats, wasted no time in adding a Red Muscat de Frontignan to this range, which co-habits on the family farm between Calitzdorp and Oudtshoorn with master distiller Danie Grundling's home-distilled spirits and liqueurs, and Susan Grundling's famous preserves and folk remedies. Though there's a new broom in the cellar, they're not neglecting their popular favourites, White Muscadel and Port. Also available, not ready for tasting, are a Colombard, non-fortified Cape Muscat, Late Harvest and a Classic Red, natural partner at table for the local speciality, ostrich.

Red Muscadel This traditional fortified dessert (and white version below), speciality of the house, vinified the 'old Cape' way. **94**, retasted mid-01, more muscatty than Red Muscat below; raisins, varnishy whiffs, some savoury notes and rose-hip all waft from the glass, tapering to a warming spiritous conclusion. Gold on local show. 18% alc. 800 cases.

Red Muscat NEW Subtitled Muscat de Frontignan. **NV**. Tawny/amber colour; very little muscat character; more overt aromas of Karoo-bush, raisin, marmalade; soft textures of caramel/molasses. Easy to drink. **Wit Muscadel** Aromatically endowed **98**, follow-up to **94**, redolent of spice, sage and grapefruit-rind, not overly grapey; palate more straightforwardly sweet with barley sugar flavours. 2 544 cases. **Cape Ruby Port** **NV** (95) individual blend cinsaut, pinotage, cab with tawny colour, geranium perfume and flavours of orange marmalade and tomato jam. Would be more accurately named 'dessert wine' than 'port'. 19% alc. ±630 cases. — *TM*

Guardian Peak

This range takes its name from the highest point on the Stellenbosch Mountain towering above the blue-chip Rust en Vrede estate, where these new-generation wines (offspring of a partnership between owner Jean Engelbrecht, winemaker Louis Strydom and marketing dynamo Neil Büchner) are currently produced, using grapes from the estate and fruit that's bought in from the Stellenbosch area and a family farm at Vredendal on the West Coast (where Jean Engelbrecht's father and rugby icon, Jannie Engelbrecht, grew up). If old and established Rust en Vrede leans towards classical restraint, these sassy, fresh-faced kids radiate new world expressiveness and accessibility, both in style and price. For tasting/sales information, see Rust en Vrede. Wines below NEW to this edition.

Cabernet Sauvignon-Syrah Blockbuster **00**; riot of spice, warm ripe red berries embellished with grain sugar; tannins, few from older Am oak, just meet struggle to keep all under control. Welcome its warming capabilities soon. 13% alc. 5 000 cases. **Merlot-Cabernet Sauvignon-Tinta Barocca** **00** combines quality with unpretentiousness; plenty savoury/earthy concentration to balance quite robust tannins (3.5 g/ℓ sugar also helps without being obvious); 44/31/21 blend, harmonised by 7 mths oak. 6 000 cases. — *AL*

Hamilton Russell Vineyards

Walker Bay (see Walker Bay map) • Tasting & sales Mon-Fri 9-5 Sat 9-1 • Cellar & vineyard tours by arrangement • Also tasting & sales of estate-matured Hemel-en-Aarde cheese • View works by artist Arabella Caccia by appointment • Views • Owner Anthony Hamilton Russell • Winemaker Kevin Grant (since 1994) • Viticulturist Stephen Roche (since 1998) • Vineyards 51.33 ha • Production 200 tons 15 000 cases 60% white 40% red • PO Box 158 Hermanus 7200 • ***Tel (028) 312-3595*** *• Fax (028) 312-1797 • E-mail hrv@hermanus.co.za*

To discover why these wines (there are only two, a Pinot Noir and a Chardonnay) are applauded by wine-show judges (Air France Top Ten and gold medal);

winewriters (92-point rating in *Wine Spectator* – highest ever for SA white), gastronomes (star turn in French foodie bible GaultMillau); and celebrities (only SA wine poured at Buckingham Palace banquet for Nelson Mandela), you have to get close – really close. To not just the beautiful HRV property loping up the Hemel-en-Aarde ridges, or the portion thereof officially delimited as the HRV Estate, but the particular wedge of soil, the site-within-a-site, that Anthony Hamilton Russell and fellow-fanatic Kevin Grant have declared their holy grail. It's taken them years of replanting, and scores of probing vinifications – and now at last they've found their essential 'HRVness'. It's not the relatively cool Walker Bay climate, they assert, nor the aspect, nor the elevation. It's their "stony, low-vigour, clay-rich, shale-derived soils". With that revelation has come a new direction and a fresh challenge: "To manage our soils is one of our most important activities," declares AHR, "we are moving organic in this area as quickly as possible." Stand by for a 'green' dimension to their mantra, 'Soil, Soil, Soil'.

⁂**Pinot Noir** 20th vintage-**00**, a small ripe crop, "winemaking milestone for HRV," believes Kevin G, "our best to date!" Followers of this internationally respected label may disagree with winemaker and prefer **97** ⁂, to us HRV's triumph of the 90s. But no question about Cape-benchmark quality of all releases of post-94 Grant era (confirmed by major HRV Pinot vertical tasting at WINPAC 01 New World Wine Show, Hong Kong – topped, incidentally, by **00**). **95** signposted new direction: first major injection of Dijon clones 777, 115, 113 and 667 (all pvs less propitious BK5 'champagne' clone); **96** with 80% new clone, some tight-on-release tannins, Wine ✲; unsurpassed **97**, again with 80% new clones; **98** big, open structure, generously ripe tannins, Wine ✲; **99** first all new clonal material. Now **00**: big wine (nearly 14% alc); stunningly scented, hints blueberries, Havana cigars, Moroccan leather, sandalwood; remarkable complexity, suppleness. Many corks will be pulled too early; for the patient, a veritable banquet of future pleasures. 9 mths small Fr oak. 3 250 cases. Best ever? Time will tell …

⁂**Chardonnay** Yearly variations ("the drama of vintage" – AHR's phrase) reflected/magnified in these wines, yet fingerprint of the site – a thrilling, tight riverstone/mineral quality, always with citrus dimension, occasionally fresh herbs – continuously present since maiden **82** (labelled Premier Vin Blanc). Vintages **95** to present stunning **00**, by incumbent Kevin G, perhaps most classically, meticulously structured of these; latest **00** again 100% barrel-fermented/sur lie 8 mths, burgundian coopers exclusively; medley spicy scents, new beeswax, toasted hazelnuts; balanced yet lively, everlasting steely/flinty finish with unheralded floral nuance. Brilliant crafting. Preview of **01** strikes as concentrated new-world, suffused with almost sweet fruit; reprise of **99**'s spring-flower character. More "drama" poised to unfold. — *DH*

Hanseret see Stellenbosch Vineyards

Hartenberg Estate

*Bottelary, Stellenbosch (see Stellenbosch map) • Tasting & sales Mon-Fri 9-5 Sat 9-3 Closed Sun, religious holidays, New Year's Day • Nominal tasting fee for groups, refundable with purchases • Vintners lunches (alfresco, weather permitting) 12-2 daily except Sun; Picnic platters in summer; Soup, vetkoek in winter Booking advisable • Views • "Great bird life including fish eagles" • Owners Fiona Mackenzie, Tanya Browne • Winemaker Carl Schultz (since 1994) • Viticulturist Frans Snyman (since 1996) • Vineyards 105 ha • Production 650 tons 40 000 cases 60% red 40% white • PO Box 69 Koelenhof 7605 • **Tel (021) 882-2541** (changing during 2002 to **(021) 865-2541)** • Fax (021) 882-2153 (changing during 2002 to (021) 865-2153) • E-mail info@hartenbergestate.com*

HARTENBERG is arguably the most visible property in the Bottelary area – which, albeit the youngest Stellenbosch ward, has rapidly established its red wine credentials. This tight-knit team can see even more clearly now the dust has settled – what with the 3 km-long driveway being tarred at last. Perfect vision had them picking well into the extended Cape summer twilights, which proved critical in a heat wave beleaguered vintage. Further foresight came from an investment in a weather station, which has already seen a 50% reduction in the usage of sprays. Seemingly against trends, 80% of their wines are still sold on the local market (with some, particularly the Gravel Hill Shiraz, reaching top prices on auction). New plantings are focused on merlot, malbec and, of course, the shiraz they've become synonymous with. The purchase of a bottling and labelling line sees them operating at full tilt, so they've doubled the oak maturation area, and also completed both the pressing cellar and new storage facility. Note: 01 versions of whites below not ready for tasting for this ed.

Cabernet Sauvignon 97 vintage, long, cool ripening period, often alluded to as most 'European' in recent years. Translates into much brighter fruit, more elegant structure; youthful sternish profile not so apparent, though no shortage of backbone. Retasted mid-01, proving to be slow developer predicted by Carl Schultz. Ripe luscious fruit now in balance with wood (20 mths oak, 40% new). Slightly medicinal, mineral tones still hiding their potential; optimal drinking couple yrs off. 2 483 cases. No **98**. **96** harmonious, good example from ambiguous year. **95** VVG a stunner. All built to last good 7-9 yrs.

Merlot 98 attractive minty nose with choc whiffs; ripe damson palate and balanced oak with choc reprising in finish. Good follow-though, length. **97**'s velvety choc-mint character growing more pronounced with time, melt-in-the-mouth tannins attuned to vintage's greater all-round intensity, persistence. **96** sweet-fruited, finely oaked. *Wine* . Not as impenetrable as massive **95** VVG, SAA, Air France trophy; but should have good 5-7 yrs' staying power. These ±18 mths Fr 225 ℓ oak, 40% new.

Pontac Only Cape bottling of this firm, dry, rustic red. Released sporadically: **97**, **96**, **95** never bottled individually. Current **98** statement wine which needs food to tame its minty/vegetal flavours. Lavishly wooded – 22 mths new Am oak.

Shiraz Schultz's favoured variety, on Hartenberg and in Cape; here shows stylistic versatility with quality, discreetly exercised power with heady snatches of scrub, fresh earth, roasted spices. **98** fuses new/old worlds in delicious, elegant expression of ripe fruit and savoury spice; generous oaking (17 months Fr, 40% new) well judged. Will benefit from ±2 yrs bottle ageing, develop until turn of decade. Cooler **97** initially tightly swaddled, now opening up; oak melding with ripe fruit. Sheer elegance of this vintage will appeal to shiraz fans. **96** intense, deep, sensuous. **95** VVG; **93-96** SAA.

Zinfandel Adventurous palates and hard-core aficionados will love **97** individual, originally held back for extra maturation at cellar. Reviewed in pvs ed, has smoothed; now sports approachable sweet rhubarb, red-berry flavours and pleasantly contrasting bitter-choc finish. 19 mths 100% Am oak, 50% new. 10% cab adds extra oomph.

Cabernet Sauvignon-Merlot 60/40 blend, 22 mths oak. None since **95**, now offering vegetal/perfumed bouquet and soft, smooth palate. Well oaked (components separately matured 12 mths, 50% new oak; blend then aged further 10 mths all-new barrels). Approaching peak, although should see out the decade.

Cabernet Sauvignon-Shiraz ✓ Formula change to 66/33 propels **99** up a good notch from pvs. Very ripe, slightly porty aromas over array of juicy red/black berries. Approachable, excellent-value red that needs no excuse to pull the cork. **98** briefer-oaked 55/45 blend.

Chardonnay Reserve From premium vyd blocks, only in great vintages. Last was **98** Michelangelo gold; fermented/matured 15 mths Fr oak, all new. **97** SAA. No **99**. Next will be **00**, released 2nd half 02. Regular **Chardonnay** "Very popular overseas," confirms Tanya Browne, "people say it's very un-South African." **99**, retasted mid-01, still on the up. Lemon/lime flavours still fresh, broadened with vanilla. Elegant. Stamina for another 2 yrs. 13,7% alc. Barrel fermented/matured 15 mths Fr oak, 20% new.

Weisser Riesling From old vines (±20 yrs), among Cape's best examples of too often overlooked variety. **00**, with 10% botrytis, beautiful floral nose melded with Granny Smith apples in soft, citrus-spicy palate with complex flavours and sweet, clean goodbye. Lighter than usual 12% alc. Ripening in bottle, plenty of life ahead.

L'Estreux Named after original Huguenot farmer. One of the less unctuous SLHs, its official designation. With departure of gewürz (vines uprooted), **00** first 100% schönberger released locally. Mid-01 presents gewürz-like litchi, rose-petal nose/palate with gentle sweetness and clean finish. Excellent match for Thai, Vietnamese and Indian cuisines.

Sauvignon Blanc **00**, maiden crop from new clone, much livelier on release, more immediately appealing than pvs. Mid-01 showing some complexity but also honeyed tones, suggesting last cases should now be uncorked – at table, where big alc (±14%) more appropriate. **Chatillon** Lovely drinking, great value **00** still going strong. Floral, earthy tones, full bodied. Fruit salad of apples/papaya with honey overtones; crisp, dry finish. 50/50 blend chenin/semillon (latter portion oaked). Also available (untasted): **Bin 9**, **Bin 6**, **Bin 3**, **NV** housewines for sale ex cellar and via mail order (also offered free with cellar's famous farm lunches); thoroughly good value, food-friendly wines, varieties/blends vary from yr to yr. — *NP*

Hartswater Wine Cellar

*Northern Cape • Tasting & sales Mon-Fri 8.30-5 Sat tasting by appointment, sales from outlet in Hartswater town • Phone ahead for cellar tours • Fully licensed restaurant with barbecue • Conference facilities • Owner Senwes • Winemaker Roelof Maree (since 1978) • Production 5 000 tons • PO Box 2335 Hartswater 8570 • **Tel (053) 474-0700** • Fax (053) 474-0975*

INDEFATIGABLE Roelof Maree is in full cry: "Half full or half empty," he declares, "it's the wine for the moment!" He's referring to their Elements range, designed to offer value for money despite being sold in slightly more expensive cork-closed packaging. But such is the ebullient winemaker's enthusiasm, he might as well be talking about their entire harvest, which rose slightly to 5 000 tons in 2001. What's new in the range? A low-alcohol Natural Sweet, with a gentle sparkle for extra refreshment in these blistering Northern Cape climes, and smart new labels. What's *not* new, it might be added, is Maree himself. Nearly a quarter century in this cellar, he's been around longer than some of his vines! The range, not tasted for this edition, includes: Elements range: **Earth** (dry red), **Rubeo**  (Natural Sweet red), **Wind** (off-dry white), **Fire** (Natural Sweet rosé); Hinterland range: **Ruby Cabernet**, **Chardonnay**, **Chenin Blanc**, **Grand Cru**, **Late Harvest**, **Jerepigo**.Overvaal range: **Sparkling**.

Haute Provence see Agusta

Havana Hills

Tygerberg • Not open to the public • Owner Kobus du Plessis & Nico Vermeulen • Winemaker Nico Vermeulen (since 1999) with Joseph Gertse (since 2000) • Viticulturist Rudi Benn (since 2001) • Vineyards 48 ha • Production 80 tons 6 000 cases 90% red 10% white • PO Box 46241 Kernkrag 7440 • ***Tel (021) 972-1106*** *• Fax (021) 972-1105 • E-mail rambo@telcomsa.net*

THIS has to be one of the most spectacular wine farm sites in the Cape. From the hilltop cellar you look down over Melkbosstrand and across the sparkling Table Bay to Table Mountain as a backdrop. Entrepreneur-turned-vintner Kobus du Plessis has taken full advantage of the perfect situation to create a stunning modern workplace for himself and partner-in-wine Nico Vermeulen. The ridges leading to the cellar have been planted with cabernet, merlot, shiraz and sauvignon. The pair's brimming enthusiasm is infectious, and they're bringing a dash of salsa to their craft and this underplayed but auspicious area. Given the constellation of stars below, it's not hard to take them seriously when they say: "We want Havana Hills to grow into one of the best wineries in SA – and the world."

Bisweni range NEW

Cabernet Sauvignon Top-of-the-range **00** evidently crafted for long haul. Core of friendly warm red-earth tones (evocative of partial Malmesbury origin); plusher roast coffee, cedary oak add complexity. Expansive, creamy mouthfeel focused by svelte mineral streak, vibrant grip. Excellent maturation potential, though all beautifully polished to deliver the goods now. Mth on skins post fermentation for better tannin integration; selection of best barrels from Du Plessis Cab below

Merlot 00 immediately declares quality/maturation aspirations through ripeness, concentration, unmissable yet integrated fine, dry tannins. Presently very tight, though all in place to realise grand maturity. Shimmers with understated class, elegance. Also real sense of 'Capeness' (rather than merely effects of modern winemaking) despite multiplicity of grape sources (Dbnville, Malmesbury, Stbosch). Doubtless meagre 100 cases will be snapped up; vinification as above: 15 mths Fr oak, 40% new.

Du Plessis Reserve range NEW

Cabernet Sauvignon-Merlot ✓ Brightest, most delicious member of this star-studded cast (and eloquent example of importance of blends in top echelon of Cape reds); **00** more than just numbers on paper (55/36 with 9% cab f): evinces sense of completeness, harmony, whole greater than parts. Confidently structured: cab's insistent, fine tannins embracing merlot's plummy rich fruit, supple texture. Lovely leafy, spicy extras - from cab f; well-paced Fr oak polish - lifts this to another distinctive level. Epitomises cellar's goal of combining Swartland's rich, if slightly rustic, profile with elegance of Dbnville. Oaked 15 mths, 40% new. 500 cases.

Cabernet Sauvignon 00 announces chic new prestige Cape cab, robed in saturated ruby/carmine hues. Sonorous black-fruited aromas accessorised with classy Fr oak lead to firm-tannined palate, dry rounded conclusion. Veneer of rich red earth, mineral thread evident in these reds lend distinctive, homogenising edge, as does seamless oaking. Probably too delectable in youth to consider ageing (which it will, beautifully). 15 mths Fr oak, 40% new. Step beyond **99**

Merlot Serious, ageworthy **00**, irresistible in harmonious youth. Nose, palate echo with deep, cedar-dusted choc plum richness, focusing fine minerality. Full-bodied. Creamy fruit concentration layered across firm, fully ripe tannin creates riveting contrast, effortlessly absorbs 15 mths sojourn in Fr oak, 40% new. Good news for those who missed meagre 250 cases of **99**: quantity quadrupled to 1 000. Dbnville/Malmesbury grapes. 13,5% alc.

Shiraz 00 more refined than swashbuckling Am-oaked **99**; retains distinctive sweet stamp of that wood (through barrelled portion downscaled to 15% vs **99**'s 100%) but punchy shiraz spice prevents sweeter notes dominating. Plentiful palate-hugging rich fruit; youthfully exuberant tannins need couple of yrs to settle, allow full play to wide savoury/spicy finish. 15 mths oak, 40% Fr new. Malmesbury fruit. 13,5% alc. 800 cases.

Havana Hills range

Cabernet Sauvignon-Merlot 00 to be blended, released only later in 02, not tasted for this ed. **99** set new-Cape tone with fashionable extra-ripe fruit, full-throated alc, mouthfilling 'sweet' flavour and melt-in-mouth tannins. Malmesbury fruit. 11 mths small oak. 2 000 cases.

Sauvignon Blanc ✓ Very fresh, Atlantic-born gooseberry/cut-grass coolness breezes off **01**; presently quieter in full, lees-padded body; finishes with soaring flavour resurgence. Powerful but refined; room to grow. Single Dbnville vyd; 19 yr old bushvines. 500 cases.

Merlot NEW ★ Pruney ultra-ripe **00**; lots of juicy flavours, generously-spread creamy texture for current drinking; definitely one to enjoy on upward curve (±3 yrs). Fr oak, 30% new. 800 cases. **Shiraz** ★ **00** bears some nostalgic shiraz farmyard smells alongside more modern new-leather, spice, choc. Elegantly rustic with good chunky, chewy substance. Great fit with beef or venison dishes, Vermeulen suggests. Yr mix Fr/Am oak, 30% new. 800 cases. **Chardonnay** NEW ★ **00** spans gap between ultra-fruity, simple styles and chardonnays treated to whole works. Tropical, pickled lime fruit aplenty, more interesting butterscotch, toasty extras; presented in juicy, supple fashion absolutely ready for current satisfaction. 70% barrel-fermented, partial malo. —*AL*

Hawekwa Peaks see Bovlei

Hazendal

Stellenbosch (see Stellenbosch map) • Tasting & sales Mon-Fri 8.30-4.30 Sat/Sun 10-3 Tasting fee R10 p/p for groups of more than 10 • Cellar tours weekdays at 11 & 3 R10 p/p (includes tasting) • Full à la carte restaurant (see Eat-out section) • Conferences • Tourgroups by appointment • Museum of Russian Art & Culture • Gift shop • Play area for children • Views • 4×4 trailing by appointment • Owner Mark Voloshin • Winemaker Ronell Wiid (since 1998) • Viticultural consultant Schalk du Toit (VinPro) • Vineyards 66 ha • Production 400 tons, 20 000 cases 70% white 30% red • PO Box 336 Stellenbosch 7599 • ***Tel (021) 903-5112*** *• Fax (021) 903-0057 • E-mail info@hazendal.co.za, restaurant@hazendal.co.za • Website www.wineroute.co.za*

"The owner just cannot understand," chuckles Ronell Wiid, "that after ordering the demolition of the old cellar, and the open cement *kuipe*, and spending millions on a modern cellar, his winemaker then buys old vats and turns them into open *kuipe* again!" Moscow-born Mark Voloshin, proprietor and rescuer of this Stellenbosch spread may not understand traditional punch-downs, or why those fabulously expensive bits of emptiness should be so dear to her oenologist's heart. But, sussed international businessman that he is, he knows when he's onto a good thing, and his Diners Club-lauded winemaker clearly is one of the best. "He's given me the freedom to try anything – so far," laughs Wiid. "He thinks I'm wonderful!" And so does the whole "incredible" team, not to mention the innumerable admirers of not just Wiid's wines, but the brilliantly executed Hazendal makeover. Until very recently this was a charming but unremarkable family *plaas*; now it's an chic arts and culinary mecca, and a magnet for the sporty and active. What's missing, concedes alarmingly forthright Ronell Wiid, is "a stunning sauvignon blanc", though her reds, she feels, "look *good*. Big, bold, black".

Cabernet Sauvignon-Shiraz Ronell Wiid quick to debate – passionately – value of shiraz, solo or blended. She would "*love*" to make a standalone (and likely standout, given her track record) version; but "the present situation makes for a better cab/shiraz blend than alone." Formula changes slightly: **98**, her Diners Club award winner, mostly shiraz; from **99** cab (55%) back in driver's seat: smoky shiraz-spiced fruit contained by bushvine cab cassis refinement, cigarbox subtlety, firm tannic support. Sample **00** richer, riper, more ample, juicy berry succulence. Likely to be a cracker. Portion 2nd fill Nadalie Am oak gives extra zest.

Merlot Now regular "but only about 1 000 cases" player. Second crop young vines **99** peppery/savoury austerity rather than meaty opulence; Ronell W trademark soft tannins temper palate – result is delicious mouthful after yr in bottle. Sample **00** similar spicy frame, firmer fruit suggests growing maturity, even more potential as young vines age.

Reserve Red ✓ Based, seemingly, on all too infrequent concept that the gravity of one's cellar is set by the quality of entry-level wines: 'Reserve' status at friendly price. **00** gregarious palate too: smoky interest, firm, chewy red-berry fruit, soft grip, easy drinking with style. Ready on release. **99** peppery spice, plump fruit, soft tannins. Unwooded, fruit-driven blend cab, merlot, shiraz from quality (incl Dbnville) sources.

Chardonnay Current **00** marking time for this label – promise of greater fruit concentration from auspicious vyds as they mature. Sensuous oak vanilla/spice to fore mid-01, clean mineral resonance in palate. Burgundian barrel-fermented/aged **99**'s wood vanilla now retiring, acquiring ripe peach/toasted hazelnut, creamy mouthful.

White Nights Brut Cap Classique Strikingly, indulgently even, packaged MCC, **98** now gaining much more oomph with appropriate time on lees. Mid-01 disgorgement offers tempting languid bead, toasted-almond breadth with richer age; still refreshing in linear style. 1st crop equal pinot noir, chardonnay, 24 mths on lees.

Blanc de Noir NEW ☻ "I need to do different things all the time to keep the 'bee in my bonnet' going" says Ronell W, who made this **01** from gentle press juice of pinot MCC run. Light, fruity, off-dry, lowish (11.5%) alc, tiny quantities for consumption at Hazendal tables this summer.

Pinotage In Kleine Hazen colours pvs ed, now 'Hazendal', exclusively for UK market. **99** tastes as 'purple' (if a colour can …) as the hue of its new livery: unequivocal unwooded pinotage, fruit pastille, candyfloss nose, packed with ripe bananas, cinnamon, clove. Easy tannins, for drinking without too much thinking. **Sauvignon Blanc** Ronell Wiid, who contemplates blends in-depth before a final decision, offered 2 samples of **01** for review: one more tense/grassy, other fuller tropical fig, both reflecting good SB vintage. **Chenin Blanc Wooded** (Bushvine) More muscle than un-oaked version, more finesse too. **00** like pvs, plumper after year in bottle: creamy vanilla nose lifted by plucky sweet-sour tang, all integrated, ready. 13,5% alc. **01** blend incomplete at tasting. 50% gets full (fermented/aged) Fr oak treatment. **Bushvine Chenin Blanc** Unwooded **00** from 30 yr old bushvines yielding only 3 t/ha, has developed golden shards, concentrated tropical (melon/pear) youth yielded to mineral stony ring, full and dry. **Konynwijn** Last/current **99** semi-sweet unwooded chenin, made for own restaurant. — *DS*

Heerenhof

POPULAR budget-priced 5 ℓ vat range from DGB. All NV.

Dry Red Juicy vin ordinaire balanced by fruit tannin for good vinous tastes; med-bodied. **Grand Cru** Foursquare med-bodied dry white from chenin. **Stein**

★★ Caribbean-fruit tones; lightish, balanced semi-dry casual quaff. **Late Harvest** ★★ Fresh, fruity semi-sweet with lower-level 10.7% alc. — *DH*

Helderberg Winery see Stellenbosch Vineyards

Helderkruin Wine Cellar

Stellenbosch (see Stellenbosch map) • Tasting & sales Mon-Fri 9-5 Sat 9-12 • Function facilities • Tourgroups • Gifts • Views • Wheelchair-friendly • Owner Neil du Toit • Winemaker Koos Bosman (since 1998) • Viticulturist Pietie Goosen • Vineyards 80 ha • Production 800 tons (200 tons 10 000 cases own label) 85% red 15% white • PO Box 91 Stellenbosch 7599 • ***Tel (021) 881-3899*** *• Fax (021) 881-3898 • E-mail helkruin@iafrica.com • Website www.helderbergwineroute.co.za*

Koos Bosman makes these wines for owner Neil du Toit (son of ex-Springbok Ben, who bought the property in 1968 and is honoured in the Special Reserve Pinotage below). Besides wine and splendid views, a good reason to visit this sunny yellow cellar high on the Helderberg is to buy the Workers Cape Port – profits from this labourer-trust-owned label are used to fund projects chosen by the community.

Cabernet Sauvignon ★★ Med-bodied, oak-aged **99**'s sweet-mulberries bouquet marred by palate's asperity. 600 cases. **Merlot** ★★ **99** mulberries, softish tannins and hint of oak, bone dry finish. 13% alc. 500 cases. **Pinotage Ben du Toit Special Reserve** Champion red wine on 1999 SAYWS; 18 mths matured in specially made Am/Fr oak barrels. **99** (unfinished sample, so unrated) shows melange of fruits over still-unyielding dry oak tannins. 250 cases. **Pinotage** NEW Oaked **00** uncompromising, very dry. Sample not rated. 13.5% alc. 1 000 cases. **Shiraz** ★★★ Variety's woodsmoke/leather aromas in **99**, Am oak aged; puckering dry finish. 13% alc. WOM Value. 600 cases. **Chardonnay** ★★ Light-toned **01**; some dried peach/haystack tastes; very firm finish. Oaked. 350 cases. **Sauvignon Blanc** ★★★ Peppery/dusty **01**, crisp sherbety finish. 13% alc. 350 cases. **Phyllis Hands Cap Classique** ★★ Blanc de blancs sparkle honouring Phyl Hands, pioneer Cape wine educator and writer. **98**, 100% chardonnay, beginning to tire (unlike namesake, who's still dancing on tables). **Workers Vintage Port** ★ Foot-crushed the traditional way, 21/24 mths oaked; **99** offers sweet leathery tastes. 20% alc. Yellow Cellar range, untasted for this ed, has included **Dry Red** (★); **Dry White** (★★), both **NV**. Discontinued: **Forté**. (Pvs **98** ★★★). — *DH*

Hendrik Boom

Feel-good range recognising the vinous contribution of Hendrik Boom, first chief-gardener of the Cape of Good Hope and founder of the original vineyard, on the 350th anniversary this year of the arrival of Jan van Riebeeck. A portion of profits will go to Help Aids Kids of Africa, a new privately-run support group. Two wines are available: a Merlot-Ruby Cabernet and a Sauvignon Blanc-Chardonnay (neither ready for tasting). Joint-venture between Cape Town businessman Maarten Venter and Dirk Jonker of Jonkheer (see also that entry).

Hercules Paragon see Simonsvlei

Here XVII

Reliable NV sparkler from the Bergkelder cellars.

Souverein ★★★ Clean, pleasant carbonated bubbly, with touch of sweetness. For everyday celebrations. Latest (01) from sauvignon, SA riesling, lowish 11.5% alc. 3 000 cases. — *IvH*

Hermanus Heritage Collection

PAUL du Toit is the energy behind this feel-good range. Five hundred sets, each with six selected wines from Walker Bay cellars, are specially labelled and boxed (artist David Errington the creative hand here) and available from Wine Village at the entrance to the Hemel-en-Aarde Valley. C/o R43 and R320, Hermanus 7200 • **Tel +27 (28) 316-3988** • Fax +27 (28) 316-3989 • E-mail wine@hermanus.co.za • Website www.wine-village.co.za

☆**Pinotage** Unwooded version; bright, fresh and food-cordial **00**. Paul du Toit recommends you drink this with waterblommetjie lamb bredie.

☆**Sauvignon Blanc 01** Complex, bracing and Loire-like; good foil for rich linefish.

Tinta Barocca ☆ **NV** Tinta on steroids; earthy, spicy, massive; easy match for venison pie and other carnivorous challenges. **Red** ☆ **NV** offers light dusty cherry flavours; chill and pop into the picnic hamper this summer. **Chardonnay** ☆ **00** bouncy peach/citrus fruits; smother the racy acidity with butter-grilled snoek. **Dry White** ☆ Flinty dry white; **01** unassuming, quaffable. — *TM/DH*

Hex see Overhex
Hexagon see Overhex

Hidden Valley Wines

Stellenbosch • Sales Mon-Fri 9-5 • Owner Dave Hidden • Winemakers Jeremy Walker (from 1996) with Guy Webber (1997/8) • Viticulturist Johan Grobbelaar (since 1999) • Vineyards 16 ha (rising to 36) • Production 45 tons 100% red • PO Box 12577 Die Boord Stellenbosch 7613 • ***Tel (021) 855-0296*** *• Fax (021) 855-0297 • E-mail hiddenvalley@mweb.co.za • Website www.hiddenvalleywines.com*

GAUTENG-BASED Dave and Margie Hidden, dynamic and eco-focused, are over the moon: last year they passed their first yearly Biogrow audit with flying colours. Concern for the environment goes into every hectare of their two prime Stellenbosch vineyards. On the Devon Valley farm, totally replanted with pinotage, cabernet, shiraz and merlot, an old block of pinotage vines is being "lovingly rejuvenated" by the vineyard team (farm manager Johan Grobbelaar thrilled with the results). The organically prepared virgin soil on their 28 Helderberg hectares awaits plantings of reds and olive trees. 'Judicious' is the rule of thumb when it comes to the use of everything from drip irrigation, to top-notch French or American oak. Down-to-earth winemakers Dave Hidden and Jeremy Walker (these wines made at Walker's Grangehurst cellar) have been mates since their Stellenbosch University days. Their first organic wines are due to be made "the natural way" next year. (They believe it'll be worth the wait. Judging by the stunning wines to date, we think they're absolutely right.)

☆☆**Pinotage** Praise-sung blueblood from fruit ex revered Devon Valley vyd, 30+ yrs old. Superb concentration of palate-coating mulberry fruit a hallmark, serious but harmonious wooding (±33% Am); touch old world minerally elegance, too. **00** barrel sample still dense, closed; anise, prune, classy cigarbox whiffs; more 'new world' than pvs: positively bursts with fruit yet HV tannic grip provides containment/structure for the long haul (though this should drink sumptuously from release late 02). **99** not back-tasted for this ed; on pvs form unusually fine-structured, fragrant, juicy; **98** marginally drier impression, less persistent finish.

☆**Cabernet Sauvignon** Maiden **99**, previewed last yr, sparked forecast of future cult status. Bottled version offers bright cassis, sweet-pepper whiffs – very juicy fruit profile. Hints cedar, mulberry, coffee round out sweet berry palate; elegant rather than muscular despite 14.3% alc. Sip from **00** barrel still densely purple; more savoury, less herbal, beautifully balanced. 10/12 yr old Helderberg, Firgrove vines provide pure blackcurrant profile, framed in 1st-3rd fill Fr/Am barriques.

Traditional vinification, including small open fermenters, basket press. On present form, could top pvs' rating. Cult wine? Let the market decide. — *TM*

High Constantia

Constantia (see Constantia map) • Tasting, sales, cellar tours by appointment • Owners/winemakers/viticulturists Bob de Villiers & David van Niekerk • Vineyards 14 ha (owned/leased) • Production 33 tons (rising to 125 tons) 88% red 12% white • Puck's Glen Groot Constantia Road Constantia 7800 • ***Tel (021) 794-7971*** *Cell 082-494-5671/083-300-2064 • Fax (021) 794-7999 • E-mail david@highconstantia.co.za*

This tiny new winery just outside the gates of the famous Groot Constantia Estate is still a hobby for owner David van Niekerk and winemaker Bob de Villiers. "But once we reach the maximum capacity of 150 tons, it'll no longer be a sideline." Financial adviser David vN is passionate about wine as an essential part of good living. At harvest time, family, friends and neighbours gather to bring in the chardonnay from the little vineyard next to the cellar and the whole thing becomes a joyful party, with meat on the braai and wine flowing until the grapes are safely in the barrels. "The wonderful thing about being a greenhorn in the wine game is that there's always plenty of free advice. Everybody is happy to share their knowledge," he laughs. His first, small vintage is ready for sale and he's faced with an agonising decision – can he afford to keep some of it back to see how it matures, or must it all go to keep the banker from the door?

☆**Sebastiaan** NEW Maiden **00** promises a standout new Cape red; cab/cab f (72/28) in beautifully realised statement of vinous elegance. Light peppery spice perfectly melded with blackcurrant/raspberry aromas, light cassia notes; mineral/earthy tones, creamy textures; ripe, soft persistent tannins. 60% new Fr oak; malo. 14% alc. Only 500 cases.

☆**Cabernet Franc** Intensely spicy with fresh youngberry fragrance; leafy, almost herbal but not green, damp forest floor/mushroom nuances. **00** gamey, high fruited – from extended maceration – despite 80% new Fr oak. **01** barrel reveals even stronger crushed leaf aromas.

☆**Cabernet Sauvignon 00** compote of black berry fruits (cassis, raspberry, wild mulberries); sweet cinnamon/molasses notes from 80% new Fr oak. 14% alc. **01** look-ahead reveals a very introverted youth; same dense textures; plummy, plump, persistent.

☆**Chardonnay** First release **99** ☆ rich and confected, massively weighty and now fully developed. Current **01** more Burgundian, grapefruit/apricot aromas, pear-drop, butterscotch in palate, lingering cassia spice. Only one cask (35 cases) barrel-fermented, malo. 13% alc. — *MF*

Hildenbrand Estate

Wellington (see Wellington map) • Tasting, sales (wine, olives & olive oil), cellar tours daily 10-6 Tasting R5 p/p if no wine purchased • Light Mediterranean meals daily, served in the 'Weinstüble' or on terrace • Klein Rhebokskloof Guest & Country House (see Restaurant & Stay-over sections), offering many amenities • Tourgroups up to 15 people • Small conferences • Walks • Views • Owner/winemaker/viticulturist Reni Hildenbrand • Vineyards 17 ha • Production 2 500 cases • PO Box 270 Wellington 7655 • ***Tel/fax (021) 873-4115*** *• Cell 082-656-6007 • E-mail info@wine-estate-hildenbrand.co.za • Website www.wine-estate-hildenbrand.co.za*

"I would like my wines to be individual and to taste of where they come from," declares Reni Hildenbrand, sounding less like the interior architect who left Gauteng in 1991 and more like the award-winning wine (and olive) grower she's become. Ensconced in the 300 year old Wellington property Reebokkenkloof, she's renovated the manor house and opened a guest lodge and restaurant. She's also planted 15 hectares (future plans include the first malbec vines), and re-commissioned the 1853 wine cellar after it had been idle for half a century. Mindful of working in harmony with nature, she's adopted eco-centric farming practices for which she was recently voted Female Farmer of the Year by the Western Cape Department of Agriculture.

★**Cabernet Sauvignon Barrique** ✓ Maiden **99**, re-evaluated yr on, maturing into something special. Sweet cassis core embroidered with warm oak, fruitcake nuances; non-overt 13.7% alc. 4-5 yrs' development ahead. 1 100 (× 6, as are all below) cases.

Cabernet Sauvignon (Unwooded) ★ Sans-barrique version popular in Germany/Switzerland, reports Reni H. **99**, unlike above, should be enjoyed in juicy, sweet-tannined youth. 13.4% alc. 360 cases. **Chardonnay** (Unwooded) ★ Silky peach fruit in easy drinking **00**; gentle finish abetted by big 13.5% alc, smoothing grain sugar. 700 cases. **Chardonnay Barrique** ★ Oaked version more overtly sweet (5.4 g/ℓ sugar, 13.9% alc); soft peachy fruit joined by suggestion vanilla. Drink now and up to 18 mths. 7 mths Fr barrelled. 350 cases. **Chenin Blanc** ★ Partially oaked **00** to us prematurely tired, though Reni H anticipates "more interest in 2-3 yrs". 20 yr old bushvines. 13.2% alc. 700 cases. **Semillon** NEW Attractive leesy wafts from soft, limey **01** barrel. Very young but showing ★ potential. First-cropped bushvines; Fr oak. 13.5% alc. 280 cases. — *DH*

Hilltop

CERTIFIED, vintage dated bag-in-the-box range by Distell, now discontinued. Last were **Ruby Cabernet** and **Chardonnay**, both **99** and ★.

Hinterland see Hartswater

Hippo Creek

VALUE range for Picardi-Rebel liquor chain. Not tasted for this edition. Previous have included: **Cabernet Sauvignon** (Pvs **98** ★), **Pinotage** (**99** ★), **Chardonnay** (**00** ★).

Honey Blossom

INTRODUCED in 1965, this Distell brand was taken off the market and re-launched some 20 years later. Consistent semi-sweet white; available in various packages.

NV ★ Similar to its cousin Virginia but plainer, not as smooth. And not as sweet as expected. — *IvH*

Hoopenburg

*Stellenbosch (see Stellenbosch map) • Tasting & sales Mon-Fri 9-5 Sat & public holidays 9.30-1 Fee R10 p/p refundable with purchases of 6 bottles or more • Cellar tours by appointment • Views • Owner/winemaker/viticulturist Ernst Gouws • Vineyards 35 ha • Production 20 000 cases 70% red 30% white • PO Box 1233 Stellenbosch 7599 • **Tel (021) 884-4221/2** • Fax (021) 884-4904 • E-mail hoopen@new.co.za • Website www.hoopenburgwines.co.za*

AFTER jump-starting a whole crop of new wine ventures, styling guru Ernst Gouws is hanging up his flying winemaker gloves and going back to what he does best – his own thing in his own immaculate Hoopenburg cellar, celebrating its tenth vintage this year. And, having charmed the global palate (from Belgium to the US), he and equally wine-centered wife Gwenda aim to grow the local market "to get a better balance" (80% of their production currently flies overseas). They're also planning to experiment with "changing the style from more elegant old-world to more full-bodied new". Supplying a leg-up is the auspicious 2001 vintage: a red wine year, Gouws predicts, with more intense and complex flavours. New in this stylish range is a Shiraz, silver medallist at the 2001 IWSC, available only from the cellar (and worth the journey).

Winemaker's Selection

✯Cabernet Sauvignon ✓ **98** developing elegantly; warm core of cassis wrapped in stylish oak; light savoury whiffs, moderate 12,5% alc. Yr new Fr barriques. Own, Malmesbury grapes, crop thinned to 6 t/ha for extra intensity. Flew with KLM Business Class, SAA. 1 000 cases.

✯Merlot ✓ **99** revisited mid-01, happily en route to peak around 05. Palate unfurling, growing plusher; whiffs of best fresh thatch; soft, sweet redcurrant finish. 14 mths new Fr/Am oak. 13.1% alc. 800 cases. **98** youthfully approachable, with ripe mouthcoating tannin.

✯Chardonnay ✓ New-barrel-fermented/aged version, classically styled. **00** among best to date; complete wine, full-flavoured, fragrant; butterscotchy core of limes/lees with heathery scents. **98**, under 'regular' label, gold medal at France's Vinalies selections. 500 cases.

Hoopenburg range

✯Merlot NEW Youthfully approachable **00** full-flavoured with ripe plums, cherries; choc nuance to slightly charry oak; best before 2004; WOM selection. 10 mths new/2nd fill Fr oak. 13.5% alc. 1 500 cases.

✯Pinotage NEW Malmesbury fruit parades in **00**, with blackberry/vanilla nuance. Clove spiciness and distinct but supple tannins make this a good option (Gwenda Gouws says) for Malaysian curries. Flavourful, but lacks depth for long cellaring. 10 mths Fr oak, some new. 1 500 cases.

✯Pinot Noir 99 heralded step up for this label; excitement continues in **00** (sample), minerally/oaky nose; smoky stone fruits; very dry tannic grip which should soften given yr/2. Massive structure (15% alc) for good med-term ageing. 8 mths 2nd fill Fr casks. 1 000 cases.

✯Shiraz NEW Debuts with panache in **00**, Muldersvlei sweet-spicy fruit tweaked for now-drinking (and up to ±6 yrs). New world feel from vanilla oak (10 mths new/older Fr), barefaced 14.4% alc, though good grind of peppermill more evocative of France. 500 cases.

Cabernet Sauvignon ✯ **00** uncharacteristically strident tannins, but countered by ripe fruit (ex Bottelary, Muldersvlei), mineral oak. Give 2/3 yrs. 1 500 cases. **Chardonnay** ✯ **99** neat wine, well proportioned; oak-dabbed limey fruit still full of verve. 2 500 cases for kitchen dinner parties. **Sauvignon Blanc** ✯ Unwooded, unaggressive example, gently dry; good standalone sip, also versatile at table. **01** (sample) med-bodied. 2 200 cases. — *DH*

Huguenot Wine Farmers

Wellington • Not open to the public • Owner Kosie Botha • Cellarmaster Bill Matthee (since 1984) • Trade enquiries Gert Brynard • PO Box 275 Wellington 7654 • ***Tel (021) 864-1293*** *• Fax (021) 873-2075*

PRIVATELY owned wholesaling company that blends, markets and distributes wines, liqueurs and spirits. The range (not assessed) includes: **Cabernet Sauvignon**, **Pinotage**, **Smooth Red** (cinsaut/pinotage), **Premier Grand Cru**, (chenin/Cape riesling), **Stein** (chenin), **Late Harvest** and **Special Late Harvest** (both chenin), **Hanepoot**, White Muscadel, Red Jeripico and **White Jeripico** (red/white muscadel), **Invalid Port**, Tawny Port, Nagmaalwyn, and carbonated bubblies Valentine Cerise (semi-sweet pink from pinot noir), Valentine Vin Doux (chenin/clairette blanche).

Hutton Ridge see Arlington, Riebeek

Icon 

SELF-styled 'unorthodox stroke of genius', by DGB. Cocks a snook at vinous convention with lurid packaging and taboo styles.

Pinotage-Chardonnay ☻ ☆ Cerise frosted bottle mirrors iconoclastic quick quaff within. Earthy pinotage nose; sweet red cherries hurtling to tangy, sort-of-dry finish. Might even last yr/2.

Chardonnay-Sauvignon Blanc ☆ Though bottle's lime-hued, chardonnay's citrus tones superseded by fruit salady flavours; definite sweetness livened by twinkling acidity. These **NV**. *— DH*

Impala see Goue Vallei
Infiniti see Stellenbosch Vineyards
Inglewood see Neil Ellis

Ingwe

Helderberg • Not open to the public • Owner Alain Mouiex • Château Mazeyres 56 Avenue Georges Pompidou 33500 Libourne France • Tel 0933 55 757-0048 • Fax 0933-55-725-2256 • Winemaker PJ Geyer (since Sep 2001) • Viticulturist Francois Baard (since 1999) • Vineyards 10.6 ha producing in 2001 • Production 45 tons • PO Box 563 Suider Paarl 7624 • ***Tel/fax (021) 858-1063*** *• E-mail ingwewine@freemail.absa.co.za*

BREEZY Schaapenberg (a tongue of low hills that licks the Helderberg basin from the fringes of the Hottentots-Holland mountains) has been buzzing with new brio. Relative newcomer Ingwe, owned by Pomerol luminary Alain Moueix – who keeps a foot in the Cape door consulting on his joint-venture with Winecorp, premium labels Naledi and Sejana – adds a dash of French cachet. With first wines made at Havana Hills winery near Durbanville, they've now moved into temporary seaside premises until the vineyard-only spread is in full swing. After a season here, winemaker Etienne Charrier returned to Ch Mazeyres; his boots have been filled by US and New Zealand-honed PJ Geyer, who will be flitting off for some French lessons in Bordeaux. In the meantime, viticulturist-manager Francois Baard is in fine fettle: "The first shiraz and cabernet were harvested in 2001 and, if this is what the rest will look like, then Ingwe is definitely in prime red wine territory!"

☆**Chardonnay** Intense but not flamboyant, persistent and food-friendly. **00** barrel-fermented, yet with fine enough fruit to transcend the oaking. Lime/grapefruit aromas; light, restrained caramel/vanilla layerings; steely citrus finish. 13,8% alc. 600 cases. First **00** similar good oak/fruit tension. These ex low-yielding Schaapenberg vyd.

☆**Sauvignon Blanc** Fragrant, not overly tropical, very elegant. **01** fuller, with pineapple/gooseberry notes, more intense than pvs. Rich yet subtle nuances (and none of the lean herbal tones of fashionably underripe 'green' wines). 13,8% alc. Maiden **00** ☆ quieter. *— MF*

Inkawu see Laibach
Interlude see Asara

International Wine Services-Pacific Wines

Manager Adam Mason • Head of winemaking Kym Milne • Production ± 850 000 cases 55% white 45% red • 5 Baring Road Beaconsfield Buckinghamshire

HP9 2NB UK • Tel (1494) 68-0857 • Fax (1494) 68-0382 • 3 Eldorado Military Road Tamboerskloof 8001 Cape Town • ***Tel/fax (021) 424-8683*** *• Cell 083-321-6884 • E-mail iwsinsa2@new.co.za • Website www.wine-info.co.uk*

ONE of the largest SA exporters to the UK (now also Scandinavia), this high-energy operation shipped about 850 000 cases of wine last year. "In line with local plantings, our product bias is slowly becoming more focused on red, up to about 45%," reveals incoming local point-man Adam Mason (Aussie John Weeks, who's run IWS in SA for 5 years, is off to southern France "to manage an exciting production project" there; UK-based Kym Milne continues to lead the international winemaking team). "I'm pleased to be back in the Cape at a time when so much development is taking place, and the industry is so vibrant and bursting with youthful talent," enthuses Boschendal and Flagstone-seasoned Mason.

Apostles Falls range

Cabernet Sauvignon These cabs 9-10 mths oaked, which apparent in tannins of **99** and more organic/herbal **00** ★, both needing time or a sturdy Bok. 13/14% alc. 2 000 cases.

Chardonnay Assertive oaked style. **99** brisk palate with peach-kernel finish; current **00** ★ honey-buttered toast and apple; nice lemony farewell which needs to be enjoyed now. 13.5% alc. 7 000 cases.

Merlot ★ Barbecue wine, says IWS team of **99**, now very relaxed, drinkable after yr in bottle; tar, woodsmoke to sniff as you fire up the Weber. 14% alc. 7 000 cases. **Shiraz** NEW **00** Not tasted. 10 mths Fr/Am oak. 13% alc. 2 000 cases.

Cape View/Winelands Reserve range

Shiraz-Cabernet Sauvignon 99 pure cassis fruit; 8 mths Fr/Am oak hidden behind scents of lavender, chaparral. 13% alc. 2 000 cases.

Cabernet Sauvignon ★ Upfront **00** features chewy cassis, slight herbal nuances. Oaked. 13.5% alc. 4 000 cases. **Merlot** ★ Stbosch grapes, unoaked in **99**; complementary savoury/plum-jam flavours. Try with cassoulet, suggests Adam Mason. 13% alc. 8 000 cases. **Pinotage** ★ Unoaked, dense-textured **00**; mouthcoating mulberry/smoked salami flavours; full 13% alc. 5 000 cases. **Cinsaut-Shiraz** ★ 70/30 unoaked blend **00** savoury, light, juicy; Italianate bitter-cherry goes with tomato-sauced pasta. 13.5% alc. 15 000 cases.

Rylands Grove range

Cinsaut-Tinta Barocca ☻ ★ Easy, antipasti-friendly **00**, bright ruby lights, sweet cherries and peppery whiffs. 80/20 unoaked blend. 13% alc. 5 000 cases. **Chenin Blanc Barrel Fermented** ☻ ★ **00** shows its age nicely in succulent petal/honey tastes. 13% alc. 20 000 cases.

Cabernet Sauvignon-Merlot NEW ★ Lightly oaked 70/30 mix. **00** soft wildberry fruit; some leather aromas; firm dry finish. 13% alc. 20 000 cases. **Sauvignon Blanc** ☆ **00** noticeable bottle age; hints of apple pie. **01** med-bodied; untasted. 7 000 cases. **Dry Muscat** ★ Funky wine for today-drinking. **00** sweet-incense bouquet; low acidity matches creamy/spicy Asian foods. Med-bodied. 20 000 cases. **Chenin Blanc-Colombard** Untasted.

Also available, not sampled: Chiwara range: **Pinotage**, **Cinsaut-Ruby Cabernet**, **Colombard-Sauvignon Blanc**; Fontein/Rivier range: **Chardonnay**; Frasers Bay range: **Cabernet Sauvignon**, **Pinotage**, **Chardonnay**, **Chenin Blanc**; Kleinbosch **Bushvine Muscat**. Plantation range discontinued. — *TM*

Iona Vineyards

Elgin (see Elgin map) • Tasting "at any reasonable hour" • Views • Mountain hikes • Owners Andrew Gunn, Rosa Kruger & Workers Trust • Winemakers Gyles Webb & Miles Mossop • Viticulturist Eben Archer • Vineyards 12 ha • Production 16 tons 60% white 40% red • PO Box 527 Grabouw 7160 • ***Tel (028) 284-9678*** *• Fax (028) 284-9078 • E-mail gunn@corpdial.co.za*

If you were a vine looking for a home, you'd be wanting to look over Andrew Gunn and Rosa Kruger's 120 hectares in Elgin. They're on a beautiful mountain plateau "with a 180° view of the valley and the peaks of the Helderberg and Franschhoek mountains to the north". And, viniferous home-seekers take note, "the cool Atlantic Ocean 4 km to the south". Not to mention the Kogelberg Floral Kingdom nearby (splendid hiking country) and a Herbert Baker-designed homestead. With a neighbourhood this alluring, the Gunns and viticultural oracle Eben Archer can afford to be ultra-selective. To date only a pair of aristocrats, merlot and sauvignon, have gained entrance to their Ionasphere. Just eight more "hand-tended hectares" are to be planted, for a maximum of 10 000 cases annually. These, the Gunns declare, will reflect "our terroir and the passionate commitment of our workers". Mirrored, also, in the inaugural release below are the signatures of Gyles Webb and Miles Mossop, who made the wine at Tokara.

⁂**Sauvignon Blanc** Undoubtedly serious, and delicious, maiden **01** offers tropical fruit/nettles; hints of complexity supported by balanced structure of savoury acidity, moderate (by today's standards) 13% alc. Only slight lack of concentration/length detract. — *TJ*

Itakane see Mouton-Excelsior

Jacaranda Estate

Wellington (see Wellington map) • Tasting, sales, cellar tours Mon-Fri 10-5 Sat 10-1 (but phone ahead). • Self-catering guest house/B&B • Cheese made, olives grown on property • 1-km "leg stretch" • Views • Owners Jan & Trish Tromp • Winemaker/viticulturist Jan Tromp • Vineyards 2,8 ha • Production 25 tons (300 cases own label) PO Box 121 Wellington 7654 • ***Tel (021) 864-1235*** *• E-mail jacranda@iafrica.com*

Jan and Trish Tromp liked our description, in last year's edition, of their farm's 'rustic charms'. So we'd like to draw your attention once again to these pastoral pleasures as we introduce Daisy (daughter of Boopsy the jersey cow, who is now officially "on pension"). Daisy is producing enough milk for both her calf and the Tromps' home-made cheeses. "The olive tree has produced a record crop and by the time the guide comes out, our 'out of this world' olives will be available once again." Yet another reason to visit the engaging Tromps and taste the wines, hand-crafted in an ingenious cellar curled up inside an old circular reservoir. The range, unavailable for tasting, includes: **Debutante 00** (cab/merlot), **Schuss 95** (chenin), **Chenin Blanc 99** (★ in pvs ed), **Jerepigo 96** (⁂).

Jacobsdal Estate

Stellenbosch • Tasting & sales at Bergkelder (see that entry) • Owner C H Dumas Trust • Winemakers/viticulturists Cornelis & Hannes Dumas • Vineyards 105 ha • Production 150-200 tons (7 000-10 000 cases own label) 100% red • PO Box 11 Kuils River 7579 • ***Tel/fax (021) 905-1360*** *• E-mail dumas@iafrica.com*

'Mr Pinotage', Cornelius Dumas (he's been specialising in the local grape since 1966), is now coaching son Hannes, who previously completed a business management course in Worcester. Their enthusiasm for pinotage continues unabated: two new hectares have been planted to replace old chenin, bringing the total pinotage area up to 22 hectares. "I'm very pleased with the recently released 98 vintage," says the modest Cornelius Dumas, whose wines are virtual shoo-ins at annual Pinotage Top 10 selections. They certainly don't have problems with marketing: half the production is exported, mainly to Norway and Sweden, and the rest is regularly sold out on the local market.

Pinotage One of the originals, still among Cape's finest, showered with awards. 25-35 yr old dryland bushvines; natural yeasts, open kuipe, freerun juice only; 12-18 mths small Fr oak. Fascinating variation between warm **98** and pvs cooler, 'European' vintage: **98** much bigger (14.5% alc vs 13.8%), classically pinotage: earthy, spicy; sweet jujube fruits with hints of variety's signature ester. Will be prized by pino-purists. 8 000 cases. **97** more rustic, not pinotagey at all, yet with own appeal – and Jacobsdal's signature restraint. — *IvH*

Jacques Pinard

International selection of wines from the greater wine producing regions of the world, sold under the name of wine negociant Jacques Pinard. Varieties/styles chosen to appeal to local consumers; the wines vary from year to year, with a red and white released annually in 1 000 ml bottles. The Merlot under this label is not from SA, it's from the Languedoc in France. By Distell.

Sauvignon Blanc-Semillon Underrated brand, deserving higher profile. Generous tropical tastes in **01**, unoaked 60/40 blend with lip-smacking tart citrus finish. 13.3% alc. 3 300 cases. — *IvH*

Janéza

Bonnievale (see Robertson map) • Tasting, sales & cellar tours Mon-Fri 9-5 Sat 9-1 • Owners Klein-Jan & Eza Wentzel • Winemaker Klein-Jan Wentzel • Vineyards 5 ha • Production 7 tons 525 cases (own label) 60% red 40% white • PO Box 306 Bonnievale 6730 • ***Tel (023) 616-2848*** *• Fax (023) 616-2848 • E-mail jan.eza@lando.co.za*

Brand new, and panting to be discovered, is this welcoming winery on a family-owned property near Bonnievale. Klein-Jan Wentzel and wife Eza, historically co-op grape farmers, had long yearned to "complete the circle" by making their own wine. Last year they got permission from nearby Langverwacht Co-op to keep back some of their best grapes to vinify for their own label. Brimming with enthusiasm, if not necessarily funds, they built what Klein-Jan Wentzel modestly calls their "scrapyard cellar" in a converted stable, dating from 1938. First up is a Sauvignon, to be followed this year by a Cabernet and, in the more distant future, possibly a Chardonnay, Merlot and Shiraz from new hillside vineyards. Eza Wentzel (daughter of KWV chair Lourens Jonker) has accessorised the tasting room in warmly rustic style.

Sauvignon Blanc Variety's grass/green pepper character uppermost in maiden **01**; fresh, tangy dry tastes with slight hint of astringency. 12% alc. 525 cases. — *DH*

JC le Roux

Stellenbosch (see Stellenbosch map) • Tasting & sales Mon-Fri 8.30-4.30 Sat 9-4 Sun 10-3 • Tasting fee R10 p/p • Cellar tours, preceded by AV show, Mon-Fri 10, 11.30, 3 • Light lunches Mon-Fri 11-3 • Sparkling breakfasts by arrangement • Conferences • Tourgroups • Gifts • Views • Wheelchair-friendly • Owner Distell • Winemaker Melanie van der Merwe (since 1994) • Farm manager/viticulturist Willem Laubscher • Vineyards 25 ha • Production 5.7 million bottles/year • PO Box 184 Stellenbosch 7599 • ***Tel (021) 882-2590*** *• Fax (021) 882-2585 • E-mail jclr@dist.co.za*

THIS temple of hedonism in Devon Valley spreads its seductions over two levels: below, a chic boutique and tasting centre; above, an oyster bar (sparkles by the glass, befitting a house dedicated to bubbles) and vistas over bright green vineyards and purple mountains. Extra allure for the energetic comes in the form of guided tours (an elevated walkway, accessible by wheelchair, affords bird's eye views of the cellar, presided over by Melanie van der Merwe). And the highlight: a tasting of the entire range including Pongrácz, the award-winning MCC that pays tribute to a flamboyant Cape pioneer of the vine.

★★**Pinot Noir** ✓ One of the Cape's top cap classiques, exceptionally well priced. In the footsteps of brilliant, still-vital **89** VVG, *Wine* ★, the new benchmark: **90**, extraordinary 10 yrs on lees, 100% pinot ex Stbosch; wonderful weighty style, rich, vinous, slightly minerally; strawberry-biscuit aromas, mouthfilling toasty flavours, endless dry finish. 11.4% alc, 9,6 g/ℓ sugar. 10 000 cases.

★**Chardonnay** ✓ Consistently excellent blanc de blancs MCC, 100% chardonnay. Classically long matured – 5-9 yrs on lees. Malo complete, bottled without sulphur additions. Current **91** yeasty/citrus tones, austere and elegant, crisp dry finish. 12% alc, 7,5 g/ℓ sugar. Pvs **90** *Wine* ★, **89** ★★, *Wine* ★.

★**Pongrácz** Excellent, consistent brut-style MCC, named after late Desiderius Pongrácz (pronounce Pon-*grats*), aristocratic Hungarian army officer who became a controversial but much-loved Bergkelder viticulturist. Winner of numerous local/international awards (including Schramsberg Trophy at IWSC). Pinot, chardonnay (60/40), min 2 yrs on lees; lowish alcs. Latest **NV** bottling honeyed, complex, creamy; long minerally finish. Very satisfying anytime bubble, well priced. 40 000 cases.

★**La Vallée** Attractive and popular semi-dry MCC (good entrée to methode champenoise style). Leaps into the upper classes with latest **99**, more complex than pvs, richer; perceptibly sweet yet invigorated by firm chalky acidity, brisk mousse. Grilled nuts, camomile and honey to savour, pre or post dinner. **98** ★ straightforward but satisfying. From pinot gris ex Stbosch, S/West. ±20 000 cases.

★**Le Domaine** Huge selling (245 000 cases) Asti-style **NV** white carbonated fizz with crowd pleasing ripe-muscat tones, lively bubbles, low alc (7,8%) for non-stop party fun. Sauvignon/muscadel. 76 g/ℓ sugar.

La Chanson ★ Hugely popular (120 000 cases) strawberry-toned sweet red **NV** carbonated fizz. From pinotage, whose (light) tannins down-tone down the sweetness (±70 g/ℓ), with splash shiraz. Low alc (7,5%). **Sauvignon Blanc** Bone-dry, crisp-finishing charmat fizz. Latest (**01**) not ready for tasting. Pvs **00** ★. — *IvH*

Jean Daneel Wines

Franschhoek • Tasting, sales, cellar tours by appointment • Owner/winemaker Jean Daneel • Production 3 000 cases • PO Box 518 Franschhoek 7690 • ***Tel (021) 876-3638*** *• Fax (021) 876-2753 • E-mail jdwines@worldonline.co.za*

"THINGS don't happen very fast in a small cellar," remarks Jean Daneel, "but I believe we're getting close to what we really want to be." And what exactly is that? we asked the Diners Club laureate, who makes his own elegant JD wines in Franschhoek between consulting to a select clientele. "The next step," he confides, "is a five-star wine under my own label, aimed at a niche market. There will be a white and a red. The exact make-up is unimportant. What's important is what is eventually in the bottle. I hope I can make a wine that will make its mark on the local and international market." He plans to produce two separate ranges, one appellated Franschhoek ("capturing the unique character of the valley"), the other Coastal, to allow him the freedom to select grapes from a variety of sites.

✵**Cabernet Sauvignon-Merlot** Elegant Medoc style red, intense yet reined-in. **99** ✵ brooding cassis notes; aromas of coffee, lead pencil, choc; very firm, almost austere finish. 22 mths Fr oak, 40% new. 1 000 cases. Less forward (13,5% alc) than spicy, exotic **98**. Bought-in Stbosch/F'hoek grapes.

✵**Merlot CWG** NEW Reserve cuvee from select Stbosch grapes, hand-crafted for Cape Winemakers Guild auction. **98** opulent mocha/choc aromas, intricate layers plum, black cherry, creme brulee. St Emilion-like restraint in fruit-tannin balance; ample texture from 26 mths Fr oak, all new.

✵**Signature** NEW Luxurious oak-fermented chenin, debuting in Diners Club yr; **01** plump with baked apple aromas, ample peach/apricot fruit lurking beneath wood caramel; soft cinnamon-cream finish. 13,5% alc. 350 cases; bought-in Stbosch grapes.

Chenin Blanc-Sauvignon Blanc ★★ Crisp, almost lean **01** (13% alc), food friendly palate with persistent citrus finish. 1 400 cases from sourced-in F'hoek fruit. — *MF*

Jean le Riche

POPULAR pair of NV carbonated sparklers from Simonsig, pioneers of cap classique. **Vin Sec** ★ Persistent bubble, attractive half-dry blend chenin/colombard and fruity aromatic varieties: floral nose, gently sweet mouthful. **Vin Doux** ★ Plumped up with sweetness; aromatic bouquet, fruity-sweet grapey palate; muscat/bukettraube complementing each other. — *DS*

John Faure see Ruitersvlei

Johnsen & Jörgensen

*Wellington • Owners Julian Johnsen & Roger Jörgensen • PO Box 57 Wellington 7654 • **Tel (021) 863-8651**/ 072 153-0627*

THIS EXPORT LABEL, created by cousins Julian Johnsen (onetime commercial manager of cricket mecca Lords) and Roger Jörgensen (of Claridge), last featured in the guide in 2000. Previous included Big Storm Shiraz-Merlot.

✵**Merlot** ✓ Soft, sweet-oaky style, thoughtfully constructed. First was **93**; Latest **99** with quirky silage whiffs, drinks nicely now. Fruit ex Klein Leeuwentuin property, plus splash Simonsberg cab. Yr Fr barriques, 33% new. 13.6% alc. 1 300 cases. — *JN*

Jonkheer

*Robertson (see Robertson map) • Tasting & cellar tours by appointment • Views • Proclaimed conservation area • Owners Nicholas Jonker & Sons • Cellarmaster Erhard Roothman (since 1970) • Winemaker Dirk Jonker (since 1992) • Viticulturists Nicholas & Andries Jonker • Farm managers Gideon van Niekerk (since 1983), André Coetzee (since 1996) • Vineyards 150 ha • Production 2 000 tons 60% white 30% red 5% rosé 5% fortified • PO Box 13 Bonnievale 6730 • **Tel (023) 616-2648** • Fax (023) 616-3146 • E-mail info@jonkheer.co.za • Website www.jonkheer.co.za*

If enthusiasm were danceable, this family spread on the Breede River would never stop jitterbugging. The fired-up Jonkers and their long-time cellarmaster, Erhard Roothman, have narrowed a previously diverse liquor business down to a fine-wine-focused operation; they've registered the property as an estate; and they're spreading their wings – internationally, through exports to seven countries, including Poland and Japan; and locally, via a new farm on promising rocky slopes next to the valley soils. Shiraz and cabernet are forthcoming attractions here; meanwhile the spotlight falls on young barbera vines making their debut next year (the first in Bonnievale). "Probably too young to venture a single varietal," Dirk Jonker speculates, "but you never know." Though their visibility remains chiefly offshore, they're raising their local profile partly through a new tasting centre, arising from the renovations to the characterful old cellar.

Jonkheer range

Pinotage Lighter, more elegant spicy/cherry style which won adherents in Switzerland, where most of **98** exported. No **99**. Latest **00** fuller than pvs (13.2%), finer; again with firm tannins needing yr/2.

Cabernet Sauvignon-Merlot Family Reserve Forceful style with densely textured tannins for keeping; **99** back-tasted mid-01 lively, succulent; initial astringency no longer evident. **00** new-leather and violets bouquet, some earthy nuances. Good maturation potential.

Chardonnay Family Reserve Serious, classically styled **00**, retasted mid-01, holding well; refined citrus tones now uppermost; fresh finish. 100% new oak fermented. Suggest drink soon while on the up. 13.7% alc.

Muscatheer New-wave white fortified dessert targeting European tastes for lower alcs/sugars. Latest version **00** sweeps into top league with elegant expression of muscat de f; spring flower fragrances, gentle acid lift; 15.3% alc just within legal limit, and all better for it; 130 g/ℓ sugar tastes smooth rather than sweet. Elegant packaging sets seal on style that deserves to be emulated. 500 ml.

Cabernet Sauvignon Family Reserve NEW **00** not tasted. **Chardonnay** Unwooded, full-bodied version; **00** tropical/citrus tastes freshened by sparkling acidity. Not for ageing. 13.2% alc.

Bakenskop range

Red Muscadel Traditional-style fortified dessert; sweet, warming, muscatty, with charm all its own. Epitomised by **98**. New release **99** more pedestrian, rustic; lacks energising acidity. 17.3% alc.

White Muscadel Billowing, raisiny fortified dessert, much loved by competition judges; **98** invigorated by tangy spirit; latest **99** deep amber-gold, more unctuous, less exciting than some pvs. 17.5% alc.

Cabernet Sauvignon NEW Lean **01** offers earthy cab qualities, strident dry tannins. 13.2% alc. **Merlot** NEW Recognisably merlot, though not the soft, approachable sort. **01**'s feisty tannin structure needs bottle ageing or suitably outgoing cuisine. 13.5% alc. Following available, not ready for tasting (pvs ratings in brackets): **Cape Riesling (00)**; **Chardonnay (00)**; **Chenin Blanc (00)**; **Colombard (00)**; **Sauvignon Blanc (00)**. — *DH*

Joostenberg Wines

*Paarl (see Paarl map) • Tasting & sales Mon-Fri 9-5 Sat & Sun 9-3 (Oct-March) Mon-Fri 10-5 Sat 9-1 Sun by appointment (Apr-Sep) Open public holidays • Cellar tours by appointment • Picnic lunches served in the tasting room garden Mon-Sun (Oct-Mar) Booking essential • Lunches also available at nearby Muldersvlei Market all year round • Home grown cutflowers for sale • Tourgroups • Guesthouse • Owner Myburgh Winery Pty (Ltd) (Philip Myburgh jnr, Tyrrel Myburgh) • Winemaker Tyrrel Myburgh (since 1999) • Viticulturist Philip Myburgh (since 1999) • Vineyards 40 ha • Production 200 tons 3 000 cases 75% white, 25% red • PO Box 82 Elsenburg 7607 • **Tel (021) 884-4932** • Fax (021) 884-4052 • E-mail joostenberg@mweb.co.za • Website www.joostenberg.com*

FIFTH-GENERATION Myburgh brothers Tyrrel and Philip Jnr made wine on their family farm in this cooler corner of Paarl in 2000 for the first time since 1947. Winemaker Tyrrel, whose talents as a triathlete are only exercised running to catch planes these days, reports that a jaunt to Japan with five local winemakers last year found a receptive market for their wines, which have started to build a "small but solid" following. A first batch was also shipped to Australia, a spin-off of Philip Jnr's ongoing connection (he's completing his Masters in wine technology and marketing through Monash University). Added expertise in the vineyards comes in the form of clued-up consultant Aidan Morton (other clients include Thelema and its neighbour Tokara). Super chef and brother-in-law Christophe Dehosse (ex Au Jardin in Cape Town) and their sister Susan recently took over the restaurant at the nearby Muldersvlei Market (still run by patriarch Philip Snr) – good news for devotees of his special brand of refined cuisine.

✪**Chardonnay Wooded** Fr oak fermented/aged, 25% new casks, 9 mths. **00** improving in bottle. Rich, deep flavours in a polished frame. **01** unfinished sample not rated conclusively; showing promise of sunny ripe lime/lemon fruit and supportive oak. ±400 cases.

Cabernet Sauvignon-Shiraz NEW **00** tasted as work in progress, augurs well; compatible plums, black cherries sprinkled with spicy oak; bought-in ex Muldersvlei. Could rate ✪ on current form. 13.5% alc. ±600 cases forming "part of the experimentation process leading to a red blend reflecting our terroir". **Chenin Blanc Wooded** Promising barrel-fermented **01** tasted pre final blending (hence unrated): ripe melon/mango aromas, peachy palate with oak deftly underplayed. Looks good. ±800 cases. **Chardonnay Unwooded** ⁂ Much more character, flavour than most of this style; **01** step up from pvs, packed full of tropical fruit. "For wine drinkers who prefer not to have planks in their chardonnay." 13.4% alc. 650 cases. **Rhine Riesling** Made dry. **01** final blend not decided on. ±200 cases. **Chenin Blanc Noble Late Harvest** ⁂ Tasted in extreme youth this **00** still undeveloped, botrytis character barely discernible though flavours already long, balanced. Potential to bloom into something special. **Chenin Blanc Natural Sweet** NEW ⁂ A revelation for Tyrrell Myburgh: "Fascinating to see how chenin starts showing itself in this style." Luscious tropical fruits in lightish, easy-sipping **00** frame (11.5% alc). "But don't take it to seriously." 200 cases of 375 ml. Discontinued: **Sauvignon Blanc** (Pvs **00** ⁑). Not retasted for this ed: **Cabernet Sauvignon** (Pvs **99** ✪) **Pinotage** (**00** ⁂).

Okha range NEW

Value-for-money wines sourced from various producers. Hence Xhosa name – loosely translated, means 'sharing your neighbour's fire'.

Pinotage 00 not ready for tasting. 350 cases. **Sauvignon Blanc** ⁂ Honest, tropical-flavoured **01**, for drinking casually with friends. **Chenin Blanc** ⁂ Baked, full-ripe **01** with some guava chopped into tropical fruit salad; could age a bit. 13.2% alc. 7 000 cases. — *CF*

Jordan Vineyards

Stellenbosch (see Stellenbosch map) • Tasting & sales Mon-Fri 10-4.30 Sat 9.30-2.30 (Nov-Apr); 9.30-12.30 (May-Oct) Tasting fee R7.50 p/p, refundable with purchases • Cellar tours by appointment • BYO picnic during tasting hours • Owners Ted & Gary Jordan • Winemakers Gary & Kathy Jordan (since 1993) • Assistant winemakers Sjaak Nelson & Johan Kruger • Viticulturists Ted & Gary Jordan (since 1982) • Production 650 tons 45 000 cases 50/50 red/white • PO Box 12592 Die Boord 7613 • ***Tel (021) 881-3441*** *• Fax (021) 881-3426 • E-mail info@jordanwines.com*

In just eight years, Gary and Kathy Jordan have become the President and First Lady of the Cape's wine meritocracy. The meticulous geologist and economist team enrolled for a crash course in wine in California before taking over the reins of the family farm in the viticulturally gilded Stellenboschkloof, and nearly everything they've touched has turned to gold – in several cases, double gold (at the annual Veritas awards ceremonies, SAA Selections et al). Recently they were named the pick of the Cape's best cellars on overall quality by SA *Wine*, and their 99 Cobblers Hill was awarded a hen's-teeth five-star accolade by the same magazine. Now they and viticulturalling patriarch Ted Jordan (who drives a mean tractor) are homing in on the flagship grape of the Rhone. Their west-facing slopes overlooking Table and False bays are perfectly suited to growing great shiraz, say the quietly confident Jordans. We say: watch these stars.

Cabernet Sauvignon ✓ Gold at 01 IWC for big, bold **98** endorses view that, whatever the vintage, Team Jordan creates a balanced wine, sure to outpace the opposition. Smoky oak, moist tobacco, aromatic cassis mark the bouquet; svelte blackcurrants hung on ripe, unaggressive tannic trellissing the palate. Altogether bigger than pvs (14% alc); requires 4-7 yrs to integrate. Extended maceration on skins after fermentation, malo, 19 mths Fr oak, 60% new. **97** understated elegance, streamlined length. WOM Value. **96**, VG. **99**, not ready for tasting, with splash cab f. 13.8% alc.

Cobblers Hill 'Reserve' (sporting natty, new worldish name) for the "ultimate expression of an outstanding wine from an exceptional vintage". **98** cab/merlot (53/47) from best (Hutton, Glenrosa decomposed granite soils) vyd, expansive, bold, generously oaked, yet without sacrificing elegance. Black as the dramatic label; cedar, roasted chestnut nose, super-ripe palate brimming with fruit, oak. 14.5% alc in like-minded company. But, success secret is in the balance. Lavished with 18 mths 100% new Nevers Fr oak. Not fined/filtered. *Wine* ✯. Substantially different to merlot-dominated maiden **97** SAA. **99** cab/merlot/cab f (52/34/14) blend, not ready for tasting.

Merlot Confirmed amongst SA's premier cadre in crowded field, geared up from **99**. Very-ripe **00** retains charm in hot vintage: ample ruby, wafts damson, mirabelle seasoned with fragrant spice, the clean oak supports, doesn't overwhelm. Juicy fruit flesh carries 14.4% alc on palate. **99** voluptuous, generous, ripe tannic frame; rich, silky texture shields supple fruit. **98** ✯ generous, not as refined. Completed malo, yr mix new/used Fr 225 ℓ oak.

Chameleon Cabernet Sauvignon-Merlot Touchstone rung between Bradgate, Cobblers Hill; contender in increasingly rare 'serious reds at less than serious price points' niche, but more striking with each vintage. Mega-ripe **00** dense ruby colour, minty-fresh berries leap out of glass, cherry fruit peppered with spice and supported by ripe tannins. 14.5% alc. **99** pleasing, bit more flesh than pvs. 49/38 mix, plus 13% cab f. 14 mths Fr oak. Ready on release, will hold up ±4 yrs.

Chardonnay Standout in veritable sea of SA chardonnay. Difficult vintage **00** as singular, delightful as always: golden, deep-toned chalky richness (step beyond mere citric fruit and creamy wood: brilliant interplay fruit/oak/structural components of palate); less bracingly dry than pvs. Has secondary mineral depth, delicious now. Not as long lived as stunning **99** ✯ with curvaceous hazelnut, citrus-peel, leesy complexity. WOM Reserve. Majority Nevers, burgundian-oak barrelled (43% new), sur lie 9 mths; malo, freshened with 17% tank fermented portion. Mature vines, mix clones (Davis, Burgundian); 13,4% alc.

Sauvignon Blanc 01 quietly authoritative herbaceous understatement when others racing after reductive, tingling edge; chalky undertones to asparagus freshness, some broader tropical/gooseberry flavours lift end-palate. A sleeper, opens with yr in bottle. 13.5% alc.

Blanc Fumé ✓ Exuberant counterfoil for slow-starting sibling above, highly individual, one of few to retain unfashionable fumé ID; rarer still: gets balance sauvignon/oak right. **00** well weighted, creamy nose (no spiky thatch), tropical melon/fig fruits made more interesting by retiring woodspice. **99** ripe gooseberries/tropical fruits, juicy. VG. 27% tank-fermented freshener for bulk Fr barrel fermented (52% new); 7 mths on lees. Multiple WOM selection.

Chenin Blanc ☆ 2nd fill barrel-fermented grapes of mature vines; **00** off-dry (5.5 g/ℓ sugar), fresh apple/peach flavours, supple spice from integrated wood. 13% alc. **Chameleon Sauvignon Blanc-Chardonnay** ☆ "Fruity wine with a creamy finish" is goal of this reliable blend, named for Cape Dwarf chameleons in cellar garden, and the "changing characteristics" of the two varieties. **01** currently quiet, tropical peach, dry lemon tones buff structured palate. Duo of grassy, citrus fruits likely to re-emerge for summer 01. Pvs just off-dry. **Rhine Riesling** ☆ Spiced lime freshness in **01** with rich, fleshy palate offers intensity beyond ubiquitous, simple floral flavours. Tangy acidity cleans up 15 g/ℓ sugar, fruit not overwhelmed by modest 12% alc. Can mature over next yr. Excels with fresh fish, spiced foods.

Bradgate range

Well priced, easy-drinking wines developed for world-wide markets, but also available locally.

Cabernet Sauvignon-Merlot ☆ Cab f retires in **00** from this light-textured, accessible blend, laced with red berries/plums, hints spice, soft tannins. Now 54/46 cab s/merlot. Rounded in Fr oak. **Chenin Blanc-Sauvignon Blanc** ☆ **01** 51/49 partnership combining tropical, pear-drop chenin charm layered onto grassy sauvignon frame; fuller than pvs, bolder (13.5% alc), not quite dry. — *DS*

Joubert-Tradauw Winery

Barrydale • Tasting & sales Mon-Sat 9-5 • Cellar tours by appointment • Traditional cuisine prepared by Beate Joubert (tel 028-572-1619/082-420-6180) and served in the garden, weather permitting. Also picnic baskets R30 p/p • Lentelus B&B tel (028) 572-1636 • Large play area for children • Tourgroups • 4×4 trailing • Mountain biking • Walks • Views • Proclaimed conservation area • Owner JA Joubert Family Trust • Winemaker/viticulturist Meyer Joubert (since 1995) • Vineyards 30 ha • Production 300 tons 80% red 20% white • PO Box 15 Barrydale 6750 • ***Tel/fax (028) 572-1619*** *• E-mail helenaj@lando.co.za, mjoubert@hotmail.com*

THEY seem to have a thing about numbers at this, the only privately owned cellar in the Barrydale area – 'they' being the Joubert family, ebulliently fronted by winemaking Meyer (brother Schalk-Willem is cellarmaster at Rupert & Rothschild near Paarl). Their wines have digits in place of names ('R62', after curvaceous and scenic Route 62, the previously 'alternative' road that's becoming a mainline tourism hit). And when it comes to a food recommendation for their Cabernet-Merlot, the Jouberts' number-crunching produces a gargantuan "700 g steak with wild mushrooms". There is, however, nothing calculated about the reception you'll get when visiting this "obligatory stop for lovers of wine, food and nature", with its brand-new tasting room and cinematic valley view. Nor are there any little grey numbers in the wine-line. Grown on four family-owned farms, the original bordeaux blend and the more recently released Chardonnay are packed with charm and personality.

☆**R62 Cabernet Sauvignon-Merlot** Dark, deep **00** warmly mouthfilling; sweet ripe fruit, soft tannins. 65% cab. Balanced, lingering, lightly supported by yr Fr oak. Partly native yeast fermentation, no fining, filtration. Alc touch lower than 14% of California-esque debut **99**, where merlot just in majority. No hurry to drink these. 3 000 (x 6) cases.

☆**R62 Chardonnay** Only 500 half-cases of single-vyd, night-harvested, barrel-fermented **00**. Refined, balanced rather than oaky blockbusterish; and rather delicious with subtle citrus flavours, hints of five-spice. — *TJ*

JP Bredell Wines

Stellenbosch (see Helderberg map) • Tasting & sales Mon-Fri 8.30-5 Tasting fee R2 • Cellar tours by appointment • Owner/winemaker/viticulturist Anton Bredell • Vineyards 95 ha • Production 950 tons 66,5% red, 22% white, 11,5% port • PO Box 5266 Helderberg 7135 • ***Tel (021) 842-2478*** *• Fax (021) 842-3124*

JP Bredell Wines

New labels from this excellent Helderberg farm (its name, Helderzicht, alludes to the views from their promontory above False Bay) are few and far between, so punters are bound to sit up and notice the bordeaux blend now confidently installed in this overwhelmingly red range. As winegrowing entrepreneur Anton Bredell's wines go, it's a fairly subdued number. More readily associated with Bredell are his 'ports', big in structure and intensity – like the man whose family took over the farm in 1965 and grew it into a world-class port house (Lower Douro-like climate and soils major quality-infusers). They've also gained fame – mostly anonymously – as red-wine suppliers to KWV. Now they're barrelling ahead with their own, highly-regarded JP Bredell label (when not relaxing on their Little Karoo game farm or on the Promontory at Pringle Bay, where the 'helderzicht' includes a vivid splash of blue). For a different take on Bredell port, see Bredell & Nel.

★ **Merlot** ✓ Maiden **98** back-tasted mid-01 ripening into fragrant mouthful of plums with hints peppermint, violets, anise. Seems bigger than 13% alc would suggest; excellent concentration augurs well for 6-8 yrs' further development. Yr new tight-grained Fr oak. Classically elegant label.

★ **Pinotage** ✓ Sampled mid-01, **98** shows reserves for further 6-8 yrs; enormous power, tightly controlled; slight savoury tone to sweet-ripe blackberry/banana and overt vanilla. This, **96**, both *Wine* ★. ± Yr oak, 50% new Fr, remainder 2nd fill Am. 13% alc. 780 cases. No **97**.

★ **Shiraz** Latest **99** reflects lighter shiraz yr; supple, fruity, good varietal aromas of smoke/pepper – all in accessible, slightly lower-keyed mode (12.5% alc) than **98** ★, with forceful, distinctive bouquet. Am oak, mostly new, 8-9 mths. **97** especially admired by *Wine* panel who rated it ★.

★ **Cabernet Sauvignon-Merlot** NEW ✓ Smooth, refined, med-bodied debut in **99**, surprisingly accessible for its youth (though great persistence finish betokens 6-8 yrs good cellaring). Fragrant; thumbprint anise whiffs plus fennel, mocha. Delicious now and something of a bargain at ±R27 ex cellar.

★ **Chardonnay** ✓ **00** features complicated vinification, wooding: 33% barrel-fermented, aged 300 ℓ oak, remainder spontaneously fermented s/steel; blended after 6 mths. Oaked portion uppermost mid-01 in sweet-vanilla, buttermilk background to lime/lemon fruit. Tasty now but better in 2/3 yrs. **99** first from this cellar (**98** made but not released). Alcs 13%.

★★ **Cape Vintage Reserve** ✓ Splendid Cape benchmark 'port' since first vintage **91**. Current **98** shows hallmarks of excellent vintage in exceptionally pure, expressive fruit, complexity. Assembled, "like a fruit bowl", from tinta, touriga, souzao, touriga francesca (50/35/10/5); separately aged 2 yrs larger Fr old-oak (500 ℓ). Initial overt wood now absorbed, revealing opulent plum/cherry fruit, mint/eucalypt wafts, marvellously tangy sugar/tannin structure. Positively criminal to uncork now; defer, desist until 2010 (**91** terrific now). 20% alc; 93 g/ℓ sugar. Notch up (but it's all relative!) on **97**, with 40% tinta, 30% each souzao/touriga, latter featuring for first time. 18.8% alc, 95 g/ℓ sugar. More promising, even, than glittering **95** Wine ★★ No **96** – released as LBV below. **94** *Wine* ★, **93** *Wine* ★★ (rarely accorded rating). These generally deserve 5 yrs min.

★★ **Late Bottled Vintage** ✓ Lighter **96** VVG did not, Anton Bredell believed, justify a Vintage Reserve, so this 'only' an LBV – but what an LBV! Rich, silky, fragrant; gaining aromatic luxuriance as it ages. On present form still decade to go. 70/30 tinta/souzao, 2 yrs Fr oak. 19,7% alc, 98 g/l sugar. *Wine* ★. Also in 500 ml. —*DH*

Kaapse Hoop see Vinfruco
Kaapse Pracht see Coppoolse Finlayson-Sentinel
Kaapse Vreugd see Coppoolse Finlayson-Sentinel
Kaaps Genoegen see Coppoolse Finlayson-Sentinel
Kaaps Geskenk see Coppoolse Finlayson-Sentinel

Kaapzicht Estate

Stellenbosch (see Stellenbosch map) • Tasting & sales Mon-Thu 9-12.30; 1.30-5 Fri 9-12.30; 1.30-4 Sat & public holidays 9-12 Tasting fee for larger groups (new bottles opened may be taken away) • Cellar tours by appointment • Restaurant/kitchen/barbecue facilities with dance floor for up to 200 people • BYO picnic (tables/chairs available) • Walks • Views • Owner Steytdal Farms • Winemaker Danie Steytler • Viticulturist George Steytler • Vineyards 136 ha • Production 1 250 tons (30 000 cases own label) 60% red 40% white • PO Box 5 Sanlamhof 7532 ***• Tel (021) 906-1620/1*** *• Fax (021) 906-1622 • E-mail kaapzicht@mweb.co.za*

One of the most charming wine farms in the Cape is tucked away in these Bottelary Hills, far from the crowds who press into the chic valley boutiques. Up a dusty track you will find the tasting room and rustic courtyard leading off to the Steytlers' home. Unpretentious, forthright and spiritual, they're comfortable in this beautiful place. But don't be fooled by the apparent tranquillity: the Steytlers (winemaker Danie, marketer Yngvild and viticulturist George) never sleep. Pumping already open international pipelines, they've grown their export business by 250% for the second consecutive year. 2001 saw German-born Yngvild at the Pro Wein show in Düsseldorf, later joined by husband Danie for their first joint marketing sortie in the UK. Meanwhile Danie's brother George is overseeing the replanting of 16 hectares of chenin with shiraz and cabernet (an additional 35 ha of young reds come on-line soon). All planned to keep Kaapzicht in its present multi-medal-winning form.

Steytler range

Honours the late George Steytler, who farmed Kaapzicht from 1946-1984.

★★**Vision** NEW **00** Assured very ripe new-world style; dense chewy fruit in balance with fairly obvious oak; potentially strident pinotage notes sensitively played. Merits ±3 yrs' cellaring to start showing its best. Pinotage, cab, merlot; yr Fr oak, all-new for merlot, pinotage; reduced to 50% for cab.

★★**Pinotage** Since stunning maiden **98**, this blindingly-medalled (VG, ABSA Top 10, Michelangelo gold, *Wine* ★★ and Pinotage Champion) 'super Reserve' a serious pretender to Cape's Pinotage crown. **98** set tone with deep perfumes, opulent fruit, massive yet controlled intensity. **99** only 20 barrels (some kept back for CWG Auction), similar dense dark hues but even better fruit/acid balance. Latest **00** unquestionably finest to date; surprisingly un-pinotagey compared with pvs: big, welcoming mulberry bouquet and open-arms flavours of black plums, ripe strawberries dabbed with choc. Well-defined tannin structure and excellent fruit/oak balance (yr new Fr Nevers).

Kaapzicht range

★**Cabernet Sauvignon** Showcases Danie S's skills beyond his beloved Pinotage. **98** bigger, more arresting than pvs, ripe and gutsy, 13,5% alc in balance. Drinks nicely now but should last ± 6 yrs. Yr Fr oak, 40% new. **97** headily perfumed, persistent. **96** *Wine* ★; **95** Air France trophy.

★**Merlot 99** ★★ an unheralded surprise; much more intense, powerful than pvs; packed with plum-pudding, meat, spice delivered in measured, already-accessible tones with good aging potential. 17 mths small Fr oak barrels. **98** reflects vintage: full, wild, muscular and meaty, big enough for both 50% new Fr oak (17 mths) and 14% alc.

★**Pinotage** The best barrels may have moved on to Steytler range above from **98** *Wine* ★, but no threat to estate's position in the Cape premier pinotage league. Latest **00** excellent tannin structure, balance between ripe fruit, wood (yr 2nd fill Fr), big alc (14%). 'Gum-baby' bouquet going into smooth palate of persistent ripe damson fruit. Drink now and until 2005. **99** ★ ripe smoky plums, banana;

slight whiffs acetone, unexpectedly hard finish. **97** VVG, *Wine* ☆; **97/98** ABSA Top 10.

☆**Shiraz** Yet another arrow in the Steytlers' quiver. **99** ☆ reserved nose though palate's more open, spicy, leathery with sniffs meat, tobacco. Full-bodied (13.8% alc). Fr oak 17 mths. **98** fruitier, pungent black pepper with lemon grass suggestions; balanced tannins. **97** VG

☆**Bin 00** classic blend 55:45 cab/merlot. Lovely ripe fruit providing necessary drinkability, though will benefit from extra yr in bottle; stamina for further 5. **99** ☆ lighter, more austere.

☆**Hanepoot Jerepigo** Deliciously decadent, either as aperitif over lemon-zested crushed ice or winter digestif, both chilled. **00** ☆ excellent balance (188 g/ℓ sugar, 17.9% alc), integration. Ample honey and musk flavours should cellar brilliantly. Pvs **98** VVG muscat essence ensconced in lemon, fresh honey. **92** VG in 1992/5.

Following **01**s not ready for tasting: **Chenin Blanc**, **Sauvignon Blanc**. Discontinued: **Kaaproodt** Last was **96** ☆.

Cape View range

Mainly for export.

☆**Merlot 99** mineral tones with sweet plummy fruit; med-bodied, choc finish; not overwooded (3 mths small Fr oak). More complex than red-berried **98** ☆ with lick charry oak.

☆**Rouge de Kaap** ✓ Name a linguistic mishmash, but **00**'s big improvement on pvs. Very good ripe fruit, bone-dry finish. Mostly cab, shiraz, splashes cinsaut, pinotage. Good for 6 yrs min. **99** ☆ undemanding, dusty. Unwooded.

Dry Red ☻ ☆ Cinsaut's sweet nose leads **00** blend with cab, pinotage, shiraz, chenin. Delicious strawberries-and-cream tastes finish sweetly.

Cabernet Sauvignon ☆ **99** choc-mint bouquet followed by vegetal palate with honey/straw flavours. Lightly oak-staved. **Cabernet Sauvignon Wooded** ☆ **98** light, fruity, smooth. Should see out 5 yrs. Yr older Fr oak. Being phased out. **Chenin Blanc** ☆ **00** old-Cape steen with pear-drops aromas, leesy fatness from monster 14.5% alc. Discontinued: **Special Late Harvest Chenin Blanc** Last was **97** ☆; **Brut** (**99** ☆), **Demi Sec** (**99** ☆).

Friesland range

Export range not tasted for this ed. Pvs included: **Cabernet Sauvignon** (☆ **97**), **Merlot** (☆ **98**), **Bin 3** (Pvs **98** ☆), **Dry Red** (☆ **99**), **Chenin Blanc** (☆ **98**). — *NP*

Kakamas see Oranjerivier Wine Cellars

Kango Co-operative

Oudtshoorn (see Little Karoo map) • Tasting & sales Mon-Fri 8-4.30 Sat 9-1 • Cellar tours by appointment • Owners 70 members • Winemaker Anton Nel (since Jan 2001) • Consulting viticulturist Willem Botha (VinPro) • Vineyards 360 ha • Production 3 000 tons ± 2 600 cases 85.3% white 14.7% red • PO Box 46 Oudtshoorn 6620 • ***Tel (044) 272-6065*** *• Fax (044) 279-1038 • E-mail antonwyn@mweb.co.za (winemaker), kango@mweb.co.za (Co-op)*

Expect the sizzle factor to increase (we're not talking only climate here) after the advent in 2001 of ex Louwshoek-Voorsorg Anton Nel, winemaker on a mission: "My goal is to place the Little Karoo on the fine-wine map," declares Nel, noting he has the active support of the 70 members, who also raise ostriches, tobacco and various cash crops. Sliding behind a busy flight deck vacated by Jaco

Potgieter (now with DGB), the new cellarmaster presides over a large and diverse domain (brandies, *witblits*, liqueurs and 'sours' also produced and bottled here, "making this a very interesting cellar to visit"). Plans are afoot to refurbish a disused cellar for vinifying and ageing small batches of red. After hours, you'll find this keen hiker on a quiet mountain trail or relaxing outdoors with his wife and baby son.

Mont Noir range

Merlot ☆ Prince Albert fruit for this, Pinotage below. **01** casual quaff with earthy tones, light tannins, fruitcake finish. Big 14.5% alc. **Pinotage** ☆ **01** red berry/earth bouqet; slight tannin, quick finish. 13.6% alc. **Chardonnay** ☆ish **01** with gentle peach/apricot textures to drink now. **Sauvignon Blanc** ☆ **00** clean, fresh, fruity; non-challenging. 13.2% alc.

Rijkshof range

These all NV. **Red Jeripigo** ☆ Red muscadel, yet tastes like pinotage. 16.8% alc. **Red Muscadel** ☆ Mahogany colour, sweet raisins and moderate (17.1%) spirit. **Golden Jeripigo** ☆ Muscat, earthy tones; surprisingly dry finish. From white muscadel. 16.3% alc. **Hanepoot** ☆ Clean muscat tastes, fragant and not too alcoholic (16.5%). **White Muscadel** ☆ Earthy, sweet, spirity. 17% alc. **Ruby Port** ☆ Earthy aromas, sweet and soft. Ruby lights. 17.3% alc. Following temporarily out of stock, so untasted: **Claret** (Pvsly ☆), **Herfsgoud** (☆), **Vin Doux** (★★).

Garob range NEW

These all **NV**. **Dry Red** Savoury-toned, light-bodied ruby cab/cinsaut. **Grand Cru** ★ Boiled sweets, honeyed tones; light dry white. **Late Harvest** ★ Lightweight; slight honeyed notes, fruity and not too sweet. **Red Muscadel** ☆ Coppery robes, full-blown muscadel; warming spirit for cold Karoo nights. 17% alc.

Vlakteplaas range NEW

Venerable range of fortifieds (first release: 1934) made by the Schoeman family on their Excelsior-Vlakteplaas property near Oudtshoorn. Bottled, marketed and distributed by Kango.

★★**White Muscadel Limited Release** ✓ This multi-young wine show award winner from same block as 'regular' below, "vinified for lightness, fruitiness"; **00** high-toned, peppery, viscous-textured. Powerfully sweet, too, with lower acid, alc. And delicious. 520 cases of 500 ml.

Red Muscadel Refined, amost ethereal style, made for early drinking as an aperitif, says winemaker. Latest **01** ★★; pvs clank with young wine show medals. 17.1% alc. 500 cases. **White Muscadel** ★★ **00** intriguing herbal/muscat aromas; clean finish. Moderate 16.8% alc. 520 cases. — *DH*

Kanonkop Estate

Stellenbosch (see Stellenbosch map) • Tasting & sales Mon-Fri 8.30-5 Sat 8.30-12.30 Closed New Year's/Christmas days, Good Friday • Traditional snoek barbecue by appointment (15 guests or more) • Owners Johann & Paul Krige • Winemaker Beyers Truter (since 1981) • Vineyards 100 ha • Production 400 tons 25 000 cases 100% red • PO Box 19 Elsenburg 7607 • ***Tel (021) 884-4656*** *• Fax (021) 884-4719 • E-mail wine@kanonkop.co.za*

Beyers Truter has the room twined round his little finger and lapping up his every word. It's a pinotage tasting for growers and some local wine-journalists, and he has the floor. "Please, ladies and gentlemen of the press," says he engagingly, I want to ask you today, on behalf of our local grape, not to use the word 'jammy'. You know, the overseas market doesn't like that term. They believe a jammy wine isn't nice. Instead, say ... (here he switches to some pretty authentic Gallic tones – he gets to practise them, after all, on the likes of Bordeaux wine-diva

May-Eliane de Lencquesaing, who's twice presented him with her prestigious Pichon-Longueville Comtesse de Lalande trophy for top blended red at the IWSC) ... say: *confiture*. It's such a nice French word, isn't it? *Confiture*. Means the same, but sounds so much nicer." Also brings down the house, of course, as it gently underlines the hugely respected winemaker's role as the Patron of Pinotage, the man who's planted SA's very own variety on the international stage and nurtured it with his understated zeal. Harvest 2002 is his 21st at this legendary estate, and for many punters Beyers Truter is King Kanonkop, too (owners Johann and Paul Krige moving and shaking, big time, mostly behind the public scenes). It's interesting to reflect, on this anniversary, that the very first 5-star laurel offered by this guide was to a Kanonkop. Two decades on, they're still the bee's knees.

★★★**Paul Sauer** Legend in its own time, Cape classic in its own right. Stayer too: **91** tasted mid-01 still vibrant; freshness balancing development of rich, tomato-cocktail claret characters. Current **98** quieter, shy on review, still with watermark herbaceous 'Kanonkop' stitched into lush blackcurrant, lifted by spearmint edge. Masterfully ripe tannins afford access now, but really will be worth waiting. Rare *Wine* ★★★. 80% cab, 10% each cab f, merlot. 25 mths new Nevers barriques. 13.8% alc. **97** ★★★ more classily elegant, but as flavoursome. **96** stunning intensity from low-yielding (4,5 t/ha), 30 yr old vines. **CWG Auction 'Kanonkop'** ★★★ Celestial blend reaching stellar prices, sparking hushed atmosphere – what's the new price barrier this year? – when it has turn in auction room. Last **97** decidedly mineral, tailored aristocrat for nurturing at least ten yrs; upcoming **98** (01) more curvaceous, bolder, higher 13.8% alc. Both emphatically sensuous, individual, outstanding.

★★**Cabernet Sauvignon** Maybe not as flash, not as headline grabbing as its siblings, but as venerable as the (avg) 32 yr old vines supplying its grapes. Newer, earlier-ripening, heatwave-shunning clones assist in retaining balance, especially in ripe harvests like big **98**. Smouldering Simonsberg smokiness unveils super mouthful of ripe (not blowsy) cassis fruit/nuts interwoven with supple, clearly ripe tannins. Lovely length, measured, balanced, treading middle road between sinuous old style and new. 13% alc. 24 mths 225 ℓ Nevers, 50/50 new/2nd fill. Cooler **97** similarly classic combination ripe fruit, elegant knitted tannins. **96** crossover of exuberant fruit-penetration with restraint; not as much stamina as pvs.

★★★**Pinotage** So certain is a full house of awards, with matching quality, consistency, that serious wine drinkers don't wait: this label barrels out of cellar on release. **99** long sold out by review time, similar power of all-conquering **98** ★★★, **97** also IWSC gold. Typically magenta purple in youth with piercing aromas of ripe damson/plum, hints banana on gutsy mineral fabric; complex palate layered with choc-cherry, cinnamon, clove; opulent creaminess. Firm but fine tannin for up to 10 yrs from harvest. **CWG Auction Pinotage** On song again in **99** after lower-key **98** – not that minor variations matter to the paddle-punters. Deeper colour, fruit concentration; more serious, finer wood than above; altogether more lavish yet restrained, longer lived selection.

★★**Kadette** ✓ Classy packaging leverages off Kanonkop splendour (which it decidedly shares, though estate's moniker appears on label in smaller font), hence no need to follow varietal-naming bandwagon. Few peers in value (as recently confirmed by US *Wine Spectator* rating among "50 great red wine values"). Current **99** ★★ eases off the authority with more overt plummy/berry fruit, less bracing tannin. For earlier enjoyment than stablemates. Diners Club-shortlisted **98** based on pinotage (55%), solid palate freshened with ripe cherries. **97** a gentle beauty; aromatic, soft tannins. Now sporting pinotage (16%) and ruby cab (12%) freshness. Subtle oak throughout. 2-4 yrs to peak. —*DS*

Kanu Wines

Stellenbosch (see Stellenbosch map) Tasting & sales Mon-Fri 10-5 Sat 9-1 (Nov-Feb) Mon-Fri 10-4.30 closed on Sat (Mar-Oct) Fee R2/wine • Owner Hydro Holdings • Sales & marketing manager Sean Griffiths • Winemaker Teddy Hall (since 1998) with Theo Brink jnr (since 1999) • Viticulturist Johann Schloms • Vineyards 45 ha (additional 60 ha leased) • Production 40 000 cases • PO Box 548 Stellenbosch 7599 • ***Tel (021) 881-3808*** *• Fax (021) 881-3514 • E-mail info@kanu.co.za • Website www.kanu.co.za*

"WE CAN GIVE the Loire a run for their money with our chenin!" has long been the rallying cry of Teddy Hall, whose wines claimed three of the top four placings at last year's Chenin Challenge – his own-label Robusto (now Rudera) came in second – and earned him a trip to France in the process. He and wife Riana went to check out the opposition. Did their wines have him eating his words? "Not at all," says Hall, who came to winemaking relatively late in life (he's currently doing his MSc in oenology). "Our best chenin is on a par with their better ones, especially at the drier end of the scale." Future excitement, he believes, will lie in the sweeter styles: "Think of our great NLH heritage. We've lost and forgotten about it." A few years back, consultant Eben Archer convinced them to follow an intensive pruning and suckering programme (Theo Brink Jnr puts in serious time in the vineyards) and they're now reaping the benefits of this "world-class advice".

✵**Keystone Limited Release** As Teddy Hall's whites are bulging with ripe fruit, so are his reds braced by soft, ripe tannins, bounds away from austerity. This 50/50 cab/merlot flagship, "keystone of all other Kanu reds" from cellar-managed Vlottenburg/Koelenhof vyds. 2nd vintage **99** opaque ruby; sensual mineral, dusty aromas plumped up by deliciously ripe, near-sweet merlot meatiness. Beauty is in rich tannic backdrop allowing access on release but will sustain maturation. **98** varietal medley of cassis, sweet-violets, ripe plums, nougat texture; will give pleasure for 3-5 yrs. 18 mths Fr barriques, some new. 3 600 cases.

✵**Cabernet Sauvignon Limited Release** Not the flagship, but the star among these reds. Next **99** as voluptuous as maiden **98**: dense purple, ethereal black-currant/raspberry scents, riveting dusty, bdx-like palate in which subtle forest-floor fruits bound up in brilliantly managed tannin-firmed structure. Sit-up-and-take-notice length of finish. 13.7% alc under wraps. **98** fragrant cedar/sweet spice; fruitcake hints contrast with savoury, chewy tannins. 5 yrs should allow full integration. 100% new Fr barriques, 18 mths. 1 200 cases.

✵**Merlot** ✓ Bold blue-black **99** smoulders with sultry floral/violet scents spiced by rosemary, full meaty sweet fruit shepherded by those ripe tannins again, late 3 g/ℓ sugar rings finish. Gutsy, applauded **98**, Air France Top 10, softening. 14,5% alc. 15 mths Fr barrels. 1 200 cases. Of Hall's suggested culinary accompaniments – including oxtail, pork rib, venison and duck – the rosemary butterflied leg of lamb gets our vote.

✵**Shiraz** Truly tasty, the smoky, savoury (marinated green-olive stuffed with almond) scents of **00** are matched in mouth by delicately poised sparring of sweet (not baked) ripe berry fruit with oak strapping, judicious tannins. Lip-smackingly good to drink, in spite of youth. **99** aromatic with firm but undaunting tannins. Push-off from oak-lavished **98** *Wine* ✵. Only 250 cases from mere 14 rows of doughty old vines on home farm. 14 mths Fr oak. 12,3% alc.

✵**Chardonnay** ✓ Sample **00** clean new oak paralleled by ripe tropical, melon, apricot fruit; good length. 13.5% alc. Gear off **99** ✵ focused, coherent, concentrated. Less boisterous than **98** which got label off to multi-podium start. Barrel-fermented/matured: yr 225 ℓ Fr oak, 60% new; 40% natural ferment. 1 000 cases.

Chenin Blanc Wooded Limited Release No room for the reticent in this burly, statement wine, Teddy H's passion and cellar's official white flagship. **99** took honours in 01 Chenin Blanc Challenge. "Explosive" suggests back-label of next **00**, verging on understatement: its flavour fills the glass, its personality the room. Big in every way, from bright flaxen colour through pungent wood, trenchant over-ripe tropical fruit ending up with emphatic 14.5% alc, 4.8 g/ℓ sugar brims over the borders of dry. Will win awards (*Wine*), shows and fans, but trifle unbridled for top rating. Free-run juice of Koelenhof bushvines barrel-fermented, 60% new Fr oak, 40% natural yeasts. Production up to 1 300 cases.

Bulkamp Sauvignon Blanc Current **01** worthy, if quieter, successor from favourable yr to stunning first **00** release, fuller, more robust than standard bottling below; youthful pale straw, penetrating nettle/white pepper leavened by rich tropical cornucopia packed into broad herbal frame. Lingering finish marked by late sweetness (4.2 g/ℓ sugar). 13.3 % alc Single "optimally manicured" Koelenhof vyd, vernacular 'Bull Camp' name alludes to pvs use of site. Limited 260 case release.

Noble Late Harvest 99 from hárslevelü, 100% new oak brilliantly absorbed in intense riesling-like bouquet; peach, pear, almond and toasted hazelnut in palate. Sumptuous, sweet and long, but bracing 9 g/ℓ acid reels in richness to thrilling conclusion. Raisined/botrytised grapes fermented 100% new Fr oak barriques, aged 15 mths. 375 ml. 500 cases.

Red **00** studded with plummy, cheery strawberry/raspberry fruit from unwooded equal parts ruby cab, cinsaut. No need for a vinous PhD to enjoy this one, more-so lightly cooled. Milder 12,5% alc. 6 500 cases.

Chenin Blanc Cheerful, flavourful basket guavas, hints candyfloss to add to the picnic fare. **01** ripe, broad 13.8% alc, off-dry. 3 600 cases. **Sauvignon Blanc** Easy **01** for "hot summer's day" drinking, "ultra-reductive" fruit-forward style, fresh nettles, juicy cut grass filled out with guava, gooseberry tints. Best fresh within harvest yr. 1 800 cases. **Spier Wine Estate Chardonnay** Not tasted for this ed. Last was **98** . — *DS*

Kaya see Coppoolse Finlayson-Sentinel
Keimoes see Oranjerivier Wine Cellars

Kellerprinz

Top-selling NV budget range by Distell.

Stein Not tasted for this ed. Pvs rating . **Late Harvest** Honeyed sweet white, some delicate muscat scents. — *IvH*

Ken Forrester Wines

Stellenbosch (see Helderberg map) • Tasting & sales at 96 Winery Road Restaurant (see Eat-out section) • Cellar tours by appointment • Luxury guesthouse • Conferences • Facilities for children • Gifts • Views • Wheelchair-friendly • Owners Ken & Teresa Forrester • Winemakers Ken Forrester & Martin Meinert (since 1998) • Viticulturists Shawn Smit & Aidan Morton • Vineyards 28 ha • Production 24 000 cases 70% white 30% red • PO Box 1253 Stellenbosch 7599 • ***Tel (021) 855-2374*** *• Fax (021) 855-2373 • E-mail ken@kenforresterwines.com • Website www.kenforresterwines.com*

"It's a paradigm shift," declares Ken Forrester, flamboyant restaurateur and chenin-vangelist, "between the traditional way of harvesting chenin unripe at 21°B to our goal of growing quality wine. That's a totally different challenge." One that the owner of gnarly old bushvines on Scholtzenhof farm in the Helderberg is mastering with his usual panache, it seems. For confirmation, hear what UK überwinewriter Jancis Robinson says of the Petit Chenin: "Possibly the best value white wine coming out of South Africa." With urbane wine-partner Martin Meinert, Forrester also styles a more serious version, which he calls "Grande Chenin", reflecting "balance, grip and drinkability." Then there's the third in the triumvirate: an opulent NLH to be sipped "as a little nightcap". As for the reds, the grenache (partnered with equally spicy syrah) is from 55 year old bushvines, probably the only block in Stellenbosch. Its style, ever-eloquent Forrester says, "evokes a vision of a sultry, raven-haired gypsy ... a seriously sexy wine to go with Moroccan spiced lamb tagine on couscous".

★**Grenache-Syrah** Individualistic, but right up the street of savoury-toothed red Rhone lovers. **00** (barrel sample) 52/48 mix, will also satisfy vinophiles who like their wines to look red – but beautiful limpid ruby rather than inkily opaque (some pvs a bit wan). Still slumbering, but suggestions of woodsmoke, new leather, cranberries promise further development, as do warm, savoury flavours tidily knit to action-packed finish. Should settle over next yr but also worth trying now with risotto al funghi. 13.9% alc. Barrel-matured yr; 300 ℓ Fr/Am oak (75/25). 2 300 cases. **99** warm, intense.

★**Merlot-Cabernet Sauvignon** Here is the out-to-please, friendly member of this red team (if the Grenache-Syrah above is too uncompromising). **99** generous ripe cherries, spicy plums; light-textured but full of honest flavours, with unpushy 13% alc. Neat tuck of truly dry tannin creates essential compatibility with food. 58/29 merlot, cab spiced with shiraz, 3.5% pinotage. 14 mths oak. 13.6% alc. 2 100 cases.

★**Chenin Blanc** ✓ Ken F calls this his "Grande Chenin", encapsulating his philosophy (to make serious, wood/bottled-aged versions to match cuisine) rather than the wine itself. In youth displays almost ethereal impenetrability, though **01** (barrel sample) shows surprising forwardness in bouquet (floral/honeysuckle fragrances), amplitude in palate (still nothing remotely flashy). This an exception, from exceptional year. Excellent potential (Forrester suggests 4-6 yrs) – though on track record, expect temporary 'dumb' phase after 2-3 yrs. 13% alc. 5 000 cases. **00** still turning on youthful charm, so enjoy now before hibernation sets in. **99** ★★ may be hitting that dip, but then doesn't really have concentration of younger siblings, both on higher plane than **98**, **97**. From 30 yr+ Helderberg bushvines, pruned for low yields.

★**Sauvignon Blanc** ✓ Sauvignon fanciers less enamoured of extreme, pungent versions will find plenty to like about carefully-crafted **01.** Forrester's deliberately food-friendly style glimmers with green fig, flinty purity, supple flavours highlighted by perfectly poised dryness. Bright juicy acids pitched to immediately stimulate another bottle. 13% alc. 6 500 cases. **00** SAA, Michelangelo gold.

★**'T' Noble Late Harvest Chenin Blanc** Gastronomically gifted Ken F never short of tempting foods or occasions to partner his wines: with **00** ★★, he suggests fried goose liver, vanilla souffle or, if sipped solo, then preferably "from a lover's navel" – in his case, presumably belonging to Teresa, Mrs F, whose qualities amply mirrored in these sizzling drops of intoxicating kumquat, fresh orange zest; taut, mercurial acid (6.6 g/ℓ); stylish botrytis embroidery. Delicious now; with time will become seduction in a (gorgeous) bottle. Barrel-fermented, 50% new 400 ℓ Fr. Somewhat higher RS than magical **98** (145 vs 84 g/ℓ) but extra brings balance not sweetness. **99** shimmering silky length buoyed with subtle oak, botrytis.

Petit Chenin ★★ "Bottled early to show the freshest fruit flavours," says back-label, whose standout green/yellow colour conveys fun aspect of this little brother to above Grande. **01** usual well-modulated food tones; accent more on weight, vinosity than full-monty fruit. Whiffs honeysuckle, hedgerows, happily bouncing along the fresh, lees-enriched palate. 100% chenin, unwooded, 13,5% alc. 15 000 cases. Discontinued: **Blanc Fumé** (Pvs **99** ☆). — *AL*

Kersfontein see Sonop
Kevin Arnold see Waterford

Khanya Wines

Durbanville • Not open to the public • Owner/winemaker Nico Vermeulen • Production 500 cases • 3 Pieter Hugo Street Courtrai Suider-Paarl 7624 • ***Tel/fax (021) 863-2048***

MOST WINEMAKERS yearn to produce own-label wines. Nico Vermeulen's dream is being realised with a little help from his mate Jackie Coetzee of Bloemendal, in whose cellar a triplet of 99s were born. Vermeulen called these 'other' children Khanya, meaning 'shine' (adored real-world offspring 'NC', Izelle and Judy, nor other half Judith forgotten – current and future releases are named after them). He now makes the range at Havana Hills, a winery overlooking Melkbosstrand which he owns in partnership with entrepreneur Kobus du Plessis. Havana Hills' own vineyards are not yet in production, so the grapes for the wines below are sourced from Bloemendal.

☆ **Cabernet Sauvignon-Merlot (NC's Choice)** Like wine below, **00** has expansive, seamless character; larger proportion cab (70%) evident only in firmer tannin structure. Picked perfectly ripe for fresh as well as supple softness feel, lengthily-chorused roast coffee, cassis, plums melange. Subtly Fr oaked, yr, 30% new. Our pronouncement – delicious – should echo until at least 08. 100 cases. 13,5% alc. First **99** introduced a serious, big yet elegant claret with ageing potential

☆ **Shiraz-Cabernet Sauvignon (Judy's Choice)** Epitomises Cape's ability (not always acknowledged) to combine European restraint, southern hemisphere ripeness. **00** homogenous 80/20 ensemble wonderfully ripe fruits; evocative aromas of freshly rained-on dark red earth, spice, choc-nut. Creamily soft with great flavour presence; bolstered for next 6-8 yrs with fine, firm tannin. Fr oak matured, 30% new, 15 mths. 100 cases.

☆ **Sauvignon Blanc (Izelle's Choice)**. Generous, sea-freshened gooseberry/cut-grass aromas breeze off **01**; full lees-padded body ends with soaring flavour resurgence. Powerful but not overblown. Single Dbnville vyd; 19 yr old bush vines. 100 cases. — *AL*

Klawervlei Estate

Stellenbosch (see Stellenbosch map) • Tasting & sales Mon-Fri 10-5 Sat 10-2 • Cellar tours by appointment • Wheelchair-friendly • Proprietors Hermann & Inge Feichtenschlager • Winemaker Hermann Feichtenschlager • Vineyards 35 ha • Production 2 500-7 000 cases • PO Box 144 Koelenhof 7605 • ***Tel (021) 882-2746*** *• Fax (021) 882-2415*

FOR YEARS irrepressible Hermann and Inge Feichtenschlager were lonely voices in the wilderness, calling (by example rather than trumpeting from a soapbox) for more enviro-cordial winegrowing at the Cape. Now that the tide is turning their way, and more wineries are embracing Mother Earthy regimes such as Integrated Production of Wine (IPW), they have the satisfaction of having been there first. And, setbacks notwithstanding (their 97 crop was a total failure), these Koelenhof eco-icons remain proud to declare their wines "Organically grown and made". The following **01** barrel/tank samples, tasted mid-01, were too young to rate: **Cabernet Sauvignon**, **Merlot** (a 98 also available) and **Chenin Blanc**.

Klawer Winery

Olifants River (see Olifants River map) • Tasting & sales Mon-Fri 8-5 Sat 9-12 Closed on Sundays & public holidays • Cellar tours by appointment • BYO picnic • Tourgroups • Conferences • Views • Bird watching • Owners 80 members • Winemaker Bob de Villiers (since Dec 2000) • Viticulturalist Klaas Coetzee (since Jul 2001) • Production 27 000 tons • PO Box 8 Klawer 8145 • ***Tel (027) 216-1530*** *• Fax (027) 216-1561 • E-mail klawerwyn@kingsley.co.za*

BOB DE VILLIERS arrived at this Olifants River co-op (from Barrydale via Groot Constantia) in time for the 2001 crush, and immediately upped the energy levels. A vine specialist was duly enlisted as part of the vision "to grow exceptionaly good grapes to produce good wines". De Villiers' own contributions were not, for the most part, ready for tasting for this edition, and Klawer fans who are curious about the new wines and the "changes that have already begun to change the face of this winery" are advised to pay a personal visit (picnicking and birding among the non-vinous attractions). Visitors should find not only a bottle to suit their tastes, but also a pecuniary attraction in the Klawer slogan: Good value for money.

Merlot ⁂ **99** sold out; new release not ready for tasting. **Pinotage** ★ Rewinding to **99** (pvs tasted was **00**); more earthy, rustic. Unoaked. 14% alc. 1 500 cases. **Grenache Blanc de Noir** ⁂ Copper-toned **00** still fairly fresh, not too sweet; lightish (11,5% alc). 1 200 cases. **Colombard 00** first 2000 vintage wine (from anywhere) on Swedish liquor shelves, very tired now. 1 300 cases. **Late Harvest NV** (00) semi-sweet chenin/colombard. 750 cases. **Special Late Harvest** Sweet dessert from chenin. 1 200 cases. **Best Wishes Cuvée Brut** Latest **NV** bottling not ready for tasting. Pvs ★. **Michelle Doux** ⁂ Amber-hued **NV** from red muscadel past her prime. 6 000 cases. **Red Muscadel** ⁑ Regular show-winner, yet latest **01** uncharacteristically unctuous, fiery mid-01; needs to meld. 18,5% alc. ±2 000 cases. **White Muscadel** ⁂ Latest **00** bit bigger than pvs (17,5% alc); similar tropical, muscat character, palate-cleansing acidity. 3 000 cases. **Hanepoot** Not tasted for this ed. Pvs **99** ⁂. Also available (not tasted): **Dry Red**.

Birdfield range

Export range, striking packaging suitably avian-themed.

Chardonnay ⁂ **01** lively, attractive tropical fruits and vanilla-oak hints. Good everyday fare. **Chenin Blanc** NEW ⁑ **01** fruity example; nip of acidity tells you it's chenin. Unwooded, med-bodied. 800 cases. **Sauvignon Blanc** NEW ⁑ Lightish **01** grassy/tropical tastes, bracing acidic tang calls for something fresh from the sea. 500 cases. Pvsly featured **Merlot** (⁂), **Shiraz** (⁑) not tasted for this ed. — *DH*

Klein Begin see New Beginnings, Vinfruco
Kleinbosch see International Wine Services, Cape Wine Cellars

Klein Constantia Estate

Constantia (see Constantia map) • Tasting & sales Mon-Fri 9-5 Sat 9-1 Tasting fee R12 p/p for groups • Cellar tours as above by appointment • Views • Owners Duggie & Lowell Jooste • Winemaker Ross Gower (since 1984) • Viticulturist Kobus Jordaan (since 1981) • Vineyards 75 ha • Production 600 tons 45 000 cases • PO Box 375 Constantia 7848 • ***Tel (021) 794-5188*** *• Fax (021) 794-2464 • E-mail kleincon@global.co.za • Website www.kleinconstantia.com*

THESE 75 HECTARES, rated (by the French, *nogal*) among the world's nine "most mythical vineyards", are getting their first major spring-clean in two decades. Recalling 1982 and the beginning of the rescue operation by entrepreneur Duggie Jooste of this more than 3 centuries old estate, scion Lowell Jooste says: "When we first started planting, we had very little experience of Constantia's potential. We're now able to fine-tune plantings more accurately. Our low, warmer north-facing slopes will remain planted with reds and the higher south-facing ones with whites. We're changing in some areas – sauvignon's now on the higher slopes in place of wind-shy chardonnay." And they're keeping pockets of riesling, adding pinot. Despite high moisture stress caused by four abnormally dry summers, 01 produced healthy reds and "fantastically ripe" whites. Jewel-in-the-crown muscat de frontignan came in a week early. Which isn't soon enough for the adoring global fanclub of Vin de Constance, cellarmaster and vini-archeologist Ross Gower's painstaking recreation of the Cape's original sweet wine. "We've planted more muscat," Lowell Jooste assures. "However it will take at least 7 years before the first wine is ready.

★**Cabernet Sauvignon Reserve** Singular product of single vyd, all new clone 163. **97** second bottling only ex farm (first barrel selection for CWG auction). Delicious, highly intense fruit/oak flavours shepherded by exquisitely tapered, elegant tannin infusion. New world fruit within Continental frame. Will grow in complexity over 5 yrs. Wine ★. 18 mths new Fr oak. 250 cases.

★**Cabernet Sauvignon** Crossover style; mix of 'new' fruitier clone infuses, expands austerity of sappy, dusty 'old' clone notes. **98** full, muscular, prominent toasted oak cloaks reticent, linear berry fruit, guarded by sinuous tannins. Not as elegant as spicy, fragrant **97**. WOM selection. Oaked 2 yrs.

★**Marlbrook** Bdx-style blend distinguished by classic cab green-walnut, cassis character. New **98** has charry oak screening sultry choc/mocha flesh, all tied up by puckering tannins. Yard off super **97** ★, best since maiden **88**. **96** and most pvs ★. From **94** cab-dominated, 50% with merlot, cab f (40/10). Fr oak 2 yrs. Alcs ±14% alcs. 3 200 cases.

★**Chardonnay** Latest **00** preserves rating after lighter **99** ★. Latest gilded ochre, mellow melange smouldering oak, nutty oatmeal complexity with ripeness, harmonious limey grip to leesy fullness. These evolve into chalky/minerally whole over 2-4 yrs. 500 ℓ Fr oak 10 mths, ±33% new, malo. 13,5% alc. **00** down to 3 000 cases.

★**Sauvignon Blanc** ✓ Who would have thought KC sauvignon, nurtured on rarefied slopes of cool Constantia, could soar to alc of 14.5%? Guts of latest **01** (sample) seamlessly woven into singular mouthful. Superbly complex herbaceous, wild scrub aromas; palate hints at gooseberry but more refined; terrific grip. Like trailblazing **86** – still a benchmark in 2000 – and successors, a stayer. Unwooded, includes 10% semillon boost since **95**. **00** full, less typically 'thrusting', preferred by Gower over **99** for its "better fruit". 19 000 cases.

★**Rhine Riesling** ✓ Perhaps management should apply 'greenback-poultice' marketing theory to this 'poor man's KC' – the higher the price, the better it must be. Because, while Sauvignon, Chardonnay price hikes get them galloping past cellar door, this undervalued gem trickles out with modest R26 swing-tag. **99** still fresh mid-straw; fruity mantle now a mineral ring; fruit-salad palate sweetness will mellow to apparent dryness over further yr/2. Off-dry finish (12 g/ℓ sugar) whets/aids gastronomy; terrific aperitif, food partner . Modest 12% alc. 2 800 cases. Secondary toastiness in **98**, WOM selection.

★**Sauvignon Blanc Noble Late Harvest** Much admired in France, where most of this gorgeous dessert is sold; reflects some Sauternes influence, though weighs in somewhat sweeter (last **98** 120 g/ℓ sugar vs sauternes' 90-100); similar oak polish intensifying spicy-sweet botrytis dimension. Small quantities (800 cases) and in 500 ml bottles, intermittently part of KC's range, at least for auctions. 14,5% alc. Yr new 500 ℓ oak.

★**Vin de Constance** Eulogies will continue to be written to this remarkable embodiment of Cape wine, reflecting legends of early glory and new struggle to recaptivate the wine world. Perhaps greatest compliment is the rush of emulating competitors – KC well placed to face challenge, not only are quality and market its own, but expeditious new plantings of muscat de f (clones as imported to the Cape in 1656 – see intro). Unbotrytised – no pseudo-Barsac/Sauternes this –

has its own, unique, riveting, complex minty, sweet lemon-honey impact. Latest **97** ✯✯ brilliantly packaged as ever; shimmering saffron heralds cornucopia of tropical scents layered with spice, creamy, freshly baked apple-pie, all deliciously cut by tart, sweet-sour citric twist in tail. Handles 15% alc with aplomb. Picked ultra-ripe (42°B) rounded 18 mths seasoned 500 ℓ oak. 2 500 cases. Pvs **95-93** all ✯✯, *Wine* ✯ or ✯✯. **91** (that's 1791!) ceremonially broached in 2001 for Duggie Jooste's 75th. "Remarkably good condition" – Lowell's Jooste's notes – "amber colour, plenty of sediment, fruit dominating, muscat noticeable – no vinegary touch; lots of sweetness. Made 2 yrs after the French Revolution!"

✯**Pinot Noir** Notch up in **00** gentle ruby complexion belies depth of truffly, earthy resonance to cherry/berry fruit flesh; super-tight tannic grip will ensure some maturation – likely to develop agricultural charm over 2-4 yrs. **98** ✯ light-textured/structured. Yr 50% new Fr oak. New clone 113. Natural yeast fermentation. 500 cases.

Shiraz ✯ Deliberate new world style continued in **99** prominent Am oak, plummy fruit-to-fore palate. 600 cases. **Brut Triple Zero** One-off **NV** ✯ MCC millennium sparkler sold out. — *DS*

Kleindal

Vinimark-owned easy-drinking range made in conjunction with local growers mainly for export to Europe.

✯**Cabernet Sauvignon 00** lightly oaked to emphasise smoothness, softness; easy yet generous cab not for laying down. 13% alc.

Sauvignon Blanc ☻ ✯ Plenty of verve in **01**, crisp fruit and chalky textures combine to vibrant effect. Definitely one to drink in flush of youth (while noting big 13,5% alc).

Pinotage ✯ Variety's rustic face to fore in **01** (sample), with dry earthy nuances. Suitably sturdy cuisine called for. 13% alc. **Rosé** ✯ Palest hue imaginable – pretty colour for prettily flavoured wine. Colombard, muscadel; ruby cab supplies the blush. **Chardonnay** ✯ Nice combination of oak and fruit in lightly wooded **01**, buttery vanilla tones to tropical palate, clean dry citrus finish. 13,6% alc. **Chenin Blanc** ✯ Lightish **01**, unpretentious just-dry quaff; lemonadey flavours designed to uncork now. — *DH*

Klein DasBosch NEW

Stellenbosch • Owner James Wellwood (Whitey) Basson • Winemaker/viticulturist Jan 'Boland' Coetzee (since 1997) • Vineyards 5.5 ha • Production 35 tons 2 800 cases (1 300 cases own label) 89% red 11% white • PO Box 826 Brackenfell 7561 • ***Tel (021) 880-0888*** *• Fax (021) 880-0999 • E-mail wine@kleindasbosch.com • Website www.kleindasbosch.co.za*

This range, with its revealing front-labels, is made at Vriesenhof by rugby-and-wine legend Jan 'Boland' Coetzee for his neighbour 'Whitey' Basson, corporate lion and grower of 51/2 bracingly scenic hectares in Stellenbosch's Blaauwklippen Valley. Enthusiastic, ambitious, Basson and his engaging family aim to produce "the best boutique wine in SA". Their varietal repertoire consists of two classics, merlot and chardonnay which, as described on their website, grow in "sumptuous vineyards bursting with delicious rich grapes begging to be made into fine wine". Local vinoscenti will find these attention-lavished, limited-release drops mainly in selected restaurants: most fly to Hong Kong and the United Arab Emirates.

Merlot Warm, rich tastes of christmas cake, plum pudding in **98**, now showing bit of age so probably best drunk in yr/2. **99** more straightford, herbal; less complex and lighter-toned (though alcs comparable: ±13.5%). ±600 cases. **Chardonnay** Bunch-pressed, oak-fermented **00**; leesy tastes and honeyed development needing to be enjoyed now. 13.8% alc. 230 cases. — *TM*

Kleine Draken

*Paarl (see Paarl map) • Tasting & sales Mon-Fri 8-12h30, 1.30-5 Closed Jewish & public holidays • Owner Cape Gate (Pty) Ltd • Vineyards 12 ha • Production ±10 000 cases • **Tel (021) 863-2368** • Fax (021) 863-1884 • E-mail zandwijk@capegate.co.za*

PAARL's current winemaking revival is clearly not going unnoticed by this specialised enclave. They've submitted their wines (made under supervision of the Cape Beth Din to super-strict Kosher and Kosher le Pesach standards) for rating in the guide for the first time in seven years, symbolic of their own reawakening. The objective of quality (re-introduction of French wood in the cellar, vineyard practices suitably fine-tuned) is paying dividends. Winemaker Neil Schnoor rose to the unique challenges of this cellar (wine is literally 'cooked' during flash pasteurisation, so delicate grape aromas and flavours can easily be lost in the process) when the former industrial chemist in him stirred. Two harvests later, this steady improvement in the range has seen a massive increase in domestic sales, new exports to Canada and the USA, with strong prospects for Israël and Germany.

Sauvignon Blanc Flash-pasteurisation no friend to fruitiness (something to consider when comparing these ratings to conventionally vinified examples): **00** just some dilute grassiness in well-balanced, clean, bone-dry and light (11% alc) package. 800 cases. **Cabernet Sauvignon** Crisp and lean; subdued plummy leatheriness in **99**, neatly built around firm structure of tannin/acid, finishing rather green. 6 mths Fr oak. 500 cases. **Kiddush** **NV** Sacramental wine from cinsaut; softly fruity; well-calculated acidity keeps from being over-cloying despite 100 g/ℓ sugar, lowish alc (11.5%). 3 500 cases. Latest **Dry Red** and **Dry White**, both **NV**, not available for tasting. — *TJ*

Kleine Zalze Wines

*Stellenbosch (see Stellenbosch map) • Tasting & sales Mon-Sat 9-5 Sun 11-4 incl public holidays except Good Fri, Easter Sun, Christmas Day & New Year's Day • Tasting fee R10 p/p refundable with purchases exceeding R50 • Cellar tours by appointment • Restaurant: Picnic platters/light lunches Mon-Sat 11.30-2.30 • Function/conference facilities • Playground for children • Wheelchair friendly • Proclaimed conservation area • Owners Kobus Basson & Jan Malan • Winemaker Willem Loots (since 1999) • Viticulturist Schalk du Toit & Jan Malan • Vineyards 280 ha • Production ±1 800 tons, 80 000 cases total (± 1 600 tons, 70 000 cases own label) 70% red 30% white • PO Box 12837 Die Boord Stellenbosch 7613 • **Tel (021) 880-0717** • Fax (021) 880-0716 • E-mail quality@kleinezalze.co.za • Website www.kleinezalze.com*

AFTER making a serious impact on some of the furthest corners of the international market, Kleine Zalze's wines are coming home. Until recently this family winery concentrated on supplying hotels, restaurants and wine stores as far afield as Poland and China. Now a new range – a red and a white – is being unpacked on local shelves. "We're aiming at the younger generation," remarks Kobus Basson, co-owner and legal-eagler (a designer golf course on the property, part of an upmarket housing and hospitality estate being further developed in conjunction with Spier, affords a different sort of eagling). Adding to the attractions are a country-style restaurant, guest lodgings and newly extended tasting room (which doubles as the clubhouse until permanent quarters in the Ritz Carlton are completed). Vinous allures include the Knorhoek range, made here for Kobus Basson's schoolmates Hansie and James van Niekerk. Fruit from their Simonsberg farm also finds its way into some of the KZ bottles below.

Vineyard Selection range

Cabernet Sauvignon Barrel Matured ✓ Pvsly reviewed, much awarded **8** drinking well, though still time to go. **99** lightly/elegantly structured. Riper **00**, altogether bigger (13.8 alc), more robust tannin. Mid-01 hiding fruit, flaunting wood; but persuasive persistence. 2 500 cases. These ex 6 ha block on KZ farm, 10 yrs old. Yr Fr wood, ±30% new.

Merlot Barrel Matured More of everything in **00** (KZ/Knorhoek vyds) than pvs: bigger, rounder, more assertive, firmer tannins. yr Fr oak. 13% alc. 900 cases. Oak dominates lightish mocha/plum cake character of **99**.

Pinotage Barrel Matured 00 deep velvety ruby; still very immature. Dusty woody nose; deep plummy flavours, big dry tannins, powerful alc (14.3%). Knorhoek fruit, yr oaked, 40% new Fr, 10% new Am. 4 500 cases.

Shiraz Barrel Matured Recent vintages not up to speed of pvs. **99** light, insubstantial. Much more powerful **00** savoury/spicy nose; big-bodied (14.3% alc), powerful tannins; finishes dusty, hard. Yr 30% new Fr, 10% Am oak. 1 500 cases.

Chardonnay Barrel Fermented ✓ **00** still very young mid-01; shy; citrus tones overbalanced by wood, massive 14.8% alc. 8 mths Fr oak. 1 200 cases. Woody finish on retasted **99** too; 'mere' 14% alc packs good fruity punch. Both gold at SAYWS.

Chenin Blanc Barrel Fermented ✓ **00** SAA retasted mid-01, coming into its own; deep honey/orange peel notes, fresh acidity, power (14% alc), good dry length, integrated Fr wood (6 mths). Knorhoek fruit. 800 cases.

Kleine Zalze range

Cabernet Sauvignon ✓ Loudly applauded **98** still unpretentiously charming; lightly wooded/structured. WOM Value. **00** deeper, riper, richer. Already tasty, though time to go; balanced despite big 14.2% alc (fruit ex Wellington); savoury acidity. Partially old-oaked. 6 000 cases. No **99**.

Gamay Noir ☻ Light and bright red **01** custom made for an elegant picnic. Mouthwatering red berries to taste. Well structured, unwooded. 7 000 cases. **Chenin Blanc Bush Vine** ☻ Immediately/powerfully forthcoming **01**, unwooded, balanced and a great pleasure (though flavours disappear rapidly). Knorhoek vyd. 13.5% alc. 10 000 cases.

Merlot Good honest stuff. **99** lightly/elegantly structured; violets/pepper tones pointed by touch of wooding. Modest 12% alc. Grapes ex Knorhoek. 3 500 cases. **Pinotage** NEW Thoroughly tasty, unpretentious; very light wooding. **00** getting unfortunately big at 14.3% alc. Knorhoek farm fruit. 4 500 cases. **Chardonnay** Unwooded **00** shy, withdrawn; lurking lemony acid-drop flavour. Just off-dry, but acidic and short. 14% alc. Gold and trophy at SAYWS. 3 100 cases. **Sauvignon Blanc** **01** notch up on pvs. Sprightly, refreshingly tart (gooseberry tart, of course), flavour packed from first to crisp last. Knorhoek grapes. 12.6% alc. 3 500 cases.

Zed range NEW

Red ☻ Ripe and rustic pleasures sometimes come wrapped in purple plush, as in this **NV** cinsaut/ruby cab blend. Have fun – but beware the 14% alc. 6 500 cases. **White** ☻ Aroma/flavour in generous light-hearted abundance in this nicely balanced **NV** dry quaffer from grape-allsorts. 12.6% alc. 5 000 cases. — *TJ*

Klein Gustrouw Estate

Stellenbosch • Tasting, sales, cellar tours by appointment • BYO picnic • Facilities for children • Tourgroups • Walks • Views • Proclaimed conservation area • Owners Chris & Athalie McDonald • Winemaker/ viticulturist Chris McDonald • Vineyards 16 ha • Production 103 tons (23 tons, ±1 250 cases own label 100% red) • PO Box 6064 Stellenbosch 7612 • ***Tel/fax (021) 887-4556***

SUDDENLY the "little-known gem" of Jonkershoek isn't so obscure anymore. Owner Chris McDonald, who as recently as last year noted the estate's relative lack of visibility, now says Klein Gustrouw has been in the news a good deal, with honourable mention by wine writers in Britain and Australia as well as complimentary reports from SA columnists. Inquiries have been received from as far afield as the US and Russia, and export orders have been flowing in from Switzerland and their "devoted following" in the UK (80% of sales are to private homes). Self-taught McDonald believes the 1999 vintage is his best ever. We concur.

- ✵**Cabernet Sauvignon-Merlot** Classic Medoc-style red, increasingly more complex with every vintage. Fine spicing of cinnamon/caramel, elusive nutmeg hints in excellent **99**, 57/43 blend, 30% new Fr oak, 18 mths, remainder yr 2nd/ 3rd fill. Moderate 12.8% alc. **98** ✵ (and pvs) leaner; some cassis, but more minty/leafy notes. 63% cab. 13,3% alc. **96**, **97** VG. First was **93**. — *MF*

Klein Optenhorst see Claridge
Klein Simonsvlei see Niel Joubert

Kleinvallei Winery

Paarl • Not open to the public • Owner Piet van Schaik • Consulting winemaker Jean-Vincent Ridon (since Jan 2000) • Vineyards 3 ha • Production 9 tons 150 cases 100% red • PO Box 9060 Klein Drakenstein 7628 • ***Tel (021) 868-3662*** *• Fax (021) 868-3130*

IN a Franco-SA rapprochement, retired stock broker Piet van Schaik and consultant winemaker Jean-Vincent Ridon make this red-only range from van Schaik's three hectares in Paarl's Dal Josafat (Dale of Joseph). And if you're reaching for a map, instead simply think of nearby Nederburg and of in-the-news Boland Kelder, where the grapes traditionally went. Vino-passionate van Schaik is proud to be Dal Josafat's first boutique vintner, and while his vineyard make-up is presently anchored in hallowed tradition – cabernet and pinotage all Cape stalwarts – he's set to expand (to 10 ha) and digress into spicier realms with shiraz, petit verdot and malbec. Both he and Ridon (whose latest, potentially seminal project is to encourage and assist microboutiques like this one) are old world-inspired, and their aim is to "make superior and interesting red wines with an emphasis on local character and flavour".

Cabernet Sauvignon ✮ Pronounced, vibrant plum/cassis aromas lead into **00**, oaky nuance in bouquet much more evident in palate (100% new Fr wood), at present overwhelming fruit. Yr/2 should bring better integration. 14% alc. 200 cases. **Pinotage Primeur** Unfinished sample **01** shows emphasis on primary fruit (partial carbonic fermentation); youthful floral/estery bouquet; palate unexpectedly (but not unattractively) muscular; feisty. Provisionally rated ✮. 3 mths oaked. 13% alc. 30 cases. — *TM*

Klompzicht

Paarl • Not open to the public • Owner Francois Klomp • Viticulturist William Noel (since Apr 98) • Vineyards 20 ha • Production 90 tons 460 cases 100% red • PO Box 130 Franschhoek 7690 • ***Tel/fax (021) 864-0085*** *• Cell 082-603-5442 • E-mail fj-klomp@mweb.co.za*

Ex PRETORIA professional Francois Klomp so loves the Cape, he owns two chunks of it – this historic property (a subdivision of La Paris, founded in 1699), and a viewsite in the Bottelary Hills which he now calls home. Clambering up the Wemmershoek Mountains, with unusual vistas, plenty of ur-fynbos and a pine grove for company, these youthful 20 hectares of cabernet, merlot, pinotage and shiraz are tended by young man-of-the-earth (and sea – he's a stoked surfer and wind-surfer) William Noel, ex KwaZulu-Natal, who snappily switched from animal husbandry to viticulture when this 'greenfields' opportunity came knocking a few years ago. The boutique-quantity wines below were made at Môreson in Franschhoek and transferred to the maturation cellarette on Klompzicht (full blown vinification/ageing facilities scheduled for 2003; tasting room already in the works). The Shibula range shares its name with a game lodge owned by Francois Klomp, who breaks away from a highly successful consulting engineering practice to play squash and sojourn with the Big Five in his beloved Bushveld. See also Zoet en Rust.

Cabernet Sauvignon Sampled from barrel, as were all these, so provisionally rated; **00** deeply tinted but lighter in palate, reflecting relative youth of vyds; still closed mid-01; hints soft red berries, vanilla oak and toughish tannins, needing at least yr to soften. 14% alc. Possible ☆ on release, as is ... **Shiraz 00** still in thrall of tannins, fruit in hiding. Should unfold in yr/2.

Shibula range

Cabernet Sauvignon Earlier maturing than above but well constructed, if uncomplex. **00** slightly minty, softly berry-fruited. Retains some composure in face of towering alc. ☆ on current form. **Shiraz** More multi-dimensional than any here, potential for eventual ☆ rating. **00** dominated by wood tannins; needs min yr for smoky cherry/plum fruit to assert itself. All above maturing in Fr oak (Taransaud cooperage); power alcs 14-14.5%; 42 cases. — *CF*

Kloofzicht Estate

Tulbagh • Owners John and Beverley Parr • PO Box 101 Tulbagh 6820 • ***Tel/ fax (023) 230-0658*** *• E-mail bevparr@icon.co.za*

"IT'S BEEN HARDCORE," says Roger Fehlmann, borrowing a word from his son's lexicon to encapsulate their years on this quirky farm. "Lots of laughter, lots of tears ... " Now he and partner Sharon are heading off for vineyards greener. Commuting Johannesburg couple John and Beverley Parr (he a filmmaker, she a graphic designer) have purchased this Tulbagh property and embarked on a major life shift. They intend developing Kloofzicht's signature red Alter Ego into a premium Cape blend, to be marketed in the next year or two. New plantings will also yield an organic range in time.

Kloovenburg

Riebeekberg (see Swartland map) • Tasting & sales Mon-Fri 9-4.30 Sat 9-2 • Owner Pieter du Toit • Winemaker Pieter du Toit • Vineyard manager Pieter du Toit • Vineyards 130 ha • Production 2 600 cases 70% red 30% white • PO Box 2 Riebeek Kasteel 7307 • ***Tel (022) 448-1635*** *• Fax (022) 448-1035 • E-mail kloovenburg@mbury.new.co.za*

A WHITE STONE WALL encircles this old Riebeek family farm, guarded by a four-legged Chardonnay. The du Toits sell most of their 1 000 tons to the local co-op, but they hold back some of the best, including pinotage, to vinify in their newly completed cellar. Since reviving winemaking with "a whole family-pressed shiraz" in 1997, the du Toits have established a growing export market in the UK and the Netherlands. Owner/winemaker Pieter du Toit is delighted with the early showing of his maiden Cabernet, to be released this year. Beyond wine, visitors are welcome to taste and buy varied produce from the olive groves, including the valley's first locally pressed olive oil.

Shiraz ✓ Harmonious and restrained, with infinitely nuanced aromas of nutmeg, pink pepper and cloves. **99** cedary, sniffs of Chinese five spice; sweet (4,1g/ℓ sugar); caramel notes from 14 mths 2nd fill US oak. **98** equally exotic, drier but no less supple. 1 000 cases.

Chardonnay Barrel-fermented, tropical. **01** grapefruit/pineapple aromas, citrus/butterscotch flamboyance; bold almost brash textures; somewhat sweet (4,4 g/ℓ sugar). 1 000 cases. At 13%, less spiritous than pvs 14% blockbuster, though both surprisingly fine; no malo to ensure greater elegance.

Pinotage ★ Easy-drinking soft-fruit style, from 30 yr old vyds. Some toasted almond, sweet vanilla (from Am oak) more evident in richer – though finer – **98**. 650 cases. More forward than herbal/mint-toned unwooded **99**. — *MF*

Knorhoek

Stellenbosch (see Stellenbosch map) • Tasting & sales Mon-Fri 10-4 Sat 10-1 • Cellar tours by appointment • Meals/refreshments for groups by arrangement • Guest house (accommodates 16) with small conference/function/entertainment area • Facilities for children Tel (021) 882-2114 • Tourgroups • Views • Wheelchair-friendly • Owners Hansie & James van Niekerk • Winemaker Willem Loots and his team at Kleine Zalze cellars • Viticulturist James van Niekerk with Corius Visser • Vineyards ± 100 ha • Production ± 800 tons (60 tons, ± 5 000 cases own label) 50/50 red/white • PO Box 2 Koelenhof 7605 • ***Tel/fax (021) 882-2627*** *• E-mail hansie@knorhoek.co.za • Website www.knorhoek.co.za*

"Beyers Truter and Johan Malan nagged us for years to start bottling Knorhoek wines," say Hansie and James van Niekerk, brothers and co-owners of 'The place where the lions growl'. Now there's no stopping them. They've just added some 32 ha of noble reds to their elevated Simonsberg vineyards, and this year they're taking in the first fruit from several young blocks, making it more necessary than ever to find a permanent production space. At present their wine is being made in the Kleine Zalze cellar by an old school friend, Kobus Basson. There's been a change in the production team with the arrival of Elsenburg-groomed Corius Visser, who takes over from Morné Kruger as viticulturist. Also promising is the first harvest from new cool climate vineyards near Cape Agulhas, established in partnership with Kleine Zalze.

Cabernet Sauvignon In its first (**97** ★★★★, VVG, *Wine* ★★★★) outing, this Simonsberg cab vaulted over the heads of many to steal the limelight locally and overseas. Follow-up **98**, back-tasted mid 01, meaty, quite developed aromas; mineral/nutty nuances, whiffs wild mushrooms distinguish this vintage from the more berry fruited **00**, though both have hints cassis, black cherry, subtle vanilla from 12 mths Fr cask ageing. No **99**.

Pinotage 98 ripening in bottle; gamey, herbal aromas, undergrowth scents melded into cloves, fruitcake, plump loganberry jam; unusual, attractive blend of earthy/fruity flavours. 12 mths oak, 50% new, 10% Am. **00** ★ barrel preview shows more herbal/eucalyptus tones. No **99**.

Sauvignon Blanc ★ **01** from tank reveals ample green fig, herbaceous aromas, delicate whiffs gooseberry, peach, lime/grapefruit; Loire-like finish. Finer than more austere **99**. 12,6% alc. 500 cases. — *MF*

Koelenhof Winery

Stellenbosch (see Stellenbosch map) • Tasting & sales Mon-Thu 8.30-1; 2-5 Fri 8.30-1; 2-4.30 Sat 8.30-12.30 • Self-catering picnics (deli nearby) • Owners 75 shareholders • Manager Helmie de Vries (since 1969) • Winemakers Andrew *de Vries (since 1997), Wilhelm de Vries (since 2001) • Production 12 000 tons (4 000-5 000 cases own label) 69% white 30% red 1% rosé • PO Box 1 Koelenhof 7605 • **Tel (021) 882-2020/1** • Fax (021) 882-2796 (to change sometime to **Tel (021) 856-2020/1** Fax (021) 856-2796) • E-mail koelwyn@mweb.co.za*

One of the oldest wine-collectives in the country, Koelenhof celebrated its 60th anniversary in 2001 with several dramatic changes. It's now registered as a company with 75 shareholders, formerly the co-op members. Indeed, it's becoming almost a family business since Wilhelm de Vries, son of manager Helmie de Vries, takes over as red-wine maker following the departure of Louw Engelbrecht for Distell. Sibling Andrew de Vries continues to look after the white wines. One of the first things this team plans for the company's future is to shift the emphasis from white to red wines. Their celebratory Koelenhof '60' is a milestone on this brave new track.

Merlot Gets super-serious in **99**, with 15% cab stiffening, oaked 14 mths new Fr barriques (cab portion 2nd fill Am). Powerful blackcurrant aromas; creamy vanilla tones in delicious, seamless palate. Good now but better in 2-3 yrs. 270 cases from Koelenhof farm Nooitgedacht. First release **98** Wine ripening in bottle; velvet colour to match smooth blackberry, cherry fruit.

Cabernet Sauvignon 99 with dollop cinsaut, oaked 14 mths Nadalie casks, Am/Fr (75/25), imparting spicy perfume to plushy black fruits. 250 cases.

Sauvignon Blanc NEW ✓ Statement **01** with bulging figgy nose, taut citrus/fig flavours and bright mouthwatering finish. At ±R17/bottle, worth driving here from Gauteng. Be sure to drink soon. 11.9% alc.

Pinotage Rosé ☻ This cellar's calling card charms with strawberry Jello tastes in **01**, lots of (natural) sweetness, usual lowish alc (11%). 490 cases. **Sparkling Sec** ☻ Delicate, bright carbonated sparkle, refreshingly semi-dry. **NV**.

Pinotage Lavish oak treatment for **00** (8 mths 2nd fill Seguin Moreau/Nadalie barriques), with 15% cab, notch up from pvs. Sweet fruited, round, pleasantly sour farewell. 13,5% alc. Just 290 cases. **Koelenhof '60'** Traditional Cape cuvee cab/cinsaut to celebrate winery's 60th. Old-Cape style, appropriately. **99** ripe, almost porty, somewhat volatile; very nostagic. Oak aged. 13.3% alc. 225 cases. **Koelenberg** Cab-merlot blend not retasted for this ed. Pvs **99**. **Cinsaut-Shiraz** Cotes du Rhone feel, **00** 80/20 blend, savoury spicy tones. 500 cases. **Koelenhoffer** Cellar's perennial top seller. Lightish, semi-dry blend sauvignon, chenin (70/30). Supple fruited **01** touch terpene/cinnamon spice. Also 1 000 ml screwcap. Good beach party fare. 600 cases. **Koelenkeur** Bukettraube in billowing, mellifluous mood, to enjoy young and fresh. Semi-sweet **01** talcum perfume, twist of grapefruit. Lightish alc, low acid. 270 cases. **Koelnektar** 100% gewürz, Natural Sweet style **01**; fragile floral, spicy bouquet; soft rosewater flavours; med-bodied. ±600 cases. **Sparkling Sec** NEW Explosive semi-dry **NV** (01) from sauvignon; bracing herbal whiffs; guaranteed to pep the most jaded palate. Lowish 11.5% alc. **Hanepoot** Traditional style **00**, unsubtle marmalade/summer-blossom qualities; powerfully sweet with rhubarb tang; lowish 16.4% alc. 200 cases. — *TM*

Koningshof see Avondvrede
Koopmanskloof see Vinfruco
Kosher see Kleine Draken

Kranskop NEW

*Robertson • Not open to the public • Owner/winemaker/viticulturist Nakkie Smit • Vineyards 35 ha • Production 700 cases 100% red • PO Box 18 Klaasvoogds 6707 • **Tel/fax (023) 626-3200***

CURRENTLY roosting in barrels, the elegant red wines of this family property in Robertson's Klaasvoogds area are set for release sometime this year. Previously all the grapes went incognito under the labels of Graham Beck and Ashton Co-op, but in 2001 owner (and keen golfer) Nakkie Smit held back some cabernet, merlot and shiraz to vinify in a converted boatshed (with expansive views). Though Elsenburg-trained and thoroughly at home in the cool, stony vineyards, Smit has never had a turn in the cellar. But with help from Jean Daneel and other seasoned hands, he's "being very disciplined and doing everything by the book", including waking up in the middle of the night to check on his fermenting 'babies'. Which had wife Helena harrumphing: "You didn't even do that for your real kids!"

Kumala see Western Wines
Kumkani see Stellenbosch Vineyards

Kupferberger Auslese

POPULAR, consistent lightish semi-sweet by Distell. **NV** ☆ Little connection with German Auslese wines, but pleasant blend chenin, dollop riesling for early/easy drinking. 12% alc. (Note, rating, from pvs ed).

KWV International

Paarl (see Paarl map) • Tasting & sales Mon-Sun 9-4.30 in Wine Centre • Cellar tours Paarl 10, 10.15 (German), 10.30 & 14.15 Tourgroups by appointment Tel 807-3007/8 Fax 807-3119 • Coffee bar for light meals/coffees • Cellar tours Worcester Brandy Cellar by appointment Tel (023) 342-0255 • Gifts • Owner KWV Group • Chief cellarmaster Sterik de Wet • Assistant cellarmasters Ian Nieuwoudt (white wines) & Thys Loubser (red wines) • Viticulturist/grape buyer Chris Albertyn • PO Box 528 Suider-Paarl 7624 • ***Tel (021) 807-3900*** *• Fax (021) 807-3349 • E-mail kwvinternational@kwv.co.za • Website www.kwv-international.com*

THIS GIANT export-focused winery is in the very safe hands of KWV stalwart Sterik de Wet, who's taken over as chief cellarmaster from Kosie Möller (now at Devon Hill). Möller can take much of the credit for giving the ranges – and KWV's image – some much-needed pizzazz. And the pace of change is likely to increase under the new driver. "We plan to double our wine sales in the next four years," he says. "A firm base has been established to produce wines that suit global consumer tastes." Each of the main brands is produced with a specific market in mind and, in line with the best cellars everywhere, the team is concentrating on obtaining the specific grapes required for each style. "We're applying state-of-the-art oenological practices to ensure that wines can develop their full potential," Sterik assures. The company recently launched its biggest ever brand-awareness campaign in order to consolidate its share of the international market.

Cathedral Cellar range

The flagship, named after the KWV's vast, domed cellar built in 1930 and now a tourist attraction – it's lined with avenues of massive vats featuring in carved form the history of winemaking in South Africa.

☆☆☆ **Cabernet Sauvignon** These cabs heaped with praise: **96** SAA, **95** VVG, SAA trophy, Concours Mondial gold, best wine at 1998 Sélections Mondiales, Canada. **94** VVG, overall champion red Ljubljana, Slovenia etc. **97** came in 2 versions (part of terroir experiment): **Paarl** more open, approachable, balanced with generous choc/mulberry tastes. **Stellenbosch** demonstrably tighter, more 'serious' with firmer tannins for long-term cellaring. Latest **98** underlying gaminess rather than cassis; whiffs lead-pencil from massive 26 mths new oak; palate concentrated but still lean, taut mid-01 with assertive tannin structure. Demands plenty of time and should cellar well (10+ yrs). Gold at Vinalies show. 13.1% alc. 6 200 cases.

Merlot Vivid contrast between **96** and **97** vintages; former silky, luscious in youth, **97** SAA, 26 mths 100% new Fr casks, tauter, needing further maturation. Potentially betters standout **95** VG, SAA, best merlot at 1998 IWSC, Air France trophy. Latest **98** outstanding. Thumbprint choc-plum richness, minty wafts in elegant, well modulated form. Ambitious 26 mths oak properly a fragrant background note. Delicious now with plenty of pleasure in store. 13.5% alc. 2 700 cases.

Pinotage Critically acclaimed label (VVG, SAA, ABSA Top Ten, golds at Michelangelo, IWC etc) Best of recent vintages undoubtedly **97**, enormous wine with wood supercharge (26 mths Fr oak, 100% new); formidable, front-of-mouth-coating tannins to blackcurrant fruit density. Pungent, high-toned, in line with cooler growing season. Warmer **98** vintage fuller, rounder, fewer strident top-notes; raspberry/strawberry fruit very well integrated with spicy oak. 18 mths oaked. 13.7% alc. 3 700 cases. Bears comparison with more accessible, lighter, **96**.

Shiraz Third-release **98** more classically styled than pvs; open peppery/smoky aromatics to black-cherry, plum-pudding flavours in rich, complex palate; super-soft tannins for instant approachability. Vinalies competition gold. 2 yrs 50/50 Fr/Am casks. 3 700 cases. Total contrast with cool-vintage **97** VVG, SAA, initially closed nose, undeveloped grippy palate needing min 5 yrs.

Triptych Formula change from bdx blend to cab, merlot, shiraz since **97** SAA. Firm cab backbone finely polished by merlot's sleekness. Very smooth, complex; excellent potential for bottle development. Follow-up **98** same varieties, oaking (100% new Fr casks, 26 mths), presently most ungenerous of these 98 reds; meaty/gamey heart sternly sheathed in savoury tannins; gorgeous array of smells (lead-pencils, cherries, mulberries), complex and subtle; will need many yrs to unfold, but will be stunning. Vinalies Gold. 12.9% alc. 1 500 cases.

Chardonnay Minimal malo sees pvs butterscotch/cream textural richness shift into somewhat crisper, zingier mode with lemon, lime fruit in sharper focus from **99**. This, below, gold at Vinalies. New-found zip continues in citrusy **00**, with butterscotch dimension present but deftly underplayed. Chardonnay du Monde. These 100% new Fr oak, 7-8 mths. 4 000 cases.

Sauvignon Blanc 98 VG flew with KLM; **99** changed tack (not totally convincingly) into herbaceous, grassy territory; finishing quick. **01** back on course with arresting bouquet of cut grass, asparagus, green fig; palate slightly less riveting mid-01, but pleasantly crisp-finishing, easy.

Port Cross-over style: sweet a la the old Cape (131 g/ℓ sugar); big alc as in Portugal (19.3%). Immensely rich, dark fruits and choc in **95**, from tinta. 2 yrs barrique-aged. 250 cases, mid-01 still brooding in KWV's cellars with all hallmarks of a classic.

KWV range

Cabernet Sauvignon Maintains high standard considering enormous quantities (100 000 cases). Latest **99** more traditional, soft-tannined, well structured but not as attention grabbing as some pvs; lighter alc (12.7%). **98** also older-Cape, albeit with vintage fatness/ripeness to compensate. **97** more elegant, vinous.

Merlot Modern, assured **99** brims with soft raspberry/mulberry tastes; similar firm but ripe tannins, sound structure as **98**, several laps ahead of **97**, hamstrung by tough tannins. Yr oaked. 13.6% alc. 45 000 cases.

Shiraz Classic styling ups the wattage in **00**, generous varietal sniffs and ripe plum tastes, soft tannins, good persistence but youthfully undeveloped, so give plenty of time to grow. Yr oaked. 14% alc. 22 000 cases. **98** sensuously aromatic, ditto **99** with pleasant mid-palate sweetness from 8 mths mostly Am oak.

☆**Pinotage** Back on rousing form in **00**; full-flavoured, complex, intelligently oaked; good now and lots of potential. 13.9% alc. Yr oak. 100 000 cases. **99** ☆ metallic, finishing short.

☆**Roodeberg** After undergoing stunning transformation from clunky pickup truck to sleek coupé with **97**, **98** ☆, both blends cab, merlot, shiraz, ruby cab, latest **99** harks back to the old Roodeberg in lovely gamey notes, soft balanced savoury tannins which equally comfortable solo or at table; pinotage, cab f replace shiraz in this well-oaked cuvee; admirable quality considering the 100 000-case volume.

Chardonnay ☆ Fuller-style **00** showing some honeyed age in mid-palate; pleasing still but should not be kept hanging about. Barrel-fermented/aged 3 mths Fr oak. 12.7% alc. 65 000 cases. **Steen** ☆ 'Old Cape' name for chenin blanc used for this bone-dry version (grain sugar distinguishes Chenin below, both 100% varietal) **01** nice and fresh, some mango with crisp lemon finish. Easy drinking. 'Only' 9 000 cases. **Chenin Blanc** ☆ SA's biggest selling cork-closed export white wine: 277 000 cases! Med-bodied **01**'s dash sugar (5,8 g/ℓ) gives really nice rich mouthfeel to ripe guava flavour. **Sauvignon Blanc** ☆ **01** lightish, grassy, swiggably fresh dry white. More character than unwooded white stablemates. 29 000 cases.

Robert's Rock range

LIFESTYLE wines aimed at foreign 'wendis' (wine enthusiasts, no disposable income) in 25-35 year age group. Robert Gordon a military man and colourful figure of the early Cape who gave his name to one of the pearl-like rocks on Paarlberg. Labels below WO Western Cape.

☆**Cabernet Sauvignon-Merlot** Lightly oaked **98** ☆ fairly firmly structured yet strong fruity presence, choc-cherry tastes in good long dry finish. 65/35 ratio. Next-up **00** well-judged combination, showcasing varieties' strengths; still quite tight, yr should do the trick. 12.5% alc. 50 000 cases.

☆**Shiraz-Malbec** Shiraz has upper hand in **00**, with gamey/red-berry tastes and soft tannins; deserves yr min for flavour spectrum to broaden. 8 222 cases. 8 mths oaked. 13.2% alc. **99**, 58/42 fusion, vibrantly fruity.

☆**Pinotage-Pinot Noir** Unusual and attractive combo; **00** round and, though light-bodied, full-flavoured; soft; ripe raspberry and beetroot tones. 2 765 cases oaked 12 mths. Pvs **98** ☆ not as successful.

☆**Chardonnay-Semillon** Unoaked **01** ☆ tasted young, still an awkward marriage but should meld with bit of time. 13% alc. 33 000 cases. **00** chardonnay portion briefly oaked for creamy finish; semillon gives savoury lime/mineral character. Can safely keep couple of yrs.

Chenin Blanc-Chardonnay ☆ Charming drink-soon everyday wine. Clever blending brings out best of both varieties in youthfully green-flecked **01**. 55 000 cases. Unfiltered.

Pearly Bay range

Cape White ☆ Straightforward everyday dry quaff; to drink soon. 170 000 cases of unwooded steen. **NV**.

KWV Fortified range

☆**KWV Maatskappywordings Vintage Port 97** marks KWV's conversion from co-op to company; 1999 SAA 'port' trophy winner; full-bodied (18.5% alc), grippy, relatively dry (102 g/ℓ sugar) blend tinta/souzao. Theatrical black depths; complex, concentrated plum, cherry fruit, some souzao minty scents which freshen, help prevent cloy; dry finish. 10+ yrs life ahead. 1 200 cases.

☆**Port** LBV style making a serious statement on its first **99** outing; cinsaut/souzao, high alc (19,5%), moderate sugar (110 g/ℓ), strapping tannin structure for keeping. Now showing sweet-violets aromas over concentrated, plums, blackcurrant/blackberry tastes, ending fairly dry; quite raw still, spirit free standing; should harmonise and improve, given 4-5 yrs. 2 500 cases.

Full Tawny Port Classic nutty nose, wonderfully balanced, soft yet lively and delicious; everything a tawny should be. Tinta, souzao aged 5-8 yrs old oak, 19,3% alc, 120 g/ℓ sugar. 5 600 cases.

Full Ruby Port Concentrated soft fruit, cherries and ripe plums in this generous **NV**; fairly dry tasting despite 131 g/ℓ sugar; tinta/souzao. 19,3% alc. 800 cases. — *CF*

Laborie Estate

Paarl (see Paarl map) • Tasting & sales Mon-Fri 9-5 Sat 9-1 (winter) Sat/Sun 9-5 (summer) Tasting fee R7 p/p • Cellar tours by appointment • Restaurant & Wine House • Picnic baskets (24 hours' notice required) • Scenic walks • Wheelchair-friendly • Owner KWV International • Winemaker Gideon Theron (since 1994) • Viticulturist Henri van Rheenen (since 1998 • Production 35 000 cases 70% red 30% white • PO Box 528 Suider-Paarl 7624 • ***Tel (021) 807-3390*** *• Fax (021) 863-1955 • E-mail therongi@kwv.co.za • Website www.kwv-international.co.za*

Two NEW varieties, shiraz and viognier, have come into production at this attractive KWV-owned estate with its beautifully preserved two-century-old Cape-Dutch manor house, and should be a feature of the cellar's wine list in due course. The popular Cape-style restaurant is under new management and several interesting traditional dishes have been added to the menu. An equally pleasurable option is to book a picnic basket to take on your lunch-time ramble through the vineyards on the slopes of Paarl Mountain. Laborie offers an attractive way of getting right into the heart of a Cape wine farm.

Cabernet Sauvignon ✓ Label with new-found verve. Open, generous texture, juicy sweet fruit and velvety finish gently contained by accessible tannins. Current **00** cedary, rich; generous blackberry tastes. Yr new/2nd fill Fr oak. 13.7% alc. 2 700 cases. **98** SAA continues upward course set by **96**, **97** *Wine*.

Merlot ✓ Persistent red fruit combines with nice grip of oak tannin and chocolatey mid-palate in latest **99**; definitely drinkable now, but probably better with ±2 yrs' softening. Oak as above. 13.1% alc. 3 000 cases. **00** preview approaching quality of Cab above: delicious ripe plum-pudding, caramel fruit; dense but beautifully packed tannins.

Merlot-Cabernet Sauvignon Bin 88 60/40 blend, yr Fr oaked. **00** (sample) more structured than pvs; firmer (but balanced) tannins carrying ripe black/red berries; give yr to settle while drinking good and ready **99**.

Chardonnay Well proportioned **00** partially barrel-fermented, which shows in subtle creamy/toasty nuances pervading pleasantly firm, not too rich body; cleverly oaked; good now and for 2-3 yrs. 4 mths small oak. 13.4% alc. 3 000 cases. Fat, flavoursome **98** upscale from **97** WOM selection.

MCC ✓ Highly rated brut, always chardonnay, pinot noir, plenty of character from ±3 yrs on lees. Latest **96** 80/20 blend showing hint black-grape savouriness, freshly-made toast; fine creamy bubbles. Seriously tasty now, potential for good bottle ageing. 2 000 cases. **95** with curious yeast/ice-cream flavour combo. More accessible than **94**, which more ageworthy. Alcs around 12%.

Pineau de Laborie ✓ Luxurious, rich dessert in Cognac tradition (grape juice fortified with spirit) – uniquely South African: made with pinotage (single vyd selection, oak-aged) with backbone of potstill brandy from pinotage. Sugars (±90 g/ℓ) not too high for comfortable solo sipping or, after dinner, with dessert or cheese. **97** in long-necked 375 ml bottle with pinotage-purple label. **98** more 'port'-like, just a shade less interesting, satisfying. 17.5% alc. 5 600 cases.

Pinotage Firmer-style **98** seemed very tired mid-01. 13% alc. 2 900 cases. **Sauvignon Blanc** **01** (sample) improves on pvs; grass/gooseberry refreshment;

full-flavoured. Easy drinking despite piercing 7.5 g/ℓ acid. 13.1% alc. 2 300 cases. **Blanc de Noir** ☆ Bottle-fermented dry sparkler from pinot noir, splashes pinot gris, pinotage. Charcuterie and smoke in food-friendly **98**; fine rose-petally mousse. Lightish 11,4% alc. 6 500 cases. Note: Granite Creek export range not tasted for this ed. — *JN*

La Bri

Franschhoek • Tasting & sales at Franschhoek Vineyards (see that entry) • Owner Robin Hamilton • Winemaker Deon Truter (Franschhoek Vineyards), Jean Daneel (consultant) • Vineyards 18 ha • Production 130 tons 60% white 40% red • PO Box 180 Franschhoek 7690 • ***Tel (021) 876-2593*** *• Fax (021) 876-3197 • E-mail info@la-bri.co.za • Website www.la-bri.co.za*

Sweeping in to help this exquisite Franschhoek property stay on target is wine deity and keen-eyed archer Jean Daneel (stalwart Deon Truter of Franschhoek Vineyards continues to make the wines at the FV cellar nearby). "Jean's valued inputs are already proving of great benefit to the quality of La Bri's wines," marvels the owner of these 18 mountain-ringed hectares, Robin Hamilton. Replanting with a higher proportion of black grapes is now complete, and the team looks forward to emulate the success of their bordeaux blend with other red varieties and styles. First in line is a Limited Release Cabernet Sauvignon 1999 (not ready for tasting at press time). Meanwhile the signature whites aren't being neglected. Now in the range are two limited releases, a Chardonnay and a Semillon, the latter from century-old bushvines.

Cabernet-Merlot Reserve ☆ Plummy, spicy dustiness to sniff in (yr) Fr oak-matured **99**; more cassis in a slightly too acidic palate. WOM Value (as were **98**, **97**). 13% alc. 3 000 cases. **Chardonnay Reserve** NEW ☆ Oak-fermented **99** hints at butterscotch/limes; genuinely dry, refreshing palate much lighter than 14% alc would suggest; finishes touch woody, acidic. 500 cases. **Chardonnay** Fr barrique-fermented/aged. Latest is **01**. It and pvs **99** untasted. 550 cases. **Sauvage la Bri** Unoaked sauvignon. **01** not ready for tasting. 1 500 cases. Pvs **99** ☆. **Semillon** Oak-fermented **01** not ready for tasting. Pvs **99** ☆. 500 cases. Discontinued: **Chardonnay-Semillon** Pvs **98** ☆. — *TJ*

La Cotte see Franschhoek Vineyards

La Couronne

Franschhoek (see Franschhoek map) • Tasting & sales daily 10-3 • Cellar tours by appointment • Continental restaurant (see Eat-out section) Picnics Nov-Apr • Luxury hotel • Tourgroups • Gifts • Conferences • Walks • Mountain biking • Views • Winemaker Miles Oates • Viticulturist Sakkie Daniels • Vineyards 15 ha • Production 80 tons 6 000 cases 80% red 20% white • PO Box 448 Franschhoek 7690 • ***Tel (021) 876-2770*** *• Fax (021) 876-3788 • E-mail winery@lacouronnehotel.co.za • Website www.lacouronnehotel.co.za*

Just like the name of their flagship, Ménage à Trois, this upmarket Franschhoek spread is a threesome of cuisine (SFW Food & Wine Competition winner in 2000), accommodation and wine. The latter is now personally crafted by the owner, ex Gauteng financial whizz Miles Oates. Encouraged by the success of an early experiment at making 'chateau le garage' at home a few years ago, he's running his own show in the refurbished cellar – and loving it. In the vineyard, additional merlot and cabernet are taking root alongside the first 4 hectares of shiraz, the goal being to raise overall production from the present 80 tons to an eventual 180. Most of the wines are exported to Europe, where they are well received – an appearance on the winelist at Wimbledon being a particular smash.

Ménage à Trois Blend 65% cab, 20% merlot, 15% cab f. **99** back-tasted mid-01 not showing initial starry form, now closer to ☆ on evidence of austere herbal tannins to the distinctive minty notes, gamey bouillon aromas, leafy tones. 1 000 cases aged 17 mths in 1st-3rd fill barrels.

Merlot Pvs was **99**. Lighter toned than many Cape examples, lightly-oaked; accessibly red-fruited. **00** not ready for tasting.

Chardonnay 99 soft, sweet vanilla oak, ripe pineapple/mango fruit for easy drinkability (though strapping 14% alc needs watching). **00** ☆ tropical cantaloupe aromas, butterscotch, oak, vanilla, mouthfilling leesy layerings, restrained lime-citrus finish. 13% alc. 50/50 tank/new Fr oak-fermented/matured. 1 000 cases.

Cabernet Sauvignon 99 ☆ shows cassis layered with notes of mint/eucalyptus. Extensive oaking (18 mths 90% new Fr casks) adds creamy textures to the black fruit/nutmeg finish. **Sauvignon Blanc** ☆ **00** food-friendly, undramatic but showing soft ripe-melon aromas, damp grass, hints of baked apple; easy-drinking and gentle. 1 000 cases. Not retasted: **Sauvignon Blanc-Chardonnay** Pvs **99** ☆. — *MF*

Ladismith Co-op Winery & Distillery

*Little Karoo (see Little Karoo map) • Tasting & sales Mon-Fri 9-1; 2-5 • Owners 95 members • Winemaker André Simonis (since 1992) • Production 9 000 tons • PO Box 56 Ladismith 6655 • **Tel (028) 551-1042** • Fax (028) 551-1930*

A GREEN WINE (not literally, of course, but eco-mindedly made, in line with the global trend) debuted in 2001 below the 'cloven' Towerkop peak, which gives its name to the small range made by stalwart André Simonis. "It's a Sauvignon," reports the winemaker, uncharacteristically in conversational mode (so we'll keep quoting him while we can), "and there are only 450 cases available." Staying with wine, their wooded 2000 Chardonnay was a class winner at the Little Karoo Show, prompting smiles and the assurance that "2001's even better". In the distillery, recent large extensions are fully productive now. "We're buying about 1.6-million litres of distilling-wine," Simonis continues, "and while most of the distillate goes to a single customer, we're delighted that other markets are picking up too. These now account for about 200 000 litres."

Towerkop Chardonnay Wooded ☻ ☆ Subtly oaked **00**, peaches-and-cream textures; toasted hazelnuts acidity for nice firmish mouthfeel. 13.5% alc not too daunting. 500 cases.

Towerkop Ruby Cabernet 01 warm climate plummy fruit, fleshy tannin; pleasant everyday swig. 13.4% alc. 3 500 cases. **Green Wine** ☆ Ushers in eco-friendlier era for this cellar; grapes from single grower, free-run juice only; very delicate, fresh, lively; some floral aromas. 12.5% alc. **Towerkop Chardonnay Unwooded** ☆ **00** lighter quaffable style; limes in palate, lemony twist in tail. 300 cases. **Towerkop Chenin Blanc** and **Colombard 00**s tired now; wait for new vintages. **Towerkop Stein** ☆ Lovely supple summer drink, soft acidity; **01** drier than many. 1 500 cases. **Elandsberg** NEW ☆ Fiery glints in **NV** fortified red muscadel; exotic camphor whiffs, not too sweet; uncertified. 17.6% alc. 500 cases. — *IvH*

La Fontaine see Long Mountain

Laibach Vineyards

Stellenbosch (see Stellenbosch map) • Tasting & sales Mon-Fri 9-5 Sat 9-1 Tasting fee R5 p/p • Cellar tours by appointment • Picnic baskets during season (24 hours' notice required) • Views • Owners Laibach family • Winemakers

Stefan Dorst (since 1997) with Francois van Zyl (since 2000) • Viticulturist Michael Malherbe (since 1994) • Vineyards 40 ha • Production 240 tons 80% red 20% white • PO Box 7109 Stellenbosch 7599 • ***Tel (021) 884-4511*** *• Fax (021) 884-4848 • E-mail info@laibach.co.za • Website www.laibach.co.za*

GLOBAL pacesetters Loni and Friedrich Laibach, a retired German industrialist, flit between their home on the shores of Lake Lugano in Italy and their winery in the Cape (followed by their extended wineloving family, of course), which rubs shoulders with Warwick and Kanonkop in the oenologically overflowing Muldersvlei bowl. No gables at this minimalist and modern cellar which was recently extended; instead you'll find a unique jetty where you can sail away on awesome views over vineyards, as far as Table Mountain. Following the European swing towards a more natural approach, 6 hectares are going that way with organic wines to be produced in the next five years. Francois van Zyl is enthused by the prospect of a season in Spain under German winemaker Stefan Dorst, who consults at Venta d'Aubert in Aragon, and hopes to pick up more organic know-how. New vineyards are coming on board with particularly good merlot clones. In the meantime, sales are "almost too good, there's not enough wine" but otherwise they're an exceptionally happy and relaxed crew.

Cabernet Sauvignon These definitely not early maturers. Step-up **99**, retasted mid-01, beginning to relax and unfold but 3-4 yrs from ready. Sinewy, nearly austere, lengthy dry finish. 16 mths Fr oak. 13.5% alc. 1 500 cases. **98** very firm on release, needed good few yrs to relax.

Merlot Initially firm, rectilinear **99** retasted mid-01 ripening into truffly maturity; still has mulberry, choc-cherry tones, light minty wafts. Though perhaps shade too much oak for slender fruit. 13,5% alc. 1 500 cases. **98** more open, luxurious. These 14 mths Fr oak, none new.

Pinotage Speciality of the house, invariably brash, broad-shouldered. **97** ABSA Top Ten selection. **98** plummy, initial oak prominence in palate calling for patience. **99** slow-starting, needing few yrs. **00** back in full flight with excellent concentration of crushed plums, exciting balance of oak and edgy fruit; whiff pinotage ester. Big 14.5% alc. 10 mths new Fr oak, ±30% new. 2 300 cases.

Friedrich Laibach Impressive flagship, blend make-up varies with vintage. To date mostly bdx blends, merlot-powered in **98** with dash cab for complexity; softer, 'sweeter' than cellar's other reds from that yr, more initially approachable. Switches to cab-dominance in **99**, 88/12 blend with merlot; beautiful cedar fragrances from 75% new Fr oak; ripe cassis core, well proportioned; mouthwatering acid; structure for 5-7 yrs' maturation. Slightly marred by perceptible sweetness in finish (3.9 g/ℓ sugar). 18 mths oaked. 14% alc. 750 cases.

Cabernet Sauvignon-Merlot Splashy **97** debut with Air France laurel; followed by darker-toned, massive **98** (14% alc) with inky plum hues, dark/bitter choc tastes, thrusting tannins. Latest **99** more rough-woven than flagship above, abrasive tannins and dusty tobacco fruit need softening. 14 mths Fr oak, ±15% new. 13.5% alc. 2 250 cases. **Cabernet Sauvignon-Merlot Unfiltered** Not tasted for this ed. Last was **97**.

Natural Sweet ✓ Exciting modern **01**, very briefly barrelled in new Fr oak for roundness rather than oak character; not oversweet thanks to racy natural acidity, lowish sugar; lovely fresh-honey tastes and German-style low alc (8%; 10 g/ℓ acid, 103 g/ℓ sugar) though variety's not the Mosel's riesling, it's chenin. 500 cases of 375 ml. Will make way for NLH in botrytis years.

Cape Classic Dry Red ☻ **00** unwooded, light-bodied pizzeria wine; sweet fruit and dry finish. Jovial combo cinsaut, cab, merlot. 500 cases.

Chardonnay **00** will please fans of a more oaky style. Delicate lemony fruit (from young vyd) currently no match for 50% new-oaked portion (remainder unwooded); perhaps time will restore balance. 14% alc. 1 100 cases. **Chenin Blanc** ☆ **01** idiosyncratic lightly Fr-oaked semi-sweet version, custom-made for Belgian restaurant market. 13% alc. 500 cases. **Chenin Blanc** (unwooded) ★★ Grassy, melony textures in **01**, dryish finish. Grapes from Stbosch. 13% alc. 1 800 cases. Pvs also under Inkawu label for export. **Sauvignon Blanc** ★★ **01** in now established non-aggressive mode; smooth, generous, tasty. 13.5% alc. 1 500 cases. — *IvH*

Lammershoek Winery 

*Swartland (see Swartland map) • Tasting/sales & cellar tours Mon-Fri 9-5 Weekends & Public holidays by appointment Tasting fee R10 p/p Free if purchase exceeds R150 • Special house platter R20 p/p indoors/outdoors Mon-Fri 9-5 • Guesthouse by arrangement • Owners Paul & Anna Kretzel, Stephan family from Germany • Winemakers Markus Huber (2000 wines) Wachau, Austria and Shaun Turnbull (since Dec 2000) • Viticulturist Anna Kretzel • Vineyards 110 ha • Production 700 tons 11 000 cases 65% red 35% white • PO Box 597 Malmesbury 7299 • **Tel/Fax (022) 482-2835** • E-mail kretzelp@intekom.co.za • Website www.lammershoekwinery.co.za*

PEEPING out from chiefly co-op-supplying vineyards in the North Perdeberg area are the enterprising Kretzel family and their Elsenburg-trained winemaker Shaun Turnbull. Fourtysomething Paul Kretzel three years ago made an early leap "from an elevated position in the corporate world into winefarming", and he and equally sporty wife Anna (one of a handful of women viticulturists in the Cape) have thrown themselves into winegrowing with gusto (long-distance partners, the Stephan family, glued to the phone in Germany). Five of their seven hundred tons go to Perdeberg Co-op (and thence into high-profile bottles like Arniston Bay), and a good dollop to high-flyers Fairview and Spice Route. The balance now proudly wears the Lammershoek colours. Vintage 2000 was made by visiting Austrian eminence Markus Huber; US-seasoned Shaun Turnbull now cellarmasters full time. The ambience here may be cosmopolitan, but the wines are distinctly Swartland: big and generous, with extra piquancy from pockets of carignan and, soon, mourvèdre. We say: watch these characterful individuals.

☆**Cabernet Sauvignon-Merlot Barrique** ✓ Lots of ripe cassis/mulberry fruit in **00**, fleshy, spicy. Slightly bitter finish no doubt a youthful peccadillo. 18 mths Fr, Hungarian oak, none new. 67/33 blend (vs 50/50 for Reserve below). 13.5% alc. 300 (× 6, as are most of these) cases.

☆**Shiraz-Carignan** ✓ Dashes pinotage, **01** shiraz add interest to delicious, spicy **00**, 65/20 blend, seamlessly oaked 18 mths in 2nd fill casks. Comfy tannins for now-drinking (satisfying wine by the glass option). "Swartland perfect for Rhone style wines," enthuses Paul Kretzel.

☆**Chardonnay Barrique** ✓ **01** in extreme youth shows bold yellow peach/apricot/spicerack attractions; full malo regime will appeal to fans of lower acid styles; Californian clone; bunch-pressed, fermented, matured 6 mths 300 ℓ Fr oak, 25% new. 533 cases.

☆**Sauvignon Blanc** ✓ Early-picked (21°B, hence refreshingly lowish 12.5% alc) but not green; **01** passionfruit/papaya tastes, cooler leafier aromas. Zesty balanced finish. 333 cases.

☆**'Noble Late Harvest'** ✓ Tasted pre-certification, extraordinary **01** hárslevelü might be released as Natural Sweet; in reality a vin de paille, botrytised while raisining on straw mats. Fr old-oak-barrelled 6 mths; excellent varietal character, 7 g/ℓ acid controls the pungent sweetness. Just 133 cases likely to be swiftly snaffled. 375 ml.

Cabernet Sauvignon-Merlot Reserve ★★ The oak-staved version. Insistent tannins in **00** need time/rustic food. 13.3% alc. 2 058 cases. **Zinfandel** ★★ **00**'s splash tinta evident in tarry touch to mega-ripe pruney/curranty zin fruit; angular tannins should smooth in 2-3 yrs; Am oak 18 mths. 222 cases. **Chenin Blanc Barrique** ☆ Brave-new-world style: oak-fermented/matured off-dry; individual. **00** fat, ripe, discernibly sweet (11.2 g/ℓ acid) though seamlessly wooded; **01** (sample) similar; full malo again, which robs freshening acidity. 1 445/866 cases. **Riesling** ☆ Cape riesling, though spice/kerosene nuances hark to the Rhine. Lemon twist in **00** med-dry finish. Yachting wine, remarks Paul Kretzel. 200 cases. **Viognier** ☆ Fr oak-fermented, 6 mths sur lie; **01** infant rich, massive (14.8 alc%), citrus/pear rather than variety's usual apricot/peach (which you'll find in Chardonnay above!). Needs time to harmonise, grow (and gain extra star luminosity). 67 cases. **Vivant** ☆ Tasty dryish med-bodied sauvignon/Cape riesling blend, unwooded; **00** assertively tropical; crisp acidity from early picked fruit. 775 cases. — *IvH*

La Motte

Franschhoek (see Franschhoek map) • Tasting & sales Mon-Fri 9-4.30 Sat 9-12 Fee R5 p/p (groups larger than 10 by arrangement) • Tourgroups by arrangement • Views • Wheelchair-friendly • Owner Hanneli Koegelenberg • Winemaker Jacques Borman (since 1984) • Viticulturist Pietie le Roux (since 1987) • Vineyards 104 ha • Production 800 tons 25 000 cases own label 65% red 35% white • PO Box 94 Main Road Paarl 7622 • ***Tel (021) 876-3114*** *• Fax (021) 876-3446 • E-mail cellar@la-motte.co.za • Website www.la-motte.com*

This well-groomed thoroughbred in the upmarket Rupert family stable belongs to Hanneli Koegelenberg (née Rupert), SA's leading mezzo-soprano, whose husband Hein Koegelenberg orchestrates the business side, including negociant house Historic Wines of the Cape. French-influenced winemaker Jacques Borman has gained something of a reputation for blending wines. Now he has a new trick up his sleeve: La Motte has dropped the estate status and he's been taking a geographical leap in a new direction (well, several). Their long-distance vineyards in cool-climate Bot River (planted mainly to shiraz with smatterings of cabernet, sauvignon, petit verdot and semillon) are being seriously developed and they're contemplating buying in grapes from Darling/Malmesbury. This will broaden the flavour range considerably - and with Borman's assured touch it's bound to hit all the right notes. The thoroughly modern cellar will be tweaked to facilitate hands-on separate vinification of small tonnage from selected vineyards. "With all this technology, we're going right back to really old-fashioned hand-crafted methods," says an enormously entertained Borman, relishing a new challenge.

☆ **Cabernet Sauvignon** Slightly dusty note along with plentiful fruit in nose of latest **98**. Substantial, ripe-fruited; firm structure of tannin/acid; sweetish finish. 23 mths oak, 60% new, 10% Am. 13.2% alc. 2 000 cases. No **97**. **96**' lighter tones reflect difficult vintage.

☆ **Shiraz** Early Cape benchmark for now fashionable variety; still very attractive. Current **98** powerful (14% alc), ripe, rich, savoury; muscular tannin/acidity needs – deserves – time. 30 yr old mountain vyd; 19 mths mostly Fr oak, 40% new. 3 000 cases. **97** as always superb food wine.

☆ **Millennium** Characteristic mineral/violet elegance, restraint in **98** cab, merlot, 10% cab f. Too young to broach. 19 mths Fr oak, 40% new. 13% alc. 4 500 cases. **97** VG benefiting from bottle age; meaty undertones to black berry fruit. **96**, **95** ☆☆, former generously built for difficult vintage.

☆ **Chardonnay** Limited release, site-specific wine from 3 clones. Current **9**[illegible] characterful bouquet; creamy texture; confident, long savoury finish still hinting at yr Fr oak, 70% new. 13.2% alc. 1 000 cases. **98** ☆ less showy. **97** rich, creamy with toasted almond flavours.

★**Sauvignon Blanc 01** firm, fruity, weighty and lip-smacking; balanced, though slightly rasping finish evidences the high (13.8%) alc. 8 000 cases. Good range of fruity/herbaceous flavour in **00** ★.

Above also under Schoone Gevel label for Belgium. Discontinued: **La Motte Blanc Fumé** Pvs **00** ★; also Roosenveldt export label. — *TJ*

Landau du Val

Franschhoek (see Franschhoek map) • Tasting by appointment • Sales Mon-Fri 9-5 • Views • Owner Basil Landau • Winemaker Jean Daneel (sauvignon blanc), Karl Lambour (semillon) • Viticulturist Jaco Schwenke (since 1992) • Vineyards 17 ha • Production 200 tons (500 cases own label) • PO Box 104 Franschhoek 7690 • ***Tel (021) 876-2317*** *• Fax (021) 876-3369 • E-mail landau@mweb.co.za*

RETIRED industrialist Basil Landau reels in two big oenological fish, Bergkelder's six-foot-plenty Karl Lambour and free-ranging heavyweight Jean Daneel, to make the wines from Landau's 17 ha vineyard, La Brie, in Franschhoek. Devotees of the Sauvignon will find the 2000 under a different label. This is because the grapes were picked at the extreme of ripeness, yielding a delicious wine, packed with interesting characters – but, oddly, no varietally typical piddling felines or racy river beds. Just "lots of exotic fruit", shrugs Basil Landau. Hence the non-standard Reserve label for one of the more interesting wines of the new millennium.

★**Semillon** Introduced with **95** *Wine* ★; invariably broad-shouldered, buttery (from barrel maturation), smooth. Latest **00** ★ with ruby grapefruit piquancy to fat, warming palate (14% alc). Mid-01 sawdusty oak evident, needing time to integrate, evolve. Ancient vyd; miserly 700 cases.

★**Reserve 00** unblended sauvignon, picked overripe, reveals hidden pleasures; huge tropical fruit salad palate, swashbuckling 14% alc, zesty dry finish. Potential to develop interestingly over 4-6 yrs. Just 700 cases. Pvs labelled **Sauvignon Blanc**; first was **95**; pvsly tasted **99** also rated ★. — *DH*

Landsdowne see Arlington

Land's End Wines

Not open to the public • Winemaker Hein Koegelenberg • Viticulturist Tienie Wentzel • Vineyards 35 ha • Production 100 tons 50% white 50% red • PO Box 14 Paarl 7622 • ***Tel (021) 876-3119*** *• Fax (021) 876-3446*

ONE of the newest accessories on chic UK wine shelves is … a lighthouse. Not a real beacon, of course, but rather the shining light in the winegrowing firmament of Elim, a new appellation near Cape Agulhas, where the Indian and Atlantic Oceans meet. Unlocking the potential of these most southerly vineyards in Africa are seven "wine-lovers and pioneers", fronted by experienced cellarmaster Hein Koegelenberg (MD of La Motte, where the wines are made). They have 35 ha on three properties (to be cultivated organically in future). Sauvignon was the first to show its colours, which are coolly crisp, as you'd expect from an area climatically reminiscent of parts of New Zealand. Semillon, merlot and cabernet followed in 2001 ("Exceptional! Lots of upfront fruit!") and in due course they'll find their way into Anthony Lane-designed bottles (emblazoned with the ultimate cool-climate status symbol, the Agulhas lighthouse), and onto the tables of the sushi generation.

Sauvignon Blanc ★ **01**, with dollop semillon, eager tropical fruit, bubblegum aromas and flavour. Pleasantly light but mid-01 rather hollow and short. 3 600 cases. — *TJ*

Landskroon Estate 

Paarl (see Paarl map) • Tasting & sales Mon-Fri 8.30-5 Sat 9-1 • Cellar tours by appointment • Self-catering cottage • Play area for children • Gifts • Views • Permanent display of Stone Age artefacts • Owners Paul & Hugo de Villiers • Winemaker Paul de Villiers jnr (since 1980), with Kobie Viljoen (since 1999) • Vineyard manager Hugo de Villiers jnr (since 1995) • Vineyards 275 ha • Production 85% red 15% white • PO Box 519 Suider-Paarl 7624 • ***Tel (021) 863-1039*** *• Fax (021) 863-2810 • E-mail landskroon@mweb.co.za • Website www landskroonwines.com*

Not many Cape winemakers can claim a history of more than 300 years of unbroken wine tradition. Yet Landskroon's De Villiers family had been vignerons before the first of their kin to reach South Africa, Jacques de Villiers from Niort in France, arrived with the Huguenots in 1689. In 1874 the first Paul de Villiers began this Agter Paarl estate's voyage into wine. Today the ninth generation, with Paul de Villiers IV at the cellar's helm, stays the course. But there's certainly no napping below deck. They're expanding their fermentation capacity "to cope with all the red cultivars" and focusing their planting programme on cabernet and shiraz. The latter, believes vineyard-watch Hugo de Villiers, "is an outstanding variety, well suited to the soils and climatic conditions of our area. We now have 40 hectares – 15% of the total". Further corroboration of their confidence in the grape recently came via UK *Wine's* tasting of 75 SA shirazes – their 1998 sailed into the top 3.

★**Cabernet Sauvignon** ✓ Steadily improving label, buoyed by newer clones, expensive new oak. Transformation began with **97** SAA; **98** denser, riper. Latest **99** ★ most satisfying of these; classic claret style with sweet berry fruits, broad soft tannins. 5 clones; 10 mths 225 ℓ casks, some new. 3 000 cases.

★**Cabernet Sauvignon Reserve** Specially bottled for Tesco. All attributes of standard version, with extra brio, personality. Latest **99** minerals, lead-pencil oak sophistication. 13.5% alc. 3 000 cases. Bemedalled **98** all-new small Fr-oak aged; VG, voyaged with SAA, Blue Train.

★**Paul de Villiers Cabernet Sauvignon** NEW Limited 500 cases honouring estate's 19th century founder (see also Shiraz below). Distinct family resemblance to above; **99** fabulous minerally oak tones, rich red-berry textures. Selected grapes; 10 mths all-new Sylvain oak. 13.5% alc.

★**Cabernet Franc** Steps up into higher league with more elegant **00** (oak-staving very well executed), herbal snatches; tangy, very dry finish. 1 700 cases exclusively for WOM Value. **98** ★ plummier, peppery with fragrant tobacco sniffs. No **99**. 13% alc.

★**Merlot** ✓ **99** ★ upscale from pvs. Fleshier; better defined fruit backed by dulcet violet sniffs, sweet-charry oak. 9 mths barriques, 15% new. 3 170 cases. For ASDA UK. **98**, itself step beyond, ready; could go yr/2.

★**Shiraz** ✓ This label really sparking from **00** ★, more bounteous and focused than pvs; spice/oak background filled by sweet, firm tannins for 5-8 yrs' very good ageing. Am oak, 20% new. ±14% alc. 5 000 cases, some to Safeway UK. No **99**. **98** *Wine* ★.

★**Paul de Villiers Shiraz** NEW More concentrated version of above; partially Am barrel-fermented/aged, remainder Fr oak-matured 12 mths. **00** with herb/wild berry snatches and gorgeous spicy oak. Tannins forward but ripe; give 1-2 yrs then dip in for up to 12. Only 500 cases.

★**Cinsaut-Shiraz** More than a bit of Cotes-du-Rhone about **00**. Finer, fruitier than pvs; nice savoury tones, dry finish, food-cordial tannin. Could go 2-5 yrs. 13% alc. 11 500 oak-brushed cases fly off UK Safeway's shelves.

★**Morio Muscat Jerepico** ✓ **01** scintillating vintage; the now familiar oriental bazaar perfumes in amazing abundance. Endless finish is thrillingly brisk, clear no hint of cloy. 18,5% alc. 1 500 hugely underpriced cases. **99** richer, more velvety.

Port ✓ Desperately needs new apparel to match shimmering array of awards. Estate's policy of 2 concurrent releases means **96**, **97** available; latter fruitier, better balanced; more 'Portuguese' (93.1 g/ℓ sugar, 18.5% alc vs 98 g/ℓ, 18%). Diners Club, Air France, Peter Schultz Trophy triumphs. **96** (three different bottlings, released from Nov 97) VVG, SAYWS champ. 2 100/4 900 cases still ungreedily priced. These last to feature triumvirate tintas b/r, souzao (future to get turbocharge from top-of-line Port variety, touriga). Upcoming **99** VVG, runner up SAA trophy, WOM selection (as was 96).

Cinsaut ☻ ✯ Always a pleasure here. **00** quaffable oak-influenced allrounder; lightish feel (despite beefy 13,5% alc) so could even partner something from the sea. 2 200 cases. **Blanc de Noir** ☻ ✯ Pinot/pinotage (60/40) in **01** formula change; velvet texture; pops with perfumed fruit which smooth rather than sweet. 13% alc. 2 000 cases. **Chenin Blanc Dry** ☻ 3 **01** refreshing as always; limpid lemon tones, zesty dry. Med/full-bodied. Suggest enjoy soon. 1 850 cases. **Sauvignon Blanc** ☻ ✯ Not a shouter, but drinkyoung **01** offers gentle, food-friendly mouthfeel, bone-dry finish. 13.5% alc. 3 140 cases.

Pinotage ✯ These need time to come round. **99** still grippy mid-01; developing smoked/roasted sour-cherry character; full-bodied (13.5% alc). 8 mths small Fr oak. 6 350 cases. **Cabernet Franc-Merlot** ✯ Low-key early drinker, though not without charm, substance. **00** med-bodied. "Braai wine", says vintner, modestly. 1 800 cases. **Chardonnay** ✯ **01** oak-influenced (first-crop **00** not oaked), lighttoned (though big in alc – 13.5%), some muted hay overtones. Workmanlike. 970 cases. **Chenin Blanc Off-dry** ✯ Light-tripping, lemonadey **01** with prickle acidity finishes smooth rather than sweet. 1 380 cases. — *DH*

Landzicht Winery

Jacobsdal, Free State • Tasting, sales, cellar tours Mon-Fri 8.30-1; 2-5 Sat 8.30-12 • Fee dependant on meal, available on request • BYO picnic • Tourgroups • Views • Owners 45 members & Min Patrick Lekota • Winemakers Ian Sieg (since 1984) & Emden Viljoen (since 2001) • Viticulturist Dirk Malan • Vineyards 325 ha • Production 3 000 tons 231 000 cases (30 000 cases own label) 60% white 15% red 15% rosé 10% fortified • PO Box 94 Jacobsdal 8710 • ***Tel (053) 591-0164*** *• Fax (053) 591-0145 • E-mail landzicht@inext.co.za*

"THERE's nothing strange about this winery, only a grind of things daily," Ian Sieg claims. But there's nothing humdrum about their first Shiraz, made last year by assistant winemaker Emden Viljoen, ex Simonsvlei, in what they promptly declared her Virgin Vintage. They also opened channels to Japan and China, and upgraded the cellar – all to ensure they keep getting called to the winner's rostrum.

Cabernet Sauvignon ✓ Light, breezy style with matching subtle oak, undaunting alc; **01** ripely fruity, light earthy/smoky touches. 2 100 cases. Gear up from **00** ✯ with uncompromising tannic grip.

White Muscadel ✓ Nearby goldfields give their colour to lustrous fortified dessert, this cellar's medal-studded signature. Latest **00** penetratingly sweet, with muscat fragrance; endless length. 17,5% alc. 950 cases. "'Springbok' label very popular in hunting season," reports winemaker.

Shiraz NEW ✯ **01** pleasurable med-bodied, everyday drinking. 13.1% alc. 1 000 cases. **Chardonnay** Lightly wooded **01** not ready for tasting. Pvs **00** ✯. **Blanc de Blanc** ✯ Formula change to chardonnay, colombard, chenin in **00**; cellar-investments in stainless steel show in crisp and zesty tones. Med-bodied. 840 cases.

Rein Blüm Not tasted for this ed; pvs **NV** (00) ☆. **Blümchen** ☆ Natural Sweet **01** from colombard, hanepoot; low alc (8.5%) "for summer pool parties and barbecues". Non-cloying. **Rosenblümchen** ☆ Delicate salmon-pink rosé; "sister of Blümchen; very popular with the ladies!" Low alc (7,5%) Natural Sweet from pinotage, colombard, hanepoot; **01**, like pvs, with plenty of character. 1 100 cases. **Special Harvest** ☆ Well made light, naturally sweet tropical sipper; **01** hanepoot/chenin/colombard. 840 cases. **Red Jerepigo** ☆ Fortified dessert from cab/pinotage/ruby cab, nice whoosh of acidity keeps sweetness at bay. 700 cases. **NV** (01). 17,5% alc. **Red Muscadel** ☆ Sweet fortified dessert with sunset shades, jasmine scents; **NV** (01) full grapey sweetness ends briskly. 17,5% alc. 1 300 cases. **Hanepoot** All these fortifieds feature big-game labels; this one's a lumbering tusker but the wine's light-tripping. **NV** (01). 17.5% alc. 700 cases.

Merlot ☻ ☆ Bright sappy/plummy mouthful in **01**, light-toned and slurpable; zesty dry finish. 13,1% alc. 2 100 cases. **Pinotage** ☻ ☆ Lightly oaked **01** engagingly soft, juicy; lightish tone though not insubstantial 13% alc. 1 100 cases. **Gewürztraminer** ☻ ☆ "Divine," rhapsodises winemaker, and we agree. Talcum/jasmine headiness in **01**; sugar well controlled by fresh acid. Very moderate 11.7% alc. **Vin Doux** ☻ ☆ Lively melon/pineapple tastes in **00** semi-sweet carbonated sparkle; light and effortless poolside/party sipping. — *DH*

Langverwacht Co-op

Robertson (see Robertson map) • Tasting & sales Mon-Fri 8-12.30; 1.30-5 • Cellar tours by appointment • Owners 30 members • Manager/winemaker Johan Gerber (since 1986) • Viticultural consultants VinPro • Production ±10 500 tons (±1 500 tons own label) 85% white 15% red • PO Box 87 Bonnievale 6730 • ***Tel (023) 616-2815*** *• Fax (023) 616-3059*

"We're thinking of planting chenin!" announces Johan Gerber and, recognising that this is counter to almost every prevailing trend, the long-time cellarmaster hastens to explain: "There will always be a demand for good chenin, and you have to have it in the ground or you lose out to the next guy. We already have quite a bit, but you never know ... " Also big in their vineyards is trusty colombard, but sauvignon and chardonnay are rising fast. At present reds account for only 5% of the 30 members' production, but the portion is doubling this year and will continue to rise with the rooting of 5 hectares of merlot. Their new red wine cellar went on-line for the 2001 harvest, as planned, and the first experimental Cabernet and Shiraz were vinified. There's no telling, though, when the first reds will appear under the in-house label, which continues to represent but a fraction of the output. Plans are afoot however, to distribute the own-brand more widely. Meanwhile their budget-priced bottles are available from the cellar, The Wine Boutique at Ashton and Branewynsdraai Restaurant in Robertson.

Ruby Cabernet ☻ ☆ **00** still R10/bottle ex cellar, epitome of affordable early sip (massive 13.8% alc rules out epithet 'swig'). Undercurrents of woodsmoke/game to more obvious juicy extra-soft fruit. 650 cases.

Shiraz NEW **01** available, not ready for tasting. **Colombard** ☆ Drink-soon **01** picnic partner with semi-dry finish and lemongrass tang. 12,3% alc. **Colombard-Chardonnay** ☆ **01** complementary combo: chardonnay provides stuffing for colombard's fruit upholstery; slightly sweet finish. 280 cases. — *CF*

Lanzerac

UNDER a gentleman's agreement, the wines below are made by Distell while a separate range is grown on Stellenbosch's historic Lanzerac property, now owned by corporate titan Christo Wiese (see next entry). Distell holds the Lanzerac trademark, however, and distributes both ranges bearing this famous name. See also Stellenbosch Farmers' Winery for tasting and sales.

Pinotage World's first pinotage, 59 vintage (released in 61) still a benchmark of this local-hero variety. **98** riper, toastier, more 'modern' than pvs. Latest **99** starts promisingly with lovely hawthorn fragrance, sweet wild-berry fruits; runs into uncharacteristically dry tannins, snatch bitterness in finish.

Rosé Hugely popular semi-sweet **NV**, consistently charming and satisfying. Mainly chenin, with clairette blanche, pinotage. Serve well chilled. — *IvH*

Lanzerac Farm & Cellar

Stellenbosch (see Stellenbosch map) • Tasting & sales Mon-Fri 9-4.30 Sat 10-2 Service fee R15 p/p refundable on purchase • Cellar tours Mon-Fri 11 & 3 • Five-star Lanzerac Hotel for stay-overs ***Tel (021) 887-1132*** *• Governor's Hall Restaurant & Craven Lounge • BYO picnic • Conference facilities • Tasting & cellar tours for tourgroups* ***Tel (021) 886-5641*** *Meals & accommodation for groups* ***Tel (021) 887-1132*** *• Views • Walks • Wheelchair-friendly • Owner Christo Wiese • Winemakers Wynand Hamman (since 1993) & Hazel Hamman (since 1997) • Viticulturist Truter Prins (since 1997) • Vineyards 50 ha • Production 350 tons 25 000 cases 90% red 10% white • PO Box 6233 Uniedal 7612 •* ***Tel (021) 886-5641*** *• Fax (021) 887-6998 • E-mail wine@lanzerac.co.za • Website www.lanzeracwines.co.za*

"IT really tickled me," smiles Wynand Hamman, even-keeled as always in the glare of some high-profile publicity for his Cabernet 1996, recently likened to California's to-kill-for icon wine, Opus One, at a tasting in the US. High praise indeed for the immensely likeable Hamman and his equally self-effacing winemaking wife Hazel (both very much hands-on in the development of owner Christo Wiese's Helderberg showpiece, Lourensford). Here at Lanzerac, where the winery shares space with a graceful five-star hotel and restaurant, Hamman & Hamman have now added a bordeaux blend to their repertoire ("Very promising"), and they're affording visitors sneak-peeks of a Cabernet Franc maturing in oak (for an at-home preview, try their Merlot 1999, featuring a 7% soupcon from these prized barrels). In the pipeline is a Shiraz from young vines and, already available, their maiden Sauvignon in a limited release. "Resembles the wines of the Loire," remark H&H, who with vine-minding Truter Prins are wowing a growing export market in, amongst others, Mauritius, where Lanzerac bottles recently were the liquid stars of a gourmet food festival hosted by renowned chef John Jackson.

Cabernet Sauvignon Classically styled **98** brooding mid-01 but promising (June 02 release); deep colour; dense texture; undomineering oak (26 mths Fr, 33% new). 13% alc. 8 000 cases. **97** touch lighter. No hurry to get these drunk – open much-bemedalled **96** now instead.

Merlot More richness, concentration in **99** pre-bottling sample than **98**; roasted coffee/plum-pudding of earlier vintage, though not its curious (and interesting) gaminess. Elegantly, firmly structured; modest alcohol (12.6% in 99), subtle wooding (2 yrs Fr oak, 66% new). 3 500 cases.

Classic NEW Softly structured bdx blend; **00** half merlot, with cabs s/f, splash malbec. Ripe plumminess; touch sugar (3 g/ℓ), balanced acidity reinforces approachability. Mid-01 dusty cedar over-evidences 15 mths new Fr oak; few yrs needed. 14% alc. 1 000 cases.

Chardonnay ☆ Elegant rather than massive; more weight/fullness in **00** than in rather insubstantial **99**; both balanced, apart from prominent wood. The younger 11 mths Fr oak – no time on lees, unlike **99**. **Sauvignon Blanc** NEW ☆ First harvest of vyd planted 98. Ripe greengage notes in **01**; mouthfilling, flavoursome, but wow! 15% alc overpowers, unbalances. 600 cases only from farm.

De Forellen range

De Forellen (meaning 'trout'), tribute to Angus Buchanan, angler extraordinaire and owner of Lanzerac in the 1940s.

Clare ☆ Refined blend cabs s/f; attractive bottle-age aromas, but light, softly wooded **97** now approaching sell-by date. 3 000 cases. **Chardonnay** ⁑ Unwooded, unchallenging, undemonstrative: some delicate pleasure in **00**, though will tire soon. 1 000 cases. **Christina** ⁑ Rare Cape example of pinot blanc; pleasantly perfumed, refreshing, light-textured **00**; burny finish. 1 000 cases. **Thanya** Dry pinot blanc/chardonnay blend, unwooded. To date only **00** ☆. **Lerato** ⁑ 'Sweet Bordeaux style' notes Wynand Hamman, and appropriately adds '!!!'. Lots of sugar in **01** rosé (cabs s/f, merlot), low 10% alc; some gently flabby charm. 750 cases. — *TJ*

La Petite Ferme Winery

Franschhoek (see Franschhoek map) • Tasting by appointment • Sales daily 12-4 • Winery tours by appointment • La Petite Ferme Restaurant (see Eat-out section) Wines below available in the restaurant or direct • 3 luxury guest suites with many amenities • Views • Mountain biking • Owners Dendy Young family • Winemaker Mark Dendy Young (since 1996) • Vineyard manager John Dendy Young • Vineyards 8 ha • Production 50 tons 3 500 cases 70% white 30% red • PO Box 55 Franschhoek 7690 • ***Tel (021) 876-3016*** *• Fax (021) 876-3624 • E-mail lapetite@iafrica.com*

WITH a second baby due just in time for the busiest restaurant season and crush, indefatigable Mark Dendy Young intends timing things just right: a quick nappy change, punch through in the cellar, snatch some sleep, then start all over again. Still, life's a peach: "It's fantastic, the cellar's right next door to the restaurant, so I toddle over, put on my gumboots, show guests how the wines still lingering on their palates are made, off with the gumboots, on with the loafers, sprint back and take their lunch orders." Plantings of merlot are destined for an easy lunch-time wine. They're completely self-sufficient now, both with grapes for production and a range of wines for the restaurant, logistically a constant juggling act in such a small cellar. But Dendy Young seems to have it all remarkably under control. Their UK order doubled, a Dutch customer (who has a Franschhoek home) is marketing them in Holland too. Now he's added coaching touch-rugby at Bridge House school to his repertoire – "I'm preparing those future Springboks early!"

☆**Chardonnay** ✓ Food-affirming, barrel-fermented; **00** youthfully gangly when sampled for pvs ed; now shows lots of very good oak, toast and marzipan whiffs grapefruit and toffee/caramel in palate. "For decadent lunches," ventures Mark Dendy Young. ±50% fermented/sur lie 8 mths new Fr oak, remainder 2nd fill 13.5% alc. 400 cases. **99** also very good; buttery melon/pear tones. 13% alc.

Merlot ☆ Eagerly aromatic **00**, fennel, bluegum, leather sniffs over plum jam and prunes; hints of choc in finish. Light-toned with some green hints, though these might be transient. 40% new oak, Fr/Am. 13% alc. 200 cases. **Shiraz** ☆ From vyd in front of restaurant. **00** tasted mid-01 savoury/gamey, clouds of varietal smoke, even some sweaty saddles in a more traditional but pleasing genre Med-bodied. Should be good, as Mark D-Y suggests, with venison. 150 cases **01** not ready for tasting. **Sauvignon Blanc** ☆ The unoaked version, individual and rather good. **01** evincing its usual gravelly tones plus some quince and a suggestion of fruit-sweetness cushioning the finish. 13,5% alc. 800 cases. **Blanc Fumé** Softer, broader version of above. Popular favourite with restaurant speciality: home-smoked trout. **01** ☆ tasted very young, shy, sherbety; the remotest hint of butterscotch and some light fruit. Should perk up with bit of time. 13% alc. 300 cases. **Semillon** ☆ **00**, re-tasted for this ed, harmonious and supple, comfortably dry; creamy texture with sweet-grapefruit, hint butterscotch. Should see in 2003. 12% alc. 300 cases. Not tasted **Chardonnay Unwooded** Last was **00** ☆; **Nectar du Val 01** not ready for tasting. — *TM*

L'Auberge du Paysan

NEW

*Stellenbosch (see Stellenbosch map) • Tasting & sales during restaurant hours (also see Eat-out section) • Cellar tours by appointment • Owners Frederick Thermann & Mike Kovensky • Consulting winemaker/viticulturist Tjuks Roos • Vineyards 2.5 ha • Production 12.5 tons 2 000 cases • PO Box 315 Somerset West 7129 • **Tel/fax (021) 842-2008***

THE rows encircling this enduring country establishment in the Helderberg aren't merely a part of the French-toned décor (though they are rather pleasing to behold, etched against the purple mountain wall). In 1998 they yielded the first young Pinotage, much sought after by the restaurant's clientele. The current release is the 1999, made by neighbour Tjuks Roos in a small cellar on the property. We weren't able to taste this gem, but Frederick Thermann and Mike Kovensky assure their aims as always are "quality and tradition" and the latest release is "no exception to excellence".

Laughing Waters see Le Grand Chasseur

L'Avenir Estate

*Stellenbosch (see Stellenbosch map) • Tastings & sales Mon-Fri 10-5 Sat 10-4 Tasting fee R10 • Group cellar tours/tastings by appointment • Luxury 9-bedroom guest lodge with pool • Own preserved/dried olives/olive oil for sale • Owner Marc Wiehe • Winemaker Francois Naudé (since 1992) • Vineyards 53.5 ha • Production 22 000 cases 320 tons 50% red 48% white 2% rosé • PO Box 1135 Stellenbosch 7599 • **Tel (021) 889-5001** • Fax (021) 889-5258 • E-mail lavenir@adept.co.za • Website www.adept.co.za/lavenir*

FORMER Pretoria pharmacist Francois Naudé firmly believes in taking a good dose of his own medicine. A few years back he made a barrel of port for home consumption simply because he "loves the stuff". Urbane Mauritian owner Marc Wiehe sipped sóme, promptly asked him to make more and the rest is history: it waltzed away with a series of young wine show awards in 1999. "I don't have any of those fancy Portuguese cultivars so I make do with cabernet," states this sure-footed winemaker. Matured for two years, the maiden Cape Vintage was released last year – though Naudé's keeping enough to make sure he never runs dry of his favourite tipple. One of the star players in the heavenly Simonsberg superbowl, there have been "fantastic" changes in quality, notably of the sauvignon blanc, from a combination of more established vineyards, improved canopy management and a cooler season. These are "magic wines" enthuses this alchemist-at-heart of vintage 2001. Happily, increased plantings will alleviate short supply, particularly of their local champion, pinotage.

☆**Cabernet Sauvignon** Francois Naudé has proven his versatility with this now reliably top-class Cape cab since nurturing it to loftier heights from **94** VVG. After further warming up with **95** VG, better-than-harvest **96**, he emphatically took the field in **97** SAA, *Wine* ☆. It gets better each vintage. **99** from super-ripe, long-hang-time fruit displaying gorgeous, expansive violets flecked with mint, classic dusty tapered cassis fruit in elegant palate. Sample **00** bursting with blackcurrant pastilles, most promising. 18 mths 33% each new/2nd/3rd fill Fr barriques, since **95**, with touch merlot – 6% in latest. Hawkish ±14% alcs. **Auction Reserve Cabernet** NEW **00** simply black, full (but classy) wood nose and beautifully structured palate – ripe tannins harbouring forest-floor fruits that need plenty of time (10 yrs min) to unfurl. Creamy finish. 19 mths all-new Fr oak, 13.8% alc. 62 cases.

Pinotage Quintessential, unambiguous, unequivocal: however one may put it, no doubt this is pinotage, and fine example at that. Wins as many fans as awards. Next **00** unlikely to be exception: dense pomegranate-seed brightness, striking purple plum character in more serious mould than pretenders, finely strung tannic core elevates finish from merely pinotage to the more serious. Louder, more hectic than **99** which finer in mouth, as good as **96** *Wine* pvsly cellar's best. Heaps of oak (±yr Nevers, 50% new) damp down assertive flavours. 4.9 t/ha yields of mainly virus-free vyds concentrates fruit further. No green bitterness that challenges many pinotages. Immunerable laurels (*Wine*, Veritas, ABSA Top Ten, IWSC, WOM). **Auction Reserve Pinotage** **00** altogether denser, more toasty, smoky, finer fruit, better oak, softer tannins than regular above. Huge wine (15% alc), less overtly displaying varietal provenance. Mere 65 cases. Proportion 35 yr old vyd fruit, 15 mths 100% new Fr casks (eschews Am oak-nurturing of so many other showstopper pinotages).

L'Ami Simon ✓ Entry-level red far ahead of following pack welcomes fruity pinotage to improve earlier accessibility from **99:** stunning colour; smoky, mineral features fleshed out by plummier palate than pvs, easy tannins which 'give' in mouth for enjoyment on release. Appetising minerally, blackcurrant mouthful of **98** a trifle harder. Now 44% each merlot, cab, balance pinotage rounded out with yr used Fr oak. **97** ; **96** VVG, SAA.

Rosé Maison Blend white/red wines (80/20), **00** delightful light pink allrounder. **01** inviting copper-salmon tints, strawberry pith laced with floral spice, uncomplicated freshness. Clairette, colombard, cinsaut, cab, pinotage blend that, we are certain, is enjoyed with gusto at the Maison. Off-dry 10 g/ℓ sugar.

Chardonnay There's a permanent nook for Chardonnay du Monde plaudits in this cellar: **00** 5th successive vintage to garner a gong, this time as gold as the potion's sheen. Continues the plump, peachy, richly oaked, weighty style favoured by Naudé as product/personal libation. Crisp tartness cuts brooding flesh of lingering finish. Latest 11 mths Burgundy casks, 20% new; long lees contact accounts for characteristic oatmeal notes. 100% barrelled only since **99**; **Chardonnay Special Cuvée** **98** 100% barrel-fermented, 40% new. On release less ready than above; stronger new world tones.

Chenin Blanc ✓ The razzmatazz is back: current **01** returns to mouthfilling offdry form licked into opulence by portion botrytis. Flaxen shimmers, ripe, tropical/soft pear theme maintained on beautifully integrated palate, not classic Loire maybe, but exceptionally tasty. 14.5% alc, 5.5 g/ℓ sugar. Award-winning style since much-praised **97** Chenin Challenge winner. **00** more classic dry food wine. **99** broad 13,8% alc. Always unwooded, 100% varietal.

Sauvignon Blanc "To drink when you're thirsty" quips Naudé. Restorative **01** maximises super sauvignon year; bright, herbaceous aromas weave best of grassy scrub with tropical melons, piercing fruit focuses any wandering attention. **00** quieter. Unwooded. 13,8% alc. **99** SAA.

Vin de Meurveur Noble Late Harvest Snappy, relatively low-sugar version of these golden desserts in **00** from colombard/Cape riesling (77/23); pebbly apricots, chalk coached to spicy complexity by Fr oak barrelling for first time. Drier 91 g/ℓ sugar than showy **97** , winner of inaugural Air France trophy, SAA, *Wine* , 144,5 g/ℓ. Alcs 13,5%.

★**Cape Vintage (Port)** NEW No probation required before the leap into red ink; **99** young wine show star sashays effortlessly onto podium in bottled form. Dense, shimmering black in complexion, dried prunes, smoky spice, moist cigars billow out of the glass. 3 yr old rebate brandy fortification still marginally separate in bracing palate, will integrate over the 10 yrs it needs. Cab not a very 'Portuguese' variety, but drier (80 g/ℓ sugar), higher-alc (19%) style is classic. 2 yrs barrelled. 275 cases.

Vin d'Erstelle ☻ ★ All-occasions, above-average quaff; **01** aromatic, floral colombard/riesling (57/43) blend, pleasurably off-dry (6,9 g/ℓ sugar) without any sugary show. Brisk finish will acquit itself well at a Thai table. Can develop riesling ring after yr or so. — *DS*

Le Bonheur Estate

Stellenbosch (see Stellenbosch map) • Tasting & sales Mon-Fri 9-5 Sat 10-4 Closed Sun • Special tastings on request • Light meals by arrangement • Owner Lusan Holdings • Winemaker Sakkie Kotzé (since 1993) • Production 435 tons 31 473 cases • PO Box 56 Klapmuts 7625 • ***Tel (021) 875 5478*** *Fax (021) 875 5624*

This glossy property (its jaunty name means 'happiness') has an enviable terroir along the slopes of Klapmuts Hill (*klapmuts* being the Dutch word for the 18th-century cocked hat, made to conveniently fold to fit into a saddlebag, that it resembles from a distance) on the northern reaches of the Simonsberg. Four years of painstaking tweaking have boosted the vineyards to optimal levels of minerals and nutrients to grow the top-performers that go into Sakkie Kotze's highly rated wines (the compact range encompasses two reds, two whites). The classic Cape Dutch H-shaped manor house, with its easy on the eye, typical of the day, ice-cream-hued exterior and rich, gleaming wood interiors, is the dream old-Cape setting for exclusive catered-for dinners.

★**Prima** Classy, much decorated yet deliciously unintimidating bdx blend. 75% merlot, rest cab in **98** which, revisited for this ed, opening out very nicely; well-ripened silky fruit ready when you are (though will wait good few yrs). Elegance a hallmark (12,5% alc), but also richness, drinkability. New (40%), 2nd fill Fr oak, 18 mths. 5 000 cases. **97** equally balanced.

★**Cabernet Sauvignon** Excellent track-record through 80s for this wine, and still very fine, roundly applauded. **98** revisited mid-01, more introverted than pvsly, fruit in hiding, though tannins markedly softer. Give yr, then monitor; might be in a trough. 4 000 cases. Brooding **97** ★★ needed time. VVG. These, anyway, not swashbucklers (alcs ±12.5%); their virtues are more subtle. Small Fr oak 18/19 mths, 60% new, rest 2nd fill.

★**Chardonnay** Always carefully constructed, nicely judged fruit and supportive oak – 4 mths Fr barrels, 50% new. **00** lime marmalade on toast, to be enjoyed, winemaker feels, "at any occasion, with or without music". This, below 3 500 cases. **99** round, understated.

★**Sauvignon Blanc** Above-average sauvignon yr serves up an ace here; **01** (sample) textbook varietal aromatics, including gunsmoke; lovely ripe-gooseberry flavour in brisk finish. 13.1% alc. More interesting than tropic-fruited **00** ★. — *IvH*

Leef op Hoop see Le Riche

Le Grand Chasseur Estate

Robertson (see Robertson map) • Tasting & sales Mon-Fri 8-5 • Cellar tours by appointment • Walks • Views • Owner/winemaker Albertus de Wet (since 1979) • Assistant winemaker Fredine Stofberg (since 2001) • Viticultural consultants

Francois Viljoen (VinPro), Freddie de Jager, Hennie de Klerk • Vineyards 250 ha • Production ± 3 300 tons 55% white 42% red 3% rosé • PO Box 439 Robertson 6705 • ***Tel/fax (023) 626-1048*** *• E-mail lgc@intekom.co.za • Website http://home.intekom.com/legrand*

THERE's a very good chance you will have tasted the produce from Albertus de Wet's farm without even knowing it. As trusted supplier to the large wholesalers, his fruit appears in all sorts of chic bottles (runaway hit Arniston Bay, for example). Now, while keeping his traditional customers satisfied, he's testing the own-label waters with a limited-quantity range under the Le GC label (the great hunter alluded to in the name is the splendid African Fish Eagle, a frequent flyer in the open-skies Le Chasseur Valley. Co-styling the range is young Fredine Stofberg, fresh out of Elsenburg College and clearly delighted to be part of this well-run family operation (owner/winemaker Albertus dW the third generation on the farm). They're brimming with fresh ideas, including a tasting centre on Robertson's main street, and very keen to take advantage of promising sites on their 1 400 hectare spread, including a separate farm, Laughing Waters, where sauvignon is champing to fly.

☆**Pinotage** Something of very ripe zinfandel about **00**, gushing sweet fleshy plums in big jammy palate. Lots of fruit, lots of character. Unoaked. 13.3% alc.

☆**Shiraz 00** ("our wine for people who understand wine") rather tasty; forthcoming varietal aromas to go with ripe berry fruits; full soft flavours redolent of oak-char and dark-roast coffee. Nice now, could age 3-4 yrs. Fr oak, 11 mths. 13.8% alc.

Fish Eagle Red ☻ ☆ (Ruby Cabernet in pvs ed). **99** shouts the variety in a most pleasing way; soft and succulent fruit complemented by minerally oak (11 mths Fr casks). Note: 14% alc. **Fish Eagle White** ☻ ☆ (Chardonnay-Colombard in pvs ed) Lovely zesty-ripe flavours of guava and peach, spicy oak overtones in med-weight, delightfully smooth **01** (sample).

Chardonnay ☆ Bright, lightish **01** features more than a soupcon vanilla, toasted hazelnuts; these background notes to zesty ripe-peach. Could go yr/2. 50% new Fr oak-fermented/sur lie 5 mths. 13.3% alc. — *DH*

Leidersburg Vineyard

Paarl • Winemakers Jan du Preez & Willie Malherbe (since 1996) • Viticulturist Jan du Preez (since 1996) • Vineyard 6 ha • Production 45 tons (1 000 cases own label) 100% red • PO Box 204 Stellenbosch 7599 • ***Tel (021) 887-9937*** *• Fax (021) 887-0566 • E-mail dupwine@intekom.co.za*

THIS attention-lavished Cabernet is grown in a scenic vineyard in Paarl and made at nearby Goede Hoop by Jan du Preez and wine-mate Willie Malherbe. Applying professional vineyard management and a higher proportion of new oak, they believe they've been able to ratchet up the quality each vintage since the first 96. Now they're looking to plant more cab, "but also looking at malbec which we think has a great future in SA".

☆**Cabernet Sauvignon** Plump, sweet-natured cab with forward blackcurrant tastes, gently firming tannins. (Back)tasting the trio of recent vintages mid-01 reveals them in good heath. Big (14% alc) booming **98** ☆ has blackcurrant confiture tones, WOM Value; **99** more classic, similar traits but more restrained; **00** (sample, unrated) different fruit spectrum (red berry/plum); generous touch of good oak tannins/tastes. These 14 mths barrique-aged, alcs ±13%. 2 000 half-cases. — *TM*

Lemberg Estate

Tulbagh (see Tulbagh map) • Tasting, sales, cellar tours daily (also Sundays!) 9-5 and by appointment. Tasting fee R5 p/p • Gourmet meals/picnics by arrangement (1-2 days' notice required) • Light lunches/cellar tours for groups Book ahead • Luxury B&B/self catering rondavel for 2-4 guests • Flyfishing • Birding • Walks • Mountain biking • Views • Owner/winemaker/viticulturist Klaus Schindler • Vineyards 4 ha • Production ± 1 000 cases 70% white 30% red • • PO Box 317 Tulbagh 6820 • ***Tel (023) 230-0659*** *cell 083 302-5634 • Fax (023) 230-0661 • E-mail schindler@lando.co.za • Website www.kapstadt.de/lemberg*

This welcoming property, neatly tucked below the Witzenberg Mountains, has become a sought-after destination, with its lakeside guesthouse set in lush gardens, excellent meals and ample picnic baskets, mountain views, country walks, bird watching, and a laid-back ambience. And if you're not completely chilled-out by all the above, the European-style wines will do the rest. The range, not available for tasting, includes: **Sensual Red** (cab/merlot), **Lipovina** (hárslevelü), **The Laughing Duck** (sauvignon), none previously rated.

L'Emigré Wines

Stellenbosch (see Stellenbosch map) • Tasting Sat 9.30-5 and during December holiday Mon-Sat • Self-catering guest cottages with fine views • Walks • Owner FV Gentis Trust • Winemakers Emile Gentis (since 1998) & Frans Gentis (since 1992) • Viticulturist Victor Gentis (since 1998) • Vineyards 55 ha • Production 500 tons (3 000 cases own label, 2 000 cases export) • PO Box 14 Vlottenburg 7604 • ***Tel (021) 881-3702*** *• Fax (021) 881-3030*

From their idyllic farm in the Stellenboschkloof, the Gentis family are acting out their motto: "To the Western World and beyond". Elsenburg-trained Emile G, whose goal is to travel and work in all the world's wine countries, can add Bordeaux's historic gem, St-Emilion, to his been-there list, having worked both the 2000 and 2001 crushes at classed-growth Ch l'Angélus. Brother Victor, who waves the marketing baton, jetted to London to open international doors. Mission accomplished, he reports. "We're proud to say our wines are being listed with some of the world's finest." Back home, they're launching a new range, Nutwood Grove, mostly for export (though small quantities will be available locally). In the vineyard, they've overgrafted 6 hectares to merlot, cabernet franc and shiraz, and established new blocks of sauvignon and shiraz. For visitors the most obvious development is the new Cape-Dutch gable atop the cellar. Like everything else here, hand-made. "It's taken 7 years," they say, "but the end is in sight."

☆**Muscat d'Alexandrie** ✓ **96** mature, extra-smooth treat, ripening delectably. Warm apricot glints (in appearance and palate), tangy marmalade finish and no hint of cloy despite very low 3.7 acid. Yrs good development ahead. 17% alc. 200 cases.

Pinotage NEW ☆ Pizza in a glass! Salami *and* garlic, lashed with cracked black pepper. **01** as far from 'typical' pinotage as is possible to imagine. 12.6% alc. More shiraz-like, even, than ... **Shiraz** ☆☆ which invariably varietally correct on this farm. **97** (still available) easy drinking, generous; med/light-bodied. **01** somewhat richer, not over-extracted. **Cimiterre** ☆☆ Back in range after short break (pvs was **95**). **01** lightish red blend (cinsaut, pinotage, malbec, cab f), soft, red fruits dusted with pepper. Approachable and undemanding, could go 4-5 yrs but perfectly good now with not too strongly flavoured cuisines. **Azure Chardonnay** ☆☆ Characterful **99** has ripened interestingly, acquired taut gravelly flavours which beg food. Vosges oak, 7 mnths. 13.7% alc. **Azure Blanc** ☆ Highly idiosyncratic style, for the adventurous. **00** developing pungent aromas, singular 'viscous' texture (not from alc: relatively low 12.6% alc); dry citrus finish. These in distinctive tall azure bottles. ± 250 cases.

Glorieux Natural Sweet ☆ (pvs was Special Late Harvest) Perfumed, petally sweetness balanced by acid; succulent orange-toned finish. From muscat d'a. **Port** ★ **98** with cellar's thumbprint peppery savouriness, improving. Tinta/cab aged yr Spanish oak. 17,5% alc. 400 cases. — *JN*

Leopard's Leap

Cape Town MD Hein Koegelenberg • Marketing Koos Jordaan • Consulting winemaker Jacques Borman • PO Box 36578 Chempet 7442 • ***Tel (021) 555-0690*** *• Fax (021) 555-0697 • E-mail kj.marketing@historicwines.co.za*

IN-HOUSE range of fine-wine maturation, labelling and distribution services company Historic Wines of the Cape.

Cabernet Sauvignon-Merlot ★ Mouthfilling, unpretentiously pleasant **99**; soft jammy fruit tastily upholsters fairly firm framework. 15 mths oak, 70% Am, remainder Fr. 13.5% alc. 2 000 currently only for export. **Pinotage-Shiraz** ☆ **00** warm, friendly welcome (more enthusiastic puppy than leopard?); then the teeth rather spoil things with sharp acid, some bitterness in finish. Partly wooded. 13.5% alc. 5 000 cases. **Sauvignon Blanc** ★ **01** satisfying mouthful crisply accented fruit; fresh, grassy, tropical overtones; dry peardrop finish. Big 13.5% alc. This, below 8 000 cases. **Semillon-Chardonnay** ★ 70% semillon unsurprisingly dominates **01** with apple/wet-wool notes; partly barrel-fermented chardonnay adds depth, roundness. Firmly structured, but essentially easy drinking. 13% alc. Export only for now. — *TJ*

Le Pavillon see Boschendal

Le Riche Wines

Stellenbosch (see Stellenbosch map) Tasting & sales Mon-Fri 8-5 • Guest house/B&B • Views • Owner/winemaker Etienne le Riche • Production 5 000 cases 100% red • PO Box 6295 Stellenbosch 7612 • ***Tel/fax (021) 887-0789*** *• E-mail lerichewines@adept.co.za*

EVERYTHING's just dandy at Etienne le Riche's winery on Leef op Hoop, translated as 'live on hope', wryly appropriate for this first solo venture, in which he's been backed up by his wife Marcelle. A guest cottage on the farm in the Jonkershoek valley, lush with fynbos, waterfalls, wineries and other allures, is a favourite hideaway for wine and nature lovers. There's "smart" new paving in front of the ingeniously renovated cellar – a working one some 30 years ago, used as a tractor shed in the interim – where the focus so far has been on grapes and barrels, not frills. "Got to keep up with the neighbours!" quips this talented winemaker, who maintains a modestly low profile but nevertheless produces one of the Cape's leading wines (the stunning Cabernet Sauvignon Reserve). It may just have to make room up there for another: last year le Riche released the limited maiden 00 vintage Cabernet-Merlot from two adjoining vineyards at a single site on old friend Roger Chennells' neighbouring property, destined for the CWG auction; next up is a single vineyard Cabernet from the same site.

☆☆**Cabernet Sauvignon Reserve** Has established itself as a leading Cape cult wine (from the least cult-conscious of winemakers) in the vintages since **97.** The array of flavours is accommodated in a supple frame where fruit engulfs tannin. Effect is one of calm elegance. Were it a touch drier and firmer, it would be more old world than new; as it is, it hovers between the two very nicely. The sound ripe-fruit/tannin balance is key, promises 10 yrs of smooth ageing. Extended oaking in 80-90% new Fr barrels, alcs ±13%, about two-thirds grapes from Jonkershoek, rest from maritime-swept Firgrove. **97** VVG, SAA, *Wine* ☆, Air France trophy. **98** ☆, *Wine* ☆☆ initially tighter; **99** fragrant, minerally, WOM selection (as was **98**); latest **00** ☆☆ more restrained, tannic than pvs, needing ±

yrs for elegant spicy fruit to unfurl. Standard **Cabernet Sauvignon** ★ Where the brooding, assertive Reserve compels more attention, there's a seamless elegance, easier drinkability in this well modulated, understated wine. **97** ★ recognisably from same hand. Pushing 13% alc. **98** untasted. **99** luscious, limpid mouthcoating pleasure; partial new oaking. WOM selection. Latest **00** biggest of these (13.7% alc); ripe cassis beautifully balanced by oak, embellished with tobacco spice; 13 mths oak, 2nd fill. Fruit from various Stbosch sites.

★**Merlot-Cabernet Sauvignon** While Etienne le R tweaks these blend proportions to play to vintage strengths, styling remains consistent – and delicious. **99** merlot/cab 60/40, cream-textured, sleek, delicate fruit very lightly, almost imperceptibly wooded; **98** cab/merlot 60/40, touch weightier but with ripe tannins, latest **00**, cab/merlot 75/25. From old, low yielding Jonkershoek vyds; open-tank-fermented; 7 mths 2nd fill Nevers, 5 mths 4 500 ℓ vats.

Leef op Hoop range

Mainly for export to UK and Netherlands.

★**Cabernet Sauvignon** A 2nd label to outclass some 1sts, and showing more of winemaker Le Riche's subtle side; soft, ripe-sweet black cherry tones in **99** make for quiet-toned charm; at 12,5% alc a touch more quaffable than **98**. Latest **00** blackcurrants, cherries and brambles, some cigarbox sniffs; "to drink when you need hope," says Etienne le R. Briefly oaked in older wood, not for long ageing. — *NP*

Libertas

Bottled for the export market, this widely distributed brand fills a modestly priced slot in the Distell portfolio.

Pinotage ☻ ★ Med-bodied, satisfying **99**, sweet-tasting berry fruit, some cinnamon-bun nuances in dry finish.

Cabernet Sauvignon ★ **99** offers warm spicy fruit in leanish frame; savoury finish to go with tomato pastas or pizza. **Merlot** ★ **99** undemanding style with light yet varietally pure fruit. Showing some ripeness, so should be uncorked soon. **Chardonnay** ★ Quickish finishing **00** perfectly pleasant, fruity, med-bodied. 17 000 cases. **Chenin Blanc** ★ **01** zingy, dry, med-bodied. To enjoy young. 12 000 cases. — *IvH*

Lieberstein

Semi-sweet table wine that revolutionised SA's wine drinking habits at launch in 1959. An instant success; by 1964 world's largest-selling bottled wine. Still model of reliable, unpretentious quaffing. By Distell.

NV ★ Honeycomb and dried herbs in latest bottling; smooth rather than sweet. — *IvH*

Lievland Estate

Simonsberg, Stellenbosch (see Stellenbosch map) Tasting & sales Mon-Fri 9-5 Sat 9-1 • Cellar tours by appointment • BYO picnic • Wheelchair-friendly • Owner Paul Benadé • Winemaker/viticulturist Jean Pienaar (since 2001) • Vineyards 65 ha • Production 350 tons 50/50 white/red • PO Box 66 Klapmuts 7625 • ***Tel (021) 875-5226*** *• Fax (021) 875-5213*

This family farm, boasting big-gun Simonsberg slopes, is headed by Cape Wine Master Paul Benadé and a brand new team – marketing manager Marlise Truter and winemaker/viticulturist Jean Pienaar – who're all fired up with enthusiasm. It's a natural progression for Pienaar, who managed the vineyards and was previously assistant to James Farquharson, now switched from after-hours to full-time winemaker at Reyneke, and acting in an advisory capacity here. While the focus of the carefully targeted range is still on blends, with viognier planted to this end last year, they're not neglecting varietal wines. Singular quality (and encouragement from visiting French winemakers) resulted in their first solo bottling of cabernet franc. They're not overlooking their flagship Shiraz either, now joined by a Reserve, to be produced only in exceptional years.

- ✯**Shiraz** Paul Benade's passion, and proud flagship of the estate. **99** closest yet to Rhone model, reveals profusion of toasty, spicy, peppery red-berry aromas; elegant yet concentrated with scrub, fennel, lavender and dark plummy flavours. Soft garnet glints. Perhaps without the staying power of pvs but fine. 13.4% alc. **00** preview darker, harder mid-01, also more expansively structured, potentially longer-lived but same fleshy plum profile. **98** big, powerful (15,2% alc), maturing with aplomb. VVG, *Wine* ✯. Fr oak-matured, 40% new ; some fermentation finished in barrel.
- ✯**DVB** Occupies deserved niche as estate's 'other' standard bearer. Cab f-dominated blend raises the bar in **99** (attention to detail in vyd bearing fruit): hallmark cab f new-thatch, cut-grass aromas uppermost as flavours expand across palate; merlot/cab's sweet ripe-plums resonate with fine tannins and spicy tobacco. **98** more integrated but less exuberantly franc-toned (here 50% to merlot's 30%, balance cab s). Immediate impression of elegant ripeness, sweet black-cherry/berry aromas, then luscious ripe fruit ending dry. Allier oak, 40% new. **97** now shows maturing potpourri, cherry, tea-leaf notes; some austerity.
- ✯**Weisser Riesling** ✓ One of the Cape's finest examples; almost-dry, beautifully harmonious and worth cellaring few years. Still-available **98** offers lime-grapefruit nuances behind spicy bottle-aged complexity and delicate terpenes. Citrus acidity interweaves with mineral flavours. Lightish 11.5% alc, 9 g/ℓ sugar. No **99**, **00** due to heat waves. **01** untasted.

> **Lievlander** ☻ ✯ Winery's best seller and still a bargain (as affirmed by amazing nine WOM Value selections). Blend of all reds on farm. **00** maintains hallmark quaffable ripe-plum profile, nice scrub/pepper tones.

Cabernet Sauvignon 00 (unrated sample, as are reds below) promising deep garnet hues and understated cassis, fennel, cigarbox aromas. Restrained dry tannins wrap around elegant, classic cab berry-flavours; still lurking, only hinting at future pleasure. **Cabernet Franc** Classic old-world red, elegantly proportioned, med-weight with refined dry tannins and touch attention-grabbing youthful astringency. **00** unexpectedly quiet bouquet – mere hint of variety's hay-field/fresh thatch bouquet – though no doubt will bloom with time. **Syrah** NEW Massively muscular, concentrated shiraz with sights set firmly on Cote Rotie, slated for Reserve status. **00** surprisingly sweet-ripe entry yielding to impressive damson, plum and choc flavours, already in harmony with spicy oak. Wonderful potential. Different fermentation from standard Shiraz above (upright fermenters vs rototanks). Watch this space for stars in profusion. Also available, not ready for tasting: **Chardonnay** (Pvs **00** ✯), **Sauvignon Blanc** (pvsly untasted), **Chéandrie** (**NV** ✯). — *TM*

Linton Park Wines

Wellington (see Wellington map) • Tasting, sales, cellar tours by appointment • Owner Linton Park plc • MD Malcolm Perkins • Winemaker Hennie Huskisson (since 2001) • Vineyard manager T C Botha • Production 500 tons 15 000 cases 60% white 40% red • PO Box 1234 Wellington 7654 • ***Tel (021) 873-1625*** *• Fax (021) 873-0851 • E-mail lpwines@mweb.co.za*

Is warm-climate Wellington a top quality sauvignon area? New chef de cave Hennie Huskisson, ex Fairview and Nederburg, intends to find out. He has special plans for this coolness-seeking variety, especially in the higher pockets on the Groenberg, where the temperature is several degrees lower than in the valley-town of Wellington. This 250 ha farm, Slangrivier (Snake River), is owned by Linton Park plc, a glossy London-listed group whose hedonistic interests run from foie gras to caviar (company HQ, a 13th century estate in Kent, gives its name to the alternative label, Capell's Court). MD Malcolm Perkins bought the spread in 1995, and with vineyard boffin T C Botha and, initially, winemaker Ian Naudé (now at Dornier), revitalised the farm and its 1809 homestead. "I'm enjoying working in my own cellar," says new-broom Huskisson, but he's not about to sweep aside the full-blooded Linton Park style, which has flown from its perch onto wine lists, terrestrial and airborne, across the globe.

✵**Shiraz** Single vyd Summer Hill super-ripe but not flabby; big oak aromas to complement rich raspberry fruit. **00** fuller, loganberry/creme brulee overtones, higher alc (14%) than slightly more tannic **99**. Both amply aromatic, grip enough on the finish. Yr oaked, 70/30 Fr/Am casks. 2 300 cases.

✵**Cabernet Sauvignon** Latest releases not quite as high-flying as off-the-wall **98** ★★★, poster kid for the anti-classicists (14.5% alc, 4 g/ℓ sugar). **99** lower alc (12,5%), drier than pvs, more recognisably claret. Powerful but quite restrained, firm-tannined, more herbal. Latest **00** fatter again, choc/coffee aromas, perhaps from more heavily toasted oak. Yr 2nd/3rd fill Fr casks. 2 750 cases.

✵**Chardonnay** ✓ Powerful, though not brash, single vineyard (Claire Division), new Fr oak-vinified. Current **00** ✵ tropical/pineapple notes, amplitude in the mouth; oaking shows as caramel and allspice; fatter than more citrusy **99** though both over 14% alc and less than 3 g/ℓ sugar. Big but not blowsy. Low volumes (1 00-1 600 cases).

Merlot ★★ Densely coloured **00**; lush mulberry aromas; uncomplicated pulpy tannins for early drinking. Soft despite yr oaking; moderate alc (12,5%); only 750 cases.

Capell's Court range

✵**Shiraz** ✓ Ripe, shamelessly forward, plenty of simple Ribena fruit, distinctly sweetish finish. **01** promising more obvious sweetness (8 g/ℓ)), less acidity than finer **00** (14% alc, 6 g/ℓ sugar) though both in the mould of super-ripe, high alc **98**. Deservedly popular with those who prefer succulent grapey aromas and a little sugar to staid vinosity.

✵**Chardonnay** Tropical though no longer full-blown (**01** ★★ 12,5% alc vs **00** 13,7% alc) and now dry; grape flavours unmediated by oak; grapefruit/lime in tangy dry finish. Noticeably more elegant than pvs heady **99** and fat, sweetish **98**. 4 000 cases.

Cabernet Sauvignon ★★ Aromatic, uncomplex, easy drinking. **00**, like pvs, light (11,5% alc), unwooded. **Sauvignon Blanc** ★★ Floral fig/herbal aromas, though **01** shows more of the grassy leanness of **00** in palate. 13,6% alc. 3 800 cases. Discontinued: **Snake River Sauvignon Blanc-Chardonnay** (**99** ★★). — *MF*

Long Mountain Wine Company

Stellenbosch • Owner Pernod Ricard SA • Group wine development director Robin Day • Managing Winemaker Jacques Kruger (since 1998) • Production 270 000 cases • PO Box 1324 Stellenbosch 7599 • ***Tel (021) 880-1688*** *• Fax (021) 880-1691 • E-mail jacques@prsa.co.za*

THIS internationally focused company – it owns the No 1 SA brand in Ireland and No 3 in the UK – disproves the old adage that too many winemakers spoil the blend. In partnership with wineries from Robertson to Rawsonville, they work closely with the viticulturists who identify the best vineyards and the winemakers who vinify the grapes at individual cellars. Now, in the pursuit of consumer-friendly wines that match their 'rich in fruit, low in tannin, acid' mantra, they're taking the whole process a step further, assisting producers to classify their best blocks and install smaller tanks to vinify the best batches. "This way, we select the best grapes," explains Jacques Kruger, the self-effacing maestro who assembles the final cuvees. He believes the 2001 vintage is "the best since 1998, with up-front fruit and soft flavours". Qualities which, one imagines, would appeal to "the very competitive and discerning French market" now being targeted by this Pernod Ricard-owned powerhouse.

Long Mountain range

Merlot-Shiraz ✓ Successful version of this rare in Cape blend. **00**, partly oak fermented/matured, leather/white pepper whiffs from shiraz, choc tastes from merlot – all well knit. 13.2% alc. **99** shiraz-dominated.

Ruby Cabernet ☻ Alluring ripe-fruit tones, smooth plumpness; light oaking for early drinking. Stock up on **99** now for your next barbeque. 13.1% alc. **Chardonnay** ☻ **01** really nice mouthful; supple melony tastes lengthened by butteriness from partial malo/extended lees lie-in. 13.2% alc.

Cabernet Sauvignon For early drinking or keeping yr/2 without losing varietal character. Spreadable plum-jam flavours in **00**; med-bodied, partly oak-fermented/matured. **Pinotage** Well-crafted example of the all-SA grape, partly oaked. **00** with sprightly beaujolais character. 13.1% alc. **Dry Red 00** not ready for tasting. **99** ruby cab/cinsaut. **Chenin Blanc** Vinified for fruit-juiciness, which **01** has aplenty, plus sherbety effervescence to maintain light, undemanding tone. 12,5% alc. **Sauvignon Blanc** No shortage of varietal character in **01**; assertive green-pea/guava sniffs; bright citrus/nettle flavours; restrained 12,7% alc. **Semillon-Chardonnay** Cleverly constructed **01**, partial malo/sur lie treatment enhances semillon's broad waxiness. Med-bodied, dry. — *TM*

Longridge Winery

Stellenbosch (see Helderberg map) • Tasting & sales Mon-Fri 9-5 Sat 9-2 Te[l] (021) 855-2004 • Owner Winecorp • Winemaker Ben Radford • Productio[n] Longridge 11 000 cases Bay View 70 000 cases • PO Box 99 Lynedoch 7603 • ***Tel (021) 881-3690*** *• Fax (021) 881-3699 • E-mail winecorp@iafrica.com*

SAND, slope or soil – avid surfer, mountain biker and winemaker Ben Radford likes to get up-close and personal with his terroir. After six vintages in the Cape, the Australian-born Winecorp cellar-head believes SA is better suited to souther[n] French varieties than "the boring old Bordeaux types." So he's looking forward to experiment with blends of viognier and shiraz ("maybe with a splash o[f] mourvèdre") when new parcels come on-stream. And he's trolling through Winecorp's holdings to find the best shiraz to join the Longridge range. "I've got all sorts of bits and pieces," he contemplates, "some petit verdot, some malbec – and young nebbiolo and sangiovese near Wellington." A mixed bag, brimming with excitement, for right hand Karl van der Merwe, who this year takes over the ranges below under Radford's supervision.

Cabernet Sauvignon 99, previewed in pvs guide, to be released during currency of this ed (as are reds below). Pvsly noted youthful edges now more smoothly polished, affording tantalising glimpses of future lofty maturity in resonant minerally cassis/brambleberry set in creamily rich texture. **98** SAA. 100% cab from single Helderberg vyd. Small Fr oak, portion new, 15 mths. Unfiltered.

Merlot Hit tracks running with maiden **95** and never looked back (except from vantage of show rostrum – four international medals in 01 alone for two most recent releases). **99** typifies vintage elegance: echoing minty/spiced-plum fragrance; fluid texture around still tight-wound core, sweeping fantail finish beautifully polished tannins. Fermented/matured Fr/Am (80/20) oak, 40% new, 14 mths. **98** SAA.

Pinotage "Made in rustic style, with no new wood to let the fruit speak," explains Ben Radford of attempt to squeeze **99** into Rhone-style shoes. Love-or-hate wine – and least ready of these reds. Retaste mid-01 reveals fruit/oak in combat, yielding gawky sweet raw-flesh tones needing yr/2 in solitary confinement. Hopefully will return to feature original attractions. 1 100 cases. Per Radford, succeeding vintages more Aussie styled. **98** vividly spicy. Partly cask fermented, oak aged 14 mths, Fr/Am (70/30), none new. Single Helderberg vyd.

Chardonnay ✓ Fine-tuning rather than wild style-swings characterises this consistent, individual Cape chardonnay. Armfuls of accolades since first **96** (including approval by many members of ABC – anything but chardonnay – brigade). Oak never dominant, even less so in **00** despite 70% new Fr barrelling; thumbprint delicacy, zest; though just post-bottling, trifle less intricate than usual; soupcon sugar (4.6 g/ℓ) gives supple, fleshy rather than sweet, balances full 13.7% alc. 5 000 cases. **99** developing some ripe grapefruit/hazelnuts complexity.

Discontinued: **Brut MCC**. Pvs **94**.

Bay View range

Most attractive quality-value wines.

Cabernet Sauvignon ✓ Least ready of these **00** reds, still-firm tannin wall, behind which queues abundant dark cassis/blackberry; antithesis of critically acclaimed **99**'s bright forwardness, and more sophisticated, bigger (13.5% vs 12.9% alc.) yet just as rewarding. Oaked, portion new, 11 mths. 11 000 cases. These, below not cold-stabilised/filtered, so sediment may form with bottle maturation.

Merlot ✓ Big, soft **00**, fleshy red berries coating every corner of mouth with warm (unjammy) ripeness. Unobtrusive oak provides extra focus, rounded finish. Partly cask-fermented/matured 11 mths, used Fr oak. 13,3% alc. 5 000 cases. **99** plummily succulent, well oaked.

Ridge Red ☻ Reliable **NV**, now all-SA cinsaut/cab blend (pvs with Fr component); vin ordinaire with more than ordinary substance. Spicy berry mouthful, firm but unintimidating tannins; balanced, dry. 5 000 cases

Shiraz Dense, soft textured **00** will appeal now to those who enjoy sweet-spicy Am oak (well supported with shiraz's chocolatey breadth); the savoury-toothed might be rewarded in further yr/2. 11 mths Fr/Am oak. 13.4% alc. 6 000 cases. **Pinotage** **00** sees the homebred grape in sassy, spicy mode; tangy profile lifted by whisper oak. Solidly dry finish, fine tannins will please modernists now and over next 3-4 yrs. 9 000 cases. **Chardonnay** **00**'s plentiful lively fruit now becoming cream-textured. Balance, length for ongoing pleasure over yr/2. Lightly oaked. 13.4% alc. 5 000 cases. **01** not ready for tasting; similarly styled. **Chenin Blanc** Bottle age adds fresh-cream/honey attractions to **00**; firm, concentrated palate elongated by soupcon balanced sugar. Best before mid-02. 10 000 cases. **01** not ready for tasting; will be in same style. **Sauvignon Blanc** **01** big (14% alc), very ripe yet agreeably dry; balanced by tropical/fig concentration, good leesy padding. Food rather than sipping wine. **Chenin-Chardonnay** Favourite in Germany, which sole market for this partly wooded blend. **01** not ready for tasting; should follow pvs crisp, well-weighted style. **00** . **Bay Blanc** Aromatic colombard, chenin, sauvignon partnership usually provides lively, dry quaffing. 5 000 cases. **01** not ready for tasting. Discontinued: **Bouquet Blanc**. *— AL*

L'Ormarins Estate

*Franschhoek • Tasting by appointment • Cellar tours Mon-Fri 10 11.30 & 3 • Owner & managing director Anthonij Rupert plus three directors • Winemaker Wrensch Roux (since 1997) • Viticulturist Danie Botha (since 1998) • Vineyards 200 ha • Production 1 300 tons 50 000 cases (800 tons own labels) 60% white 40 red • PO Box 435 Franschhoek Valley 7690 • **Tel (021) 874-1026** • Fax (021) 874-1361 • E-mail sales@lormarins.co.za*

This is not just another Cape showpiece but rather a real piece of old Cape, restored to its current glamour by the Rupert dynasty (it's been in their possession for over 30 years). The property reflects their inimitable style with no detail left untouched, no expense spared and a tasting locale that is truly special (visits by appointment). Owner Anthonij Rupert, youngest son of global businessman and conservation patron Dr Anton Rupert, has his finger on the pulse here, and in the pie at several other winelands ventures including Rupert & Rothschild and latest manifestations, Rooderust and (untasted by us) Terra Del Capo Sangiovese. The estate forms a magnificent backdrop to the inspired wines made by Wrensch Roux (the 98 Merlot now winging its way round the world on LTU, the second-largest German international airline) throughout all the seasons and especially in winter, when a waterfall cascading its way down the Groot Drakenstein adds a spectacular natural flourish.

Optima ✓ Chic, consistent merlot-dominated bdx blend, well priced for this quality (bottled-matured 2 yrs prior to release). Cabs s/f in supporting roles in beautifully elegant **97**, blackcurrant, smoked meat aromas with savoury dried-apricot (mebos) nuances; classically structured palate, fine dry minerally tannins, balanced acidity. Couple of yrs to go. 18 mths oak, 60% new. 12,8% alc. 5 800 cases. **96** something of a triumph in difficult vintage. **95** warmer vintage; supple, minty.

Shiraz Sticking to its own style (and all better for it). Cooler **97** revisited mid-01 sinewy but balanced; aromatic but in an ethereal way, almost scented; elegant leather/pepper sniffs and some fennel. Oaked 18 mths, 50% new casks. 12,9% alc.

Cabernet Sauvignon Cooler vintage leaves its imprint in more compact **97**, with Medoc-like restraint. Back-tasted mid-01 shows savoury, forest-floor characters, some cigarbox, soft dry finish. Approaching peak. 12.8% alc. 18 mths Fr oak, 60% new. **96** herby, cedary on release. Neither reaches gorgeous heights of **95**.

Merlot Ripe-vintage **98** back-tasted mid-01 holding; food style rather than standalone; soft, plummy fruit with mocha, fennel; med-weight, dry finish. **99** more concentration, structure; richer christmas-pudding tones and whiffs eucalyptus, sweet vanilla, cinnamon spice. Legs for ±5 yrs. 15 mths oak, 70% new. 12.9% alc.

Sauvignon Blanc ✓ Latest **01** textbook stuff: pungent capsicum, fig, cut-grass aromas, translating into bright nettly/figgy palate; med-weight, green freshness in dry finish. Delicious. 12.8% alc.

Chardonnay Not a shouting style, med-weight but satisfying; versatile at table. **01** (sample) delicate sweet-melon fruit, shy butterscotch hints; elegant brioche flavours. Portion new barrel-fermented/sur lie 6 mths, remainder tank/2nd fill oak matured. 13,3% alc. **Blanc Fumé** Lightly oaked sauvignon in understated, food-cordial mode. **01** elegant, balanced, not too full; tropical fruits over fresh toast, attractive spicy bouquet. Green pepper finish. 12.8% alc. **Grand Vin Blanc** Early-drinking style; lightly-oaked chardonnay with unwooded sauvignon. **00**, retasted mid-01, shy herbal tones with hints marzipan; elegant, dry, lemon rind in finish; subtle spiciness. ±12% alc. **Rhine Riesling** Latest **01** not ready for tasting. **00**. **Pinot Grigio** Name change from Pinot Gris in pvs ed consistent with the Ruperts' internationally plugged-in approach. Refined, doesn't shout. **01** spicy, pine needles/nuts bouquet; supple apricot-kernel tastes. Good food wine, unwooded, med-bodied. 15-19 yr-old vyds. — *TM*

Lost Horizons Wines 

*Tasting & sales at Simonsvlei International (see that entry) Tasting fee R5 for 6 wines • Owner Norton Cooper • General manager Jacques Jordaan • Consulting viticulturist Schalk du Toit (VinPro) • Production ±550 tons 150 000 cases 60% white 40% red • PO Box 568 Paarl 7624 • **Tel (021) 863-3848** • Fax (021) 863-3850 • E-mail horizons@global.co.za • Website www.global.co.za/~horizons/*

A joint venture between Lost Horizons, French-based Chambord et Cie and Paarl winery, Simonsvlei International, this new wave wine success story ships upwards of 150 000 cases to more than a dozen countries. Tailormade wines (from the 550-ton crush at Koelenhof or bought in from Stellenbosch, Paarl and Worcester) are bottled at Simonsvlei's state-of-the-art winery. The distinctive range is all about texture and colour, from soft, velvety reds to crisp whites, fashionably packaged in sculpted blue bottles, available in generous 'magnum' sizes, and food-friendly to boot. Their Guardian label Chenin Blanc is strutting its stuff in the growing German market for SA wines and they're looking at a local version in similar garb. Fresh-faced Quantum, the sociable white blend that's been spritzing its way to events around the country, has been joined on the guest list by a stylish new off-dry, pretty-in-pink rosé version, equally socially adroit and popular, both flying off the shelves to be quaffed by the litre.

Cabernet Sauvignon ✓ Smidgeon sugar does the crowd-pleasing trick here, along with generous scoops sweet fruit, undimmed by oak; **98** mulberries, licks blackcurrant-jam; latest **99** ripe blackcurrant and plenty of new-world juice with anise/fennel whiffs; slightly drier than pvs (4.5 g/ℓ sugar vs 5,1 g/ℓ). 6 000 cases.

Classic Red ☻ Unpretentious **99** will complement similar occasions, especially braais. Soft orange-ruby hues are easy on the eye; succulent, lightish, slightly sweet tomato-jam flavours easy on the tongue. Unwooded mix ruby cab, cab, merlot. 20 000 cases. **Quantum Petillant Rosé** NEW ☻ Of its style, one of SA's top sellers (25 000 cases); **00** excellent picnic wine with bright strawberry/cherry aromas; light, just-not-dry, delicately sparkling tastes. **Sauvignon Blanc** ☻ **01** set to win plenty of fans with non-aggressive apple/pear flavours, slight herbal tones; soft and supple. 13% alc. 6 000 cases. **Quantum Petillant Blanc** ☻ Sophisticated party animal in 1 000 ml blue bottle, chenin-sauvignon with refreshing carbonated tingle. Off-dry tastes for easy celebrating. Latest **00** haystack/cut grass aromas, zingy lemon /green apple tastes. 25 000 cases.

Cabernet Sauvignon-Merlot **99** nice plum-jam nose with hints tobacco; lighter style, slightly savoury, good dry finish tones well with pizza, tomato-sauced pasta. 13% alc. 7 000 cases Chardonnay **00** somewhat neutral, low acid, med-bodied dry white with understated peach/citrus tones, quick finish. 13.5% alc. 8 000 cases. **Chenin Blanc** Not tasted for this ed. Pvs **99**. **Classic White** Interesting dried apricot/roasted almond aromas in **00**, light citrus flavours and bone dry finish. 10 000 cases of chenin, sauvignon. — *TM*

Louiesenhof Wines 

Stellenbosch (see Stellenbosch map) • Tasting & sales Mon-Fri 9-5 Sat 9-1 (Easter-Sep), otherwise Mon-Sat 9-5 Sun 11-5 Tasting fee R5 p/p • Light meals served on terrace Nov-Mar. Booking essential • Views • Wheelchair-friendly •

Owner/winemaker Stefan Smit • Viticulturist Casper Burger (since 1995) • Vineyards 169 ha • Production ± 1 300 tons • PO Box 2013 Dennesig 7601 • ***Tel (021) 882-2632*** *• Fax (021) 882-2613 • E-mail lhofwine@iafrica.com • Website www.louiesenhof.com*

THE HEAD-TURNING wide-angle view over the Simonsberg and Stellenbosch Valley from Stefan Smit's farm, on the slopes of Papegaaiberg and spilling into Devon Valley, is enough to make you dizzy. Now you can come and take it in, ensconced on the stoep or sprawled on the lawn, or sip wines while taking in an awesome sunset. With keen conversationalist Smit, there's bound to be a stimulating discussion worth entering into: get him chatting about his brandy, sipped by serious cognoscenti, and he'll wax lyrical about his unique German distilling kettle. Mention port, and he'll describe parcels of roobernet now coming on stream. Or his talented young daughter Louie, and he'll whip out her latest masterpiece, destined for the labels on the whites. "I want people to feel they can come here, even on their own, and leave with something more than they came for!" says this warm-hearted winemaker.

Chardonnay Sur Lie Limited Release Elegantly styled **00** step up from **99**. Generous lime fruit, earthy nuances, smooth hints of integrated oak. Just off-dry, but crisp compensating acidity. 50% barrel-fermented, portion new. 13% alc. 500 cases.

Perroquet Cape Tawny Good after-dinner warmer; latest (**NV**)bottling more satisfying than pvs. Proper tawny colour, 'correct' grape (tinta), blend 93-95 vintages. High 20% alc, big acidity balance low (for SA) 80g/ℓ sugar for grippy, full-flavoured pleasure (heightened by ebony ceramic carafe, flashing come-hither looks). 500 half-cases.

Merlot Returns to guide with powerful **99**; more bones than flesh. Tarry/fruitcake aromas, moderately tannic structure, acidic finish. Oaked. 13% alc. 200 cases. **Pinotage** Back in guide with light-bodied **00**; banana-milkshake aromas suggest softness, but mouth-drying tannins meanly submerge any fruit. Yr older wood. 680 cases. **Chardonnay** New release not ready for tasting. Pvs was **99**. **Sauvignon Blanc** Occasional label. Atypical but interesting **01** taut, steely; green fig character and clean bone-dry finish. Insubstantial 12% alc. 1 000 cases. **Red Muscadel** New **00** not ready for tasting. Pvs **99**. Discontinued: **Premier Collection Cabernet Sauvignon-Cabernet Franc** (**97**). — *TJ*

Louisvale Wines

Stellenbosch (see Stellenbosch map) • Tasting & sales Mon-Fri 10-5 Sat 10-1 Fee R10 p/p • BYO picnic • Gifts • Views • Wheelchair-friendly • Owners Michael A Johnston & Hendrik Kotzé • Winemaker/viticulturist Simon Smith (since 1997) • Production 300 tons 60% red 40% white • PO Box 542 Stellenbosch 7599 • ***Tel (021) 882-2422*** *• Fax (021) 882-2633 • E-mail louisval@iafrica.com*

OVER a decade down the road at this Devon Valley winery, and Hans Froehling and Leon Stemmet were raising their glasses to the plaintive strains of distant bagpipes. The pedigreed property that they lovingly built up was sold last year to Scottish developer Michael Johnston (owner of the Carnoustie Hotel, Golf Resort and Spa, probably the toughest course in the British Open, made more so by howling winds and bone-chilling mists rolling in off the North Sea. Ernie Els, who's played in Scottish Opens held over the Angus Links, describes it as "terrifying!") and Cape Town lawyer Hendrik Kotze. London-based Master of Wine Jonathan Pedley will be developing and marketing the range. It will be a slow handover, with Froehling and Stemmet easing the transition (they've bought a smallholding in Stellenbosch to house their prized Miniature Schnauzers and Great Danes). Johnston has also acquired Stellenbosch landmark La Gratitude, which he'll be restoring. He plans to turn it into a top eatery with a 5-star hotel located behind it. Can we expect a devilish golf course next?

Dominique Flagship red, pvsly Cabernet Sauvignon-Merlot, since **97** named in honour of Hans F's & Leon S's champion miniature Schnauzer. Follow-up **98** showing good bottle development; earthy/eucalyptus wafts and hints pencil shavings; tangy sour-plum flavours in not over-extracted or too full palate; still enough structure for cellaring 4-5 yrs. Cab/merlot 65/35. 12 mths small oak. 13,6% alc. 3 500 cases. **96** VVG, **94** *Wine*.

Louisvale Chardonnay Since maiden **89**, among most consistent and best Cape chardonnays with track record for good ageing. Invariably features on Nederburg Auction. Barrel-fermented/sur lie 8 mths. **99** SAA distinctly European feel. **00** thumbprint peach/apricot tones, delicious peach-kernel dryness. More toasty, leesy than Chavant below, fuller, complex. 13,3% alc. 2 750 cases.

Louisvale Cabernet Sauvignon Comfortable, nicely-padded food wine. First was **96**, now with currant-jam aroma, stewed-fruit tastes; some honeyed tones to med-bodied palate. **97** more austere, lighter, minerally; cherries, strawberries, farmyards to sniff. **98** most overtly claret-styled of these; savoury whiffs of mince pie/smoked meat; palate-coating youthful flavours. Good now; should go good few yrs. 500 cases. These yr small-oak. Alcs 12.5-13%. Above all still available ex farm.

Louisvale Merlot Light-toned (but not -flavoured) example, from single vyd Stbosch area. **98** ripening in bottle, complex stewed-plum, savoury, damp-leaf nuances; med-bodied; varietally correct flavours with fennel finish. 500 cases. **96**, **94** VG.

Louisvale Chavant Chardonnay Began with **91** as lightly-oaked option to Louisvale Chardonnay, becoming especially popular with restaurant trade. Style continues in **00**, very full flavoured, persistent peach/apricot and hint butterscotch; well wooded (4 mths small-oak). 13.4% alc. 3 750 cases. **99** burgundian hints mushroom, lemon/grapefruit tang.

Ovation NEW Pinotage-dominated blend with merlot; juicily plush **99** light-toned and delicious. Yr small-oak. 13% alc. 500 cases. Not tasted for this ed: **LV Cabernet Sauvignon** Last was **99**; **LV Chardonnay Unwooded** Last was **99**. — *TM*

Lourensford see Wiese Portfolio
Lourens River Valley see Morgenster

Louwshoek-Voorsorg Winery

Worcester (see Worcester map) • Tastings & sales Mon-Fri 8-5 • Cellar tours by appointment • Guest cottages on Eensgevonden farm Tel (023) 349-1490 and Dwarsberg farm Tel (023) 349-1919 • Walks • 4×4 trail • Owners 32 members • Manager Gerrit van Zyl (since 2000) • Winemaker Reino Kruger (since 2000) • Consulting viticulturists VinPro • Vineyards 840 ha • Production 11 500 tons (± 2 750 cases own label) • PO Box 174 Rawsonville 6845 • ***Tel (023) 349-1110*** *• Fax (023) 349-1980 • E-mail louwshoek@xpoint.co.za*

If the wines of this Rawsonville cellar are now imbued with extra zing, that's because there's a new team infusing them with vigour and fresh ideas. Setting the faster pace is the youthful quintet of Directors, whose market-focused approach finds its counterpart in a new "cultivar plan" aimed at fine-tuning the varietal mix to the palates of the consuming public. Making it all happen is Reino Kruger, who's taken the baton from Anton Nel (now shaking up the Little Karoo from his base at Kango) and sprinting ahead with the cellar upgrade. With VinPro consultants, the 32 growers are methodically embracing new farming methods (pruning, watering and fertilisation being tweaked to produce more flavoursome grapes). Completing the clean sweep are the new front-labels for the cork-closed wines, sold under the in-house Daschbosch brand.

Daschbosch range

★**Cabernet Sauvignon** Perky-palated **01** (sample) packed with sweet red-berry, cherry fruit and green-pepper spice; good oak backing to soft tannins, clean fruity finish. For early drinking; med-bodied. Gear up from **00** ★, 9 mths oak, not as vibrantly ripe.

★**Merlot** Also stepping up is this attractive **01**, ripe plums brushed with light oak-char and very fresh, tangy finish. Pre-bottling sample shows good attack, ample fruit to cope with fairly strident tannins. For now and up to 5 yrs. 12.5% alc. 270 cases. **00** ★ less sparkly.

★**Pinotage** ✓ **01** preview ripe banana, choc/vanilla in full, round, sweet-fruited palate. Very drinkable now; enough tannin/alc for 3-5 yrs' development. 14.5% alc.

★**Nectar de Provision** ✓ This cellar's long-time signature. First local version of Cognac's classic aperitif, Pineau des Charentes; follows French methods: colombard, fortified with 5/3 yr old brandy, matured in oak. Develops rich, highly individual choc/liqueur-brandy tastes as it ages (which it deserves to). Preview of latest 00 (**NV** on label), in modern slimline bottle, finer, more sophisticated than pvs; dried apple/pear and some heathery fragrances; distinct butterscotch in palate from Nevers casking (2nd fill). ±17% alc. 179 g/ℓ sugar. 270 cases.

Chardonnay ★ Lighter-toned good everyday **01** marmalade-like flavours, well-tuned fruit/acid balance, clean apple-fresh finish. Rounded with oak chips/staves. Med-bodied. 270 cases. **Sauvignon Blanc** ★ Light, gentle **01** subdued sweet pepper nose, fresh palate with touches nettle, cut grass. 270 cases. **Port** ★ Accommodating style; light, soft, ready on release; not oversweet. Bottle age has added some attractive dried-fruit aromas to **98**, choc richness in long, smooth, spiritous finish. Old-oak. 17.5% alc. 270 cases. Discontinued: **Cabernet Sauvignon Limited Release** (pvs **99** ★), **Shiraz** (**00** ★), **Rosé** (**00** ★).

Louwshoek-Voorsorg range

Hanepoot ★ Good example of traditional SA fortified dessert. **99** very sweet yet finishing clean. 17.5% alc. — *DH*

Luddite

Walker Bay • Tasting & sales by appointment • Owners Niels Verburg & Hillie Meyer • Production 14 tons 1 000 cases 100% red • PO Box 656 Bot River 7185 • ***Tel (028) 284-9450*** *• Fax (028) 284-9617*

"I'm chuffed," says Niels Verburg of his sell-out maiden shiraz under his own label (which cocks a snook at mechanisation). Passion vinified, integrity bottled went into these wines – along with the headache of getting the packaging just right, and the crazy task of hand-numbering 6 000 bottles. All but a distant memory now. If his first 500 cases were a foot in the door, his first planting of shiraz rows on his own bit of Bot River – which he wholly believes in as red wine country – confirm that he's putting down roots. Marketing is going the niche route (he'd ultimately like to sell to people he knows on a first-name basis) with carefully selected stockists and increasing production to cover a mailing list and UK orders. Focus on shiraz – and quality – is still paramount. "It's my sincere belief that SA will make its first truly world-class wine out of shiraz," says Verburg, provocative as always.

★**Shiraz** Elegant spicy Rhone-style, more pepper/nutmeg in upcoming **01**, which fuller, smokier aromas than pvs, though both distinctly gamey, old world. Younger vintage still in cask looks more promising, with fatter fruit, raspberry/youngberry sewn with leather. More Am oak (30%), longer barrelling (30%) give standout presence compared with softer, cherry-spiced maiden **00** ✵. 14% alc. Low-cropping vyds in Bot River, Bottelary, Helderberg. 1 000 cases. — *MF*

Lusan Premium Wines

*Enquiries Garth Whaits • **Tel (021) 883-8988** • Fax (021) 883-8941 • E-mail nee@mweb.co.za*

UMBRELLA ORGANISATION for Alto, Le Bonheur, Neethlingshof, Stellenzicht and Uitkyk. Wines from these farms, totalling some 800 hectares of prime Stellenbosch vineyards, marketed by Distell. See individual entries.

Lushof Estate

*Stellenbosch (see Helderberg map) • Tasting & cellar tours by appointment as from 2002 Phone for details • Owners Steyn family • Consulting winemakers Rod Easthope & Emma Williams • Viticulturist Schalk Keyser • Vineyards 12,5 ha • Production 100 tons (2 000 cases own label, rising to 7 000 by 2003) 70% red 30% white • PO Box 899 Stellenbosch 7599 • **Tel (021) 855-3134** • Fax (021) 855-3623 • E-mail henni@icon.co.za*

IT'S BEEN FAST FORWARD at this high-Helderberg property since chemical industry businessman Hennie Steyn (who's intent on speeding things up even faster when it comes to technology) and family bought it in 1999. Briefly backtracking, their 2000 Sauvignon was awarded a gold at that year's Michelangelo awards, incentive to really put their backs into the latest vintage. Hot on the heels of producing their maiden Merlot, Cabernet Sauvignon and Chardonnay from rows replanted (Kiwi Rod Easthope and partner Emma Williams are the consulting winemakers here), was the building of the red wine maturation cellar in time for the 2002 harvest. Now they're flinging their doors open to fellow wine lovers: "We're creating the new cellar as a special, tranquil meeting place for people to come share some time with us on Lushof."

✵**Sauvignon Blanc** Statement **01** step up from pvs; fresher tasting, weightier (14% alc), brighter fruit intensity. Racy feline/wild shrub ('perdepisbos') sniffs for the olfactively adventurous. Dry finish. Maiden **00** ✭. — *TM*

Lutzville Vineyards

*Olifants River (see Olifants River map) • Tasting & sales Mon-Fri 8-1; 2-5 Sat 9.30-12 • Cellar tours by appointment • BYO picnic • Function/conference venue • Tourgroups • 4×4 trail • Owners 109 shareholders • Winemakers Jacques du Toit (since 1997) & Albie Rust (since 1989) • Viticulturist Jan Kotzé • Production 42 000 tons 95.6% white 4.4% red • PO Box 50 Lutzville 8165 • **Tel (027) 217-1516** • Fax (027) 217-1435 • E-mail lutzville@kingsley.co.za • Website www.lutzvillevineyards.com*

DOING THEIR BIT for two-way trade are the 109 shareholders of this West Coast winery, who recently took on a new skipper, Blackie van Niekerk. (Other fresh hands on deck are Chris Smit, chief of grape concentrate operations, and Hester Kriel, quality controller.) From Europe, they've imported high-tech red wine fermenters and an ultra-gentle pneumatic press, giving them denser colours without excessive tannins. By return, they've sent over wine to Europe, the Far East and North Africa. And, no doubt, toasted their trading *amis* with bottles of the new value range, Friends. The Fleermuisklip label (which derives its name locally from a massive rock, once a shelter for bats and early explorers, now a national monument) has been extended and repackaged, and sports a more contemporary look.

Colombard ☻ ⁂ Light, smooth **00** still lively and refreshing, with variety's guava tang. 800 cases.

Cabernet Sauvignon ⁑ First release **98** in danger of falling over; drink up. Yr oaked. 1 000 cases. **Pinotage** ⁂ **99** holding, with tannins to go a short while. Lightly oaked. 13% alc. 2 000 cases. **Ruby Cabernet** ⁂ Variety's savouriness shines in unwooded **00**; obvious earthy tannins. Plums from splash merlot. 13.5% alc. 600 cases. **Chardonnay Wooded** ⁑ **00** partial cask-fermentation adds smoky dimension to muted peach crispness. 13% alc. 200 cases. **Chardonnay Unwooded** ⁑ "Ideal with rock lobster," say winemakers. **01** unexpressive of variety, but pleasant enough. 13% alc. 800 cases. **Chenin Blanc Dry** NEW ⁑ **01** frisky white with attractive sherbety crispness. 1 000 cases. **Sauvignon Blanc** ⁂ **01** single vyd in Vaalkrans area; peppery, zesty casual quaff; drink soon. 13% alc. 1 000 cases. **Semillon** ⁑ Lightish **00** very crisp dry white; vinous rather than fruity. 400 cases. **Chenin Blanc Off-Dry** ⁑ Delicate, appley **01**, drier than expected, uncomplicated quick quaff. 1 000 cases. **Diamant Celebration 2000** ⁂ Light, sweetish sparkle growing honeyed, creamy. Time to drink up. Mainly colombard. 300 cases.

Fleermuisklip range

Robyn ☻ ⁂ **99** similar to Sunset below, bit more concentrated; ruby cab/cab. 13,5% alc. 300 cases.

Blanc de Noir NEW ⁂ Coral-hued **01**; candyfloss, bubblegum perfumes; sweetness cut by acid. Ruby cab. 600 cases. **Colombard-Chardonnay** NEW ★ Lightish **00** equal blend probably better in youth. 300 cases. **Bukettraube** Not tasted for this ed; pvs **99** ⁂. **Bouquet Blanc** NEW ⁑ **01** gentle, fragrant sip from moric muscat; bitterish finish. 13% alc. 600 cases. **Diamant 99** Semi-sweet, lighter-bodied 75/25 colombard/semillon blend. Untasted. **Somersoet** ★ **00** literally 'Summer Sweet', which it is. From colombard. 13.2% alc. 150 cases. **Late Harvest** ⁑ **01** from chenin; sweet, smooth. Try with Mexican cuisine, winemakers suggest. 12.8% alc. 600 cases. **Diamant Sparkling** ★ Lightish carbonated bubbly; **NV** (99) honeyed, very little fizz. 300 cases. **Muscadel** ⁂ NEW Unusual pepper/minty touches in **01**, bright-fruited, spiritous despite lowish 16.6% alc. Muscat de f. 600 cases. This replaces **Hanepoot Jerepico** Pvs **99** ⁑.

Friends range

These **NV**s in 500 ml screwtop.

Ruby Sunset ☻ ⁂ Peppers and plums on the tongue, and just enough tannins to make a good food partner. Unwooded ruby cab. 13.5% alc.

Misty Morning ⁑ Crisp dry white; blend chenin, colombard, semillon. 300 cases. **Sunny Day** ⁑ Sweet, gentle and fresh colombard. Lightish 12% alc, as is Misty above. — *DH*

Lyngrove see Baarsma

Maiden Wine Cellars NEW

Gordon's Bay • Tasting/cellar tours by appointment • MD Peter Venter • Marketing Danie Hattingh • PO Box 272 Gordon's Bay 7151 • ***Tel (021) 856-3052*** *• Fax (021) 856-5085 • E-mail mwines@mweb.co.za or peterventer@mweb.co.za • Website www.maidenwines.com*

Peter Venter & Danie Hattingh are the public faces of this young negociant company, targeting the increasingly receptive US market from an HQ on the False Bay coast. The Private Reserve below is a multi-appellation blend, a la Australia, from selected producers in the Olifants and Breede River areas.

Private Reserve ☆ Time needed to bring complex aromas/tastes into harmony with one another and the (pleasingly) dry tannin structure. **99** warm plummy tones, fennel-fragrant finish. Unfiltered; 10-14 mths oak, 50% new. Promising addition to Cape Red genre (cab/shiraz/pinotage 60/30/10). 1 000 half-cases. — *DH*

Main Street Winery

Paarl • Tasting & cellar tours by appointment • Owner/winemaker Marais de Villiers • Production 7 tons 500 cases (own label) 100% red • PO Box 2709 Paarl 7620 • ***Tel/fax (021) 872-3006*** *• E-mail mainstreet@mweb.co.za*

Turning visions into reality is the subtext of this feel-good venture, characterfully housed in the original high-beamed Schoongezicht cellar on Paarl's main street. Marais de Villiers and six other participant winemakers, all with their own labels, always hoped to someday make their own wines in their own cellar. Now they're making it happen by sharing space and some of the costs, and vinifying their bought-in grapes in a modular system designed by Marais de V. Under a label created specially by students of Cape Town's Red & Yellow Advertising School, de Villiers is launching the first Main Street wines. If these fly, it's likely more wineries will bud on the main street. "We're hoping," says Marais de V, "to inspire other enthusiasts to stop wishing and take the plunge!"

☆**Shiraz** Unmistakably shiraz, **99**'s pepperiness matched by concentrated black-cherry/mulberry fruits, integrated oak; textures still tight, need yr/2 to relax/develop. 13.8% alc. **01** seems the bigger wine, though alc's lower; aromatic, concentrated, christmas-cake flavours more in tune with spicy oak; youthfully taut but promising.

Cabernet Sauvignon ☆ Rustic tones emanate from **00** ("animal style", says Marais de V); fairly concentrated grassy/nutty aromas; very firm tannins need time. 13.5% alc. 400 half-cases. **99** old style, meaty, tight with hints of violets. **01** not ready for tasting. **Merlot** ☆ Soft red berries; whiffs coffee and slightly nutty finish. **99** subtly oaked, well structured. Preview **01** advance on **99**; riper fruit, oak still dominant mid-01; given time, should offer satisfying drinking. **Shiraz-Cabernet Sauvignon** ☆ Soft ripe mulberries/plums in **00** bouquet, transferring into more complex albeit tight-wound palate with, mid-01, slightly bitter, oaky tones that may dissipate with time. 13% alc. 300 cases. — *CF*

Makro

In-store tasting Sat 10-2 • Sales Mon-Fri 9-6 Sat 8.30-4 • Enquiries Gary Barber • ***Tel (011) 797-0664*** *• Fax (011) 803-8695 • E-mail gbarber@makro.co.za • Website www.makro.co.za*

With serious buying power and market-tuned instintcs, Gary Barber and his team constantly refine this range, distinguished by one-off specials and customised styles commissioned from selected cellars for exclusive sale through Makro outlets. Labels bought at wine shows and auctions also feature prominently in the line, along with magnum-sized offerings – great for gifts and special celebrations. All of which creates unusually high excitement for a national discount chainstore. Babbling Brook, their well-regarded value range, creates a different sort of rush, as do the easy-on-the-pocket Turtle Creek and the funky @blaauwklippen ranges.

Private Reserve range

These all exclusive to Makro, all NEW.

☆**Bouwland Cabernet Sauvignon Reserve** Succulent fruit provides the headline for **98**; deep piled, complex with sweetish tannins to go with the fruitcakey tastes. Super now and up to ±4 yrs.

✷**Overgaauw Touriga Nacional-Cabernet Sauvignon** Characterful, highly unusual blend in Cape; densely textured and firmly (but not uncomfortably) tannined; for keeping. Maiden **97** set the pace. Latest is power-packed **00**; keep for a splashy Sunday roast, mid-decade.

Louisvale Cabernet Sauvignon ⁂ Realistically priced **00** delivers lots of pleasurable sensations; pliable tannins carry them through to finish. Lightly oaked ±13% alc. **La Bri Cabernet Sauvignon-Merlot** ⁂ Pleasant, gently contrasting pepper/berry/choc tastes in **99**, 70/30 configuration for early drinking. 13% alc. **Turtle Creek Dry Red** Not ready for tasting. **Turtle Creek Dry White** ⁑ Light (11.3% alc) **01** with Caribbean fruit flavours; fresh finish. Above Turtles from Bon Courage. **Misty Mountain** ⁑ **01** vaguely tropical, lightish, unremarkable off-dry blend sauvignon, semillon, hanepoot. Ex Agusta. 1 000 ml. **Mijn Burg Pinotage** ⁂ Lively, fruity **00**, variety hardly recognisable but flavours ripe, quite soft, and should carry to maturity in 3-5 yrs. 13.5% alc.

Louisvale Chardonnay ⁂ Louisvale aren't known for quick-quaff styles, but we can't resist pinning a ☻ to **01**, with exhilarating acidic uplift to sweet, sherbety fruit. 13.1% alc. **Cellar Release Sauvignon Blanc** ☻ ⁂ **00** gathers an unlikely cast – cat's pee, lemonade, gooseberry – in a merry (but short-lived, so drink soonest) production. Ex Rickety Bridge. 13.2% alc.

Babbling Brook range

✷**Cabernet Sauvignon Reserve** Courtly **95** offers pleasing complexity, secondary cedar, pencil box, tobacco pouch. Slightly dry-oak finish suggests drink soonish, or monitor if keeping. 12.3% alc. Ex Lievland.

✷**Cabernet Sauvignon** ✓ **99** with old-Cape whiffs leather, tobacco, more modern ripe tannins for early approachability.

✷**Shiraz 00** offers piquant scrubby aromas/flavours and firm dry finish for savoury food -partnering. 6 mths Fr/Am oak, some new. 13.5% alc. From Mijn Burg.

Grand Vin Rouge ☻ ⁂ Beyond the highfalutin name frolics jovial **98**; plum-fruited, soft, easy for casual alfresco occasions. 12.8% alc. Ex Lievland.

Merlot ⁂ Ripe, sappy style with intriguing dried geranium nuances. **99** drinks easily now and could go yr/2. **Pinotage** ⁑ **99** for fans of the 'unplugged' style – raw tannins, wild banana whiffs – the whole food-craving number. With its own peculiar charms. Ex Rickety Bridge, as are Pinotage, Cabernet above.

@blaauwklippen range NEW

Exclusively for Makro by Blaauwklippen.

Pinotage ⁂ Bright-fruited **00**, recognisably pinotage with none of the variety's downsides. Mere suggestion of oak. **Pinot Noir** ⁂ **01** light, pleasant, ripe strawberry, gently dry for drinking now. "Fun wine," say vintners, aptly. **Shiraz** ⁂ Genteel, quaffable **01**; tannin structure for immediate accessibility. **Zinfandel** ⁂ **99** shiny, fragrant; velvety tannins and grain sugar for extra sleekness. Merest suggestion of oak. 14% alc. **Chardonnay** ⁂ **00** yr barrelled, giving texture/dimension to peachy fruit. Lightish; for early drinking. **Sauvignon Blanc** ⁂ **01** not much varietal character , but attractive crisp dry, easy. 13.5% alc.

Mont d'Or range

Inexpensive **NV** sparkling range by Simonsig.

Brut ☆ Fruity and unaggressive dry fizz; creamy textures and clean finish. **Vin Sec** Characterful sweetish everyday bubble; mouthfilling, with attractive minerally core. Not for ageing. 11% alc. **Vin Doux** ☆ Uncomplex but not charmless semi-sweet, floral tones complemented by ripe perky sparkle. Low 10.5% alc. — *DH*

Malan Family Vintners

COLOURFULLY and simply attired range by the Malan brothers of Simonsig, including brands listed under Simonsig in previous editions. Mainly for offshore markets, though available from selected local outlets and as housewines in some restaurant chains. See also Simonsig.

Sauvignon Blanc ☻ ☆ Decidedly tropical fullness to **01** (sample), with grass/green pea tension adding fresh interest. Invigorating.

Pinotage ☆ Bright unwooded **99**'s unambiguous baked plums leavened by ripe cherry/mulberry fruit, pvs noted bracing end softening. Pour with pasta. No **00**. **Cabernet Sauvignon-Merlot** ☆ No longer carries Adelberg label from **00**, although fondly known as such; smoky, dusty aromas, savoury/fennel flavours, tannic twist to finish. **Rouge du Cap** ☆ **NV** (00) piquant red-berry fruit ensemble laced with leather/spice. Brisk, dry, simple finish, fine for hearty hot-pots. Ruby cab, pinotage, pinot. **Chardonnay** ☆ **00** barrel-fermented, tangy, herbaceous spice notes; full, juicy with tart finish. **Blanc du Cap** ☆ **NV** (00) boasts aromatic muscat nose, grapey, firm dry finish from chardonnay, with 1/3 each riesling, colombard. **Adelblanc** ☆ Grassy crispness to **00**, fleshy mouthful, dry tail; from sauvignon, chenin, colombard. — *DS*

Marthinus see Bovlei
Maskam see Vredendal

Masters Port

Very distinguished Cape 'port': equal-parts blend of the best 500 ℓ barrels from Calitzdorp maestros, Carel Nel of Boplaas, Boets Nel of Die Krans and Tony Mossop of Axe Hill, all three Cape Wine Masters. Enquiries: Boplaas Tel (044) 213-3326 • Die Krans **Tel (044) 213-3314** • Axe Hill **Tel (021) 780-1051** • Also see those entries for tasting/sales information.

☆**Cape Vintage Reserve** Serious example, combining some diverse talents. Still-available **98** ☆☆ beautifully harmonious on retaste mid-01, approachable (but better in 4-8 yrs), balanced. Warm, ripe-fruity spread of touriga, tinta, souzao. 18 mths port pipes. 160 cases. Original **97** bit smoother on release. These *Wine* ☆; alcs ±19%; sugars ±92 g/ℓ. — *DH*

Maze Valley Wines NEW

Wellington (see Wellington map) • Tasting & sales by appointment Mon-Fri 9-5 • Owners Derek & June Holt • Winemaker Bertus Fourie (since 2000) • Vineyard manager Hendrik Laubscher (since Aug 1996) • Vineyards 30 ha • Production 150 tons 3 000 cases 75% red 25% white • PO Box 157 Wellington 7654 • ***Tel (021) 864-1154*** *cell 082 658-3866 • Fax (021) 864-1984 • E-mail doolhof@ezinet.co.za*

THE beautiful wine and stud farm Doolhof, tucked into a labyrinthine cleft between two mountains, gives this young range its name. Owners Derek and June Holt are ensconced in Scotland but their 370 hectares near Wellington are tended by man-of-the-soil Hendrik Laubscher, whose personal wine-highlight to date has been "to open a bottle produced by ourselves, and with our own label on". The vineyards – 30 ha of classic reds and whites plus pinotage – are towered over by Bainskloof and

Groenberg, "so they get less direct sunlight than the rest of Wellington", explains Bertus Fourie, who makes the wines at nearby Diemersfontein until they find their vinous feet and build their own cellar. The maiden releases were shown at a trade fair in the UK recently and pounced on by several agents.

Cabernet Sauvignon ⁑ Jammy, over-ripe style. Lightly oaked **01** sweetish to taste, 7g/ℓ sugar not masked by pleasant acidity, chunky tannins. Hot finish from 15% alc. 373 cases. **Merlot** ⁂ Massive, intense **01**; concentrated, ripe, meaty nose. Mouthfilling, but showing sweetness of 4g/ℓ sugar, with firm dry tannins. Exhausting 15.5% alc. Portion new Am-oaked. 238 cases. **Pinotage** ★ **01** overwhelmed by toasty wood (staves); fugitive fruit in warmly round palate, before roasting coffee-bean finish. 14.5% alc. 323 cases. **Shiraz** ⁑ Very toasty/smoky, some red berries trying to find breathing space. **01** massively built (15.5% alc); bright acidity, sweetish note to end with. 10% new Am oak. 208 cases. **Chardonnay** ⁑ Early-drinking **01**, orange peel/tropical fruits; dilute, flabby flavours but warmly mouthfilling from 14% alc. 500 cases. **Chardonnay (Wooded)** ⁂ **01** Experimental barrel-fermented/matured version (only 900 bottles) tasted ex-barrel. Toasty oak very apparent, but nicely textured; round and crisp; fleeting citrus flavours. 14% alc. **Sauvignon Blanc** ⁂ Undemandingly pleasant **01**; figgy/grassy character, refreshing dry palate leading to hardish pear-drop finale. 500 cases. Note: All above tasted pre-bottling; ratings provisional. — *TH*

McGregor Winery

*Robertson (see Robertson map) • Tasting & sales Mon-Thu 8-12.30; 1.30-5 Fri 8-5 Sat 9-12.30 • Cellar tours by appointment • Owners 41 members • Winemaker Pieter Carstens (since 1999) with Gerhard Swart (since 2000) • Viticulturalist Anton Laas • Consulting viticulturalist Briaan Stipp (since 1993) • Vineyards 680 ha • Production 8 473 tons 25 000 cases • Private Bag X619 McGregor 6708 • **Tel (023) 625-1741** • Fax (023) 625-1829 • E-mail mcg@intekom.co.za*

'Mystical McGregor' reads the tourist brochure, 'where time stood still'. While this may reflect the quiet hamlet "at the end of a road going nowhere", it certainly doesn't describe the switched-on, plugged-in winery on the fringe of the town, whose wines are spotted at dining tables from Poland to Sri Lanka. Already far advanced in the classification of vineyards for their various ranges, Pieter Carstens and new in-house viticulturalist Anton Laas are now looking at adding premium wines from top-performing blocks to their line of "palate-friendly styles". First up is likely to be a Cabernet, to be followed, possibly, by a Chardonnay. They're also hoping to produce more varietal Reserve in particularly auspicious vintages. Exports, meanwhile, are booming (they're now doing it for themselves in the international arena, having worked with an agent previously). Ever popular, locally and overseas, is their signature Colombard, which has found its Shangri-la in these bushvine-cordial unirrigated soils.

Village Red ☻ ⁂ Flavoursome quaff with good ruby cab character; **00** sweet strawberries and soft tannins for now and 1-2 yrs; Fr oak. 13% alc. **Colombard-Chardonnay** ☻ ⁂ **01** tropical-toned swimming pool wine, surprisingly rich with racy freshness. 60/40 blend unwooded, med-bodied. **Mystery Brut** ☻ ⁂ Lively, lightish, unpretentious sparkler with lemon-lime suggestions and mouthfilling dry mousse. **NV** from sauvignon.

Cabernet Sauvignon-Merlot ⁑ **00** tautish savoury 80/20 blend; good with sturdy food. Lightly oaked. 13.2% alc. **Pinotage** ⁂ Sweet-fruited, balanced **00** finishes briskly dry with brush of tannin. 13.5% alc. **Rosé** ⁂ Full-bodied drink-young semi-sweet from pinotage. Ripe plums and peppers in **00**, finishing crisply. 13.4% alc. **Chardonnay** ⁂ Lightly oaked **01** with understated peach/

lemon and attractive smoky whiffs. Not too dry. 13.7% alc. **Chenin Blanc** ☆ Fresh, fruity dry quaffer offering guavas and pears in **01**. Enjoy within yr of harvest, advises Pieter C. **Sauvignon Blanc** ★ Gooseberries, pepper and bracing freshness in **01**. For early drinking with food (steamed asparagus, shellfish, fresh trout among Pieter C's recommendations). **Colombard** ☆ Light muscat-like tones in off-dry **01**, crisply clean finish. "For sipping on a summer's day and picnics." **Vin Sec** ☆ Lightish sweet fizz with understated honey flavour. Carbonated. **NV**. **Red Muscadel** ★ **00** bright, fragrant fortified with delicate honeysuckle perfume; lightly chill and enjoy while young and fresh. 16.5% alc. **White Muscadel** ☆ **01** unctuous fortified to sip beside a fire. 16.5% alc.

Vrolikheid range NEW

'Jolly' wines in 500 ml six-packs. Easy, budget-priced. Name alludes to cluster of farms in the McGregor area.

Dry Red Not ready for tasting. **Dry White** ★ **01** relaxed ripe tropical tones. Med-bodied chenin, just-dry. **Late Harvest** Not ready for tasting. — *DH*

Meerendal Estate

Durbanville (see Durbanville map) • Tasting & sales Mon-Fri 8.30-5 Sat 9-12.30 Closed Sun Tasting fee R10 p/p • Function/conference facilities, call Francois Ferreira • Owner JCF Starke Trust • Winemaker/ viticulturist Soon Potgieter (since 1973) • Vineyard manager Fanie Rost (since 1996) • Vineyards 200 ha • PO Box 2 Durbanville 7551 • ***Tel (021) 975-1655*** *• Fax 975-1657 • E-mail meerendal@mweb.co.za*

This historic estate (circa 1702) has been colouring its future in decidedly rosy hues. While winemaker Soon Potgieter's belief in blends saw the acclaimed debut of their 98 Cabochon, the full range of reds have starring roles. But the whites, particularly the gewürz they're known for, aren't being left in the shade either. Trustee William Starke declares last year's dry Gewürztraminer "decidedly and deliciously" different to previous vintages. New back labels feature entertaining wine quotes: the Sauvignon's reads: "Only the first wine is expensive" (an old French proverb) – but not here, where that initial bottle and all the others that follow are sensibly priced, some of the most affordable wines around given the quality.

★ **Cabernet Sauvignon** ✓ **98** developing elegantly; oak, cassis, blackberry fruit, fine tannins all harmonious, smooth; enough stuffing/structure for 10 yrs' good ageing. 13 mths small Fr oak. 13,6% alc. Follow-up **99** not ready for tasting.

★ **Merlot** ✓ Steadily improving label. First **97** ★ easy drinking if somewhat rustic; next **98** riper; extra heft from 14,2% alc; SAYWS gold. Current **99** edging into ★ bracket. Fleshy, almost juicy; amazingly accessible for its age. Yr Fr oaked. 2 550 cases.

☆ **Cabochon** ✓ Well constructed equal cab/merlot blend, balancing latter's opulence, former's discipline. Maiden **98** weighty, contrasting blackcurrant/parma ham aromas. **99** crammed with ripe berries/choc; smooth tannic spine should easily last 6-8 yrs. 2 500 cases. These yr small Fr barriques; alcs ±14.2% alc.

★ **Pinotage** ✓ Current **98**, back-tasted mid-01, growing touch savoury, stewed fruity; suggest drink soonish. 2 500 cases. This, Shiraz below also in 1,5 ℓ magnums.

★ **Shiraz** ✓ Since **95** ★ in modern style, fruitier, seriously oaked (small Fr casks, ±yr). Notch-up **96** produced massive flavours in difficult red yr; (**97** untasted;) current **98** lower-keyed, slighter than 13.2% alc would suggest; urbane (bit like Michael Broadbent, UK walking wine encyclopaedia, quoted on back label), developing pleasing peppery/smoky tones. Drink or keep few yrs.

★ **Natural Sweet** ✓ Unblended gewürz; **98**, first dessert from estate, VG, *Wine* ★, SAYWS champ. Tasted mid-00, merited ★. Current **99** in different class:

gilded hues, freesia scents; grapefruity lusciousness. ±15% alc beautifully absorbed. 1 440 cases.

Gewürztraminer ☆ Back in guide with **01**, ravishingly dry (not for drinking on its own), petally, lightish-bodied. 2 833 cases. **Sauvignon Blanc** ☆ Returns to guide with **01**, vibrant expression of Dbnville terroir; sweet-fruited palate ends rousingly dry – strike back with braaied snoek. **Liberté Blanc NV** (99) Gewürz/chardonnay dry blend. Past best. 13,6% alc. **Blanc de Blanc** ☆ Satisfying dry med-full **01**, chardonnay/sauvignon parity, though latter's nettley zest more obvious. 2 500 cases (× 6, as are all above). Discontinued: **Navette** (not tasted for pvs ed). — *DH*

Meerlust Estate

Stellenbosch (see Helderberg map) • Tasting by appointment Fee R55 p/p (includes cellar tour) • Sales Mon-Thu 9-5 Fri 9-4.30 • Cellar tours by appointment • Owner Hannes Myburgh • Winemaker Giorgio Dalla Cia (since 1978) with Rudi de Wet (since 2000) • Viticulturist Roelie Joubert (since 2001) • PO Box 15 Faure 7131 • ***Tel (021) 843-3587*** *• Fax (021) 843-3274 • E-mail meerlust@iafrica.com*

HANNES Myburgh, eighth-generation owner of this elegant and prestigious estate, and Italian-born Giorgio Dalla Cia, courtly winemaker here for more than 20 years and an authentic Cape wine icon, won't soon forget 2001. It was the year they celebrated Dalla Cia's 60th birthday; launched (quietly, for sale ex cellar only) the first new wine in 6 years – a Sauvignon; and parted company with long-time marketing & distribution partners Distell. Much more importantly, they toasted the triumphant return of their beloved *funghi*. The previous pair of vintages had been near-complete failures: too-warm autumns, too-cold early winters. Bt last season brought respite in timely cool and damp conditions – ideal for the development of the fleshy, meaty boletus, which soon wafted their decadent aroma about the Meerlust kitchen. (Jocular) threats of leaving the country shelved, Dalla Cia revealed what he terms "the next challenge for Meerlust": viognier. They planted this famous northern-Rhone white grape two years ago (along with "lots" of cabernet, some pinot and petit verdot, among others), and Dalla Cia has already decided that he will vinify his viognier as he does the full-throated Meerlust Chardonnay: in new, heavy-toasted barrels, allowing 20 months' lees suffusion "for complexity". "There is great potential for viognier production in SA," Dalla Cia declares. How does he know his approach will work? "If you dream a lot," replies the maestro simply, "you will succeed."

☆☆**Rubicon** With pretenders aplenty, this standard bearer, pre-eminent Cape 'claret' over its 21-yr history, still holds court. Consistently fine blackberry/cassis fruit, restrained by soft ripe tannins in youth, emerges elegantly with the bottle maturation required to show its best. **98** inky black, forest-floor berries, brambles hemmed in by tense grassiness; stylish, sustained length of finish signals wonderful maturation potential. Gentle 12.7% alc despite ripe year. Notably devoid of cheery fruit, gauche Am oak. Designed to grace refined cellars: keep min 7 yrs, preferably longer. **97**'s arresting extraction demands forbearance, will bring its rewards. These par with acclaimed **95**, **91** and greats of the 80s: **89**, **87**, **86**. Slighter **96** ☆ with tannic gravitas, has Dalla Cia expecting a 20-yr life span. 70% cab, 20% merlot, 10% cab f. Petit verdot to join palette when vines mature. 2 yrs Nevers, 80% new.

☆**Merlot** Chefs of note have been known to add few shards grated, good bitter choc to game dishes' sauces. For Dalla Cia, no slouch in kitchen himself, chocolate shares some key flavour/aroma compounds with merlot. Here are all three – merlot evoking game bird, choc associations – in one (very good) bottle. **98** particularly rich, violet aromas; meaty, mocha aspects to chewy mouthful, taut finish. Delicious mid-01, will be ready on release early 02 but wants maturation to allow truffly/game characters ("pheasant breast" says Dalla Cia) to develop, as they have in compelling, minerally **97**. **96** lighter, more immediately 'charming' sweet red berries. These age well over 10 yrs. 6 t/ha from mature vyds (13-36 yrs), 80% new Nevers oak, 2 yrs. Always 10% cab. 12.8% alc.

Pinot Noir Reserve Generally fuller-bodied, less 'spiky' style from **95**, when this Reserve became estate's sole pinot label. Sample upcoming **99** in step; good colour for variety, truffly wildness backed by black cherry fruit, but touch lighter, leafier than bold **98**; effusive full-roast coffee aromas/ripe red cherries. Big, earthy wild forest mushrooms emerging from behind primary fruitiness. **97** superbly balanced, richly decadent. First vintage with some new clones for fruitier/plummier profile. Pre **94** leaner, more savoury. Regime from **96** new heavy-toast tight-grain Allier oak (±17 mths), non-standard full malo, alcs ±13%.

Chardonnay More than a decade of experimentation preceded first **95** which set new standards, defined new spectrum for SA chardonnay: weighty style, neither bold butter nor fresh citrus, rather 'fine dry white' made for table, built to mature. **99** quieter than pvs in youth, more refined, classy. Glistening flaxen colour, creamy breadth of inviting nose spiked with citric tang, feisty palate less overtly oaky, beautifully integrated: "Meursault is our benchmark" says Dalla Cia. **98** dominated by ripe fruit, big palate has crisp acid tension. **97** more settled, roast almonds, excellent length, balance; ready. Now 20 mths lees contact after 100% barrel-fermented in heavy-toast, tight-grained Allier oak, malo, regular battonage. Alcs 13.5%. 11 000 cases. — *DS*

Meinert Wines

Stellenbosch (see Helderberg map) • Not open to the public • Tasting & sales at 96 Winery Road Restaurant (see Eat-out section) • Owner/ winemaker/viticulturist Martin Meinert • Vineyards 13 ha • Production 70 tons 4 000 cases 100% red • PO Box 7221 Stellenbosch 7599 • ***Tel/fax (021) 882-2363*** *• E-mail info@meinertwines.com*

After soul-searching and agonising for months, winemaker-to-be-reckoned-with Martin Meinert (he launched Vergelegen and still makes the Ken Forrester and Sylvanvale ranges) decided not to release his 99 vintage. He's not blaming it on the vintage, even conceding that it was a bumper year for some. It simply didn't work out for him. So, true to his convictions, he's not budging on wines he doesn't implicitly believe in. With the 98 all but sold out, he found himself on a slippery slope at his prime piece of real estate, Devon Crest Vineyards. But despite this setback, tenacious Meinert ploughed ahead, focusing his efforts on the 2000 wines, to which he added a new flagship blend of all the varieties on the farm. His ultimate goal is to produce only this one cuvee, with the Devon Valley terroir and Meinert stamp strongly resonating in it.

Merlot ✓ **98** blossoming into refined expression of full, sturdy vintage. Deep smells of expensive new leather, prime fillet, cigarbox, all promising future greater complexity. Variety's silky richness fills palate with pleasing med-bodied purity; complete classic satisfaction should be achieved once taut but elegantly dry tannins have fully evolved, around 03-04. 1 200 cases. Blended with 11% cab. 13.46% alc. Used Fr. oak 18 mths. (No **99**.) **00** due first half 02, not ready for tasting. Elegant **97** cool, classically dry, probably longer maturing than **98**.

Cabernet Sauvignon-Merlot Martin Meinert feels cab is *the* variety in this picturesque valley, so from this **00** blend (with 21% merlot, 4% cab f) morphs into single varietal. On **98**'s showing, his argument is sound. Rich vinosity balanced by claret-like poise; deep blackberry, plum, lead-pencils flavours, supple fleshy texture build to climax in palate, saturate whole mouth before resolving into beautifully polished, melded dryness. Already complete, harmonious, yet could benefit from that magical 'decade of ageing'. Fermented with natural yeasts; Fr oak-matured 24 mths, 25% new. 13.8% alc. 1 300 cases. **97** enough stuffing/structure to carry many more yrs. *Wine* ✵. No **99**. — *AL*

Mellasat

Paarl (see Paarl map) • Tasting, sales, cellar tours Jan-Apr (inclusive) Sat 9-1, otherwise by appointment • Sales also through www.mellasat.com • Views • Owners Stephen & Alison Richardson • Winemaker Stephen Richardson (since 1999) with Poena Malherbe • Viticulturist Poena Malherbe (since 1996) • Vineyards 8 ha • Production 2 500 cases 90% red 10% white • PO Box 7169 Paarl 7623 • ***Tel/fax (021) 862-4525*** *• E-mail mellasat@mweb.co.za*

More deft steps have been executed at this 13 ha farm lately than by a band of nimble river dancers. There never seems to be enough space, laments Stephen Richardson, what with plantings coming into production fast and furiously. The barrelling hall completed, plans were already underway for a bottle maturation cellar. Vineyard manager Poena Malherbe, who also runs a rootstock nursery, has been kept on his toes with selecting clones and making snappy grafting decisions to optimise fruit quality. Not putting a foot wrong, further plantings of shiraz and possibly grenache are in line with Paarl's bid to become a premium area for shiraz and Rhone-type cultivars. UK connections – globehopping Stephen and Alison Richardson also farm in Norfolk – have led to a demand from niche markets there that has absorbed practically all red wine made to date. But with increased production, another step in the right direction is that they're aiming for a full range locally soon.

✵**Cabernet Sauvignon Reserve 00** vibrant fuchsia colour introduces upscale version of this Paarl cab, own fruit 30% new Fr oak-aged and still difficult to penetrate mid-01; no shortage of promise though: inky cassis/anise aromas; dense/taut structure augur well. Big 14% alc. Allow 2 yrs to harmonise. 300 cases. **99** ✵ plummy and soft, quaffable.

✵**Dekkersvlei Pinotage Reserve** Another label taking flight in **00**, very ripe just-not-jammy mulberries over gamey/smoky sniffs; sweet fruit given necessary heft by firmish tannin grip, massive 14.5% alc. 150 cases from bought-in Paarl fruit. **99** ✵ Pleasing unpretentious style.

Shiraz Reserve NEW ✵ Scented wafts of 100% new Am oak obscure **00** fruit; but beneath berries-and-cream texture lurks massed ripe fruit waiting to break out; slightly wild blackberry tones in blatantly, tastily new world example. This, above, tasted in youth so ratings provisional. 14.5% alc. 140 cases. **Dekkersvlei Chenin Blanc Reserve** ✵ **00** has come off the boil slightly (or may be in trough), mid-01 shows shy floral tones ending bone-dry. 255 cases. **Sauvignon Blanc Dekkersvlei Reserve** ✵ Commercial, appealing style, off-dry. **01** ripe tropical fruits to be enjoyed in youth. 150 cases. — *TM*

Merry-go-Round

Spruitdrift is the source of these cheerful-looking 1 ℓ NV value packs, also available on export shelves. Not retasted for this edition (previous ratings in brackets): **Grand Cru** (✵), **Stein** (✵), **Late Harvest** (✵).

Merwespont Winery

Robertson (see Robertson map) • Tasting & sales Mon-Fri 8-12.30; 1.30-5 • Cellar tours during harvest by appointment • BYO picnics • Nearby Merwenstein B&B Tel (023) 616-2806; Peet se Plek & Ou Waenhuis self catering Tel (023) 616-3151; Toy Cottage self catering Tel (023) 616-2735 • Conferences • Walks • Views • Tourgroups by arrangement • Owners 50 members • Winemakers Dirk Cornelissen (since 1983) with Charles Stassen (since 1998) • Viticulturist Charles Stassen (since 2000) • Production 9 000 tons (10 000 cases own label) 50%

*white 50% red • PO Box 68 Bonnievale 6730 • **Tel (023) 616-2800** • Fax (023) 616-2734 • E-mail merwespont@lando.co.za*

ALONG a snaking farm road, apparently to nowhere, you'll find this bright-eyed co-op, which knows exactly where it's going. With ex KWV heavyweight Eduard Beukman now in the chair (Laubscher van der Merwe, owner of Merwespont farm, having retired after a remarkable 45 years), they're looking to produce more of their own Agulhas brand, aimed at the super/hypermarket trade, and the Merwespont label, a regular on many restaurant lists. They're also courting additional joint-venture partners (current business relationships see Merwespont splashed into Craighall, S/SW and Vinfruco bottles). Internationally, they've appointed a distributor for the Benelux markets, and sent their Elsenburg trained winemaker, Charles Stassen, on another look-and-learn mission to Bordeaux. Meanwhile Dirk Cornelissen, veteran cellarmaster, keeps smiling. Vintage 2001 was "the best in my 16 years here", and the wines show "exceptional balance".

Cabernet Sauvignon ☻ ⁂ Juicy/savoury **00** has light, dry picnic-worthy freshness; plentiful red berries and modicum of oak. 1 800 half-cases.

Chardonnay ⁑ **01** notch down from pvs. Toffee-apple wafts (from oak staving), hard-edged acidic finish; light-textured but big 13.5% alc. 500 half-cases. **Special Late Harvest** NEW ⁑ Light-hearted sweetie from morio muscat; flower/grape scents in **01**, fresh despite 50 g/ℓ sugar. 260 cases.

Agulhas range

Cabernet Sauvignon ☻ ⁂ Pleasantly dry, lightish, refreshing **00**; good varietal character supported by gentle wooding. 1 000 cases. **Red** ☻ ⁂ Lightish **NV** from ruby cab/pinotage; friendly jamminess, interesting burnt-earth tones. 3 000 cases.

Chardonnay ⁑ Shy nose; medicinal flavour edged with crisp lemon. Full-bodied, dry; some wood influence. 13.5% alc. 260 cases. **White** ⁑ Light, easy-going off-dry **NV** blend, with some interesting honey notes. 1 000 cases. — *TJ*

Merwida Co-op

*Worcester (see Worcester map) • Tasting & sales Mon-Fri 8-12.30; 1.30-5 Sat 9-1 • Cellar tours during tasting/ sales hours • Merwida Country Lodge tel Diane Slabolepsky (023) 349-1435 • Gifts • Tourgroups • Conferences • Views • Owners Schalk & Pierre van der Merwe • Winemakers J 'Wollie' Wolhuter, Sarel van Staden • Viticulturist CP le Roux • Vineyards 550 ha • Production 8 600 tons (10 000 cases own label) 75% white 25% red • PO Box 4 Rawsonville 6845 • **Tel (023) 349-1144** • Fax (023) 349-1953 • E-mail wines@merwida.com • Website www.merwida.com*

THIS Rawsonville co-op has been in the Van der Merwe family for generations. A substantial amount of the prolific production here is exported under marketing companies' own brands or sold in bulk to corporates, the rest reserved for their own-label wines. Although still relatively unknown, the Merwida range is not without acclaim (the Ruby Cabernet in particular has been singled out). 'Wollie' Wolhuter and Sarel van Staden are undeniably old hands in the cellar (together they notch up over 50 years here) but they're not averse to trying something new – they bottled their first Viognier last year.

Cabernet Sauvignon-Merlot NEW ☻ ⁂ Attractive **00** well fleshed, nicely brushed with tannin; good house wine option (though high 13.7% alc needs watching). 80/20 blend, oak-chipped. 2 400 half-cases.

Cabernet Sauvignon Not tasted for this ed. Pvs **98** ⁂. **Ruby Cabernet** ⁂ Oak-chipped **00** offers plums/mulberries, plenty of oomph for fireside warming (14.6% alc). 1 000 cases. Also in 500 ml. **Sauvignon Blanc** ⁑ Light, gentle dry **01** with pretty wildflower perfumes. 500 half-cases. **Weisser Riesling** ★ Dry **00** past best. 500 half-cases. **Merwo Blanc** Not tasted for this ed. Pvs ⁑. 500/750 ml. **Cuvée Brut** ⁂ Pleasant, fruity **NV** bubbles; lightweight, gently dry. Carbonated sauvignon. 750 cases. — *IvH*

Middelvlei Estate

Stellenbosch (see Stellenbosch map) • Tasting & sales Mon-Sat 10-4.30 Tasting fee R3 p/p • Cellar tours by appointment Jan-Apr • Small conference facility (15-20 guests) • Walks • Owners Jan (snr), Tinnie & Ben Momberg • Winemaker Tinnie Momberg (since 1992) • Viticulturist Ben Momberg (since 1992) • Vineyards 130 ha • Production 1 200 tons (±800 tons crushed in own cellar) 21 000 cases own label 62% red 38% white • PO Box 66 Stellenbosch 7599 • ***Tel (021) 883-2565*** *• Fax (021) 883-9546 • E-mail info@middelvlei.co.za • Website www.middelvlei.co.za*

THIS warm extended family in wine welcomed a late-harvest arrival into their midst – Jan Jnr and Christy Momberg's baby daughter Kathleen Antonia was born in March last year, a ninth grandchild for winemaking legend Stiljan Momberg (retired to nearby Gordon's Bay but still a strong presence on the farm). Hot on her tiny heels came the much-needed rain – the year before was the driest in 21 years! The extreme conditions did have a positive spin-off though: full, concentrated and fruity red wines with "exceptional colour", according to winemaker Tinnie Momberg. The quantity of whites was halved but, with no chardonnay in 2000, last year's is something to look forward to, reports viticulturist brother Ben Momberg. A much-appreciated addition is social worker Evy Olivier, who's seeing to the farm community's wellbeing with youth programmes, educational outings (a visit to Spier's amphitheatre a recent thrill) and social events. Another milestone was the opening of a farm library, a project started by Delilah Cupido, married to Ghandi, farm manager for over 30 years. A new recycling programme is their innovative way of creating income for future projects.

⁂**Cabernet Sauvignon** Dusty black berry/green-pepper nose in **99**; jammy-sweet flavours despite lean but long finish. Balanced tannin, acid, wood. 17 mths Fr oak, 50% new. 13% alc. 2 500 cases. **98** lightish, leafy but gutsy. No **97**.

⁂**Pinotage** Modern, fruitier style unveiled with standout **94** (decried, at time, by Momberg matriarch: "Too sweet!"). Yet trio recent vintages, back-tasted mid-01, shows significant quality variance, prompting re-rate. Refined **97** ⁂, maturing well; **98** ⁂ elegant but insubstantial (11.9% alc), green; latest **99** spicily jammy; powerful tannin, alc (13.5%), acid underpinning fruit. Integrated Fr/Am oak, 70% new. 4 000 cases.

⁂**Shiraz** Hit the ground running with new-style **95** – and hasn't looked back. Upcoming **00** introverted mid-01, but massive (14.5% alc), promising. Spicy, rich, savoury; sweetness of new Am oak (30%, with 20% new Fr, rest 2nd fill Fr, 12 mths). 3 500 cases. Less enormous **99** (13.3% alc) maturing nicely.

⁂**Pinotage-Merlot** Estate's biggest seller, popular in export markets. Quiet spicy **99** nose, deep flavour carried by good balance of gentle tannin, savoury acidity. 60% pinotage. 12 mths 2nd fill Fr/Am oak. 13.2% alc. Slightly softer **98** still showing very well. 12 000 cases.

✵**Chardonnay** ✓ Rare these days, and pleasant, to find **01** combo moderate alc (13.2%), dryness, fruit undominated by wood. Butterscotch, apricot, lime sniffs confirmed in creamy, balanced palate. 30% new Fr oak-fermented, 70% tank. Drink in vibrancy of youth. **00** more massive. — *TJ*

Middlepost Wines

Enquiries Nick Dymoke-Marr • ***Tel +44 1858 57-0600*** • *Fax +44 1858 57-0601* • *E-mail nick@orbitalwines.co.uk.*

Collaboration between the UK's Orbital Wines, the Hanwood Group and the Cape's Winecorp, for British supermarket trade. Wines not retasted for this ed (pvs ratings in brackets): **Cabernet Sauvignon (99 ✵)**, **Chardonnay (99 ✵)**.

Migration

Stellenbosch • *Not open to the public* • *Owners Jan du Preez and Swartland Winery* • *Production 30 000 cases* • *PO Box 204 Stellenbosch 7599* • ***Tel (021) 887-9937*** • *Fax (021) 887-0566* • *E-mail dupwine@intekom.co.za*

Stellenbosch negociant/winemaker Jan du Preez has found a large and progressive partner in the form of Swartland Winery to expand "this exciting, futuristic range", now more widely available locally after previously being mostly for export. They're sourcing the reds from selected Swartland dryland vineyards, and the sauvignon from growers in Bottelary and Durbanville. "We want to capture the market with quality, exciting packaging and consistency," they say. Certainly, the clever and tasteful African imagery on the front-labels would be a stylish presence on any table.

✵**Pinotage** ✓ Piercing purple robes announce **01** as a flamboyant extrovert; creamy, mouthfilling banana/plum tastes; succulent, measured tannins for pleasurable drinking now with enough in reserve for 3-6 yrs. Cleverly oaked. 13. 3% alc. 8 000 cases (} 6, as are all these).

✵**Shiraz** ✓ Very expressive of the grape, oaked **00** with blackberries and gamey/herby touches; moderately intense flavours and distinct tannins containing the plum-pudding sweetness. Accessible, with enough Swartland oomph for 5-8 yrs. 13% alc. 15 000 cases.

Cabernet Sauvignon-Merlot ✵ Satisfying everyday **00**; sappy lightly oak-seasoned plums and cherries to chew, violets to nose. Undaunting 13.2% alc. 8 000 cases. **Sauvignon Blanc** ✵ Another easy/early drinker (with comfortable 12.5% alc). **01** sits comfortably on tongue, ripe nettle-toned gooseberries create a suggestion of sweetness, though conclusion is bone dry. — *DH*

Mijn Burg see Makro
Millbrook see Arlington

Mischa Estate

Wellington (see Wellington map) • *Sales Mon-Fri 8.30-5.30* • *Tasting, tours of the cellar, vine nursery (summer) and propagating sheds (winter) strictly by appointment* • *Refreshments* • *Walks* • *Views* • *Owners John & Andrew Barns* • *Winemaker Andrew Barns* • *Viticulturists Andrew & Gareth Barns* • *Vineyards 40 ha* • *Production 2 564 cases 100% red* • *PO Box 163 Wellington 7654* • ***Tel (021) 864-1019/20*** • *Fax (021) 864-2312* • *E-mail mischaestate@telkomsa.net*

"No filtering, no fining. We don't do very much actually ... put yeast into it, put it in the barrel, then into the bottle," laughs Wellington winemaker-in-progress Andrew Barns, whose 'real' job is in the well-known vine nursery on the same property. This has obvious advantages, like the backing of a seriously skilled viticultural team – they've changed pruning techniques, which will be evident this harvest, and extended plantings of cabernet and shiraz. As is his wont, he tried new things last vintage, making some terroir-specific batches with natural yeast from the area (Barns declares that while he may not be formally trained he's definitely part of this terroir), others with different yeast selections, all sticking to the minimal intervention policy. With Mischa the premium range, the alternative label, Eventide (untasted by us), offers a more accessible new world, fruity style of which his father, nurseryman John Barns (who's been growing vines here for over a quarter of a century and good-humouredly gives his son time out to pursue his winemaking passion), wholeheartedly approves: "Stop making the other stuff!" being his take on things.

Shiraz ✓ Am-casked version sold out, leaving intensely vinous, more subtle Fr-oaked **99** on centre stage. Finely crafted, heady yet unflamboyant; peppery aromas layered with raspberry (from super-ripe fruit), caramel/char from new oak. Only 150 cases made from single vyd. 14,2% alc sumptuous.

Cabernet Sauvignon Single-vyd wine, growing in bottle though inherently compactly fruited, almost austere. **99** some richer blackcurrant notes, though herbal/tannic tones dominate nose, palate. 11 mths oaking adds to grip, offering bdx-like dustiness to lead-pencil aromas. A mere 100 cases, with enough alc (14,5%) to see off the wood, release intrinsic vinosity. —*MF*

Misty Point see Barrydale
Mondial see Alphen Mondial

Monis Wines

Paarl • Tasting & sales at Oude Libertas • Owner Distell • Winemaker to be appointed • Production 24 000 cases • PO Box 266 Paarl 7626 • ***Tel (021) 872-1811*** *• Fax (021) 872-2790 • E-mail dchristowitz@sfw.co.za*

AT press time the Cape's oldest (1906) and one of the most illustrious fortified wine ranges was temporarily sans creator, ultra-seasoned Dirkie Christowitz having been tapped to look after Distell's burgeoning fruit juice operations. Fans need not be concerned, however. Consistency and continuity are synonymous with Monis, and the ambrosial desserts maturing in the cellars at Paarl will wait patiently for their new winemaker to materialise. Aside from the vintaged Tawny below, none of the wines was retasted for this edition; descriptions/ratings are from the previous guide.

Wooded Muscadel Once-off **92** fortified red dessert, from muscadel ex Breede River area, 6 yrs oaked. Hedonistic and superb. Tiny quantities.

Moscato Muscadel Current **99** lighter than pvs NVs; slightly younger and fresher; sweeter, too, though palate-cleansing spirit prevents any cloy.

Very Old Tawny Port ✓ Gorgeous, medal festooned example; latest **NV** VVG less sweet (±100 g/ℓ) than pvs, in line with modern Cape trend; non-cloying. Cinsaut, mainly ancient bushvines in Paarl area. Blend of 87, 90, 91 vintages (60/12/28). WOM Value. Now also a first **Dated Tawny Port** NEW **89** slightly sweeter than above (106 g/ℓ sugar), not as spiritous (18.9% alc) as some Portuguese examples, but beautifully refined, satisfying; tinta/cinsaut grapes from Paarlberg; 11 yrs 500 ℓ Fr barrels, none new. 2 200 cases. — *DH*

Mons Ruber Estate

Little Karoo (see Little Karoo map) • Tasting & sales Mon-Fri 9-5 Sat 9-1 • Cellar tours by arrangement • Self-catering guest area above the tasting room • BYO picnic • Gifts • Conferences • Walks • Miniature museum of artefacts from ostrich feather era • Hiking trail in proclaimed conservation area • Owners Radé & Erhard Meyer • Winemaker/viticulturist Radé Meyer (since 1990) • Vineyards 38 ha • Production 500-700 tons (50 tons own label) 80% white 20% red • PO Box 1585 Oudtshoorn 6620 • ***Tel/fax (044) 251-6550*** *• E-mail monsr@lantic.net • Website www.geocities.com/monsr_za*

NAMED after its distinctive red *koppies* (Mons Ruber is Latin for red hills) and backdropped by the dramatic Swartberg, this colourful Little Karoo farm has an intriguing history highlighted by a British Royal family visit in 1947, when the ostrich feather industry made a brief comeback (some fascinating memorabilia are on display). The pull of this semi-desert soil, ideal for making dessert wines, is strong. Just ask co-owner Radé Meyer, winemaker and "lots of other things", who left lawyerdom behind and has been happily ensconced here since. So it was not without some nostalgia that an almost 40-year-old palomino vineyard, planted when he was a child, was taken out (its swansong the first estate brandy on the farm). Asked what he's earmarked it for, he replies possibly chardonnay but they've got more than enough soil to choose from, it's water they're short of. "If only it would rain more," he laments. "The ground is as hard as a stone and the world doesn't want to get properly cold!"

Muscadel Elusivo. Utterly individual once-off **89** white muscadel, decade tucked away in used sherry vats. Deep coppery hues; 'elusive' oxidised madeira, sherry, tawny port characters; unexpectedly dry finish. Not nearly as spiritous as 21,4% alc would suggest. Low 97 g/ℓ sugar.

Cabernet Sauvignon **98** lightish soft plummy mouthful to enjoy in relative youth. **00** not ready for tasting. ±150 cases.

Conari Individual, uncertified cab from 1999 vintage; light casual quaff. 167 cases to try with pan-fried ostrich fillet. **Red Muscadel Jerepigo** Fortified dessert with unusual thatchy tones and more conventional raisins; powerfully sweet **99** still very young, needs time. 15,8% alc. 156 cases. **White Muscadel Jerepigo** **00** slightly lighter, better balanced than pvs; intense sweetness leavened with tingly spirit. 220 cases. Alternative label: Regalis. **Hanepoot Jerepigo** Raisiny sweet aromas in **98**, rich, unctuous tastes. 17,8% alc. 220 cases (siphon off bottle for next hiking expedition, recommends Radé Meyer). Alternative label: Bonitas. **Cabernet Sauvignon Jerepigo** Unusual, powerfully sweet fortified dessert; latest is **00**. 220 cases. 17.8% alc. Alternative name: Elegantia. **Sultana Jerepigo** **99** another individual Radé Meyer tinkering. Tastes powerfully of dusty sweet raisins. 18,3% alc. 220 cases. **Port** Pleasant tawny style, less sweet than most traditional Cape 'ports'; from cab; latest is **NV** blend 98, 99, 00. 18% alc. 150 cases. — *DH*

Montagu Winery

Montagu (see Little Karoo map) • Tasting & sales Mon-Fri 8-12.30; 1.30-5 Sat 9-12 • Cellar tours on request during harvest, else by appointment • Owners 70 members • Winemaker Sonnie Malan (since 1972) • Production ± 1 400 tons (± 4 000 cases own label) 97% white 3% red • PO Box 29 Montagu 6720 • ***Tel (023) 614-1125*** *• Fax (023) 614-1793 • E-mail mkwkelder@lando.co.za*

SEEMS the world's longest wine route has brought hordes of visitors winding their way down the open road (Route 62) through the soul-soothing plains of the Little Karoo. A favourite stop is Montagu, one of the best-preserved towns in the Langeberg, peopled with local characters and stories (one that persists is about legendary Oom Appeltjies, who was charged for drunken driving in his high-octane wheelchair), and rejuvenating hot water springs. Long-service awarded winemaker Sonnie Malan reports that they've considerably expanded the red wine cellar to facilitate plantings of merlot, shiraz and pinotage by the growers who feed this winery. Regulars stop at the friendly cellar to pick up their stash of wines (also available at nearby restaurants), especially the local flavour, Muscadel, to keep them in warm company when they get back home again. A not-to-be-missed annual blitz is the Montagu Muscadel Festival. The range not ready for tasting for this ed. Previous have included: **Merlot-Ruby Cabernet** (**99** ☆), **Chardonnay** (★ **00**), **Chenin Blanc** (★ **00**), **Mont Blanc** (☆ **NV**), **Vin Doux** (**NV** ★★), **White Muscadel** (**00** ★★), **Red Muscadel** (**00** ☆).

Mont Destin

Paarl (see Paarl map) • Tasting & sales by appointment Mon-Fri 8.30-4.30 • Self-catering loft apartments (breakfasts by arrangement) • Outdoor tasting area for functions max 30 people (catering can be arranged) • Private chapel for small weddings • Views • Owners Ernest & Samantha Bürgin • Consultant winemaker Stefan Dorst with Ernest Bürgin • Viticulturist André van den Berg (since 2000) • Vineyards 18 ha • Production 100 tons (7 000 cases own label) 70% red 30% white • PO Box 1237 Stellenbosch 7599 • ***Tel/fax (021) 875-5040*** *• E-mail destin@adept.co.za*

Ernest and Samantha Bürgin's thatched home, suffused with the earthy tones of Africa, has a lived-in feel, though they divide their time between here and an olive farm in Provence. Gorgeous and glossy house-trained Claudia Schiffer (their incongruously named pet pig) snuffles about greeting visitors – they've opened their doors to the public, with tasting facilities and chic self-catering loft apartments on their Paarl farm below the Simonsberg. It's a labour of love complete with a romantic chapel, a wedding gift to Samantha, which offers unique amphitheatre-style wedding ceremonies. The restaurant is getting its finishing touches, to be followed by the crux of the matter, the all-important red wine cellar. Flying German winemaker Stefan Dorst (who also consults at nearby Laibach) sees to things vinous, ably backed by on-site viticulturist André van den Berg, who brings in the goods: chenin, cabernet, merlot and pinotage, with sauvignon and shiraz coming on stream.

★★★ **Majestic Cabernet Sauvignon-Merlot** ✓ (Passioné in pvs ed) Soft, sophisticated, ageworthy bdx blend; changes to cab/merlot ensemble in **99** (82/18), 16 mths Fr oak, 30% new; claret-like aromas turning minerally in palate with plums, whiffs tobacco; supple, amazingly easy for its youth. 13,8% alc. 670 cases. **98** merlot/cab (80/20), lithely muscular with cracked pepper nuance.

★★★ **Bushvine Pinotage** NEW Modern, hedonistic style ; oozes mocha and sweet choc. Waves of conccentrated fruit, big alc (14.4%) well contained by fine fragrant tannins. 100% new, half new Am oak, remainder Fr, 14 mnths. 250 cases.

Chenin Blanc ★★★ Unoaked chenin with considerably more character than the norm. **00** fresh-fruit basket, 'smoky vanilla' tones. **01** ★★ well disguised off-dry styling; balanced, easy, for current drinking; lacks pvs' potential to acquire interest with age. 13,2% alc. 750 cases from 18 yr old vines. — *TM*

Mont Du Toit

Wellington (see Wellington map) • Tasting & sales by appointment • Owner Mont du Toit Kelder (Pty) Ltd • Winemakers Bernd Philippi, Bernhard Breuer, Pieter-Niel Rossouw • Viticulturist Alwyn Myburgh • Vineyards ±28 ha • Production ±100 tons 100% red • PO Box 704 Wellington 7654 • ***Tel (021) 873-7745*** *• Fax (021) 864-2737*

Intent on positioning Wellington on the world red wine map is Sandton-based senior counsel Stephan du Toit – but not single-handedly. The wine that had tongues wagging (second only to Rothschild/Mondavi's splashy Opus One in a tasting of joint-venture wines by UK's *Wine*) was the result of a fortuitous collaboration with top German winemakers Bernd Philippi and Bernhard Breuer (Du Toit's alliance begins with his German-born wife, Carolina, but doesn't entirely overshadow that French Huguenot heritage). The second vintage of the signature red blend, with cabernet franc a new addition, was deemed even better than the first by rule-bending Philippi. Resident winemaker Pieter-Niel Rossouw agrees, although he's "not complaining" about the latest vintage either. New plantings of cabernet sauvignon and petit verdot are to be followed by mourvèdre.

✵**Mont du Toit** First release **98**, 92 points in UK *Wine,* marked this as serious red of immense concentration, richness. Follow-up **99** ✵✵ (cab, merlot, shiraz, cab f, ±2 yrs Fr barriques, some new) finer, longer-maturing. Powerful (13.5% alc), densely ripe minerally fruit, minty texture. 1 500 cases. Likely to be trumped by upcoming **00**, with Am oak fraction, 14% alc.

✵✵**Mont du Toit Le Sommet** Cracking debut in **98**, powered by "eruptive fruit" (Bernd Philippi's phrase). Strict selection, ±4 t/ha yield, harvested 26°B plus, ±2 yrs Fr barriques, unfiltered. Only 150 cases. Next is **00** (not ready for tasting).

✵**Hawequas** Stephan du Toit's "veranda wine"; after mountain range that fills the views from said patio. Newest **00** bdx blend cab s/f, merlot, 14-16 mths Fr barriques. Unpretentious, but more sophisticated than a quaffer. 13% alc. ±1 800 cases. — *DH*

Montpellier

Tulbagh (see Tulbagh map) • Tasting by appointment • Sales Mon-Sat 8-5 • Cellar tours by appointment only • Owners Jan & Gerd Theron • Winemakers Jan Theron (since 1965) Gerd Theron (1997) • Viticulturists Jan Theron (since1985) Gerd Theron (1993) • Vineyards 40 ha • Production 400-450 tons 3 000 cases (3 000 cases own label) 75% white 25% red • PO Box 24 Tulbagh 6820 • ***Tel (023) 230-0631*** *• Fax (023) 230-0631 • E-mail jstheron@intekom.co.za*

These wines come with a pedigree as long as the Little Berg River upon whose scenic banks Montpellier farm was founded in 1714. For the past century and a half the property has been under the wing of the Theron family, who restored the gabled homestead, its vineyards and cellar. Gerd Theron and Johannesburg advocate Lucas van Tonder are spearheading a second rebirth. "Previously we were regarded as one of the three or four best white wine farms in SA," says Gerd Theron, who polishes his winemaking skills with annual crushes at Weingut Grans-Fassian in Germany's Mosel. "We're aiming to reclaim that high esteem." For 2002, they plan an extended range including a Merlot and Pinot Noir; Old Vines Chenin, Weisser Riesling, Gewürztraminer, Semillon, Sauvignon Blanc and Pinot Blanc. Three cap classiques will also be available.

Private Bin 43 ✵ Distinctly German-style riesling: early picked for elegance, lowish alcs (11.2%), slightly sweet; ethereal lemon-zest aromas and whiffs of variety's 'oiliness' in **00**, pacy acidity and light sherbety tastes. 800 cases. **01** (sample), slightly more extract, limey tastes and delicate honeysuckle scents; touch of viscosity in finish. **Chenin Blanc** ✵ Ancient block, harvested at 20-22°B in **00** for lightish 12.6% alc; understated herbal/honeyed aromas, light barley-sugar flavour with sweet-sour finish. **01** (sample) similar; almond whiffs; slightly lower sugar; easy drinking; good match with Oriental cuisines (11 g/ℓ) 600-1 000 cases. **Private Selection** ✵ Blend pinot gris, colombard, clairette blanche, **01** (sample) made off-dry though tastes nice and crisp, light; some lemony flavours – all in delicate, undemanding package with deliberately lower sulphur. ±2 000 cases. — *TM*

Mont Rochelle Mountain Vineyards

Franschhoek (see Franschhoek map) • Tasting & sales Mon-Sat 11-5 Sun (Sep-May) 11-1 Tasting fee R5 p/p • Cellar tours 11, 12.30, 3 • Summer picnics/winter warming soups (bottle of wine included) Booking essential • Tourgroups • Walks • Views • Owner Miko Rwayitare • Winemaker Justin Hoy (since 1999) • Viticulturist Alwyn Geldenhuys (since1993) • Vineyards 10 ha • Production 200 tons 18 000 cases (8 000 cases own label) • PO Box 334 Franschhoek 7690 • ***Tel (021) 876-3000*** *• Fax (021) 876-2362 • E-mail montrochelle@wine.co.za*

This jewel-like property, with its serene manor house, paddocks and vineyards regally draped over the Franschhoek Mountains, was recently sold to Congolese telecommunications entrepreneur Miko Rwayitare, who wasted no time declaring his intention "to produce wines that will be ranked amongst the top ten in SA within the next 5-6 years". In situ, and raring to put these vaulting ideals into practice, are long-time viticulturalist/farm manager Alwyn Geldenhuys and Elsenburg-schooled winemaker Justin Hoy. They'll be upgrading the cellar while scouting for sites in cool areas outside the Valley to establish ±30 hectares of classic reds, supplementing the current 9 ha (they also lease ±26 ha in the area). Extra energy will be supplied by the owner himself: Rwayitare intends to retire from his Johannesburg headquarters to the farm in 2003.

★**Pinotage** Initially tight **99** blooming in bottle, showing elegance and class in a supple frame that doesn't shout pinotage but generously offers variety's fleshy black fruits well meshed with wood. Own fruit, 18 mths Fr oak, some new. 13,5% alc. 500 cases.

★**Oak-Matured Chardonnay** Full, buttery, popular style with rich brioche aromas and wide but non-flabby tropical fruit flavours. Good toasty finish in **00**. 3 000 cases. Step-up **99** generous, full-bodied. These fermented/aged yr Fr casks, 50% new. Alcs 14% alc. **96** VG.

★**Natural Chardonnay** Would that more unwooded chardonnays tasted like this. **00** peaches-and-cream texture (partly from sur-lie maturation, 10 mths); big (14.5% alc) mouthful of plump fruit with structure that doesn't need oak. 500 cases. No **99**. **98** ★ travelled with the Blue Train. **97** developed very well.

★**Sauvignon Blanc** ✓ These usually good table companions. **01** reflects good sauvignon vintage; intense Cape gooseberry, guava and grassy/herbaceous flavours, firm flavours conclude with delicious balanced flourish. 13,2% alc. 1 300 cases.

Merlot ★ Lighter-styled **99** has softened, now shows sweet-violets/vanilla bouquet, bright fruit acidity, nice sour-plum finish. 15 mths Fr oak, none new. 14% alc. 300 cases. Not tasted for this edition: **Jacques de Villiers** Last was **97** ★, **Cabernet Sauvignon (99** ★**)**, **Blanc de Blancs (00** ★**)**. Petit Rochelle range: **Splendid Little Sauvignon Blanc (00** ★**)**. — *TM*

Mooiplaas Estate

Stellenbosch (see Stellenbosch map) • Tasting, sales, cellar tours by appointment • Owner Mooiplaas Trust • Winemaker Louis Roos (since 1983) • Viticulturist Tielman Roos (since 1980) • Production 750 tons (7 000 cases own label) 75% red 25% white • PO Box 104 Koelenhof 7605 • ***Tel (021) 903-6273*** *• Fax (021) 903-3474 • E-mail info@mooiplaas.co.za • Website www.mooiplaas.co.za*

THE brothers Roos – winemaker Louis and viticulturist Tielman – have farmed these distinguished Bottelary Hills since the early 80s, certainly qualifying for long-service awards in an industry where the seasonal shuffle is becoming mind-boggling. Wines have been made here since 1963, unbeknownst to most local consumers until they launched their own-label red-focused range a few years back. According to Louis Roos, nothing much changes here but the weather (with last year's rainy winter the best in the past five years). A cool, dry start to the 2001 season was beneficial to sauvignon, producing "a very pleasant surprise", and the pinotage (the wines from both these early ripeners have been scoring well in competitions). But soaring temperatures from mid-February put the late-season varieties under stress (likewise the Roos brothers) but with their customary patience they'll just "wait and see" how the Shiraz and Cabernet still in barrels turn out.

★**Cabernet Sauvignon** ✓ Characterised by cool elegance, fragrant raspberry, mulberry fruit. Tasting together the past 3 vintages, and being struck by the development of **97** and **98**, and the promise of **99**, prompts a re-rate. **97** ★ bdx-like structure; restrained, lightish toned with cassis, some red cherry; taut tannin balanced by yielding fruit; good for ±5 yrs. 12.6% alc. **98** flavours filling out generously; ripe-plum aromas, cassis in sweet-fruited palate, scented minerally oak. 13.8% alc. **99** (sample) already more open, rich; overt eucalyptus/mint nuance to ripe berry mid-palate; livelier tannin than above but not strident. Finest of these, potentially ✱✱. 13.5% alc. 12-20 mths barriques, **97/98** with splash merlot. ±5 000 cases (x 6, as are all these).

✱**Pinotage** ✓ Elegant, red berried example; 25 yr old bushvines on elevated n-w aspects, 250-360 m above sea level; unoaked, splash new-cask-aged merlot (10%). Local/international applause for first **98** ✱✱ (VG, ABSA Top Ten etc); back-tasted mid-01 glowed brighter than on release; excellent structure, warm-vintage generosity (14.2% alc) creates long-haul wine – should go ±10 yrs. **99**'s initial oaky richness subsiding, allowing tauter, leaner fruit profile to emerge; closer to ✱ on present showing. 13,4% alc. **00** firm tannin grip to rein in generous red fruit. Approachable but gutsy enough for some ageing. 3 000-5 000 cases.

✱**Sauvignon Blanc** ✓ Vyd atop Bottelaryberg, 380 m above sea level. Block selection, reductive vinification, favourable yr all lift **01** ✱ into new bracket; excellent concentration of sweet gooseberry, passion fruit, fresh, lingering; lovely grip of flavour in finish. ±13% alc. 1 800 cases. **00** ✱. **99**, WOM Value, mellowed into pleasing asparagus, nettle plumpness. — *JN*

Mooiuitsig Wine Cellars

*Robertson (see Robertson map) • Sales Mon-Thu 8-12; 1.30-5 Fri 8-13.20; 1.30-2.30 • Group tasting & cellar tours by appointment • Tasting/sales also from Breede River Wine Shoppe, Stormsvlei (on N2) Mon-Fri 9-5 Sat 9-1; cellar prices • Catering for large groups (up to 100-120 people) by arrangement; includes traditional cuisine • Functions/conferences/stay-overs at in-house venue, Lure Anglers Lodge. Contact Linda Claassen, linda@lure-anglers-lodge.com • Walks • Owners Jonker & Claassen families • Cellar manager Hannes Conradie • Viticulturists Adolph Jonker & Francois Claassen • Vineyards 250 ha • Production 4 500 tons • PO Box 15 Bonnievale 6730 • **Tel (023) 616-2143** • Fax (023) 616-2675 • E-mail info@mooiuitsig.co.za*

An impressive 90 000 ℓ is the size of just the ornamental khoi pond at this Bonnievale spread, where everything seems larger than life – including the welcoming smiles of Francois Claassen and wife Linda. This has been a family concern for more than 50 years, and today is one of the largest independent liquor wholesalers in SA. The business end of the operation is housed in a cellar on the Breede River (they share the premises with the Overberg Co-op). Nearby you'll find Linda Claassen's pride and joy: the Lure Anglers Lodge. It's been master-crafted from stone and antique yellow-wood, and offers upmarket reception facilities and lodgings for those who want to explore this quiet and beautiful area.

Mooiuitzicht range

Vast selection of uncertified ports, sherries, fortified reds and whites; also very wide range of reds and whites in consumer-friendly packaging. In addition, certified table wines including a **Cabernet Sauvignon 99**, **Merlot 00**, **Chardonnay (Wooded) 01**, **Sauvignon Blanc 01** (these, below, all untasted for this ed). Sweet wines: **Marsala**, **Tawny Port**, **Bonwin Ruby**, **Sweet Hanepoot**, **Old Brown Sherry**, **Red/White Maskana**, **Marsala Nagmaalwyn** (sacramental wine), **Red/White Jerepigo**, **Overberg Hanepoot**. Sparkling wines: **Mooiuitzicht Vin Doux**.

Rusthof range

Uncertified wines: **Dry Red**, **Blanc de Blanc**, **Premier Grand Cru**, **Late Harvest**. Also **Oulap** and **Potjie**, both NEW, in bright, consumer-friendly packs.

Oude Rust range

Certified dessert fortifieds: **Red Muscadel 99**, **Sweet Hanepoot 97**, **White Muscadel 99**. Also large selection of brandies, whiskies and white spirits.

Môreson Soleil du Matin

*Franschhoek (see Franschhoek map) • Tasting & sales Tue-Sun 11-5 Dec-Apr, otherwise Wed-Sun 11-4 Tasting fee R7.50 p/p Open public holidays • Cellar tours by appointment • Môreson Bread & Wine Restaurant (see Restaurants section) • Views • Wheelchair-friendly • Owner Richard Friedman • General manager/viticulturist Anton Beukes (since 1995) • Winemaker Pierre Wahl (since 1998) • Vineyards 17 ha • Production 16 000 cases 50% red 50% white • PO Box 114 Franschhoek 7690 • **Tel (021) 876-3055** • Fax (021) 876-2348 • E-mail sales@moreson.co.za • sales@pinehurst.co.za*

PIERRE Wahl is a winemaker with a sense of humour. While showing you his cellar, he likes to explain that the sediment in the MCC is known colloquially as "champagne se moer"! Even if you don't understand the Afrikaans double entendre, you won't fail to be charmed by the fresh-faced Wahl who, with ebullient general manager/viticulturist Anton Beukes, drive one of the Cape's more engaging winegrowing teams. Winkling grapes from outside their home-base Franschhoek (suddenly-starry Agter-Paarl among their newer ports of call) as well as their own 17 hectares, they're pulling one show stopper after another from their classically-inclined hat. Now they've magicked their first bordeaux blend and holding thumbs it flies as high their Pinotage, toasted by Germany's Pro-Wein and SA's Young Wine Show palates. If it does, they're sure to break out the Môreson bubbles, distributed in the UK by Pol Roger Champagne.

Cabernet Sauvignon 98 typical black cherries/cassis, but swerves from classic style with sweet suggestions (3.2 g/ℓ sugar), big 14% alc. Savoury acidity, powerful dry tannins suggest some time ahead for development. Stbosch grapes. 20 mths mostly new Fr oak. 620 cases. **97**'s expansive 'sweet' mouthful followed on **96** VG, Michelangelo gold.

Merlot Mocha/fruitcake in dark, deep **99**. Soft, mouthfilling flavour on tannic backbone, sprawling 14.5% alc and acidic finish. Integrated oak – mostly new Fr, 18 mths. WOM selection. 610 cases. **98** smooth; fresh prune/vanilla flavours. **97** VG.

Pinotage Deep, dark and ripe **00** invites with aromas of banana/vanilla. Big mouthful; bountiful fruit supported by dry tannins; acidic finish with incipient bitterness. SAYWS champion red. Mix Am/Fr oak, mostly new. 1 000 cases. Sunshine-in-bottle **99** smash in Germany.

Magia NEW Eight selected barrels (300 cases) from Paarl/Stbosch fruit for this blend cab (40%), equal cab f, merlot. **98** dark, ripe, powerful. Cedary nose; rich flavours, good structure of tannin, acid. Lengthy finish presently dominated by acid – but this wine needs time. 18 mths new Fr oak. 14.4% alc.

Sauvignon Blanc Twelve consistently top rows of fruit, hailed by show judges (**99** VG, **97** SAYWS gold). Tropical qualities underpinned by warmer honey in med-bodied **01**; crisp, clean, lingering. 450 cases.

Chardonnay **99** VVG, gold at SAYWS, now has butterscotch, leesy nose. Rich mouthful helped by residual sugar – it's just off-dry – and well integrated wood, but lots of acid and alcohol give a hard hot finish. 14.5% alc, barrel-fermented/aged 60% new Fr oak, ±yr. **Chenin Blanc** Unwooded **00**, retasted mid-01, pleasant; quiet melon/papaya scents/flavours; fiery 14.5% alc. **01** not ready for tasting. **Soleil du Matin** Extrovert **NV** brut cap classique, chardonnay, splash chenin. Latest packed with bubbles; citrusy with hint yeast; pleasant, light, crisply dry. 1 000 cases. Discontinued: **Jerepigo** Pvs **NV**.

Pinehurst range

✵**Cabernet Sauvignon** Decorated **98** followed by lower orbiting **99** ✵; flavoursome, plentiful fruit; light tannins but acidic finish which should benefit from keeping yr/2. Stbosch/Paarl grapes. Yr older oak. 13.5 alc. 2 000 cases.

Pinotage ⁂ Ripe, generous **00**; soft red berry fruit, good tannic structure. Paarl grapes, old-oak casked. 13.7 alc. 1 100 cases. **Chardonnay** ⁂ Limey **00**, vanilla from oak fermented portion; mouthfilling (14 % alc); unheralded hard acidic whoosh at end. 1500 cases. **Chenin Blanc** ⁑ Melon suggestions in quiet unoaked **00**. Soft, smooth in mouth before tart lemony finish. **01** not ready for tasting. **Sauvignon Blanc** ⁂ Exuberant tropical fruit aromas/flavours in early morning harvested **01**; crisply dry. Modest 12.5% alc. 1 400 cases. — *TJ*

Morgan see African Terroir

Morgenhof Estate

Stellenbosch (see Stellenbosch map) • Tasting & sales: In season (Nov-Apr) Mon-Fri 9-6 Sat & Sun 10-5 Out of season: (May-Oct) Mon-Fri 9-4.30 Sat & Sun 10-3 Tasting fee R10 p/p Closed Christmas Day, Good Friday, New Year's Day • Light meals daily 12-2.30 • Coffee shop daily 9-4.30 • Owner Anne Cointreau-Huchon (La Tour International Investments Pty Ltd) • Winemaker Rianie Strydom (since 1998) • Vineyard manager Pieter Haasbroek • Vineyards 67 ha • Production 295 tons 30 000 cases • PO Box 365 Stellenbosch 7599 • ***Tel (021) 889-5510*** *• Fax (021) 889-5266 • E-mail info@morgenhof.com • Website www.morgenhof.com*

THE style here is French, the ambience sophisticated, the cuisine (alfresco in summer in the centuries-old *werf*) chic and delicious. Ditto the wines, which are raised in an octagonal barrel cellar straight out of the Medoc. This is the fragrant domain of young winemaker Rianie Strydom, whose Italian- and French-polished skills now imbue the range with its signature elegance and grace. She's partnered in the vineyards by Pieter Haasbroek, in his fourth season here, priming almost 70 hectares to ensure they're ready for windfalls such as the "almost perfect" conditions at the 2001 harvest, which gave the grapes the elbow-room they needed to become fully ripe. "We're very positive about the past season," say this quietly confident team, forecasting "exceptional wines" from a favourable vintage. Setting the glossy yet unpretentious tone are sleeves-rolled-up owners Alain and Anne Cointreau-Huchon (of Remy Martin, Cointreau and Gosset family fame), whose non-wine passions include their lodge in an unspoiled wilderness reserve.

✵**Cabernet Sauvignon 99** ✵ rich ruby-red hues open to earthy nose with herbal notes and mint; clean mineral palate. 18 mths Fr oak, 30% new. Suggest age extra yr. **98** mineral/herb aromas; rich, full (14% alc); balance of cassis fruit, smoky wood (oaking as above); mild tartness in mid-palate. Probably best before 05. **Cabernet Sauvignon Reserve** ⁂ To date a **98**, untasted for this ed; at press time limited stocks still available ex farm.

✵**Merlot** Cape standout since and strong claimant to estate flagship status **93** first electrified the crowds (*Wine* ✵, SAA, golds at Vinexpo/IWSC). Latest **99** ✵ atypically austere and taut; lovely plummy fruit finishes a little hard. Will benefit from bottle age. **98** drinking very well now; tannins soft and full; ripe red-plum fruit in harmony with wood (18 months Fr oak, 30% new); structure for further 5 yrs. **Merlot Reserve** ⁂ To date a **98**, untasted for this ed; at press time limited stocks still available ex farm.

✵**Pinotage** Burgundian traits (appropriately for Fr-toned estate) of this homespun variety evident here (partly result of cool, elevated vyd). Latest **99** ✵ with dash cab, deep red glints. Sour plums and herbal/medicinal undertones that end abruptly; backbone of firm tannins quite evident, needing ageing yr/2. 18 mths Fr oak, 50% new. **98** riper, mulberry sweetness and dark choc aromas. 28 yr old vyd. **96** ABSA Pinotage Top Ten.

☆☆**Première Sélection** Taut, expensively (thoughtfully) oaked. **96** *Wine* ☆. **95** ☆☆. Blend cab, merlot, cab f (65/25/10) in current **97** VG, WOM selection; bouquet of coffee, mocha and ripe red fruit; finely tuned balance with wood (supplied by 18 mths Fr barrels, 30% new). Dark, complex wine whose secrets may be revealed only towards the end of the decade.

☆**Cabernet Franc-Cabernet Sauvignon** NEW **00** leads with cab f's 'stalky' nose (88% component); powerful tannins still only partly offset by sweet red/black berry fruit. Keep min yr to let complexity develop, tannins mellow; safe bet for another 5 yrs.

☆**Merlot-Malbec** A different, delicious take on Bdx: **00** ☆ 74/26 blend with sweet merlot fruit in nose, soft tannins and choc undertones, raspberry whiffs in ripe, chewy palate. 14 mths Fr oak 2nd/3rd fill. First was **99**, with prominent leafiness and choc.

☆**Chardonnay** Poised, with elegant acidity. **00** warm butterscotch/honey bouquet, harmonious wood/fruit. 14% alc unobtrusive but should support ±5 yrs' good development. **99** ☆ overtly oaky but not unattractive. Good chalky character with richness and toast. Fr oak fermented/matured 9 mths.

☆**Sauvignon Blanc** European firmness rather than bracing New Zealand style hallmark of **01** ☆; flinty whiffs, greengage, grapefruit flavours supported (rather than overpowered) by acidity; should see in 2004. Better structure than **00**, reflecting flavour-sapping hot vintage.

☆☆**Chenin Blanc** From venerable 32 yr old vyd, consistently excellent since maiden **96** won SA Wine's Chenin Challenge. Richly complex **99** still most attractive with cream and honey aromas over tropical fruit salad. muscular 14,5% alc adds suggestion of sweetness, touch sugar (4,3 g) suppleness; right dollop oak from 8 mths oaking. **00** ☆ another excellent effort, one of two SA wines in top ten at Tasters' Competition, Vinexpo 01 (with Paul Cluver Chardonnay). Honey-vanilla bouquet and palate, exceptional intensity from selected fruit ex 33 yr old vines.

☆**Late Bottled Vintage** One of the Cape's most 'correct' late bottled styles: nearly 5 yrs oaked, tinta, 18,9% alc and dry 88 g/ℓ sugar. Last was **95**. Latest bottling not ready to taste.

☆**Cape Vintage 98** ageing with distinction; marzipan nose and christmas cake palate. Rich, full; 100% tinta in drier (96 g/ℓ sugar) Portuguese style. Firm finish. 16 mths old Port pipes. Will continue improving until middle of next decade at least.

Sauvignon Blanc-Chenin Blanc ☆ Light-robed **01** dominated by chenin despite being junior partner (20%) in marriage; gains interest from fruit/acid balance and lemony finish. For now and up to 2 yrs.

Reserve Centenaire range

Chic 'crested'; bottles in wooden presentation casket, originally for millennium; small quantities still available.

☆**Chardonnay** Lavish wood treatment (16 mths Fr oak, 55% new) has produced big, rich wine with huge presence. Well-developed honey, butter aromas/flavours, undercurrent of citrus. Soft, elegant texture. Nearing peak; good acids suggest will still be excellent mid-decade. Gold at 2000 Mondial Selection, Brussels.

☆**Brut** MCC from pinot/chardonnay in heavyweight moulded bottle. Toast and brioche **97** VVG bouquet, medium bead; rich toasty character evokes fuller Champagne styles.

☆**Cape Vintage Reserve** Fine tinta 'port'. Pitch black **98**; meat, tar, raisins nose; uncommon intensity of flavour, spicy sniffs reverberate in ultra-smooth, velvety palate. Sweeter than Cape Vintage above (101.4 g/ℓ sugar). Aged yr old Fr barrels. Should improve until end of the decade. VVG, *Wine* ☆.

Discontinued/sold out: **Reserve Centenaire 'Reserve' (98** ☆☆**)**; **Rosé Brut** (not tasted), **L'Atrium Rouge d'M (NV** ☆**)**. — *NP*

Morgenster Estate

Stellenbosch (see Helderberg map) • Sales: Mon-Fri 10-5 • Wine Tasting by appointment only • Award winning Extra Virgin Olive Oil, Estate grown table olives & olive paste from farm • Owner Giulio Bertrand • Winemaker Marius Lategan (since 1999) • Vineyard Manager Basie Fismer • Vineyards 38 ha • 40% Merlot 35% Cabernet Sauvignon 18% Cabernet Franc and Petit Verdot • PO Box 1616 Somerset West 7129 • ***Tel (021) 852-1738*** *• Fax (021) 852-1141 • E-mail wine@morgenster.co.za • Website www.morgenster.co.za*

MORGENSTER's impressive new U-shaped wine cellar was ready just in time for the 2001 crush – much to the delight of winemaker Marius Lategan and super-consultant Pierre Lurton of Ch Cheval Blanc – with the first grapes delivered on Valentine's Day (a good omen for romanticist Giulio Bertrand). A portion could be used for bottling under the Morgenster name (wines from the still-young vineyards were previously made elsewhere, thus bottled under the second label, Lourens River Valley – by no means a reflection on the quality, rather an elegant measure of what's still to come). There's only the one classic Bordeaux-style blend. "We're very boring," says Bertrand. Not at all, say we. Morgenster's Italian-style extra virgin olive oil bowled them over with a hat-trick, winning the prestigious Orciolo d'Oro in Pezzaro for a remarkable third time in a row. Seven years down the line, cap doffed determinedly in the direction of the old world, Bertrand's cherished vision for this 18th-century estate is complete. Or is it ... ?

☆**Lourens River Valley** Exquisitely balanced, soft-tannined, elegant bdx style red. **99** ☆☆ Richer, plummier; more evident merlot fruit than pvs (62% vs 48%). Mulberry aromas, choc whiffs; superb textures; restrained, well integrated oak. Step up on maiden **98**, where younger vines, leaner and more dominant cab component delivered elegance at price of palate weight, complexity. **99** slightly more alc, wood than pvs (13%, 15 mths vs 12,6%, 13 mths). Should peak around 06-09. — *MF*

Motif see Steenberg
Mount Claire see Cordoba
Mount Disa see Coppoolse Finlayson-Sentinel
Mount Marble see Simonsvlei
Mount Maskam see Vredendal

Mount Rozier Estate

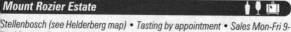

Stellenbosch (see Helderberg map) • Tasting by appointment • Sales Mon-Fri 9-5 • Views • Conservancy area • Owners Michael Rubin, Peter Loebenberg, Dave Lyddell • Winemaker Jacques Fourie • Consulting viticulturist Johan Wiese • Vineyard manager Dave Lyddell • Vineyards 45 ha • Production 2 000 cases 100% red • PO Box 784 Somerset West 7129 • ***Tel (021) 858-1130*** *• Fax (021) 858-1131 • E-mail wine@mountrozier.co.za • Website www.mountrozier.co.za*

THE ONCE QUIET hills around Sir Lowry's Pass are alive with the roar of deep-ploughing tractors preparing vineyards. Reverberating with energy, the Schaapenberg terroir is on the tip of vinophiles' tongues as a newly recognised ward within the Stellenbosch area. The Lyddells – Dave, a former civil engineer who keeps his construction instincts honed on the farm, and Rosa, planting profusions of flowers and transplanting yellowwood trees from remote corners – are running this property, now an official estate (the wines are named after Annie Rozier, who gathered wild flowers on the slopes at the turn of the century). A period of serious consolidation has seen grapes from first plantings in 98 harvested and vinified along with yield from more mature existing vineyards. Now freshly appointed winemaker Jacques Fourie (ex Wildekrans) is busy exploring every nook and cranny, and getting a handle on the serious altitude variances (some 150 m across the farm) to optimise potential. They're also planning a white-wine facility, the intent being to produce sauvignon blanc this year from a promising single vineyard on these south-facing slopes.

✿**Cabernet Sauvignon 99** improves on pvs, weightier, more generous ("Love and care given to this previously weed-strangulated vineyard seems reflected in the grape," ventures Dave Lyddell); ± 16 mths Fr oak, 50% new. 475 cases (× 6, as are all these). Good now. **98** ✿ has acquired some secondary flavours. VG. 50% grapes ex Audacia.

Merlot ✿ Pleasant, characterful **99** offers red cherries, length and balance (11 mths Fr barriques, 50% new). 5 900 cases of this "wonderful pasta wine". **Pinotage** ✿ Idiosyncratic oak-driven style, **99** finish marred by slight bitterness. 11 mths new oak, 30/70 Am/Fr. 600 cases. **Annie Rozier Red** ✿ Lighter style, easy, soft; **99** raspberry/cherry toned; 18 mths small oak. 575 cases. Merlot, cab, pinotage 40/40/20 ratio; maiden **98** 100% merlot. — *CF*

Mouton House of Wines

Cape Town • Owner Mouton House of Wines (Mouton family-owned) • Production 20 000 cases 80% red 20% white • PO Box 251 Cape Town 8000 • ***Tel (021) 426-2684/5*** *• Fax (021) 426-2728 • E-mail ucc@winejoy.com • Website www.winejoy.com*

With the world already her backyard (established markets in Europe, North America, the Orient and some sun-splashed Indian Ocean islands), wine negociant Gerda Mouton has extended the playing field further, growing German exports and tackling the Czech Republic and Russian markets last year (she's accordingly shifted her personal goalpost from aspirant Cape to British Wine Master). Keeping her company on some of those frequent international flights is the Huguenot Reserve Cabernet Sauvignon 97, now on SAA's first-class list. The three ranges, styled to her specifications by partner wineries in areas including Stellenbosch, Robertson and the Swartland, now all dwell in the newly established Mouton House of Wines, and plans are underway to develop a maturation cellar and increase production to 20 000 cases.

Mouton-Excelsior Huguenot Reserve range

✿**Merlot** NEW **99** elegant despite punchy 13.5% alc; tasty, soft choc/berry flavours; bit raw mid-01 but worth bottle ageing yr/2. Stbosch origin, 18 mths casked, some new.

✿**Shiraz** Vintage variation evident here: **98**, which upscale from pvs, rich, chocolatey; current **99**, ex Stbosch, streamlined but no less fine. Oak well woven and soft. Approachable but better in 2-4 yrs. 1 500 cases.

✿**Chardonnay** ✓ None since **98**, with burgundian tones; Fr oak fermented/aged.

Cabernet Sauvignon ✿ **97**, which flew SAA 1st class, to us ungenerous, quick (though Gerda Mouton believes time needed – 5-8 yrs). 13% alc. 1 000 cases. **Pinotage** Last was **98** ✿, attractive old-style example, big and robust.

Discontinued: **Sauvignon Blanc** Pvs **99** ✿.

Mouton-Excelsior range

✿**Cabernet Sauvignon** ✓ Switch from Stbosch to Rbtson origin in **00** ✿, yr oaked (staves/barrels), not in same league as pvs; lighter, foursquare. 5 000 cases. Pvs claret-style **97** finer, Fr barrique aged 18 mths.

✿**Merlot** Something of a house speciality; usually soft, fleshy, restrained. **98** with violet/minty fragrances; still-available **99** ✿ remains in thrall of tannin; Stbosch sweet-fruit aromas taper to sinewy palate. 3 mths Nevers. 13,5% alc. 1 000 cases.

Pinotage ✓ Non-blockbusting style, unwooded med-bodied; **98** from Darling, showed some complexity. **00** more workmanlike, not unsatisfying. F'hoek fruit. 2 000 cases.

Cabernet Sauvignon-Merlot **00** lightish-toned 55/45 assemblage ex Stellenbosch; easy commercial style, partly oaked. Good with ossobucco. 13% alc. **Chardonnay** Change to unoaked in latest **00**, ex Rbtson, uncomplicated fresh limey/lemony enjoyment. 13.5% alc. 2 000 cases. **Chenin Blanc** ★ Unwooded **00** unexpectedly tired. 13% alc. 1 000 cases.

Cape Mouton range

Sauvignon Blanc NEW ✓ Nice drinking wine, some richness in palate of **01**, fig, asparagus hints; dry, balanced mango/melon freshness.

Cabernet Sauvignon Unoaked **00** old-Cape style: compact, meaty nuances; closed mid-01. This, above, reveal Rbtson provenance in generous 13.5-14% alcs. 10 000/8 000 cases.

Itakane range

Pinotage Latest **01** not ready for tasting; pvs **99**. **Cabernet Sauvignon-Merlot** **00** 75/25 blend closed and tight mid-01; give yr/2 to develop. Stbosch fruit. 13% alc. **Chardonnay** Unwooded **01** (sample) introverted mid-01; tropical fruit lurking; should perk up to equal extroverted pvs. 13.4% alc. — *CF*

Mulderbosch Vineyards

Stellenbosch (see Stellenbosch map) • Tasting & cellar tours by appointment • Sales Mon-Fri 8-5 • Owner Hydro Holdings • Winemaker Mike Dobrovic (since 1991) with Clinton le Sueur • Viticulturist Johann Schloms • Marketing/sales Sean Griffiths • Vineyards 27 ha • Production 275 tons 18 000 cases 70% white 30% red • PO Box 548 Stellenbosch 7599 • ***Tel (021) 882-2488*** *• Fax (021) 882-2351 • E-mail info@mulderbosch.co.za • Website www.mulderbosch.co.za*

FROM winemaker Mike Dobrovic's stoep, the Simonsberg stands as a distant sentinel to this premium property, more closely guarded by his loyal companions Dog Box, Lunch Time, Marla Maples and Small Change. If Dobrovic, visionary, zealot and saviour of old vines, has a message it's still simply: "Forget quantity and without doubt go for quality". He's a fervent believer in a scientific approach to viticulture and winemaking. If he starts sounding too serious, levity is quickly restored by his ribald sense of humour (forget the French paradox – this is the Dobrovic version at work). The chardonnay crop was down by 50% last harvest (latest four-legged arrival Small Change developed a penchant for nicking bunches and eating them under the cool fermentation tanks, leaving the stems behind as evidence and straining the yield even further) so only a small quantity of Barrel Fermented 2001 was made – just about enough to cause a more than usual scramble for this sought-after wine.

Faithful Hound ✓ Isn't it just? Available, reliable, accessible in an understated manner, for drinking rather than thinking, a constant stay amongst sea-changes of other's styles, a merlot-dominated bdx blend in refined, not gobsmacker, mould. **98** brims with smoky char, deep roasted coffee beans, choc-mint hints. Excellent mineral structure dusty with red-berry fruit, juicy roast pheasant flavours. Final tannic flush reminds this is no simple wine despite characteristic drinkability. **97** restrained, red berries, clean minerally flavours in claret-type lightness. Half merlot, 38% cab, 12% malbec; 16 mths. Combo new/seasoned Fr oak.

Chardonnay Understated next to big brother below, and certainly not unwooded – intelligently crafted from third each new, used Fr oak (8 mths) and tank fermented components. Inviting wheat-ear hue to **99** packed with ripe, tropical (glistening summer melons) fruit, measured savoury oak and finely tuned late acid/tannin brace. Excellent, in line with developing **98** hazelnut bouquet, still-fresh orange zest. Rounded, nutty finish. WOM selection. Dobrovic believes this wine will last seven years in bottle; most who snap up limited 1 600 cases not that patient.

✪**Barrel-Fermented Chardonnay 99** dancing gleam to yellow crocus complexion; complex nose crammed with wood spice, creamy lees, minerals, white river-stone flint. Palate much more new world since **97** (multi-flavoured winner of Air France trophy, Wine ✪) full-frontal richness, lasting finish with a penetration that gives meaning to Dobrovic's tongue-in-cheek suggestion that it suits "formal dinner so as to dispel oedipal complexes". **98** Wine ✪ similarly fleshed out, mouthfilling appeal. New Fr oak 10 mths, half natural yeasts.

✪**Steen-op-Hout** Distinctive new-wave chenin, popular even with those who can't pronounce name! Concentrated fruit from 49 yr old dryland vines, 5% Am-oaked 4 mths. Broad **99** softer than pvs, acacia fragrance, gravelly flavours laced with sweetish finish (4.7 g/ℓ sugar) but peaking, developing stony dustiness. Mesmerising **98** *Wine* ✪, with heady, wild honey scents, remains benchmark. **97** *Wine* ✪

✪**Sauvignon Blanc** Synonymous with the cellar – and Dobrovic – since set pace for Cape sauvignons in early 90s. With home-spun philosophy, the maker suggests it suits "any occasion where sadness and depression need dispelling". Melancholy induced by excruciatingly low yields of the past few vintages, especially **99**, **00**, perhaps? **01** ✪ true to promise with tight capsicum, gassy, flinty-gooseberry spectrum, but quieter palate laced with finish in which 4.9 g/ℓ sugar shows. With **00**, slower than earlier deliciously crisp, racy vintages – **93** and **97** in particular – but legion of fans will not be disappointed. Untrellised bush vines. Regular SAA, Wine ✪ accolades.

Barrel-fermented Sauvignon Blanc ★ Individual (few wines from Dobrovic aren't), vanilla-pod sugar nose laced with sweet thatch, ripe figs; less racy, more woody but echoes of gooseberry fruit flavours in aftertaste of **00**. 60% barrel-fermented, 50/50 new/seasoned mix Fr/Am oak. Not tasted for this ed: **Alpha Centauri** (Bdx blend) Last was **98** ✪. *— DS*

Muldersvlei see Starke Wines

Muratie Estate

Stellenbosch (see Stellenbosch map) • Tasting & sales Mon-Fri 9-5 Sat 10-4 and Sun 11-3 (Nov-Mar) • Cellar tours by appointment • Meals by arrangement • Owner Melck Family Trust • Winemaker Mark Carmichael-Green (since 2000) • Viticulturist Paul Wallace (VineWise) • Vineyards 40 ha • Production 250 tons 10 000 cases 99% red 1% white • PO Box 133 Koelenhof 7605 • ***Tel (021) 882-2330/6*** *• Fax (021) 882-2790 • E-mail muratie@kingsley.co.za*

The colourful three-century history of this estate is peopled with vivid characters like Prussian émigré Lourens Campher and his wife, freed slave Ansela van der Caab (their thatch-roofed cottage still stands today), and flamboyant Georg Canitz, famous for his avante-garde paintings, lavish parties and, notably, planting SA's first pinot noir. Included in this textured past was a 134-year tenure by the Melck family's forebears. While Muratie remains steeped in history and brothers Rijk and Anton Melck pay heed to their roots, it's not caught in a time warp. Their sister Charla (fresh back from several years in Germany) has taken over the marketing and is intent on lifting the profile of this venerable estate. This spirit of rejuvenation saw the release of some new single varietal wines last year – a Merlot, Shiraz (from an old block on the farm) and Cabernet Sauvignon. "With just the one blend things got a bit stagnant," says super-keen winemaker Mark Carmichael-Green. Now new plantings are coming on stream and a massive barrel renewal programme is well underway.

Cabernet Sauvignon NEW Combining delicacy and power. **00** clean cedar-scented mulberries, cassis; sweet-violets bouquet; high (14%) alc hidden inside core of cool fragrant fruit. Far too young to drink; give ±4 yrs. 12 mths oak. 5 000 cases (x 6, as are all these).

Merlot NEW Uncompromisingly classic (as is this whole range) **00** vinous rather than fruity, cedary twists to big backbone of tannin, alc (14% alc). Yr oaked. 2 500 cases not styled for early enjoyment; cellar few yrs.

Pinot Noir SA's first pinot vines planted in these vyds ±75 yrs ago. Now low-yielding (3,5 t/ha) Dijon 113/115 clones, traditionally vinified in open fermenters, Fr cask-aged ± yr, malo in barrel. Latest pair of releases not as pleasing, complex as **98** with burgundian aromas and spicy/plummy fruit. **99**, **00** both nearer ☆. Latter smoked meat, wild strawberry whiffs; austere tannins still, deceptively light-hued. **99** re-tasted mid-01, reaching drinkability; earthy touches not unattractive. 13% alc. 2 000 cases.

Shiraz NEW Dazzling new star in the Cape shiraz firmament. Hedonistic, intensely aromatic **00** starts with savoury smoked-ham/grilled-bacon aromas, grinds pepper and spice; in palate richer mocha hints, warmly ripe blackberries and good tarry nuance are lifted by bright, invigorating acidity. Beautiful now, but patience will reap more pleasurable rewards from 2003-2008. 12 mths oak. 13.5% alc.

Ansela ✓ Stylish, well-oaked dry red blend named after a slave freed in 1695, who married the first owner of this farm and helped establish its vyds. **98** ☆ re-tasted mid-01 sappier than last, more fruit weight; powerful tannic comeback and savoury-dry finish. Cerebral wine, shows dominance of cab character (with merlot, slight touch shiraz); needs plenty of time. Punchy alc (14%) should help carry to maturity. Med/full **97** 50/50 cab/merlot; now more fragrant with cellar's trademark dryness; tannin structure still very firm. These yr Fr oak-aged.

Melck's Dry Red ✓ Cellar's earthy tones amplified here by tinta's rustic tones, with portions cab, merlot in **99**. Very dry, lightish, plenty of tannin; restrained style will appeal to classicists. ±12% alc.

Amber Forever ✓ Fortified muscat d'a, unwooded, with loyal following since the Georg Canitz era, circa 1925. **98** pine-nuts, eucalyptus in surprisingly dry citrus palate **99** botrytis-like whiffs and with delicate acidity. Lower alc than pvs (17%).

Vintage Port Outstanding example of the modern style; Portuguese varieties tintas b/r/f, souzao, 34 mths oaked, 19.5% alc. **98** opaque hue anticipates dark berry tones cloaked in vanilla oak, incense bouquet reappears in concentrated fragrant fruit; dense but supple. Many yrs from maturity. 102.9 g/ℓ sugar. 700 cases.

Isabella Superbly crafted chardonnay from grapes ex-neighbouring farm. First **98** lightish-bodied – 12,8% alc vs punchy 13.6% in latest **00** (sample) classically dry, succulent lime flavours and oak well geared to show off fruit. Hints butterscotch in full, deep-flavoured body. 6 mths Fr oak. 350 cases.

Port ☆ Tasty ruby-style **NV** with 'correct' nose and forthcoming fruitcake/prune tastes; traditional Portuguese varieties tintas b/r/f, souzao, tad shiraz, yr oaked. 19% alc, ±100 g/ℓ sugar. 1 800 cases. — *IvH*

Mystery see Wine Warehouse

Naked Truth

The ultimate no-frills range: budget-priced wines with the bare minimum of labelling, for extra cost saving. Exclusive to the Picardi liquor-store chain. Not available for tasting.

Namaqua see Vredendal

Napier Winery

*Wellington • Not open to the public • Owner GRT Farming & Financial (Pty) Ltd • Winemaker/viticulturist Leon Bester (since 2000) • Vineyards 20 ha • Production 4 000 cases • PO Box 638 Wellington 7654 • **Tel (021) 873-7829** • Fax (021) 864-2728 • E-mail napwines@iafrica.com*

Folded into a scenic vale above Wellington is this quietly dynamic winery owned by mainly US, European and some local investors, including Chris Kühn, one-time colleague of heart transplant surgeon Chris Barnard. Keeping a keen young eye on the shareholders' assets is resident "man of the roots" Leon Bester, scion of a well connected Cape wine family. The partners recently bought the next door farm, doubling the size of their holding. Now plans are afoot to replace the fruit trees on the new property with extra cabernet and merlot for the bordeaux blend, plus new syrah for an envisaged splashed-with-cab Shiraz, a la the fabled Grange (no pussyfooting here!). They're also "doing something quite extraordinary": planting chenin. This to replace a venerable parcel which is nearing the end of its productive life. Though most of the 4 000 annual cases continue to be exported (though switched-on Amsterdam wine merchant Rex Neve), some may be found locally at the Western Province Cricket Club, Kelvin Grove Club, Swartberg Country Lodge and Wine Concepts in Cape Town.

★**Red Medallion** Deep, still youthful **97** bdx blend; ripe, jammy nose. Plenty of fruit to taste, buttressed by gentle, dry tannins; big acidity. Finishes hot, thanks to massive 14.6% alc. **96** ★ less ripe; dusty, leathery tones.

Chardonnay ★ Lowish-key smells/flavours of toast/lemon in wooded **99**; powerful 14.5% alc lends fullness but, along with big acid, effects fierce finish. **Chenin Blanc** ★ Quiet **01**, honeysuckle hints mingle with tropical fruit. Firm and focused, with dry, acid-drop conclusion. 12.5% alc. — *TJ*

Natural Corporation see Cape Classics

Nederburg Wines

Paarl (see Paarl map) • Tasting & sales Mon-Fri 8.30-5 Sat 9-1 (April-Oct) Sat 9-4 and Sun 11-3 (Nov-March) Public holidays (except religious holidays) 9-5 • Cellar tours Mon-Fri (none on Sat/Sun/public holidays) by appointment, in English, Afrikaans, German, French Fee R12.50 p/p • Picnic lunches Nov-Feb R55 per person (vegetarian baskets/ children's meals on request) • Banquet facilities in conjunction with Cape Sun Intercontinental Hotel • Video/slide shows • Owner Distell • Cellarmaster Razvan Macici with Andrea Freeborough & Elunda Loubser • Farm managers/viticulturists Hannes van Rensburg, Dirk Bosman • Marketing Jeff Gradwell • Public relations Elsa van Dyk • Production 12 000 tons • 800 000 cases 55% white (including sparkling) 30% red 15% rosé • Private Bag X3006 Paarl 7620 • Tel (021) 862-3104 • Fax (021) 862-4887 • E-mail nedwines@sfw.co.za • Website www.nederburg.co.za

Razvan Macici, Nederburg's new on-the-ball Romanian-born cellarmaster (stalwart Newald Marais now overseeing an all-important initiative to develop new styles suited to the international market) is leading a revolution here. Macici's young team includes new white-winemaker Andrea Freeborough, ex Neethlingshof, and Elunda Loubser, previously an assistant in the Nederburg cellars who's taken over as stylist for the reds. Their sights are set on "a generous new-world style of wine through modern, minimalistic winemaking." Their goal, reveals Macici (wine runs in his blood: both parents work in the Dealul Mare vineyards near Bucharest) is to elevate Nederburg into "a recognised house of excellence for sauvignon blanc". And for local grape pinotage. "Chile has its carmenère and Argentina malbec. We can make our national statement very effectively with pinotage," Macici maintains.

Reserve range

☆**Cabernet Sauvignon** "Potential vehicle with which to reclaim former Nederburg finesse" gains further speed as cool-climate fruit, decent fresh oak find their way into current releases. Preview **99** electric, inky colour, perfumed rather than plummy nose, delightfully refined, lucid palate, cool blackberry fruit, gentle ripe tannins; quieter, more classy than current, ample, flavourful **98** juicy cassis, mulberry crammed into grippy package. 12.9% alc. 5 000 cases.

☆**Malbec** NEW Nano quantities of individuality, as for Petit Verdot below: **99** cedar/oak aromas plumped by damson, flashed with mint whiffs, tight tannic frame hung with plum/prune fruit, toasty richness. Interest beyond that of huge blends. 300 cases.

☆**Petit Verdot** NEW Reserve range perfect vehicle for small-volume gems like this **99**; mulberry colour intensity; individual sappy aromas of bark/cedar, succulent mirabelle, blueberry fruit intensity organised in ordered palate structure, excellent length. Needs 2 yrs. 12% alc. 280 cases.

☆**Shiraz** NEW **97** (inch off ☆) lifts label with modern confection in northern Rhone groove: perfumed oak, complex gamey notes, resounding mineral/stony ring, pimento, peppery palate. All excellently wound up in measured tannin cone, 13.6% alc assists. 'Yummy' reads our tasting notes. 2 600 cases.

☆**Chardonnay** Flamboyant modern style, not for the faint-hearted: **00** charry oak vanillins, broad melting butter dominates aromas, palate less chunky, in same mould. Tropical rather than citric, as for **99** fresh bread nose, ripe fruit with oak settling. 8 mths on lees in new Fr oak. 13,7% alc. 2 600 cases.

☆**Sauvignon Blanc** If **00** ★ "much improved" (as we remarked pvs ed), **01** singularly stellar! Razvan Macici's "baby", loaded with reductive, tingling cut grass, lancing nettles, bristling steel, more refined that standard bottling: tropical melon, sweet hay add flesh, marginally 'sweeter' finish too. Advance understated, no shortage of flavour. 2 500 cases.

Chenin Blanc NEW ★ Upgraded from Standard range. **00** shows sappy quince, guava features, palate potential restricted by tiring, trifle flabby finish. 14% alc. 300 cases.

Standard range

☆**Edelrood** Classic blend cab/merlot (56/41), dash malbec, petit verdot; for years pinnacle of Nederburg's red spectrum. At risk of neglect during development of the focus Reserve range, Razvan Macici assures eye will stay firmly on ball at this end. Modern makeover from **97** ★ with infusion new clone fruit from cooler regions, **98** notched higher, **99** in the groove: scented heather scrub, attractive blackcurrant, cherry, wafts of violets; berry fruit in tandem with tannic core. 43 700 cases.

☆**Sauvignon Blanc** ✓ **01** telegraphs Macici's team tactics: reductive cold fermentation, ascorbic acid, inert-gas treatment equals bags of flavour. Pungent nettles, steely cut-grass, capsicum clamour out of glass, ripe quince fills electric mouthful. Succulent, just-dry (3.5 g/ℓ sugar) and delicious. Entry level "visiting card" (24 500 cases) underpins more illustrious Reserve and Auction offerings, crammed with value. Splash of semillon. **00** ★ attractively fresh.

☆**Noble Late Harvest** Stylish, sumptuous, deliciously sweet, beyond its station in the range – nothing 'standard' about this better-value alternative to the auction stars below: **00** gleaming gold; ripe tropical melons, pines, toasted coconut, even spice. Terrific concentration in mouth, oily viscosity with echoing botrytis richness. Late litchi zing keeps balance. 46% chenin, 26% bukettraube, 20% muscadel, 8% semillon. 14.6% alc. 112 g/ℓ sugar. **99** good puff of botrytis, 75/25 chenin, riesling. 13,2% alc. 375 ml. 500 cases.

Rosé ☻ ⁂ Not even 'quantum' does justice to leap Team Macici has made with this unfashionable style in **01**. Emphatic transformation from frivolous candyfloss to berried, gamey mouthful, perhaps single biggest statement that there are new kids on this cellar block. As arresting as the 950 000 ℓ production. Still semi-sweet from cinsaut, gamay, but with oodles of savoury interest: a red wine drinker's rose.

Paarl Cabernet Sauvignon ⁂ Undemanding, older-style red. **99**, like pvs, victim perhaps to diversion of choice grapes to Reserve/Auction ranges. Leafy, dusty nose, tight, unyielding palate, austere tannins mask some chewy cassis fruit. 50% old-oak (mix of sizes) aged. Tagged for modernisation, although likely to be incremental: fans finish 108 200 cases a year. **Pinotage** ⁂ **99** full, ripe and unambiguous: boiled sweets, banana dominate nose, compared to more savoury **98** palate, both shored up by assertive, gum-numbing tannins, fruit gingerly peeking out from astringent cloak. 45 000 cases. **Baronne** ⁂ "I'll only continue styles I'm prepared to make," says Macici, hinting at a fruit/oak-driven upgrade for red brand stalwarts. **99** showing the way, with red berry fruit elbowing past leafy tobacco tones, hard tannins. Cab/shiraz mix (60/40). 64 000 cases. **Duet** ⁂ Cynics may not expect harmony from standard-bearers of Burgundy and Bdx, but conductor is on song: 79% pinot laced with 21% cab. **00** strong ruby colour, earthy pinot aromas and tight, youthful cherry fruit. Current tannic bite softened by gentle cooling. 12,9% alc. 40 000 cases.

Chardonnay ⁂ Immodest style, overt creamy vanilla nose heralds big, buttery mouthful, 13.5% alc weighs in too. Juicy tropical melons add to drinkability of **00**, which craves food. 46 500 cases, 50% small/large wood fermented/matured. **Paarl Chenin Blanc** Last was **99**; now in Reserve range. **Paarl Riesling** ⁑ Mr Reliable (one of SA's top-selling dry whites) gets injection of personality with Macici touch in **01** (Cape riesling). Thatchy, undemanding, like pvs, now with added flinty edge and creamy finish. 12% alc. Drink within harvest yr. **Rhine Riesling** ⁂ Petals, muscat and terpenes – aromatic style in **01**, 15% gewürz making presence felt. Racy, reductive riesling to fore on palate, lined by 9 g/ℓ sugar. Fragrant aperitif with presence or Thai culinary companion. 9 000 cases.

Prelude ⁂ Leap in production (27 000 cases) parallels expanded style for this pioneering sauvignon/chardonnay (63/33) melange in **01**; extracted vanilla (chardonnay exposed to oak staves) needs tempering at table. Full-bodied buttery fruit countered grassy tension. 13,5% alc. Exported as Sauvignon Blanc-Chardonnay. **Premier Grand Cru** ⁑ Popularity (23 630 cases) sustains dated name misnomer, rewarded in latest **NV** (01) with fresh quince flesh to grassy/hay bones, geared up from 'simple' by refreshing late brace. Chenin/colombard, soupcon semillon. **Lyric** ⁑ 720 000 ℓ a tad off the 4-million Macici made for Graça (similarities abound), but stocks still unlikely to last the yr. Sauvignon (69%) focus front-stage; grassy edge, tangy fig flesh. Still unpretentious, reliable, off-dry (7 g/ℓ sugar), but more substance in **01**. Cape riesling/chardonnay complete the package. **Elegance** ⁂ Opulent grapey nose (80% muscats) belies gravitas of **00** palate. There's sugar (11 g/ℓ), sure, but 20% (Rhine) riesling and 14% alc conspire to present robust mouthful, more so than pvs. 6 500 cases. **Stein** ⁑ For many, the 'welcome' portal to wine in general, Nederburg in particular. Mild spiciness of **00** lifts otherwise inoffensive, straightforward semi-sweet (21 g/ℓ sugar) mouthful. **Special Late Harvest** ⁂ **00** falters after luscious, minerally **99**; former damp leaf nose, sweet (33 g/ℓ), simple and uninspiring. Hopefully temporary hiccup in a stable renown for stickies. Chenin, gewürz, riesling (37/36/27). 10 000 cases.

The all-women tasting committee at the Cellars-Hohenort Hotel with its two restaurants, The Cellars and The Cape Malay, push their palates and people skills to the limit to cater to a wide range of tastes (including the Diners Club judges – they're rated tops with a Diamond award for the past two years running). Seated are the F&B team, from left: ***Inge Johansen*** *(F&B Manager) with assistants* ***Dominique Blochinger*** *and* ***Deborah Cooper****. Standing is chef-sommelier* ***Tatiana Marcetteau****, whose expert advice is usually warmly welcomed with over 350 vintages on the winelist and some 8 000 dusty finds in the cellar.*

Lorna Roos *(still finding bits of confetti in her luggage, which is ever ready and packed to accompany new husband and taster for this guide, Dave Hughes, on international wine sorties) is accomplished both on the ground (she manicures the vineyards at Sylvanvale in Devon Valley and several other notable Stellenbosch properties) and in the air (her semi-acrobatic Fuji is built for flipping upside down and other stomach-turning antics). She's also a crack shot although, she quips, it's only when she's got a good target these days …*

Modest organiser of the Cape Times V&A Waterfront Wine Festival ***Posy Hazell*** *had to have her arm twisted to appear in the guide, not sure she "deserved such an accolade". This from a whirlwind who whisks around the Waterfront so briskly when she's putting together this annual gathering of the Cape wine clans that tourists could be forgiven for thinking the force that just blew by was the Cape south-easter. With over a decade as a highly effective PR and wine consultant, like many a successful woman she has an equal achiever by her side: business partner and husband Jeremy Hazell.*

SOMMELIER
Red Wine Cellar
A Wine Cellar created for the exceptional preservation of Red Wines.
Small and silent, at home or at your favourite restaurant, it will preserve your valuable wine collection for everlasting pleasure.
No vibration
Silent - no noise
Gradual cooldown technology
Perfect maturation environment
Stable humidity
Constant temperature
Ideal for the connoisseur
National Luna
34 Plantation Road,
Eastleigh, Edenvale,
Johannesburg, South Africa.
P.O. Box 8899, Edenglen 1613
e-mail: natluna@mweb.co.za
Tel: (011) 452 5438
Fax: (011) 452 5263
www.nationalluna.com

Girls just want to have fun – well, this all-female Avontuur team certainly does, pulled together by a camaraderie and a serious underlying focus on their own chosen areas of expertise: **Carolyn Carswell** *heads up wine sales,* **Pippa Mickleburgh** *is the general manager of this lavish Helderberg spread which includes a thoroughbred stud,* **Lizelle Gerber** *is the award-winning winemaker and marketer* **Margi Schoeman** *makes sure everyone gets the message: together they mean business.*

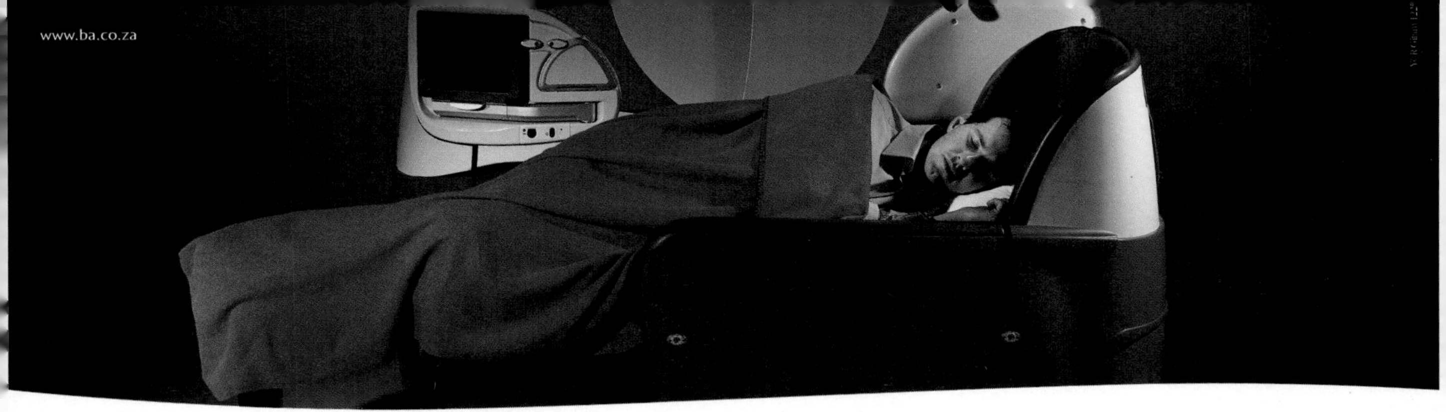

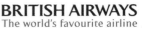

Caroline Rillema *of Caroline's Fine Wines, purveyor to palates since 1979, keeps her finger on the Cape wine pulse which decidedly flutters at her annual white and red wine reviews, where you can meet the star performers and sample the liquid golds. Branches in Cape Town's CBD and Somerset West make her elegant emporiums, stocked with local and imported wines, easily accessible.*

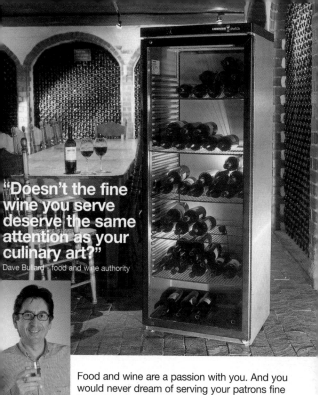

The Vineyard Connection

Stellenbosch (at Delvera cnr R44 & Muldersvlei Road Muldersvlei) • Wine tasting & sales Mon-Fri 8-5 Sat & Sun 9-4 • Hosts Lara Philp & Johan Rademan • PO Box 1484 Stellenbosch 7599 • ***Tel (021) 884-4360*** *• Fax (021) 884-4361 • E-mail info@vineyardconnection.co.za Website www.vineyardconnection.co.za*

HAVING BUILT an impressive track record as *the* exporters of wines from the Cape, they have now matured into elegant new premises, whilst retaining their enduring knowledge and passion for the wine industry. Recommended as a one stop destination for wine lovers and travellers alike. Meticulous personal service and a beautifully balanced selection of South African wines, sweeping views of the vineyards and the warmest of welcomes will leave you with a lasting impression of quality. Promises ⁂ delivery.

Sparkling range

Blanquette ⁂ Last was **95** bottle-fermented dry MCC, 100% chardonnay, 1/4 base wine barrel-fermented, 4 yrs on lees. 1 000 cases not tasted for this ed. **Premiere Cuvée Brut** ⁂ Omnipresent, SA's biggest brut likely to survive Distell's rationalisation – who could resist 50 000 cases/yr? Latest **NV** (chenin, Cape riesling, sauvignon) does everything asked of it; fresh, somewhat fruity, never sweet, late bracing stony ring primes the palate. Refreshing. Charmat method. **Kap Sekt** ✫ Style whose race seems run (potential casualty of consolidating Distell's bubbly interests in JC le Roux). Next **99** decidedly organic tones overlay flinty, toasty base. Rhine/Cape riesling, chardonnay, second fermentation in tank. **Premiere Cuvée Doux** ✫ Light, sweeter (52 g/ℓ sugar) version of Brut, shared blend. Candyfloss cut by tangy mango, spice adds substance. 1 500 cases only from farm.

Nederburg Auction wines

These made in small quantities, usually from special vyd blocks, offered in lots of ±500 cases. Originally labelled under meaningless Bin number, prefaced by letter (R indicates dry red, D dry white, S dessert and C Cap Classique); more recent vintages carry variety/blend. The Nederburg Auction, now in its 28th yr, is SA's biggest. It's open to any producer whose wine passes the selection process (Nederburg also subject to strenuous screening). The gavel is wielded by Patrick Grubb MW, inaugural and still incumbent auctioneer. 2001 saw 8 930 cases on offer from a record 70 participants, including 7 newcomers. Sales reached a new high of R6.4-million; South Africans accounted for 84% of sales; the biggest spenders once again were the Spar and Makro retail chains.

✵**Cabernet Sauvignon Private Bin R163** Vertical tasting **94**, **95**, **99** for this ed shows long-awaited fruits of investment in new/small oak, new clones/ cooler areas in late 90s. **99** ✵ hedonistic cedar, oak fragrances embroidered with savoury, black olive, pimento spice, tight-fisted mouthful harbours fruit to outlast body. Impressive, promising. 13.8% alc. 870 cases. **95** traditional old-clone mould, developed tomato-cocktail character, boxy, dusty, drying out. 12% alc. **94**, **93** both ⁂, rustically tannic. 500 cases.

✵**Merlot Private Bin R181** Wine to watch. **99** full meaty (bacon, game) core braced by delicious censer of spice. Tangy, fleshy fruit shepherded by ripe tannins, delicious accompaniment to rare roast beef. 550 cases. 13.75% alc. Ratchets up on ripe **98**, **97** modern minerally freshness; dense mocha texture lifted by cinnamon spice; firm dry tannins. 250 cases. 13,4% alc.

✵**Pinotage Private Bin R172** The trend continues. Latest **99** generous with trademark banana/clove but in measured, not opulent, blowsy style. Firm oak reins in the taut fruit, strong (13.8% alc.) not jammy. Big **98** especially savoury, judiciously structured, finishes crisply. Ripe fruit, new wood, soft tannins and Rhone spiciness initiated by **97**, superior to **95** ⁂ parsimonious with fruit, overgenerous wood. 850 cases.

✵**Shiraz Private Bin R121** Leaps and bounds away from old-style, unyielding pvs continued in **99** packed with heady milled pepper, nutmeg, cinnamon, hints clove, savoury mouthful, fruit in tandem with 13.5% alc. Sea-change started by assertive (not aggressive) **95**, delicious cinnamon-spiked fruit woven into prune/plum palate. Yr Fr barriques, 90% new. 500 cases.

✵**Cabernet Sauvignon-Merlot Private Bin R109** Carrying fresher, more modern heraldry, especially in upcoming **99** ✵: inviting nose of fresh cherries, cassis, cedar; pithy fruits, savoury twists pack palate. Excellent balance. No sacrifice to fashion: a wine to enjoy rather than do battle with. **97** (first with new Fr oak) equally inviting, more individual. **95** old style. Usually 60/40 cab, merlot.

✵**Cabernet Sauvignon-Shiraz Private Bin R103** The upgrade hasn't stopped short here, either. **99** fuller, fleshier, more inviting than earlier in the decade: plums and red berries predominate, firm structure houses enough fruit (and 14% alc!) to last the pace. **97** slightly medicinal nose, mineral/gentian core vehicle for supple fruits, gentle tannins. **94** ☆ softer than **93**, both old-style dense tannic firmness. 500 cases. ±70/30 cab/shiraz blends.

☆**Shiraz-Cabernet Sauvignon Private Bin R115** Old favourite, new substance. Beneficiary of recent fruit/oak largesse, latest offerings cross the rubicon from sinuous austerity to modernity so incisively that immediate rerating warranted. **99** heady scents of violets, crushed pepper, allspice backed by black berry opulence in minerally tapered finish. Tight, but will open. **97** ☆ richer aromatics, more complex mouthful of smoky, gamey interest, savoury depth. Thoroughbred. Both far cry from mouthcoating dusty prunes, austere tannic corset of **94** ☆. ±13.5 alcs. 550 cases.

☆**Chardonnay** Trio destined for the gavel. **Private Bin D270** Latest **01** amplifies style of Reserve range offering: big, bold, buttery but cut above, more refined elegance from juicy limey fruit balanced with integrated oak, acid/tannin backbone. **98** Complex melange of wood, candle wax, citric fruit superior to slim, trim, though not insubstantial **97**. 7 mths new Fr oak. 13.2% alc. 300 cases. **Private Bin D166** NEW **01** bin-named for muscat clone 166, aromatic muscat fragrance inescapable, clever wood exposure adds creaminess, contends with loud 14.6% alc. Frivolous fruity finish completes confection that will be popular. 5 mths new Fr oak-fermentation and lees contact, weekly battonage. 300 cases. **Private Bin DXXX (T503)** NEW **01** unwooded tank sample in bold house style but refreshing intensity of lemon/lime twist to tail. Sweetish finish.

☆**Sauvignon Blanc Reserve** NEW **01** excellent debut for Razvan Macici at auction, unwooded sibling of D234 below: Laser-beam intensity to river-stone, gunflint aromas, piercing mouthful sweetened by gooseberry flesh, complexity from month-long fermentation, exceptional length of finish. 4 t/ha harvest of single Dbnville vineyard, fine form 4 days after bottling predicts super development potential. 270 cases. **Sauvignon Blanc Private Bin D234** Emphatic oak-barrelled **01** dominated by wood at tasting mid-01, gravely, mineral penetration, full flavours bolstered by 3.7 g/ℓ sugar. Super potential. **99** herbaceous fynbos, burnt wild scrub, plus creamy oak. Fr-oak fermented, 6 mths lees, regular battonage.

☆**Edelkeur** Grand dame of SA botrytis desserts; original *raison d'être* of Auction (sales still solely via this jamboree) but not without trajectory in style, popularity. Deserted by market in 2000 (first time ever parcels left unsold) after yrs of acquisitive clamour, yet likely to regain demand with next **99** ☆ which reverts to near unctuous sweetness, richness. Drier for a time mid-90s (never-released **94** unusually so at 84 g/ℓ), **99** touches 221 g/ℓ sugar with powerfully concentrated bouquet of apricot, honeyed peach/mango, turbocharged palate of extraordinary focus, telescopic length. Outstanding. Last **98** robust acidity in drier mould 120 g/ℓ sugar. **97** rich, full-bodied, built to last (but not forever – **82** tasted mid-01 a relic). **96** classic but short on excitement. 100% chenin. 375 ml.

☆**Gewürztraminer-Weisser Riesling Special Late Harvest Private Bin S354** Blend of the exotics (65/35), misses gear in next **00** which quieter, more delicate, clean but less exciting than heady **99**: veritable potpourri; rich yet balanced palate, more finesse than somewhat ponderous pvs. 12,4% alc, 34,5 g/ℓ sugar. 250 cases.

☆**Semillon Noble Late Harvest** Buyers' value since modest debut for **97** at 2000 fiesta. Forthcoming **00** brilliant golden complexion, juicy botrytis essence, ripe, plump fruit, zesty mango/melon unfettered by wood. Successor to concentrated **99**, intensely delicious tropical fruit in measured, full, balanced palate. Lanolin richness develops with age. High 144 g/ℓ sugar, 14% alc. Unoaked. 250 cases of 375 ml. No **98**.

Weisser Riesling Noble Late Harvest Private Bin S316 "Definitely nothing to change in the style of these wines," says Macici of Nederburg stickies. Epitomised by this gem, often better value than Edelkeur on Auction day. Next **99** true to form; scintillating golden patina, rich apricot/peach pip nose, decadent botrytis viscosity checked by tart tail. Excellent, timeless finish. Superb, as is **97** intense botrytis nose, ripe pineapple core cut by litchi, pickled lime tang. Robustly strong (14,4% alc) mellowing with age. 250 cases of 375 ml.

Pinot Blanc Private Bin D250 **00** organic, vegetal nose lifted by bracing, tight palate infused with oily quince, spicy, sweet oak. 13% alc. 300 cases. **99** chalky mineral depth more complex. 12,6% alc. 500 cases. **Semillon Private Bin D266** **00** offers rich lanolin nose layered with creamy vanilla, palate unbundled, loose finish. 12.9% alc. 550 cases. **99** opening up. Fermented/matured 6 mths mix Am/Fr oak. 13,2% alc. 500 cases. **Eminence** 100% muscadel usually showing clean billowing grapey muscat, lighter, easier, not as complex as regal Edelkeur above. **00** a variant, youthful, supple grape flavours unsupported by sugar (drier at 95 g/ℓ sugar), hammered by late alcohol burn (15.4% alc.) **99** better balanced 11,6% alc. 150 g/ℓ sugar. **98** bigger within grapey/floral paradigm. No **97**. 500 cases of 375 ml. Not tasted for this ed: **Semillon Natural Sweet** Last was **99**, **Weisser Riesling Special Late Harvest Private Bin S306** Last was **97**, **Private Reserve Port** Last was **64**, **Chardonnay-Sauvignon Blanc Private Bin D218** Last was **99**, **Muscadel-Steen Private Bin S333** Last was **99**, **Private Bin C92** MCC bubbly, last was **93**. — *DS*

Neethlingshof Estate

*Stellenbosch (see Stellenbosch map) • Tasting & sales Mon-Fri 9-7 Sat-Sun 10-6 (closes two hrs earlier in winter) Also tasting/sales of Stellenzicht wines. Tasting fee R20 p/p for 6 wines (includes glass) • Cellar tours by appointment • Lord Neethling Restaurant, Palm Terrace • Farm tour with barbeque • Owner Lusan Holdings • Winemaker Philip Costandius (since 2000) • Viticulturist Danie van Zyl • Production 923 tons 66 713 cases • **Tel (021) 883-8988** • Fax (021) 883-8941 Email nee@mweb.co.za • Website www.neethlingshof.co.za*

"Look, we don't have romantic names for our vineyards," quips new winemaker Philip Costandius, "would you like the number of the block?" Settled in at his new cellar, Costandius is enjoying time in the vineyards wearing his estate manager's cap, supervising selection and planting of ±7 hectares of shiraz. He's delighted with his first vintage here, especially the "stunning" Sauvignon 01 (he immediately bottled "a special wine" for the CWG Auction – the first time Neethlingshof has participated in the prestigious event). The 'standard' Sauvignon 01 flew out of the cellar and into shoppers' baskets at Sainsbury's and Oddbins in the UK. Another highlight is "an exceptional tank" of cabernet franc 99 due to be released as a varietal in the premium Lord Neethling range. Fans will be disappointed to learn there'll again be no NLH 01 – "not a botrytis year" – though they waited until May to pick the fabled riesling-vineyard-with-no-name.

Lord Neethling Cabernet Sauvignon First release **97** full-flavoured, densely fruity yet balanced. **98** oak-dominated mid-01; cigarbox/lead-pencils aromas echo in severe, almost austere plate gripped by tannins; on present form will need 4-5 yrs' softening. 2 yrs Fr oak, 50% new. 13,4% alc. 1 174 cases.

Lord Neethling Pinotage 98 chocolate-boxy style full of 'sweetness' and soft black-plum tones; full bodied; varietal character undimmed by transfusion with 15% shiraz. 2 yrs new Am oak. More style, personality than regular version below. 1 314 cases. WOM Reserve. Maiden **97** VVG, *Wine* elegant, powered by fruit.

Cabernet Sauvignon Latest **98** delicious and very classic; gorgeous hawthorn, bramble fragrances; ripe youngberry-jam flavours (not jammy); wood woven into tight-knit, med-weight yet not unfleshy body. 2 yrs older Fr oak. 12,9% alc. 7 356 cases. **97** balanced, and perhaps still to reveal its best. **96** ✵✵ among finest from patchy yr.

✵**Shiraz** Rhone-like in style with fine firm tannins and acid, balanced with generous alc for overall silky effect. **97** supportively and unobtrusively oaked. **98** boarded up mid-01, reveals only snatches dark damson fruit, black pepper and tar; also unyielding tannins and stalky touches; on current form ✵; needs 2-3 yrs soften, grow. 2 yrs Fr/Am oak, none new. 14% alc. 2 935 cases **96** ✵ much lighter than either, quicker developing.

✵**Merlot** Past few vintages not quite as luminous as rich, mouthfilling **95**. Slight stalkiness among the black berry fruits in latest **98**, some gruff tannins need 2/3 yrs. 2 yrs Fr oak, 2nd fill to relax. **97** high toned with touch of eucalyptus. **96** ✵ less opulent (and, sensibly, less expansively oaked in response to troubled vintage).

✵**Chardonnay** ✓ Latest releases affirm this label's claim to equal status with sibling Stellenzicht. **00** exceptionally balanced, almost serene; ripe citrus, light floral scents, creamy and soft; wood all but invisible; excellent with veal dishes and other delicate cuisine. Only 50% barrel-fermented/aged, 8 mths; remainder unoaked. 3 176 cases. **99** more toasty (100% barrelled), some ageing potential. **98** cut above pvs.

✵✵**Semillon Reserve** First release **98** a new benchmark for this variety in Cape: massive and rich, with long grippy finish. Follow up **99** ✵ with splash chenin, ageing gracefully. Richness, high alc (13.7%) balanced by fresh citrus tang. Delicious now, could easily go few more yrs. New Fr oak 8 mths. 1 113 cases.

✵**Gewürztraminer** ✓ Occasion to abandon prejudice against non-dry wines. This beautifully poised and elegant, ±10 g/ℓ sugar softens rather than sweetens when well balanced by acidity, as here. **01** classic rose-petal bouquet and a less usual meaty nuance; **00** much more intensely petally, yet wears it with notable grace. **99** ✵ headily perfumed with honeysuckle. **98**, **97** SAA.

✵**Sauvignon Blanc** ✓ Delicious **01** ✵ will appeal to fans of a non-aggressive sauvignon style. Welcoming fresh-fruity aromas, then tangy flint/nettle tastes followed by tropical softness; gentle acidity ends on upbeat note. 13.3% alc. 4 763 cases. Contrast with almost pungent **00**, with crisp, long-floating tail.

Pinotage ✵ Habitually fruity, open, **98** surprises with its sullen demeanour, unyielding earthy tones. 2 yrs older wood. 13.2% alc. Not tasted for this ed: **Lord Neethling Laurentius** Last was **97** ✵✵, **Neethlingsrood** (**97** ✵); **Weisser Riesling Noble Late Harvest** (**98** ✵✵). — *IvH*

Neil Ellis Wines

*Stellenbosch (see Stellenbosch map) • Tasting & sales Mon-Fri 9.30-4.30 Sat 10-2 • Views • Owner Neil Ellis Wines (Pty) Ltd • Chief winemaker Neil Ellis (since 1986) • Viticulturist Pieter Smit (since 1989) • Consulting viticulturists Eben Archer & Johan Pienaar • Vineyards 104 ha • Production 45 000 cases 50/50 red/white • PO Box 917 Stellenbosch 7599 • **Tel (021) 887-0649** • Fax (021) 887-0647 • E-mail info@neilellis.com • Website www.neilellis.com*

Neil Ellis started 2001 on a sparkling note – a new agreement with Taittinger to distribute the range in France had him breaking out the bubbly. Some two decades ago, this grape-spotter of note pioneered seeking out highly individual sites all over the Cape and nudging growers to see things in a new light, too. He brings his booty (mainly from the Stellenbosch region including, on the doorstep, Oude Nektar Estate, owned by long-time wine-partner Hans-Peter Schröder, Groenekloof on the West Coast, where they have part-ownership of a vineyard, and the cooler Elgin valley) to their minimalist-chic cellar in Jonkershoek. His key ingredient for success in a challenging industry? Voice-of-reason Ellis advocates patience. "It just doesn't happen overnight," he says. While this industry icon is supportive of individual initiatives, he's concerned: "It takes 10 years for a winemaker to get to know a vineyard and only then can he really formulate a winemaking philosophy. Then it takes another 10 years to fine tune that." Anyone got 20 years to spare?

Neil Ellis Reserve Vineyard Selection

Single-vineyard wines, both WO Jonkershoek, for long maturation.

✯✯ **Cabernet Sauvignon Reserve** If Ellis were obliged to choose a variety to head the pack, it would be cab. This wine, even in best international company would vindicate his choice: spacious yet unextravagant; its sleek sophistication derives from ripe fruit, intuitively treated, accessorised only with suitably chic – entirely complementary 24 mths – new oak. **99** continues string of fine vintages; dark mocha/berry richness in nose, more minerally taut mouth with richness reappearing in long, intense finish. From choice cooler s-w facing Oude Nektar vyds in Jonkershoek. 13.5% alc. **98**, **97** VVG also very fine. For long – 10 yrs plus – keeping.

✯ **Shiraz Reserve** Denser, more oak-influenced version of Shiraz below; encapsulates Ellis's ability (so admired by his peers) to consistently produce wines both powerful and elegant. **99** warmly rich savoury presence with complexity suggesting the site rather than just the variety. Unquestionable maturation potential – look to ±2007 for extra delectable mellowness. 13.5% alc. All new oak. Single 9 yr old Oude Nektar vyd.

Neil Ellis Stellenbosch range

✯ **Cabernet Sauvignon** Consistency a hallmark here – fruit selection and immaculate cellar routines well established, rigorously applied since early 1990s. **99** creates triumvirate of standout vintages with **98**, **97**; latest displays yr's more obvious fruity charm: cigarbox whiffs, roasted coffee and clear, bright blackcurrant fruit all receive fair hearing without loss of structure or characteristic svelte dryness. Oaking less pronounced than in Reserves above, though 50% in new barrels. **96**, **94** *Wine* ✯.

✯ **Pinotage** Settled into modern but refined, rather than overblown, lines. **00** repeats **99**'s understatement, fine-toned brambly fruit bouquet; richly juicy though light-textured, ending on note of sleek sophistication. 13% alc. Yr in oak, 15% Am. **00** Coastal WO.

✯ **Shiraz** To emphasise Ellis can play the variety as well as the more recognised specialists, **99** followed **98** to SAA podium for triumphant two-in-a-row red wine trophy. Re-tasted mid-01, balance between elegance, complexity and enveloping richness. Fine-tuned spice livened up with luscious sweet fruit in delicious, lingering palate. **00** (tasted from cask) no less ambitious; more concentrated, riper (feature of vintage rather than vinification) which evident in deep, crimson-edged hues. Retains all-important refinement within thicker frame of alc (14.5%). 18 mths Fr oak.

✯ **Cabernet Sauvignon-Merlot** ✓ Sort of wine that inspires confidence in a whole range; reconciles opposites of 'give' and 'grip'. Variations reflect vintage conditions rather than vinification: **99** open-fruited, merlot's approachability evident in supple bridge built on cab's firm foundation. As ever, well-ordered tannins contribute to the stylish, delicious edifice. 15 mths in Fr oak provides quality backdrop, regulated to allow 5 yrs gradual maturation. 13% alc.

✯ **Chardonnay** ✓ **00** Softish, diffuse nutty bouquet, some lemony-grapefruit breadth; well-spread, flavoursome palate without great complexity but well-managed to create balance with 14% alc's riper elements. Less ageing potential than some pvs but sound, dependable as always. Fr barrel-fermented/matured 9 mths. Oude Nektar vyds.

Neil Ellis Elgin range

☆☆**Chardonnay** ✓ Poised self-confidence derives from cool upper-Elgin vyds, styled to retain fruit integrity within vintage parameters. Warmer **00** ✷ benefits from freshness-preserving partial malo, providing essential lift to broader than usual butterscotch, canned pineapple tones. If it lacks penetrating authority, greater keeping power of pvs, retains integration, polish for satisfying drinking over yr-18 mths. 14% alc. Fermented/matured 9 mths Fr oak, some new. **99** characteristically unflamboyant yet generous, crisp.

Neil Ellis Groenekloof range

Fruit ex West Coast vyd near Darling.

☆☆**Sauvignon Blanc** ✓ Anticipation of classic sauvignon from these Atlantic-influenced vyds runs high every vintage; in exceptional years such as **01**, reaches spine-tingling level – similar reaction can be expected to wine itself: incisively cool, catch-your-breath intensity infused with crisp gooseberry flinty ripeness and mouth-broadening 13.5% alc. Tops out with full-throttle, wide-angled aplomb. Breathtaking stuff. **99**, **98** *Wine* ✷.

Neil Ellis Inglewood range

✷**Sauvignon Blanc** ✓ Uncomplicated yet thoroughly enjoyable **01.** Fresh gooseberries, mown spring grass cascade across palate with juicy bounce. Balanced 13% alc.

Cabernet Sauvignon NEW ☆ Immediately appealing **00**; bright cassis/blackberry fruits with slick of mint wrapped in rounded, med-bodied frame. 9 mths oaking adds class without complication. 12.5% alc.

Chardonnay NEW ☆ Unwooded **01** with ripe pickled lime, tropical presence, persistence. Full-bodied, smoothly polished for early drinking. — *AL*

Nelson's Creek Estate

Paarl (see Paarl map) • Tasting & sales Mon-Fri 8-5 Sat 9-2 (sales also by arrangement) • Cellar tours by appointment • Restaurant meals/picnics by arrangement or BYO • Self-catering guest-house • Conference/lecture centre • Tourgroups • Views • Mountain biking • Owner Alan Nelson • Winemaker/viticulturist Richard Kershaw (since 2001) • Vineyards 44 ha • Production 345 tons (15 000 cases own label) 60% red 40% white • PO Box 2009 Windmeul 7630 • ***Tel (021) 863-8453*** *• Fax (021) 863-8424 • E-mail info@nelsonscreek.co.za*

At this progressive Paarl estate they're making sure they're ripe for the picking: a revolutionary new system, initiated by former Nietvoorbij plant pathologist Dr Gerrie Strydom, pinpoints the right moment to pick the grapes using the latest high-tech equipment. Fresh from three harvests at Mulderbosch, with international seasoning in France, Germany and Chile, Richard Kershaw joins them as estate manager and winemaker. He's already enthused the creative team at this well-rounded property – a guesthouse, crafts centre housed in traditional Xhosa huts, and facilities for weddings, picnics and conferences complement the winery. Now they're looking forward to having their own bottling and bottle maturation facilities completed in time for this year's harvest. A committed family man, senior counsel Alan Nelson is over the moon that his daughter Lisha is studying winemaking at Stellenbosch University. Last year saw them revise their marketing strategy by making their wines available in leading retail outlets to be more accessible to women purchasers, and launching their virtual wine club into cyber.

✷**Cabernet Sauvignon** Flagship label impressed with standout **95** VG. **98** later picked for bigger, riper blackberry flavour; very smooth, generous tannin; dry but non-aggressive finish. **99** potential noted in pvs edition few yrs off. Don't rush. ±Yr Fr oak. 12,5% alc. 2 800 cases.

Merlot 98 lightish-bodied (11,8% alc) but not lacking fruit; smooth, long dry exit. **99** savoury, slightly organic whiffs, lots of fine tannins that need 2-3 yrs to soften and allow fruit to develop. Small Fr-oak aged, 13 mths, portion new. **97** SAYWS gold. **95** VG.

Pinotage To date a pair of releases: **98** sappy, generous version with considerable character, style. Still-available **99** similar, but even on release less full (12.8% alc), intense. Back-tasted mid-01, nearer ; light, soft and ready to drink now. Partly oak-staved. 2 300 cases.

Shiraz These serious, thoughtfully constructed examples not for those in search of instant gratification; firm structure of tannin/oak needs some patience. Current **99** though very good, still yr/2 away from maturity anticipated in pvs ed; ripe shiraz flesh, disciplined oak augur well for development. 10% Am casks, remainder Fr, none new. 1 500 half-cases. **98** crisper, fruitier than pvs.

Albenet Characterful blend cinsaut, cab, ruby cab (34/33/33); unwooded, juicy, mellow enough to drink now. 2 000 half-cases. **Chardonnay 00** partly new-barrel-fermented; good aromatics, fruit coming slightly off the boil. 1 500 half-cases. **Sauvignon Blanc 01** carefully styled for easy drinking: lightish 12.5% alc, peachy/grassy tastes, grain sugar for extra smoothness. 2 000 cases. Following not tasted for this ed: **Chenin Blanc** (Pvs **99**); **Chenin Blanc-Chardonnay** (**99**); **Marguerite** (**99**). — *IvH*

New Beginnings Wines

Paarl (see Paarl map) • Tasting & sales Mon-Fri 9-5 Tasting fee R10 p/p for groups • Vineyard tours by appointment • Owner Klein Begin Farming Association • Winemaker Matthewis Thabo (since Jan 1998), with viticulturists from VinPro • Production 13 000 cases 60% white 40% red • PO Box 2009 Windmeul 7630 • ***Tel/fax (021) 863-8612*** *• E-mail nbwines@iafrica.com*

From its humble start in 1997, the first black-owned wine farm in SA (also known by its Afrikaans synonym, Klein Begin) has come a long way. The original land was donated by advocate Alan Nelson to farm staff who helped him transform neighbouring Nelson's Creek (a badly neglected property when he bought it some 12 years ago) into a prime winery, the rest purchased by them. Backed by intense media interest, the maiden vintage wines, made by Matewis Thabo, were snapped up. Last year, they harvested the first of their own grapes, "right out of our own vineyards which we planted ourselves," announces admin officer Danny Hurling with obvious pride. Carl Allen, who's now left Nelson's Creek, helped them make the Pinotage and Cabernet which are snug in barrels, with some mighty good 'babysitters' (Beyers Truter and Lofty Ellis) looking in on them from time to time. They now have their own modest tasting facilities on the farm and plan to build their own cellar soon. The previous labels, Classic Dry Red, Rosé and Dry White, now discontinued.

Newton Johnson Wines

Walker Bay (see Walker Bay map) • Tasting & sales Mon-Fri 9-4 Sat 9-12 • Cellar tours by appointment • Views • Owners Dave & Felicity Johnson • Winemaker Gordon Newton Johnson • Vineyards 3,5 ha • Production 5 000 cases 45% red 55% white 5% rosé • PO Box 225 Hermanus 7200 • ***Tel (028) 312-3862*** *• Fax (028) 312-3867 • E-mail capebay@netactive.co.za*

Sound, no-nonsense wines are the hallmark of this hilltop winery in the Hemel-en-Aarde Valley, with a view that goes on forever. Which is what you'd expect from the down-to-aarde Johnson family – paterfamilias Dave, soft-spoken wife

Felicite (née Newton) and sporty sons Gordon and Bevan. Winemaker Gordon has nine crushes at various wineries around the world to his credit (most recently in Bordeaux), and at press time he and some SA colleagues were leaving for some extra-fine-tuning Down Under; Bevan Johnson, in charge of marketing and export sales, is casting his net widely (recent forays include various European capitals and Singapore) while keeping his hand in with harvests at Sichel in Bordeaux. They've bought a 40 ha property in Hemel-en-Aarde, and in the next two years will be planting pinot, for which the area has gained a good reputation, Rhone varieties and sauvignon. This cool-climate fruit infusion is set to boost the already jet-propelled flagships below Sandown Bay and Cape Bay rages will continue to razzle the crowds. See also separate entries.

Cabernet Sauvignon Splashes shiraz (**99**, **00**) or merlot (maiden **98**) add salsa to these confident multi-regional cabs, oaked ±yr Fr barriques. **98** fruit ex Walker Bay; **99** Firgrove; current **00** from both areas, plus 10% Stbosch syrah. Minerally bouquet, cherry/charry tones; dry but pliable tannins. ±13% alc. 1 400 cases.

Pinot Noir NEW Sets the Hemel-en-Aarde henhouse aflutter with dream **00** debut, reeking of Burgundian truffles, smoke and cherries. Full, fleshy, supple, long charry fruit presaging excellent development. 50/50 own/insourced fruit, hand sorted; 9 mths oaked. 12.8% alc. 100 cases.

Pinotage New-generation pinotage, pvs with extra fillip of early approachability, though latest **00** still in tannic headlock mid-01; needs ±yr or, for the impatient, unshrinking food accompaniment. Firgrove fruit. 500 cases. Coming-out vintage **98** hyper-concentrated, minerally; *Wine* ✵, ABSA Top Ten plaudits. Walker Bay grapes. These ±yr oaked; alcs ±13,5% alc. No **99**.

Pour Mes Amis NEW Only congenital nice-guy Dave Johnson would dream of sharing **00**, top Walker Bay pinot in SA *Wine* 00 tasting, with his mates. Unblended pinot, 10 mths Burgundian *fûts*, fruit ex Hemel-en-Aarde (75%), Elgin. Very similar to above; marginally slimmer, firmer, charier; could age interestingly. 100 cases.

Felicité ✓ Rosé for grown-ups: flagrantly dry and food-cordial but tweaked for comfortable solo imbibing. Latest again 100% pinot ex crispy Elgin; vibrant; light tannic kick lifts **01** into upper quaffing class. 13,9% alc. 300 cases.

Chardonnay Faces some serious neighbourly competition (as does Pinot above) and comes up trumps in **00** ✵✵, as pvsly with Kaaimansgat (Villiersdorp area) fruit sparking in the engine room. Beautifully oaked, malo suppressed for mouthwatering crispness. Like pvs, super now, potentially better in 2-5 yrs. 13,3% alc. 600 cases. Fresh-faced style set with maiden **97** (unrated).

Sauvignon Blanc ✓ Cool Walker Bay fruit suffuses latest **01**, texturised with now standard dollop Fr oak fermented/matured semillon. Mouthfilling; admirable complexity, which should increase with 2-3 yrs' careful cellaring. 12.7% alc. 1 800 cases. Fatter, bit more tropical than **00**, ex Bot River, with crystalline acidity. **99** ✵ only blip since excellent **98** debut. — *DH*

Nicholaas L Jonker Estate see Jonkheer

Niel Joubert Wines

*Paarl (see Paarl map) • Tasting, sales, cellar tours by appointment • Walks • Views • Owner Niel Joubert • Winemaker Ernst Leicht (since 2000) • Viticulturist Daan Joubert (since 1982) • Vineyards 300 ha • Production 2 200 tons (220 tons own label) 60% red 40% white • PO Box 17 Klapmuts 7625 • **Tel (021) 875-5419** • Fax (021) 875-5462 • E-mail neiljoub@iafrica.com*

THE WINES from this Paarl property have been going places – London for one, where Niel Joubert entered two maiden vintages at the IWC: the Chardonnay 2000 took a silver and the Shiraz 99 was commended. Last year was the second season for Ernst Leicht who, fresh from studying at Weinberg in Germany, took up the challenge of realising the undoubted potential at the 900-hectare Klein Simonsvlei spread below the Simonsberg. About 10% of production is bottled under their own label (with long-standing ties to SFW, they still supply grapes and bulk wine to Distell). Leicht's sights are still set on reds (although the whites aren't neglected) to which end the red wine fermenting facility has been increased to 200 tons and a maturation cellar built. A tasting locale was planned to be open in time for Christmas last year. All steady signs of progress on the road to fulfilling that potential.

Shiraz NEW ✓ Low yielding (4 t/ha) Simonsberg vines impart concentration to **99**, striking deep glints, spicy (not peppery) red fruits, savoury hints. some well controlled sweet sensations (from 100% Am oak), enhanced by big 13.5% alc. Now and for 4-5 yrs. 400 cases.

Cabernet Sauvignon Lightly-oaked **99** strikes sweetly, follows with minty, dry stalky tones. Lightish bodied. 2 700 cases. **Merlot** NEW **99** unblended merlot, slurpable overripe style (appealed to WOM palates, among others); sweet entry (partly from ripely generous 14% alc), dry finish. 480 cases. **Pinotage** **98**, back-tasted mid-01, softening, tannins now more in line with dark fruit; spiciness from splash cab; 20% new oak. 2 400 cases. **Chardonnay** NEW Dab-handed partial cask fermentation leaves ample elbow room for ripe peach/tropical fruits in **00**, 8 mths on lees (though not overtly leesy). 13.5% alc. 750 cases. **Chenin Blanc** NEW **01** just off-dry, very ripe, easy pear-toned white. 14% alc. 3 400 cases. **Sauvignon Blanc** **01** lively, fresh, slight zing. Reductively vinified so muted flavours might perk up with time. 13.5% alc. 1 850 cases. Discontinued: **Cabernet Sauvignon** (Oak Aged) Pvs **98**. — *JN*

Nietvoorbij

Stellenbosch (see Stellenbosch map) • Tasting & sales Mon-Fri 9-1 • Owner ARC • Winemakers Kous Theart & Adéle Louw • Viticulturist WHL Laubscher • Vineyards 50 ha • Production 5 000 cases • Private Bag X5026 Stellenbosch 7599 • ***Tel (021) 809-3091*** *• Fax (021) 809-3002 • E-mail adele@nietvoor.agric.za*

The Nietvoorbij fruit, vine and wine research institute on the outskirts of Stellenbosch farms 50 ha of experimental vineyards; the grapes are made into wine (1 024 micro-batches in 2001!), both to check on the influences of various viticultural practices, and to probe a variety of cellar techniques. Experiments done, there's wine going begging, explains winemaker Adéle Louw. Except for the port (now cork-closed and also available in magnum), they're sold by the 6-pack – astonishing bargains all.

Kwartet ✓ Afrikaans name alludes to quartet of grapes in this classically styled bdx blend: cabs s/f, malbec, merlot. **98** open, accessible; **99** more obviously oaked, tannic, needs bit of time. 13.1% alc. 435 cases. These yr Fr barriques.

Pinotage ✓ Sophisticated **98** followed by somewhat rustic, big-boned **99** (though much admired by SA *Wine* judges, who awarded); firm fruity tannins, power alc (14.6%). Yr large/small oak and staves. 1 084 cases.

Chardonnay ✓ Fragrant, easy drinking **99** succeeded by slightly slimmer **00**, again with smoky ripe peaches (though unoaked). 13.6% alc. 989 cases.

Merlot **99** with drop cab; plummy/pruney tones, dry smoky tannins. Light/med feel despite highish 13.3% alc. Yr small oak. 508 cases. **Dry Red** NEW Three cabs (ruby, franc, sauvignon) plus merlot; unoaked. **NV** (99) ripe-fruited, supple. Screwtop. Giveway R9/bottle (also in 2 ℓ pack). 13.4% alc. 2 200 cases. Also available (not tasted): **Cabernet Sauvignon**; **Cabernet Franc**; **Sauvignon Blanc**; **Dry White**, also in 2 ℓ pack; **Semi-dry White**; **Stein**; **Semi-Sweet** In 2 ℓ; **Ruby Port**. — *DH*

Nitida Cellars

Durbanville (see Durbanville map) • Tasting & sales Mon-Fri 9-5 Sat 9.30-1 Negotiated fee for tourgroups • Proclaimed conservation area • Cellar tours by appointment • Owners Veller family • Winemaker/ viticulturist Bernhard Veller • Vineyards 13 ha • Production 125 tons (7 000 cases own label) 60% red 40% white • PO Box 1423 Durbanville 7551 • ***Tel/fax (021) 976-1467*** *• E-mail nitida@mweb.co.za*

IT's all hands on deck at this small, well-sited Durbanville family farm, says winemaker/viticulturist Bernhard Veller (his wife Peta handles sales and marketing, and parents Gerhard and Ursula Veller are also very involved). Having shed his role as MD of a business making pressure gauges, the only pressure levels he monitors now are his own at harvest time. Last season was early – and tricky – but he's very happy with the whites (volumes are picking up a bit with more sauvignon blanc to keep up with demand for this charmer). Stressing that he relies on the input of consultants in both cellar and vineyards, Veller's been delighted at the enthusiastic response to their red blend Calligraphy, thus elegantly named during an inspired night spent sharing wine with friends, as the *protea nitida* or wagon tree (still prolific here and from which the farm derives its name) had many uses in the early days of the Cape Colony, one of them making ink from the leaves (another, *fellies* or rim pieces from the wood for the wheels of ox wagons).

✵**Cabernet Sauvignon** Forward style with generous padding though backbone of healthy tannin adds classical nuance. Current **99** needs further bottle ageing to show its best; enough fruity heft to carry to maturity. 13.8% alc. ±Yr Fr oak, 50% new. ±1 000 cases.

✵**Shiraz** Never a loud wine, but lacks neither interest nor flavour; some pvs toprated by SA *Wine* panels, including **98** (✵), **97** (✵✵)). **99** quieter initially; current **00**'s plummy tastes trimmed with pepper and well managed oak. Nose blunter, less attractive mid-01 than pvs though may unfurl and earn a higher rankingt han present ✵. Grapes ex neighbour farms. 14.5% alc. 950 cases.

✵**Calligraphy** ✓ Attractive claret-style red jointly fronted by cab/cab f (35/35) in second release **99**. Classically structured, complex truffle, mulberry, cherry array in high-toned bouquet; well formed and drinkable now, but better in yr/2. 13.3% alc. 650 cases. **98** VG.

✵**Chardonnay** Yr on yr improvement for individualistic label, launched with **98** VVG, aiming for fruit expression through downsized oak influence. Which newest **00** ✓ ✵ achieves convincingly; only 30% new cask-fermented, imparting subtle but really attractive honey-buttered toast nuances to long, mouthwatering lemon-lime fruit. 13,4% alc. 1 000 cases. **99** juicy, lively but not as refined as latest. Own/bought-in fruit.

✵**Sauvignon Blanc** ✓ Pedigree stretching to **95** VVG, which put this cellar on the map. Latest **01** dazzlingly aromatic yet refined; palate presently broad rather than deep, should settle and become fuller in 2-3 yrs. ±13% alc. 1 250 cases. Acclaimed **00** probably at peak, though might hold couple of yrs. SAA (1st class), SAYWS gold. **99** VG, SAYWS gold.

✵**Semillon** NEW ✓ Distinctive and emphatic debut; **01** with Dbnville's cool climate top-tones of overgrown herb garden, heathery hill; lemon/orange blossom wafts from underlying crisp, ripe fruit. Superlative oak integration (±60% new-barrel-fermented, 2 mths sur lie; own grapes – clone GD1). 14% alc.

Pinotage ✵ Bernhard Veller's thoughtful use of oak showcases **00**'s refined, ripely fragrant fruit. Soft, varietally correct; should please fans of the grape (and cellar). 14.6% alc. 730 cases. —*DH*

Nordale Winery

Bonnievale (see Robertson map) • Tasting & sales Mon-Thu 8-12.30; 1.30-5 Fri 7.30-12.30; 1.30-4 • Cellar tours by appointment • Owners 32 members • Manager Emile Schoch • Winemaker to be appointed • Consulting viticulturists VinPro • Vineyards 580 ha • Production 5 800 tons (10 000 cases own label) • PO Box 105 Bonnievale 6730 • ***Tel (023) 616-2050*** *• Fax (023) 616-2192 • E-mail nordalewines@yebo.co.za • Website www.nordale.co.za*

THE 'Wanted: Winemaker' signs were still up on these heights behind Bonnievale at press time, prompting Emile Schoch to shrug in a resigned sort of way. More accustomed to a "consultant's role", the genial cellar manager rolled up his sleeves for harvest 01 when they first became winemakerless and has been hands-on ever since. He's also deeply involved with the marketing of the produce, still mostly earmarked for the local wholesalers but some destined for export through negociant houses. The portion that's marketed under the new spiffier in-house label is comparatively small but growing. Last year saw 10 000 cases march out of the cellar door, 40% more than previously. "We've planning to do more marketing under the Nordale brand," Schoch announces. And some expanding of the range with, among others, the smart new oak-matured Shiraz below and yet to be confirmed ideas for a red blend playfully named Double-Cab.

☆**Captain's Drift Shiraz** NEW More class, concentration, excitement than 'regular' version below, **00** shows benefit of 10 mths oak, 66/33 Fr/Am, imparting expensive fragrances to truffley black-cherry fruit. Good now, should gain suppleness (and probably extra half-star) with 2-3 yrs' bottle ageing. ±13% alc. 800 half-cases.

☆**Red Muskadel Jerepigo** ✓ **01** (sample) glows with jewel-like brilliance, ruby lights mirrored in cherry-toned palate with sweetness leavened by maraschino tang; as below, stiletto acidity to keep the sugar at bay. These can develop with distinction, though would be pity not to enjoy some of the fireworks now. 16.4% alc. ±500 cases of 375 ml.

☆**White Muscadel** NEW 'Mouthwatering' not a word that springs to mind when describing SA fortifieds, but this **01** (sample) fits the bill with delicious acidity racing through palate to invigorate and refresh. 'Borderline' (as the Wine & Spirit Board would say) 15.1% alc (15% legal min for style) helps lighten tone. 500 cases of 375 ml.

Vin Rouge ☻ ☆ Unoaked everyday drops with lots of fleshy fruit and slight tannin flick in **00** tail, telling you there's cab in this quaffable blend with ruby cab. 13% alc. 2 300 cases.

Shiraz ☆ Second-release **00** puts the variety's unwooded fruit on a pedestal: smoke, leather and warm, savoury flavours; dry, slightly tart finish could do with ±yr to soften. 12,7% alc. ±1 000 cases. **Colombard-Chardonnay** ☆ The farms Kapteinsdrift (colombard) and Nordale combine their fruit for this modest but pleasing lightly-oaked **01** blend, with soft centre, gentle wildflower perfumes. 12% alc. 3 500 cases. — *IvH*

Nuy Wine Cellar

Worcester (see Worcester map) • Tasting & sales Mon-Fri 8.30-4.30 Sat 8.30-12.30 (cases and 2-bottle packs only) Tasting fee for larger groups • Barbecue facilities • Owners 21 members • Winemaker Wilhelm Linde (since 1971) • Production 9 000 tons • PO Box 5225 Worcester 6849 • ***Tel (023) 347-0272*** *• Fax (023) 347-4994 • E-mail wines@nuywinery.co.za*

WHILE most of the production from this meticulous co-op (established 1963) goes in bulk to the big commercial wholesalers, there's enough left to quench the thirst of its many loyal fans. Medal-plated Wilhelm Linde has steered the ship for more than 20 years, and the indefatigable Diners Club double-laureate continues to keep a firm, value orientated grip on things. When in the area, miraculously untouristy still, pop in for a tasting or become entrenched in the garden, considerately outfitted with barbecue griddles to satisfy your meat-seeking desires.

Red Muscadel ✓ Beautifully poised, intense **00**, with character and charm. As with white version, moderate 16.5% alc just right for power without spiritous burn. Both too piercingly sweet for most desserts, but perfect for post-prandial contemplativeness or conversation – after bottle maturation of year or more, preferably.

White Muscadel ✓ Luxuriant raisiny fortified wine; rich, flavoursome, shot through with fresh, nervy acidity to balance massive 230 g/ℓ sugar. Latest **00** worthy heir to long line of medal winners.

Cabernet Sauvignon Tank sample of **00** offers hints of cassis, plenty of tannin. Lightly wooded. 13.5% alc. **Rouge de Nuy** Toasty notes in **99** lightly wooded blend cab/merlot; now with slightly bitter finish. Briefly wooded. 13.5% alc. **Chardonnay** Neutrally flavoured **01** has firm, dry structure; no evidence of its light wooding – or of much else. 13% alc. **Colombard** Almost steely, gently pétillant **01**, with solid flavour. Nicely balanced for early, easy downing. Dry, lightish. **Riesling** Floral aromas, but little else in watery, lowish alc (11.8%) **01** (from Cape Riesling, not the real thing). **Sauvignon Blanc** Pleasant quaffer; lightish (12.3% alc), dry and refreshing. **Fernão Pires** For undemanding light off-dry drinking. Touch lemony fruit in **01**. **Chant de Nuit** Satisfyingly racy, lemony flavours in **NV** white blend (including Ferdinand de Lesseps table variety). Dry, with lightish 11.8% alc. **Colombard Semi-Sweet** **01** sentimental sundowner; fruity, light, sugar adding richness but no cloy. **Sauvignon Blanc Sparkling** For foaming fun, **01** is gently off-dry and lightly floral. — *TJ*

Oak Valley see WhaleHaven
Oak Village see Vinfruco
Oddbins see Shoprite Checkers

Odyssey NEW

Shiny, low-alcohol Natural Sweets by Robertson Winery appealing to youth-market . 1 ℓ resealable packs splashed with flower-powerish "astral imagery". See Vinimark entry for details.

Red Sweet ripe plums and just a suggestion of tannin to give structure. **Rosé** Maidenly blushes, followed by fragile sweet tastes. **White** Fresh, vaguely fruity, light and sweet; blend colombard, muscadel, chenin. Above all **NV**. — *DH*

Okha see Joostenberg

Old Bridge Wines

Franschhoek • Not open to the public • Owner Paulinas Dal Farm Holdings (Pty) Ltd • Production 50 000 cases 50% white 50% red • PO Box 101 Franschhoek 7690 • ***Tel/fax (021) 426-1305*** *• E-mail rickety@iafrica.com • Websites www.oldbridgewines.com, www.oldbridge.co.za*

Franschhoek based, export focused producer, negociant and wholesaler sourcing wines from the Western Cape region for a variety of labels. These include Paulinas Drift International for export, and Old Bridge/Old Drift for the southern African market. Also a number of private labels for clients both locally and overseas. The wines, not available for tasting, have included: Paulinas Drift International **Cape Classic Red**, **Cape Classic White**; Paulinas Drift Premium label: **Cabernet Sauvignon**, **Merlot**, **Pinotage**, **Chardonnay**, **Chenin Blanc**, **Sauvignon Blanc**; Paulinas Drift Reserve label: **Cabernet Sauvignon**, **Merlot**,

Shiraz, **Pinotage**, **Chardonnay**, **Sauvignon Blanc**. Above, with exception of Reserves, have also appeared under **Old Bridge/Old Drift** marque.

Old Brown see Sedgwick's

Old Vines Cellars

Not open to the public • Owners Irina von Holdt & Françoise Botha • Winemaker Dominic Burke • Production 12 000 cases 100% white • 50 Liesbeek Road Rosebank 7700 • ***Tel (021) 685-6428*** *• Fax (021) 685-6446 • E-mail oldvines@iafrica.com • Website www.oldvines.co.za*

EVER the keeper of the chenin flame, Cape Wine Master (and taster for this guide) Irina von Holdt, insisting all the while that chenin should be SA's white wine flagbearer, mounted a campaign (the force of which could have launched an obscure candidate into the president's seat) that helped the Chenin Blanc Association get off the ground. She's become inextricably linked, even "married" to this once overlooked grape. Happily it's a harmonious partnership that's produced award-winning offspring. Daughter Fran Botha has been jetting around so much she hasn't had time to feel the lag: "I never thought the wine industry would make financial journalism look slow!" Hedging their bets, they export to most of Europe, Japan, Mauritius, Namibia, Dubai, Canada, the USA and more recently Hong Kong. Old Vines Chenin Blanc will soon be seen in Corney & Barrow's swishy London wine bars too. "The rest of the world is a lot more receptive to chenin than SA. Now that really fusses me," says our queen of steen, charging into the fray once more.

★**Blue White** The original unwooded dry chenin in this range, preferred by many, still in trend-setting blue bottle. Retaste of **98** mid-01 shows graceful bottle-age; silken honey, melon tones livened by variety's shiny acidity. Crystalline freshness again in new **99**, nearly as weighty (13.7% alc vs 98's 14%) but elegant. 10 000 cases. With time, could reach heights of botrytised **97** ★, beloved of 01 Chenin Challenge, WOM judges.

★**Old Vines Chenin Blanc** Sister to above, in traditional green bottle. First was **98**, lightly botrytised, weighty; though unwooded, similar taste-profile to Barrel Reserve below. **99** (sample), fruit ex Stbosch, again full-figured (13,9% alc), firm; butterscotch embrace to ripe-peach core. Structure for 3-4 yrs' bottle ageing. 2 000 cases.

★**Old Vines Barrel Reserve Chenin Blanc** Oaked version, more serious than above, deserving extra time in cellar. Tone set by **98**; second release **99** (sample) potentially finer; rich, deliciously creamy butterscotch/vanilla in generously proportioned (13.8% alc) but balanced package. Grapes ex Jordan, Kaapzicht; 2nd/3rd fill Fr casks. 1 000 cases.

Spring Valley ★ NEW Chenin/sauvignon blend, unoaked; **01** relaxed, breezy sipping, solo or (IvH's suggestion) with Cape salmon and lemon-herb butter. Stbosch vyd. 13.2% alc. 6 000 cases. **Cheerful White** To date a single **NV** ★. — *DH*

Onderkloof Vines & Wines

Schaapenberg (see Helderberg map) • Tasting, sales, cellar tours Mon-Fri by appointment • Private functions (max 20 people) Oct-Mar by arrangement • Owners Danie Truter & Beat Musfeld • Winemaker/viticulturist Danie Truter (since 1998) • Vineyards 34 ha • Production 80 tons (3 750 cases own label) 60% white 40% red • PO Box 90 Sir Lowry's Pass 7133 • ***Tel (021) 858-1538*** *• Fax (021) 858-1536 • E-mail wine@onderkloofwines.co.za • Website www.onderkloofwines.co.za*

One of the prime motivators for these premium south-facing Schaapenberg slopes to be declared an official ward, Danie Truter is well pleased with their new recognition as a sub-region on the Helderberg Wine Route. Among the early arrivals in this up-and-ready-to-fly neighbourhood (except, of course, for Vergelegen, which has been anchoring the sea-breezy appellation for over 300 years), their close relationship with a Burgundian cooper, Rousseau, gives them an edge on experimenting with barrels made to their own specifications. Facing onto False Bay (a perfect vantage point for keen sailors Truter and Swiss partner Beat Musfeld), they're subjected to the notorious south-easter, and for good reason here: it literally blows fungal diseases clean away. "What the 'Cape Doctor' takes in quantity, it gives back in quality," says Truter sagely. Their newly appointed agent in Switzerland now swallows up about 60% of production, but they're adamant they won't neglect their local clients.

- ✫**Cabernet Sauvignon** Single 1,5 ha dryland vyd on Schaapenberg the source of this unblended cab, asserting more claret qualities in **00** than pvs. Latest with ripe cassis, cigarbox whiffs; mediumweight (despite high 13.5% alc), 18 mths Fr barriques, some new. 1 000 (× 6, as are all these). More refined than **99**, with cab's 'sauvage' quality in bouquet.
- ✫**Chardonnay** Single vyd, harvested/selected by hand; Barrel preview of **01** Burgundian whiffs; creamy apple/pear tastes, immense length. 2nd fill Fr oak, Rousseau cooperage. Tasted young, ✫ but higher final rating likely. Judging from **99** with richness in reserve for 2-4 yrs, no need to rush these. ±400 cases.
- ✫**Chenin Blanc 00**, with "touch of wood", quite delicious; creamy peach/melon textures, bright acidity. Concludes with croissant-like flavours. 12.5% alc. 1 200 cases. **99** ✭✭ similar but not as rich, slightly unbalanced by heavy 13,5% alc.
- ✫**Sauvignon Blanc** Delicately constructed **01** (Danie Truter beginning to mellow?); bright, easy to drink; lowish 12% alc, even! Nice leesy French tones which, as D T says, harmonious with seafoods.

Pinotage 00 highly individual style. 18 mths Fr oak, 60% new. 13.4% alc. 600 cases. **Floreal Blanc de Blanc** ✭✭ **99** re-release. Tasted mid-01 shows lots of bottle age, terpene hints; rich, oxidative semi-dry tones which pleasant with some foods (Thai/Malay curries, traditional bobotie, Moroccan). Unwooded quartet of varieties. 13% alc. 3 000 cases. **Young Vines Cabernet Sauvignon** To date an attractive early-drinking **99** ✭✭. — *TM*

Onyx see Darling Cellars

Oom Tas

One of SA's top-selling brands (2-million cases a year, all in returnable glass). Budget-priced, has such a large, loyal following, it's produced 24 hours a day. Available only in Western Cape, where it holds over one third of the market. By Distell.

NV ✭✭ Deep amber colour looks 'sweet', but finishes decidedly dry. Light muscat fragrance; spicy hints add interest. — *IvH*

Opstal Estate

Worcester (see Worcester map) • Tasting, sales, cellar tours Mon-Fri 9-5 Sat 10-1 • Light picnic lunch by prior arrangement • Owner/winemaker Stanley Louw (since Jan 1980) • Viticulturist Kobus Theron (since Dec 1978) • Cellar assistant Jaco Theron • Vineyards 100 ha • Production 1 500 tons (20 000 cases own label) 70% white 30% red • PO Box 27 Rawsonville 6845 • ***Tel (023) 349-3001*** *• Fax (023) 349-3002 • E-mail opstal@lando.co.za • Website www.opstal.co.za*

At this Worcester estate, deep in the valley which snakes its way through the Slanghoek mountains, they've taken to scaring the living daylights out of visitors – literally, with their twilight zone Haunted Cellar Tours, followed by an evening of suitably Gothic candlelit wining (on Opstal's finest) and dining in true medieval style at long wooden tables groaning with food fit for a king and no cutlery in sight. It's the brainchild of Stanley Louw, 6th generation winemaker and owner (who dresses in monk's garb and spins a mean tale), and Suzanne Trotsky, business manager of the nearby Goudini Spa. Despite all these otherworldly shenanigans, they've still found time to collect silvers for their two reds at the Michelangelo awards.

Cabernet Sauvignon ✓ Homespun, characterful cab; **99** with smoothing grain sugar, ageing well in bottle. Following **00** dry; accessible now but probably better in 3-4 yrs. ±10 mths small oak. 13.3% alc. 6 000 cases.

Carl Everson Classic Red ☻ Now pinotage-driven, with ruby cab and cinsaut's sweetness for extra drinkability (watch that 13.5% alc); **00** oaked. 3 000 cases. **Carl Everson Reserve** ☻ Unpretentious, sluggable chardonnay/chenin blend (60/40). Med/full bodied; unwooded. 2 000 cases. **Hanepoot** ☻ Lighter, undemandingly sweet **98** fortified dessert, with variety's honeysuckle perfume and fresh finish. 16,3% alc. 600 cases.

Chardonnay Lightly wooded, full-bodied dry **00**. 13,% alc. 3 000 cases. **Chenin Blanc** NEW ★ Unwooded **00**, lightish, semi-dry, very ordinary. 1 000 cases. **Sauvignon Blanc** No **01**. **00** tasted for pvs ed, crisp cut-grass/fresh-fig flavours. — *TM*

Oranjerivier Wine Cellars

Orange River (see Northern Cape map for individual cellars) • Tasting & sales at Upington, Kakamas, Keimoes, Grootdrink and Groblershoop cellars. Tasting & sales year round Mon-Fri 8-5 Sat 8.30-12 • Cellar tours mid-Jan to March, Mon-Fri • Tourgroups up to 40 • River/vyd views from Kanoneiland • Owners ±750 members • General manager Noel Mouton • Winemakers Jannie Engelbrecht, Bolla Louw, Jurie de Kock, Chris Venter, Danie Volgraaff • Production ±100 000 tons • PO Box 544 Upington 8800 • ***Tel (054) 337-8800*** *(head office) • Fax (054) 332-4408 • E-mail marketing@owk.co.za • Website www.owk.co.za*

The Kalahari Desert might not spring instantly to mind as a wine area, but threading through its arid red soils is the Orange River, and strung out along its banks are both vineyards and this multi-winery co-op, the largest in the southern hemisphere, second largest in the world, with 750 members. They don't measure their vines by the hectare here, but by the square kilometre (about 300), producing around 100 000 tons of mainly colombard, chenin, hanepoot, ruby cabernet and sultana. A deal with the nationwide Spar chain sees their wines tickling thousands more local palates, albeit anonymously (you'll find them freshly bottled/boxed under the Country Cellars and Carnival labels). Meanwhile this large and energetic team is basking in the glow of a deserved *Grape* award for excellence in packaging.

Ruby Cabernet ★ Pale orange-ruby; hallmark herbal/thatchy aromas in light-toned **99**, to be served chilled. 13.5% alc. 5 936 cases. **Rosé** Deep salmon pink **00** with intriguing herbal, cherry-stone aromas; light-bodied, sweet, persistent cherry flavours. Chenin, ruby cab. NV. 2 739 cases. **Chenin Blanc** ★ **00** Delicate haystack/cinnamon wafts; bone-dry, steely flavours end with citrus/green-apple tang. 2 148 cases. **Blanc de Blanc** ★ **NV** (00) 3 mths oaking shows in restrained buttered-toast/lemon nuances. Low 10.5% alc. 2 100 cases. **Grand Cru** Musky and spicy aromas with hint of fig and guava; austerely dry finish makes low-alc **00** something of a challenge. 4 502 cases. **Colombard** **00** faint pear-drop/

guava sniffs, fuller than most of these (at 12.5% alc), dried apricot flavours ending with perky lift of dry acidity. 6 470 cases. **Nouveau Blanc** ☆ Lemon rind/pear-drop interests in semi-sweet **00**; popular style with low acid for extra gulpability. Blend led by chenin. **NV** (00). 15 009 cases, any of which would go well with traditional bobotie, Thai dishes. **Stein** ☆ **NV** (99) Semi-sweet chenin, shy green-herbs bouquet; palate lifted by lemongrass zing; drier than expected. Lowish 11.5% alc. 2 563 cases. **Late Harvest** ★ **NV** (00). Drinkable blend chenin/colombard with lavender/pear aromas and low acid; serve well chilled. 3 333 cases. **Special Late Harvest** ☆ Blend as above with extra sweetness; low alc still, but sugar teases out fuller flavours of guava, silky peaches. **NV** (01). 3 780 cases. **Petillement a Vin** NEW ☆ Nicely carbonated fizz offering strawberry, cherry and some good earthy tastes; not sugary. With cellar's thumbprint low alc. 1 688 cases. **Red Muscadel** ☆ **NV**. Very pale ruby/amber hues preview earthy/savoury aromas and hints of raisins; balanced sweetness and alc (17.5%). 3 880 cases. **Jerepiko Red** ☆ Attractive coppery-amber; waxy/varnishy bouquet with cherry hints; very soft, sweet but verging on dry in finish. **NV** (98) from ruby cab. 17,5% alc. 3 478 cases. **Sweet Hanepoot** ★☆ **NV** (99). Coppery gold glints introduce pungent 'dried'-muscat fruit and pleasant varnishy notes; silky palate with 17% alc well integrated. Nice winter warmer. 2 300 cases. **White Muscadel** ★☆ **NV** (99). Intense musky nose with earth/truffle snatches; peach/apricot tastes hinting at orange rind; concentrated fruit satisfies. 17% alc. 2 000 cases admired by Veritas judges. **Jerepiko White** Deep burnished gold colour looks sweet, rich; suitably luxurious potpourri scents, hints smoked meat, apricots; quite spiritous, shows bit of character. **NV**. 17% alc. 2 272 cases. **Red Port** ★ **NV** (99). Light orange-amber robes; meaty aromas and raisin whiffs; soft; traditional low-alc high-sugar style but pleasant enough. 1 890 cases. Untasted for this ed: **Bonne Souvenir**, **Blanc de Noir**, **Chardonnay**, **Therona** (these pvsly no stars). — *TM*

Organic Terroir see Sonop

Oudekloof NEW

Tulbagh • Not open to the public • Owners Paul O'Riordan & Francois Rozon • Winemakers Jan & Gerd Theron (Montpellier) • Viticulturists Arnold Hugo (since Feb 99) • Vineyards 21 ha • Production 55 tons 900 cases (own label) 75% white 25% red • PO Box 191 Oudekloof Tulbagh 6820 • ***Tel/fax (023) 230-1925*** *• E-mail oudekloof@hotmail.com*

Jan and Gerd Theron of nearby Montpellier du Sud make this range from 21 hectares owned by the bi-continental wine-partnership of Paul O'Riordan, based in Ireland, and Francois Rozon, who operates out of Canada. The property as a whole is much larger – 322 ha – and it's been managed since 99 by Arnold Hugo. The familiar varietal aristocracy (cabernet, shiraz and chardonnay) are newish arrivals here, but the terroir traditionally belongs to ancient chenin bushvines. They, judging from the star below, still have plenty of vitality to carry this property and its young range into the limelight.

★ **Chenin Blanc** Partial (Fr) oaking shows deliciously as sweetish double-cream in **00** palate; focused sweet fruit with muesli whiffs amid breakfast guava, pineapple. Stylish wine. 900 cases. — *DH*

Oude Rust see Mooiuitsig

Oude Wellington Estate

Wellington (see Wellington map) • Tasting & sales by appointment • Tasting fee R10 p/p for groups larger than 6 • Wine/brandy tours by arrangement • River Café Restaurant • Guesthouse • Tourgroups • Views • Owner Rolf Schumacher

• *Winemaker Vanessa Simkiss (since 1995)* • *Viticulturists Vanessa Simkiss & Rolf Schumacher* • *Vineyards 15 ha* • *Production 80-120 tons (2 500 cases own label) 70% white (50% for estate brandy) 30% red* • *PO Box 622 Wellington 7654* • ***Tel (021) 873-2262*** • *Fax (021) 873-4639* • *E-mail oude_wellington@kapwein.com* • *Website www.kapwein.com*

A few years ago there were only a handful of wineries on the once neglected Wellington wine route – now you can't count them on your fingers! The wines from this estate at the start of the giddy Bains Kloof Pass are slowly starting to make an impact, says Vanessa Simkiss, who's expanding the cellar to a 90-ton capacity but determined to keep it a one-woman operation. Her current flame is ruby cabernet and she's intent on keeping the spark alive: "Given the same treatment as cabernet it can stand on its own. I'm keeping at it until I'm proved right!" Retired German dentist Rolf Schumacher is the driving force in the distillery where brandy (to be released next year) and grappa are produced (if you get stuck into those after dinner, best to book into the guesthouse to recover in suitably sumptuous surroundings). Ardent foodies, chef sisters Hanlie Stepcic and Henna von Wielligh, have locals and visitors clamouring for more at their River Café on the estate.

✵**Cabernet Sauvignon** ✓ Emphatic Wellington red, big-bodied (14,5% alc) in **98** yet in **99** demonstrating that satisfaction also comes in slenderer (12.8% alc) package; similar deep flavours, some leathery and savoury whiffs, layered mouthful of plum/cassis. 14 mths Fr oak. ±250 cases to start broaching now and for 4-6 yrs.

Ruby Cabernet ✵ Reflects a rarely glimpsed side of this grape, which more usually soft and accessible (and unoaked) in Cape. Peppery **98** unfurling, showing some juice yet still tannic, dry in conclusion, needing time or food. 50% oaked in Fr barriques, all new, 12 mths. **Currant Abbey** ✵ Latest release of unoaked ruby cab reprises friendly profile of pvs; **00** smooth, sweet-fruited, very easy to drink. 13.2% alc. ±500 cases. **Rose Petal** NEW ✵ Charming name for charming off-dry blush, fragrances courtesy of gewürz (not roses, strangely, but honeysuckle, honey); colour by cab. Cross-vintage **NV** blend. **Chardonnay** NEW ✵ Pleasing debut **01** (sample) whole-bunch pressed for fruitier profile; soft, balanced peachy fruit untrammelled by oak, should appeal to even non-fans of this style. 13% alc. ±200 cases. Not tasted for this ed: **Rubignon** (Pvs **NV** ✵), **Chenin Blanc** (**99** ✵). — *DH*

Oude Weltevreden see Weltevrede
Out of Africa see Sonop

Overgaauw Estate

Stellenbosch (see Stellenbosch map) • *Tasting & sales Mon-Fri 9-12.30; 2-5 Sat 10-12.30* • *Fully equipped self-catering cottage* • *Owner Braam van Velden* • *Winemaker Chris Joubert* • *Vineyards 75 ha* • *PO Box 3 Vlottenburg 7604* • ***Tel (021) 881-3815*** • *Fax (021) 881-3436* • *E-mail info@overgaauw.co.za*

This is the natural habitat of the unashamedly big SA red. Owner Braam van Velden (the farm's been in the family since 1783) holds no truck with upfront "stadium" wines, or with marketing dictates. Statistics show the average wine is consumed within 13 hours of purchase, "not the idea I have for wine!" he states categorically. No instant gratification here, these wines of distinction should be drunk no sooner than 5 to 8 years after bottling but can be kept substantially longer with supreme reward (they recently opened a 72 Cabernet that was still in very good condition). This longevity doesn't apply only to the reds – a *Wine* vertical taste-back of Sylvaners spanning 25 years revealed serious staying power, with the 73 vintage a notable example. They've kept cases of wine from back in the 70s (and some old ports from the 50s too), so they really can put their money where their mouth is. Fittingly, Chris

Joubert's been making wines here for over a decade, with a maiden 00 vintage Shiraz-Cabernet still in the barrels for release this year.

Cabernet Sauvignon ✓ "Definite cellar wine," says Chris J, "too big to judge early." He's referring to **98**'s fruit structure rather than alc (a moderate 13% alc): intense mulberries, cherries supported though palate by firm, well-paced tannins; tobacco, fennel nuances in aftertaste. We agree: needs plenty of time. 15 mths oak, 60% new. 2 000 cases. Very similar to late-developing **95**, which needed ±4 yrs to start opening. **99** lighter, shade less complex, to sip while waiting for **98** and stunning, seriously complex **97**, with enough power, guts to absorb 18 mths 100% new Fr oak in cool vintage. Excellent tannin structure, enduring aftertaste. Still-incubating **00** most exciting of all. "Serious red," understates Chris J. No **96**.

Merlot ✓ Overgaauw a local pioneer of this grape, still among the top exponents. **99**, as above, somewhat lighter yr (though not low in alc: 13.7%), reflected in shorter barrelling (15 mths 2nd fill); no less distinguished; complex, fragrant, taffeta-textured and persistent. *Wine*, WOM selection. 4 500 cases. Standout **98** bigger (at 13,6% alc.) than **97**, more tannin, darker colour, bigger extract. Needs more time. **97** softer on release, rich, warm; emphasis on choc-cherry fruit.

Shiraz Last was exceptional **98** for 99 CWG Auction.

Tria Corda Outstanding dry red blend, featuring only the finest grapes in the finest years. **98** saw formula change: malbec replacing cab f for 60/25/15 cab, merlot, malbec blend. Spicier, darker than pvs, big, creamy; more approachable than **97**'s tight, gravelly tones. 60/25/15 cab, merlot, cab f. Above both WOM selections. **95**, slightly less cab s, more cab f, standout in exceptional red-wine yr. No **96**, **99**. Latest **00** (sample) reverts to cab/merlot/cab f configuration (65/25/10), velvety choc-slathered black cherries, whiffs pepper, mint. Reflects vintage's structure, generosity; probably finest to date. 15 mths new Fr oak. 13.5% alc. 1 700 cases.

Pinotage-Cabernet Franc ✓ **99** 65/35 ratio designed for early drinking, which it is (though there's enough substance for probably 3-4 yrs); generous, lovely sweet-fruit character. 15 mths 3rd fill Fr oak ("to protect fruit"). 13% alc. 1 000 cases. **98** 55/45 blend; spicy whiffs in plum jam palate; more forward than complex, intense 97, with sweet-ripe fruit, peppery finish. 60/40 blend. Pinotage from 30+ yr old vines.

Touriga Nacional-Cabernet Sauvignon Latest exclusively for Makro; see that entry.

Chardonnay ✓ **98** SAYWS champion wood-matured white. **99** nostalgic glance at older buttery Cape styles, emphasizing viscosity, weight. Partly achieved by natural yeast ferment (4 wks as opposed to 2 – not to be repeated as "too risky"). (No **00**.) **01** (sample) big-hearted and balanced, potentially better than pvs; oak sensitively handled to accentuate creamy ripe-peach/melon fruits. Barrel-fermented/sur lie 8 mths oak, 33% new. 13.7% alc. 600 cases.

Sauvignon Blanc ✓ Chris J moving away from reductive winemaking, allowing more lees contact than pvsly. Reflected in more intense **00**, filled with fresh green fruit, firm acids. New **01** captures all positive attributes of sauvignon-cordial vintage: ripe fruit, balance, penetrating flavour backed by delicious firmness; unusual whiff redcurrant. 2nd crop from new vyd. "Our best ever," believes Chris J. 12.1% alc. 1 800 cases.

Sylvaner ✓ The only Cape example, first bottled here in **71**. Latest **01** exceptional vintage, (and could mature into something starrier). 2nd crop from new block extravagantly aromatic, whiffs musk, sweet violets, ginger; river-pebble-smooth across palate to balanced (by dab sugar – 4.5 g/ℓ) lip-smacking finish. 600 cases, as always, good matches for Cape Malay cuisine. No **99**. **98** full bodied, touch sugar (5 g/ℓ) for smoothness.

Cape Vintage 91 lovely deep ruby robe with black heart; full, ripe-fruited, rich; generous but supple tannins, excellent length suggest another 10 yrs cellaring not far-fetched. Tintas b/f/r with souzao, cornifesto. 2 yrs 1 300 ℓ old-oak. 583 cases. **98** breathtaking intensity, lusciousness. Top Cape 'port' and rating in SA *Wine*'s tasting, WOM Reserve. These in modern drier, higher-alc style (80-90 g/ℓ sugar, 17-20% alc); Douro varieties including touriga, tintas b/f/r, souzao, cornifesto, malvasia rey. 20-24 mths old-oak unfiltered. **Reserve 97** youthfully boisterous still, slightly spiritous, acid evident though offset by delicious ripe choc-vanilla fruit. Excellent structure should see 2015. — *DH*

Overhex Vineyards

Worcester (see Worcester map) • Tasting & sales Mon-Fri 9-5 • Cellar tours for groups by appointment • Views • Owners 17 shareholders • Manager/winemaker AB Krige (since 1996) • Assistant winemaker Celeste Roberts (since 2001) • Consulting winemaker/viticulturist Rod Easthope • Production 5 000 tons 93% white 7% red • PO Box 139 Worcester 6849 • ***Tel (023) 347-5012*** *• Fax (023) 347-1057 • E-mail info@overhex.com • Website www.overhex.com*

With its 'Daring to be Different' credo and a sassy attitude to match, this once staid Worcester co-op has morphed into a plugged-in international wine company in a remarkably short time. Two of their new ranges, Hexagon and Silumku, were launched at a party in the Predator's Room at Cape Town's Two Oceans Aquarium (entirely appropriate, as consultant Rod Easthope dryly pointed out, because hitting the international wine market was "a bit like being a fish in a shark tank, if you stop moving you get eaten ..."), followed up by a similar event at London Zoo's Web of Life. Having cracked the UK market, they're now also supplying to Switzerland, Singapore, Italy and Madeira, is the feedback from motivated marketing strategist Lucy Warner. Sticking to their policy of only releasing wines that are ready to "truly deliver beyond expectations" under The Hex label, they won't be bottling the 2000 vintage intended for this premium range. Focus now is firmly on vineyard practices and plans are to replant to a 50/50 white to red ratio by 2006. Stellenbosch graduate Celeste Roberts has joined A B Krige in the cellar.

Silumku range

Dedicated to the gentleman 'father figure' of the cellar hands at Overhex.

Cabernet Sauvignon ☻ Powerful berry fruit aromas dominate easy drinking **00**; pure cassis bouquet, intensely spicy black cherry flavours, subtle oak stave notes; ripe, not flabby finish. 13,5% alc. **Chardonnay** Tropical/toasty style, fragrant rather than intense; **00** caramel overlaying peach/citrus, vanilla hints from oak staves. 13,5% alc. 7 000 cases. **Chenin Blanc** Unwooded **00**, pure fruit aromas of pineapple/apricot; rich, developed, almost smoky dry finish. 13 % alc. 8 000 cases.

Discontinued: **Pinotage**, **Sauvignon Blanc** (neither pvsly rated).

Hexagon range

Chenin Blanc-Colombar ☻ (Dry White in pvs ed) Unwooded **01**, fresh pear aromas, crisp citrus notes. Pvs **00** super-ripe fruit, lashings peach/pineapple, developed grapefruit finish. 13% alc. 20 000 cases.

Dry Red Easy drinking, soft-tannined, plump. **01** spicy cherry notes, smoky berry flavours, dry but unaggressive finish. Ruby cab/cinsaut. 13% alc. 10 000 cases. — *MF*

Overmeer Cellars

No-frills quaffing range launched in 1996 by then Stellenbosch Farmers' Winery (now Distell) to challenge the co-op and other boxed wines on price. Lately with portion non-SA grapes. Only the Late Harvest is available in glass. All NV.

Selected Red ★ Light hued vin ordinaire, earthy, very dry tasting. Med-bodied. Grapes ex SA, Spain, Argentina. **Premier Grand Cru** ★ Clean and crisp, as it should be; fairly neutral nose, furtive guava sniffs. High turnover helps ensure freshness. **Stein** ★★ Technically semi-sweet, but smooth rather than sugary; delicate grapey/tropical fragrances. **Late Harvest** ★★ Fractionally sweeter, fuller version of Stein; uncloying. — *IvH*

Paddagang Wines

*Tulbagh (see Tulbagh map) • Tasting & sales 7 days a week 9-4 Tasting fee R5 p/p • Paddagang Restaurant • Owner Paddagang Wines • Winemaker Michael Krone • PO Box 303 Tulbagh 6820 • **Tel (023) 230-0394** • Fax (023) 230-0433*

The wittily labelled 'Frog Alley' range takes its name from the characterful old-Cape restaurant on the frog route from the riverside into Tulbagh town. The eatery and adjoining wine sales/tasting locale are run, and the wines selected, by a group of friends and made by Michael Krone at Tulbagh Co-op. The labels – a play on the amphibian theme – are still among the most charming in the Cape.

✱**Brulpadda** Individual port-style fortified from ruby cab, pinotage. Latest with demerara sugar, currants; needs bit of time to integrate. Good winter warmer. ±18% alc. 300 cases.

Paddarotti ★★ Appropriately wide-girthed merlot; spicy/plummy tones finish on a high note. 13.7% alc. **NV** (as are all these). 500 cases. **Paddapoot** ★★ Fortified dessert from hanepoot; sweet but enlivened by acid/spirit. 16,8% alc. 300 cases. Also available, not ready for tasting: **Paddajolyt** (pvs ★); **Paddamanel** (★★); **Paddadundee** (untasted); **Paddasang** (★); **Paddaspring** (no star); **Platanna** (★). — *IvH*

Panarotti's

Food-friendly NV house wines of SA pizza/pasta chain, Panarotti's. Well chosen for moderate alcohol, well balanced styles. Rage not tasted for this ed. Previous have included: **Red** (★), **Dry White** (★), **Stein** (★), **Vin Doux Sparkling** (★).

Papillon see Van Loveren
Papkuilsfontein see Tukulu
Paradyskloof see Vriesenhof
Paul Bonnay see Pick 'n Pay

Paul Cluver Estate

*Elgin (see Walker Bay map) • Tasting & sales Mon-Fri 9-5 Sat 9-1 No charge for individual tasting R10 p/p for groups of 8 or more • Picnic baskets in summer • Viewing deck • Summer sunset concerts in forest amphitheatre end Oct-March • Owner Paul Clüver • Winemaker Andries Burger (since 1997) with Patrick Kraukamp (since 1997) • Vineyard manager Wayne Voigt • Marketing manager Paul Clüver • Production 120 tons 8 000 cases 50% white 50% red • PO Box 48 Grabouw 7160 • **Tel (021) 859-0605** • Fax (021) 859-0150 • E-mail info@cluver.co.za • Website www.cluver.co.za*

Günter Brözel, Nederburg's ex superstar winemaker (and still one of the winelands' most charismatic personalities) was on hand, appropriately enough, to launch the stylish new 'Arts & Crafts' front-label for this range, grown on the Cluver family's farm, De Rust, in Elgin. For its was Brözel and then Nederburg MD

Ernst le Roux who, "yearning for more excitement, more romance" in their ranges, were among the first to home in on this beautiful plateau and its potential for top-quality, cool-climate viticulture. With neurosurgeon and family friend Paul Cluver (recently voted into the chair of the SA export organisation, WOSA), they established the first rows in 1986 and, with the launch of the maiden wines in 1993, brought a rising-star area into the limelight. Now, with winemaker son-in-law Andries Burger firmly ensconced, they're ready to take the next big step: counselled by Eben Archer, they're establishing new parcels in the most auspicious sites. As Günter Brözel notes: "It might take a decade or even two to discover where the real potential lies." But the journey has begun, and it promises to be an exciting – and delicious – ride.

✵**Cabernet Sauvignon Limited Release** Individual offering from cool climes; classy, restrained yet characterful in market crowded with sameness. **98** ✵✵, much admired in Germany, probably finest to date and still improving in bottle; fruit unfurling to reveal beautiful black-cherry fragrances against oak-char and good herbaceousness; deep mulberry/blue hues and fine minerally/pebbly texture with tobacco whiffs. Lively tannins, enduring finish augur well for long development (6-10 yrs?). 13% alc. 18 mths Fr oak, 60% new. 1 300 cases (× 6, as are all these). Richer than pvs **97** ✵, slightly vegetal nose, signature pebbly, tobacco, cedar tones plus pencil shavings. Upcoming **99** still somewhat lean, reflecting difficult cab season here; needs time. **00** more fruit, extract.

✵**Pinot Noir 98** developing sensationally. Mid-01 showing restrained opulence, complexity from cherry, redcurrant, coffee nuances and sleek, fragrant oak. Delicious now, but plenty of reserves for keeping. 95% Dijon clones, with PN5; 11 mths Fr oak, 30% new. Top pinot in 99 SA *Wine* tasting. 3 500 cases. **00**, resplendent in cellar's new livery, youthfully introverted, but already silky, fragrant, very promising. Will need plenty of time. No **99**.

✵**Chardonnay** Barrel-fermented under strict temperature control for extra elegance, fruit, which reflected in current **99**, 100% new oak, confident step up from pvs. Next **00** ✵ very refined, almost reticent initially then opens fan of citrus, barley sugar, oatmeal and nascent marmalade flavours. Excellent now, potentially better in 3-5 yrs. One of two SA wines in top ten at Tasters' Competition, Vinexpo 01. 30% fermented with natural yeasts. 13,5% alc. 85% new Fr casks, 6 mths then 3 mths 2nd fill. 1 150 cases. **98** ✵, with less new oak (80%, 9 mths), creamily complex; probably at peak.

✵**Gewürztraminer** Intended as an accompaniment to fragrant cuisines (Thai dishes, light curries, traditional bobotie); **00** bright and lively, freesia/honeysuckle perfumes among the hallmark roses; technically on sweetish side of off-dry (10.7 g/ℓ sugar) but natural acidity shows quite racily. 13.5% alc. 720 cases. Continues refined style set by **99** which tastes rich rather than sweet (5.9 g/ℓ sugar), soft. No **98**.

✵**Weisser Riesling Special Late Harvest** Fragrant marmalade, pineapple more obvious now in **99** bouquet; honey overlay and generous sweetness (27 g/ℓ sugar) nicely freshened with tangy acidity. *Wine* ✵. 13.8% alc. 1 200 cases.

✵**Weisser Riesling Noble Late Harvest 99** first release snapped up at Nederburg Auction by Dutch chain Great Grapes. *Wine* ✵. **00** reserved for Auction, export, likely to be widely admired, too: floral/spicy bouquet with lime/pineapple bite; less botrytis intensity at this stage than pvs, but undoubtedly a slow starter; needs 5-8 yrs. High natural acidity (9.1 g/ℓ) ensures balanced sweetness. Basket-type press, not oaked. 14.5% alc. 280 cases of 375 ml.

✵**Weisser Riesling** Vertical tasting mid-01 reveals intriguing – always delicious – vintage variations since mid-90s, beginning with taut, austerity in off-dry **97**, with 15% botrytis complexity, shows evolved 'paraffin' tones. Lots of development potential, unlike **98** ✵, apparently marking time; very rich, almost unctuous, acidic backbone straining under combined weight of 30% botrytis, 17 g/ℓ sugar, 14.2% alc. Both WOM selections. Latest **00** (10% botrytis), returns to taut, apricot/stone-fruit nervousness; snatch savoury spice in bouquet. Dryness, penetrating acidity needs (and will aid) further bottle maturation. 13.5% alc. 800 cases. No **99** – all went into NLH/SLH.

Sauvignon Blanc Barrel Fermented ★ Popular choice on upmarket restaurant lists. **00** very subtly oaked, mere suggestion of vanilla in lemony/tropical tones; easy and satisfying. Single vyd, selected fruit. 13.5% alc. 2 200 cases. **Sauvignon Blanc** ★ **00** still youthful colours, lemony and now some tropical aromas enhancing impression of fullness, weight. Finish is bright and fresh. 13,5% alc. 2 600 cases. — *DH*

Peaks View see Bovlei
Pearly Bay see KWV

Perdeberg Co-op

Paarl (see Paarl map) • Tasting & sales Mon-Fri 8-12.30, 2-5 • Cellar tours by appointment during harvest • Owners 46 members • Winemaker Kobus de Kock (since 1989) • Vineyards 2 500 ha • Production 18 000 tons (6 000 cases own label) 60% white 40% red • PO Box 214 Paarl 7620 • ***Tel (021) 863-8244/8112*** *• Fax (021) 863-8245 • E-mail pwynk@iafrica.com*

ONLY a soupcon of this sterling co-op's production gets into bottle under the in-house label. "But only the good stuff," assures Kobus de Kock, whose arms are heavy with long-service-award gold. The winemaking stalwart obviously has a thing about these 2 500 hectares, cultivated by a cohesive 46 member corps. And so do a growing number of other savvy winegrowers, who are latching on to Agter-Paarl's dazzling potential and turning what was once an underplayed backwater into a voguish viticultural playground.

★ **Pinotage Reserve** ✓ **00** (sample) closed mid-01, allowing only glimpses of underlying red fruits, some vanilla nuances. On current form ★, but enough guts, backbone for good growth. 13,8% alc. Standard **Pinotage** ★ Unoaked **00** even bigger (14,5% alc), more open; warm Ribena aromas and ripe plummy tannins very tasty now. These 578 cases.

★ **Sauvignon Blanc** NEW **01** recalls Antipodean styles in strident green pea/ dusty sweet pepper tones, reverberating through to dry grapefruity finish. Med-toned despite heavy 14.1% alc.

★ **Hanepoot** ✓ Billows every bloom in the florist, plus litchi; underlying smoky spirit gives light, non-cloying, silky feel. **NV** (98) good with ricotta and other rich white cheeses. 17,5% alc. 578 cases.

Cinsaut ☻ ★ At over 15% alc, value-priced **00** not one to quaff standing up. Yet delightfully bouncy, extra allure from homely sweet-tomato-jam aromas. 578 cases. **Chenin Blanc Dry** ☻ ★ Still amazing value at under R10 ex-cellar. **01** quaffably fresh, as always, light-skipping lemon tastes that cunningly disguise big 14.5% alc. 578 cases.

Shiraz ★ Elegant dry **00** (barrel sample) with abundant spice, hillside scrub aromas, non-assertive, integrated tannins; savoury/earthy and sweet hints in finish ±14% alc. 578 cases. **Cabernet Sauvignon-Merlot** ★ Modern attention-seeking style; **01** (sample) plump and plummy, plenty juice with soft dark-choc/ liquorice tannins. 14.5% alc. **Semillon** NEW ★ Gutsy **01** youthfully bashful, dried-fruit whiffs and terpene/beeswax oiliness in bone-dry, full palate. 13.5% alc. 578 cases. **Chenin Blanc Semi-Sweet** ★ Individual aromatic, almost terpene nose; **01**'s sweetness neatly balanced by assertive acidity in honeyed finish. **Cinsaut Liqueur Wine** Not tasted for this ed. Pvs **NV** ★. — *TM*

Perdeberg Wines see Vinfruco
Petit Rochelle see Mont Rochelle

Philip Jordaan Wines

Worcester • Not open to the public • Owner/winemaker Philip Jordaan • Viticultural consultant Schalk du Toit • Vineyard 1 ha • Production 100% red • PO Box 55 Rawsonville 6845 • ***Tel (023) 349-1601*** *• Fax (023) 349-1581 • E-mail philipjordaan@intekom.co.za*

JUST one hectare of 11 year old vines is Philip Jordaan's stock-in-trade for his own-label wine, a stylish Cabernet Franc that hit the ground running in 98 and never looked back. The experienced Du Toitskloof cellarmaster only makes about 600 cases, but it's safe to assume a few more than usual of these corks were pulled when he recently heard he'd won his third Wine of the Month Club Best Unusual Red selection. If you're fortunate enough to have some of the 00, there's no need for follow Philip Jordaan's example, however. "You'll still be able to drink this wine in 10 years' time," he predicts.

✯**Cabernet Franc** ✓ These limited releases, full of individuality and panache, now ensconced in Cape's upper echelon. **00** expresses the variety rather exotically in fresh-peat, fernleaf aromas; minerally texture with underlying sweetness carrying through into well carpented tannin structure. 8 mths oaked. Bigger than below at 13.6% alc. Keep for drinking in 07. **99** ⁂ (but Michelangelo gold) green pepper piquancy to contrasting ripe plums. Similar to first **98**, with some emphatic tannins; dry, elegant finish. — *DH*

Pick 'n Pay

Enquiries Elsa Gray • Bahrain Drive Extension Airport Industria 7490 • ***Tel (021) 936-8400*** *• Fax (021) 934-2639 • E-mail egray@pnp.co.za*

RATIONALISATION sees this nationwide chain of supermarkets' and hyperstores' previously far-and-wide truffled range reined in to the top-selling No Name bag-in-boxes. These convient value packs continue to offer the reassurance of freshness – supplies being freshly boxed according to demand.

'No Name' range

NV 500 ml budget packs/5 ℓ bag-in-boxes sold under P 'n P's in-house brand. All ex Rbtson, unwooded.

Dry Red ☻ ⁂ Something soft and plummy for your daily goblet. Cinsaut, ruby cab blend switches easily from standalone to gastronomic.

Rosé ⁑ Semi-sweet chenin, colombard, ruby cab blend; lightish fruity casual quaffing, not sugary. **Dry White** ⁑ Plain, lightish everyday blend chenin, colombard. **Stein** ⁑ Lightish off-dry white (blend as above plus white muscadel), ripe tropical fruit core; drier than expected finish. **Late Harvest** ⁑ Guava-toned easy drinking for the sweeter-toothed. Varietal make-up as per Stein. Lightish 11.4% alc. Also available, not tasted: **Dry White Light** ⁑ Low 9.5% alc; blend as per Dry White.

The following are being discontinued (where pvsly tasted, ratings are given in brackets): 'Corporate' range: **Cabernet Sauvignon** (**99** ⁂), **Pinotage**, **Shiraz**, **Ruby Cabernet-Cabernet Sauvignon**, **Dry Red** (**99** ⁂), **Rosé** (**99** ⁑), **Chardonnay** (**99** ⁂), **Chenin Blanc**, **Sauvignon Blanc** (**00** ⁂), **Blanc Fumé** (**99** ⁂), **Blanc de Blanc** (**00** ⁂), **Johannisberger** (**99** ⁑); **Special Late Harvest** (**99** ⁑); Fab With Food range: **Fantastic with Fish**, **Chic with Chicken**, **Cool with Curry**, **Divine with Dessert**; also **Marvellous with Meat**, **Perfect with Pasta** (imports); 'Vinipak' 500 ml budget packs: **Dry Red**, **Dry White**, **Stein**, **Late Harvest**; Ravenswood budget range (2 ℓ/5 ℓ vats): **Dry Red**, **Rosé**, **Premier Grand Cru**,

Light, **Stein**, **Late Harvest**, **Johannisberger**; Paul Bonnay sparkling range: **Rouge**, **Brut**, **Vin Sec**, **Vin Doux**. — *DH*

Pierre Jourdan see Cabrière
Pinehurst see Môreson
Pinotage Company see Claridge

Plaisir De Merle 

*Simondium (see Franschhoek map) • Tasting & sales Mon-Fri 9-5. Sat 10-1 Open public holidays except religious days) • Self-guided cellar tours as above • Guided tours by appointment • BYO picnic by arrangement • Conference facilities for max 30 people with meals • Tourgroups • Gifts • Walks by arrangement • Views • Proclaimed conservation area • Owner Distell • General manager Hannes van Rensburg (since 1990) • Winemaker Niel Bester (since 1993) • Farm manager Freddie le Roux (since 1982) • Vineyards 400 ha • Production 850 tons 35 000-40 000 cases own label 75% red 25% white • PO Box 121 Simondium 7670 • **Tel (021) 874-1071/2** (wine sales) • Fax (021) 874-1689 • Cellar tel/fax (021) 874-1488 • E-mail nbester@distell.co.za • Website www.plaisirdemerle.co.za*

THE 99 Chardonnay from this showpiece winery, with its imaginative winery architecture and dramatic Simonsberg backdrop, won a gold medal at the 2001 IWC in London for Niel Bester, then repeated the performance for a Top 100 berth at the Sydney International Wine Challenge. "Best I've made in seven vintages," beams the road-running winemaker, switching easily from show-stopping whites to laying out new cabernet franc vineyards for a future red blend. Meanwhile young cabernet, petit verdot and malbec vineyards are showing "outstanding potential". In collaboration with Nietvoorbij and Ch Margaux *régisseur* Paul Pontallier, Plaisir's long-time consultant, they made an organic Sauvignon for the first time last year. It won't be released under an eco-label, however, as organic farming principles must be applied for three consecutive years before wines may be branded organic. Only once accredited by the international Société Générale de Surveillance will it get the marketing green light.

✵**Cabernet Sauvignon Reserve** NEW Striking single vyd selection from low-yielding (6 t/ha) vines, handled for max extraction, avoiding excessive tannins. Preview **99**, for release 02, young but promises excellence: dense ruby, complex, unfolding meaty, red/blackberry nose, austere tannins imprison cassis fruit mid-01, but tapered, velvety textures suggest delicious elegance will follow. Needs several yrs to achieve mature balance. 100% cab, 16 mths new Fr oak. 13,8% alc.

✵**Cabernet Sauvignon** Roller-coaster variations in form – lesser **96**, **97** ✵ followed by generous **98** ✵ – unabated with next **99**: still in cool minty/minerally mould, but palate weight lacks power of trend-setting/award-grabbing clutch after launch (SAA/Veritas selection first 3 consecutive yrs). As many fans as detractors, but current 17 000 cases appears to miss the 3 500 ℓ now standing alone as Reserve above. Cab filled out by shiraz, merlot (86/8/5) and smidgen petit verdot, mix seasoned casks. 13,5% alc.

✵**Merlot 99** cements call for re-rating signalled by **98**, edging back to lustre of maiden **95** VG, SAA trophy runner-up, which helped establish cellar's street-cred. Next **99** mild ruby support act for deliciously rich, savoury (cedar, caper, bacon) nose, finely tuned palate, still tight but promises fruit reward yr/2. Pick of this red brace. 'Milder', less severe alc (13.8%, all things being relative) than signature minty, meaty, sweet-violet **98**, with expansive 14,4% alc. Yr 2nd/3rd fill casks. 2 200 cases. **97**, **96** both ✵ less striking.

✵**Shiraz** Future stable for label undecided after Distell merger: may be absorbed in the giant's other interests (much of Plaisir's grapes delivered to

Nederburg). **00** sample combines aromatic blackberry succulence with meaty, pepper spice, searing tannins of youth. **99** ✵ on higher plane with truffles, pepper, liquorice. Fine, polished, potential to improve further. Am oak's prominent vanilla/spice absorbed into ripe choc-berries in **98** *Wine* ✵. 50/50 Am/Fr oak. 14,3% alc. 1 000 cases.

✵**Grand Plaisir** (Cape Red Blend in pvs ed) Precipitated by controversial Diners Club 'Cape Red' category. **97** cab, merlot, petit verdot (50/20/10) lean toward Bdx, but 20% shiraz re-jigs geography, adds individuality. Deeply coloured, full-roasted coffee bean aromas, ripe blackberry/cherry fullness in mouth braced by tart peppadew tang, fine-grained tannins complete, cool minty tail. 13,8% alc leaves sweetish impression. 16 mths new, 2nd fill Fr wood. 600 cases.

✵**Chardonnay** Retains broad 'weighty' style in **00**; mid-straw, back-of-spoon-coating butterscotch bouquet dramatic build-up for more elegant, lucid mouthful combining best of limey fruit, creamy vanilla, buttered croissant features. Portion stainless steel-fermented freshness lifts 85% new Fr oak (11 mths). **99** ✵ different league – "Best chardonnay I've made," avers Bester – 100% barrel-fermented, like pvs, but better quality wood adds classy smoked-oak/vanilla elegance to rich lees/lime/barley sugar. 13,8% alc. 3 500 cases.

✵**Sauvignon Blanc** Standout aromatic (unwooded) style tapered for Continental palates, marbly wild herb, spice, 'buchu' scrub on nose, succulent tropical fruits (peach, melon) in ripe **01**, full taste spectrum reinforced by grassy tang, structured racy finish. **99** aged to super creamy concentration (4 mths lees contact), gooseberry richness paced by racy acid; citrus zests finish. Alcs ±13%. 2 500 cases. **98** 10% barrel-fermented. **94-96** VG (100% oaked), all SAA.

Sangiovese 99, Petit Verdot 99 barrel samples featured in pvs ed not for release as varietal wines under this label; may feature in Nederburg reserve/auction wines. — *DS*

Plantation see International Wine Services
Pongrácz see J C le Roux
Porcupine Ridge see Boekenhoutskloof

Porterville Winery

*Swartland (see Swartland map) • Tasting & sales Mon-Fri 8-1; 2-5 Sat 8-11 • Cellar tours by appointment • Conference centre • Shady picnic spot (BYO basket) • Owners 115 members • Cellar master/winemaker André Oberholzer (since 1997) • Assistant winemaker Dico du Toit (since 2001) • Viticulturist Johan Viljoen (since 2000) • Production 15 000 tons 25 000 cases • PO Box 52 Porterville 6810 • **Tel (022) 931-2170** • Fax (022) 931-2171 • E-mail portwyn@xsinet.co.za*

If André Oberholzer and his team were in Stellenbosch, say, or Constantia, they'd have been headhunted ages ago. As it is, they're tucked into the quietest corner of the Swartland, doing their thing without fanfare or applause. So we'll leave them be, while we recognise that these as yet unscalped young heads are screwed on very much the right way. This year they made one of SA's first British Soil Association certified organic wines. Their own-label range, while on the large side, is carefully calibrated for wide appeal (there's even a dryish Rosé to accessorise your tikka chicken or Moroccan couscous); the Reserve is, properly, oaked in cask – chips (sensibly) do for the other reds. While these aren't showboating wines, they're uncomplicatedly delicious and drinkable. And at an average of about R15/bottle, amongst the best value around. These are ✵✵ easy-swiggers, the crème de la quaff, deserving of at least two smiling ☻s.

Pinotage Reserve ✓ Deep dark **00** keeps up quality progress noted in **99**. Ripe plummy fruit, chunky alc (14%), savoury acidity, yr in wood contribute to success. The cellar's really expensive wine – R22!

Pinotage **01** savoury ripe fruit, packed with verve/flavour, around framework of mild tannin, balanced acid. Mouth-drying finish – but why quibble at such value? **Enigma** Keep-em-guessing blend, which in **00** barrel preview offers usual fruity leads needed to crack the code (answer: pinotage, shiraz, cab, merlot, kept yr in old-ish wood). Unpretentious, exuberant pleasure from balanced, honest expression of the Swartland. **Vin Rouge** Plum-jammy flavours in succulent **NV** blend pinotage, cab, shiraz, cinsaut; some dry tannin, bit of wood (chip) influence adding interest. **Rosé** Latest bottling (**NV**) not ready for tasting. Pvs … Ditto **Sauvignon Blanc** (pvs **00**) and **Emerald Riesling** (pvs **00**). **Chardonnay** Unwooded **01** has notes of lime/pear-drops, in balanced, mouthfilling frame. **Chenin Blanc** Tropical fruit salad in **01**, bursting with flavour; just off-dry but kept fresh for summer by crisp acidity. **Premier Grand Cru** Fragrant, generously flavoured **NV** from colombard, bone-dry of course, mouthfilling with tropical fruit pleasure; perhaps bit less razzmatazz than previous. **Blanc de Blanc** Two blancs in latest **NV** offering – colombard, chenin. Nicely judged acidity offsets bit of sugar for soft, genial tippling. **Late Vintage** We gave up groping for words: this **NV** chenin is simply vaguely pleasant and sweetish – no more, no less. **Red Jerepiko** Current **NV** cinsaut/cab blend rather acidic, spiritous mid-01 (should quieten after some mths); but satin-textured; some interesting herby/tea-leafy overtones. **Golden Jerepiko** Imagine a rich liquid pudding of raisins, rose water and orange peel (but it works better as a wine). Latest **NV** hanepoot needs keeping yr/2 to allow spirit to integrate. — *TJ*

Post House Cellar

Stellenbosch (see Helderberg map) • Tasting by appointment • Owner/winemaker/viticulturist Nicholas Gebers • Vineyards 35 ha • Production 18 tons (1 300 cases own label) 85% red 15% white • PO Box 5635 Helderberg 7135 • ***Tel/ fax (021) 842-2409*** *• E-mail ngebers@iafrica.com*

This compact winery with its nostalgic bright-red post box (all that remains of Raithby's old post office) is proof indeed of that timeworn adage 'good things come in small packages'. There's been some expansion here though: an extended rustic maturation cellar can now accommodate another 100 barrels, and new plantings on this modest parcel of land include 7 hectares of shiraz and 3 ha of petit verdot. The latter is to be used in a new reserve blend, sure to have Nick Gebers' highly individual stamp on it.

Cabernet Sauvignon Fascinating vertical tasting mid-01 reveals progression from naiveté of **97**, rustic charm losing out to tannin/hard-pressed bitterness, to comparative sophistication of still too youthful **99**, oozing raspberry fruit/cedar. Look-ahead to **00** previews ripe tasty fruit; high 14.2% alc; massive, chewy grape tannin. Might match pvs. 35% new wood. 300 cases. **98** like trial run for **99**.

Merlot Barrel sample of **00**, deepest ruby, lots of dark cherries, earth and herbiness; aggressive tannins/acidity. 30% new oak (some Am). 14.2% alc. 300 cases. **99** was improvement on pvs.

Chenin Blanc Barrel sample of **01** suggests possible; quirky lemony richness, still oaky mid-001 from 20% new Am oak fermentation. 300 cases. — *TJ*

Prospect 1870 

Robertson • Owners Nic & Chris de Wet • Vineyards 20 ha • Production 800 cases 100% red • PO Box 141 Ashton 6715 • ***Tel (023) 615-1842*** *cell* ***082-878-2884 • Fax (023) 615-1913 • E-mail chrisdewet@hotmail.com***

RANGE not ready for tasting as the guide went to press.

Quando 

Bonnievale (see Robertson map) • Tasting by appointment • Owners/winemakers Fanus & Martin Bruwer • Vineyards 65 ha • Production 15 ton (500 cases own label) 100% white • PO Box 82 Bonnievale 6730 • ***Tel/Fax (023) 616-2752*** *cell 082-926-0805*

EVERYONE kept asking FANUS AND MARTIN BRUWER when they were going to make their own wines. So when the fruit and grape farming siblings finally relented, and produced the handsome Sauvignon below, they recalled the interminable 'whens' and decided on the name Quando. "We like the quirkiness of the Latin allusion," says Fanus Bruwer, a Stellenbosch oenology graduate, keen wine taster and cook who grows artichokes alongside export citrus and vines. Most of the grapes go to nearby Langverwacht Co-op, but a hand-picked portion is vinified in an ingeniously converted carport. "We literally are *garagistes*," laughs Bruwer with reference to the do-it-yourself micro-boutiques that are springing up in this and many other wine regions of the world. Specialising in sauvignon, the Bruwers have 12 ha on old Breede River gravels which, the brothers say, impart a Pouilly-Fumé like smokiness to the wine. "This style is rare in SA," Fanus Bruwer allows, "but sauvignon aficionados will understand."

Sauvignon Blanc ☆ **01**'s pleasantly scented, beeswaxy nose leads on to firmly crisp, well-structured mouthful; satisfying acid-drop conclusion. 12.6% alc. Attractive, elegant Italianate label very appropriate. 1 000 half-cases. — *TJ*

Quantum see Lost Horizons
Quoin Rock see Glenhurst

Raats Family Wines 

Stellenbosch (Delaire Winery) • Owners Bruwer & Jasper Raats • Winemakers/viticulturists Bruwer Raats (since 2000) & Jasper Raats (since 2000) • Vineyards 2 ha • Production 4 tons 200 cases (own label) 100% white • PO Box 2068 Stellenbosch 7602 • ***Tel (021) 885-1694*** *cell 082-902-4607 • Fax (021) 885-1270 • E-mail braats@mweb.co.za • Website www.raatsfamilywines.co.za*

THE two winemaking Raats brothers, both with full-time jobs in Stellenbosch (Bruwer at sky-high Delaire, lawyer-turned-winemaker Jasper at new glam-winery Glenhurst), have turned their lives upside down to produce these own-label wines. They've kissed their leisure hours goodbye and re-arranged family time (Bruwer Raats' third son was born last year) to indulge their passion for an old chenin vineyard, owned by a family friend. Now every spare moment is spent coaxing these 32 year old vines, between Stellenbosch and Kuils River, on a slope air-conditioned by False Bay, to reach optimal flavour. They've cut back the crop to "virtually uneconomic volumes" and invested in new oak casks. This leap of family faith will see a bottling of cabernet franc follow their maiden Chenin.

☆ **Raats Chenin Blanc** Beautifully poised, focused **00**; eager honeycomb, pine needle scents; persistent apricot acidity vivifies full (14.2% alc) just-off-dry palate. Delicious now, and one of a handful in Cape with backbone to mature fruitfully. 25% barrelled 6 mths in new oak. 500 half-cases. **01** preview more tropical, spicy; similar fine concentration, weight, vibrant acidity. — *IvH*

Radford Dale

Stellenbosch • Not open to the public • Owners Alex Dale & Ben Radford • Winemaker Ben Radford • Viticulturist Lorna Roos • Vineyards 6.5 ha • Production ±45 tons 3 000 cases 65% red 35% white • Office address: 67 Hillcrest Road Somerset West 7130 • ***Tel/fax (021) 852-3380*** *• E-mail alex@vinum.co.za*

WHO says you can't have the best of both worlds? Starting off as idealistic *garagistes*, winemaking prodigies Ben Radford (Barossa roots, Rhone benchmarks) and Alex Dale (British-born, Burgundian influenced) have brought together a balance of ol world élan and new world daring. Four vintages later it's a question of remaining quality-driven, building on growing recognition, and consistency: prices, remarkably, remain the same as from their first vintage. International inspiration comes from winemakers like Alain Graillot in the Rhone, who makes Robert Parker 93+ rated wines with every vintage, and retails consistently at £12, despite the colossal demand ("Graillot says he wouldn't pay more for his wine, so why charge more?"). They hold no truck with snobbery, there's no advertising, no shows, no tastings. They've built on word of mouth, good press from those who've found them, and loyalty of customers. With top international distribution in place, shiraz is the current focus, so expect to see that push ahead as their driving reference. And if that all sounds too serious, it's not: they have a "disproportionate amount of fun" considering the important tasks at hand.

✵**Merlot** Varietal purity with complexity the goal, so over-oaking an R-D no-no. Hence **00**'s glorious dawn-fresh blackberry bouquet – minerally, cool, profound – and begging time to permeate resistant yet fine structure, give broader mouthfeel. Correct dryness (here, in Shiraz below) antithesis of modern trick of gaining instant accessibility via dollop sugar; don't be put off: tannins perfectly ripe and elongated (through micro-oxygenation) into the wine. Already palatable with food, and presage excellent maturation potential over 5-7 yrs. Fr/Am oak (80/20), half new, 12 mths. ±13% alc. 975 cases. **99** silk-fruited with compact minerally core. Helderberg grapes.

✵**Shiraz** Satisfyingly elegant **00** ✵ convincingly debunks perception that quality Shiraz must be big, beefy and rustic. Like **99**, nods towards France rather than Barossa (R's home ground) but more complete, sophisticated. Full of subtle complexities (melted milk choc, ground black pepper) but whole much greater than parts. Deliciously savoury, not over-densely textured yet with telling crescendo of richness in back palate; rounded off by sleekest dry tannin. 13.4% alc. Unfiltered. Oak-matured 90% Fr, balance Am, half new. 275 cases. **99** leaner in youth; needing yr+ to fill out.

✵**Chardonnay** R-D believe cold cellar conditions play important role in producing quality chardonnay. **00**, from hot vintage, displays its own cool, poised profile: lemons, tropical limes, snatches incipient oatmeal, hazelnuts complexity. Palate, too, elegant, expansive yet firm; structure supportive of shiny pure fruit. New-oak trimmed to 9%, inhibited malolactic fermentation help spotlight fruit quality; less obvious wood than **99**, also excellent. Lovely now and for 2-3 years. 13.4% alc. 950 cases. —*AL*

Rainbow Nation see Cape Classics
Ravenswood see Pick 'n Pay

Remhoogte Estate

Stellenbosch (see Stellenbosch map) • Tasting, sales, cellar tours by appointment • BYO picnic • Tourgroups up to 20 people • Walks • Views • Exhibition of hunting trophies (southern African antelope) • Owner Murray Boustred Trust • Winemaker Murray Boustred with Jean Daneel • Consulting viticulturist Johan Pienaar • Farm manager Hendrik de Beer • Vineyards 35 ha • Production ± 250 tons (± 40 tons ±

3 000 cases own label) 100% red • PO Box 2032 Dennesig 7601 • ***Tel (021) 889-5005*** *• Fax (021) 889-6907 • E-mail remhoogte@adept.co.za*

FORMER property developer Murray Boustred and wife Juliet have certainly tackled the challenges of a budding wine farm with gusto. They were recently granted estate status, and they've expanded production from 3 000 cases to 10 000. The 28-year-old pinotage vines have been augmented with the planting of two more hectares. If these developments weren't enough, they've cut a joint-venture deal with Gallic superpower Michel Rolland. "Expect a bordeaux blend in the near future," they advise. Meanwhile this attractive Simonsberg estate remains a good place to visit – you're welcome to bring your own picnic and share the spectacular views. Hunting and the Bushveld are still among Murray Boustred's great loves and this is reflected in the collection of South African antelope on display at the farm.

✯**Cabernet Sauvignon** Current **99** ✯ lightish russet colour, more herbal, not as gutsy as upcoming **00** (barrel sample); riper, eucalyptus-fragranced blackcurrant/cherry fruits saved from jamminess by savoury undertone. ±13% alc. 400/700 cases.

✯**Merlot 00**, first as a registered estate, continues chunky/chewy pattern set with **98** ✯. Blackcurrant-jam aromas, wintergreen snatches in **00** sample; soft, pleasantly medicinal finish. 13.5% alc. 650 cases. **99** untasted.

✯**Pinotage** Good traditional style, consistent with old vines; **99** nostalgic savoury bouquet with whiffs woodsmoke, tar; quite fat pruney flavours; 13.5% alc. 350 cases. This and above 18-20 mths Fr barriques, 35% new. **98** untasted. **97** *Wine* ✯. *— TM*

R & de R-Fredericksburg see Rupert & Rothschild
R & R see Rupert & Rothschild
Reserve Centenaire see Morgenhof

Reyneke Wines

Stellenbosch (see Stellenbosch map) • Tasting & sales weekday mornings or by appointment • Cellar tours by appointment • Walks • Views • Uitzicht B&B cottages • Owner Reyneke Family Trust • Winemaker James Farquharson (since 1998) • Viticulturist James Farquharson with some help from Andrew Teubes • Vineyards 20 ha • Production 160 tons (±35 tons ±2 000 cases own label) 75% red 25% white • PO Box 61 Vlottenburg 7604 • ***Tel/fax (021) 881-3517*** *(after hours fax 881-3451) • E-mail wine@reynekewines.co.za • Website www.reynekewines.co.za*

THIS brave new world wine partnership is making waves. Winemaker James Farquharson (ex Lievland) is now full-time and focused, and to show it the limited range has expanded to include a Merlot and their first organically grown Pinotage (untasted). Their eco-efficient practices are no token nod at marketing dictates; rather a heartfelt and lived-in philosophy ("a paradigm shift in thinking that promotes life," is how environmental philosophy postgrad Johan Reyneke succinctly puts it). They've hauled in the local forestry department to measure biodiversity in the vineyards – well, whatever survives hunter-cat Marley's advances – and comprehensive plans involve planting indigenous 'wildlife' corridors. Grapes aren't the only things harvested on this Polkadraai Hills property: they're exporting vineyard snails to France. Part of the sustainable approach, but the irony doesn't escape them: "Like sending coals to Newcastle," chuckles feisty Farquharson.

✯**Merlot** NEW ✓ "Proves potential for elegance in Polkadraai," says winemaker, accurately. **00** generous but firm plummy mouthful (soupcon cab flexing its muscles), balanced, complex; taut still, ideally needs ±2 years (and should drink well for further 3/5) or a carnivorous date. 13 mths Nevers, Vosges, 30% new. 13% alc. 650 cases.

✵Cabernet Sauvignon-Merlot Claret-style **99** well conceived ±80/20 blend, astutely oaked 13 mths Nevers, Vosges barrels, 30% new. Now showing some pleasing herbal/tarry notes. 13% alc. 950 cases.

Cabernet Sauvignon To date a handsomely packaged **98** ✵. Not retasted for this ed. **Sauvignon Blanc** ⁂ **01** step above pvs (partly thanks to unplanned skin contact while repairing pneumatic press membrane, damaged by rats!); light, sweet candy/pear-drop tones. 800 cases (× 6, as are all above). — *TM*

Rhebokskloof Estate

*Paarl (see Paarl map) • Tasting & sales daily 9-5 including all public holidays • Formal tasting/cellar tour by arrangement, R7 p/p • Cellar tours by arrangement during tasting hours • Restaurant (see Eat-out section) • Estate grown extra virgin olive oil • Conferences • Play area for children • Tourgroups • Views • Conservation area • Wheelchair-friendly • Owner Rhebokskloof Farming & Trading (Pty) Ltd • Winemaker/viticulturist Daniël Langenhoven (since 1998) • Viticulturist Werner de Villiers (since 1999) • Vineyards ± 100 ha • Production 500 tons 60% white 40% red • PO Box 7141 Noorder-Paarl 7623 • **Tel (021) 869-8386** • Fax (021) 869-8504/393 • E-mail info@rhebokskloof.co.za • Website www.rhebokskloof.co.za*

You rarely read anything about this Paarl estate without a reference to the swans. Sadly these stately birds have sung their last song: the otters took a fancy to catching them for dinner and wiped out the entire population, a reflection of the entirely natural rhythm of life on this park-like property which borders on a nature reserve (shy rhebok still peek at you from the vineyards). The winery literally backs into the mountain, with one wall of the barrel-ageing cellar a massive chunk of granite. Keith Jenkins, anything-but-retired Gauteng businessman, along with daughter Tracey Thornycroft, keeps the people-friendly pace up. In the restaurant, German executive chef Andreas Roscher dishes up global cuisine with a Cape edge designed to complement the wines. Winemaker, viticulturist and keen cyclist Daniël Langenhoven completes the circle from vineyard to cellar.

✵Chardonnay Sur Lie ✓ Big, open, oaky chardonnay; latest **00** with leesy smoothness and, like pvs, integrated wood (barrel-fermented/aged yr, 20% new oak); massive alc (14.3%) not obvious. 1 200 (× 6 cases, as are most below). These can age few yrs, developing creamy richness.

✵Requiem ✓ Unblended riesling, unusually characterful. **98**, revisited mid-01, overt mineral/kerosene nuances, gentle sweetness, variety's signature spice. Could go 4-5 yrs. 14,2% alc. 780 cases. Underpriced.

✵Shiraz NEW Promising debut from young vyd; **00** sample shows potential to develop into ✵ over 5-7 yrs. Meanwhile team with traditional potjiekos, winemaker recommends. 18 mths oak, ±40 new. ±14% alc.

✵Chardonnay Grande Reserve More restrained version of Sur Lie above, drier, less oaky (though only new casks used; Fr/Am, 12 mths; no barrel-fermentation). **99** becoming deliciously smooth, creamy with bottle age; very ready now; nice lemon-butter finish. 13,5% alc. 900 cases.

Rhebok Dry Red ☻ ⁂ **00** quaffer features usual juicy/creamy fruits, spicy/savoury extras; light tannins for summer sloshing. Gamay, merlot, cab, pinotage, unoaked. Could be lightly chilled. 13.6% alc. 4 800 cases.

Cabernet Sauvignon ⁂ **97** has lost youthful tannic edge; ripe-fruit and tobacco/cedar fragrance starting to bloom. Oaked 13 mths, 20% new casks. 13,4% alc. 3 500 cases. **Gamay Noir** ⁂ Usually not beaujolais style (bit more guts/longevity); **01** sample juicy in palate, plenty of supple tannin. 13% alc. 400 cases. **Merlot** ⁂ Initially tight **98** beginning to show some sweet fruit; tannins still angular; give more time or smooth with a rustic dish. Oaked, some new casks. 13% alc. 5 500 cases. **Pinotage** ☆ **99** somewhat fruitier than pvs, though fiercely tannic still mid-01 (portion barrel-fermented); demands bottle ageing. 12,3% alc. 1 000 cases. **Rhebok Chardonnay** ☆ Partially cask-fermented **00** offers smooth, honeyed tastes; soft vanilla finish that needs drinking in 12-18 mths. 14% alc. 400 cases. **Rhebok Sauvignon Blanc** NEW ☆ Attractive sweet-ripe style; lighter-bodied **01** with soft deciduous fruit finish. 200 cases. **Rhebok Dry White** ☆ Easy-to-love **01**; bouncy tropical fruit to be enjoyed in flush of youth (watch that 14% alc). 5 000 cases. **Bouquet Blanc** ☆ **01** pretty summer sipper (though far from insubstantial at 14.3% alc), delicate honeysuckle fragrance. Semi-sweet chardonnay, chenin, hanepoot. 1 200 cases. **Weisser Riesling Special Late Harvest 97** past best. 13,3% alc. 1 700 cases. **Tamay Sparkling** ☆ Attractive dryish **NV** (01) sparkler; refreshingly fizzy; muscat scents from splash hanepoot (with chardonnay/riesling). 13,2% alc. 600 cases. Discontinued: **Grand Vin Blanc** (Pvs **00** ☆). — *DH*

Rickety Bridge

*Franschhoek (see Franschhoek map) • Tasting & sales Mon-Fri 10-5 Tasting fee R5 refundable on purchase • Cellar tours by appointment • Views • Owner Duncan Spence • Winemaker Wilhelm van Rooyen (since 2001) with Dawid Gqirana (since 1998) • Viticulturist Wilhelm van Rooyen • Vineyards 16 ha • Production 120 tons 65% red 35% white • PO Box 455 Franschhoek 7690 • **Tel (021) 876-2129** • Fax (021) 876-3486 •*

THEY'RE aiming ever higher at this small Franschhoek winery – all the way up the steep Dassenberg slopes with their excellent soils, where plantings will reflect their focus on Bordeaux-tinted red varieties. Plum trees have also made way for vines. Stellenbosch graduate (with Simonsig seasoning) Wilhelm van Rooyen has taken over the controls at this push-button gravity-fed cellar (which may be compact but nonetheless boasts its own bottling plant and labelling line) from Boela Gerber, who's located to Groot Constantia. Plans are to punch things up to full capacity this year, with more grapes bought in to raise volumes of these increasingly sought-after wines until their own vineyards "are really up to scratch". Channel Islands-based entrepreneur Duncan Spence checks in from time to time to make sure that everything is shipshape.

☆**Cabernet Sauvignon** Classic, well modulated cab, elegantly oaked and at times evocative of the Medoc. Vertical tasting mid-01 suggests steady line of growth. **97** ☆ showing good development, smoky cassis and gamey/bouillon tones; minerally, restrained; **98** deeper-hued; closed, cassis peeking out of woodsmoke; plumper, more mouthfilling yet also contained, lean, classic; **99** ☆ more vibrant fruit, suggestion of eucalyptus, savoury; bit oakier but balanced, satisfying. 12.5% alc. **00** (preview, not rated) hinting at change of hemisphere: overripe style, chunky; black plum depths with carmine rim; billowing toasty wood, big but fine tannins. Will make for fascinating tasting next yr. 400-1 000 cases (× 6, as are all these).

☆**Merlot** Fragrant style with clean, well judged oak. **98** re-sampled mid-01 sweetly plummy, with fennel hints in supple, rounded med-fleshed body; **99** savoury; stylish cigarbox, tobacco whiffs continue in palate. 14% alc. 15 mths Fr oak, 50% new. 700 cases. **00** (from cask) sensational crimson brilliance, firm-fruited and powerful, dark choc-plum lusciousness, well wooded. Very promising.

☆**Shiraz** This cellar's opulently-medalled signature, from single vyd on own farm. Opened for business with **96** VG and never stopped coining gold. However, to us latest **99** ☆ not quite as immediately impressive (difficult shiraz yr), mid-01 very shy; though sweet fruited, lacks fabulous concentration of pvs. 250 cases.

Wine ✵. Bung in **00** barrel hides a different animal: dense, opulent, same mouthfilling ripe black-plum fruit but bulky. Should start developing meatiness to present vanilla tones. 50% new wood, half Fr. **98** deceptively light-hued. Hallmark spice/pepper/burnt-toast all resonate in ultra-persistent palate.

✵**Paulinas Reserve 96** special release honouring farm's founder, Paulina de Villiers. Special label, bottle, individual box. 400 cases. Understated style; mid-01 shows russety robes; potpourri, leather, tobacco accents in claret-like frame with good complexity; obvious cab f aromatics (here teamed with majority cab, some merlot). At peak; drink in yr, max 2. 18 mths Fr oak, new/used. 12% alc. VVG, SAA.

✵**Chardonnay** Expansive barrel-fermented/aged style, deeply flavoured, excellent with food. Mid-01 revisited **99** could have flown in from California; massive (14% alc), ripe; sweet vanilla and grapefruit tones with asparagus; obvious but balanced butterscotchy wood. Couple of yrs to go. Yr casked, mainly new, partial malo. 400 cases.

✵**Semillon** ✓ "Best 10 casks (out of ±72), made for food – smoked trout, spicy chicken, pork ... " Current **99** retasted mid-01; ripening with distinction; fresh still, clotted cream whipped with apricot, peach, beeswax; part Am oak-elaboration imparts impression of sweetness. 13.5% alc. 200 cases. **98** fabulously complex with whiffs potpourri, dried fruits, nuts; mature – needs drinking very soon (richly sauced veal dishes terrific match). Yr Fr/Am oak.

✵**Sauvignon Blanc** ✓ **00** retasted mid-01 shows light secondary qualities; sweet supple entry followed some guava flavours; understated, a table wine. *Wine* ✵. **01** (sample) shows similar decorum with some vibrancy; pleasant sweet-sour acidity for refreshing summer drinking. 13% alc. 400 cases.

Duncan's Creek range

Classic Red ✵ Smoky mulberry aromas and grinds black pepper; plummy fruits drenched in cream from light oak; firm finish for food partnering. **Classic White** ✵ Herbal nose with touches straw, melon; clean zesty flavours and some lemon-juice in dry finish. med-bodied. These **NV**. — *TM*

Ridder's Creek NEW

Robertson • Owner George de Ridder & partners • Consulting winemaker Philip Louw (since Sep 2000) • Consulting viticulturist Briaan Stipp (VinPro) • PO Box 72 Wellington 7654 • ***Tel/Fax (021) 873-7746*** *• E-mail ridders@iafrica.com*

HAVING cut his vinous teeth at KWV and Douglas Green/Bellingham, George de Ridder and three partners have launched into the wine-merchant business with a range made to their specs by Ashton Winery. The allusion in the brand-name is to GdR's originally Dutch surname, meaning 'knight'. "Our marque is a symbol of nobility and unique character," says the enthusiastic Wellington-based negociant. Note: the wines below were tasted as unfinished samples, and ratings are provisional.

Shiraz ☻ ✵ Varietally true **01** juicy, very quaffable. Extra-soft tannins, so drink soonest, solo or with savoury foods to match the pepperiness. 13.4% alc.

Pinotage ✵ Airy feel to **01** despite power alc (14.3%); ripe fruit, some varietal ester – all highly sluggable. **Cabernet Sauvignon-Shiraz** ✵ Drink-young **01** only wooded red in this line. Oak nicely balanced by sappy fresh-fruit flavours. 13.2% alc. **Pinotage-Ruby Cabernet** ✵ Bit of tannin, supported by ripe fruit, makes **01** a good and versatile food wine, especially with savoury dishes. 14.2% alc. **Cape Red** ✵ Lightish toned **01** lively, swiggable, fruity; could be slightly chilled; lightly filtered, as are all these reds. 13% alc. **Chardonnay** ✵ **01** No complications drink-soon dry white; unfiltered; full bodied (13.8% alc). **Chenin Blanc** ⋆ **01** vin ordinaire already with some honeyed nuances; dry. 13% alc.

Sauvignon Blanc ⁑ **01** brisk casual quaffing in tropical mode; pleasant, lightish. **Chenin Blanc-Chardonnay** ⁑ Unfiltered **01** unceremonious sip; full (13.4% alc); more vinous than fruity. **Sauvignon Blanc-Semillon** ⁂ Bright, fresh, dry **01**, semillon's waxy tones add textural interest. Moderate 12.6% alc. — *DH*

Rider's Drift Wines

Stellenbosch • Tasting by appointment • Owner Rider's Drift Wine (Pty) Ltd • Production 6 500 cases 70% red 30% white • PO Box 919 Stellenbosch 7599 • Tel (021) 886-5080 • Fax (021) 886-5081 • E-mail info@ridersdrift.co.za • Website www.ridersdrift.co.za

A PRIVATE, international marketing and distribution operation specialising in customers' own-labels and house brands. Also an in-house range of consumer-friendly quaffers. These not tasted for the current edition; previous (99s) included: **Paarl Pinotage** (⁂), **Western Cape Pinotage** (⁂), **Cinsaut-Cabernet Sauvignon** (⁂), **Chenin Blanc-Chardonnay** (⁑).

Rider's Valley see Ruitersvlei

Riebeek Cellars

Riebeek Kasteel, Riebeek Valley (see Swartland map) • Tasting & sales Mon-Fri 8-5 Sat 9-2 (closed public holidays) • Cellar tours by appointment • BYO picnic • Owners 42 shareholders • Cellarmaster Zakkie Bester (since Dec 1999) • Winemaker Eric Saayman • Viticulturist Hanno van Schalkwyk (since Sep 2000) • PO Box 13 Riebeek Kasteel 7307 • ***Tel (022) 448-1213*** *• Fax (022) 448-1281 • E-mail riebeek@mweb.co.za*

TURN into this valley beneath the Kasteelberg and you are entering 'shiraz country' – just read the welcome signboards clearly posted at access roads, say Zakkie Bester and Eric Saayman, who'd like everyone to come and see what they're so excited about. Fed by vineyards from Porterville to Malmesbury, this producer of pocket-friendly wines is on a roll (and the whole of the Swartland with it). They've brushed up their act with a new corporate image that outspokenly dispels any lingering doubts that they've broken the co-op mould. Dramatically increased red tonnage naturally emphasises shiraz, with more merlot and the first petit verdot rows. Now they're adding spice with plantings of traditional port-making grapes. Committed to uplifting quality, full-time viticulturist Hanno van Schalkwyk (ex Vinpro) has got his balancing act together with a fine-tuned fruit-to-foliage ratio.

A Few Good Men range

Recognising the growers whose top performing vyds are the sources of these awarded wines. Pvsly export only, now also available from cellar.

✵**Merlot** NEW Fruitiest of these; **99** generous, sweet-violets/vanilla touches. Toothsome white-choc finish. Enough oomph to go 3-5 yrs; oak barrelling well managed here, below. 12.9% alc. 2 360 cases (} 6, as are all these) ex farm of Reenen Malan.

Cabernet Sauvignon ⁂ **99** cedary melange of berries, blue uppermost; spicy, firmish, with legs to go 3-4 yrs. 13.1% alc. 1 905 cases. **Pinotage** NEW ⁂ Good wine-by-the-glass option, with lots to think about in **99**, including soft vanilla/tannins from 10% new Am oak. Only 928 cases. **Shiraz** ⁂ **99** good varietal expression from grapes ex 'Good Man' Jaco van der Merwe, firmish tannic backbone for keeping 3-4 yrs. 1 900 cases.

Riebeek range

✵**Red Jerepiko** NEW ✓ Lightish-toned but flavour-packed **NV**. Plummy, chocolatey tastes; full-sweet but uncloying; nice fresh-turned-earth finish.

Cape Ruby NEW ✓ Brilliant, much bemedalled **NV** (Diners Club finalist, Peter Schultz trophy, Michelangelo gold) tinta, souzao (80/20) blend, portion small-oaked; ripe damson plums and choc; full, spirity length (19.8% alc). Delicious. Also in magnum.

Montino Petillant Light NEW ☻ Lively, sparkly **NV** with gentle muscatty nose; chill well for instant summer refreshment. Light 9% alc.

Pinotage-Tinta Barocca Earthy qualities, as you'd expect from varieties, **00** charry tones, too, from Fr chipping. All nicely balanced, quaffable. 13.3% alc. **Dry Red** See Cinsaut-Ruby Cab below. **Chardonnay** Leesy, smooth **01** with Granny Smith apple tail. ±13.5% alc. **Chenin Blanc** **01** pleasingly tart fruit-salad tastes, moderate 12% alc. **Sauvignon Blanc** NEW ★ **01** Demure example, some light grassy/dusty tones. Lightish 11.8% alc. **Anaïs** Lightish semi-sweet **00** mostly hanepoot, hence delicate muscat/tropical tones. Drink in yr of harvest.

Hutton Ridge range

Value for money range; allusion is to the local rich soils.

Shiraz ✓ Big, flavoursome **00** offers smoked cherries, summer berries and supple vanilla tannins from brief Fr chipping. 14.7% alc.

Cabernet Sauvignon **00** more complex than stablemates below; also firmer (but sweet-tasting), needing bit of time; lightly oaked. 13.5% alc. **Merlot** Another booming number (14.5% alc), but **00**'s well controlled, limber, ends fruitily with sweet-violet nuance. **Pinotage** Oak-chip-fermented **00** has very strong tannin platform for its (ripe) plum/banana fruits; needs a plate of something char-grilled or lightly spicy. 13% alc. 3 500 cases. Above, all NEW to this ed. **Cinsaut-Ruby Cabernet** "No evidence of wooding," say vintners. Indeed, **00**'s smooth strawberry/black pepper tones seem unblemished by oak. Exotic lantana scents to ponder. 13.5% alc. 1 800 cases.

Cape Table range

1 ℓ resealable value packs; all NV.

Cellar Red Light, fruity and very dry, so team with a braai chop. **Cellar Rosé** Coral-coloured pinotage, light, not too sweet. **Chardonnay** Firmish, good varietal character, lightish oak hints. Highest alc of these at 13%; others 9.5-11.5%. **Cellar White** ★ Simple dry chenin/semillon. **Cellar Gold Late Harvest** Lemony hanepoot/chenin duo, drier than expected. **Cellar Lite** Surprisingly flavoursome for style. 9.5% alc. — *DH*

Rietrivier Co-op

*Montagu (see Little Karoo map) • Tasting & sales Mon-Thu 8-5 Fri 8-3 • Cellar tours by arrangement • Play area for children • Tourgroups • Views • Owners 45 members • Manager/winemaker Chris-Willem de Bod (since 1999) with Petrus Bothma (since 1994) • Vineyards 300 ha • Production 4 600 tons (2 500 cases own label) 95% white 5% red • PO Box 144 Montagu 6720 • **Tel/fax (023) 614-1705** • E-mail rietrivier@lando.co.za*

"We are geared to produce high quality wines at affordable prices," says man of few words Chris-Willem de Bod. And then he's off, pausing only to add: "We're particularly noted for our Muscadel." Which of course they are, and deservedly so (at ±R12/bottle, surely they're robbing themselves?). But there's more to this limited range than luscious stickies. The Petite Blanc is a photo-finisher in the national value-swigging stakes (R5.50/bottle!), and the bubbles are so sweetly charming, they're a marriage-toast made in heaven.

Montagu Muscadel ✓ Standout in area recognised for sweet fortified desserts. Deeper hued, richer than most; **01** penetratingly sweet, soft-finishing with a warm spirituous glow. **00** billowing perfumes, cinnamon spice. Red muscadel. 17.5% alc. Also in sensible 500 ml.

Petite Blanc ☻ No-frills lightish semi-dry **NV** quaffer with peach/dried apricot charms. Colombard/chardonnay/sauvignon. 203 cases. This and Rouge below 500 ml screwtops. **Sparkling Vin Doux** ☻ Fresh, lightish, well made **NV** for bargain sweet tippling. From sauvignon. 100 cases.

Pinotage 01 Unwooded; some volatile ripe-banana characters. 154 cases. **Petite Rouge** Dry red from shiraz/pinotage. 195 cases. **NV**. **Chardonnay 00** oak chip fermented dry white. 100 cases. **Late Vintage NV** Not ready for tasting. Pvs. **Hanepoot 00** intensely spirituous fortified; some low key muscat flavours. Gold at local show. 100 cases. Discontinued: **Colombard**. — *DH*

Rietvallei Estate

Robertson (see Robertson map) • Not open to the public • Tasting & sales at Bergkelder (see that entry) • Cellar tours by appointment • Owner/winemaker/viticulturist Johnny Burger • Vineyards 142 ha • Production 2 000 tons 82% white 18% red • PO Box 386 Robertson 6705 • Tel (023) 626-4147 • Fax (023) 626-4514 • Enquiries Annelize Burger • ***Tel/fax (021) 889-8811*** *• Cell 082-338-1496 • E-mail info@rietvallei.co.za*

Bushvines, some believed to be more than 90 years old, transform Klaas Voogds' perennial sunshine into this estate's signature Red Muscadel, a frequent sighting on international drinks shelves (most recently in Sweden). Johnny Burger's grandfather planted the first vines in the area around the turn of the last century, and the present-day owner proudly perpetuates the traditional unwooded style. The other string to Burger's bow is his oak-matured Chardonnay, reflecting this Robertson ward's lime-suffused soils in its powdered-chalk tones.

Red Muscadel ✓ Among the gems of this fortified dessert style in Cape; deep flavoured, intensely sweet but seldom cloying. Bargain priced. Unusually pale coppery hues in latest **98**, belying extraordinary spice-emporium bouquet; echoes in broad, viscous palate with concluding tangy acidity that leaves you salivating for more. Bushvines, some more than 90 yrs old. Not oaked. 17,4% alc.

Chardonnay Raises bar on pvs with Burgundian **00**; minerally/chalky tones, citrus-zest and brisk acidity to match some already evident – pleasing – secondary characters. Big (±14% alc) but not obviously so. 43% oak aged ±6 mths. WOM Value. **98** sliding into decadence when tasted for pvs ed. — *IvH*

Rijk's Private Cellar

Tulbagh (see Tulbagh map) • Tasting & sales daily 9.30-4.30 Tasting fee R15 p/p • Cellar tours for large groups by appointment • Restaurant and luxury guest house (see Stay-over section) • Conference facilities • Play area for children • Tour groups • Gifts • Walks • Views • Owner Neville Dorrington • Winemaker Charl du Plessis (since 1999) • Consultant viticulturist Johan Wiese (since 1996) • Farm manager Boet Eddy (since 1996) • Marketing & sales Claire Dorrington (since 2000) • Vineyards 31 ha • Production ± 15 000 cases 80% red 20% white • PO Box 400 Tulbagh 6820 • ***Tel (023) 230-1622*** *• Fax (023) 230-1650 • E-mail wine@rijks.co.za • Website www.rijks.co.za*

Could it be the Midas touch (the deity who granted him the power of turning things to gold being none other than Bacchus, of course) or is it simply that this new Tulbagh winery has produced a range of vinous magnets attracting medals from their very first outings (Veritas, Michelangelo, SA Young Wine Show)? It's early days according to owner Neville Dorrington but, with fine young winemaker Charl du Plessis setting the pace, this cellar is certainly blowing Tulbagh's trumpet with red wine leading the latest band in this traditionally white wine valley. All this feedback translates into future promise in the form of single-vineyard and reserve wines and their first exports to Holland and the UK. A contemporary country eatery, guest house, herb garden and conference centre, all wrapped in rolling green lawns, are also in the mix.

Cabernet Sauvignon New world-toned **00** plump cassis/eucalyptus fruit; new oak nicely stitched into fabric. ±430 cases. This, below, from small blocks (=1 ha), intensively managed for ripeness. Wines reviewed here all in, or fresh from, barrel mid-01; ratings provisional.

Pinotage Rich, demonstrative pinotage; oak-vanilla/spice still prominent in **00** pre-bottling sample, though counter-weighted by prominent vibrant mulberry fruit. Banana ester, dry plum-jam finish. On present form should grow into adulthood. ±17 mths oak, Am/Fr (as are all these reds). SAYWS gold. 400 cases.

Shiraz Fruits in **00** bouquet smell sweetly ripe but taste zingy; splash cream from Am oak portion contrasts pleasingly with dry, classic palate. Some peppery, scrubby tones flaunt the varietal insignia. SAYWS gold. ±14% alc, as are all these reds. ±500 cases.

Chardonnay 00 Peach, pear and toasty bread, hint of marmalade in palate; New world style. New Fr oak-fermented/aged, 11 mths, malo. 13,4% alc. 260 cases.

Sauvignon Blanc 01 (sample) a gutsy individual. Two-fisted punch from 14% alc, mouth-expanding aromatic flavours ranging from green to organic to spicy, plus sub-tropical fruit salad. 530 cases.

Semillon Brilliantly-realised **00** glides into Cape's upper echelons on waxy tones of spice, honey, barley sugar and nuts; rounded, full, gorgeous palate, plucked from decadence by bitter-grapefruit nuance. 2 single blocks, night-harvested. Stunning (as Charl du Plessis remarks) with casseroled abalone. 100% new Fr oak, 11 mths. WOM Reserve. 13.8% alc. 260 cases.

Merlot Super-densely extracted **00** lovely deep colours, sweet bluegum bouquet with herby/smoky divertissement; palate unexpectedly astringent; needs goodly softening spell in bottle. 17 mths new Fr oak. SAYWS gold. 14.2% alc. ±500 cases. **Chenin Blanc** Charl du Plessis whips these manicured rows into taste-frenzy in **00**: pungent clouds of stewed apple scud from glass with leesy tones, which reprise in palate with almost viscous intensity; daring style, which already appears to be sliding over the edge – suggest drink soonish. 45% barrel fermented new Fr oak; technically off-dry at 4.4 g/ℓ sugar. 13,5% alc. 550 cases. — *TM*

Rite Wines see Shoprite Checkers
Rivier see International Wine Services
River Grandeur see Viljoensdrift
River's Edge see Weltevrede

Robertson Winery

Robertson (see Robertson map) • Tasting & sales Mon-Thu 8-5 Fri 8-5.30 (winter) Fri 8-6 (summer) Sat 9-3 • Cellar tours by appointment • Conference/function hall • Miniature wine museum • Owners 43 members • General manager Bowen Botha • Production manager Lolly Louwrens (since May 1995) • Winemaker Francois Weich (since Sep 1997), with Jacques Roux (since Jan 2001) • Viticulturist Anton Laas (since Nov 2000) • Vineyards ± 1650 ha • Production 20 000 tons 85% white 15% red • PO Box 37 Robertson 6705 • ***Tel (023) 626-3059*** *• Fax (023) 626-2926 • E-mail info@robertsonwine.co.za or sales@robertsonwine.co.za*

Bowen Botha well remembers the days of learning to fly solo. This winery's enterprising members, historically suppliers to the big wholesalers, had made probably the biggest business decision of their lives: unable, for competitive reasons, to continue to both service the trade and market their produce under their own label, they'd decided to follow the latter entrepreneurial route. Which meant, Botha recalls, having to build a business literally overnight, with hardly a customer from the previous era. "I used to pray all the way to work that orders had come in overnight. Man, it was scary." Fifteen years on, they're so in demand their filling lines run almost continuously; their winery, already sprawled over two street-blocks in Robertson, resembles a permanent building site. They've just completed a major red-wine upgrade and now they're adding a massive warehousing facility. Exports leapt 70% in 2000, and at press time were set to surge by an equal margin for 2001. Ensuring their combined 1 650 hectares continue to deliver internationally crowd pleasing performances is vine-magician Anton Laas, who now 'belongs' equally to this model winery, its neighbour Roodezandt and equally raring-to-go McGregor.

Wide River Reserve range

★**Cabernet Sauvignon** ✓ Modern, well-made oak-matured example, **99** with sweet-fruited strawberry mid-palate (effect enhanced by dash sugar) and pepper/charry oak. Lively acid, juicy but prominent tannins could do with yr/2's settling. 13.2% alc. Carefully-oaked **98** minerally, approachable tannins for now or 2-3 yrs.

★**Retreat Sauvignon Blanc** ✓ **01** new world mouthfilling style, with dash sugar for mid-palate fatness, high-kicking alc (14%). Most attractive, drinkable. **00** showcased pure sauvignon 'green' aromatics plus riper passion fruit. Vyd selection.

★**Almond Grove Weisser Riesling Noble Late Harvest** ✓ Standout wine of range and contender for A-league status in Cape. From Rbtson farm Almond Grove. First **99** wonderfully bright, crisp, clean. *Wine* ★. (No **00**.) **01**, labelled Reserve, huge botrytis bouquet of dried and ripe fruit, barley sugar; hints of nectarines, caramel; entrancing acidity (10 g/ℓ) contributes to somewhat leaner profile than pvs. Needs, deserves time to develop over 4-6 yrs. 9,5% alc. 375 ml.

Pinotage NEW **01** sample too young to rate. Variety fairly rare in Rbtson vyds, so will be interesting to monitor this new label's progress. **Chardonnay 01** (sample, unrated) shows improved oak management compared with pvs; lemons, limes delicately embroidered by oak, good fruit/acid balance. Wood-fermented **99**, back-tasted mid-01, too oaky for most palates.

Robertson range

★**Cabernet Sauvignon 00** smooth and soft; easy lightly-oaked style not for laying down. 13% alc.

★**Merlot** ✓ Characterful, satisfying **00**, with savoury dimension to the supple tannins; **01** preview more minerally, dry, potentially better. 12.5% alc.

★**Special Late Harvest** ✓ Consistent, delicious dessert from gewürz. **00** zippier, lemon-lime, honey, botrytis attractions melded with tangy acidity; med-bodied. **01** honeysuckle, rose petals in bouquet; rich, smooth with beautifully balanced sugar/acid; needs to be enjoyed fresh.

Pinotage ★ **01** (sample) dry, fairly earthy and rustic, better with a braai chop. 13% alc. **Chardonnay** ★ Lightly wooded **01** repeats established formula of tropical-toned buttery vanilla palate, clean dry citrus finish. 13,6% alc. **Chenin Blanc** ★ Lightish **01**, gentle, no-ceremonies just-dry swig; some lemonade tones to enjoy right now. **Colombard** ★ Made off-dry in **01**, lightish tropical/pineapple tang, smooth rather than sweet.

Late Vintage ☆ Still-fresh **00** white with gentle tropical nose, muscatty scents and smooth freshness; lightish 11% alc. Chenin/gewürz. Following trio **NV** Natural Sweets NEW, low alcs (7.5%): **Red** ☆ Sweet ripe plums and just a suggestion of structure-giving tannin from ruby cab, here partnering muscadel. **Rosé** ☆ Gossamer blush, pretty colour for a pretty wine. Ruby cab supplies the complexion, colombard/muscadel the body. **White** ☆ Colombard, muscadel, chenin in fresh, fruity mode; light and very sweet. **Red Muscadel** ☆ Muscat more to the fore now, raisins and some toffee-choc character. **99** for early drinking. 15.6% alc. **Port** ☆ **99** surprisingly youthful; shiraz-like woodsmoke (though that grape not in blend ruby cab, merlot, cab); tastes dryish, more spiritous than 16% alc would suggest.

Ruby Cabernet ☻ ☆ Seldom fails to please. Brilliantly hued **01** (sample) powerfully spicy aromas, contrasting ripe-juicy tastes. Unoaked for now-drinking. 13% alc. **Shiraz** ☻ ☆ Textbook sweet plum, woodsmoke, toast characters; **00** good follow through from bouquet, dryish tannins. Quaffably oaked. **Dry Red** ☻ ☆ Charming anytime fun wine with bright raspberry taste. Lightish ruby cab, merlot, cinsaut blend. **NV**. **Sauvignon Blanc** ☻ ☆ **01** reductive treatment from vyd to cellar delivers vibrant palate tension, good minerally threads to drink in flush of youth. Hefty 13,5% alc. **Beaukett** ☻ ☆ Delicate, pretty **01** semi-sweet from gewürz, colombard, muscadel. Lightly spiced finish.

SilverSands range

Chardonnay ☻ ☆ Fruitier, slightly less oak than 'regular' above; **00** really quaffable (so go easy on the 13,5% alc); ripe peaches, flowers; vanilla finish. Upcoming untasted **01** should be in same mould.

2 ℓ boxed range

On release, SA's first certified bag-in-box wines with varietal labels and vintage dates. Now includes two non-vintage wines.

Sauvignon Blanc ☻ ☆ **01** brazen green peppers and nettles, chopped with tropical fruit in mouthfilling dry palate; zesty finish brings you back for more. 13.5% alc.

Chardonnay ☆ Lightly oaked **00**, now with some honeyed mellowness; dry finish. 13,5% alc. **Light** ☆ Some vinous character, 'green' fruitiness; **NV** very light but satisfying. **Johannisberger** ☆ Fragrant ripe peach/guava fruit; drier than most of this style; muscadel, chenin, colombard. **NV**.

Vinipak range

Good-value, hike/picnic/beach party 'combiblocs' in 500/1 000 ml. All NV.

Dry Red ☻ ☆ Exactly what you'd expect from ruby cab and cinsaut. Light strawberry hues/tones, bell pepper whiffs, nice savoury finish. Could be chilled a bit in summer.

Dry White ☆ Lightish, smooth, undemanding. Varieties as below. **Selected Stein** ☆ Simple, light quick quaff from chenin, colombard, muscadel. **Late Harvest** ☆ Light (11% alc), pleasant, drier than expected from this style. — *DH*

Robert's Rock see KWV

Rob Roy

POPULAR 5 ℓ range from Robertson Winery. See that entry.

Robusto see Rudera
Rocheburg see Arlington
Rock Ridge see Vinfruco
Roland's Reserve see Seidelberg

Romansrivier Winery

*Wolseley (see Worcester map) • Tasting & sales Mon-Fri 8-5 Sat 8.30-11.30 • Cellar tours by appointment • BYO picnic • Conference/reception facilities for up to 200 guests • Views • Owners 43 members • Winemaker Leon Mostert • Production 6 000 tons (6 000 cases own label) 95% white 5% red • PO Box 108 Wolseley 6830 • **Tel (023) 231-1070/80** • Fax (023) 231-1102 • E-mail romans@cybertrade.co.za*

THIS range not ready for tasting for this ed. Previous have included: **Koelfontein Merlot** (**97** ☆), **Vino Rood** (**NV** ☆), **Cabernet Sauvignon-Ruby Cabernet** (**98** ☆), **Ceres Chardonnay** (**99** ☆), **Mosterthoek Sauvignon Blanc** (**00** ☆), **Grand Cru** (**NV** ☆), **Colombard** (**NV** ☆), **Ceres Vin Blanc** (**NV** ☆), **Jerepico** (**NV** ☆), **Ruby Port** (**NV** ☆), **Mosterthoek Cabernet Sauvignon** (**98** pvsly untasted).

Roodendal

LIMITED VOLUME cabernet, generally made every second year, usually in odd years. Styled to precise specs: grapes ex-Coastal region, young vineyards in light soils on higher slopes. Never advertised, and so sought after, it quickly sells out. By Distell.

Cabernet Sauvignon ☆ Small portion oaked. Med-bodied, aged 2 yrs in bottle before release. **97** good and ready; next **99** (not ready for tasting, but available this year) coincides with brand's 20th anniversary. — *IvH*

Rooderust

*Groenekloof • Owner Anthonij Rupert • Winemaker Wrensch Roux (since 1997) • Viticulturist Fanie le Roux (since 1998) • Vineyards 50 ha • Production ±350 tons 100% red • PO Box 241 Darling 7345 • **Tel/Fax (022) 492-3371***

RESHAPING this 500 ha former dairy farm in the resurgent Groenekloof area on the West Coast is Anthonij Rupert, youngest son of global tycoon Dr Anton Rupert, whose deep-pocketed passion transformed Franschhoek's L'Ormarins Estate into a temple of oenological high tech in the late 70s. Fifty hectares of existing vineyard are being redeveloped and new blocks planted with "the finest materials available", chiefly cabernet, merlot and pinotage, to take advantage of the sought-after maritime terroir.

Cabernet Sauvignon ☆ Classically inclined **98**, with splash merlot; Fr barrique aged 12 mths, which evident in ritzy oak-spice fragrance, sweet vanilla touch in palate. 13% alc. 4 000 cases. **Pinotage** ☆ Not overtly pinotage, **99** evinces zinfandel-like tones, plus eucalyptus waft; soft juicy finish. Fr small-oak, 8 mths. 13.5% alc. 4 000 cases. — *TM*

Roodezandt Winery

Robertson (see Robertson map) • Tasting & sales Mon-Fri 8-5.30 Sat 9-12.30 • Cellar tours by arrangement • Owners 65 members • General manager Abé Rossouw • Winemakers Christie Steytler (since 1980), with Elmo du Plessis (since 1999) • Consulting viticulturist Briaan Stipp (VinPro) & Anton Laas • Vine-

yards ±1 500 ha • Production ±26 000 tons (7 000 cases own label) 90% white 10% red • PO Box 164 Robertson 6705 • ***Tel (023) 626-1160*** *• Fax (023) 626-5074 • E-mail roodez@intekom.co.za*

THESE seemingly conventional vineyards are ideological hotbeds, and the 65 growers are vine-revolutionaries committed to the overthrow of viticultural practices not aligned with their newer, loftier quality goals. Stoking their zeal are Abé Rossouw, long in the GM's seat, and warhorse Christie Steytler, this year commanding his 22nd crush here. They're abetted by consulting vine-strategist Briaan Stipp, and now also by Anton Laas, dividing his time equally between these 1 500 hectares and the vineyards of Robertson and McGregor Wineries. "In-house, we're strongly focused on the 'estate within the cellar' philosophy," Abé Rossouw explains, "we manage and vinify blocks separately so we better understand their potential." Only 7 000 cases are released under the winery label, and to ensure these continue to elicit bouquets (IWSC silver medal among the recent compliments) Rossouw & Co are gradually trimming the range to a future 9 or 10. Likely to remain a prominent feature is the new spontaneous-ferment Chardonnay, slotting into the flagship Balthazar Classic range.

Balthazar Classic Cabernet Sauvignon This, below, limited releases honouring winery's long-serving chairman, Baltus Kloppers, now retired. Debut **98** VG a worthy tribute, as is current **99** with extra concentration (though alcs similar – and laudably moderate – 12.4%); bright raspberry flavours and spice from yr new Fr oak. Needs ± yr to start revealing its potential; should gain complexity over 3-5.

Balthazar Classic Chardonnay NEW Made in the increasingly fashionable 'ancienne' style: fermentation with naturally occurring yeasts (±35 days; large vats, so no obvious oak), full malo, 5 mths sur lie-maturation (without benefit of protective sulphur). Reflected in **00**'s serious, refined, almost delicate sweet-melon tones (despite big 14% alc); soft, creamy/leesy textures which delicious now and could develop with distinction (regular monitoring advised). Commendable first outing.

White Muscadel Traditional Cape dessert a regular show winner for this cellar. **00** has filled out and softened since pvs ed; bright yellow-gold shards; oily whiffs of marmalade, coconut; super-silky muscat palate with seamlessly absorbed spirit. 17,5% alc. Slightly unctuous compared with slow-starting **98**; which needed yr/2 to unfurl its charms. Still bargain priced at ±R13 from cellar door.

Red Muscadel Winter warmer with raisins, boiled sweets bouquet in **00**; deep-flavoured, fresh and balanced, carries 215 g/ℓ sugar lightly. Lovely example of the traditional style. 17% alc.

Cabernet Sauvignon Generous, quaffable **99** in lighter style, rounded yr older Fr casks. 13% alc. **Keizer's Creek** Red unwooded blend merlot, ruby cab, cab bursts with soft berry/cherry flavours. Winemaker says: "To be laid down for the future." We suggest drink now while youthfully springy. **NV** (00). 13% alc.

Colombar Well-made **01** quiet nose but lots of flavour; smooth, ripe fruit; not too dry or alcoholic. **Sauvignon Blanc** Same vyd delivers the goods every yr. **01** rounded figgy tones, ripe tastes, lowish alc for effortless drinking. **Colombar-Chardonnay NV** past best. **Special Late Harvest** Attractive flowery muscadel nose, balanced sweetness, light-bodied. **00** blend with chenin. **Sparkling Demi Sec** Carbonated fizz with sherbet and spicy muscat tastes, light alc and balanced sweetness. **Port** Confident ruby style (though in SA rather than Portuguese genre – this from ruby cab); black cherries and dark plums in integrated, easy **99** palate. Oak aged. Discontinued: **Late Harvest**. — *CF*

Rooiberg Winery

Robertson (see Robertson map) • Tasting & sales Mon-Fri 8-5.30 Sat 9-3 • Cellar tours by appointment • Light lunches/refreshments in tea garden during tasting hours or BYO picnic • Owners 35 members • CEO/exports Johan du Preez (since 1996) • Winemakers Tommy Loftus (since 1989), Eben Rademeyer (since 1996), Pieter van Aarde (since 1998) • Viticulturist Stefan Joubert (since1998) • Vineyards 720 ha • Production 150 000 cases 85% white 15% red • PO Box 358 Robertson 6705 • ***Tel (023) 626-1663*** *• Fax (023) 626-3295 • E-mail rooiberg@wine.co.za • Website www.rooiberg.co.za*

TOMMY Loftus' office, attached to the flank of this busy, buzzy, bulging-at-the-seams cellar, looks out over the peak that gives the winery its name. But the genial cellarmaster also has a view of the main Robertson-Worcester road, so he's able to set his clock, if he wanted to, by start of the Gucci Rush-Hour – the Friday mid-afternoon whoosh of upmarket vehicles en route to weekend destinations around Robertson and beyond. And it pleases him no end that the Benz & Bollinger brigade swing by the tasting room in droves, emptying the unique new self-service shelves (refrigerated whites conveniently also available). As well they might: these are among the most stylish budget wines you can buy (Team Rooiberg are the biggest supplier by volume to the Woolworths retail chain, so you know they're doing things right). And, unquietly pressing ahead, they're inspanning viticultural sages Johan Wiese and Briaan Stipp, and independent tasting panels to help them rehearse their act. On a different learning curve, cellar hand Dorothy Arendse gained some California seasoning in 2001 under the auspices of an SA Wine Industry Trust exchange programme.

- ✵**Roodewyn** ✓ Value-priced red with, inter alia, cab, merlot, pinotage, unwooded; jam-packed with ripe cherry fruit. **98** a thumping 14% alc. **99** dense, chewy, chocolatey wine. Satisfying.
- ✵**Red Jerepiko** ✓ This cellar's calling card and one of SA's perennial top unwooded fortified desserts. **96** ripening fascinatingly in bottle. Now with bouillon, smoked meat aromas and potpourri fragrance; dried fruit flavours gliding into choc-orange liqueur finish. Three VVGs since **91**. 18% alc.
- ✵**Red Muscadel** ✓ **98** developed beautifully in bottle. **99** ✵, with arresting geranium perfume, near the cloying end of sweet. Though at ±R14/bottle, who's going to be picky?
- ✵**Cape Ruby Port** ✓ These plastered with competition certificates. Currently available **95** soothing mahogany colour, rum-and-raisin tones, and though more correctly termed 'liqueur wine' than 'ruby port', altogether satisfying. Yr Fr oak. Tinta/souzao/cab f. VVG 18,6% alc.
- ✵**Port 92** LBV category winner at Diners Club 00 and an exceptional, still remarkably fresh interpretation of the traditional style; prune/fruitcake tastes and dryish feel despite fairly high sugar for this style (121 g/ℓ). 18.6 alc absolutely fused with fruit. Pinotage, souzao, tinta; 4-5 yrs old wood.

Cabernet Sauvignon ✶✶ Aromatic herbal notes in **99**, seamless flavours, good peppery dry finish. Versatile and well priced. 13.5% alc. **Merlot** ✶½ Fragrant, sinewy **98** with eucalyptus whiffs; lightish feel despite generous 14% alc. **Pinotage** ✶✶ Invariably charming example. **99** nicely oaked, fine-grained tannins, vibrant plum/mulberry fruit. 13% alc. **Shiraz** ✶✶ Ruby red **99** light, non-blockbusting, attractive. Lightly wooded. **Selected Red** ✶½ **01** cocktail of 5 varieties with very light tones, ideal for uncomplex occasions. 13% alc. **Rosé** ✶✶ Natural Sweet. Rosepetals from start to sweet finish; **00** hanepoot, colombard, ruby cab. **Chenin Blanc** ✶✶ Baked-apple tafstes and slightly gassy prickle; reliable commercial off-dry **01**. **Sauvignon Blanc** ✶½ **00** light, crisp but better in freshness of youth. **Bukettraube** ✶½ Slightly perlé **01** offers unusual sweet tea-leaf bouquet; not too sweet. **Brut Sparkling** ⁂ Frothy dry **00** showcases sauvignon's nettley tones and crisp lemony finish. Carbonated, as are all sparklers in this range. **Vin Doux Sparkling** ⁑ Real 'wedding bubble' – reassuringly sweet, pretty and slightly peachy. Light 8% alc in **00**. Not tasted for this ed: **Semillon** (Pvs **99** ⁂); **Late Vintage** (**NV** ★), **Special Late Vintage 99** (⁂).

Cape Riesling ☻ ⁂ Aromatic, lemon-zesty **01**, bracing dry freshness for instant summer rejuvenation. **Chardonnay** ☻ ⁂ **01** Charmer for fans of the unwooded, out-and-out fruity style; lime/marzipan in zippy dry palate with grapefruit twist. **Colombard** ☻ ⁂ Sweetish version of this Robertson 'invention'; **01** light-bodied, fresh and balanced. "Drink immediately," advises Tommy Loftus, who should know. **Rhine Riesling** ☻ ⁂ Delicate summer refreshment; floral/citrus tones; **01** brush of sugar wrapped in zesty acid. Moderate 11.5% alc. **Premier Grand Cru** ☻ ⁂ **NV** (00) Lightish-bodied, properly bone-dry, as always, yet easy, non-aggressive. Supple herbal/grassy tastes. **Flamingo Vin Doux Sparkling** ☻ ⁂ Wonderfully frivolous sparkle with allspice/dried flower bouquet and almost-dry finish. **NV**. Low 8,5% alc won't dampen your party spirit. Yes, it's flamingo pink. — *TM*

Rosenburg see Uiterwyk

Rozendal

Stellenbosch (see Stellenbosch map) • Sales by appointment • Luxury auberge with restaurant and many amenities • Owners Kurt & Lyne Ammann • Winemaker Kurt Ammann • Production 2 000-3 000 cases 100% red • PO Box 160 Stellenbosch 7599 • ***Tel (021) 883-8737*** *• Fax (021) 883-8738 • E-mail rozendal@mweb.co.za*

We first alerted wine drinkers to restaurateur Kurt Ammann's red in this guide's 1984 edition. An 83 blend was his debut vintage. By 1990 this description had blossomed, like the wine, into "If you can lay your hands on an 83 Rozendal, do not pass up the opportunity. Even better, drink it." We asked Ammann how he'd made this gem. "I don't know," he said, disarmingly, "I'm still trying to find out." In the case of his wine then and since – the awards and acclaim have continued to roll – perhaps Rozendal is better experienced than dissected. Try to squeeze it into a tobacco pouch or spice rack and you reduce its individuality, render the mysterious banal. The current release not available for tasting. But ... in the spirit of our recommendation a decade ago: find it, sample it (at the Ammanns' auberge with their immaculate food, maybe), judge its star quality personally.

Rudera Wines

Not open to the public • Owner/winemaker/viticulturist Teddy Hall • Vineyards 3 ha • Production 6,5 tons 60% white 40% red • PO Box 2868 Somerset West 7129 • ***Tel 083 461-8111*** *• Fax (021) 881-3514 • E-mail winemaker@kanu.co.za*

A bureaucratic snafu sees Teddy Hall's critically acclaimed own-label, Robusto, rebranded and expanded under the equally rugged sounding name Rudera. The reigning chenin king – cellarmaster at Kanu, his wines took three out of four top positions at last year's Chenin Challenge with the Robusto placed second – Hall was a pioneer of the swing to own-label wines, and an already emulated new style of barrel-fermented chenin. This groundbreaker is now taking things a step further with a barrel-fermented Shiraz and a Cabernet under the new label. Sticking to his uncommercial guns (despite funding the venture lock, stock and barrel), Hall believes in letting specific vineyards rather than market pressures dictate the style of his own-label wines and trying to make the best wines possible without any shortcuts. "I make wines I like to drink, not to win competitions –

if a wine convincingly expresses the terroir and vintage, I'm sure I'll find customers around the world who'll like to drink it too ... "

✵**Chenin Blanc** Teddy Hall's maverick belief in this variety amply vindicated by results of 01 Chenin Challenge (see intro). This **00** and trophied Kanu half-sibling, both bear distinctive Hallmarks. Developing gold shot with lime; rich tropical/spicy nose; boisterous, fully ripe peach/pear/guava fruits spar with bouncy 14.5% alc; there's even space for 15 g/ℓ sugar in the melange. Plump and luscious; not classic but singularly emphatic. 5 t/ha cropped from Hall-manicured old Koelenhof bushvines, fermented/aged 7 mths Fr barriques. 300 cases. — *DS*

Ruitersvlei Estate

Paarl (see Paarl map) • Tasting & sales Mon-Fri 8.30-5.30 Sat 9-2 • Belgian/French restaurant/bistro open daily for lunch & dinner (closed Sun evening/Mon; closed Tue during winter) Tel/fax (021) 863-3959 • Guesthouse/B&B Tel (021) 863-1517 • Gifts • Views • Wheelchair-friendly • Owner Faure Holdings (John Faure) • Marketing manager Belinda Faure-Griessel • Bottling manager Riaan Richter (since 1999) • Winemaker Dominique Waso (since 1999) • Assistant Winemaker Johan Stemmet (since 2001) • Vineyard manager Sheryl Butler • Vineyards 300 ha • Production 1 500 tons 60 000 cases 50% red 50% white • PO Box 532 Suider-Paarl 7624 • ***Tel (021) 863-1517*** *• Fax (021) 863-1443 • E-mail ruitersv@iafrica.co.za*

"Our great-grandfather made wine, our grandfather made wine, our father made wine," say the Faure sisters on their website. "What do you expect from us – *melktert*?" (traditional milk tart). They run the show here, supported by dad John Faure, who's content to background-manage this Paarl spread (which includes adjoining Vrymansfontein). The youngest Faure, Sheryl, handles production, Nicki's the bean counter and Belinda does the marketing. "People phoning to speak to the winemaker are often taken aback when I answer, they're expecting a female voice," chuckles Dominique Waso, happily surrounded by women in wine (his wife is involved in wine exports). Crystal-gazing ahead, Waso sees a great future for shiraz, soon to be added to the premium reserve range. New plantings are thick on the ground with whites diminishing year by year. Contrary to fashion dictates they're planting more cinsaut – seems they can't get their hands on enough for their popular blend. Funds from the special Destiny label finance projects like the daycare centre, run by warm-hearted pre-school teacher Tannie Susie.

✵✵**Cabernet Sauvignon Reserve** Concentrated Paarl cab, classically Fr barrique-aged, 14 mths; low-crop vyds yielding around 4 t/ha. **99**, classwinner at Paarl/national young wine shows, savoury extensions to blackcurrant fruit; interminable finish. 13.5% alc. **98** decadent ripeness buttressed by polished tannins. **96** VVG.

✵**Shiraz** Balanced, tangy **00**; sappy blackcurrants, hillside scrub fragrance. Med-bodied (12% alc). Am oak (9 mths, some new casks) subtly handled. Preview of **01** punchier (13% alc), fruitier, potentially finer.

✵**Merlot Reserve** Behind pale exterior lurks considerable intensity, plushness. **98** ✵ VG overshadowed by more refined **99** (14.3% alc hardly noticeable), with liquorice twist and oak perfume. 14 mths barriques, ±15% Am.

✵**Cabernet Sauvignon-Merlot** ✓ 60/40 blend, only on selected restaurant lists. **00** ✵ continues elegance announced by **99** in somewhat slighter form; gamey/savoury whiffs, refined fruit tannins (unoaked).

✵**Rider's Valley Shiraz-Merlot** ✓ Most is exported, though small quantity to be released locally "at later stage". **99** soft/substantial enough for early drinking or in 2-4 yrs. Shiraz oaked 9 mths Am casks. 12.5% alc.

✵**Four Sisters** Classically styled MCC brut sparkle, pinot noir from next-door Landskroon. **NV** (97). Extended bottle ageing imparts good appley leesiness; slightly earthy finish. 12% alc.

★½ **John Faure Port** ✓ Light LBV style (though **NV**), low cropped tinta from 96/97 vintages and "dash very old port"; smoked ham, tarry hints; dry finish (66 g/ℓ sugar). 18.3% alc.

Pinotage ★ Friendly, fruit-pastille style **00**; finishes effortlessly with mere suggestion of tannin. Lightly oaked. 13% alc. **Chardonnay Reserve** ★ Obvious oaky/butterscotch aromas, toffee tastes in **00**, fanning into surprisingly crisp finish. Mainly Fr, some Am casks. **Chenin Blanc** ½ **01** dry white with green-melon/pear flavours. Mediumweight despite bulky 14.5% alc. **Mountainside White 01** not ready for tasting. Pvs **99** ★. **Late Harvest** NEW ★ Among better examples in Cape. **01** appealing blend colombard, hanepoot, chenin (50/25/25) with bright honeysuckle/fruit salad tones; balanced sweetness. 12.5% alc. Note: No **01 Sauvignon Blanc**. Pvs **00** ★½. Discontinued: **Paarl Riesling** (crouchen blanc). Pvs **99** ★½.

Cinsaut-Cabernet Sauvignon ☻ ★ Mainly for export; small quantities "available locally from time to time. Very popular". **01** sappy nouveau style; ethereal despite mighty 14% alc. 75/25 blend. **Mountainside Red** ☻ ★ Interesting unwooded blend cinsaut with dabs ruby cab, tinta, carignan; **NV** (00) easy campfire quaff (14% alc ensures early night) or, lightly chilled, summer sip. Grain smoothing (rather than sweetening) sugar.

Destiny range

Profits donated to Ruitersvlei Children's Charity.

Tinta Barocca ★ Simple but juicy, **00** shows variety's attractive inky tarriness. Food wine – Belinda Faure-Griessel recommends carpaccio or hearty casseroles. 14% alc. **Chenin Blanc-Chardonnay** ★ **00** 60/40 blend; pungent stewed apple tones. 12.5% alc. — *TM*

Rupert & Rothschild Vignerons

Simondium (see Paarl map) • Tasting & cellar tours by appointment • Owners Anthonij Rupert & Baron Benjamin de Rothschild • Marketing manager Debra Savage • Winemakers Schalk-Willem Joubert (since 1997), Clive Radloff (since 1997) • Viticulturist André Pentz • Production 90% red 10% white • PO Box 55 Simondium 7670 • ***Tel (021) 874-1648*** *• Fax (021) 874-1802 • E-mail info@fredericksburg.co.za • Website www.fredericksburg.co.za*

THIS NEW-GENERATION partnership between the scions of two leading wine families (Benjamin, son of the late Baron Edmond de Rothschild and Anthonij, son of Dr Anton Rupert) is global networking at its finest. Throw into the imposing blend an immaculately-restored historic Cape farm, Fredericksburg, Pomerol winemaking guru Michel Rolland; and a very enthusiastic team of young winemakers, all locals with fresh ideas: Schalk-Willem Joubert (protégé of La Motte's master blender Jacques Borman), Clive Radloff and Yvonne Schröder, fresh from the University of Stellenbosch and crushes at Springfield and De Wetshof (Yaan Buchwalter accepted a permanent post at the Rothschilds' Ch Clarke), and you have an all-star mix. They were recently awarded the ISO 14001 Environmental Management Certification, the first winery in South Africa and one of only a handful in the world to have achieved this.

★★½ **Baron Edmond** Magnificent addition to Cape's burgeoning bdx pantheon. Latest **99** 75/25 cab/merlot blend (vintage rather than formula dependent) more pulse-racing than contemplative, cerebral **98**, (60/40 merlot/cab) with tighter, drier profile. Latest is hedonistic, opulent, weighty (14% alc), but the drama's matched by refinement – tantalising clove, dark forest berries aromas; textural richness reined in by supple, ripe tannins; taut, pulsing persistence. Effortlessly absorbs 26 mths new Taransaud/Demptos barrelling. Delicious, but destined for greater heights over min 7/8 yrs. Grapes selected in prime vyds, blended during vinification. 4 500 cases.

✰**Classique** Elegant, agile Left Bank mix cab/merlot; **99** encapsulates claret epithet even with substantial alc (14%). This, **98** similar; younger wine sweet-fruited, succulent, further lifted by dab spicy cab f; abundant fine tannins create sophistication with accessibility, complexity. 18 mths Fr oak, 1/4 new. 16 000 cases. **98** ✰ (all new oak) revisited mid-01 shows balanced refinement but lacks weight/spine to cope with food or develop more than 2/3 yrs.

✰**Baroness Nadine** Sure hands make this chardonnay, ones who understand classicism as much achievable in Cape as in Burgundy. Both **99**, **98** convincing, complete; demanding (in local terms) because of plentiful oak, intensity; but ultimately satisfying. **99** bigger wine, youthfully exuberant, tangy; slightly sweet from 14% alc; yr/2 needed for creamy hazelnuts, subtle oak tannins to develop more savoury mellowness. 1 500 cases. Longer lived than decadent **98**, with 100% new oak extravagance (vs **99**'s 60%), now close to peak. These barrel-fermented/aged 11-14 mths, 100% malo. Pine Ridge, West Coast vyds. —*AL*

Rustenberg Wines

Stellenbosch (see Stellenbosch map) • Tasting Mon-Fri 9-4.30 Sat 9-12.30 • Sales Mon-Fri 8-5 Sat 9-12.30 Closed Sun, Good Friday/Easter, Christmas • Cellar tours by appointment • Wheelchair-friendly • Owner Simon Barlow • Winemaker Adi Badenhorst (since Dec 1999) • Assistant winemaker Randolph Christians (since 1995) • Viticulturist Nico Walters (since Nov 1999) • Vineyards 100 ha • Production 600 tons 46 000 cases 70% red 30% white • PO Box 33 Stellenbosch 7599 • ***Tel (021) 809-1200*** *• Fax (021) 809-1219 • E-mail wine@rustenberg.co.za • Website www.rustenberg.co.za*

In the unofficial heavyweight bout of 2001, Lennox Lewis wove into the winelands and this supremely cultured Stellenbosch spread, with vineyards promenading the ridges of the Simonsberg. The former world champion, fêted at a tasting among the vines, was double-whammied – by the views and the wines. Then it was off in a fleet of six helicopters, but not before ordering some of the elegant bordeaux blend for friends in the US. Throughout its history, this exquisite farm has drawn the wealthy and powerful, including visionary old-Cape Prime Minister John X Merriman, who bought and revivified the farm after the 19th century devastation of phylloxera, and is now honoured in the renamed Rustenberg Stellenbosch label. Meanwhile the Stellenbosch Chardonnay is being served by the Lord Mayor of London for official functions and, at home, sites are being prepared for, among others, Rhone staples mourvèdre, roussanne and viognier. And new clones of shiraz, cabernet and merlot will be making their SA debut via the in-house nursery at Caledon. "Very exciting!" beams Nico Walters, viticulturist and Elsenburg classmate of cellar-induna Adi Badenhorst who, with Randolph Christians, deliver their own impressive punches.

✰**Peter Barlow** When Robert Parker, America's – if not the world's – most powerful wine critic, says "may be the finest red wine I have ever tasted from South Africa", as he did of **96** ✰, it's worth noting. Raging mountain fires during 00 harvest affected prime single vyd cab site supplying grapes for this dedication to Simon Barlow's late father; hence no release. Secure some of the 1 200 cases of **99** if you can. Scintillating deep indigo hues, perfumed violets/pencil lead, cedarwood, cigarbox aromatics; currently closed, firm but ripe ascendant tannins cloak plush fruit; time needed in bottle/glass to unveil all its class. 14.2% alc, 20 mths Fr oak, 100% new Fr. **98** in similar mould; pencil-shaving aromas interleaved with floral violets; understated, ripe, never blowsy. Favourite of SA *Wine*, US *Wine Spectator* palates.

✰**Rustenberg Stellenbosch John X Merriman** Previously minimalist by name, this elegant bdx blend gains JXM moniker in carefully considered response to export markets' call "for a name". Quite a mouthful, like the wine. **99** exquisite dense imperial purple, fantastic bouquet tobacco/leather intertwined with blackcurrant fruit; super black cherry, cassis concentration battened down by bristling tannic/acid/alcohol stays. Worthy of its Prime Ministerial allusion. Now merlot-dominated (64%), cab in back seat (23%), 13% cab f. 20 mths oak, all Fr, 50% new. 13.5% alc. 5 500 cases. Pvs **98** similar tobacco scents; riper, near-chunky red berry fruits. Slow-ripening vintage **97** ✯ suits refined style; notch up on medalled maiden **96**.

✯**Five Soldiers** Only 500 cases from single chardonnay vyd guarded by five tall stone pines; 100% natural yeast fermentation, 100% new wood, 100% malo, for more complexity, more viscosity. **00** due for release only mid-02, not tasted. **99** tropical melons, broad buttery richness, endless length regenerated by tart crispness. Extrovert **98** ✯ bold, lashings of lime, butter melting on hot toast. Both brawny 14.5% alc, differ from initial understated **97**.

✯**Stellenbosch Chardonnay** Some cellars aim for fruity citrus, others for broad butter. Here they just aim high. Firm, ripe and assertive, confident style melding best from cool Helderberg terroir of sibling farm, Nooitgedacht. **00** butterscotch cut by lemon twist, very ripe fruit but organised mouthful belies hyperactive components: 14.3% alc, 4.8g/ℓ sugar, 100% barrel-fermented, 50% new Fr, partial malo, 10 mths on lees. 3 000 cases. **99** zippy lemon/lime fruit supports rich, creamy palate, simultaneously minerally and fleshy. 13,8% alc. **98** boldly scented, flavoured.

Stellenbosch Sauvignon Blanc Not retasted for this ed; pvs 99 ✯; neither was **Stellenbosch Brut NV** (97) ✯).

Brampton range

Good value label; flamboyant fruit-driven, market-led whites, fleshy reds; focus firmly on varietal fruit.

✯**Old Vines Red** ✓ Old vines maybe, but modern fruit wrapped in contemporary clothing – a wine writers' house red! Latest **00** merlot, cab, dash cab f. Glowering, smoky-nightclub nose, juicy coffee/meaty fruit hemmed in by energetic tannins mid-01; should settle within yr. 15 mths 2nd/3rd fill oak. 13,5% alc. 2 000 cases. **99** lighter with tobacco leaf aromas.

✯**Cabernet Sauvignon-Merlot** Not quite entry-level pricing, but bags of fruit for your money: succulent, juicy, jammy, expansive red blend in Antipodean mould. Barrel sample **00** concentrated colour; trenchant fruit. **99** jam-packed with red/black cherries. Near equal parts blend, Am oak, 40% new, malo. 13,5% alc. 5 500 cases.

✯**Chardonnay** ✓ Incisive chardonnay – but pvs showy style tempered in largely tank-prepared **01**; bulges with clean citrus lemon/lime, orange zest; athletic palate kept tight by limited wood exposure (mere 8%, old oak), no malo. Deliciously restorative finish. 13.6% alc. 1 200 cases. **99** loaded tropical melons, citrus, all tightly bound.

✯**Q F 3** Third in series of rich, weighty NLH-style desserts, name alludes to Friday afternoon diversion to the cellar for a 'Quick Fix' after the week's work. **01** (sample) saffron-shot gold; billowing tropical mango, pines, over-ripe apricot, peach; velvet viscosity coats palate, intensely sweet – 10.4g/ℓ acidity battles to contain 220 g/ℓ sugar. 13.5% alc. Partially botrytised sauvignon yielding 3 t/ha, Fr oak. 670 cases due 3rd quarter 02. Pvs **Q F 2** (**00**), from sauvignon, and original **Q F 1** (**97**) *Wine* ✯ from fully botrytised chardonnay, listed in pvs ed under 'formal' range. Such boisterousness more appropriate with Brampton ...

Sauvignon Blanc ☆ **01** (sample) packed with ripe tropical melons/pines, cling peach; ritzy mid-palate with refreshing crescendo. Cool, protective handling, neither skin nor wood contact. 13.6% alc. 9 000 cases. **Port** ☆ **94** was, and will be, last. — *DS*

Rust en Vrede Estate 

Stellenbosch (see Stellenbosch map) • Tasting & sales Mon-Fri 9-5 Sat Oct-Apr 9-4 May-Sep 9-3 Public holidays 9-4 • Owner Jannie Engelbrecht • Winemaker Louis Strydom (since 1998) • Production 280 tons 20 000 cases 100% red • PO Box 473 Stellenbosch 7599 Annandale Road Stellenbosch 7600 • ***Tel (021) 881-3881*** *• Fax (021) 881-3000 • E-mail info@rustenvrede.com • Website www.rustenvrede.com*

BOLDLY navigating the way ahead while keeping an eagle eye on the specifics at this first-class estate is former airline pilot Jean Engelbrecht – father (and famed Springbok rugby wing in his day) Jannie Engelbrecht handed over the controls a few years ago. Stratospheric team Engelbrecht and Neil Büchner spend more than a third of the year away from the farm on marketing sorties. Bearing testimony to this high-flying international diplomacy is the soaring status of these wines. The 1996 Estate Wine made US *Wine Spectator*'s Top 100 Wines of 2000 list, the first SA red to do so (bringing them even closer to their ultimate goal of a single flagship blend). This wine has also been seen in some lofty company – it's currently served in the British House of Lords. Further room to spread their wings comes with 15 additional hectares (originally part of R&V according to the history books) purchased from a neighbouring property. Back on the ground (but only just), golden winemaking couple Louis Strydom and his wife Rianie (Morgenhof) welcomed their second-born son, Jacq, into the world.

Rust en Vrede Estate Wine If R&V team keep any vintage in mind when considering their goal of single *grand vin*, they won't go wrong with superb **98**. Echoing berry, spicy, savoury depths with restraining firm tannin, fresh acid spine; beautifully proportioned. No stragglers in this blend, always led by cab (53%) with shiraz, merlot (29/18), though whole much greater than parts; reflecting new and old worlds but ultimately – gratifyingly – with own (R&V?) personality. 18 mths new Fr/Am oak. Delicious in infancy, more so towards 06-08. 13.5% alc (at lowest end of Louis Strydom's ideal range). 2 500 cases. Slighter **97** reflects cool, old-clone disfavouring vintage (though VVG, as was **95** – these, pvs, widely lauded by local/overseas palates). Arresting **96** among top reds of (challenging) yr.

Shiraz Variety closely associated with R&V since **79**, Jannie Engelbrecht's first vintage. Elegant rather than robust, though never short of depth; latest **98** warming smoky fragrance, perked up with Am oak-spice, cedary resonance. Lightish texture belies richness, creamy length, showing benefit of input from some young virus-free clone. Comforting savouriness should increase over 5-7 yrs. 13% alc. 1 800 cases 16 mths, 50/50 new Fr/Am barrels. Am -oaked **97** among R&V's finest.

Cabernet Sauvignon Bdx-like **98**, from splendid yr, back on top form after less noteworthy **97**. Virus-free vines (50% of barrels) making mark with suave ripe-berried dimension (though cellar's hallmark sophisticated elegance remains). Harmonious interplay between ripe vinosity, structural poise, enhanced by med-bodied feel of 13% alc; dry finish, classy polish of 16 mths new Fr barriques. Excellent; staying power until at least 06. 6 000 cases.

Merlot ✓ **00**'s rich ruby gloss heralds another celebrity-status vintage. Opulence continues throughout with swathes of thick, ripe fruit sheltered by vibrant, dry tannins; poised acid spine adds all-important freshness. 15 mths used Fr oak. 13.2% alc. **99** silky, succulent, enhanced by ripe, wrap-around tannins; poised acidity provides welcome length, elegance. 1 200 cases

Tinta Barocca 00 follows footsteps of pvs duo of restyled vintages. Lively macerated cherries, spice with subtle oak vanillin lift. Juicy, fat feel, solid holding tannins; fresh, balanced despite hefty 13.5% alc. Unfussy style will swing along happily with like-minded dishes. Edges rounded by 15 mths older Fr barrels. 13,8% alc. 1 200 cases. — *AL*

Rusthof see Mooiuitsig
Rylands Grove see International Wine Services

Sable View

EXPORT aunched in 1990, marking then Stellenbosch Farmers' Winery's re-entry into the international market. Now part of the Distell portfolio.

Cabernet Sauvignon 98 upped the charisma here. Back-tasted mid-01, still balanced, satisfying. **99** less magnetic. Warm, raisiny fruit.
Pinotage NEW Good advertisement for variety. **98** summer pudding and pleasing tarry touches; fullish, packed with ripe fruit, balancing tangy acid.
Muscat d'Alexandrie Specially for Asian market. Still-fresh **00** glides across palate trailing garlands of exotic flowers and fruits. Though sweetish, ends crisply clean. Lowish 10,7% alc. ±5 000 cases.
Chardonnay Last tasted was **99**. **Sauvignon Blanc 01** demure version of variety, guaranteed not to offend. Floral, med-bodied, easy. 4 000 cases. — *IvH*

Sandown Bay

Passionate foodies Dave and Gordon Johnson style and make these wines for relaxed enjoyment, rather than knock-your-socks-off impact. The Sandown label completes the range produced at Johnson's winery in the Hemel-en-Aarde Valley, and fits comfortably between the budget Cape Bay label and the flagship Newton Johnson wines (see separate entries).

Chardonnay **01**'s lightish creamy/leesy texture blends well with salads, smoked foods. Bright lemony finish freshens the palate. 1 300 cases.

Cabernet Sauvignon Comfortable **01**, pepped with 15% merlot, nice charry tannins from partial Fr oaking. 13.1% alc. 1 500 cases. **Pinotage** **01**'s sweet ripe plums are from Firgrove and Bot River; charry oak from France; serving suggestions (lamb breyani, Thai curry) straight from Dave and Felicity Johnson's well stocked kitchen at Hermanus. 13.4% alc. 2 300 cases. — *DS*

Savanha 

Stellenbosch (see Stellenbosch map) • Tasting & sales daily 9-5 at Spier Wine Shop (see Spier Cellars), or by appointment Tasting fee R12 p/p • Cellar tours by appointment • Owner Winecorp • Winemakers Stéphane de Saint Salvy (reds) Christo Versveld (whites) • Consultant (Naledi, Sejana) Alain Mouiex • Viticulturists Gerrie Wagener (Afrika Vineyards), Johan Smit • Production 15 000 cases • PO Box 99 Lynedoch 7603 • ***Tel (021) 881-3690*** *• Fax (021) 881-3699 • E-mail winecorp@iafrica.com • Website www.winecorp.co.za*

A stylised magic drum, evoking an African myth of fertility and rebirth, is the stamp on this very glossy Winecorp-owned range (distributed in Europe and the USA by the same company that handles Romanée-Conti). A refined, more old world style is the mission here, both in the Savanha range and the two top labels, Naledi and Sejana (the names mean 'star' and 'trophy' in Sotho, both presciently chosen in light of their gushing international reception – no shortage of local plaudits, either: Air France-Preteux Bourgeois, *Grape* Packaging Award are just two panels that recently beheld or tasted and succumbed). Lending extra lustre is Alain Moueix, from a fabled Bordeaux wine-aristocracy, here in role of "guide and mentor" to the Naledi/Sejana winemaking team – now ensconced in the modern cellar at Spier where select, contract-grown grapes are vinified under the Australian-trained eye of cellar chief Ben Radford.

Naledi Cabernet Sauvignon Like its partner below, **00** carries thumbprint of hot, dry vintage. This the fresher: characteristic mint/cassis aromas with minerally undertones and well-absorbed new Fr oak (40%). Very youthful, lively palate bears 13.7% alc lightly. Brusque though fine dry tannins spoil overall picture with hint of untoward bitterness. As pvsly, Dbnville/Paarl grapes, vinified separately; yr barrelled, 30-40% new. 2 200 cases. **99** characterised by minerally freshness, well-judged oak, polished dry tannins.

Sejana Merlot This, above, arouse much discussion, controversy, as much about their lofty prices (R175 locally) as the wines themselves. Designed with quality old-world wines in mind (fitting, then, that Air France 01 competition's Fr judges loved **99**, **98**, voting both into top 10). Yet reactions differ greatly, and doubtful if latest **00**, from hot, dry year, will forge greater consensus. Intensely ripe (porty?) dusty, meaty tones with matching sweet palate. All-important structural tannin less mature, very dry, unyielding. This very different Cape style now in extreme youth, so difficult to predict how/if will age. Yr Fr barriques, 30-40% new. 2 200 cases.

Savanha range

Merlot ✓ If Fr-inspired **99** puzzled many local winelovers, **00** should give them only pleasure. Exudes charm, refinement in unique SA style (indefinable cross between old, new worlds); generous plum/mulberry ripeness fleshed out with choc richness wrapped in vibrant but unaggressive tannin. Balanced current drinking, though best around 05/06. Yr Fr oak, 35% new component well judged. 13.4% alc. 1 000 cases.

Cabernet Sauvignon Fine array cigarbox, spicy cassis, walnut fragrances in refined **00**. Palate distinguished by similar fluidity, fruit definition as above wine but tannic bitterness diminishes appeal. 13.5% alc. Fr oak 12 mths, 40% new. **Shiraz** Pliable tannins, silky texture, delicate choc-mint-spice flavours enhanced by carefully judged oak, lend youthful appeal to **00**, best enjoyed before these attractions give way to serious but presently integrated 14.8% alc. Fr oak, 40% new. 1 500 cases. **Chardonnay** No **01**. Pvs **00** sold out. **Semillon Reserve** NEW **01** (sample) convincingly different from following wine; rich vinosity complemented by sophisticated fresh honey, lemon character; ripe, weighty feel with good oak integration. Should mature min 2/3 yrs. Helderberg grapes. Possible. Barrel-fermented/matured 7 mths, 40% new. 300 cases **Semillon** Early, unfinished sample **01** shows bold build though lesser fruit potency despite barrel fermentation, 3 mths lees enrichment. From F'hoek grapes with non-aromatic lemony, waxy flavours often associated with area's semillon. 13,8% alc. 1 000 cases. **Sauvignon Blanc** **01** usual brisk flinty herbaceous style associated with Dbnville. Unlike **00**, this generously proportioned (13.3% alc), intense, dry. Best partnered with well-flavoured fish or white meat dishes. 3 000 cases. —*AL*

Savisa see Sonop
SA Wine Cellars see Distell

Saxenburg

Stellenbosch (see Stellenbosch map) • Tasting & sales Mon-Fri 9-5 Sat 9-4 Sun 10-4 (Oct-May) Tasting fee R1,50 per wine • Cellar tours by appointment • Guinea Fowl Restaurant • Gifts • Conferences • Views • Lunchtime pony rides for children Sun & public holidays • Variety of small game permanently on view • Owners Adrian & Birgitte Bührer • Winemaker/viticulturist Nico van der Merwe (since 1991) with Koos Thiart (since 2000) • Vineyards 70 ha • Production 350 tons, 50 000 cases (300 tons, 25 000 cases under own label) 80% red 20% white

• PO Box 171 Kuils River 7580 • ***Tel (021) 903-6113/6313*** *• Fax (021) 903-3129 • E-mail saxfarm@iafrica.com • Website www.saxenburg.co.za*

"Some critics say Saxenburg is hovering. Well, we're happy hovering!" declares feisty Nico van der Merwe, who levitates between this respected Kuils River spread and 16th-century Ch Capion, near Montpellier, both owned by Adrian and Birgit Bührer. After six vintages at Capion, vdM's learned a little French and a lot about coopering. "In France you're close to heaven. If you can't find the right barrel in Bordeaux, you simply hop to the next area. There are endless options." Here at Saxenburg, they've installed extra fermentation tanks to handle new plantings of cabernet, pinotage, shiraz and sauvignon. They're also looking to further increase the vineyard to 90 hectares by the end of the year. After a lean, dry 2000 vintage, a relieved vdM reports that wines with greater elegance, flavour and finesse are emerging out of cooler 2001. Watch out for some outstanding reds, including this winemaker's signature shiraz. Which, he ventures, "is best grown in neglected old vineyards – ask the French."

Private Collection Cabernet Sauvignon "Bad comments from Wine & Spirit Board, good comments north to south at pre-release tastings," rues vdM, reflecting something of the mismatch between perspectives of officialdom and the consumer. One of the Cape's grandest; critically applauded single vyd selection from S'burg soils gets vintage fillip in big **98** opaque vermilion, nose packed with wood spice, cassis; palate stacked with fantastic juicy blackcurrant, mulberry fruit, classic supporting oak and measured tannins. Super length, still classy in bolder frame, big brother to elegant, linear **97** reflecting cooler vintage. **96** ready, open herbaceous charm. Yr Fr barriques, 80% new. 1 200 cases. **Guinea Fowl Cabernet Sauvignon** Less serious, more fruity/accessible; "poolside/sport wine" in vdM's book. **99** offers sappy succulence, taut grassy fruit shielding red/black berries in youth, energising, unrestricting, tannin support. **98** more open, developed. 20% bought-in fruit, Yr Fr barrels. 13% alc. 2 500 cases. Enjoy **96**, **98** while waiting for **97**, **99**.

Private Collection Merlot VdM lists "Top sales!" as the awards attracted by this wine; **97** a standout, **98** wowed European markets. **99** in more tapered elegant mould, redolent of roasting coffee, fine Belgian chocolate, densely stacked, supple tannins need time to soften – up to 10 yrs will reward. Richer, more supple sheen, less overtly savoury than version below. **98** a brooder, for further contemplation, not instant gratification. **97** refined, dark-fruit opulence. From **95**, 100% S'burg grapes, cooler slopes planted 1990. 70% new, Fr oak adds spice to underlying richness. 5% cab for structure. 13% alc. 1 500 cases. **Guinea Fowl Merlot** Gears up a refined ratchet in **99** after big, plummy **98**; latest super savoury character, hints coriander/beef fillet, evokes biltong-in-preparation! Tweak more tannin grip than usual for range, no loss of fruity identity; 1/2 yrs will bring fuller harmony. 10% cab. 13% alc. Yr Fr oak. 3 000 cases.

Private Collection Pinotage "Best vintage yet from this single vyd," avers vdM of **99,** striking in its refinement rather than elementary fruitiness: purple tints to rich colour; pared plum, beautiful but measured Am oak, conspire with embroidered tannins to offer concentrated mouthful. Rich, concentrated **98**, more traditional pinotage sweetness. Yr 80% Am oak, rest Fr. 13,5% alc. 1 300 cases. Guinea Fowl **Pinotage** VdM avoids varietal bitterness in **99** sultry damson, clove nose driven on by ripe fruit palate woven into tense frame; requires bit more time to reach comfortable drinkability. **98** smoky, dried-fig/nuts, wrapped in vibrant juicy structure. Warm-fermented, seasoned Am oak. 13% alc. 2 000 cases.

Private Collection Shiraz No 'regular'/Guinea Fowl version, nothing standard about this PC label, farm's flagship. Only regularity is consistent, riveting brilliance. **99** potency poised with restraint, composition far more complex, integrated, restrained than individual elements of its analysis may suggest. From leather spice, seasoned sandalwood through gently juicy fruit to powerful tannic palate, unfolding waves of class. 13.5% alc. **98** heralded coming-of-age; amazingly rich, concentrated (14% alc). **97** seductive, Rhone-like. **96** SAA (runner-up red wine trophy) peaking. Oaking now Am casks, 30% new. 40% bought-in Stbosch grapes. 3 500 cases.

Saxenburg Shiraz Select Fondly known as 'SSS', particularly to the few who have it: 180-200 cases, portion for CWG auction, remainder only from farm at R350/bottle; vyd/vintage selection that starts in the PC mould above, but soon leaps into an orbit of its own. Black ink complexion, intense herbal essence of rosemary, sage on spicy nose, fantastically tight, tapered palate shows/confines juicy fruit that will be allowed out to play over next decade. Last **98** worthy follow-up to Hermitage-like **97** – as massive, demanding. Needs until at least after Athens Olympics. Stbosch grapes from gravel soils; used Am oak-fermented for extra fruit concentration, then ± yr Fr oak, ±50% new. 13.5-14.5% alc.

Gwendolyn First, best in blended range named after Bührers' children (younger daughter Gwendolyn) "to celebrate the millennium & the future" Third-vintage **99** aromas reflect whimsical packaging: smoky, cracked pepper spice allure, but gravitas from rich savoury shiraz fruit folded into waves Am-dominated oak. 'Sweet' compote finish, but bone-dry. **98** reflected generosity of warm vintage. Distinguished partnership 55% home shiraz, rest Stbosch-sourced cab. Yr Fr/Am oak. 13% alc. 2 000 cases.

Manuel Evenly moulded 70% (coastal, bought in) cab, 30% S'burg merlot named after Bührers' eldest son. **99** ripe blackberry nose, ethereal before compact, grassy palate; glimpses juicy merlot belted in by fine, dry tannins. **98** Needs 18 mths in bottle, but may drop fruit thereafter. **97** fine-boned, mineral, blackcurrant freshness, 3 yrs further maturation potential. Yr Fr new/used oak. 13% alc. 1 000 cases.

Private Collection Chardonnay Graduation from regular to higher-toned PC range from **99** sustained in latest **00** which reflects harvest heat: muted citric nose, pebbly depth to broad palate, ripe, just-dry 4 g/ℓ sugar calls for some tighter acid strapping. For earlier enjoyment than overtly tropical, supple **99**. 100% barrel-fermented/matured 11 mths, 50/50 new/used Fr oak. Usually 13,5% alc. 1 200 cases.

Private Collection Sauvignon Blanc ✓ 01 drum-roll comeback for label after unreleased 00 (failed to make stringent PC quality cut): unambiguous ripe, pulpy gooseberry, asparagus, pea-soup features, bold rather than racy; more emphatic sauvignon fruit than many more bristling, reductive examples. Excellent finish, style demanding food. 99 elegant, tropical. 13,0% alc. 2 000 cases.

Adrianus next **99**, **Appolonia 99** (white blend featuring viognier, chardonnay, marsanne, roussanne) and **Fiona 99** (red blend) set to complete the above 'Family' concept range in 2001; untasted. **Grand Vin Rouge** Light-bodied quaffer, designed as easy entry into world of wine. **NV** French/SA marriage (90% Capion grapes, 10% S'burg). Latest vinous all-sorts: syrah, cabs s/f, merlot, grenache, cinsaut, carignan. Baked fruit, dry, dusty mouthful. **Grand Vin Blanc** Novel cross-equator **NV** blend 50/50 S'burg chenin/Ch Capion chardonnay, rich beyond its station with integrated chalky lime resonance for ripe tropical guava/ melon fruit. Soft, flavoursome; sufficient presence for food. 5 000 cases. **Private Collection Natural Sweet Le Reve de Saxenbourg** Lightly coloured, textured **NV** (01) non-botrytised dessert, equal parts chenin/sauvignon. Pungent pine~apples, citrus scents; 80 g/ℓ sugar finish. WOM selection. 5 000 cases of 375 ml. **Private Collection Le Phantom Brut Cap Classique** Lightish; energetic bead in line with crisp foil to chalky, yeasty body, developing moderate richness. Brut **NV** sparkler from 50/50 bought-in chardonnay/pinot, min 48 mths on lees ("an expensive ongoing hobby"). 300 cases. — *DS*

Scali

Paarl (see Paarl map) • Tasting & sales by appointment • Owners/winemakers Willie & Tania de Waal • Viticulturist Willie de Waal • Vineyards 5 ha • Production 15 tons 850 cases 100% red • PO Box 7143 Noorder-Paarl 7623 • ***Tel (021) 863-8349*** *• Fax (021) 863-8340 • E-mail info@scali.co.za • Website www.scali.co.za*

ENTHUSIASTIC couple Willie and Tania de Waal, who've pitched a tent in both the old wine world (the vineyards of the Rhone and Burgundy harvests French highlights) and the new (Australia), have brought backpacks brimming with inspiration to their family farm, Schoone Oord, in Paarl. Traditionally their grapes were supplied to Boland Kelder but they eventually succumbed to their passion for winemaking and were granted permission to keep back 10 tons of their finest grapes (upped to 15 last year). They've been unstoppable ever since. From their renovated stone cellar with its newly installed open wooden fermenters, they crafted their first highly individual Pinotage (the maiden 99 vintage, released last year) and tried their hand at a Syrah (still in the barrel) for the first time last harvest.

☆**Pinotage** Individual, superlatively-packaged contender (inexplicably overlooked by Grape 2000 Packaging Award judges); brims with personality; boutique quantities: 940 half-cases. Debut **99** more shiraz- than pinotage-like, but fine intensity; warm, mouthcoating flavours. **00** ☆ will appeal greatly to traditionalists: more overtly varietal, more confiture character, estery snatch; finishes with vanilla twist from 25% Am oak (rest Fr, 12 mths, 50% new). Alcs ±13%. — *TM*

Scarborough see Cape Point Vineyards
Scholtzenhof see Ken Forrester

Sedgwick's

VENERABLE Cape brand, now owned by Distell.

Old Brown Sherry ☆ The original SA old brown (first produced 1886), and still the fisherman's favourite warming drop. Actually a jerepiko/sherry blend; rich, sweet; now with warm nutty aromas. **Government House Port** Not tasted for this ed. Pvs rating ☆. These **NV**. — *IvH*

Seidelberg Estate

Paarl (see Paarl map) • Tasting & sales Mon-Fri 9-5 Sat/Sun/public holidays 10-4 Tasting fee R6 for 5 wines • 'Sunset tastings' on lawn in front of tasting centre (advance booking essential) • Cellar tours by appointment • Olive & Vine Restaurant (see Eat-out section) • Conference/function centre • Tourgroups • Gifts • Walks • Views • Helipad • Owner Roland Seidel • Winemaker Nicolaas Rust (since 1999) • Assistant winemaker Stephan Basson (since Dec 2000) • Viticulturist Conré Groenewald (since 1999) • Vineyards 85 ha • Production 20 000 cases 80% red 15% white 5% muscadel • PO Box 505 Suider-Paarl 7624 • ***Tel (021) 863-3495/6*** *• Fax (021) 863-3797 • E-mail ebr@new.co.za • Website www.seidelberg.co.za*

A HIKING PATH on Paarlberg behind the winery, sunset wine tastings on the terrace (nocturnal genets and porcupines occasional, pleasing, distractions), a helicopter pad and a wedding reception hall are just some of the delicious new charms of this 17th century estate, known as De Leuwen Jagt in the early days when the big cats still roamed. Then there's Nicolaas Rust, himself a tourist attraction as he holds a malolactically-fermenting merlot to his ear and asks: "Can you hear it talking? Now that's what I call a symphony in the glass!" The red soils of Seidelberg produce big red wines with "wonderful extract, intense colour and unbelievable up-front fruit", says Rust who, with Hamburg-born owner Roland

Seidel rooting from the wings, is upping the wattage in this reawakening Agter-Paarl area. Flying in from Elsenburg via an extended Iberian tour is new assistant-winemaker Stephan Basson, scion of a winegrowing family from Malmesbury.

Roland's Reserve range

★**Cabernet Sauvignon 00** firmly in estate's densely extracted mode: dark brooding colours/tastes with sweet cassis and cigarbox from 9 mths new Fr oak, well controlled. Fennel/liquorice in chewy departure. Big 13.8% alc. 600 cases. **99** more compact, firmly tannic.

★**Merlot** Massive ripe-fruited style unveiled with **99** continues in follow-up **00** (sample); vibrant plum and savoury tones, very smooth sweet flavours following through into well fleshed mid-palate, fruity finish.

★**Shiraz** NEW Promising crossover style evoking aromatic European examples with smoke and truffles, some game/garrigue whiffs but also Antipodean fruit-oaky tones with brazen redcurrants; **00** (sample) very nice wine, controlled, potential to develop into ★ with time.

Pinotage 99 ★ not retasted for this ed. No **00** (released as Seidelberg below).

Seidelberg range

★**Chardonnay** Pungent mango, pear-drop aromas in wide-bodied **00** ★ tending towards overweight now; bit of dried-apricot tang just not enough to offset massive 13,8% alc. Better with rich food (Nicolaas Rust's eclectic suggestions – abalone, foie gras, lemon shark, croc tail – could all work); 6 mths Fr oak, 50% first fill. 700 cases. **99** still the better wine: lively, fruit-driven, balanced.

Pinotage NEW ★ Good middle of the road style, well constructed. Warm forthcoming **00** brambly, slightly smoky aromas pervade fleshy mulberry fruit; ripe, sweet, med-bodied with soft dry finish. 9 mths Fr oak. 1 000 cases. **Un Deux Trois** NEW ★ Bdx blend of equal portions cabs s/f, merlot, 8 mths aged in Fr barriques. Concours Mondial 01 judges loved overripe **00**, awarding a gold medal. Highly idiosyncratic that will appeal to some, though probably not classicists. 13.5% alc. 1 500 cases. **Cabernet Sauvignon-Merlot** ★ **99** 65/35 blend appears prematurely aged; pungent green olive/herbal smells in somewhat austere frame with underlying greenness. 100% new oak, 7 mths. 13.5% alc. 1 500 cases. **Chenin Blanc** ★ **01** (sample) creamy stewed guava tones balanced by bright refreshing acidity; super food wine, well priced. 900 cases. **Sauvignon Blanc** ★ Textbook varietal aromas in **01** (sample) plus some youthful guava; crisp, luminous fruit, passion fruit and lime in bone dry finish; med-bodied. Not tasted: **Sauvignon Blanc-Riesling** Previous **99** rated ★.

De Leuwen Jagt range

★**Red Muscadel** ✓ Latest incarnation of sophisticated **NV** fortified dessert raises the star quality with hyper-intense aromas of jasmine, apricot and succulent raisins; very sweet flavours; choc notes and energetic combo of high acidity, alc to power away any suggestion of cloy. 18,5% alc. **NV**. 2 000 cases to sip now or keep.

Merlot ★ **00** reviewed for pvs ed has softened, unfurled into tasty drink with suave blackcurrant bouquet and nice chewy fruit flavours. Unwooded, bought-in grapes. 13,2% alc. 1 000 cases. **Shiraz** ★ Food-inclined **00** offers good peppery/tobacco aromas over blackberries, turning good and dry in finish. Unwooded. Could go few yrs. 13.5% alc. 800 cases. **Nuance** ★ Delicate muscadel, Cape riesling mix, **01** (sample) tastes off-dry with rose petals and light terpenes over tasty ripe fruit. 1 000 cases. Not tasted: **Cabernet Franc-Merlot** (Pvs **99** ★), **Chardonnay (98** ★), **Chenin Blanc (00** ★), **Sauvignon Blanc (00** ★). *— TM*

Sentinel see Coppoolse Finlayson-Sentinel

Seven Falls see Barrydale

Shibula see Klompzicht

Ship Sherry

Not 'sherry', but a jeripigo-style fortified – a trusted companion, especially among bluecollar workers in the Eastern Cape. By Distell.

NV ☆ Somewhat neutral but clean; raisiny, decidedly sweet. — *IvH*

Shiraz Company see Claridge

Shoprite Checkers

National wine buyer Stephanus Eksteen • PO Box 215 Brackenfell 7561 • ***Tel (021) 980-4000*** *• Fax (021) 980-4075*

A panel of winemakers, wine experts and consumers meets every month to select the Oddbins in-house range for the nationwide retail stores Shoprite and Checkers. "They're usually a very enthusiastic bunch!" laughs wine buyer Stephan Eksteen, divulging that the brand has been growing by leaps and bounds "as consumers become accustomed to the fact that these are quality wines at affordable prices". Inside Oddbins bottles are limited-edition varietal wines, sourced directly from estates and cellars. Bin numbers change as batches are replaced buy new parcels, which helps ensure that contents are fresh and consumers stay interested.

Oddbins range

Ruby Cabernet-Pinotage NEW ☻ ☆ No Bin number at time of sampling for gluggable blend offering the spice and juice of ruby cab, cherry fruit of pinotage; **01** harmonious, supple, tasty.

Cabernet Sauvignon-Merlot Bin 117 ☆ Stbosch fruit gives **99** a leg-up; surprisingly big/good cab character for med-weight wine; good sappy fruit quaffs easily. 13,5% alc. **Pinotage Reserve Bin 36** ☆ Paarl origin of this nostalgic **00**, with textbook hi-toned ester, banana tones, old-style blustery tannins. Traditionalists, stock up! **Chardonnay Bin 108** ☆ Zesty tones underpin dusty aromas mixed with tropical fruit; good everyday fare and not too full-bodied. 13% alc. **Sauvignon Blanc Bin 124** ☆ Tropical aromas and guava tastes in lively **01**, lightish mouthful with brisk finish. WO Rbtson. **Chenin Blanc-Chardonnay Bin 46** ☆ Light-bodied vin ordinaire with slight tropical tones and very dry citrus finish. **NV** ex Rbtson. **Colombard-Chardonnay Bin 66** ☆ From the 'home' of colombard, Rbtson, as pvsly, and it shows: fresh guavas, sweet herby wafts, enough citrus tang to keep things lively and easy to drink. **NV** with lightish 12% alc. Also available, not tasted: **Shiraz-Cabernet Sauvignon**; **Merlot** (Bin numbers unallocated at press time; vintages unknown). Some of these recent releases might still be available: **Cabernet Sauvignon Bin 85 (99** ☆), **Cabernet Sauvignon-Merlot Bin 86 (95** ☆), **Ruby Cabernet-Cabernet Sauvignon Bin 142 (00** ☆), **Ruby Cabernet-Merlot Bin 146 (00** ☆), **Chenin Blanc Bin 137 (00** ☆), **Sauvignon Blanc-Chardonnay Bin 139 (00** ☆), **Stein Bin 39 (00** ☆).

Cellar Reserve range

This replacement for the Rite house-brand of 5 ℓ boxed easy drinkers is made by Vredendal Winery. The range, untasted for this ed, includes a **Dry Red**, **Rosé**, **Grand Cru**, **Stein** and **Late Harvest**. — *DH*

Signal Hill 

Cape Town • Tasting & sales 50 Kloof Street at the Wine Concepts shop in Cape Town • Owners Ridon Family Vineyards (Pty) Ltd • Winemaker Jean-Vincent Ridon (since 1997), Lawrence Buthelezi (since 1999) • Viticulturist Marietjie Marais • Vineyards 4,5 ha • Production 3 500 cases 70% red 15% dessert 15% white • 24 Scott Street Cape Town 8001 • ***Tel (021) 461-9590*** *• Fax (021) 465-0342 or +33 1 53013167 • E-mail ridon@iafrica.com • Website www.winery.co.za*

HARVEST 2001 found energetic Frenchman Jean-Vincent Ridon happily – albeit temporarily – ensconced in a Waterfront winemaking facility next door to Flagstone. With his usual infectious enthusiasm, Ridon now seems intent on creating a posse of urban winemakers. "There are lots of advantages to having a small unit in the city," insists this irrepressible émigré, who keeps his wine in an old stone cellar below Bree & Loop streets ("My wine is in a safe and spiritual place – and it reminds me of Burgundy"). On which subject, he wonders: "In France, it's said that terroir is more important than the winemaker. But is that true here?" asks Ridon, who micro-vinified pinot from 14 different Cape sites and is ageing them separately to see how each evolves. The goal of all this effort is to help fellow pinotphiles access the better terroirs and graftings. Food for his Gallic soul was hearing his label had made the wine list in Alain Ducasse's 3-star restaurants back on his home terroir.

✵**Cabernet Sauvignon** ✓ An individual ("SA cab with French flair – no Aussie style"), aromatic and elegant. First was **97** *Wine* ✵; **98** with ripe-banana nuance; **99**, liked by Paris International judges, whiffs of creosote; latest **00**, ex mature Simonsberg bushvines, milk-choc and extra-ripe fruit, plump tannins. Delectable now and, as Ridon says, probably for shorter-term enjoyment; 12 mths mainly Fr oak, 25% new. 13.8% alc. Sample shows ✵ potential. 300 cases.

✵**Petit Verdot** NEW Vibrant fruit a hallmark of this range, here thrillingly expressed as sweet-grassy plums, bitter choc; luxurious cigarbox wafts, too, about **00** sample, oaked 18 mths 2nd fill Fr barriques. Fruit ex Stbosch, Wellington (latter's generosity reflected in 14% alc). 100 cases. **99** similar; some gamey whiffs.

✵**Pinotage** NEW Limited release, cleverly architectured for elegance within the modern idiom. **00** (from barrel) vanilla hints, light pepperiness in finish, persistent; 16 mths Fr oak, 2nd fill. 13.% alc. Savoury/mulberry aromas to try with J-V R's exotic food suggestion: guinea fowl lasagne. 30 cases.

✵**Pinot Noir Barrel Fermented** Inaugurated with experimental **98**, burgundian; **99** similar; gunpowder, gamey tones; **00** skipped. **01** barrel reveals shiny new world infant: in-your-face, red-fruited, popping with promise. These barrel-fermented/aged on lees; F'hoek fruit. Alcs ±13%.

✵**Vin de l'Empereur** Deliciously different golden Natural Sweet from Simonsberg hanepoot, unbotrytised. **98** *Wine* ✵; **99** ★ organic, earthy. Latest **00** ✵ floral/grapey; amazingly weighty, almost jerepiko-like (though unfortified – 13% alc), yet elegant. 500 cases.

✵**Vin de Glacière** NEW Unctuous **00** icewine with enormous bouquet of dried flowers and fruit; wonderfully smooth across the tongue; barley candy tastes add to the unbridled hedonism. 400 bottles.

✵**Crème de Tête** Luscious/lustrous botrytis dessert ex 40 yr old Simonsberg hanepoot bushvines; oak aged. Latest **00** ✵✵ beautiful wine; waves of cool acidity sweeping aside the sweetness (214 g/ℓ sugar), wonderful persistence. Low 11% alc. Just 80 cases (375 ml) which absolutely beg for foie gras. No **99**. **98** *Wine* ✵, Michelangelo gold.

Gamay Noir NEW ★ Quaffable juicy-fruity style, yet not frivolous; good palate weight to fill out shy plummy aromas. Ex Polkadraai, unwooded. 700 cases.
— TM

Silumku see Overhex

Silversands see Robertson Winery

Simonsig Estate

Stellenbosch (see Stellenbosch map) • Tasting & sales Mon-Fri 8.30-5 Sat 8.30-4 Tasting fee R5 p/p • Cellar tours Mon-Fri 10, 3 Sat 10 (max 8 unless by arrangement) • Owners Malan family (Simonsig Estate Partnership) • Winemaker Johan Malan (since 1981), with Van Zyl du Toit & Debbie Burden • Viticulturist Francois Malan (since 1980) • Marketing Pieter Malan • Vineyards 286 ha • Production 2 100 tons 150 000 cases 50/50 red/white • PO Box 6 Koelenhof 7605 • ***Tel (021) 888-4900*** *• Fax (021) 888-4909 • E-mail wine@simonsig.co.za • Website www.simonsig.co.za*

After celebrating the 30th anniversary of the Stellenbosch Wine Route, brainchild of patriarch Frans Malan, this estate Simonsig last year toasted another landmark: 30 years of making Kaapse Vonkel, SA's first cap classique. On hand to break out the bubbles was winged superstar Michael Johnson – appropriate for an estate that, since 1968, has consistently kept ahead of the Cape pack. Winemaking remains a family concern for siblings Johan, Pieter and Francois and their very much hands-on wives and children. Each brother has his own domain (respectively winemaking, marketing and viticulture), and these "are big enough for the three of us," laughs Johan M. At wine tastings, they like to pass around a jar of soil from their Rooibult vineyard, home-ground of their acclaimed Redhill Pinotage. "It's the ultimate expression of the Simonsig terroir," remarks Johan M. For their other site-specific star, Merindol Shiraz, they're experimenting with two options: the sandy loams of the old orange orchard, and a site behind the cellar. "Astounding how different they are," marvels Johan M, whose quiet excellence is the epitome of Simonsig.

✵**Shiraz** General quality improvement of Cape shiraz mirrored in the Malans' 'standard' bottling. Others emphasise pepper spice – which this has – but the focus here is a penetrating smokiness. **99** fleshed out with red berries, hint cassis, palate marked by earthy brawn, sinuous structure, 13.5% alc. Modern style, but individual 'farmyard' character. WOM Reserve. **98** cracked peppercorn, redcurrant whiffs, full mouthful. Oaked 87% Fr, 34% new, 15 mths; pvs 33% Am oak; 25% new, 19 mths.

✵**Merindol Syrah** We used to flinch at three-digit price tags, especially ex cellar, now they seem commonplace. Nothing 'common' about this single vyd selection, as premium as its price. **99** Full plummy colour, billowing vanilla-pod aromas, sensuous milled black pepper, coriander spice links to tense palate in youth. Ripe fruit pumped up with delicious Am oak (100% new, 21 mths), but with restraint – not big/blowsy. **97** combined ripe 'Australian' fruit, Rhône hillside scrub, 18 mths new Fr, some Am. *Wine* ✵, as was **98** VG, Michelangelo gold. 500 cases.

✵**Pinotage Red Hill** Serious red wine, with attitude. Unlike standard unbarrelled version below, the grape's often loud character only part of the orchestra here. Standout vyd (40 yr old bushvines) and barrel selection, empowered in **99** by 100% new Fr oak, 18 mths. Fragrant, sensuous, rich and delicious, more refined, complex interplay raspberry fruit/spice, oak than second release **98** which saw 80% Am oak, one third new, 20 mths. Broader grain in mouth. **97** SAA. 480 cases. Multiple WOM Reserve selections.

✵**Pinotage** Not long ago oaking pinotage was novel, now it's the reverse. This stalwart has never seen wood and it's none the worse for it – more typical even. **00** bursts with tastebud-thumping ripe, baked plums/prunes, asphalt, wet leaves, spicy/nutmeg edge. Tannic grip firm enough without wood. 14% alc. **99** concentrated curranty, mulberry fruity punch to juicy palate. 13,6%

alc. Individual, parochial even, but certainly South African. **98** US *Wine Spectator*, WOM, best value selections.

✪**Tiara** Accessible, palate-friendly, excellent bdx blend: sample **99** super ruby, plump cherry/meaty/smoky notes, fleshy palate braced by soft tannins, 14% alc. Johan M's favoured petit verdot creeps up to 9% of blend (with 52% cab, 39% merlot). **98** smoky, earthy, elegant sweetly tuned fruit. Muscular 14% alc. For the long haul. Oaking now 3:1 Fr:Am, 40% new, 20 mths.

✪**Frans Malan Reserve** While protagonists debate what makes a 'proper' Cape Red, Simonsig's emphatic contribution honours family patriarch Frans Malan, far-sighted Cape wine pioneer. Pinotage retains centre stage (supported by cab, merlot) in sample **99** bursting mulberry colours, bouncy plums, bananas, cassis tagged by cloves, wood spice. Assertive, youthful palate shows predominance of Am oak (68%, 23% new). **98** complex smoky, plum pud characters, finely judged Fr/Am, new/2nd fill oak; fine-grained berry flavours. Up on **97** ✰.

✪**Chardonnay** Cape benchmark with proclivity for gold awards from **96**, next **00** ✪ marginally dented by hot harvest, retains lime pickle/nut-brittle tension, albeit in quieter form. 13.6% alc adds breadth. **99** powerful citrus/butterscotch, dense, juicy lemon with toast. Barrel fermented/aged 11 mths Fr oak, 33% new. Better vintages can develop hazelnut/marzipan complexity with age. **98** VVG, **97** IWSC gold.

✪**Gewürztraminer** ✓ SLH style (though not labelled as such) glowing gold, thumbprint rosepetal/peeled-litchi aromas, ripe melon flavours. **00** drier than pvs (25 g/ℓ sugar), trifle muted, ends a touch bitter (a varietal bite). **99** elegant, WOM selection. **98** greater length.

✪**Cuvée Royale** Distinguished, incisive MCC, 'prestige cuvee' to mark Frans Malan's pushing the limits three decades ago. Golden hues of **92** punctuated by needlepoint bead, buttered-croissant nose still fresh, bone dry, firm acidity regenerates lengthy finish. Wonderful condition, further maturation potential even, from classic 7 yrs on lees. 84% chardonnay leads charge, 16% pinot. WOM Reserve. **91** marked 30 yrs of Simonsig wines.

✪**Kaapse Vonkel** Avant-garde 30 yrs ago as first local commercial bottle-fermented bubbly, the 'Cape Sparkle' keeps glistening. Current **97** sees pinot meunier squeak into blend (2%): pearly primrose hues; developed creme anglaise, butterscotch aromas; full mousse delicate blend of chardonnay (53%) creaminess and pinot body. Satisfying finish. **96** sported 15% pinotage adding local colour, black grape body/fruit. WOM selection. 4 yrs on lees, plus bottle maturation give more weight, complexity, ready for enjoyment on release. Around 7 g/ℓ sugar.

✪**Vin de Liza** Bukettraube NLH named for revered Malan matriarch, Liza. Fetching, elegant packaging, striking slim 375 ml bottle. **99** delicate potpourri dried peach, apricot, mebos, whiff honey, botrytis; not too sweet (96 g/ℓ sugar), departure from older-style 'sticky nobles'. **98** even drier (85 g/ℓ), more substance.

✪**Port** NEW **94** LBV-style bottled Dec 97, 100% pinotage. Though grape's not classic for port, structure is (18.6% alc, 75 g/ℓ sugar). Dense ruby; layers smoke/dried prune/leather nose, plump grape provenance bounces across tense, slightly spiritous palate. One-off, from farm only.

Chenin Blanc ☻ ✰ US market favourite, and with cause. **01** deliciously tangy compote of soft peach, ripe melon, strung with racy acid. 14% colombard adds dimension; drink in flush of youth.

Cabernet Sauvignon ✰ Sheet anchor for forays into bigger, flashier, riper, artfully oakier territory (see siblings above). Older style without sacrificing fruit: **99** sappy, cedar nose, mulberry/plum fruits, supportive 20 mths older oak, mainly Fr. **Sauvignon Blanc** ✰ **01** striking, unfettered varietal identity. Delineated thrusting nettles, cut grass, flint, green pea. Arresting, firm and dry. Alc. back under 13% after weighty **00**. **Vin Fumé** ☆ Amongst the first Cape wooded sauvignons, one of few still bearing the 'fumé' tag; popular in restaurants, with caterers, due to culinary versatility/fair price. **00** lightly oaked, fruit salad, gooseberry mix, firm, food-friendly finish. Consistency smoothes out vintage variation. **Weisser Riesling** ☆ Just-dry **99** swansong for one of Cape's few standouts, now discontinued. **Mustique** ☆ Seductive, aromatic bukettraube-driven blend laced with muscats (morio, ottonel) and splash riesling. **00** confirms welcome drier trend, letting ambrosial scents impart interest, 9.4 g/ℓ sugar. **Franciskaner** ☆ **00** 36 g/ℓ sugar, wafts of spice, nicely cut sweet fruit, from bukettraube, gewürz, shake of chenin. *— DS*

Simonsvlei International

Paarl (see Paarl map) Tasting & sales Mon-Fri 8-5 Sat 8.30-4.30 (also Sun 11-2. 30 Dec-Apr) Fee R8 for 6 tastings • Cellar tours (German, French, English or Afrikaans) by appointment Fee R15 (incl. 6 tastings) • Luncheons Wed-Son 12-3 Tel (021) 863-2486 • Tourgroups (guided tours including meals available) • Function/conference facilities • Views • Wheelchair-friendly • Owners 73 shareholders • Consulting viticulturist Kobus van Graan (VinPro) • Vineyards 1 400 ha • Production 220 000 cases 80% white 20% red • PO Box 584 Suider-Paarl 7624 • ***Tel (021) 863-3040*** *• Fax (021) 863-1240 • E-mail info@simonsvlei.co.za • Website www.simonsvlei.co.za*

Simonsvlei International, one of the first old-style Cape co-operatives to emerge as a modern, market-honed business, is now focused on farming for quality in the vineyards. In the past few vintages, their meticulous team has tasted through the 65 members' vineyards with a view to assigning each block to the appropriate tiers within the Simonsvlei range, explains MD Kobus Louw. Individual vinification of these allocated lots enabled farmers to gauge the quality of their vineyards, gleaning invaluable insights into managing their farms better in the process and, of course, ultimately fetching higher prices for upgraded grapes. A computer system keeps track of where each batch of wine was grown. A real win-win situation in the making for the Simonsvlei brand and the growers alike.

Hercules Paragon range

☆ **Cabernet Sauvignon 98** unusually streamlined modern Paarl cab; savoury/earthy with tobacco whiffs over minerally strawberry fruit. Ripe but firm tannins suggest could age further. Yr new oak. 12.9% alc. 2 000 cases.

☆ **Merlot** Med/light-bodied **98** ready for your enjoyment; savoury mellowness now a hallmark which much liked by *Wine* panel, who awarded ☆. 100% new oak, 70% Fr, remainder Am. 1 000 cases.

☆ **Shiraz** Initially-austere **98** has ripened in bottle, acquired fuller plummy profile plus signature varietal aromas of woodsmoke, clove, cinnamon. Ready now, should go few more yrs. 10 mths Fr/Am (80/20) casks. 13.4% alc. 1 000 cases. 13% alc. Michelangelo gold medal. **97** VVG, SAA, wine mail order club selection.

☆ **Sauvignon Blanc** Nod to the old world in austere, bone-dry **00** with spread 'green' flavours; peaking, drink (with food) within 12 mths. Med/full-bodied. 700 cases.

Simonsvlei range

☆ **Shiraz** ✓ Attractive lightly-oaked example with richer, plummier textures in **00** than pvs herby/savoury **99**. Bigger alc (13.5%) in **00** doesn't upset balanced, accessible style. 2nd fill Fr oak.

☆ **Cabernet Sauvignon-Merlot** ✓ Improved claret-style **00** with minty/gummy dimensions; 50/50 blend yields approachable fruity palate with ample soft minerally tannins for now or 4-6 yrs. Partly oaked. Lowish 12% alc. **99** sweetly ripe palate and soft dry finish; without pretensions.

✵**Humbro Red Jerepico** ✓ Well fleshed **NV** winter warmer from red muscadel, fortified to 17% alc. Balanced sweetness. WOM selection.

✵**Humbro Hanepoot** ✓ Latest **NV** bottling raises quality stakes (and value – still ±R13 ex winery!) Perfumed honeysuckle, freesia bouquet; sweet and spiritous yet light and refreshing. Lightly chill for unadorned enjoyment, or pour over ice for a fragrant summer cooler.

✵**Premier White Muscadel** ✓ Invariably excellent unctuously sweet fortified; released in tiny parcels and premium priced. More luscious than jerepigos above. Current **96** golden robed, developing fragrant nutty/peach-kernel tones in lengthy honeyed conclusion. Moderate 17.4% alc. Pvs **95** *Wine* ✵.

✵**White Port** Individual example and one of small handful in Cape. **99** not ready for tasting. **98** curious spread of sensations, tropical fruit to hazelnuts to peppery vanilla. Chenin, developing well in bottle.

Cabernet Sauvignon ⁂ Undemanding med/full-bodied **00** with signature rhubarb twang, well toned tannins. Full-bodied (13.6% alc) and lightly oaked, as is ... **Pinotage** ⁂ Drink-soon styling, lightish bodied; **00** unremarkable with bone-dry finish needing rustic food companions. **Chardonnay 01** not ready for tasting. **Premier Chenin Blanc** ⁑ Explosion of fruit turns bracingly dry in palate of **01**, lightish bodied and needful of a rich food contrast. **Sauvignon Blanc** ⁑ Light-bodied **01** very fresh, zippy, dry. **Premier Bukettraube** ⁑ **01** uncomplicated semi-sweet; lightly floral with zesty acidic finish and lightish 11.5% alc. **Port** ⁂ Old-style fortified; pinotage with shiraz/tinta. **97** gaining marked savouriness, nice lifting spirit in finish. **96** similar smoky/ savoury prune aromas.

Mount Marble range

Vin Doux ☻ ⁂ Sherbety sweet carbonated sparkler with bright, mouth-filling foam; straightforward yet satisfying. Low ±8% alc.

Simonsrood ⁂ Popular everyday red combo cinsaut, cab, ruby cab. Med-bodied **NV**. Nice-and-easy 12.3% alc. **Blanc de Blanc** ⁑ **NV** Bone dry and austere chenin. **Riesling** ⁑ Recognisably Cape riesling; dry-hay tones in lightish, crisp finishing **01**. Suggest drink early. **Stein** ⁑ Light bodied off-dry **NV** marries chenin, colombard, Cape riesling. Finishes with citrus twist. **Late Vintage** ⁂ **NV** Supple, sweet flavours and honeyed/floral scents. Lightish no-frills chenin with enough acidity for now – but not for keeping. 3 000 cases.
Discontinued: **Semillon** (Pvs **99** ✵), **Bouquet Blanc** (**NV** ⋆), **Special Late Harvest** (**99** ⁑). — *DH*

Simunye

Joint-venture label between California's outstanding lady of wine, Zelma Long, and her viticultural consultant husband Phil Freese. Made in the Backsberg cellars, distributed in SA and the US. To date a Sauvignon Blanc (**98** ✵, **99** ✵); grapes from Durbanville. This label eventually will adorn bottles with the Long and Freese grapes grown on their joint-venture vineyards with Michael Back at Paarl. The vineyards, planted in 1998, will be devoted to the two cabernets and merlot and have been established with exceptional care.

Sinnya

Afro-accented brand ('Sinnya' the San equivalent of 'Breede River'), grown by various Robertson winefarmers and owned/marketed by Vinimark.

Pinotage ☆ Nice juicy mouthful. **00** youthful banana/mulberry fruits, vibrant tannins. 13% alc. **Merlot-Cabernet Sauvignon** ☆ **00** with splash ruby cab, lightly oaked. Minerally, softly fruity. Med-bodied. **01** preview (sans ruby cab) similar, attractively charry. **Chardonnay** ☆ **01** quieter than pvs; gentle; some vanilla tones. **Colombard-Chardonnay** ☆ **01** light, dry pineappley quaffer. — *DH*

Siyabonga

Wellington • Not open to the public • Owners Graham Knox & Alain Moueix • Winemaker Etienne Charrier (since 2000) • Viticulturist Francois Baard (since 1999) • Vineyards 12 ha • Production 5 000 cases (1 350 own label) 60% red 40% white • PO Box 1209 Wellington 7654 • ***Tel (021) 864-3155*** *• Fax (021) 864-1744 • E-mail doolhof@mweb.co.za*

Not so long ago Siyabonga (it means 'we give thanks', and if you're Africa-seasoned the traditional accompanying double handclap instantly comes to mind) was a supplier of grapes to Bovlei Co-op. But this farm, in a tiny Wellington valley completely ringed by mountains, had a few terroir tricks up its sleeve. Pomerol supremo Alain Moueix pinpointed a few in a 97 study: deep, well-drained Malmesbury shale soils rich in clay (mostly on steep slopes, not without practical problems which involved building new roads as vehicles tended to slip-slide away in wet weather); a high rainfall with underground water drainage all year round; consistent exposure to moderately strong south-easterly winds; less hours of direct sunlight and extended twilights in summer, as the sun rises and sets over the mountains; a longer winter and later harvests. All this means crops are left absurdly small, wines suitably striking. Vineyards also produce well into old age – many are around 30 but try a 90-something semillon vineyard for longevity! Close to Graham and Diane Knox's hearts is the SA Wine Industry Trust-funded literacy, life-skills and empowerment programme, a model for the valley, opening up new worlds and opportunities for workers and their dependents.

☆☆ **Cabernet Sauvignon-Merlot** NEW Striking **00** bears assured claret profile (real Fr influence derives from winemaker, Etienne Charrier; elevation under watchful eye of Bordelais Alain Moueix. Regrettably also entire production exported to France). Immediately distinctive with sustained minerality topping elegant, streamlined cedary, berry smells (though variety plays second fiddle to style in this 50/50 blend). Beguiling soft entry, layers tobacco, cassis, leaves unfold with deliberate understatement yet absolute satisfaction. Deliciously savoury, long tannins remind of necessity for min 6-8 yrs' further maturation. Own chenin-overgrafted vines, 20+ yrs old. 13.5% alc. Fr oak, 40% new, 13 mths.

☆ **Pinotage 00** same genre as statement **99**; attracts attention with swathes of massive ripe fruit – prunes, plums, mulberries (purer pinotage than many overly made-up with new oak). Rich, muscular palate with recurring layers sweet red fruits, more unusual savoury finish; extraordinarily smooth, elastic tannins ensure youthful pleasure, provide guts to improve good 5 yrs. Low-yielding (4 t/ha) vyd on own farm. Partly barrel-fermented/aged yr new/2nd fill Fr oak.

☆ **Severney** One of few to focus on *premium* white blend ("rest of the Cape chases after varietal sauvignon, chardonnay or chenin," explains Graham Knox). Tastefully crafted equal mix barrel-fermented semillon, chardonnay, chenin freshened with unwooded chenin, sauvignon. **01** ☆ unusual herbal, tropical, grassy nose/flavours create unique profile ("subtle enough to make excellent partner with Japanese cuisine"); sinewy, chewy, firm, smoothly dry. 13% alc. Pvs **00** quietly delicious. — *AL*

Slaley Cellars 

*Stellenbosch (see Stellenbosch map) • Tasting by appointment • Sales Mon-Fri 9-4 Sat & public holidays by appointment • Owners Hunting family • Winemaker Christopher van Dieren (since 1998) • Vineyard manager Jaco Mouton (since 1999) • Vineyards 80 ha • Production 450 tons (150 tons/12 000 cases own label) 90% red 10% white • PO Box 119 Koelenhof 7605 • **Tel (021) 882-2123** • Fax (021) 882-2798 • E-mail chris@slaley.co.za • Website www.slaley.co.za*

It's full steam ahead for the enterprising Hunting family, marine and aeronautical constructors by tradition and latterly, with prime landholdings in Stellenbosch's gilded Simonsberg area, vintners by meticulous design. With Bordeaux-trained Christopher van Dieren at winemaking helm, they've charted a course to stylistic classicism and restraint, Lindsay Hunting stating: "We're not at all convinced that a new world philosophy is the way to go in SA. We need to return to proven old-world values while developing our own individual styles." Their approach chimes with the latest international trends, so it's unsurprising that they're reeling in plaudits at wine selections (a prestigious gold medal at the Hong Kong IWC for their Cabernet-Merlot one recent example; closer to home, a rare SA *Wine* ✰✰ rating for their Slaley Shiraz) as well the admiration of consumers world-wide for their flagship Slaley label and strikingly packaged Broken Stone range. Neither ready for tasting for this edition; previous have included **Hunting Family Shiraz**, **Hunting Family Merlot**, **Hunting Family Chardonnay**; Broken Stone range: **Cabernet Sauvignon-Merlot**, **Cabernet Sauvignon-Shiraz**, **Cabernet Sauvignon**, **Pinotage**, **Sauvignon Blanc**.

Slanghoek Winery 

*Worcester (see Worcester map) • Tasting & sales Mon-Fri 8-12.30, 1.30-5.30 Sat 10-1 • Cellar tours by appointment • Grietjiesdrift Guesthouse & Restaurant 100 m from cellar, open daily • Tourgroups • Walks • Views • Owners 25 members • Winemakers Kobus Rossouw (since 1993), Henri Swiegers (since 1996) & Christo Pienaar (since 1998) • Viticulturist Francois Nel • Vineyards 1 600 ha • Production 24 000 tons (12 000 cases own label) 82% white 18% red • PO Box 75 Rawsonville 6845 • **Tel (023) 349-3026** • Fax (023) 349-3157 • E-mail slanghoek@lando.co.za • Website www.slanghoek.co.za*

The team from this Worcester cellar traipsed back to the picture-perfect Slanghoek Valley after last year's National Young Wine Show clanking with awards: the Pietman Hugo trophy, awarded to cellarmaster Kobus Rossouw and his crew for the fifth consecutive year; the trophy for the SA Champion Noble Late Harvest (third year in a row); and the SA Champion Muscat Fortified Wine crown, proudly worn by the Red Muscadel Jerepigo. These royal results pay tribute to the vines that now languish in five-star comfort at the 25 members' vineyards, with neutron water-sensors and weather stations monitoring their every need. If you're the outdoors type, try the scenic Slanghoek hiking trail but be warned, you could land up in hot water – it leads to the Goudini Spa (and a welcome mineral soak for tired muscles). If that doesn't warm you up enough, their very pocket-pleasing Port will do the trick.

✰**Camerca** NEW Promising classically styled bdx blend, this cellar's first; equal portions merlot, cabs s/f; attractive thatch/redcurrant scents and some good taut tannins in **99**. For now and 3-4 yrs. 600 cases.

✰**Chardonnay Private Reserve** Deftly handled **00** maturing harmoniously; delicious refined brioche/pineapple tones which should be enjoyed soon. Fr barrel-fermented. SAYWS class winner. 600 cases. 13.5% alc.

✰**Natural Sweet** NEW **00** delicate mouthful of peaches, scented flowers; luscious sweetness balanced by bright fruit acids. For delicious starter, try with prosciutto-wrapped melon. VG. 200 cases.

Noble Late Harvest ✓ At its best one of SA's finest botrytised desserts. **99**, SA champion NLH, and first release **98** both from riesling. Formula change to 50/50 chenin/hanepoot in **00** and upcoming **01**. Back-tasted mid-01, **00** up to speed of pvs after pedestrian start. **01** preview appears less characterful. Botrytis less obvious; fruitier, lighter toned/weighted. Consider rating provisional, however – track record suggests these improve in bottle. 350 cases (375 ml).

Port ✓ Since **97** in more modern style, less sweet than pvs. **98** from cinsaut, Ruby Port category winner at 2000 Diners Club; mature strawberry jam aromas, hints of forest footpaths; med-dry at 113 g/ℓ sugar. 17.5% alc. 400 cases.

Chenin Blanc ☻ Attractive fruit-salady **01**; pear-drops and peach tones; refreshing cut of acid. Med-bodied, just off-dry. 1 000 cases. **Sauvignon Blanc** ☻ Complex, harmonious **01** from cool vyd site, which shows in citrus crispness; med-bodied, dry finish. 800 cases. **Chardonnay-Sauvignon Blanc** ☻ Intriguing marzipan whiffs and exotic spices in full-bodied, fruity **01** just-dry white. As pvsly, 50/50 blend with low-altitude 11,5% alc.

Cabernet Sauvignon Obvious vanilla-spice in **99** will appeal to fans of an oakier style. Yr 1st fill Fr barrels. 13.5% alc. 800 cases. **Pinotage Private Reserve** Light-textured (though big – 13.8% alc), easy drinking **00**, not a 'Reserve' style. Gamey sniffs, med-weight spicy palate; 3 mths Fr oak. 800 cases. **Shiraz Private Reserve** Plum/prune aromas in refined **00**, step up from pvs; appears med-bodied though alc is high (13.8%); Rhone-like spice, potpourri wafts; well handled oak. 800 cases.

Riesling-Semillon Hugely popular, inexpensive 50/50 blend crouchen, semillon; straw, honey nuances in **01**; lemony dry finish. Lowish 11,5% alc. 1 500 cases. **Vinay** Supple, light off-dry quaffer; **NV** blend sauvignon, chenin, colombard. 1 000 ml. 2 000 cases. **Special Late Harvest** Candy, jasmine scented **01**, sweet, light, fruity mouthful; good sugar-acid tension for effortless sipping. 100% hanepoot. 800 cases. **Sparkling Wine NV** Sweet sparkling not available for tasting. Pvs . **Vin Doux** Moscato d'Asti style **NV** delicate grapey carbonated sparkler; refreshingly frothy, not too sweet. Low 10.5% alc.

Red Jerepiko Penetratingly sweet fortified dessert. **00** showcases pinotage's aromatic red fruits, plus choc-cake/plum flavours. SAYWS gold. 18.4% alc. 600 cases. **Red Muscadel** NEW Good **00** winter warmer, though not typically muscat; unusual linseed oil/terpene character. 17% alc. 600 cases. **Sweet Hanepoot** This cellar known for delicate, elegant muscat fortified desserts; latest **98** unusually full, sweet, spiritous. Intense, almost 'oily' musk/honeysuckle bouquet; atypical but should age well. 16.7% alc. 500 cases. — *TM*

Snake River see Linton Park

Somerbosch Wines

Stellenbosch (see Helderberg map) • Tasting & sales Mon-Fri 9-5 Sat 9-1 • Cellar tour by arrangement • Views • Wheelchair-friendly • Owner Roux family • Winemakers Marius & Japie Roux • Viticulturist Marius Roux • Vineyards 80 ha • Production ± 700 tons (250 tons 15 000 cases own label) 60% red, 40% white • PO Box 12181 Die Boord 7613 • ***Tel (021) 855-3615*** *• Fax (021) 855-4457 • E-mail enquiries@somerbosch.co.za • Website www.somerbosch.co.za*

This family farm may be midway between Somerset West and Stellenbosch but don't expect any halfway measures. Living life at full tilt are winemaking brothers Marius and Japie Roux, who see to the burgeoning range of wines in the cellar (in between fishing expeditions to out of the way places). They released their previously export-only Pinotage Reserve (the 99 vintage) locally for the first time last year. The range isn't the only part of the extended Somerbosch family that's growing: Marius and Yolande Roux's second son, Tiaan, was born during last year's harvest, and Japie and Sally Roux's first baby, Amy, made her appearance the spring before – all suitably seasonal for a family living and working in such close harmony with nature.

Cabernet Sauvignon ✓ Returns to form in **00**, sweet ripe fruit more in mode of succulent **98** than stricter, herbal **99**. Latest pleasantly firm, well supported by yr oak, mainly Fr, 10% new. Best in 3-5 yrs. 13.7% alc. 2 100 cases.

Merlot ✓ Invariably good here. Latest **00** with 10% new oak fillip and enormous 15% alc, buoyantly fruity. Youthfully exuberant tannins need time (and will see wine to likely maturity in 3-5 yrs). Yr Fr/Am oak. 2 000 cases. **98** markedly softer in youth.

Pinotage ✓ Settling into its own style: full, almost brash, uncommonly aromatic. **99** with tomato-jam quirkiness; **00** sample, when tasted mid-01, unyielding; needed bottle ageing to get up to speed. 50% new oak, balance unwooded. 1 000 cases.

Seugnet Blanc (Say: soo-*nay*) Bright outdoorsy tipple with pre-packed picnic of tropical fruit, tinned asparagus. Med-bodied, dry.

Cabernet Sauvignon-Merlot Reserve Occasional label; to date maiden **95** (unrated); **97** which evolved into smooth, satisfying food wine. **Seugnet Rouge** Partly-oaked cinsaut (60%), cab blend; **00** soft, easy, with hint of tannin for standalone or tableside sipping. 13.6% alc. 3 000 cases. **Chardonnay** For early pleasure. Ripe, fresh peach/tropical fruit in **01** preview, enervating crispness. **Chenin Blanc Reserve Natural Sweet** NEW Soft yet balanced **00**, not oversweet; exotic fruit flavours evolve nicely in palate. Suggest enjoy soon while blossom-fresh. 87.5 g/ℓ sugar; 13.5% alc. 375 ml. 600 half-cases. **Chenin Blanc** Unwooded **01** not ready for tasting. **Sauvignon Blanc** Comfortable, light-toned **01**; ripe gooseberries in crisp dry finish. 13% alc. 1 200 cases. **Port** Cape rather than Douro-inspired **NV** from cab; pleasant, undemanding; good spicy/spiritous qualities. ± 18% alc. 450 cases. —*DH*

Sommelier's Choice see Wine Concepts
Sonnigdal see Goue Vallei
Sonop see African Terroir

Southern Right Cellars

Walker Bay • Tasting & sales at Wine Village (see Hermanus Heritage Collection) • Owners Anthony Hamilton Russell & Kevin Grant • Winemaker Kevin Grant (since 1994) • Viticulturist Stephen Roche (since 1998) • Vineyards 23 ha • Production 140 tons 10 000 cases 70% white 30% red • PO Box 158 Hermanus 7200 • ***Tel (028) 312-3595*** *• Fax (028) 312-1797 • E-mail hrv@hermanus.co.za*

VINTAGE 2001 was a milestone for the Anthony Hamilton Russell and Kevin Grant-owned venture, currently operating out of the HRV cellar in the Hemel-en-Aarde Valley but soonish to get its own "simple, small and focused" (on pinotage, the all-SA diva here, co-starred by sauvignon) vinification facility. Rows on their 113-hectare farm neighbouring HRV came into production in 01, as did two joint-venture pinotage plantings in the Walker Bay area. "It was tremendously exciting to see the highly individual character and wonderful quality of fully-ripe, clay-grown, cooler-climate pinotage," enthuse the pair. "Our Pinotage will certainly be 'something different' and, we hope, a new direction for the future." Meanwhile the Sauvignon is growing apace and finding a popular place in upscale eateries (including moveable feasts such the recent Robben Island fundraiser featuring Hillary Rodham Clinton and Bill Cosby). Their reactions are undocumented, but probably echo British super-palate Steven Spurrier: "... a sophisticated, ripe wine."

Pinotage Always a top contender, this label steps up with drop-dead-gorgeous **01**, assured, suave-textured, expressive in the less challengingly austere style unveiled with **99**. No lack of classicism, however: nervy riverstone coolness runs though massed, sweet-oaky ripe cherries/plums, trailing Indian spice and signature ripe banana. Sample tasted; projected 12 mths casking. W/Bay, Stbosch fruit. 2 800 cases. **99** better fleshed than pvs, with no pinotage acetone or bitterness. **98** as big as these (14% alc) but tighter on release. **97** ABSA Top 10, *Wine*.

Sauvignon Blanc Complex cool-climate sauvignon, super-reductively made (latest **01** picked from 3 am!; "literally hundreds of kg of dry ice used") – all worth the effort, happily. Real oyster-zing from nose to tail, smoothed by slightly sweet nettle/gooseberry fruit. W/Bay, Overberg fruit. 12.8% alc. 6 500 cases. **00** more sappy, demandingly fresh than pvs. —*JN*

Spar

PO Box 1589 Pinetown 3600 • ***Tel (031) 701-8401*** *or (012) 998-4737* • *Fax (031) 701-2030 or (012) 998-4738* • *E-mail saexvino@mweb.co.za; ray.edwards@spar.co.za*

"There's a friendly Spar wherever you are", reads the marketing slogan of this national supermarket group. Beyond a wide selection from some leading wineries, Spar offers its own Country Cellars and Carnival ranges (see separate entries). These are selected and managed by an independent wine panel according to very specific styles. The recently-launched Spar Wine Club sources special wines for its members including lots from the Nederburg Auction, where Spar buyers have been snapping up record quantities for two years running.

Spice Route Wine Company

Swartland (see Swartland map) • *Tasting & sales at Fairview (see that entry)* • *Cellar tours by appointment* • *Owner Charles Back* • *Winemaker Eben Sadie (since 1998)* • *PO Box 645 Malmesbury 7299* • ***Tel (022) 487-7139*** • *Fax (022) 487-7169*

"I'm married to this terroir," says committed winemaker Eben Sadie (so passionate about the subject he looks for the exit sign before he starts discussing wine in case he rubs someone up the wrong way), though he's been around the world to find his own rhythm. He currently fits in a second harvest at Clos Martinet in Priorato, an isolated mountain region in Spain, that "speaks with magnitude" – small wonder, with wines up to a hefty 18% alcohol by volume. Back in the Swartland, he's more than found his stride with four vintages behind him and wines that, in turn, speak with eloquence of this region's undoubted class. His goal now is to be able to present a minimum of five consistently excellent vintages to tasters and buyers internationally. The wine world is pumping, according to this fervent surfer and he's ready to ride the wave. "There are people out there who make a special wine just to go with their lunch. I want to learn from them. But some day I'm going to take a holiday that doesn't involve wine, just go surfing in Indonesia ..."

'Flagship' range

Syrah One of thrilling new-genre SA shirazes, smilingly approved by Gérard Chave, probably world's greatest exponent of Hermitage (syrah): "Very good, fine expression of syrah." Superb **99** (accorded further Fr recognition via Air France 01 judges, who placed it among top ten reds; also hailed by IWSC) drawing together individual threads displayed yr ago, though still very much (delicious) infant. Encapsulates power/grace of variety; concentrated opulence, overall 'darkness' of character (black spice, roasted meat, savouriness) add to richness, veiled complexity. "Will take years to mature – 15?" speculates Eben Sadie. 18 mths Fr barrelled, 30% new. Perfectly balanced 14.5% alc, 6.1 g/ℓ acid. For all sophistication, has warm, 'big bear' personality of **98** *Wine* ✵.

✵✵ **Merlot** Also drew plaudits from Gérard Chave: "More expressive of grape than in America; very good". Striking **99** ✵✵ developing broad meaty tones, now augmenting area's red earth nuances, underpinned by macerated red plums, dark bitter choc. Soft, resonatingly rich yet concentrated/structured; firm, dry tannins enhance echoing, spicy intensity. Assured follow-up to impressive **98**, Air France finalist. Sympathetically, thoughtfully oaked (as are all these): 18 mths, all Fr, 50% new. 14,3% alc.

✵✵ **Pinotage** More obvious varietal character of **99** ✵✵ now retreating, giving way to complex savoury richness with toasty Fr oak influence, offsetting overall viscosity, creaminess. In same genre as massive, inky **98**, thoroughly modern, classy individual. Despite size, concentration (minuscule 2.5 t/ha yield) and assertive (though glossy) tannins, nothing vulgar, out of place with this individual. *Wine* ✵✵. 13,5% alc. 18 mths Fr barriques, 40% new.

'Standard' range

✵ **Shiraz 00** most assured, personality-driven of 3 vintages to date (though **99** no slouch); gives tantalising hint of future form of 00 Flagship above. Resonating roasted meat, savoury spice, warm red earth; repeated in palate with breadth, richness yet utmost delicacy. Finest, driest tannins, minerally focus allow full expression of (Swartland) fruit; complemented by Am oak. Deceptively approachable; will reward with further complexity over next 6-8 yrs. 14% alc. 1 800 cases. 14 mths Am oak, 33% new. **99** brooding Fr style: deep, dark, minerally, savoury; bolstered by 14,5% alc.

✵ **Pinotage** Each pinotage here has own identity – though all display uncommon tannin/fruit refinement. Here, smoky spicy infusion of quality Am oak creates subtle interplay with pinotage's similar fruitiness, though overall impression is of European sophistication. **00** of same family as **99**; gorgeous, silky concentration; light-textured with dry, filigree tannins; total absence of bitterness. Colours here tempo with general elegance: brilliant, saturated. Unheavy 14% alc. Worth cellaring 6-8 yrs. Magnificent double-trophy at IWC 01: Best Value Red, Pinotage of Year. 14 mths Am oak, 45% new. 4 500 cases.

✵ **Cabernet Sauvignon-Merlot 00** returns to more outgoing mode of **98** *Wine* ✵ after subtlety, restraint of **99**; also reflects hot, dry vintage's spectrum meaty, red earth generosity, emphasises sense of Swartland origin more than just its varietal make up. Perhaps also not too soon to identify cellar's thumbprint purity, finely manicured, dry tannins, sensitive oaking. 14% alc. Like others, should cope with/benefit from 6-8 yrs maturation. 14 mths Am oak, 40% new . 2 000 cases.

✵✵ **Chenin Blanc** Integrity of this label, whole range enhanced by refusal to release vintage, as in **00**: "not up to high standard set by the others". **99** ✵ less extrovert than dazzling **98** though lacks nothing in style, personality; could well out-live predecessor. Ripe canned mango, passion fruit, pineapple, overlaid with some oxidative decadence; palate similarly linear, tight, emphasises purity of fruit, also sturdy 14% alc. **98** similar treatment, analysis; more lushness. Both barrel-fermented, older Fr oak, 8 mths sur lie. From 36 yr old bushvines. Unfined/ filtered.

✵ **Viognier** Having pvsly dangled carrot with **00** one-barrel wonder, we'd hoped to bring news of larger quantities of **01**; sadly "birds damaged the isolated vineyard to such an extent, there was not even one berry in sight, let alone enough to make one barrel," Sadie reports. On upside, bigger vyd starts bearing this yr. Maiden **00** electrifying, subtly scented with dried apricot, wild flowers, herbs; richly textured, graceful yet packed with spicy vibrancy, power. Concentration from minuscule yield – 1 bunch per vine – from less than 1 ha. Barrel-fermented, 3rd fill Fr oak.

Andrew's Hope range

Sauvignon Blanc ✓ 01 perfectly fits entry level bill (as do all these) for drinkers wanting honest wine at honest price; readily recognisable herbaceous, asparagus freshness comfortably stretched over lees-padded palate. Ripe, properly dry finish completes easy-yet-interesting profile. Enjoy while youthfully charming, before end 02. 5 500 cases.

Pinotage NEW Introduced for "those who need meatier entry level red". From young vyds. Pleasantly restrained smoky/sweet fruit; bigger feel than blend below, featuring pinotage's assertive though fine tannins, approachable lush juiciness. 13% alc. Combo Fr oak staves/barrels. 2 500 cases. **Cabernet Sauvignon-Merlot 00** uncomplicated but not simple red fruits laced with oak spice, vanillins; throat-hugging silkiness resolving into easy yet firm, dry finish. 50/50 blend, Fr oak staves. 13,8% alc. Well priced. 5 500 cases. —*AL*

Spier

'BATTLE of the Spiers resolved' announced the headlines recently, ending a protracted legal duel between the proprietors of the 'Spier' resort complex on Stellenbosch's Lynedoch road and the owners of the name 'Spier Wine Estate', operating from the Polkadraai Hills farm Goedgeloof, over custodianship of this famous old-Cape name. After much Spier-rattling it's been agreed the resort will buy the marque and, in due course, rebrand its Spier Cellars/IV Spears wine ranges. 'Spier Wine Estate', meanwhile, will go forward with their own successful brand, Kanu (see also separate entries). "Now that agreement over the name has been reached," read the official statement, "both farms are able to focus their energies into the continued production of quality wines." Moving on ...

Spier Cellars

Stellenbosch (see Stellenbosch map) • Tasting & sales daily 9-5 Tasting fee R6 p/p informal tasting, R12 p/p conducted tasting • Cellar tours by appointment • Jonkershuis & Taphuis restaurants, also Farmstall • Luxury hotel • Tourgroups • Conferences/banqueting • Gift shop • Conservation area • Facilities for children • Vintage train • Walks • Views • Wheelchair-friendly • Owner Winecorp • Winemaker Frans Smit (since 1995) • Viticulturist Gerrie Wagener (Afrika Vineyards) since 2000 • Vineyards 75 ha • Production 2 800 tons 40% red 60% white • PO Box 1078 Stellenbosch 7660 • ***Tel (021) 809-1143*** *• Fax (021) 809-1144 • E-mail francoisvdw@spier.co.za • Website www.spier.co.za*

IT would be easy for the Spier range of wines to be upstaged. Often a first winelands stop, the Spier complex has burgeoned into a veritable village, with an annual summer programme of rare and stirring performances in the open-air amphitheatre, one hotel built, another soon to follow, a Peter Matkovich-designed golf course, a vintage train, cheetah park, multiple restaurants, gourmet picnic baskets to spread out on the lawns, ducks to feed, ponies to ride, local arts and crafts to snap up. Then the upgraded cellar now produces 2 500 tons under Winecorp's auspices and acts as HQ for the viticulture services through Afrika Vineyards, overseen by Gerrie Wagener (four vineyards, including 100 hectares, mostly replanted with sauvignon blanc, chardonnay, cabernet, merlot, pinotage and shiraz, at Spier; 25 growers). But the wines certainly aren't showing any signs of lack of attention: Smit continues to keep his focus on the range as sharp as ever.

Private Collection

Cabernet Sauvignon *Wine*, VVG accolades for pvs **98**, classic Cape style with excellent ageing potential (5-7 yrs). Following **99** more forward, less attention-grabbing. Open, sweetish, though some unripe tones don't suggest seriousness implicit in wine's price or good Fr oak input. May gain integration if not more gravitas with further yr/2. Yr 70% new Fr oak. 13% alc.

Merlot 99 fruit-focused (typical of vintage) but plenty of stuffing (and new oak) for weightier, cellar-worthy profile. But alluring red plum robe, spicy accessibility, integrated tannins, overall balanced demeanour will cause many corks to be pulled soon. Age should see more savoury development, though expect 5 rather than 10 yr wine. 13.5% alc. **98** *Wine*, VVG. These 14 mths 100% new Fr oak.

Sauvignon Blanc ✓ 01 as intoxicating as sauvignons can get. Oozes class from shimmering steely glints to cool, tingling finish. In between, pure ripe fruit glides purposefully across palate; powerhouse of gooseberry/minerals intensity. Balance rounds off wine which should be up with yr's best. 13.6% alc. 3 000 cases. Technically off-dry **00** success story in less-than-storied vintage.

Noble Late Harvest 98 now upgraded, quite rightly, to PC range. Maturing gracefully; nutty richness brings further delicious dimension to spice, dried-apricot bouquet with botrytis undertones. Perfect pairing of silky opulence, zippy freshness matched by clean, spicy length. Harmonious partnership should continue for several yrs. Surprisingly delicate feel for 13,5% alc, 138 g/ℓ, 18 mth spell in used Fr oak. From old-vine bukettraube. 8 g/ℓ acid.

Regular' range

Cabernet Sauvignon Frans Smit's answer to achieving accessibility in difficult, dry **00** is to leave teaspoon sugar. Works in showing off ripe briary fruit, minimising severer tannins (though purists looking for dryness will dislike sweet tail). Light chilling could benefit all. Well-proportioned **99** modern version of traditional Cape style. 13% alc. 20 000 cases.

Chenin Blanc Barrel-fermented ☻ Subtle oaking in **00** highlights delicate floral/honey nuance; firm, flavoursome; gains length rather than sweetness from soupcon sugar. Moderate 12.5% alc. **Bouquet Blanc** ☻ **01** blend (riesling, semillon) somewhat offbeat, but result no oddball: sophisticated fusion lime/pepper/honey in broad, luscious palate. Tangy fruit tail lengthened by poised acid; well camouflaged sugar.

Merlot NEW Follows approachable lightly-oaked style of rest of range; **00** gentle plum/chocolate scents; charm curbed in palate by greenish slightly bitter tannins. Probably best over next 12-18 mths with richer dishes. 13.5% alc. **Pinotage** **00** in summery mood; lighter feel than even 12.5% alc would suggest; straightforward red plums/currants bouquet, flavours. Picnic fare such as salami or other rich sausage will alleviate characteristic astringency. 30% Fr oak-matured, 8 mths. **Chardonnay** **00** uncomplicated crowd-pleaser. Cellar's usual aromatic melange of spice, citrus, toast, obvious but well balanced. Fat and juicy; generous chilling should help cut rather cloying sweet vanilla finish. 60/40 cask/tank-fermented. 13% alc. **Sauvignon Blanc** **01** sparks with lively grassy aromatics; green theme continues in palate but in austere rather than weighty mode; bracing dry finish. 13% alc. Discontinued: **Symphony** (pvsly unrated). —*AL*

Springfield Estate

Robertson (see Robertson map) • Tasting & sales Mon-Fri 8-5 Sat 9-4 • Cellar tours by appointment • BYO picnic • Play area for children • Walks • Views • Owners Abrie & Jeanette Bruwer • Winemaker/viticulturist Abrie Bruwer • Vineyards 150 ha • PO Box 770 Robertson 6705 • ***Tel (023) 626-3661*** *• Fax (023) 626-3664 • E-mail admin@springfieldestate.com • Website www.springfieldestate.com*

Gifted, congenitally restless iconoclast Abrie Bruwer likes to quote his late father Only those who do, foul up. Since parting with SFW in 1995 and going solo Bruwer Jnr's certainly been unafraid to *do*. His ever-bolder tweakings have made him a winemaking icon locally and abroad (but don't look for show medals Springfield seldom enters competitions). Tenaciously pursuing softer, less manipulated styles, Bruwer now ferments all but his sauvignons with naturally occurring yeasts. Such envelope-pushing inevitably results in some defeats (hence the openly admitted stock of vinegar from failed ferments) but also triumphs (see below, and watch for the upcoming Méthode Anciènne Cabernet, a ☆ in the making). Admiring sister (and sussed business partner) Jeanette Bruwer sometimes wonders why Abrie's well, … Abrie. "His father's genes," shrugs their still vigorous mother, whose sculpted Mercedes (a ricked neck makes reverse manoeuvres especially hazardous) is part of a well-seasoned fleet. "We'd rather spend money on the wines," explains Jeanette Bruwer unapologetically.

☆**Whole Berry Cabernet Sauvignon** ✓ **99** actualises long desire to revert to 'lost tradition' of whole berry winemaking (fermentation by wild natural yeasts of whole, uncrushed grapes). "Does it make any difference?" consumers will ask. The answer: "Plenty". Instant re-rating demanded by cream/mineral bouquet, unforced blackcurrant/raspberry concentration, but mostly by incredibly gentle, baby's-bottom-soft tannins. Unique, and in crowded market, uniquely underpriced. 3 wks maceration, 2 wks fermentation, 3 mths malo, yr new/2nd fill Fr oak; bottled unfiltered/stabilised. 13.6% alc. Pvs **98** ☆ shade less compelling, but chiming with Abrie Bruwer's resolute classicism.

☆**Méthode Anciènne Chardonnay** Winemaker's philosophy ("rather make a monumental stuff-up than a huge quantity of mediocre wine") taken to extreme in high-risk 'ancient Burgundian' practices: cool night harvesting sans sulphur, must oxidation, nerve-wracking 55 day native yeast fermentation, yr on lees in oak, bottled un-everything (-filtered, fined, -stabilised). Result in **99**, only 2nd successful attempt in 5 (**9**… SAA), utterly beautiful. Extraordinary. Fussy detail on how to store/serve dictated by market potentially offended by natural precipitates. We say Risk it! 14 mths 300 ℓ Vosges casks, 80% new, full malo. 13,5% alc.

☆**Wild Yeast Chardonnay** ✓ Unwooded version; natural yeast fermentation imparts extra floral dimension to usually beautiful ripe fruit. Single vyd, tank-fermented (3 mths), yr on fermentation lees sans sulphur. **99** swiftly snaffled; **0**… not ready for tasting – get it while/when you can!

☆**Special Cuvée Sauvignon Blanc** Muscular unwooded style, distinct from 'extra-flinty' version below; stamp of mature vines, particularly in **01**; creamy plump gooseberry texture, bracing but not as overtly reductively racy as sib ling, some contenders. Promise of gunpowder/flint in 2 yrs. **98** rated Top 1… on British shelves by *Weekend Telegraph*.

☆**Life from Stone Sauvignon Blanc** Abrie Bruwer considers sauvignon estate's hallmark (certainly put it on map); no more individual, strikingly differen… than this elixir eked from 70% quartz rock. **01** harvested day after Valentine' ("earliest ever"); green pepper power; passion fruit to fore, yet far more measured than others of good vintage. 12.5% alc modest by comparison, toc Pace set by maiden **99**, listed by several international carriers.

Discontinued: **Colombard-Chardonnay** (**00** ☆). — *DS*

Spruitdrift Winery

Olifants River (see Olifants River map) • Tasting Mon-Fri 8.30-4.30 • Sales Mon-Fri 8-5 Sat 8.30-12 • Cellar tours during harvest Mon-Fri 10 & 3 • Conference centre for up to 40 delegates. Book ahead • Owners 85 members • Winemaker Driaan van der Merwe (since 2000) • Consulting viticulturist Jeff Joubert (since 1996) and Pieter Daan Koegelenberg (since 2001) • Production ± 30 000 tons • PO Box 129 Vredendal 8160 • ***Tel (027) 213-3086*** *• Fax (027) 213-2937 • E-mail spruitdrift@kingsley.co.za*

This West Coast co-op, established in 1968, produces wines with a built-in quaffability factor. They're best enjoyed in the full bloom of youth so polish off now, secure in the knowledge that the next vintage holds fresh pleasures. Driaan van der Merwe, ex Franschhoek Vineyards, now fills the vinous boots here. At time of going to press, serious discussions of a merger between Spruitdrift, which has its members' vineyards stretching along the Olifants River, and nearby big brother Vredendal Winery were well underway.

★★★ **Hanepoot Jerepiko** Warming fortified drop for misty/rainy days. **99** scented with muscat, honey and sweet spice. Soft, unctuous but bright-finishing. 17.5% alc.

Cabernet Sauvignon ★★★ **00** still satisfies; red-fruity/savoury tastes with toasty nuances. 13,5% alc. Suggest drink soon. **Merlot** ★★★ Current **00** still quite tannic (though matched by ripe fruit); drink soonish with game or other full-blooded food. 13,9% alc. **Pinotage** ★★ Unwooded **00**; like pvs, unripe banana aromas, astringent tannins needing (and good with) robust casseroles etc. 13,5% alc. **Rosé** ★ Delicate coral-hued **NV** (00) past prime. Insist on new bottling. **Chardonnay** ★★ **00** hints of peach, but more vinous than fruity characters; serious acidity. 13% alc. **Chenin Blanc** ★ **00** honeyed and bracingly fresh; this – and all these whites – for drinking within yr of vintage. 13% alc. **Premier Grand Cru** ★★ Bright, tropical fruity **NV** (00), properly dry. 13% alc. Also with screwcap. **Rapsodie** ★★ Light/med-bodied semi-sweet **NV** (00); colombard/white muscadel; smooth and quite sugary. **Late Harvest** ★ Simple, honeyed semi-sweet; chenin/colombard. Lightish **NV** (00) also with screwcap.

Also available, not ready for tasting: **Cabernet Sauvignon** and **Merlot** Reserves; **Ruby Cabernet** (Pvsly rated **98** ★★★); **Shiraz** (unrated); **Sauvignon Blanc** (unrated); **Special Late Harvest** (**99** ★★★); **Sparkling Doux** (**NV** ★★★). — *DH*

Spur

This popular family steak restaurant chain links its house wines to its cow-punching Western theme. Food friendly NVs with lowish alcohols; not tasted for this ed. Previous have included: **Buffalo Red** (★★), **Desert Moon** (★★), **Autumn Rain** (★★), **Sparkling Rain** (★★).

S/SW

South/South West – "easy-drinking, sociable" wines from African Wines & Spirits in fashionable 1 000 ml bottles. S/SW geographical reference to Cape wine country.

Ruby Cabernet-Pinotage ★★★ Juicy, smooth, friendly **00**; fruitiness uncomplicated by any wooding. Pvs **99** was blend ruby cab, merlot. **Chardonnay-Chenin Blanc** ★★★ **00** Easy-going, flavoursome 50/50 blend, chardonnay adding citrusy interest; touch sugar gives softness. 13% alc. These 50 000/80 000 cases (× 6). — *TJ*

Starke Wines

Stellenbosch (see Stellenbosch map)• Tasting & cellar tours by appointment • Sales Mon-Fri 8.30-5 • Luxury B&B • Views • Owner/viticulturist Julian Starke • Winemakers Ian & Julian Starke • Vineyards 30 ha • Production 90 tons 3 500 cases 90% red 10% white • PO Box 66 Muldersvlei 7607 • ***Tel (021) 884-4433*** *• Fax (021) 884-4324 • E-mail wine@muldersvlei.co.za • Website www.muldersvlei.co.za*

A SELF-TAUGHT winemaker, 21-year-old Ian Starke was born to be just that: the spark was ignited by a winemaking book picked up at school, fanned by his first crush at the ripe old age of 18, and turned into an eternal flame by his stylish maiden 99 Pinotage. It runs in the blood: his grandfather and great-grandfather both made wines here but the equipment eventually became so out-dated that his father elected to sell the grapes to Simonsvlei (vines were first planted in 1814 and the cellar dates back to the early 1800s). Julian and Helen Barnes are delighted with their son's winemaking bent. "He's an incredibly intuitive winemaker," says his dad, pleased as punch, and modestly downplaying his own role of bringing in the prime fruit, managing the dairy and fruit orchards (where the young winemaker puts in time when not in the cellar), and generally smoothing the way.

✵**Pinotage Reserve** ✓ Whole-berry vinification in **99**, previewed mid-01 now showing suave cherry-nuanced fruit, grilled bacon touches in palate-cloaking flavours. Barrelled 14 mths, no new wood. 12.5% alc. Standard **Pinotage** Concurrently-reassessed **99** developing into exotic version of the home-grape. Mocha/toast aromas, gamey mulberries with cigarbox and sweet fruit; all very pleasing, if unorthodox. 13% alc. 13 mths oaked, no new wood. 250 cases. **00** barrel sample more recognisably pinotage; shows some comfortable rusticity.

✵**Shiraz** ✓ Steps up a rung with **00**, aromatically endowed with pepper, leather, braaivleis char. Slightly fuller, more measured than maiden **99** ✵ bricking, now almost rosé-hued yet not ephemeral in mouth. These in restrained style, mid-weight (alcs ±12.5%), evoking older Cape styles. ±13 mths older oak. 1 500/500 cases.

✵**Juliette** ✓ Interesting perspective on the above varietal bottlings from vantage of this blend of shiraz/pinotage (50/50), oaked 13 mths 3rd fill casks. Pvsly-featured **99** now with savoury touches to cherry perfume, some very nostalgic sweaty saddles. Med/full-bodied. 200 cases still full of juicy fruit, so could go into cellar or straight to table.

Chenin Blanc 00 not tasted. — *MF*

Stark Wines

Stellenbosch (see Stellenbosch map) • Tasting & sales by appointment • Owner Schröder Family Trust • Winemakers José Condé & Pieter Smit • Viticulturist Pieter Smit • Vineyards 40 ha • Production (own label) 10 tons 3 000 cases 80% red 20% white • PO Box 389 Stellenbosch 7599 • ***Tel (021) 887-3665*** *• Fax (021) 887-4340 • E-mail wine@thecapeco.com*

IT'S A LONG LEAP from the big skies of the American Midwest to Stellenbosch's craggy Jonkershoek, and from there to the top of the Cape wine table, but José Condé has made the transition with the poise of a Zen master. Recognising that "the field is still wide open for quality-focused SA producers", Kansas City-born Condé and father-in-law Hans-Peter Schröder, high-powered owner of Oude Nektar farm at Jonkershoek, launched Stark Wines in 1998 (the name a tribute to Francesca Stark, late matriarch and inspiration for the Schröder family). The first two vintages, with Schröder's wine-partner Neil Ellis consulting, went almost exclusively to one client in Japan. But last year saw the brand, with its bold in-house designed packaging, introduced to a wider export market as well as selected SA restaurants and retailers. Now the winery has its own home in a small cellar on Oude Nektar ("emphasis on very traditional winemaking – no stainless steel here!"), and its own new premium label, Condé, initially featuring a single-vineyard Cabernet and a Pinot Noir.

Cabernet Sauvignon Dream debut for this label, exuding confidence, class in wonderfully refined **98** bouquet of black-cherries, truffles, coffee; suggestions of mint and char, and the pièce de résistance: finest Japanese silk tannins – sustained, soothing, superb. Pretty much irresistible now, should improve over 5-7 years. Elegantly barrel-matured 20-22 mths. 13.5% alc. 300 cases.

Pinotage Braai wine for billionaires. Clever, well groomed yet unpretentious – gulpable, even; if only more pinotage would taste this way. **00** distinct varietal bouquet, in palate extra interest and sophistication from sleek red fruit, lightest charry touch from understated oak. Manageably proportioned (12.8% alc). 600 cases.

Chardonnay 00 new-world style with structure, balance; 50% unwooded portion creates breathing space for both the sweet fruit and the oak (Fr barrique-fermented, aged 9 mths); good leesy fullness, lemon touch in tail. Good now but better in 18-24 mths and for up to 5-6 yrs.. 13.5% alc. 400 cases.

Sauvignon Blanc ✓ Sushi-friendly **00** ripe gooseberries broadened by tropical/guava; crisp but not jarring, gentle steely/flinty bite to finish. Great now, should get better with few yrs' bottle age. Own, Darling, vyds. 13.5% alc. 400 cases. — *DH*

St Clements see Frost Vineyards

Steenberg Vineyards

Constantia (see Constantia map) • Tasting & sales Mon-Fri 8.30-4.30 Sep-Feb also Sat 9-1 Tasting fee R5 p/p for tourgroups • Cellar tours by appointment • Cape-Continental restaurant • Five-star Steenberg Country Hotel • Championship golf course • Owner Johnnies Industrial Corporation (Johnnic) • Winemakers John Loubser (since Nov 2001) & Christa von la Chevallerie (since 2000) • Viticulturist Herman Hanekom (since 1990) • Production 500 tons 38 800 cases 60% white 40% red • PO Box 224 Steenberg Estate 7947 • ***Tel (021) 713-2211*** *• Fax (021) 713-2201 • E-mail info@steenbrg.co.za or sales@steenbrg.co.za • Website www.steenberg-vineyards.co.za*

Teeing off in the cellar at this upper-crust property with its golfing estate, chic country hotel, Conran-inspired restaurant and immaculate young vineyards, established by viticultural virtuoso Herman Hanekom, is accomplished winemaker John Loubser. Most recently at Graham Beck's Robertson cellar, Elsenburg-trained Loubser (top student of his year) has been fulfilling all that earlier promise, with stints at Môreson and De Wetshof Estate behind him too. Easing him into the swing of things on his new turf will be Christa von la Chevallerie (ex Kaapzicht). Former winemaker Nicky Versfeld, an integral part of this showpiece winery in the cool Constantia valley's success (accolades by the score, clamourings both here and abroad for these elegant wines, particularly the champion Merlot and Shiraz), is stepping into the production director role at Vinfruco.

Steenberg range

Merlot This winery's charismatic queen-pin, recognisable by consistent minerally peppermint-cream distinction, combination new world flair/old world solid modulation. **00** (sample) similar dimensions as **98** but more expansive, gutsy, persistently savoury. Despite generous alc (±14%), always pleasingly endowed with fine, very dry tannins. **99** reflects vintage's mellifluous, forthcoming nature. **98** best merlot worldwide on 2000 IWSC; dense, vibrant yet soft. Yr Fr barriques, mix new/2nd fill. **CWG Merlot 00** for 01 Auction maintains family ties with standard label though grander oaking provides richer, more viscous feel. Extra tannin currently barricades usual fruit flow; will need yr/2 longer than above to attain similar pleasurableness, probably around 2006. Selection four new Fr oak barriques.

Catharina After Catharina 'Tryn' Ras, feisty four-times-widowed first owner of this historic (1682) farm; stylish and classy. **99**, immediately post bottling, oozes obvious fruity charm deriving from vintage, merlot's leadership in blend with cab, shiraz. Sound structural backing will allow it to settle, shed few sweet edges, develop the more striking complexity and savouriness of **98**. Latter (42/40/15 blend with 3% cab f) will probably outlive new release. These barrel-matured separately (yr new Fr oak), and as blend (6 mths 2nd fill). Alcs 13.5-14%. Maiden **97** cab/merlot (70/30) merges strength with elegance.

Cabernet Sauvignon Should appeal to those who find Merlot, Catharina too new-worldy. **99** and unfinished sample **00** reflect quiet sophistication of **98**; svelte insinuating cassis/cigarbox bouquet; ripeness in more ample but light-textured palate. Fine dry tannins round off most agreeable, honest cab which should provide satisfaction, if not vaulting complexity, over next 3 yrs. 13.4% alc. ±Yr Fr oak, 50% new. Also in magnums.

Pinot Noir Latest **00** alluring, providing immediate gratification thanks to lush juiciness, bright raspberry/cherry appeal squeezed into moderate body. All contained by comfortable tannin. Yr Fr oak-matured. 12.9% alc. Agreeable drinking while demonstrative **99** bides time.

Cabernet Sauvignon-Merlot-Shiraz NEW Stepping stone between Motif, Catharina in price/style, though make-up (60% cab, equal merlot/shiraz) results in individual flavour spectrum. **00** (pre-bottling sample) shows cab/shiraz combo more dominant than merlot, provides rich savouriness; merlot supportive. The whole wrapped in amicable chunky tannin. Will command both affection and respect over next 3/4 yrs.

Chardonnay (Wooded) **00** simpler, softer than more serious **99**. Confected vanilla, buttered toast flavours; apparent (though not actual) sweetness probably due to high alc, low acid (13.7%, 4.8 g/ℓ) in robust vintage. Best drunk soon with well-flavoured white meat dishes. No **01** (grapes from drastically reduced crop channelled into bubbly below).

Sauvignon Blanc Reserve ✓ Consistent quality reflected in unbroken string of awards (SAA First Class every vintage since **98**, among noteworthy gongs). Doubtless **01** will emerge from youthful cocoon to similar acclaim; probably biggest to date (in breadth, concentration rather than alc – ±13.5% as usual), but all well proportioned, balanced. Trademark power combined with grace, pure minerally persistence. WOM Reserve. **00** reflects richness of vintage. **99** SAA white wine trophy. Regular **Sauvignon Blanc** Referred to in-house as 'Loire style', from Fr clones exclusive to this label. Distinct from Reserve, more forward, luscious; **01** big, intense with compelling cool chalky thread focusing ripe figgy fruit; less ready than usual, though obviously star in making. 13.5% alc.

Semillon (Wooded) ✓ After expansive **00**, new **01** returns to tauter, grassy style reminiscent of **99**, though generously structured. Same grapes as unwooded version below but barrel fermented; oak influence tempers wilder tendencies, gives richer feel. Barrel sample tasted mid-01 should outpace all previous vintages; good 3-4 yrs' maturation potential. 13.7% alc. Fr oak fermented, some new.

Semillon (Unwooded) **01** mainly export label for Holland; almost sauvignon-like aromatic intensity, filled out with distinctive 'sweet' lemon/honeycomb richness, finishing incisively clean, dry. Deliciously modern; better balanced, focused than ultra-ripe **00**; 12.6% alc vs blustery 14%.

Steenberg 1682 Brut Second release of this **NV** cap classique equal blend of the 99/98 vintages, 70/30 chardonnay, pinot noir. Chardonnay's delicate creamy, bready nuances apparent in bouquet; pinot's bright raspberry tones enrich palate; together, strike elegant partnership, tickled to life by a fine, effervescent bubble, softening 6 g/ℓ sugar. Maiden bottling impressed with champagne-like rich, toasty lees, creamy persistence. Also in magnums.

Shiraz ☆ **00** (sample) follows elegant footsteps of pvs, with vintage's more scrumptious fruit further spiced with soupcon Am oak (majority Fr). Generosity of 13.5% alc matched by mouthfilling pepper-and-violets flavours. **Nebbiolo** ☆ Instantly recognisable red, characterised by increased colour/fruit in **00** though, overall, reflects austerity of pvs. Earthy fresh bouquet lifted by violets/cherry-kernel fragrance; gentle fruit sweetness alleviates palate's dry astringency; natural partner to richer not too strongly flavoured dishes. Yr Fr oak, 10% new; 13.5% alc. **Chardonnay** (Unwooded) ☆ For those who want to experience what chardonnay fruit (rather than oak) really tastes like, **01** offers zingy limes, ripe melons, softened by smoky, oatmeal savouriness. Richly mouthfilling, with balancing firmness and dry length. Excellent food style. 13,7% alc. Best within 18 mths of harvest. **Catharina** ☆ White bdx might be inspiration for this sauvignon/semillon blend, but profile is very Steenberg; goal is flagship white blend partner to red above. **01** (pre-bottling sample) not dominated by either component, 10% barrel-fermented semillon should become more influential with time, impart complexity, depth which currently absent.

Rosé Sec ☆ **00** has aged deliciously with sprinkling ground black pepper savouriness to ripe strawberry fruit. Attractive glimmering hue, food-friendly dryness. **01** will be composed along similar lines, from cab/shiraz; unblended at deadline. **Rosé Semi-Sweet** ☆ **01** untasted; will be same wine as above, but around 18 g/l sugar; **00** balanced, pleasant summer sip (though lacks individuality of dry version). Discontinued: **Sauvignon Blanc-Muscat**.

Motif range

Rouge Sec ☻ ☆ Not so ordinary everyday red; consistently offers quality, extra value from whole (rather than chopped/chipped) barrel ageing. Latest **00** from blockbuster yr, very ripe, juicy bdx blend cab/merlot/cab with suggestion of farm's distinctive choc-mint. Solid, dry finish. Best around mid-02. **Blanc Sec** ☻ ☆ Sprightly, medium-bodied **01**; unflamboyant mix sauvignon, semillon with subtle muscats f/a infusions. Finishing burst of fruit set off by dab sugar (3.5 g/ℓ). — *AL*

Stellekaya

Stellenbosch • Tasting by appointment on Fridays • Owner Dave Lello • Winemaker Peet le Roux (since 1998) • Viticultural consultant Eben Archer • Vineyards 18 ha • Production 50 tons 750 cases own label 100% red • PO Box 12426 Die Boord 7613 • ***Tel/fax (021) 880-1200***

With a tribal shield and the Southern Cross as motifs, this is an eclectic Afro-Italian hybrid ('Stelle', from Stellenbosch, also meaning stars; 'kaya' the Xhosa word for home). Proprietor Dave Lello is chief of a listed IT group. His passions include northern Italian art, architecture and wine (in characteristic multi-mode, he once wrote SFW's grape-procurement software). After buying part of the old Stellenrust farm in 1998, he retained Jan 'Boland' Coetzee to make the first Merlot (from an Italian clone, naturally) at nearby Vriesenhof. Subsequent vintages were vinified in Stellekaya's cellar by in-line viticulturist Peet le Roux, power-assisted by Beyers Truter. Consultant man-about-vine Eben Archer is overseeing new red plantings to join 11 hectares of mature merlot and pinotage. The top range will eventually include a blend; a second line, Emerald Glen, will follow in time. Coming soon, a Mediterranean-theme village to complete the transformation.

✪**Merlot** European style, not plush or jammy. Taut, bright **First Release 99**, fine tannic backbone to plummy/savoury tones, choc-fennel finish. 18 mths oaked. 13.5% alc. 750 half-cases. Partially barrel fermented **00**, previewed mid-01 in gangly youth, gutsier, more assertive. Some (doubtless transient) green/volatile nuances. — *TM*

Stellenbosch Farmers' Winery (Adam Tas facility)

See Stellenbosch map • Tasting & sales Mon-Fri 8.30-5 Sat 10-1 • Cellar tours Mon-Thu 10 & 2.30 Fri 10 only. Booking essential ***tel (021) 809-7599*** *• Oude Libertas Restaurant* ***tel (021) 809-7429*** *(see also Eat-out section) • Oude Libertas Amphitheatre for summer twilight concerts • Cellarmaster Callie van Niekerk • Winery manager Jan le Roux • PO Box 184 Stellenbosch 7599 •* ***Tel (021) 809-7000***

Stellenbosch Farmers' Winery has merged with Distillers Corporation to form the Distell group, yet most of Farmers' (as it was affectionately known) popular and long-lived brands – Chateau Libertas, Grand Mousseux, Graça, Sedgwick's Old Brown Sherry, Autumn Harvest Crackling, Tassenberg, Zonnebloem et al – continue. And the buzzy Stellenbosch visitor centre, with its leafy tasting area, vaulted restaurant and alfresco theatrical venue still throws open its welcoming doors. See Distell for a complete list of products featured in the guide. — *IvH*

Stellenbosch Vineyards

Tasting/sales at Welmoed and Helderberg Mon-Sat 9-5.30 Eersterivier Mon-Fri 9-5.30 Sat 9-3 Welmoed Sun 10-4 • Meals and refreshments at Welmoed (021) 881-3310 and Helderberg • Cellar (021) 842-2012 • Cellar tours by appointment • Welmoed and Eersterivier Tel (021) 881-3870 • Helderberg Tel (021) 842-2370 Fax (021) 842-2373 • Managing director Hermann Böhmer • Winemaking team at Stellenbosch Vineyards comprises of Chris Kelly (Chief Winemaker) Elizabeth Augustyn (based at Helderberg Winery) Carmen Stevens (Welmoed) and Morné van Rooyen (Eersterivier) • Viticulturist Francois de Villiers • Vineyards 2 400 ha • Production 11 000 tons (rising to 16 000 by 2006) 700 000 cases 52% red 48% white • PO Box 465 Stellenbosch 7599 • ***Tel (021) 881-3870*** *• Fax (021) 881-3102 • E-mail info@stellvine.co.za • Website www.stellvine.co.za • Viticultural info www.geocities.com/stellvine*

"Many people looking for us under Stellenbosch Vineyards can't find us on your maps," bemoans Hermann Böhmer. So allow us to set the record straight: if you're looking for a physical address, you'll find the nerve-centre of this thoroughly modern Cape dynamo (transformation of a handful of Stellenbosch cellars into one entity) on the Welmoed property (whose cellar-door sales outlet is being turned into a showcase for all the SV lines). In line with their new corporate emphasis, the front-labels across the range will now reflect the kinship among the established 'winery' brands – Welmoed, Helderberg, Eersterivier – and newer 'corporate' marques such as the flagship Genesis and super-popular Versus. In-house winemakers Elizabeth Augustyn, Carmen Stevens, Morné van Rooyen and Kiwi team-leader Chris Kelly might be based at the separate wineries but all are involved in creating the portfolio. Which, Kelly reveals, is being extended with a bevy of newcomers to the premium Kumkani range. "Increased plantings by our contract growers, particularly of noble reds," Kelly continues, "will better enable us to select prime grapes and make wines that show consistency and reliability."

Genesis range

☆☆**Merlot** NEW Current Cape mantra – ultra-ripe fruit – scales new heights here, absolutely brimming with sweet berry/cherry tastes, deep-layered with herbs, mint and something dry-undergrowthy. Enormous alc (14.6%) further distends palate. Attention-grabbing **99** tastes very good now and is poised for good development over 5/6 yrs.

☆**Shiraz** Kelly & Co seem to be specialising in fanfare wines; this is another. Maiden **97** Diners Club finalist hotly pursued by concentrated, richer **98**, achieving extra wattage yet also polish, finesse. Latest **99** ☆☆, though massive (14.2% alc), glides fairly elegantly on cherry/plum palate with cracked pepper hints, sweet-ripe flow enhanced by luxurious choc to dry finish. Yr oaking in Fr/Am (80/20) barriques well judged.

☆**Chardonnay** Worthy white counterpart to above flagships, characterised by meticulous vinification: single vyd; 40% spontaneously fermented; yr small-oaked 100% new casks. Launched with **99** which successfully walks tightrope of generosity, elegance. **00** ☆☆ patently in same mould – and higher league; beams personality from yellow-gold robe, wonderfully rich, almost comforting citrus-vanilla array; ever-present understated sweet-oak. Gorgeous. You'll want to drink it all now, but pacing the pleasure over 3/5 yrs would be the better option.

Kumkani range

☆☆**Pinotage** NEW ✓ This debutante sweeps into the ballroom with a stylish **99**, dripping luscious summer fruits and vanilla oak in style calculated to captivate. Fresh, vibrant, immediately drinkable, with some half-hidden reserves which will grow more interesting over 7/8 yrs. 14 mths barrelled, 30% new wood. Stbosch fruit. 13.4% alc.

☆**Shiraz** NEW Opaque glowerings introduce ultra-concentrated **00**, fruit-powered with downplayed savouriness. Sweet tannins control waves of cherry/plum flavours with hints of sweet-spice from 30% Am oak (remainder Fr). Mouthfilling yet balanced, even elegant, within a massive frame (14.5% alc). 2 000 cases.

☆**Merlot-Cabernet Franc** NEW Stylish, compatible and downright delectable blend (ratio undisclosed) specially for fans of aromatic styles: Provencal kitchen (plus its herb/flower garden) fragrances in **00**, cake-mix tastes and bold but supple tannins to mature 7/8 yrs. Sprig mint in the exit. Helderberg grapes barrelled in Fr oak, 60% new. 14% alc. 2 000 cases.

☆**Shiraz-Cabernet Sauvignon** ✓ After successful kick-off with **98** Diners Club finalist, **99** weighs in with plenty of guts, power (13.6% alc) but, sampled mid-01, a fruit-engine that's yet to engage fully (which it should do, given time). Meanwhile some earthy, savoury, spicy tones for the impatient to chew over. Helderberg fruit rounded 13 mths in Fr oak, 50% new.

☆**Sauvignon Blanc** ✓ Our enthusiasm for **99** *Wine* ☆ undimmed after tasting next-up **01**, featuring "secret!!" vinification techniques. Everything we liked about pvs reprised: confident intensity, fruity succulence, fresh integrated acid verve. Cool, clean feel, balanced with plenty flavour. Refreshingly manageable 13.1% alc. 2 500 cases. Ex Helderberg.

Infiniti range

☆**Shiraz MCC** ✓ First commercially available red of its kind in SA, an **NV** cap classique with plenty of personality and difference; not quite dry, yet tastes smooth rather than sweet (so comfortably partners many richly sauced meat/poultry dishes). Lively, expansive mousse exaggerates ripe berry/black cherry fruits with nuances of oak and dark choc; creamy, persistent. Drink now and over 2-3 yrs. Base-wine aged yr in Fr casks, none new. 13.1% alc.

☆**Brut MCC** ✓ Maiden **99** ripening deliciously in its rather stylish bottle, chardonnay character dominant (as it should be in 95/5 blend with pinot). Creamy biscuity mouthfilling mousse, nice toasty lees and smidgeon sugar (5 g/ℓ) cannily calibrated to give dry but-not-too-grippy feel. Good for a few yrs. 12.5% alc.

Versus range

Red ☻ ☆ Too late for inclusion in pvs guide, companionable quaff debuts here with juicy, sweet-fruited **00**, unwooded and delightful solo or with just about anything (lightly chill if necessary). Blend merlot, cab, shiraz in hugely popular 1 000 ml 'superbottle' pioneered by sibling below. Note: 13.7% alc.

White ☆ Extraordinary value available here, as zillions of devotees well know. Now in relaxed, tropical mood with honeysuckle/gooseberry extras. **01** as pvs, smooth rather than sweet. Night-harvested chenin, sauvignon.

Welmoed range

☆**Cabernet Sauvignon Reserve** ✓ Serious yet unintimidating, and hugely enjoyable company. **00** ☆ superior to pvs **99** ☆ in every way. Latest complex, fragrant; spicy/charry oak well controlled for firm, classic feel with enough juice for 4/6 yrs. Elevated yr in Fr oak. 4 000 cases.

☆**Shiraz Reserve** ✓ Varietal vibrancy a hallmark here, especially in **00**, leaning towards fruit-essencey style. Big wine (14.2% alc) but contained, not too blockbusting. Fr-barrelled. **99** with, again, plenty of grape to chew on. These good partners to Cape Malay dishes.

☆**Merlot Reserve** Latest **00**'s fruity/floral tones, soft tannins and sweet-ripe finish ought to be enjoyed now while fresh, or at most in 2/3 yrs. 12 mths Fr oak. 14% alc. Ultra-ripe **99** ☆ also for current drinking.

☆**Sauvignon Blanc Reserve** ✓ Brims with ripe figs, passion fruit in spotlessly clean, persistent **01**. As always, virtually irresistible on release with lots of octane in tank for few yrs' cellaring. 13% alc. So crustacean-friendly, should come with crayfish on a neck-tag. **00** "precision harvested" for success in difficult vintage.

Sauvignon Blanc Selection ☻ ☆ Latest **01** trumpets ripe tropical fruits and gooseberries; bouncy persistence ensures second bottle is opened immediately. 4 600 cases. **Chenin Blanc Selection** ☻ ☆ **01** almost defines gulpability with fresh Granny Smith apple and lemonade juiciness. Fairly voluminous alc (13,4%), soupcon sugar make for extra-smooth quaffing.

Helderberg range

☆**Cabernet Sauvignon** ✓ Reflects vim now found among all these ranges. **00** ripe-fruit-driven, bouquet of strawberries comes with some pleasing earthy tones; no wood evident; soft tannins for overall sappy effect. 13.2% alc. **99** ☆ refined, fresh, mouthcoating though not heavy.

Merlot-Cabernet Sauvignon ☻ ☆ Gentle lightish red with ripe plum, sweet choc tones in **00**. Non-interfering tannins sufficient to stand up to most rustic meat dishes, develop ±2 yrs. **Sauvignon Blanc** ☻ ☆ Juicily upbeat **01** with crushed nettle tang smoothed with ripe fruit and smidgeon sugar. 13.7% alc high but not bothersome. For current drinking.

Pinotage ☆ Instantly recognisable redcurrants softened with touch flattering oak. **00** light-textured, pleasant fruity bite, roughish finish of pvs ed has smoothed, become tastily toasty. 13.2% alc.

Eersterivier range

Pinotage ✓ Juts into a higher plane in **00** after **99**'s uncharacteristic dip (★). Lovely sappy, almost pastille-like fruit, slightly wild notes and dry but balanced tannin to remind this isn't soda-pop. Unwooded. 13.4% alc.

Sauvignon Blanc Cream-soda possibly imbibed by pickers during night-harveting of **01** reappears in glass with bright, tasty sauvignon fruit. Unassertively dry and delicious, so watch the 13.7% alc. **Chenin Blanc** A fruit salad spread with lemonade in **01** crowd-pleaser; succulent lemon flavours and vanilla-like tastes (though unwooded). 13% alc.

Cabernet Sauvignon-Merlot Notches up in easy, very satisfying **00**, tempting with berries, flowers and a bit of spice. Tannin structure, big 13.6% alc should provide limited longevity (3/4 yrs). Lightly wooded.

Following not tasted for this ed: Genesis range: **Cabernet Sauvignon** (Pvs **98**); Welmoed range: **Pinotage Reserve** (**00**), **Pinotage** (**99**), **Chardonnay Reserve** (**00**), **Chenin Blanc Reserve** (**99**); Helderberg range: **Cinsaut-Cabernet Sauvignon** (**99**), **Chardonnay** (**00**), **Chenin Blanc Reserve** (**00**), **Chenin Blanc** (**00**), **Chenin Blanc-Sauvignon Blanc** (**00**), **Blanc de Blanc** (**00**), **Port** (**97**); Eersterivier range: **Cabernet Sauvignon** (**98**), **Muscat d'Alexandrie** (**00**); Stellenbosch range – pvs included **Radiant Red** (**97**), **Blanc de Noir** (**99**), **Dry Steen** (**00**), **Weisser Riesling** (**99**), **Special Late Harvest** (**00**), **Jerepigo** (**NV**/99), **Ruby Port** (**NV**); Hanseret range (all **NV**): **Claret**, **Edelblanc**, **Bouquet Blanc** (unrated), **Special Late Harvest**. — *DH*

Stellendrift

Stellenbosch • Tasting & sales at Louiesenhof (see that entry) • Owner/winemaker/viticulturist Fanie Cilliers (SHZ Cilliers/Kuün Wines) • Vineyards ± 12 ha • Production 1 250 tons • 100% red • PO Box 6340 Uniedal 7612 • ***Tel/fax (021) 887-6561***

Small-scale producer Fanie Cilliers (winemaker of origin Breede River Valley, now Stellenbosch-sited) has been making a Cabernet Sauvignon under the Stellendrift label, with its nostalgic horse-drawn barrel-laden cart, since 1996. Now he's released a portion of his 99 Cabernet under his new Cilliers Cellars label. Grapes from his own Vlottenburg vineyards are vinified at Louiesenhof winery (where his wines can be tasted) and aged at Tjuks Roos' Rust en Vrede farm, opposite Eikendal, where the Rostberg bottling plant is conveniently housed. Seems this keen distance runner's been doing a winemaking marathon: he also produced his maiden Merlot in 2000 and first Pinotage in 2001, both to be released early this year.

Cabernet Sauvignon Among more interesting cabs around; two vintages available: **98** with Ribena-like gushy fruit, attractive volatile touch contrasting with unexpectedly dry, densely extracted palate. Rustic but charming. ±20% new oak. Follow-up **99**, with dab merlot, very light (11.6% alc), aromatic; some resinous notes, bits blackberry/cassis in bouquet turning into sour-cherry palate with wild-herbs farewell. Sounds a mishmash, but works with food, especially pasta. Could even be chilled. Yr barrelled. — *TM*

Stellenryck

Top-notch range from Bergkelder, reserved for classic varieties and better vintages, and now moving to a vineyard focus, with emphasis on good fruit selection. Tasting/sales at Bergkelder (see that entry).

★**Cabernet Sauvignon** Ageworthy cab; selected vyds vinified & raised separately. **93** announced more modern, approachable style. Fast-forward to **98**; all best cab qualities – ripe cassis, cedar, lead-pencil – present and already quite open in bouquet; palate steelier, tannins tight but fine, merely needing time (4-5 yrs, probably). 18 mths Fr oak, 80% new. Alc 13.4%. 5 000 cases. **95** (reviewed for pvs ed) also wound-up initially, though fruit-packed. **94** ⁂ one of top cabs of vintage.

⁂**Chardonnay** ✓ Refinement within new world context seems mantra here. Towering alc (14.4%) all but invisible in **00**; ditto tucked-away oak (regime not disclosed) for classic, even restrained profile. Always with something interesting to sniff: glamorous lime-honeysuckle in this latest, marmalade buttered toast in pvs barrel-fermented **99** ★, with good maturation potential over 2/3 yrs, like delicious and elegant **98**.

Sauvignon Blanc Not tasted for this ed. Pvs **00** ★. Before **96** wooded, labelled Blanc Fumé. — *IvH*

Stellenzicht Vineyards 

Stellenbosch (see Stellenbosch map) • Open for visits and sales – phone for details (sales also at Neethlingshof Estate until Jan 02 – see that entry) • Owner Lusan Holdings • Winemaker Guy Webber (since 1998) • Vineyards Jaco van den Berg (since 1998) • Production 626 tons 50 000 cases 70% red 30% white • PO Box 104 Stellenbosch 7599 • ***Tel (021) 880-1103*** *• Fax (021) 880-1107 • E-mail nee@mweb.co.za*

"WINES are like lovers," states Guy Webber, "some are great for a one-night stand; others last a lifetime. It all depends on what you're looking for." And whatever you seek, this easygoing winemaker might add, you're likely to find among this three-tiered range from one of the Cape's most celebrated cellars. If you've a yen for a long-term relationship, start with their iconic Syrah (gold at IWSC 2001, double-gold Veritas for the 98 just two of a trophy roomful of awards). If you're inclined towards something less enduring, the Golden Triangle wines (allusion to the farm's fabled Helderberg terroir) could be a stylish choice. And for instant gratification there's the Stellenbosch range of drink-now drops. Firmly in the saddle after three harvests, Guy Webber says he's building up a profile of every site on the property. The consistent excellence of, among others, the vineyard known as Plum Pudding Hill, leads him to an early conclusion: "This is shiraz country!"

⁂**Founder's Private Release Cabernet Sauvignon** Never-to-be-repeated **97**; just 420 cases of unblended cab given very respectful treatment in cellar – 90% new oak 26 mths! Specially selected fruit. Revisited mid-01 unexpectedly relaxed, open, revealing fleshier-than-anticipated core of rich, supple, toasty fruit, though in subtle, keenly balanced framework. Beautiful wine. Given apparent accelerated maturation, would be a pity to miss any of the fireworks, so perhaps indulge in smidgeon then monitor regularly and pleasurably. 13.3% alc.

★**Merlot** Easy, clean-fruited succulence a hallmark of this label; latest **97** ★ provides more of same; juicy if uncomplex, dryish finish. (Used oak 30 mths, 13,4% alc.) 3 700 cases. **95** VVG, SAA continues to bloom. Perfumed with violets, ripe plums; richly flavoured with more plums, hints tobacco, coffee. ±6 mths Fr oak.

⁂**Syrah** A Cape icon since **94** introduction and probably first (non-auction) Cape red to break the R100 barrier, back in 1995/96. Catapulted to fame after upset win over Australia's fabled Grange (91) – judged by international panel at Oz-SA Wine Test in 1995. Lavishly decorated (at Sélections Mondiales, Michelangelo, *Wine*, Veritas etc). Key contributor is the terroir – single mature vyd, called Plum Pudding Hill. Outstanding **95**. (No **96**). **97** great, **98** ⁂ a stunner, nudging a whopping 15% alc but excusable in such beautifully weighted showcase. Should grow into a **94**. Current **99** 14 mths oak, 87% new, mainly Fr. Back-tasted mid-

01, less peppery than pvs; opaque depths harbouring gorgeous mocha/dark-choc nuances, balanced persistence; fruit starting to evolve, though very much an adolescent still. **00** blend not completed at press time. 1 500 cases.

Stellenzicht Billed as property's second red flagship – after Syrah above; thrilling cab-led bdx blend with merlot, cab f and, since standout **97**, dash malbec. Only prime own-fruit, fermented separately. Barrel-aged, 100% new oak. Current **98** assembled for final 56/22/13/9 configuration, 26 mths (!) barrelled. Coolly sensuous; presently showing cab's hauteur: very dry, mouthfilling texture; need plenty of time. 13.2% alc. 500 cases.

Chenin Blanc NEW "Experiment which turned out very well." Single vyd on Neethlingshof, fermented/aged 100% new Fr oak; partial malo. **00** ripe fruit and spicy oak background; bold flavours strike positively and carry into persistent peachy finish. 13.8% alc. 200 cases.

Semillon Reserve Highly, widely acclaimed, including **99** whose lime-rich finish, uncompromisingly dry palate confirm its niche – a singular food wine (specially for frontal-fruit-averse drinkers). With potential to grow, given 5-6 yrs. Current **00** lime piquancy complemented by superb wooding (a Guy Webber speciality); vaulting 14.8% alc. **98** another muscled dreamboat (15%+ alc). Cask-fermented/aged new Fr oak, 8 mths; partial malo.

Not tasted for this ed: **Sauvignon Blanc-Chenin Blanc** Last rated was **99**, **Sauvignon Blanc-Semillon** (**99**). Discontinued: **Cuvée Hans Schreiber** Last was **98** (), **Merlot-Cabernet Franc** (**97**), **Fragrance** (**99**), **Weisser Riesling Noble Late Harvest** (**98**).

Golden Triangle range

Cabernet Sauvignon After vintage-associated dip in **96**, this label back up to earlier elevated standard. **97** compact, vinous rather than fruity; dry cedary tannins wrapped in fairly cerebral package – yet not inaccessible, or mean. Will be much prized, in fact, by classicists. 17 mths Fr/Russian casks/vats. 12.9% alc. 4 800 cases.

Merlot Easy, clean-fruited succulence a hallmark of this label. Latest **98** with curranty juiciness which deliciously approachable but not formless thanks to integrated oak tannins (23 mths barrelled, 35% new); firm dry finish. Best in 2-3 yrs, and then with turkey and sage stuffing. 13.1% alc. 4 300 cases. **97** well fleshed but relatively simple.

Pinotage Back-tasting mid-01 of still-available **99** finds it unexpectedly introverted; pvs boldness (not just function of thrusting 14.5% alc) somewhat dimmed, on present form. Sweet, crushed-plum fruit still lurks, with unintimidating tannins, so give bit of time to revive. Yr Am/Fr oak, 22% new. WOM selection. 1 800 cases. First **98** *Wine*.

Shiraz Excellent show record for this label, invariably characterful and rewarding as in **99**, mouthwatering roasty notes, ripe morello cherry/strawberry sap, firm but unintimidating tannin. Delicious, especially with guinea fowl potjie. 15 mths 2nd fill casks, nearly all Fr. 14% alc. 1 700 cases. **98** rounded, complete, bereft of coarse tannin.

Chardonnay Barrel-fermented/matured. Laudatory performances by **97** and pvs. Most recent not quite so acclaimed. **99** ample, 'correct' rather than exciting. Latest **00** unintimidating, almost retiring (though not diminutive at 13.9% alc); subtle peachy nuances, creamy texture. Mainly Fr oak, 70% new. 3 300 cases.

Sauvignon Blanc 01 classically austere, flinty, firm. More varietal character than multi-site cousin below, gutsier. 1 700 cases. **00**, result of difficult, hot, fruit-sapping vintage.

Stellenbosch Series

Inexpensive range, blends of grapes/wines from Lusan's various Stellenbosch vyds.

✵**Sauvignon Blanc** Composite of 4 Stbosch vyds (of Lusan's five, only red wine Alto missing). **00** weighty example, attractively fruited. **01** ★ more commercial, undemonstrative. Hake-and-chips wine, with price tag to match. 13.4% alc. 13 000 cases.

✵**Triplet** Morphs into quintuplet in **99**, merlot-driven (with shiraz , cab f, cab, malbec). Distinctive classicism; nice dry savoury tannins. 13.8% alc. Combo vats, barriques 16-18 mths, none new. 7 000 cases. **98** ★ simpler but also nice.

Chardonnay ★ Barrel-fermented, briefly aged **00** has acquired decadent bouquet palate contrastingly firm, disciplined. Best in yr/2. 8 600 cases. 13.5% alc. — *IvH*

St Elmo's

PIZZA and pasta demand food-friendly, uncomplex wines, and the successful St Elmo's restaurant chain offers family diners value for money with this NV range by Simonsig.

Dry Red ⁑ Ruby cab, pinotage, pinot blend, offering piquant raspberry fruit, leather, spice. Dry, simple finish won't detract from the pizza. **Blanc de Blanc** ⁑ Aromatic grapey nose, firm but pasta-friendly dry finish from chardonnay, with 1/3 each riesling, colombard. **Semi-Sweet** ⁑ Aromatic varieties including buket, gewürz in popular semi-sweet style; wafts of spice, sweet fruit, uncomplicated appeal Undemanding 12% alc. — *DS*

Stettyn Wine Cellar

Worcester (see Worcester map) • Tasting by appointment • Owner Stettyn Winery Co-op (3 members) • Winemaker Albie Treurnicht (since Nov 2000) • Viticulturists Hendrik & Johannes Botha (Stettyn) with Schalk du Toit (VinPro) & Hendrik Griessel (Die Hoek) • Vineyards 250 ha • Production 3 340 tons 85% white 15% red • PO Box 1520 Worcester 6849 • ***Tel/fax (023) 349-4220*** *• E-mail stettyn@xsinet.co.za*

BACK in the guide after a 10 year break, this small co-operative is again selling wines under its own label. A Pinotage, Cape Blush (off-dry rosé) and Sauvignon Blanc are available from the cellar, which is folded into a scenic valley between Worcester and Villiersdorp. To follow, reveals ex Romansrivier winemaker Albie Treurnicht, is a premier range consisting, possibly, of their Worcester Young Wine Show class winning Shiraz-Cabernet, a Vin de Paille, organic Pinotage and "a super-Chenin". The three members, farming a total of 250 hectares, plan a marketing blitz this year to establish their brand in the top-quality market segment.

Steytler see Kaapzicht

Stille Waters

DISTELL trademark, sold exclusively to one customer in the Netherlands. Currently a Steen and a Cape Red, untasted.

Stonecross see Deetlefs

Stonewall Wines

Stellenbosch (see Helderberg map) • Tasting & sales Mon-Fri 9-5 Sat 9-1 • Cellar tours by appointment • Guesthouse • Owner De Waal Koch • Consultant winemaker Ronell Wiid (since 2000) • Viticulturist De Waal Koch • Vineyards 80 ha • Production 400 tons (2 500 cases own label) 80% red 20% white • PO Box 5145 Helderberg 7135 • ***Tel (021) 855-3675*** *cell 083 310-2407 • Fax: (021) 855-2206*

THE characterful old *ringmuur* (low farm wall) on Happy Vale farm, a landmark in the Helderberg, inspired fifth-generation grower De Waal Koch when he decided to launch his own label in the mid-90s. The wines, mostly red, mostly exported, are made the time-honoured way in open fermenters by Diners Club laureate Ronell Wiid, here in after-hours care-giver role (she midwifes full-time for Hazendal). An old-world ambience envelops the property – the rustic cellar dates back to 1828 and the old stables house a quaint tasting-room. Even the nostalgic sepia wine labels are affixed by hand using a homemade contraption straight out of Heath Robinson's handbook of bizarre gadgets.

✵**Cabernet Sauvignon** The house style emphases power, concentration, but usually not without some refinement. **98** fairly grippy on release, needing time. Tannins better managed in **99** ✵, for earlier approachability. Incipient dark-choc richness. 18 mths oaked. 13.5% alc.

✵**Pinotage** NEW ✓ **00** booms dramatically from opaque depths; smoky, spicy dimensions to sweet palate (viscosity enhanced by 14% alc); firm finish. 5 mths oak. Potential to develop into ✵ over 4-6 yrs. *Wine* ✵.

✵**Ruber** Forceful red blend; more powerful than elegant, yet flavourful, structured for good keeping. Newest **99** ✵ more balanced than pvs, sturdy but sweet tannins already approachable (49% merlot, remainder cab); should carry 6-7 yrs. 13.5% alc. **98** perceptibly oaky on release, needing yr/2 to settle.

✵**Chardonnay** ✓ Latest **00** ✵, with floral, lime, butter touches, notch up on pvs. Full butterscotch palate; drinkable now but better in 3-4 yrs. 13% alc. No **99**. **98** with contrasting toast, sweet-melon flavours.

Sauvignon Blanc ✵ **01** preview shows no obvious oak (pvs was lightly wooded); zingy-fresh grass/nettle flavours, leesy hints. Give ±yr to settle. — *DH*

Stony Brook

Franschhoek (see Franschhoek map) • Tasting & sales Mon-Sat 9-1 Tasting fee R5 p/p refundable with purchase • Facilities for children • Views • Owners Nigel & Joy McNaught • Winemaker Nigel McNaught • Consulting viticulturist Paul Wallace (VineWise) • Vineyards ±14 ha • Production 70 tons 5 000 cases 70% red 30% white • PO Box 22 Franschhoek 7690 • ***Tel/fax (021) 876-2182*** *• E-mail mcnaught@iafrica.com*

On this tree-shaded Franschhoek property the vineyards, planted in 1995, have been subjected to some intensive care (a country doctor in a former life, Nigel Mc Naught still moonlights at the local clinic). Now that they've come into full production, certain character traits in certain blocks are clearly recognisable: "A bit like getting to know a child as they develop!" Healthy new siblings are mourvèdre and additional shiraz; the chardonnay's been pulled out (01 the last, although they may buy in grapes). New releases include their first single bottling of Merlot 00, and the Semillon is starting to confirm their high hopes for this progeny. Quizzed as to what else is new, Mc Naught cryptically states "Well, the chickens all died," followed by a dry "and we got a new cross ridgeback labrador, named Wente (Chinese for 'big problem')." No co-incidence: "Anyone with space and no livestock nearby is welcome to apply!" With not enough wine to meet demand, they're concentrating on exports and direct sales from the farm – worth a visit for the informal, highly entertaining tastings (mad dogs and all).

✵**Cabernet Sauvignon Reserve** Applause for first release **98** VVG, *Wine* ✵, wine mail order club selection, which set this powerful, densely extracted cab rolling. Excitement continues in **00** with thumbprint eucalyptus/mint fragrance, abundant ripe red berries, obvious sweet oak and tannins. More massive than pvs (14.5% alc), will need time to develop. Own, Stbosch fruit. 270 cases. These ± yr oak, 50% new. No **99**. Regular **Cabernet Sauvignon** ✵ Blend own, Agter-Paarl fruit in **99**, commendable follow-up to maiden **98**. No **00**.

✵**Pinotage** Regains form of **98** *Wine* ✵ with latest **00**, Swartland fruit providing classic ripe-plum/banana bouquet and more unusual dry straw; very smooth;

choc/vanilla from 11 mths Am/Fr oak; big 14% alc a slightly-sweetening rather than aggressive presence. 600 cases. **99** ☆ chewier, needing time to come round.

☆**Merlot** NEW **00** more refined, gentler than any of these reds (despite muscle-bound 14% alc). Clean ripe berry fruit, delicate sweet-violets scents and juicy tannins spiced with cinnamon, ground coffee. Yr mainly new Nevers. 355 cases best matured yr/2, then drunk over 4-5.

☆**Shiraz** Pvs love-or-hate **98**, **99** featured some aggressive, animal-like smells; curiously attractive. Latest **00** more conventional, better in every way; rich, choc entry; ripe plum backing; pepper/liquorice woven with smooth sweet tannins. Accessible now but better in 2-5 yrs. Brawny 14.5% alc. 11 Am/Fr barrels, none new. **99**, **00** WOM selections.1 100 cases.

☆**Reserve** Debut **99** mainly cab, merlot, dashes petit verdot, malbec. **00**, from own fruit, with dab cab f, more minerally, lead-pencil tones. Much bigger wine (14.5% alc vs 13,3), drying, firmer; needs 5 yrs min to show potential, peak probably ±10. "Released early with understanding will be cellared," says Nigel M, disarmingly, "to help pay my bills!" 650 cases. These 11 mths Fr barriques, some new.

Chardonnay ☆ **00** partly wild-yeast-fermented in barrel, subdued melon/mango hints, quite dry and short. 13% alc. 320 cases. **Semillon** ☆ **98**'s lanolin smoothness; honeyed bottle age, flavoursome dry palate should be enjoyed now while at delicious peak. 14% alc. 8 mths Fr casks, some new. **Sauvignon Blanc** NEW ☆ **00** Pleasant tropical/flint combo; smooth, dry and clean; 650 cases for everyday drinking. 14% alc. Not tasted for this ed: **Rose de Vert** (**98** ☆), **Annie's Wine** (**97** ☆). Discontinued: **Sophie's Choice** (**NV** ☆); **Vert** (**99** ★). — *DH*

Stormberg

Wellington • Not open to the public • Owner/winemaker Koosie Jordaan • Partnership vineyards 32 ha • Production 2 500 cases 100% red • Winery at Onverwach Estate Wellington PO Box 2907 Paarl 7620 • ***Tel 082 776-3540*** *• Fax (021) 872-4912 • E-mail kooskit@mweb.co.za*

Anything-but-tempestuous Koos Jordaan makes these wines in the Onverwach cellar at Wellington for the international and local speciality wine trade and upscale restaurants. When not stumping for his own label, this dab-handed marketer wins friends and influences people on behalf of the wine-services group Historic Wines of the Cape, which represents a select clientele (including deep-piled Rupert & Rothschild) as well as its own label, Leopard's Leap (see that entry).

☆**Barrel Select** NEW Powerful blend merlot, cabs s/f. **98** savoury from start to finish; attractive meaty/herby dustiness leads to lip-smacking palate with good fruit, firm, well-balanced tannins and (natural) acidity. 14.2% alc. **99**, though similar assemblage (56/37/7), more ripely fruity (less interesting!); touch lighter, drier; also satisfying. 19 mths older Fr oak. 1 200 unfiltered cases .

Cabernet Sauvignon-Shiraz ☆ All-occasions red; med-bodied **99** with sweet berry fruits sitting easily in light, well-constructed frame. 18 mths older wood. 1 200 cases. Very pleasant now, but not for long haul, which ampler **98**s literally were: they flew with BA. — *TJ*

Sumaridge

Walker Bay, Hemel en Aarde Valley (see Elgin/Walker Bay map) • Tastings & sales Mon-Fri 9-5 Sat 9-2 • Cellar tours by prior arrangement • Owner Lorraine Cellars (Pty) Ltd • Winemakers Bartho Eksteen consulting, with Auguste Natter (since 2001) • Viticulturist Greg de Bruyn, advised by Vaatjie Jacobs • Vineyards 28 ha • Production 85 tons 4 000 cases 50% white 50% red • PO Box 1413 Hermanus 7200 • ***Tel (028) 312-1097*** *• Fax (028) 312-2824 • E-mail gregdb@itec.co.za*

THE FURTHEST wine-producing farm in the Hemel-en-Aarde fold, the first mature harvest from these four-year-old vines last year was the latest in the valley ("long after everyone else had finished"), nail-biting stuff although fortunate: cool, dry conditions ensured exceptionally healthy fruit and a smaller than predicted yield. Flying French winemaker Auguste Natter, (from Sancerre, he cooks such a mean *potjie* it has local masters blushing) teamed up with Walker Bay consultant Bartho Eksteen and Reginald Muphamolu to test-drive everything in the modern cellar, ready in the nick of time, for the first laps – "not always with the expected results!" Luckily resident architect and Cape Wine Master Greg de Bruyn knows his way around a building site (and a vineyard) and remained relatively unphased throughout. Finishing touches were in process by winter and they've now opened their brand new doors to the public.

Sauvignon Blanc Slow-starting maiden **00** needed ±yr to begin to unfurl, so try not to rush delicious, step-up **01** with massive, ripe, glazed-fig, crushed-nettle bouquet, whistle-clean pineapple farewell. Bracing freshness a signature here, via 100% natural acidity; differential picking for complexity within cool, exciting frame. 12.7% alc. 2 200 cases.

Chardonnay NEW Pristine pear-drop, peach aromas in **00**, supported by elegant oaking; bright skein of acidity cushioned by grain sugar. Pleasing style which will appeal to admirers of fruit-led chardonnay. 50% cask-fermented, 6 mths, half new Fr, rest 2nd fill Am. 13.2% alc. 500 cases.

Merlot NEW Could be subtitled Driveway Block – this single vyd on own farm origin of **00** with warm smoked-meat, wild-berry tastes and snatch fennel; wood prominent, so give bit of time. 14 mths oak, 50% new. 13% alc. 250 cases for "serious occasions," says Greg de Bruyn, "wakes, insolvencies, divorces etc"!

'Dry Red' NEW Name undecided at press time for **NV** from pinot noir, unusual and delightful drops for *unserious* occasions. Delicate rosé-like pinot colour, dusty cherry nose/palate, merest suggestion of oak. Chill lightly and drink with copious quantities of carpaccio. 13.5% alc. — *TM*

Swartland Wine Cellar

Swartland (see Swartland map) Tasting & sales Mon-Fri 8-5 Sat 9-12 • Owners 102 members • Production head Andries Blake • Winemakers Andries Eygelaar, Abrie Beeslaar & Hugo Truter • Marketing manager Marius Kotzé • Quality control Gerda Eygelaar • Production 1,2-million cases 70% white 30% red • PO Box 95 Malmesbury 7299 • ***Tel (022) 482-1134/5/6*** *• Fax (022) 482-1750 • E-mail swartland@swwines.co.za*

ANTEDATING all the hoopla about the Swartland and its world-class viticultural potential is this large and enterprising winery (the first co-op to do all its marketing in-house), established in 1948 by 15 growers around the town of Malmesbury. The numbers have changed (they're crushing an enormous 23 000 tons from more than 90 farms, making them the third-largest co-op – in volume – in SA and the biggest where production, bottling and marketing take place under one roof), but their knowledge of the good Swartland earth and their high percentage of now-fashionable bushvines give them an edge on the newcomers that have swarmed all over this swooned-over terroir. Their fruit is from a 'golden circle' around the original Doornkuil farm, where the cellar was built in 1950. Modernised and extended, it remains a landmark amid the wheat fields and a welcoming stop for tastings and sales just 3 km outside the town.

Reserve range

Only made in exceptional years.

Cabernet Sauvignon-Merlot ✓ Serious red in any company ('antique green' bottle to match). Warm-country generosity suffuses **00**, liquorice and basket of berries, black choc; wood well woven with flesh; tannins still abrasive but should soften with yr/2. Concentrated, as was **99**, ripe tannins giving just the right firming grip to juicy/spicy fruit. WOM selection. These 70/30 blends, 4-6 mths small-oaked; alcs ±13%.

Pinotage ☆ Med-bodied **00**'s tannins have softened since tasted for pvs ed; lacks exuberance of unwooded version below, but has own warm pruney appeal. Some pvs have been excellent: **96** ABSA Top Ten.

Indalo range NEW

☆**Sauvignon Blanc** Impresses with deep varietal flavours, crisp tones, general confident mien achieved without effect. **01** dusty sweet peppers, generous fruit, brisk but non-aggressive finish. Med-bodied.

Chenin Blanc ☆ More gravitas than stablemates, extra concentration imparted by 33 yr old vines, unwooded; **01** very ripe, broad (rather than long) (14% alc), some spiciness, richness; soft acidity, so probably not a stayer.

'Standard' range

☆**Cabernet Sauvignon** ✓ Hugely appealing (especially to fans of the nearly-unadorned style – 3-6 mths small oak more a rounding than flavour-imparting exercise). **00** back-tasted for current ed offers stuffed green peppers (complete with meat!), pine needle freshness. Tannins still bit abrasive so better now as table partner rather than solo drink. Pvs **98** harmonious, balanced. Great bargain at R20 ex-cellar.

☆**Pinotage** ✓ Pinotage unplugged! **01** showcases everything you love (or hate) about the local yokel: high-toned estery bouquet; perfumed sweet-sour tastes; big body (13.9% alc). Exuberant unwooded show-off, well priced. **00** ☆ less flagrantly varietal.

☆**Shiraz** ✓ Time, surely, to elevate to Reserve range? **00** gorgeous, fragrant, achieves pleasure quotient of pvs **99** without uppercut alc; ripe mocha and prunes mingle with soft vanilla tannins in sleek palate; handsome black-velvet looks. 13% alc. 6-8 mths small oak. Strapping **99** decidedly warming at 15% alc but balanced, not unmanageable. **97/99** *Wine* ☆. Dryland bushvines.

☆**Colombard** ✓ Having impressed with exceptionally expressive fruit in **00, 01** ☆ strangely subdued on nose (probably just youthfully shy); palate up to usual speed: light, lively, delightfully crisp and dry.

☆**Red Jerepiko** Traditional old-Cape flavours of sweet baked prunes and raisins; smooth and warming. Balanced **NV** from pinotage. 17,6% alc.

☆**Vintage Port** Tasty and satisfying, with its own styling, not quite Portuguese but not old-Cape either. Latest **99** ☆ more LBV feel than Vintage: very ready, mellow flavours of coffee, dusty earth and christmas cake, full-bodied and dense; long nutty finish. Tinta, cab, shiraz. 17% alc. 2 yrs small oak. Bit sweet but uncloying. **97** oaky/tannic in youth (but *Wine* ☆

☆**Ruby Port** ✓ Modern, focused ruby; pleasing red-plum fruit in big, spiritous frame with lots of personality. Sugar well calibrated to avoid cloy. 100% tinta. 19% alc. Very well priced at around R16 ex cellar. **NV**.

Merlot ☆ Small step down from pvs; **00** not quite as giving, though pleasantly fruity, dark brambly hints in med-weight chassis; absolutely dry; 6 mths oaked. 13,% alc. **Tinta Barocca** ☆ Quintessential boerewors wine. **01** as always expansive, full-bodied, with clean-cut mocha flavours and no hint of portiness. Bushvines "planted all over the Swartland", unoaked. 13,8% alc.

Rosé ☆ **NV** from mostly chenin; pinotage contributing alluring coral-pink hue; nice savoury red-wine tones; not too sweet so should appeal to more serious drinkers, too. Try with grilled linefish. 13,5% alc. **Blanc de Noir** ☆ For the sweeter-toothed. Lightish **00** with pear/quince and some spun-sugar nuances. From pinotage. WOM Value.

Chardonnay Barrel Fermented 'Icon' NEW Serious contender in cask-fermented stakes. Very promising. Ripe **01** full of mouthwatering tropical flavours;

sweet-spicy oak youthfully prominent (sample tasted; unrated); should settle soon enough. 20% Am, rest Fr oak, 20% through malo. 16 yr old vines. 14% alc. **Chardonnay** ☆ Won't ruffle any feathers; pleasantly fruity **00**, rounded, balanced; subtly oaked. Non-overt 13.6% alc. **Light** ☆ Good lunchtime tipple with low alc of 8.75%. Low keyed, off-dry. **NV**. From fernao pires. **Riesling** ☆ **00** re-tasted mid-01, showed developed 'sea breeze' bouquet; lightish, dry. Good with plate of calamari. Gentle dry finish. **Blanc de Blanc** Not tasted for this ed. Pvs **NV** ☆. **Bukettraube** ☆ Soft semi-sweet **01** with variety's floral perfumes. Light 10,6% alc. **Stein** ☆ Lightish semi-sweet chenin, touches of honey/pineapple, unusually sugary for this label. **NV**. **Late Vintage** Not available for tasting. Pvs **NV** ☆. **Natural Sweet** ☆ **NV** Pleasantly sweet chenin; lightish 11.5% alc adds to clean, soft feel; ends with mouthwatering pineapple tang.

Hanepoot ☆ (certified) **99** Thatch and barley sugar bouquet with honey and touches pineapple; rich, mouthcoating, not as sweet as ... **Hanepoot** ☆ (uncertified **NV**) Absolutely billows muscat; intensely sweet yet irresistible. 19% alc. WOM Value. **White Jerepiko** ☆ **NV**. Thatchy, malty tastes in powerfully sweet palate, not fully integrated mid-01. 19.5% alc.

Cinsaut ☻ ☆ Variety at its most quaffable; **01** (sample) med-bodied and popping with juicy, lightly savoury fruit, no tannins to speak of. **Dry Red** ☻ ☆ Probably best advertisement for the Swartland, ever. Downright delicious, warm-hearted; generous meaty/fruity tastes, earthy touches and hardly a tannin in sight. Moderate 12.5% alc. Unoaked **NV** blend pinotage, cab, tinta. R14/bottle ex cellar deserves extra ☻. **Steen** ☻ ☆ Perennial favourite in top form; **01** exuberant guava, cut-grass succulence, pleasingly ripe; clean acidity and lowish alc make this a lovely standalone gulp. **Sauvignon Blanc** ☻ ☆ **01** light-bodied version of this crowd-pleaser; spread of good 'green' flavours, bone-dry finish and lively green pepper aftertaste. **Premier Grand Cru** ☻ ☆ Crisp and dry, as befits style, but unaggressive; very pleasant **NV**; lightish mix chenin, colombard, clairette blanche. **Bouquet Blanc** ☻ ☆ **NV** smooth, delicate, pretty wine from buket, hanepoot, colombard.

Sparkling range

Carbonated NVs, budget priced and subtitled Special Reserve.

Cuvée Brut ☆ Sauvignon in unusually creamy guise; pleasantly full (12% alc), holds its own in elevated company. **Demi Sec** ☆ **NV** Sauvignon, hanepoot; soft, semi-sweet, easy drinking. Lowish 11,7% alc. **Vin Doux** ☆ Sweeter version of Demi-sec above; fullish uplifting bubbles for a rainy day. Sauvignon/hanepoot. **Rosette** ☆ Pretty pink fizz; sweetish, light and delicious over fresh strawberries. Low 8.% alc. Pinotage, here with mostly chenin, hanepoot.

Boxed range

Untasted for this ed, but on track record, solid ☆/☆ quality. 5 ℓ casks: **Grand Cru**, **Blanc de Blanc**, **Stein**, **Late Harvest**; 2 ℓ: **Grand Cru**, **Stein**, **Late Harvest**. *— IvH*

Sylvanvale Vineyards

Stellenbosch (see Stellenbosch map) • Tasting & sales daily 9-6 Fee R5 p/p refundable on any purchase • Cellar tours by arrangement • Vineleaf Restaurant with children's menu (see Eat-out section) • Picnics by arrangement • Luxury 40 room hotel • Conferences • Tourgroups • Play area for children • Gifts • Walks • Views • Owner David Nathan-Maister • Consultant winemaker Martin Meinert (since 1999) • Consulting viticulturist Lorna Roos (since 1998) • Vineyards 6 ha • Production 2 500 cases 50% red 30% white 20% rosé • PO Box 68 Stellenbosch

7599 • **Tel (021) 882-2012** • fax (021) 882-2610 • E-mail devon@iafrica.com • Website www.sylvanvale.co.za

HOTELIER David Nathan-Maister couldn't wait to tell us about new developments at the tiny vineyard surrounding his Devon Valley Hotel. A lover of the Italian Amarone styles, he was wondering how they could produce something vaguely similar here. Then they hit on it: vine-dried wines. Over to clued-up Lorna Roos and her vineyard team for some time-consuming and tedious work, which involved snapping the stems with long-nose pliers to stop sap from getting to the bunches so they'd dry out on the vine (with the disgruntled harvesters moaning all the while that the unaccustomed action hurt their hands). All worth it in the end though: the Vine-dried Chenin Blanc and Pinotage (a very small experimental batch, available only from the hotel where it's jokingly referred to as 'Pinorone'), made by Martin Meinert at his cellar, are truly unique. No vine-drieds were made last year as conditions weren't perfect (the process requires a long, slow harvest). But they certainly intend repeating the dose.

Pinotage Reserve Outspoken, charismatic style with own select fanclub. **00** being Fr oak-tamed when previewed for this ed; hugely concentrated; closed, mere hint of cinnamon-dusted fresh raspberries in lavishly textured palate. All seems in place for long haul. Very promising, more appealing than presently wild (slightly feral?) **99** with tropical punch-cup exaggeration; open, lush sweet-spicy flavours; spicier, more grippy finish. Can take, probably benefit from 3-4 yrs maturation. 13.2% alc. 500 cases. Single vyd ±30 yrs old. Yr Fr oak, 30% new.

Laurie's Vineyard Chenin Blanc ✓ 01 long-awaited follow-up to **98**, in much same vein. Fully ripe, rich aromas (honeysuckle, dried mango); plenty fleshy viscosity to soak up high alc, acid (14.5%, 6.5 g/ℓ) and still have balanced, bone-dry conclusion. Better with spicy foods (eg Thai chicken) than solo. ±20 yr old vines. Unwooded. 350 cases.

Vine Dried Chenin Blanc Scintillating dessert wine – neither NLH nor vin de paille but containing elements of both, plus own quirky singularity. **00** 375 ml power-packed essence of chenin, further concentrated after 18 mths new Fr oak, (revealed in finishing snatch toasty richness). Soars through mouth with fabulous intensity; flashes white peach, dried apricot, nutmeg and much else besides; sets every known (and unknown!) taste bud aquiver; irresistibility enhanced by low, though still vinous, 10.8% alc, 230 g/ℓ fruit-saturated sugar, fully effective 8 g/ℓ acid. ±30 yr old vines, harvested at 43°B, bunch stalks pinched to stop sap flow; berries left to desiccate. 200 cases.

Vine Dried Pinotage Casts fascinating and positive new light on pinotage taken to extremes of ripeness (though fits general gutsy ambit of range); viticultural methods as above, **00** harvested at lower 29°B, fermented with own yeasts to whopping 15.8% alc! Difficult to compare with anything local; internationally has similarities with Amarone. Profound caramelised nuts, cinnamon base with resonating buchu-like top notes; intensely ripe without ugly in-your-face sweetness; glycerol viscosity high enough to drown/smooth over more youthful alcohol and tannin exuberance/abundance; glides to amazingly poised conclusion for such a big wine. No need to hurry over drinking this one, stamina for many years. 500 ml.

Dry Pinotage Rosé Occasional bottling. To date only **99**. —*AL*

Table Mountain

THIS RANGE by Distell was first released into the Japanese market in 1997 and fast became a top seller. Following are available (not tasted for this ed, pvs ratings in brackets): **Cabernet Sauvignon 98** (), **Chardonnay 99** ().

Table Peak

Export wines for Matthew Clark, UK, by Vinimark (see also that entry).

Ruby Cabernet ☻ ✯ Brilliantly hued **01** (sample) powerfully spicy aromas, contrasting ripe-juicy tastes. Unoaked, ready to drink now. 13% alc.**Colombard** ☆ Off-dry **01**, lightish tropical/pineapple tang, smooth rather than sweet. — *DH*

Talana Hill see Vriesenhof

Tassenberg

Among the biggest-selling reds in SA, launched 1936; associated with good times by generations of South Africans. Current blend includes Spanish fruit, carefully chosen to resemble the SA cinsaut originally used. By Distell.

NV ☻ ✯ Now rather more Mediterranean than classic Cape, but warmly satisfying, tangy, med-bodied. — *IvH*

Taverna Rouge

Lightly sweet (unusually for Cape red), budget-priced NV from Distell. Now a blend of oak-matured wines from Spain/SA. Not tasted for this ed; on track record ✯.

TenFiftySix Winery

Franschhoek (see Franschhoek map) • Tasting by appointment • Owner Michael Falkson • Winemaker Gerda Willers (since 1999) • Viticulturist Toll Malherbe • Vineyards ± 3 ha • Production ± 3 500 cases 50/50 red/white • PO Box 244 Milnerton 7435 • ***Tel (021) 551-2284*** *• Fax (021) 551-2487 • E-mail charbrey@new.co.za*

When businessman Michael Falkson first moved to the idyllic Franschhoek valley he planned to relax and enjoy country life on his piece of it, portion 1056 (from whence it takes its name). But, as luck would have it, a field lying fallow next to the house was just begging to be planted, which he duly did with cabernet sauvignon a decade ago. Now this self-taught winemaker and freelancer Gerda Willers produce a mainly-for-export range covering several vinous bases. New additions are the first Rosé and a blend of semillon and sauvignon. Remainder of the range not tasted for this ed; previous have included: **Cabernet Sauvignon (99** ✯**)**, **Sauvignon Blanc (00** ✯**)**, **Blanc Fumé (99** ✯**)**, not previously tasted/rated: **Chardonnay 99**, **Chenin Blanc 97**, **MCC 98**.

Tesco see Vinfruco

Teslaarsdal Winery

Overberg (Walker Bay) • Not open to the public • Owners JJ & WS Malherbe • Winemaker Willie Malherbe • Marketing manager Rufus Scheepers • Vineyards 2 ha • Production 1 000 cases 100% red • 6 Stemmet Street Hermanus 7700 • ***Tel 083 258-0952*** *• Fax (02831) 23591*

Adding extra cool-climate gloss to the Cape's changing viticultural complexion is the Malherbe family, grape-farming below the Akkedisberg between Hermanus and Caledon. Fronted by winemaker Willie Malherbe, they grow cabernet and merlot near the hamlet of Teslaarsdal, which gives its name to the winery and its dinky two hectares. Their first release is an amalgam of own fruit and grapes ex Stellenbosch and Villiersdorp. Closed to the public at present, they're raring to build a tasting centre and expand the vineyards and cellar. And promote Teslaarsdal as a vinotourism destination "to increase jobs in the area".

Grand Rouge ☆ Good kick-off with lightish merlot-dominated (40%) **NV** blend. Charry black cherries; earthy/peppery nuances from equal dollops cinsaut, shiraz. Deserves yr/2 to smooth out. Unoaked. — *DH*

Thandi Wines

Elgin (see Elgin/Walker Bay map) • Tasting & sales at Paul Cluver (see that entry) • Winemaker Patrick Kraukamp (since 1996) with Andries Burger • Farm manager Jan Jansen with Karin Voigt • Consulting viticulturist Eben Archer • Vineyards 26 ha • Production 8 000 cases 54% red 46% white • PO Box 594 Grabouw 7160 • ***Tel (021) 859-0547*** *• Fax (021) 859-0482 • E-mail thandi@cluver.co.za • Website www.cluver.co.za*

'With Love We Grow Together' is the motto of this uplifting joint-venture in Elgin, established in 1995 among the black forestry and farmworkers' village of Lebanon, threatened by privatisation, by eminent neurosurgeon and local farmer Paul Cluver, and parastatal forestry company SAFCOL. Initially focused on fruit farming and forestry to create wealth for the stakeholders, the initiative has since diversified into a wine brand, Thandi. The maiden vintage flew off the shelves of UK supermarket chain Tesco in 1999, followed by larger quantities of 2000. Now an exciting new stage is being entered with Tesco agreeing to mentor the project in conjunction with Vinfruco, the SA export powerhouse. Kromco, the Elgin fruit packer, and Capespan, international marketing organisation, now also form part of a "network of caring supporting organisations". Remarks Paul Cluver Jnr: "Given the project's growing success, we envisage it will eventually be possible to extend the brand benefits beyond the Thandi community to the surrounding areas in Elgin."

☆**Chardonnay** Two versions. For Benelux/German markets: **Cape of Good Hope 00** good notch up from pvs; better balance, more citrus-tangy zip for overall lighter, more polished feel. Barrelling well managed. Fr oak, 30% new, rest 2nd fill. 4 500 half-cases. For UK market: **Elgin 99** mellowing and picking up slightly sweet bouquet though tropical/citrus fruits still taste bright and lively; 2-3 yrs life ahead. 1 940 half-cases. Alcs 13,5%.

Pinot Noir ☆ **00** with plummy bouquet and spicy/earthy tones; good sappy fruit and some sweet sensations concluding dry with parting tannin flick. 13.5% alc. **Cabernet Sauvignon** ☆ **97** first release ripening, plummy fruit emerging from herbaceous/vegetal cocoon; dry tannins better with a sturdy food partner. 12,5% alc. — *DH*

Thelema Mountain Vineyards

Stellenbosch (see Stellenbosch map) • Tasting & sales Mon-Fri 9-5 Sat 9-1 • Tourgroups by arrangement • Views • Wheelchair-friendly • Owner McLean Family Trust & G H Webb • Winemaker Gyles Webb • Assistant winemaker Rudi Schultz (since 2001) • Viticulturist Aidan Morton • Viticultural consultant Phil Freese • Vineyards 50 ha • Production 350 tons 25 000 cases 60% white 40% red • PO Box 2234 Stellenbosch 7601 • ***Tel (021) 885-1924*** *• Fax (021) 885-1800 • E-mail thelema@adept.co.za*

'THELEMA' is Greek for 'will', the operative word here. Winemaking eminence Gyles Webb has twice been Diners' Club Winemaker of the Year and won numerous other awards (if there was an award just for winning them, Thelema would doubtless have won that, too). All this praise is justly earned through a combination of sheer hard work, total commitment and vision. Not one to let the grass grow under his feet (rather it grows between the vines to limit vigour and concentrate flavour), he simply couldn't resist taking on production at neighbouring Tokara as well ("to keep me fully occupied"). Webb reports that the eight new alfresco red fermenters "work beautifully", come mountain mist, rain or shine. The vineyards are under sound management of Mathew Castle and Aidan Morton (former vineyard manager, he now consults from his own business), with Californian inspiration from consultant Phil Freese. Future promise comes from the new blocks of shiraz, more merlot coming on-stream and additional sauvignon to be planted.

⁂**Cabernet Sauvignon** Years ago established Cape cult status and style, as did Gyles Webb's early mentor, Joe Heitz's California cab in the 70s (earlier Thelemas' hallmark minty whiffs tipped hat to above's Rutherford profile). Now more harmonious ("huge amount of work in the vineyards on canopies to get proper ripeness"); always deeply plum-robed, intense brambly, cassis bouquet with complex mocha, fennel nuances. **98** ★ with splash merlot, still shy, lurking potential with subtle cigarbox, plum, vanilla aromas and muscular, tense minerally blackcurrant fruit. Long, firm, chewy finish suggests min 2 yrs' bottle ageing required. 14% alc. 18 mths Fr oak, 40% new. **97** ⁂ velvety, less claret-like; minty imprint less aggressive than pvs. *Wine* ⁂. Upscale from earlier-drinking **96** ★, *Wine* ★. **CWG Auction Reserve** Firmest, finest, densest cab selected for this prestige label. Preview of **99** reveals huge structure with endless dense cassis and plum fruit. Same recipe: dash merlot, 40% new Fr barriques, 18 mths. Stunning ⁂ potential.

★**Merlot** Unusually in Cape, rivals cab in this winery; always stylish, impressively firm, suggesting few yrs' ageing. Yet even in youth, ripe with property's watermark plush berry bouquet; fleshy warm palate, poised finish. Preview **99** classic restraint, gravelly structure and trademark potent berry fruit very much to fore. **98**, with 10% cab, bright mulberry whiffs, arresting dark-choc, fennel flavours blanketing palate with enormous persistence. Intriguing savoury notes add spice, complexity; sweet finish well reined in by tannin. Fr/Am oak, 20% new. **97** more muscular, gamey. **96** herbaceous, less meaty, for early drinking. **CWG Merlot** Departure from Webb's propensity to offer cab at auction. Last was **98**. **Merlot Reserve** ⁂ 100% merlot, all-new Fr wood; **99** staggering even in youth; voluptuous spicy plum, mocha, cocoa whiffs over palate already on course for spectacular development. All manner savoury, vanilla, creamy flavours lurking in black-fruity depths. Near-perfect balance of ripeness and solid tannins.

★**Pinotage** "First – and last!" Gyles Webb declared of **98**. But intention to abandon local icon now itself abandoned ("Couldn't resist another crack in such a fine pinotage year"), so expect an **01**, from sourced-in Stbosch fruit, in yr/2. Meanwhile, stocks of pvs long snaffled.

★**Chardonnay 00** returns to more classic style of **97** *Wine* ★ after two higher-alc vintages. Latest ripe melon, marmalade, apricot fruit framed in brioche-fragrant oak with toasty extras – just enough wood (11 mths Fr) to add substance, spice to taut flavours. Bone dry, 13.5% alc integrated. More than nod to Burgundy here; ageworthy, too. Tantalising 'woodsmoke' hint (from 00 Simonsberg bushfires?) **99** emphatic, rich, palate-filling (partly from just-dry 4 g/ℓ sugar, 14,4% alc) **98** with 15% alc late-palate rush (and *Wine Spectator* 91-point rating). **Reserve Chardonnay 97** ⁂ wowed 00 Nederburg Auction with stratospheric R250/bottle.

★**Ed's Reserve** Front-label says 'A Dry White' under sepia photo of cherub which must be matriarch Edna McLean ("that's me – unplugged!"), shareholder and tasting room captain, as wee bairn. Back label tells you it's pukka chardonnay (though unusually exotic, spicy wafts from special 166 clone confuse the Wine & Spirit Board on occasion). All-new barrel-fermented **00** shows even more honey than usual and complex, toast and butterscotch take-no-prisoners oak frame around rich tropical fruit. 'Moderate' 13.5% alc – **98** staggered in at a whopping 15,6%. **97** (14% alc), encouraged Webb to showcase its boisterous charms solo. First was **96**.

☆**Sauvignon Blanc** ✓ After series of tricky sauvignon vintages, cooler **01** sees numbers of fine examples; few more impressive than this. "Best since **97**," beams Gyles W (that benchmark vintage's now bottle-aged delights generally eschewed by winemaker in favour of "drink soon" policy). Latest, too, will gain with few mths' rest: presently tense, mineral, grapefruit flavours, considerable palate weight (13.5% alc). **00** saw off Simonsberg fires, drought with commendable freshness; notch up on **99**, impacted by searing heat.

☆**Rhine Riesling** ✓ One of few in Cape in dry style, elegant and long-lived (maiden **88**, slightly sweet, back-tasted recently, still delicious). Current **99** attractive bottle-maturation aromas, honeysuckle hints, terpene complexity; full, dry peach/grapefruit palate (2.8 g/ℓ sugar). Upcoming **00** ☆ shyer, lemon-zest/grapefruit bouquet, haystack hint and taut, controlled citrus fruits. Deserves extra plaudits for offering top-class alternative dry white for current drinking or cellaring. 6/800 cases.

☆**Muscadel** Fortified **NV** dessert with golden amber, nutty tastes. Rich, not too sweet/weak. Pvs blend 93, 96 vintages; next 98, 00; created in sherry-like maturation system – shows in rich 'oloroso' style (arresting very cold). Not available at present: only bottled "when I feel like it"!

Shiraz Bit-champing punters need to be patient for while longer while **00**, **01** incubate (in Fr/Am barrels). Both fabulously fragrant with cracked peppercorn and dusty scrub to ripe cassis. Unlike Pinotage above, these could become regulars judging from Webb's quiet enthusiasm. **Rhine Riesling Late Harvest** NEW ☆ **98** from super-ripe crop, offers above Riesling's honeysuckle, shy terpene whiffs; alluring beeswax/pollen character in supple, succulent peachy palate. Sugar delicately balanced by acidity. **Muscat de Frontignan** ☆ **01** elegant, off-dry grapey mouthful with rose petal, jasmine aromas; rich passionfruit flavours. Refreshing chilled, with spicy food. — *TM*

Theuniskraal Estate

Tulbagh (see Tulbagh map) • Tasting & sales by appointment Mon-Fri 9-12, 1-5 • Cellar tours by appointment • Winemakers Kobus & Andries Jordaan • Viticulturists Rennie, Kobus, Andries & Wagner Jordaan • Vineyards 130 ha • Production ± 1 500 tons ± 20 000 cases 87% white 13% red • PO Box 34 Tulbagh 6820 • ***Tel (023) 230-0687/88/89/90*** *• Fax (023) 230-1504 • E-mail info@theuniskraal.co.za • Website www.theuniskraal.co.za*

With the release of their first red, the Jordaan family of Tulbagh now proudly cater for both ends of your meal, and the in-between bits too. The delicate Natural Sweet, new in this venerable range, could get your juices going or, if you're a dry-drinker, the ever-popular Riesling. With the meal, the light Cabernet (named Symphony, perhaps with a future blend in mind) or the dry Semillon-Chardonnay. Afterwards, the low-alcohol sweet is the obvious choice. And if you prefer your vinous companion to look chic and contemporary, then the Jordaans can help you too, with smartened-up versions of the nostalgic old-Theuniskraal label.

☆**Riesling** ✓ This (Cape) riesling something of an SA icon: first 'estate' white – 54 yrs on market and still a big seller (16 000 cases/yr). Current on-song **01**, fresh, lively, bone-dry; excellent alfresco drink, solo or with salad buffet. Med-bodied. Though winemakers recommend "drink as soon as possible", won't keel over immediately. **00** untasted. **99** ☆.

☆**Semillon-Chardonnay** ✓ Interesting counterpoint to above – richer (in estate's restrained context), fuller (13.1% alc), riper fruit in **01**; satisfying, yet without the keen frisson of acid. Unoaked equal blend, vs **00**'s 56/44 partnership. ± 4 000 cases

Symphony NEW ☻ ★ Estate's first red is a cab and, though hardly recognisable as such, delicious and quaffable now. **00** lightly oaked, lightish-bodied, savoury. 115 cases.

Natural Sweet NEW ★ Charming, fragile newcomer to this growing category. Lowish alc, consistent with house style, soft, pretty **00** blend buket/gewürz. — *IvH*

Three Rivers see Bon Courage

Tokara

Stellenbosch (see Stellenbosch map) • Tasting, sales, cellar tour hours to be announced • Restaurant (please call (021) 808-5959) • Views • Owner GT Ferreira • Cellarmaster Gyles Webb • Winemaker Miles Mossop (since 2000) • Farm manager Eddie Smit (since 1997) • Vineyards 43 ha • Production 700 tons max 60% red 40% white • PO Box 662 Stellenbosch 7599 • ***Tel (021) 808-5900*** • *Fax (021) 808-5911 • E-mail wine@tokara.com*

WHERE are the eagerly anticipated wines we predicted would be ready mid-2001? Still in the vineyards of this swish Helshoogte property, with its angel's eye views and celestial restaurant. A full dress rehearsal saw a small amount of wine made last year (not for public release, however). After its first test run, the designer cellar gets rave reviews from young winemaker Miles Mossop (son of port-producing Cape Wine Master Tony Mossop). High-powered owner GT Ferreira and cellarmaster Gyles Webb are patiently waiting for exceptional quality to come from the vineyards (3-5 years old). Consultant viticulturist Aidan Morton is spending an "inordinate amount of time" nurturing these young vines, according to Mossop, who is optimistic that wines will be released in the near future. "If not, you probably won't be speaking to me for the next guide," says Mossop with a cherubic grin, despite the mounting pressure. Some things in life simply can't be hurried.

Topaz Wine

Helderberg • Sales & cellar tours by invitation • Owners Clive Torr & Tanja Beutler • Winemakers Clive, Mark, Ian, Tanja & Grant • Consulting viticulturalist Dirkie Morkel (Bellevue) • Vineyards 0.04 ha • Production 25 cases 100% Pinot Noir • 26 Topaz Street Heldervue Somerset West 7130 • Tel (021) 855-4275 • Fax (021) 855-5086 • E-mail topazwines@mweb.co.za

IN TRUE *garagiste* tradition, pinot is made at canny Cape Wine Master Clive Torr's Heldervue home with its fledgling vineyard by a bunch of friends who share a passion for natural wines and a back-to-the-earth approach. A long-standing love affair with Burgundy turned Torr on to a different way of thinking, one that takes into consideration biodynamics and sways with ancient wisdom and planetary pulls. The first barrels made in 1997 turned out so well, they were all the encouragement Torr and partner Tanja Beutler, who runs the show and prunes the vines, needed – now friends are demanding more wine than they can produce. Although he insists winemaking is just a hobby, a partnership between Canadian Philip Holzberg and Torr saw them slip through parochial Burgundy's tight controls to buy a vineyard in Ladoix – admittedly not the first stop of pinotphiles – where they conjure up a notable pinot under the tongue-in-cheek Domaine de Clivet label.

Clive Torr Pinot Noir Burgundian-style **01** too unfinished to rate conclusively, but classic qualities present in generous quantities, hinting at ★. potential. Bright ruby lights; cherry fruit on fresh toast; silky dry palate dominated by mocha oak; undergrowth/game nuances to finish. 17 mths 2nd fill oak; Stbosch fruit. 12 9% alc. 152 cases. **Clive Torr Shiraz 01** not tasted. — *TM*

Towerkop see Ladismith
Tradouw see Barrydale

Travino Wines

*Olifants River (see Olifants River map) • Tasting & sales Mon-Fri 8-1; 2-5 • Phone ahead for cellar tours • Owners 47 members • Manager Eben von Waltsleben • Winemaker Alkie van der Merwe (since 1995) with JC Coetzee (since 1995) • Consulting viticulturist Jeff Joubert (VinPro) • Vineyards ±600 ha • Production 8 817 tons 85% white 15% red • PO Box 2 Klawer 8145 • **Tel (027) 216-1616** • Fax (027) 216-1425 • E-mail travino@kingsley.co.za*

Growing wine in a warmer climate has its advantages and rewards, as Alkie van der Merwe is quick to point out. "We are the cellar that's probably the first to harvest!" says the high-spirited winemaker, who always speaks with at least one exclamation mark. "In 2001 we started on January 7th with chardonnay, closely followed by sauvignon. Being so early, we get lovely fruity, crisp wines – but none of the mid to late-season heatwaves and the stress that goes with them!!" Which would tend to explain the infectiously upbeat tone here, which extends to the names they give their wines. Deciding that common or vineyard 'Port' is far too ordinary, they've plumped for Matador ("bullfight!!").

Merlot ☆ **00** delivering on early promise: full, ripe-fruity tastes, persistent. Wholesome everyday drop, partly oaked. 13,1% alc. **Pinotage** ‡ Lightly wooded **00** full, vinous; some savoury tastes end firmly dry. 13% alc. **Shiraz** ☆ Varietal character shows in **00**'s smoky plums, but some aggressive tannins present too, needing down-toning with (AvdM's suggestion) "*lekker* slab of beef". 13.8% alc. **Grand Rouge** ‡ "There's a niche for an off-dry red," insists AvdM, though latest **NV** (00) (equal pinotage/ruby cab) tastes bone-dry. Astringency, massive ±14% alc call for rustic food antidote. **Chardonnay** ☆ Unwooded **01** bone-dry, somewhat leavened by sweet peachy fruit. 14.3% alc. 800 cases. **Sauvignon Blanc** ☆ **01** improves on pvs. Sweet-fruited, zesty, for splashing with the day's catch. 12.2% alc. 800 cases. **Blanc de Blanc** ☆ Unwooded **01** (sample) pick of these whites; equal sauvignon/chardonnay in med-bodied, semi-sweet, harmonious partnership. **Classic Dry White** ‡ **01** step above pvs NV. Pleasing tropical tastes, fresh non-aggressive finish. **Special Late Harvest** ☆ Attractive, unusual **NV** (00) semi-sweet chenin dessert; high raisin content adds dimension, interest. 12.9% alc. **Muskateer** ☆ Fortified dessert from muscat de f, oaked 12 mths. Latest **00** rich marmalade sweetness. Lowish 16,5% alc. 500 cases. "'Red Muscadel' too uninteresting for our label!" **Matador** NEW ☆ Ruby style 'port' from ruby cab, 7 mths oaked. **00** lively, fresh, sweet. 200 cases. — *DH*

Trawal see Travino

Tukulu

*Darling • Tasting & sales at Oude Libertas, Stellenbosch • See Stellenbosch Farmers' Winery • Owners SFW, Leopont 98 Properties, Maluti Groenekloof Community Trust • Winemaker Mlindeli Metshane • Vineyards to be expanded to 330 ha • Enquiries Carina Gous **tel (021) 808-8237***

Transkei-born Mlindeli Metshane (nicknamed Wellington by a teacher) travelled a circuitous route to land up in the region of his namesake Boland town. Based at the Nederburg cellars outside Paarl, where he'll continue making red wines under cellarmaster Razvan Macici, he's the newly appointed winemaker for Tukulu. It's the brand of leading empowerment initiative Papkuilsfontein Vineyards, a join venture between a Gauteng group of black businessmen, Distell and the local community. Metshane's climb started as cellar assistant at then Gilbeys; next rung was SFW, and an edge acquired assisting in the company's experimental cellar. As the very first recipient of the Patrick Grubb Scholarship, Metshane also worked a northern hemisphere harvest in Bordeaux, and in cellars in St Emilion and the Medoc, in 1998. "The classical approach gives an excellent foundation, a platform from which to grow and create a stamp that is unique. Right now I'm learning the soil at Papkuilsfontein. When people drink Tukulu I want them to have a sense of its origin," says Metshane, whose dream is to make a blend from cabernet, pinotage and shiraz.

Pinotage Bushvines on Groenekloof's Contreberg produce these sonorous, black pinotages with fruit cordial-like concentration, charry vanilla oak background and long, spicy tannins. Introduced with wildly acclaimed **99**, Yr small 25% Am casks; power alc (14%). Opaque **00** similarly flamboyantly structured; arresting sweet-incense bouquet turning tangy and then pruney in palate; fleshy, perfumed tannins.

Chardonnay NEW Full-bodied modern style, just-dry but – refreshingly – fruit-rather than oak-focused. **01** (sample) nuanced citrus tones, sweet vanilla-oaky background. High 14% alc not too demanding.

Chenin Blanc Red Tukulu soils – first identified on a KwaZulu-Natal farm of same name – and ancient, low cropping vines produce extraordinary chenins. **01** (sample) fragrant, floral with Loire-like mimosa/quince aromas and flavours of baked apple; concentrated; suggestion of sweetness (partly from very high 14.5% alc). Food-match with lightly curried West Coast mussels in creamy sauce. **00** rich, intense yet admirably restrained. Maiden **99**. — *IvH*

Tulbagh Co-op

*Tulbagh (see Tulbagh map) • Tasting & sales Mon-Fri 8.30-5 Sat 9-1 Closed religious public holidays • Views • Owners 70 members • General manager Marius Burger • Public relations Madeleine du Toit • Winemaker Michael Krone (since 1997) with Stefan Smit • Vineyards 1 000 ha • Production 10 000 tons • PO Box 85 Tulbagh 6820 • **Tel (023) 230-1001** • Fax (023) 230-1358 • E-mail tkw@tulbaghwine.co.za • Website www.tulbaghwine.co.za*

THE TULBAGH vineyards are brimming with vitality and, not to be outdone, these 70 co-op winefarmers are adding some fresh touches of their own. They've tapped Marius Burger to general-manage the operation, bringing with him experienced gained most recently at Franschhoek Vineyards (Michael Krone, from the valley's most famous winegrowing family, and Stefan Smit continue in their roles as cellar commander and adjutant). And in keeping with the current emphasis on affordability and value, they've launched the Village Collection labels to cater for the budget portion of the market.

Cabernet Sauvignon NEW Unpretentious everyday stuff; supple tannins make the strawberries/blackcurrants very easy to swallow. Med-bodied. 2 500 cases. **Chardonnay** Partially wood fermented **01** bouncy, sappy and balanced; spring flowers bouquet undimmed by oak. Watch the 14% alc as you tuck into the 2 700 cases.

Merlot Latest **00** unexpectedly astringent (6 mths oaked) compared to unwooded pvs ripe, rounded profile. Give yr/2 to soften. 13,7% alc. 3 000 cases. **Cabernet Sauvignon-Merlot** (Camelot in pvs ed) **00** 55/45 unwooded blend not as ripely charming as pvs; savoury, very dry; med-bodied. 600 cases. **Brut** Sauvignon's rocky riverbeds team with good aggressive bubbles in **NV** (00) styled, remarks vintner, "for celebrations or just for the hell of it". Lightish

(10.7% alc). 1 500 cases. **Vin Doux** ☆☆ Ruby cab imparts the coral hues colombard/chenin the sweet, unexpectedly refined flavours. Carbonation does the rest. Light 10,5% alc. **NV** (00). 2 000 cases. **Hanepoot** ☆ "For cold winter nights", Michael K envisages; and with the generous 2 ℓ **NV** (97) 'barrel bags', he must be anticipating some particularly lengthy chills. 16.8% alc. 2 000 cases. Discontinued: **Seminay Blanc** (Pvs **00** ☆).

Tulbagh Magnums

NEW

Merlot ☻ ☆☆ **99** good unpretentious quaffing; balanced vinification for informal dinner parties, barbecues etc. 6 mths oaked. **Vin Rouge** ☻ ☆☆ No home should be without this **NV** (01) unoaked pinotage/ruby cab blend; cheerful dry glugging at a bargain price.

Cabernet Sauvignon ☆☆ **98** bit more serious than above (though Michael K's still thinking "big party"); fragrant cedar whiffs from brief oaking. **Chardonnay** ☆☆ **00** unembellished by oak; sappy, dry and unpretentious. 13.6% alc. **Blanc de Blanc** ☆☆ Med-bodied, just-dry blend chenin, colombard, sauvignon, unwooded no-worries quaff. **NV** (01) **Natural Sweet** ☆☆ "Specially for people of the old Transvaal," Michael K explains. We predict fine-strung **NV** (01), from chenin/hanepoot, will appeal much more widely. Good expression of this style.

Village Collection

NEW

NVs in 2 ℓ 'barrel bag', 750 ml and 500 ml screwtops.

Classic Red ☻ ☆☆ Not-so-classic varieties (pinotage/ruby cab), but no lack of spicy high-toned flavour (or alc: 14% – take note), sour-cherry piquancy. Unwooded. 5 000 cases.

Blanc de Blanc Chalky/honeyed everyday dry lubrication. Med-bodied. 5 000 cases. **Extra Light** ☆ Modestly flavoured off-dry blend fernao pires/clairette blanche. 9.3% alc. 10 000 cases. **Stein** ☆ Demure, quick finishing semi-sweet white, chenin/colombard. 5 000 cases. **Late Harvest** Sweeter version of above; lightish, undemanding. 5 000 cases. — *IvH*

Tulbagh Mountain Vineyards

NEW

Tulbagh • Owners Jason Scott & George Austin • Vineyards 15.5 ha • Production 6-8 tons/ha (target) • PO Box 19 Tulbagh 6820 • ***Tel (023) 231-1118*** *• Fax (023) 231-1002 • E-mail tmw@tulbagh.com • Website www.tulbagh.com/tulbaghmountainvineyards.htm*

Fired by safaris to some of the world's premier vineyards, British wine buddies and financial market operators Jason Scott and George Austin scoured Europe, the US and Australia before settling on 180 hectares on the boundary of the choc-box pretty Great Winterhoek wilderness sanctuary near Tulbagh. Their goal is to "create one of the best red wines in the world", and if your first reaction is to splutter into your chardonnay, they're betting the farm their "15.5 ha of organically grown vines and Malmesbury shales will tell their own story in 2003". The Scott-Austin weapons of global domination are shiraz, cabernet and mourvèdre, and an infectious passion that borders on chutzpah (the wine person they'd most like to meet is über-arbiter Robert Parker ("*after* our first release, to show him that SA can produce the goods"). Stand by for fireworks when the balloon – and a 200 ton cellar – go up towards the end of the year.

Twee Jonge Gezellen Estate 

Tulbagh (see Tulbagh map) • Tasting & sales Mon-Fri 9-4 Sat 10-2 • Cellar tours Mon-Fri at 11 & 3; Sat at 11 • Closed Sundays, 1 January, Good Friday, 24, 25, 26 & 31 December • Casual tastings: No charge Formal tastings: Fee on request Large/tourgroups: by appointment • Views • Owner/winemaker Nicky Krone (since 1970's) • Vineyard 120 ha • Production 1 200 tons • PO Box 16 Tulbagh 6820 • ***Tel (023) 230-0680*** *• Fax (023) 230-0686 • E-mail tjg@mweb.co.za*

THERE's always something fresh happening at this historic wine estate in the pioneering Tulbagh valley. Multi-faceted winemaker Nicky Krone (first to night harvest, first underground MCC sparkling wine cellar in SA, first preservative-free MCC bubbly) has been considered eccentric at times ("Who, me? Couldn't be!") but that simply translates into way ahead of the pack. "Everything we do at TJ is aimed at making our products in as healthy a way as possible – if that is eccentric, then I'm happy because I see a lot more people in the wine industry trying to become *eccentric* ... " Now they're bottling a new Beaumes-de-Venise-style wine ("So far, everyone has loved the samples," says Mary Krone, who likens the estate to a swan: "Graceful on top, paddling like anything underneath"). Book a *sabrage* session, an impressive party trick in anyone's book – those brave enough to lop the head off a bottle of bubbly get to go home with a certificate (it's also an indemnity form, laughs Mary Krone). Although bubblies remain the Krone's true love, reds have been replanted, with shiraz the focus.

✲**Krone Borealis Brut** Astonishment among Air France Classic 00 judges at quality, longevity of these fine, subtle, preservative-free cap classiques, 50/50 chardonnay/pinot. "We hadn't realised," said all-French panel, "wines such as these could be made outside of France" (they awarded a selection of Krones spanning vintages from **93** onwards the class gold medal *and* next three places). Nicky Krone no stranger to winner's enclosure: 95 Diners Club awardee; top-rated by bubbly savant Tom Stevenson). Now Krone offers his latest **98**; wakes with classic 5 am-bakery aromas, then lovely, creamy appley fruit, departs with clean, almost austerely dry finish. Very young-tasting still, beautiful balance between fermentation qualities and fruit; unlike pvs, no apparent mid-palate sweetness. Energetic, persistent mousse. 8 000 half-cases.

✲**Viognier** NEW Experimental first release **01** individually styled, steely profile (despite 100% malo) rather than more usual opulence. Mouthful of complexity with thyme hints; 'sweet' fruit touch well contrasted with invigorating dry finish. Med-bodied, unoaked. Interesting wine. 100 cases sure to be pounced on by collectors.

Pinot Noir NEW ★ **00** (tank sample, as are all wines below, so may rate marginally higher on release) Individual unoaked version with some authentic farmyard, strawberry tastes; aggressively dry, tannic. Will probably need lots of time. 1 600 cases. **TJ 39** ✲ Blend riesling (39 is clone number), sauvignon, chardonnay, chenin good dry white aperitif, table companion. **01** with lunchtime-lightish alc (±12%), delicate lemony nose, perky-fresh palate. 5 200 cases. **TJ Schanderl** ✲✲ Perfumed, smooth, off-dry **01** billows fresh muscat de f flavours. Lightish 12% alc. 5 200 cases. **TJ Light** ✲✲ Way-low 8% alc, but more charisma than many 'lights'. **01** "blend of early ripening, fruity varieties", daintily perfumed, gentle, fairly dry brisk finishing. Acknowledged by Heart Foundation. 5 200 cases. **TJ Night Nectar** ✲✲ Becomes Natural Sweet from **01** (pvs officially Semi-Sweet); still mostly chenin, spattering riesling, sauvignon. Honeysuckle and guava tastes; clean, soft. For curry nights. 7,5% alc. 2 600 cases. **NC's Night Cap** NEW ✲✲ Whimsically subtitled Oupa se Dop, lowish-alc fortified muscat de f with enough sweetness to keep grandpa dancing on his bedside table! Sweet melon, muscat bouquet; fresh spirity finish with unorthodox heathery/peaty aftertaste. **Engeltjipipi** Delicate botrytis notes in **01** (sample, unrated), Natural Sweet dessert with 15.5% alc. 2 500 cases. **TJ Rose Brut** ☆ Light salmon hues to this "designer sparkling wine", pinot/chardonnay, unwooded, with extended lees stay-over for authentic yeasty effect. Light tastes of candied/baked apple, perked up with explosive, mouthfilling bubbles to short, crisp finish. Feathery texture enhanced by lowish 11,7% alc. **NV**. 2 600 cases. — *DH*

Two Oceans

Even if the eye-catching labels wrongly claim that the Atlantic and Indian oceans meet at Cape Point, this is a good value range. Now with extra verve. By Distell.

Semillon-Chardonnay ☻ ☆ For connoisseurs on a budget. Not too full lemony body in **00**; firm but round texture which versatile at mealtimes (lemon-buttered cob would be a good match).

Cabernet-Merlot ☆ 65/35 blend, unwooded. Soft, slightly sweet Aussie-style **01**, decent everyday red (155 000 cases made, so go ahead and enjoy), fairly priced. 13% alc. **Rosé** ✩ Lightish **01** cab/pinot partnership tastes earthy, dusty; drier than ±10 g/ℓ sugar would suggest. Needs a good chill. **Sauvignon Blanc** ☆ Shouts sauvignon in **01**; well-formed flavours in not-too-alcoholic frame. Very fresh, satisfying. — *IvH*

Uiterwyk Estate

Stellenbosch (see Stellenbosch map) • Tasting & sales Mon-Fri 10-4.30 (Oct-Apr) Mon-Fri 10-12.30; 2-4.30 (May-Sep) Sat 10-4.30 year round • Tasting fee R10 p/p for groups 10+ • Cellar tours during harvest by appointment • Owners De Waal family • Winemakers Chris de Waal (white wines, since 1978), Daniël de Waal (red wines, since 1990) • Marketing Pieter de Waal • Production 1 000 tons ±20 000 cases 50/50 red/white • PO Box 15 Vlottenburg 7604 • ***Tel (021) 881-3711*** *• Fax (021) 881-3776 • E-mail info@uiterwyk.co.za • Website www.uiterwyk.co.za*

It's Rhone on the range at this Stellenboschkloof winery, with a maiden Shiraz that was fermented on viognier lees a la Cote Rotie. Oenologist Daniël de Waal (one of the ninth-generation brothers here) selected his site to replicate Rhone conditions, planting in poor gravelly soils on a warm north-facing slope. Both varieties were grafted onto old chenin rootstock for a turnaround time of only one year instead of the usual four. A single bottling of cabernet franc is another step in their new direction. Red wine cultivars are encroaching at a dizzying rate, but white wine specialist Chris de Waal doesn't feel in the least bit threatened: some south-facing slopes and soils are so perfectly suited to sauvignon and chardonnay that whites will always feature. And the Sting in the tale? Pieter de Waal thought he was seeing things when the British megastar popped in unannounced (and uninvited!) at a tasting on the terrace of a Cape Town hotel. But, a true-blue marketer, he didn't miss a beat and immediately persuaded him to try a glass of their Pinotage.

☆☆ **Top of the Hill Pinotage** World-class red, showered with awards, released only in exceptional vintages. Since first **96** ☆☆, always single vyd selection, ±45 yr old vines, new Nevers oak-barrelled ±22 mths, racked half-yearly. **97** ABSA Top Ten, *Wine* ☆. **98** and, now, **99** not up to usual standard, so bravely 'declassified'. No doubts, however, about pedigree of **00** (pre-bottling sample): fabulous dense hues, reserved yet spicy bouquet, superb fruit-packed, creamy flavours – all hallmarks of a champion (to rival **96**?).

☆ **Pinotage** Critically acclaimed stablemate to above 'Reserve'; gentle-tannined fruit from lower-cropped younger vyds; usually dash merlot for extra softness (though most need min 4/5 yrs to reveal their charms). **00** preview less oak-influenced than above (only 50% new barrels), so pure varietal fruit shines: spicy plums; hallmark palate-coating mulberries. Super-ripe (13.8% alc). Current **99** ✵ lighter; similar traits plus darker burgundian forest floors. Elegant maturation potential. **98** extra-concentrated, more tannic, plush fruit delivering less obvious spiciness than some pvs, reflecting the de Waals' stylistic evolution. WOM Reserve.

✵✵**Estate Cape Blend** Outstanding cab-based cuvee, proudly waving SA flag with routine infusions local-grape pinotage (max 35-40%, mandated by variety's feistiness). **99**, due 02, regrettably not ready for tasting. **98** ✵ big (13,5% alc), robust; showcases Daniël de Waal's dazzling blending skills: leafy, spicy fragrance from cab f (45%, highest to date), stronger bdx character from 30% merlot. 22 mths Fr oak, 60% new. WOM selection. **97** recently hailed as "a revelation" by Swiss *Basle-Zeitung*. **94-99** featured cab f (cab s rejected as clashing with other components); will change from **00**.

✵**Merlot** Now one of Cape's more serious contenders; heightened complexity, harmony from wide variety of vyd aspects, soils. Already-complex **99** (sample) bright cassis fruit; mineral and rich chocolatey notes with leafy nuances. Potential ✵. Downsized new Fr oak (30%) allows fruit to blossom. Showier form inaugurated with **96** *Wine* ✵. Build, tannins demand cellaring good 3-4 yrs. **97** WOM selection.

✵**Shiraz** NEW ✓ Complicated, forelock-tugging (to France) winegrowing behind maiden **99** (see intro). Revisited just prior to mid-01 release, shows stunning bottle development; fairly reeks of the Cote Rotie (dense liquorice, cassis, cracked peppercorn) but also, in palate, waves to the warmer Antipodes in protracted sour-plum, redcurrant, chocolatey spice. (This bi-hemispheric persona much loved by UK critics.) Very elegant, doubtless first of many fine examples. 5 mths Fr oak, 30% new. 13.4% alc. 600 cases.

✵**Cabernet Franc** NEW Just 400 cases of **00**, from stalwart 10 yr old vyd previously infusing Estate blend. "We are so excited about this quality, we're bottling some on its own," enthuses Daniël de Waal. Hallmark sweet cinnamon, fresh thatch, ripe berry characters all present in incredibly dense, chewy form; yet overall effect is soft, supple; fine-drawn grape tannins ensure long, velvety curtain-call. Deserves time to settle, develop. Fr oak, 20% new.

✵**Viognier** One of handful in Cape of this aromatic Rhone speciality white. **01** bouquet closed, yet palate surprisingly rich, powerful, dry; creamy apricot fruit partners deluxe alc structure (13.5%), enhancing subtle viscosity. This, bright (6.5 g/ℓ) acidity fine foils for Asian cuisine. Portion maiden vintage **99**, new Fr oak matured, reappeared in **00** (both rated ★). None shows overt varietal perfume, but should age well in bottle.

Cabernet Sauvignon Last was **98** ★. **Sauvignon Blanc** ★ New **01** retains fresh, brightly fruited profile of pvs – all green grass, gooseberry, dusty pear-drop whiffs. Conservative 23°B harvest translates into mid-weight 12.5% alc, bracing lemon-sherbet freshness in assertive finish. **Chardonnay** ★ 15 mths heavy-toast new Allier oak supercharges **99**; with full-cream butterscotch lushness contrasting pleasingly with firm, very dry palate. 13.5% alc. **Chardonnay Reserve** Last was **98** ★.

Rosenburg range

For UK restaurants; also sold locally. **Cabernet Franc-Pinotage** Not tasted for this ed; **97** pvsly rated ★. — *TM*

Uitkyk Estate

Stellenbosch (see Stellenbosch map) • Tasting & sales Mon-Fri 9-5 Sat & Sun 10-4 • Picnics in summer season • Owner Lusan Holdings • Winemaker Estelle

Swart (since 2000) • Manager & viticulturist To be appointed • Production 869 tons 62 796 cases • PO Box 3 Elsenburg 7607 • **Tel (021) 884 4416** • Fax (021) 884 4717 • E-mail nee@mweb.co.za

THIS venerable old Cape estate, with its magnificent neo-classical manor house, has entered a fresh new era. "Whatever the techniques used to make a wine, whatever the concept that the producer has of it, terroir is always the master," is the conviction held by brand-new winemaker Estelle Swart, who's taken over in both cellar and vineyards from Theo Brink, now retired. No easy task but she's well equipped (Aussie seasoning at Tatachilla, California know-how from Simi in Sonoma, and stints as assistant winemaker at sister farms Neethlingshof and Stellenzicht). The 'best student in oenology and viticulture' in her Stellenbosch university days, Swart will be applying all that knowledge to further developing the already pedigreed vineyards. Another new addition is the tasting centre, housed in an 18th-century cellar building remodelled by architect Mark Rosenbaum. Like everything here, it's a clever combination of modern lines and historic dimensions, with plaster removed in places to reveal the original stone and brickwork.

Cabernet Sauvignon Venerable Cape institution, long-standing 'Carlonet' epithet dropped from **98**, but this, pvs, always 100% cab so no change in make-up. **98** mirrors vintage generosity; positively laden with cassis, sundry dark berries, carnation-scented tannins sweep aside richness for stunning classic conclusion. 13.8% alc. 18 mths Fr oak, 50% new. **97** firm tannic structure, lurking fruit needing few yrs' development. **96** vegetal twist in difficult Cape yr; VG, *Wine*, WOM Reserve. **95** stunning 'sweet' profile, super-supple.

Cabernet-Shiraz Chunky, chewy **98** initially strikes as savoury; meaty tones travel unimpeded through palate until ripe fruit/tannins kick in towards finish. Suggest wait yr/2 to integrate/develop, then serve with traditional hearty beef potjie. Equal blend; 18 mths Fr oak. 14,2% alc. **97** Cherry, cedar and medicinal notes; big dry tannins.

Sauvignon Blanc Latest **01** tasted just post bottling still finding its pace; delicate meadow-flower bouquet, soft tropical fruit, gentle acid. Nice food wine/by-the-glass option. Melon, highly unusual uncooked pumpkin aromas in **99**; balanced and rich. **98** almost baroque richness, power. Effusive gooseberry, figs, grass in **97**.

Chardonnay Reserve Old-worldy dank cellar hints developing in delicious step-up **00**, firm but ripe, full; variety's lemon/limes paired with buttered toast and butterscotch; lovely chalky dry finish. **99** creamily rich, spiced with cloves and dominated by oak (11 mths new Fr). — *IvH*

Uitvlucht Winery

Montagu (see Little Karoo map) • Tasting & sales Mon-Fri 8.30-5.30 Sat 8-12 • Cellar tours by appointment • Owners 45 members • Winemaker Kootjie Laubscher (since 1993) • Production 7 000 tons 15 000 cases 95% white 5% red/dessert • PO Box 332 Montagu 6720 • ***Tel (023) 614-1340*** *• Fax (023) 614-2113*

RANGE not ready for tasting for this ed. Pvs have included: **Cabernet Sauvignon**, **Merlot**, **Ruby Cabernet**, **Sauvignon Blanc**, **Blanc de Blanc**, **Colombar**, **Chenin Blanc**, **Late Harvest**, **Vin Doux**, **Vin Sec**; **Red Muscadel**, **White Muscadel** (these also in 250 ml); **Muscat de Frontignan**, **Port**.

Upington see Oranjerivier Wine Cellars

Upland Estate

*Wellington (see Wellington map) • Tasting, sales, cellar tours by appointment • Self catering cottages Tel (021) 864-1184 • Walks • Views • Owners Edmund & Elsie Oettlé • Winemaker/viticulturist Edmund Oettlé • Vineyards 13 ha • Production ±700 cases 100% red • PO Box 152 Wellington 7654 • **Tel (021) 082-731-4774** • Fax (021) 873-5724• E-mail edmund@oettle.com • Website http:\\oettle.com*

Edmund and Elsie Oettlé lead a healthy lifestyle on their small fruit, nut and wine farm against the Hawequa slopes near Wellington. They've adhered to organic principles (half the farm is pristine fynbos) for the last 7 years and just received international certification ("a costly business!"). A practicing vet (he sees his four-legged patients by referral only in the evenings), Oettlé's a keen falconer: he has his own frequently-flown hunting bird, Guinevere. He also breeds peregrines and black sparrowhawks. He's a dab hand in the kitchen and, of course, the low-key cellar. He made and welded his own steel tanks, saving a small fortune in the process. And when he decided to make brandy out of the existing chenin and riesling grapes, he constructed his own distilling plant too_ last year saw the first release. Oettlé started making 'house' wine in high school, and with this experimental edge still in evidence, he's now made a traditional grappa.

✵**Cabernet Sauvignon** Flew from the Oettlés' wonderfully Durrell-esque farm straight into the hearts of Michelangelo judges with second release **99**; sturdy, but less muscle-bound than massively chunky, tobacco-dusty **00** (tank sample rated ⁂); big dry oak tannins overwhelm fruit (though only older barrels used) in coarsely fleshy palate. Beware 14.5 alc.

Merlot ⁂ Approachable **98** shows choc-coated cherry fruit, medicinal sweetness perhaps from Am. component of yr new oak. Marked acidity complements corpulent 14% alc. — *TJ*

Uva Mira Vineyards

*Stellenbosch • Tasting by appointment • 3 self catering, fully serviced guest cottages • Views • Owners Weedon family • Consulting viticulturist Paul Wallace • Vineyards 18 ha • Production 5 000 cases 80% white 20% red • PO Box 1511 Stellenbosch 7599 • **Tel/fax (021) 880-1682** • E-mail uva.mira@softswitch.co.za*

This eyrie property bordering the Helderberg Nature Reserve is proving it can be as eco-friendly as the neighbour. In the hands of owner Denise Weedon and family, the property is switching to organic grape production. They're also planting cabernet franc and shiraz, to join existing blocks of noble varieties and wildcard roobernet in what vine-cordial Paul Wallace, the new consultant here, identifies as "excellent cool-climate sites". Nurturing the vision of late patriarch Des Weedon, his family plans to erect a cellar once the vineyards have been registered and certified. Meanwhile the 'Special Grapes' para-glide to nearby Stellenbosch and the cellars of Bergkelder. Pvsly tasted were **Chardonnay 00** (✵), **Sauvignon Blanc 99** (⁂).

Van Loveren

*Robertson (see Robertson map) • Tasting & sales Mon-Fri 8.30-5 Sat 9.30-1 No tasting fee • Owners Nico & Wynand Retief • Winemakers Bussell Retief (since 1993) & Phillip Retief (since Dec 98) • Viticulturists Hennie Retief (since 1991) & Neil Retief (since 1998) • Production 3 000 tons 153 000 cases • PO Box 19 Klaasvoogds 6707 • **Tel (023) 615 1505** • Fax (023) 615 1336 • Email vanloveren@lando.co.za*

Just beyond the tranquil tasting area – a *rondavel* amid lush gardens – hums the Retief family's bee-busy winery, fronted by the four cousins whose faces now smile from their handsome and popular 1 500 ml bottles. All are boundlessly energetic (patriarchs Nico and Wynand, and hands-on wives no less so), and wildly successful, annually sending more than 150 000 cases trundling down their apricot-kernel strewn farm road to markets locally and abroad (Muscadel Blanc de Noir already stocked by most UK supermarket chains "and sales just keep growing"). So popular is their River Red, they're having to fill fresh batches every 30 days; their Sauvignon, to guarantee crispness, is bottled 16 times a year. Having made the big leagues, they're now going small with micro-vinifications, under a Limited Release label, of Cabernet, Chardonnay and Shiraz (they're especially proud of the latter, from vines ex another grower's cancelled order – "Their loss, our gain!").

Limited Release Shiraz NEW **99** serious example, deeply layered with fruit, vanilla-oak and tannin, but not at expense of house's thumbprint approachability. 6-7 yrs to peak. 6 000 individually numbered bottles.

Cabernet Sauvignon-Shiraz Standout **99** quite earnestly structured, firmer than most range-mates yet balanced. Oak-staved **00** much lighter/softer, earlier maturing. Gulpable strawberry/smoky-shiraz tastes. 5 000 cases.

River Red Deserved success for this unpretentious, affordable everyday drink. Unoaked ruby cab, merlot, pinotage (60/30/10). **01** soft and pleasantly balanced as ever. 13,3 alc. Can be chilled in summer. 35 000 cases. Also in 500 ml screwcap. **Four Cousins Natural Sweet Rosé** NEW Sweet but non-cloying **01**; gentle red cherry/fairground candy flavours; very low alc (7.5%) for easy sipping. 4 000 cases in striking high-shouldered 1 500 ml bottles, as are ... **Four Cousins Dry White** Thimble muscadel adds intrigue to **00** lightweight pool-party playmate; colombard, sauvignon (60/30) softened by suggestion sugar. 4 000 cases. **Cape Riesling** Canny commercial style, invisible sugar filling all the spaces in **01**. Lowish 11.5% alc. 2 000 cases.

Limited Release Cabernet Sauvignon NEW Lighter-toned than LR Shiraz above; **00** fruity, fairly dry tannins hugging the juicy cherry/plum flavours. 4 000 numbered bottles. **Pinotage** NEW **01**, tasted young, already soft, accessible; whiffs banana, woodsmoke from oak stave fermentation. 13% alc. 10 000 cases. **Merlot** NEW **01** unrated sample showcases winery's signature drinkability; soft red-berry/choc tastes and tannins, empathetic oaking. 13.5% alc. 4 000 cases. **Four Cousins Dry Red** NEW Clone of River Red in generous 1 500 ml. Current release is **01**. 4 000 cases. **Blanc de Noir Shiraz** Lovely onion-skin colour; **01** soft, rounded, well constructed and dry enough to bring to table. 13% alc. 4 000 cases. **Blanc de Noir Red Muscadel** The sweet version; huge in the UK. **01** light (11% alc), sweeter tasting than pvs but balanced. For drinking now or sooner. 50 000 cases. **Reserve Chardonnay** Six mths Fr-oaked **00** generous limey flavours, which delicious now and for another yr. 13.5% alc. 1 000 cases. Will make way for a Limited Release from 01. **Spes Bona Chardonnay** Unwooded version. **01** closed when tasted mid-01, but nicely balanced; should perk up in time for festive season. 14% alc. **Pinot Gris** Crowd-pleasing style, grain balancing sugar; easy, ripe; some asparagus flavours in **01**. 14% alc. **Sauvignon Blanc** Grassy, just-dry **01**'s assertive freshness needs food now or short calming spell in bottle. 12.5% alc. 25 000 cases. **Blanc de Blanc** Racy **01** usual colombard/sauvignon blend; fresh, fruity and just-dry. 10 000 cases. Also known as ... **Vino Blanc** in 500 ml screwcap. **Colombar-Chardonnay** 50/50 blend, fruitily/florally aromatic; **01** with firm acidity which good with rich linefish like yellowtail. Lightly oaked. 2 000 cases. **Colombar** "Smell those guavas!" Bussell & Phillip Retief exclaim. Smallest crop ever delivers unusually bouncy **01**, with lots of acid to balance the 12 g/ℓ sugar. 2 000 cases which should be enjoyed soon. **Semillon** ☆ Sherbety figs in unwooded, dry **01**, which unexpectedly short (possibly a function of super-reductive vinification). 2 000 cases. **Fernão Pires** ☆ **01** graceful muscat scents, mango tastes – all balanced, lightish and not too dry. 1 500 cases. **Rhine Riesling** ☆ **00** shows some pleasing beeswaxy development, nonaggressive dryness. **01** not ready for tasting. 2 000 cases. **Special Late Harvest Gewürztraminer** ☆ Gorgeous potpourri bowl in **01**; light, not too sweet (41 g/ℓ natural sugar well balanced by acid). 3 500 cases. **Red Muscadel** ☆ Translucent rose-amber **01**, scented candyfloss aromas, delicate muscat tastes. Not oversweet. 17% alc. 1 000 cases.

Papillon range

Colour-coded butterflies feature on these budget priced, lowish alc **NV** (00) carbonated bubblies. The range includes **Brut**, **Demi-sec**, **Vin Doux**, each ☆, 10 000 cases. — *CF*

Van Zylshof Estate

Robertson (see Robertson map) • Tasting & sales Mon-Fri 8.30-12.30 & 2-5 Sat 9-1 • Owners Chris & Andri van Zyl • Winemaker/ viticulturist Andri van Zyl (since 1983) • Vineyards 30 ha • Production 450 tons 99% white 1% red • PO Box 64 Bonnievale 6730 • ***Tel (023) 616-2940*** *• Fax (023) 616-3503 • E-mail vanzylshof@lando.co.za*

This is the smallest estate in the Robertson Valley: just 40 hectares amble up a gentle rise from the Breede River to the van Zyl family home looking out over Bonnievale village. The winery is appropriately diminutive, yet focused and, now, even more welcoming after a revamp of the cellar-attached tasting area. Third generation Andri van Zyl, recently joined by lanky son Chris, has a palette of cabernet, merlot, chardonnay, chenin and sauvignon, which he applies with pointillist precision: "I will never oak my chenin", he declares, "it will always be crisp and fruity, Loire-style." Chardonnay, likewise, "must never be woody", so only a soupcon is oaked. All in service of his philosophy – "You must be able to drink a bottle and look forward to another the next night" – which has earned him an enthusiastic following locally and in Europe and America.

☆**Cabernet Sauvignon-Merlot** NEW ✓ Bright debut for estate's first red; **01** (in youth) big mouthful (13.6% alc) with scents of violets and roses; understated, already-integrated oak enhances promise of further development over 3-4 yrs.

Chardonnay ☆ Friendly, approachable style; some complexity from partial Fr oak barrelling. **00** honeyed, leesy/buttery tones, for early enjoyment. 13,9% alc. **Sauvignon Blanc** ☆ Not as energetic as some pvs. **01** bits of green grass and some tropical tones; lowish alc (11.6% alc).

Chardonnay Riverain ☻ ☆ Unwooded version. **01** pure expression of estate's fragile pear flavours; briskly dry conclusion with fresh-lemon aftertaste. 13.7% alc. **Chenin Blanc** ☻ ☆ Lightish **01** bounces with ripe guava aromas, sunny tropical fruit; lemon-zesty finish. — *DH*

Vaughan Johnson's Wine & Cigar Shop

Cape Town • Sales Mon-Fri 9-6 Sat 9-5 Sun 10-5 • Owner Vaughan Johnson • Victoria & Alfred Waterfront Pierhead Cape Town 8001 • PO Box 50012 Waterfront 8002 • ***Tel (021) 419-2121*** *• Fax (021) 419-0040 • E-mail vjohnson@mweb.co.za • Website www.vaughanjohnson.com*

Uniquely placed to track trends in both hemispheres, Vaughan Johnson's been reading the Cape wine thermometer at his Waterfront emporium and its sister store in Dublin's super trendy Temple Bar. South African shiraz is red hot, solo or in blends, reports this debonair pamperer of palates, while the cooler 2001 vintage is "great to sell", particularly sauvignons. Barrel previews of reds "look set to herald a new era of ripe tannins," ventures Johnson, who sees a dramatic improvement in quality compared to the late 80s and early 90s (he's been setting a stylish example for over a decade). Americans are discovering Cape wines in a bigger way and are "totally wowed by the quality". Before foreign interest creates a stampede though, long-term loyalty from producer to retailer to customer is still the only way to successfully build a quality name – short-term greed has no place in this equation, cautions Johnson.

Seriously Good Plonk (White) ☻ ☆ What it says. Cheerful, perky semi-dry white from Stbosch chenin (70%), sauvignon. Unpretentious screwtop (also red version below). 12,5% alc.

Sunday Best Red ☆ Paarl's sun-drenched fruit in latest mouthfilling version of this well-priced *every*day drink. Merlot and (surprisingly full-throated) carignan, Paarl origin. 14% alc. **Good Everyday Cape Red** ☆ Berries, smoked meats, herbs folded together for versatile full-bodied sipping; Paarl tinta/shiraz, all 01. Value. **Seriously Good Plonk (Red)** ☆ If you prefer a bit of tannin in your plonk, this one's for you. Strawberry/savoury touches and enough tannin to cut fatty barbecues. Might even go yr/2. Stbosch cinsaut/pinotage. Screwcap. **Good Everyday Cape White** ☆ Sells for under R12, but nothing cut-rate about the enjoyment; refreshing, dry; quartet of grapes ex F'hoek, all 01. 13% alc. New versions of the following not ready for tasting: **Really Good Red** Pvs ☆ chic, expensive-smelling, really good, in fact. **Sunday Best White** Pvs ☆ easy and versatile, comfortably dry; **Really Good White** Pvs ☆ mouthfilling and crisply dry; equally good solo or with seafood.

Waterfront Collection

Nautical labels distinguish this reasonably priced, quaffable duo.

Captain's Claret ☆ Honest everyday fare. Lightish; sweet jammy flavours neatly balanced by touch tannin. 50/50 shiraz/merlot from Paarl. **Great White** ☆ Nothing sharp about this fresh tropical chenin from Paarl, with coolly dry lemony finish. Med-light bodied. All above **NV**. — *DH*

Veelgeluk see West Coast Vineyards
Veelverjaaght see Bowe Joubert

Veenwouden

Paarl (see Paarl map) • Tasting, sales, cellar tours by appointment • Tasting fee R100 p/bottle if no purchase made • Max 6 people per tasting – "we are a small cellar" • Owner Deon van der Walt • Winemaker Marcel van der Walt (since 1995) • Viticulturist Charles van der Walt (since 1990), with Marcel van der Walt (since 1993) • Production 80 tons 5 500 cases 100% red • PO Box 7086 Noorder-Paarl 7623 • ***Tel (021) 872-6806*** *• Fax (021) 872-1384 • E-mail veenwouden@intekom.co.za*

This small, specialised Paarl property is owned by Zurich-based South African tenor Deon van der Walt, who regularly flies back to the close-knit family fold, laden with liquid inspiration from all corners of the wine world for them to taste: brother Marcel is the winemaker here, father Charles the farm manager and mother Sheila the one who "really holds it all together". Last year saw the debut of their Thornhill Shiraz 00 (the maiden vintage was made from a neighbour's bought-in grapes while their own vines mature). They're expecting fruit for this year's harvest from their 4,5-hectare vineyard, planted with shiraz and cabernet. While some may find the R125 per bottle tasting fee hard to swallow, it's not exorbitant in the grand scheme of things: the prices *do* hit the high notes (R100 for

Vivat Bacchus, R180 for Chardonnay) but so do the wines, they're limited in quantity and all very special. While there'll be no 'good value' indicators in the red print, it's all relative – they represent great value, especially if you had the foresight to buy some and stash them.

☆☆☆**Merlot** Upstaged at times by Classic below, as rousing but altogether more fleshy, palate-friendly and lip-smackingly delicious. **99** reflects cellar's passion for quality – "only the finest, cleanest, ripe fruit" – ruthless selection (4-5 t/ha yield). Oozes concentration, flavour, class: huge ruby colour; forest berries jostle with mocha under cover of firm, palate far too young to unveil its considerable charm. Hallmark is stylish, measured penetration in the mouth, deliberately understated rather than immediately opulent. 8% cab adds electricity. **98** greater individual personality, more echoing concentration yet nothing obtrusive, overdone. Oaked 2 yrs 80% new Fr barriques. 14% alc. 2 500 cases.

☆☆☆**Classic** Termed classic: it is. **99** follows big shoes of dramatic **98** ☆☆☆. More muscular than stablemate Merlot (due to powerful 52% cab, with 38% merlot, 10% cab f), demands more patience. Squid-ink black; oak char, perfumed red berries, fresh-ground coffee beans cajoled out of currently closed nose, palate riveting – gently layered cassis fruit, unobtrusive oak, ripe tannins and incisive 14% alc all warming up for the main act – another 4 yrs required for authoritative tannins to release sumptuous underlying fruit, will go 10 with ease. **98** bolder albeit within linear paradigm of taut pencil-lead, blackcurrant and dusty spice. New Nevers cooperage adds final polish to bdx-like aura. 2 300 cases. Impressive award haul includes gold Bdx International Challenge du Vin, Air France trophy. 80% new Fr oak, 20% 2nd fill. 2 000 cases.

☆☆**Vivat Bacchus** Frivolous, naïve packaging depicting scene from Mozart's *Abduction from the Seraglio* belies gravity of the contents. Styling from **98** similarly to above wines, next **99** in the slot: smoky nose redolent of seasoned leather, tobacco leaf, akin to a venerable, panelled, book-lined study. Palate firm, full, brambly fruit cosseted in mineral tannic shroud. Excellent length. 65% merlot, rest malbec, cab f, bulk 2nd fill barrels, 20% new. 14% alc. 1 000 cases. **98** retains malbec's distinctive minerally character, deep, supple flavours finely framed by tannin.

☆☆**Thornhill Shiraz** NEW **00** launches another arrow from the vdW quiver, likely to reach cult status of siblings from the start. Grapes (90% shiraz, 10% cab) bought from neighbour of new 4.5 ha vineyard in Wellington ("just 7 km from Veenwouden" – own rows due to bear in 02). Dense colour concentration, reticent nose in spicy frame; ripe aromas of mulberry, nutmeg, savoury wood with caper twist; clearly fruit-forward, big style (14% alc.) but avoids blowsiness. 14 mths Fr oak, 20% new, rest 2nd fill. 300 cases.

☆☆☆**Chardonnay Special Reserve** One may gasp (in local context) at R180 swing ticket, but with only 45 cases made in **00**, and at this quality level, value is relative. Current **00** singularly brilliant, crosses threshold of being just 'chardonnay' and becomes 'great dry white': shimmering gilts to straw colour, plumes of earthy, apple-pie richness herald classic palate – mineral fruit bundled with elegant oak – neither citric nor buttery, timelessly stylish. Understated finesse of enduring finish mark of class. **99** uncommon breadth and structure. Reluctantly-released maiden **98** classically barrel-fermented/aged, new Fr oak. — *DS*

Vendôme

Paarl (see Paarl map) • Tasting & sales Mon-Fri 9.30-4.30 Sat 9.30-12.30 • Cellar tours by appointment • Cheese platters by arrangement • Views • Wheelchair-friendly • Owner Jannie le Roux • Winemaker Jannie le Roux jnr • Vineyards 40 ha • Production 2 000 cases own label 75% red 25% white • PO Box 36 Huguenot 7646 • ***Tel (021) 863-3905*** *• Fax (021) 863-0094 • E-mail lerouxjg@icon.co.za • Website www.wine.co.za/vendome*

THIS delightful farm, with its leafy old-Cape ambience and characterful tasting room, features two Jannie le Rouxs: Snr is the owner and chair of critically-acclaimed Boland Cellars (also a power-figure within KWV); son Jannie is the 10th generation to farm here on a tributary of the Berg River just outside Paarl (a French namesake, Jean, was the first le Roux on SA soil: he arrived as a 17-year-old with the Huguenots in 1687). Jannie Jnr, the winemaker, is young, ultra-keen and showing an increasingly assured touch. Meet the men themselves and taste their wines when next you visit Paarl – the property is conveniently near the N2 highway and, if you call ahead, they'll spread a cheese platter to enjoy, weather permitting, outside in the shade.

Cabernet Sauvignon ✓ Barrique-aged **00** in different league to pvs; fruit riper, purer; minerally oak more overt but well managed; tannins moderately firm but ripe. 6-8 good yrs ahead. 12 mths Nevers casks. 13.9% alc. 500 cases (} 6, as are all these). Maiden **99** simpler, more rustic.

Chardonnay Classique ✓ Well made **00** peaches-and-cream texture, balanced, finishing clean. Ready, should go 3-5 yrs. Barrel-fermented, aged 5 mths, Nevers cooperage. 13.5% alc.

Merlot-Cabernet Sauvignon ☻ Unwooded **00** pleasingly ripe, fruity; just-perceptible tannins and sweet finish add to the enjoyment. 13.5% alc. 400 cases.

Chardonnay Unwooded NEW Comfortable **00** with peach/lime bouquet, soft and ready to drink now. 13% alc. 500 cases. Discontinued: **Cabernet Sauvignon-Cabernet Franc-Merlot** (pvs untasted) **Red Blend** (untasted); **Chardonnay-Chenin Blanc** (pvs **99**). — *DH*

Vera Cruz Estate see Delheim
Verdun see Asara

Vergelegen

Stellenbosch (see Helderberg map) • Tasting & sales daily 9.30-4.30 (including Sun during season), except Christmas, Workers' Day (May 1st), Good Friday. Tasting fee R5 p/p • Guided winery tours daily 10.30; 11.30; 15.00 • Lady Phillips Restaurant, Rose Terrace (see Eat-out section) • 'Interpretive Centre' depicting farm's history • Gifts • Tourgroups • Walks • Wheelchair-friendly • Owner Anglo American Farms • Winemaker André van Rensburg (since 1998) • Viticulturist Niel Roussouw (since 1995) • Vineyards 105 ha • Production 43 000 cases 58% red 41% white 1% NLH • PO Box 17 Somerset West 7129 • ***Tel (021) 847-1334*** *• Fax (021) 847-1608 • E-mail eturner@vergelegen.co.za • Website www.vergelegen.co.za*

"You know," a cocktail-party guest recently confided to André van Rensburg, "I love your wines. But I have to say, I really dislike you." Even the famously outspoken Vergelegen cellarmaster admits this unprovoked revelation left him gobsmacked – with admiration! "I wish I could be that forthright," marvels the man who's been known to tell hard-shelled customers "to go and buy their wine from the local co-op". How could vR possibly want to become more frank, when already he's considered Cape wine's most notorious iconoclast? "If, as a wine industry," he reflects, "we want to make our mark on the world, we need to cut out the bull and address the critical issues honesty and without fear. Complacency is death." Which is why, within his own very large and internationally respected domain, he's constantly pushing the limits. Here consistency and uncompromising quality are the mantras. And focus: with owners Anglo American now wholly committed to this one property (sibling spread Boschendal up for sale), Team vR have the green light to plant 50 additional hectares – to make, paradoxically, fewer wines: "Ultimately we'll have only two labels: a red and a white that will stand with the world's top handful." The red version, known simply as Vergelegen, has already established its class; the white, a Graves-style blend, is about to fly. Like its maker, it may arouse controversy. But it won't be ignored.

Cabernet Sauvignon One marvels at the man's versatility: from sauvignon through semillon and chardonnay, then the plethora of reds, AvR doesn't miss a beat. He's spot on with this beautifully crafted, classically styled cab: blue-black, utterly textbook tobacco leaf, cigarbox, cassis nose, superbly refined, elegantly textured palate displaying lovely ripe tannins. Approachable, but tragic not to allow further development. 13% merlot adds tad flesh to bone. Also dashes cab f and merlot (7%, 6%) for complexity and quantity in relatively munificent **98** (5 000 cases compared to paltry 500 in **97**); deserves more time: 10 yr+ lifespan. 24 mths Fr oak, 55% fresh, rest 2nd, 3rd fill. 14% alc.

Cabernet Franc-Merlot (Show Reserve in pvs ed) What Schaapenberg is to the whites in this range, super-vyd Rondekop is to the reds, including this stratospheric cuvee for auction only. Bold (comes easy to AvR) ensemble orchestrated, unabashedly, to leverage max cachet. Few get to taste the wine, as ultra-scarce in **99** (just 200 cases) as **98** (250). **99** squid-ink black, cab franc-led electric herbaceous aromas echoed in palate by savoury flavours, mineral backbone. Mastery is in the perfectly ripe Belgian-lace tannins. Stunning length. Equal portions cab f, merlot, 12% cab s., "Standard" cellar treatment. 14% alc.

Vergelegen "The wine is a meal," says AvR of the property's flagship, which maiden **98** garnered the Pichon Longueville Trophy for best bdx red blend at IWSC; also SAA. Follow-up **99** shares breeding, class of Rondekop vineyard; vibrant deep garnet shimmer, fine-grained cedar, tobacco-leaf scents with hints of cassis; palate arresting in both succulence of coffee/berry fruit, tannin and refinement of structure, like dressed stone. Comfortably follows the act of **98** riveting complexity, balance, intensity. Both for deepest corner of cellar. 80% cab, rest merlot from warmer, northerly Rondekop vyd, 3-4 t/ha yield. 26 mths 100% new Fr oak after natural fermentation and mth on skins. 14% alc. 2 000 cases.

Merlot 98, first release since **95**, almost not followed by **99**: strong winds performed natural pruning and reduced yields to 2-3 t/ha. Full plum complexion leads clean, minty, floral violets nose, delicious choc/berry fruit napped in marvellously ripe tannin. Impressive – accessible yet firm – structure (dash cab f) requests couple yrs in bottle. **98** rich plummy red, mocha nose, ripe berry fruit intensity. 20 mths Fr oak, 50% new. 14% alc. 4 000 cases.

Mill Race Red ✓ 'Bottom of the range', but then it is some range, isn't it? **99** broaches the bigger leagues; bright garnet; sleek black berries and aromatic wild scrub, choc sheen to ripe fruit, tannins; super balance, more intensity than pvs. Cab, merlot, cab f (44/44/12), 16 mths Fr oak, 40% new. 12 000 cases. **97-99** all SAA. Not quite the bargain basement of pvs, still good value.

Chardonnay Reserve Prodigious chardonnay meticulously crafted from celestial single vyd on lower Schaapenberg hill. Parsimonious 2,5 t/ha yield in **01** sees supplies limited to only 400 cases. Nothing mean about the wine: green-flecked straw; rich, minerally core padded with creamy fruit intensity; not bigger than regular label below, simply better, more concentrated, intense and lingering. 13.8% alc fully integrated. **99** *Wine* initially more oaky than **98**, star of 01 Nederburg Auction. **96** VG, SAA White Wine of 98. All whole-bunch-pressed, 31/2 month natural yeast fermentation, yr 100% new oak. **Chardonnay** ✓ Suave and sensual, elegance to match serious treatment: gentle handling, 100% barrel fermentation, 10 mths on lees add richness but no sacrifice of fresh citrus fruit focus. **00** emollient lemon butter nose, beautifully measured ultra-long palate with perfect tension between citric fruit and toasty butter, mineral core the base. 13.8 alc. Acclaimed **99** all-Vergelegen grapes for first time. 60% bunch-pressed, 100% Fr oak 10 mths, 40% malo.

Sauvignon Blanc Reserve (Schaapenberg Sauvignon Blanc in pvs ed) From illustrious Schaapenberg vyd (now registered as trademark, to be used for Auction wines in upper Loire, Pouilly-Fumé, wooded style). "Very standard, no wood," says AvR of the winemaking in rare moment of understatement: result is emphatic, dramatic, powerful sauvignon, among best in Cape, characterised by flinty-fruity raciness and varietal purity. Tightly coiled, smouldering at first, needs time to show its best. Meagre 4 t/ha, so minuscule 500 case production highly contested. **01** with ripe bluegum, asparagus, fig bouquet; astoundingly concentration of flavour, mineral weight in tapered, curvaceous yet flinty palate. **00** big, gusty (14%), stylistically closer to steely **98**, showered with awards. These tighter than **99** SAYWS grand champ, which more profusely flavoured, riper. **Sauvignon Blanc** ✓ Far from 'standard', rather standout in heady crowd in **01.** First offering exclusively Vergelegen grapes, nettle, fig aromas, broad green pepper succulence, spice in excellently concentrated palate, brilliant intensity in finish. Near-viscous mouthfeel (partly from now standard 9% semillon). Unlike single vyd bottlings at Nederburg/CWG auctions, doesn't require a second bond. **00** shyer, softer than racy **99**. 12 000 cases plastered with show awards.

Vin de Florence Keenly priced off-dry white omnipresent in better establishments; hugely quaffable, now gently sweeter (10,8 g/ℓ sugar). Forthcoming **01** all bought-in grapes: fragrant, grapey nose, sultana sunshine with ginger spice intrigue. Clearly sweet but balanced. Chenin, hanepoot, sauvignon blend, vintaged from **99**. **00** had proportion Vergelegen chardonnay, semillon.

Noble Late Harvest Semillon Signal, full-sweet botrytised dessert, deeply flavoured, invigoratingly fresh. **00** riveting aperitif, gaining honeyed luxuriance. Amazing elegance considering flavour concentration, sweetness, high alc (14,5%). New techniques: unwooded, sweeter at 120 g/ℓ sugar, botrytis character more restrained, peach-pip, apricot intensity fluted by delicacy. Different to instantly sumptuous **99**, oak-fermented/finished, big, relatively dry (14,5% alc, 100 g/ℓ sugar).

Not retasted for this ed: **Pinot Noir** To date single **98**; **Syrah** Single **99**, mostly for CWG auction. **Show Reserve White** (Semillon) To date a **99**. *—DS*

Vergenoegd Estate

Stellenbosch (see Stellenbosch map) • Tasting & sales Wed 2-5 Sat 9.30-12.30 • Views • Owners Vergenoegd Wine Estate (Pty) Ltd (shareholders John Faure and Strauss Family) • Winemaker/viticulturist John Faure • Vineyards 100 ha • Production 600 tons (5 100 cases own label to be increased from 2001 vintage) 100% red • PO Box 1 Faure 7131 • ***Tel (021) 843-3248*** *• Fax (021) 843-3118 • E-mail enquiries@vergenoegd.co.za*

"I TAKE it all with a pinch of salt," says 6th-generation winemaker John Faure, who's been quietly raising the profile of this historic wine farm with its unique terroir ('coastal' here means almost on the beach). At this low-key, even lower altitude estate (only 9 m above sea level in places, with False Bay so close you can taste the ocean tang), Faure has been pulling out all the stops, from vineyards to cellar. The watershed 98 vintage heralded the fruits of a new approach, which includes strict barrel selection (and 100% new oak for all wines that year, subsequently reduced), choosing sites more scientifically, harvesting bunches from blocks in waves two or even three times, and a 10-year replanting programme that's transforming the vineyards. With this all-out effort, Vergenoegd is really starting to shine. "We're lifting the bar a little each year," is the way Faure, who has now joined forces with the Strauss family (the very one rugby player Tiaan Strauss is part of) from the Northern Cape as co-owners of the business, sees it.

✪**Cabernet Sauvignon** Back on par with acclaimed **95** VG, *Wine* ✪ after **96** difficult vintage, lightweight **97** (both ★). Latest **99** ⁂ big yet refined; cassis/ black cherry aromas and eucalyptus waft; sweet-fruited with cinnamon/clove spice, distinct pepperiness in finish from splash cab f (13%); expertly wooded (Fr oak, 75% new). 1 125 cases. **98** attractively scented, potentially long-lived.

✪**Merlot** Tight, restrained style capable of good ageing; fragrant, always with hint of mint. **98**, revisited mid-01, has ascended into higher league; softening, lovely black-plum flavours coming into their own, joined by sweet violet, touches vanilla, eucalyptus and mint; ripe, smooth with big but sweet tannins. Give another 1-2 yrs, drink for 4-5. Latest **99** ripe plum and whiffs heather, eucalyptus, mint, sweet vanilla; still-lively tannins need few yrs. Improvement on **97**, which richer than more eucalyptus-like **96** VG.

✪**Shiraz** Steady improvement culminates in exceptional **99** ⁂, featuring 50% infusion of cleaned-up clone SH21 from new block ("not particularly auspiciously sited," remarks John F, "drainage is not as good as it could be. But turned out very well"). Explodes in mouth with dark cherries, ripe plums and the whole herbarium – truly amazing bouquet: complex, aromatic, exciting. New-oak portion (Fr) sensitively notched down to 70%, preserving fruit. ±1 000 cases that will drink earlier than pvs but probably age longer. **98** old-Cape blockbuster, lashed with new oak. **97** ★ earlier approachable; *Wine* ✪.

✪**Reserve** ✓ Flagship blend, understated (and so perhaps underrated by market currently more attuned to big, showy styles); initially tight but develops very well. Latest **99** ⁂ shade more forward, concentrated than some pvs, but will be accessible earlier (2/3 yrs); wild herb redolence with red berry/cassis and eucalyptus complexity; blend cab, merlot, cab f (75/22/3); new Fr barrels, 18-20 mths. 900 cases. **98** powerful yet restrained; firmly structured but balanced. 60/20/20 cab, cab f, merlot. **97** ✪ softer initially, reflecting higher proportion merlot (32%, with cab 50%, cab f 18%). **96**, from lighter yr, not as rich as standout **95** ⁂ VG, *Wine* ✪.

✪**Port** Nods to the Douro with dry profile (90 g/ℓ sugar), intense flavours from 'correct' grapes (100% tinta, though supercharged from **01** with dash touriga). **98** ⁂ one of their best; spirity bite to ripe cherries, plums and licks sweet milk choc, cinnamon; still youthfully fiery, tannic, give 4-5 yrs min. 400 cases. **97** already smooth, lovely sweet-clove finish. Also dry (83 g/ℓ sugar) but quite sweet tasting; **96** rich, complex fruitcake tones, chocolatey finish. These 2 yrs used barriques. Potential for long, fruitful maturation. — *DH*

Versus see Stellenbosch Vineyards

Vignerons du Monde

This range by wine-partners Graham de Villiers (ex Mont Rochelle) and Achim von Arnim (Cabrière) discontinued. Sole release a **Sauvignon Rouge 99** ★.

Viljoensdrift Wines

Robertson (see Robertson map) • Sales at new cellar Mon-Fri 9-4 • Tasting & sales Sat 10-2 at river raft/tasting area – Breede River cruises Sat 12 (weather permitting) or by appointment – Adults R20, children under 12 R10 • Picnic baskets by arrangement • River raft/tasting area for groups of 15 or more by arrangement • Small conferences • Owners Viljoen family • Winemaker Fred Viljoen • Viticulturist Manie Viljoen • Farm manager Jaco Kotze (since 2000) • Vineyards 70 ha • Production 1 000 tons (33 000 cases own label) • PO Box 653 Robertson 6705 • ***Tel (023) 615-1901*** *• Fax (023) 615-3417 • E-mail viljoensdrift@lando.co.za • Website www.viljoensdrift.co.za*

This is a wine experience you shouldn't miss: taste either on terra firma (in a welcoming Breede riverside tasting room), or on a double-decker raft, 'Uncle Ben', navigating an unspoiled stretch of water; picnic baskets an optional extra. These are just some of the attractions introduced by the enterprising Viljoens (brothers Fred and Manie and Fred's wife Lindy, née Bekker, sibling of Boschendal cellar chief 'JC') since they reactivated the 180 year old family winegrowing tradition in 1998. Most recently they turned their energies to the cellar close by, revamping and expanding it virtually out of all recognition. Tucked inside is a new visitor centre which spills out onto a deck, affording lovely views of the valley. This is a good spot to taste the new River Grandeur range, featuring the high-flying (in their Cessna 182) Viljoens' excellent new Shiraz.

Pinotage ✓ Minerally, plummy **01** unwooded, highlighting the plentiful sweet fruit; 14% alc. 4 885 cases (× 6, as are all these). **00** gold on SAYWS.

Shiraz Sweetish tones from ripe fruit make well-oaked **01** very easy to drink; nice bone-dry finish with hints of smoke/Karoo-bush aids food partnering. 14,2% alc. 1 000 cases.

Cabernet Sauvignon ☻ Fresh, vibrant **01** mulberry, black-cherry tastes unobscured by oak; gulpable braai wine. 13.5% alc. 1 330 cases. **Colombar-Chenin Blanc** ☻ Delightful, juicy, lightish **01**, jasmine-fragranced and gently dry. Chill and quaff today. 12,5% alc. 2 000 cases.

Chardonnay **01** light smoky/vanilla whiffs from fermentation on oak-staves; clean lemon-lime flavours and some lees; finishes quite firmly. For early enjoyment. 13.5% alc. 3 335 cases. **Semillon** Fred & Manie V pull out all stops in vyd, cellar to capture fruit freshness; reflected in **01**, from young vines: light, very pleasant, easy; still reductively shy when tasted – might fill out with time. 1 000 cases.

River Grandeur range NEW

Cabernet Sauvignon Very soft and accessible **00** doubtless will be enjoyed early but has potential to improve over 4-6 yrs. Good minerally tones, spicy oak backing flatters ripe red-cherry fruit. 1 355 cases.

Shiraz ✓ Deservedly chosen to represent Rbtson at recent wine-media briefing; **00** a standout among new-wave Cape shirazes: mega-ripe (picked 27°B for final alc of 14.8%), chock-full of sweet fruit (though technically dry) – dark cherries, choc, cinnamon spice, some wild scrub whiffs and light savouriness to offset the ripeness; yet lively, not ponderous, porty or overly oaky, partly from back-blending dash unoaked 01. Lots of healthy tannin hints at good future. Open fermenters, 85% Fr/Am oak. 813 cases.

Chardonnay 01 ripe peachy nose backed by cream-butterscotch texture from partial Fr oak fermentation; apple-zest finish. Smidgeon sweetness in palate. Nice now, could go yr/2. 14% alc. 555 cases.

Chenin Blanc ☻ Lovely effortless **01**; zesty fruity acids, tangy apple finish; drink soon. Ex high Langeberg farm, Wildepaardehoek. 13.9% alc. 1 110 cases.

Sauvignon Blanc **01** assertive varietal nose and good flavour flow of grass, passion fruit; pleasant and quaffable. Easy 12% alc. 1 110 cases. — *DH*

Villiera Wines

Paarl (see Paarl map) • Tasting & sales Mon-Fri 8.30-5 Sat 8.30-1 • Self-guided cellar tours during tasting hours • Guided tours by appointment • Annual cellar function • Owners' Annual St Vincent's Day dinner closest Sat to 22nd Jan • Owners Grier family • Winemakers Jeff Grier (since 1984) with Anton Smal (since

1991) • Viticulturists Simon Grier (since 1983) & Christie Franse (since 1990) • Vineyards 300 ha • Production 1 800-2 500 tons 105 000 cases 45% white 35% red 2% rosé 18% sparkling • PO Box 66 Koelenhof 7605 • ***Tel (021) 882-2002/3*** *• Fax (021) 882-2314 (possible change in tel numbers) • E-mail wine@villiera.com • Website www.villiera.com*

"YOU GET in touch with a lot of things with a good bottle of wine," chuckles Jeff Grier, a winemaker with a sense of humour as dry as his Brut Natural, the newcomer to this remarkably consistent, admirably affordable range. "Wine takes you to a village in the Loire (courtesy of winning SA *Wine*'s Chenin Challenge) – and this stony slope here in Paarl," he continues wryly. Wine brings people to Villiera every harvest, too – Jean Charles Villard from Chile assisted in 2001 ("the best-quality harvest since 1997", maintains Jeff G). The Brut Natural 1998 – naturally fermented, sulphur-free, from eco-benign vineyards – was so well-received, they're releasing another. Then there's the winery's first NLH (inspired by Grier's trip to the Loire) – watch out for the sticky sequel "made with lots more skin-contact and love". Also new are the Cellardoor Reserves, from quality blocks vinified and bottled separately. Looking ahead, Villiera is planting more shiraz, pinotage and some touriga to add to their Port. With a current emphasis on red wine, they've expanded fermentation and maturation capacity, specifically for merlot. Rumoured, but probably untrue, is a name-change for their super-starry Chenin, to Sharon Steen.

✵**Merlot Reserve** ✓ **99** underlines authority, stepped-up quality/gravitas achieved with first **98** release (as always within Villiera's assured, comfortable style, where vintage allowed to speak for itself). **99** captures fruity fluidity within perfectly proportioned body. Plush dark chocolate/plum attractions add more classic profile than **98**'s obviously minty tones; breed enhanced by classy oak (13 mths, new Fr barrels). Thoroughly enjoyable now (another Villiera characteristic) but can be laid down 5-7 yrs with confidence. 13.7% alc. Single vyd. 600 cases. **97** being held back for further maturation. Regular **Merlot** More forward, less complex but reliably serves up own level of satisfaction. Sample **00** shows effect of Griers' 'picking at full ripeness' mantra: not merely whopping 14.8% alc, but waves ripe plum-jam (30% fermented as whole berries for fruit emphasis) and, all-important mature tannins. 8 500 cases, which frequently fly with SAA.

✵**Shiraz** ✓ Engaging, out-to-please style highlighting variety's fruit and yielding texture. **00** ✵ sturdily constructed with pleasantly soft core; white spice/clove features over-effusively sweetened with Am oak, diminishes overall attractiveness. May gain more savoury dimension with yr/two; currently will make non-combatitive partner to Griers' food suggestion of rosemary-spiked lamb or roast pork. 13.8% alc. **99** stiffened with 10% cab, deep flavoured, yielding tannins. No **98**. **97** also delicious. Single bushvine vyd. 500 cases.

✵**Merlot-Pinotage** ✓ Happy marriage continues in **99**, though 20% of often unruly pinotage lowest of 3 vintages to date. Both grapes still compatible; merlot offering quality, richness, pinotage flashes of spice. Lovely supple mouthfeel, stroked by tender tannins. 14% alc. 500 cases. Fr/Am-oaked ±yr. After price hike, still seriously good value. Convincing candidate for 'ideal' Cape Blend: **98**, 73/27 mix, winner of Paarl Vintners' Wineland Red Blend challenge; thoroughly modern (Cape?) feel but not lacking old-fashioned backbone. Pinotage from 20 yr old dryland bushvines, low yielding.

✵**CWG Auction Reserve** NEW **00** assembled for 01 Auction; pinotage, merlot, shiraz blend (36/40/24) richly influenced by 15 mths new Fr oak. Harmonious trio, no one variety taking lead in youth; big, mouthfilling wine, very ripe (though lacking jamminess associated with 14%+ alc), balancing vibrant tannins. Designed to keep; bottle-age should benefit individuality. 50 cases.

✵**Cru Monro** ✓ Cab-merlot fusion remains on its flagship pedestal despite challenge of Merlot Reserve above. Appreciated by many fans for consistency, quality, ability to out-mature others with more lofty ambitions (10 yrs often no idle boast); amazing value. **99** also appreciated for claret-like countenance; cab plays greater role (62%) as in **98**, imparts compact, savoury-dry tannin structure though also reflecting vintage's visible fruity charm. 13% alc. Yr in Fr oak, 50% new. 5 000 cases. **98** tight in youth; plenty rich, dark-berried fruit waiting to harmonise. **97** fine minerally texture, dense but non-aggressive tannin.

Chenin Blanc ✓ Tends to disprove theory that you can't please all the people all the time. Loved by winedrinkers, for both astonishing price/quality ratio (±R17 ex farm!) and consistency. Equally praised by judges; regular top 5 appearance in *Wine*'s Chenin Challenge (**98** overall winner), SAA (**99**) and WOM Reserve. (Loire chenin producers have also been known to covertly admire this rich, weighty style, bolstered with 40% barrel-fermented portion.) **01** promises no disappointments; delectably ripe yet fresh chenin nose – melon, banana, twist zesty tangerine-peel – bouncy palate, long fruity tail. Carries substantial 14.5% alc with great verve. 7 000 cases.

Cellardoor Reserve Chenin Blanc NEW Grier cousins masters at selecting vyds to create specific styles (cf their sauvignons). Now they've spotlighted chenin: trio top vyds, grapes fully ripe to handle 100% barrel-fermentation. Supercharged **01** (unfinished sample) shows chenin's fine floral/tropical tones layered with richness rather than intrusive oak flavour (Jeff Grier's usual deftness revealed); dimension/succulence from extended lees maturation. For all richness, substantial alc (14.5%), ends with fruity flourish.

Bush Vine Sauvignon Blanc ✓ Consistency/quality, with little help from scarcity value (single 25 yr+ vyd produces max 1 500 cases), makes this – deservedly – one of SA's few cult sauvignons. **01** should enhance exclusive status, emulate successes of pvs; vivid pale straw brilliance sets tone; sonorous fumé/flinty depths still youthfully unevolved, resound around weighty, luscious palate; decisively clean, vivid length. After short settling period should develop, hold over 3-4 yrs. 13.5% alc. **00** slow-motion explosion of passion fruit/gooseberry, echoing finish. **99** SAA, WOM Reserve, sumptuous, long, complex.

Sauvignon Blanc ✓ Always good barometer for health of vintage (usually early out of starting blocks). **01** in fine form; intense but not intimidating ripe fig aromas; weighty, concentrated palate with fine-thread fruit-lifting acid. Maintains status in local sauvignon front-row. 13.3% alc. **00** difficult year, touch lighter, more zesty but no less satisfying. Trellised vyds. 10 000 cases. **99** SAA full of herbaceous fragrance, tropical touches.

Blanc Fumé ✓ **01** follows usual stylistic route of fully ripe old-vine fruit, partially barrel-fermented for extra spice, mouthfeel. **01** different, more sophisticated (equally captivating) profile: dry, flinty, smoky notes with complementary toasty oak dimension. Firmly built, richly vinous, slow flavour build-up to long, solid, dry finish. Best with food – BBQ chicken a tempting partner; should develop well over 3/4 yrs. 13,9% alc. 2 000 cases. **00** succulent, WOM Value; **99** ripe, concentrated.

Rhine Riesling ✓ **01** (sample) offers breakaway in style for this always characterful riesling; made totally dry – punters can thank Cape Wine Master and taster for this guide Tony Mossop, long-time advocate of the Alsace style, whose most recent public appeal chimed with Jeff Grier's own inclination ("plus, the vintage played ball"). No sweet accoutrements necessary: natural acid tension revs up, counterbalances fullish 13% alc, adds daintiness to pure though presently restrained spicy lime fruit, with peppery tang. Begs laying down until at least 04, with much longer maturation curve (and likely higher rating) projected. 1 000 cases.

Tradition Rosé Brut ✓ Only pleasant, non-challenging images conjured up by this whisper-pink **NV** MCC bubbly – fun-filled summer days, strawberries and cream, poolside fiestas. Current (99) gorgeous ripe strawberry/brandy-snap appeal, fuller than pvs (terrific black-grape input from 30% each pinot, pinotage), even more seductive. Still deliciously, dreamily light, clean tangy finish. Most demanding thing about this wine would be reaching out for 2nd bottle. Invisible 8 g/ℓ sugar. 2 500 cases.

☆**Monro Brut Première Cuvée** ✓ Top-of-the-range (yet unpretentiously-priced) bubbly, combination of pvs Carte d'Or (three SAA MCC trophies) and Vintage Tradition. Latest **96** bouquet displays pinot's fine fruit contribution, palate chardonnay's creamy breadth; both interwoven by persistent pin-prick mousse. Will benefit from further ageing. Classically brut at 8 g/ℓ sugar. Five-star packaging. Equal partnership pinot, barrel-fermented/matured chardonnay, min 4 yrs on lees. 1 500 cases.

☆☆**Brut Natural Chardonnay** NEW ✓ Near additive-free as is possible (including pesticide-free vyds), only concession yeast used to inoculate bubble-forming fermentation. **98** introduced to loud applause; incredibly pure yet complex aromas, flavours: baked apple laced with cinnamon, warm toast; sleek, smooth feel for such unrelenting dryness (no sweetening either) aided by drifting creamy mousse. Early tasting of **99** suggests similar style/pleasure. Note: Because of their lack of protective sulphur, Jeff G advises these should be enjoyed within 2 yrs of disgorging, ie drink **99** before end 2002.

☆**Tradition Brut** ✓ Enduring **NV** favourite. Captures imagination with consistency, affordability and local character thanks to presence of pinotage (with pinot, chenin, chardonnay (40/25/20). Latest (**99**) alluring yet dainty red-fruit nose; slightly more ample fruity flavours, some ginger-biscuit richness should develop tastily over yr/2 – creamier mousse with trademark elegance. Med-bodied, hint of citrus and non-sweetening dash sugar add to overall perk-me-up/aperitif style. Also available in 1,5 ℓ and 375 ml. 13 000 cases.

☆**Inspiration Chenin Blanc Noble Late Harvest** ✓ Sparked by Jeff G's Loire travels (courtesy of winning Chenin Challenge); label an inspiration of Anthony Lane (Villiera's Man of the Year at their annual St. Vincent's Day celebrations). Honey-hued **00** with nose of sun-warmed orange blossom, rich botrytis tones; waves silky fruit threaded with riveting acid. Harmonious, yet still far off undoubted grand maturity (Grier now guesses up to 30 yrs!). **01** untasted, for release end 2002. Fermented/aged 10 mths in new/older Fr barrels. 13% alc, 149 g/ℓ sugar, 9.8 g/ℓ acid. 2 475 cases of 375 ml.

☆**Port** ✓ Jeff Grier in bi-hemispheric mode with this tasty, accessible LBV dessert: Portuguese styling (higher alc at around 20%, lower sugar at ±90 g/ℓ) yet SA-orientated varietal mix of mainly pinotage, shiraz, gamay. Result is individual, 'authentic' example with properly dry finish. **97** ☆ still available, in no hurry to lose creamy choc-nut-berry features; pleasant grip, warmingly long; 21/2 yrs in barrel. Top LBV style in *Wine*. Pvs **96** austere but not lean; **95** ☆ VVG, *Wine* Top Ten.

Blue Ridge range

Mainly for export, but available in some stores and from farm. Good Value.

Rouge ☻ ☆ All-round inviting drinkability captured in Rhonish-toned **00**; shiraz with carignan, splash gamay, offers plenty fruity vibrancy, savoury length. 2 000 cases. **Blanc** ☻ ☆ **01** booming chenin/sauvignon aromatics, full juicy flavours. Generous 13.6% alc balanced by vivacious, palate tingling freshness, fruity length. 12 000 cases. **Sonnet** ☻ ☆ Reliable, charming off-dry quaff with subtle muscat enticement; fruit intensity in **01** balanced by smoothing grain sugar. Satisfies sweet and dry-toothed. Muscat ottonel laced with chenin. 1 000 cases.

Cabernet Sauvignon ☆ **99** in usual mild-mannered mode; well-defined ye quiet cigarbox/cassis; yielding palate with sweet-fruited accessibility, persistence. Good now but substance to hold for 5 yrs. 12.6% alc. Oak-aged, one yr 6 000 cases. **Pinotage** ☆ 'Don't know/like pinotage' brigade should try appealing, ready-to-enjoy **00**, smoky/spicy aromatics, fruity succulence and dried-fig richness, beautiful savoury finish with quality Am oak sheen, well-tailored tannins. 13.6% alc. WOM Value. 1 300 cases. **Chardonnay** ☆ Quietly stylish chardonnay; oak invariably used to flatter rather than dominate fruit. **01** with tank fermented portion to lift fruity finesse, partial malo preserves freshness essential in big, luscious vintage. Forward but not simple creamy rounded palate. 14.% alc 2 000 cases. **Gewürztraminer** ☆ Gentle rosepetal, litchi fragrance in **01**; big smooth mouthful, fruity attractions slightly dimmed by discernible 7.6 g/ℓ residual sugar, touch of characteristic bitterness. Best over next yr with spicy Thai chicken, lamb curry. 1 900 cases. *—AL*

Villiersdorp Co-op

Worcester (see Worcester Map) • Kelkiewyn Farmstall, Main Road, Villiersdorp • Contact person Mrs Lauritha Burger • Tasting & sales Mon-Fri 8-5 Sat 8-1 • Cellar tours by appointment only • Breakfasts, light meals, coffee/tea Mon-Fri 8-4.30 Sat 8-12.30 • Conference facilities for 30 delegates • Farmstall • Dried fruits • Gifts • Owners 60 Grape members • Cellar Manager/Winemaker Danie Conradie • Assistant Winemaker W S Visagie • Production 7 000 tons 97% white 3% red • PO Box 14 Villiersdorp 6848 • ***Tel (028) 840-1120/1151*** *• Fax (028) 840-1833 • E-mail vilkoop@freemail.absa.co.za*

Temporarily winemaker/managerless when our previous guide went to press, the 60 growers of this scenically situated cellar looked no further than the nearest vineyard for a successor to gone-farming stalwart J P Steenekamp. Tapping incumbent viticulturist Danie Conradie, they implicitly endorsed the now fashionable-in-Cape philosophy that good wine is made in the vineyard. And with sites confettied over an very large area, Conradie and right hand W S Visage have no shortage of options with which to make good wine. Even the traditionally monochrome palette here is rapidly gaining colour, as classics planted since the late Steenekamp era bring the proportion of reds closer to the target 30%.

☆**Hanepoot Jerepiko** ✓ Orange-peel tang, hanepoot's signature honeysuckle in still-vigorous **NV** (99), now with warming spiritous finish. 18% alc. 250 cases.

Cabernet Sauvignon ☆ Fr oaked **00** (sample) improves on pvs with ripe plummy fruit, dry but balanced tannins for satisfying everyday gulping. **Merlot** NEW ☆ Lightweight, attractive **01** (sample) lightly oak influenced; downy tannins for effortless tippling. **Pinotage** NEW Not ready for tasting; neither was **Ruby Cabernet** (**99** ☆). **Rosé** ☆ Invariably good here; coral prettiness tweaked with bit sugar and lowish alc (11,9%) for easy alfresco sipping. Gently crisp finish. **NV** ±250 cases. **Chenin Blanc** ☆ Semi-dry, med-bodied **01**, quiet nose as usual but friskier guavaish palate. Enjoy in bloom of youth. 903 cases. **Colombard** ☆ Drink soon **01** with fresh guava taste, suggestion of sweetness. Lightish 11.9% alc 640 cases. **Sauvignon Blanc** ★ These for early drinking. **01** competently made but one-dimensional; some light dusty tones. 13.3% alc. 537 cases. **Blanc de Blanc** NEW ☆ Trusty colombard/sauvignon partnership (66/34) does service in **01**, very light tropical fruits and quick, bracing finish. 287 cases to be opened with food. **Late Vintage** ★ **01** (sample) light tropical fruit, sweet in sugary rather than fruity way. 316 cases. **Demi-sec Sparkling** Latest **NV** not ready for tasting. Pvs ☆. **Port** ☆ Blend of Portuguese grapes, yet more liqueur wine than port character; soft, sweet, gentle-on-eye ruby hues. Low (for style) 16.9% alc. Some of above also in 5 ℓ boxes. Discontinued: **Cabernet Sauvignon-Merlot** (Pvs **98** ☆), **Colombard-Chardonnay** (Pvs **00** ☆). *— DH*

Vinfruco

Stellenbosch/London • Vinfruco (UK) Farnham House Farnham Royal Buckinghamshire SL2 3RQ England • Tel +44 (1753) 64-7093 • Fax +44 (1753) 81-8821 • Vinfruco (SA) Oude Molen Distillery Road Stellenbosch 7600 • ***Tel (021) 886-6458*** *• Fax (021)886-6589 • E-mail dalena@vinfruco.co.za • Website www.arniston-bay.co.za*

APPEARING to be all over the show (blending and final processing cellar at Perdeberg winery, barrel maturation cellar at Koopmanskloof), leading exporter Vinfruco is anything but (annual turnover in excess of R100-million, recipient of two President's Awards for Export Achievement). In a consolidating move, this slick operator purchased and occupied the historic Oude Molen premises – complete with extensive warehousing and dispatch facilities, bang on the mark for its strict on-time delivery discipline. They also launched easy-drinking Arniston Bay (one of the biggest SA labels in the UK and set to expand by two new reds and a bubbly – untasted) on the local market. Swapping roles in this tableau is Anton du Toit, now marketing director, with accomplished winemaker Nicky Versfeld (ex Steenberg) in his previous production director position. Besides making wines for its export ranges and in-house brands, Vinfruco also represents Paul Cluver, Koopmanskloof, Mooiplaas and Thandi in the international market. In the thrust to place the no-longer-nebulous SA wine brand firmly on it, they established a presence in Japan and are tapping into North America's potential, too.

Arniston Bay range

Cleverly packaged brand with wide appeal.

Ruby Cabernet-Merlot ☻ ✰ Gulpable style; **00** plenty of juicy mulberry fruit; mouthfilling (13,6% alc); firmish dry finish. Not oaked. 69 000 cases (× 6, as are all these).

Shiraz NEW ✰ Successful extension to this big-hitting SA brand. **00** new world style, partial oaked, earthy/spicy tones with sage, pepper hints. 13.1% alc. 20 000 cases. **Pinotage-Cinsaut** NEW ✰ **00** totally upfront, totally fruit-driven blend, almost pastille-like succulence; 80/20 blend carefully calibrated for maximum pleasure (to which 14% alc may or may not add). 20 000 cases. **Rosé** ✰ Charming, quaffable pinotage-based dry pink; jasmine scents, nice pinotagey tastes in **01**. Excellent lunchtime sipping (with an eye on the generous 13.3% alc). 40 000 cases. **Chenin Blanc-Chardonnay** ✰ SA's 2nd biggest label in UK. **01** pulpy peach fruit, feathery texture (partly from brush of sugar). Light, breezy impression despite big 13.5% alc. 4 000 cases.

Oak Village Premier Barrel Selection

Specially chosen casks from catch-all Coastal appellation.

✰**Cabernet Sauvignon** Textbook cassis bouquet, expansive mulberry fruit in **97** palate developing well, showing complexity in plush vanilla/liquorice tones. Med-bodied. 16 mths Fr casks. 4 000 cases.

✰**Shiraz 00** notch above pvs. Aromatic shiraz tones but well behaved, not too alcoholic; quite European flavour silhouette (though 13.8% veers to new world). Yr Fr/Am (60/40) casks. 4 000 cases.

✰**Chardonnay** NEW Showy new world-style **99** VVG has held well, but should now be drunk, before creamy butterscotch textures turn decadent. Fermented/aged new Fr casks. 13.3% alc. 2 000 cases.

Pinotage NEW ✰ Plump, full-bodied, out-and-out commercial-style **99** will turn many onto variety. Nice tannic grip. New/2nd fill Fr oak seamlessly woven. 13.% alc. 3 000 cases.

Oak Village range

Cabernet Sauvignon NEW ☆ Well modulated. **99** quiet, dusty/savoury tones verging on herbal; partially oaked. Med-bodied. 26 000 cases. **Pinotage** ☆ Modern, plush, fruit driven style; **00** unwooded, med-bodied. Stbosch/Paarl fruit. 13.3% alc. 40 000 cases. **Vintage Reserve** ☆ Maintains quality despite massive (in Cape terms) 100 000 case production. **00** European-toned, balanced; good with food. Cab/merlot with cinsaut, shiraz; appears med-bodied despite high 13.5% alc. **Chardonnay** (unoaked) Not tasted for this ed. Pvs **99** ☆. **Chenin Blanc** ☆ Casual quaffing **01** with creamy peach/pear texture; appealing to those who don't enjoy their wine with too much zip. 13.5% alc. 15 000 cases. **Sauvignon Blanc** NEW ☆ Good middle of the road sauvignon. **01** med-bodied, unaggressive herbal/nettle, light fig tastes; crisp finish. 50 000 cases.

Groot Geluk range

Exclusively for Netherlands market.

Cinsaut-Shiraz ☆ Solid quaffing style; **00** with some sweet/savoury flavours; unoaked 60/40 blend with big 14% alc. 6 000 cases. **Premium Cabernet Sauvignon-Merlot** NEW ☆ Popular, undemanding 67/33 blend, partially oaked. Versatile at table. Soft, round **99**, med-bodied. 3 000 cases. **Chardonnay Premium** ☆ Barrel fermented/aged **00**, from Stbosch grapes, not as interesting/complex as expected; some shy, dusty candyfloss notes in med-bodied palate. 2 000 cases.

Kaapse Hoop range

For Dutch market.

Chenin Blanc NEW ☻ Unwooded, so all **01**'s peach/honeysuckle aromas and delicious fruit-salad tastes shine through. 13.4% alc. 6 000 cases.

Droë Rooi NEW ⁑ Light cinsaut/pinotage blend, very pleasant; goes nicely with pasta. Sweet, slightly jammy cherry fruit. 3 000 cases. **Eerste Pluk Rosé** ☆ Comfortable, lightish, just-dry **01** from pinotage; vibey pink hues; muted strawberry perfume; nice with a range of foods (you'll find smoked salmon or asparagus good matches, winemakers predict). 3 000

Rock Ridge range

Exclusive to Marks & Spencer, UK.

Cabernet Sauvignon ☆ Old-style **00**, comforting plum-jam aromas; mouthful ripe stewed fruit. Yr Fr barrels. 13.5% alc. 26 000 half-cases. **Pinotage** ☆ **00** crowd pleasing style, generous, sweet-fruited; 8 mths Am barrelling well absorbed. 13,3% alc. 9 000 cases. **Chardonnay** ☆ Modern, partially cask-fermented chardonnay; **01** bright peaches-and-cream flavours, sweetish finish (partly from mouth-expanding 14% alc). 45 000 cases.

Eikestad

Cinsaut-Shiraz ☆ Light bodied, food friendly **00**, strawberry finish. Unoaked 75/25 blend. 12 000 cases. **Chenin Blanc** ☆ Delicate guava/peach aromas waft from **01**, medium palate with attractive slightly sweet-sour finish which good with Thai food. 13.4% alc. 4 000 cases.

Other ranges/labels available, not ready for tasting: For Marks & Spencer, UK **Bin 121 Merlot-Ruby Cabernet, Perdeberg Sauvignon Blanc**; Klein Begin range, to be relaunched; pvs included **Cabernet Sauvignon, Pinotage, Sauvignon Blanc-Chardonnay**; Koopmanskloof range: **Cabernet Sauvignon Pinotage, Chardonnay**; Tesco range: **Cabernet Sauvignon, Merlot Cinsaut**. — *TM*

Vinimark

Directors Tim Rands, Cindy Jordaan, Guys Naudé • PO Box 441 Stellenbosch 7599 • **Tel (021) 883-8043/4** *• Fax (021) 886-4708 • E-mail info@vinimark.co.za (export enquiries: richard@vinimark.co.za) • Website www.vinimark.co.za*

Stellenbosch wine merchants styling various ranges, including Kleindal, Cullinan View and Table Peak (see those entries) for export in conjunction with local partners.

Vinum

Stellenbosch • Not open to the public (wines made at Onderkloof winery, Sir Lowry's Pass) • Owners Alex Dale, Edouard Labeye, Martin Gebers, Christophe Durand • Winemaker Edouard Labeye (since 1999) with Gus Dale • Viticulturist to be confirmed • Vineyards 9.5 ha • Production 65 tons 4 500 cases 67% red 33% • Postnet Suite 124 Private Bag X15 Somerset West 7129 • **Tel (021) 842-0001** *• Fax (021) 842-0002 • E-mail alex@vinum.co.za*

This micro-producer has taken off like the proverbial bat (Oddbins in the UK, Disney in the USA, Carnival Cruises in the Caribbean, a top mail-order catalogue in Germany, high-end gastronomy in Holland) with marketing radar that's spot on: high quality contents in stylish packaging, all at very reasonable prices. "It's not really that clever, just sensible among such general greed!" laughs marketing powerhouse Alex Dale. Robert Parker also rated their 99 Cabernet (twice) as one of the greatest value wines in the world and "arguably with the year's best wine label". Causing, unsurprisingly, a minor stampede with the 2000 sold out at bottling, (demand in their export markets has so far outweighed supply but happily they're going to make some wine available in SA, solely via direct marketing). But the Vinum crew, a remarkable blend of nationalities, wits and culture with one overriding passion, are intent on remaining humble "We know we can get a lot better, and the vineyard is currently being jacked-up for precisely that."

Cabernet Sauvignon ✓ Modern style that will keep traditionalists happy too. Bright, sassy **99** scooped by **00**, which bigger (13.5% alc), more serious; mouthfilling and ripely vinous. Polished dry tannins pervade the wine rather than conclude bluntly (benefit of Edouard Labeye-advocated micro-oxygenation). ±Yr casked, Fr/Am oak (80/20), 50% new; unfiltered. Helderberg/ Devon Valley vyds. 550 cases.

Chenin Blanc NEW Stylish packaging (feature of range) mirrors steely brightness of **01**; expressive, delightfully individual; piquant flint, lemongrass, oak-spice subtleties preceed almost unbelieveably delicate lemony intensity, neutralising the 14% alc. Best in freshness of youth. Single old Helderberg vyd, yielding 39 hl/ha. Slow fermented, partially in Fr oak barrels; 4 mths on lees. *—AL*

Virginia

"The wine for men who enjoy being men" seems to have gathered quite a female following too, with the actual male to female consumption ratio about 3:2. One of SA's largest-selling whites for many years, it's sold in glass; the old gallon jar now metricated to 4,5 ℓ. By Distell.

Semi-dry **NV**, surprisingly fresh aromas; soft, smooth, swiggable. *—IvH*

Vlakteplaas see Kango

Vlottenburg Winery

Stellenbosch (see Stellenbosch map) • Tasting & sales Mon-Fri 8.30-5 Sat 9-12.30 • Tasting fee R5 • Owners 22 members • Winemaker Kowie du Toit (since

1973) with PG Slabbert (since 1997) • Viticulturist PG Slabbert (since 1997) • Vineyards ± 1 000 ha • Production 8 000 tons 55% white 45% red • PO Box 40 Vlottenburg 7604 • ***Tel (021) 881-3828/9*** *• Fax (021) 881-3357 • E-mail vlottenb@netactive.co.za*

When they say Limited Release here they really mean it – the minute a new vintage is made available, those in the know screech up to the cellar doors to fill their boots with the bounty from this Stellenbosch co-op that's got its act together, even more so now with extensions to the red wine fermentation and maturation facilities complete. All this means increased quantities going into the Vlottenburg label (the bulk of production is routed to Distell for their various ranges) and winemake. Kowie du Toit, himself vintage 1973 at this model winery, hopes they'll now have wines available at the cellar all year round.

Cabernet Sauvignon Limited Release ✓ **97** special release peaked prematurely, but **98** appears to have ascended a quality notch: soft tannins, black cherry richness with liquorice whiffs. Yr 100% new Fr oak. Standard **Cabernet Sauvignon** Plushy **00** cigarbox/lead pencils bouquet from yr Fr oak, 30% new; not quite matched by palate which closed mid-01, with puckering finish needing ±yr to soften.

Merlot ✓ **98** introduced new, more serious style with riper fruit, richer profile. Follow-up **99** choc-minty black cherry palate, well meshed tannins. Yr 300 ℓ Fr oak, 10 % new. 13.8% alc. **00** preview bigger (14.3% alc) but still closed mid-01, difficult to gauge.

Pinotage Limited Release NEW ✓ Maiden **99** shows multi-layered liquorice, black cherry, banana bouquet and just enough of its yr all-new Fr casking. Potential to improve over 3-4 yrs. ±13% alc. Regular **Pinotage** Pure-fruited **00** with banana/black cherry succulence, really attractive and well oaked. Value at R21/bottle. 13.3% alc.

Shiraz ✓ After promising debut in **98**, follow-up **99**, latest **00** maintains well-structured, fragrant style with abundant but soft tannins; **00** good now, legs for 2-3 yrs. 13.6% alc.

Reserve ✓ Stylish, snappily packaged shiraz/cab cuvee. **98** 60/40 ratio with mint/high-toned touches and big ripe tannins. **99** 50/50 blend edgier, needs 2 yrs to relax. 12 mths Fr oak, some new. 13.1% alc.

Chardonnay ✓ For fans of richer styles, **99**, **00** offered buttered toast/leesy tones. But 100% new oak (8 mths) seems better integrated in **01** (sample); butterscotch weight countered by lime for balanced effect. 13.1% alc. We echo winemaker: "Don't age more than 2 yrs".

Muscat de Hambourg ✓ First-class example of this unusual in Cape variety. Fuchsia-pink **00**, made jerepiko style with no fermentation, intensely floral with savoury palate. Very sweet but not cloying; pleasingly tingly finish. Extra-low 15.7% alc. **99** developed well in bottle.

Rouge ☻ Latest **NV** unwooded bottling again epitome of quaffability. Banana-fritter tastes from 50% pinotage component (remainder cinsaut); silky tannin. 13.1% alc. **Blanc de Blanc** ☻ "Drink as regularly as possible," recommends Kowie du Toit. Unpretentious tropical-fruited **NV** from sauvignon/chenin. Off-dry. This, above 1 000 ml screwcap.

Chenin Blanc Off-dry sociable sip finishes cleanly despite generous dash sugar; soft guava/sherbety tones in **01**. 13.2% alc. **Sauvignon Blanc** Nice grassy/figgy mix in crisply dry **01**. Given its 14% alc, could develop interestingly over yr/2. **Gewürztraminer 00** sold out and **01** won't be released. **Late Harvest** Relaxed, uncloying semi-sweet ("made to sip beside your Weber," winemaker reveals); latest **NV** much fuller than pvs (13.4% vs 10%), now from sauvignon. Discontinued: **Hanepoot NV** Pvs ★. — *CF*

Von Ortloff

Franschhoek (see Franschhoek map) • Tasting, sales, cellar tours by appointment • Owners/winemakers/viticulturists Georg & Evi Schlichtmann • Vineyards 15 ha • Production 100 tons (60 tons 3 500 cases own label) 55% white 45% red • PO Box 341 Franschhoek 7690 • ***Tel (021) 876-3432*** *• Fax (021) 876-4313 • E-mail vortloff@mweb.co.za*

If, as former BMW executive Georg Schlichtmann says, his home is his castle then it's a mighty stylish one, with everything designed or restored by his acclaimed architect wife Evi: a 300-year-old cottage, all modern and minimalist. After a bountiful 2001 harvest, they entered terra incognita in the cellar (fortunately with their mentoring winemaker only a call away) with open, wooden fermenters, where the natural yeast waited until a Saturday night to start fermentation – and shook Schlichtmann awake on Sunday morning when he realised what a 'solid cake' really meant: "I've always tried to avoid warlike activities against the precious red nectar, but I had to break this – four times a day – until my back almost broke." Still idealistic, although nerves have been worn a bit thin, they weathered last year's rainy winter and are "almost home and dry" for the next season, with their share of the growing German thirst for Cape wine secured. Their trilogy complete – vineyards, winery, manor house – irrepressible Schlichtmann announces that maybe he should write a book next.

★**Cabernet Sauvignon-Merlot** Tight-wound inaugural **96** followed by friendlier, more approachable **97**, with higher fraction merlot. Next was **98** ★, encompassing both these styles. 99's merlot component too small (14%) for certification under this label, so appears as the wine below.

★**Cabernet Sauvignon** Easy modern international-style **99**, waving flag of ripe fruit, big alc (14.5%), toasty wood (19 mths, all new Fr). Immediately accessible; substantial cushiony tannins, plummy fruit, but should keep. 2 375 half-cases.

★**No 7** ✓ Softly styled, ingratiating merlot since **97** (maiden **95**, **96** sterner); choc/cherry notes in very ripe **00**. Smoothly graceful, gentle tannins. 9 mths Fr oak, 20% new. 1 980 half-cases. **99** ★ seductive and accessible.

★**Chardonnay** ✓ Elegant barrel-fermented example since first **93**. Delicately flavoured **00** shows toasty evidence of casking (9 mths Fr oak, half new). Insubstantial mouthfeel despite 14% alc (hence ★ rating), forcefully crisp dry conclusion. 1 110 half-cases. **99** lighter/fruitier than **98**, with 'dark' butterscotch/fudge spectrum.

No 5 ★ Generously forthcoming with flavour, from sauvignon, **01** round, rich, though plenty acid/alc (13.5%) in finish. Brilliantly stylish packaging, like No 7, an asset to any dinner table! — *TJ*

Vredendal Winery

Olifants River (see Olifants River map) • Tasting & sales Mon-Fri 8-5.30 Sat 8.30-12.30 (tasting venue closes half-hour earlier) • Cellar tours 10, 5 during harvest • BYO picnic • Fully-equipped conference centre for ±45 delegates • Audio-visual presentation • Gifts • Owners 160 members • Winemakers Alwyn Maass (since 1997), Len Knoetze (since 1999), Pieter Verwey (since 1999) • Viticultural consultant Jeff Joubert • Vineyards 3 300 ha • Production 70 000 tons • PO Box 75 Vredendal 8160 • ***Tel (027) 213-1080*** *• Fax (027) 213-3476 • E-mail vredwine@kingsley.co.za*

Swift and sure, this winery works exceptionally hard to be first on the overseas market with their wines (Gôiya Kgeisje with its stylised Bushman image on the label fittingly means 'first wine'). And just as hard to ensure that, as exporters of note, quality and pricing remain consistent. The largest winery under one roof in SA, it's an integral part of this flourishing West Coast town, with a sprawling 3 300 ha of vineyards to choose from. They've installed a charmat process plant with a view to exporting tank-fermented bubbly. At time of going to press, serious discussions of an amalgamation between Vredendal and nearby Spruitdrift, which would become a purely red wine operation, were underway. Together they'd be the biggest in both size and volume in the southern hemisphere and provide a central force for the Olifants River region.

Maskam Cabaret ✓ Friendly, well made, drink-now red blend cab/ruby cab. Last was **97**. Follow-up not ready for tasting. **96** VG. **94** Jan Smuts Trophy for best SA wine of year, *Wine* Top 5 co-op selection.

Mount Maskam Shiraz NEW Refined, tasty **00** with warming fruit, sweetish entry turning peppery/savoury mid-palate; Am oak (8 mths) deftly handled. 13% alc. 1 000 cases.

Namaqua Rosé NEW ☻ Jazzy pink **NV** (01) blend colombard/pinotage (60/40); fruity, med-bodied, semi-sweet yet food-cordial. 1 000 cases. **Mount Maskam Colombard-Chardonnay** NEW ☻ **01** opens austerely, then develops succulent peach/guava favours before tailing off to racy finish. 13% alc. 2 000 cases. **Mount Maskam Chenin Blanc** NEW ☻ Sweet-melon ripeness in **01**; peachy acidity cuts the 17 g/ℓ sugar for drier, fresher feel. 13% alc. 2 000 cases. **Gôiya Kgeisje** ☻ Pronounced Hoya-heyshe, joined by firm click. Winery's top seller (500 000 cases annually). Equal chardonnay/sauvignon blend, unwooded, just off-dry (6 g/ℓ sugar). Effortlessly quaffable **01**, as always meant to be uncorked as fresh as possible to catch the delicate tropical tones. 13% alc. **Spumanté** ☻ Captivating low-alc (8%) **NV** carbonated fizz with bergamot and lemon fragrances; gently sweet and madly drinkable. 2 000 cases.

Mount Maskam Merlot NEW Unsubtle but satisfying **00**; sweet-ripe nose, obvious vanilla spice from 8 mths Fr oak; lightish feel despite strapping 14% alc. 1 000 cases. **Gôiya G!aan** Literally, 'wine red'; **01** tasted very young, more Med-styled than previous; bright cerise; smoky plum/crushed mulberry fleshiness. Unoaked ruby cab, pinotage, merlot. 13% alc. 300 000 cases. **Namaqua Dry Red** Latest bottling not ready for tasting. Pvs **NV**. **Mount Maskam Chardonnay** NEW Assertive, unusual **01** with wintergreen snatches; unwooded; not heavy despite 13% alc. 2 000 cases. **Namaqua Grand Cru** Steely-dry chenin needs a rich food partner like lemon butter sole. **NV** (01). 12,5% alc. 1 000 cases. **Namaqua Selected Stein** Billowing honey-fruity **NV** (01) from chenin, finishes drier than 17 g/ℓ sugar would suggest. 12,5% alc. 1 000 cases. **Namaqua Late Harvest** Mellifluous, sippable semi-sweet chenin; **NV** (01) tangy finish goes well with sweet-and-sour pork. 1 000 cases. **Namaqua Johannisberger** NEW Fragrant floral/terpene **NV** (01), simple, lightish and sweet; try with pineapple pizza. 1 000 cases. **Maskam Port** **NV** (98) from ruby cab, among driest at 70 g/ℓ sugar; full bodied (18% alc). Very well priced at R13 ex-cellar. Good partner for blue cheese. 500 cases.

Discontinued: **Namaqua Selected Red** (**99**), **Namaqua Dry White** (**NV**), **Maskam Red Muscadel** (**98** ★), **Maskam Hanepoot Jerepiko** (**99**). — *TM*

Vredenheim Wines

Stellenbosch (see Stellenbosch map) • Tasting & sales Mon-Fri 9-5 Sat 9.30-2 Fee R1/wine • Barrique Restaurant for lunch/dinner Tue-Sun • Reception/conference hall (catering included) • Play area for children • Tourgroups • Views • Walks • Wheelchair-friendly • Owner/viticulturist C Bezuidenhout • Consulting winemaker Johan le Hanie • Vineyards 80 ha • Production 3 000 cases 50% red 50% white • PO Box 369 Stellenbosch 7599 • ***Tel (021) 881-3878*** *• Fax (021) 881-3296 • E-mail trendsetter@vredenheim.co.za • Website www.vredenheim.co.za*

THIS 300 year old cellar – frequently hired out for weddings, birthdays and other celebrations – is an engaging venue, with Angus cattle, horses, sheep, antelope and the odd ostrich to greet you. You can eat outdoors in summer (the Barrique Restaurant offers picnic lunches in season by arrangement), and there's a play area for children. Stellenbosch artist Piet Grobler designed the quirky and colourful labels on Vredenheim's wines. These were not ready for tasting for this edition; previous included: **Cabernet Sauvignon** (**97** ⁑), **Merlot** (⁂ **98**), **Vredenheim 208** (**97** ⁂), **Dry Red** (★ **96**).

Vriesenhof-Talana Hill-Paradyskloof 

Stellenbosch (see Stellenbosch map) • Tasting & tours by appointment • Sales Mon-Thu 8.30-1; 2-5 Fri 8.30-1; 2-4 Closed on weekends and public holidays • Owner/winemaker Jan 'Boland' Coetzee • Production 21 000 cases 80% red 20% white • PO Box 155 Stellenbosch 7599 • ***Tel (021) 880-0284*** *• Fax (021) 880-1503 • E-mail vriesen@iafrica.com • Website www.vriesenhof.co.za*

HANNES COETZEE, who attended Boland Agricultural School, is a natural-born farmer: his first word was *trekker* (tractor) and he gained early infamy when his father, wine veteran Jan 'Boland' Coetzee, smuggled a few cuttings of chardonnay into the country in his nappy. Last year young Coetzee spent a month in Eger, where pinot noir is finding its place in Hungary. This notoriously fickle variety has been an enduring passion for former Springbok flanker JBC: his first was bottled in 1978 (he declares it still smooth and drinkable) and he's been tinkering about with it ever since. So it was with immense satisfaction that the first Pinot from a young Vriesenhof vineyard was bottled last year. Hannes Coetzee's been increasingly involved in managing Vriesenhof farm, single-vineyard Talana Hill and the various blocks that go into the easy-drinking Paradyskloof label (suburban creep saw them secure several neighbouring vineyards). He also shouldered much of the responsibility for last year's harvest under his father's sage guidance. JBC compares it to the benchmark 97 (when he made some of his "best ever" reds) – promise of big wines to come.

⁂**Vriesenhof Cabernet Sauvignon** Deep hues of latest **99** equal to profound aromas of smoky plum and whiffs fennel, tobacco, cigarbox. Elegant bdx profile underpinned by textbook Vriesenhof structure: challenging now but promising stellar complexity with time (7 yrs, says JBC). **98** ⁂ more vegetal tones with the tobacco, sensitively oaked (20% new Fr, balance 2nd fill). Longer-lasting probably than **98** Kallista, but shorter legs than **97**, with dense cassis in firm palate.

⁂**Vriesenhof Pinotage** Burgundy beckons from **99** glass in red berries, forest floor before turning full-frontally local with ripe mulberries in almost aggressive envelope of juicy acidity and fruit tannins. Gamey flavours need game on the plate, says winemaker. **98** more traditional huge tannins, generous banana tones with medicinal sniffs. **97**, 20 mths new-oaked, engineered for the long haul.

⁂**Vriesenhof Pinot Noir** NEW Consider rating for this long-gestated infant provisional: **00** sampled just post bottling mid-01 so still unsettled, yet flashing some rather good looks from Anthony Lane-tweaked label. 22 yrs' tinkering preceded this leap of faith, but it's worth the effort/wait: wonderfully structured, layered and fragrant wine, carefully constructed from Dijon clones in differing soils (tasting components and then completed puzzle a fascinating and pleasurable exercise). Firm oak treatment complements vibrant cherry and ripe strawberry flavours, with farmyard whiff in background. Includes dash first-crop 99 from young vyd.

Vriesenhof Kallista Flagship bdx blend; firmly structured for long-term pleasure rather than instant gratification. Yet **99** develops more approachable style of **98**, with billowing claret cassis, choc and fragrant herbal counterpoint of cab f (10%, with 50/40 merlot/cab). Taut, mineral frame surrounds ripe red-berry fruit; elegant vanilla-spice finish from 18 mths Fr oak, 33% new. "Our long-term goal is to marry the cooper and the vineyard," notes JBC. Merlot's dominance lends earlier drinkability without sacrificing considerable cellaring potential of pvs. **97**, with 50% cab, gravelly, elegant, needing more time than leaner **96**. Older vintages show some herbaceous austerity – prized by traditionalists.

Talana Hill Royale Long-established bdx blend shows huge step up in **99** on lean **98** ☆☆. Ripe new-world cassis and smoky choc aromas carry to rich, supple sweet-fruited palate; savoury 25% cab f adds spice to more dominant, concentrated merlot. Subtle fragrance from 18 mths Fr oak, new/2nd fill only, more heavily toasted than for others in range.

Talana Hill Chardonnay Single-vyd **00** continues tense style of **99** with shy toasty brioche notes and finely-drawn minerals. Both show weighty lime flavours, finish with austere persistence. Less perfumed than peach/pear-nuanced **98**. These worth cellaring few yrs.

Paradyskloof Pinotage ☆☆ Stewed plum and cocoa aromas lead seamlessly to elegant mid-weight palate, showing peppery tones with juicy dry finish. Blend from two vyds. **Paradyskloof Cabernet Sauvignon-Merlot** ☆☆ Returns to guide with **00** light, bright ruby hues and laid-back strawberry/green olive scent. Light bodied; simple red-berry fruit and touch green fennel in finish. 8 mths older wood. **Vriesenhof Chardonnay** ☆☆ Somewhat retiring creamy melon-tinged nose belies gutsy citrus flavours in cleverly-wooded bone-dry **00** sleeper – should develop layers of complexity in 1-3 yrs. **Paradyskloof Sauvignon Blanc-Chardonnay** ☆☆ Intriguing marzipan dimension to more conventional grapefruit in **00**; full dry palate offers some bottle development and muscles plenty with 13.4% alc. — *TM*

Waboomsrivier Co-op

*Worcester (see Worcester map) • Tasting, sales & cellar tours Mon-Fri 8-5 Sat 8-10 • Views • Owners 50 members • Winemakers Chris van der Merwe (since 1987) & Wim Viljoen (since 1991) • Consulting viticulturist Schalk du Toit (VinPro, since Sep 2001) • Vineyards 883 ha • Production 11 360 tons (60 tons, 4 000 cases own label) 62% white 38% red • PO Box 24 Breede River 6858 • **Tel (023) 355-1730** • Fax (023) 355-1731*

"Nee wat, hier het niks verander nie – alles maar nog dieselfde," reports long-time winemaker Chris van der Merwe, and while his 'sorry, no news – nothing's changed' may not be may a journalist's dream, it must surely please this co-operative's many fans locally and in Canada, Holland and Switzerland (doubtless the eagle-eyed will have spotted a new face in the personnel roster above: VinPro's Schalk du Toit, who takes over from Pierre Snyman, now vine-magicking full-time for Brandvlei). Just 2% of production is sold in bottle under the in-house Wagenboom label; the rest goes to the merchants in bulk. The range, not tasted for this ed, includes: **Cabernet Sauvignon** (Pvs **99** ☆☆), **Pinotage** (**99** ★), **Ruby Cabernet** (**99** ☆☆), **Blanc de Blanc** (**00** ☆), **Perlé** (**NV** ☆), **Chenin Blanc Late Harvest** (**99** ☆), **Rubellite Sparkling NV** (99) ★, **Port NV** (95) ☆☆.

Wagenboom see Waboomsrivier

Wamakersvallei Winery

Wellington (see Wellington map) • Tasting & sales Mon-Fri 8-5 Sat 8.30-12.30 • Picnics by arrangement • Gifts • Owners 45 members • Winemakers Bennie Wannenburg (since Dec 2000) with Chris Roux (since 1970) • Consultant viticulturist Dricus v/d Westhuizen (since 2001, VinPro) • Vineyards 1 600 ha • Production 11 500 tons (10 000 cases own label) 65% white 35% red • PO Box 509 Wellington 7654 • ***Tel (021) 873-1582*** *• Fax (021) 873-3194 • E-mail sales@wamakers.co.za • Website www.wamakersvallei.co.za*

THEIR logo may be a wagon wheel, fitting for this 'valley of the wagonmakers', but there's no slow creaking along here. New winemaker Bennie Wannenburg previously pushed the pace at West Coast winery Goue Vallei. Famous for his kudu-neck potjie, which he deems the perfect partner with which to swig their Cabernet, he's teamed up with viticulturist Dricus van der Merwe and fishing legend Chris Roux. They've been busy re-designing the ranges, with additions to the own-label line and a new brand of red-blooded wines, now quietly resting in barrels.

✵**Merlot** ✓ Oak-influenced **99** still lively; sappy coffee-toned fruit, very full (14.5% alc), good dry finish (signature of this winery's reds). Well priced at R20 ex cellar. 2 220 cases.

✵**Duke of Wellington Muscat d'Alexandrie** ✓ Fortified **99** dessert with pale looks belying piercing muscat bouquet; not overly alcoholic at 17.4%. 1 000 cases.

> **Cinsaut** ☻ ⁂ Speciality of this winery. Unusually deep colours; bright strawberry fruit carrying to gently tannic **00** finish. Quaffable, so watch that 14.3% alc. 2 200 oak-influenced cases. **Celebration 2000** ☻ ⁂ Fragrant muscat/tropical fruit happily billow in lightish-bodied, smooth, semi-dry sparkle from sauvignon. 2 000 cases.

Cabernet Sauvignon ⁂ Oak-touched **99** still tasty, sweet-savoury, light-bodied. 2 200 cases. **Pinotage** ⁂ Value for money **99** (R18/bottle) with ripe plums, slice banana, touch tannin. Lightish-bodied and very good, according to winemaker, with lasagne. 2 200 cases. **Duke of Wellington Victory Red** ⁂ Cellar's flagship **99** with sweetish strawberry fruit, powerful tannins needing time. Lightish body, oak-brushed. 4 200 cases. "Taste and be conquered" says label. **Chardonnay** NEW ★ Unwooded dry white with bracing acidity. 13.2% alc. 2 200 cases. **Chenin Blanc** ✧ **01** pleasant everyday drink, modestly fruity, non-aggressively dry. 13,6% alc. 2 300 cases. **Sauvignon Blanc 01** not ready for tasting. Pvs ★. **Stein** ✧ Ripe fruit salad/honey in sweetish **NV** from chenin. Lightish, easy. 2 200 cases. **Late Harvest** ✧ Soft, honeyed semi-sweet from chenin. **NV**. 2 200 cases. **Fishermans Jerepigo** ✧ Fortified **NV** to warm a sea dog's soul. Very sweet yet delicate hanepoot. 17,5% alc. 1 000 cases. **Jagters Port** ✧ **NV** 'Hunter's Port' from cab, perfect for campsite quaffing; suitably 'wild' tastes, decidedly warming finish (19.8% alc). 1 000 cases. —*DH*

Wandsbeck see Agterkliphoogte

Warwick Estate

Stellenbosch (see Stellenbosch map) • Tasting & sales Mon-Fri 10-4 Sat 9-1 Nov-Apr • Cellar tours by appointment • Closed Sundays, Christmas, Family Day, New Year's Day & Easter Sunday • Nominal tasting fee refundable with purchases • Mediterranean picnic baskets under the oak trees Oct-Apr (advance booking essential) • Magnificent views of Simonsberg • Walks/hikes by arrangement • Owners Ratcliffe family • General manager Michael Ratcliffe • Winemakers Louis Nel with Norma Ratcliffe • Winegrower/viticulturist Nicholas Dowling (since

*1998) • Consultants Philip Freese & Johan Pienaar • Vineyards 75 ha • Production 350 tons, 15 000 cases 90% red 9% white 1% rosé • PO Box 2 Elsenburg 7607 • **Tel (021) 884-4410** • Fax (021) 884-4025 • E-mail cellarinfo@warwickwine.co.za • Website www.warwickwine.co.za*

INFECTIOUS enthusiasm, always brimming from the Ratcliffe family property in the Muldersvlei bowl, positively booms now that scion Michael is running the show. Taking the helm from seafaring father Stan (whose parting advice was: "shut up when competitions don't go your way, but make sure you make a hell of noise when they do!"), Ratcliffe the younger is leaving his fingerprints all over the place. "Specialisation is the name of the game," he maintains, "and team effort and – though we're not trying to reinvent the wheel – cellar technology." New wielder-in-chief of said technolgy is Louis Nel, ex Neil Ellis, stepping into the winemaking shoes of departing Anna-Mareè Mostert. In the vineyard, resident vine-man Nicholas Dowling and super-consultants Phil Freese and Johan Pienaar are stepping up the pace. During harvest 2001, they reaped the benefits of a new irrigation system, use of pre-harvest aerial photography and an array of temperature sensors that collect vineyard data at 15-minute intervals every day. Great strides were made by 'batching' single vineyards in smaller 3 000 ℓ tanks – one block of merlot was picked six times over a fortnight to ensure ripeness!

✵**Trilogy** Marked by triple antique marriage cup motif and fine, understated style. Latest **99** continues downsize of cab f component to perfunctory 5%, with nearly equal cab, merlot (if trend continues, name must surely be in order – to Duality?). Herbal nose, tart sour-cherries in palate, good structure of acid/tannin for extended ageing. Juicier, fruitier than cab-dominated **98** (54%, with merlot 39%, cab f 7%). Violets bouquet and intriguing aloe nuance amid the blackcurrants and choc. Seminal **97** restrained blackcurrant fruit eased by meaty merlot (39%), sappy 7% cab f. Michelangelo gold. **96** variant of generally lighter vintage, full of well-fleshed fruit. Pvs ±60/30/10 cab/merlot/cab f. 18 mths Fr small-oak, 30% new.

✵**CWG Auction Reserve** Special new-oak-aged selection of Trilogy barrels offered at auction under Femme Bleue label. Most recent were **95** dramatic, scented, cinnamon spicy; **96** a cracker, new-oak vanilla, aromatic savoury cherry fruit, dominant cab intensity in palate; **97** oak-toasty, concentrated, needing plenty of time; latest **99** ✵✵ blend from oldest cab f vyd (20 yrs), 20-yr-old cab, vinified separately, 19 mths Fr barriques. Intense, perfumed bouquet with pyrethrum hints, mineral ring with massive tannin platform to sweet bramblу/curranty fruit. Expansive wine (13.5% alc), needs yrs to develop; potential to grow into ✵✵, given enough time.

✵**Three Cape Ladies** Features pinotage – rightly, many would argue – albeit in non-starring role – ditto – with cab, merlot. Maiden **97** now drinking very well; balanced, with pronounced toasted hazelnuts tastes. 40/40/20 ratio of cab, merlot, pinotage. Follow-up **98** slightly stronger cab contribution (50/30/20), nuts, plums, choc flavours; chewy ripe-fruit character. Should go 10 yrs. ±2 yrs Fr oak.

✵**Cabernet Franc** Run of quality started with landmark **94** *Wine* ✵✵, continued with **95** SAA, *Wine* ✵, IWSC Dave Hughes Trophy; **96** earthy, more rustic, quiet. **97** ✵✵ initially closed but ripe, needing time to show its true excellence. **98** fleshier, but currently in transition from big tannins to velvet complexity; sharp edges need extra yr/2 to soften. **99** leads with variety's stalky/brambly aromas and terse, abbreviated palate; huge tannins demanding time to soften, let raspberry/redcurrant flavours through. Should last 10 yrs. 100% varietal (except for **93**). ±20 mths Fr oak, 30% new.

✵**Old Bush Vine Pinotage** At-risk millennium vintage – hit by devastating Simonsberg fires – fortunately in good health: **00** sweetly ripe, round black-cherry palate with choc finish. **99** now shows very ripe, chewy, pastille-like fruit concentration; acetone wafts. Purple-hued **98**, with dash merlot, more obvious boiled-sweets, banana, liquorice nuances. **97** more retiring. **96** *Wine* ✵ new-wave style. From old bushvines, low yields.

✵**Merlot** After pair of concentrated vintages, **99** ✵ in lighter, more herbal mode, harking back to **96**, which featured splash cab. Latest features good red-fruit qualities and choc finish, though altogether less intense than big, ageworthy **98**, with tangy fruit in elegant tannin structure. **97** more delicate with fine tannins.

✵**Cabernet Sauvignon** Latest **99** ⁂ takes this label up a good notch with massive sweet ripe fruit and matching round tannins, promising extraordinary development. **98** similar ripe-fruit profile plus pepper, mixed spice, though in somewhat scaled-down form; good mouthfeel, balance. Lots of ageing potential. Easier, more relaxed than **97** ⁂ with tense acid/tannin structure. These average 5 t/ha, 14 mths new/2nd fill med-toast Nevers/Allier oak.

✵**Chardonnay** Recent vintages showered with awards: **98** *Wine* ✵; **99** triumphant in Cowra Tri-Nations Chardonnay Challenge, SAA First Class, Michelangelo gold. **00** excellent balance, length, complexity. Rich toasted hazelnuts, honey tones with limey au revoir. **01** ⁂ precociously elegant, balanced; fruit melded with creamy vanilla from just enough wood (4 mths new Fr) to match the stunning ripeness. Racy citrus acidity promises min 5-yr lifespan. **97** initiated new style, more modern and drinkable than maiden **96**. — *NP/DH*

Waterford

Stellenbosch (see Stellenbosch map) • Tasting & sales Mon-Fri 9-4 No fee • Landowners Jeremy & Leigh Ord • Company owners Jeremy & Leigh Ord, Kevin Arnold • Winemaker Kevin Arnold (since Nov 1997) • Assistant winemaker Gunther Schultz (since Sep 2001) • Viticulturist Bob Hobson (since 1999) • Production 20 000 cases 70% red 30% white • PO Box 635 Stellenbosch 7599 • ***Tel (021) 880-0496*** *• Fax (021) 880-1007 • E-mail waterfordhil@icon.co.za • Website www.waterfordwines.com*

From clementine orchards and beds of lavender to clever design using local stone and timber, this venture evokes the south of France, stylish and serene with easy aesthetics. Everything centres on the square with its fountain, so guests go with the flow, lolling about in comfort in the tasting room or leaping up to play a game of boule in the courtyard. It's all about quality time here, especially for the families involved: Didata's Jeremy and Leigh Ord, Kevin and Heather Arnold and their broods. Gunter Schultz (ex Morgenhof) has joined Arnold as assistant in this super-clean cellar, where everything runs on smooth wheels (including the mini-forklift). With only three years behind them in this infinitely desirable Stellenbosch Mountain neighbourhood, there's growing clarity on the stratification of the range. Most significantly, seven varieties bearing this year, to be added to the existing cabernet sauvignon, herald the beginning of Waterford's 'icon' wine, the real business here: "The crux of the Waterford investment ... our vision for the future," says Arnold.

✵**Cabernet Sauvignon** Vyd focus is on future 'icon' wine incorporating tempranillo, mourvèdre, barbera etc... and cab. For now, this varietal label is Waterford flagship. Fascinating **98-01** vertical tasting shows pendulum swing from Fr to Am dominance and back again – as Kevin Arnold seeks perfect balance. **99** Am oaked (at 60%, highest of these); quieter than maiden **98** ✵ now integrating; ripe blackberry fruit weaving threads with spicy oak into soft tannic elegance. Juicy, tasty. *Wine* ✵. Barrel samples **00** richly fragrant, firm cassis core (50/50 Fr/Am), **01** delicious tapered berry fruit, fine tannins (70% Fr) show increasing vyd maturity, vinous complexity. Home fruit supplemented by Helderberg grapes. 3 000-8 000 cases.

⁂**Kevin Arnold Shiraz** When you put your name to it – and those of your children – it had better be good. It is. Reviewing **99-01** at one sitting confirms just how good. Next-to-market **99** 'Lloyd Francis', an Arnold son (maiden **98** 'Robert Charles', the eldest, *Wine* ✵) softened to succulent decadence with extra yr under cork. Piercing peppercorn, deep roast coffee, fantastic savoury intensity in firm, full palate. Utterly riveting, simultaneously delicious. **00** 'Ashleigh Anne' (Jeremy O's eldest) purple colour intensity, spice-spiked red-berry fruits in dense palate, anchored by soft tannic stays. Excellent long haul prospects. 700 cases. Barrel sample **01** (turn of A daughter Nadine) as intense, concentrated, yet lip-smackingly inviting – beautiful ripe tannin management the key. 2 000 cases. Grapes sources Stellenbosch Kloof, Helderberg northern slopes. Shift in oak predominantly from Fr (64% in **99**) to Am (70% in **01**). Alcs 13-14%.

✵**Chardonnay** Like sauvignon below, 'in-between' style (not fence-sitting, rather integration between fruit, oak – with elegance). **01** (sample) lime fruit resting under luscious wood. 2 700 cases; **00** already unfurled into balanced beauty; gravelly palate with smooth, ripe melon fruit. **99** (with dash 98) fully mature, starting to show bottle age. Barrel fermented.

✵**Sauvignon Blanc** 4th vintage **01** (sample) hints at future style: understated, neither blowsy tropical nor rapier reductive; finely judged grip for food accompaniment. 2 100 cases. **00** now less melon/pear fruity, more flinty; better balance than pvs **99**, with massive 14% alc.

Pecan Stream Cabernet Sauvignon NEW ☻ ★★ "The wines of Kevin Arnold" (under)states **00** back-label: his stamp is indelible. Full ruby colours, creamy berry-fruit scents, preserved with softest tannic grip. Excellent balance at this price level. Own fruit. 750 cases.

Pecan Stream Chenin Blanc-Chardonnay ★★ Foxily packaged, subliminally branded 'Waterford' by motif (label, cork) rather than word. 86% bought-in chenin, polished by own chardonnay (new-oak lavished ±6 mths). **01** (sample) boasts tropical fruit breadth, citrus tang to refreshing palate. 5 000 cases. — *DS*

Webersburg

Stellenbosch • Not open to the public • Owner Fred Weber • Viticulturist Braam Steyn (since 1996) • Consulting Winemaker Giorgio Dalla Cia (Meerlust) • Vineyards 40 ha • Production 60-80 tons 3 500 cases 100% red • PO Box 3428 Somerset West 7129 • ***Tel (021) 851-7417*** *• Fax (021) 852-5280 • E-mail weber@iafrica.com*

"You've got to work to be able to afford to farm with grapes!" quips amiable businessman Fred Weber – owner of this boutique against the prime red Helderberg slopes – of his sidelines, which include a game farm (they head off to the bush when those wet Cape winters really set in). Wine may not be his only concern but he's paid it his full attention right from the start: varieties were expertly selected by master winemaker Giorgio Dalla Cia (Meerlust) and consulting viticulturist Johan Pienaar. A cellar and wine tasting area will materialise this year, soon followed by a Merlot and a blend.

★★**Cabernet Sauvignon** ✓ Not a wine that flaunts itself in youth: **98** (for 02 release) still tight in its shell in mid-01. Touch more powerful than **97** and should match its herb-tinged silky firmness. 14 mths Fr oak, 80% new. 1 500 cases. Both vintages restrained, classically styled; good structure of tannin, savoury acidity, long dry finish. Single 8 ha vyd. — *TJ*

Welgegund Wines

Wellington • Not open for tasting/sales • Guest-house/B&B Tel Ron Spies 082-453-4787 • Owners Alex & Sheila Camerer • Winemaker Hendrik de Villiers (Bovlei Winery) • Viticulturist Ron Spies (since 1995) • Vineyards 28 ha 63% red

37% white • Production 12000 bottles • PO Box 683 Wellington 7655 • ***Tel (021) 864-1185*** *• Fax (021) 873-2683 • E-mail rac@icon.co.za*

After "many discussions and many blending sessions", long-range vintners Alex and Sheila Camerer have decided to add a "splash shiraz" to their trademark Carignan, vinified to their specs at nearby Bovlei. "If grenache had been more freely available," the Gauteng eminences explain, the decision would probably have gone that way. In the event shiraz is grown on the farm and fitted in well." Coinciding with this development, the "rather old-fashioned front label is being tarted up" and a new back-blurb on "the unheralded carignan variety" introduced.

Carignan ☆ Now with 10% shiraz and bit more (ripe) tannin, imparting extra gravitas to oak-influenced **01**. Still the hallmark brilliant purple lights; zesty baked plum flavours, dry finish good, the Camerers assert, with pastas, goatsmilk cheese. — *DH*

Welgemeend Estate

Paarl (see Paarl map) • Tasting & sales Wed 2-4 Sat 9-12.30 or by appointment • Owner Hofmeyr family • Winemaker Louise Hofmeyr (since 1991) • Manager/viticulturist Ursula Hofmeyr • Vineyards 12,6 ha • Production 3 500 cases • PO Box 1408 Suider-Paarl 7624 • ***Tel (021) 875-5210*** *• Fax (021) 875 5239 • E-mail welgemeend@worldonline.co.za*

This is the real thing – an honest-to-goodness working farm with dogs (all boxers, adored beyond measure) and a true passion for making and drinking good wine. "I don't make alcoholic blockbusters that jump into your mouth and kill your palate," says assured winemaker Louise Hofmeyr of these restrained wines, echoing her late father: Billy's métier was a contained European style. They have an established and faithful following, and aren't on the competition circuit, so there's no impressing with showy wines. In fact, there's nothing that will get up your nose the wrong way here, including the prices. Abraham Fuse, who's been on the farm for 18 months, flew off to France last year to work and study, courtesy of that country's government and the SA Wine Industry Trust, in what is hoped becomes an annual sojourn under the Burgundy Viticulture Exchange Programme. "You don't get anyone in return though," laughs Hofmeyr, who was deeply delighted even though faced with bottling sans her resident expert in that line.

☆☆**Estate Reserve** ✓ **98** and **97** yr on, revealed new high for this, the first Cape bdx blend cab, merlot, cab f, and one of few with established track record of consistently expressing its terroir origins. Latest **99** ☆ shy but complex; savoury aromas with tobacco hints; concentrated red fruits and thumbprint nuances of coffee, flint, green olives; Fr oak, ±30% new, 18 mths. **98** concentrated, rich but elegant; triumphant supple balance. Alc unusually bold at nearly 13%, reflecting hot vintage. **97** more restrained but very fine. Recommendation: tuck above vintages away at least 5 yrs (this label noted for ability to age) and enjoy early-matured **96** simpler, lighter (but not lightweight), thoroughly pleasant.

☆**Amadé** ✓ Remarkably successful, uncopied Cape interpretation of Rhone blend: equal portions shiraz, grenache, (now mostly non-estate) pinotage. Extraordinary value for serious (though not grand) wine, with ability to age interestingly. **99** wild, untamed version – barnyard sniffs and savoury mushroom flavours; whiffs saddle-leather; powerful tannins needing cellaring (best drinking around 2005). Older oak maturation, 18 mths. **98** ☆ added herby richness to fine tannin structure.

☆**Douelle** A different nod to Bdx, malbec dominating (with cab, merlot, cab f). 98 beguiling wildness – particularly appreciated by foreigners, here and abroad.

Fresh, elegant, firm but non-aggressive tannins. More inward-looking 99 3 needs time; firm tannins; flinty/mineral texture with faintly medicinal conclusion.

✵**Soopjeshoogte** Shows that barrels not quite good enough for the top wines still offer very satisfying, excellent value drinking. Estate Reserve's virtues here in slightly reduced form. Latest **99** savoury/meaty bouquet with hints of sweet ripe fruit. Palate vinous rather than fruity; minerally/flinty texture; dry finish. Cab, merlot, cab f aged 18 mths Fr oak, none new. Harks back to more austere **97** ★, with dried fruit, fennel, nutty qualities. **98** fleshier, in line with yr. — *NP*

Wellington Co-op 

Wellington (see Wellington map) • Tasting & sales Mon-Fri 8-1; 2-5 • Owners 50 members • Winemaker Gert Boerssen (since 1980) & Koos Carstens (since 1991) • Assistant winemaker & viticulturist Bertus Albertyn (since 2000) • Vineyards 1 530 ha Production 10 500 tons 20 000 cases 55% white 45% red • PO Box 520 Wellington 7654 • ***Tel (021) 873-1163/1257*** *• Fax (021)873-2423 • E-mail wellwyn@iafrica.com*

After switching tempos – red varieties are now playing a bigger part – the seasoned duo of Gert Boerssen and Koos Carstens has been joined by new assistant winemaker and viticulturist Bertus Albertyn. The red wine facilities have accordingly been upgraded to fit the new bill. While most of the production here finds its way into the bottle under third-party labels, a portion is retained for the characterful in-house brand, which sings of such good value and drinkability it has consumers in several countries dancing in the aisles.

✵**Shiraz** ✓ Inky **00** with tar/crushed pepper aromas; some liquorice in well-wooded (as elsewhere in range) palate. 9 mths casked. 14.1% alc. 1 200 cases (× 6, unless indicated). Upscale from pvs **97** ★.

✵**Hanepoot Jerepiko** NEW ✓ Delicate, charming **01** fortified dessert with perfume-counter bouquet, supple honey sweetness underlain by damp straw tastes. 17% alc. 284 cases (× 12).

Pinotage ☻ ★ Oak-aged **99** mulberry-and-cream aromas, jelly-baby juiciness and very generous 14.5% alc. 1 580 cases. **Cinsaut-Ruby Cabernet** ☻ ★ Round, soft, succulent **00** quaffs easily (14.5% alc cunningly hidden), finishes with sour-cherry twang. 1 148 cases.

Cabernet Sauvignon ★ Oak-matured **99** good varietal expression, minerally tones, woody edges which should soften with extra yr in bottle. 13.5% alc. 1 175 cases. **Merlot** ★ Strawberry-cream aromas in **99**, contrasting very nicely with tangy fruit-acid. 9 mths oaked. 14.5% alc. 1 200 cases. **Chardonnay** ★ **01** trumps pvs release with sappy mouthful melon, fresh hay; low acid (4.7 g/ℓ) and expansive 14% alc calibrated for maximum smoothness. 446 lightly oaked cases. **Chenin Blanc** ★ Guava/melon fruits in lightish **01**, piercing green-apple acidity demands a culinary companion. Neither **Sauvignon Blanc 01** nor **Stein 01** ready for tasting. — *TM*

Welmoed see Stellenbosch Vineyards

Weltevrede Estate 

Robertson (see Robertson map) • Tasting & sales Mon-Fri 8-5 Sat 9-3.30 • Cellar tours by appointment • Traditional lunches Mon-Sat 12-2.30 or BYO picnic • Farmers market every Sat moning • Self-catering cottages • Play area for children • Tourgroups • Gifts • Walks • Conservation area • Mountain biking • Views • Owner Lourens Jonker • Winemaker Philip Jonker with Riaan Liebenberg (since 1999), Sam Davids (since 1972) • Viticulturist Philip Jonker with Herman Kitshoff (since 1995) • Viticultural consultant Francois Viljoen (VinPro) • Vineyards 100 ha • PO Box 6 Bonnievale 6730 • ***Tel (023) 616-2141*** *• Fax (023) 616-2460 • E-mail info@weltevrede.com • Website www.weltevrede.com*

LOOKING out over the family farm at Bonnievale, Philip Jonker grows pensive. Blocks are due to be replanted and he must decide which varieties to establish. "An incoming generation really has only one shot an placing their thumbprint on the vineyards. So I have to be extra careful about what I do." Here is a young man who's clearly thought long and hard about his role as new custodian of the Jonker spread (father Lourens, stalwart of KWV, taking a back seat). Philip J's decision, when it comes, will be measured, and informed by wider, international perspectives as well as an osmotically-absorbed knowledge of Weltevrede farm and its customers. Plus a firm belief in the truism that wine is grown in the vineyard. Adding their own perspectives are Jonker's wife Lindelize ("my main winemaking inspiration"), and engaging winemaking assistant, Riaan Liebenberg, who's traded the stark beauty of a Karoo sheep farm for a residency at this gentle spread beside the Breede River.

Oude Weltevreden range

✵**Chardonnay** The estate's limited-release barrel-fermented flagship, grapes selected (on taste) from more than 10 separate blocks. First was **98** VG, *Wine* ✵; Current **00** ✵ very full and rich, almost viscous with pear/apricot, some butterscotch, unusual clove-spice finish. Will appeal to adherents of a softer, lower-acid style. Though Philip Jonker believes will hold "another few yrs", we suggest drink soon while acid's still in balance. 9 mths Fr oak. 13.5% alc. 380 cases. **01** sample reveals pear aromas and good length, auguring well.

Merlot-Cabernet Sauvignon ✵ First dry red from this estate, traditionally vinified in open fermenters, basket-pressed. **98** SAYWS gold. Latest **99** savoury tones with bell peppers and hints of spice; still tannic and tight, needs time. 55/45 blend, oaked 16 mths Fr casks. 13,5% alc. 380 cases.

Weltevrede range

✵**Chardonnay** Altogether convincing in **98**, fine balance of citrus/tropical fruit and vanilla oak. Similar, albeit in reduced intensity, in **00** ✵ (difficult chardonnay yr); delicate peach/mango tastes in big (13.5% alc), soft body. Barrel-fermented/aged 9 mths Fr oak. Malo. 700 cases. **01** preview more structure, flavour.

✵**Philip Jonker Brut** MCC from chardonnay. **98**, released in time for 'real' millennium, holding; energetic mousse sets lively pace, joined in palate by bright acidity balancing the richer honey/butterscotch tones. 370 cases, Philip J ventures, to dip into today: "Think of everything that is wonderful and create an occasion to celebrate life!"

✵**Cape Muscat** Benchmark jerepigo-style muscat de hambourg, opulent and concentrated, handsomely packaged. From venerable vyd, traditionally vinified. Pvs was **98**. Current **01** ✵ gorgeous fuchsia glints, complex fragrant malty nose; intense sweetness combines with very low alc (15%) to slightly unctuous effect, which pvs avoided. 750 cases of 375 ml.

Sauvignon Blanc ✵ Ripe gooseberry aromas in **01**, palate tasty and, though presently uncomplex, may develop more depth with time. Philip J notes: "This is a *vine* selection, individually identified on taste and harvested separately." 12% alc. **Riesling** ✵ Easy floral off-dry **00**, WOM Value, Rhine riesling with delicate lemon/pineapple tastes; fuller bodied than pvs **98** SAA. 13% alc. 620 cases. **Gewürztraminer** ✵ Lots of varietally correct aromas billow from **00** glass, off-dry and very gentle in the mouth. "Pure roses, spice and Turkish Delight!" says Philip J. **Privé du Bois** Popular chardonnay/sauvignon blend returns to the guide in **01**, 60/40 ratio, 6 mths Fr oak. Sample too unformed to rate, but pvs have been regular wine mail order club selections. **Ovation Rhine Riesling Natural Sweet** ✮ Single-vyd dessert, only made in botrytis yrs: "Looking for a unique style – drier than NLH". Which current **99**, at 32 g/ℓ sugar, undoubtedly is, though beginning to taste sweeter than when sampled last yr as initial freshness fades. Suggest drink soon. 12,5% alc. 750 cases. **Oupa Se Wyn** ✮ Flavourful fortified dessert from red muscadel, portion of grapes from vyd planted 1926, now a national monument. Latest **00** powerful sweetness, enduring length; ethereal tangerine/raisin aromas. Bigger alc than pvs (17%). 2 800 cases of 375 ml. **Ouma se Wyn** ✮ Consistently delicious fortified from white muscadel. **00** SAYWS reserve champion intense incense and honeysuckle perfumes; rich, viscous palate suffused with sunny sweetness. Lightish 15% alc. **97** VVG. 1 300 cases of 375 ml.

River's Edge range NEW

Blanc de Noir ★ From red muscadel, fairly sweet in **00** with vague muscat aromas. Stocky frame (13.9% alc) for such delicate robes. 1 700 cases. **Cape Riesling** ★ Variety not known for aromatic pyrotechnics; **00** delicate apple, pear tones, lightish 12% alc. 1 500 cases. **Chardonnay** ⁑ Unwooded summer standalone or casual lunch partner. **01** with pear/melon tastes. 1 100 cases. 13.5% alc. **Colombard** ⁑ Fresh, lightish off-dry **01**; gentle undemanding partner with salads and lighter dishes. **Sauvignon Blanc** Varietal gooseberry/grassy tones in med-bodied **01**, tank sample too young to rate. Lightish 12% alc. 2 700 cases. **Blanc de Blanc** ★ Colombard, chenin blend in **00** with melon, pear tastes and quick finish. Lowish 11.5% alc. 4 200 cases. **Muscat-Colombard** ⁑ Apple and pear tones in **00** lightish off-dry easy quaff. 700 cases. —*JN*

Weskus see Winkelshoek

West Coast Vineyards NEW

Paarl • Not open to the public • Owners Bennie van Rensburg, Kosie Möller & Jannie Vermeulen • Winemaker Kosie Möller (since Mar 2001) • Production 100 000 cases 50% red 50% white • PO Box 1317 Suider Paarl 7626 • ***Tel (021) 863-1471/2862/2864*** *• Fax (021) 863-1473 • E-mail westco@iafrica .com*

RISING-STAR negociant house based in Paarl, which makes its own ranges for the local market and export, sources SA wines for international brands such as Assegai, Beste Wense, Veelgeluk and Western Wines, and provides marketing services to several local cellars including Simonsvlei, Du Toitskloof, Bonnievale and Slanghoek. See also Devon Hill. The wines below were tasted as work in progress and therefore not rated.

Celiwe range

Shiraz Stylish **01** spotlights agreeably tart black/red fruits, contrasting with luxurious spicy oak. Tasted in extreme youth, already balanced, auspicious. 13.3% alc **Chardonnay** Honest peachy fruit stars in **01**, delicious vanilla-oak in properly supportive role. As below, granule sugar, big alc (13.7%) ensure Aussie-style swiggability.

Rising River range

Cabernet Sauvignon 01 sample still dauntingly tannic; stalky, dry; lurking mulberry fruit needs time to develop. 13% alc. **Merlot 01** muscular style with rippling alc (14.5%), dense fruit and mouthcoating tannin. **Pinotage** Toasty, roasty qualities uppermost in atypical **01**; mere suggestion of variety's high toned sweetness; good plummy-dry finish. Promising. **Ruby Cabernet** Massive (14.8% alc), pulpy **01** rescued by firmish tannin for vinous rather than fruit-juicy feel. **Shiraz** Embryonic **01**

(barrel sample) already showing breed; polished black fruit, fine-textured tannins; high but not unmanageable 13.3% alc. **Chardonnay** Lightly oaked **01** with Aussie-style grain sugar for luscious peaches-and-cream effect. High 13.5% alc enhances fatness. **Chenin Blanc** Unwooded, quaffable **01** offers spicy touches to vibrant fruit; pleasantly tart green-apple finish. Med-bodied. **Sauvignon Blanc** Well behaved **01** has none of variety's wilder qualities; soft tropical fruit, bone-dry finish; moderate 12.7% alc.

Something Else/Ietsie Anders range

Cape Red Cinsaut (90%), ruby cab in soft, extra-drinkable mode; unoaked **01** sweet mouthwatering red-cherry fruit, downy tannins. 13.5% alc. **Chenin Blanc** Easygoing, fruity **01**; very ripe, appley; modest in most respects. 13.1% alc. Not wooded. *— IvH*

Western Wines

*Not open to the public • Winemaker Rhyan Wardman • Production 1 000 000-1 200 000 cases • Western Wines Ltd (Inc in the UK) PO Box 769 Stellenbosch 7600 • **Tel (021) 882-8177** • Fax (021) 882-8176 • E-mail manager@westernwines.com • Website www.western-wines.com*

"WE'VE kept a low profile," smiles James Reid, cherub-faced local lynchpin for this hugely successful wine exporter, explaining why most SA vinophiles are unfamiliar with the company and its UK-conquering brand, Kumala. Powering from 81 000 to 1,2-million cases in just four years, Kumala is the top SA wine brand in Britain and, according to statsmeisters Nielsen, the No 7 UK brand overall. Now WW is entrenching its position, with Kiwi winemaking chief Rhyan Wardman headquartered in the Cape (he also makes and blends the group's wines in Italy, France and Spain), and by ex Goudini winemaker Ben Jordaan. They like "to get right into the nitty-gritty", working with partners from the Breede River to the West Coast on block selection and vinification. What comes next? "We're looking at the SA market," Reid confides. Watch this space.

Kumala range

✵**Cabernet Sauvignon Reserve** Heavily (but not over-) extracted Stbosch fruit in **00** (sample); dense, chewy, herbal/leafy whiffs with snatches eucalyptus. Fr barrels, some new. ±3 800 cases. **99** equally weighty, extra complexity from splash merlot.

✵**Merlot Reserve 00** (sample) again Stbosch fruit, but very different profile: shy, sweet plums and some pleasant leafiness. Wood (Fr casks, some new) delicately handled. 13% alc. 1 080 cases. **99**, with dab cab, ripely plummy.

✵**Cabernet Sauvignon-Shiraz** Strawberry jam (not jammy), sweet cinnamon spice in latest **01** ⁂; cab gives structure without compromising drinkability. 30% Allier casked. ±130 000 cases. Standout **00** fuller (13% alc vs **01**'s 12.5), riper.

✵**Colombard-Chardonnay** Pleasurable drink-young style. Partly oak-fermented **01** ⁂ seems shyer than pvs, light-bodied. ±144 000 cases. **00** more extrovert.

✵**Chardonnay Brut** NEW Biscuity complexity in **00** MCC sparkle, plus lemon-cream hints; acidity well controlled for soft, gently dry finish. 11% alc. Partner for oysters, fresh line-fish. 5 000 cases.

Merlot-Ruby Cabernet ☻ ⁂ Stylish, satisfying everyday drink. **01** (sample) sour-plum aromas, nice sweet dark-choc farewell. Portion Fr-oaked. ±40 000 cases. **Ruby Cabernet-Merlot** ☻ ⁂ Good on its own or with food, thanks to broadband flavours (savoury, organic, herby); **01** very ripe, mouth-filling (13% alc). Partly Fr-oaked.

Pinotage NEW ☆ Boldly fruity style; pleasing tarry whiffs, sweet farewell to med-bodied **01**, partly Fr oaked. 15 000 cases. **Pinotage-Cinsault** ☆ Swiggable, well-crafted **01** (sample); sweetish mulberry tastes for those who prefer an undemanding style; part Fr-oaked. ±136 000 cases. **Cinsault-Cabernet Sauvignon** NEW ☆ Light-robed **01** partly Fr-oaked; supple almost fruit-cordial tones, med-bodied. Well executed commercial style. 85 000 cases. **Chenin Blanc** NEW ☆ Cleverly made off-dry **01**, waxy breadth and apricot flavours. Some ageing potential, so no need to rush. Med-bodied. 45 000 cases. **Semillon-Chardonnay** ☆ Elegantly fruity **01**, aromatic peach/apricot tones, twist of ripe pear; 30% new Fr oak-fermented. **Chenin Blanc-Chardonnay** ☆ Peachy, full-bodied **01** summer picnic wine or partner for Thai curries. 20% new oak-fermented. ±47 000 cases. **Sauvignon Blanc-Colombard** ☆ Crisp, lemony **01** med-bodied, dry. Good solo sip. 13 900 cases. — *TM*

WhaleHaven Wines

Walker Bay (see Walker Bay map) • Tasting & sales Mon-Fri 9.30-5 Sat 10.30-2 Closed Sun & religious holidays • Tourgroups by appointment Fee R10 p/p • Owners Storm Kreusch, Robert, Maryke & Nick Middlemann, Dr Alberto Bottega • Winemaker Storm Kreusch (since 1995) • Production 6 000 cases • Private Bag X14 Suite 10 Hermanus 7200 • ***Tel (028) 316-1633*** *• Fax (028) 316-1640 • E-mail whwines@hermanus.co.za*

THOUGH the children's animal-farm attached to tasting room has had to make way for a new vineyard, this charming Walker Bay winery lives up to the name 'haven'. In winter, Chardonnay the full-bodied ginger cat curls up on a sofa in front of a blazing log fire. "The rest of the time she lives on my lap," laughs Storm Kreusch, the nurturing winemaker who is mother to a pair of young daughters, and a "much-aligned" press named Yellow Submarine and a destalker called Spitnick, aged 2. No longer en famille is their Sauvignon, which has had to be discontinued because the bought-in grapes have become prohibitively expensive. Better news for admirers is that the Cabernet Franc 97, intended as a once-off (subsequent crops going into the popular Baleine Noir), might be revived with the auspicious 01 vintage. This cellar's signature Pinot Noir also benefited from the 01 season, "a lovely, low-cropped vintage with great colour and body." Best buy it at the cellar-door: the 96 sold for R38 ex farm in 1998, and R150 per bottle at the 01 Nederburg Auction!

☆☆ **Oak Valley Pinot Noir** Elegant, restrained, in more classic than new world manner, but also succulent and marvellously undisguised by excessive wood (mix of new/older Fr oak). Entirely from new-clone grapes since **97**, which topped local pinot tastings for *Wine* ☆ (as did **96**), travelled with the Blue Train. **98** with raspberry aromas, gamey hints, voluptuous palate of velvet. **99** similar, leathery whiffs among the raspberries; good oak and firm tannin structure auguring particularly well for good ageing. These, anyway, amply reward few yrs' patience. 16 mths Fr oak, 20% new. 1 180 cases. Maiden **95** ☆ (pure BK5 clone) and more complex **96** ☆ (14% BK5), both drinking well; earthy, farmyardy sweetness.

☆ **Cabernet Franc Chélene** To date a 'once-off' **97**, though at press time it seemed there might be a sequel **01** (see intro).

☆ **Oak Valley Merlot** Minty choc and fruit-cake the signatures of this wine, grapes ex Elgin, 14 mths Fr oak in latest 99 4, bigger, bolder than pvs, almost sweetly ripe yet firmly controlled, properly dry; potential 5 yrs beneficial development. 1 800 cases. Medicinal quality in 98 leads to fleshy, slightly baked, soft-tannin palate. 97 ☆ shade less rich and structured.

☆ **Chardonnay** Grapes from Kaaimansgat near Villiersdorp; fermented/matured mix new/older oak, yr on lees in latest **00**; big, soft, open with citrus, tropical fruit and hint of butterscotch. Integrated silky palate, lingering crisp finish.

±13,2% alc. Intelligently wooded, as always. 550 cases. **99** ☆ more restrained in all respects. **98** panoply of lovely, almost perfumed, aromas.

☆**Cabernet Sauvignon Oak Valley** Choc-minty cassis and green pepper, hint rose petal in **98**, plenty of fruit but also more tannin than pvs, needs 2/3 yrs or, as Storm K suggests, pepper steak, curry or braaied sosatie. 22 mths oak, 18% new. 13.5% alc. 1 100 cases. **97** ☆.

Baleine Noir ☻ ☆ Wine "for any occasion which is fun and happy!". Whiffs peppery cinnamon, red berry in lightish **NV** (98), soft fruit-laden tannins and just a hint vanilla from light oaking. Very easy to drink; chill in summer, especially over lunch. 1 300 cases. — *DH*

Wide River see Robertson Winery

Wiese Portfolio

Megapreneur Christo Wiese now runs his considerable vinous interests – wine farms Lanzerac and Lourensford, future flagship blend Christo Wiese, and bigger volume brands Forellen, Five Heirs and Caap Mooi – under this organisational canopy. At full production in 2006, the operation will produce 1.7-million litres, 70% for export. About 1/3 of output will be top-table wine, much of it made at Lourensford on the Helderberg. Here some 250 hectares, in 10 individually managed sites, are being developed and a 2 500 ton cellar built in time for harvest 2003. See also Lanzerac Farm & Cellar.

Wildekrans Estate

Walker Bay (see Walker Bay map) • Tasting & sales daily 8.30-5.30 at Orchard Farm Stall on N2 near Grabouw • Tasting & sales at the Cellar on Wednesdays 8. 30-5.30 (summer only) or by appointment • Tasting for tourgroups by appointment • Cellar tours by appointment. • Breakfast, lunch, snacks, farm produce available at Orchard Farm Stall, or BYO picnic • Play area for children • Proclaimed conservation area 'The Koegelberg Biosphere Reserve' • Owner Bruce Elkin, EK Green • Winemaker Bruce Elkin • Viticulturist Barry Anderson (since 1990) • Vineyards 50 ha • Production 400 – 500 tons, 10 000 cases (150 tons, 8 000 cases own label) 60% red 40% white • PO Box 200 Elgin 7180 • ***Tel (021) 859-5587*** *• Fax (028) 284-9872/ (028) 284-9902 • E-mail houw@mweb.co.za*

Wildekrans followed *Decanter*'s 1997 billing as 'one of the 21 hottest New World wineries' with a curtain call as one of 50 cellars worldwide to crack the nod to its glossy Rising Stars Fine Wine Encounter in London last year, where the Osiris garnered four stars. As an encore, the *Washington Post* rated their Barrel Selection Pinotage the best of this SA variety. Not that they're being ignored back on their stomping ground: the Cabernet Sauvignon was selected for the Nederberg Auction. At their Bot River property bordering on the Koegelberg Biosphere Reserve, additions to the vineyards include 2 ha each of shiraz and merlot. Then there's a new hectare of shiraz on their farm in Elgin. "We anticipate an interesting blend, with it being much cooler up there," says owner Bruce Elkin (who was a dentist in Sea Point in a previous life). Elkin will now be taking over as winemaker, a prospect he's excited at, though he wryly mutters: "This year's vintage will be the proof of the pudding."

☆**Pinotage Barrel Selection** First release **98** ☆☆ introduced a new benchmark for Walker Bay. **99** on release and, back-tasted mid-01, reveals deep layered fruits, complex tannic finish; merits laying down 4-5 yrs. Only 408 cases from low-cropping (3 t/ha) bushvines, 11 mths new Fr oak. 14% alc.

☆**Pinotage** Densely fruited, forward, uncomplex **00** ★ pungent herbal notes, black cherry, varnish and minty whiffs. Lighter, tighter than pvs **99**, with red berry, cloves and liquorice. 9 mths 2nd/3rd fill Fr casks. 14% alc. 1 000 cases.

☆**Cabernet Sauvignon** Fragrant, firm-tannined, spicier and more herbal than most Medoc examples. **99** sweet praline notes, cherry/youngberry aromas, taut yet sappy finish. 9 mths 2nd/3rd fill Fr oak. 13,5% alc. 1 000 cases. Standout **98** more cassis, less herbal, with chunkier, more mineral textures. VG. **97** initially steely, consonant with yr. **96** trophy winner at SAYWS.

☆**Merlot** Succulent plummy **99**; mulberry/greengage/youngberry aromas, fine subtle oak notes, more allspice than vanilla. At 14% alc, bigger, richer than most. "A wine to dine your mistress," suggests winemaker. Less textured than plumper **98**, though just as food friendly. 550 cases.

☆**Osiris** Winemaker describes this bdx blend, half cab and equal dashes merlot, cab f, as a "stunner", though to us latest **99** ★ not up to the more flamboyant, internationally highly rated **98**. **99**'s more herbal, with drier tannins, greener notes, more forward pine/eucalyptus whiffs. Pungent yet austere, less of the forward fruit, spicy oak of pvs. 9 mths barreled. 13,5% alc. 250 cases.

☆**Semillon** ✓ Pvs was **99**, full-bodied, serious, figgy whiffs a la Australia's Margaret River. Follow-up **00** immediately post-bottling reticent on nose, palate more alive with leesy flavours; good acid backbone that augurs well. 70% Fr casks, some new. 400 cases.

☆**Chenin Blanc** Harmonious, lightly oaked, very stylish 01 combo pear/apricot/peach, layered with hints creme brulee, hazelnut, dried-fruit compote. 2 mths in wood. Complex; worthy successor to elegant yet flavoursome **00** ★.

Cabernet Franc-Merlot ★ 90/10 blend with peppery green-olive aromas, black cherry notes, sweet redcurrant fruit through to finish. **00** easy, fun red "for poolside drinking with a block of ice", suggests winemaker; ready accessibility belies ample flavour to complement spicier red meat dishes. Cab f portion 6 mths 3rd fill Fr oak. 1 200 cases. **Chardonnay** Last was **00**, barrel sample rated ★. 6 mths new/2nd fill Fr oak. **01** not ready for tasting. **Sauvignon Blanc** ★ **01** green fig, slight smoky herbal tones, light lime/herbaceous layerings in finish; food friendly, styled for rocket and feta cheese. 12,5% alc. 2 000 cases. Less intense than pvs and only vaguely reminiscent of Loire-like **99**. **Caresse Marine** ☆ Flinty dry white, mineral notes, unassuming dry finish. **01** blend semillon/sauvignon/chenin. — *MF*

Wilhelmshof

Stellenbosch • Not open to the public • Owners Nico & Petra van der Merwe • Winemaker Nico van der Merwe • Production 25 tons 2 000 cases 100% red • PO Box 12200 Stellenbosch 7613 • ***Tel/fax (021) 903-9507*** *• E-mail wilhelmshof@xsinet.co.za*

Already flying a high profile with two winemaking portfolios – Saxenburg and Ch Capion in the south of France – self-confessed maverick Nico van der Merwe decided it was time to fulfil his own-label dream. And, true to character, prove a point by sourcing grapes for the maiden Robert Alexander Shiraz from a "non-traditional" area – the largely undiscovered Trawal Valley, an oasis in the semi-desert Olifants River region. Confounding first-time tasters as to its origin, response was so favourable that Travino Wines (where brother Robert Alexander vdM cellarmasters) approached him to produce a Merlot and Chardonnay, to be followed by a Cabernet and Pinotage, under this label – strict supervision a given. The flagship Mas Nicolas Cape gives him the chance to shine with his signature grape, syrah. Next up are their own vineyards and cellar (wine-motivated wife Petra is a partner in the venture) – not a long shot, he already owns undeveloped land in quiet Bot River where he's bound to make some noise.

Mas Nicolas Cape First release **99** shiraz/cab quintessential Nico vd Merwe: rich, polished, balanced. Deep colour, reticent mineral spice, wild scrub tones consistent with structured youthful mouthful of berry fruit, bound up in tannin corset. Deliberately neither shiraz nor cab, rather fine red wine. Statement stuff, understated. R150/bottle will raise eyebrows, ditto elegant packaging. Needs 8 yrs to peak. 60/40 Kuils River shiraz, Stbosch cab. Yr Fr oak, 60% new. 13,5% alc. 500 cases.

Robert Alexander Shiraz Initial disbelief that this a product of solar-rich Olifants vyds mollified by savoury mouthful of note. Ex cooler Vredendal slopes, made to vdM's specs by brother Robert Alexander ('Alkie'), Travino cellarmaster. Next **00** stylish, smoky, savoury green olive, pimento characters, bold but supple tannins. First **99** spicy, savoury. Yr used oak; bottled at Saxenburg. 13.5% alc. 1 500 cases.

Robert Alexander Merlot NEW VdM family expands Trawal-sourced range in **00** with, as Nico vdM says, "fine merlot from an undiscovered region matured in French oak for a pleasant surprise". That it is: sweet wood mingles with cool minty plums; in the mouth, pears-in-red-wine spiciness infuses ripe berry fruit. Also crafted by RA vdM up the West Coast. More open than above; good now, for 2-3 yrs. Yr used oak. 13.5% alc. 1 000 cases.

Robert Alexander Chardonnay partially wooded **01** will be first; not ready for tasting. — *DS*

Windfall

Robertson • Owner Eddie Barlow • PO Box 802 Robertson 6705 • ***Tel/fax (023) 626-4498***

CRICKETING legend Eddie Barlow has been convalescing on his wine farm in the secluded Agterkliphoogte valley, after a stroke brought him home prematurely from his appointment in Dhaka as coach to the Bangladesh cricket team. He's looked after by his wife, Cally, who's ever at his side. They had an exceptionally good harvest last year (a decision was still to be taken at time of going to press whether to bottle it or not) and winemaker 'Robbie' Roberts, who's an integral part of the Robertson winemaking landscape. Sadly, the farm is now up for sale and the Barlows are patiently waiting for the right buyer.

Windmeul Co-op

Paarl (see Paarl map) • Tasting & sales Mon-Fri 8-12.30; 13.30-5 • Cellar tours by appointment • Owners 54 members • Manager/winemaker Danie Marais (since 1999) • Winemaker Hugo Lambrechts (since 1999) • Viticulturist Paul Wallace (VineWise) • Production 9 200 tons (1 500 cases own label) 70% white 30% red • PO Box 2013 Windmeul 7630 • ***Tel (021) 863-8043/8100*** *• Fax (021) 863-8614 • E-mail windmeul@iafrica.com*

THOUGH production of this Paarl co-op's increasingly red own-label range (the rest travels incognito in other people's bottles) has doubled up to 3 000 cases, wines have been selling a storm from their newly spruced up visitor-friendly tasting locale, so followers may soon be left panting for more. The cabernet/merlot blend gets snapped up "like nothing else" says winemaker Hugo Lambrechts, who works closely with farm manager Danie Marais. These new brooms have made sweeping changes in the few seasons they've been here. The cellar's been expanded to handle the increased red wine production, and a classification system (viticultural consultant Paul Wallace watches over the vineyards) has been implemented to sort the A-blocks from the Bs for separate vinification. All this effort is reaping results but man-on-a-mission Lambrechts shows no sign of slowing down: "There's always room for improvement."

Cabernet Sauvignon-Merlot ✓ String of VGs for this well made, unpretentious new world style red, amazingly low-priced. Fresh excitement heralded by **98**. Follow-up **99** less immediately accessible, as is **00**; big (14% alc), minerally, voluminous sweet tannins needing 2-3 yrs. Fr casks, 12 mths. 500 cases.

Cabernet Sauvignon ✓ **98** set crowd-pleasing forward-fruity tone. Latest **00** yr Fr oaked, fruit ex Perdeberg area; cinnamon/clove spice in deep-flavoured, expansive (13,8% alc) palate. Bigger tannins, too, than pvs; will need 4-5 to fully soften/develop. 500 cases.

Merlot ✓ **00**, revisited for this ed, ready; violet perfumes, sappy ripe-plum flavours, more accessible tannins than above reds. Could go another 1-3 yrs. Yr Fr oak. 13,5% alc. 500 cases. Pvs **98** mineral-textured.

Chenin Blanc ☻ ★ Vibrant Agter-Paarl fruit in **01** tastes tropically fresh, ends zippily dry with no hint of big 13,5% alc. Unwooded. 800 cases.

Sauvignon Blanc NEW ★ Night-harvested, reductively made **01** tastes softly dry; full-flavoured (and pleasingly moderate 12.5% alc), sweetish grass/nettle palate. Nice. 550 cases. Following not tasted for this ed: **Pinotage** (pvs unrated), **Merry Mill Red**, **Chardonnay**. — *DH*

Winds of Change see Sonop

Wine Concepts

Cape Town • Tasting & sales Mon-Fri 9-6 Sat 9-2 • PO Box 1 Cape Town 8000 • ***Tel (021) 465-8707*** *• Fax (021) 465-8709 E-mail sales@wineconcepts.co.za • Website www.wineconcepts.co.za*

INFUSING this Cape Town consulting/retailing business with savvy and spice (the fabled Blue Train a long-time customer) are wine impresarios Mike Bampfield-Duggan and Murray Giggins, partnered by local architect Derrick Henstra. Their in-house budget range, Sommelier's Choice, was temporarily out of stock at press time. But M & M were attempting their first harvest, "so watch this space for new releases", available from new retail premises in Kloof Street.

Winecorp

Chairman Faisal Rahmatallah • CEO Johan van Reened • Group winemaker Ben Radford • Vineyards & viticulture Gerrie Wagener • Marketing manager Renske Minnaar • National sales manager Bryan Culhane • PO Box 99 Lynedoch 7603 • ***Tel (021) 881-3690*** *• Fax (021) 881-3699 • E-mail winecorp@iafrica.com • Website www.winecorp.co.za*

Listed group producing some 600 000 cases of wine a year, mostly under its own internationally recognised brands – Longridge, Bay View, Savanha, Spier and Capelands, as well as Naledi and Sejana (with Bordelais luminary Alain Mouiex) – chiefly for export to Europe and North America. See separate entries, and Winecorp PLS below.

Winecorp Private Label Services NEW

Franschhoek • Not open to the public • Owner Winecorp Limited • Head winemaker Johan le Hanie (since 2000) • Assistant winemaker Lelanie Germishuys (since 2001) • Consultant "flying winemaker" Clive Hartnell (since 1999) • PO Box 62 Simondium 7670 • ***Tel (021) 860-1300/01*** *• Fax (021) 860-1334 • E-mail general@winecorppl.co.za*

New division of Winecorp (see entry above), focused on buyers' own brands (BOBs) for supermarket groups, private importers and distributors in the UK, Holland, Germany, Belgium Denmark, the US, Canada, Japan, Thailand and SA.

Grapes come from selected private cellars and cooperatives around the Cape, and are vinified at Ashwood's mega-modern facility near Franschhoek, complete with a line capable of filling up to 40 000 bottles a day. Experienced Johan le Hanie (one-time Blue White winemaker) is assisted by Lelanie Germishuys and 'flying' consultant Clive Hartnell, who makes the Chapel Hill wines in Hungary during one of his three (!) annual crushes.

Ashwood range

Cabernet Sauvignon ☆ Robust, rustic **00**; pleasant, straightforward blackcurrant juiciness cut short by grippy tannins, sharpish acid. May benefit with yr-18 mths in bottle. 10 mths oaked. 13% alc. **Pinotage** ★ NEW Unashamed full-frontal raspberry/banana aromas in **00**; light-textured, juicy, though variety's gruff tannins dampen immediate appeal. Tame now with winemaker's suggestion of braised spiced duck or watch development over next 2-3 yrs. 13.5% alc. Barrel-matured 9 mths. **Chardonnay** ★ **00** combines limey liveliness with subtle butterscotch, juicy pineapple broadening; all integrated/balanced for current agreeable drinking. Portion oak-fermented. 13% alc.

Cheetah Valley range

Five percent of sales of this range are donated to the non-profit Cheetah Conservation Fund, under whose auspices the cheetah breeding programme at Spier is run (see that entry). Produced for importer Rafiki Wine Company, of Minnesota. Following all NEW to this ed.

Merlot ★ Moreish **00** uncluttered by oak, full of variety's ripe plum fruit, flesh. Full-bodied, any heaviness deflected by spicy clean finish. 13% alc. **Pinotage** ★ Unpretentious everyday drink. **00** balanced mix sprightly red berry, juicy texture rounded off by complementary tannins. Med-bodied. Briefly oaked. **Ruby Cabernet-Pinotage** ☆ **00** on pale side for two such colourful grapes. Pretty quiet on fruit front too, otherwise offers balanced drinking. Unwooded 60/40 blend. **Chardonnay** ☆ **00** full-bodied, soft-textured with gentle, insinuating buttercream, melony notes. Partly barrel-fermented. 13.2% alc. **Chenin Blanc** ★ Fresh spring flower aromas in **01**; gains appeal, suppleness, from 30% oaked portion. Successfully styled as both aperitif and food partner. **Port** ★ **97** veering towards Ruby style, from tinta. Generous, mouth-enveloping flavours enhanced by lowish 93 g/ℓ residual sugar. 18.5% alc.

Dumisani range

QUAFFING WINES with a Xhosa flavour – from the name (Dumisani: praise) to the labels, which feature translations from Xhosa praise songs. Joint-venture with Winecorp's UK agent Private Liquor Brands; now also listed in the US.

Pinotage NEW ★ **01** boasts pinotage's vivid purple/crimson hue. Big, soft, juicy; subtle oaking, though unfinished sample still lacks integration. **Cinsault-Merlot** NEW ★ Unwooded 60/30 blend with dash ruby cab. **01** remarkably drinkable for such an infant; soft generous fruit, mere squeeze of tannin. Good summertime red, slightly chilled. **Ruby Cabernet-Merlot** ☆ **00** shows ruby cab's wildness on nose; palate fleshier, less coarse; would probably make happy partner to suggested dish of spicy sausages. Unwooded. **Chardonnay** NEW ★ Whiffs spice from oak and fruit (60% oak-fermented). **01** med-bodied, refreshing balanced acid padded with lees enrichment. Should provide satisfying, if straightforward, enjoyment. **Chenin Blanc-Chardonnay** ★ Juicy canned pineapple laced with spicy cinnamon in **01**. Non-exhausting 12.5% alc, quaffability enhanced by balance, sound fruity dry finish. 60/40 blend, portion oaked. Some of above were sampled unfinished, and ratings are provisional. Discontinued: **Cabernet Sauvignon** and **Pinotage** Reserves. —*AL*

Winelands see International Wine Services

Wines of Charles Back

Portmanteau for some of SA's most stylish and portable brands, including Goats do Roam and Spice Route, from Charles Back, third-generation winemaker at Fairview. See separate entries.

Wine Village see Hermanus Heritage Collection

Wine Warehouse

*Tasting & sales at Enoteca outlets (Cape Peninsula) Newlands: Mon-Fri 10-9 Sat 9-7 City (Buitengracht Street): Mon-Fri 9-8 Sat 9-5 • Tourgroups • Gifts • Conferencing • "Definitely no mountain biking!" • Monthly Wine Fair • Regular tutored tastings • Owner Oscar Foulkes • Production 30 000 cases • PO Box 16571 Vlaeberg 8018 • **Tel (021) 424-4060** • Fax (021) 424-9196 • E-mail oscar@wine-warehouse.co.za*

Oscar Foulkes has been uncharacteristically low-key of late. Our international man of Mystery (his fast-moving, easy-drinking range) has decided to stop chasing around the world focusing on exports and concentrate instead on what he does best – keeping the local market happy: "More than ever we're into value. Consumers simply have a lot less money to spend." He and equally wine-tuned wife Andrea are paying particular attention to Cape Town and their chic Enoteca outlets. Part of getting with the new programme was a wine-blending workshop with the rugby Springboks in Plett (could this have been the secret of their recent improved form?), which led to developing a team-building and creative workshop, Taste Buds. "I still think that South Africa could be producing better quality wines at almost all levels," concludes Foulkes, as direct as ever.

Cabernet Sauvignon Reserve ✓ "Phenomenal bargain!" gloats Oscar F, correctly. Delicious, mature **97** packed with sweet, smooth fruit; bit of tannin makes seamless transition from patio to table. 13% alc. Fr oak-aged, mostly new. 1 500 cases.

Mystery Dry Red ☻ Recipe change to ruby cab/tinta leaves tried-and-true **NV** super-quaffing formula intact. Unoaked, slurpable (though 13,5% alc needs watching), not averse to light chilling. 4 800 cases. **Mystery Dry White** ☻ Gulpability galore in latest (**NV**) incarnation of dry-tasting unwooded colombard/chardonnay blend, yours for under R10/bottle. 13% alc. 4 800 cases.

Mystery Reserve Sauvignon Blanc Latest **01** not ready for tasting (neither was **00**). **Mystery Melon** Simple but tasty semi-sweet **NV**, fresh, non-cloying and practically on the (ware)house at sub-R10 price. 2 000 cases. **Mystery Vonkelwyn** Bilingual labelling for this energising, lightish **NV** sparkle from sauvignon. Fruit origin, appropriately, a mystery. 1 500 cases. "Taking a break": **Oscar's Easy Red** Pvs **NV** . — *DH*

Winkelshoek Wine Cellar

*Piketberg (see Swartland map) • Tasting & sales Mon-Fri 8-5 Sat 8-1 Tasting fee R1 p/p • Restaurant daily 8 am-9 pm • Gifts • Owners Hennie Hanekom & Jurgens Brand • Winemaker Hennie Hanekom (since 1984) • PO Box 395 Piketberg 7320 • **Tel (022) 913-1092** • Fax (022) 913-1095 • E-mail winhoek@intekom.ca*

This cellar's easy drinking Weskus range is available for tasting and sale from the restaurant/visitor centre at the N7/R44 intersection near Piketberg. The wines, untasted for this ed, include **Vin Rouge**, **Grand Cru**, **Blanc de Blanc**, **Late Harvest**, all **01**s.

Withoek 

*Calitzdorp • Not open to the public • Owner Koos Geyser • **Tel (051) 432-4748***

CONSTRUCTION engineer Koos Geyser indulges his abiding passion for wine on this small property just outside his old hometown, Calitzdorp. Now Bloemfontein-based, Geyser's been tapping outside expertise since 1996 to help him make mostly fortifieds and a red blend from tinta, ruby cab and pontac. A strong advocate of traditional methods (open *kuip* fermentation, basket pressing straight into cask among his mantras) he believes the wine makes itself in the vineyard during the season. "I'm just the facilitator who helps it into the bottle."

Dry Red ☆ Italianate **00** casual swig with ruby lights; dry vanilla/plum tastes, generous grind of the peppermill. Natural partner for pepperoni pizza. 13.4% alc. 120 cases. **Ruby Port** ☆ Comfortable fruity style with shy but 'correct' bouquet, bright plummy fruit, integrated spirit; coffee/choc and toast to finish. Vintaged (**99**). ±200 cases. — *TM*

Woolworths

*Category manager (wine/beverages) Howard Kotze tel (021) 407-2530 • Selection manager (wine/beer) Allan Mullins **tel (021) 407-2777** wwamu@woolworths.co.za • Assistant selector (wine/fresh juices/beer) Jenny Ratcliffe tel (021) 407-2956 wwjrat@woolworths.co.za • Buying manager (food/beverages) Ivan Oertle tel (021) 407-2762 wwioe@woolworths.co.za*

THE IDEA of 'supermarket wines' could conjure up a rather dreary picture of little grey numbers chosen randomly off a list and plonked unceremoniously on a shelf. This quality retail chain's range is different, and to discover why you need look no further than the high-energy Cape Wine Master who selects them – 'select' being a woefully inadequate term for the truffling, sniffing, tweaking and dealing that goes on between Allan Mullins and his personally anointed suppliers who, by no coincidence, represent the crème de la crème of SA winemaking. The inimitable Mullins encourages them to put their best foot forward and they invariably oblige – sometimes making even more interesting wines than for their own ranges. Excitement is key, Mullins maintains, and to keep it palpabale he and senior buyer Ivan Oertle (now masterminding logistics for all Woolworths' food and beverage products) and assistant selector Jenny Ratcliffe (wine-steeped daughter of Norma and Stan of Warwick), constantly introduce fresh labels and ranges. New for 2002 is the first Organic range from a local retail chain, plus a selection of exclusives under the excellent limited-release Signature, Reserve and brand-new Durbanville ranges. Non-SA wines aren't neglected. On the shelves now or in the near future are personal selections from Italy, Spain and Australia. And, from France, a special Veuve Clicquot champagne to ring in the New Year.

Signature Series

Flagship range, only in exceptional vintages.

☆☆☆☆ **Cabenert Sauvignon-Merlot** NEW Classic Warwick understatement in **99**; cool leafy/spicy aromas, slender fruit tapering to languid, tangy finish.

☆☆☆☆ **Danie de Wet Limestone Hill Chardonnay** NEW ✓ Unsullied by oak, **00**'s core of chalky fruit carries scintillating array of flavours (lemon, lime, some peach, lees) through to bold, fleshy finish. Outstanding example of this style. VVG; exclusive to Woolworths.

Pinotage NEW ☆ Front label of **99** co-autographed by Allan Mullins, but it's Beaumont's Niels Verburg's signature that's inside: massed damson fruit, parma ham, big smoky oak. Somewhat marred by bitterness in finish. Pvs was **Cabernet Sauvignon 99** ☆☆☆ ex Flagstone.

Reserve range

Exclusive to Woolworths; all in suitably smart livery featuring imported bottles.

✵**Cabernet Sauvignon** ✓ Current **98**, back-tasted mid-01, open textured, ready (especially for the impatient, though we would keep few more yrs). Marginally fuller, richer than pvs **97** ✵, also from Villiera, though both classically restrained. Latter *Wine* ✵.

✵**Pinotage** Reintroduced to range with power-ranging **98** by Danie Steytler of Kaapzicht. Follow-up **00**, from Bellevue, showcases Dirkie Morkel's singular essence-of-pinotage style: super-ripe, exotically perfumed, crammed with cashmere tannins. Try not to open for 2 yrs. So disctintive, deserves place in Signature range below. 13.4% alc.

✵**Groenekloof Shiraz** NEW Open textured, sunny **99**, accessible now (feature of all these reds), ample flesh and backbone (14.5% alc) for ageing min 5 yrs. Ex Darling Cellars.

✵✵**Cabernet Sauvignon-Merlot** ✓ Now in its rightful place among the Reserves. Latest **99**, from Neil Ellis, dazzles with fabulous silky texture (chiming with vintage); hallmark aromas of rare roast beef, cool cedar; dense yet elegant. 43/42 blend, with 15% cab f, 18 mths Fr oak. 13.1% alc. Pvs **98** with typical Neil Ellis restraint.

✵**Cabernet Sauvignon-Shiraz** ✓ Classicist Jacques Borman of La Motte constructed **97** for the long haul; mid-01 still taut (but not unbalanced); some extra-dry savoury/tangy flavours which need something carnivorous now or further spell in bottle.

✵**Grenache-Syrah Reserve** Individual, food-empathetic style with loyal fan club. **01** preview reveals similar piquant tones as pvs **99**. Plenty of tangy, southern French flavours that end pleasantly tartly. From Ken Forrester.

✵**Chardonnay Reserve** ✓ This berth in range 'reserved' for Neil Ellis since **97** (of which two versions: Elgin, available 97/98; Stbosch, available 98/99). **98** selection of Stbosch barrels, as was standout **99** ✵✵, gracefully complex, balanced. Latest **00**, again Stbosch fruit; boldly structured, leesy, hazelnut enriched, though touch less elegant than pvs (13,8% alc). Fr oak-fermented/aged 9 mths.

✵**Barrel Reserve Chenin Blanc** Deliciously ripe **00**'s chalk-textured palate resonates with flavours of apple/quince; hint of oak adds sheen to already polished feel. Excellent now and for minimum 3 yrs.

✵**Constantia Reserve Sauvignon Blanc** ✓ Cooler, sauvignon-favouring yr yields this cracker **01** ✵✵ from Buitenverwachting; widescreen aromas (including Loirish blackcurrant piquancy); breathtaking concentration, lusty freshness invigorating sweet ripe fruit. Deserves ample time in which to develop. No **99**, so **00** 'rushed in' (from above source) to meet demand.

Noble Late Harvest Chenin Blanc Barrel Reserve Latest not ready for tasting. Pvs (**99** ✵) partly barrel matured, lightly botrytised. Lively acidity, lowish sugar for crisp, uncloying pleasure at either end of the meal. **Fields of Gold** ★ **NV** Arrestingly sweet unbotrytised dessert from Ashanti; attractive, if somewhat offbeat, flavours. 500 ml.

Pvs included **Wild Yeast Chardonnay 98** ✵ from Springfield.

Durbanville range NEW

✵**The Shiraz** Somewhat sullen mid-01, but all correct characters waiting to unfurl: intensity, malleable tannins; full body; **00** drinkable now but much better in 2-3 yrs.

✵**The Blend** Pristine cool climate fruit, mainly cab/merlot/cab f, dash shiraz; delicious and sleek, mouthwatering acidity buoys the clean-cut cassis/crushed red cherry fruit; unobtrusively oaked.

Limited Release range NEW

Merlot ★ Villiera source of open woven **99**, slight coloured but not insubstantial; smoky black-cherry fruit with cellar's hallmark poise. 13.5% alc. **Pinot Noir** ★ Earthy/savoury rather than berry bouquet in love-hate **01** sample; off-beat pomegranate/spice rack nuances, sweet-sour finish. Pour at wineclub and watch them squirm. Ex Jordan. **Gewürztraminer** ★ Textbook **01** seems freshly plucked from the rosegarden; gorgeous petally textures; though soft acidity somewhat overwhelmed by power alc (13.5%). Ex Bergsig.

Organic range NEW

These made by Sonop.

✵**Shiraz** Unusually pure expression of ripe berry fruit in **00** (no smoking shrubs, leathery saddles). Clean, fleshy, sensitively oaked; almost serene. 13.7% alc.

✵**Sauvignon Blanc** Radiates sweet healthy grapes; **00** concentrated yet graceful; extended gently dry figgy finish. 12.7% alc.

Millennium Collection

Discontinued except for **Millennium Collection Brut Reserve**, now under MCC range below. Pvs were: Celebration range: **Cabernet Sauvignon-Merlot 98** ✵; **Sauvignon Blanc 00** ★; **Cuvée Brut NV** ★; Millennium Collection range: **Shiraz-Cabernet Sauvignon Reserve 98** ✵; **Chardonnay Reserve 98** ✵.

Terroir range

All except Cabernet Sauvignon-Merlot (now in Reserve range above) to be discontinued. At press time, limited stocks of **Cabernet Sauvignon 97** ✵; **Merlot 97** ★; **Semillon 99** ✵ still available.

Premium range

✵**Shiraz** Rbtson's welcoming warmth suffuses **00**; oaked tucked into eiderdown of smoky red fruit; voluptuous 13,6% alc adds to final sweet impression. From Rooiberg.

✵**Chardonnay-Pinot Noir** Cream-textured food wine from Cabrière; peach-kernel/spicerack sophistication in step-up **01**; brilliant with sushi, piquant terrines. **00** ★ showed fruitier side of this stylish off-dry marriage.

✵**Rhine Riesling** ✓ Youthfully charming but ageworthy off-dry example from Villiera. **00**, yr on, shows some good development; spicy/terpenoid touches; assertive flavours; weight rather than sweetness. Could age further. 12.8% alc.

Merlot ★ Made by La Motte. Buy **01** now and put away for winter 2003 potroasts, by which the upright tannins should have slumped into a comfortable position. 13% alc. **Grand Rouge** ★ **99** cab/merlot blend, tasted yr on, ready; seamless dry savoury tastes, tangy finish. From La Motte.

Premier range NEW

Bush Vine Shiraz ★ Robust **00** red awash in sweet, sun-drenched fruit. Roasted/toasted nuances are natural partners for rustic cuisines. Ex Swartland. **Merlot-Cabernet Franc** NEW ★ Simonsvlei made this velvety mouthful mulberries, crushed leaves; oaked **01** juicy but not simple; husky 13.9% alc nuzzles rather than bites.

Sauvignon Blanc ★ Herbaceous **01** extra dry, tart; needs full bodied rejoinder like butter-basted yellowtail. Ex Darling Cellars.

Discontinued: **Cabernet Franc-Merlot** (Pvs ★ **99**).

Vins de Cuvée

Mid-priced cork-closed range; 750 ml bottles (though some also in 'Flexible' range below).

✵**Pinotage** ✓ Customer favourite from Rooiberg. Latest **99** with cassia/tar/roast beef to think about; unobtrusive oak to calm the riot of sweet fruit. 13.7% alc.

✵**Chardonnay-Semillon** NEW ✓ Complex mouthwatering **01** from Delheim. Flint (from dash sauvignon), lanolin, squeeze lemon add zest to vanilla-custard oak. Med/full-bodied. Sample rated.

Cabernet Sauvignon ☻ ⁂ Invariably good early quaffing. Lightly oaked **99** from Bergsig, med/full-bodied, savoury/tangy dry tannins. **Chardonnay** ☻ ⁂ Soft, creamy **01** beckons with delicate lemony/yellow peachy fruit; spicy tail. 13.5% alc needs watching. Also in 500 ml, 1 ℓ, 2 ℓ 'flexibles'; from Robertson Winery. **Cape Riesling** ☻ ⁂ **00** (with generous splash Rhine riesling) ripening in bottle, growing broader, spicier. Try with crispy roast pork or age a bit more. From Weltevrede. **Muscat-Colombard** ☻ ⁂ **00** spicy, muscat-smooth off-dry ex Weltevrede. Generous 13.5% alc.

Maison Rouge ⁂ Sociable everyday red, lightly oaked. Spicy-sweet aromas; plump maraschino fruit; dry finish. **NV** varietal foursome ex Winecorp PLS. **Rosé** ⁂ Villiera has this semi-dry style taped. **00** lightish but full flavoured; partner for warm duck salad with orange dressing. **Blanc de Noir** ⁑ Unserious semi-sweet **01** sample; demure but not ungenerous flavours. **Chenin Blanc** ⁑ Full-bodied off-dry **01** for enjoying in youthful prime, when fragile tropical tones still fresh, lively. From Rooiberg. **Sauvignon Blanc** ⁂ Commercial style with enough varietal character to appease the purists. **01** bone dry, not over-alcoholic. Also in 500 ml, 1 ℓ, 2 ℓ 'flexibles'; from Robertson Winery. **Blanc de Blanc** ⁂ Balanced, zesty dry white; apples/pears to taste, though big 13.6% alc makes this a weekender rather than power-luncher. Ex Villiera.

Discontinued: **Chenin Blanc-Chardonnay** (pvs **00** ⁂).

'Selected' range

Dry Red ⁂ Soft, friendly, fruity. Sip (rather than slosh – 14.1% alc!) with shaved biltong while watching rugby. **NV** from Simonsvlei; also in 1 ℓ 'combibloc', 5 ℓ box. **Cape White** ⁑ Off-dry, very easy drinking **01**. Colombard ex Rooiberg. Constitution-friendly 11.5% alc. **Late Harvest** ⁑ Cheerful sunny semi-sweet from Simonsvlei; finishes zestily. **NV**; also in 1 ℓ 'combibloc', 5 ℓ box.

Three Springs range

Discontinued. Pvs were **Red NV** ⁂; **White 00** ⁂.

'Lite' range

Bianca Light ⁑ Never insipid, as low-alc wines can be. **01** slightly fuller (10% alc) than pvs, more generous tropical flavours. Lively off-dry from Delheim.

Nouveau range

Gamay Noir ⁂ Invariably delicious and gulpable; newest **01** again with suggestion of sweetness to match the pulpy, perfumed, lightly peppery fruit. 12.2% alc. Not made to age. From Villiera.

Discontinued: **Blanc** (pvs **00** ⁂).

'Zesties'

These friendly, affordable sips for wine-newcomers have become Woolies' top sellers since their launch in 2000 (close to 30 000 cases a year). NEW is a **Rosé** from Winecorp PLS (not ready for tasting).

Juicy Red ☻ ☆ Good red-wine flavours in smooth, if somewhat quick, form. Lowish 12.1% alc for unproblematic quaffing. **Zesty White** ☻ ☆ Lightish but satisfyingly curvaceous, smooth rather than zesty, semi-dry. These **NV**s ex Winecorp PLS.

Cap classiques

Made to Allan Mullins' specs by long-time campaigner, Villiera's Jeff Grier.

☆**Vintage Reserve Brut** 5 yrs on lees, 18 mths on cork, pinot/chardonnay (60/40). Latest **94** thrillingly fresh still; ozone bouquet; vigorous dry mousse with toasted hazelnut nuances; chardonnay's excellent length. Pvs **93** biscuity, briskly dry. These make elegant table partners, contemplative sippers, anytime morale boosters. This, below 12-12.5% alcs.

☆**Millennium Collection Brut Reserve** Authoritative, even slightly daunting **NV**; febrile but firm mousse; complex and pleasurable palate interplay between sappy, lactic and dry biscuity textures.

☆**Brut** ✓ Assured, unintimidating new world style, rounded and delicious; flies off the shelves. Pinot, chardonnay, pinotage, chenin blend; moderate 12,5% alc. **NV**.

☆**Brut Rosé** ✓ Gorgeous shell pink. Latest disgorgement (**NV**) with meaty tang, cream texture, added weight of black grapes; should age well. Pinot noir/chardonnay, pinotage imparts colour.

Basic sparklers

Spumanté Rosé ☆ Coral-pink semi-sweet fizz; tropical/pomegranate aromas, sweet-sour tastes. Low 9,5% alc. From red muscadel. **Brut** ☆ Enduringly popular perky bubbles from sauvignon. Dry but soft (courtesy grain sugar); lowish 11.5% alc. **Spumanté** ☆ Evergreen low-alc (8.8%) sparkler; sweetness offset by bracing effervescence. Gewürz/chenin. These **NV**s all ex Rooiberg.

Bag in boxes/'Flexibles'

Filled on demand for freshness.

Merlot ☆ Warm, open-textured **00**, easy drinking, med-bodied dry red. 1 ℓ, 2 ℓ 'flexibles' from Simonsvlei. **Dry Red** ☆ **NV** 1 ℓ 'combibloc', 5 ℓ box; same as Selected Dry Red above. **Chardonnay** and **Sauvignon Blanc**: Vintage dated 500 ml, 1 ℓ, 2 ℓ 'flexibles'; see under Vins de Cuvée above. **Blanc de Blanc** ☆ Crisp Granny Smith apples; bone dry finish. Med-bodied. **NV** 1 ℓ 'combibloc' ex Simonsvlei. **Premier Grand Cru** ☆ Sea breeze tones, palate-cleansing crispness; med-bodied dry. Best seller in range (though Red closing in). **NV** 5 ℓ box from Simonsvlei. **Bouquet Blanc** ☆ Pretty floral/muscat scents; delicious; smooth rather than sweet. **NV** 5 ℓ box ex Simonsvlei. **Stein** ☆ Lively, if very shy; drier end of semi-sweet scale; **NV** 5 ℓ box from Simonsvlei. **Late Harvest** ☆ **NV** 1 ℓ 'combibloc'; same as Selected Late Harvest above. Also, popular **Glühwein**, **Sangria** and various wine coolers. — *IvH*

Yellow Cellar see Helderkruin

Yonder Hill

*Stellenbosch (see Helderberg map) • Tasting, sales, cellar tours by appointment • Views • Owners Naudé Family • Winemaker/viticulturist David Lockley (since 1998) • Vineyards 10 ha • Production 100 tons 8 000 cases 97% red 3% white • PO Box 914 Stellenbosch 7599 • **Tel (021) 855-1008** • Fax (021) 855-1006 • E-mail wines@yonderhill.co.za • Website www.yonderhill.co.za*

Each vintage is "one big experiment" for mechanically minded winemaker David Lockley. With all the rain last year he's been focusing on canopy management "drastically". His constant drive to make the best wines possible is matched by an insatiable need to tinker. He deliberately didn't irrigate a cabernet block last year (it took such a knock, friends phoned to express their concern), resulting in a "deep blackberry tannic wine, an excellent building block!". He also produced a unique once-off Shiraz-Merlot blend (from bought-in syrah). Next, he'd like to see shiraz, cinsaut and cabernet as his contribution to the quest for a quintessential Cape blend, so watch this cellar space (which they've been turning into a more environmentally friendly one, hence the "very important" new CD system acquisition, classical music for the wines, Deep Purple when it's time to clean up and go home). They've planted more French-clone merlot, his winemaking raison d'être, "a difficult wine to make, it needs the same kid glove focus in the vineyards as sauvignon," and keeps Lockley constantly on his toes.

Cabernet Sauvignon Elegance the hallmark of these cabs, aged 18-23 mths Fr oak. Maiden **98**, with green pepper/mulberry tones, needed time to soften. New **99** plum cake/game pie complexity, some leathery whiffs; firm minerally textures. Should age well. Alcs 13-13,5%.

Merlot This cellar's signature, always showing some restraint in manageable alcs, fine tannins, understated oak. **00** (sample), again with splash cab, streamlined, polished. Choc/cassis joined by tobacco, liquorice whiffs from already well-knit wood. 13.5% alc. 900 half-cases. **99** mouthfilling, promising excellent development over 5-6 yrs.

iNanda Meaning 'beautiful place', characterful blend cab, merlot, cab f, proportions depend on vintage – 68/19/13 in latest **99**, 23 mths Fr oak. More complete than pvs, astutely oaked. Educated wine. Closed mid-01, but set to unfold deliciously. 13% alc. 3 000 half-cases. **98** and pvs balanced, restrained; deserving time to grow.

Shiraz-Merlot NEW **00** (sample) makes a powerful peppery statement; 75/25 assemblage with arresting scrubby finish, mouthwatering dried-fruit flavours. Taut still, might need 2-3 yrs (during which could well grow into). Own fruit & bought-in Stbosch shiraz, 2nd fill oak. 400 half-cases.

Chardonnay Now in breezy unoaked style (and none the worse for it). **01** lightish (12.5% alc), crisp; water-white and lightly leesy. 300 half-cases to enjoy, David Lockley chuckles, "iced, in tall glasses, with your curry and rice". — *TM*

Zanddrift Vineyards

Paarl • Not open to the public • Owner Zanddrift Investments International Singapore • PO Box 1302 Suider-Paarl 7624 • ***Tel (021) 863-2076*** *• Fax (021) 863-2081*

This Singapore-owned Paarl winery's vineyards were virtually wiped out by 'black goo' (which, while it may sound like some science-fictional sludge, is a particularly deadly fungus that has devastated vineyards worldwide), resulting in all the vines – mainly white varieties with pockets of pinotage – having to be ripped out. On the bright side, the disease can be contained and the soil treated. The farm will then be totally replanted with reds. Zanddrift is expected to remain out of the production loop for the next three to four years. Previous labels featured in the guide included: **Cabernet Sauvignon 98** ★; **Pinotage 98**; **Chapel Cellar 'Route 303' 00**; **Semillon Reserve 00**; **Tuscany Spring**; **Capella Reserve 00**; **Chapel d'Or 98**.

Zandvliet Estate

Robertson (see Robertson map) • Tasting & sales Mon-Fri 9-5 Sat 9-1 • "Lots of friendly dogs for friendly children" • Tourgroups • Gifts • BYO picnic • Views • Owners Paul & Dan de Wet • Winemaker Johan van Wyk (since 2000) • Viticulturalists Dan de Wet & Wouter Theron • Vineyards 176 ha • Production 1

500 tons 50 000 cases 50% red 45% white 5% rosé • PO Box 36 Ashton 6715 • ***Tel (023) 615-1146*** *• Fax (023) 615-1327 • E-mail shiraz@lando.co.za • Website www.zandvliet.co.za*

"MY FATHER," recalls Paul de Wet, "had a remarkable eye for a good-looking filly, and he always said: 'With Shiraz, we have a romance'." A quarter-century later, Paul and sibling Dan still have the hots for the Rhone's sexiest siren. "We run a wine farm with lots of different grapes," they say, "but if you peel off the layers, you get to the core. And the core of Zandvliet is Shiraz." If you plotted the heart of this big-sky farm on the map, you'd site it in two only recently developed *côtes*: a north-facing (*rôtie?*) aspect below Dan de Wet's home; the other a cooler southerly ridge above a farm dam. These chalky parcels are now vinified – and from vintage 2001 may be bottled – separately ("our emphasis is on site exclusivity from earth to glass"). The other wines previously under the flagship Zandvliet label – Cabernet, Merlot and Chardonnay – are being phased out or rebranded in the new Equus colours. And joining the face-lifted Astonvale value range is the Old Paddock, with its own equine 'terroir' indication. It's a blend of cabernet and … shiraz. The romance continues.

☆**Kalkveld Shiraz French Oak Matured** Renewed sense of purpose here, with Paul & Dan de Wet taking bit between teeth and galloping fast as each vintage will allow. They've decided Fr oak (not necessarily all new) is best partner for new shiraz from chalky tiers ('kalkveld') behind farm. So, fast-forward to **01**, where site-vinification lets terroir suddenly, positively identify itself (Bo-dam – southern slope – elegant, violet-toned; Northern Slope, richer, more 'grunt'). Rewind to **96**, first of new era. (No. **97**.) **98** ☆, satisfying but overshadowed by more expressive younger wines; upcoming **99**, more compact, darkly spicy, savoury. 13.7% alc. **00** preview broader shouldered, extra concentration from maturing vines. Leitmotifs here are elegance and a pure fruit core ("thread of minerality"), not as dramatically evident in … **Kalkveld Shiraz American Oak Matured** ☆ Demonstrative new world style, entirely Am barrelled (latterly 100% new casks), more extrovertly 'sweet' than above. Now sacrificed on altar of the de Wet's terroir ambitions: "friends and media invariably preferred Fr oak option in blind tastings". So only **98, 96** released.

Shiraz ★ Cellar's traditionally-styled shiraz since maiden **75**. Blend all farm's vyds, 100% old-oak matured. **99** with laid-back (but not feeble) woodsmoke, leathery whiffs; smooth, light-textured (but not ethereal – 13.7% alc) palate. To be discontinued: **Chardonnay** Last was **99** ☆, superseded by Equus below.

Equus range

☆**Cabernet Sauvignon-Merlot-Shiraz 99** re-tasted mid-01, retreated into quieter mode than when assessed for last yr's guide, especially on nose. More evident sweet fruit on palate, though still unevolved; elegant, savoury tannins require 3-4 years to fully effect their binding, mellowing influence. Expansive 14% alc well contained by minerality. 23 different single-vyd parcels, individually oaked, portion new casks; assembled for 60/40/20 final ratio.

☆**Equus Chardonnay** Akin to Astonvale below, but **00** more chicly garbed (50% barrel fermented/matured). Exhales air of gentle accessibility; chalky, tropical, lemon melange plumped by smooth creaminess, all cleverly harnessed by minerally acid. 13.5% alc.

Shiraz ★ Unwooded to highlight grape's full wild berry, savoury richness. **00**'s immediacy further enhanced by low tannins, medium body. Presence to partner wide range flavoursome dishes. **Ruby Cabernet** NEW **01** unavailable for tasting. **Old Paddock Cabernet Sauvignon-Shiraz** NEW ★ Broad, pure-fruited **00**; both varieties get good hearing in blackberry/savoury combination; sound tannin to keep yr/2 if absolutely necessary. Small portion cab oaked. 13.3% alc. **Chardonnay Unwooded** ☆ One of few unwooded versions with presence, individuality. Sunny lemony brilliance in **01**; matching ripe but refined smoky, flinty tones. Full-bodied, good dry persistence. 13.5% alc. **Sauvignon Blanc** ☆ **01** with bright flinty/grassy attack; full-bodied concentration, invigorating 7.2 g/ℓ acid.

Astonvale range

Marketed by Bar Valley Wines, PO Box 55 Ashton 6715. Tel/fax as for Zandvliet. All wines Rbtson origin, reasonably priced ex-farm.

Colombard ☻ ☆ **01** shows off grape at its quaffing best: ripe guava, herb, pear cut into stimulating, clean, med-bodied frame. **Crème** ☻ ☆ Colombard-sauvignon blend with full, intense wild Karoo scrub, ripe papaya backing in **01**; juicily flavoursome, not too heavy. Attractive hot-weather sipping. *— AL*

Zandwijk see Kleine Draken
Zevenrivieren see Zevenwacht

Zevenwacht Estate

Stellenbosch (see Stellenbosch map) • Tasting & sales Mon-Fri 8-5 Sat & Sun 9.30-5 R12.50 (includes international tasting glass) Tumbler & tasting R9 • Cellar/vineyard tours by appointment • Restaurants, picnic basket/barbeque baskets etc • Cheese tasting on request • Guest cottages • Conference centre • Banqueting facilities • Traditional 'lapa' for outdoor functions • Helicopter pad • Children's play park • Cheese factory • Professional Chef's School • 4×4 trail • Views • Owners Harold & Denise Johnson • Winemaker Raymond Greyling • Viticulturist Kevin Watt • Production 1 100 tons 75 000 cases 50% red 50% white • PO Box 387 Kuils River 7579 • ***Tel (021) 903-5123*** *• Fax (021) 903-3373 • E-mail sales@zevenwacht.co.za • Website www.zevenwacht.co.za*

THERE's been a changing of the guard at this revivified estate with its umpteen enticements (helipad, scenic 4×4 trail, children's play park, country-flavoured restaurant, school for professional chefs and modern cheesery). After a five-year stint, winemaker Hilko Hegewisch stepped out to set up his own consultancy. Marching in for harvest 2001 was Raymond Greyling (like Hegewisch, ex Boschendal) with an about-turn approach: planning the wine from the marketing strategy all the way back to the vineyard, where he'll "identify specific blocks and treat them to make specific wines". A new red fermentation section has been installed, and semillon, merlot, shiraz and pinotage have come into bearing under the watchful eye of new consultant viticulturist Kevin Watt (of Rustenberg repute). New *fromagère* Helga Beukes (ex Lancewood cheesery in George) came back from a UK foray fired up with fresh ideas for products to join the champion Farmhouse Cheddar.

Zevenwacht range

☆**Cabernet Sauvignon** ✓ Latest releases in different league to pvs. **00** warm vintage picked ripe, minerally rich, generous; long tannins for 5-6 yrs' ageing. 50% Fr oaked, 7 mths. 13% alc. 4 300 cases. **99** soft, spicy; some not unpleasant volatile whiffs. **98** ☆ less juicy, needing time.

☆**Pinotage** ✓ Sweet-choc richness developing in **00**, skillfully handled (only 40% casked) to showcase intense black fruits, ripe banana whiffs. 13% alc. 4 160 cases. **98** ☆ Ribena-like juicy fruit, soft tannins. **97** *Wine* ☆.

☆**Shiraz** ✓ The celebrity here since dramatic **97** *Wine* ☆. Keynotes are intensity, spicy warmth, promise of fine development. **98** with alluring pepperiness, ripe fruit. Current **99**, 10 mths new-oaked, sinewy, massively tannic; demanding bottle ageing. On present form nearer ☆. But **00** barrels harbour a corker:

incredibly dense fruit crammed into powerful (14,5% alc) spicy/peppery frame, with whiffs thyme, sage. Future ★?

★**Chevalier** ✓ Satisfying bdx-style equal blend cab/merlot, undramatic but flavourful. Cab tones uppermost in **99** and **00**; this latest, sampled ex cask mid-01, tight, tannic. **99** by contrast, lush, finely padded with mulberry fruit, poised to grow into ★ over 7-8 yrs. 10 mths Fr oak, none new. 13% alc. ±3 800 cases. **98** SAA, WOM selection; **96** SAA, *Wine* ★.

★**Zevenrood** ✓ Unvarying quality/value blend, easy drinking, mainly cab with merlot, splash shiraz. Current **NV** (00) pops with ripe-fruit juiciness, untrammelled by oak. Mediumweight 12.5% alc. 11 400 cases.

★**Chardonnay Private Reserve** ✓ NEW to this ed. Promising **99** with austere chalkiness, acidic grip. Lemon blossoms/toasty oak in elegant embrace. Potential to develop into ★ over 3-4 yrs. 14% alc. Only 370 cases. No **00**. Standard **Chardonnay** glides into seductive sweet-oaky mode in generous **01** (sample), 40% small Fr oak-fermented. ±2 000 cases. Pvs **00** ★ fruitier, only 10% "delicately oaked" 6 mths, Fr barrels.

★**Chenin Blanc** (Unwooded) ✓ Semi-dry **01**, mouthfilling, vividly flavoured, easy to drink. 5 g/ℓ sugar. 13% alc. 3 430 cases.

★**Chenin Blanc Private Reserve** (Wooded) NEW ✓ The dry big brother (14.1% alc); only 10% lightly Fr-oaked, preserving lemon-lime friskiness. Drink **01** now (with, suggests winemaker, roast pork and stir-fried veg), and keep some for extra pleasure in 2-3 yrs. ±1 000 cases.

★**Sauvignon Blanc** ✓ **01** shows benefit of cool ripening season in vibrant crisp fruit with herbal, muscat attributes. 13,5% alc. Delicious now, but should develop over 2-3 yrs. 4 300 cases. **00** ★ mirrors warmer yr.

Bouquet Blanc ☻ ★ Real feel-good wine. Suave petally perfume, sweet fruity acids to enjoy on their own or with Oriental cuisines. Best in yr of harvest. **01** trio of varieties plus hanepoot. 12.3% alc. ±5 000 cases.

Merlot Not ready for sampling. **99, 00** pvsly untasted/rated. **Blanc de Blanc** ★ Refreshing, well priced dry sip with more character/interest than big volumes would suggest (±16 000 cases). Latest is **01**. 13.3% alc. Discontinued: **Blanc de Noir** (Pvs **00** ★).

Zevenrivieren range

From Harold Johnson's Banhoek vyds, vinified at Zevenwacht.

★**Cabernet Sauvignon** ✓ Solid, ungreedily priced cab, partly oaked to preserve softer fruit from youngish vines. **99** difficult yr ably handled. **00** beefier, more tannic, needs yr/2; life for 4-5 yrs. 13% alc. 2 460 cases

★**Chardonnay** ✓ Lighter-toned than sibling above (though doesn't lack body, flavour). **00** barrel-fermented/aged 8 mths, no new casks. **01** (sample) same oak regime, bigger (14.3% alc), generous; attractive chalky nuance; balanced. ±1 100 cases.

Sauvignon Blanc ★ Reflects more conducive **01** vintage; sweet fruit freshened by lemonadey texture. 13,2% alc. ±2 000 cases. — *DH*

Zoet en Rust NEW

Stellenbosch • Not open to the public • Owner Adila Klomp • Viticulturists William Noel • Vineyards 4 ha • Production 70 cases own label 100% red • PO Box 130 Franschhoek 7690 • ***Tel/fax (021) 864-0085*** *• Cell 082-603-5442 • E-mail fj-klomp@mweb.co.za*

This Devon Valley eyrie (Hartenberg roosts next door) is owned by consulting engineer Francois Klomp, who now resides here after recently migrating from

Pretoria with his family. The limited release Merlot below is from a slip of a vine yard on the property (cabernet makes up the other portion), vinified and mature on contract by SAWISA. See also Klompzicht.

Merlot Sampled as infant, **01** appears to have structure to develop into ✯ adult. Plentiful, persistent black cherry, mulberry and truffle flavours over alread soft tannins augur well. Fr oak-aged. 14.5% alc. Only 70 cases. — *CF*

Zomerlust

Budget range in 2/5 ℓ casks by Robertson Winery for Vinimark.

Dry Red ☻ ✯ Fruity varieties make for delicious sappy tastes/textures, savoury finish works with a wide range of lightish foods, especially pizza/tomato-sauced pasta. Lightly chill in summer.

Blanc de Blanc ✯ Lightish, smooth, undemanding dry white. **Selectec Stein** ✯ Trio of varieties in this simple, light, not too sweet quaff. **Late Harvest** ✯ Pleasing, light (11% alc), not as sweet as you'd expect from this style These all **NV**. — *DH*

Zonnebloem

Stellenbosch • Tasting & sales at Oude Libertas See Stellenbosch Farmers' Winery • Owner Distell • Cellarmaster Callie van Niekerk • Winemakers Michae Bucholtz (reds) • Louw Engelbrecht (whites) • Winery manager Jan le Roux • Production 212 000 cases 65% red 35% white • PO Box 46 Stellenbosch 7599 • ***Tel (021) 808-7911*** *• Fax (021) 883-2603 • E-mail gedge@sfw.co.za • Website www.zonnebloem.co.za*

This ubiquitous, consumer-cordial brand has had a new-blood transfusion and is now pumping to the double-beat of oxygenated Michael Bucholtz, maker of SFW/Distell's avant-garde wines since 1996, now styling the reds, and Louw Engelbrecht, ex Koelenhof with priming at Delheim, supercharging the whites. Plugged into the new-generation philosophy of more natural, minimally manipulated wines, the duo have the added advantage of a spanking high-tech cellar dedicated exclusively to Zonnebloem, with more than double the previous capacity. Here they can do their big-canvas thing (the larger-quantity brands fly off shelves at the rate of well over 200 000 cases a year) as well as create the miniature masterpieces that find their way into Fine Art Collection bottles under labels by leading SA visual artists. Bringing his own surfer-cool to the mix is brand manager Chris Edge: "We've broadened the fine art concept to include more complex single-vineyard wines with prominent varietal flavours, while making the mainstream wines more accessible with a softer palate."

Fine Art label

Ch Mouton-Rothschild -inspired limited-edition range launched 1996, featuring unique front-label paintings by local artists.

✯**Pinotage** NEW Ancient bushvines on venerable Stbosch farm Libertas supercharged with vanilla-oak in thoroughly modern **00**. Enormous concentration of blackberry fruit, approaching fruit-cordial intensity, sumptuous mouthfeel with overt but stylish oak, some liquorice-allsorts nuances – all somehow controlled, not completely over the top.

✯**Cabernet Sauvignon-Sangiovese** NEW Here's the unheralded star of this range: a local 'supertuscan', 50/50 blend from 2 Simonsberg vyds and a supremely harmonious marriage: **00** lovely clear-cut black-cherry fruit, touches tar and smoke; very subtly oaked; full flavoured, firm but ripe tannin for early approachability and, we'd say, shorter-term ageing. Densely fruity but not overblown. Maturation probably of only academic interest: this cork will be pulled immediately, though will be shame not to keep some to see how it develops. 6 000 ℓ.

Pvs included: **Cabernet Sauvignon** (**99** ✵), **Merlot 99** ✵✵, **Shiraz** (**99** ✵✵), **Sauvignon Blanc 00** ✵✵.

Standard range

✵**Cabernet Sauvignon** ✓ Unflashy food-friendly style, remarkably good considering the large quantities. **99** classic Cape cab: mulberry, spicy hints, some tobacco aromas; clean-cut flavours, no fuzziness; very dry finish. 86% oaked, variety of woods. 13.6% alc. **98** warmer, more generous vintage; ready. **97** ✵ shade less intense, some initially austere tannins.

✵**Merlot** ✓ Very attractive **99**, soft-tannined for earlier drinking; sultry liqueur cherries, black chocolate tastes in full (13,9%), fleshy body. Lengthy fine-grained dry tannins. **98** possibly finest to date under this label. Mouthfilling and subtly oaked (as are all these reds). **97** ★ undomineering, good at table.

✵**Pinotage** ✓ One of the Cape's more reliable, flavoursome pinotages. Diffidently-oaked **99** with cellar's signature tarry note, spicy whiffs; sweet fleshy fruit reined in by tight tannins for balanced, good vinous effect. 13.7% alc. **98** (exceptional red vintage for cellar) full, ripe, instant roundness with longer-term keepability. **97** not tasted. **96** ✵ tangy, seamlessly oaked.

✵**Shiraz** Urbane, well behaved **99** shows good vinous qualities; soft, supple tannins with pleasingly light tarry touches. Large/small oak-matured. 13.5% alc. Electrifying **98** ✵✵ generous but refined, early accessible yet enough structure for keeping. **97** suave, understated.

✵**Lauréat** Stylish understated bdx blend, usually cabs s/f with merlot. Formula for latest **99** 62/13/25; lots of presence; oak noticeable (which unusual), cab's cedar/sweet pepper melded with dark choc in full (14% alc), dry but not austere palate; tannins fairly disciplined but sweet. Give 1-2 yrs, then drink over 4-5 with roast beef and Yorkshire pud or rare fillet. Partially oaked in variety of woods. **98** closed on release, quite tannic, needing yr/2. **97** more approachable, earlier maturing.

✵**Chardonnay** ✓ Steady improvement sees this pvs support player now ensconced among the stars. **00** combines silky mouthfeel with gorgeous toasty oak and fresh, focused lime fruit. Wood nicely melded in not-too-full body (13.4% alc). 17 000 cases. As in **99**, partially barrel fermented/aged, imparting butterscotch/lees character without dominating bone-dry lime piquancy.

✵**Sauvignon Blanc** ✓ Stringent vyd selection provided extra octane in **00** for broad, gusty satisfaction. **01** ★ more middle of the road, gentle sauvignon flavours. 13.2% alc. 13 000 cases.

✵**Blanc de Blanc** 85/15 chenin/sauvignon mix, uncommonly concentrated in **00**, super-fresh profile (partly from careful reductive handling). **01** ★ recognisably chenin, peachy, curvaceous rather than sparky, smoothly mouthfilling. Best within yr of harvest. 13.3% alc. 17 000 cases.

Premier Grand Cru ☻ ★ Familiar colombard/chenin (50/50) mix in charming, delicately rounded **01**; gentle – no aggressive acidity often associated with this style. Lightish 12% alc. 9 000 cases.

Not tasted for this ed: **Pinot Noir 97** ✵, **Rhine Riesling** (Pvs **00** ✵), **Special Late Harvest** (**98** ✵), **Noble Late Harvest** (**96** ✵). — *IvH*

A-code numbers

Many wines appear on the market under brand names, with, at first glance, no reference to their producers or purveyors. However, consumers need not buy 'blind', and may trace a wine's provenance by checking the official 'A-number that appears on the bottle or pack. This identity code tells you either who has produced the wine, or who has acquired it. In the latter case, an enquiry to the purveyor should elicit the source. The list keeps growing and being revised, and the version below is the latest supplied by the National Department of Agriculture, Liquor Products Division. An extensive update was underway as the guide went to press, and some details were not yet available. For the latest information, contact Albert Smith, tel (021) 809 1682, fax (021) 887-6396, e-mail alberts@nda agric.za.

B/dale = Barrydale **B/West** = Beaufort West **Bfn** = Bloemfontein **Bhspruit** = Bronkhorstspruit **Bkfl** = Brackenfell **Bnvale** = Bonnievale **C/dorp** = Calitzdorp **Citrd** = Citrusdal **Const** = Constantia **Cpt** = Cape Town **Dbnville** = Durbanville **Dur** = Durban **Els** = East London **F/hoek** = Franschhoek **Fgrv** = Firgrove **G/Bay** = Gordon's Bay **G/wood** = Goodwood **Grj** = George **Grt D/stein** = Groot Drakenstein **Hmsdrp** = Humansdorp **Hwhse** = Halfway House **Jnb** = Johannesburg **K/dorp** = Krugersdorp **K/hof** = Koelenhof **K/River** = Kuils River **K/voogds** = Klaasvoogds **Kim** = Kimberley **Klny Gdns** = Killarney Gardens **Kmtn Prk** = Kempton Park **K/Dorp** = Krugersdorp North **L/doch** = Lynedoch **Lw Rdg** = Lynnwood Ridge **M/bury** = Malmesbury **M/gdns** = Montague Gardens **M/vlei** = Muldersvlei **Mtgu** = Montagu **N/Paarl** = Noorder-Paarl **Ouh** = Oudtshoorn **P/ville** = Porterville **Pbz** = Plettenberg Bay **Plz** = Port Elizabeth **Pta** = Pretoria **Pzb** = Pietermaritzburg **Rbg** = Randburg **Rbktl** = Riebeek Kasteel **Rbtson** = Robertson **Rw/ville** = Rawsonville **S/bosch** = Stellenbosch **S/paarl** = Suider-Paarl **S/ville** = Sinoville **S/West** = Somerset West **Smdm** = Simondium **T/Valley** = Tyger Valley **Tbgh** = Tulbagh **Utn** = Upington **V/dal** = Vredendal **V/dorp** = Villiersdorp **Veng** = Vereeniging **Vltburg** = Vlottenburg **Wdville** = Wadeville **Wlnton** = Wellington **Wstr** = Worcester

Code

A001-A017 A046 Cancelled **A018** E W Sedgwick & Co, Cpt **A019** Gordon's Dry Gin Company (S A), Wdville **A020-A022 A024 A027-A028 A030-A031 A033-A039 A041-A044** Distell, S/Bosch **A023** Die Bergkelder, S/Bosch **A025** Drostdy Winery, S/Bosch **A026** Castle Wine & E K Green, S/Bosch **A029** Henry C Collins & Sons, S/Bosch **A032** Paarl Wine & Brandy Co, S/Bosch **A040** Durbanville Hills Wines, Dbnville **A045** Martell & Co (Sa), Cpt **A047** Erven Lucas Bols, Cpt **A048** Zonnebloem Wines, S/Bosch **A049-A055 A057-A058** Distell, S/Bosch **A056** Plaisir de Merle, S/Bosch **A059** Bonnievale Farmers Winery, Bnvale **A060** J C Botha, Wlnton **A061 A078** DGB, Wlnton **A062 A082** Kersaf Investments, Rbg **A063-A067 A079** Guinness UDV South Africa, T/ Valley **A068-A077** Distell, S/Bosch **A080 A083 A085 A087** Cancelled, **A081** Henry Taylor & Ries, Florida **A084** Ladismith Co-Op Winery & Distillery, Ladismith **A086** Saxenburg Wine Farm, K/River **A088** Natal Wholesale Wine & Spirit Merchants, Dur **A089** Distell, S/Bosch **A090-A094** Cancelled, **A095** D D Joubert & C J W Joubert, Vltburg **A096** Superior Imports, Cpt **A097** Boland Co-Op, Paarl **A098** Rustenberg, S/Bosch **A099** Mooiuitsig Wine Cellars, Bnvale **A100** KWV, S/Paarl **A101 A126 A128 A133 A153 A178** Cancelled, **A102** Culbemborg Winery, Wlnton **A103** Brockmann & Kriess SA, Lw Rdg **A104** Jonkheer Farmers Winery, Bnvale **A105** Langeberg Associated Wineries, Rbtson **A106** Anglo American Farms, Grt D/Stein **A107** Blue Ridge Vineyards, K/Hof **A108** The Round House, Camps Bay **A109** Cellarmaster Wines Tvl, Troyeville **A110** Simonsig Wine Estate, K/Hof **A111** Mecklenberg, Jnb **A112** Liquor Born, Bfn **A113** E

Snell & Co, Isando **A114-A115** Drop Inn Group, Plumstead **A116** Oude Kaap Wine & Brandy, **A117** Benny Goldberg's, Bramley **A118** South Western Tvl Agricultural Co-Op, Jacobsdal **A119** Seventh Light Anti-Aircraft Regiment, Cpt **A120** Romansrivier Wine Cellars, Wolseley **A121** Boland Wine & Brandy Merchants, Huguenot **A122** Magnum Liquordrome, De Tijger **A123** Vlottenburg Wine Cellars, Vltburg **A124** Rooiberg Wine Cellars, Rbtson **A125** Fairview, S/Paarl **A127** Regiment University, S/Bosch **A129** Simondium Wine Cellars, Smdm **A130** Kanonkop Cellars, M/Vlei **A131** Koelenhof Winery, K/Hof **A132** Constantia Negociants, Garden View **A134** Weltevrede Estate, Bnvale **A135** Simonsvlei Wine Cellars, S/Paarl **A136** Roodezandt Winery, Rbtson **A137** Backsberg Estate, Klapmuts **A138** Retief Bros, K/Voogds **A139** Bottelary Winery, K/Hof **A140** Stellenbosch Vineyards, L/Doch **A141** Bainskloof Wine Cellar, Breërivier **A142** Vaalharts Co-Op, Hartswater **A143** Hamilton Russell Vineyards, Hermanus **A144** Swartland Winery, M/Bury **A145** Spruitdrift Wine Cellar, V/Dal **A146** Clairvaux Wine Cellar, Rbtson **A147** Perdeberg Wine Farmers, Paarl **A148** Badsberg Wine Cellar, Rw/ Ville **A149** Groenkloof Wholesalers, Darling **A150** Slanghoek Wine Cellar, Rw/Ville **A151** Landskroon, S/Paarl **A152** Nuy Wine Cellars, Nuy **A154** Botha Wine Cellar, Botha **A155** Goudini Wine Cellar, Rw/Ville **A156** Blaauwklippen, S/Bosch **A157** Brandvlei Wine Cellar, Wstr **A158** Aan de Doorns Winery, Wstr **A159** Merwida Winery, Rw/Ville **A160** Barrydale Winery, B/Dale **A161** Drie Berge Farm Cellar, Mtgu **A162** Lievland, Klapmuts **A163** Louwshoek Winery, Rw/Ville **A164** Picardi Hotels, De Tijger **A165** Allied Shippers, Isando **A166** Tulbagh Winery, Tbgh **A167** Waboomsrivier Winery, Breërivier **A168** Marcows Cellars, Cpt **A169** Whitby Distillers & Liquor Wholesalers, Grabouw **A170** Southern Cape Vineyards (Boplaas), C/Dorp **1** Aufwaerts Winery, Rw/Ville **A172** Wellington Wine Farmers, Wlnton **A173** Neethlingshof Estate, S/Bosch **A174** Kango Co-Op, Ouh **A175** Franschhoek Vineyards, F/Hoek **A176** Mon Don Estate, Rbtson **A177** Bon Courage Estate, Rbtson **A179** Rietrivier Winery, Mtgu **A180 A181 A183 A199** Cancelled, **A182** Oude Nektar Estate, S/Bosch **A184** Douglas Co-Op, Douglas **A185** Ashton Winery, Ashton **A186** Le Grand Chasseur Estate, Rbtson **A187** Du Toitskloof Winery, Rw/Ville **A188** Calitzdorp Fruit & Winery Co- Op, C/Dorp **A189** De Wet Theron & Sons, Tbgh **A190** Danie De Wet (De Wetshof Estate), Rbtson **A191** Eikendal Vineyards, S/ Bosch **A192** Kaapzicht Estate, Sanlamhof **A193** North West Liquor Merchants, V/Dal **A194** Stettyn Winery, Wstr **A195** J Parker, Dbnville **A196** Baumker's Hotel (Alexander Hotel), Caledon **A197** Woolworths, Cpt **A198** Namakwaland Winery, Klawer **A200** Zevenwacht Estate, K/River **A201** Team Liquor World, **A202** Opstal Estate, Rw/Ville **A203** Mouton Excelsior, F/Hoek **A204** De Wet Winery, De Wet **A205** Simonsig Sales (Coastal Wines), K/Hof **A206** Die Krans, C/Dorp **A207** Kersaf Investments, Rbg **A208** C J Meyer & Son, Ouh **A209** Whitby Distillers & Liquor Wholesaler, Grabouw **A210** Lutzville Vineyards, Lutzville **A211** De Doorns Winery, De Doorns **A212** Stellenbosch Vineyards, Vltburg **A213** Buitenverwachting, Const **A214** Soetwyn Farmers Co- Op, Mtgu **A215** Winkelshoek Winery, Eendekuil **A216** Moralis (Vaughan Johnson), Northlands **A217** Spiko Hotels, Els **A218** Chasapy, Wstr **A219** Porterville Cellar, P/Ville **A220** Morgenhof, S/Bosch **A221** Stellenbosch Vineyards, Fgrv **A222 A226 A229 A231 A233 A235** Cancelled, **A223** Citrusdal Liquor Merchants, Citrd **A224** Citrusdal Winery, Citrd **A225** Vredendal Winery, V/ Dal **A227** Mcgregor Winery, Rbtson **A228** Agterkliphoogte Winery, Rbtson **A230** Groot Eiland Winery, Rw/Ville **A232** Vinotec, Jacobs **A234** Uiterwyk Estate, Vltburg **A236** Wamakersvallei Winery, Wlnton **A237** Cancelled, **A238** Saxenburg Wine Farm, K/ River **A239** Montagu Winery, Mtgu **A240** Delaire Wines, S/Bosch **A241** Klawer Winery, Klawer **A242** Makro, Jnb **A243** Van Riebeeck Cellars, Wlnton **A244**

Rozendal Farm, S/Bosch **A245** Pinetown Bottle Store, Pinetown **A246** Oranjerivier Winery, Utn **A247** Rooiberg Liquor Merchants, K/River **A248** **A249 A251 A253 A256** Cancelled, **A250** Riebeeck Wine Farmers, Rbktl **A252** Clos Cabriere, F/Hoek **A254** Domein Doornkraal, De Rust **A255** Cape Vintners, S/Bosch **A257** Vredenheim Estate, S/Bosch **A258** Loopspruit Estate, Bhspruit **A259** Edelstahl Wine Prmotions, Parow **A260** Bovlei Winery, Wlnton **A261 A264-A267 A269 A273** Cancelled, **A262** Trawal Winery, Klawer **A263** Standard Liquor Market, Wstr **A268** Delheim Wines, K/Hof **A270** Villiersdorp Moskonfyt & Fruit Co-Op, V/Dorp **A271** Frank Joao Co, De Deur **A272** Zandwijk, Paarl **A274** House Of Bacchus, K/Dorp **A275** Hartenberg, K/Hof **A276** Highveld Bottle Store, Ermelo **A277** Brockmann & Kriess Sa, Lw Rdg **A278** Rust En Vrede Estate, S/Bosch **A279** Vinimark, S/Bosch **A280** Robertson Winery, Rbtson **A281** Mocoma Caterings, Hmsdrp **A282 A283 A288** Cancelled, **A284** Premier Liquor Wholesalers, Veng **A285** Rhebokskloof, Windmeul **A286** Ever Grace Farm, S/Bosch **A287** Onverwacht Estate, Wlnton **A289** Du Toit Bros, Herold **A290** Distell, S/Bosch **A291** Jmb Liquor Cellars & Distributors, G/Wood **A292** Charles et Charles, S/Bosch **A293** Lug-A-Jug, **A294** OK Bazaar, Jnb **A295** D J Nel & C C Nell Partners, C/Dorp **A296** Klein Constantia Estate, Const **A297** Downtown Liquors, Cpt **A298** Prestons Liquor, Els **A299** E S Ratcliffe (Warwick Estate), M/Vlei **A300** Vintage Liquor Distributors, Silverton **A301** Glen Garlou Vineyards, Klapmuts **A302 A305 A361 A389** Cancelled, **A303** D C Van Velden, Vltburg **A304** De Wet Bros, Ashton **A306** Karoo Wine Distributors, Cradock **A307** La Rochelle Wine Depot, Bnvale **A308** Constantia Nek Restaurant, Const **A309** Wine Distributors, Benmore **A310** B Truter, K/Hof **A311** Kaapsche Wijn & Brandewijn, S/Bosch **A312** Expo International Liquors, S/Bosch **A313** J P Coetzee (Bloemendal Estate), Dbnville **A314** Diemersdal Farmers, Dbnville **A315** Heughn Ronald Jacobs, Athlone **A316** Mcleod's Wines & Spiritis, N/Paarl **A317** G J Jardim, S/Ville **A318** Southern Cellars Franchise Holdings, Silverton **A319** John Platter, S/Bosch **A320** Overhex Winery, Wstr **A321** Twee Jonge Gezellen, Tbgh **A322** NMK Schultz, Jnb **A323** Muratie Wine Farm, K/Hof **A324** Avontuur Winery, S/West **A325** Neil Ellis Wines, Dennesig **A326** J P W Jonker, Albertinia **A327** Merwespont Winery, Bnvale **A328** De Lucque & Dieu Donne Vineyards, F/Hoek **A329** Hemel-en-Aarde, Hermanus **A330** Prof R K Belcher, S/Paarl **A331** Clos Malverne, S/Bosch **A332** Groot Constantia Estate, Const **A333** A H Pillman, Botrivier **A334** Pick 'n Pay Hypermarket, Bkfl **A335** Big Daddy's, Centrahill **A336** Vinafrica Import & Export, Jacobs **A337** Fenshaw Wines, Dur **A338** Gala Import & Export, Jnb **A339** Jardim G S, S/Ville **A340** Woodlands Liquor Company, Waterkloof **A341** R Fehlmann, Tbgh **A342** J R C Jorgensen, Wlnton **A343** Loop Wholesalers, Sea Point **A344** Kangra Holdings, Rbtson **A345** Wimex Wine Import & Export, Troyeville **A346** EBR Products, S/Paarl **A347** Breeriver Valley Wine Distributors, Wstr **A348** Aan de Doorns Winery, Wstr **A349** Mulderbosch Vineyards, S/Bosch **A350** Montestell, S/Bosch **A351** Villiersdorp Liquor Merchants, V/Dorp **A352** Bordelais Distributors, Wittebome **A353** Mooivallei Wines, Wstr **A354** Eikehof Wines, La Motte **A355** Tollgate Vintners, Wynberg **A356** D Retief, Wlnton **A357** Lateganskop Winery, Breërivier **A358** DSA Liquor Wholesalers, Hwhse **A359** Rob's Liquor, Els **A360** Aroma Fine Wine Centre, Bkfl **A362** Jumbo Liquor Mart Dayton Centre, Bluff **A363** Anglo American Farms, Grt D/Stein **A364** Longridge, S/Bosch **A365** Stellenbosch Oak Liquor Store, S/Bosch **A366** HSJ Coetzee, Ficksburg **A367** Klein Gustrouw, S/Bosch **A368** Storm Creek Bottling Company, Pinetown **A369** Kruger Wine Estate, Klapmuts **A370** A & M Distillers & Vintners, Benoni **A371** Vinfruco, S/Bosch **A372** Chris van der Spuy Loubser S/Cape Liquors, Waverley **A373** The Form Organisation, Cpt **A374** Grande Provence, Vltburg **A375** Vinicor International

Wine & Spirit Corporation, Howard **A376** Vriesenhof, S/Bosch **A377** Grangehurst Winery, L/Doch **A378** Grestemar International, S/West **A379** E W Sedgwick, Cpt **A380** Berghof Wine & Guest Farm, Paarl **A381** Sonop, Windmeul **A382** Hazendal, S/Bosch **A383** Manikas Trading, Brixton **A384** Bacchus Bros, Newlands **A385** Niblock Properties, Elgin **A386** Fredericksburg, Smdm **A387** Diamant, S/Paarl **A388** Henry J Beans Holdings, G/Wood **A390** Torbix, S/Bosch **A391** Stillwater, Barkley West **A392** S A Cultural History Museum, Rayton **A393** Wine of the Month Club, Const **A394** The Hyperama, Jnb **A395** Carecor Distributors, Parow East **A396** Robertson Winery, Rbtson **A397** Watergang, K/Hof **A398** L'Avenir, S/Bosch **A399** Cape Chamonix, F/Hoek **A400** Constantia Uitsig, Const **A401** Zanddrift, F/Hoek **A402** Louisvale, S/Bosch **A403** Worcester Museum, Wstr **A404** Goedverwacht Estate, Bnvale **A405** The Wine Company, Jnb **A406** Vanderbijlt International, S/Bosch **A407** La Petite Ferme, F/Hoek **A408** Nietvoorbij, S/Bosch **A409** Yonder Hill, Helderberg **A410** Mixed Doubles Coktails, Umgeni **A411 A429-A430** Totpak Manufacturing, Ventersdorp **A412** Jordan Vineyards, Vltburg **A413** Vinexpo, Pinelands **A414** Trauve Estates, F/ Hoek **A415** Napier Winery, Wlnton **A416** Senator Liquor Store, Jnb **A417** Spier Winery, S/Bosch **A418** Paddagang Vignerons, Tbgh **A419** Winmark, S/Bosch **A420** Wine Industries International, Airport Industria 2 **A421** Vineyard Graphics, S/West **A422** Haute Provence Vineyards, F/Hoek **A423** Davritch Trade, Dur **A424** Von Ortloff Estates, F/Hoek **A425** Van Zylshof Estate, Bnvale **A426** Loubser Du Plessis, S/Bosch **A427** Jakowet Wines, Rw/Ville **A428** Mont Fleur, S/Bosch **A431** Windmeul Co-Op, Windmeul **A432** Omni Liquor, Cpt **A433** Cilliers Park Cellars, Welkom **A434** Veenwouden, N/Paarl **A435** Simonsvlei Liquor Merchants, S/Paarl **A436** J P Bredell Wines, Helderberg **A437** Shoprite Checkers, Parow **A438** Worcester Co-Op, S/Bosch **A439** Pre-Mix, Kmtn Prk **A440** Totpak Natal Midlands, Pzb **A441** Albertinia Poort Farms, Albertinia **A442 A443** J M B Liquor Distributors, Klny Gdns **A444** Hermanusriver Wines, Botrivier **A445** Seabreeze Bottling, Grabouw **A446** Coastal Liquor Distributors, Plz **A447** Regional Marketing Organisation, Fochville **A448** Williston Liquor Wholesalers, Williston **A449** Mooiuitsig/Overberg Co-Op, Bnvale **A450** Sabasco Wholesalers, Jnb **A451 A460** Moreson, F/Hoek **A452** Noordkaap Cellars, Hartswater **A453-A455 A457** J M B Liquor Distributors, G/Wood **A456 A484** Liquor Management & Marketing, Bergvliet **A458** Bellmount Liquor Store, Ceres **A459** Huguenot Wine Farmers, Greyville **A461** La Motte, Paarl **A462** Morgenzon, Vltburg **A463** Boschendal, Grt D/ Stein **A464** P J T International, Pta **A465** Grundheim Wines, Ouh **A466** Thambazimbi Liquor Store, Thabazimbi **A467 A481** La Lucia Liquor Shop, La Lucia **A468** Winelands, Dur **A469** Midmar Liquor Store, G/Wood **A470** Thelema Mountain Vineyards, S/Bosch **A471** The Cape Wine Link, Cpt **A472** Krugels Buiteverbruik, Lydenburg **A473** Allan Nelson Vineyard, Windmeul **A474** Horncastle Wholesalers Unit, Pzb **A475** Southern Cellars, Silverton **A476** Bodega Farm, K/Hof **A477** Tanbee Properties, K/Hof **A478** Cawood Liquor, Plattekloof **A479** Connoisseurs Wine Club, Rivonia **A480** Jacaranda, Wlnton **A482** Somerbosch, S/Bosch **A483** La Brie, F/Hoek **A485** Irina Botha, Rosebank **A486** Perdeberg Vineyards/Sonop Wine Farm, Windmeul **A487** Doherty Wine Distributors, Bredell **A488** Jade Liquors, Atlantis **A489** Stellenbosch Wines Direct, S/Bosch **A490** Springfield Estate, Rbtson **A491** Meerdendal Estate, Dbnville **A492** Papegaaiberg Cellars, Windmeul **A493** Imandi Cellars, Windmeul **A494** Kersfontein Farm, Windmeul **A495** Beaumont Wines, Botrivier **A496** Cloete Wines, S/West **A497** United Distillers Imports, Claremont **A498** Excelsior Farm, Rw/Ville **A499** Ruitersvlei Estate, S/Paarl **A500** Ralton's Restaurant, Bkfl **A501** Pernod Ricard, S/Bosch **A502** Penaltembe, Turffontein **A503**

Goedehoop, K/River **A504** Dawilla Mampoer, Pta **A505** Kenbu Investments, N1 City **A506** Steppe Buzzard Partners, Dbnville **A507** Wine Mecca, K/Dorp **A508** Cape Wine Cellars, Wlnton **A509** Central Liquor Store, B/ West **A510** M & M Liquor Cellars, Houghton **A511** Orchard Cellar, Windmeul **A512** De Breede Worcester, Wstr **A513** Savanha Wines, Cpt **A514** Robertson Valley Wines, S/Bosch **A515** Nampini Cellars, Bfn **A516** Coppoolse & Finlayson, Old Oak **A517** Leo's Producers, Boons **A518** L'Ormarins Estate, S/Paarl **A519** Helderenberg, S/Bosch **A520** Cape Classic Wines, Dur **A521** United Distillers, Claremont **A522** La Lucia Liquor Shop, La Lucia **A523** Windhoek Beer, Windhoek **A524** Paarl Bottling Trust, Paarl **A525** Ardevi International, Rosenpark **A526** Watervliet Farm, Smdm **A527** Wilreza, Jacobsdal **A528** Premier Liquors Marketing, Sir Lowry Road **A529** Johann de Wet & Son, Rbtson **A530** Steenberg Vineyards, Steenberg **A531** Orion Agencies, Greyville **A532** Almin Bottle Store, Strand **A533** Steven Rom Liquor Merchants, Sea Point **A534** Royal Africa Intnl, Pzb **A535** Cape Vinex, S/Bosch **A536** Cantot, Silverton **A537** Langverwacht Wine Cellar, Bnvale **A538** Van Nyathi, Falcon Ridge **A539** Nu-Ced Liquor Distributors, Hatfield **A540** Lemberg Estate, Tbgh **A541** Hard Rock Liquor Store, Witbank **A542** Tropicana Liquor Distributors, Glenvista **A543** Marico Valley, Groot Marico **A544** Whalehaven Wines, Hermanus **A545** Simonstown Bottle Store, Simonstown **A546** Hawekwa Cellars, Wlnton **A547** Walker Jb/Lelievlei Estate, Wolseley **A548** W & G Wholesale Liquors, Cannon Rocks **A549** Etienne le Riche Wines, S/Bosch **A550** Diamond Discount Liquor, Maitland **A551** Bravo International Liquor Merchants, Howard Place **A552** Rozendal Distillery, S/Bosch **A553** Chapmans Peak Liquor Store, Cpt **A554** Exclusive Label & Liquor Gifts, Kocksvlei **A555** Fruit Processes Africa, Strand **A556** Boland Estate Wine Distributors, S/Bosch **A557** Brown Forman Beverages, Rondebosch **A558** Packaging Excellence, Wierda Park **A559** Lanzerac Wines, S/Bosch **A560** Ernst Estate, Leeudoringstad **A561** Fairseat Cellars, Kenilworth **A562** Paarden Eiland Beverage Bottlers, Paarden Eiland **A563** Camberley Wines, S/Bosch **A564 A579** Stilwater Distributors, Bfn **A565** Mooiplaas Estate, K/River **A566** King Shooters Beverages, Observatory **A567** Afriprobe, Pta **A568** Hermitage Van Zyl Family Trust, Swellendam **A569** Mont Rochelle, F/Hoek **A570** Spurwing Liquor Wholesalers, Wynberg **A571** Peninsula Liquor Distributors, B/Ville **A572** Tandi International, Epping **A573** Amani Farm, Vltburg **A574** Bot River Hotel, Bot River **A575** Liquors For Africa, K/Dorp **A576 A586 A587** Celestine's Liquor Distributors, Ferrierastown **A577** New Cape Africa, Dur **A578** Good Success Farm, S/ Bosch **A580** Weltevrede Estate, Rbtson **A581** Stellenbosch Vineyards, L/ Doch **A582** Elsenburg Wine Cellar, S/Bosch **A583** Bonnievale Wine Cellar, Bnvale **A584** Eugene Kruger & Co, Zeerust **A585** Devonhill Winery, S/Bosch **A588** Lebensraum Estate, Rw/Ville **A589** Biggest Sa Trading, Dur **A590** G S Incorporation, Veng **A591** Calba Liquor Merchants, Stikland **A592** Bloupunt Wines, Mtgu **A593** Paul Cluver Wines/De Rust Estate, Grabouw **A594** Wine Direct, Rivonia **A595** Lost Horizons, Paarl **A596** Fort Simon, K/River **A597** De Villiers Wines/ Nantes Farm, N/Paarl **A598** Boschkloof Cellar, S/Bosch **A599** Happy Valley Farm, S/West **A600** Jmb Cellars & Liquor Distributors, G/Wood **A601** The Company, Umkomaas **A602** Hoopenburg Wines, S/Bosch **A603** Madotta Distillers, Alma **A604** Du Preez Wines, S/Bosch **A605** Kleine Zalze, S/Bosch **A606** R Manson Trading, Steenberg **A607** D'em Distributors, Hwhse **A608** Hamlin House, S/Bosch **A609** Table Liquor, Helderberg **A610** Gilhar Service Centre, Parow **A611** Bebida Distillers, Maitland **A612** R J Superior Liquors, Silverton **A613** Bavaria Brau, Centurion **A614** Oude Wellington Estate, Wlnton **A615** Green & Gold, Pta **A616** Ocean Traders International, Prince Albert **A617** Channel Clipton Liquor Wholesalers, Pbz **A618**

Forresters Winery, Pbz **A619** Bar-Valley Wines, Rbtson **A620** Jack William Mudd/Nayati Pools, Hoedspruit **A621** Cape Vineyards, Rw/Ville **A622** Cape Bay Wines, Hermanus **A623** Anchor Liquor Distributors, S/West **A624** Philadelphia Liquor Suppliers, Klein Dassenberg **A625** Purlikur, B/Ville **A626** Henniges & Henniges, Cpt **A627** Cape Vintages, S/West **A628** Ashanti, Klein Drakenstein **A629** Cape Viticultural Holdings, K/Hof **A630** Johannes Erasmus, Ventersburg **A631** Withoek Cellar, C/Dorp **A632** D & H Liquors, Kraaifontein **A633** De Meye Wines, Elsenburg **A634** Larlornie Distributors, Krost Park **A635** Bayside Liquors, Jacobs **A636** Jacsel Liquor Store, Paarden Eiland **A637** Vinotec Liquor Distributors, Grj **A638** Nobunto Liquor Wholesalers, Rw/Ville **A639** Helderfontein Mampoer, Pietersburg **A640** Somerset Wine & Spirit Company, S/West **A641** Perseverance Liquors, Swartkops **A642** Shavo Food & Beverage, S/Ville **A643** Remhoogte Wines, Dennesig **A644** Drowsy Moon Liquors, Wynberg **A645** Glover Family Trust, Vyeboom **A646** Viljoensdrift Farm, K/Voogds **A647** Die Baken Farms, Wlnton **A648** Tansiedor Een, S/Bosch **A649** Awethu Liquor Wholesalers, Rivonia **A650** Independent Liquor Company, Blue Route **A651** Masakhane Liquors, Wynberg **A652** J C Liquor Distributors, B/Ville **A653** Duplenia Farms, S/Bosch **A654** The Spice Route Wine Company, M/Bury **A655** Luca De Luca, Jnb **A656-A660** Ready Tot, Honeydew **A661** Namakwa Foods, V/Dal **A662** The Beverage Business, Westville **A663** Excelsius Wines, V/Dal **A664** Middelvlei Estate, S/Bosch **A665** Clear Mountain Wines, Dennesig **A666** Neil Joubert, Klapmuts **A667** Intra International Trading, Westlake **A668** South Western Free State Liquor Wholesalers, Jacobsdal **A669** Genetic Beverages, Jnb **A670** Rietrivier Distributors, Jacobsdal **A671** Bonnie Wines, S/Bosch **A672** Haskins Bottle Store, Hmsdrp **A673** Terrace Road Trading, Cpt **A674** Black Sheep Brewery, M/Gdns **A675** Diamonds Discount Liquor, Maitland **A676** Wine Concepts, Cpt **A677** Bonsteen Wholesalers, Bloubergsands **A678** Groene Cloof Estate, Darling **A679** The Spar Group, Pinetown **A680** Midmar Liquors, Parow **A681** Long Chan Distillers, Bfn **A682** Mijn Burg Wines, Klapmuts **A683** Calvinia Drankwinkel, Calvinia **A684** Mellasat Wine & Fruit, Paarl **A685** Cederberg Kelders, Clanwilliam **A686** African Wine & Spirits, Const **A687** Nordale Winery, Bnvale **A688** Liquor Ranch Goodwood, G/Wood **A689** Die Kelder, Calvinia **A690** S A Fine Wine, Ale & Spirits Merchants, Plz **A691** Audacia Wines, S/Bosch **A692** District Township Bottle Store, K/Dorp North **A693** Calba International, Grj **A694** Parade Café, S/Bosch **A695** Metro Cash & Carry, Jnb **A696** Hildenbrand Estate Wines, Wlnton **A697** Liquor Link, Gallo Manor **A698** Mountain Range, Cpt **A699** West Coast Wholesale Liquors, K/River **A700** Wel d'Mer Winery, S/Bosch **A701** Pakata Liquor Wholesalers, M/Gdns **A702** Hoopenburg Wines, S/Bosch **A703** J B C Liquor Distributors, Bothasig **A704** Clos Du Toit, **A705** Darling Cellars, Darling **A706** Ben Nevis Cellar, Clocolan **A707** Frangelo, Jnb **A708** Roodezandt Winery, Rbtson **A709** Silver Hill Wines, S/Paarl **A710** B S A Wholesale & Bottling, Midrand **A711** Pacific Distributors, Cpt **A712** Matlaplan Architects, Hatfield **A713** Old Rock Wine & Liquor Wholesalers, Roodepoort **A714** Eastern Cape Liquor, Plz **A715** Akho Property Investments, F/Hoek **A716** Paulinas Dal Farm Holdings, F/Hoek **A717** Z S Wines, Plankenbrug **A718** Vintage Liquor Merchants, Centurion **A719** Retail Brands Interafrica, Wdville **A720** The House of Coffees, Jnb **A721** Drews Brew, Milnerton **A722** Free State Distillers, Fauresmith **A723** Starpack, Alberton North **A724** Southern Liquors, Cpt **A725** Oasis Liquor Wholesalers, Benoni **A726** Leebri Wholesalers, Jnb **A727** Windsor Discount Liquor, Windsor Glen **A728** De La Querre, S/Bosch **A729** Fixtrade 253, Midrand **A730** Dyasonsklip Wine Cellar, Dyasonsklip **A731** Northern Natal Liquor Distributors, Newcastle **A732** The Avondale Trust, Paarl **A733** G & M Manufacturers, Prieska **A734** Bulmer Sa, Centurion **A735**

De Wet Cellars, Bfn **A736** Gewalisa Bottlers, Pinetown **A737** Kevin Kitley, S/ Bosch **A738** Rolon Beverages, Glendale **A739** Stormberg Trust, Wlnton **A740** Totpak Distributors, Bfn **A741** Plodimex Liquor Wholesalers, Benoni **A743** Breevallei Co-Op, Wstr **A744** Onderkloof Estate, Sir Lowry's Pass **A745** Herberts Associated Berries, Kmtn Prk **A746** The Wine Village, Hermanus **A747** Davnat Liquor Wholesalers, Jnb **A748** Mahers Bottling, Grj **A749** Donkerhoek Fruit Syndicate, F/Hoek **A750** Klein Karoo Wines, B/Dale **A751** Maiden Wines, Kmtn Prk **A752** Nicholson Smith Agencies, Rbg **A753** Bafana Wines, Dbnville **A754** Gants Wholesale Liquor, Strand **A755** Vaalharts Brewery, Hartswater **A756** Yonder Hill, S/West **A757** Winkelshoek Cellar, Piketberg **A758** Overberg Wholesale Liquor Distributors, Sunnyside **A759** Wine Village, Hermanus **A760** Von Regen Wines/Geelkop, Keimoes **A761** Vendôme, Huguenot **A762** Bag-O-Vino, S/West **A763** Midlands Distillers, Pzb **A764** The Rock Wholesale Liquors, Paarl **A765** Jordaan Broers – Theuniskraal Partnership, Tbgh **A766** Springbok Liquor Store, Plz **A767** Cormard Spirit Blenders, Dur **A768** Hennie Reynecke, K/Voogds **A769** Central Liquor Store, Fraserburg **A770** Reserved for Waterford Wines, **A771** Black Sheep Beverage Distributors, M/Gdns **A772** Liq 'O' Mac, Utn **A773** Kapland Wines, G/Bay **A774** Foxi Snax Lowveld, White River **A775** New Cape Wines, Wstr **A776** Greeff's Liqueurs, Mowbray **A777** P R Kelder, Prieska **A778** Monate, Brits **A779** Tokara, S/Bosch **A780** Diablo Trade 200, Jnb **A781** Bilton Wines, L/Doch **A782** Divan's Mcgregor Liquor, Mcgregor **A783** The Real McCoy Products, Pinetown **A784** Mafilas Liquor Stores, Jnb **A785** Swartland Wines, M/Bury **A786** Cape Perlé Wines, G/Bay **A787** Highway Tavria, Dur **A788** Embiteni Wholesalers, Nelspruit **A789** C B C International Trading, Parow **A790** Millennium Liquors, Kmtn Prk **A791** Intombi Liqueurs And Fine Foods, Dur **A792** Ultramix 21, Cpt **A793** Concordia Liquor Store, Bfn **A794** Mega Wholesale Liquors, Observatory **A795** Independent Liquor Marketers, Elandsfontein **A796** Thirsty Now Beverages, Centurion **A797** Hanzet Muti (Distillers), Vredefort **A798** Emerald Glen Vineyards, S/ Bosch **A799** Esancha Liquors, Van Riebeeckstrand **A800** Verdun/Asara, Vltburg **A801** F C Distributors, Kim **A802** High Constantia, Const **A803** Stellenbosch Bottling Co, L/Doch **A804** Appelsdrift Winery, Rbtson **A805** Brenthurst Winery, S/ Paarl **A806** Bowe Vineyards (Stellenbosch), S/Bosch **A807** Myburgh Winery, M/Vlei **A808** De Heuvel Estate, Tbgh **A809** Bernheim Winery, N/Paarl

Complete general index

This is a summary of wines featured in the A-Z section.
NT = not tasted; **NR** = not rated

Drostdy, Du T'kloof, F'hoek Vyds, G Constantia, Hildenb, Hpnburg, IWS 00 (+1), Kaapzicht, Klnvallei NEW, Kpzicht NEW (+1), La Couronne, Libertas, Linton P, Long Mntn, L'Ormarins 97, Makro, Mouton 00, Ndrburg, Neil E NEW ☺, Onderklf, Overhex ☺, Post House 00, Rdezandt ☺, Rhebklf, R'hoogte 99, Riebeek (+1), Rooderust NEW, Rooiberg, Sandown, Savanha, Savanha 00, Slnghoek, Smnsig, Smnsvlei, Spier 00, Sprtdrift, Stlndrif, Sxnburg, Thnskraal ☺, Tulbagh NEW ☺ (+1), Upland 00, Villiera, Vljsdrift ☺, Vlrsdorp, Vltnburg, Waterford NEW ☺, Wlworths ☺ ★★½ Bodega, Cop-Fin, Country C, Kaapzicht, L'zicht 00, Main Str NEW, Mouton, M'pont ☺ (+1), Niel J, Nuy, Spier 99, Thandi, Vinfruco NEW (+1), Wamakers, Wlington ★★ Ashwood, Cape Clas, Cape Gab, Cape Wine C, Lutzville, Maze NEW, Mouton, M Ruber ☺ (+1), Devon H NEW (+1), Hldrkrn ★ Brnheim **NT:** Avoca NEW, Baarsma, Blue M NEW, Breëvallei NEW, Brenthurst, Cape Wine E, Clovelly NEW (+1), Cltzdorp, Cop-Fin, Die Poort, Fairview, F'hoek Vyds, Flgstone (+1), G'dveld, Groot E, Hippo, Huguenot, IWS, Jonkheer NEW (+1), Kaapzicht, Louisvale, Mdlpost, Merwida, Mrgnhof, M Rochelle (+1), M'uitsig, Ntvbij, O-Bridge (+1), Romans, Slaley, Sprtdrift, Starke, Stbosch Vyds, TenFiftySix, Uiterwyk, Uitvlucht, Vinfruco (+2), Vrdnheim, Waboom, West Cst **NR:** Anura NEW, Ashton NEW, De Zoete, Klvrvlei, Lievland, New Begin, Roodendal, Table Mtn, Thelema, Van Lvrn NEW

Carignan

★★★ Fairview, Welgegund

Chardonnay

Unwooded

★★★★ Bouchard

★★★½ B'punt ✓, Delaire NEW, De Wetsh ✓, M Rochelle

★★★ Cape Bay, Clmborg, C-Uitsig, G'vertouw, Hildenb, Jonkheer, Linton P 01, Makro ☺, Mouton (+1), Neil E NEW, Ntvbij 00, O-Wlngtn NEW, Prtrville, Riebeek, Rooiberg ☺, Sandown ☺, Smrbsch, Starke, Van Z'hof ☺, Vendôme NEW, W Village, Zndvliet ★★½ Blue M NEW, Botha, Brandvlei, Breëvallei NEW, Cape Wine C, Country C, Die Krans, G'verwacht, Ridder's, Stnberg, Travino, Tulbagh, Van Lvrn, Yonder ★★ Bon C, Cape Clas (+1), Darling C, Dieu D, Gecko, Kleine Z, Ladismith, Lanzerac, Lost H, Lutzville, Maze NEW, Shoprite, Vrdndal NEW, Wltvrede ★½ Avoca NEW, Boplaas, Kango, Sprtdrift ★ Wamakers NEW **NT:** Baarsma (+1), Bovlei, Excelsior, F'hoek Vyds, G'dveld, Goue V, Hrtswater, IWS (+1), Jonkheer, Louisvale, Montagu, Oranje (+1), Padda, Seidel, TenFiftySix, Vinfruco (+1) **NR:** Table Mtn

Wooded

★★★★½ Avontuur, Bouchard, C-Uitsig, De Wetsh 00, Fleur dC NEW (+1), Glen C, HRV, Neil E ✓, Newton J 00, R&R, Sprgfield, Stbosch Vyds 00, Stlnryck ✓, Veenwdn, Vrglegen, Warwick 01, Wlworths NEW, Wlworths 99 NEW

★★★★ Afr Terroir, Amani ✓, Asara 00, Beaumnt, Bschndal, B'wachting, Chamonix, Clos du C, Delaire, De Meye, De Wetsh NEW (+1), Edonia NEW, Eikendal, Fairview (+1), Fort S ✓, Frost NEW, G Constantia, Glen C, Hpnburg ✓, Hrtnberg, Jordan, JP Bredell ✓, KWV, La Motte, La Petite F, L'Avenir, Le Bonh, Linton P 00, Longridge 00 ✓, Louisvale, Mdlvlei ✓, Meerlust, Mrgnhof (+1), M Rochelle, Mulderb (+1), Muratie, Neil E ✓, Nitida 00 ✓, Nthlshof ✓, Overgw ✓, Paul C 00, Radford D, Rhebklf ✓, Rickety, Rstnberg (+1), Sprgfield ✓, Stnwall 00, Thelema (+1), Uitkyk 00, Vljsdrift NEW, Vrglegen ✓, Vrsenhof, Whlhaven, Zonneblm ✓, Zvnwacht

★★★½ Afr Terroir NEW (+2), Agusta, Ashton, Bksberg 00, Bon C ✓, Boschklf, Bouchard 00, B'punt ✓, Brgsig ✓, Brydale, Cape P'nt, Cape Vyds, Cdrberg, Chamonix, Cordoba, Darling C, Deetlefs, Delheim, De Wetsh NEW (+2), D-Hills, Eikehof ✓, Fat B, Goudini ✓, Graham B, Groote P, Hazendal, High C 01, Ingwe, Jonkheer, Joubert-T, Kanu ✓, Klvnburg, K Constantia, Kleine Z 00 ✓, Laborie, Lwshoek NEW ✓, Louiesen, Louisvale, Môreson, Ndrburg NEW (+3),

Onderklf 00, Oranje NEW, Plaisir, Rdezandt NEW, Rhebklf, Rietvallei, Rijk's, Rstnberg ✓, Slnghoek, Smnsig 00, Smridge NEW, Stark NEW, Starke, Sxburg 00, Thandi, Vendôme ✓, Vinfruco NEW, Vltnburg ✓, Von-O 00 ✓, Vrsenhof, Waterford, Wltvrede 00, Zndvliet, Zvnwacht

★ Afr Terroir (+1), Amani NEW, Ashwood, Bksberg, Cape P'nt NEW, Cape Vyds, Douglas G 00, Du T'kloof, Elephant, Goede H, G'verwacht, Havana H NEW, Hermanus H, Hildenb, Hpnburg, Hrtnberg, KWV, La Bri NEW, La Couronne 00, Ladismith ☺, Laibach, Lanzerac, Le Grand C, L'Émigré, Long Mntn ☺, Longridge, L'Ormarins, Lwshoek, Makro, Napier, Ndrburg, Nelson, Rtrsvlei, Seidel 00, Stlzicht 00 (+1), Swrtland, Uiterwyk, Van Lvrn, Van Z'hof, Villiera, Vinfruco, Vljsdrift, Wltvrede 00, Wlworths ☺ (+1), Bdsberg, Claridge, Cul-View, Dieu D, Dumisani NEW, Glnwood NEW, Goue V, IWS 00, Klawer, Kleindal, Libertas, Maze NEW, McGreg, Môreson, Niel J NEW, Overhex, Rbtson ☺ (+1), Sinnya, Spier, Stnberg 00, Stony B, Tulbagh ☺, Vinfruco, Wlington ★ Boland, Cheetah V NEW, De Vlrs, De Wet, De Zoete, Hldrkrn (+1), Klein DB NEW, Lutzville, Malan, M'pont (+1), Nuy, Rbtson, Rhebklf ★ F'hoek Vyds NEW, Goue V, Lndskrn, Opstal *No star:* Rietrivier **NT:** Agtrklip, Avondale, Baarsma (+1), Bksberg, Cape Wine E, Clovelly NEW, Cltzdorp, Cop-Fin, Country C, Darling C, Dellrust, D-Hills, Fairview, Flgstone (+1), Groot E, Hippo, La Bri, Lievland, L'zicht, Mdlpost, Mouton, M'uitsig, O-Bridge, Romans, Sable V, Savanha, Slaley, Smnsvlei, Stbosch Vyds (+1), Uva Mira, West Cst (+1), Wldkrans, Wlhlmshof, Wndmeul **NR:** Altdgdcht, Bllevue NEW, Blngham, Dmrsdal NEW, Rbtson, Swrtland NEW, Zvnwacht NEW

Chenin blanc

Unwooded, dry

★ Old Vines

★ Avontuur NEW ✓, Deetlefs, M Destin, Old Vines, Sylvnvle, Zvnwacht

★ Beaumnt, Boland ☺, Brandvlei ☺, Brgsig ☺, Cape Bay, Cape Wine C, Delaire, Delheim, Groene C, Hazendal, Kanu, Ken F, Kleine Z ☺, Laibach, Libertas, Lndskrn ☺, Napier, Ndrburg NEW, Prdeberg ☺, Seidel, Stbosch Vyds ☺, Swrtland ☺ (+1), Van Z'hof ☺, Vaughan J, Vljsdrift NEW ☺, Wndmeul ☺ ★ Bovlei ☺, Clmborg, Du T'kloof, Gecko, Goue V, KWV, Long Mntn, Riebeek, Smnsig ☺, Starke, Vinfruco ★ Bdsberg, Blue M NEW, Bon C NEW, Bovlei, Breëvallei NEW, Cape Clas, Cop-Fin, Country C, Cul-View, Die Krans, Drostdy, Du T'kloof, Groote P, Klawer, Kleindal, Lutzville NEW, McGreg, Mellasat, Môreson (+1), M'pellier NEW, Overhex, Rbtson, Rtrsvlei, Smnsvlei, Wlington ★ Brnheim, Cop-Fin, Smnsvlei, Vlrsdorp, Wamakers ★ Mouton, Opstal NEW, Oranje, Ridder's, Sprtdrift *No star:* Ladismith **NT:** Capelnds NEW, Cape Wine E, Fair Valley, Goue V, Groot E, Hrtswater, IWS, Jonkheer, J'randa (+1), Kaapzicht (+1), Lost H, Nelson, O-Bridge, Seidel, Smrbsch, Stbosch Vyds (+1), Stille W, TenFiftySix, Uitvlucht, West Cst (+1) **NR:** Klvrvlei

Unwooded, off-dry/semi-sweet

★ Sylvnvle

★ Rudera

★ Goudini ✓

★ Bksberg ☺, Bschndal, Cape Gab, Cdrberg ☺, Dellrust ☺, Lndskrn, Stbosch Vyds ☺, Vrdndal ☺, Wlworths ★ Botha NEW, Hazendal, KWV, Ladismith, McGreg, Overmeer, Prdeberg, Prtrville, Rooiberg, Smnsvlei, Vinfruco, Vltnburg, Vrdndal, Western NEW ★ Clmborg, Drostdy, Heernhf, Padda, Slnghoek ☺, Swrtland, Virginia, Wlworths (+1), Country C, Lutzville, Niel J NEW, Oranje, Prtrville, Zomerlust ★ Cape Gab, Grünb **NT:** A Harvest, Delheim, Die Poort, F'hoek Vyds, Goue V, Huguenot, K'prinz, Merry, Montagu, Ntvbij, Romans, Rooiberg, Shoprite, Swrtland, Waboom

White
★★★★Du T'kloof ✓
★★★½Bdsberg ✓, Sprtdrift, Vlrsdorp ✓
★★★ Brandvlei, Goue V, Prtrville ★★½ M Ruber (+1), Swrtland, Wamakers ★½ Kango
NT: Die Poort (+3), Huguenot (+1), J'randa, M'uitsig, Romans, Stbosch Vyds
NR: Oranje

Kosher wines
★★½ K Draken Cabernet ★½ K Draken Kiddush, K Draken Sauvignon **NT:** K Draken Dry Red, K Draken Dry White

Late Harvest
★★★ Rtrsvlei NEW, Thelema NEW ★★½ Ashton ☺, Clmborg, Overmeer, Vltnburg, Vrdndal ★★ Boplaas, Drostdy, Heernhf, Lutzville, Pick 'n P, Riebeek, Wlworths (+1), Rbtson, Wamakers, Zomerlust ★ Carnival, Country C, Kango, Oranje, Sprtdrift *No star:* Klawer **NT:** C Cask, Delheim, De Zoete, Die Poort, G'dveld, Goudini, Hrtswater, Huguenot, McGreg, Merry, M'uitsig, Shoprite, Uitvlucht, Waboom, Wnklshoek **NR:** Tulbagh NEW

'Light' & low-alcohol wines (some labels duplicated elsewhere)
★★★ 5th Avenue, De Wetsh, Douglas G ☺ (+1), Grünb, JC le R (+1), L'zicht, Twee JG, Vrdndal ☺ ★★½ Boplaas ☺ (+1), Breëvallei ☺, Cinzano, Fleur dC, Grand Msx, Rbtson, Rooiberg ☺, Wlworths ★★ Boplaas, Brgsig, Cinzano, Clmborg, De Wet, Drostdy, Riebeek, Tulbagh NEW, Wlworths ★½ Pick 'n P, Swrtland
NT: Cltzdorp, Country C, F'hoek Vyds

Malbec
★★★½Bllevue, Fairview ✓, Ndrburg NEW
★★★ Bksberg

Merlot
★★★★★Spice R 99, Thelema 99
★★★★½Avondale NEW, Cordoba, Eikendal, Havana H, Kaapzicht, KWV, Overgw ✓, Stbosch Vyds NEW, Stnberg (+1), Veenwdn
★★★★Afr Terroir NEW, Asara 98, Avontuur 99, Bschndal (+1), B'wachting (+1), Delaire, De Traf, D-Hills, Fleur dC, Havana H, Hpnburg ✓, Hrtnberg, Jean D NEW, Jordan, JP Bredell, Kanu ✓, Klnhof 99, KWV, Lanzerac, Lndskrn 99, Longridge, Meerdal 99 ✓, Meerlust, Meinert ✓, Plaisir, Radford D, Reyneke NEW ✓, Rickety, Rtrsvlei, Rust en V ✓, Savanha ✓, Seidel, Smnsvlei, Sxnburg, Thelema, Villiera ✓ (+1), Vrglegen, Vrgnoegd, Whlhaven ✓, Yonder, Zonneblm ✓
★★★½Amani ✓, Bilton 99, B'klippen NEW, Bksberg, Blngham, Bodega 99, Boplaas, Botha ✓, Bschndal, Country C, Darling C ✓, Delheim, Dellrust, D-Hills NEW (+1), Dmrsftn NEW, Douglas G NEW, Edonia NEW, Elephant 99, F'hoek Vyds NEW, Fort S, Frost NEW, Gracelnd ✓, Hazendal, Hpnburg NEW, Johnsen, Kaapzicht, Kleine Z, Laborie, Laibach, Longridge ✓, L'Ormarins, Louisvale, Lwshoek, Môreson, Mouton NEW, Mouton 99, Mrgnhof 99, Muratie NEW, Ndrburg, Nelson, Nthlshof, Rbtson NEW, R'hoogte 00, Riebeek NEW, Smrbsch ✓, Spier, Stbosch Vyds, Stkaya, Stlnzicht, Stlzicht 97, Stony B NEW, Sxnburg, Uiterwyk, Vltnburg ✓, Von-O 00 ✓, Wamakers, Warwick 99, Western, Wldkrans, Wlhlmshof, Wndmeul ✓
★★★ Agusta NEW, Assegai NEW, Boeken, Boplaas, Boschklf, Bovlei, Cape Wine C, Clmborg, C-Uitsig 99, Devon H NEW, Dieu D, Dmrsftn NEW, Drnkraal, Drostdy, Du Preez NEW, Du T'kloof ☺, Eikehof, Fleur dC 99, Fraai U, Graham B, Groote P, G'verwacht NEW, Havana H NEW, IWS, Klawer, Klein DB 99, Kleine Z, La Petite F, Linton P, L'zicht ☺, Maze NEW, M Rochelle, M Rozier, Padda, Post House 00, Riebeek, Rijk's, Savanha 00, Seidel, Smridge NEW, Sprtdrift, Travino, Tulbagh ☺, Upland, Vrdndal NEW, Wlington, Wlworths (+1), Botha, Cape Clas, Cheetah V NEW, Cop-Fin, Country C, Excelsior NEW, IWS, Libertas, Louiesen, Main Str NEW,

Pontac

★★★★Hrtnberg

'Port'

Red

★★★★★Axe Hill ✓, JP Bredell ✓

★★★★½A'verloren ✓, Boplaas ✓, Bredell & Nel, Die Krans ✓ (+1), JP Bredell, KWV (+1), Masters 98, Muratie, Overgw (+1), Vrgnoegd 98

★★★★Boplaas NEW (+1), Die Krans ✓, Die Krans 99 ✓, Glen C, KWV, L'Avenir NEW, Lndskrn, Monis (+1), Mrgnhof, Riebeek NEW ✓, Rooiberg

★★★½Alto, Botha ✓, Brgsig ✓ (+1), Dellrust NEW, Die Krans ✓, Drnkraal ✓, G Constantia, Louiesen, Mrgnhof (+1), Padda, Rooiberg ✓, Rtrsvlei ✓, Slnghoek, Smnsig NEW, Swrtland ✓, Swrtland 99, Villiera 97

★★★ Beaumnt, Boplaas (+1), Cheetah V NEW, De Zoete, Du T'kloof, F'hoek Vyds, KWV, L'Émigré, Lwshoek, M Ruber, Muratie, Rbtson, Rdezandt, Rstnberg, Smnsvlei, Smrbsch, Travino NEW, Vrdndal, Withoek NEW ★★½ Aan de D, Avoca NEW, Boland, De Wet ★★ B'trams, Clairvaux NEW, Gr'dheim, Vlrsdorp, Wamakers ★½ Ashton, Bdsberg, B'klippen, Kango ★ Bovlei, Hldrkrn, Oranje *No star:* Brnheim, Goue V **NT:** Cltzdorp, Die Poort, Douglas G, G'dveld, Goudini, Huguenot (+1), M'uitsig (+1), Ndrburg, Ntvbij, Romans, Sdgwick's, Stbosch Vyds (+1), Waboom

White

★★★½Asara NEW, Smnsvlei

★★★ Boplaas, Die Krans **NT:** Die Poort

Red blends

Cape 'bordeaux'

★★★★★Havana H ✓, Knkop, Vrglegen

★★★★½Asara 98, Bllevue, Boschklf, Bschndal 98, B'wachting, Cordoba, Gr'hurst, Meer'dal ✓, Meerlust, Mrgnhof, Mrgster 99, Overgw, R&R, S'bonga NEW, Veenwdn, Vrglegen, Vrgnoegd 99, Warwick 99, Wlworths NEW

★★★★Avontuur, Baarsma (+1), Bksberg, Boschklf, Camberley, Claridge, Coleraine, Delaire, De Toren, Devon H NEW, Glen C, Goede H, Graham B NEW, High C NEW, Hrtnberg, Jordan, JP Bredell NEW, Kaapzicht, Khanya, Klein G 99, KWV (+1), La Motte, Le Bonh, Le Riche, Lievland, L'Ormarins ✓, Louisvale, M Destin ✓, Meinert, Môreson NEW, Mrgnhof NEW, Mulderb, Ndrburg 99, Neil E ✓, Nitida ✓, Rickety, Rstnberg, Smnsig, Spice R, Stbosch Vyds NEW, Stlnzicht, Stnwall 99, Swrtland ✓, Veenwdn, Villiera ✓, Vrsenhof, Warwick, Welgemnd 99 ✓, Wndmeul ✓, Yonder 99, Zonneblm

★★★½B'klippen, Bon'vale NEW ✓, Bouwland 00, B'trams ✓, B'wachting, Cape Bay ✓, Clos M, Dmrsdal, Eikendal, G'verwacht ✓, Havana H, Jean D 99, Jonkheer, Jordan, Joubert-T, Kanu, K Constantia, Ken F, KWV, Laborie, Laibach (+1), Lanzerac NEW, Lwshoek NEW ✓, M du Toit, Napier, Ndrburg, R&R, Reyneke, Rstnberg ✓ (+1), Rtrsvlei 00 ✓, Slnghoek NEW, Smnsvlei ✓, Stony B, Strmbrg NEW, Sxnburg, Van Z'hof NEW ✓, Vrglegen ✓, Vrsenhof, Welgemnd ✓ (+1), Wlworths NEW, Zvnwacht ✓

★★★ Agusta, Blngham, Boschklf, De Vlrs, Dieu D, Dmrsdal ☺, IWS NEW, La Bri, La Couronne 99, Leopard's NEW, Lndskrn, L'Ormarins, Merwida ☺, Migration, Mouton, Ntvbij, Prdeberg, Shoprite, Spice R, Stbosch Vyds ☺ (+1), Stnberg ☺, Vendôme ☺, Vinfruco NEW, Wldkrans 99, Wltvrede, Wlworths NEW (+1), Craighall, Lanzerac, Lwshoek NEW, Makro, Malan, Mouton, Padda, Seidel (+1), Sinnya, Tulbagh, Two Oceans, Vrsenhof ★★ Devon H NEW, McGreg ★½ Nuy **NT:** Bksberg, Brenthurst, C-Uitsig, Goue V, J'randa, Kaapzicht, Klnhof, Lemberg, Nthlshof, Rozendal, Seidel, Slaley, Smrbsch, Vrdnheim **NR:** Ashanti NEW, Avondale NEW, Brnheim NEW

Red blends with pinotage

★★★★★Clos M 98

★★★★☆Afr Terroir NEW, Darling C, Gr'hurst, Kaapzicht NEW

★★★★Clos M, Dellrust NEW, G Constantia, Knkop, Overgw ✓, Smnsig, Uiterwyk 98, Villiera NEW (+1), Warwick

★★★☆B'klippen NEW, Kaapzicht, L'Avenir, Mdlvlei, Rooiberg ✓, Welgemnd ✓

★★★ Afr Terroir ☺ (+2), Ashanti NEW, Baarsma (+1), Boland, Carneby L, Cdrberg, Country C, Du Preez ☺, Goue V ☺, Graham B, Icon ☺, Kaapzicht ☺, Louisvale NEW, Maiden NEW, Prtrville, Rhebklf ☺, Ridder's, S/SW, Shoprite ☺, Swrtland ☺, Tulbagh ☺, Van Lvrn NEW (+1), Vltnburg ☺ ★★☆ Ashton, Boland ☺, Bon C ☺, Capelnds ☺, Clairvaux NEW, Drostdy, Fort S 00, L'Émigré, M'pont ☺, M Rozier, Opstal ☺, Prtrville, Riebeek, Tulbagh NEW ☺, Vinfruco NEW, Vrdndal, Western ★★ Cape Clas ☺, Carnival ☺, Cop-Fin, Country C ☺, Douglas G NEW, Leopard's NEW, Malan, St Elmo, Travino, Vinfruco NEW ★☆ Avontuur, Bovlei, Cheetah V NEW ★ Glnview *No star:* Rietrivier **NT:** Baarsma (+1), Cop-Fin, Flgstone, Goue V, Huguenot, Oranje (+1), Spur, Uiterwyk **NR:** Drnkraal NEW

Other red blends

★★★★★Rust en V 98

★★★★☆M du Toit (+1), Avondale ✓, Bschndal, Clos M, De Traf, Eikendal NEW, Glen C, Hazendal, Hrtnberg, Khanya, Makro, Mrgnhof 00, Sxnburg, Wlhlmshof, Wlworths NEW, Zndvliet, Zonneblm NEW

★★★☆Annandl NEW, Bon C ✓, De Meye NEW, Fairview ✓ (+2), Lwshoek NEW ✓, Lndskrn, Long Mntn, Muratie 98 ✓ (+1), Ndrburg (+1), Plaisir, Rtrsvlei ✓, Stbosch Vyds ✓, Stnberg NEW (+1), Uitkyk, Van Lvrn, Vltnburg, Vrdndal ✓, Wlworths ✓ (+1), Yonder NEW, Zvnwacht ✓

★★★ Afr Terroir NEW ☺, Avontuur ☺, Botha ☺, Brandvlei ☺, Brgsig ☺, Brydale ☺, Bschndal, Cape Bay ☺, Cape Vyds, Ch Lib ☺, Clmborg ☺ (+1), Cordoba ☺, Darling C ☺, Dellrust ☺, Douglas G ☺ (+1), Drnkraal, Fairview, Goudini NEW, Guard P NEW, Kanu ☺, Klnhof (+1), Laibach ☺, Lievland ☺, Lutzville ☺, Main Str NEW, Makro ☺, Ndrburg (+1), Nelson, Nordale ☺, Oranje, Pick 'n P ☺, Rdezandt ☺, Ridder's, Rtrsvlei ☺ (+1), Stbosch Vyds ☺, Strmbrg, Tassenbrg ☺, Teslaarsdal NEW, Vaughan J (+2), Vinfruco ☺ (+1), Wamakers, Western ☺ (+1), Western 01, Whlhaven ☺, Wine Wrhs ☺, Wldkrans, Wlworths ☺, Zndvliet NEW ★★☆ Bon'vale ☺, Bovlei ☺, Cape Wine C, De Wet, De Zoete, Drostdy, Dumisani NEW, Du T'kloof ☺, F'hoek Vyds, Gecko NEW, Guard P NEW, IWS ☺ (+1), Kleine Z NEW ☺, Longridge ☺, Lost H ☺, Ntvbij, Rbtson ☺ (+1), Ridder's, Riebeek (+1), Smnsvlei, Smrbsch, Sxnburg, Vaughan J (+1), Villiera ☺, Vinfruco (+1), Withoek NEW, Wlington ☺, Wlworths (+1), Zomerlust ☺ ★★ Bksberg, Boplaas, Clairvaux, Cop-Fin, Dumisani, Eikendal ☺, Heernhf, Overhex, Riebeek, Rooiberg, Western NEW, Wlworths ★☆ Aan de D, Avoca NEW, Cape Gab, Overmeer *No star:* Kango **NT:** Asara, Baarsma, Bovlei, C Cask, Clovelly NEW, Cltzdorp, Coleraine, Delheim, Die Poort, F'hoek Vyds, Flgstone (+1), Goudini, Goue V, Hrtswater, Kaapzicht NEW, Kango, Klawer, Long Mntn, Makro, McGreg, Montagu, M'uitsig NEW (+1), Nthlshof, O-Bridge, P'rotti's, Rider's, Romans (+1), Shoprite (+2), Stille W, Sxnburg, Taverna, Vaughan J, Vinfruco, Vrdndal, Vrdnheim, West Cst, Wnklshoek **NR:** IWS

Red muscadel (fortified)

★★★★☆Monis

★★★★Du T'kloof ✓, Gr'dheim, Monis, Nuy ✓, Rietrivier ✓, Rietvallei ✓, Seidel

★★★☆Aan de D ✓, Ashton, Boland ✓, Bon C 01, De Wet, Jonkheer, Nordale ✓, Rdezandt, Rooiberg 99

★★★ Kango, L'zicht, McGreg, Rbtson, Twee JG NEW, Van Lvrn, Wltvrede ★★☆ Avoca NEW, Lutzville NEW, Slnghoek NEW ★★ Kango, Klawer, Ladismith NEW ★☆ Kango, Oranje **NT:** Agtrklip, Drnkraal, G'dveld, Huguenot, Montagu, M'uitsig, Uitvlucht

Red, sweet (unfortified)
✪Sylvnvle ✫ Avontuur **NT:** C Cask, G'dveld

Riesling
Cape or SA
✪Thnskraal ✓
✯ Bschndal, Lwshoek NEW, Swrtland, Wlworths ☺ ✯ Rooiberg ☺, Van Lvrn ✫ Boland, De Wet, Fleur dC, Goudini, Ndrburg, Smnsvlei ✫ Nuy ★ Bon C, Du T'kloof, Wltvrede *No star:* De Vlrs **NT:** Bovlei, Jonkheer

Emerald
Prtrville

Rhine or weisser
✪De Wetsh, G Constantia, Hrtnberg, K Constantia ✓, Lievland, Paul C, Rhebklf ✓
✪Bwachting 01, Thelema ✓, Villiera ✓, Wlworths ✓
✯ Deetlefs NEW, Jordan, Ndrburg, Smnsig ✯ Bksberg, M'pellier NEW, Rooiberg ☺ ✫ Van Lvrn, Wltvrede ★ Merwida **NT:** L'Ormarins, Starke, Stbosch Vyds, Zonneblm

Rosé
Dry
✪Fairview ✓, Newton J ✓
✯ Blngham, De Zoete ☺, Stnberg ✯ Ashanti, Vinfruco (+1) ✫ Kleindal ★ Country C **NT:** Afr Terroir, Asara

Off-dry/semi-sweet
✯ Darling C ☺, Delheim ☺, Douglas G ☺, Goudini ☺, Goue V NEW, L'Avenir 01, L'zicht, Ndrburg ☺, Swrtland, Vlrsdorp, Wlworths ✯ Bdsberg NEW, Dieu D, Graca ☺, Klnhof ☺, Lanzerac, Lost H NEW ☺, McGreg, Vrdndal ☺ ✫ Avontuur, Bksberg, Gecko, Grünb, Lanzerac, O-Wlngtn NEW, Pick 'n P, Riebeek ✫ Clairvaux, Oranje, Two Oceans ★ Avoca NEW (+1), Sprtdrift *No star:* Brnheim, Cape Gab **NT:** G'dveld, Groot E, Prtrville, Shoprite, Stettyn

Ruby cabernet
✯ Afr Terroir ☺, Drostdy, Edonia NEW, Le Grand C ☺, Long Mntn ☺, Lutzville, McGreg ☺, Merwida, Rbtson ☺, Table Peak ☺ ✯ Country C NEW, Lutzville ☺, O-Wlngtn ✫ L'wacht ☺, O-Wlngtn ✫ Avoca NEW ★ Oranje **NT:** Agtrklip, Capelands, G'dveld, Goudini, Hrtnberg, O-Wlngtn, Sprtdrift, Uitvlucht, Vlrsdorp, Waboom, West Cst, Zndvliet NEW **NR:** Ashton, Ladismith

Sauvignon blanc
Unwooded
✪✪Vrglegen 01
✪✪D-Hills NEW, Fleur dC, Neil E, Spier ✓, Stnberg ✓, Villiera ✓, Wlworths ✓
✪Afr Terroir, Avondale ✓, Bartho E, Bschndal (+3), B'wachting (+1), Clos M ✓, C-Uitsig 01, Darling C 01 ✓, Delaire 01, Delheim, Devon H, D-Hills (+1), G Constantia, Groote P 01, Havana H ✓, Hermanus H, K Constantia ✓, Khanya, M'plaas 01, Mrgnhof 01, Ndrburg NEW (+2), Newton J, Nthlshof 01, Overgw 01 ✓, Plaisir, Smridge 01, Spice R ✓, Stark NEW, Stbosch Vyds ✓ (+1), Stlnzicht, Stnberg ✓, Sxnburg ✓, Uitkyk, Villiera ✓, Vrglegen ✓, W Village
✪Afr Terroir, Avontuur, Beaumnt, Boeken, Brydale, Cape P'nt, Cdrberg, Devon H NEW, Dmrsdal, Drknsig NEW, Eikendal ✓, Fleur dC ✓, Fort S, Ingwe, Iona, Jordan, Kanu, Ken F ✓, Klnhof NEW, KWV, La Motte, Landau, L'Avenir, Le Bonh, Lwshoek NEW ✓, L'Ormarins ✓, Lushof, Môreson, Mouton NEW ✓, M Rochelle ✓, Mulderb 01, Ndrburg ✓, Neil E ✓, Nitida ✓, Onderklf, Prdeberg NEW, Rbtson ✓, Rickety ✓, Rijk's, Smnsvlei, Southern R, Sprgfield (+1), Swrtland, Waterford, Wlworths NEW, Zvnwacht ✓
✯ Afr Terroir NEW (+2), Altdgdcht, Assegai NEW, Baarsma (+1), Blngham, Boland, Bonfoi NEW, Bouchard, Bovlei, Cape Bay, Cape P'nt, Cul-View ☺, De

Wooded

🦋Delaire, Jordan ✓, Villiera ✓

🦋Amani ✓, Bksberg, Bschndal, De Wetsh, Elephant

✲ Chamonix, Eikendal, L'Ormarins, Mulderb, Paul C, Smnsig 🦋 La Petite F **NT:** Flgstone, Fort S 🆕, TenFiftySix, Uva Mira

Semillon
Unwooded

🦋 Bksberg, Prdeberg 🆕 ✲ Van Lvrn, Vljsdrift ✲ Glnwood 🆕, Lutzville **NT:** Rooiberg, Stony B

Wooded

✲Fairview

✲Boeken 00 ✓

✲Bschndal, C-Uitsig, Fleur dC 🆕, Green on G 🆕, Nthlshof 99, Rickety ✓, Rijk's, Stlnzicht, Stnberg, Wldkrans ✓

🦋Deetlefs, Eikehof ✓, Fairview ✓, Nitida ✓

✲ Eikehof, Glnwood 🆕, Landau 00, Ndrburg, Stony B 🦋 Savanha *No star:* Drnkraal, F'hoek Vyds **NT:** La Bri, Vrglegen **NR:** Savanha 🆕

Shiraz

✲Delheim 98, Gilga, Muratie 🆕, Sxnburg SSS

✲Afr Terroir 🆕 (+1), Ashanti, Bartho E, Boeken, Bschndal 99, Fairview, Hrtnberg, KWV, Lndskrn 99 🆕, Spice R, Stbosch Vyds 99, Stlnzicht, Vljsdrift 🆕 ✓, Vrgnoegd 99, Waterford

🦋A'verloren ✓, Avondale ✓, Beaumnt, Blngham, Bovlei 🆕 ✓, Bschndal 🆕, B'trams ✓, BWC, Coleraine, Darling C ✓, Delheim ✓, De Traf, D-Hills, Drknsig 🆕, Fairview ✓, Glen C 🆕, Goede H ✓, Graham B (+1), Havana H, Hpnburg 🆕, Kaapzicht, Klvnburg, KWV, La Motte, Lievland, Linton P, Lndskrn 99, Luddite, Mdlvlei, Meer'dal ✓, Mischa (+1), Neil E (+1), Niel J 🆕, Radford D 00, Rust en V, Smnsig, Spice R, Stbosch Vyds 🆕, Stlnzicht, Stony B, Swrtland ✓, Uiterwyk 🆕, Wlworths, Zonneblm

★★★Afr Terroir, Altdgdcht, Assegai NEW ✓, B'klippen NEW, Bksberg, Boeken, Boland, Bon C NEW (+1), Cape Clas ✓, Clos M NEW, Cop-Fin, Country C, De Heuvel NEW, De Meye, Devon H NEW, Dmrsdal 99 ✓, Dmrsftn NEW, Domaine B NEW, Du Preez NEW ✓, Du T'kloof, Edonia NEW, Eikehof ✓, Fleur dC, G Constantia, JP Bredell 99, Kanu, Kleine Z, Kpzicht NEW, Le Grand C, Linton P ✓, L'Ormarins, Main Str NEW, Makro, Migration, Mouton, Ndrburg (+1), Nelson, Nordale NEW, Plaisir, Rhebklf NEW, Rickety 99, Riebeek ✓, Rijk's, Rtrsvlei, Seidel NEW, Smnsig, Smnsvlei ✓ (+1), Stbosch Vyds ✓, Van Lvrn NEW, Veenwdn NEW, Villiera 00 ✓, Vinfruco NEW, Vljsdrift, Vltnburg, Vrdndal NEW, Wlhlmshof, Wlington ✓, Wlworths NEW (+2), Zandvliet (+1), B'klippen, Blue M NEW, Bon'vale ☺, Boplaas, Botha, Bovlei ☺, Breëvallei NEW, Cape Wine C, Deetlefs, De Vlrs, Glnwood NEW, Havana H, K Constantia, Kpzicht NEW, La Petite F, L'Émigré, Longridge, L'zicht NEW, Makro, Mellasat NEW, Nitida 00, Nordale, Nthlshof 98, Prdeberg, Rbtson ☺, Ridder's, Riebeek, Rooiberg, Savanha, Seidel, Slnghoek, Stnberg, Vinfruco NEW, Zandvliet (+1), Zvnwacht 99 ★★ Botha, Cop-Fin, Hldrkrn, Travino, Wlworths NEW ★ Maze NEW **NT:** Agtrklip, Baarsma, Cordoba, Darling C, Flgstone, Fort S, Groot E, Klawer, L'wacht, Overgw, Slaley, Sprtdrift, Vrglegen, West Cst (+1), Ashton NEW **NR:** Brnheim NEW, IWS NEW, Lievland NEW, Thelema, Topaz NEW

Sparkling
Méthode Cap Classique

White

★★★★JC le R ✓

★★★★Avontuur ✓, Bschndal (+2), Cabrière (+1), Graham B (+1), JC le R ✓ (+1), JC le R 99, Laborie, Mrgnhof, Smnsig (+1), Twee JG, Villiera NEW ✓ (+1), Wlworths (+1)

★★★Bon C, Bschndal, B'wachting, Chamonix, Hazendal, Rtrsvlei, Stnberg, Villiera ✓, Western NEW, Wltvrede, Wlworths ✓ (+1)

★★ Cabrière (+1), Môreson

★★ Sxnburg ★ Hldrkrn (+1), Ndrburg (+1), Rstnberg, TenFiftySix

Red

★★★Stbosch Vyds ✓

★★ Graham B

Rosé

★★★Cabrière, Villiera ✓

Non-MCC

Pink (dry)

★★ Stnberg ★★ Laborie, Twee JG **NT:** Stnberg

Pink (off-dry/semi-sweet)

★★ 5th Ave Cold Duck, Brgsig, Drnkraal, Swrtland, Wlworths ★★ Rooiberg ☺ ★ Bon C **NT:** Huguenot, Waboom

Red (off-dry/semi-sweet)

★★ JC le R ★ Cinzano **NT:** Grand Msx

White (dry, often carbonated)

★★★Brgsig ✓, Stbosch Vyds ✓

★★ Eikendal ☺, F'hoek Vyds (+1), Here XVII, JC le R, McGreg ☺, Rhebklf, Swrtland, Wine Wrhs ★★ Boland ☺, Bovlei, Delheim, De Wet, Du T'kloof ☺, Goue V, Makro, Merwida, Ndrburg, Rooiberg, Wlworths ★ Blngham, Brandvlei, Goudini, Ndrburg, Tulbagh ★ Lutzville **NT:** Gecko, Klawer, Van Lvrn

White (off-dry,/semi-sweet)

★★★JC le R

★★ Botha, Rietrivier ☺, Smnsvlei ☺, Vrdndal ☺, Wamakers ☺ ★★ Aan de D, Agusta NEW, Boplaas, Bovlei, De Wet, Goudini NEW, Grand Msx, Klnhof ☺,